THE CAMBRIDGE HISTORY
OF AMERICAN LITERATURE

The Cambridge History of American Literature addresses the broad spectrum of new and established directions in all branches of American writing and will include the work of scholars and critics who have shaped, and who continue to shape, what has become a major area of literary scholarship. The authors span three decades of achievement in American literary criticism, thereby speaking for the continuities as well as the disruptions sustained between generations of scholarship. Generously proportioned narratives allow at once for a broader vision and sweep of American literary history than has been possible previously, and while the voice of traditional criticism forms a background for these narratives, it joins forces with the diversity of interests that characterize contemporary literary studies.

The *History* offers wide-ranging, interdisciplinary accounts of American genres and periods. Generated partly by the recent unearthing of previously neglected texts, the expansion of material in American literature coincides with a dramatic increase in the number and variety of approaches to that material. The multifaceted scholarly and critical enterprise embodied in *The Cambridge History of American Literature* addresses these multiplicities – the social, the cultural, the intellectual, and the aesthetic – and demonstrates a richer concept of authority in literary studies than is found in earlier accounts.

THE CAMBRIDGE
HISTORY OF
AMERICAN LITERATURE

Volume 7

Prose Writing

1940–1990

General Editor

SACVAN BERCOVITCH

Harvard University

CAMBRIDGE
UNIVERSITY PRESS

PUBLISHED BY THE PRESS SYNDICAT͘ ͘ ͘ ͘ ͘ ͘ ͘ ͘ ͘ ͘ ͘ ͘ ͘)F CAMBRIDGE
The Pitt Building, Trumpington Street, Cambridge, United Kingdom

CAMBRIDGE UNIVERSITY PRESS
The Edinburgh Building, Cambridge CB2 2RU, UK   http://www.cup.cam.ac.uk
40 West 20th Street, New York, NY 10011-4211, USA   http://www.cup.org
10 Stamford Road, Oakleigh, Melbourne 3166, Australia

First published 1999

Printed in the United States of America

Typeface 11/13 Garamond 3   *System* QuarkXPress™   [HT]

A catalog record for this book is available from the British Library

Library of Congress Cataloging-in-Publication Data

The Cambridge history of American Literature.
Includes bibliographical references and index.
Contents: v. 1. 1590–1820 — v. 2. 1820–1865 — v. 7. Prose Writing 1940–1990
1. American literature—History and criticism. I. Bercovitch, Sacvan. II. Patell, Cyrus R. K.
III. History of American literature.
PS92.C34 1994   810.9   92-42479

ISBN 0-521-49732-9 hardback

CONTENTS

ACKNOWLEDGMENTS

FROM THE GENERAL EDITOR

My thanks to Harvard University for its continuing support of this project. I am grateful for the assistance of Anne Sanow of Cambridge University Press and for the steady support of Eytan Bercovitch and Susan L. Mizruchi. Finally, it is my great pleasure, personal and professional, to register the contributions in this volume of three scholars of a new academic generation – three outstanding young Americanists trained in the eighties who bring to our common venture the particular concerns, perspectives, and insights of the past decade of literary and cultural criticism: John Burt, author of "After the Southern Renascence"; Cyrus R. K. Patell, author of "Emergent Literatures"; and Margaret Reid, who wrote most of the second part of the Introduction, summarizing the connections between the different sections of this volume.

Sacvan Bercovitch

FICTION AND SOCIETY, 1940–1970

I am grateful for the patient encouragement and valuable comments of the editor, Sacvan Bercovitch, and the collaborative efforts of fellow contributors, John Burt, Cyrus R. K. Patell, and Wendy Steiner, whose own fine work enabled me to concentrate on the writers who most engaged me. I profited from the insights of numerous critics of postwar fiction, including John W. Aldridge, Leo Braudy, Robert Bone, Malcolm Cowley, Chester E. Eisinger, Josephine Hendin, Irving Howe, Stanley Edgar Hyman, Peter G. Jones, Frederick Karl, Alfred Kazin, Thomas Hill Schaub, Mark Shechner, Ted Solotaroff, and Gore Vidal, and from broad historical studies of postwar American life by William H. Chafe, John Patrick Diggins, Godfrey Hodgson, Kenneth T. Jackson, William E. Leuchtenburg, William L. O'Neill, and James T. Patterson. I learned much from graduate students in my courses on postwar fiction, among them, Peter Mascuch and Bill Mullen. As usual, Lore Dickstein's enthusiastic support made all the difference.

Morris Dickstein

AFTER THE SOUTHERN RENASCENCE

My first acknowledgment is to Sacvan Bercovitch, who helped me with this project from the beginning and whose conversations with me show through many of my readings in this text. Morris Dickstein also helped me a great deal in sorting out my thoughts and in getting a sense of this project as a whole. He, like Sacvan Bercovitch, also read my section carefully and provided thoughtful criticism and advice. Rosanna Warren, James A. Grimshaw, and William Bedford Clark have enlightened me tremendously. I have also had the benefit of conversing with wonderful colleagues and students at Brandeis University about this project, most especially Eugene Goodheart, George Franklin, Susan Staves, William Flesch, and Laura Quinney. The astute and discerning criticism of Jo Anne Preston has stood me in good stead here and everywhere, as always.

John Burt

POSTMODERN FICTIONS, 1970–1990

It is seldom the case that an encyclopedia entry has changed its author's life as decisively as this account of contemporary American fiction has affected mine. Its scope coincides with my adulthood, and thus the fateful assignment that came to me from out of the blue in a telephone call from a stranger, Sacvan Bercovitch, was nothing short of the imperative to learn my world. The stranger soon became a generous friend and advisor, so that by now, *gratitude* is far too limited a word to describe what I feel toward him. Part of his gift to me was an introduction to the most talented Americanists of my generation who, with the erudition of literary historians and the courage of liberal reformers, have reconstructed the canon of American literature in these volumes. I feel privileged to be included among them. Over the years, discussing the ideas of "Postmodern Fictions" in my courses at the University of Pennsylvania, I have learned much from my students, both graduate and undergraduate. I am grateful for their stimulation, and for the unfailing support of the institution itself, which provided leave time and research funds for me to carry out my work – most particularly, the Richard L. Fisher Chair in English. Finally, I would acknowledge with much love my children, Emma and Emil, who grew into life as I grew into my intellectual inheritance. It has not always been easy for us to tolerate each other's stalls and spurts, but who of us three would have it any other way?

Wendy Steiner

EMERGENT LITERATURES

My interest in the dynamics of emergent literatures began to take shape during my tenure as President's Postdoctoral Fellow at the University of California (UC) at Berkeley from 1991 to 1993. I am grateful both to the UC president's office and to the Department of English at Berkeley for providing me with the resources necessary to begin the research published here. I am also grateful to New York University's (NYU) Research Challenge Fund, which provided a summer grant that enabled me to complete the final draft of my contribution to the *Cambridge History*.

I want to thank the various editors at Cambridge University Press with whom I have worked on this and other volumes of the *History*: Andrew Brown, Julie Greenblatt, T. Susan Chang, and Anne Sanow. Their belief in the importance of this project has helped its contributors get through many moments of doubt and frustration.

One of the lessons that I have learned while working on this project is that scholarship at its best is a collaborative enterprise. My account of emergent American literatures would simply not have been possible without the foundations laid by the work of the following scholars, some of whom I have had the good fortune to meet personally, others of whom I know only through their superb writings: Rodolfo Acuña, Barry D. Adam, Paula Gunn Allen, David Bergman, Homi K. Bhabha, William Boelhower, Juan Bruce-Novoa, Joseph Bruchac, Hector Calderón, Sucheng Chan, George Chauncey, King-Kok Cheung, Stephen Cornell, John D'Emilio, Roger Daniels, Mary V. Dearborn, Martin Duberman, Thomas J. Ferraro, Phillip Brian Harper, Marlon K. Hom, Frederick Hoxie, Abdul JanMohamed, Jonathan Katz, Elaine Kim, Arnold Krupat, Paul Lauter, Shirley Geok-lin Lim, Kenneth Lincoln, Amy Ling, David Lloyd, Lisa Lowe, Francis Mark Mondimore, Nancy J. Peterson, A. LaVonne Brown Ruoff, José David Saldívar, Ramón Saldívar, Catharine Stimpson, Claude J. Summers, Dana Takagi, Ronald Takaki, Bonnie TuSmith, Andrew Wiget, Hertha D. Wong, Sau-ling Cynthia Wong, and Robert J. Young. Where possible, I have included their works in the bibliography for this volume.

Elizabeth Fowler encouraged me to take up this project when the opportunity first presented itself and helped me to refine its conception in its crucial early stages. Her devotion to intellectual rigor remains an inspiration for me. The following colleagues and friends generously took time out to read drafts of the manuscript and offered suggestions that have proven to be invaluable: Nancy Bentley, Una Chaudhuri, Josephine Hendin, Suzanne Keen, Ellyn Lem, and Blakey Vermeule. I am particularly indebted to Werner Sollors, who not only read and critiqued a complete draft of the manuscript but also invited me to test my ideas in his undergraduate seminar on ethnicity.

My colleagues at NYU have supported my interest in emergent American literatures at every step of the way: I am grateful to Anthony Low, Josephine Hendin, and Jeffrey Spear for enabling me to shift my graduate teaching into this area. The students in my courses on emergent contemporary American literatures have been a joy to teach: their enthusiasm has been infectious and they have consistently challenged me to articulate and defend my evolving views. Among the many students whose conversation and papers have influenced the account presented here, I would like to cite in particular Bridget Brown, Loretta Mijares, Jae Roe, and Deanna Turner.

I have been fortunate enough to have had inspirational teachers at every stage of my life. My deepest gratitude is owed to Mary Evelyn Bruce, Thomas Squire, Gregory Lombardo, Gilbert Smith, Donald Hull, John V. Kelleher, Warner Berthoff, Leo Marx, and Philip Fisher for schooling me in the joys of learning and scholarship.

I have also been fortunate in my friends. Cabot and Mollie Brown, Joseph Hershenson, Jonathan and Irit Kolber, Anne Corbett, and Andrew Whitney – far flung though they may be – are never far from my thoughts. It's heartening to know that old friendships can survive divergent career paths and professional interests.

My family, both near and far, have always been a source of inspiration to me. My aunts Banoo Patell and the late Frainy Patell and my uncle Noshir Patell have provided me with models of perseverance, dedication, and faith. I am deeply grateful to my aunt Diana M. Patell, who has supplemented love with financial assistance, including the gift of the laptop on which the early drafts of this project were written. I cherish the memory of her husband, my late uncle Minocher K. N. Patell, fellow scholar and professor. My sister, Shireen, a fellow literary scholar, has read this manuscript as it evolved, offering guidance and encouragement; her belief in my abilities keeps me strong in moments of doubt. My parents, Rusi and Estrella Patell, instilled in me the importance of education at an early age and sacrificed much to provide me with the best education imaginable; they continue to be my safe harbor when the seas get rough. My wife, Deborah L. Williams, challenges me every day to be the best that I can be: intellectually, spiritually, and emotionally, she completes my world.

Sacvan Bercovitch has been both teacher and friend to me and has shown me the kind of unconditional support that one expects only from family. Fourteen years ago, he gave me a new lease on intellectual life. For that, and for countless other moments of scholarly inspiration, I will always be in his debt.

Finally, my contribution to this volume of the *Cambridge History of American Literature* is dedicated to my grandmother Francisca D. Raña, who emigrated to the United States from the Philippines in 1971 and who became an American citizen twenty-five years later at the age of 92.

Cyrus R. K. Patell

CHRONOLOGY

Christopher Bigsby, Wendy Steiner, Adam Weisman, and especially Morris Dickstein and Cyrus Patell made valuable suggestions and corrections to the literary chronology. I thank them all. I owe particular thanks to Sacvan Bercovitch; my work here and elsewhere has benefited greatly from his sage and patient counsel. Finally, I thank Elizabeth Miller for her constant support and companionship.

Jonathan Fortescue

INTRODUCTION

THIS MULTIVOLUME HISTORY marks a new beginning in the study of American literature. The first *Cambridge History of American Literature* (1917) helped introduce a new branch of English writing. *The Literary History of the United States,* assembled thirty years later under the aegis of Robert E. Spiller, helped establish a new field of academic study. This *History* embodies the work of a generation of Americanists who have redrawn the boundaries of the field. Trained mainly in the 1960s and early 1970s, representing the broad spectrum of both new and established directions in all branches of American writing, these scholars and critics have shaped, and continue to shape, what has become a major area of modern literary scholarship.

Over the past three decades, Americanist literary criticism has expanded from a border province into a center of humanist studies. The vitality of the field is reflected in the rising interest in American literature nationally and globally, in the scope of scholarly activity, and in the polemical intensity of debate. Significantly, American texts have come to provide a major focus for inter- and cross-disciplinary investigation. Gender studies, ethnic studies, and popular-culture studies, among others, have penetrated to all corners of the profession, but perhaps their single largest base is American literature. The same is true with regard to controversies over multiculturalism and canon formation: the issues are transhistorical and transcultural, but the debates themselves have often turned on American books.

However we situate ourselves in these debates, it seems clear that the activity they have generated has provided a source of intellectual revitalization and new research, involving a massive recovery of neglected and undervalued bodies of writing. We know far more than ever about what some have termed (in the plural) *American literatures,* a term grounded in the persistence in the United States of different traditions, different kinds of aesthetics, even different notions of the literary.

These developments have enlarged the meanings as well as the materials of American literature. For this generation of critics and scholars, American literary history is no longer the history of a certain agreed-on group of American masterworks, nor is it any longer based on a certain agreed-on historical perspective on American writing. The quests for certainty and agreement continue, as they should, but they proceed now within a climate of critical decentralization – of controversy, sectarianism, and, at best, dialogue among different schools of explanation.

This scene of conflict signals a shift in structures of academic authority. The practice of all literary history hitherto, from its inception in the eighteenth century, has depended on an established consensus about the essence or nature of its subject. Today the invocation of consensus sounds rather like an appeal for compromise, or like nostalgia. The study of American literary history now defines itself in the plural, as a multivocal, multifaceted scholarly, critical, and pedagogic enterprise. Authority in this context is a function of disparate but connected bodies of knowledge. We might call it the authority of difference. It resides in part in the energies of heterogeneity: a variety of contending constituencies, bodies of materials, and sets of authorities. In part it resides in the critic's capacity to connect: to turn the particularity of his or her approach into a form of challenge and engagement, so that it actually gains substance and depth in relation to other, sometimes complementary, sometimes conflicting modes of explanation.

This new *Cambridge History of American Literature* claims authority on both counts, contentious and collaborative. In a sense, this makes it representative of the culture it describes. Our *History* is fundamentally pluralist – a federated histories of American literatures – but it is a pluralism divided against itself, the vivid expression of ongoing debates within the profession and the society at large about cultural values, beliefs, and patterns of thought. Some of these narratives may be termed celebratory, insofar as they uncover correlations between social and aesthetic achievement, between technological and stylistic innovation. Others are explicitly oppositional, sometimes to the point of turning literary analysis into a critique of (even attacks on) pluralism itself. Ironically, however, the oppositional outlook here marks the *History*'s most traditional aspect. The high moral stance it assumes – literary analysis as the occasion for resistance and alternative vision – is grounded in the Romantic reverence of Art and the genteel view of High Literature. That view insisted on the universality of ideals embodied in great books. By implication, therefore, and often by direct assault on social norms and practices, especially those of Western capitalism, it fostered a broad ethical-aesthetic antinomianism. The result was a celebration of literature as a world of its own, a sphere of higher laws that thus provided (in Matthew Arnold's words) a standing criticism of life. By mid-twentieth century, that approach had issued, on the one hand, in the New Critics' assault on industrial society, and, on the other hand, in the neo-Marxists' utopian theory of art. The new oppositionalism, including that of the counterculture critics, is inextricably bound up with these legacies.

The complex relationship this makes between advocacy and critique speaks directly to the problem of nationality. This has become a defining problem of our time, and it may be best to clarify what for earlier historians was too obvious to mention: that in these volumes, *America* designates the United States, or the territories that were to become part of the United States. Although several of our authors adopt a comparatist trans-Atlantic or pan-American framework, although several of them discuss works in other languages, and although still others argue for a postnational (even post-American) perspective, as a rule their concerns center on writing in English in the United States – "American literature" as it has been (and still is) commonly understood in its linguistic and national implications.

This restriction is a deliberate choice on our part. To some extent, no doubt, it reflects limitations of time, space, training, and available materials; but it must be added that our contributors have made the most of their limitations. They have taken advantage of time, space, training, and newly available materials to turn nationality itself into a *question* of literary history. Precisely because of their focus on English-language literatures in the United States, the term *America* for them is neither a narrative donnée – an assumed or inevitable or natural premise – nor an objective background (*the* national history). Quite the contrary: it is the contested site of many sorts of literary-historical inquiries. What had presented itself as a neutral territory, hospitable to all authorized parties, turns out on examination to be, and to have always been, a volatile combat zone.

America in these volumes is a historical entity, the United States of America. It is also a declaration of community, a people constituted and sustained by verbal fiat, a set of universal principles, a strategy of social cohesion, a summons to social protest, a prophecy, a dream, an aesthetic ideal, a trope of the modern (*progress, opportunity, the new*), a semiotics of inclusion (*melting pot, patchwork quilt, nation of nations*), and a semiotics of exclusion, closing out not only the Old World but all other countries of the Americas, North and South, as well as large groups within the United States. A nationality so conceived is a rhetorical battleground. *America* in these volumes is a shifting, many-sided focal point for exploring the historicity of the text and the textuality of history.

Not coincidentally, these are the two most vexed issues today in literary studies. At no time in literary studies has theorizing about history been more acute and pervasive. It is hardly too much to say that what joins all the special interests in the field, all factions in our current dissensus, is an overriding interest in history: as the ground and texture of ideas, metaphors, and myths; as the substance of the texts we read and the spirit in which we interpret them. Even if we acknowledge that great books – a few configurations of language raised to an extraordinary pitch of intensity – have transcended their time and place (and even if we believe that their enduring power offers a recurrent source of opposition), it is evident on reflection that concepts of aesthetic transcendence are themselves time bound. Like other claims to the absolute, from the hermeneutics of faith to scientific objectivity, aesthetic claims about high art are shaped by history. We grasp their particular forms of beyondness (the aesthetics of divine inspiration; the aesthetics of ambiguity, subversion, and indeterminacy) through an identifiably historical consciousness.

The same recognition of contingency extends to the writing of history. Some histories are truer than others; a few histories are invested for a time with the grandeur of being "definitive" and "comprehensive"; but all are narratives conditioned by their historical moments. So are these. Our intention here is to make limitations a source of open-endedness. All previous histories of American literature have been either totalizing or encyclopedic. They have offered either the magisterial sweep of a single vision or a multitude of terse accounts that come to seem just as totalizing, if only because the genre of the brief, expert synthesis precludes the development of authorial voice. Here, in contrast, American literary history unfolds through a polyphony of large-scale narratives. Because the number of contributors is limited, each of them has the scope to elaborate distinctive views (premises, arguments, analyses); each of their narratives, therefore, is persuasive by demonstration, rather than by assertion; and each is related to the others (in spite of difference) through themes and concerns, anxieties and aspirations, that are common to *this* generation of Americanists.

The authors were selected first for the excellence of their scholarship and then for the significance of the critical communities informing their work. Together, they demonstrate the achievements of Americanist literary criticism over the past three decades. Their contributions to these volumes show links as well as gaps between generations. They give voice to the extraordinary range of materials now subsumed under the heading of American literature. They express the distinctive sorts of excitement and commitment that have led to the remarkable expansion of the field. Finally, they reflect the diversity of interests that constitutes literary studies in our time as well as the ethnographic diversity that has come to characterize our universities, faculty and students alike, since World War II, and especially since the 1960s.

The same qualities inform this *History*'s organizational principles. Its flexibility of structure is meant to accommodate the varieties of American literary history. Some major writers appear in more than one volume because they belong to more than one age. Some texts are discussed in several narratives within a volume because they are important to different realms of cultural experience. Sometimes the story of a certain movement is retold from different perspectives because the story requires a plural focus: as pertaining, for example, to the margins as well as to the mainstream, or as being equally the culmination of one era and the beginning of another. Such overlap was not planned, but it was encouraged from the start, and the resulting diversity of perspectives corresponds to the sheer plenitude of literary and historical materials. It also makes for a richer, more intricate account of particulars (writers, texts, movements) than that available in any previous history of American literature.

Sacvan Bercovitch

Every volume in this *History* displays these strengths in its own way. This volume does so through its engagement with a particular challenge in contemporary literary studies. In addressing the historical dimensions of modern and postmodern American literature, the five authors of this volume confront a resistant subject. History seems to be elusive in the literature of these decades. Critics have often discussed post–World War II writing as a sequence of stylistic changes – innovations in form, experiments in language and genre. Yet the authors in this volume reveal that every writer responds in some deep sense to surrounding cultural conditions even when espousing self-conscious detachment from society. Thus they may be said to write history in its richest sense – dense with layers, resonant with voices. In their readings of some of American literature's most deliberate statements of isolation and withdrawal, they demonstrate that the value of literary history goes far beyond its capacity to uncover parallels and commonalities between art and society. The declared distance between literature and society is here read as a cultural myth of its own accord. As a result, we see here how, from 1940 to 1990, the dynamics of anxiety and protest – drawn from the *in*congruities between mainstream America and its literary cultures and subcultures – have provided perhaps the richest dialogues on record in this century between literature and society.

Christopher Bigsby's discussion of drama deals with these dialogues directly. His narrative centers on a literature that avoids the general historical trends of postwar national optimism. In his study of American dramatists from Tennessee Williams to August Wilson, Bigsby shows how innovations in theater – such as repetitions in dialogue, constraints in set design, and representations of the materiality of memory – provided the country with an alternative view of contemporary life. Amidst widespread celebrations of American democracy and its promises for the future, mid-century drama turns to anxious inquiries into the past – in all of its horror – including the Holocaust. These voices of anxiety anticipate a world of emerging countercultures. Morris Dickstein registers this development in the growing awareness of social and communal identity belonging to the solitary wanderer – both author and character. Here, that ostensibly autonomous self is not emptied of connection; rather, it is so inflected with varieties of the social past as to drive one into a denial of fundamental connections. Here cultural *dis*engagement bears witness to the powers of history on the individual consciousness. The burdens of memory that this entails consistently have been a major preoccupation of the literature of the American South. John Burt's analysis adds a new layer of interpretive complexity to this dilemma of representation. For Burt, recent Southern literature is a mythic descendant both of the post–Civil War era and of a later generation of scholars who established the terms of Southern regionalism. Mid-twentieth-century issues such as Cold War politics and the growing civil rights movement become central contexts for fictions experimenting with new freedoms from old prejudices. Wendy Steiner, too, takes as her subject both literature and the influence of its critical reception. Whereas formalist concerns have generally shaped critical discussions of postmodernism, Steiner emphasizes the need for a new vocabulary consistent with the social dynamics implicit in postmodern aesthetics. Steiner addresses the limited, and limiting, terms through which the postmodern era has been remembered. Her narrative revives a sense of the interplay (rather than the opposition) between such formal categories as traditionalism and experimentalism. Cyrus R. K. Patell's subject is the fitting complement to Steiner's revaluation. His critical reflections bring new vitality to alternative writings, hitherto considered regional, parochial, or otherwise marginal. As he profiles the strong voices of resistance in America that have come from the emergence of Native American, Asian American, Chicano, and gay and lesbian authors, Patell finds a mandate for the revision of the categories in which they have been set apart from American traditions for so long. Together these five narratives compel us to consider the dynamics of history in literary traditions grounded in an imagined flight from history.

Christopher Bigsby approaches his subject through in-depth analyses of major American dramatists. In Eugene O'Neill, Tennessee Williams, and Arthur Miller, Bigsby presents the writer as a social critic whose public art form conveys messages of private discontent. His analysis reveals that changes in theater during the 1940s–50s reflect not the traditionally remembered American values but bleak suspicions about American experience. By discussing drama as a ritual replaying of experience, Bigsby draws attention to the values embedded in these staged representations of cultural history, the movement (or stagnation) of time and place. The isolation of Tennessee Williams's tragic women (Laura of *The Glass Menagerie,* Blanche of *A Streetcar Named Desire*) epitomizes the dangerous fragility of a world enamored of beauty but repelled by time. The plays of this era are filled with characters whose lives are caught within preordained plots. Their histories, often unlearned but ever present, are solidly material in form. This material representation of history holds true as well in later plays, and Bigsby addresses its changing forms in the works of Edward Albee, Sam Shepard, and David Mamet (whose *American Buffalo* is performed on the cluttered stage of a Chicago junk dealer's store). American drama since World War II is a literature craving connections to history. This is most palpable in works of socially committed dramatists, drawing upon the traditional political power of the theater. Bigsby's history includes discussion of radical experiments in authority, context, and of boundary-crossings that characterized Joseph Chaikin's Open Theatre and Richard Schechner's Performance Group. Not relegated only to performance issues, political concerns also dominate the challenges to ethnic identities and race relations in the work of African American dramatists (Lorraine Hansberry's *A Raisin in the Sun,* James Baldwin's *Blues for Mister Charlie*). Bigsby details the emergence of black drama through the works of LeRoi Jones (Amiri Baraka) and those influenced by him, particularly August Wilson. He explores the politics of gender through women's theater groups of the 1970s and 1980s, particularly the work of Marsha Norman, Beth Henley, and Wendy Wasserstein. Throughout, Bigsby's method is to emphasize the broad scope of theater in America – its growing decentralization and multiplicity of voices, from the radical plays of Cuban-born Maria Irene Fornes to Asian American explorations of history and identity.

For both Bigsby and Morris Dickstein, literature provides a rich subtext from which to reread the rapidly paced story of national development to review a time marked by extraordinary violence and haunted by threats of apocalyptic change. Dickstein's narrative establishes surprising parallels in the fiction of two American cultures shaped by war: America after World War II and America after involvement in Vietnam. The literary voices of these cultures are deepened and complicated by Dickstein's coverage of fiction of the home front as well as of the battlefield; in both cases, the specter of war is the spirit of the text. Between these two periods, Dickstein finds the "road novel" to be among the strongest achievements in American fiction, and with this common center, he connects writers as diverse as Jack Kerouac, John Barth, and J. D. Salinger. In one of his most richly detailed sections, Dickstein elucidates history through incisive close readings of some of the country's most defiant literary outsiders, drawing particularly upon African American and Jewish American writers, whose ethnicities highlight a double conflict. These authors tell of internal struggles resulting from both the social marginality of the group and the psychic stress of constructing a particular individualized identity within the group. In James Baldwin, Norman Mailer, and Saul Bellow, Dickstein finds a paradox of social reflection built on self-examination. The condition of rebellion, implicit or explicit, takes form here in the inward turn – a movement away from a world of violence into the traumatic issues of individual identity – where historical forces are internalized in the troubled memories of authors and characters. Ralph Ellison's *Invisible Man* is a key work here, presenting as it does the vast and multiple dimensions of African American life in the context of the larger American culture. Ellison, Dickstein argues, presents both African American experience and American identity as fundamentally improvisational constructions of the personal intertwined with the cultural. Dickstein shows that the results of such tensions in establishing identity prompt a variety of major shifts in literary representation. In the works of Truman Capote, Vladimir Nabokov, and John Updike, among others, the idea of a strong individual self based on old standards of active heroism becomes a figure of nostalgia and familiar hero tales are obsolete. The alternative to such tales is the psychological parable, whereby even a form as familiar as the war novel centers on entirely new questions, specifically those unanswered by the ideals of valor and patriotism: what sort of person can kill? Who are those lost to the killing? Finally, what happens to human consciousness confronting the prospect of nuclear apocalypse?

Not nuclear destruction but the annihilation of regional identity faces the writers in John Burt's narrative. Burt first recounts this cultural anxiety through detailed discussions of the works of Robert Penn Warren, Carson McCullers, Flannery O'Connor, and Eudora Welty. The specter of modernization threatened the very essence of the old South. Yet, that same sense of threat brought promises of freedom and renewal. Burt's narrative demonstrates that for Southern literature, modernization meant a chance to escape the sorts of traps experienced by William Faulkner's characters, such as the obsession of living and telling the same story over and over again. To some extent, then, the new modernity of Southern literature offered a possible end to the nightmares of collective guilt and family curses. Burt, however, presents this notion of escape as yet another layer of the shared mythic history of the South. Where solutions are imagined, new problems take on familiar patterns. For example, in his discussion of two crime novels, Faulkner's *Intruder in the Dust* and Harper Lee's *To Kill a Mockingbird,* Burt sees not the solution to racism but the substitution of class for race as the mark of the Southern scapegoat. A clean break from the familiar Faulknerian story would mean abandoning a tangled web of definitions, and the writing itself shows a tacit awareness that this would entail a *loss* of freedom. Even if such escape were possible, the Southern authors seem to say, this break with the past would be nothing more than a recoding of memory. Ironically, then, the freedoms won by late Southern authors bespeak a continued entanglement with the past. Nostalgia is now heightened, having been revived by the *illusion* of broken connection. Burt concentrates on authors and works that experiment in redrawing the boundaries of identity for postrenascence Southern literature. Margaret Walker, William Styron, and Ernest J. Gaines provide important perspectives for understanding the legacy of reconstruction, and Walker Percy, Reynolds Price, and Peter Taylor provide diverse views of the South's legacy to American memory. The recent literature of the American South, it turns out, is a story of the varieties of literary *resistance* to historical change, from history's incomplete burials in O'Connor or Welty to its imperial dominance in the tradition reaching from Faulkner to Price.

Historical change may be both represented and resisted in stylistic innovations, and these experiments are central to many of the fictions of postmodernism. But for Wendy Steiner, stylistic experimentation involves far more than aesthetic choice. Her history covers American fiction from about 1970 to the present, and as she organizes her material, her narrative reopens the study of this period by first complicating the relations among the long-standing standard categories of postmodernist discourse. Steiner enriches the inherited categories she identifies: she challenges the divisions of traditionalism, experimentalism, and feminism. In this way, she establishes the need for a more dynamic model of critical memory – specifically, a model that acknowledges the social concerns of literature. Her revised sense of historical vision emphasizes the overlappings and mutual dependencies of traditional, experimental, and feminist voices in postmodern American fiction. These hybrid forms become new vehicles for postmodern realism, which demonstrates its cultural engagement by reflecting on contemporary experiences of ambiguity. Thus Steiner shows that an intellectual concern with the confusion between history and fiction becomes *experientially* central – central to the fabric of everyday life – as American audiences sort through the press accounts of the Vietnam War. In both literature and culture, such confusion issues not in newly credible documentaries but in the increasingly relativistic perceptions of truth and value. Steiner's analyses are based on her strong claim for the frequently overlooked differences between contemporary and modernist art forms. She argues compellingly that the foundational postmodern claim is the rejection of the fetish, explaining – by reference to texts such as John Hawkes's *Innocence in Extremis* – how the postmodern author locates the fetish as folly, as nothing more than the deluded faith in the possibility of real compensation for loss. The power of the fetish depends on an almost religious belief in the capacity of the symbolic object to compensate fully for some profound loss of the real. By rejecting this faith, postmodernist fictions expose the false shadows of that modernist promise in critiques of fetishistic forms of replication. In this new and more limited sense, the postmodern text may be considered a fetish itself, and as such, reveals its own complex historicity. Steiner's approach here may be termed the perspective of recovered history. She discloses the political significance of all aspects of postmodern art, from the conservative premises of the experimental novel to such (ironically) radical traditionalism as that of Toni Morrison's uses of personal history in fiction.

For Cyrus Patell, postmodern fiction makes its strongest historical claims in that insistence on the importance of personal experience. Patell's history recovers that subjectivity among a powerful group of newly recognized literary traditions. These traditions may be newly visible as they emerge in a changing relationship with dominant ideologies, but, Patell emphasizes, they must be considered as voices with strong traditions of their own. Focusing on what has been the most neglected literature of this period, he ascertains the key roles played by Native American, Chicano, Asian American, and gay and lesbian authors in the recent literary history of the United States. His approach is comparative, delineating similarities among these literary voices, and yet his method maintains the importance of difference. Patell shows that minority identity defies quiet submission to mainstream discourse, both in language and in history. He illustrates this with texts as diverse as the Chicano narrative ballad, the *corrido,* and literary representations of the tensions between first (*Issei*) and second (*Nisei*) generation Japanese Americans. By reference to Raymond Williams's categories of historical analysis – residual, dominant, and emergent – Patell brings to light a dramatic paradigm shift. These authors are not token voices of diversity. Quite the contrary: they enact a fundamental design underlying the evolution of a national literature. In the voices of these once marginal groups over the past decades, Patell sees the emergence of central issues in American identity. This is not to say that their radical power is co-opted within a national ideology; rather, they are newly contextualized within as well as against an increasingly broad set of national traditions.

This volume presents American literature of the past half century in a dramatically new light. Here this literature is remembered in its capacity to make focused, critical reflections on the intricate patterns of social context from which it has been produced. This is not reflexive representation – not a mirror of society – but it is no less historically engaged for its critical voice. It directs us toward the tensions between representational and resistant theories of the relations between art and society. The five authors in this volume uncover history in unexpected places, and in doing so, they historicize the very idea of literary resistance in fresh and provocative ways. Directly and indirectly, they argue that the social engagement of art does not depend on its coherent synchronicity with the mainstream voices of the culture. History, especially in the catastrophic forms it took near mid-century, may have been too much to bear as the center of the literary subject. Together, these five authors explain how the dissonance between literature and society may define a particular and profound layer of cultural expression, formulated in the artistic negotiations with the hidden and often overwhelming powers of historical memory. Through an often cultivated distance from social matters, American literature of the past half century – in all of its remarkable variety – expresses those surprising depths of engagement. Working from historically recalcitrant literary sources, this volume allows us to see that every work of literature that has achieved its voice through its designed distance from society has achieved a lasting and resonant voice *within* American culture at large.

Margaret Reid
Sacvan Bercovitch

THE DRAMA, 1940–1990

Christopher Bigsby

I

INTRODUCTION

THE UNITED STATES emerged from the Second World War with a powerful economy, a restored faith in capitalism, and a society rededicated to national myths of material advancement and moral and ideological purity. It also emerged with three major dramatists, in Eugene O'Neill, Tennessee Williams, and Arthur Miller, who appeared to dissent from this consensus.

There was a confidence about prewar theater that, for the most part, did not survive the conflict. The social dramas of Clifford Odets were predicated on the possibility of change; the comedies of Philip Barry and William Saroyan, largely on a contentment with the given. Thornton Wilder celebrated familiar pieties in *Our Town,* and although *The Skin of Our Teeth* suggested a more radical revisioning at the level of style, the ironies were never allowed to disturb a fundamental equanimity. Lillian Hellman's plays relied on a disruption of the moral world finally contained by the structure of melodrama, and if Robert Sherwood, equally drawn to melodrama, offered a lament for the collapse of democratic and Christian values that brought him to the edge of an affecting paradox, he then turned with apparent relief to the banalities of plot for a reassurance that had no place in the logic of his drama. Indeed, his case became, in a sense, paradigmatic. Aware of the dislocations of social and moral purpose, he offered faith and a kind of desperate belief in human goodness that he could never adequately dramatize but only assert. To be sure, his early pacifism crumbled under the pressure of war, but in its place he put militant idealism, as his most successful play celebrated the resistant qualities of a national hero – Abraham Lincoln. The resounding speeches that he gave to Lincoln easily elided with those he gave to president Roosevelt when he became his speechwriter.

For Maxwell Anderson, too, the triumph of evil on the stage was unthinkable, and drama essentially a moral force. His idealism, together with that of Elmer Rice, Susan Glaspell, and Sidney Kingsley; the fantasy world of Marc Connelly and Paul Green; and the comedy of S. N. Behrman and S. J. Perelman, suggested the power of continuity, the persistence of values, the reality of a redemptive humor, and the recuperative power of a theater in which the existence of community was a presumption as well as a necessary precondition. There were powerful exceptions. Elmer Rice's *Street Scene* and Sidney Kingsley's *Dead End* had exposed a social world of occluded desire and frustrated aspirations while the vision of Eugene O'Neill was darkening toward a bleak irony, but, for the most part, the harsh realities of Depression America inspired a theater confident in its structures, expansive in its aims, and optimistic in its social vision. The Federal Theatre Project, as exciting an artistic experiment as any ever conducted in the United States, suggested that drama could confidently engage an oppressive economic and political reality and play its role in transforming society. A new solidarity was proposed, demonstrated, and vindicated.

Little of this survived the war. It might have been presumed that America, emerging triumphant from its engagement with the manifest evils of fascism, would have greeted the return of normalcy and the triumph of democracy with a celebratory theater. The American dream of material prosperity and spiritual contentment seemed once more just a step away, as ever beckoning on a nation with a profound investment in the future. The fact that it did not turn out that way was partly a result of what was quickly revealed as the ambiguous heritage of that war and partly a consequence of writers who had been formed in another time.

It is true that the United States quickly retooled its industry from wartime production to domestic needs. Austerity gave way if not to immediate abundance then to an increasing confidence in a country that could not only generate wealth for its own citizens but also redeem a bankrupt Europe and democratize its former enemies. There were, however, several causes of alarm. The hot war quickly gave way to the Cold War. Nuclear terror, legitimized as a weapon to secure peace in the Pacific, suddenly made the continental United States frighteningly vulnerable. Democracy, it appeared, had not emerged so triumphant after all. Meanwhile, at home there were apparently those prepared to betray their country in the name of an ideology that had once seemed to have attractions to the disaffected poor and the alienated intellectual; that made the past deeply suspect. The 1930s simply could not be unambiguously claimed. Not only had the war drawn a line across American experience but a decade that had nudged the country toward what anywhere else in the world would have been called a form of state socialism now seemed contaminated by the more recent history of that experiment abroad.

The theater, meanwhile, was dominated by three talents whose personal roots were very decidedly in the past. Eugene O'Neill's last plays all looked back to his youth and beyond. In the midst of a personal crisis, withdrawn from the world and afflicted with a disease that threatened to deprive him of the ability to write, he created a series of plays that expressed his sense of the tragic and even absurd nature of human life. Arthur Miller, a bright new talent, emerged on the scene with a play about the burden of good fortune *(The Man Who Had All the Luck)*, the betrayal of idealism and the corrupting power of a material dream *(All My Sons)*, and the spiritual aridity of familiar American pieties *(Death of a Salesman)*. Tennessee Williams offered a similarly bleak view of the social world and of the individual's ability to survive its assault intact *(The Glass Menagerie)* and a portrait of the slow disassembly of private fictions by public realities in a play *(A Streetcar Named Desire)* in which time proves no less threatening to the South, where it is set, than it does to the woman who seems its victim. America might celebrate the individual, free of history and of social obligations beyond the family; its major playwrights saw the individual crushed by time, threatened by coercive myths, and adrift in a world whose declared values seem at odds with human need. Indeed, the family, a central icon, becomes itself the origin of self-deceit, deformed values, and an oppressive tyranny. Arthur Miller has suggested that an animating theme of American writing is not only the inadequacy but the collapse of the American dream, and the evidence for that does seem strong. But the problem goes deeper. The failure of experience to fall into line with enabling myths, which does indeed lie behind much American writing, hints at a more radical disjunction between the self and its context, the individual and his or her imaginative projections. Certainly the major playwrights of postwar America, Miller included, have chosen to dramatize something more than the frustrated hopes of latter-day Horatio Algers. Their ironies bite down harder. In a culture that had always assumed that time was on its side, time becomes the enemy. In a society committed to liberating itself from history, the past reaches out toward the present. Nowhere, perhaps, were these ironies so apparent as in the last plays of America's first great playwright, Eugene O'Neill.

❧

The tragic sensibility has never been particularly in tune with American values. Herman Melville's Lear-like Ahab first struck a chord in European ears. His misanthropy proved as difficult to take at home as did Twain's. O'Neill, whose tragic sense of life had literary as well as psychological origins, was aware that he was out of tune with his times. The last, great plays were first withheld from the public and then, when released, were not received with enthusiasm or understanding. The bleakness of *Hughie,* so close to that of Beckett, whose contemporary he was, seemed too rigorous to embrace.

To enter these plays is to move into a hermetic world, to stand in an echo chamber as phrases are repeated, experiences replayed, lives reenacted as parody. His characters stare into mirrors rather than look through a clear glass into the future. They fear process. The dominant trope is performance. Mary Tyrone, in *Long Day's Journey into Night,* dresses up in her wedding clothes; Con Melody, in *A Touch of the Poet,* in an old military uniform. They replay their own early lives and are trapped, as Tyrone had been (and O'Neill's father, on whom he was based), in the roles they play as a defense against a reality that terrifies them. These are storytellers, doomed to repeat their stories not as a means of redemption or expiation but out of the actor's need to generate meaning out of repetition. These are characters who exist in and through their memories because memories can be carefully crafted and, once repeated, can become reassuringly inert, abstracted from a natural process that implies decay. They have ceased to live. Life lies in the past, in which they had once played active roles, generating their own meaning out of experience. Now that past must be drained of whatever surviving energy it may have had. It must be turned into an aesthetic object that can be held in the hand, no longer organic.

For the most part, these characters are now static. They rarely leave a single room; when they do, as in *The Iceman Cometh,* they recoil in terror. They cling to those who torment them, dramatize themselves, restage their lives secure in the knowledge that they thereby insulate themselves from process. In *The Iceman Cometh,* the dominant tense is the past, and since the tense of the theater is the present, an irony seeps into the resulting space. Urged to project their past into the future, to extend themselves along the line of their lives, they are as terrified as Beckett's characters by the threat of renewed life. Immunity from the absurd requires a denial of hope. In this play, in which Hope and Tomorrow are the names of two self-deceiving has-beens, survival depends upon a refusal to imagine such a transformation.

❦

In *Long Day's Journey into Night,* the theater becomes the condition of being for all the characters. James Tyrone is a literal actor, but in that he is scarcely distinguishable from the rest of the family. His drunken son, Jamie, recites lines by an array of writers and plays the role of drunk the more easily to avoid a reality that can only destroy him. He becomes a stereotype, a literary figure, because thereby he secures a provisional immunity. He is fixed, typed, relieved of the pressure to be. So, too, Mary Tyrone, who takes herself out of time by resort to morphine, plays a series of roles designed to protect herself and others from a knowledge of mortality. In a play in which O'Neill looks back to his own past – it is set in 1912, the year of his attempted suicide – she looks back to hers, performing herself as young girl, eager lover, and, finally, bride, in a desperate attempt to deny the present and refuse the possibility of the future. Performance is the condition of their being. It is also the essence of their torment in that they can no longer escape the roles that once they chose but that now inhibit the human contact for which they long. The fourth character in the play is, effectively, O'Neill himself, now locked securely in a roomful of ghosts, listening to voices from the past and as determined to use that past as a defense as any of his characters.

Yet process cannot be denied. The prevailing note is one of decay. The back room of *The Iceman Cometh* is run down; the faces of the Tyrones betray the power of time; the hotel lobby of *Hughie* is crumbling; the splendid military uniform in which Con Melody dresses, in *A Touch of the Poet,* cannot conceal the collapse of his hopes or the erosion of his physical grace.

These plays, written during the war and produced after it, in the 1940s and throughout the 1950s, are startlingly different in tone and effect from those which preceded them. The exuberant energy and invention of O'Neill's early plays, which restlessly experimented with form, explored the plenitude of theater, investigated the possibilities of style, dislocated character, staged the social and political as expressionist sketches or carnivalesque cavalcades, now stilled. It was not that he had exhausted his inventiveness or reached the end of his investigation into theater's potential, but that he felt the undertow of a prevailing irony, and saw in the theater itself not so much a mirror to reflect society as a perfect paradigm of experience. Here, on stage, incarcerated in a foreordained plot and required to repeat words and gestures processed through other minds and other bodies or simply echoes of their own former selves, are a group of individuals whose only choice is to continue to perform: each day repetition, each present word or action necessarily a memory, so many ghosts in a machine.

By now this was O'Neill's fate, too, as he sat and wrote with a shaking hand, alone save for those he summoned into existence from his own past, seeking in some way the forgiveness that he retrospectively extended to those at whose hands he felt himself to have suffered. The result was a series of plays of astonishing power, plays whose lyricism paradoxically lies in the stuttering incompletions and fragmentary dialogue of those who distrust the words they speak, aware, as they are, of their own capacity for deceit, of the power of language to exacerbate the pain of being. These plays, in which the visual tableaux formed by the characters express simultaneously the spaces that separate them from one another and the shared nature of that separation, are among the greatest achievements of American postwar theater. Their naturalism is charged with a symbolic power. The stasis that they dramatize is the essence of their vision. The melodramatic tinge, which was seldom absent from his work, was a sign not that he was reverting to the nineteenth-century theatrics of his father, which he deeply despised, but that in his work character is placed under intense pressure, language heightened by storytellers desperate to detach words from experience, while degradation and despair bring the self into a confrontation with the reality of human need, a confrontation whose avoidance thus becomes the sole purpose and function of their being.

It seems incredible that critics and public, prepared to acknowledge the disturbing achievements of Samuel Beckett, should for so long have remained unreceptive to the work of a man who once almost single-handedly invented modern American theater and who in the last years of his life created plays whose tensile lyricism and rigorous integrity place them in the forefront of twentieth-century art.

❦

Both Tennessee Williams and Arthur Miller had their roots in the 1930s. They were formed as writers by the Depression, influenced by the radicalism of a committed decade, and carried forward in their work a sense of the fragility of American myths. Williams worked for a radical theater group in St. Louis and wrote a series of plays during the 1930s that were politically if not theatrically challenging. They staged the losing battle between the free individual and a social system implacable in its cruelties and destructive in its banality. Miller, enthused by the Marxist tone of student politics at the University of Michigan, wrote a series of plays about labor disputes, corporate venality, and, like Williams, the coerciveness of the prison system. In both cases these plays, written over some ten years, pre-date those for which Williams and Miller are known and the supposed start of both their careers.

For Williams, the frontal assault was restaged in his postwar work as a battle between the romantic bohemian-artist and a public world tainted with money and power, stained by a sexual, and occasionally racial, corruption. Arthur Miller, abandoning the ideological neatness of his thirties dramas, chose to explore the nature of private and public morality, the extent to which the individual can be held morally and socially responsible for his or her actions. Past and present are brought into dialectical relationship, both theatrically and in terms of plot, because the causal connection between event and consequence is seen as the essence of personal and social meaning no less than the basis of ethics. Miller's protagonists tend to be consumed by guilt, dimly aware of their capacity for betrayal, and desperately anxious to infuse their identities with dignity and meaning in the face of a world that seems to conspire to deny them both. Williams was drawn to the pure heart, broken on the rack of time, the free individual caged by convention, trapped by need and a coercive modernity. Both, however, remained true to their radical origins either in their celebration of the rebel, their portraits of those crushed by the myths no less than the realities of national life, or in their assumption that the writer retained a crucial role as social critic.

2

❦

TENNESSEE WILLIAMS

TENNESSEE Williams felt himself to be an outsider. His particular sexuality was expressly forbidden by law; his avocation as a writer seemed to put him at odds with a society that plotted its priorities along different axial lines. He came from a part of the country that seemed to have been abandoned by a nation whose model of the twentieth century had little use for those whose eyes were fixed not only on the past but on a fantasy reworked as myth. Even in the South, however, he felt out of place, aware, as he was, of its prejudices and of the violence that existed just below the veneer of civility. It is perhaps hardly surprising, therefore, that he wrote a series of plays that focused on the plight of those left behind by the bright lights and noise of the *Twentieth Century,* that symbol of modernity, the cross-country train that used to roll across America and that Hart Crane turned into a powerful metaphor in a poem, part of which Williams was to use as an epigraph to *A Streetcar Named Desire.*

His first public success, *The Glass Menagerie,* drew deeply on his own family situation. Indeed, he himself appears as Tom (his own name was Thomas), a young man torn between responsibility for his crippled sister (Williams's own sister, Rose, was mentally damaged) and a free life as a writer responsible to no one but himself and to nothing but his craft. It was a play of considerable honesty and great subtlety. The guilt that in part generated the play (Williams was away from home when his mother had Rose lobotomized) is apparent, too, in the person of Tom, whose mind constantly reverts to these events, who summons the play into existence.

Laura withdraws from society. She has nothing in common with its language or its rhythms (she cannot keep up with the pace of her stenographic course). An arranged date leads only to new humiliations. Conscious that she is different from others, she steps into her own imagined world, the fragile realm constituted by her collection of glass animals. There, at least, she feels secure, but there, too, she is immured against process, abstracted from the world that so terrifies her. The play ends as we see Laura and her muddled – and in some senses cruel – mother, Amanda, silently sitting together, reconciled only in the mind of Tom, who brings them into being to still his conscience, and by the fact that they have anyway moved beyond a language that would pull them into time. For a moment, frozen into a tableau and viewed through the glass of the window, they are released from the corrosive reality that has terrified them both in different ways, but they become like the glass animals, abstracted from the world.

Williams made a similar move. If Laura animated her glass menagerie, choosing to inhabit her imagination in preference to a bruising world, then so, too, did he. His insistence that there are no lies except those thrust down the throat by the "hard-knuckled fist of need" could apply equally to the lies of art. Himself neurotically obsessed with the passage of time, he had the romantic's faith in the incorruptibility of art. On the other hand, the terrible stasis in which his sister was trapped (she spent the rest of her life in a mental hospital, her mental age fixed forever), was evidence that this could offer no ultimate solution.

The fluid theatrical form of *The Glass Menagerie* – the narrator summons moments from his memory – besides proving influential on Arthur Miller (in *Death of a Salesman, A View from the Bridge,* and, later, *After the Fall*), reflected that "plastic" theater for which Williams worked. As a spokesman, in and outside his work, for the imagination in its one-sided struggle with a brute facticity, he created a style that would be commensurate with his characters' need to sustain the alternative reality to which they are connected. Williams's impressionism was not only an attempt to capture a reality not accessible to the naturalistic writer; it was an assertion of value. It has the same glasslike fragility as Laura's world, but this vulnerability was one of his essential themes. Perhaps that is the reason that he chose to focus on the figure of the romantic and to make women the protagonists of his early work.

Williams has written some of the finest roles for women in the American theater. One reason for his placing them at the center of a number of his plays seems to be his sense that time is a greater enemy to women. Amanda's awareness of her own fading looks sends her back to memories of her youth, whereas her fears for Laura turn on her belief that the window of romantic opportunity will be only a brief one. She herself may sell subscriptions to romantic magazines and color her memories with sentiment, but she is acutely aware that a clock is ticking.

So, too, is Blanche in *A Streetcar Named Desire.* Her options have closed down one by one. She has smelled corruption behind the social myths of the South, detected decadence behind the elegant mask in which style has substituted for substance. She is a fox run to ground. She can only turn and fight or step into a world of pure fiction. She uses what weapons she has left, a brittle sexuality and the power of a desperate imagination. Arriving in her sister's New Orleans apartment, she sets out, with all the skills of a playwright, to set a stage for her own drama. She softens the light with a shawl, arranges the stage, and plays a whole array of roles with perfect conviction, hoping to remain secure behind the images that she projects – yet time is running out for Blanche. Her beauty is fast disappearing, or so she fears, and she has become the thing that shocked her. Like the owners of the family plantation, Belle Reve, whose name underlines its mythic status, she has engaged in epic fornication; in marrying her homosexual husband, she had looked for a momentary immunity, blotting out thoughts of death with desire drained of content.

In one sense, she becomes an embodiment of the South, refusing the logic of time, constructing a myth that will ensnare and inter her. She offers the same civilized mask and presents a pretense of manners and elegance, becoming, in effect, a character in a play of her own invention. She denies her history of defeat, as the South denies its own, but in that reflexiveness, that narcissism, lies some ultimate sterility. Her affairs are with young boys and a homosexual man. By contrast, her sister bears a child. Her Bourbon blood mixes with that of the new man, Stanley Kowalski, a descendent of European immigrants and literally a salesman for the new America. As in Hawthorne's *House of the Seven Gables,* the curse is lifted – but not for Blanche.

In *Streetcar,* the hard-edged realism of Stanley, who inhabits a tangible world in which people line up for the bathroom and hurl meat and radios around a literal apartment, is confronted by the fictive skills of Blanche. She sees the world symbolically, he realistically. *Streetcar* stylistically embodies the conflict at its heart.

Tennessee Williams was in essence a poet. Not merely did he deal in dramatic symbols but his imagination worked by bringing unlikes into confrontation, creating powerful social and metaphysical images. The confrontation between Blanche and Stanley, like that between Alma and John Buchanan in *Summer and Smoke,* generates a meaning central to his work, a meaning born out of a division in Williams himself, that between mind and imagination, the material and the spiritual, the male and the female.

In *Orpheus Descending,* a character describes a bird with no legs that survives only so long as it stays on the wing. To touch the ground is to die. Blanche DuBois is already in free fall when she enters the play. A witness to the corruption of the world in which she had once felt secure, she had begun a series of rearguard actions that have finally brought her to her sister's apartment. With no further retreat possible in a tangible world of reality, she attempts to invent a world, to move beyond the reach of those who occupy the prosaic present and thereby to secure some limited protection, but her poetry is broken on the prose of Stanley Kowalski. Beyond that lies another disabling irony, an irony that destroys a whole series of Williams's protagonists.

If flight represents one possible avenue of escape, then human relationships, usually sexual, represent another — but these solutions are incompatible. To stop, to reach out in love, is to be wholly known and hence wholly vulnerable. To move on is to deny the one true consolation on offer on the Camino Real, the royal or real road, down which they all travel. His plays are thus about a losing game in which fate can only be deferred, never evaded. As a result, an extraordinary number of them end in death, literal or symbolic. Laura, in *The Glass Menagerie,* and Blanche, in *A Streetcar Named Desire,* are lifted out of life, becoming fictive figures who can survive only in the fictions that eventually claim them, the one moving into the inanimate world of her glass animals, the other leaving the play, having become her own invention. That logic is pursued in *Camino Real* in which the characters are literal fictions, characters from literary texts, as later, in *Outcry,* in which the performing self is the only self he can envisage. In similar fashion, Williams described his own public face as "an artifice of mirrors." Meanwhile, the flame and the blade await those who think to beat the game of life with a temporary alliance of lost souls.

For the most part, his women, like Carol Cutrere in *Orpheus Descending,* are "not built for child bearing." They are the end of something, the remnants of a world that has exhausted its possibility. Sexuality still glows, but its power to light up the world is fading. A new kind of power is loose, at its most vital, if primitive, in Stanley Kowalski, but more usually corrupt and corrupting. Boss Finley sets out to emasculate Chance Wayne in *Sweet Bird of Youth,* Brick is sexually disabled in *Cat on a Hot Tin Roof,* Val in *Orpheus Descending* is emasculated by a blowtorch. Kilroy in *Camino Real* is turned into a clown, Shanon in *Night of the Iguana* is tied up while a group of Nazis celebrate the victory of the machine over man. In the later plays *(The Seven Descents of Myrtle, Red Devil Battery Sign),* civilization itself is seen in total collapse and human lives are reduced to parodic gestures. In *Outcry,* two characters perform a play in an empty theater, a play that echoes their own empty lives.

Williams was a Southern writer and had the Southern writer's fascination with the gothic, a romantic concern to replace experience with language and a suspicion of process that has its roots in both personal psychology and regional history. He was no sentimentalist, however, when it came to dramatizing a world that had set limits to its own possibilities. His aristocrats, like Faulkner's, are corrupt; the new South, for the most part, is peopled by amoral, sexually inert materialists.

Williams's plays sometimes have the trappings of realism. The pressure of the social world is evidenced by sets that hint at the shrinking space for personal action. Tenement buildings loom in a world he describes as "sick with neon." The truth that interested him, however, was not accessible through direct representation. The stage is refashioned as metaphor. The lighting up of a house of death in *Orpheus Descending* is emblematic of the new life that momentarily throbs at its heart. The dried-up fountain in *Camino Real* is a symbol of the aridity of personal and social relationships. The house built over a chasm, in *Period of Adjustment,* is an image of contingency, as it is again in *The Seven Descents of Myrtle.* The list could be extended. Nothing appears in a Williams play as a mere detail of social living. Every prop, every piece of scenery, is less concerned to serve plot than theme, and what is true of the set is true also of character. Increasingly, these emerge as archetypes, elements of a morality play in which contending forces confront one another: the pleasure principle and the reality principle (in *Streetcar*), the pure at heart and the deeply corrupt *(Orpheus Descending),* the spiritual and the physical *(Summer and Smoke),* those who represent life as opposed to those who represent death *(Cat on a Hot Tin Roof, Suddenly Last Summer).* In particular, Williams stages that confrontation which lies at the heart of Lawrence's work, between a world of spiritual sensitivity, physical pleasure, and human tenderness on the one hand, and a material, mechanistic, and sterile world on the other. The "incontinent blaze" of live theater was to play its part in this, for it was, in Williams's mind, a place for "seeing and feeling." In other words, it already represented that physical and celebratory element he wished to endorse.

His plays are, accordingly, charged with sexuality. That was and remains part of their shock. Outside of O'Neill, the American theater had not previously produced a playwright for whom the subversive power of sexuality was quite so central. The offstage rape in *Streetcar* retrospectively sends a shockwave back through the play, as the hints of sadomasochism, a curious blend of homosexual and heterosexual display, make *Suddenly Last Summer* so disturbing. In a sense his roots go back to nineteenth-century American fiction, to Hawthorne, Poe, and Melville, who recognized the disturbing power of the libido and its significance as an image either of regeneration or social dislocation. It is tempting, indeed, to relate Williams's tendency to stage sexual melodramas within buildings threatened by imminent collapse to Poe's *Fall of the House of Usher.*

As with Poe, too, that sexuality coexists with violence. If the offstage rape sends a tremor through *Streetcar,* the strangled cry of an emasculated Val Xavier, in *Orpheus Descending,* performs a similar function. Civility is provisional in Williams's plays. The individual psyche and the social world alike threaten at any moment to crack open, to devolve into mere anarchy. If, in Freudian terms, the self and civilization are both built on compromise, a series of repressions necessitated by social living, that compromise seldom holds in Williams's work. The sound we hear is of a world breaking apart along fault lines in the self and society alike. His plays disturb precisely because they threaten us at a level beneath that of intellectual analysis. Like Strindberg, he allows anarchy to surface and chooses sexuality as its expression. His belief that the essence of life "is really very grotesque and gothic" finds its correlative in plays whose lurid shocks are contained only by his control of language, a lyricism into which his characters often self-consciously escape and hence a language touched with artifice, shaped as a defense against the inexpressive but brutally direct prose of those who command history.

There can be no doubt, either, as to who does command history, in the sense of representing social logic, the processes of power, and the possession of space. Those characters whose affecting defeat he tends to celebrate have few possessions, no hold on the world they inhabit. They occupy one-bedroom apartments, sleep on the floor, in hotel rooms, in hammocks. They constantly have to be moving on. They watch the social drama from the wings. Neither is there any doubt where history is leading. The apocalyptic strain in Williams's work, strong from the beginning, intensifies until, in *Red Devil Battery Sign,* humankind is left to scrabble around amid the ruins of the planet, having reverted to the animal state, unredeemed and unredeemable.

To his mind, *Suddenly Last Summer,* with its prevailing image of cannibalism, was rooted in his conviction that people devour one another in the sense of "using one another without conscience." Conscience, indeed, is the missing element in Williams's work. It is not simply those in possession of power who feed off those they abuse; so, too, do his desperate protagonists. Blanche has no conscience about deceiving Mitch, the lumbering mama's boy whom she hopes will rescue her from despair. Chance Wayne, in *Sweet Bird of Youth,* shamelessly clings to a fading movie star as she does to him, hoping to regenerate herself with his energy. Lady, in *Orpheus Descending,* forces Val Xavier to stay with her – at the ultimate cost of his life. They may be victims, but they are not without complicity in a process that seems inevitable.

Art cannot slow such a process. In *Orpheus Descending,* Lady attempts to control and contain the anarchy she witnesses through art, much as Williams saw himself as doing, but though painting may provide her with some apparent consolation, it does not deflect her fate. In just the same way, Williams has said, "I don't think that any play, any playwright, or any work of art is going to make any difference in the course of history. History is inexorable in its flow and I think the flow of history is towards some form of social upheaval." His essays and interviews are full of references to "moral decay" and "moral collapse," elements that are powerful in his work. His late play, *A House Not Meant to Stand,* was very self-consciously offered as "a metaphor for society in our times," but his own confession of the powerlessness of art made it in some way complicit and that complicity surfaces from time to time. The mannered lyrics of Sebastian, in *Suddenly Last Summer,* are generated by the same destructive sensibility that he sees still latent in the individual psyche, that disordered self which art can only momentarily conceal. His description of the stage set for that play, indeed, is close to being a statement of his own vision of the unregenerate nature of the human animal:

The set may be as unrealistic as the decor of a dramatic ballet. It represents part of a mansion of Victorian Gothic style in the Garden District of New Orleans on a late afternoon, between late summer and early fall. The interior is blended with a fantastic garden which is more like a tropical jungle, or forest, in the prehistoric age of giant fern-forests when living creatures had flippers turning to limbs and scale to skin. The colors of the jungle-garden are violent, especially since it is steaming with heat after rain. There are massive tree-flowers that suggest organs of a body, torn out, still blistering with undried blood; there are harsh cries and sibilant hissings and thrashing sounds in the garden as if it were inhabited by beasts, serpents and birds, all of savage nature.

Here, art is not simply the ego that attempts to control the jungle of the id; it is its willing collaborator. Elsewhere, it is simply overwhelmed by the hard-edged nature of the real and by time.

The artist in *In the Bar of a Tokyo Hotel* is destroyed, whereas the doctor in *Small Craft Warnings,* in many ways an image of Williams the artist, has lost his license to practice. Those who generate the plot and dialogue of a play out of their own lives in *Outcry* do so to an empty theater and have no connection with the world beyond that theater or lives beyond their own. As Williams remarked, "I always had the same problems as the people in my plays: no connection to the outside world. I was trapped within myself." The comment is a paraphrase of Val Xavier's similar remark. There is little doubt that apart from the unconvincing optimism of *The Rose Tattoo* and *Period of Adjustment,* that description could apply with equal force to virtually all of his protagonists.

He liked to claim that his plays displayed an essential optimism. Writing in 1957, he had, he insisted, never written anything as "gloomy" as *Long Day's Journey into Night.* He hoped that his audiences would "admire the heroic persistence of life and vitality," that they would "feel the thwarted desire of people to reach each other through this fog, this screen of incomprehension." This was the violet growing in the rock in *Camino Real* with the power to split the granite in which it is rooted, but the persistence of which he spoke gradually became evidence first of irony and then of absurdity as his career progressed. Increasingly, there was little sign of real vitality. The enormous energy of Big Daddy in *Cat on a Hot Tin Roof* is subverted by the cancer eating away his body; that of Maggie, in the same play, is sapped both by her husband's refusal to confront the truth and, ultimately, by the demeaning object toward which her energy is directed.

In the 1940s and 1950s, Williams's rebels had a social and political edge to them. Dissenters from the new consensus, subverters of power, they denied the imperatives of a material society. Outsiders, they represented an implied critique of a society in which power was claimed as a value and sexual and social conservatism were extolled as primary virtues. The shock of his characters lay in their refusal to accept the repressions regarded as the basis for private and public life. They were sexual beings with no concern for the Puritan ethic, little desire to claim the rewards of the American dream. Few, if any, of his protagonists had a job. They were itinerants, traveling in a direction at a tangent to that of a society on the make. They were close kin to those other natural existentialists of the fifties, the Beats. They shared something with Steinbeck's bums and drifters, though without his sentimentality. They staked a claim for another world, a world of feeling, of passion and fragile hopes. They sought to sustain at least the illusion of civility and style. They were the ones who sang, carried musical instruments, painted, wrote poetry, or simply bent language into shapes that gave a certain elegance and rhythm to experience, redeeming it from mere functionalism – which is to say that what they primarily denied was the real, or rather, what they set out to do was redefine the real in such a way as to include their needs, hopes, and inventions. They fought to legitimize the body as they did the poetic imagination. In a conformist decade, in which America was defined in such a way as to exclude the dissenting voice, they generated meaning out of refusal. They were romantics claiming the romantic's right to oppose system and repression with language and the imagination, and their subversiveness is the source of the plays' energy. By the same token, the destruction of these rebels, their immolation, edged his work in the direction of tragedy. Indeed, in some ways their fate echoed that of many in society who found themselves vilified and reduced to penury for having challenged the orthodoxies of capitalism.

Time outstripped him, however. In the 1960s, the rebel became the culture hero. The dissenter, the dropout, the wandering musician, the sexually liberated were apotheosized. The body, displayed at rock concerts, used as a public gesture to oppose the mechanical logic of militarism, or presented on stage by groups for whom nudity and simulated sexuality were the essence of a new freedom, became a central icon. Even the style of government changed as power moved to a younger generation and sex entered the White House. The dark gothicism of the South now came under national scrutiny, where it was demythologized as institutionalized bigotry wedded to random violence. Now the bohemian, the addict, the underclass themselves accreted a kind of power that placed a bland conformist power system under pressure – and the theater reflected this. Jack Gelber's *The Connection* offered a group of junkies awaiting their fix as a paradigm of American society. Edward Albee's *The Zoo Story* turned the Beat into an aggressive and dominating apostle of love with responsibility to redeem a sexless and enervated middle class. Black dramatists reduced the white establishment to stereotype in James Baldwin's *Blues for Mister Charlie* and LeRoi Jones's *Dutchman* and *The Slave*.

Williams's broken souls – his powerless rebels without a cause – no longer seemed culturally central. Besides, in the middle of a personal crisis, he turned to drink and drugs and created a series of plays that lack any conviction. Audiences began to drift away. He found it increasingly difficult to stage his work and spent much of his time reworking plays or writing works that were parodic versions of his earlier successes. His 1961 play, *Night of the Iguana,* in which a defrocked priest finds himself tied up in a hammock, unable to function, proved prophetic in that Williams spent part of the decade in a straitjacket or confined to a mental hospital. Unsurprisingly, the plays from this period have a grotesque, nightmare quality, as he created a series of apocalyptic gestures that reflected his sense of personal decline.

He did, however, emerge from this period of degradation, reprocessing his experiences into art. *Small Craft Warnings* and *Outcry,* the best of these, are imperfect works, but it is possible to feel behind them the desperation of someone afraid that he is losing his ability to write, as he had patently lost the loyalty of his audience. His last plays, *A Lovely Sunday for Crevecoeur* and *Vieux Carré* among them, took him back to his youth and explored the experiences that had once been the source for plays of genuine power and moving lyricism. The signs of recovery were there as he reached far back in an attempt to reestablish contact with a talent he had come close to destroying. It was a process suddenly halted by his ironic death; as a man obsessed by what he had always assumed to be his fragile health and terrified of the solitariness he nonetheless perversely sought died alone in a hotel room, having choked to death on the plastic cap of his medication bottle. As Arthur Miller has said, "the story of American playwrights is awfully repetitive – the celebratory embraces soon followed by rejection or contempt, and this without exception for any playwright who takes risks and does not comfortably repeat himself." Though Williams did eventually repeat himself, he was by nature a risk taker, exploring the possibilities of theater and celebrating the lives of those pressed to the margin of the social and political world. At his best, he created a drama informed by a powerful sense of paranoia. His characters inhabit a world hostile to their needs and unreceptive to their hopes. In part, that paranoia had its origins in a public world that did indeed define his sensibility as deviant and his art as destabilizing the equanimity of social values. To that extent, the radicalism of his thirties' plays simply reconstituted itself as a drama that staged the conflict between the free self and a threatening materialism. More fundamentally, however, it had its roots in his sense that the individual is a victim of a cosmic conspiracy. Seen thus, life becomes a doomed struggle against the logic of time, the temporary alliances forged along the way serving only to underline an essential solitariness. It was out of that battle and those alliances that he created plays of disturbing power and a dark poetry.

3

❦

ARTHUR MILLER

TENNESSEE Williams's sense of an oppressive social world, of the diminishing space available to the embattled self, was a product partly of conscience and partly of paranoid vision, but it was shared by his fellow writers. O'Neill's Yank, trying to embrace the animal when his body is bent to adjust to the mechanical; Miller's Willy Loman, scattering his seed – literal and symbolic – on the stony ground of his backyard; and Laura Wingfield, defeated by the typewriter and retreating to the cold purity of her glass animals, are all examples of the human defeated by the mechanical. It is a matter, too, of space: the cage and the stokehold of O'Neill, the enclosed backyard of Miller, and the cellular living units of Williams all embody a drastic shrinking, a radical diminution of possibilities that lies at the heart of the work of all these writers. American rhetoric is one of expanding frontiers, proliferating possibilities, unformed selves, economically and politically free individuals. American reality, as portrayed in their work, is constrictive, disillusioning, and deforming.

America is a failed utopia, an impossible project, built on a Puritan rhetoric of recoverable innocence and an enlightenment polemic of perfectability. It is the grandiloquent nature of America's promise to itself, and to a world to which it offered itself as a great experiment, that provoked a literature of disillusionment and betrayal. That strain is strong in a drama characterized by its oppositional stance. Thus, O'Neill suggests that his plays have in essence been concerned with the sacrifice of individual to material values; Williams, that his characters are romantics in an unromantic world. Arthur Miller, meanwhile, has engaged the American faith in attainable innocence and a dream of material success.

Miller's imagination is repeatedly drawn to images of a broken contract, a fundamental breach, not only in the codes of civilized behavior, but in terms of human coexistence. The Depression was one concrete example of this, as banks reneged on formal obligations and, under the pressure of need, civilities and humanities were abrogated. The early strike plays – *They Too Arise* and *Honors at Dawn* – detail the denial of human by commercial values, as does *All My Sons.* There was a more fundamental denial, however, that alarmed him, the first signs of which appear in *The Half-*

Bridge, written during the war, a play that quite literally transplanted to America the Nazi denial of Jewish humanity.

❧

Arthur Miller did not serve in the Second World War (neither did Tennessee Williams), but he did know what it meant. *The Crucible* is his equivalent to *The Trial.* It is concerned with a world in which the irrational is ruled rational and reality is defined by the profoundly paranoid. John Proctor died in seventeenth-century Salem, but Miller knew that he died again in twentieth-century Auschwitz. His offense was not to have sinned (paradoxically, the court refuses to countenance his confession of actual adultery); it was to deny reality as defined by those who presumed themselves to know the real. The Puritans needed their witches as the Nazis needed their Jews. In both cases, the innocence of the accusers depended on the supposed guilt of the accused.

In Primo Levi's telling phrase, the entire history of the Third Reich was "a war against memory." Perhaps Miller's insistence on the centrality of memory is an expression of his Jewishness. In play after play, he insists that history has to be given its due. That conviction runs throughout his autobiography, but it suffuses virtually everything he has ever written. America's primal sin is to deny its past, except as myth.

Arthur Miller has given America an existential drama in which the protagonist's concern for his own identity is seen to be an act of bad faith so long as it is not rooted in an understanding that the individual is the sum of choices made and actions performed. It is a drama in which guilt is to be transmuted into responsibility.

Miller's characters are never more insistent on individual identities than when they are denying them. So Willy Loman, John Proctor, and Eddie Carbone shout out their names precisely when their identity is most threatened. The common experience, stamped on their lives like a genetic code, is betrayal. Only incidentally is this a betrayal of others; at its most ironically destructive it is a reflexive treachery that turns back on itself.

All My Sons may reveal that blend of Marxism and transcendentalism that made *The Grapes of Wrath* simultaneously a radical and a conservative document, but Miller has never been concerned to promote a model of the self designed to dissolve into a generalized community of selves. Steinbeck's fascination with the biological metaphor of single-celled marine organisms that bond together to form communal beings would chill a writer for whom the individual was ultimately where the buck stopped. The community of Steinbeck's Joad family has to defer to the community of man as private ownership had to defer to communal rights.

Although Joe Keller had to learn that the rest of society were all "his sons," however, responsibility rested with the individual. Miller, by this stage in his career, did not want to dissolve the family any more than he wanted to dismiss capitalism. Clifford Odets may have wished (rhetorically rather than literally) to dismantle the family unit ("Marx said it, abolish such families") as an impediment to change; Miller did not.

Eddie's crime in *A View from the Bridge* is primarily against the community, a community that continues to survive, hidden away beneath the rush and bustle of the traffic on Brooklyn Bridge. It is precisely the rush of time up on the bridge – the accelerating world of contemporary America – that blinds us to the tragic, to the significance of the individual, to the binding force of personal traded in for commercial relationships. Now, personal relationships have an exchange value. Miller, like Williams, deals with the shift from gemeinschaft to gesellschaft, community to society. That is the root of the process that he makes his subject, as it is at the root, too, of many of O'Neill's and Williams's plays.

Arthur Miller, in many ways so different from O'Neill and Williams, is not without his similarities to them. He, too, has staged the conflict between the self and its setting, acknowledges the pressures that seem to conspire against the individual, and sees the sensibility as deeply divided between a desire for material and spiritual contentment. He, too, has been concerned with a debate as to the nature of the real and has challenged the paradox of national myths expressed through coercive social facts, an American reality seeking sanction in the American dream.

There is a controlled anger in Miller's early plays. His wartime melodrama, never produced, called *The Half-Bridge,* describes as the ultimate offense the removal of buoys marking the safe passage between concealed rocks in the North Atlantic. The notion is that certain betrayals strike at a fundamental human contract. To deny the terms of that contract is to deny the basis of moral action and undermine that notion of human solidarity which is the foundation of civilization. That, of course, was precisely what he saw happening. If the Depression seemed to deny the promise that America had held out to itself, to break some agreement rooted deep in the national psyche, events in Europe suggested a more profound flirtation with anarchy. Miller, a Jew, watched the denial of humanity itself. An early play, *The Golden Years,* ostensibly about the confrontation of Montezuma and Cortés, had been prompted by the prospect of European countries mesmerized by the power of Hitler. Domestically, his novel *Focus,* published in the immediate aftermath of the war, emphasized an anti-Semitism at home, and though it was not until 1964, with *After the Fall* and 1965, with *Incident at Vichy,* that he was able to address the question of the Holocaust, it is not unreasonable to see its shadow on *All My Sons* and *The Crucible,* or to feel its presence behind his continued fascination with betrayal as subject and theme.

Thus, if in one sense the title of his first Broadway success, *All My Sons,* seemed an echo of 1930s radicalism, the human solidarity demanded in Steinbeck's *The Grapes of Wrath* or Clifford Odets' *Waiting for Lefty* and *Awake and Sing,* it was born, too, out of other urgencies. Written during the war but produced after its conclusion, it dramatized the consequences of a denial of moral and social responsibility not simply by showing its social results but by presenting its impact on the self. Joe Keller, an industrialist who has allowed faulty aircraft parts to be supplied to the air force, with fatal results, has justified his actions to himself by reference to business and familial priorities. Confronted with his wider responsibility, he can no longer sustain his sense of himself. The play's suggestion that the individual has no meaning outside the social world of which he is ineluctably a part was to prove a central conviction lying at the heart of virtually all of Miller's plays. Tennessee Williams may have celebrated the alienated self, in flight from the demands of society; Miller will not let his protagonists walk away. Indeed, his dramatic strategy is to bring them to the point at which they are forced to acknowledge the logic that connects event to consequence, past to present, and private experience to public fact.

During his university studies, Miller found himself reading Greek dramas alongside the work of Ibsen. From the former he derived the belief that drama is in origin a society's method of confronting its history and acknowledging its tensions. It is a public art that relies on the fact, as he himself was to put it, that the chickens always come home to roost. From Ibsen he learned a similar lesson: past and present are pulled together to forge an existential link between causality and meaning, and the individual is seen as wrestling with competing responsibilities. If he learned from the Greeks that a flawed self could be productive of tragedy, from Ibsen he learned that it could be the root of social dislocation and moral chaos.

All My Sons seemed, and in part was, a realistic play. Its sets were solid, its plot carefully crafted. Its process involved a gradual revelation of suppressed truths. Like a surgeon laying bare successive layers of tissue, it works its way down to the heart of the disease. There are truths to be discovered. Joe Keller was guilty of implicitly approving the defective parts. He did allow his partner to take responsibility (as did the parallel character in Ibsen's *The Wild Duck* on whom he seems in part to have been modeled). His eldest son, Larry, did commit suicide on learning of his father's actions. There are, however, other elements in the play that disturb a simple reading. Joe Keller is not the only one guilty of betrayal. His partner's children have turned their backs on their father. Joe himself is forced to confront his guilt by his second son, Chris, not because he is dedicated to truth but because he wishes to liberate himself from the past. Chris destroys his mother's fantasies (Kate believes her air force son may still be alive) not out of concern for her but because he wishes to marry his brother's fiancée. His self-righteous accusation is designed to deny the complicity of which he is guilty. Miller himself has even suggested that Kate's suppression of her knowledge of Joe's guilt is paradoxically an expression of her desire to revenge herself on her husband, driving him physically to his knees and to suicide. Indeed, he has wondered whether the essence of the play may not lie in "the return of the repressed," as the past bursts through the membrane of the present, reminding us that whenever "the hand of the distant past reaches out of its grave, it is always somehow absurd as well as amazing," as an "unreadable hidden order behind the amoral chaos of events as we rationally perceive them" becomes apparent. His conviction that "there are times when things do indeed cohere" is a key to his moral position and theatrical strategy alike, but not the least fascinating aspect of his remarks is the emphasis they place on the irrational route to rational process. Miller's comments were offered in the context of a defense of the play's coincidences, the sudden and convenient revelation of long-suppressed truths, but it is precisely his insistence on the existence of a concealed text in the apparent randomness of experience that explains the nature of his drama.

The most powerful presence of the play is that of a man who never appears–Keller's dead son. As in Eugene O'Neill's *Hughie* and Samuel Beckett's *Waiting for Godot,* that absence proves definitional. It also symbolizes other absences, as Joe Keller fails to realize the space that has opened up between his language and his actions and between himself and his family, the family in whose name he has violated his social responsibility. There is a moral void at the heart of the play that it is the play's purpose to fill. That void is the gap between the demands of a social life and the isolating egotism of a self that refuses all commitments. The play ends with a pistol shot as Joe Keller translates a new sense of responsibility into guilt.

Death, indeed, was to provide the final punctuation to all Miller's plays of the 1940s and 1950s (the single exception being *The Man Who Had All the Luck,* the unpublished novel version of which did end with the death of its protagonist). It is as though the force of revealed truth were so powerful as to require underscoring by human sacrifice. Even though the plays of the 1960s through the 1980s offered a new grace, with characters permitted to resolve their moral dilemmas without the added force injected by such sacrifice, both *After the Fall* and *Incident at Vichy* explore authenticity in the context of mortality.

All My Sons was extremely successful. Its assertion of human solidarity was in tune with a postwar optimism, as it had been with wartime necessity. The other issues contained within the play – the tainted nature of idealism, the disturbing pressures of capitalism, the dark side of innocence – remained largely unexplained and unexplored.

All My Sons, Miller has explained, "exhausted my lifelong interest in the Greco-Ibsen form." Now "more and more the simultaneity of ideas and feelings within one and the freedom with which they contradicted one another began to fascinate me." It is an interesting remark, for although he was looking back from the distance of forty years – in an autobiography that itself explored such simultaneity, bringing together events distant in time but emotionally or causally related – *Death of a Salesman* did represent a radical break. Its stylistic experiment grows out of a recognition of the theater's power to bring discrete moments into confrontation. Feeling that in *All My Sons* he had allowed language to carry too great a burden, he set out to create a play in which the central character can never allow his anxieties to make their way into language, a man for whom the past is a continuous present.

In *Death of a Salesman,* the past is not narrated, it is presented. Past and present collapse into the same space, a space defined by the disordered mind of its protagonist. Willy Loman is a salesman whose life has fallen apart in his hands. Derided by the buyers on whom he depends, alienated from his son, Biff, no longer in touch with his life, he plans a suicide that will redeem him. A believer in the dreams paraded as social realities, he finds himself holding nothing that will give meaning to his life, so he revisits his past, searching for the moment when promise had turned to failure, when the myth that had provided his life with structure and purpose had collapsed.

Willy's desperation is partly socially generated. The encroaching city has closed down dreams born in another time and place. Personal relationships in business have devolved into alienated encounters; language has been denatured by advertising to the point where he is bemused by its failure to define experience. His confusion also derives, however, from the failure of his inner resources. He has too completely absorbed the values of a world that fails to touch on his inner needs and has fought to pass this tainted inheritance onto his sons.

At the heart of his life, indeed, is this relationship, especially that with Biff. Once, they gave him the respect the world denied him; now he believes that their success may neutralize his failure. Biff, however, has turned his back on the world that Willy had taught him to reach for. Discovering his father in a Boston hotel room with another woman, he rejects his values and denies his love – yet so powerful is the dream that destroys Willy and that he has worked so assiduously to bequeath to his sons that, even now, Biff is pulled back to the family home. The tension of the play derives from Biff's desperate need to liberate himself from his father, to seize his own fate, and Willy's equal and opposite need to claim Biff, to assuage his guilt by passing to him, as his inheritance, a dream whose corruption he cannot acknowledge. One must leave, the other must prevent him from doing so, and the meaning of both their lives is in the balance. Those productions that cast a strong Willy Loman and a weak Biff miss the point.

Willy's two sons, Biff and Happy, represent two different attitudes to life. Biff is the poet, alive to the beauty of the natural world, conscious of the inadequacy of his life. It is his moral conscience that disables him, just as it is his anguished self-doubts that immobilize him. Happy is self-deceiving, a simple materialist for whom no passion cuts deep. They are, in effect, two sides of Willy's own warring personality, for he is something more than a product of the myth to which he is drawn. He, too, responds to a natural world now rendered null by an encroaching modernity. He, too, is left with a discontent that is more than the residue of failed dreams.

Behind this, however, lies the question of reality itself, for the play in part concerns itself with competing versions of the real. After all, are Willy's reveries less substantial than the myths proposed by society or the rural idylls embraced by Biff as he leaves the play, retracing his steps against the tide of history?

Death of a Salesman was something more than a minority report on the materialism of postwar America, though Miller did hope that it might also prove a time bomb "under the bullshit of capitalism, this pseudo life that thought to touch the clouds by standing on top of a refrigerator, waving a paid-up mortgage at the moon. Victorious at last." It was more even than a play about the gulf between the generations and the extent to which the sensibility may be deformed by ideology. It explored the subjective nature of reality, the degree to which memory shapes the present as the present selectively reconstitutes the past. The stage conventions that he establishes – whereby at times the house is substantial, defining the limits of Willy's possibilities, and at other times insubstantial, merely the context for a life whose vital concerns cannot be precisely located – directly bear on the play's theme. Willy Loman is his own construction. The lies he tells his wife, Linda, are the lies in which he himself desperately needs to have faith. He is a simple drummer, a salesman who has to believe that he is a frontiersman, "knocking them dead," proving himself in a world touched with glamour. As Miller once said, his problem is that he believed the stars projected on the clouds from the rooftops were real stars. He goes to his death still fatally illusioned but, in doing so, he is attempting to invest his life with meaning and his name with dignity. He acts out of terror, the terror that his life may amount to nothing. No wonder this play, which seems born out of a particularly American experience, has proved of such universal appeal.

Miller's play was not about capitalism. He even creates portraits of two compassioniate and successful products of capitalism in Willy's neighbor Charlie and his son Bernard. It is, however, concerned with those who allow their inner lives to be invaded and deformed by values external to human needs. Linda is baffled by Willy's suicide at the very moment when they have paid off the mortgage on the family home, but a Willy Loman content to be satisfied with this would be a Willy Loman without the redeeming quality of self-doubt. The play does not end with his death. The dilemma is projected forward as Biff rejects the dream that hounded his father to his death and Happy dedicates himself to it. The spiritual and the material remain in tension. O'Neill once said that the fundamental theme of his work could be expressed in the biblical question: "What can it profit a man if he should gain the entire world and lose his soul?" In some essential way, it was to prove Arthur Miller's central theme too.

The real force of the play, though, lay in its method, in a use of time that opened up process and compacted past and present into the same space. How fantastic, Miller said to himself, "a play would be that did not still the mind's simultaneity, did not allow a man to 'forget' and turned him to see present through past and past through present, a form that in itself, quite apart from its content and meaning, would be inescapable as a psychological process and as a collecting point for all that his life in society had poured into him." As he explained, there were three categories of time in the play: surreal time, psychological time, and the time created by the play as it is perceived by the audience. Searching for a way of presenting these so that they became the fiber of the play, he arrived at a structure generated by the state of mind of his central character but bearing directly on a historical consciousness that related the American present to the American past. If *All My Sons* had its roots in a recognizable dramatic tradition, *Death of a Salesman* was a wholly original creation.

❦

America might have emerged from the war confident in its values and assured as to its future, but, if so, this situation changed rapidly. The explosion of a nuclear bomb by the Soviet Union and the fall of China to communism made the United States vulnerable to external attack and increasingly concerned with internal subversion, and that placed it at odds with its own past. The radical decade of the 1930s was now seen as the breeding ground for treachery. Communism, once presented as twentieth-century Americanism, was now revealed as diabolic, and the Right saw its opportunity to take revenge on the perpetrators of the New Deal. Senator Joseph McCarthy, a self-publicist, seized the moment, turning an obscure Senate committee into an inquisitorial court that had its parallel in the House Committee on Un-American Activities. At first, these encountered resistance from the executive branch of government, but eventually it bowed to the populist appeal of those who prospered in the paranoid atmosphere of Cold War politics. Suddenly anyone with a radical past, anyone who had proved to be, in one of the revealing phrases of the time, a premature antifascist, was at risk. Those who had signed their names to the manifestos, petitions, and declarations that were the currency of 1930s dissent were liable to find themselves called to account, clearing their own names by offering others. A republic born of dissent now insisted on rigid conformity to values defined by reference to their opposite. The central crime was to be un-American, a piece of Orwellian newspeak whose irony could hardly be savored by those who found themselves thus excluded not only from the body politic but from employment. Along with State Department officials, blamed for the "betrayal" of Yalta, writers, actors, and directors were asked to justify their work and their associations, their public visibility guaranteeing the media interest sought by their persecutors.

It was in this context that Frederic March and Florence Eldridge approached Miller to adapt Ibsen's *An Enemy of the People* for Broadway production. The story of a man who detects harmful organisms in the water of a town that depends on its reputation as a spa, it dramatizes the conflict between the truth-telling individual and a society whose fear for its existence leads to demands for "loyalty" and conformity. Such loyalty in this case requires the central character, Stockmann, to betray scientific as well as personal truth. The subtlety of the play, however, derives from the fact that he himself is flawed, guilty of naïveté and hubris. In the context of early 1950s America, such ambiguities deferred to the obvious parallel whereby betrayal becomes the price of loyalty for the citizen who wishes to claim the benefits of citizenship. Miller himself was unhappy with aspects of the Ibsen play, in particular its social-Darwinist assumption that truth is the prerogative of an elite, but he found in it a defense of the role of the artist as a preserver of values in the face of intimidation. Thus, he recalled telling a "meeting of Marxists years earlier that an artist has the duty to claim new territory, and that if I had obeyed either the Party line or the shibboleths of the national press during the war, I could not have written *All My Sons*. Ibsen-Stockmann was simply making the artist's immemorial claim [to]

point man into the unknown." The response to the play, perhaps pre-
dictably, was uneasy and for Miller, personally, it opened up what he himself called his "time of confusion," for the fact was that a gap was rapidly
opening up between him and the audience he would address.

❦

His response was to write "something that would heat up the atmosphere a
little more" – *The Crucible.* Set in Salem in 1692, it focused on the literal
witch-hunts of Puritan New England. As he has explained,

> the reason . . . I moved in that direction was that it was simply impossible any
> longer to discuss what was happening to us in contemporary terms. There had to
> be some distance. . . . We were all going slightly crazy trying to be honest and
> trying to see straight and trying to be safe. Sometimes there are conflicts in these
> three urges. I had known this story since my college years and I'd never under-
> stood why it was so attractive to me. Now it suddenly made sense. It seemed to
> me that the hysteria in Salem had a certain inner procedure or several which were
> duplicating once again, and that perhaps by revealing the nature of that procedure
> some light could be thrown on what we were doing to ourselves.

The play concentrates on the dilemma of John Proctor, a man who is
almost politically and religiously agnostic. An affair with a servant girl,
Abigail, generates a sense of guilt that comes close to immobilizing his
moral being. When terminated, the affair provokes a jealousy in Abigail
that finds its expression when witchcraft is suspected in the village. She
accuses Proctor's wife, Elizabeth. In trying to defend her, Proctor implicates himself but is offered absolution if he will betray others. He is
tempted but ultimately refuses.

Elizabeth is not the only victim of a hysteria, sanctioned by the law and
religion, that conceals as duty what in fact has its origins in envy, vindictiveness, and simple fear. For Miller, who in the 1950s saw

> people . . . being torn apart, their loyalty to one another crushed and . . . com-
> mon decency . . . going down the drain . . . nothing [seemed] to be sacred any
> more. The situations were so exact it was quite amazing. The ritual was the same.
> What they were demanding of Proctor was that he expose this conspiracy of
> witches whose aim it was to bring down the rule of the Church, of Christianity. If
> he gave them a couple of names he could go home. And if he didn't he was going
> to hang for it. It was quite the same excepting we weren't hanged, but the ritual
> was exactly the same.

For British playwright John Arden, the play "moved the theatrical recreation of history forward in one great stride of English language, and

thereby made it as important a vehicle for enacted ideas as were Brecht's not dissimilar and roughly contemporary plays *(Mother Courage, Galileo)."* In particular, it made it possible, he claimed, for him to write his own historical dramas. In some sense, the strict historical parallels have been marginalized by time, and though it has not lost its political edge, its power, perhaps, lies elsewhere. As Tom Wilkinson, who played John Proctor in the National Theatre's 1990 production, observed, "He's not defending an abstract principle. He's defending an idea of himself, or rather he thinks he's defending a principle for a good part of the play but is finally confronted with who he is. And that's not something that one ever wants to happen to oneself." For the play's director, Howard Davies, the stress also lay elsewhere: "In any power struggle, within any society or community, what you name to be real, or relevant, or significant, if you're in authority, is what becomes significant and relevant. It then takes a major upheaval, the sounding of a common voice, before that reality is changed, those names are re-named or re-defined. To reduce it to McCarthyism would be a mistake. In a sense it is a play about power, about people who find themselves forced into playing roles which they had not asked for."

The Crucible, whose precise control of language owes something to the fact that it was written first in verse, is centrally concerned with signification. "What signifies a needle?" asks Proctor, in a society in which the right of interpretation is claimed by those in authority. In Salem, in 1692, there is a contest over meaning and the nature of the real. For the state, witches and spirits are substantial and the world a battleground between good and evil. To inscribe a personal meaning by signing one's name to a document contesting state authority or by claiming the right to interpret experience for oneself is to dissent from truth, to challenge the single authorized text. *The Crucible* is full of texts: warrants, depositions, confessions, in which individuals attest either to personal or to officially sanctioned truths. The battle is thus in part for the linguistic high ground. It is not simply a contest between truth and falsity but a debate over the degree to which we are the authors of our own lives. For the Puritans, there could only be one text, one version of moral history, one source of interpretation. John Proctor, under pressure, finds that he cannot trade his name on a piece of paper for his life. He will not subscribe to a text in which he has no belief and that is the denial of his being. They want his name, but, in offering it, he comes to realize that he will have drained it of meaning and content. To offer the names of others is both to sanction a reality in which he does not believe and to forfeit the integrity without which his individuality is devoid of meaning. Elizabeth, too, in the words of Zoe Wanamaker, who played the part in the National Theatre production, "learns to read her heart."

There was no space in Puritan theology for the ambiguities of human nature, for the fallibility that is as much evidence of our humanity as the ideals that at times we are capable of serving. Truth was a concept drained of human content. When Elizabeth Proctor stood before her Puritan judges and told a lie to save her husband, she inadvertently betrayed him only because they had no capacity to understand that human necessity which now drove her and which in that moment redeemed her from the coldness into which an absolutist religion had previously driven her.

The Crucible opens in the house of the Reverend Perris through the "narrow window" of which sunlight streams into a room whose colors are "raw and unmellowed," a world of "clean spareness." It ends in the dirt and disorder of a prison cell as the sunlight spills through a "high barred window" onto the face of Elizabeth Proctor while "the drums rattle like bones in the morning air." The two images are separated and united by the action of a play that exposes the cruelties of those who seek to create a clean, spare society by applying a raw, unmellowed spirit, and embraces the muddled, besmirched dignity of those whose humanity resides in their fallibility. *The Crucible* is as much a triumph of symbolist writing as Nathaniel Hawthorne's *The Scarlet Letter,* to which it is related by more than setting.

In 1956, wearing an unaccustomed suit and looking like a cross between a Harvard professor of mathematics and a basketball player, Arthur Miller appeared before the House Committee on Un-American Activities. It was a summons he had waited many years to receive. Elia Kazan, director of *Death of a Salesman,* and Lee J. Cobb, who had created the part of Willy Loman in that play, had both already been subpoenaed and both had succumbed to its intimidation.

Miller himself would be a bigger catch. After all, he had written a play widely perceived as an attack on the committee's methods, morality, and very existence – and then there was his relationship with Marilyn Monroe. Had he agreed to the committee chairman's being photographed alongside Monroe, then the most famous and enticing woman in America, the case against him would have been dropped. Such was their seriousness in pursuing enemies of the people. Arthur Miller was not interested in such games, nor, to her credit – under Miller's tutelage – was Monroe.

By one of those ironies that sometimes disturb our sense of the real, Miller was actually driving back from Salem, where he had been completing research for what was to be *The Crucible,* when, on the car radio, he heard Kazan naming names. When his own turn came, he made his position clear. "I could not use the name of another person and bring trouble on him." Willing to take responsibility for everything he had done, he refused to take responsibility for others.

They were familiar sentiments for those with memories of *The Crucible,* for in that play, John Proctor, also offered absolution at the price of betraying others, had replied, "I speak my own sins; I cannot judge another." Reminded of the similarity, in a later interview, Miller replied, "Well, there was only one thing to say" – but of course, there was not. Others bought redemption with a name. He did not. There was nothing self-righteous about it. He understood the pressures that made others break. Of Lee Cobb, he remarked, "Whoever said the artist has to be strong?" When, years later, Kazan was offered as director of his play *After the Fall,* he refused to block the appointment, because "that would be like operating my own blacklist" and besides, "he was the best." It was simply that the writer whose characters place so much weight on their own names, shouting them out in the face of logic and history ("I'm not a dime a dozen. I'm Willy Loman. . . . I am John Proctor still. . . . Eddie Carbone, I'm Eddie Carbone") could hardly offer somebody else's name to propitiate the gods of the moment.

The Crucible's appeal was not limited to the 1950s. It is his most produced play. In China, it was seen as offering a comment on the Cultural Revolution, as youth, in alliance with age, exacted its vengeance on the rest of society. In central and eastern Europe, there was a ready audience for a play about informers, show trials, and the punishment of those whose definition of the real differed from that of a ruling orthodoxy. According to Miller, it regularly frames South American revolutions, being staged immediately before and immediately after coup d'états and rebellions.

Nonetheless, it undoubtedly had a special force in 1953. Senator McCarthy, holding aloft a sheaf of papers supposedly inscribed with the names of traitors, flourished an implied history from which he offered to liberate America. Still other lists summoned people before his inquisition, denied them livelihoods, removed their names from the credits of films or the doors of offices. What's in a name? Suddenly, everything. To declare your innocence it became necessary to assert the guilt of others (in the words of a character in *After the Fall*: "To maintain our innocence we kill most easily"). Ironically, this was a mirror image of that other world to which many of the victims of McCarthy had once, two decades earlier, pledged their faith – the Stalinist hell in which betrayal was likewise regarded as the ultimate test of citizenship. Miller was not finished with the theme of betrayal.

His next play, *A View from the Bridge,* had the same tragic aspirations, but now Miller set himself to dramatize the life of a man who does betray, who offers up the names of others not to save his life or secure his social position but in defense of what he needs to believe is his own innocence. Eddie Carbone is a longshoreman who hides two illegal immigrants, his wife's cousins, in his own home. When his niece, Catherine, falls in love with one of them, however, his world threatens to collapse, for although he can never acknowledge it, he loves her. It is not simply that he sets out to destroy a rival, however. The truth of his feelings can never be faced, must never make its way into words; thus, he wants to stop the biological clock, to deny her sexuality, for thereby he can deny both reality and the force of his own passion.

Written first as a one-act play and then extended for its London production, *A View from the Bridge* is a radical experiment because it takes as its central character a man who not only cannot articulate his inner desires but cannot even allow them to enter his consciousness. As such, it is more successful than O'Neill's similar experiments insofar as he finds a way to communicate Eddie Carbone's feelings, to articulate tensions within the house, without reliance on the mannered dialogue of *The Hairy Ape* or *Anna Christie*. The moment when he humiliates his niece's fiancé by kissing him on the mouth has a traumatizing force. His inner weakness is expressed in a scene in which a parlor game (he competes in trying to lift a chair by holding only one of its legs) turns, wordlessly, into a trial of more than physical strength. A boxing lesson similarly transforms into real and wordless aggression. As Michael Gambon, who played Eddie in the National Theatre production, remarked, "His actions are all instinctive. He doesn't understand why he's doing what he does, and he can't express himself very clearly – so the actor playing him has to get inside him perhaps more than other parts where the words tell the audience what the character is thinking."

❦

In 1956, Miller found himself in a curious position. Indicted for contempt of Congress after his refusal to cooperate with the House Committee on Un-American Activities, and confronted with a somewhat calamitous decline in the popularity of his plays, he was nonetheless at the center of attention as the husband of the most famous woman in America, Marilyn Monroe. For a number of years, much of his emotional energy was to be taken up with dealing with her deepening emotional and psychological crises. The nine-year silence, as far as the public stage was concerned, that then ensued was a more direct consequence of his loss of an audience. The man who had seen his plays produced on Broadway in 1944, 1947, 1949, 1953, and 1955 now fell silent. His own convictions were so much at odds with a ruling orthodoxy that he no longer felt he had anything to say to those who supported the American theater. He was, in short, a misfit, and it is not too fanciful to see the film of that name – the only new work by Miller produced between 1955 and 1964 – as an expression of his situation. Gay, an aging cowboy, captures wild horses in Nevada. He brings the same skills to the task, the same integrity as he always has, but now these are degraded by a society out of touch with its values. The muscular grace of the horses is rendered down to manufacture animal food. In one sense, it can be seen as an account of the process whereby all the effort of composition is destroyed by the crude response of critic and reader/audience. Indeed, he has said of his relationship to both, at that time, "it's not that it was difficult to relate; it was totally impossible."

Returning from England, where he had been working on the original short-story version of *The Misfits,* Miller faced the fact of his alienation:

A play title that occurred to me at the time, *Music for the Deaf,* might symbolize my feelings about our return to the States and what followed. Beethoven conducted the Ninth Symphony's premiere after he had gone totally deaf and during the performance lost the tempo; so there he was waving his arms and hearing what he was hearing while the audience heard something quite different. I could not hear the tempo of the time anymore; the theatre and the country seemed to confuse art with self-indulgence, as though the naive alone had truthfulness in it. On some days there was the flowery whiff of nihilism in the air, but who was I to level judgements?

It is possible that if Off-Broadway had been fully functional in the mid-1950s, he might still have found an audience, or that if he had had the Group Theatre to write for, as had Clifford Odets, he might have found those willing to support a writer so plainly at odds with his society. Lacking such alternatives, he simply withdrew, though hardly into a secure private life. The theater, meanwhile, seemed to him to concern itself with what he characterized as "devastation," which is not the same, he insisted, as tragedy. This was a reference to the theater of the absurd. Perhaps – especially as a Jew, in common with Saul Bellow – he felt that this colluded with that antinomianism which had, to his mind, facilitated the Holocaust and of which the Holocaust was an archetypal expression. He himself, however, was in no mood to return to the theater and challenge its ruling metaphors.

Nevertheless, America was changing. The election of John F. Kennedy, in particular, gave him some hope for the sixties. Kennedy's death, therefore, was a double blow, killing present and future in one go. It was a death that "pushed a finger through the delicate web of the future. With Kennedy's assassination the cosmos had simply hung up the phone."

When he did return, in 1964, it was with a play that sought in the past some explanation for this collapse of hope, some grounds for reopening a path into the future. He originally planned a play about Hiroshima and his own willingness at the time to sanction the dropping of the bomb, a play that was to be in blank verse. In the process, however, he arrived at another theme, the extent to which guilt incapacitates the individual, the extent to which it is possible to live with a knowledge of private and public fallibility.

Three experiences seem so to have marked Miller's consciousness that he repeatedly returns to them in an attempt to exhaust their meanings: the Depression, the Holocaust, and the House Committee on Un-American Activities. Each exerted a pressure on the individual and the group that made certain questions unavoidable: What do we owe to ourselves and other people? May we with any legitimacy walk away? Is betrayal an unavoidable aspect of human nature? Can innocence exist? In 1964, he returned to the American theater with *After the Fall,* an attempt to pull all those threads together.

The action takes place inside the mind of the play's central character. Its processes replicate those of that mind as memories and ideas flare in his consciousness and sudden connections are forged between moments separated in time. That central character, Quentin, is, depending on your point of view, a lawyer who comes to plead his case before an absent judge, a penitent in an empty confessional, or a patient who generates the analyst who will offer a benediction that will make future life possible. At the time, it was seen as an autobiographical work that explored Miller's own relationship with Marilyn Monroe. More than three decades later, it is clear that that is the least interesting aspect of the play (the National Theatre production, neatly sidestepping the issue, cast a black actress as Maggie, the part once seen as exclusively related to Monroe). The central problem that it addresses is: With religion defunct, ideology bankrupt, national myths exposed, in the name of what does one lead one's life, except a deeply suspect self? And could it be that the betrayals of which we are all guilty are of a piece with the betrayals that have blighted our public history? As Quentin sorts through a private and public past, as he assiduously edits and reformulates events, the one constant is provided by the need to defend oneself by denouncing others, to pronounce racial purity by finding impurity in others, to lay claim to innocence by declaring the guilt of others. To go forward as an individual whose most personal relationships have failed, as a society that has chosen to take vengeance on its own history, as a race that has been both victim and victimizer, it is necessary to confront the past – and to do that, it is necessary first to construct that past.

In its anxious ransacking of the national psyche and of human frailties, *After the Fall* is what amounts to a psychoanalysis cast in a theatrical form. The past may be sacred, but it is not immutable. We are the product not of the past but of what we chose to make of that past, and that is the grace that this play offers and his earlier works did not. This is the first play in which Miller does not consign a major character to death. Quentin is redeemed not merely by virtue of acknowledging his own guilt but by accepting guilt itself as a part of human experience.

After the Fall is a play in which Miller seems to have laid some personal ghosts. It is the first of his plays in which the characters are confessedly Jewish. Without this play, he has admitted, it would have been impossible for him later to have created the figure of Solomon, the eighty-nine-year-old comic Jewish furniture dealer in *The Price*. It is also a play in which he felt able to acknowledge the guilt of the survivor and that history of personal failures which we all carry. It ends with Quentin about to marry a woman who has herself lived through the nightmare of Nazi Germany, a marriage that will offer both the grace they seek. Miller himself had contracted just such a marriage, to Inge Morath, whose own sufferings during the war he documents in his autobiography.

An attempt to wed the scope of epic theater to the intensity of psychological drama, it brought two worlds into direct confrontation. As he explained.

The way I see life is that there are no public issues; they are all private issues. We have gotten divided. We are political men or private men. I can't see the separation . . . it's all one to me, and the attempt, in *After the Fall,* was to unify both worlds, to make them one, to make an embrace that would touch the concentration camp, the Un-American Activities Committee, a sexual relationship, a marital relationship all in one embrace, because that's the way it really is.

In 1964, its emphasis on events one, two, and three decades removed from the present, and what was seen as a private attempt at self-justification on Miller's part, led to its being poorly received, as was a play that was in some ways its companion piece, *Incident at Vichy* (1965). His anxieties were rooted in a history that was not one that a newly politicized black drama or a somewhat truculently ahistorical avant-garde wished to address. Moreover, at a time when rhetorics of all kinds, other than those sanctioned by revolutionary politics or avant-garde aesthetics, were regarded with suspicion, he chose to create a deeply rhetorical play in which a professionally articulate protagonist struggles to define in language the nature and extent of betrayals born outside of words. *After the Fall* was an intellectually demanding play produced at a moment when articulateness and rationality were treated with some suspicion by a theater that looked for authentication in feeling and conviction. The American theater had other priorities. It was now flirting with the absurd, albeit ironically, in the form of Edward Albee's *The American Dream* and Arthur Kopit's *Oh Dad, Poor Dad*; engaging the immediate realities of the racial situation, in Lorraine Hansberry's *A Raisin in the Sun,* James Baldwin's *Blues for Mister Charlie,* and LeRoi Jones's *Dutchman* and *The Slave*; and exploring theatricality in a contemporary context, in Jack Gelber's *The Connection* and Kenneth Brown's *The Brig.* For all his commitment to experimentation, for all his concern to deconstruct historical and psychological reality, Miller was increasingly praised for the plays of the forties and fifties and ignored as a contemporary. It was an extraordinary misjudgment and one not made elsewhere in the world. In the 1980s and 1990s, Britain, in particular, staged those of his plays of the previous three decades which had failed to secure popular or critical support in America, in a series of impressive productions.

The fact was that in his plays Miller continued to insist on the significance of the past at a time when America was self-consciously announcing the necessity to liberate itself from history. The 1960s were a decade in which music, art, politics, and personal style were to be improvised out of an encounter with the present. In one sense, it culminated in 1968, the year of the revolutions, with America's cities ablaze, the universities in rebellion, and the undeniable signs of a coming debacle in Vietnam, where the country's youth and minorities were being sacrificed to a politics born of another age. What was perhaps less apparent was that the language of rebellion itself has a history, as does that of a liberated consciousness, and that burning cities and invaded embassies were a culmination rather than a denial of historical process. They were the price to be paid not only for the tangible realities of the past but still worse for the process whereby that past is reconstituted as myth.

Miller's 1968 play *The Price,* therefore, far from being a throwback to Ibsenesque psychodrama, was a work that registered the shock of a past made suddenly unstable as the pressure of change retrospectively sends shock waves back through the years. As a time traveler's incautious bruising of a blade of grass may change his own subsequent reality – logic reassembling itself along new paths – so Miller's characters are made to travel back through memory and discover the false step that changed their consciousness. A play whose set – a tangled pile of furniture – seems to hint at a truth that lies in the accumulation of details, a naturalist's faith in the physical evidence of lives lived externally, proves a work of considerable subtlety in which the door to the future lies through the past.

The Price explored the extent to which we retrospectively invent our own history: two brothers enact old hostilities and come to recognize their complicity in their own fate. Wildly comic and deeply moving by turns, it explores the nature of memory as time slowly unwinds the coils of self-deceit.

Nearly ten years later, with *The Archbishop's Ceiling* (1977), a play set in a baroque palace in eastern Europe, he created another timely drama of teasing social and metaphysical sophistication that debates not only the responsibility of the writer but the extent to which reality is composed of a series of performed gestures. The characters meet in a room that may or may not contain concealed microphones. They do so to debate the responsibility of the writer. A dissident has to decide whether to leave his country. At stake is his survival as a writer and a citizen. His fear is that either decision may represent betrayal. Those who advise him, meanwhile, themselves have ambivalent motives perhaps not wholly apparent even to themselves, for the fact is that the possible presence of the concealed microphones transforms them all into performers, acting out their dramas for an invisible audience. This situation was entirely familiar to those with any experience of eastern Europe, or, indeed, for those in America who had followed with fascination the revelations of Watergate in which the president of the United States had turned the Oval Office into a form of theater as he alternately recalled and forgot the microphones that he, too, had concealed. *The Archbishop's Ceiling* was not simply offered as a timely response to a current reality ignored by other American playwrights, however. It was a drama that deconstructed the supposed reality of social behavior and raised questions of metaphysical no less than psychological interest. If *The Price* had exposed the insubstantial nature of the past, then *The Archbishop's Ceiling* did the same for the present. It is not that Miller set aside his commitment to character and social process but that increasingly he chose to explore the extent to which these are the product of memory or the consequence of performance.

He took this a step further with two related plays presented under the title *Two-Way Mirror;* one spare, almost Becketian in its severity, the other a detective story of sorts in which the line between paranoid fantasy and physical reality constantly threatens to dissolve. In the first play, *Elegy for a Lady,* a man is seen, motionless, as yet devoid of character, function, or identity, like the first words written on the page by a dramatist. He encounters a woman who is also at first motionless. A story is generated as they are brought together, before the woman becomes motionless again and the man leaves the stage. It is a play that mimics its own writing: the characters are born out of the story that they jointly elaborate. Like actors seen first in the wings who become themselves by entering the stage, they act their lives into being, much as had the figures in *The Archbishop's Ceiling.*

In the accompanying play, *Some Kind of Love Story,* a detective visits a woman who may or may not possess the key to a crime that he is investigating. Former lovers, they meet now only in the context of the crime whose plot the detective struggles to understand. The meaning of their encounter comes from their roles – as lovers, as investigator and witness – and from the story that unites them. They have other roles, however. He has a wife; she is a schizophrenic who alternates between catatonia and a succession of identities, from prostitute to sophisticate.

Together these plays, as their joint title suggests, imply Miller's increasing fascination with the nature of character, the power of story, and the substance of reality. For those eager to dismiss him as an incorrigible realist, wedded to a liberal view of history and committed to an outmoded model of dramatic structure, these plays were hard to assimilate. Most critics did not try; *The American Clock,* the play with which he responded to the truculent capitalism of the 1980s by returning to the 1930s, seemed to reinforce this image of Miller. Even here, though, his epic drama restages American history as a vaudeville, a kaleidoscope of images, a pointillist portrait of a culture acting out its myths while struggling to locate an underlying human reality.

Arthur Miller is not a man to deny the existence or significance of the real. Without an agreed reality, there can be no moral values, no shared assumptions about right actions. Where once, in his early plays – those he wrote in the 1930s – he believed that reality could be easily identified and defined, that the mechanism of society could be spread out for inspection like the parts of a car, he has long since come to feel that we move in a world less easy to pin down – not that reality was ever as stable or assured in his work as perhaps we assume. The moral and social certainties of *All My Sons* proved to have little predictive force. In *Death of a Salesman,* Willy Loman, in common with his society, believed that the myths he embraced were as real as the refrigerator in his kitchen or the car in his drive. In *The Crucible,* John Proctor inhabited a world where those in authority deemed witches to be real and those who denied this to be agents of the devil. A similar incubus was alive in the America of the 1950s when, as Miller observed, the Right had created "a new objective reality," an objective reality by means of which, as he showed in his adaptation of *An Enemy of the People,* public corruption and political ambition would present themselves as civic duty. More recently, though, his sense of the fragility of character and the deceptive nature of the real has intensified, particularly in such works as *The Archbishop's Ceiling* and *Two-Way Mirror.* He has confessed to an increasing concern with the mystery of time, "memory, self-formation," the degree to which "we're all impersonators . . . impersonating . . . ourselves," the extent to which "we've all become actors." Now the questions proliferate. Is memory rooted in the mind or the imagination? Do we exist independently of the roles we play or the roles we coerce others into playing? Can a world that is substantially the sum of private interpretations and public myths be said to be real? If we live in a house of mirrors, will we ever see anything but a reflection of our own needs, desires, and illusions?

In *Some Kind of Love Story,* there are realities: a man is dead; someone killed him. It is necessary to cling to those realities. The difficulty, for the audience no less than for the characters, is to plot a path to those realities. Not long after writing *Two-Way Mirror,* Miller remarked that while "I can't say that I believe that you can ascertain the real, I do believe in the obligation of trying to do so," since to abandon the attempt is to surrender, too, any sense of causality or responsibility until "everything becomes a question of taste, including the hanging of innocent people" (interview with Miller). The characters in these plays may inhabit a house of mirrors, but somewhere, it seems, there is a door. The problem is to find it.

Miller has never been the simple realist that some critics have proposed. It was not only in the 1970s and 1980s that he wrote texts in which character is unstable and social reality a fragile artifice. He was from the beginning a writer concerned about generating a theatrical style commensurate with his distrust of the banality of surfaces. The present is seldom secure in his plays, character is rarely stable, and language is always bending away from a literal accuracy. A moralist rather than a moralizer, he has looked for a structure of meaning in experience, believing that to be the artist's function no less than the individual's responsibility. His conception of the real, however, was never simplistic, from *Death of a Salesman* through *The Crucible* to *After the Fall, The Archbishop's Ceiling,* and *Two-Way Mirror.* If he does indeed believe, in the words of *After the Fall,* that the past is holy, his plays acknowledge that the route to the past lies through the transforming mind and confused emotions of the individual whose present self is already deformed by the past that it summons into being.

For Miller, the 1990s proved a period of intense activity. In 1991, he opened *The Ride Down Mount Morgan* in London. He followed this with *The Last Yankee,* in 1993, and *Broken Glass,* in 1994. This last won England's Olivier Award as best play of the year and was filmed for television. This, in turn, was followed by *Mr. Peter's Connections* in 1998.

The Ride Down Mount Morgan is an ironic comedy in which the bigamously married Lyman Felt is confronted by both wives when they rush to his hospital bedside after an accident. Lyman is a man who believes he could have everything, that indeed everyone benefits from his marital arrangement. In some ways a response to 1980s America, in which greed and self-interest appeared to predominate and to be sanctioned by a culture that elevated the self as a primary value and by presidents who derided the notion of mutual responsibility, *The Ride Down Mount Morgan* is carefully balanced between humor and serious moral concern.

The Last Yankee can also be seen as a response to a society that Miller saw as continuing its commitment to the dream of success at the cost of those individuals who accepted such a dream as a social and psychological imperative. Set in a state mental institution in which a number of women are being treated for depression, it explores the relationship between a carpenter, Leroy, and his wife Patricia, and that between a highly successful local businessman and his wife Karen.

Though it is the women who are being treated, it is apparent that the men who come to visit them are also baffled, if not by their lives, then by those to whom they are married. They meet across a gulf that is only in part defined by gender. More particularly, they see the world differently. Patricia comes from an immigrant family and has internalized that need to succeed that once drove her family across the ocean and that has already destroyed her brothers. Leroy comes from older stock and has older values, building his life stolidly, as he constructs objects with his hands, caring little for material rewards – yet his failure is not simply material. For all his efforts, he has not yet fully understood the nature of his wife's pain. The play ends, however, with the possibility of a new beginning – and other possibilities are also hinted at. Karen, too, begins to reclaim her life, but it is by no means clear that her husband will offer the support she needs. Meanwhile, throughout the play, another woman lies motionless on a bed, unvisited, for much of the time ignored, and the lights do not fade with the exit of Patricia and Leroy, moving out into the world, but with this woman, inert, unchanging, lying on the bed, an expression simultaneously of the need for change and the difficulty of accomplishing it.

Broken Glass, likewise, leaves audiences delicately balanced, committed to possibility but aware of how fragile is the hope they are offered, for history offers an ambiguous lesson. Set in 1938, the year of Kristallnacht, when Nazi thugs attacked Jews and synagogues and thereby foreshadowed the fate of six million, the play concerns Sylvia Gellburg, who suffers from a sudden and unexplained paralysis, and her relationship with her husband Phillip, Jewish but anxious lest he prejudice his success in the non-Jewish world in which he works. The play explores the roots of her paralysis, which seem sunk partly in private and psychological concerns and partly in a sudden disabling sense of the gathering irrational forces that threaten her and others. Unable herself to intervene, and seeing

others equally unable or unwilling to do so, she rationalizes that incapac-
ity. There are equally personal tensions at work in her life and that of her
husband, however.

Broken Glass is an exploration of broken relationships, private and public. The bonds that held individuals and communities together seem to
have disintegrated. The doctor, to whom she is drawn and on whom she
depends, is unable to address a problem that goes deep into her psyche and
deep into a world that seems to have betrayed fundamental principles of
civility, to have destroyed the very foundations of mutuality. Miller thus
takes us on a journey that involves the past, suppressed truths, and denied
identities. Sylvia cannot stand because there is no longer anywhere to
stand, no place of security, no certainty about human nature and its possibilities. She struggles to rise but cannot do so until her husband suffers a
heart attack and necessity drives her up. The play ends with her standing,
uncertainly, wonderingly. Yet does it take his death to liberate her? Is she
free because he has inadvertently released her? Meanwhile, this is 1938, a
year of political and military paralysis on the part of America and Europe
as all stand immobile, transfixed by the effrontery, the sheer fact of Nazi
power. If that will change, ahead lie the camps in which Jews will have
their lives permanently stilled. The eventual victory, as much a part of the
audience's awareness as the events played out before them, would not end
paralysis in the face of power: the writing of this play was concluded, its
rehearsals conducted, its first performances offered as the former
Yugoslavia reenacted the cruelties of World War II, "ethnically cleansing"
the country as the world stood by, immobile.

Miller's first public success, *All My Sons,* had turned on the question of
moral responsibility. The Second World War was equally an offstage fact
in whose shadow the action took place, but the war was no more the subject than Kristallnacht is here. His concern then, and now fifty years later
in the 1990s, was with the failure of individuals to acknowledge full
responsibility for their own lives and hence for the lives of others. There is,
in Miller, a natural existentialism in that he sees identity as the product of
decisions made or refused and insists on the connective tissue that links
private actions to public events. The title of that first successful play, *All
My Sons,* could equally well have stood as the title of a play about a woman
disturbed by events in a faraway Europe while struggling to understand
the link between herself and the world she inhabits. By the same token,
something could be said to be broken in all his plays, some thread that
connects cause to effect, action to consequence, individual to community.
His work, in all its stylistic variety, tragic perception, and humorous tone,
has been dedicated to repairing the thread that stitches together past and

present, self and society. Always rooted in a sense of character dense with ambiguity and finally unknowable in its complexity, his drama nonetheless proposes the necessity of stepping into that shadow in search of those truths consciously or unconsciously suppressed, denied in the mistaken belief that denial relieves one not simply of awareness but of responsibility. That, in the end, is what interests him: not guilt, which is the pointless residue of wrong actions, but responsibility, which is the key to identity and the possibility of change.

4

❧

EDWARD ALBEE

A T THE END of the 1950s, the American theater seemed to have lost
its direction. Miller, it appeared, had ceased to write. Tennessee
Williams was on the verge of annihilating himself in what he was
later justifiably to call his "stoned decade." The initiative seemed to have
shifted to the other side of the Atlantic. Where earlier, those in the British
theater had been enthused and challenged by the remarkable flowering of
American dramatic talent that had marked the decade from 1945 to 1955,
now they generated their own talents, who brought a new energy and purpose to that theater. In America, the dominance of Broadway was undermined by its peremptory economics, a declining urban setting, and the
increasing power of a dwindling number of newspaper reviewers. An audience that had once supposedly been homogeneous now showed signs of
fragmenting. As is often the way, decay concealed new life, however. By
1959, Off-Broadway had become a significant force. For the first time, the
Ford Foundation began to put money into the theater and a number of
productions pointed the way forward into the 1960s and beyond. As political power began to move to a new generation, so also did theatrical power.
In 1959, Arthur Miller was forty-four, Tennessee Williams was forty-
eight, and Eugene O'Neill was six years dead (though *Long Day's Journey
into Night* had not been produced until 1956 and *A Touch of the Poet* and *A
Moon for the Misbegotten* until 1957, with productions of *Hughie* still lying
ahead in 1964 and of *More Stately Mansions* in 1967). In that same year,
however, came *A Raisin in the Sun* from twenty-nine-year-old Lorraine
Hansberry, *The Connection* from twenty-seven-year-old Jack Gelber, and *The
Zoo Story* from Edward Albee, thirty-one. In terms of the Kennedy rhetoric
of the time, the torch had been passed to a new generation.

Edward Albee has always liked to present himself as his own Platonic
creation, springing fully formed into existence as a writer with *The Zoo
Story* (1959), but that image is not strictly true. For a decade, he had been
sketching plays, several of them in verse, and that latter commitment to
the rhythms of language, sometimes at the expense of character or plot,
intensified as his career developed. He has the poet's fascination with linguistic precision, with metaphor and symbol. Indeed from *Tiny Alice*

onward, it was possible to detect the influence of a particular poet, T. S. Eliot, whose plays and poems increasingly became the source of ideas, images, and even characters, but there were other influences. *The American Dream* was an echo of Ionesco, *The Sandbox* of Beckett; *The Death of Bessie Smith* was offered as a gesture at social commitment, albeit not yet fully assimilated to his personal style. With *The Zoo Story,* however, he found his own voice in what is one of the finest one-act plays ever written by an American. He followed it with a play, spitefully denied the Pulitzer prize that it patently merited – the witty, articulate, and urbane *Who's Afraid of Virginia Woolf?*

He followed this with a challenging, if somewhat gnomic, venture into metaphysics, *Tiny Alice,* and the accomplished *A Delicate Balance,* which was rewarded with a Pulitzer prize, as were his later plays *Seascape* and *Three Tall Women.* However, as the seventies gave way to the eighties he seemed, for a while, less central to the theater he had so manifestly helped to reanimate. In part this was perhaps a product of fashion; in part it was a reflection of his own occasional hermeticism, his interest in language which seemed at times detached from those who deployed it. To a degree, though, this in turn was an expression of his growing sense that language had itself been eroded, hollowed out by a history of betrayal, evacuated of the humanity that engendered it. Certainly the brittle texts made to collide with one another in *Quotations from Chairman Mao Tse-Tung* suggested as much. It was also, though, to some degree a reflection of Albee's own arcane imagination, a sensibility that itself responded to language as an object, drawing attention to its angularities. The overconcern with linguistic precision evidenced by some of his characters seems as much an expression of Albee's own schoolmasterly fussiness as of their own desire to imply the ordered nature of the world, which they hope to pin down with words.

The fact is that for over twenty years his plays failed to strike a response from the public. Few writers, however, have chosen to enter the territory into which he moved in exploring the nature of religious conviction, the intertextual realm that constitutes our reality, and the terrible consonance between individual and national decline. Edward Albee is a poet who tries to accomplish in prose what Eliot attempted in verse. Perhaps his primary failure was not to recognize that such experiments are likely to suffocate on Broadway or to acknowledge the contradiction involved in calling for a renewal of human commitment in a language that no longer carried the smell of humanity – but at the beginning of his career, things had seemed very different. Later, with *Three Tall Women,* they did again.

The Zoo Story was a perfect Off-Broadway play with only two characters and a single set that required nothing more than two park benches and a tree. Peter, middle class, middle-aged, and blond, is seated on one of the benches reading a book. Defined purely in negative terms, "neither fat nor gaunt, neither handsome nor homely," he is effectively a nonperson in retreat from human contact. Contact, however, is forced upon him by Jerry, disheveled, physically dissolute, a man who has something of the convert's disturbing enthusiasm. First verbally and then physically, he assaults the alarmed Peter, who responds with a feigned disinterest rooted in fear. The dramatic tension derives from his desperate desire to be free of his assailant and his assailant's almost religious zeal to detain him until he has communicated the truth that this encounter will reveal.

The *Zoo Story* is a play that elaborates the metaphor on which it rests, a story that justifies the indirections of story. Here, Jerry is the storyteller, the playwright; Peter, the passive audience to be provoked, intrigued, and transformed. Jerry deploys the full range of narrative and dramatic skills, from simple storytelling to metaphorical parable to physical action. The mystery with which he seeks to intrigue Peter is equally what holds the playwright's audience.

The Zoo Story was the first evidence of Albee's almost musical control of rhythm as the play moves through a carefully orchestrated and dramatically functional series of crescendos and diminuendos, a technique at its most accomplished in *Who's Afraid of Virginia Woolf?* Indeed, in some ways it communicates as much through rhythm and through sheer emotional power as it does through speech. The threat that Jerry poses to Peter is felt viscerally by the audience no less than by its victim. Language, in the play, is oblique. Words are aggression. There is a grammar to the relationship that goes beyond the exchange of lexical meaning. Jerry's attempts to communicate by indirection are equally those of the playwright; thus, he offers exemplary tales in a play that is itself an exemplary tale.

So it is that the play's title hints at the double lesson that Jerry has learned and that he tries to pass on to the enervated Peter. He has been to the zoo, discovering in the caged animals an expression of the human isolation he had experienced, that he had claimed as a means of securing immunity from the complexities of relationship, but he also sees in the animal vitality of these caged creatures a quality drained out of a society, which can be adequately represented by Peter.

There is perhaps a sentimentality at the heart of the play: Jerry offers a gospel of redemptive love underlined by a Christian iconography. However, the muscularity of the language and the expressive power of the dramatic action mitigates what was to become a sixties piety. The one flaw, acknowledged by Albee, lies in that very nullity from which Peter is to be redeemed. The play requires that he be stripped of a third dimension. The absence of that dimension makes it difficult to feel the pressure of the humanity that it invokes, but seldom has a playwright begun his career with such an original and powerful work or with one that offers so much to the actor.

Albee's next play, *Who's Afraid of Virginia Woolf?*, has deservedly attained classic status. All the qualities revealed in *The Zoo Story* are apparent in a work that condenses wit, excoriating language, and a bruising emotional force to offer an insight into what Albee sees as a collective failure of national will. The play focuses on the relationship between George, a professor of history at a small New England college, and his wife Martha, the blustering daughter of the college president. On one level this is a Strindbergian drama of marital distress that stages the mutual incompatibility of men and women, but Albee's claim to be a "demonic social critic" is justified: the history of their marriage reenacts a national history of betrayed values, failed dreams, and dissipated ambition.

George and Martha, named after the first president and his wife, are childless, but unable to accept such a bleak reality, they invent a fantasy child whom they invest with a detailed reality. It is a fiction designed to give meaning and direction to their lives but one that divides them instead. Out of touch with reality, they are out of touch with one another. So, too, Albee implies, a country that prefers myth to substance, that elevates a dream to the status of national icon, must similarly founder. His intellectual protagonists may spar with brilliant verbal agility, but they are, as they confess, merely walking what is left of their wits. Language has become not a means of communication but a mechanism of evasion.

Albee seeds the play with apocalyptic images and references. The township of New Carthage where the play is set is related, through Spengler, whose *Decline of the West* George pointedly reads, to its classical counterpart, as it is, significantly, to Sodom, Gomorrah, and Illyria, Shakespeare's fantasy country. It is quite as much a play about betrayal as any of Arthur Miller's, but the betrayal here is born of a nation's preference for dream over reality and of the characters' substitution of performance for being. George and Martha are actors. Like Blanche DuBois, they invent their own play. They create a son and give him lines to speak in absentia. They enact his death. They themselves exist only in and through the language they speak, carefully constructed arias and elaborate jokes that draw attention to the ambiguous function of words. As the supposed parents of the fantasy child, they reduce themselves to characters in their self-created drama and perform in front of an audience, a young faculty member and his wife, Nick and Honey, who are themselves conscious of their role as audience. Style replaces substance; language stands in place of action. George and Martha meet only as role players.

The play never leaves the room, which is the stage on which they perform. Theirs is a hermetic world designed to be sealed against process, for they are as much afraid of time as O'Neill's or Williams's characters are, but they are trapped in the logic of their own fiction. The fantasy child is about to attain his majority. The occasion of the play is the eve of his twenty-first birthday. Since he has grown in real time, their invention is about to self-destruct, their play about to end. They must either let him leave or break their own rules. The play ends with George and Martha stripped of their function, bereft of an audience, deprived of their defensive wit, and almost denied language. O'Neill's characters in *The Iceman Cometh,* brought to a similar moment, choose to continue as actors rather than chance themselves in a frightening world of reality. Albee has Martha parody an O'Neill line. Tennessee Williams has his characters choose fiction over reality. Albee has George parody a Williams line. Stripped of pretense, George and Martha have the chance to reach out to each other and confront the painfully ambiguous world they inhabit; though Albee insists that he did not preempt their decision, the logic of a play that moves from aborted gestures of contact to a moment of contact, from a defensive verbosity to monosyllabic simplicity, seems to suggest a resolution in which at last the actors lay aside their masks.

For Albee, this was very much a play that expressed the mood of a particular period. Its apocalyptic overtones were a product of Cold War anxieties (George invokes the defense of Berlin); its implied accusation of liberal equivocation, a withdrawal from political life, was offered as a comment on the decade just concluding. By the same token, the optimism implicit in an ending set against the light of a new dawn was a response to the Kennedy years, an optimism shortly to disappear from Albee's work. In *A Delicate Balance,* staged only three years later, the return of the dawn becomes merely an ironic comment on the ease with which truths confronted in the small hours are discarded with the return of the day. Certainly his apocalypticism was to become more evident and more unrelenting as his career continued. In *Box* and *Quotations from Chairman Mao Tse-Tung* (1968), he peered beyond the moment of nuclear annihilation into a world in which an offstage voice comments on an empty stage, itself evidence of the failure of art no less than of human commitment.

Edward Albee writes about loss. It is tempting to see such a concern as intensely personal. For the adopted son of a multimillionaire theater owner, whose home life was anything but happy, to write about the failure of love, childlessness, those who prefer theater to commitment, and the collapse of communality might seem too close to the bone to be ignored.

Whatever its origin, though, Albee's diagnosis of alienation is offered as a social and political truth, as an account of a society that, in inventing itself, also invented the collapse of real values that is the price to be paid for choosing to inhabit a myth.

His plays are full of failed relationships, a decayed sexuality, and broken families. Physically, his characters show signs of age; they are spiritually depleted and emotionally scarred. Compassionate gestures are repulsed and language attenuated to the point of translucence. His is a world that in the title of one of his plays, seems *All Over.* In *Who's Afraid of Virginia Woolf?*, George and Martha, whatever their human failings, are vibrant, three-dimensional. Thereafter, his characters drift toward abstraction: his work seems invaded by the very virus he claims to detect in the world he drama-tizes and that his plays might be presumed to attack. Their language is deracinated, whereas they barely move, remaining seated in a chair *(A Delicate Balance),* lying immobile on a bed *(All Over)* or beach *(Seascape),* sta-tic on a stage defined by nothing but the outlines of a cube *(Box).* It is as though all energy is leaching out of the system. There is no longer any resistance to a process characterized by decay. The ordered grace of the gar-den in *Listening* has collapsed into tangled disarray; the text of the poem, in *Quotations from Chairman Mao Tse-Tung,* is broken open by self-pitying monologue and political diatribe. His characters all seem to be waiting for the end, not only unable to deflect it but themselves part of the logic of dis-solution. It is not only in *All Over* that a character is dying. The same is true of *The Lady from Dubuque,* which, like *Box* and *Quotations,* seems to be a postapocalyptic reverie.

This is a terminal generation, Albee finding in frustrated sexuality an image of a world drained of generative energy. George and Martha and Nick and Honey are childless in *Who's Afraid of Virginia Woolf?*. Julian, in *Tiny Alice,* is a lay brother on the verge of surrendering sexuality and mocked for his desire to embrace the chimerical Alice. Tobias, in *A Delicate Balance,* spills his seed and ceases to sleep with his wife. Virtually all mar-riages are presented as sterile, devoid of love or fulfillment. Even his early plays – *The American Dream* and *The Zoo Story* – offered parodic versions of the family and an account of sexual contact as a meaningless gesture.

Something else also seemed to drain away from Albee's work: a vivify-ing and in part redemptive humor. It is powerfully present in *Who's Afraid of Virginia Woolf?* and though touched with ambiguity, implicated as it is in the complex strategies of evasion, nonetheless lifts George and Martha above the humorless representatives of the next generation, by turns vapid and threatening. It is there, too, in *A Delicate Balance,* but in *Tiny Alice,* this becomes a thin and sardonic wit; in *A Delicate Balance,* a mannered weariness; in *Box* and *Quotations,* an irony born of contingency; in *All Over,* merely arch condescension.

If Albee has a direction, it is toward the other side of comedy, beyond a transitive language that speaks of possibility. The danger was that in moving into this territory he was breaking a link between himself and his audience. Thirty years on from the beginning of his career, his characters began at times to seem little more than instruments orchestrated by Albee, deprived of any dimension save that of voices scored for their harmonies and dissonances. The powerful theatricality of his early work appeared to give way to thin, almost antitheatrical gestures. *Listening* was initially written for the radio. Increasingly, this seemed a natural medium for plays that less and less required the vivifying physicality of the theater. His own lament over the decay of form and the collapse of private and social structures seemed to have been reflected in plays that themselves had become attenuated to the point of mere verbal gestures, notes without a stave.

❦

Then came *Three Tall Women,* which won him his third Pulitzer prize and put him firmly back on the theatrical agenda (which, in truth, he had never left, if we judge by performances of his work in Europe and Latin America, in particular). The play turns on a central conceit, which generates much of its humor. Three actresses, who in the first act play separate characters – an elderly, incontinent, and apparently fast-fading lady; her nurse; and a young lawyer – in the second act become three versions of the same woman, captured at different stages of her life. The only other character is a young man, who has no lines.

Albee has admitted that the play is effectively a portrait of his adoptive mother, a woman he disliked both for herself and for what she, as a rich, right-wing Republican, represented. By the same token, the young man is Albee himself. Less interesting than whether the play is a belated act of reconciliation and forgiveness, for a woman anyway beyond such gestures, having died some time before, is the wit generated out of the interplay between the various women. Each has a different level of awareness of how events will unfold. Youthful naïveté debates with middle-aged experience, which in turn is confronted with the cynicism of old age. Hope is met with disillusionment; confident youth, with the embarrassments of decrepitude.

It is a play not without cruelty, but equally not without compassion. Beyond anything, it is a play of genuine wit and perception. If Albee was indeed hostile to a woman whose values were so at odds with his own, he manages to create a multiple portrait, Picasso-like, that presents a woman who is more than the butt of humor, more than the victim of her decaying body.

The American production opted for a mannered acting, which stressed the artifice of the play; the British offered something closer to realism, albeit in the context of that kind of baroque realism that Maggie Smith, who played the oldest of the three, prefers.

The success of *Three Tall Women* immediately led to successful revivals of a number of his plays in London and New York (a production of *Who's Afraid of Virginia Woolf?* moved from the former to the latter). In 1997, Maggie Smith appeared in a revival of *A Delicate Balance*. In 1998, *The Play About the Baby,* which had been commissioned by an Austrian theater, opened in Britain to enthusiastic reviews. A play that in some ways recapitulated themes from his earlier work, it offered a witty debate about the way we constitute the reality we inhabit. Two new plays were announced. The "new hope" for the American theater announced in 1959 remained a principal voice in that theater forty years later, once again surprising audiences with his wit, invention, and moral purpose. To look back from the perspective of forty years is to be struck by his integrity, his commitment to experiment, and his refusal to settle for easy popularity. If his plays register the pressures of private fears and public anxieties, if they are burdened with a knowledge of decline and decay, they are also expressions of his belief that the greatest tragedy lies in an unexamined life. The real may be problematic, an arena for debate, the site of contention, but the struggle to apprehend and engage it remains a central commitment for the individual and the theater.

5

❦

SAM SHEPARD

Edward Albee had his roots in Off-Broadway. With *Who's Afraid of Virginia Woolf?*, he moved to Broadway. Despite the deserved success of that play, it was not where he belonged. It is arguable that his work would have found a more receptive audience elsewhere. Certainly, an increasing number of writers turned not to the large-scale and increasingly expensive midtown theaters but to the Off-Broadway and Off-Off Broadway venues that sprang up, from the early 1960s onward. In a decade that privileged youth, that increasingly saw a challenge to conventional social structures, that witnessed social fragmentation along lines of race and gender, and that was defined by political and aesthetic revolt, the theater, as image and fact, seemed the natural focus of change. It was to be a theater that challenged the distinction between performer and audience, that stepped outside Cartesian logic and tapped into the unconscious as it redis-covered the expressive power of the body. Groups such as the Living Theatre, under the direction of Judith Malina and Julian Beck, and the Open Theatre, whose director was Joseph Chaikin, set themselves to explore the potential of the theater by deconstructing it into its component elements – movement, sound, the dialectics of performance. Their emphasis was on the actor. They were interested in liberating the voice, stressing physicality, generating powerful images, improvising, transgressing the supposed limits of theatrical expression. The audience they addressed was not one that attended Broadway plays. There was to be an element of risk in visiting an Off-Broadway or Off-Off Broadway theater, a threat of finding yourself incorporated into the theatrical moment or being assaulted, as in the Living Theatre's production of *The Brig* (1964), by a concatenation of sound and movement deliberately designed to intimidate and shock.

The cross-genre experiments represented by "happenings," in which visual art, dance, music, and performance had been combined, had subse-quently influenced a theater committed to the denial of boundaries of all kinds. There was an intimacy, particularly to Off-Off Broadway, consist-ing, as it did, of small performing spaces in cafés, church halls, and lofts, that became part of its methodology. The emphasis on the actor, on perfor-mance and theatricality – in a decade in which all those qualities were embraced by a culture enacting its politics and social conflicts self-consciously on the streets, in demonstrations, on television, and at rock concerts – made the theater seem a central cultural form. Writers who might once have been drawn to poetry or the novel now saw in it a route into the sense of community that was increasingly embraced as expressive of the cultural ethos of a decade of revolt, social regeneration, and utopian politics. The theater group seemed a perfect expression of the communitarian impulse so strong in a generation in rebellion against the alienation, urban angst, and vapid materialism that many saw as having characterized the previous decade. To those who inhabited a society whose increasing secularism offered little to the supposed inheritors of a nation born of a commitment to spiritual fulfillment, there seemed a sense of spiritual renewal in the self-conscious generation of theatrical ritual and ceremony. There was a great deal of naïveté and self-delusion and not a little hubris about this movement that would eventually impact against the considerable realities of the political and economic system against which it was in revolt. Other commitments would eventually lead some of its talents away from the theater or toward another definition of drama, but for the best part of ten years it fostered a number of remarkable writers, from Jean-Claude van Itallie, Lanford Wilson, Rosalyn Drexler, and Terrence McNally to Rochelle Owens, Adrienne Kennedy, Paul Foster, Megan Terry, and Maria Irene Fornes. Of all the writers whose careers were born in the small but productively empty spaces of Off-Off Broadway, however, the one who emerged as the most multitalented and impressive was Sam Shepard.

Shepard arrived in New York from California in 1963. Working as a waiter at the Village Gate, he wrote his first plays for Ralph Cook at the Theatre Genesis, at St. Mark's in-the-Bowerie. That same year, he met Joseph Chaikin and went on to attend workshops at the Open Theatre.

Shepard is a rootless man. The son of a man who moved the family from one air force base to another, he fills his plays with similarly deracinated figures. His father in particular haunts his plays, most particularly *The Curse of the Starving Classes* and *Fool for Love*. An alcoholic, and randomly violent, he had been psychologically maimed by his war service. One day, Shepard walked away from him – but what was easily accomplished physically was not so easily accomplished psychologically. The width of a continent proved insufficient. It was the need to leave his family that made him a playwright, but, as a playwright, he returned to the mystery of the family and the ambivalent passions that attract and repel the men and women who constitute it. His plays are full of corrosive families who exist in a state of constant tension, menaced by violence from without and within. For men, relationships seem a trap, a compulsion to be resisted, a snare to

be escaped by moving outside society entirely. For women, such relationships are the source of danger, their passion pulling them toward a vortex
that threatens their very being. Beneath the surface, buried in a shallow
grave, are anxieties, dark memories, a gothic abyss of psychological terror.
The world they inhabit lacks all coherence. If relationships fragment and
splinter, so, too, does the logic of social living. An early, abandoned play
had been influenced by Tennessee Williams, and it is not hard to see the
similarities. Shepard creates a series of marginal characters, restlessly wandering across a landscape with few features, inhabiting decaying houses,
motel rooms, anonymous suburban homes, remote cabins, or the bleak,
uncommunal spaces that define the lives of those he groups together in
sullen resentment and hostility.

   His early plays, however, were different. They were powerful extended
images, by no means wholly subject to rational control. He was part of the
drug culture of the sixties, which alone may explain the gnomic quality of
some of the work he did at this time. The influence of Open Theatre exercises seems equally apparent, however, in plays in which character seems
unstable and meaning is subordinate to action. The plays had the irrational, associative quality of the dream, something in common with
Kerouac's scat writing, each sentence generating the next as though it were
an improvised sequence of notes. Shepard had no background in theater,
Beckett being one of the only playwrights whose work he had read, so he
brought few preconceptions to his writing. He himself has said of *Chicago,*
which opened at Theatre Genesis in April 1965, that "the stuff would just
come out, and I wasn't really trying to shape it or make it into any big
thing. I would have a picture and just start from there." Directors and
actors confessed to bafflement in the face of his texts, responding instead to
the images and the music of the prose. Michael Smith, who directed
Icarus's Mother (1965), has explained that

the meaning of his work was never defended. It was somehow important not to
bring it up. It was uncool. Somehow, as soon as the meaning of a work was
brought up, the work would somehow dissolve, and it was going to slip away. . . .
I had that feeling for a long time and it was true of a lot of Sam's early work,
that it was very unclear about what's happening. To say that the plays don't
mean – they do – is a kind of a cop out. It was a style of the time not to be
direct about content. I don't mean it's better to be rational or obvious. But it
sort of went on various levels at the same time and it made it very hard for the
actors to figure out what they were doing.

That statement is no less revelatory of the mood of the sixties than of
Shepard's plays.

In a time of experimentation, trust was demanded of audiences; it was explored in the acting exercises of the Open Theatre. There is something to be said for an approach that asks the audience to submit to such plays without subjecting them to rational analysis. The route is directly from Shepard's subconscious to that of the individual member of the audience. As one of his characters remarks, concentrate on the road – never mind where it's going. In *Icarus's Mother,* which takes place in a park on July fourth, the energy of the play is unlocked by a series of oblique references to nuclear apocalypse, which in turn rhymes or establishes a harmonic with cataclysms on a more personal level. The recourse to the vocabulary of music, poetry, and art is not irrelevant, for these early works do find their point of reference outside the theater. Mostly one-act plays, they are offered as intense and concentrated experiences to be decoded largely at a nonrational level. *La Turista* (1967) deals, at the level of plot, with an attack of dysentary suffered by two American tourists. That skeletal structure, however, is the basis for a play in which character devolves into myth and reality slides away into the fantastic. The play ends with a character leaping, cartoonlike, through the rear wall, much as the artist Jim Dine had once jumped through his own canvas. Again, almost everyone involved confessed bewilderment as to the play's meaning but responded to its rhythms, images, and the dissociative power of a language released from the burden of sustaining either character or plot.

In a political decade, Shepard was interested in other kinds of subversion, withdrawing as screenwriter for Michelangelo Antonioni's film *Zabriskie Point* when it began to take a political direction. His radicalism was of a different order. Indeed, when he wrote *Operation Sidewinder,* in which the myths of popular culture interact with those of Native American rituals, his portrait of a group of black radicals caused offense. The play concerned an air force computer, in the shape of a huge snake, that escapes into desert country and becomes the object of a battle between the military and a band of black revolutionaries who intend to use drugs to take over the country. Instead, the snake falls into the hands of an Indian tribe, who incorporate it into their ceremonies, thereby neutralizing its destructive power. The play ends with the arrival of aliens from outer space who rescue the pure in heart. Because of protests from black students at Yale, it opened not at the Yale Repertory Theatre but at Lincoln Center. Suddenly, Shepard, a pure product of Off-Off Broadway, found himself at what was designed as a showpiece of the American theater. The play failed but is not without interest. Shepard, a drummer with a group called the Holy Modal Rounders, introduced songs, performed by that group, into the play, trying to integrate music into a work that itself staged a battle between two kinds of rhythm, the mechanical and the organic.

Then, in 1971, Shepard left America. Personal crises to do with relationships and drugs, a career that seemed momentarily stalled, and the desire to pursue his ambitions in rock music took him to England, where he stayed for three years, writing plays for the Hampstead Theatre Club and the Royal Court Theatre, revelling in actors who were not "paranoid about their technique." The two principal plays of this period are *Geography of a Horse Dreamer* and *The Tooth of Crime*. The former grew out of his new enthusiasm for greyhound racing and concerns an individual with the power to dream winners, an echo of *Melodrama Play,* in which a songwriter is under similar pressure to be successful. It is tempting to see in this a symbol of Shepard's own situation: he was expected to add to his earlier successes. *The Tooth of Crime* staged a style war, a battle between a rock star and his rival, a conflict with mythical overtones: they defend their territory like two gunfighters. Brilliantly effective, its barely suppressed violence is communicated through a language whose aggressions are compacted into images or displaced into song. Shepard has always been fascinated by mythic figures. The cowboy recurs in his work (his first play was called *Cowboys*), as do movie stars (Marlene Dietrich and Mae West are featured in *Mad Dog Blues*) and rock singers. Myth, ancient and modern, rural and urban, provides the focus; character moves from stereotype to archetype.

From the mid-1970s onward, however, he became more interested in the variousness of character, the multiple and contradictory selves locked up in the individual. British director Peter Brook reportedly advised him to engage the complexity of character more than he had in his early work and directed him to the writings of G. F. Gurdjieff. Ellen Oumano quoted a telling passage from Gurdjieff's *Meetings With Remarkable Men* that not only accords, as she points out, with the philosophy behind the Open Theatre's "transformation" exercises, in which actors would abruptly jump from one version of a character to another, but also anticipated the concerns that would dominate Shepard's imagination when, on returning to the United States, he collaborated with Joseph Chaikin on a number of performances. According to Gurdjieff, "We think if a man is called Ivan, he is always Ivan. Nothing of the kind. Now he is Ivan. In another minute he is Peter, and a minute later he is Nicholas. . . . You will be astonished when you realize what a multitude of these Ivans and Nicholases live in one man." The problem is to find meaning in a plurality of selves. So, in 1977, Shepard wrote to Chaikin, saying that he felt "like writing in a new way now" and that he had "been thinking about words emanating from many different sources in a character. Each like a different voice, without having to explain or justify their connection necessarily." His description of *Tongues* (1978), a joint project with Chaikin, seems to point directly back to Gurdjieff: "We wanted to construct a piece that had voices coming up, sort of visiting a person. The age-old idea is that a character evolves along a line, and any deviation from that has to be explained somehow. But I feel that there are many different people in one person, so why shouldn't they have a chance to come out."

In one sense, he wanted to explore the potential of language detached from its prosaic functionalism, as he had done in his early work: "I'm still obsessed with this idea that words are pictures and that even momentarily they can wrap the listener up in a visual world without having to commit themselves to revealing any other meaning. The sounds and rhythms seem to support those images and bring feeling into it." He also remained fascinated with "an attempt to find an equal expression between music and the actor . . . environments where the words and gestures are given temporary atmosphere to breath[e] in, through sound and rhythm." These concerns were then explored in a work that also introduced an element that became his subject throughout the 1980s. Thus, *Savage/Love,* the oblique stroke of whose title relates rather than separates the title's two words, investigates the contradictions of love.

Savage/Love and *Tongues* took Shepard back to the West Coast, to the newly founded Magic Theatre in San Francisco. In a decade in which regional theater took over many of the functions of Off-Broadway, he chose to launch his plays there, as David Mamet chose to stage his in Chicago and August Wilson to stage his in Minneapolis, but there was more to it than that. Increasingly, he was drawn to the West and Southwest and away from the urban alienations of the East. As writer and actor, he chose to stage relationships against a background of heartland America or West Coast myths. His career was on the verge of change.

Where once he had believed in spontaneity, he now began to revise and rewrite, to read the work of modernist writers (including, interestingly, William Faulkner), listen to Vivaldi, and star in movies *(Days of Heaven, Resurrection, Frances, Raggedy Man, The Right Stuff, Country)*. The plays that followed proved more appealing to a wider public. *Buried Child* (with echoes of Eugene O'Neill's *Desire Under the Elms* as well as Harold Pinter's *The Homecoming* and Tennessee Williams's late plays) even received the Pulitzer prize. His approach remained oblique, but he was now, perhaps following Peter Brook's advice, more directly concerned with character. He was certainly opposed to the enthusiasm for conceptual theater that had proved one of the fascinations of the 1970s, rejecting it as barren and void of meaning, insisting that if theater is to have any meaning, "it must touch people where they live, not where they think they think. True thought only comes from opening up areas of experience that ordinary thought is too dull to grasp." In *Savage/Love,* these areas had to do with love and its contradictions. Much the same could be said of the plays that followed.

Shepard's is an American landscape, but raw, stripped down. His protagonists encounter one another in a space that is psychological rather than literal. Character is provisional, fragile. Moods swing abruptly. These are neurasthenic figures, living on the edge. Their lives have focused to a sharp point. They are frequently seen in a state of shock. Writing in 1983, Shepard said that he had come to be increasingly fascinated with a sense of loss that "only makes sense . . . in relation to the idea of one's identity being shattered under severe personal circumstances. . . . I don't think it makes much difference . . . whether it's a trauma to do with a loved one or a physical accident . . . the resulting emptiness or aloneness is what interests me. Particularly to do with questions like *home? family?* . . . A Haunted state but *not* from the dead. A living ghost hunting now in the present for a life that is always escaping."

That proved an accurate description of his plays of the 1980s. There is something of the dream about them, some hidden force that presses against the surface of character. They are charged with a disturbing energy for which present actions offer inadequate explanation. Something has happened. The bullet has struck; what we witness is the second the pain registers. Sound, light, emotion are all amplified in a world in which feeling dominates thought and violence exists like static electricity ready to earth through bodies that become the expression of pure need. The past is a wound whose scar is still fresh. It is crucial not, as in Arthur Miller's work, as a key to moral being or, as in Tennessee Williams's, as an ironic comment on a degraded present, but as the source of trauma. That shock is primarily delivered through a love, destabilizing, all-consuming, that sears his characters with its heat and chills them with its cold obsessiveness. In *Fool for Love* (1983), set, like *Paris, Texas* and *True West* (and, perhaps not incidentally, like Williams's *Camino Real*), on the edge of a desert, he stages the drama of two people, Eddie and May, isolated by their setting, who find it equally impossible to live together or apart. They are like the divided parts of a single personality (true, also, of the brothers in *True West*) at war with itself. As May remarks, "I can smell your thoughts before you even think 'em." They prowl around one another like wounded animals longing for the contact which torments them.

Much the same tension is evident in *Paris, Texas,* the film he made with Wim Wenders, in which a man searches for the wife from whom his violence has separated him. The film climaxes with an extended scene in which they talk to each other from either side of a peep show's one-way mirror, which symbolizes the transparent but implacable barrier that seems to exist between so many of his characters. Indeed, seen through the glass, which acts alternately as window and mirror, the husband and wife become fantasies, by turns offering back reflections of the self and images of the other, as love both embraces the real and projects fictions, the fictions that it is the heroine's duty to enact for the lonely men who come to her for the simulation rather than the substance of sexual contact. The narcissism implicit in such reflections is underlined, in *Fool for Love* and *Buried Child,* by hints of incest. Eddie and May, in the former, are half brother and half sister, whereas the buried child is possibly a result of an incestuous relationship. Even the characters in *A Lie of the Mind* seem as much brother and sister as man and wife. The breaking of taboo serves to isolate such characters in their passion, as Quentin had sought to isolate himself with his sister Caddie in Faulkner's *The Sound and the Fury.*

The pressure of emotion finds its correlative in the play's theatricality. In *Buried Child,* the realism of the set is deformed and subverted by his approach to character and plot. In *Fool for Love,* concealed microphones in the set exaggerate sound as blinding lights are directed at the audience (an echo, perhaps, of Jean-Claude van Itallie's *America Hurrah!,* also set in a motel, in which two oversized mannequins destroy one another in a sexual frenzy and in which lights are similarly turned on the audience). Indeed, the realism is disrupted more profoundly by the presence on stage of a third figure, rather as in Harold Pinter's *Old Times.* This character is both past memory and present fact, a projection and a reality and thereby a reminder of the boundaries that the characters themselves transgress.

Fool for Love is not without its weaknesses. A fourth character, Martin, is little more than a comic stereotype, a plot device that creates a stylistic interference pattern. The real force of the play subsists in the very hermeticism that drives from their lives all other thoughts, all other feelings, all other commitments. They are trapped in a desperate ritual that seems about to return to its beginning: contact is followed by desertion and desertion will in turn give way to contact.

These are figures for whom language is inadequate, indeed somewhat beside the point. In *Buried Child,* a character had wandered into the desert and "lost" his voice. In *Paris, Texas,* the trauma of his own violence and his broken relationship with his wife sends the protagonist on a similar double journey as he walks off into the wilderness and goes spinning into aphasia. He is exiled from speech as he severs his links with the woman he both loves and victimizes, leaving society and setting out across the desert. The course of the film plots his return to society and his recovery of language, two related acts of restoration, but when he locates his wife and chooses to redeem her – reuniting her with their child – he opts for silence once again. He listens, mostly without interruption, to what is in effect an extended monologue from the woman behind the film of glass and then retreats, driving out of the city toward the desert. Everything that matters to these characters exists outside the words that can never even approximate their feelings.

In *A Lie of the Mind* (1985), whose set is to give the "impression . . . of infinite space," Beth is shocked into aphasia by a literal beating at the hands of her husband. The very force that brings them together seems to create an equal and opposite reaction. In Shepard's work, there is something almost of a scientific law about this rhythm of attraction and repulsion.

Shepard is America's poet of decline. His plays are often set in a landscape that once provided the setting for its moral tales of male endeavor – the John Ford country of the Western myth, the Hollywood of sanctioned dreams – and focuses on the family, which provides the foundation and justification of American ambition. He writes of love, but there is a countercurrent pulling in the direction of anarchy. Psychosis presses myth toward parody. Violence is not the purifying weapon of ethical consciousness or the punctuation of national advancement, nor is love a redeeming sentimentality. His is a world in which repressions are removed, a world in which character is at war with itself and language retains a fragile hold on experience. His characters are borderline in a number of respects. They are often described as living on the edge of desert country. They exist at the extreme edge of society, like Tennessee Williams's spiritual vagrants, and they tread the boundary of insanity. Their own self-definition is insecure. On one level he seems to offer a vision of America that he once described as "cracking open," a world of alienated individuals and discarded images. The nervous energy of urban living shades into paranoia as sexuality is denatured into pornography. Beyond that, however, lies a model of the self and its incompletions, a space at the core of identity that may be filled with love or with violence, both of which seem to stem from the same source. Estrangement is the condition of being, abandonment a natural impulse, yet it is precisely the paradox whereby we desert what we value, contaminate love with jealousy, alienate ourselves from our inner needs, and betray at the level of language what we would embrace at the level of emotion that fascinates him. He listens for the assonance within dissonance, tries to detect a harmony within the apparent discord. If that hints at a potential sentimentality, then it is not hard to see that sentimentality in the ending of *A Fool for Love, Paris, Texas,* or even *A Lie of the Mind,* the first concluding as we hear Merle

Haggard's "I'm the One Who Loves You" playing in the darkness, the second with the reuniting of mother and child, and the last with a reference to "fire in the snow." In each case, however, the consonance is shot through with, but not wholly defined by, irony. Some hint of harmony is also present in the music that accompanies many of his plays and offers to close the spaces opened up by plot and character.

In his early work he had been interested in fragmentation, as social fact and aesthetic principle. His plays were brief, a series of images or actions that staged lives lived as performed gestures. Later, that fragmentation began to seem the root of a modern malaise, an estrangement evident in social behavior and personal relationships alike. By 1988, he was regretting the fact of individuals' alienation from one another, from their setting, and from themselves. Now he looks for some kind of consonance. The urgency of that seems to have left him with the compulsion not only to stage the anarchy that he detects but to seek behind it what he has called "a story that's already been told." In other words, he has increasingly looked for archetypal shapes in a modern formlessness, sought to establish some sense of continuity in a discontinuous experience. He becomes the romantic, offering the grace of art to stabilize the anarchy of history and personal psychology alike.

Fool for Love and *A Lie of the Mind* are about an obsessive passion that isolates his characters, who become mirror images of one another (in *A Lie of the Mind,* they do so almost literally – Beth and Jake assume stances that, a note tells us, are "almost identical"). On one level, they cannot escape the society of their family, any more than they can the language that is an expression of a shared situation, but their lives eventually narrow to that *egotism à deux* of love, an autism in which passion isolates them, a monomania or a psychosis that deforms them. It is indeed difficult to describe such characters without recourse to the language of madness, for, on another level, his portraits of men and women, so like one another, so different, fused together by passion, pulled apart by differing needs, offer a schizophrenic model of the self, part male, part female, an androgyny that leaves the self divided against itself. His characters meet as strangers. In *Buried Child,* members of the family no longer recognize one another.

He has said that in his plays he is looking for "the invisible part of things." Memories become present realities; suppressed feelings crystalize into action. Certainly his sets, sometimes apparently solidly realistic, sometimes no more than impressionistic gestures, represent the surface he wishes to crack open. His is a world in which the earthquake has already happened; his characters have to live within the tangled wreckage, the broken structures, the aftershocks. The nuclear apocalypse of *Icarus's Mother* is later reflected as personal cataclysm, a violence that he sees as "the main source of tragedy . . . an incredibly hopeless pit we can't seem to escape from." The world he chooses to inhabit is an interior one in which dream, fantasy, and myth form an inner landscape. Like Eugene O'Neill, whom he admires, he allows the disordered self to project its environment; like Beckett, he stages a drama in which that self is the origin of its own pain. These are also plays in which the passion that proves so mutually destructive lifts his characters out of the grayness of simple existence, however. They live with an intensity that is literally unbearable, but it is this that gives his plays their disturbing force. If he cuts deep through the sensibility and psychology of the individual, he performs similar surgery on a culture built from a passionate idea, whose history he sees as stained with violence and whose present is characterized by an alienation neutralized by synthetic myths. Sam Shepard is virtually the only American playwright who has succeeded in carrying forward from the 1960s a concern with the irrational and the power of the image, a commitment to exploring analogies with music and art, with disassembling character and language, and who has continued to forge from those elements compelling drama.

❧

In the 1990s, Shepard's interest seemed to shift somewhat from male–female relationships to that between men, whether it was the baffled couple in his film *Far North,* aware of their redundancy because a shift in the system of power that has left them stranded, or the surreal pair in *States of Shock,* Shepard's response to the Gulf War, who are traumatized, by turns truculent and bewildered. In *Simpatico,* likewise, first staged in 1995, he explores the relationship between two men, yoked together by crime, yet hostile to one another, a mock marriage in which, as in *True West,* the men eventually exchange roles and identities.

States of Shock, first produced by the American Place Theatre in 1991, is set in a café. A man and woman sit, like Duane Hanson figures, witnesses to an unfolding drama from which they detach themselves, their self-absorption being reflected in a masturbatory gesture. Patently rich, but pallid "like cadavers," they watch as the Colonel, dressed in a strange outfit consisting of scraps of military uniforms from past wars and different services, wheels in Stubbs, a former soldier now confined to a wheelchair, "mutilated" in the way that a figure in *Far North* claimed to be "born injured," a state common enough to Shepard characters. In the course of the play, these two reenact the moment of Stubbs's wounding, largely oblivious to the domestic routine of the café. Meaning, for them, lies in the existence of an enemy who gives them purpose and at least the appearance of solidarity, simultaneously threatening their very survival.

Explosions punctuate the action as the waitress and her other two customers struggle to maintain a sense of normality, though their normality is
itself bizarre. The Colonel and Stubbs, meanwhile, may well be father and
son, and the play ends as the latter raises a sword to strike the former.

The title *States of Shock* accurately describes the condition of the central
characters, as it does virtually all Shepard characters, whose traumas lie
somewhere back in the past. It also seems to hint at Shepard's own anger at
America, whose latest war precipitated the play. Stubbs suffers a patent
sense of loss, but then so do the other characters, loss being, ironically, the
thing that unites Shepard's characters. This is an empty world in which
routine and violence coexist and the generations bequeath one another a
dubious heritage.

In *Simpatico,* women once again exist on the margin of a relationship
between two men. They drift in and out of their lives, but the men are tied
to one another more securely than they are to any women. Involved in the
past in racecourse scams, Carter and Vinnie had framed a commissioner of
racing with incriminating photographs. They themselves, however, were
forced to take steps to escape detection. Carter has subsequently become
rich and pays his fellow conspirator to change his name and keep on the
move. Vinnie now decides to take his revenge and, in the course of the
play, the two exchange roles, though, as in *True West,* it seems they may be
no more than two extremes of the same sensibility.

Though *Simpatico* is set in places that are real enough, strung out along
the San Bernadino Freeway in California, it opens in a cheap apartment
that looks out onto blank space, with no trees, no buildings, and no landscape. There is something primal about the contest between the two men,
a contest that may take place in an identifiable America, which has
betrayed its values and its past, but that is also located in a more timeless,
less precisely located context. The blank desert is never far away in
Shepard's work. Sometimes it is the desert of American myth, sometimes
the featureless sand of Samuel Beckett against which characters enact dramas that expose truths about the disproportion between human needs and
human satisfactions. Where Beckett's humor is merely ironic, however,
generated at the expense of characters who fail to understand that they are
the butt of a cosmic joke, in Shepard's plays the humor is often consciously
deployed by characters for whom such ironies are recognized for what they
are. They, too, persist with hope when the grounds for hope seem to have
disappeared, but they play their hand for what it is, and redemption, often
in unlikely forms, remains a possibility.

Shepard is drawn to the myths he exposes. He creates blank spaces and
fills them with movement, identifies loss and offers momentary consola-

tion. Relationships, in his work, may be broken, assurances denied, confidences betrayed, but there are still values to be acknowledged and necessities to be served. Men and women may simultaneously be drawn together and thrust apart, the bond between men may easily be broken, but the need for relationship frequently transcends the knowledge of such failures, such fractures in experience. Out beyond the window is the desert, the blank face of an unknown and unknowable world, but in the temporary refuge of a motel room, in the passing contact of solitary selves, Shepard is as prone to acknowledge a momentary epiphany as was Tennessee Williams. Like García Lorca, on whose work Shepard was raised, he sees passion as flecked with blood, but like García Lorca, he acknowledges that it is not, therefore, rendered without meaning.

6

❦

DAVID MAMET

AVID Mamet is no less fascinated by personal and national psychosis than Sam Shepard. His America also is cracking apart. Like Shepard, he is drawn to a male world of encoded violence and stresses the all but unbridgeable gulf between the sexes. He, too, is fascinated by myths that have collapsed into fantasy, finds in Hollywood a paradigm of tainted dreams, and offers bleak portraits of American alienation. Like Shepard, he peoples his stage with urban cowboys and dramatizes the collapse of language in the face of experience. *Sexual Perversity in Chicago* has something of the brittle energy of *The Tooth of Crime; The Woods* offers a requiem for love not very different in spirit from *Fool for Love.* Mamet's characters, like Shepard's, inhabit a burned-over land in which the past exists only as buried fragments, echoes of half-forgotten myths. Shepard's *True West,* in which two brothers trash their mother's home, is echoed in Mamet's *American Buffalo,* in which a character trashes a junk store. The peep show in *Paris, Texas* is reminiscent of that in *Edmond.* There are also clear differences, however.

There is, behind Mamet's *American Buffalo* and *Glengarry Glen Ross,* a consistent critique of American values, of a promise that has become the basis of betrayal, of a spirit of enterprise that has degraded in the direction of crime. History exists and is invoked but has no functional value. Something has disrupted a moral continuity. His America, once invented by a gentleman farmer, is now reinvented by petty criminals *(American Buffalo),* depressives *(Edmond),* and confidence tricksters *(Glengarry Glen Ross* and *The Shawl).* The brutalism of the language his characters speak reflects that of the lives they live and the world they inhabit, yet it is also a defensive screen thrown up to hide their genuine needs. The stories these characters tell and the myths they embrace serve much the same function. Mamet, indeed, is fascinated with storytelling, sometimes a positive function – as fears are contained and anarchy is refashioned as order – and sometimes a mechanism of deceit. The theater itself was to be a means of exploring the collapse of community and a mechanism for recuperating community.

Critics have suggested that Mamet writes plotless plays, but, in fact, he dramatizes the lives of plotless people. They live in the moment. The spine has been removed from their culture. It is in a state of collapse. In *American Buffalo*, police cars circle the block; in *Edmond*, the protagonist moves from peep show to brothel; in *Sexual Perversity in Chicago*, men and women deploy the degraded language of pornography as they brush against one another like the strangers they are. Somehow, though, behind the dislocations and dysfunctions, behind an aggressive language that seems to deny the possibility of intimacy, there is a surviving instinct for trust, a desire to reach out toward those strangers, which may be the source of vulnerability and the agency of betrayal but is also evidence of a vestigial humanity. The rhetoric of his character is a jumble of American pieties and obscenities – the former an echo of past ironies, the latter an expression of a degraded present – but there are moments when that language shapes itself into a kind of consonance, when the characters combine to generate stories, to restage their lives as drama, to suggest a level at which need may find its free articulation. There is a suggestion that the alienations generated by social decline and moral decay may be neutralized by an imagination still capable of redeeming a degraded reality.

David Mamet has said that the "simple magic of the theatre rests in the nature of human perception – that we all want to hear stories. And those stories we like the best are those told the most simply." It is an observation that explains much of his work, from the deceptively simple fable of *Dark Pony* to the spontaneous inventiveness of the confidence tricksters in *Glengarry Glen Ross*, *The Shawl*, and *House of Games*, who, knowing the compelling need for story, make it the agent of their power. Mamet writes about the theater in his essays, and his characters are frequently self-conscious performers – directly so in *A Life in the Theatre*, but no less convincingly in *Glengarry Glen Ross*, in which a group of salesmen stage plays for their clients and weave their commercial imperatives into narratives. These have a simplicity that comes from the need for reassurance that is built into story, from the fairy tale to the elaborate fictions of Dickens. As with fairy tales, though, or with Dickens, there are shadows that potentially poison that consolation. Such ambivalence has always intrigued him.

David Mamet is fascinated with the processes of theater. He has taught actors; in his work, he explores the implications of the theatrical imagination. Many of the things he says about theater in his essays are equally applicable to the world with which it has an ambiguous relationship. Speaking of realism as a concern with "minutiae as revelatory of truth," he observes that in our own time we have "sickened of the Material" and need "to deal with things of the Spirit." We must, he insists, "lay aside our boring and fruitless pursuit of the superficial and dedicate ourselves to Action, which is to say to Will as the expression, as it is, of the Spirit." His plays turn on precisely this conviction, which amounts to a social and moral imperative rather than simply a piece of theatrical advice. As for the actor, he or she needs "to *elect* and to do what we elect to do." Just so, he reminds us, Stanislavski once wrote that the actor should "play well or play badly, but play truly" in pursuit of "discipline" and simplicity. In the context of his observation that "our society has fallen apart and *nobody* knows what he or she should be doing," no wonder the theater appears in his work as the source of redemption as well as of deceit.

Perhaps curiously, his own taste in novelists runs to Theodore Dreiser, Sinclair Lewis, and Willa Cather, who might be thought to have had the realist's concern for detail, but all three were writers who set out not merely to catalog an external reality but also to find a correlative for social process. Thus, Cather's narrative strategy mimicked the making of one America and the unmaking of another, whereas Dreiser and Lewis found in the businessman and the salesman an image of an America investing in the material and disinvesting in the spiritual. It is in this sense that Mamet sees himself as a realist, like the actor who seeks not the "reducible and copyable" but a "realistic vision," a phrase that instructively yokes together style and image. Indeed, he defines realism as that which "responds to some of our *preconscious* views of the world." In other words, it touches on a truth felt on the pulse before it makes its way into a language that may deny that instinctive knowledge.

When he speaks of the corruption implicit in a theater "which misuses the audience's trust in order to gain money," he could be describing the action of the salesmen and confidence tricksters he presents from *American Buffalo, The Shawl,* and *House of Games* to *Glengarry Glen Ross.* Trust offered, trust demanded, trust betrayed proves the fundamental theme of his work, yet even the manipulators believe in the reality of the need that generates that desire for trust. Beneath the evidence of an attenuated moral and physical world, below the tangle of deceit and the cluttering detritus of a material existence that has seemingly traded any idea of transcendence for immediate satisfaction or consoling fictions, there are human realities whose survival he celebrates and without which his work would be drained of irony.

Mamet's plays tend to focus on men. There are no women in *Duck Variations, American Buffalo, Lakeboat, A Life in the Theatre,* or *Glengarry Glen Ross.* In his essays he has written about a number of predominantly male activities, from poker playing to pistol shooting, and the sheer pleasure of male comradeship. The episode of the television series *Hill Street*

Blues that he wrote included only two women, one bringing a false charge of rape, the other offering an ineffective criticism of the all-male hunting party around which the action turns (and that admittedly collapses into parody). The myths he explores are themselves essentially male. The salesmen in *American Buffalo* and *Glengarry Glen Ross* are urban frontiersmen, enacting rituals and deploying the language of a society that once chose to see its own making as coeval with the unfolding of a male identity. His salesmen are the descendents of Daniel Boone; his petty criminals, of Jessie James. They speak the half-remembered and now degraded language of Manifest Destiny, frontier individualism, American idealism, and the male existentialism that had defined the self in terms of an encounter with nature. This is a world in which language has detached itself from its referents. The obscenities his characters utter take the language of physical intimacy and turn it into aggression in a world in which genuine sexual intimacy is rare. Men and women in his plays encounter one another out of different needs, express themselves in a different language, need one another in a way that their social lives seem to have incapacitated them to understand. When he does address that relationship directly, in *Sexual Perversity in Chicago* and *The Woods,* it is to confess to a gap in perception, needs, and language that is either unbridgeable, as in the former, or bridged only within the fictions that men and women agree to give the force of reality.

Mamet is a Chicago writer. He lists his own play *Sexual Perversity in Chicago* in a catalog of Chicago works that includes *The Pit, Sister Carrie, An American Tragedy,* and *The Man with the Golden Arm,* all of which are written, he claims, by authors who see the city as "a manifestation of him or herself." Certainly his dissonant cities reflect the dislocated characters who inhabit them, but where in those other works they had existed as the source of a certain implacable power to which the individual was drawn, now they are no more than the origin of a random energy generated out of dissolution: Chicago is represented by the alienated rhythms of the singles bar and a downtown junk store, and New York, by a careless violence and the seedy trappings of sexuality institutionalized as pornography.

❧

The first of Mamet's plays to achieve public attention was the provocatively but appropriately named *Sexual Perversity in Chicago.* That perversity does not subsist in the dramatization of obscure sexual practices. It lies in what has become of sexuality in a late twentieth-century America frozen in the callow attitudes of adolescence. Men and women speak the language of a frank physicality but in fact stare at one another across a void and displace into fantasy the sexual encounters they dramatize to themselves as battles for dominance.

Bernie Litko regards himself as having a black belt in sexual relationships. A natural product of a city which had given the world *Playboy* magazine, with its suggestion that women are readily available, his values are rooted in the metonymic fantasies of pornography. He acts as teacher to Danny, an "urban male," and together they attempt to pick up two women in a singles bar, women who are as alienated from themselves and the opposite sex as are the men. What is missing from their world is any intimacy, any shared perception of the possibilities generated by relationship. The denatured language they speak shapes their values. Contact is momentary, self-consuming. The play's structure – it consists of a series of short scenes – is partly a product of the revue style to which Mamet had been exposed while working at Chicago's Second City but partly a reflection of the discontinuous lives his characters live and the fragmented identities they deploy. When Danny finds himself in a real relationship with a woman, he has no idea how to conduct himself, no sense of how sexuality might be related to other experiences. The leftover language of 1960s liberation leaves his characters stranded on the beach as the tide of true relationships and true community retreats ever further.

Sexual Perversity in Chicago is brilliantly funny and scatological. Once called a "disco dance of death," it enacts a Strindbergian sexual battle against the fast-paced rhythms of a society in which the logic of capitalism – possession and consumption – is extended to personal relationships. The very seductiveness of those rhythms, however, implicates the audience, which responds to the sheer energy of a play that mimicks the urban style that is its subject.

David Mamet appeared on the scene when American drama seemed to have taken an inside track. The barricades of the 1960s had been dismantled. Writers were drawn to private anxieties, to a concern with that isolation forced by illness or disability – stroke, blindness, deformity, cancer – in such plays as Arthur Kopit's *Wings,* Mark Medoff's *Children of a Lesser God,* Bernard Pomerance's *The Elephant Man,* and Michael Cristofer's *The Shadow Box.* Edward Albee's plays had taken an increasingly inward direction, while the avant-garde was exploring the nature of consciousness (Robert Wilson, Richard Foreman, Lee Breuer) and the monologue (Spalding Gray). Even Sam Shepard had abstracted his characters from the social world.

By contrast, Mamet offers himself as a social critic, if scarcely only that, and writes essays full of the language of liberal responsibility. His metaphors of urban alienation suggest a betrayal of values that lies further back than the birth of the city. A culture that made a virtue of its dispossession of the Native American and the rapacity of individuals unleashed to subdue nature, a process cloaked in the language of moral enterprise, has left a doubtful heritage. Thus, *American Buffalo* turns on Veblen's analogy between business and crime, as later did *Glengarry Glen Ross*. Mamet's characters take entirely seriously what they see as the basis of American enterprise. The ironies of history invade *American Buffalo* at every level. The junk store, which is its setting, implies a naturalism that is finally beside the point. Its true force is metaphorical: it is shaped by Mamet into a powerful image of history reduced to rummage sale and a present that subsists in secondhand language and values. The various bits and pieces that fill Don Dubrow's secondhand store are not simply the discarded remnants of a generalized history, however; they date from a precise moment. Along with a pigsticker, a device to hold pigs' legs open while the blood drains out (a reminder of Chicago's past and, incidentally, a harbinger of the violence to come) are the trinkets from Chicago's Century of Progress Exposition of 1933. Irony nestles in irony. The celebration of American progress four years into a crippling depression already suggested the failure of a particular model of progress. The distance between that moment of civic pride and a degraded present is a mark of still further decline. The nineteenth-century association of history with progress is thus reversed. Now the culture of enterprise can be adequately represented by a group of petty criminals planning a robbery that they lack the will, the ability, and the courage to carry out.

When a customer pays an excessive price for a buffalo-headed nickel, they assume that he has taken advantage of them as they would wish to have taken advantage of him. Even the reference to buffalo carries an echo of history insofar as they now arm themselves to pursue the buffalo quite as though they were the legitimate descendents of those frontiersmen for whom nation-building was simultaneously an act of faith. Mamet's social critique, in other words, extends back in time as the mutual suspicions generated by greed result in a violence entirely familiar from America's past. The difference is that the frontier has closed. The open plains have shrunk to this cluttered room in a run-down junk store. Masculine independence has withered into a crazed mysogyny and the language of American liberalism has been so hollowed out by time as to be merely ironic when it is not meaningless.

There is no action in *American Buffalo,* if we mean that the characters fail to act, in the sense of accomplishing their objective. That, however, *is* the action. These are characters living their lives without a plot, as ironized by their failure to fulfill the action they plan, as Vladimir and

Estragon in Beckett's *Waiting for Godot,* where the injunction "Let's go" comes up against the implacability of a stage direction that says, *"They do not move."* There is, though, another sense in which they do act. They play the roles of the fearless thieves they wish to see themselves as being. They invest their sense of self in performance quite as much as do Tennessee Williams's characters. They are never so active as when they mutually perform their fantasies or shape their paranoia. Like Eugene O'Neill's derelicts in *The Iceman Cometh,* however, they can sustain their roles only so long as they are not tested in a world of reality.

In other words, those critics who saw in *American Buffalo* a glimpse into the lives of the underclass and who praised or attacked it for the accuracy of its scatological language and its expressive staging missed the point, as they did when they lamented the lack of specific action. Although Mamet admires the naturalists, that kind of detailed accuracy is not the primary function of his theater. What he offers is a metaphor for America's failed promises, a critique of a system that deployed language as cover for rapacity and greed. His characters have no inner resources. They are performers. There is no tension between the self and its moral, linguistic, and social environment. All are in a state of disrepair. They use the vocabulary of friendship, teamwork, moral enterprise, and liberal endeavor but betray the meaning of the words they speak at the moment of utterance. Some force that used to maintain the social world has gone, as has the power that sustained the grammatic structure, the syntactical logic of speech, and this collapse reminds us that Mamet is not simply a social dramatist. Though the cityscapes of his plays are identifiably American, the dislocations that he stages, the space that has opened up between the self and its social projections, hints at a more profound level of absurdity than the merely social.

A few years later, he returned to the 1933 Exhibition in *The Water Engine.* Originally commissioned as a radio play, it in part mimics a 1930s radio melodrama, staging the story of a man who invents an engine that runs on water. The villains are the capitalists who see this as destroying their profits. They first try to buy and suppress the engine and finally resort to simple murder, but not before the secret has been passed on. This parable of commercial venality is interfused with other rhetorics: the voice of a chain letter promising wealth and threatening vengeance: that of a public orator commenting on the collapse of the American ideal. In *The Water Engine,* fictions collide, creating ironies and disturbing their own coherences. The very neatness of the melodrama is a clue to its falsity, just as the slogan "A century of progress" invites a skepticism born of its own rhetorical pretension. The figures who perform the radio play in front of microphones are themselves, of course, contained within the frame of

Mamet's play, and inevitably, this metatheatricality draws attention to the factitious nature of theater, which itself offers to present truth through deception, a notion explored directly in *A Life in the Theatre* and indirectly in *Glengarry Glen Ross.*

A Life in the Theatre brings together two actors, one established and even, perhaps, over the hill, the other brash, on the rise. These are people who perform not simply in the series of plays that they enact, however, plays that parody different writers and genres, but in the life they live outside the theater. To act is to replace one mask with another. They are as concerned about their "authenticity" in the one role as in the other. The play ends as they perform themselves in an empty auditorium, rather as do the characters in Tennessee Williams's *Outcry* and with much the same Becketian overtones. Just as actors' lies have to be presented with total authenticity if they are to believe in their own truth, so it is, too, in the wider theater of public life.

Dark Pony, Duck Variations, A Life in the Theatre, The Woods, and *Oleanna* each consist of two characters. *Sexual Perversity in Chicago, American Buffalo, Lakeboat, Glengarry Glen Ross,* and *Speed-the-Plow* for much of the time focus on two people in conversation. *Speed-the-Plow* and *American Buffalo* have only three characters; *Sexual Perversity,* four. It is as though this were the critical mass. Theater comes into being at the moment there is a speaker and a listener, a storyteller and an audience, and there is a sense that at the heart of all his plays is a concern with the stories we tell ourselves and other people. The void between two people proves extraordinarily difficult to cross, however. Even in their fictions, they have difficulty in sharing. So, in *The Woods,* the woman invokes an imagery of completion and commitment, the man an imagery of discontinuity and freedom. In *Dark Pony,* a father tells his daughter a fairy story that is designed to calm and annihilate anxieties but into which intrude his own insecurities. Sometimes, though, story is the one place where his characters do connect. In *Glengarry Glen Ross,* a group of real estate salesmen effect their sales by providing a fictive structure in which a mere house becomes a solution to needs that go deeper than that for shelter. The irony is that, for all their cynicism, they are most alive in their own performances, most perceptive about human need when they construct the fictions designed to capitalize on that need.

Glengarry Glen Ross is the most accomplished play of an accomplished writer. On one level, it looks back to *American Buffalo.* Once again, a link is established between business and crime. This time, the robbery actually takes place: a real estate agent steals the addresses of potential clients in order to secure his own job. Here, however, the indictment is, if anything, more direct, as the salesmen's employers establish a competition that neatly summarizes the peremptory ethics of capitalism. The one who sells most properties wins a Cadillac; the runner-up, a set of cutlery. The loser is fired. Mamet's interest, though, lies elsewhere, in the confidence trickster salesmen, descendents of Melville's confidence man, who, for all their deceits, are Protean as they become hucksters for the very security they themselves so desperately seek, traders in a human commodity market holding out to others the very gleaming possibilities that motivate them. They seek to ensnare their customers in language but are no less its victims themselves, one of them accusing his supposed friend of complicity because he "listened." There is a further irony, however, in that in order to succeed as salesmen they have to understand those they would deceive. They become hypersensitive, like the confidence trickster in *The Shawl* who masquerades as a psychic and who is convincing precisely because he is aware of the desperation, the fear, and the need that drive his client into his hands. In a way, that shared knowledge begins to provide what that client yearns for, which is something in which to believe. In an apparent contradiction, those who can best connect two isolated people are those who deploy the falsities of fiction. The salesmen in *Glengarry Glen Ross* and the psychic in *The Shawl* are indicted for their deceptions, deceptions of which they, too, are victims, but embraced for their awareness of a surviving need for trust and connection and admired for the performances generated out of their own desperation. Mamet's theater does no less, for it is in those fictions that we meet.

Mamet has brought to the American theater a demotic prose that he refashions into aphasic arias of affecting power. The scatological language that his characters speak is the linguistic detritus of reified lives, while those lives are presented as the product of a society that has traded values for hard cash. At the heart of his work are a series of metaphors – a dark pony, an American Buffalo, a water engine, a lake boat, the theater – that the plays themselves elaborate. He writes with a comic energy, but his characters have no access to humor. They remain unaware of the ironies generated by the discrepancy between their language of self-sufficient enterprise and a reality that is diminished and diminishing. Mamet, however, is not Beckett. At the heart of his plays is a will to connect that is seldom completely negated by the exploitative instincts of characters who have too completely absorbed the values of their society. He writes plays whose comic effect relies on the survival outside his drama of the moral discriminations that inside are shriveling to a nullity. Mamet, as much as Miller, is a moralist. He is something of a civics teacher, invoking the high hopes of the Great Experiment if only as a means to stage the betrayal of those hopes. He is also, however, himself a confidence trickster, exposing the fantasies and manipulative tactics of his characters in dramatic fictions that respond to that very need for story, coherence, and mutual trust that gives them such power. He is an actor who admires other actors, a playwright who responds to the fictive skills even of those who spin their stories only as a web in which to capture their victims.

Both *Speed-the-Plow* (1987) and *Oleanna* (1993) were concerned, at some level, with a recurrent subject in Mamet's work: power. In both plays, that power is intertwined with sexuality: in the former, in the context of a comic look at a Hollywood in which the language of idealism comes up against the reality of exploitation; in the latter, in the context of a serious clash of values, of differing perceptions of the real.

Oleanna was seen at first as purely a response to the then current debate over political correctness. A young woman student comes to see her professor because she fails to understand his classes and feels inferior. He is preoccupied with his own affairs – the purchase of a house, a strained marriage. She seems barely in control of her language, adrift in a world in which she is out of place. He offers her perfunctory advice and an apparently consoling hand on her shoulder. In the second act, she is transformed. Her language is now that of political correctness. She invokes a group to which she belongs and that has plainly offered her an interpretation of her situation and of her relationship to her professor. She now brings charges of sexual harassment against him that, as the play continues, slowly wreck his career and marriage until, in a final act of anger, he strikes her, thus validating the very charges he has been resisting.

It is hard not to feel that Mamet's thumb is securely on the scales. The professor can legitimately be accused of callousness and indifference and the audience is forced to reassess his gesture in offering an apparently consoling arm, but the student is so plainly captured by the language she uses, so irrational in her apparently determined rationality, so vindictive as she systematically destroys a man who, if guilty, is guilty of nothing more serious than self-absorption and professional inadequacy, that sympathy shifts to the man who is now securely caught in a web, his struggles merely snaring him more securely. What interests Mamet, however, is not the rights and wrongs of this clash but the mechanisms of power, the manner in which language creates reality, defines relationships, shapes our perception of experience. There is no escape in side-stepping words, for his final gesture of violence follows his linguistic exhaustion. The irony of that ending lies not simply in his springing her final trap but in the degree to which the damage has already been done, the extent to which language itself is not merely an expression of power: it is power itself. We are spoken by the words we use.

Mamet followed *Oleanna* with *The Cryptogram* (1995), a play in which he explored his own past. A young boy watches, uncomprehendingly, as the relationship of those around him changes, a shifting code that he cannot read, a dilemma in which the audience is equally implicated.

Mamet's power in the theater lies in the language that he manifestly invents rather than transcribes (critics, at first, were inclined to praise him for the realism of his dialogue), a language whose fragmented nature is a reflection of characters only barely in touch with themselves and the world they inhabit. It lies in his fascination with power, which sometimes finds a correlative in a violence more imminent that actual, in his creation of compelling metaphors for a society in which the language of idealism comes back as a faint echo from the broken buildings and broken dreams of a world unmaking itself. It lies in his exploration of the relationship between men and women, who seem to inhabit separate, if parallel, universes, and in his fascination with the relationship between men, who are constantly suspicious of one another yet drawn together like figures around a fire. It lies in his sense of the deceits and betrayals of virtually all his characters but the simultaneous belief that such betrayals can exist only because of a persistent need for relationships, for something in which to believe. Indeed, at some deeper level, I suspect, there is in his work a growing fascination with the subject of faith itself. His film *Homicide* is the most direct expression of this, though even here a final twist ironizes this search for belief, as though he cannot finally – or as yet – bring himself to acknowledge the seriousness of his own commitment.

7

❦

CHANGING AMERICA:
A CHANGING DRAMA?

I N THE 1960s, change was an imperative. Signaled politically by a generational shift, it was reflected socially in an economically empowered
youth movement whose spending power began to shape popular culture.
The civil rights movement, kick-started in the late 1950s, now became the
principal domestic issue, while the Vietnam War provoked a resistance that
politicized a generation. Authority was challenged; formal structures were
questioned. Politics became street theater, a series of publicly enacted gestures. Individuals underlined the integrity of their beliefs by physical presence and dramatized their faith by offering to levitate the Pentagon or place
their bodies in front of munition trains as a symbol of the body's vulnerability to the military machine as well as a pragmatic strategy of resistance. The
body, indeed, became an expressive force, sexually liberated by the birth control pill, publicly deployed as a provocation to a society presumed to be
simultaneously puritanical, materialistic, and aggressively technological.
This was life lived metaphorically, and, perhaps logically, the theater, which
deploys the body as a primary instrument of signification and works through
metaphor, became a focus and means of revolt.

For those committed to transformation – personal, social, political –
where more natural to turn than to a form in which transformation was of
the essence? In an age of performed gestures and specially staged events,
the theater had a persuasive symbolic force. In a period in which the slave
was shown transmuting into the rebel, the self being reborn, and history
being restaged as paranoid vision, the theater seemed to offer itself as paradigm. Certainly sociologists (most notably Erving Goffman) and literary
critics (particularly Richard Poirier) found in it a persuasive model of
social action. When the Odeon Theatre in Paris proved the center of revolt
in 1968, it merely seemed a confirmation of theater's central significance.

Transformations, however, took different forms. The Living Theatre, the
Open Theatre and the Performance Group set out to investigate the nature
of theatricality. Language, movement, and sound were explored and the
authority first of the writer and then of the director was challenged. The

Living Theatre's commitment to modernism in the 1950s, a concern that had already manifested itself in a fascination with such metatheatrical works as Luigi Pirandello's *Tonight We Improvise,* led to Jack Gelber's Pirandello-like *The Connection* in 1959, and Kenneth Brown's more radical *The Brig* in 1964. The latter showed the impact of Antonin Artaud's *The Theatre and Its Double,* which had appeared in translation for the first time in 1958. This challenged the primacy of language; stressed the significance of movement, sound, and spectacle; denounced the tyranny of dramatic tradition; and resisted the coercive power of the writer. In subsequent works, therefore, the Living Theatre chose to break open the texts they used, legitimize the personality of the actor, and seek, in the generation of powerful stage images and a renewed physicality, a visceral response from audiences. The body was unclothed as an image of the liberation it proposed as theatrical means and social ends. Politicized by Vietnam, the theater's members spilled onto the streets, provoking the reaction they sought to expose. At heart pacifist anarchists, they nonetheless developed a theatrical approach that could be aggressively dogmatic; their revolts took an increasingly programmatic form. Nonetheless, there was, for a brief moment, a symbiosis between experiments generated out of a commitment to theater and commitments generated out of social experiments. If the Living Theatre was ultimately overtaken by the change it had sought to provoke, this is perhaps a testament to its credentials as a handmaiden of change.

Joseph Chaikin's Open Theatre was also committed to transformation, but Chaikin's emphasis was more directly on the development of acting skills. One of those exercises, indeed, was specifically to do with transformation: actors switched abruptly from one character to another, a technique put to use in Jean-Claude van Itallie's *America Hurrah!* Where the Living Theatre turned to the plenitude advocated by Antonin Artaud, however, Chaikin preferred the aestheticism of Jerzy Grotowsky, whose concept of a poor theater combined a strict discipline with a commitment to theater as ritual. Though Chaikin lacked Julian Beck and Judith Malina's political beliefs, the Open Theatre, too, was changed by the Vietnam War, producing Megan Terry's *Viet Rock.* Lacking the Living Theatre's suspicion of the writer, it welcomed the collaboration of playwrights who worked with actors to create texts.

Richard Schechner's Performance Group was an altogether more brash affair. Having cofounded the Free Southern Theatre, which had taken drama to poor black communities in the South, he scarcely needed Vietnam to politicize him, but it did serve to give a social edge to the works that he chose to stage. Thus, a play such as *Dionysus in 69,* which showed the same fascination with nudity expressed by the Living Theatre, that same care to erode the barriers between audience and performer that was an implicit claim to a continuity between the theatrical and the social stage, was in essence a debate about the legitimacy and nature of power. Everything was suddenly in the public arena.

In later years, the cinema was to become obsessed with the morally corrosive effects of the war and did address it obliquely throughout the 1970s, but the theater also responded quickly. Not only did the war, as we have seen, transform those groups whose commitment had initially been to more purely theatrical concerns but it prompted a number of plays, from Megan Terry's *Viet Rock* and David Rabe's *Sticks and Bones* to Toby Cole's *The Medal of Honor Rag* and Lanford Wilson's *The Fifth of July*. Rabe, in particular, recreated the moral half-light of the war in a play in which nightmare erupts through the bland surface of an America hooked on life as soap opera, its style replicating the collision of two worlds, two modes of experience.

Vietnam continued to haunt Rabe. It is at the center of *Sticks and Bones* (1971), *The Basic Training of Pavlo Hummel* (1971), *The Orphan* (1973), and *Streamers* (1976), but the violence that flickers in those plays – verbal and physical – is no less apparent in *In the Boom Boom Room* (1973), in which a woman struggles to receive some recognition of herself in a world that offers her little but a reductive role.

America, then, was remaking itself in the 1960s and nowhere more obviously than in its redefinition of ethnic identity. A resurgent civil rights movement pressed for full integration, the abolition of restrictive laws, and the full enfranchisement of all citizens. In 1959, Lorraine Hansberry's *A Raisin in the Sun* perfectly caught that new sense of commitment. A late-fifties *Awake and Sing,* like Odets' play it stresses the spiritual suffocation of those pressed to the edge of society and contained within a spiritually airless environment. Also as with that play, its dramatic logic propels its characters out of that world with the assistance of a plot contrivance as the proceeds of a life-insurance policy make possible a challenge to the white world that would presumably have been impossible without it.

The Younger family are middle class, at least in ambition, but the male head of the house, Walter Younger, has been crushed and humiliated, rendered impotent by an environment that allows him no control over his fate. His wife's planned abortion is a symbol of aborted hopes. By default, the family is sustained by its women. Even the decision as to how the proceeds of the fortuitous insurance policy are to be spent is in the hands of Walter's mother. Desperate to buy himself some dignity, Walter squanders part of it on a high-risk project. He and the family are redeemed, though, by their decision to move into a white housing area. Threatened with violence, they close ranks and decide to challenge the system to which they had previously submitted.

There is much that is naïve about the play, and Lorraine Hansberry's own comparison of it with *Death of a Salesman* is a reminder of how great the gap is between Walter Younger and Willy Loman, but it caught the mood of the moment. It placed squarely before the American people the price of bigotry and staged the reconstruction of social purpose and spiritual will that was the objective of the civil rights movement. If it was a pure Broadway product in its sentimentalities, it was nonetheless a moving statement of black resiliency that placed on stage the black lives that had previously found little reflection in the work of white playwrights. Significantly, for example, there is scarcely a black face to be seen in the work of the South's major playwright, Tennessee Williams. Precisely because *A Raisin in the Sun* was an accurate gauge of the mood of turn-of-the-decade America, however, as the civil rights strategy changed and a new mood of militancy became apparent, so other voices, less modulated, less redolent of compromise and sentimentality, made themselves heard, though not before another writer turned to the theater as the natural arena in which to debate the nature of race relations in America. His name was James Baldwin.

A certain level of performance had always been required of black Americans, whose every gesture was liable to be seen as a coded threat by the white world. For centuries, body language, facial expression, and tone of voice had had to be carefully calculated and composed to fit the role in which they had been cast. The price of a bad performance could be death. That role, moreover, was always that of supporting actor, never the principal. Now the plot was changing, but role playing still remained crucial in the drama of race relations in the United States. Not for nothing had African Americans excelled in performance arts: sport, religion, music. It was not simply that this was the territory in which they were allowed to operate but that the actor, in whatever sphere, moved outside the realm of daily reality, performing in a contingent space in which any threat was contained, ritualized. Now, in a society itself increasingly theatricalized, the membrane between performance and social transformation became more permeable.

For Baldwin, theater performed a special function. As a writer, he drew on a heritage that went back not through W. E. B. DuBois and Frederick Douglass but Ralph Waldo Emerson, Henry David Thoreau, and Henry James. His rhetoric was shaped by the King James Bible and John Wesley. His sentences were perfectly balanced, each semicolon bespeaking a double commitment rooted in a profound ambivalence. That tension left him suspended between black and white, male and female, word and act as in another way he was torn between two continents, Europe and America. The distance that he sought to maintain between himself and experience, as a key to the objectivity of the writer-commentator, was a distance that increasingly he and others felt to be the basis of a social and moral failing. Theater might close that gap.

His essays were so finely constructed, so rhythmically precise, so rhetorically persuasive that they excluded nothing but the raw experience they affected to engage. His anger was so completely finessed into art that it was hard to believe that it was rooted in any soil deeper than that constituted by a literary sensibility which had trained itself to transmute the motion of fact into the texture of art. For Baldwin, black speech was "a kind of emotional shorthand," a system of hieroglyphs that contained a history. It was not his natural language – not anymore, not after years spent in Paris, after years spent addressing another audience. Insofar as he offered himself as an explicator, a decoder of the cipher of black suffering, he was increasingly seen by his fellow blacks as a betrayer. He therefore had to find his way back to a language that was more organically related to experience, to deny the aestheticism that insulated him from the rough edge of reality.

At the heart of the problem was language. His own observation that the price a black writer has to pay for becoming articulate is to find himself at length with nothing to be articulate about goes to the core of the dilemma, for language is precisely what placed a barrier between him and those whose lives he wished to express. Articulateness itself was suspect.

The aesthetic came to be distrusted. The written word, carefully sculpted, composed in isolation, sealed between the covers of a book, lacked the authenticating power of the spoken word preached from the pulpit, shouted from the soapbox, snatched from the mouth by the wind on the streets, which alone closed on the centers of power. Only gradually did he begin to feel that he had an argument with language. Early in his career, he reveled in its possibilities as he distanced himself from his black identity; later he felt the pressure of a language complicit with the forces that had oppressed him. The key solution lay in forsaking his own voice and liberating the voices of characters who could lay claim to a directness that he had eschewed.

He abandoned the voice of the essays, whose aesthetic control had hinted at the possibility of a social compromise to be won by negotiation, for that of his characters, trapped within the grammar of their own prejudice. In *Blues for Mister Charlie* (1964), the stage is split into "blacktown" and "whitetown," as his characters are divided by the myths they separately embrace. History precipitates a residue of hatred and suspicion. Richard, embittered and angry, returns from the North only to encounter the sullen resentment of a South on the lookout for a challenge to its power. When he truculently responds to a white woman, the consequence seems predetermined by their past. He is murdered. At the trial, forced only on the intervention of a white liberal, the community divides along racial lines, and even the liberal compromises his values. Melodramatic, perhaps as befits its subject, it stages a stark battle against a background of the civil rights movement. The result is a curious ambivalence. It is not only Richard's father, a minister significantly named Meridian, who balances between the Bible and the gun; Baldwin himself seems committed to opposing values. Thus, the discredited liberal is permitted to join a civil rights march whose pursuit of justice he has just negated, whereas Richard himself is killed when he is persuaded to abandon his gun and seek redemption through love. Not untypically, Baldwin found himself committed to two mutually exclusive responses. The conscious division of the stage thus reflects a division that went deep in Baldwin as he simultaneously embraced Old Testament wrath and New Testament love. Though the play is based on an actual murder – that of Emmet Till – it is hard to believe in characters who represent divisions within Baldwin's sensibility as much as polarities in society. The white liberal, in particular, is little more than a dramatic expression of his will to indict the very readers/audience to whom much of his work was directed, to whom this play, indeed, was addressed, since its title refers not to the black man who dies but the white man whose detachment turns into complicity.

Blues for Mister Charlie was Baldwin's last work for the theater, except for a script left unrevised at his death, but that same year, 1964, marked the appearance of a man who was to have a considerable impact on the emergence of a powerful black drama in the United States. His name was Leroi Jones, poet, part of a New York bohemian intelligencia, and married to a white Jewish wife. In the mid-1960s he suddenly abandoned that life for a new one as a black cultural nationalist and founder of the black arts theaters that began to spread throughout America. The pressure of the racial situation was such that it broke his marriage as it snapped his links with the white literary world. The two plays that received their premiere in 1964, *Dutchman* and *The Slave*, may have been produced with the assistance of Edward Albee and have contained an ambiguity that accurately reflected that of their creator, but they also indicated the urgencies that would shortly turn LeRoi Jones into Amiri Baraka.

Dutchman is set in the "flying underbelly of the city," on a subway train, a location that hints at the subterranean myths and subconscious impulses that it explores. Indeed, its dreamlike quality suggests that what we are offered is something of a psychoanalysis of culture. In ritual form it plays out the equally underground tensions that divide whites from blacks and blacks from their own consciousness. Clay is an assimilated black man, with buttoned down collar and buttoned down attitudes, who is confronted by Lula who is white, attractive – an apple-eating temptress. She is the nemesis that historically has awaited any black man drawn to a white woman, an expression of desire he is supposed to feel and the fate reserved for him if he does. Her provocations are calculated moves in an ancient ritual. She wishes to transform him into the dangerous and sensual being of white fantasies and then punish him for his transformation. For a moment he responds, emerging as a powerful and dominating figure, but abandons this stance for what he believes is the safety of words. She responds by killing him. Her silent fellow passengers, the detached white fellow travelers, collaborate in the disposing of the body before the next victim enters and the ceremony of death can be repeated, their very detachment turning them into collaborators.

A powerful metaphor, *Dutchman* accurately reflected LeRoi Jones's, and, incidentally, the black movement's dilemma. The objective of integrating into white society – a logic implicit in Lorraine Hansberry's play – was being abandoned by many in favor of an assertion of black values and a black identity defined in terms of opposition and resistance. Jones's character seems caught in a double bind, faced with literal or metaphorical destruction whichever path he takes. He chooses safety in language, but that turns out to be no safety at all. Jones had done no less and increasingly felt that he had merely become complicit in a process that, were integration even successful, would ensure the annihilation of his identity.

Dutchman, and its companion piece, *The Slave,* catches LeRoi Jones at a moment of transition. They were the last of his plays that would carry his old name. His next collection would announce their revolutionary provenance and be the product of an emergent Amiri Baraka. Meanwhile, in a skillfully choreographed drama, he pushes forward a character who enacts a dilemma that was essentially his own and that turns on two myths, one rooted in a history reprocessed as paranoid vision, the other in a story of eternal repetition, that of the Flying Dutchman, in which a man who had blasphemed is condemned to sail the world forever. The logic of this latter myth implies the implacability of the former. The moment of pure violence as Clay strikes out suggests, however, that such a logic may be ruptured. The brutal directness of his later plays, indeed, asserts that art itself, indirect, subtle, ambiguous, may have to be broken open under the pressure of need if it is to effect social change, that aestheticism may come to seem the enemy of a social action that becomes not the by-product of art but itself the only form of art worth endorsing. For the moment, though, he was poised in genuine hesitation, so both *Dutchman* and *The Slave* capture a moment of real self-doubt. For a brief moment, just before LeRoi Jones transmutes into Amiri Baraka, he explores his own contradictions in two related plays whose oscillation between violence and debate proves as expressive of a historical moment as it is of a career in the balance.

The second of these two plays, *The Slave,* is thus characterized by a functional irony. It begins with the figure of a shambling field slave, suddenly transformed into a black rebel, leading an assault on an American city. It is as though the fact of the former was bound eventually to generate the reality of the latter, but the play implies that there is another cause for this transmutation, namely white equivocation and liberal detachment. The rebel, Walker Vessels, returns to his ex-wife's apartment on the eve of battle and confronts her and her white liberal university professor husband. The real question, though, is why he should have chosen to abandon his troops in order to debate his position with those against whom he is ostensibly in rebellion. The fact is that in some essential way he remains a slave, a slave to the intellectual and literary traditions of which he, in common with Jones, is in part a product. He and the white man he confronts meet within the culture they share, just as they meet within the context of Jones's drama, whose own models are recognizably part of a white Western tradition. Vessels, indeed, has to smash the sophisticated structures of that tradition with force in order to give birth to something new. This was essentially what the black theater was about to do, breaking open character, disdaining formal ambiguities, and forging out of the stereotype exemplary figures, brutally direct portraits not easily accommodated to the modernist tradition that Vessels and Easley, the university professor, share. The play concludes as Vessels shoots the man who represents his other self and the battle for the city begins. Within the wreckage of the house whose destruction they have jointly precipitated, we hear the cry of the children whom Vessels had fathered, a future in the balance.

For LeRoi Jones, heir to the same double tradition, the articulate spokesman for a group that distrusted such articulateness as a sign of power and laid claim to other values, other ways of structuring the world, the dilemma was scarcely resolved merely by addressing it in drama. Warning against the temptation of becoming "fluent in the jargon of power," he nonetheless deployed that jargon in a play whose fluency, whose dialectical method, and whose powerful metaphor of a society imploding on its own contradictions located him in the very world from which he struggled to escape. What was required was a drama of praxis, a play that offered itself as a form of action. *Dutchman* and *The Slave,* subtly exploring myths and lives braided together and torn apart by history, were not that — or at least they seemed not to be when performed Off-Broadway to an audience who laid claims to the values with which they debated. After all, these plays deployed the very techniques – the pared-down language of the poet, the mythic references, the elaboration of dramatic metaphor – with which they seemed in contention. Moved to Harlem, however, the same plays became threatening. Performed on the street, they became subversive. The ambiguities were blunted by context as Walker Vessels became less an ambivalent actor in his own psychodrama and more a revolutionary plotting the direction of the future. LeRoi Jones moved in much the same direction. He divorced his white wife, set himself to create a black revolutionary theater whose directness would prove instructive, and changed his name. What followed were his revolutionary plays, which lacked all the ironies of *Dutchman* and *The Slave* and proposed a model for social action. Brief agitprop sketches, they created exemplary black heroes and warned against the corrupting power of white society. Theatrically unadventurous, they sought their validation in their social impact. In time, he came to feel the inadequacy of this approach, not because he sensed the weakness of such work from a purely dramatic point of view but because of a change in political outlook. He came to feel that a purely racial interpretation of experience failed to address a problem that had its origins in economics and class – the black control of inner cities for which he worked in Newark providing no solution. Accordingly, he became a Marxist-Leninist and created plays, such as *The Motions of History,* that did little to advance his reputation or his cause. Marxist-Leninist playwrights hardly fared well anywhere in the 1970s and 1980s. In America, they condemned themselves to obscurity. There are few playwrights whose claim to attention rests on as narrow a base as that of Amiri Baraka, but there are few playwrights who have written two plays with the honesty and theatrical force of *Dutchman* and *The Slave.*

Baraka was important not simply because of his plays but because of the impact he had on others. It was his inspiration which led to the establishment of black theater groups in America's major cities; it was his inspiration in particular that led Ed Bullins to write, though in many ways the shape of his career was the opposite of Baraka's. His early works were consciousness-raising exercises, brief, cautionary dramas. The essence of his achievement lay ahead, in a cycle of plays that detailed the struggle of characters not to define themselves against an implacable white world but against the almost equally implacable world of their own environment. The naturalistic drive behind such works as *In the Wine Time* and *The New England Winter* was, though, modified by an imagination that pulled in the direction of impressionism. His is a world in which sexuality is both promise and threat, an avenue of escape and a dead end blocking off the possibility of transcendence. Violence flickers, flares into fierce intensity, and then fades against the underlying music of relationships that form, fragment, and reform. His characters' lives have a poetry that leaves them discontented with a prosaic reality, just as the naturalistic surface of his plays is attenuated to the point where fact refashions itself as image. There is an epic pretension to works that move us through the psychic history of black Americans in the 1950s, 1960s, and 1970s, without seeing the black experience as mere pathology or as rendering up its meaning solely through confrontation with a white world. There is also, however, a personal intensity that gives depth to that engagement with social process. The fantasies that weave their way into the minds of some of his characters (*In the Wine Time, The Duplex*) also work against the physical determinism of lives seemingly defined by alcohol, drugs, and a willing surrender to brutality and sexual need. The shaping power of the dramatist becomes an expression of that resistant spirit that survives in his characters and that lifts them out of a defining context.

The black cultural nationalists of the sixties and seventies made black Americans the center of their own dramas. They were not the first to do so, but in the context of a changing political and social world, their work assumed a centrality that earlier writers had not been able to claim. Their plays were offered as elements in a national debate. The black theater group was a demonstration of the potential and power of black cooperation, the black play a statement, an intervention, an articulation of black needs and possibilities. These were the pathfinders dropping flares to light up the target. The pressure they exerted was partly theatrical, partly social. Some plays, like those of Amiri Baraka, were crude components of a dialectic, the other half of which was constituted by the unarticulated assumptions and prejudices of the white world; others engaged the ambiguities that accompanied a revolt against a particular view of language and a particular view of the self.

One man who was involved in this movement and who benefitted from it was August Wilson, cofounder, in 1968, of the Black Horizon Theatre in Pittsburgh. Curiously, it was to be more than a decade before he would emerge as a writer, but when he did so, he proved the most successful black playwright not only of the 1980s but of all time. He himself has claimed that his early efforts foundered on his inability to construct credible dialogue. In common with a number of writers in the black theater movement of the sixties, he allowed his characters' speech to be shaped by the rhetorical demands of the moment or modeled on the suspect articulateness of mainstream theatre. On moving, in the late seventies, from Pittsburgh to St. Paul, Minnesota, he found a new sense of distance that enabled him to gain a perspective on the black community and on its rhythms of speech. Perspective began to matter to him in another sense, too, as he located the lives of his characters against the unfolding drama of black life in America in the twentieth century. His first play, *Jitney,* was set in 1971, his second, *Fullerton Street,* in 1941. By the time of *Ma Rainey's Black Bottom,* set in 1927, what had at first been inadvertent became a deliberate strategy as he set himself to write the history of an emerging race and a crystalizing identity. What followed was a conscious attempt to write that history, decade by decade, as he set himself to tell the emotional, psychological, and spiritual story of a people previously written out of the national narrative, displaced from the central drama of America. His was to be an act of recuperation and celebration.

His characters are not exemplary figures, self-confidently engaging the world. They are neither rebels nor purely victims. They live their lives within the contradictions of a social system that is not elaborated and in the interstices of political events that are seldom referred to or articulated. His characters have other priorities. These are plays about the struggle to survive with dignity on the edge of history.

Ma Rainey's Black Bottom is set in a recording studio in the 1920s. The white recording company gathers together a group of musicians to play with the blues singer, Ma Rainey. On one level, this is a story of the exploitation of black talent, but August Wilson is less interested in this than in the lives of the musicians. The racial tension is implicit in a stage set that places the representatives of a white record company in an office above the basement where the black musicians rehearse, but, for the most part, that racism is not expressed directly. It is simply the condition of being within which his characters have to feel their way to personal meaning.

At the heart of the play is music for the blues, which the whites see simply as entertainment to be reshaped for public taste, grew out of real experience. It is a music with its own history that encodes the lives of those who play as well as those who listen. In Wilson's words, that music is what enables them "to reconnect"; it is "a way of understanding life." The members of this band are divided, however, so separated by private ambitions and experiences that their solidarity is corroded by violence. The white world remains aloof as black turns against black.

In *Fences,* set in 1957, Troy, the son of a sharecropper who had left home at the age of fourteen and turned to crime, is now a garbage man. Such meaning as he finds in his life he discovers in his relationship with his wife, but an increasing bitterness begins to destroy him. Once he had been a baseball star but was refused admission by the white baseball leagues. Now he deals with his collapsing self-esteem through an affair with a married woman and by frustrating his son's ambitions, partly out of a baffled love, partly out of jealousy. In one sense, this is pathology. Troy's life winds down and eventually stops as he is practicing a swing with his baseball bat, an irony that focuses the forces that have destroyed him. That is not, though, the note on which Wilson leaves us, for he has said that he finds in Troy a willingness to live life with zest and vibrancy, precisely the qualities he detects in the blues, and the play ends with a series of reconciliations.

The past cannot be unambiguously claimed by black Americans. It contains the echo of humiliations. Once, they were literally the invention of whites who gave them names and required them to inhabit those names. The move to deny "slave names" in the 1960s was a conscious rejection of one model of history. Those who chose to replace that name with the letter X were making the slave's mark of illiteracy a badge of honor and crossing out a record of subordination, but there was another history, a history inscribed on the body. That history looked backward beyond slavery to Africa, to that community ruptured by the diaspora, and it is toward that source that he presses in his next play, *Joe Turner's Come and Gone.*

Set in a boardinghouse, it brings together a scattering of individuals all on journeys of one kind or another, looking to reunite themselves with those they have lost, to discover some solidarity whose need they instinctively feel but whose form they find unclear. The dominant image of the play is of a lost harmony. These are individual voices looking to sound together, dislocated lives seeking for a consonance they can claim. Selig is a white man, a salesman, who accepts commissions to discover the lost; Bynum is a black man who insists on his power to bind people together. In a play in which the other characters are in search of a lost wife, a lost lover, a potential bride, they have a central function, expressed through an imagery of music. Song becomes a metaphor for identity as a literal dance brings the characters together, responding to the rhythms that Wilson, in a note, reminds us have their origins in the "shouts" of slaves. It is in that sense that Africa and the African heritage presses more directly on this play than on its predecessors.

What Selig and Bynum do as characters is what August Wilson does as a playwright, identifying, as he does, with "this attempt to bind together." What is true of individual plays, in which characters struggle toward some relationship with one another and their own past, is true equally of the entire cycle. Each play stands alone. Each play gains through being seen in relation to the others. For a people who, like one of the characters in *Joe Turner's Come and Gone,* have been "wandering a long time in somebody else's world," the reestablishment of a chain of being – the assertion of a continuity of thought, experience, and imagery – is simultaneously an assertion of community.

Like Tennessee Williams, Wilson describes sets that are simultaneously literal and symbolic, as he creates characters who contain, compacted within them, a personal history and an archetypal experience. In narrative terms, he is drawn to fable and myth, just as, in thematic terms, he is attracted to music and image. The set of *Ma Rainey* is both a literal recording studio and a visual representation of a power system; the fence, which Troy slowly erects in *Fences,* is an accurate expression of a psychological and social state. The rooming house in *Joe Turner* implies a spiritual isolation that parallels the physical. Meanwhile, the action is played against a background of music whose mutual expressiveness is both his dramatic strategy and his subject.

Two Trains Running (1990) moved the action on to the 1960s, to Pittsburgh in 1969. Black power is in the wings but, once again, Wilson is less concerned with confronting history head on than with studying those who live their lives in the interstices of public events. Set in a restaurant across from a funeral parlor, the play engages issues of life and death, the two symbolic trains of the title, as the real trains run back to the South, from which one of the characters has come.

These are people who have found ways of making it: an undertaker who relies on the reliability of death, a restaurateur who knows that people have to eat, a petty criminal who, having returned from jail, tries his hand at the numbers. Suspicious of political slogans, they put their faith in chance, in a wise woman, in anything that will lift them out of their trap. They plot and bargain their separate fates, and yet there is also a sense of community that makes them support one another as well as compete. Once again, Wilson creates a living tapestry, a group portrait, a dance. The very simplicity of character, plot, and language underlines the extent to which he is dedicated to creating a modern myth more powerful than the public history that so seldom finds space for those who constitute it.

In *Two Trains Running,* he brings together a handful of stories about the past and the future, the memories and dreams of those who watch the world go by, aware of change that threatens them and of the pressures that hold them in a place that is both home and an alienating setting. They are survivors, and here, as in the other plays of the cycle, he dramatizes the strategies by which they live and die, giving them a centrality in his drama that they lack in the society they did not make but have made their own.

Black drama in the 1960s was an urban affair, and it spoke an urban language of alienation, despair, and provocation. Violence leaped across racial gaps or looped back on the self that generated it. Relationships were temporary or placed under extreme pressure. The past existed only as the source of a wound, or as explanation for trauma. It was to be set aside in the name of a future where alone lay the possibility of recovery. August Wilson plots his plays along different axes. The language is not only urban. Alienation exists, but so does the desire to deny it. Above all, history is not only an implacable fact; it is the source of redemption: the logic that connects moment to moment also links individual to individual until patterns begin to emerge and the past becomes something more than explanation. There is a tensile strength, a resiliency that is clear only when plotted through time. It becomes possible to understand identity not through a series of confrontations with present realities but by rediscovering the substance of past experiences. The theater becomes an arena in which time is annihilated. Brothers meet across time as well as in the present and in so doing come to understand the nature of their kinship. Theater offers community within the present tense. Wilson's drama offers community by creating a past tense that looks toward that present.

❦

Just as the Black Power movement, in fighting injustice and racism, had a tendency to be blind to its own prejudices, being guilty at times of anti-Semitism and sexism, so black revolutionary theater, as exemplified by Amiri Baraka, proposed a model of women as willing collaborators in their own irrelevance or supportive adjuncts to their black warrior men. Those black female playwrights who had done much to place the dilemma of the black American on stage tended to be marginalized. Alice Childress was one such playwright. An actress who had made her name with the American Negro Theatre in the 1940s, she became the first black woman to secure a professional performance of one of her plays on the American stage. *Gold Through the Trees* was first produced in 1952. Her plays, largely realistic, engaged the problems of black artists struggling to invest the roles they play with meaning and dignity (*Trouble in Mind*) and to generate images of black life that have integrity rather than expediency. Adrienne Kennedy similarly found herself at odds with a new orthodoxy that sought exemplary figures or deployed stereotypes in the service of political policy and a commitment to community theater. Part of the Off-Broadway, avant-garde, she had other commitments, in particular to stylistic experiment, exploding language, and generating images that had their origins in the subconscious rather than the tangible realities of urban life or racial prejudice. *Funnyhouse of a Negro* (1962), *The Owl Answers* (1963), and *A Rat's Mass* (1966) stood in contrast to the expressive gestures of James Baldwin, Amiri Baraka, and Ed Bullins. *Funnyhouse of a Negro,* first produced at Edward Albee's workshop, drew on her experience in West Africa, but was rejected by many of those in the black arts movement as "irrelevant." Interestingly, it and others of her plays also inspired criticism from those who objected to her work because there were heroines in her plays who were "confused," a response that anticipated a reaction that was to become more widespread in the 1970s and 1980s as female playwrights began to make their presence felt.

The fact of theater's power to offer representations of the self, to explore the politics of social role, and to act as a focus for group solidarity was not lost on others. If women had not found it easy to operate within the context of black cultural nationalism, they were ready to draw conclusions from the success of black theater in presenting a public model of social performance and racial identity. They also learned a lesson from the rediscovery of the body that had been such a feature of performance theater in the 1960s. The problem was that the point of reference tended to be the male experience and the male body. That was about to change.

The women's movement had always seen an analogy between racism and sexism and hence between a civil rights movement designed to secure rights for a racially unprivileged minority and what, by the early 1970s, tended to be seen as a sexually unprivileged majority. For race read gender; and there were, of course, those who found themselves doubly disadvantaged or, alternatively, heirs to a double tradition. One such was Ntozake Shange, who had encountered racism as a child but been sensitized to sexism as a student of women's studies in California, refusing to join the Black Panther Party because of its unwillingness to concede equality to women. Her interest in dance, meanwhile, led her to stress the physical correlative of racial and gender identity. *For colored girls who have considered suicide/when the rainbow is enuf* (1976) is a choreopoem that explores the very qualities that are the basis of stereotype: natural rhythm, sensuality, intuitive perception. At the same time, its own structure and style was an act of resistance to formal social constructs and its emphasis on flow, movement, and harmonics was an implicit claim to a mode of being that was not the one defined by Arthur Miller or Amiri Baraka. "Writing is for most people a cerebral activity," she explained, but "for me it is a very rhythmic and visceral experience. Dance clears my mind of verbal images. . . . I am not bogged down with the implications of language."

Women made their presence felt in the Off-Off Broadway world of the 1960s, but it was not until the mid-1970s that women's theater groups began to proliferate as black theaters had earlier. It was a movement that seemed to peak in the mid 1980s, thereafter declining. The creation of these theaters put the stage at the service of writers who might earlier have found it difficult to secure production. The elaboration of feminist theory and the publication of feminist manifestos gave a context for work that could otherwise have seemed private. Some groups were programmatic, enforcing an orthodoxy that led to a criticism of all those writers who had succeeded in a male world, from Lillian Hellman and Lorraine Hansberry to such emerging talents as Marsha Norman, Beth Henley, and Wendy Wasserstein. Nonetheless, the energy released by these theaters created a new environment and a new audience for the woman writer.

Rochelle Owens's priorities were rather different. A product of Off-Off Broadway, she wrote plays of considerable stylistic originality. Often bizarre and frequently impenetrable, they deal in wild images and surreal conjunctions. Only later did she begin to discover in that work (*Futz, The String Game, Istamboul, Beclch, Emma Instigated Me*) a latent feminism that resided in her challenge to familiar theatrical modes and in images that bypass a narrow rationalism.

Cuban-born Maria Irene Fornes was similarly committed to radical experimentation, working for a time with Joseph Chaikin's Open Theatre. The characters in *The Successful Life of 3* (1965) and *Promenade* (1965) have no substance and generate a language that fragments and oscillates between poetry and prose. Claimed by feminists, she suggests that such a description is applicable only to the extent that, in her play *Mud,* she places a woman at the center of the stage and that the play is generated out of the mind and sensibility of a woman. Perhaps her battle with realism, however, could be seen as an attempt to break open structures of thought as much as styles of presentation in much the same way that Susan Glaspell had done in the early decades of the century and with the same implications for women battling against other determinisms.

For all the public nature of the women's movement, a fair number of the plays women created addressed private issues. The insecurities that now bubbled to the surface had to do with the threat of illness, of desertion, of broken relationships. They explored the relationship between mother and daughter, as O'Neill and Miller had that between father and son. They responded to the de-centering of women's experience by placing it at the heart of their work; if this was not a drama that engaged public issues in the way that works by Baraka, Miller, Mamet, or Wilson had done, the validation of these private issues was seen as a public act.

Nor was the public element wholly absent. Wendy Wasserstein's exploration of the unfolding identity of her protagonist in *The Heidi Chronicles* takes place against the background of changing social, political, and economic values. Meanwhile, Emily Mann shaped her first play, *Annulla: An Autobiography* (1977) out of interviews with survivors of the Holocaust, whereas her *Still Life* (1980) concentrated on a Vietnam veteran and *Execution of Justice,* on the trial of the murderer of San Francisco's mayor and city supervisor. The pressure of that external reality indeed was such that it forced its way into her drama in the form of documentary material.

Marsha Norman was a product of regional theater and in particular of Louisville's New Plays Festival, which was also to give a start to Beth Henley. Though she established a public reputation with her Pulitzer prize–winning *'Night, Mother,* her first play, *Getting Out* (1978), was more powerfully original in its stagecraft and as relentless in its emotional force. Its central character has just been released from prison, where she had been incarcerated for murder, but the "getting out" of the title refers to more than her emergence from jail. She has now to escape from her own past, from the persona in which she has entombed herself, and from the roles projected on her by others. The daughter of a family of criminals, she has drifted into crime and prostitution. She has the paranoiac's hostility toward the world but has reached a moment in her life when she knows that she must make a choice. She can return to the streets, brutal, degrading but empowering, offering her the possibility of wealth and a kind of sexual revenge, or choose the reliable, safe, bland existence that will come from taking a secure job in the kitchen of a café. That debate is externalized as the two sides of a fractured sensibility claim their separate voices.

The two versions of Arlene are in effect her former and her present self, one defiant, vulgar, angry, obscene; the other self-doubting, insecure, uncertain, bewildered. Other voices intrude, particularly those of authority figures who have sought to define her identity and plot her future, but the essence of the play lies in the dispute waged within the self. Nor is Marsha Norman's thumb on the scale. There is a vitality to Arlie, the younger self, as she challenges the world with all the force of her language and molds an identity out of conflict, which sharply contrasts with the apparent inertia of Arlene. She has to contend with male violence, but she also struggles with the given insofar as she is a product of her circumstances. The adult Arlene is seemingly more passive, more resigned, less inclined to wrestle the world to a standstill, but is this mere capitulation? The choice is not simple.

The theme of the play is survival. Arlene struggles to define the terms on which she can effect a truce with the world and with her own competing needs. In a play whose strength lies partly in Marsha Norman's orchestration of the two voices, played against one another though sharing the same key signature, Arlene fights to hear the authentic note of a fractured self. The irony is that, for her, a bland existence may represent the redemption which she seeks. For all its considerable emotional power, *Getting Out* is a subtle drama whose theatricality is generated out of character and theme alike.

Her next play, *Third and Oak* (1978), took a favorite concern of women's theater – abandonment – but explored it in terms of its differing meaning for men and women. A play with comic overtones, it manages nonetheless slowly to strip away the assurances of social roles to expose a shared experience of pain. It was, however, with *'Night, Mother,* which opened in Cambridge, Massachusetts, in 1983 and moved to Broadway the following year, winning a Pulitzer prize, that she emerged on the national scene.

The play could hardly be simpler. On a single set, a mother and daughter, Thelma and Jessie, confront one another. The daughter has decided to commit suicide. The gun awaits in an adjoining room. Her mother must try to prevent her daughter from opening the door. If that tension provides the dramatic force of the play, its ironies stem from something more than a Freudian melodrama in which a child attempts to return, symbolically, to the womb and an accompanying oblivion. The fact is that Jessie Cates sees the suicide as offering her the dignity and meaning that her life has lacked. In taking her life, she will at last be assuming responsibility for it. The set becomes not merely the context for the action but an essential element in Norman's dramatic strategy. When Hedda Gabler slams the door behind her in Ibsen's play, she is in effect claiming her life in the act of sacrificing it; society has no role to offer her, no protection against a dissolution of the social self. Jessie makes what is effectively the same decision, though here the moral and spiritual victory are won at the literal cost of her life. Hedda Gabler challenged the world of male presumption encoded in social practice and sexual relationships. Jessie challenges her own surrender of will and imagination. Like Hedda, she has in part been the victim of male assumptions. Her marriage has collapsed and her own son is a stranger, but this is not the heart of the play. That lies in the ambiguous relationship between mother and daughter.

In a curious way, though they have previously been so separate from one another, encased in their mutual incomprehension, they are brought together by the tension of these last minutes. As the pressure increases, old barriers are broken down. The urgency of the situation drives out pretense and defensive evasions. Blame gives way to a desire to offer and receive absolution as Jessie acknowledges the responsibility she feels for the mother she is abandoning. In terminating her own future, she tries to secure Thelma's. The very conversation that is the basis of the play, however, underlines Jessie's need for justification and her desire to absolve herself of the guilt that her new self-confidence should have obviated. Declaring her independence of those whose lives she has shared, she is perhaps not as free as she would wish to believe.

On the face of it, 'Night, Mother is an entirely naturalistic play, but the single room in which it is set transforms into an image of those experiences, values, and attitudes that have trapped both Jessie and Thelma. The door that must open may redeem more than just the daughter. Indeed, that relationship fascinated Marsha Norman precisely because the mother is an image of both past and future. She represents those attitudes that Jessie inherits just as she stands for the future that she must reject. In walking through the door, Jessie will be rejecting her mother's passivity, refusing the destructive compromise that she has made with her life – but the ironies remain. If the two voices for which it is scored do occasionally sound out in harmony, there is a dissonance, too, that is generated out of character and out of differing perceptions of the world.

For a number of feminist critics, not only was *'Night, Mother* the story of a defeat – as yet another neurotic woman convinces herself that the only solution to her problems lies in suicide, a capitulation to the world rather than a decision to reconstruct it – it stood as a drama that succeeded only because it offered confirmation of female stereotypes. It was a wrong step along the path of liberation. The door that opened to Jessie and to Marsha Norman alike signaled the death of a particular set of possibilities for the woman writer. It is hard to agree with such critics. Norman is no more unaware of the falsity of the choices that confront her characters in *'Night, Mother* than she had been in *Getting Out,* whose title carries the same irony. Liberation in her work is not the result of epiphany or unclouded by ambivalence. Her commitment is not to didacticism, to consciousness raising, or to the elaboration of tales of emancipation. She does place women at the center of her work, but they speak in different voices, voices whose rhythms, tone, and timbres express differing experiences of the world. They have suffered in their relationships with men, but the choices that face them are the more complex because a simple declaration of independence will not suffice and whichever choices they make can only commit them to new dilemmas.

Beth Henley, also a product of Louisville, suffered similar attacks, not least perhaps because a suicide also lies at the heart of her most successful play, *Crimes of the Heart,* which opened at Louisville before moving to New York, where it won the New York Drama Critics Circle Award and the Pulitzer prize in 1981. Three sisters, a long way removed from Chekhov's, share the distant trauma of their mother's death, a death that grows out of a desperation equally familiar to them in that their lives, too, have come apart in their hands. They have all failed in one sense or another, but this is a new generation. When one of them is caught, by her politician husband, having an affair with a young boy, she shoots her husband instead of killing herself. Somewhat surprisingly, given its subject matter, *Crimes of the Heart* is a comedy. That comedy is itself an assertion of changed values, of a refusal to capitulate in the face of experience. Disabling irony is transformed into enabling humor. Just as Henley herself sees writing as a way of containing anger and neutralizing pain, so her characters permit themselves the grace of a redeeming detachment, and into that space between experience and its perception comes a humor that makes self-destruction impossible. There is more than a touch of the Southern gothic about Beth Henley, but that results not in lurid grotesques but in a comedy generated out of disproportion. Her characters are survivors who refuse to be the victims of their own or other people's expectations.

Wendy Wasserstein, likewise, deals in comedy, but her characters are for the most part seen outside the context of the family. In a sequence of plays –

Uncommon Women and Others (1976–7), *Isn't It Romantic* (1981), and *The Heidi Chronicles* (1988) – she plotted the course of individual lives against a changing social and political world. Private and public ambitions are contrasted with the reality of compromise and adjustment. She, too, attracted the hostility of some feminist critics precisely because she acknowledged the conflict between ideal and reality, because, in terms of individual characters, she recognizes the competing demands of career and family, sisterly solidarity, and individual development. Her young college girls move confidently into a world that they expect to prove responsive to their energies and to accommodate itself to the rhetoric of liberation. Stage by stage, as the decades pass, they push the date of personal fulfillment further into the future. These are plays essentially about America and its ability to generate dreams that will frustrate and disillusion. They are about women and their struggle to survive in a world that they promised themselves would be different but that proved less susceptible to the transforming imagination than they had imagined. The humor of these plays is two-edged. In one sense, it is a defensive tactic deployed by characters who generate a brittle comedy to conceal their sense of failure and even despair. In another, it is, as Wendy Wasserstein has said, "a life force." Speaking in the late eighties, she remarked that "women playwrights fall into a trap because the audience goes in expecting a 'woman's play' with a feminist sensibility. Nobody goes into a man's play and thinks, 'I want a man's point of view on this.' . . . That is never asked of men. . . . As a playwright, first and foremost you must be true to your characters. It's the character's motivation; not me speaking for womankind." On the other hand, she confessed to writing *Uncommon Women* "so that women's voices could be heard," believing that "nine girls taking a curtain call can be seen as political." Her ambivalence was an expression of the ambiguous position of the female playwright moving into the 1990s.

The territory Wendy Wasserstein occupies has in part been cleared by others. She herself credits Marsha Norman with opening doors (ironically so, given the plot of *'Night, Mother*) so that it no longer proves so necessary to declare extra theatrical loyalties. On the other hand, drama in America has a history against which emerging writers tend to find themselves defined. Thus she has remarked that "we are all playwrights. I think that is very important. But for now, any minority group must be labeled. Our idea of a playwright is a white male . . . then all the others are separated into subsets: black playwrights, gay playwrights, women playwrights, and so on. The point is we are all in it together." She adds, however, that "I listen to my plays . . . and I still think, 'A Woman wrote this.'" It is a revealing addendum, and one that applies to a later play, *The Sisters Rosensweig* (1992), a comic drama, albeit one that its author thought her most serious.

The three middle-aged women at its center, vulnerable and searching for love, stand in contrast to the men, lightly sketched, amusing, but the background noise to lives whose ironies, strengths, and weaknesses derive in large part from the literal and symbolic sisterhood of which they are a part. A woman also takes center stage in her later play, *An American Daughter* (1997) in which she engages the political world more directly.

❦

Writing in 1982, the Chinese American playwright David Hwang announced that the American theater was beginning to discover Americans, by which he meant that a pluralistic culture was at last starting to acknowledge the lives of those who constitute the basis of its pluralism. The black theater of the sixties had been in part a political challenge but in part also a declaration of difference. With the collapse of consensus came a renewed interest in an identity not defined by reference to a presumed homogeneity. The debacles of Vietnam and Watergate seeded doubt about those centripetal values presumed to forge a disparate people into one. In a decade in which explorations of the self became if not imperative then at least legitimate, the fact of ethnicity was increasingly seen as a key to identity. The fragmentation of the theater, initially a response to economic realities, lent itself to the proliferation of plays that both expressed and addressed a minority audience defined in terms of ethnic or national origin. What was born out of the urgencies of political change became the basis for an investigation of cultural meaning. Thus the Chicano theater, which began as an adjunct of political action with brief consciousness-raising agitprop sketches created by Luis Valdez, later focused on the question of cultural identity. That in turn drew Valdez, in particular, to the past, not least because the Chicano identity is itself a racial amalgam that carries the marks of its history. The myths and ceremonies that he staged were not the reconstructions of East Coast intellectuals eager to plug into the energy sources of the Third World but were implicated in the processes of Chicano experience and thought. If Valdez was also committed to theater in a broader sense, a commitment that led him to the Mark Taper Forum, with *Zoot Suit* in 1977, and subsequently to Hollywood with *La Bamba,* he continued to draw, as he did in these two works and in ways not always initially obvious, on the Mayan myths that he saw as a vital element of Chicano experience.

Chicano theater reaches out toward two linguistic traditions, often blending English and Spanish in the same play as a thematic gesture rather than as simply a reflection of the linguistic intermixture of southern California. That was equally true on the other side of the country, where the Hispanic theater has its roots in Spain, Cuba, Puerto Rico, and South

America. Originally largely Spanish speaking, by the 1970s and 1980s it performed in both languages as complex negotiations between periphery and center redefined the nature of the center. Where once the surrender of language was the price willingly paid for inclusion in the American enterprise, now that language was increasingly seen as part of the dowry brought by the immigrant and his or her descendents. How, anyway, could one gain access to the past except through language; how could one gain access to the present except through the past?

That proved no less true for Chinese American writers David Hwang and Laurence Yep or for Japanese Americans Wakako Yamauchi and Philip Kan Gotanda. A crucial moment in the work of all four is that in which denial of the past is no longer seen as a route to success in the present. David Hwang's *The Dance and the Railroad*, set in 1863, stages the dilemma of an immigrant who carries his own past into the New World, as Laurence Yep, in *Pay the Chinaman*, creates a character who distrusts his own experience as the source of meaning. Hwang's *M Butterfly* examines the fantasies that Chinese and Americans seem content to substitute for the reality of human relationships as his characters meet within another fantasy, that conjured up by Puccini's *Madame Butterfly*. As this implies, Hwang is as interested in interacting theatrical forms as in the dialectic of cultures.

The theater is a public rite. It is a mechanism for addressing anxieties, for seeking to locate form in the randomness of events. It is also, however, an expression of its society and has historically perpetuated those social caricatures that are the mechanism of power. Just as Hwang chose to see theatrical stereotypes as a clue to the damaging misapprehensions that in turn become the basis for social action, so, in *Yankee Dawg You Die*, Philip Kan Gotanda stages a debate between two actors who discuss the stereotypical roles offered to Asians. In other words, these are plays that acknowledge the theater's power either to confirm or resist the reductivism that lies at the heart of prejudice. It was in that spirit, perhaps, that the Kiowa playwright Hanay Geiogamah chose to reclaim in the theater the right to define a Native American identity that otherwise had been enrolled, by theater and cinema, in the myths of American expansionism. In another direction, gays sought either to redeem themselves from the high-camp irrelevance to which they had been sentenced or to inhabit the stereotype offered to them and find in that an energy that might itself be the source of value.

The most striking gay playwright of the 1990s was undoubtedly Tony Kushner. His first play, *A Bright Room Called Day*, was staged in 1985 but it was *Angels in America* that established his reputation as one of the most exciting of contemporary writers.

In fact his first play is itself an impressive work. Written in response to Bertolt Brecht's *Fear and Misery in the Third Reich,* it is set in Germany but with two time scales—the 1930s and the 1980s. Experimental in form, deeply political in intent, it sought to suggest a parallel between the rise of Nazism in Germany and the nature of Ronald Reagan's America. The very outrageousness of the proposition was intentional and defended by Kushner in an interview as he refused to be intimidated by the seemingly unique and implacable nature of the Holocaust. The Right, he implied, was far from dead. The ghosts of the past still walked the world. Overstatement became an aesthetic.

This was no less true of *Angels in America (Millennium Approaches,* 1990; *Perestroika,* 1992), a work in two parts which he suggested was concerned with the need for individuals to neutralize entrapping myths by generating their own. A carnivalesque exploration of America, at a time of plague—literal and symbolic—it combines myth and fantasy with an acute analysis of the social, political, and sexual pressures potentially destroying both the individual and a sense of community. The play moves through time, bringing together seemingly disparate elements in a synthesis whose coherence is perhaps at odds with its methods. Gender lines are blurred, Jew meets Mormon, black meets white, and conservative engages liberal. Beyond the specifics of its concern with AIDS, it is a celebration of that pluralism most suspect in 80s America (the play is set in 1985).

Though a dying man lies at its heart, it is a play, finally, about redemption, a redemption that lies in the simultaneous acknowledgment and transcendence of history. It is a play that takes America's claims for itself entirely seriously while deploying a deliberately camp ostentation. A comedy rather than a farce, it edges toward epiphany.

The two parts of *Angels in America* received multiple awards. It was followed in 1994 by *Slavs,* a contemplation of history and of the implications of the collapse of order in the 20th century and particularly in the Soviet Union, and subsequently by *Hydriotaphia or the Death of Dr. Browne.*

꘎

So it is that the theater continues to be the place where America debates with itself. Henry James's question about the nature of American identity remains a central one, and certainly from the 1960s onward, the theater has provided the arena for that debate. Where else would the distinction between role and identity be explored? Where else would the creation of group solidarity be enacted? Where else would those who wished to see acknowledgment of their role in an unfolding national drama turn but to the theater? If, as O'Neill, Miller, Williams, Albee, Mamet, Wilson, Rabe, and

Shepard all separately suggest, some communality, some essential cohesiveness has disappeared from the modern experience, where else to signal the necessity for the possibility of reconstruction than in that most public of the genres, the theater? The economics of the cinema dictate a blandness that is consequent on a need for the mass audience. The theater, for all its vulnerability to economic pressure, can live more dangerously. The film is a product that cannot be modified by the viewer. The theater, however, is an experience in which the audience is an active participant with the power not only to observe the transformation of actor into character but to become an essential part of that transformation. In the 1960s, theater burst out of the buildings that contained it. It has never quite been forced back inside again, either literally or metaphorically. In some senses, indeed, it has always been America's central metaphor. Manifest Destiny itself presupposed that America was a stage on which was to be enacted the principal drama of civilization that the rest of the world would watch and applaud as an eager audience. That particular hubris might have been diminished, if scarcely destroyed, by time, but the legitimacy of theater as an image of social process continues to be acknowledged. It should scarcely surprise us, therefore, if the writer with an eye on social change chooses to pursue that logic in the direction of drama.

The American theater emerged from the Second World War as the most powerful and influential in the world. No other national drama could boast such talents as Eugene O'Neill, Tennessee Williams, and Arthur Miller in the 1940s and 1950s. The American musical proved an innovative and often socially aware form that found an international audience. In the 1960s, the experiments of the New York avant-garde proved influential and compelling, and Sam Shepard and David Mamet, in the 1970s and 1980s, were among the most impressive playwrights working in the English language. For all its growing decentralization, Broadway was not without its impact. William Inge's poignant and sentimental dramas of middle America touched a nerve in the mid-fifties, just as Neil Simon's knowing comedies of urban angst bridged the second half of the century, compelling not only in their humor but in the moments in which they seem to acknowledge an experience resistant to that humor.

Talent existed in depth. Lanford Wilson, a product of Off-Off Broadway, moved to New York's Circle Repertory Company and from such experimental works as *The Madness of Lady Bright* and *The Rimers of Eldritch* to a series of plays that explored family life against the background of a changing world. In *The Hot l Baltimore* (1973), he explored the lives of a group of transients in a broken-down hotel on the verge of demolition. In *The Mound Builders* (1975), he exposed the tensions within a group of people excavating the past as the present collapses around them. His studies of the Talley family – in *The Fifth of July* (1979), *Talley's Folly* (1979), and *Talley and Son* (1985) – dissected the values of a family drawn to greed and exploitation. With *Burn This* (1986) and *Redwood Curtain* (1992), he consolidated his position as one of America's principal playwrights.

John Guare's success with *The House of Blue Leaves* (1971), successfully revived at Lincoln Center in 1986, was matched by that of *Six Degrees of Separation* (1990). In between, he wrote a powerful and poetic series of plays – *Lydie Breeze* (1982), *Gardenia* (1982), and *Women and Water* (1990) – that explore the fate of a utopian community that mirrors the flawed utopianism of America itself. Guare's plays have a startling originality. Although some are little more than sketches – *The House of Blue Leaves* is a farce that perhaps never cuts as deep as it might – there is a lyricism to his work that has few equals in the American theater. *Lydie Breeze,* in particular, recalls the poetic language and metaphoric richness of early twentieth-century Irish theater and those American playwrights, such as Susan Glaspell and Eugene O'Neill, influenced by that theater. A. R. Gurney found humor in his dissection of upper-class WASP life. Christopher Durang satirized everything from religion to American film. Richard Nelson was equally drawn to satire in *An American Comedy* (1983) and *The Return of Pinocchio* (1983) but along with comedies has written a powerfully political play, *Principia Scriptoriae* (1986), as well as plays that explore the nature of history – *Misha's Party* (1993), *Columbus and the Discovery of Japan* (1994) – and theatricality – *Some Americans Abroad* (1989), *Two Shakespearean Actors* (1990). The list could be extended and yet, curiously, that dramatic literature, that theatrical history, that catalog of artistic achievement has found little room in histories of American literature or studies of American culture. Critics who have responded to the achievements of American poetry, brought considerable analytic skills to a consideration of the American novel, and explored the nature of critical theory have given little attention to a genre in which, from the perspective of other countries, America excels. Certainly British drama, so widely respected in America, can hardly hope to compete with the accomplishments of a theater that in the last fifty years has produced such classics as *The Iceman Cometh, Long Day's Journey into Night, The Glass Menagerie, A Streetcar Named Desire, Cat on a Hot Tin Roof, Death of a Salesman, The Crucible, A View from the Bridge, The Zoo Story, Who's Afraid of Virginia Woolf?, Fool for Love, Buried Child, American Buffalo,* and *Glengarry Glen Ross.* The fact that eight of these, however, were not thought worthy of the Pulitzer prize perhaps suggests that the underestimation of American drama is not the exclusive prerogative of academic critics.

FICTION AND SOCIETY, 1940–1970

Morris Dickstein

I

❦

WAR AND THE NOVEL: FROM WORLD
WAR II TO VIETNAM

E VEN MORE than World War I, in which American participation
had been brief and casualties relatively light, the Second World
War was a watershed, a turning point, in the social history of the
nation. In the second war there were five times as many American dead,
over half a million in a period of almost four years. This was a total war
effort that mobilized virtually every segment of American society. Men
and boys from sleepy towns in the Midwest, segregated farms and ham-
lets in the Deep South, and large ethnic enclaves in the North were
thrown together in a huge, highly organized fighting force and sent to the
bloody beaches and killing fields of France, Italy, North Africa, and especially the Pacific islands. On V-J Day in August 1945, America had
nearly twelve million men under arms; more than sixteen million had
served in the course of the war.

Novels written about the war invariably emphasize the shock of a new
kind of experience, the social and personal dislocation as well as the shock
of blood and carnage. They show how recruits were forced to adjust to the
army before they had to face the war itself. To many, the hierarchy and discipline of military life cut against the American grain. Individualism gave
way to a harsh, demanding group experience. The men they encountered
and the distant places they were sent catapulted them out of the life they
knew and thrust them into a larger world.

If these soldiers were transformed socially, exposed to other ways of life,
they were also influenced morally by being exposed to killing and dying at
an early age. In battle, young men in the prime of life, at their peak of
health and strength, were faced with danger and death at almost any
moment. The foxholes produced instinctive existentialists, young men
caught between adventure and dread who suddenly became aware of the
fragility of life and their own vulnerability.

The home front was almost as dramatically affected as the men who
went to war. Despite the new mobility made possible by the automobile,
despite the new mass culture of tabloids, newsreels, films, and radio,
despite the gradual migration from towns to cities, many Americans still

lived in isolated, relatively homogeneous communities, including those in the black and immigrant ghettos of large cities. Foreshadowing the new mobility of the postwar years, the war drew many women into the factories, blacks from the South to the war plants of Detroit, and showed other Americans a way of life they had barely imagined and might never otherwise have seen. It sent Japanese Americans from their homes to detention camps, in a perverse echo of the racism of America's foes. Forties films about small-town America, such as *Our Town, The Magnificent Ambersons, Shadow of a Doubt,* and *It's a Wonderful Life,* edged in darkness, were bittersweet elegies to an earlier way of life.

If the poverty of the war zone made men appreciate American abundance, the risk and excitement cut them loose from their solid moorings of class and morality. One of the first significant novels of World War II, John Horne Burns's *The Gallery* (1947), deals with the impact of life in wartime Naples and North Africa on an assortment of Americans who seem at times like innocents abroad confronting Mediterranean decadence, or small-town "grotesques" out of *Winesburg, Ohio,* at sea in a different world. On some, the effect is horrifying; on others, liberating. Of one Red Cross worker we're told, with transparent venom, "She'd never think of the word parasite in the future without modifying it by the adjective, Italian."

An American GI, however, drunk with Neapolitan sensuality at a performance of *La Bohème,* seems happy for the first time in his life: "What was there here in the sweetness of this reality that he'd missed out on in America?" Boozily, lyrically, he sets love and feeling against the power of commerce: "He saw for the first time in his life that the things which keep the world going are not to be bought or sold, that every flower grows out of decay, that for all the mud and grief there are precious things which make it worth while for us to leave our mothers' wombs." Here we feel the heavy hand of the author laying in his themes, as we do when so many of these characters come to a bad end.

If the war made individual Americans less insular and parochial, it also made American culture more cosmopolitan. Americans went abroad, as they had in 1917, but this time foreigners also came to us, as America became the refuge for a vast intellectual emigration that altered many of our arts and sciences. Just as Einstein and other Europeans transformed American physics, surrealists such as Matta, abstractionists like Josef Albers and Hans Hoffmann transformed American painting, helping to create the new abstract art through which New York would displace Paris as the world art capital.

Already in the 1930s, émigré filmmakers, though chafing under the constraints of the studio system, had begun to transform how American movies were made. Literary intellectuals helped spread the influence of Franz Kafka and other European moderns. Such political intellectuals as Hannah Arendt, along with widely read writers like Orwell and Koestler, developed theories of totalitarianism that contributed to postwar anti-Communism. Émigré psychoanalysts helped foster an inward turn that saw Americans shift from the social concerns of the Depression years to the therapeutic ideas of the postwar period.

The writers who drove ambulances in World War I, who fled to Paris for artistic and personal freedom during the 1920s, were disillusioned by the contrast between Wilsonian ideals and wartime brutality. They saw a nation that seemed largely unaffected by the war, a nation of hucksters and boosters dominated by small-town values and middle-class morality. The protagonist of Hemingway's "Soldier's Home" (in *In Our Time,* 1925) returns to a world of boys and girls courting, parents pressuring him to snap back to normal, to look for a job. Always out of step, he cannot talk about what he has gone through, cannot fall back on routines that have gone dead for him. He is far from rebellious; it is just that he cannot seem to make the effort:

Vaguely he wanted a girl but he did not want to have to work to get her. . . . He did not want to get into the intrigue and the politics. He did not want to have to do any courting. He did not want to tell any more lies. It wasn't worth it.

He did not want any consequences. He did not want any consequences ever again. He wanted to live along without consequences. Besides he did not really need a girl. The army had taught him that.

The numb repetition of small words and simple syntax reflects the state of mind of a man deadened by his experience, a man not understood by those around him. He is someone for whom the bright bustle of America, all this active willing and doing, has grown meaningless. Krebs he is called, for crabbed he is. "I don't love anybody," he finally blurts out to his pious, sentimental mother, only to retreat quickly from the flood of her tears. America was no place for those who, having seen the war, had seen through everything.

The suffering and endurance of ordinary Americans during the Depression made such a detached attitude untenable. When the money in Paris ran out, the expatriate writers came home physically; soon enough, they also tried to come home spiritually, though the results did not always feel authentic. Even those writers who had remained in the States, relishing the satiric barbs of H. L. Mencken and Sinclair Lewis, were propelled by the Depression toward journalistic curiosity, radical commitment, and gestures of solidarity with the poor and dispossessed. Hemingway himself signaled his new commitment by involving himself publicly with the cause of the Spanish republic, and having a dying Harry Morgan, his rum-running hero of *To Have and Have Not* (1937), spit out at the end, "No man alone now . . . a man alone ain't got no bloody fucking chance."

One result of this change was to make American literature more insular again, more focused on the struggle for survival at home, and less bleakly pessimistic. The cause of the common man, the bright revolutionary future, made sophistication and formalism seem passé, self-indulgent, and this gave naturalism, moribund since Dreiser's prime, a new lease on life. A handful of writers, such as Nathanael West, preserved the mocking spirit of the twenties but found few readers. Henry Miller, who remained abroad, was as wildly funny in his affirmations as West was in his nega-tions, but the single-minded cry of the flesh kept his work apart from pro-letarian pieties, as it kept it from publication in this country. Another interesting exception, William Saroyan, also wrapped his populism in a prickly individualism. Like Miller he was a kind of anarchist, rejecting the current political formulas for his own common-man vision.

The war put an end to these social commitments and antisocial adven-tures as effectively as it ended the Depression itself. Taking its cue from the cherished myths of the thirties, the war novel substituted the common sol-dier, the ordinary grunt, for the common man, and put the hiking army, wallowing in mud, in place of the bonus marcher, the hobo, the unem-ployed drifter, the migrating family. Reporters such as Ernie Pyle, cartoon-ists like Bill Mauldin, and photojournalists such as Robert Capa and Margaret Bourke-White became the new laureates of the American experi-ence, lending a gritty, heroic cast to the tribulations of the common man.

The war also contributed to the masculinization of American writing. It gave a central place to the Hemingway themes of courage and risk in situa-tions of testing and crisis. In the aftermath of the war, a much more conser-vative view of gender roles became dominant. Depression unemployment often made women the economic and emotional mainstay of their family, and wartime employment brought them into the factories, mills, and war industries. The return of the fighting men, though, left little room for Rosie the Riveter, and the migration to the suburbs kept women domestic as they raised increasing numbers of children. Gender stereotypes returned with a vengeance, replacing the more liberated images of women that had developed between the wars, as Betty Friedan showed in *The Feminine Mystique* (1963). In turn, the major figures in postwar fiction for more than two decades were nearly all male, with rare exceptions, such as Flannery O'Connor, Carson McCullers, and Eudora Welty in the South; the brilliant and brittle Mary McCarthy, who emerged from the bosom of the New York intellectuals; *New Yorker* writers like Jean Stafford, Hortense Calisher, and Shirley Jackson; and Grace Paley, writing in a woman's voice of rare subtlety and delicacy among American Jewish writers. It was not until the sixties sparked a revival of feminism that women reclaimed their vital position in the American novel.

The war also marked a closure for many literary careers. We can scarcely understand postwar fiction without seeing how few writers from the prewar years actually survived the war itself. Some died literally, and others simply lost their creative edge in the changed conditions of the postwar world. West and Fitzgerald died on successive days in 1940, Sherwood Anderson in 1941 (along with Joyce and Virginia Woolf, whose greatest influence in America was yet to come), Dreiser in 1945, Gertrude Stein in 1946, and Willa Cather in 1947. Most of the proletarian writers disappeared after one or two books, some to Hollywood or *Time* magazine, which both remained sympathetic to social melodrama, others into children's writing, historical fiction, or pulp fiction. The rise of McCarthyism made their lot even more untenable.

There was no successor to Henry Roth's *Call It Sleep* – Roth's next novel, really a free-form memoir, would not begin to appear for sixty years – to Daniel Fuchs's Williamsburg novels, to Robert Cantwell's *The Land of Plenty* or Jack Conroy's *The Disinherited*. Committed social novelists who remained prolific were unable to regain the élan of their best work. Steinbeck would never again write anything to match the urgency of *In Dubious Battle* (1936) and *The Grapes of Wrath* (1939); James T. Farrell and John Dos Passos would never equal the social grasp and personal intensity of their Depression trilogies, *Studs Lonigan* (1932–35) and *U.S.A.* (1930–36). Their naturalist methods, which required an immense piling up of realistic details, and a minute verisimilitude, seemed unable to encompass the complexities and absurdities, to say nothing of the social changes, of the postwar world. Along with the expansive, egocentric Thomas Wolfe, who had died prematurely in 1938, their impact on the wartime generation remained great.

Other naturalists lost touch with America by leaving it behind. Living in Europe in the late forties and fifties, Richard Wright remained essentially the author of *Native Son* (1940) and *Black Boy* (1945). His later writing, influenced by European existentialism, became more abstract and lost touch with home – and with his own talent. (The same fate would befall James Baldwin after 1963.) Only the ravages of age or alcoholism and the fragility of genius could begin to explain the decline of the greatest writers of the interwar years, Hemingway and Faulkner, which set in just as their earlier work was gaining them readers, fame, and increasing literary influence. Hemingway's important work ended with his last great stories in 1939 and *For Whom the Bell Tolls* in 1940, though *The Old Man and the Sea* and *A Moveable Feast* would show something of the old hard brilliance.

Faulkner last achieved real power with *The Hamlet* in 1940 and *Go Down, Moses* in 1942, just before he left once more for Hollywood to earn his bread. Most of his later books are sequels that fill in details of the Yoknapatawpha County saga. Despite the Nobel prize that reached them too late, as it eventually reached T. S. Eliot and even Steinbeck, neither Hemingway nor Faulkner did major work on the postwar scene, when young writers revered them, along with Fitzgerald, as the very definition of the modern American novelist.

Finally, the novelists of manners, who had prospered as a conservative counterweight to the radical writers of the Depression, had great difficulty sustaining themselves as postwar writers – outside the best-seller market, where their work continued to thrive. J. P. Marquand, James Gould Cozzens, John O'Hara, John Cheever, and Louis Auchincloss were the diminished heirs to what once had been a major tradition in American fiction. They were the writers from New England and the Northeast who closely documented the lives of the upper and professional classes. In the hands of Henry James and Edith Wharton, this WASP novel of manners was still rooted in the New England moral tradition and the Hawthornean fable. It had not yet devolved into a mere social record or documentation of the status anxieties and sexual or professional problems of a declining elite. Their only real postwar successor was John Updike, a great admirer of Cheever, though he came from a much humbler Pennsylvania background. His brilliant, dexterous prose, scrupulous realism, and bold focus on sex, marriage, and family life gave the novel of manners a different kind of vitality.

By the 1930s, when O'Hara published *Appointment in Samarra* (1934) and *Butterfield 8* (1935), and Marquand, fresh from his success with a Japanese detective, Mr. Moto, turned to serious social comedy with *The Late George Apley* (1937) and *Wickford Point* (1939), American writing was already turning more ethnic and pluralist. John Cheever's published journals refer frequently to the novels of Saul Bellow, for Cheever feels their colloquial and demotic energy eludes him. Writers from the small towns and larger cities of the Midwest had already staked a major claim to national attention in the twenties. Now Southern writers, Jewish writers, and black writers were finding their voice, as they increasingly would after the war. The Depression had weakened the social position of the upper classes and redirected literary attention to the marginal and the dispossessed, so that even a writer as critical of the rich as Fitzgerald was attacked by the literary left and neglected by the magazines that were once so eager to publish his work.

O'Hara, for example, had gone to school with both Hemingway and Fitzgerald, emulating one for his hard-boiled style, built on spare but pregnant dialogue, the other for his gift of social observation. He was more the straight reporter than either of them, however. He shared Fitzgerald's fascination with success but showed little of Fitzgerald's strong emotional identification with his characters. He had very little interest in psychology, not much more in advanced fictional technique, but an insatiable appetite for social and sexual detail. His brief, anecdotal, understated stories were almost the definition of *New Yorker* fiction in the thirties and forties, when they were praised by Lionel Trilling, for their "exacerbated social awareness." But after the war, his novels, once far more disciplined, swelled into an unselective, unrefined record of the material culture of the upper middle class, and critics found it harder to take him seriously.

Ironically, the whole phenomenon of a declining gentry fallen on hard times would gradually lose its basis in social reality during the postwar economic boom, when even the old rich became richer. Yet these writers, caught in a narrowly realist aesthetic, were increasingly trapped in minute social documentation of a numbing and trivializing sort at a time when manners themselves became less important. Affluence was the great economic surprise of the postwar era, since many had predicted that a severe contraction, perhaps even a return of the Depression, would follow the end of war production and the shift to a peacetime economy. Instead, Americans went on an economic binge, stimulated by the savings that had accumulated during wartime and the vast consumer demand that had been pent up since the onset of the Depression. The birth rate soared along with the boom in consumption.

General Motors' immensely popular Futurama exhibit at the 1939 World's Fair was a promise of abundance whose fulfillment was cruelly postponed by the war, then achieved beyond our wildest dreams. (Though many were incredulous, it boldly predicted that there would be a staggering 38 million cars on American roads by 1960. There were actually 74 million.) The show confidently anticipated technological triumphs that were achieved only in wartime military research and were later adapted to peacetime use. Scientific advances ranged from telecommunications and jet propulsion to atomic power and antibiotics. Meanwhile, the economies of Europe and much of Asia were shattered by the war, making the United States the supplier and producer for the whole international system. As Godfrey Hodgson wrote in *America in Our Time,*

In 1945, the United States was bulging with an abundance of every resource that held the key to power in the modern world: with land, food, power, raw materials, industrial plant, monetary reserves, scientific talent, and trained manpower. It was in the war years that the United States shot ahead of all its rivals economically. In four years, national income, national wealth, and industrial production all doubled or more than doubled. . .

In 1947, with postwar recovery under way everywhere, the United States produced about one half of the world's manufactures: 57 per cent of its steel, 43 per cent of its electricity, 62 per cent of its oil. It owned three quarters of the world's automobiles and was improving on that show by manufacturing well over 80 per cent of the new cars built in the world that year. The American lead was greatest in precisely those industries which contributed to the power to wage modern war: aviation, chemical engineering, electronics.

If the American economy provided a basis for world power, it also made possible a consumer society and a new leisure culture that radically altered American life, and this was reflected in American literature and art. Very few postwar novelists could sustain the large-scale social visions of a Dreiser or a Faulkner. *Freud* replaced *Marx* as a catchword not only for writers and intellectuals but for a self-seeking new middle class. In a culture of affluence, in which more and more people were entering the middle class, therapeutic ideas gradually took the place of class consciousness. As American society turned inward, toward the nuclear family and the house in the suburbs, American novels also turned inward, focusing more on private life and individual experience. Novels grew shorter and avoided modernist experiments with time, consciousness, and narrative fragmentation.

A handful of thirties writers, such as Henry Roth, William Faulkner, and Nathanael West, had written their books under the immediate impact of *Ulysses* and *The Waste Land,* as well as the French surrealists and the German expressionists. Henry Miller had been inspired by writers as different as Whitman, Rimbaud, and Céline. The major influence on postwar fiction, however, was Henry James, whose work was just then being revived. James was appreciated less for his ambitious social canvas or his attention to manners than for his formal rigor and his minutely detailed aesthetic and psychological discriminations.

The war novel was the major exception to this Jamesian wave, with its pull toward analysis, reflection, and formal control. If the James revival was a reaction against the proletarian excesses of the thirties and the shocking facts of the war, the war novelists looked back unashamedly to different influences: the social outlook and conservative technique of Theodore Dreiser, John Dos Passos, and James T. Farrell; the autobiographical novels of Thomas Wolfe; and the masculine crucible of Hemingway and other novelists of the previous war. Without the example of such books as *In Our Time, A Farewell to Arms, The Enormous Room,* and *Three Soldiers,* but also of such Depression novels as *Studs Lonigan* and *U.S.A.,* the major novels of the Second World War would be unimaginable. In some essential ways, the war novel was a brilliant offshoot of Depression writing, the last big explosion of naturalism in American fiction.

Unlike popular works of novelized history (like Herman Wouk's *The Winds of War*), which tried to swallow the war whole in one episodic piece of fiction, most serious novels of World War II, even very long ones, dealt with only a handful of incidents, a small corner of the conflict, usually one the writer himself had witnessed. Harry Brown's *A Walk in the Sun* (1944), which became famous for the movie version directed by Lewis Milestone, was a tour de force in the style of *The Red Badge of Courage* that described a grisly day in the campaign to establish a beachhead in Italy. Both Norman Mailer's *The Naked and the Dead* (1948) and James Jones's *The Thin Red Line* (1962) were about the invasion and conquest of a single Japanese-held Pacific island. Yet in unfolding a single action, from the anxieties of landing through all the stages of combat, each novelist managed to portray the whole shape of the war.

But other major novels scarcely dealt with combat at all. Jones's *From Here to Eternity* (1951), still the best of all the novels about the Second World War, is set within the regular army in Hawaii in the months leading up to Pearl Harbor, while Cozzens's *Guard of Honor* (1948) is built around a racial incident at an air force training base in Florida. Mailer, Jones, and Cozzens use flashbacks to fill in the civilian lives of the men in uniform. Circumscribed by the classical unities of time, space, and action, their big novels become microcosms not only of the war but of a larger American society in transition. At its best, the war novel was not simply about the conflict, graphic as it was, but about much of the world that preceded and would follow this war.

Prewar writers, including Michael Gold, Roth, Steinbeck, Wright, and Faulkner, had turned the spotlight on ethnic and regional characters; war writers brought these types together in close quarters under the pressure of extreme conditions, as the war itself had done. Proletarian writers had focused on class conflict in American society; they had drawn special attention to the drifters, the lumpen, the dispossessed of the Depression years, or they had written alarming fables about the dangers of Fascism. War novelists transposed these very themes onto the authoritarian hierarchy of the army. The dictators and plutocrats of Depression fiction were now obtuse, capricious officers; the common man riding the freights became the common soldier hiking through the jungle mud.

Some of the outstanding war novels, such as *The Naked and the Dead,* were actually political novels, novels of ideas. They were written not in the trenches but during the sobering transition between war and peace, between hot war and the cold war. They reflected the writers' fear that victory over Fascism abroad had been purchased at the cost of intolerance and regimentation at home. These war novelists' nightmare was a world threatened not by foreign tyrants and obvious villains but by large, impersonal social organizations. Thus novels like *The Naked and the Dead* led directly to the widely read social criticism of such men as David Riesman (*The Lonely Crowd*), William H. White, Jr. (*The Organization Man*), C. Wright Mills (*White Collar, The Power Elite*), and Vance Packard (*The Hidden Persuaders, The Waste Makers, The Status Seekers*).

American society had been fragmented by the Depression, which exacerbated class consciousness and widened the chasm between the haves and the have-nots. Attacks on the rich were staples of the 1930s, not only in left-wing polemics but in such social satires as Marquand's *The Late George Apley,* screwball comedies like *My Man Godfrey* and *Easy Living,* and congressional investigations into arms profiteering. The pressure to win the war overrode these social divisions, however, as it overcame the Depression itself. For the duration of the war, a sense of unified purpose linked workers and businessmen, Communists and capitalists, farmers and city dwellers, women in factories and men in uniform. To win the war, unions agreed not to strike, businesses accepted price controls, minorities agreed to mute their grievances.

By the end of the war, this artificial unity had turned America into a more patriotic, less tolerant place, more devoted to organizational values and social conformity, more homogeneous in its stated ideals. This helped produce a malaise, an uneasiness that was reflected in the best novels, the darkest films and plays. Since nearly all the war novels were written *after* the war, the writers projected their sense of the postwar world back onto the war, their anger at bureaucracy onto the army, their new fears of nuclear annihilation onto earlier scenes of mortal combat. For all their surface realistic grit, the best war novels were really parables about American life.

Jones's *The Thin Red Line,* a remarkable achievement for a combat novel, shows how a work of limited scope could encompass a large part of the war. Its subject, the invasion and conquest of Guadalcanal in 1942, was a turning point in the morale of Americans in the Pacific, the first offensive action after Pearl Harbor and the first American victory in the Pacific theater. It begins with the landing of men, including some longtime regular soldiers, who have never been in combat, and takes us through every stage of fear, disbelief, exhaustion, camaraderie, battle-tested numbness, injury, unheroic victory, and removal from the war. In Jones's trilogy, the novel is flanked by two books that deal with the prewar military (*From Here to Eternity*) and the postcombat fate of wounded men in a military hospital back home (*Whistle,* 1978).

The last of these, *Whistle,* was a tired novel, written when Jones was already seriously ill, and published posthumously; it reflected the much more downbeat post-Vietnam atmosphere of the 1970s. Full of illness and injury, including the physical and psychological wounds that had lifted the author himself out of combat 35 years earlier, it portrays the war and the larger world from the point of view of the hospital, another "enormous room" like e.e. cummings's World War I detention camp. The war still unfolding far away seems remote and distant but also, in the injuries the men have suffered, an ever-present physical intrusion. The book's links were not with combat stories but with such grim postwar rehabilitation films about damaged human beings as *The Best Years of Our Lives* (1946) and *The Men* (1950), as well as their successors of the 1970s, such as Hal Ashby's *Coming Home,* which turned the spotlight on Vietnam veterans just as Jones's last novel was being written.

The first two novels of Jones's trilogy, *From Here to Eternity* and *The Thin Red Line,* however, are among the most impressive works of American realism. Jones's main rival as a war novelist, Norman Mailer, paid grudging tribute to both books in essays sharply attacking most of his other rivals. In *Advertisements for Myself,* he described Jones as "the only one of my contemporaries who I felt had more talent than myself," called *Eternity* "the best American novel since the war," and said later (in *Cannibals and Christians*) that *The Thin Red Line* could be used as a training manual for an infantry campaign. Perhaps Mailer meant to underline the books' limitations, yet both novels do convey an overpowering sense of actuality.

Though it is as deftly structured as a five-act drama, *From Here to Eternity* unfolds incrementally in the most unforced manner imaginable. Set in and around the Schofield Barracks near Honolulu, where Jones himself had served, the novel creates characters who seem fully alive and a setting that feels like an authentic world. The thirty-year-men we see at Schofield, and later in the concentration camp-like stockade, are refugees from an economically depressed, socially constricted small-town America, as Jones himself had once been. "Most of them had bummed around the country at least once, before they finally enlisted," says Jones. They were "jerked loose from ties by the Depression and set to a drifting that had ended finally in the Army as the last port of call."

Hewing not only to the literary technique but to the social outlook of the 1930s, Jones gives us an outsider's perspective, a grunt's-eye view of the army in *From Here to Eternity,* then of the war itself in *The Thin Red Line.* His achingly proud, taciturn hero, Robert E. Lee Prewitt, a coal miner's son from Harlan County, is a figure out of the proletarian novel, like his mentor in the stockade, Jack Malloy, a veteran of the old Industrial Workers of the World (IWW), who preaches passive resistance. Where the hero of proletarian fiction is usually initiated by some hardened Communist into an understanding of the class struggle, however, Prewitt, as his name indicates, is more of a romantic rebel, doomed, self-destructive, caught between his love of the army and his inability to accept its harsh, often unfair discipline, a Kid Galahad living by his own stubborn code of honor. In his boxing, which he abandons after blinding a man, and his near-magical bugling, which is snatched away from him by officers trying to control or break him, Prewitt is also a sentimental portrait of the artist as the sort of ornery individualist whom no mass organization – and few proletarian novels – could easily accommodate.

Initially a misfit, Prewitt eventually becomes too much the white knight, the prickly hero incapable of compromise. His unbending code of morality makes trouble for others, not just for himself. This stern behavior, which he often regrets, leads to catastrophe in his and other people's lives, including Bloom's suicide, Maggio's imprisonment, and finally his own death. He spoils everyone's lax tolerance for the way things are. There is a laconic stoicism and youthful integrity that make him a figure out of Hemingway – the writer who, along with Stephen Crane, lies across the path of every modern war novelist. Like Mailer, Jones builds on Hemingway's feeling for extreme situations. He explores the special intimacy that develops among men separated from women even as he exposes the corruption of the institutions that bring these men together. Jones's other hero, Sgt. Warden, as ornery as Prewitt, refuses to accept a commission, though it spoils his love affair with his captain's wife.

Though he deals with the regular army, Jones takes a jaundiced, outsider's view of the military character. Officers are nearly always assholes in Jones's novels: petty, ambitious, time-serving careerists who put their own interests first. Their methods parallel those of the bosses and politicians in the civilian world: they exercise power selfishly, arbitrarily, or sadistically. The brutalities of the stockade, as overseen by small-time fascists like Fatso Judson, come more from the chain-gang movies of the 1930s than from the author's insight into Nazi-like violence. The stockade becomes a metaphor for the mass organization's efforts to stamp out resistance and individual identity. Another parable about totalitarianism, *1984,* had been published only a year or two before Jones's novel appeared; Hannah Arendt's book, *The Origins of Totalitarianism,* also came out in 1951. As the Cold War deepened, the whole subject was very much in the air.

Jones's evocations of sadistic brutality bring to mind the striking parallels between *From Here to Eternity* and Mailer's *The Naked and the Dead.* Like Jones, Mailer brought to the army an outsider's viewpoint, in his case that of the middle-class Jew, the Harvard man, the aspiring young literary intellectual. He had joined the army not to fight Fascism (like some of the left-wing writers) or to exit the Depression (like Jones and his characters) but to write the great American novel, deliberately choosing the Pacific theater to avoid the cultural complications of a European setting.

Unlike Jones, though, Mailer was fascinated by everything in his Texas outfit that was not himself – not Jewish, not Ivy League, not liberal or intellectual. He even developed an occasional Texas drawl in imitation of the rednecks who ragged him. His liberal surrogate, the Harvard-educated Lt. Hearn, comes off as honorable but also weak and vacillating. In his clumsy, unbending resistance to evil, he is almost as self-destructive as Prewitt, but his death at the hands of the two fascist types, Gen. Cummings and Sgt. Croft, carries little of the tragic poignance that echoes lyrically through Jones's handling of Prewitt. Mailer's two Jews, Goldstein and Roth, are almost anti-Semitic caricatures of sensitive weaklings, too eager for acceptance, as uneasy in their own skin as in a man's army.

Mailer's real equivalent for Prewitt was his lower-class soldier parallel to Hearn, a tough anarchist named Red Valsen, yet another character straight out of the novels of the thirties. He can still sing "Brother, Can You Spare a Dime?" and he believes "they ain't a general in the world is any good. They're all sonsofbitches." The "Time Machine" chapter that fills in his background is a pastiche out of proletarian fiction and *Studs Lonigan,* a book that influenced not only Mailer's style but also his whole sense of men in groups. (Mailer once described the book as "the best single literary experience I had had.") At the end, in a neat symmetry, Valsen is humiliated by Croft just as Hearn had been humbled by Cummings: this is Mailer's sour epitaph for the humane but naïve liberalism of the Depression era.

In an ironic twist, Cummings and Croft, the figures who represent power rather than conscience, are also confounded. Cummings's chessboard strategy proves as pointless as Croft's superhuman, Ahab-like drive to conquer Mt. Anaka. All their effort, all their brutish cunning, in the end are useless. Instead, the island campaign is won quite accidentally by the doltish Dalleson, a cautious, blundering fool. In tune with the existentialism of the late forties, which had itself been generated by the violence and extremity of war, Mailer's ironic conclusion deflates heroic designs and points to the forces of history and chance over which people have no con-

trol. As the novel ends, brilliantly but anticlimactically, a postwar sense of
the absurd displaces the prewar social consciousness.

Mailer himself saw very little of the war: as the injured Jones left the war
early, Mailer, finishing at Harvard, came to it quite late, while the campaign for the Philippines was being waged and won in 1945. Like many of
his characters, Jones joined the army before the war as a way of escaping not
just the Depression but the responsibilities of civilian life. "The Jones man
is essentially a vagrant," wrote Wilfrid Sheed, a little too sardonically in
1967, "which means that his life has been a compound of freedom and feckless dependency. The army is the ideal nest for him, a place where he can
wave his finger at authority and lean on it at the same time."

Jones saw the army and the war from the viewpoint of the thirty-year
man, the professional soldier but also a loner who is contemptuous of
draftees and officers alike. Mailer, on the other hand, already the political
novelist, was fascinated by those who have the power of decision and command. Jones's officers are time-serving careerists and opportunists, organization men stroking their own vanity. The contemptible Capt. Holmes,
who gave his wife gonorrhea within months of their marriage, becomes the
army's instrument for trying to "break" Prewitt. Like Cummings in *The
Naked and the Dead,* he tries to govern by instilling fear and leveling resistance. To him, Prewitt is a pocket of anarchic individualism, a challenge to
his power and a passport to his next promotion. Both Prewitt and Mailer's
Red Valsen are holdovers from the rural-proletarian thirties, the good soldiers allergic to the Organization, incapable of simply getting along.

Mailer's Cummings, on the other hand, is the grand strategist, the
philosophical-minded officer schooled on Carlyle, Nietzsche, and Spengler
who sees men as the intractable raw material for his larger designs. He first
takes Hearn as his audience, his accomplice, his protégé, only to turn on
him (when he resists) with all the venom of a spurned lover. This part of
the book, a psychosexual novel of ideas, is a crude rehearsal for Mailer's
later fictions about ego, power, and dominance. (Cummings is Mailer's
Citizen Kane, as Kane himself was Orson Welles's prototype for his many
later versions of overweening power and ego. In a beautiful twist, Welles
would play General Dreedle, Joseph Heller's send-up of Cummings, in
Mike Nichols's tamely respectful film version of *Catch-22.*)

With its scheming general and its representative platoon stocked with
every regional and religious stereotype, the first part of *The Naked and the
Dead,* like so many war movies, mirrors the Popular Front fiction and
drama of the late thirties. Its "Time Machine" flashbacks are borrowed
from the biographical interludes of Dos Passos's *U.S.A.* The novel rises to
real distinction only in the latter half, the gripping account of the long

patrol dominated by Sgt. Croft, the best character in the book, a purely instinctive, almost animal version of the cerebral Cummings. Here Mailer's interest shifts to the physical and mental testing of men under stress, driven beyond the limits of exhaustion by an obsessive figure. The sensory and visceral details of this part of the story would make it the master text for later writers dealing with jungle warfare, especially the Vietnam War novelists. (Its effect can still be felt, for example, in the opening chapters of Tim O'Brien's *Going After Cacciato* [1978], easily the best of the Vietnam novels.)

Here finally, in this test of endurance, Mailer's ethnic and regional stereotypes come to life as they are cruelly pressed by a single man's will. Mailer's formal sympathies are with the ordinary men but his inner attraction draws him to the Nietzschean overreacher, the kind of character who would help him find his real strength as a writer.

Thus, Mailer and Jones wrote the same novel from opposite points of view. Jones remained the thirties anarchist whose hatred of the organization would take on a new meaning in the Organization Man world of the 1950s, when the social rebel of the prewar years would become the prickly nonconformist of such works as *The Catcher in the Rye* and *On the Road.* Mailer, despite his use of the trappings of the social novel in *The Naked and the Dead,* was already the postwar Freudian and existentialist, more interested in power than in justice, drawn to instinct and will rather than social improvement. In his later fiction and journalism, however, he went on to do some of the best political writing of the postwar era, exploring the erotic rather than the institutional dimensions of power. Jones, on the other hand, like a true thirty-year man, was incapable of adjusting his literary lens to civilian life, though he did write one strong, shapeless, underrated novel, *Go to the Widowmaker* (1967), set largely in the Caribbean, an autobiographical work about masculinity and sexuality perhaps too reminiscent of both Hemingway and Mailer.

Jones's best book after *From Here to Eternity* was his only combat novel, *The Thin Red Line* (1962), essentially a tighter, more disciplined rejoinder to *The Naked and the Dead.* Compared to Jones's limpid and authoritative treatment of the island campaign, with its vivid sense of actuality, *The Naked and the Dead* was the most literary of all war novels; it echoed a score of the best modern writers. Mailer's stereotypes include the vicious sergeant, the college-educated lieutenant, the pompous general, the cringing Jews, the beefy farmboy, the lascivious Southern redneck, the guilt-ridden Irishman, the frightened Mexican, and so on. Filling in their backgrounds clumsily with "Time Machine" chapters, he imitates overripe Southern writing for the redneck Wilson, F. Scott Fitzgerald for the WASP

Hearn, Farrell for the Irishman Gallagher, proletarian fiction for the drifter Valsen. But this is only the beginning of Mailer's anthology of literary echoes: Hearn's sudden death comes from E. M. Forster, Croft's obsession with Mt. Anaka mingles Shelley's "Mont Blanc" with *Moby-Dick,* Martinez kills a Japanese soldier in a scene out of *Man's Fate,* the fetid jungle atmosphere reminds us of *Heart of Darkness,* Wilson's wounded body is borne along and swept away like Addie's corpse in *As I Lay Dying,* Roth's masochistic sense of humiliation is pure Dostoyevsky, Cummings's reflections on war and history echo *War and Peace* – the list could go on. These numerous and classy literary debts, along with the clumsy, mechanical structure of the book as a whole, help explain why many readers have felt some inauthenticity about *The Naked and the Dead,* though it was surely a tour de force for a 25-year-old writer.

Jones's response to Mailer in *The Thin Red Line* is to tell the same story straight, reducing it to the barest essentials. More interested in the psychology of the group than in the individual soldier, he mobilizes a huge cast of characters, including most of the key figures of *From Here to Eternity,* and, in a strange move, gives them all monosyllabic names, paring their personalities down to a few key traits. Thus, Prewitt becomes Witt, Warden becomes "mad" Welsh, and Stark becomes Strange, all mere kernels of the people they once were. Moreover, he ruthlessly purges the Kid Galahad romanticism that had surrounded Prewitt's rebellion and death, his love affair with Lorene, the martyrdom of Maggio in the stockade, the affair between Warden and Karen Holmes. Instead, he substitutes an emphasis on courage and fear, the crushing fear of men new to combat, and, most of all, the utter cowardice of a new, largely autobiographical character, Fife, whose experiences and reactions closely follow the author's own.

Jones's unheroic, often comic view of war and violence partly reflects the period when it was written: the late fifties and early sixties, exactly the time of *Catch-22.* (Jones and Heller had been in a writing class together shortly after the war.) The absurdism of both books, though – far more marked in Heller's – could already be found in the last part of *The Naked and the Dead.* An existential view of war informs Mailer's novel and, more obliquely, creates a feeling of bottomless sadness and futility just beneath the lyrical glow of *From Here to Eternity.* It is at the core of Harry Brown's short novel *A Walk in the Sun,* published before the end of the war: a sense that the conditions of combat, the physical trials, the arbitrariness of instant death, opened up a moral and metaphysical abyss that was as ridiculous as it was tragic, as ironic as it was horrific. This kind of black humor had been a strong presence in war novels going back to Stephen Crane, Jaroslav Hašek's *The Good Soldier Schweik,* and, above all, Céline's

Journey to the End of Night, with its bitter, mocking sarcasm, a tradition Heller would bring to a kind of apotheosis. The interminably dying Wilson, carried along like some intolerable human burden, was but one thread of Mailer's novel; the dying Snowden became the core of *Catch-22,* an image not to be set aside, a continuous reminder of the softness of mere flesh, the fragility of human life.

By the time *The Thin Red Line* appeared in 1962, Heller's book made it look tame. Like Heller, Jones had the notion of writing a "comic combat novel," and many early scenes, such as Bead's gruesome struggle with a Japanese soldier who comes at him when he is emptying his bowels, are bizarre set pieces, strange, unexpected events demonstrating the absurdity of war. At odd moments, the stringent naturalism of Jones's novel seems more like the magic realism of sixties writers like Pynchon and Vonnegut than the verisimilitude of Theodore Dreiser. These later writers, in line with the mocking spirit of the 1960s, belong to a long antiheroic tradition that goes back to Shakespeare's Falstaff, to the Battle of Waterloo as seen in Stendhal's *Charterhouse of Parma,* and to the raw recruits of *The Red Badge of Courage.* This is essentially a comic tradition, though it evokes a disrupted, endangered, and topsy-turvy world. In other war fiction of the 1960s, we find atrocity (the bombing of Dresden in Kurt Vonnegut, Jr.'s *Slaughter-house-Five*), contingency (the London blitz in Thomas Pynchon's *Gravity's Rainbow*), absurdity (everywhere in Joseph Heller's *Catch-22*), moral ambiguity (Vonnegut's *Mother Night*), and paranoia (in all of the above).

Jones's book is less stylized than any of these, yet odd, unheroic things keep happening, especially in the early stages of the campaign, when the men are going through their clumsy, intense, fantastic rites of passage. The novel turns more conventional as it goes on – it becomes almost straight and documentary – but it never falls back upon the old romantic idea of war. We see that tactics and strategy still matter, as in the old war fiction, that even terrified men, turned numb to fear, can stumble into amazing feats, but also that those who survive come out not as heroes – their heroism is always either savage, unthinking, or quite accidental – but simply as changed men. The crucible of combat has made them different, besides showing them stark, unforgettable things about who and what they are.

Like the war novels of Stendhal, Stephen Crane, and Hemingway, Jones's *The Thin Red Line* is finally a bildungsroman, the tale of how a raw youth all too quickly becomes a man. But by making this a collective story – the story not of a tragic Prewitt but merely of Fife, Bead, Doll, and other truncated characters – and stressing their fear and inexperience, by making the officers such knaves and fools, Jones undercuts all patriotic resonance and conventional machismo. Other combat novels are more harshly antiheroic, but none conveys so well the ordinariness of men in extraordinary situations.

Knowing something about Jones's meager war record, his success in getting *out* of the war, Hemingway had angrily rejected *From Here to Eternity,* much as he turned on all the writers who worshiped and threatened to overtake him. (Jones was the last discovery of Hemingway's own editor at Scribner's, Maxwell Perkins.) Had Hemingway lived to read *The Thin Red Line,* it would surely have confirmed his feeling that Jones was cowardly and neurotic, a recalcitrant outsider to the combat he described. "I spotted him for a psycho and not a real soldier," he wrote to Scribner's in 1951. By 1962, though, Jones was in close touch with the insecure feelings that an earlier Hemingway, free of bluster, had helped him understand. In *The Thin Red Line,* he focused not on the quixotic integrity of a Prewitt but the smell of fear, the horrified sense of disbelief, of smaller characters like Fife and Bead. This does not keep them from becoming swaggering brawlers when they grow inured to battle.

Bead is vetted into combat in the most ridiculous way imaginable, when the Japanese soldier comes at him as he is taking a crap. Clumsily, unheroically, almost involuntarily, he nearly beats the man to death before bayoneting and shooting him, all the while trying to keep his pants on. "My god," he thinks, "how much killing did the damned fool require? Bead had beaten him, kicked him, choked him, clawed him, bayoneted him, shot him. He had a sudden frantic vision of himself, by rights the victor, doomed forever to kill perpetually the same single Japanese." He kills the man clumsily out of a sheer savage reflex of survival, as Jones himself had once done at a similar moment. When he must return to the corpse to look for his glasses, the scene modulates from horrific comedy to existential absurdity:

The faceless – almost headless – corpse with its bloody, cut fingers and the mangled hole in its chest, so short a time ago a living, breathing man, made him so dizzy in the stomach that he thought he might faint. . . . Bead wanted to turn and run. He could not escape a feeling that, especially now, after he'd both looked and touched, some agent of retribution would try to hold him responsible. He wanted to beg the man's forgiveness in the hope of forestalling responsibility. . . . Suddenly Bead had a mental picture of them both with positions reversed: of himself lying there and feeling that blade plunge through his chest; of himself watching that rifle-butt descend upon his face, with the final fire-exploding end. It made him so weak that he had to sit down. . . . Bead saw himself spitted through the soft of the shoulder, head on, that crude blade descending into the soft dark of his chest cavity. He could not believe it.

This passage, with its sense of vertigo and horror, its involuntary empathy, is typical of the serious combat novel, and it makes *The Thin Red Line* especially fascinating as a transitional work, a book anchored half in the documentary spirit of the late forties, half in the surreal climate of the early sixties. Beginning with a meticulous naturalism, the report of a wild and dangerous adventure, these lines modulate into metaphysical irony, a sense of utter disbelief, suggesting that such matters of life and death could not be encompassed by any documentary approach. Along with war novels, works like Malraux's *Man's Fate* had highlighted the sense of fleshy human vulnerability that also would prove crucial to *Catch-22*. (Closer to home, a spirit of grotesque comedy, complete with gothic touches, was an important part of the work of such earlier American naturalists as Stephen Crane and Frank Norris.)

Thus, the war novel, which seemed at first to look backward toward the social fiction of the Depression, also looked forward to the black humor, the anguished sense of alienation of the postwar years. If Mailer and Jones, in their first novels, had looked at the army as the Organization, a possible harbinger of postwar Fascism, soon, thanks to the postwar economic boom, the regimental spirit they feared would emerge in a much blander yet more pervasive fashion. A new sense of community had come out of the war. No doubt it made many Americans feel good to pull together, but to the social critics and filmmakers of the fifties it seemed intolerant, conformist, an "invasion of the body snatchers," an enforced Americanism rooted in the homogeneity of the small towns and new suburbs. The new comic and existential novels about World War II that began appearing in the late fifties, such as Thomas Berger's *Crazy in Berlin* (1958), Heller's *Catch-22* (1961), and Vonnegut's *Mother Night* (1962), along with *The Thin Red Line,* were reactions to that peculiar mixture of social intolerance, boosterish optimism, and metaphysical angst that marks the late fifties.

Some of the changes in how writers saw World War II were based on simple distance and the passage of time. As the impact of the war faded, including the immediate feeling of joy and relief, the deeper horror of the war's aftermath began to seep in: the news of the Holocaust, the new technology of mass destruction that began with Hiroshima, the swift beginnings of the Cold War and the arms race, with periodic crises such as the Berlin blockade and airlift in 1948. Though many Americans felt as righteous in prosecuting the Cold War as in opposing the Nazis, to others our position in the world – even our behavior during the war – became morally ambiguous. What had the Holocaust revealed about human nature, ourselves included? What did it mean for us to have been the first to use atomic weapons? How far would our opposition to Communism carry us? In the new balance of terror, with its mutually assured destruction, what would it mean to "win" a nuclear war?

Eventually, our conflicts over Vietnam crystallized many of these doubts, but World War II became the screen on which these postwar concerns would first be projected. The new war novel of the 1960s was less about the war than about the Holocaust, the Cold War, fear of atomic war, and finally the ongoing war in Vietnam. This second wave reflected a sense of national vulnerability we felt at the peak of our world power, as well as our loss of the moral certainty we had briefly enjoyed – that confident, Wilsonian sense of righteous innocence so deeply ingrained in American history.

The history of these doubts and losses can be traced all through the war writing of the sixties and seventies, both in fiction and reportage, from *Catch-22* and *Mother Night* to Michael Herr's *Dispatches* and Tim O'Brien's *Going After Cacciato.* Indeed, it would not be too strong a statement to say that the history of the whole postwar era could be examined through its changing perspective on war, since the whole period was shadowed by memories of war and by Cold War fears of its recurrence in even more unspeakable forms.

This emphasis on absurdity and moral ambiguity was an intensification of how war had long been portrayed rather than an invention of the 1960s; it can be found already in the 1940s but was deeply rooted in the whole literature of war. There is an ambiguous sense of horror in the vivid vio- lence of the *Iliad,* the antiwar satire of Aristophanes, the "modern" cyni- cism of Euripides, the savage mockery that runs through Shakespeare's *Troilus and Cressida.* The antiheroic currents in these works spoke power- fully to the forties generation, as many critical writings show, beginning with Simone Weil's classic account of the *Iliad* as a "poem of force." As much a prose poem as an essay, it was widely admired here after it was translated into English by Mary McCarthy. Following the disillusionment of World War I, which undercut all heroic ideals, this existential point of view became the dominant way of writing about war.

Thus Robert Rossen's adaptation of *A Walk in the Sun,* filmed in 1945 by Lewis Milestone, became almost a film noir about World War II. It was based on an extraordinarily direct and simple novel by Harry Brown that tried not only to show how combat felt but also to distinguish it from stan- dard movie heroics. Its emphasis on fear, on the testing of men, its portrayal of their uncertainty and vulnerability, would greatly influence later combat novels, especially Mailer's. The oddity and strangeness of *A Walk in the Sun,* a book that often edges toward the surreal, would become essential to a novel like *The Naked and the Dead,* where some of the major twists of plot serve to deflate the action. Any moderately talented editor could have told Mailer that the triumph of the doltish Dalleson and the final irrelevance of the long patrol, which continues when the battle for the island has already ended, were ridiculously trivial ways of resolving the campaign for the island. Only a silly hornet's nest, not a sense of rational restraint or the limits of human endurance, finally thwarts Sgt. Croft's obsession with the mountain long after it has lost all strategic meaning. Mailer aimed to show how strategy and command fall prey to ego and the need to dominate.

What were simply odd, disorienting touches in Brown and Mailer become the whole novel in *Catch-22,* a World War II fable in a class by itself and one of the most original novels of the whole postwar era. Though one soldier in Brown's *Walk in the Sun* could talk repeatedly about fighting the battle of Tibet in 1956, this surreal touch is grounded in an actual situation: combat weariness, grim pessimism, a sense that the war will drag on forever. Mailer undercuts the characters in his novel with an ironic anticlimax, but he never abandons the view that this is a true campaign, a chapter of a real war. Heller burlesques Mailer's view of the war; for him the war and the army display a pervasive sense of unreality, an element of insanity.

Where Mailer begins his novel with a map of an invented island, Heller begins his with a note on a *real* island that "obviously could not accommodate all of the actions described." Starting (like most combat stories) with the ethnic and regional stereotypes of naturalistic fiction, Mailer thickens his characters with invented histories, psychological profiles, and circumstantial details. Heller, beginning with an even larger cast of the stereotypes, each with a chapter to himself, exaggerates them instead into cartoons, putting them through the paces of stand-up comedy and Road Runner farce.

Similarly cartoonish elements can be found in the ingenious reversals and doublings of Vonnegut's *Mother Night,* in the Candide-like hero and the science fiction trappings of his *Slaughterhouse-Five, or, The Children's Crusade: A Duty-Dance with Death* (1969), and the dizzying multiplication of bizarre plots and oddball characters of Thomas Pynchon's *Gravity's Rainbow,* which wraps the war in comic and paranoid versions of pop-culture myths. This is a novel in which the new technology, including the U-2 rocket, has reduced the characters to ciphers and rendered them almost irrelevant. Pynchon's book is more abstruse and yet more like a comic book view of the war than anything in Heller's and Vonnegut's works. Those older men belonged to the same generation as Mailer and Jones, though they told their stories much later; Pynchon (born in 1937) was not a witness to the war but an inspired, occasionally kitschy fantasist whose overdetermined plots fasten on rocketry and technology as a nexus between sex, extinction, and apocalypse.

Like Vonnegut, Pynchon is interested less in the conduct of the war than in the Nazis, whom he sees through the lens of German Romantic kitsch and post-sixties paranoia and apocalypse, as filtered through writers like William Burroughs, with his dangerous twilight world of the "Zone." What we learn in reading his book is that "this War was never political at all, the politics was all theatre, all just to keep the people distracted . . . secretly, it was being dictated instead by the needs of technology . . . by a conspiracy between human beings and techniques, by something that needed the energy-burst of war" [ellipses in original]. The lesson to be learned from the Germans is that "love, among these men, once past the simple feel and orgasming of it, had to do with masculine technologies, with contracts, with winning and losing." For Nazis like Weissmann, the war, embodied in rocketry, is simply an erotic Götterdämmerung, "a love for the last explosion – the lifting and the scream that peaks past fear," the last big bang. This has little to do with World War II and everything to do with the high-tech war in Vietnam and the sexual-conspiratorial fantasies of the 1960s.

The galloping disillusionment with the Vietnam War all through the 1960s made a revisionist view of World War II inevitable. As reports of atrocities like My Lai began filtering out of Vietnam, survivors of the Holocaust also began to break their near silence of two decades. Their horrendous stories, told in memoirs, documentaries, novels, and fictionalized films, made the old combat novels seem remote and superficial. Starting with a small handful of works by writers like Primo Levi, Elie Wiesel, Hannah Arendt, and Jerzy Kosinski, the Holocaust narrative would eventually displace the combat narrative as our principal vision of the Second World War. As these and other wartime atrocities – and the irrationality and insanity of war in general – became central, as Vietnam shattered our sense of our own purity, it was inevitable that our own behavior in World War II would also be brought into question. The popular view of the war as a simple struggle between good and evil would lose much of its credibility.

By portraying the army in *Catch-22* as a structure of illusion, a vast PR operation, Heller anticipated Don DeLillo's vision of history as virtual reality, the manipulation of appearances. This is an army that would rather move the bomb line than bomb the target, with officers prepared to sacrifice down to their very last enlisted man, officers whose goal is to *look* like officers, to enforce the rules, and to raise the number of required missions rather than to defeat the enemy or win the war. In Heller's war, *every* officer is like Mailer's Dalleson, the comical figure of a total bureaucrat who would rather plan the parade afterward than the battle beforehand, or like Jones's "Dynamite" Holmes, the brutal time server climbing the rungs of promotion and self-promotion.

For Heller, Pynchon, and Vonnegut, writing in a later period, this has become a static war, a war in which nothing happens. This is reflected in the fictional structures they develop – and the individual characters who fail to develop. Both Mailer and Jones, though working close to the events they described – in a sense bearing personal witness – were writing historical novels. The campaigns they worked out had beginnings, middles, and ends; they were microcosms of the war as a whole and sometimes of the whole society that was waging war. In the late writers there is no real sense of unfolding history, no sequential pattern, and little relation between causes and consequences. Their books are circular rather than developmental; they are antihistorical novels. Their characters are pawns rather than agents. No longer hoodwinked by our official war aims, they look to survival, not mastery or heroism, and they are constantly being overwhelmed by larger forces they scarcely understand.

Thus Vonnegut in *Slaughterhouse-Five,* in trying to make sense of his most searing memory – the firebombing of Dresden, which haunted him for 25 years – makes his hero a shell-shocked simpleton, the last of a long line of innocent nobodies caught in the swirling currents of history, politics, and warfare. The book's lugubrious tone can be wearing; its numbing, fatalistic refrain ("so it goes") is repeated when anyone dies, when anything awful happens. This seems to reflect the depressive mood of the author as much as the muted anguish of his Everyman protagonist. By giving us someone who "comes unstuck in time," however, someone whose experiences seem to be happening all at once, whose memories cannot be sorted out or exorcised, Vonnegut at last finds a way of writing about the unthinkable – events that surpass the limits of "realism" and unhinge a novelist's usual approach to character and individuality.

In an aside, the author tells us that "there are almost no characters in this story, and almost no dramatic confrontations, because most of the people in it are so sick and so much the playthings of enormous forces. One of the main effects of war, after all, is that people are discouraged from being characters." This may be too blatant and explicit, yet the word *discouraged* is well chosen: the courage to become a character and lead a coherent life is beyond Billy Pilgrim and his friends. Instead, his role in the book is to show how the shock of history has nullified individual agency. Even after the war, this Pilgrim's "progress" is studded with mental breakdowns, marked especially by a failure to feel, combined with an inability to forget. His behavior seems anesthetized, mechanical, just as Vonnegut's style is nerveless and repetitive. Billy is outwardly adjusted yet inwardly haunted, numb, and mentally disturbed, revealing the survivor mentality that has since become a familiar feature of Holocaust memoirs and oral history.

Vonnegut finally finds a way of telling the story of the Dresden bombing through a "character" who is utterly ordinary yet permanently blighted by it. Thanks to the dubious moral authority of our actions in Vietnam, Vonnegut chooses to focus *his* war on an Allied atrocity; of German ancestry himself, he uses the "good" war to question all war. Billy Pilgrim's later breakdowns convey some of the horror of what was repressed behind the placid and prosperous facade of the postwar world.

Some of the same elements can be found in other post-1960 novels about World War II, such as *Mother Night, Catch-22,* and *Gravity's Rainbow*: a comic-book atmosphere of sheer lunacy and brutality, the reduction of individuals to nonentities by large organizational and technological forces. In the Pavlovian world of *Gravity's Rainbow*, Pynchon's nominal protagonist, Tyrone Slothrop (who bears much of the author's own family history, going back to the Puritans), is wired and conditioned, down to his very erections. In the twilight world of the Zone, he disappears from the novel long before the end, "broken down . . . and scattered." By then, the individual self is barely an object of nostalgia; only a few "can still see Slothrop as any sort of integral creature any more. Most of the others gave up long ago trying to hold him together, even as a concept." Unselved, Slothrop has been dismembered into postmodernism. As Vonnegut dropped into science fiction to unspring our sense of time, sequence, and causation, Pynchon used technology and the pop stereotypes of spy fiction to flatten his characters, to render them absurd and ineffectual.

If Pynchon's characters dash about in circles like experimental rats, Heller's equally two-dimensional characters are the punch lines of jokes, yet they convey a serious point about the war. In the opening chapters of his first novel, *Journey to the End of Night* (1932), Louis-Ferdinand Céline had virtually invented a form of delirious black comedy about war. He gave his hero, Bardamu, whose only goal is to survive, a scabrous ebullience in flaunting his cowardice, his hatred of officers, his loathing of all official and heroic values. Through this first-person protagonist, exploding with rancor and bile, who is hard to distinguish from the author himself, Céline portrays the war as a scene of lunacy and apocalypse, a world saturated with casual death. Instead of the unreliable narrator, Céline creates the hyperbolic narrator, whose nihilistic exaggerations, far from making him less trustworthy, imprint his perceptions like a burning brand. At the edge of madness, he presents himself as the last sane man in the world. For him "this war, in fact, made no sense at all," yet all around him there are madmen determined to fight it: "With such people this infernal lunacy could go on forever. . . . Why would they stop? Never had the world seemed so implacably doomed. Could I, I thought, be the last coward on earth? How terrifying! . . . All alone with two million stark raving heroic madmen, armed to the eyeballs?"

According to Céline, it takes some imagination to understand the horror, to grasp the death happening all around you: "When you have no imagination, dying is small beer; when you do have an imagination, dying is too much. . . . The colonel had never had any imagination. That was the source of all his trouble, and of ours even more so. Was I the only man in that regiment with any imagination about death? I preferred my own kind of death, the kind that comes late. . . . A man's entitled to an opinion about his own death."

Borrowing this tone of slashing anarchic humor, Heller fashioned his own comedy about death, cowardice, and survival. His Yossarian is a more somber variation on Céline's Bardamu, just as Vonnegut's Billy Pilgrim is a doleful, shell-shocked version of Czech writer Jaroslav Hašek's Good Soldier Schweik, the quintessential Little Man caught up in a big war. Despite their real-life origins, as revealed in a 1998 memoir *Now and Then,* Heller's soldiers are not people so much as cardboard cutouts who strike an attitude. Clevinger, for example, is one of those who know everything but understand nothing about the war:

Clevinger knew everything about the war except why Yossarian had to die while Corporal Snark was allowed to live, or why Corporal Snark had to die while Yossarian was allowed to live. It was a vile and muddy war, and Yossarian could have lived without it – lived forever, perhaps. Only a fraction of his countrymen would give up their lives to win it, and it was not his ambition to be among them. To die or not to die, that was the question, and Clevinger grew limp trying to answer it.

In Heller's world, this verbal shell game conveys the existential absurdity. Clevinger is Heller's broad burlesque of Mailer's Lt. Hearn, the Harvard-educated intellectual – reflective, yet also an activist, a doer – whose knowledge masks a real ignorance and whose skills prove essentially useless. "Everyone agreed that Clevinger was certain to go far in the academic world. In short, Clevinger was one of those people with lots of intelligence and no brains. . . . In short, he was a dope." Later, he gets his comeuppance in a chapter that begins: "Clevinger was dead. That was the basic flaw in his philosophy." In Heller's world, death alone provides critical perspective.

In *Catch-22,* Heller brings off a knockabout farce and creates a madcap reality that eventually becomes unbearably poignant and grim. He seduces us with mocking laughter only to take us beyond the jokey one-liners, structuring the book with lightning reversals, comic-book changes of fortune, brilliant riffs of language, and, like Vonnegut, widening circles of disclosure that gradually carry us from comedy to horror. Instead of unfolding chronologically, as if there were a real sequence to the men's

wartime experiences, the book is anchored by arbitrary points of reference
– Yossarian's stays in the hospital, the number of required bombing missions. In this intricate pattern, characters who are already "dead" in one
chapter are still alive in a later chapter, pinned all the more ineluctably to
their determined fates. These characters function more as leitmotifs than as
real people, since individuality would do little to alter what happens to
them. As in Vonnegut's works (but in a more explosive rhythm), everything in the book seems to be happening continuously: throughout,
Snowden is dying, the dead man in Yossarian's tent is "dead," and the
Soldier in White – faceless, almost bodiless, his being no more than a surreal exchange of fluids – leads his ghostly existence between the animate
and the inanimate, between farce and horror.

The characters' "real" life is not necessarily the same as their official life;
the man in Yossarian's tent is dead ("his name was Mudd") but has never
officially arrived, whereas Doc Daneeka, though alive, has officially died.
Heller's satire on bureaucracy – on the insanity of the organizational mind
– links the book with his later novels, such as *Something Happened* (1974)
and *Good as Gold* (1979), which do for business and government what
Catch-22 had done for the army.

In its way, Heller's book is as literary as Mailer's. The life history of a
character like Major Major is a send-up of the biographical baggage in
Mailer's "Time Machine" sections. It is built up entirely out of Borscht
Circuit shtick:

Major Major had been born too late and too mediocre. Some men are born
mediocre, some men achieve mediocrity, and some men have mediocrity thrust
upon them. With Major Major it had been all three. . . .

  Major Major had three strikes on him from the beginning – his mother, his
father and Henry Fonda, to whom he bore a sickly resemblance almost from the
moment of his birth. Long before he even suspected who Henry Fonda was, he
found himself the subject of unflattering comparisons everywhere he went. . . .

  Major Major's father was a sober God-fearing man whose idea of a good joke
was to lie about his age. . . . His specialty was alfalfa, and he made a good thing
out of not growing any. The government paid him well for every bushel of alfalfa
he did not grow. . . . Major Major's father worked without rest at not growing
alfalfa.

Each of these paragraphs goes on like a theme and variations, a comic verbal riff – mercurial, paradoxical, outrageous – with satiric swipes directed
at both the army and the larger American society. As Heller builds up
Major Major into a major comic nonentity, we laugh at the army yet begin
to feel sorry for this useless cog in its silly machinery, which barely leaves
room for even the smallest measure of humanity. Major Major's endless tri-

als and humiliations, beginning with his birth and name and climaxing with his promotion to major – which makes him a pariah to the enlisted men – demonstrate Heller's inspired comic adaptations of Dostoyevsky as well as his affinity with shlemiel humor, the serious comedy of victimization that links Jewish jokes to Jewish American fiction.

Heller takes the edge of anxiety built into most combat fiction and makes a comic universe out of it. This is a world saturated with death but made more poignant by his compulsion to joke about it. In this inverted world, for example, Heller's Yossarian prefers the decorum of death in the hospital to the unpredictable turns of death outside the hospital:

There was a much lower death rate inside the hospital than outside the hospital, and a much healthier death rate. Few people died unnecessarily. People knew a lot more about dying inside the hospital and made a much neater, more orderly job of it. . . . They didn't explode into blood and clotted matter. They didn't drown or get struck by lightning, mangled by machinery or crushed in landslides. . . . Nobody choked to death. People bled to death like gentlemen in an operating room or expired without comment in an oxygen tent. There was none of that tricky now-you-see-me-now-you-don't business so much in vogue outside the hospital, none of that now-I-am-and-now-I-ain't.

Alone among these writers, Heller turns a joke into an outlook on life; he transforms anxiety from a stoic situational fear, indigenous to the war novel, into an acrid, cynical sense of vulnerability that becomes the very principle of existence. Thus, *Catch-22* is the apotheosis of the war novel even as it transcends it, since war for Heller is merely a heightened instance of how life will always conspire against you, scheming to do you in. Years later, when Heller himself was stricken with a nearly fatal illness and temporarily paralyzed from the neck down, he was uniquely equipped to milk it for sickly but hilarious comedy in a book appropriately called *No Laughing Matter* (with Speed Vogel, 1986).

Heller's savagely funny sense of the ironies of life was grounded not only in his war experience but in his Jewish outlook and upbringing (as satirized in *Good as Gold*), in his stint as an organization man with Time, Inc. in the 1950s (which formed the basis for *Something Happened*), and in the popular existentialism of the period. It helps explain why *Catch-22*, like other black-humor novels about World War II, remains such a static book. Heller's view of war, like his view of the corporation, the government, and the neurotic Jewish family, is that nothing *can* happen: all involved are stuck in their own rut, perpetual parodies of themselves, acting out roles assigned long ago, a laughable reduction from the fully human. Heller's saturnine outlook, with its conservative sense of possibilities of human development, is reminiscent of haughtier satirists, such as

Evelyn Waugh in *A Handful of Dust,* who entrap their hapless characters in their own pervasive sense of futility.

Something Happened is a postwar pendant to *Catch-22,* using the same comic strategies and verbal riffs in a way that is no longer funny but full of desperation, cruelty, and self-loathing. The nearly anonymous Bob Slocum, surrounded by corporate characters with names like Green, Brown, White, and Black, is merely a voice, ranting at us, suffocating us for nearly 600 pages. A diagrammatic illustration of David Riesman's "other-directed" personality, caught on a middle rung of the corporate fear ladder, Slocum hates his wife and children as much as he hates his job yet is powerless to get away from them. *Something Happened* is as statically uneventful as *Catch-22* is inertly stuffed with reams of "plot." Both are dark books, specimens of gallows humor, but where the earlier book charms us, turning its nihilism into a gradually darkening source of comedy, the later novel, more rigorous in its way, never tries to be ingratiating.

❧

Heller wrote other books of considerable interest without ever matching the brilliance of these first two novels, yet in the sixties and seventies, his cynicism perfectly matched the mood of the times. *Something Happened* was quickly displaced by the work of such writers as Raymond Carver, which achieved the same grim, almost suicidal impact with far greater economy of means. Carver's followers learned to punish readers by withholding from them rather than battering and overwhelming them, and *Something Happened* was set aside as an unpleasant piece of verbal virtuosity that need never be repeated. But *Catch-22* seemed perpetually relevant, especially after Vietnam and Watergate. After Jimmy Carter, American politics took a laughable turn: Ronald Reagan, with his little anecdotes borrowed from old movies, and George Bush, with his fractured syntax and gee-whiz attitudes, could both have been Heller inventions.

The Vietnam writers were especially influenced by Heller's absurdist treatment of war, as well as the magic realism popularized by Latin American writers. Vietnam was exactly the war Heller had anticipated, utterly meaningless to most of its participants yet fraught with a sense of anxiety and waste, the sense of a war machine run amok. The best writers and filmmakers who dealt with Vietnam tried to convey feelings of phantasmagoria that go back in their literary lineage through Heller to Mailer, Harry Brown, and *The Red Badge of Courage.* In Tim O'Brien's best-known novel, *Going After Cacciato* (1978), Cacciato's surreal flight from Vietnam toward Paris is a distant echo of Yossarian's flight to Sweden and Brown's anticipation, there on the Italian coast, of some future Battle of Tibet.

On the other hand, the efforts to deal with combat in Vietnam in a more documentary fashion, such as John Del Vecchio's *The 13th Valley* (1982), proved more earnest than effective. With no clear sense of a front or an enemy or a purpose in fighting, with little prospect of victory and little sense of honor, Vietnam was not a war that would yield to realistic treatment or conventional heroism. Instead, young American conscripts, drenched in monsoon rains and jungle heat, constantly exposed to inept allies and to a tormented civilian population almost impossible to distinguish from the enemy, were saturated with drugs and rock music that meshed with their anxiety but further disoriented their sense of reality.

Every good book or film about the Vietnam War tries to convey its nightmarish qualities, its hellish sense of unreality. Between the ignominious end of the war in 1975 and the early eighties, these long-delayed works probed an untreated wound in the American psyche. Two powerful memoirs, Ron Kovic's *Born on the Fourth of July* (1976) and Philip Caputo's *A Rumor of War* (1977), showed how gung-ho soldiers, passionately committed to the American mission and the American dream, could be transformed into anti-war veterans, maimed in body or mind, who loathed everything our country had tried to do in Vietnam. In *Dispatches* (1977), Michael Herr developed a nervous, explosive, rifflike style, suffused with dread, rhythmically influenced by drugs and rock, to convey a sense, as the best war correspondents had always done, of being there on the ground, being *in* the war:

> The ground was always in play, always being swept. Under the ground was his, above it was ours. We had the air, we could get up in it but not disappear in *to* it, we could run but we couldn't hide, and he could do each so well that sometimes it looked like he was doing them both at once. . . . You could be in the most protected space in Vietnam and still know that your safety was provisional, that early death, blindness, loss of legs, arms or balls, major and lasting disfigurement – the whole rotten deal – could come in on the freakyfluky as easily as in the so-called expected ways. . . . The roads were mined, the trails booby-trapped, satchel charges and grenades blew up jeeps and movie theaters, the VC got work inside all the camps as shoeshine boys and laundresses and honey-dippers, they'd starch your fatigues and burn your shit and then go home and mortar your area. Saigon and Cholon and Danang held such hostile vibes that you felt you were being drysniped every time someone looked at you, and choppers fell out of the sky like fat poisoned birds a hundred times a day.

In the edgy flow of his run-on sentences, studded with slang, charged with arresting images, Herr works the feeling of the war into the texture of his prose. His metaphors cut like a knife, and the cutting edge is always fear: "It is a small trench, and a lot of us have gotten into it in a hurry. At the end farthest from me there is a young guy who has been hit in the throat, and he is making the sounds a baby will make when he is trying to work up the breath for a good scream." Herr makes each image count. The "fat poisoned birds" stand for America itself, with its excessive and nearly help-less technology, while the gurgling, choking baby is the hapless soldier, the strangled innocent, a vulnerable human element in that machine.

Soon afterward, filmmakers as different as Hal Ashby (*Coming Home*), Michael Cimino (*The Deer Hunter*), Francis Ford Coppola (*Apocalypse Now*), Stanley Kubrick (*Full Metal Jacket*), Brian De Palma (*Casualties of War*), and Oliver Stone (*Platoon, Born on the Fourth of July*) made movies that tried in different ways to capture the sense of entrapment, horror, and moral ambi-guity that had become basic to our view of the Vietnam War. O'Brien's *Going After Cacciato,* on the other hand, was a much more musing and ellip-tical work that, by going back to the more unconventional novels about World War II, managed to see the Vietnam quagmire in a fresh way. As in *Catch-22* or *Slaughterhouse-Five,* the time structure of O'Brien's novel splin-ters the relationship between past and present, as if no sequential treatment could do justice to the surreal feeling of the war. The book mixes realistic chapters set in the war with whimsical, picaresque chapters about tracking a missing soldier, Cacciato ("the hunted one"), all the way from Vietnam to Paris – chapters as much indebted to the Road movies of Bob Hope and Bing Crosby as to any literary models. These are punctuated by short, intro-spective chapters called "The Observation Post," set in the mind of the book's protagonist, Paul Berlin, during a tour of guard duty.

In these inward musings, the whole meaning of the war (and of the novel itself) passes in review. Nothing actually happens in these chapters, though each is carefully marked by a moment in time from midnight to 6 A.M., the period of Paul's watch. In a sense, though, this is where the whole novel takes place – in Paul Berlin's mind, which takes us alternately back into the war, including his own first day of combat, and out of the war, in a reverie about trekking after the missing Cacciato through Delhi, Mandalay, and Tehran to a Paris that is not a place but a "state of mind," a soldier's dream of careless peacetime pleasure. Thus, the book begins exactly where *Catch-22* ends, with Yossarian leaving the war, though it is written not from Yossarian's viewpoint but from that of another man who is trying to imag-ine why he left, where he has gone, what might have become of him.

Like *Catch-22,* the book has a circular structure. Beginning and ending with chapters that give us a handful of "facts" about Cacciato's disappear-ance, it weaves backward and forward from grim or funny memories of the war to the larky possibilities of life away from the war. In the long opening chapter, the "factual" chapter, many of the minor characters have already died, but as in *Catch-22,* they live again in flashbacks or as leitmotifs, sometimes comic, often troubling, invariably bizarre. For example, there is Billy Boy Mitchell, who (we are often told) "had died of fright, scared to death on the field of battle." Only much later do we discover that this Snowden-like figure died of fright only after his leg had been blown off by a mine. O'Brien learned from Heller and Vonnegut how to combine the comic with the horrific. He makes war all the more real, as they did, by making his characters less real. They are cutouts, like cartoon figures who have been run over by a steamroller. Caught in a vise that flattens them, squeezes the reality *out* of them, they have been turned into "war stories" – the oddities of what a soldier might happen to remember, or embroider – just as the Cacciato stories are the "battlefield dreams" of "men figuring how, if suddenly free, they would deploy the rest of their lives." Thus, the retrospective and the prospective meet in a multilayered structure of description, fantasy, and reflection, in a book that explores not so much the war itself as the mind of the war – above all, the mind's need to get away from the war.

O'Brien's subject is not simply war but how to write about it, to make sense of it, to find some closure for it. If the postmodern is the realm of the indefinite, the ambiguous, the open ended, then Vietnam epitomized postmodern warfare. O'Brien pursued this postmodern strategy just as effectively in a superb collection of stories, *The Things They Carried* (1990), and in a seemingly more conventional novel, *In the Lake of the Woods* (1994), which deals with the traumatic aftermath of the war, the return of the repressed.

The evolution of the war novel from the late forties to the late seventies is a measure of how the attitudes of American writers changed not only toward war but toward American society. In their own ways, Mailer and Jones were both outsiders, one an intellectual and a Jew who used the war as vehicle for a novel of ideas, the other an aimless Midwesterner, a romantic anarchist who could never quite adjust to the army life he loved and observed with such keen attention. Both were political writers who looked back to the radical causes and literary methods of the 1930s; both wrote under the influence of Hemingway, who treated war as a test of masculinity and courage, of manhood under stress.

For the writers of the sixties and seventies, whether they wrote about World War II or Vietnam, there was no longer even a trace of nobility about going to war. Like many Americans, these writers had lost their faith in the promise of American life; the goals for which we fought no longer had much credibility. The dubious war aims and official lies about Vietnam, the rise of media politics, and the exposure of political malfeasance in the Watergate affair all contributed to a critique of America different from the old political one. The new threat was not Fascism but a public life of sham and unreality.

For such a theme, the outrageous exaggerations of the black humorists and the magic realism of the Latin American writers proved more useful, more authentic and honest, than did the tightlipped, brutally restrained realism of Hemingway. Tim O'Brien's constant concern in *Going After Cacciato* is the relationship of the observer to the thing observed, the fine line between fact and fantasy, memory and dream. Vietnam is the war that eludes those who fought it and even those who write about it. Sequence and order elude Paul Berlin; chronology puzzles him. "Focus on the order of things," he says to himself in one of his musings; "sort out the flow of events so as to understand how one thing led to another, search for that point at which what happened had been extended into a vision of what might have happened. Where was the fulcrum? How did it tilt from fact to imagination? How far had Cacciato led them? How far might he lead them still?"

Some of these sentences might have come from books of the early sixties, such as Pynchon's *The Crying of Lot 49,* but Vietnam and Watergate seemed to have confirmed them. As postmodernists were fond of pointing out, the culture of the image, the reign of "virtual reality," had taken hold. From a sixties viewpoint, Yossarian and Cacciato, like their predecessor, Holden Caulfield, are rebels against authority, tender misfits who step outside the official frame. By the late seventies, however, rebellion had been transformed into isolation, skepticism, and unbelief, as if society were no longer real enough to rebel against.

Compared to the World War II novels, the books about Vietnam take place in a vacuum. The sense of the world back home that Mailer and Jones tried to provide, that even Heller and Vonnegut evoked in a more comical and formulaic fashion, had been completely dissipated. It appears only as the false promises that soldiers unlearn in the hellish context of the war itself. In the world we see here, patriotism is little more than the illusion that unhinges us, that seduces us toward destruction. The Vietnam stories, fiction and journalism, film and memoir, are all about disillusionment, loss of faith, a grim awakening. In these works, we cut through seeming knowledge to find uncertainty, cut through a tissue of lies to reach the heart of darkness. The characters find that they have risked their lives for what they were taught in grade school. The greatest illusion, it seems, is that their leaders were honorable, their cause was just, and that this society can ever command anyone's unambiguous loyalty.

THE NEW FICTION: FROM THE HOME
FRONT TO THE 1950S

THERE WERE OTHER war novels besides those set in the armed forces or at the front, novels that dealt with World War II more obliquely or were set on what was then called the home front. A number of these books anticipated the direction of postwar fiction more acutely than did the combat novels. Though ambitious young writers like Norman Mailer and James Jones dreamed that the war could provide material for the Great American Novel, the naturalist methods of the early war novels were discarded when American society, without reverting to isolationism, turned in upon itself during the Truman and Eisenhower years. The new writers were influenced less by the war than by rapid onset of the Cold War and of nuclear weapons so soon after the shooting war, which fostered anxieties that America's victories abroad might otherwise have laid to rest, and by the new therapeutic culture of psychoanalysis, which gradually replaced the social consciousness that had driven much of American literature and visual art during the Depression. As American power and prestige expanded outward across the world, at home artists and writers looked inward, sometimes boastfully, often fearfully, to explore the existential dilemmas of selfhood. Europe had been broken as a dominant political and economic force, but strands of European culture, from modernism and surrealism to existentialism, had migrated to America. As America entered an era of prosperity and international dominance, American artists and writers grew pessimistic and introspective, like troubled prophets brooding darkly at the banquet of national celebration.

Two first novels published toward the end of the war foreshadowed the conflicting directions that would be taken by later fiction writers. In contrast to the gargantuan size of some of the combat novels, Chester B. Himes's *If He Hollers Let Him Go* (1945) and Saul Bellow's *Dangling Man* (1944) are hardly longer than novellas. Both are first-person novels that end with the narrator's induction into the army; both are preachy, self-concerned, argumentative. Here the similarity seems to end, for though the two books emerge from newly articulate ethnic groups – the blacks and Jews who would have the greatest impact on postwar fiction – their characters find different ways of coping with their lives. Himes and Bellow were almost archetypes of the outsiders who had already begun to play significant roles in American fiction before the war. Both writers came of age against the background of the Depression. Bellow was born in Lachine, Quebec, Canada, in 1915, grew up in a lower-middle-class Jewish family in Chicago, the scene of some of his best fiction, and studied anthropology at the University of Chicago and Northwestern University. Himes, whose parents were schoolteachers, was born in Jefferson City, Missouri, in 1909 and dropped out of Ohio State University after one semester. Arrested for armed robbery in 1928, he served eight years in an Ohio penitentiary, which turned him into a writer. He published his first story in *Esquire* in 1934 while still in prison.

If *He Hollers Let Him Go,* his first novel, could not have been written without the incendiary example of *Native Son,* the book that dramatically undermined America's illusions about racial harmony. These misconceptions had not been seriously challenged by the more genial, more accommodating writers of the Negro Renaissance, who were strongly supported by white patrons, or even by such powerful prewar works as James Weldon Johnson's *Autobiography of an Ex-Colored Man,* Jean Toomer's *Cane,* Langston Hughes's *The Ways of White Folks,* and Zora Neale Hurston's *Their Eyes Were Watching God.* Himes's hero, Bob Jones, is a more reflective, better educated version of Richard Wright's Bigger Thomas, a man seething at the daily slights his color imposes on him. He has worked through two years at Ohio State by waiting on tables, and his girlfriend Alice is the light-skinned daughter of a wealthy, prominent black physician. He supervises a black crew as a "leaderman" at a wartime shipyard in Los Angeles, a position of responsibility that he loses early in the novel for cursing out a white Southern woman who calls him nigger. His almost uncontrollable fury over the way he is treated as a black man propels him to the brink of rape and murder. His rage is a new tonality in African American writing.

Like Bigger Thomas, Bob Jones careens through the novel boiling with anger, ready to explode, struggling constantly with his fear and hatred of the white world. Though he destroyed himself, Bigger achieved some kind of purgation and freedom through violence, and finally through self-acceptance, dispelling a nameless force that had oppressed his every waking moment. In the same way, Bob Jones dreams constantly of striking an arbitrary but massive blow that will somehow liberate him. But unlike Bigger he is a highly self-conscious character, analyzing his own situation acutely, bitterly. Each time he moves to act out his violent fantasies, he sees with perfect lucidity exactly how it will ruin his life.

Bob Jones is pulled in every direction: toward the accommodation that works so well for his girlfriend and her middle-class family, toward the white men and women he would like to kill or rape yet would also like somehow to emulate, and toward the generous and gentle black woman whose house he shares, who is kinder to him than anyone else in the novel. Nursing a baby, nurturing the men around her, she stands for the honest, authentic life he never succeeds in creating for himself.

With all these figures, Bob's fantasies are almost entirely sexual. His girlfriend, who could pass for white, lends him dignity and class while trying unsuccessfully to soften his edges and make him over. The white woman is the classic bitch of film noir, pure poison, a perfect male nightmare. ("When I thought about Madge that cold scare settled over me and I began to tremble. Just scared to think about her, about living in the same world with her. Almost like thinking about the electric chair.") Though she treats him like dirt, he is drawn to her whiteness, her pure cracker hatred of him, until she finally ruins him by accusing him (falsely) of rape. In contrast, his poor black woman friend, living with another man, stands for sex mainly as nurture and domesticity – which is not nearly enough for him.

Chester Himes would later become famous in France, and finally in America, for his detective novels published in the *Série noire*, but *If He Hollers* is already a classic hard-boiled novel, acrid, taut, atmospheric, and menacing – a cross between Richard Wright and James M. Cain, between a social novel about black rage and a seedy romantic thriller. The *Postman* aura of Los Angeles noir lends a mood of fatality to Bob Jones's obsession with race. His girlfriend warns him that "you're insanely belligerent" and "if you continue brooding about white people you are going insane," but he is hooked on his daily dose of fear and humiliation, which gives the book its amazing psychological intensity.

If He Hollers was exactly the kind of pulpy protest novel that critics of the forties and fifties would belittle or ignore. James Baldwin cut his teeth as a writer by reviewing many of these books including Himes's *Lonely Crusade*; he finally denounced the whole genre in his celebrated attack on Wright and Harriet Beecher Stowe ("Everybody's Protest Novel," 1949). But such novels, often written by beleaguered survivors of the proletarian movements of the thirties, would lead an underground life all through the postwar years in cheap paperbacks, well below the dignified purview of "literature."

As a social novel about race and sex, status and prejudice, written in the low-life proletarian mode influenced by Hemingway, *If He Hollers* seems to look backward. *Dangling Man,* on the other hand, cast as a journal, with its action entirely internalized and reflective, anticipates the more private world of postwar fiction, drawing away – but not *too* far away – from the old social and political themes, much as its protagonist detaches himself from all his former commitments. *Dangling Man* even begins with an attack, in the same spirit as Baldwin's, on the "era of hardboiled-dom," which the writer identifies with the active masculine style of both the Depression and the war years. As he uses it, however, the term also embraces the politics of the Communist Party, which has ostracized the narrator for dropping out, and the larger ethos of America itself, the literary and social code embodied by Hemingway, "the code of the athlete, of the tough boy – an American inheritance."

By keeping a journal, the narrator, Joseph (a name out of the Bible by way of Kafka), will pursue a slightly subversive, European mode of self-interrogation. *Dangling Man* gives an American accent to the gloomy, cerebral fiction of ideas that would help displace the kind of naturalistic social novel that loomed large in American writing from the 1890s through the 1940s. In its different incarnations, this introspective approach would become the major current in postwar fiction. For all their differences, though, the Himes and Bellow books were two rivulets from the same source, Dostoyevsky's *Notes From Underground*, the master text for all modern portraits of the thwarted, angry, alienated outsider chewing nervously on his own bitter thoughts.

Dostoyevsky's feverish portrait of a self-tormenter proved irresistibly attractive to black and Jewish writers alike. To blacks it provided some wonderful metaphors for marginality – the whole notion of the underground, for example, and the closely related theme of someone who feels invisible, who is not even noticed by those whose very being oppresses him, as Dostoyevsky's protagonist is elbowed aside by a man on the street who does not see him, for whom he simply does not exist. (Richard Wright and Ralph Ellison performed their variations on Dostoyevsky's themes in "The Man Who Lived Underground" and *Invisible Man*, respectively.) Jewish writers like Bellow, on the other hand, would be most taken with the anxiously brilliant, unstable, fretfully intense manner of the man who translates his marginality into neurosis. Looking for slights and quarrels, brooding endlessly about revenge, the Underground Man messes up his relations with everyone around him. He gnaws away at himself with paranoid imaginings and overwrought self-analysis, living in his agitated mind more than in the actual world. *Dangling Man* hardly measures up to Dostoyevsky's original, but in its musing, low-key fashion, almost stripped of novelistic action, it is an impressive sketch for Bellow's best later novels, *Seize the Day* (1957), *Herzog* (1964), and *Humboldt's Gift* (1975).

Even before his journal opens, Joseph, waiting for his army service to begin, has gradually separated himself from the life around him, quitting his job at a travel agency, distancing himself emotionally from wife, friends, and family. With his induction delayed, he has been "dangling" for months, and in the course of the book he quarrels with nearly everyone around him, very much like Bob Jones in *If He Hollers*. Joseph lives in the *pensées* of his journal, where his life contracts to the reports he makes of it. Finally, at the end of his rope, he puts himself up for immediate induction, canceling his burdensome freedom and solving his problems in one stroke. The self-examination he touted in the opening paragraphs has run its course.

It would be far too easy to reduce these two versions of Dostyoevky to black and Jewish stereotypes, to say that the core of Bob Jones is his emotional violence, his sexual fantasies, his constant sense of humiliation, whereas Bellow's Joseph, almost a caricature of the pure intellectual, turns everything in his life into ideas. In fact, Bob Jones is a virtuoso of self-analysis, though he also behaves like a man under unbearable pressure, and Joseph, for all his philosophical distance, is almost as irritable and quarrelsome as Himes's alter ego. But Himes's book, though it is an intense exploration of Jones's mind, also has an explosive and timely social subject – race. Joseph's mind, on the other hand, runs toward the metaphysical: his ruminations anticipate Bellow's later reflections on the self and the universe, on the general condition of man. They are the meditations of a restless intellectual who is essentially a version of Bellow himself, as all of Bellow's protagonists after Herzog would be.

In contrast to Himes's focus on race, and even to the ethnic punctuation of Bellow's later books, there is only one passage in *Dangling Man* that explicitly treats Joseph as Jewish. This comes when Joseph tries to account for his touchiness, but even here the word *Jew* is never mentioned: "I have known for a long time that we have inherited a mad fear of being slighted or scorned, an exacerbated 'honor.' . . . We are a people of tantrums." But he goes on to attribute such behavior to a previous self, the "old Joseph," still ethnic and benighted: a social being who had yet to transcend these petty feelings, the very feelings that are the subject of Himes's book.

For all the delirious extremity of its mental atmosphere, *If He Hollers* – like Himes's longer, more diffuse, more ambitious second novel, *Lonely Crusade* (1947) – is firmly set in wartime Los Angeles, with its mixed population of Southerners drawn to the defense industry, working side by side with blacks and women taking advantage of unheard-of job opportunities. It is a workplace full of newcomers thrown together in a racial and sexual tinderbox, under wartime production pressure as well as a new federal antidiscrimination order. Like the shipyard itself, Bob Jones is less an individual than a social emblem for Himes. Along with many other Californians he is a man from elsewhere, tossed into a bubbling urban cauldron.

In the course of the war, the issue of race and prejudice rapidly came to a head in American life. The racial rhetoric of the Germans and Japanese, the racism directed *at* the Japanese, and the string of nasty incidents at military bases and in neighboring towns raised the level of racial tension in America. Though blacks made up only ten percent of the population, they made up sixteen percent of the still segregated armed forces. Many of the bases were in the South, where the presence of black soldiers provoked whites, just as their frequent mistreatment evoked violent anger among blacks back home, who felt that their contributions to the war effort were being discounted. To many blacks, they were fighting for the rights of others abroad while their own rights were being violated at home. There were a number of racially motivated murders that led to black protest marches; even small clashes and rumors of racial incidents affecting black soldiers mushroomed into serious race riots in Detroit and Harlem. The war exacerbated the fever about race in a world already hot with violent conflict.

In "Notes of a Native Son" (1955), one of his best essays, James Baldwin vividly described the 1943 Harlem riot, which coincided with the death of his preacher stepfather. He recalled how the funeral procession had moved somberly through the surreal devastation of the ghetto. Ralph Ellison used a similar scene for the dramatic climax of *Invisible Man.* The zoot-suit riots in Los Angeles, in which white soldiers and sailors beat up young Mexican Americans, come up as part of the background in *If He Hollers,* along with the federal antidiscrimination efforts. The transplanted Southerners in the novel feel personally aggrieved that in California they cannot simply lynch Bob Jones – for disrespecting a white woman with dubious morals and low credibility.

In *Lonely Crusade,* set in 1943, Himes casts a wider net. Though much of the novel focuses on the hero's attraction to white women and his betrayal of his long-suffering black wife, Himes also deals unflinchingly with black anti-Semitism and with the duplicity of Communists doing union organizing, who feel free to sacrifice their own or even sabotage the cause if they cannot control it. Both the Communists and the law *do* try to frame or lynch the protagonist, Lee Gordon, but their vicious antics, devoid of moral principle, help make a man of him. Embittered from the beginning, hating himself as much he hates and fears white people, yet cursed by an internal, prickly sense of pride, he ultimately recoils when other blacks use race to excuse failure and justify violence. Gradually (if not wholly convincingly), he develops an Orwellian commitment to basic human decency, and at the end of the novel, as the police try to smash an organizing march, he picks up the fallen banner of the union, perhaps at the cost of his life. To redeem himself, he must take up the standard of something larger than himself.

～

This sense of a larger society, superficially unified by wartime goals but wracked with internal tensions, is completely missing from *Dangling Man*. Joseph has stepped away from all this. He belongs with the alienated intellectuals: his detachment, his "dangling," defines his position or lack of one. The shocking force of Himes's novels is grounded in a social psychology, not an individual one; it is focused on the lurid intersections of race, sex, and the desperate need for manhood or respect. Bellow's novel looks to a different kind of fiction in which the important conflicts will be personal or cosmic, not social. This longer view makes Joseph quite conservative – in his taste in clothes, for example – since "he wants to avoid the small conflicts of nonconformity so that he can give all his attention to defending his inner differences, the ones that really matter." The thirties romance of political commitment and even of an assertive bohemian individualism seems distant and distracting. Bellow's fundamental conservatism came through early.

Like Bellow's later intellectual protagonists, including Herzog and Mr. Sammler, Joseph preaches a sense of metaphysical limits as well as of individual obligations. Through Joseph's jottings in his journal, Bellow argues that "we suffer from bottomless avidity," from an exaggerated "Sense of Personal Destiny." We ask ourselves, "shall my life by one-thousandth of an inch fall short of its ultimate possibility," for "we have been taught there is no limit to what a man can be." Bellow would pick up this theme again in his next novel, *The Victim*. "Everybody wanted to be what he was to the limit," he says. "You couldn't expect people to be right, but only try to do what they must. Therefore hideous things were done."

Ironically, the economy of growth and abundance that developed after the war did more than anything to dispel the sense of limits that had been built up during the Depression and enforced by wartime rationing. The surge of consumerism would convince social thinkers and political leaders that we had genuinely transcended social conflict, that only Communists and fellow-traveling liberals still believed that there were significant class issues in American life. This emphasis on consensus went back to the war. Wartime propaganda had fostered an artificial unity – a resurgence of Americanism and a suspicion of dissent – that did much to drive class issues out of American politics. Harry S. Truman's successful populist campaign in 1948 as an underdog candidate was the last hurrah for the rhetoric of the New Deal, though the Democrats would still cling to it with diminishing force in future elections. This was the year that Truman, over intense opposition, finally integrated the armed forces. A strong civil rights plank became part of the Democratic platform, provoking a Dixiecrat rebellion led by diehard segregationists like J. Strom Thurmond of South Carolina.

Yet all through the late 1940s, before McCarthyism took hold, there were powerful novels and films, still rooted in the naturalism of the 1930s, that dealt with race, anti-Semitism, and the darker side of urban life – sometimes boldly and honestly, yet often luridly and formulaically. Ira Wolfert's *Tucker's People* (1943), Ann Petry's *The Street* (1946), Willard Motley's *Knock on Any Door* (1947), and Nelson Algren's *The Man with the Golden Arm* (1949), like Himes's *Lonely Crusade,* upheld a waning style of urban realism identified with Richard Wright and James T. Farrell; they conveyed a feeling for the stifled and oppressed, for the mean streets of the neighborhood; they exposed the traffic in power and corruption, the difficulty in preserving one's humanity.

Meanwhile, the crackling films noirs of the late forties, including work by such directors as Edgar G. Ulmer, Nicholas Ray, Joseph Lewis, John Huston, Billy Wilder, Robert Siodmak, and Jules Dassin, translated the harsh outlook of hard-boiled fiction into memorable film imagery: shadowy, menacing interiors; rain-swept, dimly lit streets; seductive but treacherous women whose behavior still reflected the sexual tensions and fantasies of the war years. For all their stylized urban settings, a mood of cynicism and paranoia ran through the ingeniously twisted plots of these films, which were dominated by themes of official corruption, moral depravity, and personal betrayal. Though made in Hollywood, they became a kind of official nay-saying counterculture of the late 1940s.

There were other dissenting notes in the upbeat social climate of the era. After the war, there was a short-lived vogue of social problem stories focusing on outsiders and victims. Sometimes these victims seemed interchangeable, as when the murdered homosexual in Richard Brooks's novel *The Brick Foxhole* became the murdered Jew in Edward Dmytryk's effective film noir adaptation, *Crossfire* (1947), and the psychologically damaged Jewish veteran in Arthur Laurents's play *Home of the Brave* became a black man in the film version. Even the Western could be turned into a timely parable about race relations. Delmer Daves's *Broken Arrow* (1950), made from a screenplay by Michael Blankfort – soon to be blacklisted, like many other Hollywood leftists who worked on these films – centers on the lethal hatred and warfare between white men and Indians. The conflict is eased by the mediation of a brave white scout (Jimmy Stewart) who, rather too easily, gains the trust and friendship of the fierce Apache chieftain, Cochise (Jeff Chandler) and the love of an Indian woman.

After evoking troubling issues, these stories too often tilted toward pat conclusions and happy endings. *Broken Arrow* preached mutual respect, the brotherhood of man; it gave the individualism of the Western hero a liberal twist. The films about disabled veterans like *The Best Years of Our Lives* and *The Men* preached adjustment over brooding resentment, socialization (at all costs) over prickly individuality. They made short work of the surly loner who, for whatever understandable reasons, nurses his hurt and anger, like Himes's Bob Jones, or stays outside the norms of the group, like Marlon Brando's embittered paraplegic veteran in *The Men*. In many of these films, like *Home of the Brave* and *The Men,* a doctor serves as a therapeutic mediator to bring these men back into harmony with the group. Eventually, this defense of community and conformity became the dominant "social ethic" of the 1950s, as critical observers like William H. Whyte and David Reisman would show in their widely read works of social criticism.

Besides the early work of Chester Himes, novels touching on racism and anti-Semitism after the war included books as different as Faulkner's *Intruder in the Dust* (only the second Faulkner novel made into a film); Laura Z. Hobson's popular but superficial *Gentleman's Agreement,* which became far better known as a film, directed by the ubiquitous Elia Kazan and starring Gregory Peck; Sinclair Lewis's *Kingsblood Royal*; and the young Arthur Miller's 1945 *Focus,* published before his success as a playwright. Both the European and Pacific war had sensitized the public to racial issues, which figured significantly in such war novels as James Gould Cozzens's *Guard of Honor* and Irwin Shaw's *The Young Lions,* written from sharply opposed conservative and liberal viewpoints. Saul Bellow's second novel, *The Victim* (1947), arose from the same set of forties concerns, which also produced such landmark studies of prejudice as Gunnar Myrdal's *An American Dilemma* (1944), the classic study of American race relations, as well as T. W. Adorno's *The Authoritarian Personality* (1950) and Hannah Arendt's *The Origins of Totalitarianism* (1951), both dealing with anti-Semitism. Beginning with its title, *The Victim* is almost a parody of the literature of social protest. But like *If He Hollers,* it also confronts the ethnic identity that was so muted and oblique in Bellow's first novel.

The strong concern with victims and outsiders in the postwar years also created an opening for writers to deal more frankly with homosexuality, another issue heightened by wartime changes in living patterns. Two of the literary sensations of 1948, both by writers in their early twenties, were Gore Vidal's *The City and the Pillar,* an unexpected best-seller, and Truman Capote's first novel, *Other Voices, Other Rooms,* an exercise in style that, along with his early stories, catapulted him to sudden fame. Neither book is a problem novel that reduces the homosexual to society's victim. Both are coming-of-age fables, psychological parables, that substitute sensibility and point of view for social protest. Though Vidal's book is strictly realistic, even oversimplified, and Capote's is often shimmeringly surreal to the point of being opaque, both anticipate the 1950s fascination with troubled adolescents that would soon be exemplified by J. D. Salinger's *The Catcher in the Rye* and films like *The Wild One, The Blackboard Jungle,* and *Rebel Without a Cause.*

Already in the early forties, Malcolm Cowley, who had once been a strong defender of radical and proletarian writing, anticipated this turn toward the personal and the psychological. Looking back in 1943, he observed that "the social realism of the 1930s had proved to be a less fertile movement than many writers had hoped. . . . People had begun to feel the need of books with more warmth, inwardness, and freedom." Warmth and freedom, however, were not the emotions that echoed most strongly after the war, but rather a gloomy inwardness, spiced with a strong sense of fatalism. This mood showed itself in the cynicism of the films noirs, which gave a deep psychological twist to the urban realism of the Depression, often showing the hidden links between cops and criminals, victims and villains. Other films noirs (such as Nicholas Ray's *In a Lonely Place*) concentrated on psychologically damaged war veterans; still others *(They Live By Night, Gun Crazy)* dealt poignantly with thwarted, doomed young outlaw couples, a theme that carried over from such grimly deterministic Depression-era works as Edward Anderson's Bonnie-and-Clyde novel *Thieves Like Us* and Fritz Lang's second American film, *You Only Live Once* (both from 1937).

Like Himes's books, Bellow's second novel, *The Victim,* gives us a literary variant on the nightmarish urban atmosphere of film noir. At the most superficial level, Bellow's protagonist, Asa Leventhal, feels put-upon and harassed by the anti-Semitic Kirby Allbee, who accuses Leventhal of depriving him of his job years earlier and putting his life on a downhill slide. At the same time, Leventhal feels responsible for a sick nephew, since his sister-in-law is desperate, irrational, and his brother is unaccountably out of town. These two threads of "plot," such as they are, barely serve to hold the novel together. Set in the stifling atmosphere of a sweltering New York summer, *The Victim* is a Kafkaesque novel about a man who (like Himes's self-lacerating heroes) feels deeply uncomfortable in his own skin.

If Joseph anticipates the intellectual surrogates of Bellow's late novels, Asa Leventhal foreshadows the blocked feelings, the sense of entrapment and asphyxiation of the hapless Tommy Wilhelm in *Seize the Day,* whose whole life comes unstuck in just twenty-four hours.

Such Russian writers as Dostoyevsky and Gogol had focused obsessively on clerks, bureaucrats, and minor functionaries who live pinched lives, hounded by their superiors and their creditors, tormented even by their families (if they have families). Jewish writers as different as Sholom Aleichem and Kafka were strongly drawn to these stories, which often transformed the social disabilities or frantic insecurities of their luckless protagonists into morose shaggy-dog comedies of survival. Thanks to the Kafka vogue right after the war, agonizing versions of such Little Man stories reappeared among Jewish writers like Arthur Miller (in *Death of a Salesman),* Bernard Malamud (in his short stories and in *The Assistant*), and Bellow. (*Seize the Day* would be Bellow's masterpiece in this suffocating yet spiritual "Russian" vein.)

These tales shifted the attention of Jewish writing from typical Depression subjects; exploited workers and poor immigrants gave way to lonely salesmen, loveless clerks, and long-suffering shopkeepers. The postwar writers moved away from social problems toward metaphysical concerns about identity, morality, and man's place in the larger scheme of the universe. In some sense they were all Holocaust novels, starting with *The Victim,* though the murder of Europe's Jews is scarcely mentioned in them. It was as if the Nazi genocide had eclipsed not only the social outlook of the Depression but the social character of anti-Semitism itself, offering us instead a terrible glimpse into the human heart.

The details about the Holocaust that became known only in 1945 no doubt account for some key differences between *Dangling Man* and *The Victim,* which climaxes with Kirby Allbee, the down-at-heels descendant of America's WASP patriciate, turning on the gas in Leventhal's kitchen, perhaps hoping to kill them both. (He "tried a kind of suicide pact," Leventhal tells someone, "without getting my permission first.") Asa Leventhal and Allbee are alter egos, each the oppressor, each the victim. Just as *Dangling Man* is a more lighthearted version of *Notes From Underground, The Victim* crosses *The Double* with a plot borrowed from another Dostoyevsky novella, *The Eternal Husband,* a story of early middle age, about a "worn-out man" who discovers his own inadequacies.

To make sure we understand the doubling effect, Bellow reminds us that "it was supremely plain to [Asa] that everything, needlessly everything without exception, took place as if within a single soul or person." Much like the characters who are cruelly paired in Malamud's fiction, Asa and Allbee are doppelgängers who plague and harass one another as if each is the suppressed part of the other's being. Bellow's point, never fully conveyed by the murky details of the story, is that we all have the capacity for cruelty, for self-exculpation, and that we are all inseparably responsible for one another. Thematically, *The Victim* reminds us of many less imaginative postwar works that yoke Freud's pessimism to notions of sin and human imperfection coming down from Paul and St. Augustine by way of Reinhold Niebuhr. Bellow refuses to see even the Holocaust as a tale of good and evil. Avoiding any easy division into victims and villains, Bellow's fable turns the protest novel inside out.

Besides Dostoyevsky, the other main influence on *The Victim* was Kafka – not the Kafka who was then seen too simply as a prophet of totalitarianism but the Homer of Jewish insecurity, the lyric poet of the soul's profound uneasiness with itself. Asa is dominated by a nameless malaise, a vaguely unhealthy nervous excitement. Analyzing everything, brooding about what people think of him, Asa begins "to feel unsure of his ground," to fear that "the lowest price he put on himself was too high." Just as Kafka's characters are complicit with all that oppresses them, with the terrible circumstances they feebly protest, Asa never understands why he permits intolerable demands to be made of him, why he allows Allbee to insinuate himself into his life, even to move into his home.

Kafka showed Bellow how to give a dreamlike credibility to the improbable and implausible, but Bellow uses this device to develop a moral theme – that men are accountable to each other, that debts must be paid – to wives, to children, even to strangers:

After all, you married and had children and there was a chain of consequences. It was impossible to tell, in starting out, what was going to happen. And it was unfair, perhaps, to have to account at forty for what was done at twenty. But unless one was more than human or less than human . . . the payments had to be met.

This refers to Leventhal's brother, who manages somehow to be absent while his young son is dying in a hospital, but Allbee, too, belongs to this "chain of consequences." A reflux from the past, he is like the intrusive Trusotzky, the Nemesis figure in Dostoyevsky's *Eternal Husband*. Allbee is not only a buried part of Asa himself but also the Other, the accuser, the figure with whom he must somehow come to terms. In Bellow's novels, early and late, all human debts must eventually be paid. During the same period, in such much-admired stories as "A Tree of Night," "The Headless Hawk," and "Shut a Final Door," the precocious Truman Capote was developing a glossy gothic version of the same haunting motif, but without Bellow's moral weight.

Bellow developed this doubling pattern in rather academic terms; his ideas seem independent of the novel's minimal plot. In later years, Bellow was fond of saying that in these two books he was paying his dues to get into the club — that *Dangling Man* was his master's thesis, and *The Victim,* his doctoral dissertation. By then, however, he had become a voluble critic of the "cant of alienation," the "Wasteland outlook"; he was perhaps embarrassed to have begun his career with two such pinched, depressive books. But *The Victim* was as prophetic of postwar fiction as *Dangling Man.* It helped shift fiction from the social subject to the private subject, from naturalism to the Hawthorne/Kafka mode of fable, from politics to themes of personal growth and identity.

This was the moment when a publisher, under pressure from a leading book club, subtracted Richard Wright's political history from his autobiography and turned *American Hunger* into *Black Boy,* yet another story of growing up. It was a moment when the two most ambitious postwar political novels, Robert Penn Warren's *All the King's Men* (1946) and Lionel Trilling's *The Middle of the Journey* (1947), shifted the emphasis from their political protagonists (based on the charismatic figures of Huey Long and Whittaker Chambers) to their ambivalent observers, instinctive metaphysicians who are more engrossed with sin, fate, and human destiny. In these two books, as in Norman Mailer's *Barbary Shore* (1951) and *The Deer Park* (1955), we can see the novel of ideas swerving from the stresses of politics toward the mysteries of personality and moral choice.

In such quasipolitical novels, the public world is still part of a dialogue with the troubled reflections of the private man. But in many of the most widely discussed books of the late forties, touted by critics as the "New Fiction," the public world disappears completely and we are plunged into a vortex, a metaphysical abyss. Even in *The New Yorker,* that weekly offshoot of the novel of manners, long famous for its flippant and light-hearted view of life, such writers as Jean Stafford, John Cheever, Shirley Jackson, and Hortense Calisher began turning away from the social text toward an interior castle of personal trauma and dysfunction, the familiar terrain of such young Southern writers as Carson McCullers and Eudora Welty. Closely linked to them in sensibility were the daring new gay writers, Vidal, Capote, Paul Bowles, and Tennessee Williams, who managed at once to be outlaws and celebrities, media favorites and cultural villains. Consciously posing for a group portrait as a new literary generation, they were friendly rivals then, mainly Southern but not exclusively regional, mostly homosexual but also immensely gifted at portraying indelibly original female characters.

Ten years before Norman Mailer turned from fiction to brilliant self-projection in *Advertisements for Myself,* Vidal and Capote, cultivating an aura of notoriety and sexual ambiguity, began promoting their work by projecting their own personalities. The feline, sybaritic figure lounging on the jacket of *Other Voices, Other Rooms* eventually became the fey talk-show personality that would completely displace the writing. A new culture of outrage and provocation was waiting in the wings. Vidal was another performing self who would later make a specialty of literary feuds and cutting attacks beginning with his well-publicized "feud" with Capote. The challenge, as he said in one novel, was to capture the spotlight and hold it forever. Ultimately, like his despised rival Mailer, he would prove more consistently gifted as an essayist than a novelist. Reviewing Williams's memoirs, introducing Bowles's or Williams's stories several decades later, he would become the historian and publicist of the group, rehearsing their happier moments, retelling old stories in which he always comes off well, angling for a place in literary history.

The difference between *The City and the Pillar* and *Other Voices, Other Rooms* is somewhat like the difference between Himes and Bellow. Where Vidal, still under Hemingway's influence, is flat and literal, Capote grows shadowy and metaphorical; where Vidal is concrete, Capote's early work trembles, not always convincingly, with dark symbolic relationships, doublings, in the manner of *The Victim* (though borrowed more directly from Carson McCullers, especially from *The Member of the Wedding,* 1946). Just as *If He Hollers* was almost a handbook of bruising racial encounters, filtered through the pores of a thin-skinned black protagonist, Vidal's novel was a Baedeker of gay life, from growing up in Virginia to making one's way in the armed forces, or in the demimonde of Hollywood, New Orleans, and New York. With the war as a distant background, Jim Willard explores each of these fugitive scenes, trying to find his identity and come to terms with his homosexuality. But the author's real purpose is to enlighten the audience on the range of homosexual behavior, feelings, even terminology:

Jim discovered their language, their expressions. The words "fairy" and "pansy" were considered to be in bad taste. It was fashionable to say that a person was "gay." A person who was quite effeminate, like Rolloson, was called a "queen." A man who could not be had, who was normal, was called "jam." The rough young men who offered themselves for seduction but who did not practice were known as "trade"; sometimes they prostituted themselves for money; more often, however, they were homosexuals who had not yet realized it themselves. Among the homosexuals there was a saying that "this year's trade is next year's competition."

Vidal's ambition to become the Virgil of homosexual underworld is admirable, even courageous. (Many years later, Edmund White and Armistead Maupin would take on a similar role in exploring the more uninhibited gay scene of the 1970s.) Vidal aims to show his readers that homosexuals are anything but monolithic: like straight people, their personalities, their sexual styles and social practices, vary immensely. Jim is cast as the innocent, as yet uncertain of his identity, who encounters gay characters ranging from effeminate queens to famous writers to seemingly virile Hollywood stars. This documentary aspect of the book is the fictional counterpart of the first Kinsey report, *Sexual Behavior in the Human Male,* a study that caused a sensation when it appeared just a few months later, in part because it revealed – and perhaps exaggerated – the extent of homosexual experience among American men. But such an instructional approach, though socially admirable, does real damage to the novel. Vidal permits characters to lecture each other over drinks on the origins of homosexuality and the dominance of castrating women in American culture. Most of *The City and the Pillar* is written in a numbingly simple declarative style, punctuated by Dick-and-Jane dialogue in which everyone sounds alike and no one, not even a sailor, ever curses or uses slang.

Vidal had begun his career with *Williwaw* (1945), a spare war novel written under the Hemingway influence, and this uninflected manner persists in *The City and the Pillar,* but without Hemingway's wealth of reverberation and implication. After Jim's idyllic sexual initiation and his stints in the navy and in Hollywood, a vague malaise settles over the second half of the novel, in which very little occurs. Unhappiness is the one common denominator among the people Jim meets and sleeps with. Their unfulfilling lives are meant to build up a 1940s gay equivalent of *The Sun Also Rises,* with its wounded or dissatisfied expatriates living aimlessly, for pleasure, but cut off from their own feelings. But this part of the book falls flat, drifting forward on a style so muted, so lacking in color or emotional atmosphere that it takes us nowhere.

As an acute observer of the literary scene, Vidal was very much aware of the stylistic options available to him; but he must be pulling our leg, or his character's, when he has a woman say: "You know, I'm really thrilled to see Henry James coming back. I think we are all tired of those short ungraceful sentences of the thirties. It will be nice to read books with lovely long sentences about *real* people." Henry James *was* coming back, but not in this novel. Someone else responds that "it takes something more than long sentences to create great literature" and that there is "a lot to be said for the staccato style." This allows the author to have it both ways while satirizing the literary chitchat of the moment.

The real failure of the novel comes not from its style, however, which Vidal himself later renounced, or its documentary approach, and certainly not from its sympathetic portrayal of the problems of homosexuals, but from its basic timidity, especially if we compare it to a genuinely outrageous later book like *Myra Breckinridge* (1968), the work of a more freewheeling era. Gore Vidal set out in *The City and the Pillar* to show that homosexuals, far from being strange or exotic creatures, could be as ordinary as anyone else. Just as Laura Z. Hobson cheated in *Gentleman's Agreement* by making the victim of anti-Semitism a gentile in disguise, Vidal's protagonist is a handsome, tennis-playing young athlete from Virginia, an all-American boy out of an Andy Hardy movie. But Jim is an anachronistic figure: in the Freudian climate of postwar America, Andy Hardy was turning into James Dean. Jim is unhappy with his life and turned off by the subterranean gay cultures he encounters. "He liked young men his own age who, like himself, were not effeminate or unnatural." As in so many of his later novels and essays, Vidal wants to be transgressive and popular at the same time. Attracted only to the most civilized outcasts and scoundrels like Julian the Apostate or Aaron Burr, he is always courting outrage while exercising a safe kind of daring.

To take *The City and the Pillar* seriously as a work of imagination, not simply a documentary of gay life, we would have to accept the unconvincing premise that Jim Willard's goal in life is to recapture the magic of a single adolescent experience with a heterosexual friend. According to Vidal's memoir *Palimpsest* (1995), the friend was based on the only man he ever really loved, a brilliant young athlete named Jimmie Trimble who was later killed in the war. A nostalgically remembered scene of awkward initiation has since become a commonplace of gay fiction, but the weight it is forced to bear in *The City and the Pillar* damages the novel's credibility.

The tangled memory of Jim's thwarted infatuation is meant to make him a gay figure with whom everyone else can identify – not someone motivated by simple hatred of his father, fear of women, or strong repugnance toward their bodies. In a wildly improbable and lurid conclusion that Vidal rewrote two decades later, Jim is reunited with his old friend eight years afterward and kills him when his sexual overtures are rejected. (In the 1965 version, he merely rapes and abandons him.) Thus, Vidal's first searching critic, John W. Aldridge in *After the Lost Generation* (1951), complained that as a character Jim was not a person but *only* a homosexual, simplified to make a social point, as in the contemporaneous protest novels about blacks and Jews, in which the characters were often merely social types.[1]

Later, in novels like *Burr, 1876,* and *Lincoln,* Vidal would bring a stylistically richer version of his no-frills approach to well-researched but thinly imagined historical fiction. He began in 1964, after a decade away from fiction, with a distinguished novel about Julian the Apostate, probably inspired by Robert Graves's crisply written Claudius novels. Vidal portrays Julian as a genuinely civilized figure in a society of power-hungry Caesars, a tolerant, enlightened classicist amid small-minded Christians.

But Vidal also tried, to match the disillusioned wit of Henry Adams, and starting with *Washington, D. C.* (1967) he began writing a sardonic history of America in fictional form, achieving commercial success by appealing to a more disillusioned age. At best his transparent style followed Graves in wiping away the cobwebs and museum clutter from the historical novel. Trying to write a fictional chronicle of American politics, he could do no more than assemble a collection of venal politicians – plotters, scoundrels, and corrupt scalawags – faceless avatars of the American empire whom he attacked repeatedly in his witty essays. Simply as a storyteller, he did more justice to Burr and Lincoln and American politics than to Jim Willard and homosexuality. His novels tried to serve both the Hollywood-fed imagination of the mass audience and the patrician cynicism of his own political outlook. He exploited the roguish charm of his heroes as pendants to his own public personality, which he cultivated on talk shows, in occasional movie roles, and in many cutting and entertaining essays.

Vidal himself had made an effective but quixotic run for Congress from New York in 1960, doing well as a Democrat in an entrenched Republican district. He drew upon his Washington background and his knowledge of the mechanics of American politics in a hit play and film, *The Best Man* (1960; 1964), then in *Washington, D. C.* The novel holds a special place in his fiction because it is so autobiographical, saturated with his own boyhood in Washington during the New Deal era. Vidal had politics in his blood. His maternal grandfather was a blind senator from Oklahoma, Thomas P. Gore, and his father was a New Dealer who had become well

---

[1] In his afterword to the 1965 revised version, Vidal argued that the novel had always been misunderstood, since the character had been intended as a *negative* example: "I intended Jim Willard to demonstrate the romantic fallacy. From too much looking back, he was destroyed, an unsophisticated Humbert Humbert trying to re-create an idyll that never truly existed except in his own imagination. Despite the title, this was never plain in the narrative." This intention was belied by the autobiographical emotion that Vidal invested in Jim, feelings that still echo through Vidal's 1995 memoir, where he even looks forward to being buried near his boyhood friend. In the novel, the incident is portrayed lyrically; the afterword comes more from the more cynical, technically adroit older writer half acknowledging the weaknesses of the book.

known as a star athlete and coach at West Point and as an aviation pioneer. Taking us from the beginning of FDR's second term in 1937 to the heyday of McCarthyism in the 1950s, *Washington, D. C.* includes portraits of his adored grandfather as a "flawed idealist," his mercurial mother and handsome father, and his own callow but sharply observant younger self, with secondary characters based on such familiar legends of the Washington scene as Alice Roosevelt Longworth and the closeted columnist Joseph Alsop. The novel is powered by Vidal's essayistic intelligence, his insider's knowledge of Washington life, his moral seriousness, and his smoothly adroit handling of the levers of conventional fiction. It even recaps, more realistically, the sexual initiation portrayed so lyrically in *The City and the Pillar* without pursuing the earlier novel's homosexual theme. But *Washington, D. C.* loses strength when its central character, a rising young politician and fake war hero, turns into a hollow pastiche of John F. Kennedy. Vidal had a family connection to Jacqueline Kennedy – they shared a stepfather – but he had grown to detest her husband after being banned from the White House in the early 1960s. The personal thrust of his need for revenge undermined the fiction, but the book did initiate Vidal's unique chronicle of American history, which he would carry through five additional novels, from *Burr* (1973) to *Empire* (1987) and *Hollywood* (1990).

❧

The best contrast to the well-meaning but pedestrian treatment of homosexuality in *The City and the Pillar* can be found in the stories of Tennessee Williams and the fiction of Paul Bowles. Born in the same year, 1911, Bowles and Williams were more than a decade older than Capote and Vidal, and both had significant careers outside their work in fiction. Something of a prodigy himself, Bowles, as a protégé of Aaron Copland, Virgil Thomson, and Gertrude Stein, found success as a composer before turning to fiction, whereas Williams was the most renowned American playwright of the late forties and early fifties. (This helps explain why his fiction went virtually unnoticed as he was doing his best work.) Neither had the genius for self-promotion of Vidal and Capote, though they were bolder, more dangerous writers.

All four writers were dependent on style to the same degree that many thirties writers depended on *not* having a style, on not embracing the merely aesthetic during a time of social suffering. Vidal's style – crisp, direct, intelligent – was the most readable and least original of the four, serving him better in the essay form than in the novel, carrying us along on the intimately conversational yet mandarin flow of his voice, entertaining us with the twists and turns of his clever mockery and self-regard. Yet

Vidal would later be generous to the writers of the late forties – Williams, Bowles, John Horne Burns, even Mailer – who shared his moment of literary history. Introducing Williams's collected stories, for example, he says incisively: "These stories are the true memoir of Tennessee Williams. . . . Except for an occasional excursion into fantasy, he sticks close to life as he experienced or imagined it. No, he is not a great short story writer like Chekhov but he has something rather more rare than mere genius. He has a narrative tone of voice that is totally compelling."

Aside from telling us how much Vidal learned from Williams, this puts a finger on the paradox of Williams's neglected but wonderful prose fiction. At a time when the well-made story was the dominant mode – thoroughly plotted, oblique, full of irony and complexity – Williams's memory stories and anecdotal fragments were a sharp departure, almost doomed to be undervalued. They seem dreamed or hallucinated rather than formally composed. At moments they feel like erotic reveries, written solely for the writer's own satisfaction. Frequently Williams loses interest in them a few pages before the end and simply races to a conclusion. They are storyteller's stories, pieces of an ongoing life, and they resist all closure, yet they are kept afloat by a remarkable vividness: it is virtually impossible to put them down. Even Williams's late, eccentric *Memoirs* (1975) have this mesmerizing, irresistible quality: they are the inimitable sound of one man talking.

Like many of his fine autobiographical sketches (such as "Grand" and "The Man in the Overstuffed Chair"), the *Memoirs* clarify the handful of intense relationships that lay behind both the plays and the stories: the overbearing mother captured so well in *The Glass Menagerie,* the alcoholic and mercurial father who mocked his son as a sissy, the maternal grandparents, the Reverend and Mrs. Dakin (his beloved "Grand"), the sister who was his inseparable companion until adolescence separated them and a frontal lobotomy destroyed her mind, and the young girl who was the other female companion of his childhood. These early connections eventually gave way to his life as a writer and his discovery of his homosexuality, to travel, love affairs, cruising, addictions and breakdowns, and always an iron devotion to the daily call of his work. When Williams had nothing new to write (Gore Vidal reports), he simply sat down in the morning to retype something he had already done.

The later forties were a time of fictional experimentation. As Bellow reflects the impact of Kafka and Dostoyevsky, as the early Vidal uses the spare manner of Hemingway without its suggestive depths, so Williams and Bowles reflect opposing facets of the work of D. H. Lawrence, early and late. In Williams's hands, Lawrence's vision remains earthy, lyrical, and celebratory, whereas Bowles explores the dark side, the sense of drugged self-surrender in the pursuit of the primitive. In "The Mattress by the Tomato Patch" (1953), Williams too easily creates a female Zorba, the woman as life force, strong and indestructible compared to the men around her, whereas in the weakest part of his masterwork, *The Sheltering Sky* (1949), Bowles yields to a masochistic fantasy of erotic surrender, sexual enslavement, and the descent into madness, all motifs from Lawrence's later work, including *The Plumed Serpent, St. Mawr,* and "The Woman Who Rode Away."

The common coin of the New Fiction was the allegorical fable, which the writers used as a Freudian vehicle for tapping into the unconscious, but like all *literary* fables, they worked best with an abundance of realistic detail. Good fiction is nothing if circumstantial, full of what Irving Howe calls "gratuitous detail." Bowles became famous (or notorious) for his remarkably concrete horror stories – "A Distant Episode," "The Delicate Prey," "Pages from Cold Point" – in which frightful events were narrated in a detached, neutral, almost clinical manner. He dedicated his first collection, *The Delicate Prey and Other Stories* (1950), to his mother, "who first read me the stories of Poe."

Williams worked entirely from experience as rearranged by memory and fantasy. As Vidal remarked, he spent "a lifetime playing with the same, vivid ambiguous cards that life dealt him." He reworked his stories tirelessly, sometimes in new versions, often as plays, seeking fresh emotional truth as he rearranged details, bringing a different intensity to each transformation. For him, writing was an act of recovery that began with the experience of unhappiness and loss. In one of his most autobiographical stories, "The Resemblance between a Violin Case and a Coffin" (1949), he describes a young man's loss of his childhood as he grows alienated from his beloved sister and feels the first confused promptings of his own homosexuality:

And it was then, about that time, that I began to find life unsatisfactory as an explanation of itself and was forced to adopt the method of the artist of not explaining but putting the blocks together in some other way that seems more significant to him. Which is a rather fancy way of saying I started writing. . .

Williams sees art as a way of reassembling blocks of experience to yield new structures of emotional meaning. Yet this passage itself, so typical of Williams, is a rather clumsy piece of "explaining" that sounds more like an excerpt from an essay than lines from a story. If Williams seems gauche and uneven, this is inseparable from the marvelous spontaneity of his writing. As he compares an idyllic past with the conflicts and losses that came afterward, Williams endlessly wrestles his experience into meaning, not by any literary strategy, certainly not through form, but by whatever means language affords – sometimes discursively, often confessionally and self-accusingly, always emotionally. Williams writes out of an intense yearning to retouch and reshape a handful of unforgettable experiences.

Williams's stories feel at once repetitive and strikingly different. Two stories about his sister, "Portrait of a Girl in Glass" (the source for *The Glass Menagerie*) and "The Resemblance between a Violin Case and a Coffin," are like an artist's rendering of the same scene or the same model at different moments of recollection. As a writer, Williams is driven by a relentless dissatisfaction, or simply an inability to let anything go; for him to finalize his memories would be to cast them aside. Thus, "The Mysteries of Joy Rio" (1941), about furtively looking for love in the balcony of an old movie theatre, is transformed twelve years later into "Hard Candy." Because they belong to the culture of the closet, haunted by a mixture of fear and desire, pleasure and embarrassment, Williams's stories of gay sex seem strikingly complicated, brave, and (unlike *The City and the Pillar*) unformulaic. "Two on a Party" (1951–2) must be one of the best stories of the hustling life ever written. Entirely unpredictable, it portrays the bond of affection between a male hustler and slightly older prostitute who team up and go looking for trade together. Above all, it is suffused with Williams's own comic affection for marginal characters and their sordid, insecure lives, over which he never sits in judgment.

Another of his best stories, "There Players of a Summer Game" (also 1951–2) – the source for his play *Cat on a Hot Tin Roof* – takes place in a completely different world, a Peter Taylor world of rich social memory, in which money and class are no defense against emasculation, cancer, alcoholism, or unhappiness in love. An unhappily married man has an affair with a recently widowed woman, but it ends badly for both of them when his determined wife gets the upper hand. The story centers on this strange love triangle fraught with social disapproval, personal weakness, and even a kind of vampirism. Williams's special touch is that this is all observed from the point of view of two children who mainly remember the period as a magical summer, not as the misfortune that adult life might have in store for them as well.

Williams's darker material foreshadows the whole Grove Press school of underground writers – such as John Rechy in *City of Night* (1963), and Hubert Selby, Jr. in *Last Exit to Brooklyn* (1964) – yet his work is as fluent, unforced, and forgiving as theirs is violent and sensational. Occasionally his work comes closer to theirs, as in the famous "Desire and the Black Masseur" (1946), one of his rare horror stories in the lurid vein of Capote, Bowles, and the last pages of *The City and the Pillar.* Williams's stories

scarcely underline his personal links to the Southern gothic manner of
Eudora Welty and Carson McCullers that are writ large in the early
Capote. Like many writers who dramatize the conflicts of the closet,
Williams deals frequently with sexual confusion, guilt, and repression, but
"Desire and the Black Masseur" is one of his rare fictional excursions into
sadomasochism and allegory. Bowles, on the other hand, explores the edges
of civilization as a twilight zone in which these dark and forbidden needs
are repeatedly acted out. Where Williams naturalizes homosexuality and
its conflicts into a narrative of lyrical recollection, Bowles is the first of the
transgressive writers whose bleak nihilism and lurid atmosphere open
doors for the James Baldwin of *Giovanni's Room* and *Another Country* and
the William S. Burroughs of *Naked Lunch.*

Each of these writers came from seriously dysfunctional families.
Williams's parents were hopelessly mismatched, as he never tires of showing in his work. Vidal's and Capote's mothers were alcoholics; Capote's
mother quickly realized that her unreliable husband would never manage
to support her, and she farmed her son out to her family for years until she
remarried and brought him north. In "The Frozen Fields" (1957), a rare
autobiographical story, Bowles, the precocious son of a well-to-do Queens
dentist, portrays his father as a sadistic tyrant bent on crushing and humiliating him, and shows up his mother as a woman too weak to stand up for
him. The summers the boy has spent on his grandparents' farm are an
"enchanted world" to him, an escape into his own imagination, but the
presence of his father threatens him, "because it was next to impossible to
conceal anything from him, and once aware of the existence of the other
world he would spare no pains to destroy it."

His father objects when the family fusses over the boy and showers him
with Christmas gifts, and he in turn imagines his father's being carried off
by a wolf who embodies the terrifying forces that lurk outside the safe circle of society. In a horrendous scene, his father – who is concerned (as
Williams's father was) that the boy was too sensitive and unmasculine –
forces him to take a walk in the snow and, in a fit of anger, rubs the snow
in his face and down his neck. "As he felt the wet, icy mass sliding down
his back, he doubled over. His eyes were squeezed shut; he was certain his
father was trying to kill him. With a desperate lunge he bounded free and
fell face-downward into the snow."

Deftly, the story takes an existential turn typical of Bowles. Instead of
fighting his father, the six-year-old boy, "his mind empty of thoughts,"
takes a mental leap into a land of unfeeling, where he finds his freedom.
"An unfamiliar feeling had come to him: he was not sorry for himself for
being wet and cold, or even resentful at having been mistreated. He felt

detached; it was an agreeable, almost voluptuous sensation which he accepted without understanding or questioning it." Nearly every wrinkle of Bowles's imagination can be found in this story. If the father stands for the despotic power of respectable society and the patriarchal family, the wolf is the lure of what lies outside the town gates, outside the limits of the conscious mind. Between these two extremes Bowles gains the almost inhuman detachment of the sensitive yet fatalistic observer. As he says of his surrogate, Port Moresby, who is observing an ugly quarrel in *The Sheltering Sky,* "He was determined to remain wholly on the periphery of this family pattern; the best way of assuring that, he thought, would be to have no visible personality whatever, merely to be civil, to listen."

This detachment became not only Bowles's social mask but his literary physiognomy as well. Along with Poe and Lawrence, Conrad's *Heart of Darkness* is the tutor text of all Bowles's best work. Bowles was drawn to Morocco and then into the Sahara as Mr. Kurtz and then the Marlow of *Heart of Darkness* were drawn into the Congo, fathoming the limits of civilization in themselves and those around them. "I think one is always writing about oneself," Bowles once wrote, but added that "writing is, I suppose, a superstitious way of keeping the horror at bay, of keeping the evil outside." Williams writes in order to get in touch, to actualize his memories, fantasies, and desires more vividly in his mind, on paper, or on stage. Bowles, on the other hand, felt the pressure to *dis*engage, to outline his fantasies with a cool precision very far from the adjectival vagueness of Conrad's portentous evocations of the horror of the unknown.

Bowles's stories and novels reject the father without sentimentalizing the wolf. The wolf crystalizes everything that is violent, primitive, and devouring yet still somehow attractive to him. Modern literature is full of versions of the wolf, Rilke's sleek panther, for example, or Kafka's leopard, which every day invades the courtyard of the temple to drink up the blood on the altar. Kafka's leopard, the force of the irrational, can scarcely be resisted but it can somehow be domesticated, included in the ceremony, made part of the ritual. Freud's system, though less fatalistic about the power of the unconscious, in effect aims at achieving the same result. For Bowles, however, the wolf – the irrational, the primitive, the unconscious – represents the irresistible attraction of letting go.

Bowles's protagonists seek the outer limits of a civilization they detest; deliberately or unconsciously, they yield themselves up to forces that will dissolve or destroy them. "A Distant Episode" could be the title of many of Bowles's stories, just as "The Delicate Prey" describes their lurid, sado-masochistic material, which the writer develops in the crisp, neutral style of an anthropological observer. The title "Pages from Cold Point" could almost be a motto for this detachment, though it also refers to the chilling, predatory traits of the characters. In a remote part of a Caribbean island, a young man, by all appearances a paragon of innocence, seduces and black-mails his own father, who is himself a repressed homosexual with some buried scandal in his past. In "A Distant Episode," a professor, a linguist, has his tongue cut out by nomadic tribesmen who imprison him and make him their mascot and buffoon. In "A Delicate Prey" a trusting young mer-chant traveler is robbed, mutilated, raped, and then murdered by a desert outlaw, whose crime is then grotesquely avenged by the victim's kinsmen.

Whether the narration is oblique, understated, and brilliantly sugges-tive (as in "Pages from Cold Point") or graphic and lurid (as in "A Distant Episode" and "The Delicate Prey"), Bowles's strategy is the same. His sup-posedly "civilized" characters, like Mr. Kurtz in Conrad's story, are drawn to the heart of a void, a solitude, which then enfolds and envelops them, exposing their secret wishes and vulnerabilities. Port and Kit Moresby in *The Sheltering Sky* have come to Africa, just as Paul and Jane Bowles had done, to find a resonant backdrop for their own estrangement. Obscurely, they hope to overcome the sexual dissonance, the failure of feeling, that has overtaken their twelve-year marriage, but they have also brought along a companion, Tunner, as a distraction, a defense against intimacy, and he makes it harder for them to find each other. Even before he seduces Kit on a nightmarishly crowded train, the boringly normal Tunner, with his casual, conventional masculinity, serves as a buffer between them, making it almost impossible for them to be alone. His sharp will accentuates their vague aimlessness, their immense fatalism.

It is not at all clear what the couple is seeking in Morocco as they move ever more deeply into the Sahara, even as Port falls dangerously ill with typhoid. Bowles himself was making the same journey as he wrote the book, turning to drugs to write the difficult scene in which he knew Port would have to die. For Port, as for Bowles, Africa is a way of sloughing off the decadence of the West, with its residue of oppressive morality. "Pages from Cold Point" begins with a Spenglerian vision of decline keyed to the nuclear age – "Our civilization is doomed to a short life. . . . The bigger the bombs, the quicker it will be done" – but this vast claim will be quali-fied by our sense of the narrator's personal failings as a husband, brother, and father. Kit's problem is that she wants Port, wants him back, but can-not empathize with what Port needs, since it diminishes and frightens her. Part of him is oriented to the void rather than to humankind. At a key moment, they cycle out at sunset to some remote rocks overlooking an empty landscape, which highlights the gap between his longing for the abyss and her inescapable fears:

It was such places as this, such moments that he loved above all else in life; she knew that, and she also knew that he loved them more if she could be there to experience them with him. And although she was aware that the very silences and emptinesses that touched his soul terrified her, he could not bear to be reminded of that. It was as if always he held the fresh hope that she, too, would be touched in the same way as he by solitude and the proximity to infinite things. . . . And now for so long there had been no love, no possibility of it. . . . The terror was always there inside her ready to take command. It was useless to pretend otherwise.

In such ruminative passages, Bowles steps not only beyond the descriptive, detached manner of the stories but also outside the novel itself, providing discursive touches of motivation that are otherwise elusive; they seem to come from his own mind and marriage. Early critics like John W. Aldridge complained that the characters "move without motive from sensation to sensation" and that Port "is driven by a compulsion which neither he nor we can formulate," but this ignores the *kind* of novel Bowles is reinventing: the prewar existential novel (like Sartre's *Nausea* and Camus's *The Stranger*) in which hollowed-out characters, devoid of feeling and clear motivation, move obscurely through vacant landscapes of alienation. (This helps explain why *The Sheltering Sky* became a cult book in Europe, and why Bernardo Bertolucci would eventually direct a faithful film version, with the aged Bowles in a cameo role.) Long before the French discovered this way of developing the theme, Hemingway in *The Sun Also Rises* and *In Our Time* had created a pared-down, shell-shocked style of the unspoken, with characters drifting aimlessly, almost devoid of affect or purpose, a style that relied heavily on inference and suggestion. More convincingly than Gore Vidal, Bowles creates a 1940s equivalent of Hemingway's mood of postwar disillusionment.

The Sheltering Sky remains powerful and convincing as long as Bowles stays with the Moresbys' marriage, their descent into the Sahara, and Port's illness and death. In the predatory Lyles, mother and son – vicious, bigoted, thieving, paranoid, and probably incestuous – Bowles provides the reader with a comically horrible foil for the Moresbys. Early in the novel, Bowles distinguishes between tourists and travelers, between mere sightseers collecting experiences and true voyagers who submit to the alien strangeness of their surroundings. Armored in their Mercedes, following the same route as the Moresbys, bickering over their hotel bills, the Lyles are contemptuous of the Arabs and impossible to each other. The Dickensian solidity of these sharply drawn characters contrasts very effectively with the growing metaphysical vagueness of the Moresbys. The underlying strain in the Moresby marriage is set into high relief by the satirical intensity of the Lyles' incessant quarreling.

As the Moresbys leave the last vestige of European influence behind, Port's health deteriorates, as if in direct consequence of his descent into the Sahara. While her husband falls into fever and hallucination, Kit is increasingly drawn to the exotic and sinister Arab men around her. Feeling imprisoned by his illness, tied to a person she now scarcely recognizes, she is gradually transformed, seeking out the self-obliterating transcendence he had sought for himself. Distracted but no longer fearful, she yields to the primitive void all around her. While Port dies, she is off with Tunner, but afterward she wanders into the desert, where she is picked up by a tribal caravan.

Repeatedly ravished, lost in an erotic haze, Kit willingly becomes the kind of sex slave we encounter in Victorian orientalist pornography, such as *The Lustful Turk*. As Port yields himself to death, to the gray emptiness he had perceived behind the blue, sheltering sky, Kit takes on his vast fatalism: instead of remaining the character we knew, she acts out the author's fantasy of masochistic submission, which also lay behind the cocky professor's enslavement and humiliation in "A Distant Episode." Both characters surrender themselves with huge relief and resist only when their submission ends. When the professor's numb stupor begins to pall, he angrily rebels; similarly, Kit recoils and grows disoriented when her rescuers, including the persistent Tunner, manage to bring her back into civilization, a return that she (or her madness) is unable to accept. Like some late Lawrence characters, they have known the ecstasy of self-surrender and self-immolation. A return to sanity and the trials of individual existence feel unbearable to them.

So long as the book rests on its autobiographical foundation – the strange marriage of Paul and Jane Bowles – it remains haunting and resonant. Despite Paul's nihilism and fatalism, his recoil from Western civilization, despite Jane's lesbian promiscuity and neurotic fears, the two were a devoted and dependent couple. Their life together, difficult as it was, seemed to liberate and inspire him, and he did little significant writing after her death in 1973. Especially during this short period in the late 1940s, his fantasies and memories were chillingly concrete. The same cannot be said of the other most celebrated practitioner of the grotesque during this period. Capote's early stories and novels show up the weaknesses of postwar gothic in its most banal and aestheticized form. For the celebrity journalism of the period, in the pages of such glossy magazines as *Life* and *Vogue,* Capote himself became the precocious, sexually ambiguous child who appears throughout his early fiction. But Capote's writing was more authentic than his clippings, not as a designer version of gothic horror but as growing-up stories that anchor the New Fiction in a child's-eye view of the world. Capote was a fashionable tourist in the lower depths but his work was only a step or two away from the imperishable adolescent complaint of *The Catcher in the Rye* and the kinky Old World lust of Nabokov's *Lolita,* with its refined attraction to the robust vulgarity of youth.

More chic but less touching than these later works, entirely lacking their comic concreteness, *Other Voices, Other Rooms* (1948) and the horror stories in *A Tree of Night and Other Stories* (1949) give us fragile fantasy without resistance, sexual anxiety and dysfunction without solidly grounded detail. Whether they deal with orphaned children in search of their parents (as in *Other Voices*) or impish children as evil spirits, wreaking revenge on the adult world (as in "Miriam"), whether they are set in the rural South, a land that time forgot, or in fashionable New York, Capote's fiction is spun out like a gossamer web from the viewpoint of the child who is not quite ready to grow up, whose fantasies recoil from sexual differentiation and adult behavior. (Capote developed a mellower, more benign version of this Peter Pan fantasy in *The Grass Harp,* 1951.) Even when the protagonists are adults, as in "The Headless Hawk" or "Shut a Final Door," they are people who never really grew up, who certainly never resolved the conflicts that plagued them as children. Haunted by mysterious doubles representing suppressed parts of themselves, locked in emotional isolation, as little able to give as to receive love, they come to grief like shipwrecked boats on the raw, unintegrated parts of their own personalities.

If Bowles is always writing variants on Conrad's *Heart of Darkness,* the distant ancestor of Capote's early fiction is Hawthorne's greatest story, "My Kinsman, Major Molyneux," the archetypal American coming-of-age fable. Both Bowles and early Capote are also literary descendants of Poe, but Bowles is astringently precise and detached where Capote remains watery, vague, and self-pitying. In the light of its theme, a young man's search for his father, Capote's style in *Other Voices* is far too mannered and involuted, too lyrical. As Alfred Kazin wrote not long after it was published, "I am tired of reading for compassion instead of pleasure," adding, "This demand on our compassion is not limited to the quivering novels of sensibility by overconscious stylists."

There is something exquisitely artificial about Capote's early fiction, as if he were too young to have experienced any of the things he wrote about, except for the feelings behind them. Aldridge complained in 1951 that "the real world behind the nightmare which Capote gives us has been refined almost completely out of existence. . . . Joel, the central figure in *Other Voices, Other Rooms,* is neither a boy nor a caricature of a boy. He is a creation entirely of Capote's talent for the grotesque." The same point could be made about James Purdy's more accomplished but strangely airless growing-up stories of the 1950s and 1960, such as "63: Dream Palace" and *Malcolm*. Like *The City and the Pillar* and several of Williams's best stories, *Other Voices, Other Rooms* is about discovering and coming to terms with one's homosexuality. But its reliance on gothic devices and its hothouse atmosphere and stylistic extravagance seriously undercut the genuine feelings of loneliness, homelessness, and personal confusion that give the novel some authenticity. We have the testimony of writers like Cynthia Ozick and Alfred Chester about its powerful impact on them when the book first appeared, but its affected manner made it largely an exercise in style, a throwback to the decadence and aestheticism of the 1890s.

Like McCullers's *The Member of the Wedding*, Capote's novel centers on the dreamy world of a young adolescent. Thirteen-year-old Joel Harrison Knox journeys from New Orleans to a remote, moldering mansion called Skully's Landing in search of his lost father, Edward Sansom, who turns out to be a drooling, helpless, mentally incompetent cripple rather than the strong Samson figure he desperately seeks. Instead, he finds a tomboy, Idabell, who rejects his very tentative sexual advances, and his stepmother's cousin Randolph, a Wilde-like transvestite who, despite his own miserable experiences, enables Joel to accept his own inchoate homosexual identity. This is curious, since identity itself is portrayed by Capote as fluid and mercurial: the book's title refers metaphorically to different identities and alternative selves. In a rather willed conclusion, we see the sensitive boy turning unconvincingly into the precocious author: "'I am me,' Joel whooped. 'I am Joel, we are the same people.' And he looked about for a tree to climb: he would go right to the very top, and there, midway to heaven, he would spread his arms and claim the world." But this has nothing to do with the sad and uncertain boy we have known, only with the ambitious claims registered by the author's style. It does nothing to resolve the deep sense of lovelessness and homelessness that give Capote's early stories their bleak and horrifying edge.

What enabled the self-destructive author to survive as long as he did – he died shortly before his sixtieth birthday in 1984 – was not the newly integrated personality he asserts at the end of the novel but, as in Bowles's case, the writer's steely detachment, even cruelty, in the face of his own lurid material. Admirers of his later journalism, such as Mark Schorer, applauded Capote's "progression from the wholly private psychic world into the world of objective social realities." Though Capote removed the trappings of gothic fantasy and childlike bewilderment and, beginning with *The Muses Are Heard* (1957), became a solid reporter in the best *New Yorker* manner, real life would provide him with material even more garish than his youthful fantasies. Capote the reporter, still the bright, attentive child, became indistinguishable from Capote the voyeur, the social butterfly, the malicious gossip, the cold melodramatist.

Looking always for *le mot juste,* he set down all he saw and heard in a neutral manner that concealed his own wounds. "From a technical point," he later wrote, "the greatest difficulty I'd had in writing *In Cold Blood* was leaving myself completely out of it." The two psychopathic killers in *In Cold Blood,* however, are found versions of the confused waifs and grimly haunted adults of his early fiction, and Capote, for all his surface detachment, identifies with them far more than he identifies with their "innocent" victims. Similarly, the gossipy, back-biting world of his last, unfinished novel, *Answered Prayers,* is a keenly observant child's malicious report on what society is. Capote himself had the killer instinct, and, like the precocious child accustomed to being forgiven and rewarded, he was amazed when his tale-bearing was not applauded by its victims.

Other Voices, Other Rooms today seems like a passing phase for its author and a minor moment in American fiction, yet it epitomized many of the qualities of the New Fiction that would develop in the decades after the war. Its emphasis on inwardness and style foreshadowed much of the psychological fiction of the 1950s, just as its focus on a boy's coming of age anticipated the direction of the new youth culture that would lead through the Beats to the counterculture of the 1960s. Capote himself was a fastidious writer who famously described *On the Road* as typing rather than writing, yet his phantasmagoric treatment of homosexuality paved the way for Burroughs and the Beats. Adept at manipulating the publicity machinery, Capote himself became very much an insider despite his homosexuality. Nevertheless, the figure of the delicate young outsider in his early work anticipated the sensitive, alienated misfits – young, black, gay, Jewish, or simply unhinged by contemporary life – who would establish a main line in American fiction from Salinger to Vonnegut, a line that joined the underground writers to the more acclaimed and established talents.

The major alternative to the New Fiction would be offered by one of its early practitioners, Saul Bellow, who, along with such black writers as Ralph Ellison, would take the new style of personal fable in a more social, moral, and ethnic direction, away from the violent aestheticism and lurid primitivism foreshadowed by Capote and Bowles. The nightmares of the black and Jewish writers seem more historical, less purely personal, for they were grounded in real traumas, the cultural legacies of their people. They certainly had no sense of a lost innocence; like Kafka, they felt they were born guilty, born under a curse or at least a burden. They understood how their quest for identity had strong social roots, but they were as concerned with survival as with identity, and they looked more to be integrated into society than simply to transgress its norms.

If the new gay and bisexual writers were the immoralists of postwar fiction – bold in exploring a dangerous new terrain, lyrical in evoking both a lost innocence and a utopia of personal freedom – Jews and blacks were the moralists, weighing the inexorable cost of the historical horrors and psychic traumas their characters had experienced. There was no Jewish equivalent to the emotional poetry of Tennessee Williams's plays, to the willed horror or sense of loss in Capote's evocations of childhood, or to Bowles's shocking variations on Poe and Conrad. Since they were intellectuals as well as fiction writers, Bellow and Mailer would respond strongly to the effects of politics, war, the Holocaust, and the bomb, as the more self-concerned Capote and Williams did not. Their ruminations about history and personality, about all the catastrophic twists of modernity, would give their own work a deeper moral and metaphysical cast that would in turn be reflected in the work of the many younger writers whom they would strongly influence.

3

🐦

ON AND OFF THE ROAD: THE
OUTSIDER AS YOUNG REBEL

D ESPITE the emergence of writers who were moving in new directions, the late 1940s was hardly a stellar period in American fiction. Very few major novels were produced. Most of the important
books, as we have already seen, either dealt with the war or reflected its
aftermath, since very few events altered American life as much as this
global conflict. Many novels that were much acclaimed at the time, such as
The Naked and the Dead, All the King's Men, The Young Lions, Guard of Honor,
and *Other Voices, Other Rooms,* seem flawed or dated today; in some cases their
authors (Mailer, Capote) went on to make their mark in strikingly different
styles. The plays of Tennessee Williams and Arthur Miller and the hard-
boiled films noirs of the era seem stronger today than the fiction of the
period. The work of some novelists who were just beginning to write then,
including Mailer, James Jones, Saul Bellow, Flannery O'Connor, Ralph
Ellison, and James Baldwin, still feels vital and impressive today, yet their
work belongs primarily to the literary scene of the next decade.

Nevertheless, the forties were the testing ground for everything that
happened in American writing for the next twenty years. As the
American economy moved from Depression and war production to affluence, consumerism, and worldwide geopolitical dominance, writers
turned away from economic and social concerns to engage more with
spiritual and personal issues. The radical politics and progressive social
views that were so important between the wars lost favor, despite Harry
S. Truman's unexpected victory over Thomas E. Dewey in 1948. With
much of the world's economy in ruins, America entered a period of
booming economic growth and relative social peace, marked by
expanded job opportunities, a high birth rate, migration to the suburbs,
new upward mobility and, thanks to the GI Bill of Rights, a vast expansion of higher education. To some it seemed that American society had
entered a new golden age, but very few writers shared this expansive outlook. Instead, they reflected a deep sense of malaise that contrasted with
the surface buoyancy and optimism.

The cultural mood, influenced by the horrors of war, grew receptive to European existentialism and crisis theology. For many intellectuals, the sense of sin and evil in Søren Kierkegaard and Reinhold Niebuhr, which found a secular equivalent in the psychology of Freud, supplanted the pragmatic social hope and faith in reform that marked the work of John Dewey, though Dewey himself lived until 1952. In fiction, the social novel of the 1930s gave way to stylized fables that brought forth the prismatic figure of the outsider, the misfit, the madman, or the primitive. As America's official values grew more conservative, this outsider character would give a radical edge, a mood of brooding alienation, to work that no longer had any clear public agenda. It would link this new fiction with the Beat poet, the abstract painter, the Method actor, the jazz musician, and the youth-oriented rocker. As economic growth leaped ahead dramatically in the two decades after the war, this outsider character emerged in fiction, poetry, movies, and music as one of the great nay-saying figures in American culture.

Not all thirties writers were naturalists or Marxists, but nearly all of them, even those who were modernists influenced by James Joyce and Marcel Proust (including John Dos Passos, William Faulkner, and Henry Roth) saw the texture of society, of city life, or of America as a whole as their inescapable subject. For them, the marginal characters who mattered to their fiction were *social* misfits, immigrants moving haltingly into a new culture, Wobblies laying down their idealistic challenge to American capitalism, poor white trash like the Snopeses making a new order out of their own predatory needs. The writers who followed in the forties and fifties, however, were influenced more by *Heart of Darkness, The Interpretation of Dreams,* and *Civilization and Its Discontents* than by *The Communist Manifesto* and *Das Kapital.* They were obsessed more with Oedipal struggle than with class struggle, concerned about the limits of civilization rather than the conflicts within civilization. Their premises were more Freudian than Marxist.

Auschwitz and Hiroshima had set them thinking about the nature and destiny of man, and relative affluence gave them the leisure to focus on spritual confusions in their own lives. Just as the burgeoning consumer society sanctioned a new selfishness, so the growing therapeutic culture, buoyed by affluence, invited a focus on "relationships" that would have seemed a luxury or irrelevant to earlier generations. At the same time, the beginnings of the Cold War and the development of McCarthyism, which aimed to root out the remnants of Depression radicalism, encouraged writers to turn away from politics to domestic problems and personal relations. The war itself had brought ordinary Americans together, heightening their patriotism and their intolerance of dissent. The crusading, provincial, and suspicious atmosphere of the Cold War contributed to a new conformity and materialism. This in turn deepened the spiritual malaise of the post-war years and made some of the best writers feel even less at home in America than the radicals of the 1930s, who put a noble *idea* of America and a belief in its promise and possibility at the center of their work.

Thus, at a moment when America seemed more triumphant than at any time in its past, when we had just fought and won a "good war" and much of the world (including our leading economic and political competitors) lay in ruins, a deep streak of disaffection set in. As advertising became more pervasive, as television began to enter every home, some serious artists felt swamped by the growth of mass culture, though others welcomed it as an expression of the native energy. During this period, Robert Hughes wrote, "the real artist was the one who worked against the grain of American vulgarity, who aspired to a European complexity and subtlety and felt alienated at home." Artists also felt politically alienated. Communism and Fascism were the gods that failed, yet to many writers, American society seemed disoriented, confused; they sought a vantage point outside it. This is reflected in the brutal fantasies of pulp fiction, which exploded in the 1950s from such writers as Jim Thompson and Mickey Spillane, and in the dark patterns of film noir, where the outlook is often so bleak, the milieu so dark and corrupt that the appointed czar of the film industry threatened to forbid the export of American movies for fear of tarnishing our image abroad.

The Catcher in the Rye, which J. D. Salinger had been working on since the last days of the war, seemed a harmless and beautifully crafted book about adolescence when it first appeared in 1951. But with a baby boom developing in tandem with a spending boom, adolescence would prove to be a more potent and far-reaching subject than many realized at the time. Meanwhile, Marlon Brando arrived on the stage as one of Tennessee Williams's dangerous primitives in *A Streetcar Named Desire,* but in his first film, *The Men,* he played a paralyzed war veteran, surly and morose, who must be coerced – by his peers, by doctors, by women – into rejoining the community. Brando's acting combined sullen toughness with hints of strong emotion, a smoldering physicality with a bruised sensitivity. At once masculine and feminine, his style, like Salinger's, helped usher in a new mood of youthful rebellion.

Within a few years, in *The Wild One* (1953), Brando was playing the leader of a motorcycle gang that terrorizes a small community. By then much of America was up in arms over a new youth culture, marked by supposedly antisocial comic books, media violence, and juvenile delinquency. The older generation in small towns, cities, and newly affluent suburbs found their values rejected by their own children. With a surge of economic growth, social and geographical mobility, and consumer spending, more Americans were moving into the middle class. As the fruits of plenty and of world power dispelled memories of deprivation that went back to the Depression, many of the young turned away from the ethic of upward mobility, finding their parents' lives stodgy, unadventurous, and materialistic. Soon the culture industry discovered a potent new market among adolescents. They made films and songs *for* the young, not simply about them, and rock 'n' roll became the official music of adolescent rebellion, much to the horror of the older generation. In films like *The Wild One* and *The Blackboard Jungle,* the sociological study of delinquency turns into an anthem of generational revolt. The pride of the fifties was the nuclear family, nurturing, wholesome, and patriarchal, celebrated in such television sitcoms as *Father Knows Best.* But movies like Nicholas Ray's *Rebel Without a Cause* (1955) exploded such families as dysfunctional – distorted by neglect, parental discord, and repressed sexuality – with adults unable to understand the simplest needs of the young. The kids in the movie, led by a very insecure James Dean, must form a more nurturing alternative family among themselves. In the hands of "sensitive" new actors like Brando, Dean, and Montgomery Clift, maladjustment itself became a form of rebellion, even if its goal was obscure. Asked what he was rebelling against in *The Wild One,* Brando answered famously, "Whad'ya got?"

❦

Soon the widespread concern over juvenile delinquency, which led to congressional hearings like those on organized crime, gave way to the media's fascination with the antics of the Beats. *Time* saw them as good copy, combining moral titillation with public spectacle. But besides their promotional gifts, which were reminiscent of earlier avant-garde movements such as Dada and surrealism, the Beats conveyed to their young followers a new social spirit, communal, antinomian, and sexually liberated. Among the Beats, the values previously associated with advanced art were played out in bohemian enclaves of voluntary poverty and spirited exhibitionism. With the beginnings of the civil rights movement and later the Vietnam War, student protest activities burgeoned on a scale unseen since the Great Depression. This new radicalism in turn helped fuel the rise of the sixties counterculture, whose focus on community, poverty, drugs, and sexual experimentation acted out a criticism of American values and behavior, ranging from puritanism and competitive individualism to anti-Communism and the worship of technology.

Artistically, the Beats had strong links to two movements whose permanent achievements would prove greater than their own. One was jazz, which was undergoing a revolution in the forties, turning from large swing bands playing dance music to the amazing virtuosity of bop artists like Charlie Parker, Dizzy Gillespie, and Thelonious Monk. It was their improvisational freshness, complexity, and spontaneity that the Beats would try to recreate in their prose and poetry. The other movement was abstract expressionism, the reigning avant-garde of the late forties and early fifties, whose gestural, performative manner and large spiritual ambitions also influenced the Beats. For these artists, painting was an act, an event, an experience rather than a crafted, finished object or the direct representation of a recognizable image. "What was to go on the canvas was not a picture but an event," said Harold Rosenberg, the critic who coined the term *Action Painting.* The purpose of art, as Meyer Schapiro wrote in 1957, had become "more passionately than ever before, the occasion of spontaneity or intense feeling." In the work of such abstract painters as Jackson Pollock, the tangible buildup of the paint on the canvas reminds us constantly of the physical action and movement that put it there. "The work of art," said Schapiro, defining the abstract aesthetic, "is an ordered world of its own kind in which we are aware, at every point, of its becoming."

In both jazz and abstract painting, as in Beat writing, the fluidity, energy, and subjectivity of the creative process become signifying elements of the work itself. This self-consciousness points to the Americanization of modernism in the postwar years. Challenging the more conservative culture of the fifties, these kinetic arts supplanted traditional forms with a vehement expression of personal energy; they became part of a growing counterculture that appealed strongly to alienated intellectuals and to the rebellious and discontented young.

Many contemporary observers described the fifties as the Age of Anxiety. Because of the Cold War, the widespread fear of nuclear annihilation, the Korean War, and finally the war in Vietnam, American society had remained, psychologically at least, in a wartime frame of mind. To all this, a large segment of the young said no, first through the music, then eventually with drugs, political protests, campus rebellions, and freer sex. By and large they were children of affluence, moved by the guilt and boredom that comes with privilege, not the anguish born of deprivation. Even their leaders, many of them children of thirties radicals, abandoned the rhetoric of class conflict that had fired up their parents. The colorful circus of generational conflict appealed to the media far more than the quiet persistence of class conflict. From the surly Brando and the troubled James Dean to the raucous Abbie Hoffman and the clownish Jerry Rubin, the restless young exposed a widening fissure in American life that novelists and filmmakers were among the first to exploit.

Novels and films rarely found a public language to deal with social conflicts over race, war, McCarthyism, Communism, or any other issues that divided an otherwise triumphant America in the decades following World War II. By integrating the armed forces and supporting civil rights legislation, the Truman administration had briefly put race at the top of the American agenda, provoking a Southern revolt, but the brief vogue of social protest films and novels in the late forties effectively died by 1950, and the tough, shadowy style of film noir lasted only a few years longer. The public lost interest in the problems of the returning soldiers, especially when most of those veterans, taking advantage of the education offered through the GI Bill of Rights, began to thrive in the booming postwar economy. By the 1950s, as anti-Semitism diminished, thanks to a spasm of guilt over the Holocaust, race and poverty became subjects few still cared to discuss. Some social scientists and historians, often former radicals, began emphasizing consensus rather than conflict, status anxieties rather than class divisions, and portrayed America as a country that had largely solved its most pressing problems.

Novelists and filmmakers, on the other hand, were drawn to stories that reflected the darker side of American life. The fifties saw a vogue of low-budget horror and science-fiction films that reflected pervasive anxieties about the Cold War, nuclear war, and the blight of timidity that spread in this atmosphere of fear. These works expressed such themes as the fear of invasion by an alien force, fear of the invisible, delayed effects of nuclear radiation, and (in the case of Don Siegel's *Invasion of the Body Snatchers,* 1956) fear that, beneath a veneer of normality, the Cold War itself would undermine American traditions of dissent and individuality.

Again and again, such novelists as Ralph Ellison, William Gaddis, and Thomas Pynchon would deal not so much with the contour and clash of personalities, like most earlier novelists, but with the loss of personality in a world that trivialized individual differences. Some of this effacement of personality had already been a theme of war novelists such as Norman Mailer and James Jones, who saw the repressive and brutal aspects of army life as an intimation of postwar fascism. But McCarthy, the kind of figure their novels anticipated, proved to be a demagogue and a clown rather than a Fascist, and the threat came more from what William H. Whyte, Jr. called the "social ethic," the spirit of suburban and corporate conformity, than from political repression. Although Mailer would argue in 1957 that the concentration camps and the atom bomb had visited untold psychic havoc on the postwar world, the new prosperity had a deadening effect at least as widespread as any anxious concern about survival. The fifties were at once a period of complacency, of getting and spending, and an age of anxiety, a time for doubt and self-questioning, as shown by works like David Riesman's *The Lonely Crowd* and Hannah Arendt's *The Origins of Totalitarianism.* With such writers as Riesman, Whyte, Vance Packard, C. Wright Mills, John Kenneth Galbraith, and finally Paul Goodman and Betty Friedan, social criticism became a major growth industry in an apparently self-satisfied society. Much of the fiction of the fifties, including such popular novels as Sloan Wilson's *The Man in the Gray Flannel Suit* and Cameron Hawley's *Executive Suite,* belongs to this vein of critical self-examination.

❧

It is hard to think of J. D. Salinger as any kind of radical. His best-known hero, the superbright young prep-school dropout, Holden Caulfield, and Holden's even brighter and cuter sister, Phoebe, live comfortable middle-class lives on New York's Park Avenue, where Salinger himself spent his adolescent years. The son of a prosperous Jewish cheese importer and a Scottish-born mother, Salinger was born in 1919 and, after an indifferent academic career, served in the army from 1942 to 1946. Before he joined the literary community surrounding *The New Yorker* in 1948, the army was the family to which he became most strongly attached. From the breakdown he describes in his 1953 story "For Esmé – With Love and Squalor," it appears that the emotional problems he experienced during the war impelled him to look for a way to recapture the lost innocence of childhood and adolescence. His work would become one of the literary keys to a world in which adolescence was becoming an overriding concern.

Though earlier writers like Henry Roth in *Call It Sleep* (1934), Jean Stafford in *The Mountain Lion* (1947), and Truman Capote in *Other Voices, Other Rooms* (1948) had written intensely lyrical growing-up stories, Salinger was the first to tap emotionally into the new youth culture created by America's growing adolescent and college-age population after the war. The economic boom enabled Americans to keep young people out of the job market for a much longer period; meanwhile, increasing affluence turned the young into consumers with cultural values distinct from those of their elders, whose needs had been shaped by immigration, depression, and war.

The stresses of the period from 1929 to 1945 had created a cautious, culturally conservative middle-class generation whose values, at least initially, were invested in home, family, and maturity. Thanks to the GI Bill, returning soldiers received college degrees that gave them an advantage in the increasingly specialized postwar economy. But the massive influx of blacks and Hispanics into the large cities drove newly affluent whites to garden suburbs organized around single-family homes, shopping malls, and the automobile. When many of their children took up rock music and Beat styles, with their roots in the ghettos and in black culture, they were embracing the milieu and the values their elders had left behind.

Salinger's work is the most polite, well-bred version of adolescent rebellion, yet it is founded on a sweeping dismissal of grown-up life as inauthentic, pompous, and moralistic. Holden Caulfield is the first of a long postwar line of fictional naifs who see through everything, whose lives are an epic of thwarted sensitivity, who feel stifled by the hypocrisy of adults, the stupidity of their peers, the betrayal of those they trust, and the manipulations of all figures of authority. In the course of the novel he is misunderstood, patronized, verbally abused, beaten up, even propositioned by a trusted teacher, all described in the same bright-eyed tone of shocked wonderment and premature sophistication.

Like dozens of later novels from *On the Road* and *Slaughterhouse-Five* to *Portnoy's Complaint* and *Bright Lights, Big City,* Salinger's *Catcher in the Rye* is not a growing-up novel but a *not*-growing-up novel, focusing on a young man's refusal to assume the social responsibilities the world is too eager to impose on him. All these novels go back in different ways to *The Adventures of Huckleberry Finn,* one of the *ur*-texts of postwar fiction, with its emphasis on the inner life of troubled boyhood, and Huck's need to escape the corruptions of the adult world. This had a special point in the fifties, when *maturity* and *adjustment* were cultural watchwords, bolstered by a pop Freudianism. To Holden Caulfield, everyone from his teachers to the actors he sees on the stage are "phonies." Thrown out of yet another school, Pencey Prep – modeled on a well-known military academy where Salinger himself had spent two years – Holden is a genteel urban Huck Finn who dreams of taking to the road but instead, in his few days of adventure in New York, is actually in the midst of having a breakdown. The book thus brings together three of the main tropes of the fifties counterculture: the youthful misfit, the road, and mental illness as a form of social maladjustment and intuitive wisdom.

Where the growing-up novel, even in the hands of a writer as unsentimental as Jean Stafford or Nabokov, often expresses itself in nostalgia for a lost world, Salinger's stories rediscover the vernacular of childhood and youth as a language of endangered innocence. A wicked satirist with a cool eye and a perfect ear, Salinger lampoons the vulgarity and duplicity of adults while endowing his powerless young with amazing verbal virtuosity. Some of Salinger's best and worst stories, from "De Daumier-Smith's Blue Period" and *Catcher in the Rye* to the five long stories about the Glass family published in *The New Yorker* between 1955 and 1965, are essentially extended comic monologues that cleared a path for the picaresque writers of the 1960s, including Roth in *Portnoy's Complaint,* who, with some impetus from Céline, helped bring this tradition to its climax. One of Truman Capote's early mentors had called *Other Voices* the "fairy Huckleberry Finn," but *The Catcher in the Rye* was more truly in the colloquial Huck Finn tradition. Only Salinger successfully captured the exact accent and rhythm of the adolescent voice and sensibility; only in his work did the young recognize themselves as they were or as they dreamed of being.

Unlike the writing of Twain or Ring Lardner, Salinger's theme is spiritual: his young people and his sainted dead (especially Seymour Glass) are eternal innocents who cannot adjust to society or accept its compromises. "A Perfect Day for Bananafish" (1948) is the prototype for Salinger's later, more garrulous fiction. The main character besides Seymour Glass is an infinitely wise, articulate child named Sybil. He meets her on a Florida beach, and she provides him with a momentary respite from his gossipy wife Muriel ("Miss Spiritual Tramp of 1948," according to Seymour), whom we see polishing her nails and chatting with her mother on a long-distance telephone call. Caught between an unrecoverable innocence and a vulgar vitality, Seymour commits suicide – the founding moment of the Glass dynasty. Holden Caulfield and the shell-shocked soldier in "For Esmé – With Love and Squalor" are spiritual descendents of the martyred Seymour, while Holden's bright sister Phoebe and the young Esmé belong to the oracular mode of the bright young Sybil.

As we see in the later Glass stories and occasionally in Beat writing, such fictions can easily turn precious and narcissistic, reposing on a sentimental vision of the elect, but with little sense of the society that frustrates their needs. Salinger's later work needs more Muriel and less Sybil, more of the world's variety and less obsession with saintliness. In Holden Caulfield's sojourn in New York, though, Salinger still has his ear tuned to wider frequencies: roommates, parents, prostitutes, college boys, taxi drivers, elevator operators, spoiled mentors, all the people who fail Holden on his way down. The key to Holden is that at sixteen he is still virginal, presexual, like the falling children he dreams of rescuing as "the catcher in the rye." He has a grown-up mind trapped uneasily in an adolescent's awkward body. Holden's problem with sex is a more concentrated version of his problem with the adult world: that it seems unspiritual, crude, a violation of the perfect sympathy he feels only with children:

If you want to know the truth, I'm a virgin. I really am. I've had quite a few opportunities to lose my virginity and all, but I've never got around to it yet. Something always happens. For instance, if you're at a girl's house, her parents always come home at the wrong time – or you're afraid they will. Or if you're in

the back seat of somebody's car, there's always somebody's date in the front seat –
some girl, I mean – that always wants to know what's going on *all over* the whole
goddam car. I mean some girl in front keeps turning around to see what the hell's
going on. I came quite close to doing it a couple of times, though. . . . The thing
is, most of the time when you're coming pretty close to doing it with a girl – a
girl that isn't a prostitute or anything, I mean – she keeps telling you to stop. The
trouble with me is, I stop. Most guys don't. I can't help it. You never know
whether they really *want* you to stop, or whether they're just scared as hell. . . .
Anyway, I keep stopping. The trouble is I get to feeling sorry for them. . . . They
tell me to stop, so I stop.

This sexual embarrassment is the material of stand-up comedy, but it is
more than a riff: it remains wonderfully in character. Holden's adventures
in New York are really a series of Jewish jokes, at once sad, funny, and self-
accusing. Like Philip Roth, Salinger is an inspired mimic. When Portnoy
complains that he feels caught in the middle of a Jewish joke, he's following in Holden's footsteps. Though little of Salinger's work belongs explicitly with the Jewish American novel, there is a touch of the schlemiel
about Holden's fumbling adolescent self-consciousness, about the way he
is prone to disaster, doomed to disappointment at every turn. Holden's
haplessness arises from a mixture of anxiety and good-heartedness; his failures attest to his nobility and single him out for a special destiny.

As Twain did with Huck Finn, Salinger concentrates on the flow of
Holden's voice, the starts and hesitations that echo his behavior. Voice –
volatile, immediate, and seductive – was the secret weapon of fifties writers
against the postwar resurgence of gentility and good form. Where more formal writers depend on a stable sense of identity, the picaresque narrator,
like the jazz performer or Action Painter, seems to be making himself up as
he goes along. Holden is not only a great storyteller but also a compulsive
fibber and fantasist, living more easily in the identities he assumes than in
the ones imposed on him. He lies out of an excess of imagination, and as a
way of avoiding unpleasant confrontations. He is verbal and judgmental
but never grasping or deliberately cruel. He understands sex only as violation – as a way of using someone and spoiling what is perfect about them.
For Salinger, this makes him not just confused and unhappy but morally
superior to the world around him. Holden foreshadows a counterculture
that will be less about sex than about innocence; its ideal would be a kind
of sainthood and spiritual election in a fallen world.

The youthful rebels and misfits who followed in the fifties and sixties
were generally less funny than Holden and far less attentive to the nuances
of a world they found oppressive. Their cultural or moral revisionism takes
the place of the social revolts of previous decades; it aims to escape the
demands of society rather than to change society. Their unorganized

protests occur not in a Depression world of crisis, suffering, and upheaval but in a triumphant world of postwar affluence and economic growth, a world they find soulless rather than exploitative. They are truly rebels without a cause. The terms of their radicalism are existential, not political; they seek inner satisfaction and identity, not social justice. Thus James Baldwin and Ralph Ellison reject the work of their mentor, Richard Wright, as "protest novels" or as works that fail to do justice to either the richness of African American life or the hollowness of the larger society.

If the protest novel, in Baldwin's sense, was political, propagandistic, and its moving force was a burning rage at injustice, the new kind of novel of the 1950s was not only personal, it was lyrical. Lyrical novels were not so much critical of society as indifferent to it, in flight from it, subjecting it to a dismissive mockery. These novels were often colloquial, written in the first person (like *Huckleberry Finn*), loosely structured, seemingly spontaneous. Their heroes, always in flight, lay claim to the Emersonian freedom to create and remake themselves that many Americans consider their birthright. The alternative to the lyrical novel in the 1950s is the ironic novel, tightly patterned, intricately written, in which such freedom proves to be a delusion, because society will never permit it and life itself makes it unattainable. Here the protagonist, much less identified with the author, becomes an object lesson in frustration or failure.

Versions of the lyrical novel include the road novel, the adolescent novel, the adventure novel, the first-person picaresque. The sensitive protagonist is always trying to escape from social regimentation, from the nuclear family, especially from the domesticating power of women, and trying to find his own path within an overorganized society. The ironic novel, on the other hand, often took the form of the Jamesian social fable or the Kafkaesque metaphysical parable. It centered on plots that created a sense of entrapment or futility, on characters caught in webs of circumstance not of their own making, or in contradictions set deep within their own personalities. Fatalistic works like Bellow's *Seize The Day* or Malamud's *The Assistant* show us a world not at all shaped to a person's needs or likely to bend to his will.

The ironic novel belongs to the conservative, quiescent strain of American thought after the war: the darkly shaded Freudianism of such critics as Lionel Trilling, the sense of sin of theologians like Reinhold Niebuhr, the anti-utopianism of historians like Arthur Schlesinger, Jr. and Richard Hofstadter, the critique of liberalism and progressivism of the work of these and other writers and thinkers, including Schlesinger in *The Vital Center* (1949), Niebuhr in *The Irony of American History* (1951), and Hofstadter in *The Age of Reform* (1954). As Morton White showed in *Social*

Thought in America (1949), the darkly shaded mood of existentialism had displaced the spirit of progressivism; the influence of Dewey had given way to the ghost of Kierkegaard. In Trilling's *The Liberal Imagination* (1950), a sense of modernist complexity and tragic realism undermines the old faith in reform. Nearly all these intellectuals remained liberals, but their social faith had a tragic, anti-utopian cast.

This recoil against liberal optimism was influenced by both the failures of Communism in the 1930s and the barbarities of Fascism in the 1940s. It was a neoliberalism that had little confidence in human nature and the benign power of the human will; it looked back not to Emerson but to the founding fathers, with their suspicion of democracy and irrationality and their insistence on checks and balances to keep human nature at bay. Its literary roots were more European than American, for its outlook was grounded not in Emerson, Thoreau, and Whitman but in the social determinations of the realistic novel and the ironies of literary modernism.

The ironic novel, the kind of novel in which people are defined by who they ineluctably are, not by what they want or need, became the specialty of Jewish writers such as Saul Bellow and Bernard Malamud, of Southerners like Flannery O'Connor, and blacks like James Baldwin, writers who came from groups that had known defeat and oppression and had experienced the direct impact of history on their collective and personal lives. The idea of man's unbounded freedom had little resonance for them except as a misguided form of hubris. It didn't belong to their own experience. The goal of their characters was survival, decency, the chance to get along: the recognition of their humanity, not the giddy intensities of self-invention. People in their novels who do try to reinvent themselves, like Tommy Wilhelm in *Seize the Day* (1956), are invariably thwarted, humiliated, even destroyed, though not without moments of tragic self-understanding. Lyrical novelists, on the other hand, brought American fiction closer to native traditions of transcendentalism and pragmatism. Emerson's work was their scripture, Whitman and Twain their literary inspiration. The oral richness of American humor spoke to them more strongly than the ironic reverberations of Kafka or Freud or the social structures in Balzac and George Eliot. Their novels, so often autobiographical, were personal effusions more than social canvases, though they were scarcely free of ironic details, and often conveyed a sharp sense of the social limits they fiercely resisted. These were utopian novels, dreamers' novels, even when (as in *The Catcher in the Rye*) their well-meaning characters came to grief. They appealed most to young people, and in the fifties and sixties they became an important vehicle for an emerging counterculture as well as a momentous turn in American fiction.

The novel that had the greatest impact after *The Catcher in the Rye* was Jack Kerouac's *On the Road,* completed the same year *Catcher* appeared (1951) but not published until six years later. In the interim, Kerouac wrote nearly a dozen books in what became his autobiographical saga, the Duluoz legend, but none would be as readable as *On the Road,* nor would any of his other novels match its mythic status as a founding text of the Beat movement. Born in 1922 in the mill town of Lowell, Massachusetts, where his French Canadian father worked as a printer, Kerouac did not even speak English until he was five or six, and his later celebrations of the American heartland were the work of a keen observer rather than a confident insider. For Kerouac, Lowell and his mother's home represent a Catholic tradition of family values, while the great empty spaces of the West, which he discovers for the first time in *On the Road,* offer undreamed-of possibilities of freedom that leave him feeling ecstatic but deeply ambivalent.

Kerouac's more traditional first novel, *The Town and the City* (1950), was written in the expansive autobiographical mode of Thomas Wolfe. A high school football star, Kerouac had left Lowell in 1939 for a year of prep school in New York before taking up an athletic scholarship at Columbia. After a disastrous hitch as a merchant marine in the U.S. Navy, he returned to New York, where his real life in the city began. In his first novel, the hometown and the large nuclear family based on Lowell were set off against the exciting bohemia of the city, peopled by characters based on Allen Ginsberg, then still a Columbia freshman, and William Burroughs, the Harvard-educated black sheep of a wealthy St. Louis family – Kerouac met both of them in 1944. Their world, on the fringes of the university, attracted the young writer, essentially an autodidact, to whom art was as darkly appealing as sin. This alternative family offered the hope of self-transformation through a new kind of community: close-knit but transgressive, morally adventurous, marginally criminal, and wonderfully creative.

The Town and the City is a benign version of the "revolt from the village" novels of the 1920s, typified by Sherwood Anderson's *Winesburg, Ohio* (1919) and Sinclair Lewis's *Main Street* (1920), in which the writer's autobiographical surrogate tries to flee the stultifying intimacy of the small town to seek fulfilment in a wider world, usually the big city. The genre was ill suited to Jack Kerouac, who, just beneath his bohemianism, had a deeply conservative cast of mind, as his later life would repeatedly show. It was only by escaping *from* the city that he found the subject that truly ignited his literary imagination.

On the Road is based on a series of cross-country trips that Kerouac himself had made, mostly with Neal Cassady, between 1947 and 1950, at the very moment other Americans were rediscovering the mobility they had lost during years of Depression and wartime. There would soon be an explosion of cars on the road, sped along by the sleek new highways of Eisenhower's Interstate Highway System, the major federal achievement of the 1950s. Best-selling books like Whyte's *The Organization Man* (1956) would show that Americans were becoming a rootless people, thanks to migrations from rural areas to cities, from cities to new towns and suburbs, and from stable manufacturing jobs to corporate white-collar positions that repeatedly transferred them to different parts of the country. Though *On the Road* seemingly turned its back on the world of marriage, families, and jobs, it was very much in tune with the new mobility that peace and prosperity afforded to many Americans in the 1950s. The jobless, penniless drifters of the Depression were turning into the white-collar transients of the postwar world; Cassady and Kerouac, one rootless, the other restless, were pushing their way past a door that was already swinging open.

The genius of *On the Road* was to attach the new restlessness to the classic American mythology of the road, and to use it to express a subversive set of values – exuberance, energy, spirituality, intensity, improvisation – that would challenge the suburban and corporate conservatism of the 1950s. The road represents the expansive, footloose spirit of America after the war yet also the need to escape from the constraints of the new domesticity and work ethic. Dean Moriarty, Kerouac's hero, based on Cassady – his name combines James Dean with Sherlock Holmes's chief villain – is everything from a charismatic con man and cocksman to a "HOLY GOOF" with the tremendous energy of "a new kind of American saint." As a self-made man, he is much better at holding down a job and supporting a family than the pampered Kerouac, raised on mother love. But this saint lives for kicks and preaches a gospel of irresponsibility that makes everyone around him miserable, especially the long-suffering women. In the eyes of Sal Paradise, the fearful but enamored narrator (based on Kerouac), the kinetic Dean, fleet runner, legendary driver, virtuoso lover, is everything he himself is not: comfortable in his own skin, free of moral hang-ups and family ties. Where Sal, like Tom Sawyer, never breaks the umbilical cord connecting him to his aunt, Dean is a modern Huck Finn who was "actually born on the road" and grew up with his wino father on skid row in Denver, an abused child and orphan who learned early on to fend for himself.

In *On the Road,* the likable but impossible Dean is the daemon who presides over the Road; he is the tutelary spirit of the West, even of the pioneers Kerouac also had in mind as he repeatedly tried to tell the story of his "life on the road." He runs and drives like a figure out of Greek myth or black magic. The American tradition of the Road is built into the scale of the continent itself, the endless migration made possible by the frontier and the great open spaces of the West, a migration that extends the "westering" movement that first brought the colonists to the New World. In biblical and Christian imagery, this westward movement is always renovating and apocalyptic, offering the promise of a fresh beginning, a new life, as John Steinbeck understood when he took his family of Okies on a biblical trek across the desert to a green and promising land. In *On the Road,* as in early Westerns like *The Virginian* and its many film offshoots, the East represents a stale, unhealthy, ossified civilization, an indoor civilization out of touch with nature, while the West is a brave new world, full of explosive energies and dangerous possibilities.

Road novels and movies were especially important in the 1930s when so many Americans were uprooted by the Depression. From *I Am a Fugitive From a Chain Gang* (1932) and *Wild Boys of the Road* (1933) to *U.S.A., The Grapes of Wrath,* and *Sullivan's Travels* (1941), the hobo and the drifter became icons of the era, staples in fiction, photography, and Depression journalism as well as film. Even earlier, Whitman had eulogized the open road as the emblem of a truly American freedom and Mark Twain had turned the Mississippi into an escape route that rescues Nigger Jim from slavery and Huck Finn from the brutality of his drunken father and the tyranny of small-town respectability. As the novel ends, Huck decides famously "to light out for the territory" when the adults threaten to "sivilize" him. Jack London had collected the memories of his tramping life in the 1890s into another apotheosis, rich with hobo slang, *The Road* (1907). "I became a tramp – well, because of the life that was in me, of the wanderlust in my blood that would not let me rest," wrote London, whose adventurous ways had already made him a legend. "I went on 'The Road' because I couldn't keep away from it; because I hadn't the price of the railroad fare in my jeans." Immensely literary and self-conscious about his work, Kerouac responded strongly to plebeians like London and to vernacular writers who experimented with the American idiom, including Twain, Sherwood Anderson, Hemingway, Ring Lardner, Nelson Algren, and William Saroyan – the same writers who most impressed the young Salinger. Most of these were writers whose work emerged out of the great oral tradition of American humor, storytelling, and mimickry.

In Kerouac's work, going on the road is less a matter of economic need, as it had been during the Depression, more a myth of rebirth, as in literary and religious parables. Almost from the beginning, the narrator feels eerily estranged from himself: "My whole life was a haunted life, the life of a ghost. I was halfway across America, at the dividing line between the East of my youth and the West of my future." This is not so much a destination as a dream of pure movement, directionless, propulsive, unreflective. To the more conventional Sal, Dean's "frantic" travels eventually come to seem "maniacal" and "completely meaningless," but at certain times they make him ecstatic; their manic intensity projects him into a realm of pure spirit. Kerouac himself was afraid of driving, terrified of flying, uncomfortable with women, afraid of falling under the tracks of trains – all the spheres in which Dean, with his amazing physical dexterity and con man's irresistible charm, performed with such ease and confidence.

At about the same time Kerouac was mythologizing Cassady, the publicity apparatus of American culture, especially *Life* magazine, was mythologizing another rugged son of the West, Jackson Pollock. He was hard drinking, taciturn, intensely physical, and often worked on a grandiose American scale. He had studied with Thomas Hart Benton but then gone his own way, though the swirl and flow and size of Benton's compositions influenced his work. Though he rejected the stylized realism of the thirties muralists, he said he wanted to create "large, movable pictures that will function between the easel and mural." Keeping the canvas on the floor so that he could get *into* it, throwing paint at the canvas and letting it drip, sometimes adding tactile, angular bits of gravel and pebbles, he created a thickly layered grid, a complex impasto of paint that was almost a road map of the energy and intensity he had put into it. (Like Kerouac he was attracted by the improvisional energy of jazz.) For Pollock, the canvas itself was his way of being "on the road," of taking off on an explosive free-form adventure of his own. Until one drunken night on New York's Long Island in 1956, he wrapped his car around a tree, killing himself and one of the women with him. Like James Dean in his silver Porsche the previous year, he was yet another casualty of the road.

At about the same time, another great visual artist, the Swiss-born photographer Robert Frank, also took to the road to create a document of American life. When his pictures were collected in *The Americans* (1959), with an introduction by Jack Kerouac, they not only captured the look of postwar America but reshaped the legacy of Depression photography. Where Walker Evans and Dorothea Lange had portrayed an America suffering extreme privations with exquisite dignity and determination, Frank showed the world a casual, backwater America, tending its small-town rituals, caught up in the undramatic business of everyday life.[2] Unlike their Depression counterparts, Frank's "Americans" had multiple histories, not just one big brush with History. In line with their subjects, his pictures

---

[2] Frank, working with Alfred Leslie, memorialized the downtown world of the Beats and the New York painters with the same random attention in a largely improvised film, *Pull My Daisy* (1959), that was pulled together by Kerouac's inspired narration.

had a drab throwaway look that broke sharply with the artful composure of previous American photography. They seemed to have a deceptively amateur quality, as if the image just happened to come together, like some of Kerouac's prose of which Paul Goodman complained that "nothing is told, nothing is presented, everything is just 'written about.'"

But unlike Frank's sad, eerie images of an American wasteland, Kerouac's novel has a figure at the center to energize his portrait of America. At first Sal relishes the simple pleasure of being with Dean, the sense of putting all entanglements behind him, of leaving even himself behind. He feeds on Dean's explosive energy, his sheer physicality. Dean is the spirit of the West, life in the raw; he is the orphan boy without a superego, ready at any moment to pull up stakes and jettison his life. Friends, jobs, wives, children mean something to him only so long as he feels impelled to stay with them. A kind of centaur, perfectly fused to his four wheels, Dean believes in movement simply as a way of going with the flow, cutting any knot that binds him and complicates his life.

"Whooee!" yelled Dean. "Here we go!" And he hunched over the wheel and gunned her; he was back in his element, everybody could see that. We were all delighted, we all realized we were leaving confusion and nonsense behind and performing our one and noble function of the time, *move*. And we moved!

As time goes on, however, Sal, with his Catholic feeling of guilt, his middle-class sense of family, recoils from Dean's habit of simply picking up and moving on. Like Dean's wives and girlfriends, Sal flinches from the irresponsibility that attracted him in the first place. In one memorable scene, many of the women in Dean's life, wives of his old buddies, have their say: we see the Pied Piper from the point of view of those who were left behind, who nail him for living solely for "kicks." To Sal, as to these jealous upholders of civilization and domesticity, Dean's energy has become more like madness than exuberance; it evokes Sal's deep-seated anxieties as much as his sense of wonder. For him, Dean's sainthood and irresponsibility are all mixed up. Dean is like the unfathomable Gatsby seen through the grudgingly respectful eyes of Nick Carraway; he's the obsessed Ahab conjured up in lightning flashes by his chronicler, Ishmael.

Curled up in the back of the car, expecting an imminent smash-up, Sal tries to sleep. Soon, in Dean's hands, his mortal fear gives way to resignation:

As a seaman I used to think of the waves rushing beneath the shell of the ship and the bottomless deeps thereunder – now I could feel the road some twenty inches beneath me, unfurling and flying and hissing at incredible speeds across the groaning continent with that mad Ahab at the wheel. When I closed my eyes, all I could see was the road unwinding into me. When I opened them I saw flashing shadows of trees vibrating on the floor of the car. There was no escaping it. I resigned myself to all. And still Dean drove.

As Dean's character thickens into moral ambiguity, Kerouac's prose becomes less wide eyed and innocent, more Melvillean. This "road unwinding into me" is also the Buddhist or Tao road of cosmic submission, the tranformation of fear into individual purpose. "What's your road, man?" he imagines Dean saying to him, "– holyboy road, madman road, rainbow road, guppy road, any road." The enigma of Dean, the message of Dean, even Dean's style – these are what the book is all about. Soon after he completed *On the Road,* Kerouac would write another book, *Visions of Cody* (1973), his most free-flowing and experimental work, simply to fathom his friend's character.

The run-on spontaneity of Cassady's talk and letters influenced Kerouac's writing much like the improvisational flow of jazz riffs, which Kerouac worked hard to imitate in language. Kerouac's "spontaneous bop prosody," as Allen Ginsberg called it in the dedication of *Howl and Other Poems,* was yet another version of the "road," the flow, the book's organizing metaphor. So was the physical manuscript of the final version, which Kerouac produced on a single long roll of paper in three weeks of nonstop composition in April 1951. As he wrote to Cassady a few weeks later: "I've told all the road now. Went fast because road is fast . . . wrote whole thing on strip of paper 120 foot long (tracing paper that belonged to Cannastra.) – just rolled it through typewriter and in fact no paragraphs . . . rolled it out on floor and it looks like a road" (*Selected Letters,* 22 May 1951). Truman Capote quipped that Kerouac's style was not writing but typing. Yet Kerouac's typing, with its uncensored, unshaped remembering, was one of the few spheres in which he could match the speed and intensity of Cassady's driving, running, screwing, and verbal riffing. His style, shaped by this nonstop flow of memory, reflects the aimless spontaneity of their cross-country travels.

Kerouac's three-week marathon was his literary breakthrough. *On the Road* is somehow a great book without being a good novel. Too much in the book happens mainly because it happened, with little dramatic buildup or consequence; too many minor characters are there just because they really were there at the time. Even the style often falls into cliché; the much-edited syntax, the punctuation "improved" by the publisher, too often goes lame. There is a gushing adolescent enthusiasm that does not entirely belong to Kerouac's narrator, Sal: "I licked my lips for the luscious blond." "The nights in Denver are cool, and I slept like a log." On apple pie and ice cream: "I knew it was nutritious and it was delicious, of course." But neither the clichés nor the publisher's insistence on conventional punctuation really damages the *lilt* of Kerouac's prose or the propulsive energy and feeling behind it. Shapeless at its worst, incandescently evocative at its best, Kerouac's prose became a landmark in the poetics of improvisation that gave the counterculture its distinct character. At its frequent best, this style, influenced by eruptive writers like Céline, would free up countless others, beginning with his friends Ginsberg and Burroughs, and then Norman Mailer, all of whom were still working in a far more conventional vein in 1951. If we compare Burroughs's straightforward *Junkie* to *Naked Lunch* or Ginsberg's formal early poems to *Howl*, Kerouac's influence on them becomes immediately clear. Kerouac taught writers from Ginsberg to Bob Dylan to go with the flow, to avoid censoring outlandish images, to tap their fantasies as they shaped their memories, and to ride the shape of their own breath, as the surrealists preached, the Buddhist masters taught, and jazzmen instinctively practiced. The flow of this style, the cascade of details that Kerouac recalled astonishingly well – Ginsberg called him "The Great Rememberer" – meshes with Dean's kinetic personality to give the novel its unusual kind of strength.

Ultimately, *On the Road* was more important as a myth, as a cultural marker, than as a novel. As Holden Caulfield became the first literary protagonist of the new youth culture, Dean Moriarty would become the patron saint of the counterculture, to be followed closely by the Ginsberg of *Howl*, the Mailer of "The White Negro" (1957), the Paul Goodman of *Growing Up Absurd* (1960), and, among literary characters, the ultracool Randall McMurphy in Ken Kesey's fable *One Flew Over the Cuckoo's Nest* (1962) and many others throughout the 1960s. (Before his death in Mexico in 1968, Cassady himself would drive the bus for Kesey's perpetually stoned group of Merry Pranksters, as tediously recorded in Tom Wolfe's sixties chronicle, *The Electric Kool-Aid Acid Test* [1968].) Thomas Pynchon's *V.* (1963) zanily crosses the offbeat drifter world of Kerouac with the precise plotting of Conrad and Graham Greene. In later years, Ginsberg would mythologize Kerouac as a Beat legend, as Kerouac had mythologized Cassady, and as Norman Mailer, the promising but reserved young novelist, would revamp himself into a hip adventurer, an existential legend, in "The White Negro," "The Time of Her Time," and *Advertisements for Myself* (1959).

Because of Kerouac's sense of himself as an outsider, *On the Road* is ultimately a sad book rather than merely an exuberant one. Where Mailer mythologized blacks as figures of impulse and violence, Kerouac, in the most notorious passage in the novel, projected his loneliness onto the black ghetto of Denver, imagining it as a scene of warmth and belonging from which he feels excluded. Sal is disappointed with Dean, cut off from everyone else, locked in his own shyness and inhibitions. Feeling abandoned, he dreams of exchanging worlds with "the happy, truehearted, ecstatic Negroes of America." They represent the vitality, spontaneity, and human connection he himself had despaired of achieving except in fugitive moments, as in the brief affair with a Mexican girl described so touchingly in *On the Road.* For Kerouac himself, this sense of being stranded and cut off was prophetic, for the success of the book made his world a living hell.

Kerouac was deeply ambivalent about the fame he had sought and found, which made him feel even more isolated. Nearly all his important work was written before *On the Road* was published. His chronicles ranged from early love affairs retold in strikingly different styles in *Tristessa, Maggie Cassidy,* and *The Subterraneans,* which brought out some of his tenderest writing, to accounts of the Beats themselves, his substitute family, in books like *The Dharma Bums,* written quickly to capitalize on the success of *On the Road,* and in *Desolation Angels* (1965), his last good book.

In his final years – he died of alcoholism in 1969 – he became almost as reclusive as Salinger. The two writers also shared a deepening interest in Buddhism, and both obsessively devoted their later energies to shaping a family saga. Like the fictional Holden Caulfield, who idealizes his dead brother Allie as a dreamy legend, Kerouac wrote worshipfully of an older brother, Gerard, whose death in childhood left him feeling half amputated, a mere survivor. *Visions of Gerard* (1963) was the peculiar shrine he erected to this departed saint. Kerouac played off another childhood legend in *Dr. Sax* and described a nervous breakdown brought on by fame, drink, and drugs in *Big Sur.* Publishers showed little interest in his carefully composed Buddhist scrapbook, *Some of the Dharma,* an ambitious collage of poems and meditations that did not appear in full until 1997. The last book he published in his lifetime, *Vanity of Duluoz* (1968), was a more directly autobiographical version of *The Town and the City.* As Salinger's last published story, "Hapworth 16, 1924" (1965), was written in the precocious voice of a seven-year-old Seymour Glass, Kerouac's posthumously published *Pic* (1971), an early experiment in first-person storytelling, was narrated in dialect by a black boy of ten.

It would be foolish to extend the parallel between Kerouac and Salinger too far. Even with the solipsistic excesses of his Glass stories, Salinger remained a fastidious writer in the *New Yorker* mode, crafting each sentence as if it were his last. Kerouac was in every way a looser, more spontaneous stylist, a good travel writer with an evocative sense of place, experimenting with different techniques from book to book, running the gamut from solid naturalism to undifferentiated stream of consciousness depending on the subject and his state of mind. One of Kerouac's most improbable admirers was a younger *New Yorker* writer, John Updike, mandarin stylist, heir to Nabokov in lexical playfulness and metaphoric dazzle, yet also a conscientious realist, dutiful husband and father, and protégé of John Cheever as chronicler of the suburban middle class. In a 1971 interview excerpted in *Picked-Up Pieces* (1975), Updike singled out Salinger, Kerouac, and the virtually unknown Harold Brodkey, his Harvard contemporary, for having broken the mold of the well-made story they had inherited in the 1950s.

According to Updike, "It's in Salinger that I first heard, as a college student in the early Fifties, the tone that spoke to my condition," something he had not heard in the short stories of such hard-boiled or "wised-up" writers as Hemingway, John O'Hara, or Dorothy Parker. "Salinger's stories were not wised up. They were very open to tender invasions. Also they possessed a refreshing formlessness which, of course, he came to push to an extreme, as real artists tend to do."

He goes on to praise Brodkey's work for going "deeper into certain kinds of emotional interplay than the things written by older writers" and Kerouac because "there is something benign, sentimentally benign, in his work." When the interviewer expresses astonishment at any link between Updike, the polished craftsman, and the fluent Kerouac of the printer's roll, Updike insists that "Kerouac was right in emphasizing a certain flow, a certain ease. Wasn't he saying, after all, what the surrealists said? That if you do it very fast without thinking, something will get in that wouldn't ordinarily."

Updike's comments are virtually a manifesto for the lyrical novel by someone not usually associated with the first-person picaresque or with any kind of countercultural self-assertion. They suggest that Kerouac's and Salinger's importance even to the most buttoned-up writers was not simply a matter of form or style but a whole approach to experience. The arrival of the sensitive male in American fiction followed quickly on his appearance in film and drama. The formal breakthrough of the writer also represents the physical freedom many young people were seeking in a transitional era of severe but rapidly eroding moral constraints. American society still stigmatized sex and stressed the value of home, family, and work, but this was a rear-guard position within a growing culture of consumption and abundance. "Maturity" was the albatross of the postwar generation; Salinger and the Beats helped their readers see beyond it, to find the sensitive child, the thwarted adolescent in themselves. This in turn connected them to the newly emerging values of personal fulfilment, individuality, and unlimited consumption.

In remarks in *Esquire* in 1945, Salinger himself had criticized the hyper-masculine war novels for showing "too much of the strength, maturity and craftsmanship critics are looking for, and too little of the glorious imperfections which teeter and fall off the best minds. The men who have been in this war deserve some sort of *trembling melody* rendered without embarrassment or regret. I'll watch for that book." Here, Salinger speaks rather self-consciously for those for whom the war was a trauma rather than a triumph, a desperate challenge or a breakdown rather than an adventure. His aim is to write the emotional history of the war genera-tion, to give us characters who, in Updike's revealing phrase, are "very open to tender invasions."

Salinger, Kerouac, and Updike thus represent in their different ways the inward turn of the postwar novel, its feminization, so to speak. They look beyond masculine worlds imagined by Hemingway, the social map minutely drawn by John O'Hara. They look beyond sophistication toward the lost innocence of childhood, the paradise approximated by sex or drugs, the freedom associated with the road yet also the tenderness of fam-ily life. Families are their subject yet families also bring out their most ambivalent feelings. Families represent at once the remembered scene of childhood, the site of tender relationships, and the maturity trap they are anxious to escape. Sometimes they reject home and marriage only to exper-iment with new families, as with Kerouac and his Beat friends or Updike's Rabbit in *Rabbit Redux,* whose house becomes a kind of sixties communal pad, an irregular family, after his wife has left him.

Transgressive writing had flowered briefly with such homosexual authors as Tennessee Williams, Gore Vidal, and Paul Bowles in the late forties, but in the fifties and sixties a dream of freedom, a sexual and moral utopianism, beckoned to nearly every important American writer. Saul Bellow's chilling novella *Seize the Day,* a masterpiece of ironic fiction, dra-matizes the failure of one man's bid for freedom, but it is preceded and fol-lowed in Bellow's work by two wildly lyrical novels, *The Adventures of Augie March* (1953) and *Henderson the Rain King* (1959), essentially road novels exploring limits of both well-made fiction and social convention. Ralph Ellison's great *Invisible Man* (1952) is the most surreal of autobio-graphical novels. Its form takes on the classic picaresque pattern of Voltaire's *Candide* or Nathanael West's *A Cool Million,* in which the eter-nally hopeful hero, like a rubbery cartoon character, repeatedly takes it on the chin from a crude and brutal world. *Invisible Man* carries us through Ellison's Oklahoma childhood, his encounter with the South and the ideas of Booker T. Washington at Tuskegee Institute, his arrival in Harlem in the late 1930s, and his disillusioning attachment to the Communist party.

For the anonymous protagonist, as for many other black migrants, this road takes him nowhere, toward a Dostoyevskian underground room where he nurses his final cynicism. The strategy of his patrons is simply to manipulate him, to wear him out with the appearance of movement and progress: "Keep this nigger boy running."

Even compared to Bellow and Ellison, Updike is the most improbable of road novelists, the one most anchored to suburban life and a conventional literary career. At a time when so many young couples married so they could have sex and conceived children largely because they were married, Updike and his first wife were raising four children while still in their twenties. His literary mentor, John Cheever, seemed every inch the country squire, the well-mannered *New Yorker* stylist with the moral weight of his New England Puritanism behind him. But early on, Cheever began writing, in a deceptively light tone, about seriously dysfunctional families — emasculating mothers, failed fathers, murderous fraternal rivalries — and from *Falconer* (1977) to his posthumously published *Journals* (1991), he raised the curtain on a secret life of dark bisexual hedonism and marital misery on an epic scale. Another errant son of New England with a troubled family history, Robert Lowell, made the breakthrough much earlier and more daringly in the autobiographical prose and verse fragments of *Life Studies* (1959), contrasting his famous family name and genteel but impoverished background with his tortured mental history.

Compared to Cheever and Lowell, Updike's family origins were strictly lower middle class. His father, memorably portrayed in *The Centaur* (1963), was a high school math teacher and his mother, the central figure in *Of the Farm* (1965), was a frustrated writer who actually began publishing fiction late in life. Born in 1932 and raised in rural Pennsylvania, Updike attended Harvard on a scholarship and spent a year in Oxford as an art student before joining the staff of *The New Yorker*, where he became a lifelong contributor. His alter ego in fiction, Harry "Rabbit" Angstrom, is his notion of what he might have become had he never left southeastern Pennsylvania. The two main settings of Updike's fiction are the Pennsylvania towns where he grew up (the suburb of Reading he calls Olinger or Mt. Judge) and Massachusetts shore towns like Ipswich (called Tarbox in his novels) where he brought up his growing family after 1957.

Updike's work blends social chronicle with invention and autobiography, but like most lyrical novelists, his writing has a deeply personal core. Besides *The Centaur* and *Of the Farm*, two of his most effective and heartfelt works, he wrote remarkable sequences of stories about his boyhood and youth (collected in his *Olinger Stories,* 1964); his travels and his life as a writer (transmuted into *Bech: A Book,* 1970); and his first marriage, separation, and divorce (brought together memorably in *Too Far to Go,* 1978), collections that read like loosely sutured autobiographical novels. His first great commercial success, *Couples* (1968), was an epic of suburban adultery lightly salted with spiritual longing. But the core of his work can be found in the life history of Rabbit Angstrom, a sensual man trapped in marriage, family, responsibility yet always hungering for something beyond, a perfection he once experienced as a high school athlete.

Free of the showy stylistic filigree of Updike's early work and the lumbering, pedantic manner of some of his late books (such as *Roger's Version,* 1984, and *Memories of the Ford Administration,* 1992) and written in the vivid immediacy of the present tense, the Rabbit novels become Updike's personal history of America over four decades. His scenes from a marriage are keyed to the mood of the country at large: rebellious but frustrated in the late fifties, apocalyptic in the late sixties, smugly materialistic in the late seventies, disintegrating by the late eighties. Since Rabbit is not an intellectual, not a writer but a sentient animal who lives most in his body, the novels are full of vividly observed details, a flat poetry of the ordinary that gave rise to the Kmart school of fiction (by such lower-middle-class writers as Bobbie Ann Mason) in the seventies and eighties. But the Rabbit novels, especially *Rabbit, Run,* are also the history of a spiritual quest that does not always mesh well with Rabbit's unreflective nature. Though Rabbit eventually becomes prosperous, making love to his wife in a bed of Krugerrands in *Rabbit Is Rich* (1981), the novels unfold a long history of decline, foreshadowed from the first page of *Rabbit, Run.*

The Rabbit tetralogy begins and climaxes with the same scene: a bit of sandlot basketball in which the sometime star athlete tries to turn the clock back, to show the kids (and himself) that he still has the moves. In *Rabbit, Run,* eight years out of school, already past his prime at 26, Rabbit impresses the kids, who have no idea who he is; in *Rabbit at Rest* (1990), ailing, fat, out of shape, he reaches for the rim one last time but suffers a massive heart attack that has been coming on for two decades. Yet the subject of the books, especially of *Rabbit, Run,* is not Rabbit's fall so much as his inchoate quest, his effort to shape his life to the fleeting glimpses of glory he once had – occasionally still has – as an athlete and lover. Though Rabbit's instinctive middle-American conservatism seems a world away from the Beats, we can see here how Updike, a serious Christian, was influenced by Kerouac in crafting a fable about the frustrating constraints of family life, the deadening spiritual limits of adulthood, maturity, and civilization itself.

Along with Richard Yates's neglected *Revolutionary Road* (1961), *Rabbit, Run* is the classic novel of middle-class disappointment in the late Eisenhower years, when the social confidence of the fifties was breaking up, when John F. Kennedy was building his presidential campaign on a sense of national malaise, on the contrast between Republican stagnation and his own well-projected vigor. Although his opponent, Vice-President Richard Nixon, accused him of "downgrading America," he offered a new beginning, with a historic sense of passing the torch to a new generation. Though his private life did not become public till long after his death, he and his young wife even then conveyed a sense of sexual as well as political potency that contrasted with the avuncular Eisenhower and the devious, sinister Nixon. Updike, like Mailer before him, like Philip Roth, his exact contemporary, also projected a sense of male energy at bay, caught in a world swamped by mediocrity and routine.

Rabbit, Run is built on images of blockage, frustration, baffled vitality. *On the Road* had begun with the end of Sal's marriage, the start of his life on the road. Updike's novel begins with Rabbit married two years, with a son at home, a child on the way, a crummy job, and a wife who drinks too much, who watches children's programs on television, and no longer attracts or responds to him much in bed. "Just yesterday, it seems to him, she stopped being pretty." Her pregnancy "infuriates him with its look of stubborn lumpiness." In one recurring metaphor, Rabbit feels meshed in a "net" that keeps tightening around him, "a net he is somewhere caught in," not the hoop of his glory on the court but a web of routine and responsibility. He "senses he is in a trap." Surrounding the town there are still "hundreds of acres of forest Mt. Judge boys can never wholly explore," a dark wood just outside the line of civilization, the mountains where Rabbit continues to run as the novel ends.

Work and marriage have made Rabbit claustrophobic; his instinctive solution as an ex-athlete is to run, sometimes on his own two legs, often on wheels: "Harry sits wordless staring through the windshield, rigid in body, rigid in spirit. The curving highway seems a wide straight road that has opened up in front of him. There is nothing he wants to do but go down it." Not long after the novel begins he takes to the road for the first time, impulsively, after a quarrel with his wife Janice, getting all the way to West Virginia before turning back. Soon he is living with a part-time whore, Ruth, who also becomes pregnant, but he comes back home when he learns that his wife is in labor, leaving Ruth as abruptly and unthinkingly as he had left his wife. When he runs out again on Janice, she accidentally drowns their baby, in one of the most painstakingly horrific scenes in recent fiction. After another reconciliation, and after the baby's funeral, he rejects the guilt others seem to be heaping on to him and takes off again, running for his life.

Summarized in this way the novel seems flimsy and repetitious. As a middling sensual male with a positive gift for messing up his life, Rabbit hardly seems worth the writer's loving attention. His two women are more real than their counterparts in *On the Road* but they remain essentially male projections: Janice the resistant female, the intractable wife who has lost her sexual appeal; Ruth the compliant female, the tough but tender broad who has been around, who knows the score. Sex is no hang-up for her, though she has grown cynical about the way men use her to get it. When Rabbit demands and receives oral sex – a signal moment in the sexual history of the American novel – she feels humiliated only because he is bent on humiliating her, bringing her to her knees, where she must prove herself by servicing him. (A briefer, less explicit scene of oral sex in Mailer's *The Deer Park* [1955] had caused the original publisher to drop the book.) The next morning, Rabbit's wife gives birth and he guiltily leaves Ruth behind, having in a sense gotten all he wanted from her.

As Rabbit rattles his chains, the two women remain passive objects of his need and anger. His real antagonist in the novel is another man, the Reverend Eccles, who becomes his persistent goad and confidant, working tirelessly, despite his own troubled marriage, to bring Rabbit and Janice together again. Superficially sympathetic but meddlesome, Eccles is a version of the therapeutic figure who had been reappearing in plays and films since the late forties, especially such social-problem dramas as *The Best Years of Our Lives, Home of the Brave, The Men,* and *Rebel Without a Cause.* He is Updike's mordant comment on this new authority figure of postwar culture, the doctor, minister, psychiatrist, or social worker who began offering post-theological solutions to the sense of alienation – the seismic shifts in social relationships – that had shaken American life since the war. Eccles is a vehicle for Updike's larger ambition: to make *Rabbit, Run* more than a documentary take on the miseries of married life, to turn it into a novel of ideas. Eccles stands for a therapeutic liberalism that blatantly intrudes into other people's lives; his religious skepticism deifies social and personal bonds over any higher powers. To Updike, Eccles represents the vaunted religious revival of the fifties, humanistic instead of dogmatic, this-worldly rather than otherworldly, altogether enlightened and reasonable but spiritually null. Eccles's technique for saving souls is manipulative, not authoritarian. His own soul is in a questionable state; perhaps it has been replaced by his social conscience, which Updike sees as a subtle will to power. By befriending Rabbit and bringing him back to Janice, disastrously, he bears some responsibility for the death of their child.

To Rabbit, it is his flight, his "sin," even his need for sex that must surely be to blame for his daughter's death. In relation to *On the Road,* Rabbit is at once the guilty, conflicted Sal and the amoral Dean, for Updike has taken the cry for liberation at the heart of the lyrical novel and enmeshed it in the fateful and ironic consequences of the fiction of relationships, the fiction of entrapment. "There is a case to be made for running away from your wife," Updike told an interviewer in 1969. "In the late Fifties beatniks were preaching transcontinental travelling as the answer to man's disquiet. And I was trying to say: 'Yes, there is certainly that, but then there are all these other people who seem to get hurt.' That qualification is meant to frame a moral dilemma." (In 1995, in an introduction to a one-volume edition of all four Rabbit novels, he framed the point even more moralistically. *Rabbit, Run,* he says, "was meant to be a realistic demonstration of what happens when a young American family man goes on the road: the people left behind get hurt." But he acknowledges that "arriving at so prim a moral was surely not my only intention: the book ends on an ecstatic, open note that was meant to stay open. . . . The title can be read as advice.") In *On the Road* the same moral issue, framed by women but also by Sal, only highlights Dean's terrifying spontaneity, his amoral charisma. It affirms Dean's mythic status but offers little counterweight to the lure of the road. "Funny," thinks Rabbit near the end of the novel, "how what makes you move is so simple and the field you must move in is so crowded."

If Rabbit is ambivalent like Sal, he is also a quester like Dean, a confused, propulsive id who lives in his body yet seeks something beyond, a transcendence that other people scarily discount. Here, the earthbound Eccles is his antagonist. When they play golf together *(golf!)* Rabbit, growing too articulate, feels the pull of a world behind the visible: "there's something that wants me to find it." When he lands a shot, when the ball "with a kind of visible sob takes a last bite of space before vanishing in falling," he says triumphantly: "That's *it!*" Eccles is skeptical, however. To him, "all vagrants think they're on a quest." "That was all settled centuries ago, in the heresies of the early Church," he tells Rabbit. "It's the strange thing about you mystics, how often your little ecstasies wear a skirt." Rabbit's half-articulated goal, which Eccles mocks, is what Kerouac in *Visions of Cody* calls "the Go – the summation pinnacle possible in human relationships." "I'm a mystic," Rabbit says jokingly of himself. "I give people faith." Still, his simple story resists taking on this cumbersome freight.

It is typical of the younger Updike to give a slightly allegorical cast to an essentially realistic novel, to seek God in the suburbs, to allow his characters (not wholly convincingly) to debate theological issues on the golf course, and to put someone like Rabbit at the center of such a conversation. Eccles speaks for maturity, adjustment, the sober, hard-nosed realism cherished by social thinkers of the 1950s, but Updike makes Rabbit his unlikely spokesman for a keen spiritual and sexual hunger. To Eccles, Rabbit should come to grips with life's limits, should accept the "muddle" of diminishment as other couples do. Rabbit demurs: "After you're first-rate at something, no matter what," he tells Eccles, "it kind of takes the kick out of being second-rate. And that little thing Janice and I had going, boy, it was really second-rate." Though no postwar novelist writes more lyrically about married love than Updike, *Rabbit, Run* is grounded in the male sense of enclosure, the loss of sexual freedom and variety – a sense of being weighed down by family, no matter how much loved, and having one's wings clipped. "If you're telling me I'm not mature," Rabbit tells Eccles, "that's one thing I don't cry over since as far as I can make out it's the same thing as being dead."

But by giving us a Rabbit who does not simply want to be free but has a longing for something beyond, Updike attaches the novel to the utopian discourse that emerged in the late fifties, which marked a path for the counterculture of the next decade. In its own way, *Rabbit, Run* is a Christian version of not only the violent sainthood of the Beats but also the spiritual-sexual mythology of Herbert Marcuse's *Eros and Civilization* (1955); Norman Mailer's "The White Negro"; Norman O. Brown's apocalyptic *Life Against Death* (1959), with its appeal to Christian mystics like Boehme and its radical reading of Freud; and Paul Goodman's *Growing Up Absurd,* which famously interpreted both the hell-raising of delinquent youth and the bad-boy behavior of the Beats as a cry of existential anguish, an inchoate quest for meaning. Updike connects sex to theology, physical grace to spiritual grace. *Rabbit, Run* is at once a fifties recoil from maturity, a male outcry against being domesticated, a Freudian rebuff at the instinctual sacrifices that make civilization possible, and a Christian dream of unfallen perfection. This is a terrible weight for any novel to bear, but Updike's book, with its wonderful surface realism, its plenitude of sharply observed details, carries it off from scene to scene, as if the physical world itself had great sacramental purpose.

Rabbit, Run relocates the road novel in middle America, at the heart of American marriage, far away from the voluble sophistication of Salinger's precocious young or the bohemianism of Kerouac's self-consciously marginal rebels. Unlike some of Updike's more pretentious or experimental novels, the Rabbit books are grounded in the ordinary, the concrete, whatever their spiritual or historical themes. Rabbit gets away, but Updike never lets him get off easily and he allows him moments of complex awareness beyond what the character can bear. Even before his daughter dies, Rabbit is surprised when someone "seems oblivious of the gap of guilt between Harry and humanity." He experiences the recognition of limits that Eccles has been projecting at him. "He feels the truth: the thing that had left his life had left irrevocably; no search would recover it. No flight would reach it. . . . The fullness ends when we give Nature her ransom, when we make children for her. Then she is through with us." This is Updike's thinking, not Rabbit's.

In *Rabbit Redux,* the situation of the previous novel is reversed. His wife Janice leaves him – *she* is having the affair – and we see the world at least initially from her point of view. Instead of chafing at his static surroundings, Rabbit, grown increasingly conservative, has turned pensive and downhearted as the world explodes around him. The scene is the summer of 1969, the summer of the first moon landing, Ted Kennedy's fall at Chappaquiddick, and riots in the streets of American cities. In a culture saturated with casual sex, desire has leaked out of Rabbit like the air from a balloon, or his rapidly fading memories of early success. He has grown passive, become a working stiff whose job in a print shop will soon be lost to automation. After Janice takes off, he lives at home with his teenage son, then takes in an 18-year-old runaway girl and a young black fugitive who has been to Vietnam and now dreams of becoming the black Jesus. But Rabbit's amorphous politics recoil at everything the newcomers represent: the new youth culture, the antiwar movement, and the hopped-up rhetoric of black nationalism. Though this is Updike's most topically attuned novel, trying too deliberately to take in the whole sixties scene, Rabbit seems more than ever the ordinary man: he is no longer dreaming of special ecstasies, and his stubborn, almost shell-shocked recalcitrance prefigures the sullen American backlash against the counterculture, which lies just over the horizon.

Like Philip Roth's *American Pastoral* twenty-five years later, *Rabbit Redux* relies on stereotypes to evoke the era, especially the figure of the violent, wayward, aimless child, the angry adolescent; yet it was a prophetic book, less about the sixties than about their impact on middle America. Once, Updike had found a metaphor for his own sense of restlessness in Kerouac's evocation of the road; now Rabbit's own mother, almost paralyzed by Parkinson's disease (a "movement disorder," as doctors call it), urges him to leave, to run away, but there is nowhere he wants to go; he already feels old, wasted. The road seems closed to him. Now that the moral world that once confined him has broken up, he misses its stability. The sexual freedom he coveted is everywhere, not simply among the young but in the suburbs, as Updike had already demonstrated in *Couples* (1968). Surrounded by the cacophonous bacchanal of the late sixties, Updike, still in his thirties like Rabbit, writes a precocious novel about middle-aged depression. As America grows absurdly younger, Rabbit ages prematurely.

The even more spent and tired protagonist of *Rabbit Is Rich* and *Rabbit at Rest* is a much coarser figure, reunited with his newly independent and self-sufficient wife, battling viciously with his son, even sleeping with his daughter-in-law. Like the narrators of other late novels such as *Roger's Version,* Rabbit becomes the rancorous, disappointed shadow of his increasingly distinguished author, the vehicle of Updike's pet peeves as he had once been the earthy dreamer of his visionary hopes. Retired to Florida, Rabbit observes the mores of aging Jews with distaste but feels reassured by having a Jewish surgeon tinkering with his defective heart. At the same time Updike is perfectly aware of Rabbit's limitations, and he laces *Rabbit Is Rich* with strategic references to Sinclair Lewis's *Babbitt.* The novels themselves grow longer, becoming more like reportage, an accumulation of realistic details about a changing America, with little of the allegorical cast, the young writer's wild ambition, that gave another dimension to *Rabbit, Run.* Accepting an award for *Rabbit at Rest,* Updike paid tribute to the tradition of realism descending from William Dean Howells, who had not previously been his household god.

Rabbit's inexorable decline speaks to a sense of loss at the heart of Updike's imagination, an empathy with failure at odds with his own carefully managed, beautifully evolving career, which seemed to go from strength to strength in every department of writing: novels, innumerable stories, light verse, brilliant book reviewing, art criticism, memoir, the whole terrain of the man of letters. The key lies undoubtedly in Updike's sense of the past, of life unfolding in time and inexorably running down, as indeed it must. Despite Updike's fluent ability to conceptualize a book and will it into being, the core of feeling in his work is lyrical and autobiographical, as it finally is in the works of Cheever and Nabokov as well. Nothing in Updike's work can quite match the emotional intensity of such stories as "Flight" and "The Blessed Man of Boston, My Grandmother's Thimble, and Fanning Island," both in *Pigeon Feathers* (1962) or the closely related novella *Of the Farm* (1965) and its 1990 sequel, "A Sandstone Farmhouse," collected in *The Afterlife and Other Stories* (1994). They pay a mixed tribute to his difficult mother, who believed in his future even when he was a boy, who told him thrillingly that he was "going to fly," and they evoke the final years of his maternal grandparents, whose lives open up a vista of historical time he feels he must preserve, and finally his mother's own death. At the same time that he deals with the paradoxes of growing up and growing old, Updike, like Salinger and Kerouac before him, feels an immense tenderness toward every aspect of his own experience – every tangle of relationship, every nuance of perception, every observed or imagined fact.

In *Of the Farm,* the protagonist, on a visit to his mother's farm, feels emotionally estranged from his new wife when he begins to see her through his mother's judging eyes, the eyes that first helped him see and feel. "You've taken a vulgar woman to be your wife," his mother tells him, almost mesmerizing him with her force of will – but the younger woman, like the city to which he must return, belongs to the life he has chosen, the grown-up world he loves and needs. His mother must let go, as he must let go of her and of the farm, of the whole dreamy boyhood preserved so perfectly in memories that the farm itself brings flooding back. His mother has a spell of illness that foreshadows her death and the sale of the farm. "I saw her, now, as an old woman. Always before she had appeared to me as a heavier version of the swift young mother outsprinting my father from the barn. . . . In sleep my mother had slipped from my recognition and blame and had entered, unconsciously, a far territory, the arctic of the old." As Charles Thomas Samuels remarks of the Updike paradox: "Definition requires that we keep faith with our past; freedom demands that we move beyond it."

Memory takes on an even more sublime cast in "The Blessed Man of Boston. . . ," a tryptich about all the stories he could write, the people he could recreate, the memories he could turn into words if he had world enough and time. Written in an almost magical style that brings to mind the play of memory in Wordsworth's *Prelude,* the story shows us an Updike in almost an ecstasy of involuntary recollection. Finding a silver thimble, his grandmother's wedding present, he falls down a Proustian well. With this "stemless chalice of silver" between his fingers, "the valves of time parted, and after an interval of years my grandmother was upon me again." He must "tell how once there had been a woman who now was no more, how she had been born and lived in a world that had ceased to exist, though its mementos were all about us." In the story's most ecstatic moment, he recalls lifting the sick, brittle old woman, in the full pride of his young strength, and whirling her dangerously around the room: "Had I stumbled, or dropped her, I might have broken her back, but my joy always proved a secure cradle. . . . I was carrying her who had carried me, I was giving my past a dance, I had lifted the anxious caretaker of my childhood from the floor, I was bringing her with my boldness to the edge of danger, from which she had always sought to guard me." The young man is about to step out on a date, the vibrations are intensely sexual, but the erotic anticipation of his immediate future spills out onto the vivid relics of his past, a world he hugs to his heart even as he is leaving it behind. The narrator's exhilaration comes from making the past live, from lifting aged forebears into one last dance, momentarily reversing the flow of time. Updike's sense of decline, like Wordsworth's, is grounded in the luminous plenitude but also the concreteness of the remembered past. Of "A Sandstone Farmhouse," which deals with his mother's death, Updike himself commented that "by keeping the focus on the house – its stones, its smells, its renovations – I hoped to convey the dizzying depth of life its walls have contained. . . . The story is about *things* – how they mutely witness our flitting lives, and remain when the lives are over, still mute, still witnessing."

❧

Though the later Updike would often grow cerebral, recruiting stuffy pedants, or the pedant in himself, to narrate some of his novels, his deepest affinity as a writer was not only with the gorgeous prose, the profligate imagination, of predecessors like Vladimir Nabokov, but with the sense of lost radiance that gives their narratives such a poetic charge. In the brief preface to *The Stories of John Cheever* (1978), the collection that finally gained him unassailable stature as a modern classic, Cheever remembers a "long-lost world when the city of New York was still filled with a river light, when you heard the Benny Goodman quartets from a radio in the corner stationery store, and when almost everybody wore a hat." Cheever tells us how he chanted aloud some passages in which the best stories spin off into sublimity – bursts of poetic gusto he finds as thrilling to recall as they were to indite. Cheever's higher flights, which disconcerted his editors at *The New Yorker*, were as essential to his work as were his powers of social observation. In their flow of images, occasionally in their pull toward fantasy, Cheever's stories veer from a level realism toward glimpses of paradise that break through a fog of misery or depression.

Though he is oddly known as a cheerful chronicler of suburbia, and as Updike's precursor as a keen social historian, Cheever, born in 1912, writes about the suburbs as a state of mind, almost an imaginary place, a pastoral utopia that seems as cut off from history and memory as from suffering and tragedy. Yet behind the spacious houses, well-trimmed lawns, inviting swimming pools, and perfectly groomed children, behind the façade of a community built on wealth and exclusion, behind the impeccable manners and decorum, Cheever's stories give us glimpses of alcoholism, lust, family combat, and melancholia. One character thinks wistfully, "How sad everything is!" but the line could come from almost any of the stories, with their inextricable sense of "the pain and sweetness of life."

In view of his light tone and his long connection to *The New Yorker*, which broke down as his work grew darker and less simply realistic, it is remarkable how much unhappiness we find even in Cheever's early work, how much bitterness, disappointment, and latent violence, whether he is writing about the Massachusetts in which he grew up, the New York he lived in during the late thirties and forties, or the Westchester County, New York, towns where he raised his children. This is the kind of bad news that comes in over "the enormous radio," unhinging a woman who is armored in her innocence and gentility yet, like the writer himself, obsessed with other people's secrets. Though some stories seem infused with a willful bleakness, others glow with longing, shimmer with Edenic recollections of summers past and boyhood dreams. Like Updike's Rabbit, Cheever's characters are divided souls, schooled in duty, discretion, and self-restraint, fueled by lust and passionate longing, wracked by unappeasable melancholy. Despite these conflicts, their lives are redeemed by moments of transcendence in love, in nature, in language, or in some lovely pocket of the past, miraculously unspoiled, at least in memory. Cheever's 1978 preface points to three privileged moments, composed aloud in a frenzy of inspiration, in which his own language turns poetic and incantatory: the conclusion of the fratricidal "Goodbye, My Brother," in which two women, the narrator's wife and sister, rise naked out of the sea; the opening of "The Housebreaker of Shady Hill," which begins almost with a chant; and the close of "The Country Husband," a tale of deep marital and social discord, which signs off exuberantly in the magical language of romance: "It is a night where kings in golden suits ride elephants over the mountains."

Cheever's often unconvincing endings were his way of escaping unhappiness and redeeming misery and self-division into art. The endings are foreshadowed by Cheever's deceptively bright tone, which fits in rather too well with the decorous cheeriness and the limited social spectrum of the old *New Yorker.* Acordingly, the stories were persistently undervalued; their core of darkness was scarcely taken in (though Alfred Kazin shrewdly observed that "his marvelous brightness is an effort to cheer himself up"). Such superb collections as *The Enormous Radio and Other Stories* (1953) were tarred by reviewers who disliked the self-satisfied tone of the magazine, with its focus on upper-middle-class manners. Cheever collaborated with this misunderstanding by sanitizing his family history in *The Wapshot Chronicle* (1957), though every theme of his work – including his grim sense of Puritan origins, his fierce rivalry with his brother, his parents' painful marriage, his father's feeling of being rendered superfluous, and even his own fear of turning homosexual – is tucked into the narrative with unobtrusive charm. (He was especially proud of including a four-letter word that alarmed his genteel publisher.) Scattered into storylike episodes, the book is a warm tribute to his failed father; it combines nostalgia for a lost Eden with the sense of a world gone terribly awry. The book was a great success for the wrong reasons: a wistful poetry of recollection somehow allays any temptation to despair.

The stresses that seem so attenuated in the novel are powerfully compressed and controlled in the three stories singled out in Cheever's preface. "Goodbye, My Brother," the perfect overture to the collected stories, contrasts the gloomy, puritanical brother, harsh in his judgments, morosely indifferent to his family and his past, with the life-affirming narrator who, looking out at the sea, finds beauty and rebirth where his sibling sees only death and decay. The narrator, Cheever himself in his most exalted vein, extends his tolerance to everyone except his brother, without realizing how much he resembles him in his own self-righteousness. Like many Cheever stories, it turns on an act of transgression when the narrator, exasperated by his brother's saturnine gloom, murderously strikes him from behind, in a sense expelling him from the family and subduing his own dark alter ego. For this moment at least, a violent gesture restores the family to the summer and the sea and a sense of paradise regained. The story, with its Cain-and-Abel theme, its tincture of fantasy and the breach of the social code, becomes a way of facing down the writer's own despair and recapturing an unspoiled sense of nature.

The other two stories, both among Cheever's best, are about another form of trouble in paradise: the quiet misery of suburban marriage. Losing his job, disappointed in his family, which seems impervious to his problems, the husband in "The Housebreaker of Shady Hill" takes to stealing from his neighbors. "The Country Husband" is not much more realistic in dealing with family discord. It begins with a cinematic sequence about an air crash, in which Francis, the husband, is nearly killed; but when he gets home he finds the family too preoccupied to pay any attention to what has happened to him. Feeling that he is taken for granted, that his needs do not really matter, Francis manages to be rude to the town's social arbiter, to blacken the family's standing with its conforming neighbors, and to fall in love absurdly with the baby-sitter. In both stories, the husband feels his wife, children, friends, and neighbors do not understand him, as Cheever himself repeatedly complained in his journals. In both stories, he commits a transgression that represents his very tentative bid for freedom, his attempt to regain the state of joy he once knew and still dreams about. In both, the husband and wife quarrel and almost separate but are quickly reconciled. In another story, "The Cure," the couple actually does separate, but the husband then sinks into a misery so complete that he grasps desperately at restoring his marriage. This seems to have been much the story of Cheever's own marriage, with his bisexuality left out.

In Cheever's world, freedom, including sexual freedom, is an abstract good and a pressing need, but not quite as strong as the need for family bonds and social acceptance, however narrow and hollow they may sometimes seem. "The Country Husband" is full of touches that point to a larger moral and historical world, images of challenge and adventure including memories of the war, symbolized by a French maid whose head was shaved for consorting with Germans, but also points to romantic passion, symbolized but also mocked by the husband's infatuation with the baby-sitter. (Her father is brutal and alcoholic – she cries on Francis's shoulder when he drives her home.) The allusions to the war are unusual for Cheever, despite his years of military service, and utterly unthinkable in the sheltered world of Shady Hill. "The war seemed now so distant and the world where the cost of partisanship had been death or torture so long ago. . . . The people in the Farquarsons' living room seemed united in their tacit claim that there had been no past, no war – that there was no danger or trouble in the world." The Farquarsons' living room stands not only for Shady Hill but for postwar America, where the sense of Edenic happiness seems built on the denial of social misery and historical tragedy.

In "The Country Husband," Francis rediscovers the joys of being deliberately rude and chafes at "the strenuousness of containing his physicalness within the patterns he had chosen." Its title alludes to Wycherley's 1674 erotic farce, *The Country Wife,* in which a man feigns impotence in order to seduce unwary women. The country husband, on the other hand, really is impotent, trapped in a world of straitlaced conventions and sublimated needs. Francis rediscovers passion but is unable to act on it any more than he can talk to people about what happened after the war, since "the atmosphere of Shady Hill made the memory unseemly and impolite." They are, however, the customs *he* had chosen, as Cheever himself, on the evidence of his journals, had done as well, and in the end these rebels invariably choose to return home, even when (as in "The Swimmers") that home is now empty and deserted.

This is where Cheever, who seems to celebrate home and family, oddly fits in with the postwar direction of the road novel as well as the closely related fiction of youth and transgression steeped in the Freudian tension between civilization and its discontents. Behind the façade of manners in Cheever's world is a dream of freedom along with a steady accumulation of misery. Later recollections of Cheever, including Updike's numerous tributes, highlight his youthful energy and buoyancy, for which he never found sufficient outlet; his despondency, which made him suicidal and alcoholic; and his family feeling, which forced him to curb and contain himself.

Cheever's journals frequently explore the anarchic sexual itch, especially the homosexual feelings, that remained masked but essential in his fiction, but also the strong needs that restrained him from exposing them, even to his closest friends, or acting on them. "But then there are the spiritual facts," he writes in his journal in 1962: "my high esteem for the world, the knowledge that it is not in me to lead a double life, my love of perseverance, a passionate wish to honor the vows I've made to my wife and children. But my itchy member is unconcerned with all of this, and I am afraid that I may succumb to its itchiness." Typically, the attraction is to another man, and as time passed, Cheever succumbed more openly and frequently, all the while maintaining his tempestuous marriage, marred by his narcissistic demands for unconditional love and approval from his long-suffering wife. And the more he succumbed, the more his work changed. His stories grew more surreal and, in a more permissive cultural climate, his novels (especially *Falconer*) began exploring more dangerous terrain: homosexuality, incarceration, fratricide.

Cheever belongs with Updike not simply because he influenced him, they admired each other, and both explored the troubled suburban marriages of white Protestant males. If they seemed equally at home in lyrical and mandarin prose, in the sensuous and the Apollonian, it was because both of them were riven by the conflict between sex and marriage, between the pull toward freedom and call of home, between instinctual need and family life. Between them, they domesticated the themes of the road novel. Like the larger popular culture of the 1950s, Cheever's work is divided between a celebration of the nuclear family, however dysfunctional, and an attraction to the figure of the outlaw, the deviant, however self-destructive. "There does seem to be, in my head some country," wrote Cheever in his journals, "some infantile country of irresponsible sexual indulgence that has nothing to do with the facts of life as I know them."

Ironically, "the facts of life" refers here not to the birds and bees but the concrete facts of social and family life, the settled domestic world that keeps the road runner at home, that keeps this fiction writer wedded to the quotidian, not the apocalyptic. Once, Cheever even puts this in the form of a small parable, inspired perhaps by Kafka's retelling of Greek and Hebrew myths:

He could separate from his red-faced and drunken wife, he could conceivably make a life without his beloved children, he could get along without the companionship of his friends, but he could not bring himself to leave his lawns and gardens, he could not part from the porch screens and storm windows that he had repaired and painted, he could not divorce himself from the serpentine brick walk he had laid between the side door and the rose beds. So for him the chains of

Prometheus were forged from turf and house paint, copper screening, putty and brick, but they shackled him as sternly as iron.

All the tensions in Cheever's work come to a head in this self-conscious fragment. He sees himself with fallen grandeur as Prometheus the light bringer, the rebel, but also as the victim bound in chains of domesticity, the willingly shackled adventurer who never left home. Instead, Cheever became the bard of suburbia, the explorer of the joys and trials of middle-class marriage. His transgressive impulses he largely reserved for his tortured private life; in fiction, he became the superlative celebrant of the joys of the quotidian. An unlikely admirer, Vladimir Nabokov, was charmed by the wealth of circumstantial detail in his stories, and pointed out that "The Country Husband" was "really a miniature novel beautifully traced." Cheever in turn admired Nabokov but saw that his own style was as different as his origins: "The house I was raised in had its charms, but my father hung his underwear from a nail he had driven into the back of the bathroom door, and while I know something about the Riviera I am not a Russian aristocrat polished in Paris. My prose style will always be to a degree matter-of-fact."

※

Nabokov, of course, was forced to leave home. He was born in Russia in 1899; his father was a distinguished liberal and reformer who was imprisoned by the czar, chased and scorned by the Bolsheviks, and finally assassinated by Fascist thugs in Berlin in 1922. For Cheever and Updike, nostalgia for lost boyhood was an aspect of temperament, a way in which they remained "open to tender invasions." For Nabokov, this remembered radiance was produced by physical exile and the dislocations of modern history. For all his privileged upbringing, which he celebrates with great sensuous immediacy, far from being "a Russian aristocrat polished in Paris," he led a penniless, hand-to-mouth existence in Berlin in the twenties and thirties, supporting himself by writing for émigré journals and for publishers with a minuscule readership.

One of the most moving of the autobiographical essays that appeared mainly in The New Yorker between 1948 and 1950 – collected in Conclusive Evidence (1951) and, in revised form, in Speak, Memory (1966) – is his account of how, as a Cambridge student, he went about reconstructing the Russian culture, language, and literature he had taken for granted in his cosmopolitan home: "The story of my college years in England is really the story of my trying to become a Russian writer. I had the feeling that Cambridge and all its famed features – venerable elms, blazoned windows, loquacious tower clocks – were of no consequence in themselves but existed merely to frame and support my rich nostalgia." When fully

assembled and revised in 1966, the book became an album of fifteen portraits, only very loosely chronological, richly portraying the figures and
settings of his youth: his mother, his father, his colorful tutors, his Russian
education, his English education, and an early love interest.

The loving detail of these reminiscences, the almost hallucinatory intensity with which he conjures them up, impels us to question Nabokov's customary rejection of realism, his insistence that his art is essentially a
magician's game, a set of artful tricks. Both his early work in Russian and
English and such late, self-indulgent works as *Ada, or Ardor* (1969) are
marred by a hothouse atmosphere of strained allegory, an oppressive literariness. Nabokov himself insists on the unreality of the "real" world around
him – always very concretely described! – as compared to the superior reality of memory, fantasy, and mental invention. "'Reality,'" he says in the
afterword to *Lolita*, is "one of the few words which mean nothing without
quotes." "I open Nabokov," Cheever wrote in his journals, "and am
charmed by this spectrum of ambiguities, this marvellous atmosphere of
untruth." For Nabokov, the matter-of-fact world so beloved by Cheever, or
imposed on him by his spare origins, carried no charge of emotion except as
material for satire or invitations to murder, while the remembered world
was suffused with nostalgia, and charged with psychic energy. In his 1951
album and the novels and stories that followed, however, Nabokov, perhaps
drawn by the mainstream audience of *The New Yorker*, made a pact with
common life, inspired by his new American setting as he had been by his
Russian past. Though he was the least sentimental of émigrés, he achieved
his greatest power, in *Lolita*, by fusing memory and desire, nostalgia and
impossible longing. His autobiography is a key to his published work,
inaugurating his most passionate and accessible decade as a writer. It was
followed by *Lolita* (1955), *Pnin* (1957), the short stories in *Nabokov's Dozen*
(1958), and the diabolically clever *Pale Fire* (1962).

Like many lyrical writers, including Salinger and Updike, whom he
always singled out as the current American authors he most admired,
Nabokov's work is heightened with an intense feeling that makes his style
luminous and incandescent yet utterly precise. But he was also an ironist
whose work is a hall of mirrors, a multitude of deceptive masks, tricky and
problematic, with stylized characters full of Dickensian vitality, ranging
from the harmlessly eccentric to the maniacally obsessive. His past in
Speak, Memory is the sun-dappled garden of the country estates around
Petersburg. His descriptions are full of remembered pleasure but also shot
through with darker anticipations: his father's murder, his mother's wid-
owhood and poverty, and his separation from his siblings, his social position, his beloved language, and his country.

Art is Nabokov's method for recreating a perfect, unchanging past. One of his metaphors for art – and the subject of the most charming and revealing chapter of *Speak, Memory* – is his passion for butterflies, which he began collecting and identifying at the age of seven and continued to pursue and classify for the next seven decades; this was a love affair (like Humbert Humbert's) that was also a fierce obsession. The mounted butterfly, like the book itself, is nature under glass, a timeless, flawless reality armored against contingency and disintegration. Nabokov writes of the butterfly's protective coloration as a cunning device, gratuitously "carried to a point of mimetic subtlety far in excess of a predator's power of appreciation. I discovered in nature the nonutilitarian delights that I sought in art. Both were a form of magic, both were a game of intricate enchantment and deception." Nabokov's self-image, often belied by the work itself, is that of the writer as a conjuror, not a passive recorder, using mimetic effects that are a form of enchantment rather than realistic representation.

Along with Alfred Kazin's *A Walker in the City* (1951), Mary McCarthy's *Memories of a Catholic Girlhood* (1956), and Robert Lowell's *Life Studies* – a collection of poems that includes his prose memoir "77 Revere Street" – *Speak, Memory* is one of the essential autobiographies of the 1950s, not only an album of recollections but a work like Wordsworth's *Prelude* that interrogates the nature of time and the sinuous process of remembering. One of Nabokov's favorite ideas was that time was really a form of space – what Wordsworth called a "spot of time" – part of the lush terrain of our mental life, to be revisited at will. "The act of vividly recalling a patch of the past is something that I seem to have been performing with the utmost zest all my life," he said. Nabokov recalled how his parents did it before him, repeatedly memorializing vital moments of experience almost as a hedge against future losses. Of his mother, he wrote:

As if feeling that in a few years the tangible part of her world would perish, she cultivated an extraordinary consciousness of the various time marks distributed throughout our country place. She cherished her own past with the same retrospective fervor that I now do her image and my past. Thus, in a way, I inherited an exquisite simulacrum – the beauty of intangible property, unreal estate – and this proved a splendid training for the endurance of later losses.

Just as Wordsworth constantly insisted that the fullness of memory had more than compensated him for the loss of his sensuous childhood, Nabokov endows the past with an unsentimental poignance that anticipates deprivations to come. Instead of chronology, he gives us (as his title suggests) a dialogue with memory, a series of visits to corners of the past as conserved in his own mind, rescuing characters who had already been transformed in his fiction, shuffling different periods like a pack of scattered cards, reconstituting "things that fate one day bundled up pell-mell and tossed into the sea, completely severing me from my boyhood."

But this loss, he insists, is a source of imaginative strength, far superior to a banal, uneventful continuity, to whit, an American experience innocent of the tempests of history ("a smooth, safe, small-town continuity of time, with its primitive absence of perspective"). As his lost Russian past would remain a source of intense emotion, the vulgar American present would become the object of frenzied, cruel, but curiously loving and minutely attentive satire.

Nabokov had nothing but scorn for the czarist émigrés who mourned the loss of wealth or privileges. He himself had come into an estate and become wealthy barely a year before the revolution, but this, he insists, meant nothing to him. *His* losses and gains, like Humbert Humbert's, are Proustian, not material. *Speak, Memory, Lolita,* and *Pnin,* all written between 1948 and 1955, form a trilogy on the inner life of the émigré, in which *Lolita* is the delirious comic inferno, *Pnin* the mild and wistful purgatorio, and *Speak, Memory* the paradise of the past recaptured, pinned and mounted under glass. We might say that what the past represents for the nostalgic biographer as he contemplates his blissful childhood, Lolita, the downy nymphet, incarnates for Humbert Humbert, who is Nabokov's most ingenious mask.

Lolita is *Speak, Memory* as a hall of mirrors, an uneasy tissue of obsession and deception that connects remarkably to the cultural themes of America in the 1950s. Where Nabokov the autobiographer seems to have surmounted his losses, imaginatively reconstructing his past within him, Humbert's loss of his first young love (named after Poe's "Annabel Lee") has left him tormented by predatory sexual needs, fixated on the transient moment when childhood is turning into adulthood. Where Nabokov could turn his harmless mania for butterflies into a mixture of aesthetic passion, adventure, and scientific pedantry, Humbert is enslaved to the fantasies he projects on this one specimen of America's coarse but energetic new youth culture.

No one, however morally censorious, can fail to be moved by the baroque language of Humbert's passionate attachment to his nymphet, around whom he weaves a solipsistic plot as rich as any writer's imaginative flights. As in other lyrical novels (though far less colloquially), Nabokov uses all the tricks of voice to give Humbert an overwhelming presence – to make us complicit with his feelings and needs, even as he himself describes them with wicked relish. But Humbert's is also a tale of self-loathing, the fable of beauty and the beast from the beast's point of view, as written in the archly euphemistic language of both romantic love (with Lolita as the bewitching demon child) and Victorian pornography (with Lolita as the coyly seductive victim of a besotted sexual predator).

Again and again, Humbert describes himself as a pervert, a maniac, the depraved victim of his own revolting lust, an enchanted hunter manipulating (and being manipulated by) his prey. On the very first page, he even attributed his gloriously arch European prose to his kinkiness and criminality: "You can always count on a murderer for a fancy prose style." By the end, after he loses her, he recants almost convincingly, killing a farcical rival even more sordid than he is, feeling redeemed only by the fact that he loved her: "It was love at first sight, at last sight, at ever and ever sight." "I loved you. I was a pentapod monster, but I loved you. I was despicable and brutal, and turpid, and everything, *mais je t'aimais, je t'aimais!*"

As Lolita is the product of the youth culture that gave us Holden Caulfield and James Dean, her strange admirer is the neurotic, maladjusted, but feelingful male who runs like a thread through postwar culture: the returning war veterans unable to adjust to a peacetime world; the disaffected young misfits, represented by Brando and Dean, who can find nowhere to channel their surly individuality and sexual energy; the outright madmen of Mailer's "The White Negro" and Yates's *Revolutionary Road,* whose psychopathic gaze pierces the timid rationalizations of the "normal" world. As Humbert's sexual compulsion and lack of moral inhibition distantly connect him to the priapic Dean Moriarty, so *Lolita* is a send-up of the lyrical novel that, in a sense, parodied *On the Road* even before it appeared.

Both were transgressive works that in different ways challenged moral as well as fictional norms; both were rejected repeatedly by publishers, appearing in America only years after they were written. But where *On the Road* is an Emersonian celebration of anarchic personal freedom, turning its hero into a countercultural myth, *Lolita* masquerades as a case study in deviance and abnormal psychology, satirizing the roadside America that Kerouac effusively celebrates. For Kerouac, the road is a metaphor of movement, of breakthrough; through Humbert's European eyes, it stands for aimless flight, a feigned sense of "going places," an illusory progress through a phantasmagoric landscape of cultural kitsch and inward fixation. Nabokov's book is a tissue of ironies, a modernist hall of mirrors; Kerouac's is as innocent of irony as it is of any sense of evil. The young who would adopt *On the Road* as one of their canonical books were also the young who were mercilessly lampooned as teenage cretins and stealthy masturbators in Nabokov's novel.

Kerouac's America is a cartoon seen through the eyes of worshipful, sad, and sheltered observer; Nabokov's America is a cartoon of natural wonders, impoverished humanity, and purblind compulsion. "We had been every-where. We had really seen nothing. And I catch myself thinking today that our long journey had only defiled with a sinuous trail of slime the lovely, trustful, dreamy, enormous country that by then, in retrospect, was no more to us than a collection of dog-eared maps, ruined tour books, old tires, and her sobs in the night – every night, every night – the moment I feigned sleep."

From *The Catcher in the Rye* to *Portnoy's Complaint,* a favorite device of the lyrical novel is the psychiatric monologue, the confession of the unhappy outsider who, after a life of conflicts and confusions, finally lands on the couch. With its clever, well-defended hero and his made-up dreams, *Lolita* mocks the therapeutic language of 1950s analysis and criminology. It begins with a Swiftian mask, a burlesque preface by "John Ray, Jr., Ph. D." whose "scientific" and moralistic language and laughable air of authority are exploded by the passionate metaphorical language of the work itself, and by Humbert's brilliant mockery of those who try to explain him. A tongue-in-cheek work from start to finish, *Lolita,* unlike many of Nabokov's other novels, breaks through to real feeling in its portrayal of the schemes and sufferings that flow from Humbert's fixation – which a later generation might describe clinically as a form of incest and child abuse, as Lolita herself (and the obtuse Dr. Ray) already do.

Nabokov always believed that fiction was neither moral, social, nor psychological but a sensuous exercise in style that (as he says in his 1958 afterword to *Lolita*) leads to a state of "aesthetic bliss." His curmudgeonly essays and interviews deride social novelists like Balzac and Stendhal and ridicule Freudians as Viennese quacks who substitute cheap formulas for experience. John Ray is one such scientific charlatan, like the mad and meddlesome editor, Kinbote, in *Pale Fire,* yet Humbert, as his assumed name indicates, is something of a humbug himself, though both speak at moments for the elusive author. Despite their modernist tricks and games, however, Nabokov's stories, memoirs, and novels from the late forties to the midfifties are also his closest encounter with realism, his most open and direct works. (Compare them to his previous novel, *Bend Sinister* [1947], a clotted *1984*-ish allegory of totalitarianism.) In *Lolita,* faced with erotic obsession on the one hand and American vulgarity on the other, the writer transcends himself, escaping the airless world of some of his other novels to achieve a burning intensity in dealing with both love and the American landscape.

Lolita is a road novel but also an antinovel, a metafictional tissue of literary allusions (besides Poe, to literally dozens of writers) and parodic names (characters like Humbert Humbert, Harold Haze, and Miss Opposite; places like Lake Climax, Insomnia Lodge, or "the township of

Soda, pop. 1001") that belong to savage farce and undercut our reference to the "real" world. Nabokov's bent for caricature reminds us of satiric writers as different as Dickens, Sinclair Lewis, and Nathanael West, as well as his friend Mary McCarthy and his student Thomas Pynchon. His mixture of cruelty, disgust, and Flaubertian sense of outrage focuses rather than blurs his attention to detail. The author's peculiar blend of empathy and disdain for Humbert, his love-hate relationship with America, enable the book to escape his control and to become a uniquely fresh comment on American life.

From the very beginning, Humbert's monologue follows directly from the nostalgia and timelessness so central to *Speak, Memory*. A nymphet, as Humbert defines her, is a creature in whom time is suspended, "an enchanted island" between the ages of nine and fourteen "surrounded by a vast, misty sea." "Ah, leave me alone in my pubescent park, in my mossy garden," he says. "Let them play around me forever. Never grow up." In this respect, nymphets resemble mounted butterflies, or chess problems, or crossword puzzles – Nabokov created the first ones in Russian – or for that matter the past itself, perfect and unchanging. But Lolita, like any particular nymphet, does not quite fit this prototype, for not only will she soon turn into an ordinary woman, a bovine adult, losing her perilous magic, but her very nature is mixed, open to the immediate and the contingent. "What drives me insane," says Humbert, "is the twofold nature of this nymphet – of every nymphet, perhaps: this mixture in my Lolita of tender dreamy childishness and a kind of eerie vulgarity." Lolita is not only immature but, unlike her mother, with her French affectations, she is the complete product of American popular culture, the teenage consumer for whom the ads were written, the movies were filmed, the candy bars confected, the roadside attractions promoted. In enslaving himself to Lolita and escorting her forcibly across the country, Humbert, like other fifties runaways, is both escaping and discovering America.

Though Humbert is a haughty, fastidious émigré exuding a Frankfurt-style disdain for American popular culture, *Lolita* is no more a version of Henry James's international theme, as some early readers saw it, than of *On the Road*. Humbert's nefarious designs upon "the child," which include the dream of killing her mother and various schemes of how to drug and deflower her, point deceptively to a contrast between European decadence and American innocence. Instead, Lolita, already deflowered by a precocious 13-year-old at camp, playfully initiates *him,* in one of the novel's most tender and troubling scenes. "In my old-fashioned, old-world way, I, Jean-Jacques Humbert, had taken for granted, when I first met her, that she was as unravished as the stereotypical notion of the 'normal child,'" he writes in his posthumous brief. Instead she instructs him in a "game she and Charlie had played." With Humbert rather than Lolita as the protagonist, the novel gives us a satiric reverse angle view of the coming-of-age materials of Vidal, Capote, Jean Stafford, and Salinger.

As Humbert sums up his mock sexual initiation, "Suffice it to say that not a trace of modesty did I perceive in this beautiful hardly formed young girl whom modern co-education, juvenile mores, the campfire racket and so forth had utterly and hopelessly depraved. She saw the stark act merely as part of a youngster's furtive world, unknown to adults." Here, Humbert the European moralist allows himself to be shocked before giving way to Humbert the lover, who allows himself to be consumed by "the perilous magic of nymphets."

Both sexually and as a consumer, Lolita reflects the directions of the postwar youth culture, which Nabokov observed as an outsider who idealized his own very different childhood. When he was young, he tells us in *Speak, Memory,* even mutual masturbation was unthinkable and "the slums of sex were unknown to us," for all sex was airy romantic fantasy. As a young émigré writer in Berlin, Nabokov, like another displaced writer, Samuel Beckett, belonged to the first generation that fully assimilated the impact of Joycean word games, Proustian recollections, and Kafkaesque themes of entrapment and paranoia, all of which figure in the shaping of his novels. Beckett's self-exile was voluntary, but he, too, achieved a breakthrough by shifting to another tongue, freeing himself of the literary associations and daunting precursors of his native language. But where Beckett's fiction and drama move relentlessly toward a pared-down, timeless space, Nabokov's American novels develop into a comic dialogue between European modernism and a New World culture of consumerism, progressive education, youthful autonomy, fussy academic careerism, and small-town provincialism.

Nowhere is Nabokov's gift for ridicule (or penchant for disgust) more sharply etched than in his account of Humbert's cross-country travels with Lolita. Nathanael West in *Miss Lonelyhearts* and *The Day of the Locust* had uncovered a pathos, almost poignant, at the heart of America's cultural wasteland, but Humbert writes about America's roadside and motel culture like the proverbial visitor from Mars, astonished at the strange enormity of it all. Roadside America becomes the incongrous backdrop for his overheated passion and the raw material for his overcharged style. Like West he is a master of the grotesque, yet his account is also punctuated by Kerouac-like paeans to the "smooth amiable roads" that radiated "across the crazy quilt of forty-eight states" and to "the lyrical, epic, tragic but never Arcadian American wilds." He finds them "beautiful, heart-rendingly beautiful," with their "quality of wide-eyed, unsung, innocent surrender" that lacquered Swiss villages and the overpraised Alps no longer possess.

Despite such moments of celebration, *Lolita,* far from being a lyrical novel, turns in upon itself like Ellison's *Invisible Man,* to disappoint all its characters' hopes – indeed, in this case, to kill off the characters themselves. In the form of a criminal's confession, a pervert's guilty plea to judge and jury, the novel is actually a network of correspondences that reveal the all-powerful control of that playful artificer, the one Humbert calls "McFate," which in turn connects destiny with the manipulations of the author, whose own hands are never too far from the puppet strings. As Humbert's aimless travels with Lolita give way to his stalking of Clare Quilty, who has lured Lolita away from him, and as Humbert tracks down and farcically murders him, *Lolita* is transformed into a mock detective story full of hunters and hunted, crime and punishment. Were it not for Peter Sellers's nimble performance as the almost unkillable Quilty in Stanley Kubrick's 1963 film version, this darker second half of the novel would be far less remembered than it is today. Yet it brings home what we should feel from the start – that Humbert is both an unreliable narrator and a moral monster; there is the devil to pay for both the pleasures he stole from his 12-year-old mistress and for the laughs we enjoyed in the great comedy of seduction and betrayal.

Along with *Invisible Man, Lolita* foreshadows both the dark, scarbrous comedy of the novels of the sixties and the paranoid vision that makes them so intricate, so rich with menace. If black humor is comedy about the forbidden, comedy that negotiates moral boundaries and shatters taboos, *Lolita* epitomizes it. The work of Pynchon, Heller, Vonnegut, and Philip Roth can hardly be imagined without *Lolita*'s boldness, the uneasy mixture of comedy and horror in its perpetually unstable tone. Humbert's possessiveness and jealousy toward Lolita makes him her jailer as well as her adoring lover, but like so many later fictional characters – in Heller's *Something Happened* (1974), for example, another autobiography of a heel, or Pynchon's *Gravity's Rainbow* (1973) – he is also the slave of his own obscure compulsions, enjoying at best an illusory freedom.

In *Lolita* the road novel takes on an uproarious but troubling agenda and implodes. The youth culture of the fifties is at once idealized (in Humbert's infatuation with Lolita) and satirized (in the cultivated European's view of America). The lyrical novel of Emersonian self-assertion turns into the ironic novel of Kafkaesque entrapment and self-loathing confession, a transgressive work that remains genuinely shocking yet, in its playfulness, still somehow liberating. First read as a piece of sexual scandal, a glimpse of the author's own darkest impulses, the book has been transformed by academic readers into an elegant set of tricks and allusions, a postmodernist exercise in self-reflexive writing. What was lost was the novel's encounter with its own age, with an exploding popular culture, a rampant consumerism, and a rambunctious younger generation that represented both a new market and the rapidly changing sexual values of a prosperous, permissive liberal culture.

Lolita's mixture of seductive innocence and brash vulgarity was typical of the ambiguous outlook of the new culture, which would soon turn into the counterculture. American culture in the fifties was staid and repressive at the center, in its treatment of women, for example, or its range of political debate, but there was also a liberal idealism that survived from the New Deal and the war. This culture was also highly self-critical – pop sociology and psychology were virtual cottage industries – and alive with change at the margins. Not only were long-forbidden works soon to be published (*Lolita, Naked Lunch, Lady Chatterley's Lover, Tropic of Cancer, Tropic of Capricorn*) but much of the popular culture – from the seamy small-town setting of *Peyton Place* to the family melodramas of Douglas Sirk, such as *Written on the Wind* and *Imitation of Life* – took on a lurid, feverishly troubled cast. Where many today look back nostalgically at the fifties as a golden age, the filmmakers, writers, and social critics of the period saw trouble in paradise: anomie, conflict and tense uncertainty amid suburban prosperity. While some writers had used the road novel to declare their turn from the American mainstream, others invented a kind of anti–road novel to explore these tensions and uncertainties, to show how hard they might be to resolve. Two dark, ironic works, John Barth's *The End of the Road* (1958) and Richard Yates's *Revolutionary Road* (1961), offer a counterstatement to the kind of self-liberation celebrated by Kerouac, mythologized (soon afterward) by Ken Kesey, explored ambivalently by Updike and Cheever, and transformed into deviant or criminal passion by Mailer and Nabokov.

❦

Of all the practitioners of the first-person novel in the 1950s, few have a more distinctive or more astringent voice than John Barth. Born in Cambridge, Maryland, in 1930, Barth often returned to the Maryland shore as his intricately textured local world, his native ground, as O'Hara and Updike created a social microcosm out of the small towns and cities of Pennsylvania. But Barth's interest in society was much more limited than theirs. He was the most cerebral of novelists, building his plots less out of milieu than from an interrogation of the nature of fiction. If Nabokov turned the road novel into the anti–road novel, making the road a timeless locale of forbidden passion, Barth turned it into the antinovel, an experiment in the problem of fictional representation.

Barth's fastidious manner sometimes resembles Nabokov's, especially in his habit of dealing with sex in a tone of educated circumlocution. While remaining impeccably "literary," both writers echo the elevated diction of classic pornography, skillfully deploying an arch manner that titillates the reader yet eludes the censor, including the moral censor in the individual reader. But where the scheming Humbert Humbert is helplessly dominated by his obsessions, Barth's manipulative, coldly calculating heroes are more theoretical in their motives and hence more repugnant specimens of humanity. Once upon a time, Barth's protagonists played the game of emotional entanglement, the old drama of needs and relationships; later they learned to look beyond it, to use other people for their own purposes.

In Nabokov there is a plangent emotional core behind the satiric disgust and cultured rage. Barth uses the first-person narrator for the least lyrical aims imaginable, just as he plays with the confessional mode with scarcely any tincture of Freudianism. His heroes are either the typical innocents of picaresque fiction, such as Ebenezer Cooke in *The Sot-Weed Factor,* or hardened cynics who have turned their default of feeling into a bottomless nihilism. They can manipulate and even torment people, but essentially they are indifferent to them. *The End of the Road* is Barth's best novel because it beautifully explores the personal cost of such a failure of feeling. The novel wreaks vengeance on Barth's heartless hero as he wreaks havoc on everyone around him. It gives us a brilliant anatomy of this recurrent character type, whose philosophical indifference and detached, almost inhuman intellectuality preside over Barth's whole body of work.

Barth's early books come in pairs, but whether they are seemingly realistic novels like *The Floating Opera* (1956; revised 1967) and *The End of the Road* (1958), or mock-historical novels like *The Sot-Weed Factor* (1960; revised 1967) and *Giles Goat-Boy* (1966), or sequences of metafictional texts like *Lost in the Funhouse* (1968) and *Chimera* (1972), or even an epistolary novel synthesizing (or burlesquing) all the preceding works (*Letters,* 1979), their real subject is the nature of narrative. Barth is fascinated by earlier, more naïve forms of storytelling, such as the Greek myths, the *Arabian Nights,* or the picaresque novels of the eighteenth century, which take us "back to the original springs of narrative." He idealizes the storytelling past the way Nabokov cherishes the lost world of his own past. But his nostalgia for the mesmerizing qualities of these old stories, their power to induce belief, does not prevent him from deconstructing them into postmodern narratives, laying bare their stereotypical qualities. What draws him most is not the stories themselves but the framing devices that loosely link such collections as *The Thousand and One Nights, The Canterbury Tales,* and *The Decameron,* or the direct address to the reader that punctuates the picaresque novels, always reminding us that fiction is a constructed artifact. Todd Andrews, his narrator in *The Floating Opera,* tells us from the outset that he is no novelist. He jumps backward and forward in chronology, and his cold, witty tone, his analytical precision, so typical of Barth's protagonists, can read more like legal brief or an investigative report than a personal history.

"Storytelling isn't my cup of tea," he says, not simply because he cannot resist digression but because his mind-set, along with his clinical view of character and personality, is austerely factual and skeptical. He is reporting to us, almost twenty years after the fact, about a day in 1937 when he changed his mind, when he decided not to kill himself. But he also thinks, human behavior should always be logically defensible and organized around rational choice. "I tend, I'm afraid, to attribute to abstract ideas a life-or-death significance," he says. Yet life and death have repeatedly found ways of nullifying his conscious choices. He confesses that he has experienced a strong emotion only five times in his life – the specific number is typical of him – and each time he responded by completely altering his approach to the world, adopting a new "mask" and essentially becoming a different person. In each case, whether he behaves for years as a rake, an ascetic, or an utter cynic, he lives his life as a conscious project, first adopting a pose out of some unexpected burst of feeling, then rationalizing it in abstract terms like a man who pretends to know exactly why he does whatever he does.

These roles, even the role of the cynic, finally collapse for him, so he decides quite reasonably to commit suicide. But when he realizes that even suicide is a meaningless choice, that Hamlet's question has no answer, he decides (in good Dorothy Parker fashion) that he might as well live. From then on, he spends his time pursuing an elaborate *Inquiry* into his father's suicide, with little confidence that anyone can truly explain anything. Like the novel itself, this inquiry becomes a metaphor for the limits of knowledge. It thus comes to resemble David Hume's *Inquiry* in its skeptical account of causality. After years of reading and thinking, he decides that "there is no will-o'-the-wisp so elusive as the cause of any human act. . . . [A]s Hume pointed out, causation is never more than an inference."

Such an intellectualized view of behavior and motivation seems like very unpromising material for a novel; actually, it is a perfect recipe for the kind of antinovel or postmodern novel that Barth already anticipated in the 1950s, with its sense of a decentered self and its view of the world as a "mirror-maze" (as Barth would later call it in *Lost in the Funhouse*) in which everything is a representation. Like the picaresque writers of the eighteenth century, Barth gives us novels whose busy, involuted plots undermine their apparent realism, novels without any clear cause and effect: all action with little character development or psychological "depth." Barth's characters do not grow or change like those in Shakespeare's plays or in nineteenth-century novels. Instead, they simply alter their existential project, moving on to the next stage. Todd Andrews and Jacob Horner, Barth's first two heroes, are early examples of decentered selves, completely constructed personalities always defined by the masks they assume. Barth's early novels turn Sartrean existentialism into a form of intellectual play. It was Sartre who had pointed to the option of suicide as the ultimate source of man's freedom, Sartre who had insisted that existence precedes essence and people are defined by what they do, not by who they "are."

Barth turns this notion of an arbitrarily constructed, radically contingent self into a comedy of nihilism and a subversive exploration of the form of fiction. For a fabricated personality like Todd Andrews, life itself is an occasionally gorgeous but discontinuous spectacle that engages him only intermittently and ironically. His metaphor for this is the "floating opera," the showboat that moves up and down the river providing the audience on shore with no more than discontinuous glimpses of what is being performed on board. Born with the century in 1900, Todd gives us just such glimpses of his own life: his service in the trenches of World War I, his chronic heart and prostate conditions, his modest legal career, his father's suicide in 1930, his ascetic home life in a geriatric residence hotel, his long affair with the wife of a client and friend, and his efforts in court to salvage a large inheritance for his friend from the man's eccentric father. Except for his experience in the trenches, which first convinced him of the sheer animal meaninglessness of life, Todd describes every one of these experiences, especially his affair and his suicide plans, with cynical detachment, as if life itself were a game in which the actual moves mattered very little. His defective heart is a metaphor for his defective humanity, but also for the brute contingency of life itself. (He often reminds us he might die before finishing the chapter.)

Barth turns the melodramatic material of ordinary novels – paternal abandonment, wartime violence, courtroom strategy, an adulterous love triangle – into a *virtual* plot that highlights its own fictional nature. The more story we get – as in overstuffed later books such as *The Sot-Weed Factor* and *Giles Goat-Boy* – the more constructed it seems, giving substance to Todd's theory of behavior as a sequence of masks. Salinger and Kerouac were drawn to the antinomian qualities of picaresque fiction, its metaphors for escape, personal freedom, and irresponsibility, its shaggy-dog version of one man's progress. The casually constructed road novel, especially when written in the first person, establishes the claims of individual voice against the pressures of literary form as well as social convention. This sound of innocent outrage, with its wounded sincerity, is what eventually made *The Catcher in the Rye* and *On the Road* such canonical texts of sixties youth culture.

The lyrical novel turns sincerity into an instrument of social protest, but sincerity is the last thing we would expect in a Barth hero. Barth is drawn instead to the antiquarian aspects of the picaresque, its rogue hero, its sheer accumulation of detail, which takes him back to a period before romantic individualism grew dominant, and enables him to link the premodern to the postmodern. If the lyrical novel achieves authenticity by way of the personal voice, Barth parodies the first-person novel by telling his story in a voice so dry, so antiseptic in its illusionless clarity that it makes personality, psychology, and motivation seem like outworn remnants of nineteenth-century narrative.

But Barth's novels also capsize themselves and turn harshly against their protagonists. Despite his insistence that all behavior is a social mask, without a "real" self behind it, Todd Andrews finds himself periodically upstaged by his own emotions, from the wave of fear he feels in the trenches to the surge of self-disgust that finally propels him toward suicide. This is where *The End of the Road* – the "companion-piece" to *The Floating Opera* (both were written in 1955) – "completes the earlier novel and gives it a tragic dimension. *The End of the Road* is an inversion of the road novel, a reversal of its kinetic energy and movement; its hero, Jacob Horner, like his proverbial counterpart, is stuck in a corner, afflicted with complete immobility. The story is framed by his treatment at something called the Remobilization Farm, a curious send-up of the whole therapeutic and progressive culture of the fifties, which put its faith in personal improvement through socialization. At this farm, with its Progress and Advice Room, Horner is treated by a brilliant quack – one of the innumerable mad doctors of fifties fiction, like Dr. Benway in Burroughs's *Naked Lunch* – whose methods flow from the theory of masks of the preceding novel.

To this doctor, life is simply performance, motion rather than emotion, the challenge of playing a part as if you believed in it. What he calls Mythotherapy is a form of dramaturgy: stereotyped role playing that at least serves to get you moving. Like so many well-rewarded vendors of positive thinking in the 1950s, the doctor urges his patients to take charge of their own story. As Dean Moriarty in *On the Road* solved all personal problems simply by moving on, leaving friends, jobs, and lovers behind, Jake Horner, paralyzed by sheer immobility, is urged to become the protagonist of his own drama, to get a life, as if he were writing a novel or casting a play.

But the life that Jake Horner simulates has a devastating effect on other people, largely because he invests so little feeling or humanity in the roles he plays. *The End of the Road* gives a deeper cast to the most frivolous and satiric of all fifties genres, the academic novel. Like Todd Andrews, Horner has an affair with a friend's wife, but this leads not to the enlightened civilities of *The Floating Opera,* where all the parties pride themselves on being tolerant and open-minded, but to her miserable death on an abortionist's table. Andrews was frank about seeking sex "without falsifying it with any romance." "The truth is," he explains, "that while I knew very well what copulation is and feels like, I'd never understood personally what love is and feels like." Todd's detachment could be interpreted as fear or despair on the few occasions when he has ever experienced a genuine emotion, but the games he plays do not have much impact on anyone's lives. Jake's manipulations, on the other hand, destroy other people's lives and cripple his own.

Jake begins his course of mayhem by callously wounding an older woman he picks up at the beach, making his contempt for her all too clear and virtually forcing her to beg for sex, which he performs with barely contained ill will, even disgust. "It was embarrasing," he says, "because she abandoned herself completely to an elaborate mood that implied her own humiliation – and because my own mood was not complementary to hers." Besides, "I was always uneasy with women who took their sexual transports too seriously." In this kind of novel, as in the road novel, the woman generally becomes the victim, whether of male lust or male indifference, of male wanderlust or male conventionality.

Jake's destructive behavior with this woman prefigures his clinical detachment during his affair with his colleague's wife. Much as he tries to avoid any messy emotional entanglement, however, this is an attitude he cannot sustain. Finally stirred to action by his pregnant mistress's suicidal anguish, Jake frantically arranges for her to have an abortion. Following her gruesome death, he collapses into a terminal apathy that puts an abrupt end to his experiment in remobilization. Like Todd Andrews in *The Floating Opera,* he has been unable to play a single "role" consistently, giving way instead to "irrational flashes of conscience and cruelty, of compassion and cynicism." Like Andrews, too, he is undermined by bursts of spontaneous humanity that his theory denies. But such moments of compunction only worsen the damage he has already done through cynicism and indifference. If the road novel uses movement as a metaphor for freedom, *The End of the Road* shows how movement alone, without a moral or emotional compass, leads to a dead end, to paralysis, to Jake Horner's dark corner. By the end he is a full-time patient, like Holden Caulfield, with nothing to do but tell his story. As he takes leave of that story, his final word to the cab driver, "Terminal," nicely catches the ambiguity of the fate. He can go to the station to catch the train, even rejoin his mad doctor, but he has nowhere to go. His case is terminal.

The paradoxes of identity and movement also provided the material for Barth's experimental short fiction in the 1960s. The stories in *Lost in the Funhouse* are all comic turns on going nowhere, on being caught between an unmediated "reality" that is no longer available, at least to this writer, and various forms of role playing or fictional representation that will be quickly paralyzed by self-consciousness. The title story, "Lost in the Funhouse," is one of several that never quite gets told; it is interwoven with a pedantic handbook on fictional technique. Ambrose and his family are off on an excursion to "the funhouse," the hall of mirrors of all representation. But the narrator's infernal dithering, his fondness for cliché, and his acute awareness of narrative choice constantly retard the narration, preventing any suspension of disbelief and reducing the story to mere words. This was a game Laurence Sterne played long ago in *The Life and Opinions of Tristram Shandy,* backtracking and digressing to make us wonder whether his hero would ever manage to get born.

Barth's often cogent comments on fictional technique point up the fact that he was one of our first writers to study in a creative writing program – there were only two in the United States when he enrolled at Johns Hopkins University in 1947 – and one of the first to make his living as a full-time professor of creative writing, initially at Pennsylvania State University, where he taught English from 1953 to 1965, then in Buffalo, New York, until 1973, when he finally went back to Johns Hopkins. His excess of concern about fictional form, his nostalgia for a period when storytelling was a simpler matter, bespeak a certain professorial relation to the study of fiction. "Plot and theme: notions vitiated by this hour of the world but as yet not successfully succeeded" ("Title"). But the influence of Beckett has overlaid the example of Sterne: "The final question is, Can nothing be made meaningful. . . . And I think. What now. Everything's been said already, over and over; I'm as sick of this as you are; there's nothing to say. Say nothing." (Think of Beckett's "you must go on, I can't go on, I'll go on.") In *Lost in the Funhouse* and *Chimera* Barth's genial narrators soon grow as heartily sick of this self-consciousness as we do. He even tells us that his wife and adolescent daughters "preferred life to literature and read fiction when at all for entertainment. Their kind of story (his too, really) would begin if not once upon a time at least with arresting circumstance, bold character, trenchant action."

In these short texts, the problems posed by fictional technique lead to the same paralysis that beset the heroes of his first two "realistic" novels; there, too, self-consciousness and emotional distance had entrapped his characters and kept them from really living their lives. Barth's nostalgia for storytelling is a nostalgia for more spontaneous living, and his obsession with fictional technique becomes a metaphor for an arrested emotional life, for a shyness or coldness that inhibits his characters from making real contact with other people. "I was cursed," Jake Horner said, "with an imagination too fertile to be of any use in predicting my fellow human beings: no matter how intimate my knowledge of them, I was always able to imagine and justify contradictory reactions from them to almost anything." Horner's problem in writing the script of his life becomes Barth's problem in writing a story while feeling swamped by an excess of possibility. At one point in *The Floating Opera* Barth's hero, methodical as ever, perfectly in character, actually advances the plot by drawing up a two-page list of all the ways the action might develop.

Barth's protagonist is a figure who recurs in postwar fiction: the intellectual whose springs of feeling have dried up, whose whole existence is a simulation of living, a series of abstract choices. In this social masquerade, reminiscent of Melville's *Confidence Man* or Gaddis's *The Recognitions* (one of the secretly influential texts of postwar fiction), Barth's writing becomes "Another story about a writer writing a story! Another regressus in infinitum!" – which seems to weary him as much as the reader. Barth is a forerunner of postmodernism, not simply in his formal experiments but in portraying an inevitable loss of affect within a culture in which all the stories have already been told, the plot gambits tried, the forms exhausted from repeated use. His longer books are as removed from spontaneous storytelling as his characters are cut off from spontaneous interaction. They become no more than "novels imitating the form of the Novel, by a writer who impersonates the role of the Author." Barth thus anticipates the French theorists for whom the so-called author became simply a formal construct, the "author function," a convenience of literary discussion.

❦

There could hardly be a writer more different from Barth than Richard Yates. At a time when the realist aesthetic was waning, or simply migrating from literature into film and television, Yates emerged as one of the last of the scrupulous social realists. As other members of the World War II generation – Mailer, Styron, Heller, even James Jones – shifted toward history, apocalyptic fantasy, myth, and black humor – Yates emerged as the faithful chronicler of the lives of his contemporaries. His characters were men who fought in the war but were not war heroes, who married too young, had children too young, and were swallowed up by the suburbs and the large corporations. Born in 1926, Yates was a prep-school boy who saw infantry service in World War II; he was the archetype of the aspiring writer who spent the postwar years in journalism or on Madison Avenue dreaming of writing the great American novel. Remarkably, he came close to doing it. His finely crafted stories, eventually collected in *Eleven Kinds of Loneliness* (1962), drew critical admiration all through the fifties, but with *Revolutionary Road* in 1961, Yates wrote the definitive history of a part of his generation.

The popular version of Yates's story had already been told by William H. Whyte in *The Organization Man* (1956) and in novels like Sloan Wilson's best-selling *Man in the Gray Flannel Suit* (1955). *Revolutionary Road* rewrites Sloan Wilson's novel as tragedy, as it also gives us a perfect mirror image of *On the Road*. In Yates's novel the title is wholly ironic: the road that beckons becomes the road not taken. The book tells the story of the would-be rebel, the imagined free spirit, who never leaves home, never quits his job – the man who, more typically than Sal Paradise, seeks his pastoral utopia not in the American West but in the suburban towns of Connecticut. Like *The End of the Road,* it ends catastrophically with a botched abortion – this one is self-inflicted – and it leaves the novel's male protagonist, Frank Wheeler, as little more than a ghost of himself.

The young suburban couple we meet at the beginning of the novel, Frank and April Wheeler, despite the buoyant lilt of their names, are already people with diminished expectations. After rebelling against his virile, defeated father, Frank had eventually joined the same IBM-like corporation. He had lived most intensely as a soldier, as an undergraduate intellectual at Columbia University, and as a Greenwich Village bohemian after the war. There his affair with April had first begun. Now he feels the smoldering discontent of many prematurely sober young professionals of the 1950s. April, once a drama student, now a mother of two – Revolutionary Road is their suburban address – remains the keeper of what is left of Frank's artistic hopes, which soon crystallize in a quixotic plan to sell the house, leave the job, and move the family to France, where he can fulfill his youthful dream of becoming an artist. (Her own talents, of course, have long since been subsumed in his, almost as an extension of her motherhood.)

As this possibility arises, Frank, for one brief moment, is exhilarated, but unconsciously he is appalled. He has no real desire to live out his old fantasy, or to take up the freedom to be poor and creative (rather than comfortable and stultified). Soon April is pregnant again and he manipulates her into carrying the child while he himself carries on a little affair in the city. "Paris" is Frank's road, his dream of escape, but this is a road novel in reverse, with the hero secretly unwilling to go anywhere, except to the next rung of the corporate ladder. For Frank, bohemianism is the pipe dream still cherished by his wife, since it made him the man who first attracted her; she is the keeper of his earlier self, with which he has secretly lost faith. Unable to be frank with anyone, not even himself, Frank mouths glib clichés attacking conformity, adjustment, security, and togetherness, those familiar staples of fifties social criticism. Meanwhile, he maneuvers his wife into a suburban domesticity that shields him from his own sense of diminished horizons.

In *The Man in the Gray Flannel Suit,* Sloan Wilson finesses these conflicts and lets his hero, Tom Rath, have it both ways. He is a war hero with few regrets about the blood he spilled; indeed, the war and the romance that came with it provided the only real excitement of his life. He discovers that he has an understanding wife who encourages him to support the child he had by his Italian mistress. Soon it turns out that he even has a sympathetic corporate mentor who treats him as a surrogate son and allows him to turn down the rat-race job he himself had once pressed on him. Tom is also helped by a benign Jewish judge who enables him to inherit his grandmother's property and turn it into suburban housing. In short, the novel takes up the problem of the organization man and resolves it through wish fulfillment. "I don't think I'm the kind of guy who should try to be a big executive," he tells his boss, who has damaged his own life by choosing the same options. "I'll say it frankly: I don't think I have the willingness to make the sacrifices." Tom can have it all: can take responsibility for his wartime past, support his mistress but also rekindle his marriage. By just saying no, he can keep his job yet preserve his integrity and his family life – all by an act of personal choice. With a timely theme yet also a happy ending, the novel – and the film version starring Gregory Peck – became immensely popular.

Connecticut real estate also figures significantly in *Revolutionary Road,* beginning with the title, but it offers no easy solution to Frank Wheeler's problems. Like Tom Rath, he is nostalgic for the desperate excitement, fear, and romance of the war years, which his wife imagines they can recapture as twenties-style expatriates in Paris. During the war, he tells her, "I just felt this terrific sense of life. I felt full of blood." Now he wants to recapture that feeling, to break out of the cellophane bag that envelops his life. This could have been anyone's story in the 1950s: suburbia, family life, the corporate ladder, the loss of brave possibility once glimpsed in the war. It is too archetypal, too fraught with generational significance. But Yates adds a daring touch that transforms the novel. Through their real estate agent, Helen Givings, the town busybody, the Wheelers are exposed to a schizophrenic young man, her son, who eventually strips away their lies and self-deceptions and triggers the disaster that befalls them.

If *Revolutionary Road* impresses us with its verisimilitude and social realism, John Givings seems like a mutant, a strange interloper from a novel by Céline, Burroughs, or Kerouac. He is brilliantly mad: grievously damaged but lucid, dysfunctional but clairvoyant. A one-time mathematician whose face and memory have been scarred by too many electroshock treatments, he is the tragic demon the suburbs are designed to repress, the bad news no one welcomes in this pastoral utopia. His chirrupy mother, a master of denial, is adept at papering over cracks, looking at the bright side of everything; his stolid, impassive father deals with her by turning off his hearing aid. Mrs. Givings, who sells the Wheelers their house and then sells it again after April's death, is the very spirit of the suburbs in her obtuse and meddlesome cheerfulness, like a character from one of John Cheever's more sardonic stories:

The Revolutionary Hill Estates had not been designed to accommodate a tragedy. Even at night, as if on purpose, the development had no looming shadows and no gaunt silhouettes. It was invincibly cheerful.

After the Wheelers have departed, she is indignant that they failed to keep the house up, and prefers the "*really* congenial people" who have taken their place.

But while they were there, she sensed their difference – their tolerance and vulnerability – and so guessed that she could take the risk of initiating them into her private tragedy: the institutionalized son whose condition, we soon understand, reflects strains in the "normal" family that produced him. The young man first adopts Frank and April as surrogate parents, identifies with their planned escape to Europe, but turns on them brutally when they back out. As he sees it, April's new pregnancy, which binds them to Connecticut, can only spawn an unloved, unhappy child like himself. He alone in the novel sees through Frank's cowardice and manipulation, but he makes Frank's wife see through him as well. "You got cold feet, or what?" he says to Frank. "I wouldn't be surprised if you knocked her up on purpose, just so you could spend the rest of your life hiding behind that maternity dress." To April he says, "you must give him a pretty bad time, if making babies is the only way he can prove he's got a pair of balls."

Givings's role as madman and truth teller is so audacious that it ought to shatter the economy of the novel. Instead it shows us how much even realist fiction has changed since the start of the decade. The mad seer is really a figure from the Laingian counterculture of the sixties – who belongs to novels like Ken Kesey's *One Flew Over the Cuckoo's Nest* (1962) – not from the sober and sensible 1950s. Yet Salinger, Nabokov, Barth, and even Cheever had focused on characters who break down out of emotional turmoil, and Kerouac had portrayed Neal Cassady as an inspired madman, a kind of saint or "Holy Goof" who, like the egregious Randall McMurphy in Kesey's book, helps liberate his more timid friends. So Yates prophetically imports Givings into the Wheelers' life as a return of the repressed, a perverse product of suburban optimism, and a distorting mirror that reflects back the compromises and denials that enabled the Wheelers to construct their little world.

Givings has had shock treatments to short-circuit his emotional conflicts, but the therapy also obliterated his mathematical gift. "It's awful for anybody to forget something they want to remember," April tells him. But her husband, by his dishonesty, has also muffled his feelings and talents, emptying himself out all on his own. From the beginning she had collaborated "by telling easy, agreeable lies of her own, until each was saying what the other most wanted to hear." The truth was that at bottom, behind the self-deceptions, he was simply ordinary, not the stifled artist he imagined. Her self-induced abortion is a gesture of harsh honesty that she turns on herself.

In the end Yates's message was not very different from Salinger's or Kerouac's. The world of Revolutionary Road, like Cheever's Shady Hill, stands for the life Holden Caulfield mocks for its phoniness, the world the Beats left behind, the premature home-and-family trap Updike's Rabbit tries hard to escape. Frank and April Wheeler are another version of the bright, well-meaning young liberal couple whose good intentions get rough treatment in so many postwar fictions, from Trilling's *Middle of the Journey* to Barth's novels, from Cheever's stories to the cycle of marriage stories Updike collected in *Too Far to Go*. But with John Givings, *Revolutionary Road* crosses the WASP novel of manners and personal relationships with the Beat novel of spiritual accusation and salvation, to frame perhaps the most comprehensive indictment of the whole decade. For Yates, the corporate jobs and garden suburbs that crystallize the American dream are also the bland settings in which America has lost its memory and misplaced its adventurous, risk-taking soul.

To many historians, the fifties were an era of prosperity and tranquility – an island of stability in a century of violent change – but the novelists, filmmakers, and social critics of the period saw it differently. They looked at youthful rebellion and dysfunctional marriage as evidence of deep social malaise. With the spread of xenophobia and McCarthyism, the pervasive anxieties connected with the Cold War and atomic weapons, such fears were very close to the surface. Critics also saw a timid conformity, even a spiritual poverty, at the heart of America's prosperous economy and spectacular growth, with its emphasis on home and family and its conservative view of women's roles. When Frank Wheeler tries to convince his wife that she is emotionally disturbed, even unnatural, for not wanting to bear his next child, he is substituting a kitsch Freudian language of mental health for the patriarchal authority he resented in his father; the effect is the same. At the end he is merely an empty shell, like Barth's and Nabokov's hero-villains.

From Salinger and Ellison to Yates, the best writers of the fifties identified with the outsider, not with a dominant culture they found hollow and oppressive. They saw rebellion, neurosis, and madness as forms of lucidity, and portrayed adjustment and sanity as symptoms of deadly compromise. In her great story "A Good Man Is Hard to Find," Flannery O'Connor could even identify with the Misfit, an escaped and demented criminal, as a violent bearer of unpleasant truths to foolish people. Where O'Connor traffics comically in mass murder, other writers use failed abortion, tormented youth, or the death of children (as in *Rabbit, Run* or Joseph Heller's *Something Happened*) as an indication of social failure and loss of humanity.

Never did so triumphant a period produce such a mass of angry criticism, which accelerated toward the end of the decade with Beat writers like Kerouac and Ginsberg; mordant novelists such as Nabokov, Barth, and Yates; and the trenchant social commentary in C. Wright Mills's *The Power Elite* (1956), Galbraith's *The Affluent Society* (1958), Mailer's *Advertisements for Myself* (1959), and Paul Goodman's *Growing Up Absurd* (1960), which was itself a critical synthesis of the new youth culture. Even in the political realm, the winds of change were finally stirring. The end of the Korean War and the death of Stalin in 1953 led to the first of a series of thaws and détentes with the Soviet Union that softened the atmosphere of intolerance at home. With such works as Arthur Miller's *The Crucible* (1953) and Don Siegel's *Invasion of the Body Snatchers* (1956), liberals struck back at McCarthyism, and McCarthy himself was censured and effectively destroyed by his fellow senators in 1954. He died in an alcoholic haze in 1957, an embarrassment even to his diehard supporters.

Soon cracks began appearing in the blacklist, but also in the moral blacklist that barred any frank treatment of sexuality in books and films. Nabokov, D. H. Lawrence, Burroughs, and Henry Miller became hot new authors, though their books had been written, suppressed, and published elsewhere years earlier. The Supreme Court's unanimous 1954 decision in *Brown v. Board of Education of Topeka* took the nation on its first halting steps toward desegregation and racial equality, and in the late 1950s, the young civil rights movement under Martin Luther King, Jr., turned to direct action with bus boycotts and lunch-counter sit-ins in Southern towns and cities.

In the 1958 midterm elections, an eager class of young liberals were elected to Congress, where the Democrats controlled both houses by almost two-to-one margins. By 1960, John F. Kennedy could mobilize the widespread discontent of the late fifties into a political campaign that stressed youth, energy, change, and, in its final moments, social justice for black Americans. A child of privilege, the son of a political fixer, and raised in an increasingly right-wing Catholic family, the young candidate ironically inherited the mantle of expectations created by Brando and Mailer, James Dean, and Jack Kerouac – in short, by all the angry, wounded, mysterious, and sexually charged young men of the 1950s. Soon, by the narrowest of margins, the political outsider was president and a new era would begin, burnished by a stirring rhetoric of social responsibility, a turbulent decade of confrontation and social change for which the critical culture of the fifties had helped pave the way.

4

❦

APOCALYPSE NOW: A LITERATURE
OF EXTREMES

Historian E. J. Hobsbawm has described the twentieth century as the age of extremes. In a strange way, no quarter of the century had to grapple with extremity, or its terrible aftermath, more than the seemingly tranquil decades after the Second World War, which some Americans still look back on as a golden age. Though the war had spared the North American continent, its effects were brought home as Americans emerged from their traditional isolation. Besides coming to terms with the general carnage on an unheard of scale, and moving rapidly toward the reconstruction of Europe and Asia, the postwar world had to assimilate the most shocking news of the war, perhaps of the century as a whole: the details of Holocaust and the effects of the atomic bomb. The Holocaust and the bomb do not often explicitly appear in the literature of the forties and fifties, perhaps because writers found them too large to encompass and too remote from their direct experience. Despite this eerie silence, they contributed to an undercurrent of anxiety that was freely reflected not only in poems and novels but in the popular culture, including horror films, science fiction, and the new vogue of ghoulish comic books that alarmed the moralists and psychologists of the period. Along with peace and prosperity came a heightening of anxiety and insecurity.

Ordinary Americans, insulated from immediate knowledge of the worst horrors of the war, recoiled after 1945 into an island of normalcy, a world of getting and spending, as they had done after the First World War. There was an emphasis on family and domesticity, on traditional gender roles, and on a new culture of consumption made possible by rapid economic growth. The war industries retooled to produce consumer goods, beginning with new homes and cars. But the impact of the bomb, the Holocaust, and the mass destruction caused by the war was widely felt, along with other changes that were transforming the world at midcentury: the spread of Communism to eastern Europe and China and its strong influence in western Europe, the rise of other forms of totalitarian and military dictatorship, the new bipolar world created by the Cold War and the fear of nuclear annihilation, the elaboration of the welfare state, the constantly increasing effects of technology on daily life – from new weapons systems and new domestic appliances to new forms of instant communication – the dismantling of outright colonialism and its replacement by subtler forms of economic and cultural domination, the major upheavals in race relations – first in America, then in western Europe – and a gradual resurgence of nationalism and religious conflict in areas previously attached to the former empires.

It is perhaps too easy to see the arc of the century, from 1914 to the 1990s, beginning and ending in Sarajevo, a city of varied inhabitants – Serbs, Moslems, Jews – that would come to symbolize the murderous ferocity of ethnic hatreds. The "ethnic cleansing" of the former Yugoslavia was part of a vicious process of fratricide and displacement that ran through much of the century. It is certainly no exaggeration to take the religious violence and the uprooting of whole populations on the Indian subcontinent in the late forties as a prologue to the second half of the century, which would be marked by lethal struggles between Jews and Arabs, Greeks and Turks, Asians and Americans, Irish Catholics and protestants, Bosnian Christians and Moslems, Hutus and Tutsis, black and white Americans.

Though writers must stay close to what they know, the American novel at its best reflected the pressure of these fears, hatreds, and passions. The neglected American masterpieces rediscovered and reinterpreted at mid-century – the works of Melville, Hawthorne, Whitman, Emerson, Thoreau, and Emily Dickinson – themselves compose a literature of extremes, as do the modern classics that gained a wider readership in the postwar years: the dark fables of Kafka and Beckett, the encyclopedic social canvases of Joyce and Proust, the inquiries into the heart of darkness in Conrad and Thomas Mann, or into the mainsprings of sexuality in Lawrence and Freud. The influence of existentialism and crisis theology worked against earlier traditions of American optimism. Emerson, Whitman, and the pragmatists looked dated and naïve to many American intellectuals after the war; the tragic vision of Melville and Hawthorne, Kafka and Dostoyevsky seemed more in tune with a world gone amok.

Very few American writers were equal to these challenges, but even fewer remained wholly unmoved by them. The travail of uprooted people in their futile attempt to find a place for themselves can be traced in stories as different as Nabokov's "Signs and Symbols" (1948), about an old émigré couple whose misery is reflected in their brilliant and demented son; Flannery O'Connor's "The Displaced Person" (1954), which savagely portrays the insularity of a Southern community through the fate of one refugee family; and Bernard Malamud's "The German Refugee" (1963), a story of maladjustment that ends in suicide. Modernist writers like Joyce made exile a metaphor for their sense of estrangment from ordinary life; later writers like Vladimir Nabokov and I. B. Singer dealt with the literal effects of exile and dislocation. By the end of the century, the upsurge in immigration would lead to a large hyphenated literature of cultural displacement.

It would be easy to put too much emphasis on the obvious fault lines within postwar American literature: between the cautious small-scale novelists and poets of the fifties and the more apocalyptic writers of the sixties; between the writers who applied a Jamesian irony to social issues and those who took on more metaphysical themes with an Emersonian expansiveness; between WASP authors who wrote about America in homogeneous or regional terms and the new ethnic and homosexual writers who helped decenter American literature in line with a shifting population and changing social values. In the long run, the more complacent and conservative writers of the period have been forgotten; they were looking back nostalgically to a vanishing way of life. It would be futile to resurrect the legion of genteel *New Yorker* fiction writers and humorists of the forties and fifties except as documents of their class and times. Those who are still read, like John Cheever, S. J. Perelman, or Jean Stafford, make deeper claims. By the sixties, the well-made story or poem, the well-bred novel of manners, came to seem irretrievably dated. What survived best from the fifties had an undertone of hysteria, as in the desperate pathos, the sense of entrapment in Saul Bellow's *Seize the Day,* the fecundity of imagination in Ellison's *Invisible Man,* the mournful sense of fear or loss in Malamud's *The Assistant* and *The Magic Barrel,* a riveting confessional authenticity of the kind that burns in James Baldwin's early essays, or the exaggerated, often futile assertion of freedom, as in the road novels discussed in the previous chapter.

It is hardly an accident that many of these writers were black or Jewish, for race and ethnicity had situated them on painful ground, the point of contact between the social marginality of the group and the psychological stress of constructing one's identity as an individual. ("It was enough to make a man pray to God to remove his great bone-breaking burden of selfhood," thinks Bellow's Herzog.) At a time when more Americans then ever were becoming middle class, the humble, even despised origins of these writers gave them a classic American story to tell: the tale of the outsider straining to get in, the divided soul struggling to come together, but someone who has a privileged view of the society not as a seamless whole but as an arena of conflict and difference. For the ethnic writer this was best expressed not by an omniscient narrator and a smooth linear fiction but by explosive parables (as in Malamud and Baldwin), constantly shifting styles (in the work of Mailer and Ellison), and emotional extremes reflected in unstable characters and equally unstable mixtures of comedy, tragedy, and pathos (see Bellow's *Herzog,* for example, or virtually any of the sixties black humorists). Unless these writers were eaten up by their anger, as Baldwin was in his later work, it mattered little whether they were creatively inspired by the eruptions of the sixties, as were Philip Roth, Norman Mailer, and even John Updike, or condemned them root and branch, as did Saul Bellow in *Mr. Sammler's Planet* (1970). Bellow's sweeping moral censure was as apocalyptic as Mailer's ambivalent celebrations of sexual and political excess.

Because of the underlying continuity of postwar culture, it no longer feels useful to contrast the best writers of the fifties with those who flourished in the sixties. Often they were the same people, moving restlessly from one style to another. Despite some striking changes after the mid-fifties, the quarter of a century after the war seems more like a single sweep of time. Beneath the surface calm of the fifties we can now feel the seismic rumblings of discontent; it was the cosseted children of the fifties, the children of social mobility, suburban affluence, progressive education, and Cold War anxiety, who became the shock troops of the civil rights movement, the antiwar protests, the campus uprisings, and the sexual revolution. Some, like Philip Roth, would later recall the postwar years as a time of innocence, Edenic and uncorrupted, but this was not how the best writers experienced them at the time. The sense of metaphysical irony in a work like *Invisible Man* foreshadows the apocalyptic mood of the fiction of the 1960s. There is a despairing innocence about Salinger's *Catcher in the Rye* that feels very different from Philip Roth's deliberate, even cartoonish outrageousness in *Portnoy's Complaint.* Yet both are therapeutic monologues, wounded confessions full of anguished protest; both are good-boy's books, fundamentally moral, at bottom rather childlike, as eager to please and ingratiate as to complain. Many of the lesser writers of the fifties were abnormally mature, cautious in their limited goals, grown up before their time, and they were heavily criticized even then for their timidity. Among the writers whose work still matters, the quest for a presocial innocence, the quest for absolution, unites writers of the fifties and sixties in their focus on harsh subjects and extreme states of mind.

Other links emerge clearly as we look at the whole period between 1945 and 1970, as the preceding pages show. The reliance on realistic technique connects most of the war novelists of the forties to the naturalists of the thirties. But there are also moments of riveting absurdity or keen political insight in *The Naked and the Dead* or *From Here to Eternity* that looked forward to the war novels of the sixties. Mailer's dark revolutionary novel, *Barbary Shore* (1951), and his fascinating Hollywood novel, *The Deer Park* (1955), develop connections between politics and sexuality that are obscure but remarkably prescient, anticipating the Nietzschean or apocalyptic turn of sixties culture. The gay and bisexual writers of the late forties, such as Tennessee Williams and Paul Bowles, seem especially prophetic of the transgressive literature that began with Burroughs and the Beats and became a major element of the literary culture of the sixties. Ellison's *Invisible Man* not only anticipated the black humor and black nationalism of the sixties but developed notions of cultural identity that would make a new impact in the debates over diversity and multicultural-ism in the 1980s and 1990s. Even aside from traditional literary forms, the fifties and early sixties saw a major boom in social criticism as the widely read work of David Riesman, Hannah Arendt, Vance Packard, John Kenneth Galbraith, William H. Whyte, and Betty Friedan gave way to the psychosexual speculations of Herbert Marcuse, Norman O. Brown, and Paul Goodman. Relentless self-criticism, not complacency, was the real key to postwar culture.

MAILER: THE FIFTIES AND AFTER

Among the literary figures who gained fame before the fifties ended, the most prophetic, most attuned to the cultural eruptions soon to come was Norman Mailer, followed closely by Ellison, Baldwin, Bellow, Nabokov, Roth, and Updike. If the postwar literature of extremity can be said to have crystalized in a single work, it would be Mailer's feverish essay "The White Negro" (1957), with strong competition from Allen Ginsberg's dithyrambic manifesto *Howl,* published the previous year. As *Howl* focuses on the madness that was an undercurrent of the enforced sanity of the fifties – the same demon that haunts works as different as *The Catcher in the Rye* and Robert Lowell's *Life Studies* (1959) – "The White Negro" explores the sources of that insanity through the figure of the hipster – the cool, murderous misfit who incarnates it. Like Ellison and Baldwin before him, Mailer understood that race, not class, would become a major metaphor of social identity in the postwar years. By turning the Negro into a psycho-sexual metaphor for the hipster, however, Mailer ran the risk of distorting the actuality of race in America, which was already fraught with half-acknowledged sexual myths and fantasies.

Among the sources of Mailer's existential portrait, he insists, were the pervasive threat of the bomb and the unbearable knowledge of the death camps, which nearly all American writers, even the Jews, had managed to avoid confronting. What the war in Europe and Asia had revealed about human nature, the more bland American culture of the fifties had some-how managed to suppress. The hipster had taken this knowledge upon himself, not suicidally, not as illness (like Carl Solomon, the subject of *Howl*), but as a Nietzschean challenge to live dangerously. The hipster, by his example – and Mailer, by his writing – tempts us to go beyond the strict limits of middle-class life, to explore the existential risk of sex and violence as both our damnation and our salvation.

Where other writers saw the genocidal cruelties of the war as a blinding revelation of the human potentiality for evil, a confirmation of original sin, Mailer saw them as a leap into the irrational, a challenge to the bland lies of civilization, the compromises and adjustments of middle-class life in the 1950s. For him the Holocaust and the bomb are not pointers toward the moral abyss so much as they are prototypes of the modern form of collective death, death by technology, that robbed death of all personal meaning or heroism. Mailer himself, like Philip Roth, grew up as the beloved young prince of a middle-class Jewish family. He had an incubus of respectability that he needed to shake off. Though he got his literary education at Harvard, not in prison, "The White Negro" was his manifesto as a moral explorer in the tradition of outlaw writers like de Sade and Genet, or writer-adventurers like Hemingway and Malraux.

Mailer's first three books had been written when "the novel" still existed in its traditional form, as an arena of huge ambition for young writers. The passion for film that developed in the sixties and seventies was still fixed upon prose fiction in the years after the war. Despite its absurdist touches, *The Naked and the Dead* had essentially been a conventional novel, grounded in the prewar naturalism of Farrell and Dos Passos. Mailer had planned the novel as a student at Harvard; its literariness clashed with its vivid sensory intelligence. But no American writer since Melville had made such a sharp turn away from his initial success. *Barbary Shore,* Mailer's Marxist political allegory, and *The Deer Park,* his brilliantly sordid Hollywood novel, pleased neither the critics nor the public, though they were important steps in his gradual transformation from a writer concerned with social themes to a cultural radical exploring a new psychosexual terrain.

The Deer Park begins as a novel in the prewar tradition of Hollywood gothic – the mode of Nathanael West and Fitzgerald; it portrays Hollywood as a swamp of moral corruption dominated by tyrannical studio chiefs, personified by the egregious Herman Teppis, a Louis B. Mayer–like figure, and his son-in-law Collie Munshin. Before long, the blacklist becomes a key theme. Mailer's protagonist, a longtime director named Charles Eitel (pronounced "I tell"), at first refuses to cooperate with the congressional committee, but then makes his peace and returns to work, only to find that his talent has been dissipated in moral compromise. If this were all that happened in *The Deer Park,* Mailer would have remained true to the thirties-style anti-Fascism of *The Naked and the Dead* and the book would resemble other novels and plays of the fifties attacking the blacklist. As it proceeds, however, and as Mailer revised it from its original conception, it focuses much more on the sexual complications of its characters than on their political wrongdoing. Eitel's reluctant decision to name names and his consequent return to work at the studio not only undermine him morally and politically but damage him as a lover and an artist – Mailer insists on these parallels.

Eitel's love affair with Elena Esposito (a character loosely based on Mailer's wife at the time, Adele Morales) had enabled him to retreat from politics, to give up the world and concentrate on his creative work. When he falls into the smooth professionalism of the studio hack, he becomes as coolly calculating in love as in his writing. This is not only Mailer's verdict on Hollywood, it is his view of the compromises of the 1950s, the morally fatal concessions of middle age, and the sinister ease of the well-oiled literary career, the safe commercial path Mailer himself had been unable or unwilling to follow.

At Mailer's novel is not content with telling the story of Eitel and Elena. In the final version of *The Deer Park*, two other figures struggle to emerge: a Nick Carraway–like narrator, Sergius O'Shaugnessy, who served as Mailer's surrogate in several works in the 1950s, and Marion Faye, Mailer's first portrait of the hipster, a psychopathic moral adventurer who tests the limits of experience by killing all compassion in himself. A study in sexual ambiguity, a pimp who, much like the studio bosses, crystallizes the stew of corruption that intrigues Mailer in Hollywood – a world in which sex, work, and people themselves are constantly bought and sold – Marion signals Mailer's own shifting interest from a politics of altruism and compassion to a psychopathology of human nature. "The White Negro" would become Mailer's hypnotic commentary on his portrait of Marion Faye, the remarkable creature whom he had introduced but not really integrated into *The Deer Park*. (Later, he would try again by adapting the novel into a play.)

In his conception of Sergius O'Shaugnessy, the other character grafted onto *The Deer Park*, Mailer tried to create another kind of moral outlaw, the handsome, swaggering fake Irishman who is the author's inverted tribute to his own Jewish origins. At one time, Mailer projected Sergius as the hero of a huge eight-part novel, a modern *comédie humaine,* but *The Deer Park* and a few pieces of fiction in *Advertisements for Myself,* including Mailer's two best stories, "The Man Who Studied Yoga" and "The Time of Her Time," are all that remain from this grandiose plan. Sergius is an off-stage presence in "The Man Who Studied Yoga," which Mailer intended as the prologue to the eight novels. He figures as Cassius O'Shaugnessy, psychopath and sinner, political adventurer and avant-garde writer between the wars, who later enters a monastery.

"The Man Who Studied Yoga," like *The Deer Park,* is about the compromises of middle age, the onset of tepid sex, tepid politics, and tepid art which Mailer identifies with the gray atmosphere of the early 1950s. Sam Slovoda, the protagonist, is Mailer's Rabbit, his version of what he himself might have become had he settled unprotestingly into the groove of middle-class marriage and routine work. But a Dr. Sergius also is mentioned as Sam's shrink, the very oracle of the kind of psychic adjustment Mailer detests about the liberal, therapeutic culture of the period.

Written in 1952, the story is unlike any other fiction Mailer published. In its deliberately flat, musing manner, it reads like the solemn, half-satirical fables about intellectuals that we find in Delmore Schwartz's best book, *The World Is a Wedding* (1948), or the fiction Saul Bellow began writing with his first novel, *Dangling Man* (1944). What distinguishes Sam from Mailer's other protagonists is his lack of distinction, the matter-of-factness of his whole being. He is neither ordinary nor extraordinary, young nor old, tall nor short. Once he dreamed of becoming a great novelist, but now he's writing continuity for comic strips. Once he belonged to the Party, dreamed of redeeming suffering humanity, but that too is little more than a memory. He has some sense of himself as a great lover, but in the story this devolves into an evening with old friends watching a crudely made porno film, then making love to his wife after the friends depart. In his passivity, Sam even feels he is psychically a Jew, though he is only one-quarter Jewish. In short, Sam is everything the Mailer of the fifties is trying to escape yet fears he essentially *is.* As Mailer later described it in *The Armies of the Night,* among his many selves was "a fatal taint" of "the one personality he found absolutely insupportable – the nice Jewish boy from Brooklyn. Something in his adenoids gave it away – he had the softness of a man early accustomed to mother-love."

To Mailer during this period, psychoanalysis was simply another version of the dance of adjustment that had long enabled Jews to survive but had become for him an unbearable form of capitulation. It reeks of the caution that had destroyed the previous literary generation. "Defeated by war, prosperity, and conformity," he wrote in *Advertisements for Myself,* "the best of our elders are deadened into thinking machines, and the worst are broken scolds who parrot a plain housewife's practical sense of the mediocre – worn-out middle-class bores of the psychoanalytical persuasion who worship the cheats of moderation, compromise, committee and indecision, or even worse, turn to respect the past." He says of his own World War II generation, on the other hand: "The past did not exist for us. We had to write our way out into the unspoken territories of sex – there was so much there, it was new, and the life of our talent depended upon going into the borderland."

The same animus against psychoanalysis colors "The White Negro." Mailer writes of his hipster hero: "The psychopath is ordinately ambitious, too ambitious ever to trade his warped brilliant conception of his possible victories in life for the grim if peaceful attrition of the analyst's couch." A few lines later, in the essay's most notorious passage, Mailer eulogizes the courage, if not the therapeutic value, of two 18-year-old hoodlums who murder a candy-store owner. He does not mention that the storekeeper, like the psychoanalyst, is likely to be Jewish, representing a rejected part of his own identity. (Mailer's maternal grandfather kept a grocery in Long Branch, New Jersey, besides being the town's unofficial rabbi. The writer himself was born there in 1923.)

This was hardly the first time Mailer identified with the perpetrators rather than the victims of violence. His secret fascination with sex, power, violence, and irrationality was an undercurrent in his first three novels, beginning with the characters of Croft and Cummings in *The Naked and the Dead,* but with "The White Negro," it emerged in a wholly new style as the major direction of his work. The essay, which makes painful reading today, followed the critical and commercial failure of *Barbary Shore* and his long effort to complete and publish *The Deer Park,* but it also came out of other stresses: his struggles with pot and Seconal, with the new Beat phenomenon that changed the course of his work, with his own Jewishness, with writer's block, with the exigencies of conventional literary form, and with the gray cultural climate of the 1950s. For too many reasons this period was not a happy one for Mailer; his obsession with violence became his way of defying and exorcising it.

The famous *Partisan Review* symposium on "Our Country and Our Culture" in 1952 has often been seen as a turning point, marking the postwar reconciliation between the once-alienated writer and American society. Mailer's contribution, however, was an angry, dissenting one:

This period smacks of healthy manifestoes. Everywhere the American writer is being dunned to become healthy, to grow up, to accept the American reality, to integrate himself, to eschew disease, to revalue institutions. Is there nothing to remind us that the writer does not need to be integrated into his society, and often works best in opposition to it?

Between 1952 and 1957, Mailer turned from this stereotyped rhetoric of alienation to a more radical resistance that synthesized all the countercultural themes of the 1950s. He evolved the self-promoting, self-lacerating confessional stance that would carry him through the next decade and a half. In place of the "healthy manifestoes" that accepted the American reality, "The White Negro" is a deliberately *un*healthy manifesto in the surrealist tradition, a feverish text that sings the praises of criminality as an antidote to totalitarianism and (like the surrealist manifestoes) rarely bothers to distinguish lurid metaphor from literal prescription. Mailer's proclaimed goal is "to encourage the psychopath in oneself," "to try to live the infantile fantasy," and always to seek "an orgasm more apocalyptic than the one which preceded it."

Some of the essay is simply Reichian boilerplate. As the outlaw analyst expelled by Freud, who put so much stock in the healthy release of sexual energy, and who finally died in a federal prison, Wilhelm Reich was a major influence on dissident writers in the fifties and sixties. Some of Mailer's language is recycled from the antinomian tradition that runs through Blake, Nietzsche, D. H. Lawrence, and the Beats, a language of energy against reason, movement over stasis, physical intensity over civilized reflection, self-expression over repression. Some of it – the portrait of the Negro as the violent, jazz-soaked primitive, the fumbling vocabulary of Hip – is simply embarrassing, a primitivist myth left over from prewar modernism. Yet for all its overheated rhetoric and dubious moral outlook, it marks not only a new phase of Mailer's career but also a momentous shift in American literary culture, a turn toward the dark side, the rebellious and the demonic. Renouncing the Apollonian program of postwar society, Mailer also turns away from conventional literary form, toward a prose that mingles fact and fiction, social criticism and confession, cultural prophecy and personal therapy.

᷈

Already in *The Deer Park,* Mailer seemed at odds with fiction as a literary medium. Though the minor characters (Teppis, Munshin) and the Palm Springs setting come through wonderfully, all the major male characters – Eitel, Faye, O'Shaugnessy – were projections of Mailer himself or his developing ideas; the pimp Marion Faye, the book's devil figure, animates two or three scenes brilliantly, but only Eitel and Esposito are fully realized characters. (The second half of the novel breaks down under the weight of Mailer's ideas, anticipating his search for greater immediacy in discursive writing.) Mailer's next book would not be a novel but a collage assembled out of the blockage of his career as a novelist. The sinews of *Advertisements for Myself* – the confessional prose that knits the book together – came from "The White Negro," which had been published separately two years earlier. The remarkable persona that Mailer shaped for this book, the figure of the risk-taking yet disaster-prone moral adventurer, the maladroit, ambivalent existential hero, dominates his next novel, *An American Dream* (1965), as well as the great first-person journalism that would soon make him one of America's most influential writers. The sixties would redeem for Mailer what the previous decade had nearly destroyed.

After turning away from early success as a conventional novelist, Mailer found that he worked best in a jam: when he was feeling pressed for money, in despair about his reputation, blocked as a writer, or out of touch with his audience and his times. *Advertisements* was the prototype for how he turned his losses into strengths, his sense of failure, neglect, or misunderstanding into cultural meaning. One model for the book was undoubtedly "The Crack-Up," Fitzgerald's three *Esquire* essays of 1936 around which Edmund Wilson had built a posthumous collection in 1945. The thirties had been a bad decade for Fitzgerald in much the same way the fifties were for Mailer; Fitzgerald too had tried to recoup his losses by way of confession, which appalled many of his friends, including Hemingway. "I'd started off with the idea of a collection of stories and articles," Mailer recalled in 1985, "but discovered that my collection would have no meaning unless I threw in a lot of the worst pieces. Because where I had failed often offered the most interesting revelations." Subtly, apology gave way to self-projection. "Unconsciously I was trying to take inventory. I was trying also to end a certain part of my literary life and begin anew. I wanted to declare myself, put myself on stage firmly and forever."

Mailer had long been searching for a hero, dogged by the Hemingway view that heroism was at best elusive in the modern world, that heroes were now the sum of their damages. In *Advertisements,* amid the wreckage of his hopes, he found himself as his own flawed but exemplary protagonist. Mailer was scarcely the only one to look to the self in search of cultural meaning. James Baldwin had already probed his own experience in his deeply introspective reports on race in America, which marked a major shift from the naturalistic approach of many earlier black writers. His essays, first collected in *Notes of a Native Son* (1955), had staked out new territory for the fiction writer. Robert Lowell, partly inspired (like Mailer) by the Beats, made a parallel turn toward the confessional in the poetry and prose brought together in *Life Studies* (1959). This shift was not well grasped by their many imitators, since both Lowell and Mailer had an almost Augustan sense of decorum, a high degree of self-consciousness, and a mordant, civilized wit that were hardly duplicated by those who followed them along the confessional path. Mary McCarthy was another novelist who had strayed into autobiography and published essays and memoirs almost indistinguishable from her fiction. Together, McCarthy,

Baldwin, and Mailer did much to erode the lines dividing the novel from the essay. Together they helped make the essay a major literary form, first by importing fictional techniques, then by rescuing the essay from the whimsical voice of the eccentric gentleman – the wayward musings of an E. B. White still writing in the tone of Charles Lamb – and infusing it with a sense of personal immediacy and social crisis. Out of this was born the New Journalism, the quintessential literary form of the eruptive 1960s.

Mailer's gift was to match his own problems with his intuitive sense of the moment. *Advertisements* was put together at a time when the sexual discretions of the fifties were breaking up; the book's most celebrated and reviled story, "The Time of Her Time," was one of the most daring pieces of erotic writing of the decade. Sergius O'Shaugnessy would personify Mailer's role playing in the fifties, much as the character called Mailer (in *The Armies of the Night* [1968]) or Aquarius (in *Of a Fire on the Moon* [1971]) would personify it in the sixties. In "The Time of Her Time," the shy narrator of *The Deer Park*, traumatized by war and (also in the Hemingway mold) wounded in his sexuality, would be transfigured into the Irish stud who would wield his "avenger" to ignite the sexuality of Denise Gondelman, a bohemian Jewish princess.

Nothing brought Mailer more grief from such later feminists as Kate Millett than this curious story of sexual conquest. Like Stephen Rojack subduing his late wife's German maid in *An American Dream,* Sergius humbles and excites Denise by attacking her from behind. Yet he sees himself as an infinitely generous lover, determined to give pleasure – and to reap the psychological rewards of that pleasure – even by way of pain and humiliation. He has the vanity as well as generosity of the saint, he tells us. "I was the messiah of the one-night stand, and so I rarely acted like a pig in bed, I wasn't greedy." Though he is fired by his "rage to achieve" and his need to "lay waste to her little independence," he is less a sexist than a sexual utopian, eager to lead a recalcitrant, domineering woman to the promised land of orgasm, eager for "those telepathic waves of longing" that would surely accrue to him over the years "because I had been her psychic bridegroom."

Where Denise's Jewish analyst and passive Jewish boyfriend have failed, Sergius will succeed, pushing her excitement over the edge at the crucial moment by calling her a "dirty little Jew." His only fear is that "some bearded Negro cat" would get there before him, "would score where I had missed and thus cuckold me in spirit." At the end, Mailer, at least as giving as his hero, allows Denise to turn the tables on Sergius by calling him a "phallic narcissist" and repressed homosexual. But this neat reversal hardly diminishes the author's identification with his character. Coming together in this story are Mailer the fantasy fascist – the scourge of milk-fed Jews, assertive women, and intellectuals who chat about T. S. Eliot – and Mailer the sexual metaphysician, who evolves an exquisitely complex style to gauge the most minute vibrations of sexual power and energy that pass between people. This emphasis on sex as an arena of power eventually earned Mailer the hatred of many feminists, yet it also became an ax they would wield in their own analysis of the relations between the sexes.

Advertisements for Myself salvaged Mailer's career by turning him into a cultural figure, another prophet of the orgasm, substituting the author and his Napoleonic ambitions for the conventional novels he could not write, novels that were no longer anyone's royal route to fame. The winds had shifted from a literary culture to a media culture, a celebrity culture in which Mailer would thrive as much as Byron or Hemingway did in their own time. Mailer's career as a New Journalist appropriately began with a landmark report on the 1960 convention that nominated John F. Kennedy, the essay in which Mailer surprisingly turned the telegenic young senator into the hipster hero whose advent was announced in "The White Negro." Mailer might not have known of Kennedy's sexual adventures, but he was drawn to the candidate's youth, vitality, and energy, his seeming emancipation from the liberal catchphrases Mailer had often mocked. He saw the sentimental candidacy of Adlai Stevenson, ignited by Eugene McCarthy's eloquent nominating speech, as the last gasp of the old, tired, puritanical liberalism. Kennedy's, on the other hand, was a liberalism of power and realism, an image-oriented liberalism that played into Mailer's Carlylean quest for heroes, his great-man theory of history.

Writing about the public world for *Esquire,* Mailer had a new career before him, a wider field for his personal metaphysics. With Kennedy, Mailer sensed that the drab political atmosphere of the fifties was a thing of the past, that the dynamics of the Democratic and Republican parties could become as interesting as the dynamics of the sexual underground. Mailer picked up where another keen observer of political conventions, H. L. Mencken, one of the granddaddies of the New Journalism, had left off. It turned out to be a very close election; Mailer was both pleased and shocked by the influence of his piece, which "had more effect than any other single work of mine," or so he wrote in his second collection of essays, *The Presidential Papers* (1963), published just weeks before the assassination. He discovered a new power in writing a kind of fiction about real people, something not to be found in fiction as he had known it. "I was bending reality like a field of space to curve the time I wished to create."

Kennedy was elected, and Mailer enrolled (in his own mind, at least) as court wit, jester, and advisor to the new president, determined to save him from "intellectual malnutrition." But the self-destructive furies of the

1950s caught up with Mailer, and almost terminated his new career before it began. Soon after Kennedy was elected, Mailer stabbed and nearly killed his second wife, Adele Morales, after a disastrous party meant to launch his candidacy for mayor of New York. "My pride is that I can explore areas of experience that other men are afraid of," he told the court. "Your recent history indicates that you cannot distinguish fiction from reality," responded the judge, who committed him to Bellevue for psychiatric observation.

The stabbing, which seemed like a page out of "The White Negro," proved to be an exorcism that marked the end of a bad period for Mailer. Though he continued to explore the dark side of the psyche in his next major piece of journalism, "Ten Thousand Words a Minute" (1962), an *Esquire* account of the first Sonny Liston–Floyd Patterson boxing match, and especially in *An American Dream,* he soon emerged less as the scrapper than as the distinguished gentleman of American letters, a writer who would carve his own niche by sheer intelligence and self-projection, outside accepted literary categories. Above all, through his uncanny instinct for the Zeitgeist, he would be able to connect with the turmoil of the sixties as he had not been in tune with America since the years right after the war. The existential self-creation he had projected onto Sergius and admired in Kennedy would flourish in a period of personal and political theater, which looked to the self as an Emersonian field of creative possibility.

Mailer's first boxing piece set the pattern of his work of the next decade, which would prove to be the peak of his career. In *Advertisements* he had written freely of himself for the first time, shaping a personal legend out of the loose ends of his occasional writing. In "Ten Thousand Words a Minute" he becomes a novelistic character, the protagonist of a larger public story. When the bad boy of boxing, Sonny Liston, knocked out Floyd Patterson in the first round of their title bout, reporters were left with a nonevent as unpalatable as it was insubstantial. Mailer shapes his immensely long piece as an attack on journalism, with its "excessive respect for power" and its failure to find the truth amid "a veritable factology of detail." He shifts the dramatic center of the piece from the Liston–Patterson match, which ended almost before it began, to a stunning account of an earlier bout in which welterweight Emile Griffith killed Benny Paret in one of the most horrific displays of ferocity in boxing history:

Paret died on his feet. As he took those eighteen punches something happened to everyone who was in psychic range of the event. Some part of his death reached out to us. One felt it hover in the air. . . . He went down more slowly than any fighter had ever gone down, he went down like a large ship which turns on end and slides second by second into its grave. As he went down, the sound of Griffith's punches echoed in the mind like a heavy ax in the distance chopping into a wet log.

There is an almost unbearable dream logic to these slow-motion images, which interpret the event even as they visualize it; there is an almost feral intelligence on display here. Mailer's subject is never simply the event itself but its psychic resonance, brought home to us through arresting, indelible metaphor. This account leads Mailer into a defense of boxing as a reflection of some primitive "religion of blood, a murderous and sensitive religion which mocks the effort of the understanding to approach it." Nowhere is Mailer closer to Ernest Hemingway and D. H. Lawrence than in his portrayal of boxing as an existential encounter with violence and death; nowhere do bad ideas inspire such electric writing.

For the Liston–Patterson match itself, however, Mailer takes a different literary tack. He concentrates on his own antics as he tried to give a press conference afterward, then offered to promote a rematch, and even tried to pick a fight with Sonny Liston. This is the reader's first encounter with Mailer as inept scene stealer, the buffoon with grandiose ideas who tries to project himself into the center of the event. This is the Mailer of infinite bravado and questionable judgment, who achieves in his prose what he could not bring off in real life. The Hemingway–Lawrence Mailer would shortly write *An American Dream* in eight monthly installments for *Esquire.* But the buffoonish Mailer would soon reappear, with spectacular effect, when, after many setbacks, he would find a way to step back from his own legend. He would create himself in the third person as a comic character swept up by history in *The Armies of the Night,* his best book, and in *Miami and the Siege of Chicago,* his best piece of convention reportage, both published in 1968 as the conflicts of the sixties came to a boil.

Just as "The White Negro" and *Advertisements* developed out of *The Deer Park, An American Dream* is closely linked to *The Presidential Papers,* and especially the Kennedy essays. In Mailer's view, the writer, the politician, the hipster, and the boxer are all (at their best) adventurers, self makers on a quest into the unknown. Unlike the reporter, who is "close to the action" but "not *of* the action," who is inhibited "by a hundred censors, most of them inside himself," and "learns to write what he does not naturally believe," the real writer "discovers something he did not know he knew in the act itself of writing." In line with this faith in self-discovery, Mailer evolved a prose of Carlylean complexity, a cumulative, periodic style designed to convey a sense of risk, the sense of a mind in motion as it examines the world from every angle. The serial composition of *An American Dream* added another element of contingency to the book's Dostoyevskyan pretensions. Stephen Rojack is fictionally tied to Jack Kennedy – they were both war heroes and entered Congress together – but where Rojack turned to explore the dark side, to pursue his "secret frightened romance with the phases of the moon," Kennedy remained the kind of rational liberal Mailer himself had once been, the political actor whose personality is built over a void. Rojack and *An American Dream* become bold (or foolhardy) vehicles for Mailer's pulp fantasies about murder, espionage, and the spidery tentacles of wealth and power in America.

No book of Mailer's divided critics as violently as *An American Dream.* Those who expected a realistic novel with credible, rounded characters and a well-structured plot were angry and disappointed. Mailer had stabbed his own wife only a few years earlier, and now he was indulging himself in a shapeless tale of "crime without punishment" that begins with a man strangling his wife. But *An American Dream* was written under the influence of Burroughs and Céline, not Farrell and Dos Passos. (Mailer was testifying for Burroughs in an obscenity trial over *Naked Lunch* as he was writing his book.) *An American Dream* is more a nightmare, a hallucination, than a realistic novel. It projects the mood of Mailer's "mad" period of the late fifties onto the public hubris of the Kennedy era, when America pumped up its imperial pretensions and, in a high-stakes confrontation over Soviet missiles in Cuba, came chillingly close to nuclear war. *An American Dream* is the nightmarish underside of Camelot, a twilight zone girded by Mafia connections and CIA plots, by a paranoia that sees a web of evil behind every event.

In personal terms *An American Dream* is also a book about the sour feelings of middle age; Mailer had just turned forty when he began writing it. Like Sergius in "The Time of Her Time," Rojack is haunted by the men he killed during the war, by the darker side of his own heroism. He is lacerated by a core of violence in his soul, which he exorcises in the course of the book, and he passes through murder, sexual aggression, megalomania, and madness to emerge "something like sane again" in the final lines.

Ever since the heyday of gothic novelists and Romantic poets, the emblematic image of the dark side, of what we sometimes call lunacy, has always been the moon. Behind *An American Dream* is a residue of the Greek myth of Endymion, the shepherd who falls in love with the moon. Rojack kills a wife who represents every kind of human rot; he is drawn instead to the moon in constant suicidal tests of irrational male daring. But by challenging himself, by walking close to the edge in every way, by walking a parapet thirty floors above a city street, he expels his demons and becomes a new man, or so at least we are meant to believe. This theme of personal transformation is exactly what Mailer would pursue again in *The Armies of the Night,* but as comedy and history rather than pulp fantasy. The Mailer of *An American Dream* plots out a Dostoyevskyan idea of spiritual renewal using the noir techniques of Jim Thompson, James M. Cain, and Mickey

Spillane. *Armies* would transfer the same idea into a larger public arena, linking the 1960s, with comic-epic extravagance, to the figure of a recalcitrant, unheroic, middle-aged Mailer.

❧

We would have to look back to Byron to find a precedent for the comic turn Mailer takes with his own long-cultivated legend in *The Armies of the Night*. Like Byron when he wrote *Don Juan*, Mailer was already a known quantity, not entirely respectable, a "semi-distinguished and semi-notorious author," as renowned for his disorderly life, truculent temper, and naked ambition as for his literary achievements. A sense of scandal attached to both men, who had pursued fame, as Hemingway did, by nurturing a personal myth and becoming a public character. Now, however, like Byron in *Don Juan*, Mailer steps back from the ego and its metaphysics, examining his own legend with a poised urbanity that freshens and restores it. Byron's *Don Juan* is perfectly modern in being a poem largely about itself: its structural principle is digression; its form allows the writer to include anything that crosses his mind. This is true for *Armies* as well, but with a difference: here the antihero, the old lion who has already fought his battles, who is long beyond his angry radicalism and grown attached to his comfortable life, must answer the call of the historical moment, the 1967 Pentagon march protesting the Vietnam War. *Armies* is not just about Mailer but about the sixties with "Mailer" as protagonist. Written in the third person, like *The Education of Henry Adams*, *Armies* is also a very American book, steeped in millennial patriotism but also in the self's hunger to kidnap history and become its agent.

As in the Liston essay, Mailer begins by attacking conventional journalism – in this case, *Time* magazine's account of his loutish behavior – for exploiting his notoriety while distorting what really happened. As Lowell had done in his latest poetry, Mailer sounds the confessional note, full of small, seemingly trivial details, making the reader his intimate collaborator, almost his co-conspirator. He fabricates personal drama out of his unwillingness to get involved at all, and makes gossip of his jealousy of other writers at the march, including Lowell and Paul Goodman. This is Mailer's old self-indulgence in its most relaxed, conversational form. Situating himself at some distance from the event, he stresses his distaste for both the middle-aged radicals who have organized it and the young rebels and hippies, so different from him, whose spirit shapes it; they somehow seem to be carrying history in their bones. Mailer had been an ideologue of sex, a theorist of Hip, but these are kids who "conceived of lust as no more than the gymnasium of love." As far as the older radicals, the pacifists, "Mailer could feel no sense of belonging to any of these people. They were much too nice and much too principled for him." To Mailer, "the modest everyday fellow of his daily round was servant to a wild man in himself," an exigent brute perhaps responsible for the worst and best in his work, the Mr. Hyde he had no wish to kill off.

If "The White Negro" and *An American Dream* give us the psychopathology of the brute, *The Armies of the Night* and the last forty pages of *Miami and the Siege of Chicago* celebrate the emergence of a more Apollonian Mailer, reasonable but newly courageous, dignified yet as protean as ever. The middle-aged Mailer, now more Burkean than Marxist, a "left conservative" who holds onto his sense of sin, is redeemed from inertia by the younger generation he had scorned at the end of his report on the 1960 convention, the Puritans and defeated idealists who made a last stand for Adlai Stevenson. In both the Pentagon and Chicago pieces, the old war novelist inspects his ragged troops and, to his own satisfaction at least, leads them into battle.

With *In Cold Blood* (1966), Truman Capote had made much of writing a "nonfiction novel," but he had kept himself out of the picture and confined his story to a single crime. It was the ultimate *New Yorker* article, vivid yet coolly detached, exquisitely calibrated in tone and detail. Tom Wolfe and other magazine journalists had been using fictional techniques to great effect in evoking the carnivalesque uproar of sixties culture. But only Mailer, conflating fiction, journalism, and autobiography, had made himself the protagonist of the story, filtering history through the prism of his own ambivalence and harnessing the whole decade to his own comically refurbished legend. By stepping back from "Mailer," setting him in a larger public world, the author, like Henry Adams, projected his personal quirks into a dialogue with America at one of its defining moments.

In the journalistic works that followed *Armies,* including *Miami and the Siege of Chicago, Of a Fire on the Moon* (on the astronauts and their moon landings), and *The Prisoner of Sex* (on the new feminism), Mailer tried time and again to renew this exchange between the perceiving self and the national destiny, with gradually diminishing results. His prose sang, but beginning with the moon book, his real involvement waned. Mailer's persona, with his Emersonian ambitions – the initial hesitations, unflagging intelligence, and predictable heroism – began to grow tired, predictable, like a trick worked up once too often. With *The Fight* (1975), a pedestrian account of the George Foreman – Muhammad Ali match in Zaire, the personal anchor faltered definitively, though Mailer could still summon up sharp memories of the fight for a documentary film twenty years later. By the midseventies, though, American culture itself had grown less interesting. Its public life offered no characters of the size of the Kennedys, King, or Malcolm X, the martyred figures of the sixties. Instead Mailer, always drawn to personal myth and mystery, began to channel much of his energy from journalism into biography – first with such literary predecessors as D. H. Lawrence and Henry Miller in *The Prisoner of Sex,* then with full-scale portraits of Marilyn Monroe (1973), Gary Gilmore (1979), Lee Harvey Oswald (1994), Pablo Picasso (1995), and, most surprisingly, Jesus Christ (1997). By and large, these books were more workmanlike than inspired, the product of Mailer the professional writer rather than the driven artist. The first three used materials assembled by an entrepreneurial researcher, Lawrence Schiller; the Monroe and Picasso books were criticized for their undue reliance on the work of other biographers. All were highly readable, ambitiously explanatory, but in some degree derivative, written to make money yet elaborating at too great a length on old Mailer obsessions, which sometimes obstructed our view of the subject.

The great exception was the longest of them all, the Gilmore book, *The Executioner's Song,* the most untypical of Mailer's masterpieces, a book that meets *In Cold Blood* on its own flat Midwestern ground. Where Capote's book was limited by its *New Yorker*-ish detachment, its blandly even tone, which belied Capote's almost excessive involvement with his subjects, Mailer's book was clearly saturated with Mailer's own themes, though they never break into the narrative. Mailer had been fascinated by men like Gary Gilmore from the beginning, psychopathic killers who are not Hip but who *are* unstable containers of a violence that could erupt at any moment. On the surface, *The Executioner's Song* is as objective and impersonal as Mailer's previous books had been steeped in ego, or scored with pet ideas coming down from "The White Negro." Described as a "true life novel," the book pursues the greatest challenge of any novel: the writer's empathetic identification with people very different from himself. With his silly accents and strange fictional masks, Mailer had always tried to be everything but what he was. "Mailer" the literary character and Sergius the fake Irishman were the opposite of "the nice Jewish boy from Brooklyn," yet they let loose a torrent of Jewish introspection and ambivalence, a riot of self-analysis that enabled him to recoup in prose what had eluded him in dealing with people. But in the Gilmore book Mailer really sets himself aside, not by assuming a mask but by feeling his way into the mind of this character, the other, as he had rarely done since *The Naked and the Dead.* "I'm not as interesting to myself as I used to be," he told an interviewer in 1981.

To do this he develops yet another style: quick declarative sentences, short paragraphs, the prose equivalent of documentary filmmaking yet free of the careless megalomania that ruins the films he actually made. Mailer's closest approach to Gary Gilmore had come, oddly, in his book on the astronauts, for there too he was extending himself to take in another America, the middle American world of the Faustian WASP, untouched by inwardness and self-doubt, insulated by scientific know-how and emotional cliché – the square, patriotic, ramrod American that Tom Wolfe would capture very well in *The Right Stuff* (1978). Gary Gilmore had anything but astronauts' commanding confidence, but he was the ominous underside of the same flat Midwestern landscape, the misfit and loser who eventually fired back the violence that had been pounded into him as a child.

Whatever fantasies Mailer had once spun around the violent criminal as existential hero are redeemed by this harrowing account of the nine months between Gilmore's release from prison in April 1976 and his execution for murder – the act that restored capital punishment in the United States – in January 1977. During this time he became an unguided missile seeking out a target, a lethal weapon simply bound to explode. Mailer creates Gilmore, his girlfriend Nicole Baker, and dozens of other characters by immersing us in a steady accumulation of details as he had submerged himself in thousands of pages of interviews, letters, and court documents. "I came to know him better than almost anyone in my life," Mailer later told an interviewer. "I began to see that he was a man easily as complex as myself."

The book is a collage of viewpoints told from within, that Mailer carefully shapes without intruding himself. With a colorless prose accented by an occasional touch of slang, Mailer looks for clues to how these people think, how they look at the world. Perhaps there is something mannered about the way the story is told from inside the minds of people below the literary horizon, free of the authorial commentary that might dispel their mystery. Despite its thousand-page length, the book has an affinity with the spare blue-collar minimalism of such lockjawed writers as Raymond Carver and Joan Didion; their work, like Mailer's earliest fiction, is ultimately rooted in the stark, unpolished writing and broad social sympathy typical of the Depression years.

Like those Depression writers, Mailer sees Gilmore as the product and victim of all the forces that created him. Mailer's old belief in personal freedom gives way here to a brooding sense of how the unvaried landscape, Mormon culture, and dysfunctional families resonate in people's lives without fully explaining their behavior. The book reverts to a less formulaic version of the determinism that shaped the characters in *The Naked and the Dead,* where each of them was simply emblematic of his background, and the whole mix was America. Some of the life goes out of the book halfway through when Gilmore has been captured, tried, and sen-

tenced, but until then Mailer recreates a real piece of American life, frightening in its blind unreasoning force, prophetic of the explosive white violence and frustration that would later haunt the nation. This white male
anger would show itself in the renewed popularity of capital punishment,
the bitter battles over gun control, and the festering growth of right-wing
militias that culminated in the bloody bombing of the Alfred P. Murrah
Federal Building in Oklahoma City in 1995.

MALAMUD AND BELLOW: THE JEW AS PARIAH

Mailer's brief foray into environmental determinism, his exploration of a
grim Utah landscape of gas stations and convenience stores and ex-cons,
makes *The Executioner's Song* one of his most "American" books, even more
than *An American Dream* and *The Armies of the Night*. With its impressive
qualities of realistic observation, the book shows that Mailer might have
become our Zola rather than a restless reincarnation of Hemingway. But it
also links Mailer to such Jewish writers as Malamud and Bellow, who have
very little of his belief in personal freedom, who pride themselves in being
moralists and humanists and dark ironists of the human condition. For
Mailer the Holocaust and the bomb were horrors because they nullified
personal heroism and individual destiny. For Malamud and Bellow the
Holocaust is an extreme example of mankind's inhumanity, confirming the
sense of entrapment that Jews had always understood and tried to evade.

After 1945, very few American writers thought they could make much
sense of history. They focused instead on small epiphanies in private lives;
this was the only reality they felt they knew. But from his portrayal of
Cummings and Croft in 1948 to his work as a participatory journalist of
the late 1960s, Mailer, the Orson Welles of American literature, creates
hugely egocentric characters who try to meet history on their own terms.
Malamud's work is exactly the opposite. His "hero" is an Americanized
version of the schlemiel figure out of Yiddish literature and Jewish
humor, darkened by an implicit knowledge of how the Jews were
uprooted, tormented, and murdered during the war. Malamud's subject is
the ironies of character and fate, which few can evade, and the occasionally redemptive nature of suffering, which sometimes allows us moral victories in spite of worldly defeats. If Mailer was the lyrical writer who
emerges defiantly from the repressive culture of the 1950s, Malamud was
the doleful, ironic writer who retrieved some dark humor out of two
thousand years of Jewish persecution.

Born in Brooklyn in 1914, almost a decade earlier than Mailer,
Malamud was shaped by the economic struggle of the Depression rather

than by Harvard and the war. The small shopkeeper's world of *The Assistant* (1957), his best novel, was a poetic transposition of where he grew up; it turns his father's store into a harsh, isolated dramatic setting for the whole human condition. For Malamud, people are locked in by the unalterable past, by economic necessity, by the jocular ironies of fate, and by the inexorable weight of their own character. The fate of Morris Bober in *The Assistant* is to suffer, as the fate of his young helper, Frank Alpine, is to assume gradually the moral burden of that suffering, to redeem himself from a life of drifting and petty crime by becoming a Jew. To Frank, Jews are "born prisoners," people who shut themselves up "in an overgrown coffin" of self-denial. But the novel centers on Frank's redemption, the apprenticeship in suffering through which he discovers his own moral nature, "the self he had secretly considered valuable."

Mailer too was a Jewish moralist, in the same way a Satanist is an inverted Christian. "I don't consider myself moral at all," he once told an interviewer. "I see myself as a man who lives in an embattled relation to morality." The expansive form and loose texture of his books convey his sense of unlimited human possibility, his need to defy received conventions of form and behavior. He is interested in how people shape – or fail to shape – their own destiny. Malamud's form, on the other hand, is always more closely knit, more constricted. Like Flannery O'Connor, he uses symbols, images, and recurring plot motifs to load his stories with significance but also to convey the burden of necessity that weighs on his characters. His belief in craft and form reflects his severe morality.

The Assistant is as tightly written as a prose poem. In Malamud's early books and stories, no writer is farther from the picaresque – the form whose fluidity and mobility proclaim a typically American assertion of freedom. Unlike Mailer, Malamud prefers not the grandiose personal history or the Napoleonic biography but the Kafkaesque short story, with its knifelike ironic twists and turns, its pinched scope, which so well suits a writer whose imagination insistently humbles all personal pride. (Even his more picaresque heroes, such as Levin in *A New Life* [1961] and Fidelman in *Pictures of Fidelman* [1969], looking for satisfaction far from home, must go through endlessly humbling experiences.) *The Assistant* is an extended short story, more realistic in texture but similar in outlook to the wonderful stories collected in *The Magic Barrel* (1958). At the end of his career, he turned, like Mailer, to biography, and even wrote a long novel about a biographer, *Dubin's Lives* (1979), but his late stories about Virginia Woolf and Alma Mahler, though carefully researched, are scarcely half a dozen pages long, and are written in a staccato mode from which all expansiveness and flow have been harshly expunged.

Malamud's stories, even such novels as *The Assistant* and *The Tenants,* are two-character pieces, densely written chamber compositions rather than orchestral works. Where Mailer, who once described himself as a "Nijinsky of ambivalence," puts all his dialectics into the individual ego, Malamud focuses on the interplay of self and other, now literal, now symbolic, to bring his characters toward some kind of self-understanding. His stories begin with swift, hard strokes, like rap sheets on people whose lives can be reduced to a few phrases attached to their names. Always they seem pinned to the destiny that has already overtaken them, or to one they are desperate to evade:

Feld, the shoemaker, was annoyed that his helper, Sobel, was so insensitive to his reverie that he wouldn't for a minute cease his fanatic pounding at the other bench [from "The First Seven Years"].

Manischevitz, a tailor, in his fifty-first year suffered many reverses and indignities. Previously a man of comfortable means, he overnight lost all he had, when his establishment caught fire and, after a metal container of cleaning fluid exploded, burned to the ground [from "Angel Levine"].

Henry Levin, an ambitious, handsome thirty, who walked the floors in Macy's book department wearing a white flower in his lapel, having recently come into a small inheritance, quit, and went abroad seeking romance [from "The Lady of the Lake"].

Fidelman, a self-confessed failure as a painter, came to Italy to prepare a critical study of Giotto, the opening chapter of which he had carried across the ocean in a new pigskin leather brief case, now gripped in his perspiring hand [from "The Last Mohican"].

Even if "The First Seven Years" were not loosely based on the story of Jacob and Laban, there would still be something biblical about these sharply condensed openings, which have the generalized quality of fairy tales ("he overnight lost all he had"). We feel the heavy clang of fate in such terse accounts of the bare details of these lives. Malamud's hapless protagonists are either older men, already ground down by the unforgiving hardness of their immigrant lives, the reverses or illnesses that have hemmed them in, or else younger men of the next generation, Malamud's own, who still dream of a new life in which early failures can be avoided or undone. The old men tend to be cranky, bitter, rigid, and blind to their own shortcomings, but the younger men are even more cold-hearted in their dreams of love and fame. In the stories, they invariably encounter their opposite – their demon and alter ego – often a slightly magical figure as mercurial as they are unbending, as emotionally labile as they are walled up in themselves, who exposes their limitations but also gives them a glimpse of their own stifled humanity.

Some of these "others" are simply people in need – the love-smitten helper in "The First Seven Years," the evicted tenant in "The Mourners" – whose humanity must be recognized before their tormentors can gain access to their own. Others are the fixers, con men, and ghetto operators who fascinate Malamud – Salzman, the marriage broker in "The Magic Barrel"; the slightly sinister, endlessly intrusive Susskind in "The Last Mohican," who finally destroys Fidelman's Giotto manuscript ("the words were there but the spirit was missing"); the shadowy real estate agent Bevilacqua in "Behold the Key"; the black guardian angel out of Frank Capra in "Angel Levine." These men are almost a mirror of the protagonists' deeply repressed needs and wishes. Where the heroes are stiffly "American" – pale intellectual products of the second generation, with its never-ending ordeal of civility – their alter egos are colorful ethnics, black, Italian, ghetto Jewish, like a reflux of some disreputable vitality the Americanized characters have suppressed in themselves.

Bellow too is fascinated by the unruly vitality of small-time crooks, con men, and wheeler-dealers, the dense underbrush of urban life. But Malamud's nimble tricksters, like Ellison's Rinehart, also have a good deal of the fantastic about them. They materialize unexpectedly but are hard to find when you look for them. Their office is "in the air"; they work out of their own socks. Behind them is the tradition of the wonder rabbi but also the black market: Jewish survival in the cracks of a civil society that scorned them. In this encounter between the famished heart and its repressed double, Malamud takes the material of Depression literature and Yiddish fiction – the cost of living, the brutal lot of the tradesman, the apprentice, the greenhorn, the refugee – and gives it a touch of magic realism, turning away from the economics of poverty toward the metaphysics of human loneliness and longing.

For all their realistic detail, their poetic authenticity of speech and feeling, Malamud's best novels and stories are parables rather than documents of immigrant life. Their abrupt poetry and folkloric characters give free play to Malamud's superb sense of comic incongruity. Often the time and setting are dreamlike and unspecific. *The Assistant* seems be set in Brooklyn during the Depression, but its world is a handful of houses, stores, and families that reflect the constricted lives and limited horizons of the people caught in it. Even this bleak world has room for a wraithlike figure who offers to burn down the wretched store for the "insurinks." "I make a living," he says. "I make fires." The world of Malamud's novel has no mayor, no governor, no president – and no respite from its own moral intensity. The life that persists in it is a burden, and its people are honored bitterly for bearing that burden. "He was, through the years, a hard man to move," Morris Bober's wife feels. "In the past she could sometimes resist him, but the weight of his endurance was too much for her now." The grocery store to which Bober is chained is metaphorically, almost literally, a prison, as are nearly all of Malamud's settings right up through *The Fixer* (1966), which is actually set in a prison, and in a Russia that is simply a much larger prison, at least for poor Jews.

But alongside this parable of suffering is a parable of redemption. Morris Bober dies, but not before finding a surrogate son to make up for the son he lost long ago, someone to whom he can pass on his strenuous moral example. The rabbinical student in "The Magic Barrel" will face up to his scarcely acknowledged sexual need, the longing that bedevils his failed spiritual vocation, in the fallen daughter of the marriage broker. ("This is my baby, my Stella, she should burn in hell," says Salzman in tears.) Thus the marriage broker becomes the instrument of Leo Finkle's fall as well as his redemption. By facing up to the "evil" in his own nature, the lure of the forbidden, Leo may overcome the coldness and emptiness at the heart of his own stunted humanity.

But Salzman is also the ghetto Jew whom the rabbinical student has subdued in himself, the past he is so eager to overcome. In a more schematic story, "The Lady of the Lake," Henry Levin has even changed his name to Henry Freeman as a way of asserting his freedom from the burdens of Jewish identity. He imagines that "a man's past was, it could be safely said, expendable." Being Jewish? "What had it brought him but headaches, inferiorities, unhappy memories?" Abroad, he finds love and beauty in a mysterious Italian woman, almost an apparition, but she turns out to be Jewish herself, a survivor of Buchenwald. "I can't marry you," she says to him, not quite credibly, before he can undo the erasure of his own identity. "We are Jews," she adds, before flitting away. "My past is meaningful to me. I treasure what I suffered for." Like Fidelman in "The Last Mohican" and Carl Schneider, the primly moralistic graduate student in "Behold the Key," Freeman has turned himself into a brittle construct, a hollow self-made man who can neither find himself nor find his way in a society in which the past still matters.

In "The Silver Crown," the best of Malamud's later stories, Albert Gans seeks out a wonder rabbi to heal his desperately ill father. As a rational man, however, he is also dogged by his inability to trust anyone, his fear of being taken in, which also betrays the limits of his love for his father, whom he secretly detests. When he ceases to put any faith in the miracle cure, when his suspicions take over, his father expires, done in by his son's failure of imagination and failure of feeling. If the older generation, in its struggle to survive, is shady, colorful, devious, and cunning, the younger generation's advanced worldly wisdom has made it spiritually sterile.

Like "The Magic Barrel," "The Silver Crown" shows Malamud's close kinship with the work of I. B. Singer, who also found imaginative truth in fantasy, superstition, and rabbinical lore. The well-received publication of *A Treasury of Yiddish Stories* (1953), edited by Irving Howe and Eliezer Greenberg, and Singer's *Gimpel the Fool and Other Stories* (1955) helped create a market for stories more closely rooted in Jewish magic and folklore than the naturalistic fiction produced by such American Jewish writers as Abraham Cahan, Anzia Yezierska, Ludwig Lewisohn, Michael Gold, and Meyer Levin before the war. This was part of the postwar shift from Marx to Freud, from the mechanics of society to the dynamics of the unconscious. Malamud's work shows how much the fiction of the fifties was internalized into myth and psychological fable. But because of the unforgettable facts of persecution and discrimination, ethnic writing also maintained an important social base. It was impossible for a black or Jewish writer to focus on the self without also writing about the social conditions that assaulted and helped define it. Such black writers as Ralph Ellison and James Baldwin would turn away from the naturalism of Richard Wright while remaining grounded in the problems of the community, which were reflected in their own search for identity. Purely personal writing was a luxury the ethnic author could scarcely afford. As long as social acceptance remained problematic, as long as people could be hated or excluded because of the color of their skin or the shape of their nose, an "American" identity could never fully substitute for ethnic and communal roots. However much they might try to escape it, Jews and blacks were indelibly marked by their own history, which had been imprinted on them from the beginning of their lives.

❧

Saul Bellow's career was more varied and expansive than was Malamud's; his books were longer, more American, often less emphatically Jewish. But his most deliberately American work, *The Adventures of Augie March* (1953), was his most confected and least authentic, though its picaresque form and nimble, vernacular prose were a major breakthrough for Bellow. *Henderson the Rain King* (1959) was a more unified and ingenious picaresque fantasy, a high intellectual comedy set in an Africa that derives from the movies and from Bellow's anthropological reading, but it was also infused with his meditations on the modern self and its destiny. Both these upbeat books proved to be dead ends for Bellow. Between them, astonishingly, he wrote a great novella, *Seize the Day,* a classic of Jewish American writing, a failure story very close in spirit to Malamud's or Singer's work.

Like Henry Freeman (né Levin) in Malamud's "The Lady of the Lake," Bellow's Tommy Wilhelm, formerly Wilhelm Adler, has tried to alter his destiny by changing his name. Instead of going to Europe like Freeman, he had gone to Hollywood, the dream factory that embodies the American idea of an infinitely malleable identity, the belief in new beginnings. "Tommy Wilhelm" was his bid for freedom, which failed in Hollywood and fails definitively in the day-long course of the story. To his cold, dignified, censorious father, Dr. Adler, who lives in the same residence hotel on Manhattan's Upper West Side, he remains Wilky, the inarticulate son who embarrasses him, whom he refuses to "carry." "He had cast off his father's name, and with it his father's opinion of him." His father tells him, "I want nobody on my back. Get off! And I give you the same advice, Wilky. Carry nobody on your back." But hapless Wilky carries the weight of the world on his back.

Since the Jewish novel is almost synonymous with the family novel, and since he himself is being squeezed for alimony payments by his estranged wife, Wilhelm's rejection by his selfish father is perhaps the worst blow he receives in the course of the day, though not the final one. It is comparable to the concluding scene of Kafka's story "The Judgment," in which Georg Bendemann's enfeebled father rises titanically from his bed and condemns him to death by drowning, a sentence he quickly executes on himself. Rather than drowning, Tommy Wilhelm is suffocating. He is clogged with feeling, congested with a sense of inarticulate desperation as his life comes apart. Just as the tragic quality of *The Assistant* is grounded in Morris Bober's bad luck – and the good luck of insensitive neighbors like Karp, the liquor store owner, who thrives wherever Morris stumbles – *Seize the Day* is about the "flavor of fatality" that draws Wilhelm unerringly toward disaster. *Seize the Day* is a Jewish joke turned dead serious, a schlemiel fable about real people. More obliquely than *The Assistant,* it is also about the redemptive power of suffering.

"Maybe the making of mistakes expressed the very purpose of his life and the essence of his being here," Wilhelm thinks. Perhaps, he wonders, his suffering has more meaning than the prosperity of those around him. The instruments of Wilhelm's downfall are not simply his pitiless wife and father but also his surrogate father, a trickster figure named Dr. Tamkin. The con man as Emersonian philosopher, Tamkin convinces Wilhelm to "seize the day" and venture everything on the commodities exchange (which he scarcely understands) in one last bid for freedom. When he hits bottom and loses his last $700 on a wild investment, Wilhelm is reduced to that bedrock of humanity, the tormented heart, that remains Bellow's ultimate ground of value. In the story's famous ending, he wanders into the funeral of someone he does not know and begins weeping:

> Soon he was past words, past reason, coherence. He could not stop. The source of all tears had suddenly sprung up within him, black, deep, and hot, and they were pouring out and convulsed his body, bending his stubborn head, bowing his shoulders, twisting his face, crippling the very hands with which he held the handkerchief. His efforts to collect himself were useless. The great knot of ill and grief in his throat swelled upward and he gave in utterly and held his face and wept. He cried with all his heart.

At this impersonal, wholly unexpected moment, the emotional block within him finally gives way. The other mourners, awed by this show of grief, take him to be a close relation. As a fellow human being, in a sense he is. Swept away by a flood of feeling he grieves for himself, for everyone, or for no one in particular, yet moves "through torn sobs and cries toward the consummation of his heart's ultimate need."

Critics have questioned whether the clumsy, ill-fated Wilhelm is entitled to the author's sympathy or to his final moments of ecstatic transcendence. Like Malamud in *The Assistant,* Bellow sees his protagonist's worldly failure as some kind of spiritual triumph, especially as compared to his father's self-love, professional success, and bitter resentment that his less worthy son will survive him. Tamkin, on the other hand, one of those fantastic eccentrics who play bit parts in all of Bellow's novels, is a grand burlesque of the sympathetic figure Wilhelm vainly seeks in his own father. Bellow stacks the deck against Tommy Wilhelm, shows him suffering blow after blow, many of them self-inflicted. Criticizing Bellow's book in *Advertisements for Myself,* Mailer complained that "it is not demanding to write about characters considerably more defeated than oneself," but he praised the ending as an indication "that Bellow is not altogether hopeless on the highest level." Certainly, the ending foreshadows the spiritual themes that emerge in Bellow's later fiction, including the speculations about "the future of the moon" in *Mr. Sammler's Planet* (1970), the streak of mysticism and the meditations on death in *Humboldt's Gift* (1975), and the concluding pages of *The Dean's December* (1982), where the hero, climbing up into the unearthly interior of the great telescope on Mt. Palomar, feels in touch with the icy spirit of the cosmos, with "its power to cancel everything merely human."

Perhaps it was Mailer's criticism, along with developments in his own life, that fostered Bellow's great shift in the 1960s toward a more autobiographical protagonist. More than most novelists, Bellow had always been an intellectual as well as a fiction writer. His first novel, *Dangling Man,* was an almost plotless novel of ideas, the musing of a wartime intellectual in the spirit of Dostoyevsky's *Notes from Underground.* In *Herzog* (1964) Bellow tackled the subject of the Jewish intellectual much more directly, using the clever device of Herzog's unsent letters to convey the comic extravagance of his breakdown and to expand upon his own vision of the larger breakdown of the modern world. Though *Seize the Day* was Bellow's most controlled and perfectly executed piece of fiction, the core of his nature work can be found in *Herzog, Mr. Sammler's Planet,* and *Humboldt's Gift,* which could be described as the *Purgatorio,* the *Inferno,* and the *Paradiso* of his modern *commedia. Seize the Day* and *Henderson the Rain King* were the last books in which Bellow was not essentially his own protagonist, as Mailer would become in much of his later work.

Tommy Wilhelm and Moses Herzog are two of Bellow's exemplary sufferers, though Herzog's disintegration is florid and operatic where Wilhelm's is choked with feelings he can scarcely express (not choked enough for his father, who tells him, "There's no need to carry on like an opera, Wilky.") "Well, when you suffer, you really suffer," Herzog's friend and lawyer Sandor Himmelstein says to *him.* "You're a real, genuine old Jewish type that digs the emotions." *Herzog,* awash in Herzog's tempest of feeling, his sea of grievance, has perhaps the thinnest plot of any major postwar novel. Herzog has been betrayed by his wife, Madeleine, with his best friend, Valentine Gersbach – the most trite story imaginable. (It seems clear, though, that the worshipful Gersbach wants little more than to be like Herzog, to *be* Herzog.) By filtering this old triangle through Herzog's tormented memories, his endless self-analysis, his grandiose intellectual constructions, however, Bellow creates a different kind of novel, formally in the third person yet subjective, rueful, hyberbolic, unstable – shifting constantly between past and present, theories and feelings, internal monologues and actual events.

Herzog is not a novel of action but a state of mind. As a desperately personal work, it seems grounded in two motives generally fatal to fiction: self-pity and the desire for revenge. Bellow's friends could recognize every character and detail, could see exactly where he distorted and fantasticated, but *Herzog* is much more than a roman à clef, for Bellow's animus sharpens his powers of observation. The novel is fired by indignation yet transcends mere retaliation. In a passage that echoes a celebrated image from Kafka, Bellow writes:

It's fascinating that hatred should be so personal as to be almost loving. The knife and the wound aching for each other. . . . Some cry out, and some swallow the thrust in silence. About the latter you could write the inner history of mankind.

Thanks to this luminous hatred, everything in *Herzog* – the characters, the settings, the feelings – glows with preternatural intensity. Herzog feels used and abused, deceived by trusted friends, passive and helpless before the women who fatally attract him, whose love is indispensable to his male pride. Like Wilhelm, Herzog is said to have a "talent for making a fatal choice," but this is simply Bellow's way of deflecting responsibility – giving him a subtler sense of victimization. The emphasis on Herzog's foolishness and depth of feeling is meant to mitigate his self-absorption. He is "foolish, feeling, suffering Herzog," an "eager, hasty, self-intense, and comical person." He is weak, good-hearted, a co-conspirator with those who take advantage of him. Everything here suggests that Bellow is writing about himself, taking stock of his own life but also transforming it in the telling. *Herzog* is one long Hamlet-like soliloquy, antic, tormented, and highly self-conscious.

Like Mailer and other novelists in the early sixties, Bellow turned from distanced, ironic, carefully structured fictions toward mercurial self-portraits, using himself as a prism through which the cultural moment could be refracted. Much of what Bellow says about Herzog's character reads like oblique self-description. Herzog's taste for paradox has been honed by Kafka and seasoned by Dostoyevsky. "He dreaded the depths of feeling he would eventually have to face, when he could no longer call upon his eccentricities for relief." When Bellow analyzes Herzog's "feminine" passivity, his "psychic offer" of "meekness in exchange for preferential treatment," it makes sense only as self-analysis, at once a display of injured innocence and an apology for becoming more aggressive and self-protective. Only his bruised vulnerability makes this egotism bearable. Beginning with *Herzog,* Bellow, like some latter-day Montaigne, would never tire of exploring the complications of his own nature. In later novels like *The Dean's December* and *More Die of Heartbreak* (1987), this inner portraiture leaves fiction behind, focusing entirely (and almost plotlessly) on the author's increasingly cranky life and opinions. But in the richly developed *commedia* of the sixties and seventies, before he received the Nobel Prize in 1976, Bellow maintains a lively balance between the self absorbed hero and the actual world.

There is a broad streak of misogyny and paranoia in Bellow, as in Norman Mailer and Philip Roth, a fierce resentment of the power women have over him. An injured male narcissism gives his work its tremendous emotional energy. The actual murder of Rojack's wife in *An American Dream* is only a more literal version of the murderous feelings of Roth's alter ego in *My Life as a Man* (1974) or the lethal characterization of Madeleine in *Herzog.* But where Roth's book, obsessed with blaming the other, remains caught up in his sense of victimization, his need for self-vindication, Bellow turns the raw material of autobiography into cultural diagnosis. The affair between Madeleine and Gersbach comes to represent a larger breakdown of decency and civility, just as Herzog himself embodies the ineffectuality of the intellectual: humane yet deeply vulnerable, brilliant but pretentious and confused, exploring with his talented mistress the same sexual freedoms he roundly condemns in his wife.

Herzog is an apocalyptic novel that disdains apocalypse, a novel of ideas that mocks intellectuals. Herzog sees the sixties, then still just beginning, as a season of moral anarchy, animated by a dream of erotic salvation of which his mistress Ramona is an early prophet. Later, the much more exaggerated forms of this new freedom would become the sour subject of *Mr. Sammler's Planet.* "She has read Marcuse, N. O. Brown, all those neo-Freudians," says Herzog of Ramona. "She wants me to believe the body is a spiritual fact, the sinstrument of the soul." He sees Ramona as "a sort of sexual professional," full of knowledge that could be learned only through experience, as well as theories from which his patriarchal Jewish being recoils. Being an incorrigible theorist himself, he turns his attraction to her into an ironic dialogue between Jewish suffering, morality, and discipline and the immediate promise of an erotic utopia. An evening with Ramona becomes an escape from the burden of history, the constraints of tradition, the inhibitions of character.

As a figure in a novel, Herzog is saved by his contradictions. "He might think himself a moralist but the shape of a woman's breasts mattered greatly. . . . When he jeered in private at the Dionysiac revival it was himself he made fun of. Herzog! A prince of the erotic Renaissance." The novel ends wishfully in Ramona's love nest, where good food, good sex, and good conversation – and perhaps the writing of this novel – have begun to heal Herzog's wounded narcissism, his damaged male pride.

Much of the strength of *Herzog* can be found in the vividness of the minor characters and the spiritedness of the book's zany intellectual comedy: Madeleine with the medieval Russian tomes she lugs to bed with her, the guilt she feels about her aborted conversion to Catholicism; Gersbach as a "second Herzog," a cheap, fawning imitation of the genius himself, with his crude, proletarian Yiddish, his easy male swagger, and ultimately his saving tenderness toward Herzog's young daughter as he gives her a bath, which prevents the crazed father from shooting him; Mady's divorced bohemian parents, themselves a small chapter of American cultural history; Herzog's assorted friends and academic colleagues in Chicago, including a professor who gives mouth-to-mouth resuscitation to a tubercular monkey. All are drawn with Bellow's sure feeling for the low-down and the eccentric.

Yet Herzog-Bellow's strength of observation is surpassed by his power of memory, the sentimental pull of Napoleon Street in Montreal, where he grew up. Long after the Bellow persona, the Bellow outlook, had overwhelmed every other element in his work, he could still write remarkable stories – "The Old System" (in *Mosby's Memoirs and Other Stories,* 1968), "The Silver Dish" and "Cousins" (in *Him with His Foot in His Mouth and Other Stories,* 1984) – exploring the tangled web of Jewish family relationships. In *Herzog* this pull of memory is the core of the book, the cultural memory expressed in Herzog's letters, family memory in his childhood recollections. Just as Herzog cannot fathom how three thousand years of discipline, suffering, and sacrifice have led him to Ramona'a bed, he cannot imagine how the kid from Napoleon Street, the "bookish, callow boy" who could not see that his own mother was dying, became the grown man who married Madeleine and was betrayed by Gersbach. His whole life feels like a falling away from some authentic point of origin, which is identified with being Jewish and being his parents' son.

Like Kerouac in *On the Road* and Roth in *Portnoy's Complaint.* who are also consumed by the contrast between where they came from and what they became, Bellow sees his identity as a novelist as bound up with the power of remembering, the curse of not forgetting, which seems like an obsession to ordinary people. When a childhood friend, now an early hippie, avoids him on the street, he thinks the man is running away from "the power of his old friend's memory." "All the dead and the mad are in my custody," he imagines, "and I am the nemesis of the would-be forgotten." To his memories of Napoleon Street ("rotten, toylike, crazy and filthy, flogged with harsh weather") Herzog's mind is still "attached with great power. Here was a wider range of human feelings than he had ever again been able to find." "What was wrong with Napoleon Street?" he wonders. "All he ever wanted was there." Herzog recognizes something unhealthy about this plangent longing, which was so common to Jewish writers as they endlessly relived their warm and crazy childhoods. "To haunt the past like this – to love the dead! Moses warned himself not to yield so greatly to this temptation, this peculiar weakness of his character. He was a depressive. Depressives cannot surrender childhood – not even the pains of childhood."

Herzog's brilliant, often incoherent letters are an equally neurotic and yet necessary way of not surrendering his intellectual past. They convey Bellow's brief against the apocalyptic temper of the times, the reign of Romanticism and individualism, the emphasis on self-development at all cost, the rise of "plebeian envy and ambition," the glorification of the erotic, the "confusion between aesthetic and moral judgments," the expansion of violence on a mass scale, and most of all the doctrinaire pessimism in the wake of European existentialism – "the commonplaces of the Wasteland outlook, the cheap mental stimulants of Alienation, the cant and rant of pipsqueaks about Inauthenticity and Forlornness."

Herzog's recoil from the modern world would only sharpen in Bellow's later work, when Bellow grew close to the jaundiced outlook of such Straussian friends at the University of Chicago as Allan Bloom. Yet Bellow's rejection of modernism, partly grounded in the feeling that his generation of writers had been unfairly overshadowed by their predecessors, was itself a modernist gesture, a fierce declaration of independence. Despite his piety toward the past and his own reserved temperament, Bellow felt a deep affinity for such wild, confused, out-of-control personalities as Von Humboldt Fleisher, modeled on his friend, the doomed poet Delmore Schwartz. Like the critic Lionel Trilling, Bellow, despite (or because of) his own quiet life and muted personality, was attracted to charismatic and crazy geniuses who spoke to his buried self, from which his imagination drew surprising energy.

Bellow's work falters when the superego in him, the hateful moral censor, gets out of hand. *Herzog's* hero is a divided soul, deeply implicated in all he condemns; the novel is powered by its ambivalence. In *Mr. Sammler's Planet* Bellow writes from the more lofty perch of the sage. Herzog's hatred is sharp and specific, laced with self-irony. Mr. Sammler's loathing is vague and sweeping, constantly in search of emblems to objectify it, like the exposed penis of a lordly black pickpocket or the sexual habits of Sammler's daughter Shula and niece Angela. As in *Herzog,* not much happens in *Mr. Sammler's Planet.* While his nephew lies dying in a hospital, an old man travels up and down Manhattan's West Side, still brooding about his own freakish survival in a Polish forest during war. His outlook is European: he is "an Anglophile intellectual Polish Jew and person of culture," once an acquaintance of H. G. Wells, that apostle of human progress.

In a tone of detached hauteur, Sammler takes the long view of the rebelliousness of the young and the anarchy he feels in the streets of New York, where at moments he sees a collapse of civilization comparable to the barbarism of the Nazis. At the end his nephew dies and he eulogizes him, despite his flaws, as a man who "did meet the terms of his contract. The terms which, in his inmost heart, each man knows." Much more than *Herzog, Mr. Sammler's Planet* is a jeremiad, a sharp rhetorical rather than fictional performance, a hyperbolic vision of the 1960s through the lens of Western culture under siege – in other words, yet another extreme attack on extremist thinking.

One difference between the two novels can be seen in the treatment of women. Madeleine is a man-eating monster but her opposite number,

Herzog's mistress Ramona, is a nurturing tutor in the new dispensation of erotic freedom. Both characters are male fantasies – woman as gorgon, woman as love goddess – but Herzog sees the high comedy of being drawn to what his nature regards with deep suspicion. In the higher synthesis of *Mr. Sammler's Planet,* sex belongs only to a constellation of moral degeneracy that centers on women, blacks, and young people in general. Sammler constantly thinks of women in terms of their foul odors, their corrupt natures, their unclean organs, "the female generative slime." There is no indication of what personal crisis may lie behind this insistence, but no writer since Swift has built his work on such a fascinated repugnance toward female odors and female organs, or expected them to bear the onus of representing a whole culture in decline. In an astonishing summary of the sixties as seen by a cultivated émigré, Bellow links the sexuality of women with the criminality of the black pickpocket as well as the anti-authoritarianism of the young, the neoprimitivism of the intellectuals, and the antinomianism of advanced art:

From the black side, strong currents were sweeping over everyone. Child, black, redskin – the unspoiled Seminole against the horrible Whiteman. Millions of civilized people wanted oceanic, boundless, primitive, neckfree nobility, experienced a strange release of galloping impulses, and acquired the peculiar aim of sexual niggerhood for everyone. Humankind had lost its old patience. It demanded accelerated exaltation, accepted no instant without pregnant meanings as in epic, tragedy, comedy, or films.

Bellow, who once edited a magazine called *The Noble Savage,* includes even Native Americans (or white myths about them) in his heinous catalog, though they were hardly part of the sixties cultural revolution. Since women are thought to embody nature rather than culture, they stand with young people, blacks, redskins, and artists in the vanguard of the new erotic utopia. With this "sexual niggerhood" as its subject, *Mr. Sammler's Planet* can be read as an inversion of "The White Negro," inspired by the same fantasies and imagery. But Sammler gives Norman Mailer's argument (and William Blake's language) a racist spin: "The labor of Puritanism now was ending. The dark satanic mills changing into light satanic mills. The reprobates converted into children of joy, the sexual ways of the seraglio and of the Congo bush adopted by the emancipated masses of New York, Amsterdam, London."

Like Trilling, who gave a more modulated account of the "adversary culture" in his late essays and interviews, Bellow saw the sixties as a literal fulfilment of the modernist vision: "The dreams of nineteenth-century poets polluted the psychic atmosphere of the great boroughs and suburbs of New York." Most at fault for undermining civilization were "its petted intellectuals who attacked it at its weakest moments – attacked it in the name of proletarian revolution, in the name of reason, and in the name of irrationality, in the name of visceral depth, in the name of sex, in the name of perfect instantaneous freedom." Bellow connected the morality of the young with their politics of protest. "For what it amounted to was limitless demand, refusal of the doomed creature (death being sure and final) to go away from the earth unsatisfied. A full bill of demand and complaint was therefore presented by each individual. Non-negotiable. Recognizing no scarcity of supply in any human department." This is what Irving Howe had called the "psychology of unobstructed need," an infantile need for self-gratification. By portraying the new erotic utopia as an offshoot of the culture of modernism, Bellow ignores a much more immediate source, the consumer culture of the postwar years – and even the dreams and aspirations of the immigrant parents, who looked to a better life, unhampered by grim necessity, for their "American" children.

For all the crisp intensity of Bellow's writing, *Mr. Sammler's Planet* often reads more like a polemic than a novel, for it is punctuated by little discursive volleys, puritanical, patriarchal, and intolerant, delivered by Bellow through the figure of the aged intellectual who has seen everything. Yet Bellow's genius in his late work, beginning with *Herzog* and especially with his great 1967 story "The Old System," was precisely to take the long view, to step back and see the whole cycle of birth, nurture, passion, and death through the eye of eternity yet fully grounded in human detail and razor-sharp prose. "The Old System" sets the pattern for Bellow's later work by giving us simply a man remembering – the author's surrogate, a distinguished geneticist, thinking back with pleasure about some recently deceased relatives whose unquiet lives suddenly matter to him, whose deaths seemed to resonate with unspeakable poignance. But the almost scientific detachment that works so well in "The Old System," that lends universality to ordinary family history, feels duplicitous in *Mr. Sammler's Planet,* where an aura of olympian neutrality scarcely masks a mood of bottomless revulsion. Bellow shrouds his anger in the measured cadences of the European sage, the cold, world-weary wisdom of the elderly survivor. Surrounding Sammler with caricatures rather than characters, Bellow's harsh indictment brooks no viewpoint different from his own.

❦

Ironically, Bellow well understood the utopianism of the young, the apocalyptic temperament of artists and intellectuals. He had been there. Along with other *Partisan Review* writers who came of age between the two world wars, he had cut his teeth on modernism and revolutionary socialism. He was also typical of his generation in rediscovering his suppressed Jewish identity in middle age. Donning the mantle of a scornful Hebrew prophet, Bellow sees the sixties as a revival of paganism, a return to the worship of nature, exactly what the original prophets denounced among the ancient Hebrews. But the other half of the prophetic message is missing: the appeal for social justice, the denunciation of merchants and princes, the identification with the poor and despised (as echoed by the Jesus of the Gospels). As Bellow had named Moses Herzog after the biblical lawgiver rather than the liberator, he has Sammler question "whether release from long Jewish mental discipline, hereditary training in lawful control, was obtainable upon individual application."

Beginning with *Dangling Man,* Bellow always had shown a weakness for lofty judgments and sententious pronouncements, but this was always off-set by his feeling for the manic energy of characters coming apart, like Herzog and Humboldt. This balance is lost in *Mr. Sammler's Planet,* beautifully regained in *Humboldt's Gift,* then lost definitively in the discursive ramblings of *The Dean's December* and *More Die of Heartbreak,* both written after the author was crowned with the Nobel prize in 1976.

Mr. Sammler's censoriousness has been compared with the cold disdain of Dr. Adler, Tommy Wilhelm's unbending father. For all his show of detachment, his Oxonian airs, however, Mr. Sammler is deeply fascinated with the whole scene he condemns, beginning with the sex organs of the black pickpocket ("great oval testicles, a large tan-and-purple uncircumcised thing – a tube, a snake") and the lordly expression of his face ("not directly menacing but oddly, serenely masterful"). In its own way, which can be seen as racist and misogynistic, Bellow's synthesis of the sixties is both astute and covertly sympathetic. The period both inspires and unhinges him. The bemused erotic experiments of Herzog lead directly to the excesses that outrage Mr. Sammler. But even Sammler objects helplessly when his brutal son-in-law smashes the black pickpocket, whose wordless eloquence had deeply impressed him.

The cultural turbulence of the 1960s inspired little first-rate fiction but much attitudinizing. Updike's *Rabbit Redux* and Malamud's *The Tenants* ran aground in their portrayal of young people and blacks, much as Updike's *Couples* grew mechanical in depicting suburban adultery, that other half of the sexual revolution. Two strong generational novels anchored in an earlier period, Joyce Carol Oates's *them* (1969) and E. L. Doctorow's *The Book of Daniel* (1971), conclude with emblematic events of the 1960s – the urban riots in Detroit in 1967, the student uprising at Columbia University in 1968. Much later in *American Pastoral* (1997),

Philip Roth would portray the young radicals of the sixties as simply ranting, obnoxious, and demented in their hatred of grown-ups, indifferent to
human life, and quite damaged by their permissive liberal upbringing.
Bellow does better than this. Paradoxically, his apocalyptic view sharpens
his picture and makes *Mr. Sammler* one of the few reactions to the era that
matches it in intensity. Though Sammler reflects that "New York makes
one think about the collapse of civilization, about Sodom and Gomorrah,
about the end of the world," Bellow's portrait of the city itself, his sense of
the streets, is even more vital than in *Seize the Day.* This is New York as
many experienced it, as a scarily exciting jungle.

The self-righteousness of *Sammler* borders on moral cant, but Bellow's
hunger for significance is deeply felt. In his greed for meaning, Bellow
made Sammler both a survivor of the Holocaust and a witness to Israel's
Six-Day War. He should certainly not have compared the moral liberties of
the sixties to the Holocaust or implied that the Jews' trauma as fugitives
and partisans in the Polish forests had earned them the right to be pitiless
toward the next generations, which had not been tested in the same way.
Bellow used the war years as a club to beat the callow young. But only
Mailer in *The Armies of the Night* – and perhaps Thomas Pynchon in *The
Crying of Lot 49* – managed to put the sixties together as powerfully as
Bellow did in the embittered pages of this novel.

Bellow's rancor made the benign turn he took in his next novel,
Humboldt's Gift, all the more impressive. The story is virtually a memoir of
Bellow's friendship with Delmore Schwartz, compatible in almost every
detail with James Atlas's biography of the poet. Schwartz's golden promise
in his early years, his later descent into paranoia and madness, his quarrels
with virtually all his friends, and finally his miserable, anonymous death in
a cheap midtown hotel in 1966 – his body lay unclaimed for several days –
must have triggered Bellow's sense of mortality. This feeling was already
on view in "The Old System" and *Sammler,* since the first was a set of post-
mortem reflections, and the latter was framed by a death watch of an old
man who has himself passed through death and lived, yet himself feels
long dead.

Deeply touched by Delmore Schwartz's death, Bellow in *Humboldt's Gift*
is nostalgic and self-critical rather than reproachful. Instead of seeing the
world through a single lens, he splits his protagonist into the self-destructive poet Humboldt and the self-serving, successful playwright, Charlie
Citrine, the Bellow surrogate who is not all-knowing, and feels a weight of
guilt toward his troubled friend. After Citrine had had a great success on
Broadway in the early fifties – around the time Bellow himself had a major
breakthrough with *Augie March* – Humboldt had accused him of plagiariz-

ing his personality, even threatening to picket the play if he did not receive a share of the royalties. A few weeks before Humboldt died, Citrine had spotted his estranged friend on the street and avoided speaking to him, as Bellow himself had done with Delmore. Far better than *Sammler,* the novel deals with both the meaning of death and the complicated feelings of the survivor.

Despite Humboldt's zaniness and paranoia, there may have been something to the charges he levels, as Citrine acknowledges. Bellow *did* make a breakthrough in *Augie* around a character of manic energy very different from himself, to which he would return repeatedly with figures like Herzog and Humboldt. Delmore Schwartz had even acclaimed the novel in *Partisan Review.* It is not far-fetched to give some credit to him for what was best in Bellow's later fiction. Where would the self-accusing survivor, Citrine, be without Humboldt, his wild, undisciplined Other, the *poète maudit* who galvanized his imagination? Citrine himself describes this as a kind of authorial cannibalism, combining fierce admiration and envy with the novelist's gift for absorbing other people:

I did incorporate other people into myself and consume them. When they died I passionately mourned. I said I would continue their work and their lives. But wasn't it a fact that I added their strength to mine? Didn't I have an eye on them in their days of vigor and glory?

Some of Bellow's most heartfelt writing can be found in terse obituary pieces for such writer friends as Isaac Rosenfeld and John Berryman. In these essays, collected in *It All Adds Up* (1994), the sense of loss is always inflected with the inner satisfaction and guilt of the survivor. *Humboldt's Gift* is an immense version of such a fond farewell, a reckoning that is also an assertion of life, an appropriation, an ingestion.

Citrine shares many qualities with Bellow's earlier protagonists. He gets involved with petty gangsters. He is hounded by his ex-wife and put upon by an assortment of other women. He has a mistress, Renata, who is a reincarnation of Herzog's Ramona. But unlike Joseph (in *Dangling Man*) or Herzog or Sammler, he does not let himself off easy. He is a sellout who is redeemed in the course of the book, but also a spiritualist deeply involved with the ideas of Rudolf Steiner — as benign toward the world's frailties as Sammler was judgmental. For once Bellow gives the Deep Thinker a rest. The book is rueful, exuberant, and playful; it can be read as an apology for Bellow's recent political furies, especially in *Mr. Sammler's Planet.* Citrine endorses Tolstoy's admonition "to cease the false and unnecessary comedy of history and begin simply to live." His regret for the angry mood in which Bellow wrote *Sammler* is unmistakable. Citrine has experienced "the light," some access of spiritual wisdom, and this has given him "an altogether unreasonable kind of joy. Furthermore, the hysterical, the grotesque about me, the abusive, the unjust, that madness in which I had often been a willing and active participant, the grieving, now had found a contrast."

Besides this new tolerance and spiritual joy, the other element of Citrine's redemption is Humboldt himself, the gift of the title, the legacy of a jointly conceived story that now becomes a successful film. Implicitly, this stands for Delmore's legacy to this novel, the gift of his own character to a work that lifts Bellow out of his misanthropic slough of the late 1960s. Humboldt helps restore Bellow to the busy life of the particular that he had slighted in *Sammler,* including the "noisy bumptious types" like Ricardo Cantabile, a Chicago hoodlum who (like Humboldt) represents Bellow's "weakness" for characters who are "demonstrative exuberant impulsive destructive and wrong-headed." Humboldt allows Bellow to reclaim his own boisterous fictional territory after the scorched earth of *Mr. Sammler's Planet.* Even the few familiar jibes at advanced sex or the advanced intellectuals ("the educated nits, mental bores of the heaviest caliber") are remarkably good-humored. *Humboldt's Gift* lacks the discipline and intensity of *Seize the Day, Herzog,* or *Mr. Sammler's Planet,* but it is Bellow's most purely enjoyable book, tolerant, self-critical, and humane. In this vein of mellow reminiscence Bellow finds a respite from his personal furies, as he would again in the ruminative mood of some of his later stories.

NATIVE SONS: JAMES BALDWIN AND RALPH ELLISON

The fallout from World War II had created a rough parallel between Jews and blacks. Western shame over the Holocaust dealt a serious blow to long-standing American patterns of genteel anti-Semitism, including social discrimination against Jews, quotas in higher education, and exclusionary barriers in the major professions. Similarly, blacks at home complained and even rioted over the treatment of their soldiers in the segregated armed forces, where they were assigned to menial duties, barred from combat, harassed in and around Southern bases, and humbled when they returned to civilian life. But black soldiers, like so many other Americans, were also introduced by the war to a wider world. Fighting against racial hatred abroad, they became more conscious of their second-class status at home. "I went into the Army a nigger; I'm coming out a *man,*" said a black corporal from Alabama in 1945.

As prejudice against blacks and Jews came unstuck in the late forties, ethnic writers found a wider audience and an opportunity to influence the nation's changing attitudes. If Malamud and Bellow presented Jews as exemplary sufferers, emblems of both their people's history and of humanity as a whole, Ralph Ellison and James Baldwin were determined to avoid portraying blacks mainly as society's victims. All four writers were alike in giving their characters and stories a symbolic more than a sociological cast.

Both Ellison and Baldwin had begun as protégés of Richard Wright – Ellison in the 1930s when Wright, who was then a Communist, encouraged him to write first for his own short-lived Harlem magazine, *New Challenge,* then for the Communist *New Masses*; Baldwin in the 1940s when the older man, then at the peak of his fame, took him under his wing shortly before departing for Paris, where his rebellious disciple soon followed. At his best in *Native Son* (1940), *Black Boy* (1945), and the posthumous *American Hunger* (1977), Wright was no mere naturalist or protest writer. Ellison was drawn to him because of their mutual interest in modernist writing, and he vividly recalled Wright's frequent battles with his Party comrades and patrons who resented his independence. Wright's memories of growing up in the Jim Crow South and his feeling for life in the Chicago ghetto had almost a hallucinatory intensity, but his connection to his material diminished abroad while younger black writers opened themselves to new influences. Acclaimed by French intellectuals as an avatar of existentialism, cut off from the scenes that had nurtured his work, Wright's fiction grew abstract as he emerged as a lonely but influential public figure.

Baldwin's damaging depiction of *Native Son* in his own manifesto, "Everybody's Protest Novel" (1949), and again in "Many Thousands Gone" (1951), dealt a major blow to Wright's reputation. It cleared the ground for writing that was far more personal than Wright's, more metaphysical, more concerned with individual identity, including sexual identity. This was in line with the inward turn of other postwar writers, and it connected Baldwin especially to the Jewish writers and editors who admired his work and first published it in *Commentary, Partisan Review,* and *The New Leader.* But neither Baldwin nor Ellison ever challenged one essential tenet of Wright's – that the experience of African Americans was deeply conditioned by the traumatic facts of racial separation and discrimination. However, they insisted that this alone was insufficient to account for the varied ways that blacks had accommodated to their treatment and the complex lives they had shaped for themselves despite the humiliating often degrading conditions to which they were subjected.

Born out of wedlock in 1924, Baldwin was the son of an adoring mother who bore eight more children after she married a fiery preacher. But his harsh stepfather, whose name he bore, could barely support the family, and he grew increasingly demented and suspicious of white people before he died in 1943. One of Baldwin's most extraordinary essays, "Notes of a Native Son" (1955), interweaves his stepfather's death with the Harlem riots that just preceded it; the debris of this conflagration still littered the streets through which the funeral procession passed. The great revelation of *Native Son* had been the rage and despair that festered in the black urban ghetto, sometimes concealed behind the smile of acquiescence, friendship, or humility. Baldwin's rancorous father wore no such ingratiating mask, though his fear of whites suffused and poisoned his life. "He could be chilling in the pulpit and indescribably cruel in his personal life and he was certainly the most bitter man I have ever met," Baldwin recalls. "He had lived and died in an intolerable bitterness of spirit and it frightened me, as we drove him to the graveyard through those unquiet, ruined streets, to see how powerful and overflowing this bitterness could be and to realize that this bitterness now was mine."

Baldwin, just turning nineteen, had been away from home for a year when his father died, and in that time he had "discovered the weight of white people in the world." Working in New Jersey, he behaved almost suicidally in his encounters with Jim Crow racism on the job and in public places. In restaurants he is repeatedly told that "we don't serve Negroes here," and when he finally explodes, bringing the frustrations of the whole year to a head, he barely escapes with his skin. The next day he returns home to face his dying father ("lying there, all shriveled and still, like a little black monkey"), with whom he had always quarreled, and sees the Harlem neighborhood ignite like a vast projection of his father's (and his own) bitterness and rage.

Just as Baldwin's essays on *Native Son* helped create an opening for his own more inward kind of writing, his "Notes of a Native Son" and his largely autobiographical first novel, *Go Tell It on the Mountain* (1953), showed that writing at its best. As he explains in *The Fire Next Time* and enacts in the novel, Baldwin at fourteen had undergone a religious conversion and become an impassioned storefront preacher, which shielded him from the temptations of the Harlem streets, from his father's cruelty and power, and from his own strange new sexual feelings. At almost the same time, however, he entered an elite white high school, where he was surrounded by skeptical Jews "who laughed at the tracts and leaflets I brought to school." Reading those tracts himself, he too began to find them "impossible to believe."

Baldwin's fictional version of this conflict between faith and doubt comes in the wonderful opening pages of the last section of *Go Tell It on the Mountain* when the young protagonist, John Grimes, falls to the floor in an ecstatic trance, overwhelmed as if by some gigantic physical force. Yet even as those around him – his loving mother, his seething father, his dying aunt, and the young sexton, Elisha, who physically attracts him – are helping him through and seeing to his salvation, a "malicious, ironic voice" in his head keeps telling him to rise from the filthy floor, to get up from this "heart of darkness," which is reflected in his father's coal-black face, and "to leave this temple and go out into the world." This is just what Baldwin himself would eventually do.

It is hard not to see this as a parable of the contradictions of Baldwin's whole writing life, caught between the prophetic impulse, expressed in the cadences of the born preacher, and the ironic outlook, a kind of second sight, that enabled him to step outside his own feelings and analyze them with astonishing precision and eloquence. (Ellison remarked that like himself, Baldwin was "not the product of the Negro store-front church but of the library.") For fifteen years, from the time he wrote his report "The Harlem Ghetto" for the Jewish editors of *Commentary* in 1948 to the near-apocalyptic *The Fire Next Time* in 1963 (which caused a sensation when it first appeared in *The New Yorker*), Baldwin was both a first-rate novelist and a native informant, an interpreter of the black psyche for white America.

During this period Baldwin was living primarily among whites yet reporting in depth from regions of his mind. Whether he was returning to Harlem, venturing into the Deep South, living among the French in an interracial Paris, or finishing his novel in a Swiss village that had never seen a black person before, the passion he brought to racial issues was tempered by the detachment of the reporter and the introspection of the fiction writer. Never for a moment forgetting that he was black – an amnesia, he felt, that had befallen the expatriate Wright – Baldwin brought to his own life a sense of inner mystery, as well as a capacity for irony, that was perfectly in tune with the postwar scene.

His message was anything but reassuring. Like W. E. B. Du Bois and Richard Wright before him, he was an anatomist of black rage – the toxic effects of racism – and the "double consciousness" through which blacks adapted to it. He found in himself – and in virtually every black person he knew – a lacerating, soul-destroying anger scarcely visible to whites, and he understood how it could overwhelm him, as it had already poisoned his father's life. A cutting irony was Baldwin's rhetorical weapon of choice; his seeming detachment had a sardonic edge:

It is hard . . . to blame the policeman, blank, good-natured, thoughtless, and insuperably innocent, for being such a perfect representative of the people he serves. He, too, believes in good intentions, and is astounded and offended when they are not taken for the deed. . . .

Negroes want to be treated like men: a perfectly straightforward statement, containing only seven words. People who have mastered Kant, Hegel, Shakespeare, Marx, Freud, and the Bible find this statement utterly impenetrable.

These excerpts are from "Fifth Avenue, Uptown" (collected in *Nobody Knows My Name*, 1961), a valuable sequel to his 1948 report from the Harlem ghetto. They show how the sardonic mode enabled Baldwin to sidestep the sentimental pitfalls of social protest. Irony sharpened Baldwin's message and directed it to a literate public – neither rednecks nor homeboys but enlightened liberals who might have mastered Shakespeare, Marx, and Freud but understood next to nothing about race. It was a universal human message, not that Negroes want to be loved as Negroes or as neighbors but simply that they "want to be treated like men." The best response to color is to be color-blind, to grant blacks a full measure of humanity. This was a simple message, but eventually Baldwin would find it almost impossible to sustain.

Even before Baldwin published his first novel, his liberal outlook could be gauged from an odd bit of ventriloquy we find in some early essays. In "Many Thousands Gone," for example, he freely borrowed the first-person plural from Lionel Trilling's essays to speak for the sentiments of the *white* world, often with surreal results: "Our dehumanization of the Negro," he writes, "is indivisible from our dehumanization of ourselves: the loss of our own identity is the price we pay for our annulment of his." Or "Time has made some changes in the Negro face. Nothing has succeeded in making it exactly like our own." This is not Baldwin trying to pass – he was already becoming known as a young black writer of promise – but a white-identified Baldwin speaking hopefully as the voice of the larger society in the act of questioning itself. It shows the awkwardness of a man eager to belong, to make a difference, someone writing in the acceptable voice, anxious to speak from the center yet deeply uncertain about where he stands.

By the early 1960s, however, in the long novel *Another Country* (1962) and in *The Fire Next Time,* this liberal message began to be crowded out by another view, more strident in its rhetoric yet also prophetic of the stresses of the coming decade. Even before a resurgent black nationalism used the slogans of black pride and Black Power to challenge the integrationist faith of the civil rights movement, Baldwin himself was changing. As long as he kept the ironic and prophetic voices in balance, his inner conflicts lent drama to his fiction and dialectical strength to his remarkable essays. But as his anger took hold, exactly as he predicted, as success and acclaim freed him to vent his bitterness, his prose turned preachy, his characters became ciphers of his argument. Rufus, the self-destructive jazz musician in *Another Country,* and Ida, his even angrier sister, become vehicles for the writer's denunciation of white people. Even as the novel preaches a gospel of love, Baldwin uses Ida to express a bitter contempt:

They keep you here because you're black, the filthy, white cock suckers, while they go around jerking themselves off with all that jazz about the land of the free and the home of the brave. . . . Some days, honey, I wish I could turn myself into one big fist and grind this miserable country to powder. Some days, I don't believe it has a right to exist. . . .

I used to see the way white men watched me, like dogs. And I thought about what I could do to them. How I hated them, the way they looked, and the things they'd say, all dressed up in their damn white skin, and their clothes just so, and their little weak, white pricks jumping in their drawers. . . . I used to wonder what in the world they did in bed, white people I mean, between themselves, to get them so sick.

It would be too much to say that this highly sexualized hatred speaks unequivocally for the later Baldwin, who began to warn of an impending racial apocalypse in *The Fire Next Time.* Still, Rufus and Ida's all-consuming anger showed the direction their author was taking. In *The Fire Next Time* he was able to sustain a complicated mixture of feelings for perhaps the last time, at once mocking and applauding the separatist demonology of the Nation of Islam.

Like Ralph Ellison in his portrayal of the Marcus Garveyite figure of Ras the Exhorter in *Invisible Man,* Baldwin had often shown how seemingly extreme and irrational views within the black community spoke to something every black person had experienced in a life of second-class citizenship and demeaning discrimination. Baldwin was brave in trying to enlighten white readers about those prejudices and where they came from. Even in 1948, publishing his first lengthy essay in *Commentary,* Baldwin had been candid about black anti-Semitism. Glimpses of Baldwin's growing interest in black nationalism could be seen in a 1961 essay, "East River, Downtown," where he first develops his sympathetic but critical treatment of the Black Muslims. Although he rejects the Muslim faith in black supremacy as no more sensible than white supremacy, he notes that "it is quite impossible to argue with a Muslim concerning the actual state of Negroes in this country – the truth, after all, is the truth. This is the great power a Muslim speaker has over his audience. His audience has not heard this truth – the truth about their daily lives – honored by anyone else."

From his years as a preacher, Baldwin was adept at holding an audience. And because of his homosexuality, he felt as much a sexual as a racial pariah, especially in the uncertainty of early manhood. He explored these feelings separately in *Go Tell It on the Mountain* and *Giovanni's Room* (1956) before blending them in the heated atmosphere of *Another Country,* his last genuinely effective novel. Together they cover the three phases of his life up through the early sixties – the uptown life of his boyhood in Harlem, the expatriate life of his Paris years after 1948, and his downtown life in Greenwich Village in the late fifties. All three are novels of conversion and personal transformation: John Grimes in the throes of adolescence, at the threshold of maturity; David in *Giovanni's Room* resisting and finally acknowledging his own homosexuality; and, finally, all the characters in *Another Country,* black and white, gay and straight, finding ways to love and forgive each other after the suicide of Rufus, their troubled friend, brother, and lover.

With many postwar writers, Baldwin always believed, as he said in 1959, that "the private life, his own and that of others, is the writer's subject – his key and ours to his achievement." Like Bellow, Malamud, and Ellison, he rejected the documentary realism prized by the thirties generation. As Renoir said he painted with his prick, Baldwin wrote with his emotions even if they were raw and confusing. He never truly took possession of the form of the novel, never reshaped it to a vision of his own, as Wright and Ellison did. He depended too heavily on flashbacks and on melodrama to plumb what he took to be the mystery of all human relationships, "the dreadful human tangle, occurring everywhere, without end, forever," as he described it in *Giovanni's Room.* The solid world of *Go Tell It on the Mountain* – the Harlem streets, the great migration that brought its people there – was something he would rarely recapture in his fiction, though it remained part of the social fabric of his essays for another decade. The descriptive and visual sense of Paris in *Giovanni's Room* is strong, but the anguished flow of introspection is really the author's own, for it goes beyond the characters as we know them. In *Another Country* the loss of control is even greater, for the novel's plot, involving five or six major characters, never fully objectifies the tangled mass of feelings the writer brings to it.

By contrast, there is an almost mechanical element of form in *Go Tell* and *Giovanni's Room* that keeps these stories *too* tightly structured. The former takes place on a single day in 1935, John Grimes's birthday, the day he receives the Lord's call. Enclosed between the two steps of his conversion are three novellas centering on his aunt, his stepfather, and his mother. Each of them migrated to Harlem from the South; all three made terrible choices that pinched and choked off their lives; all three made a life for themselves not much better than what they left behind. Baldwin's prose does little to suggest the different contours of their minds, the personal imprint of each of their recollections.

As Eliot and Joyce shaped their stories around ancient myths and literary allusions, Baldwin reworks his own family history around biblical motifs. Thus John Grimes becomes Ham, "the accursed son of Noah," father of the Negro race, who fell into sin and shame when he looked on his father's nakedness, and also Ishmael, despised son of the bondswoman Hagar, rejected by the patriarchal father. This Oedipal struggle with the violent, paranoid father may remind the reader of Henry Roth's *Call It Sleep*: both are growing-up stories about boys who are detested by their fathers and feel like outsiders in their own home. In Roth's story, too, the father rejects a son he sees not as his own but as a child of sin; there too the boy, much younger but also troubled by new sexual feelings, undergoes a spiritual conversion that breaks his father's terrifying grip on him.

John Grimes's fate is left open at the end, but there is hope he can evade the disasters that befell the family members who have witnessed his transformation. All of them grew up in oppressive surroundings, battered by poverty or constrained by a frigid respectability, deprived of a beloved parent or hemmed in by their own bad choices. Each of them reached for freedom and love; none succeeded except for heartbreakingly brief periods. His aunt, now gravely ill, had abandoned her mother, loathed her brother, and driven her free-spirited husband away; John's stiff-necked father, torn between carnal feelings and moral inhibitions, had turned his back on the woman carrying his child, whom he never acknowledged, and then married another woman out of self-mortification rather than love; John's mother had seen her young lover destroyed by despair and anguish, then had married mainly to give her son a name. None of them remained true to their feelings; none could hold on to the kind of love that, to Baldwin, was the only salvation that mattered.

Baldwin's strength in *Go Tell,* as in his essays, comes from his emotional intelligence, which outweighs the novel's structural flaws and literariness. When Baldwin writes about his characters' hopes and disappointments, especially in love, or about the weight of the past in their lives, he can be piercingly eloquent. Elizabeth's vividly remembered feelings about the mother who dies on her; the father who abandons her; the cold, unfeeling aunt who takes her in; the lover, Richard, who sweeps her off her feet but cannot stand on his own; the harsh man she marries; and finally the son she hopes to shield – these empathetic details have precisely the strength of Baldwin's essays at their best. But the story does not unfold in an emotional vacuum. Because of who these people are, the rough and painful world they live in, the way race has affected all their lives, the novel also has an encompassing social framework. Young Richard, for example, loses his moorings after he has been unfairly imprisoned, abused, and grudgingly released. His suicide, like Rufus's in *Another Country,* is the act of a man at the end of his rope, a victim of both society and his own corruscating despair.

Unfortunately, the lessons in love we get in Baldwin's next two novels, *Giovanni's Room* and *Another Country*, really do take place in a world void of nearly everything but personal feeling. *Giovanni's Room* was partly inspired by the famous Beat murder case in the early forties in New York, in which Lucien Carr, a friend of Jack Kerouac's, was jailed for killing an unwanted homosexual suitor. (Kerouac himself was imprisoned briefly as an accessory after the fact.) Baldwin's plot, centering on Americans in Europe, is a sexualized version of Henry James's international fables, such as *The Ambassadors*, with added touches of the expatriate world of *The Sun Also Rises* and the sexual self-discovery of *The City and the Pillar*, but without Hemingway's chic despair or Vidal's earnest didacticism.

The bisexual Giovanni, an Italian peasant turned Paris bartender, stands for the kind of guilt-free Mediterranean sensuality that the American protagonist, David, can neither resist nor accept. David's fiancée Hella, though patient and understanding, stands plainly for the dull satisfactions of conventional marriage. Almost against his will, David falls into a passionate love affair with Giovanni, but he is tormented by guilt feelings and eventually pulls away, as he had once done in a youthful escapade with another young man. Torn apart by ambivalence and fear, he finds it impossible to be honest with himself or with his lovers of either sex. When he finally comes to terms with his feelings, it is far too late. After David's retreat, Giovanni falls into a sordid world of predatory old queens, which propels him, all too melodramatically, to murder, and then to execution on the guillotine. So David loses both his lover and, in due course, his fiancée, without quite rising, like Lambert Strether in *The Ambassadors* or Isabel Archer in *The Portrait of a Lady*, to the misguided dignity of a Jamesian act of renunciation.

Besides the contrast between European worldliness and American inhibition, *Giovanni's Room* has another Jamesian quality characteristic of postwar fiction: not much longer than a novella, the book is tightly coiled around a single metaphor, Giovanni's room. The room stands for Paris itself, where an American far from home can find or lose himself; small and squalid, it also represents the perilous appeal of forbidden love. For David it threatens to become a prison of sexual difference, a trap that will separate him from normal life forever, like the cell in which Giovanni awaits execution. David finds the room's clutter and disorder frightening. "I was trembling. I thought, if I do not open the door at once and get out of here, I am lost." Writing about love, Baldwin falls readily into the clichés of romance fiction: "But I knew I could not open the door, I knew it was too late. Soon it was too late to do anything but moan. . . . With everything in me screaming *No!* yet the sum of me sighed *Yes.*"

For Baldwin himself the room stands for the irresistible pull of the private life, the risky search for identity, which strikes fear into David but offers Baldwin an escape from the racial climate in America. But the room also is the void into which Baldwin's fiction could fall in the quest for love apart from a wider sphere to give it meaning. *Giovanni's Room* can be evocative – a love letter to the streets of Paris, where Baldwin felt he could breathe free air – but expatriate Paris is a small world grafted onto the life of a great city; the tumultuous ongoing life of the French capital barely appears in the book. The streets contain little but cafés, bars, and rented rooms. They do not resonate like the hieroglyphic streets of Harlem that he was leaving behind. Like Richard Wright, Baldwin seriously risked losing touch with his American material during his Paris exile.

Yet *Giovanni's Room* is a brave portrayal of the confusions of sexual identity. It is a book about self-discovery, like *Go Tell It on the Mountain* and *Another Country,* but this is thwarted by David's emotional knot, his conflicts over his own desires. Feeling like an outcast, David despises himself, but his homosexuality washes over him like the religious conversion in the previous novel (which also had a sexual subtext). *Giovanni's Room* is less a defense of homosexuality, like *The City and the Pillar,* than a brief for honesty, for attending to intimations of love wherever they appear. *Another Country* develops this theme on a much larger scale, interweaving the racial and sexual motifs that had been kept apart in the first two novels.

❧

The main characters in *Another Country* include Rufus Scott, a jazz musician who vents his growing fury first on his white Southern girlfriend, then on himself; Ida, his tempestuous sister, who takes on his sulfurous anger after he kills himself; Vivaldo Moore, an aspiring white novelist, first Rufus's friend, then Ida's often frustrated lover; Cass Silenski, wife of a glibly successful novelist; and finally Eric Jones, an actor, also white and Southern, who is returning from some contented years in France, where he lived with a man he loved, to take a part in a Broadway play. In the course of the novel, these characters sleep with each other and deceive each other in various combinations, black and white, gay and straight, almost never for kicks but as a way of breaking the ice floe that blocks them from living happy lives.

This search for self-fulfilment makes the novel something of a high-toned soap opera. Despite its considerable daring and racy Greenwich Village setting, the novel's round-robin of relationships follows the pattern of popular bestsellers of the 1950s – it is a *Peyton Place* of interracial bohemia instead of small-town New England. Rufus's story, added by Baldwin in his final draft, is almost a free-standing novella that serves as the book's prologue. The other lives are acted out over his corpse: his friends feel they have somehow failed him, and his sister feels an inchoate need to avenge him, to take up where he left off. The other bookend is Eric, the expatriate actor, who enters the novel when it is almost half over. His early life is yet another fable about growing up gay in America, coming to terms with being different, seeing yourself as others see you. Eric's French life reflects the quest for happiness of Baldwin's own expatriate years. His return to America galvanizes his friends to connect with each other and with their own feelings. If Rufus represents the self-destructive rage they must get beyond, Eric stands for the love and release they must somehow find. Eric is a salvific figure who puts them all on a path to self-forgiveness.

Unfortunately, Eric is more a figment of fantasy, even self-idealization, than a credible character. He is not only a great lover, generous to both men and women, but a model of emotional honesty, the very quality his friends need to sort out their lives and break through in their work. We first see Eric sitting naked in an Edenic garden overlooking the Mediterranean together, with his young French lover, Yves (Eve?). Their hard-won serenity is threatened, for Eric is about to leave for Paris and New York, where he will have to deal with a world he fled years earlier. Once there, this is exactly what he does. Sleeping with Cass, he will enable her to stand up to her insensitive husband and put her marriage on a more honest footing. Sleeping with Vivaldo, he will somehow empower him to reach out to Ida with a new depth of feeling. Thus, Eric is not only a mechanism to resolve the novel's plot but also a vehicle of the author's evangelical belief in salvation through love, especially homosexual love. (To Eric, man-woman love is only a form of "superior calisthenics.") Both Cass and Vivaldo are white and heterosexual and therefore, according to the novel, uptight, uneasy in their bodies, and out of touch with their feelings. The bisexual Eric is their liberator, their bountiful instructor, like Ramona in *Herzog*. In the process Eric also saves himself. When Yves finally joins him in New York, they will find that the hothouse bloom of their love can flower in the real world.

This belief in redemption through love, and especially through a polymorphous sexuality, situates *Another Country* firmly in the period that produced Mailer's *The Deer Park* and "The White Negro" and Norman O. Brown's *Life Against Death,* that saw the first American publication of D. H. Lawrence's *Lady Chatterley's Lover,* Henry Miller's *Tropic* novels, Vladimir Nabokov's *Lolita,* and William S. Burroughs's *Naked Lunch.* As a Jamesian who at bottom was aesthetically and morally conservative, Baldwin officially disapproved of these books, as he made clear in his essay on Mailer in *Nobody Knows My Name.* Yet *Another Country* is itself a product of the existential 1950s, with its quest for personal authenticity, its fascination with the hipster, and its effort to break down rigid barriers between races, genders, and sexual identities. This utopian strand comes through most clearly in passages of unfortunate sexual description, invariably between men: "Eric felt beneath his fingers Yves' slowly stirring, stiffening sex. This sex dominated the long landscape of his life as the cathedral towers dominated the plains." When Vivaldo, feeling strange yet comfortable with another man's body, suddenly turns passive, and allows himself to be taken by Eric, Baldwin's run-on prose turns purple and utopian: "Vivaldo seemed to have fallen through a great hole in time, back to his innocence, he felt clear, washed, and empty, waiting to be filled." As if trembling on the brink of a religious revelation, he becomes as a child again, an empty vessel "waiting to be filled." A moment later he feels "fantastically protected, liberated. . . . All of his hope, which had grown so pale, flushed into life again."

Baldwin makes up for passages of dreadful writing about sex with lightning shafts of perception about people and their behavior: Cass's dawning realization of the emptiness of her marriage, Vivaldo's insight into the block that keeps him from giving life to his fictional characters, young Eric's gradual recognition of his sexual difference, which is confusing to him yet clear to everyone around him. Significantly, these are all interior changes, like the famous chapter in *Portrait of a Lady* in which Isabel Archer, in one long fireside reverie, understands her marriage from just a glimpse of her husband with another woman. Baldwin was a lifelong Jamesian. But where James could lend drama to a character who is simply thinking, Baldwin invests himself almost too copiously in his people, reducing them to aspects of himself. "The sharp outlines of character are dissolved by waves of uncontrolled emotion," complained critic Robert Bone. "The author does not know where his own psychic life leaves off and his characters' begins."

Another Country proved to be a turning point in Baldwin's inexorable shift from the ironic to the prophetic voice. Much more than *Giovanni's Room,* it showed the intrusion of Baldwin the essayist into the work of the novelist, with every major character at some point speaking for him, either as an artist, a black man, or a homosexual who had loved both men and women. Rufus's anger and frustration, Ida's bitterness, her sense that white people do not actually *see* her, Vivaldo's conflicts over his writing, and Eric's feelings about being an expatriate, coming to terms with being gay, and finding meaning through love – all these (except the homosexuality) are autobiographical motifs better developed in Baldwin's essays. The greatest overlap is with *The Fire Next Time,* Baldwin's last major essay, the one that reads most like an inspired sermon, apocalyptic yet highly personal.

If Baldwin's best work reflects his ambivalence, the Jamesian complexity of his inner life, this essay was the last time he could keep the interior dialogue in balance. It is a rhetorical masterpiece, mesmerizing in its prose though often contradictory in its point of view. Telling the story of his religious conversion at fourteen, Baldwin takes us back to the setting of *Go Tell It on the Mountain,* but the essay itself belongs to the new racial landscape of the 1960s, which Baldwin was the first to explore. In one passage describing the music of the church, for example, Baldwin reaches back to the rhythms of the pulpit to convey a sense of unearthly beauty invisible to the white world:

It took a long time for me to disengage myself from this excitement, and on the blindest, most visceral level, I never really have, and never will. There is no music like that music, no drama like the drama of the saints rejoicing, the sinners moaning, the tambourines racing, and all those voices coming together and crying holy unto the Lord. There is still, for me, no pathos quite like the pathos of those multicolored, worn, somehow triumphant and transfigured faces, speaking from the depths of a visible, tangible, continuing despair of the goodness of the Lord.

This is warmly nostalgic, with Baldwin the preacher lending eloquence to Baldwin the writer, yet it also foreshadows the new sixties discourse of pride in the black experience. Once Baldwin had fled Harlem and the church for the freedom he could find only downtown; now he transfigures their pathos and despair into beauty, agency, and communal emotion. The world Baldwin tried to escape had also marked him for life. Just a few pages earlier, Baldwin had written about the church as his "gimmick" for transcending the ghetto, and later he describes the hypocrisy of the church, the lack of any real love in it: "It was a mask for hatred and self-hatred and despair." But here, recalling the emotions, the drama, the spectacle, the language, he lets his ambivalence shade off into incantation, even sentimentality. For the moment at least, the church takes possession of him.

The Fire Next Time, like the great March on Washington of August 1963, commemorated the anniversary of Lincoln's Emancipation Proclamation in 1863, which was also, understandably, the historical reference point in Ellison's *Invisible Man.* Thanks to the nonviolent protests organized by such civil rights organizations as Martin Luther King, Jr.'s Southern Christian Leadership Conference (SCLC), the Student Nonviolent Coordinating Committee (SNCC), and the Congress of Racial Equality (CORE), as well as the court actions brought by the Legal Defense Fund of the National Association for the Advancement of Colored People (NAACP), the racial situation in the South was beginning to change. The burning of churches, attacks on civil rights workers, and heavy-handed resistance by white Southerners were drawing national attention. In June 1963 President Kennedy, appalled by televised scenes of the police in Birmingham, Alabama, assaulting black women and schoolgirls with attack dogs and water hoses, came out strongly in support of new civil rights legislation, which his successor would shepherd through Congress after his assassination.

Baldwin's text straddles the line between the integrationist views of civil rights leaders and the angry militance soon to come. He connects his own experience in the church with the separatist teachings of the Black Muslims; in an uncanny way, they anticipate themes of black pride, black rage, black separatism, and black power that were shortly to dominate the race issue. At the end, Baldwin turns against Muslim notions of racial superiority, arguing that "the value placed on the color of the skin is always and everywhere and forever a delusion," but it is too late, for the whole thrust of the essay has been to explore the anger and pain, the history of mistreatment and dehumanization that make the appeal beyond color, an appeal to universal human standards, seem beside the point.

Earlier in the essay, Baldwin had caricatured whites for being "terrified of sensuality," for imitating jazz singing so badly "that one dare not speculate on the temperature of the deep freeze from which issue their brave and sexless little voices," and even (the low point of the essay) for "the blasphemous and tasteless foam rubber" they call white bread. In both *Another Country* and *The Fire Next Time,* Baldwin follows Mailer in upending racist clichés about black sensuality by turning them into hip virtues. In the years to come, these inverted stereotypes would become a staple of black nationalist rhetoric, along with a rhetoric of violence, of African origins, of separatism, and of communal pride, themes pushed hard by the puritanical Muslims.

In his earlier discussion of the Black Muslims in "East River, Downtown," he had quoted a "prominent Negro" saying, "I am not at all sure that I *want* to be integrated into a burning house." In *The Fire Next Time* he repeats this question in his own voice, with less qualification, and makes it his central theme: "Do I really *want* to be integrated into a burning house?" Yes, answered one critic, if it is the only house you have. Baldwin anticipates this reply by saying that "the Negro has been formed by this nation, for better or for worse, and does not belong to any other – not to Africa, and certainly not to Islam." On claims of black superiority, he writes, in the spirit of his earlier work: "The glorification of one race and the consequent debasement of another – or others – always has been and always will be a recipe for murder." Such sensible second thoughts carry little weight, however, beside the book's apocalyptic warnings. In a sentence that foreshadows the urban race riots of the 1960s, Baldwin writes: "The Negroes of this country may never be able to rise to power, but they are very well placed indeed to precipitate chaos and bring down the curtain on the American dream."

Baldwin's vision of a bloody racial conflagration combines biblical imagery ("the fire next time") with repeated references to the Holocaust. His life till then had been bound up with Jewish teachers, Jewish friends, Jewish editors, Jewish magazines. He had grown up in a literary scene in which Jews played a pivotal role. He had alluded to the Holocaust in previous essays as evidence of what an advanced Christian civilization could perpetrate on its designated scapegoats. Like the Jews of Europe, a Negro initially "just cannot *believe* that white people are treating him as they do," for it "has nothing to do with anything he has done," simply with what he is. Now Baldwin feels for the first time that whites actually intended to destroy black people, that the ghettos of our great cities may be little different from the European ghettos in which Jews were rounded up for slaughter. In the opening essay he writes to his nephew that "this innocent country set you down in a ghetto in which, in fact, it intended that you should perish." He qualifies this, however, as being "the root of my dispute with my country," that is, a family quarrel.

The Fire Next Time oscillates unsteadily between such dire predictions and less eloquent qualifications. Describing the world's passivity before the murder of the Jews, he imagines the same indifference "on the day that the United States decided to murder its Negroes systematically instead of little by little and catch-as-catch-can." Baldwin bolsters his fears with evidence from his own encounters with racism and from recent history, especially the mistreatment of colored soldiers during and after World War II. Spiraling downward into self-destructive rage, caught in the powerful whirl of his own style, he projects a vision of the coming doom of American and Christian civilization: "Time catches up with kingdoms and crushes them, gets its teeth into doctrines and rends them; time reveals the foundations on which any kingdom rests, and eats at those foundations, and it destroys doctrines by proving them to be untrue." In such passages of empty eloquence, Baldwin put his mind to rest and allowed his prophetic cadence to take over.

ও

Baldwin's newfound militance, his conversion to protest and anger, was lauded by Irving Howe in his controversial 1963 essay "Black Boys and Native Sons," which harshly criticized Baldwin's earlier attacks on Richard Wright. But it did little to endear Baldwin to the young black militants of the sixties, who attacked or dimissed him, and it seriously damaged his work, which at its best was grounded in introspection, not angry rhetoric. Baldwin's latest conversion was also mocked by Ralph Ellison in his celebrated reply to Howe, "The World and the Jug," his best-known essay, in which he wittily disparaged Baldwin for "out-Wrighting Richard" and minimized his own Oedipal relationship to the author of *Native Son.* "Wright was no spiritual father of mine," he wrote. "I rejected Bigger Thomas as any *final* image of Negro personality." Ellison explored the relationship much more affectionately in a lecture about Wright a few years later, revealing how close he was to his mentor at least until 1940. "I read most of *Native Son* as it came off the typewriter, and I didn't know what to think of it except that it was wonderful. I was not responding critically."

In this tribute, Ellison mobilizes Wright to make his own case against "the mystifications of racism," black and white. He emphasizes Wright's conflicts with his fellow Communists, who had no respect for the autonomy of art and little understanding of the actualities of black life. But he also shows how Marxism, and Wright's own confidence as an artist, enabled Wright to escape the poverty of merely racial analysis. He admired Wright as a combative figure, fearless in his integrity: "In him we had for the first time a Negro American writer as randy, as courageous, and as irrepressible as Jack Johnson."

In such essays as "The World and the Jug" and "Remembering Richard Wright," Ellison picks up where Baldwin faltered, insisting on the variety and complexity of black life and the range of influences, from Ernest Hemingway and T. S. Eliot to jazz, that can be enriching for a black artist. Ellison was immune to the destructive effects of black nationalism, perhaps because in *Invisible Man* he had already shown his mastery over every facet of black life, from folklore and dialect to urban hustling and pan-Africanism. This was why he reacted so strongly to Howe's well-argued but prescriptive essay. It seemed to confine the black writer to a path of anger, protest, and victimization. To a man who had aspired to write the Great *American* Novel, this was a much narrower role than the one he wished to play.

Ellison's response to Howe and Baldwin anticipated all the attacks that younger black writers would level against him in the late sixties and seventies. With considerable empathy, his novel had already sent up just such ideological currents in black life, from the Marxism of the thirties to Black Power notions that would flourish only more than a decade later. Born in Oklahoma in 1914, not long after its transition from Indian territory to statehood, Ellison had studied music at Tuskegee Institute between 1933 and 1936 before migrating to Harlem, where he began to write under Richard Wright's insistent prodding. Thus, he not only knew black life in the West, in the South, and in the largest northern ghetto, but at Tuskegee was exposed to the accommodationist ideas of Booker T. Washington ("the Founder"), which he would wickedly satirize throughout *Invisible Man*. All these, including his close links with the Harlem branch of the Communist party, are among the autobiographical strands out of which his novel is loosely woven. But these experiences appear even more directly in the essays that, as we now can see, form a major part of Ellison's literary legacy.

When Ellison first brought together his essays, reviews, lectures, and interviews in *Shadow and Act* (1964), they were reviewed respectfully as revealing adjuncts to his novel and as a promissory note for the fiction yet to come. A second collection, *Going to the Territory*, which appeared with no fanfare in 1986, seemed even more an act of propitiation. Well before the posthumous *Collected Essays* of 1995, however, it was becoming clear that this impressive prose was not simply an assortment of personal opinions but a major body of cultural criticism that had already inspired other black intellectuals and had begun to influence the national outlook on race, as Du Bois's critique of Booker T. Washington had done at the beginning of the century, as Wright had done for the 1940s, and as Baldwin had done for the fifties and early sixties. The key to Ellison's approach is his distinct way of exploring his double consciousness, his sense of identity as a Negro and as an American. His answer to Baldwin's question about being integrated into a burning house would surely have been "Yes, because it's *my* house" – and because not all of it is burning, not all the time: the property is still rich with undeveloped possibilities.

Of all African American writers and intellectuals, Ellison stakes the greatest claims – not for a separate black culture or literary tradition, but for an inestimably great role within *American* culture. He acknowledges a debt to Jewish American writers but insists that they did not escape provinciality until they saw their experience in American terms – not simply in ethnic or personal terms but as a characteristic feature of a larger world. Instead of simply exploring his own memories, the Jewish writer first "had to see himself as American and project his Jewish experience as an experience unfolding within this pluralistic society. When this was done, it was possible to project this variant of the American experience as a metaphor for the whole."

Where others pay lip service to "diversity," Ellison shows in fascinating detail how different currents have merged into the mainstream of our culture – not simply how Anglo-Saxon culture was altered by the folkways and speech of outsiders but how the children of immigrants and slaves adapted remote customs to their own usage. Cultural appropriation is the great theme of Ellison's essays, which explore the mixed origins and improvisational forms of both black and American identity. Through half a century of lecturing and writing, Ellison never tired of describing how different cultural forms, high and low, classical and vernacular, Eastern and Western, Northern and Southern, were braided together into an authentic American creativity. In the varied tradition of the early W. E. B. Du Bois, John Dewey, Horace Kallen, Randolph Bourne, and Alain Locke, Ellison's is a classically pluralist defense of cultural diversity. In a revealing tribute to Locke, Ellison stressed the danger of becoming "unconciously racist by simply stressing one part of our heritage," the genetic, racial part:

You cannot have an American experience without having a black experience. Nor can you have the technology of jazz, as original as many of those techniques are, without having had long centuries of European musical technology, not to mention the technologies of various African musical traditions. . . .

What I am suggesting is that when you go back you do not find a pure stream; after all, Louis Armstrong, growing up in New Orleans, was taught to play a rather strict type of military music before he found his jazz and blues voice. Talk about cultural pluralism! It's the air we breathe; it's the ground we stand on.

Part of Ellison's story was how a culture could be created by people who were neither free nor equal, by despised immigrants or oppressed slaves. In one example, he describes how slaves adapted European dance fashions brought over by their masters:

First the slaves mocked them, and then decided, coming from dancing cultures, that they could do them better – so they went on to define what is surely the beginnings of an American choreography.

He goes on to show that what began in rags in the slave yards eventually found its way into Negro dance halls and juke joints until it finally reached the stage. In Ellison's picture, popular and vernacular culture, located at the fringes of the social hierarchy, provides the pores through which the main body of culture breathes and renews itself. Blacks had "the freedom of experimentation, of trying out new things no matter how ridiculous they might seem," because "there was no one to take them too seriously." Oppression and dislocation had imposed "a great formlessness" on Negro life. They needed to experiment, to develop a new language, because they were forced into corners where they *had* to improvise, to re-create themselves, and because the cultural mainstream reflected no honest images of their own lives – or mirrored them only in distorted or one-dimensional forms, as in minstrel culture or in Hollywood movies.

To Ellison, white Americans have always "suffered from a deep uncertainty as to who they really are." On one hand this has forced them to seek a unified identity by scapegoating "outsiders," But the same national uncertainty gives these outsiders exceptional leverage – politically, to recall the majority to its professed ideals; culturally, to work within the many popular forms of expression that make America different from an ancient and traditional culture. "On this level," says Ellison, "the melting pot did indeed melt, creating such deceptive metamorphoses and blending of identities, values, and life-styles that most American whites are culturally part Negro American without even realizing it." He shows how, beginning at least as far back as *Huckleberry Finn,* the black presence led to "certain creative tensions" that had a decisive effect on the high culture as well.

In the opening piece of his second collection, "The Little Man at Chehaw Station," Ellison wrote a definitive (if idealized) meditation on the American audience, which he saw embodied in the little man behind the stove at a small railroad station near Tuskegee – the random individual whose judgment matters, who sees through the bogus performance, whose culture is at once eclectic and classical, popular yet demanding. If *Invisible Man* had a single ideal reader, it would be this man, completely ordinary yet protean and adventurous. "Possessing an American-vernacular receptivity to change, a healthy delight in creative attempts at formalizing irreverence, and a Yankee trader's respect for the experimental, he is repelled by works of art that would strip human experience – especially American experience – of its wonder and stubborn complexity." Whether or not such a man actually exists, for Ellison he is a paradigm of democratic life, in which culture and education have flowed through mysterious channels and "certain assertions of personality, formerly the prerogative of high social rank, have become the privilege of the anonymous and the lowly."

Such a figure, as Ellison sees it, can also become the agent, not simply the recipient of culture; in this guise he reappears later in the essay as a classic "American joker," a cool ghetto customer who performs some astonishing bits of personal theater before delighted onlookers outside Ellison's home on Riverside Drive. After describing this street-smart character's antics, including his flamboyant dress and body language, Ellison calls him "a home-boy bent on projecting and recording with native verve something of his complex sense of cultural identity." This man – or Ellison's projection of him – represents culture as pragmatic improvisation, for he is putting together his own personality out of bits and pieces of different traditions. Making himself up as he goes along, he demonstrates "an American compulsion to improvise upon the given." He "was a product of the melting pot and the conscious or unconscious comedy it brews." To Ellison, Americans have "improvised their culture as they did their politics and institutions: touch and go, by ear and by eye; fitting new form to new function, new function to old form."

In this kind of cultural analysis, focusing on eclectic American forms of self-invention, Ellison is at once expounding the technique of *Invisible Man,* situating it within American culture, and perhaps explaining why it was so hard for him to complete his second novel. Two years later he developed these ideas in an autobiographical lecture, "Going to the Territory," the title piece of the same collection. Here Ellison gave one of the most forceful descriptions of how our culture and identity have been shaped by creative tensions and a constant process of cultural assimilation. The very title alludes to Huck Finn's metaphor for reclaiming his freedom. Recalling his own school days in Oklahoma, not long after the territory had become a state, Ellison describes young black kids learning European folk dances, a sight that some might find "absurd" but to him was part of a necessary process of appropriating the Other, making creative use of what seems alien. Rather than expressing "a desire to become white," we were narrowing "the psychological distance between them and ourselves," as well as "learning their dances as an *artistic* challenge." This skill, this discipline, would be the black children's secret weapon as well as their key to an unnoticed freedom – "our freedom to broaden our personal culture by absorbing the culture of others," something that could develop and grow even "within our state of social and political unfreedom."

This might be seen as special pleading out of the writer's own autobiography, but to Ellison what he received was a gift, for it introduced him "to the basic discipline required of the artist." His music education also enabled him "to grasp the basic compatibility of the classical and vernacular styles which were part of our musical culture." This in turn would eventually shape his vision of American literature as the cultural correlative of democracy, an ongoing process of transformation mediated by the vernacular. The vernacular is not simply "popular or indigenous language" but a "dynamic *process* in which the most refined styles of the past are continually merged with the play-it-by-eye-and-by-ear improvisations which we invent in our efforts to control our environment and entertain ourselves." On one level this is a demotic version of Eliot's "Tradition and the Individual Talent," with its account of how the tradition is constantly being transmuted by new voices and creative departures. On another level, it is a beautifully articulated example of a fluid and functional pragmatist aesthetic within a democratic culture, an aesthetic of improvisation, spontaneity, and continuous transformation.

Far from seeing the vernacular as a dumbing-down of high culture, a view common among critics of popular culture in the 1950s, Ellison sees it as part of an ongoing process of cultural self-renewal. Arguing that "there is no necessary contradiction between our vernacular style and the pursuit of excellence," Ellison describes the vernacular as the medium in which we experiment with the languages and forms that will best express us. "While the vernacular is shy of abstract standards, it still seeks perfection in the form of functional felicity. This is why considerations of function and performance figure so prominently in the scale of vernacular aesthetics." This, of course, is nothing less than a description of jazz, for Ellison the very epitome of how vernacular artists refine and transform traditional materials. But it applies equally well to a writer like Twain, who showed how to turn regional speech into art "and thus taught us how to capture that which is essentially American in our folkways and manners."

Ellison's accounts of Twain, of jazz and the blues, and of his early musical education are also accounts of the creative process that shaped *Invisible Man* and made it an archetypal American novel. In his 1953 speech accepting the National Book Award, Ellison gives prime importance to the book's "experimental attitude," a phrase out of the pragmatist lexicon that would apply equally well to a modernist or a jazz aesthetic. Explaining why he turned away from the language of naturalism (including the hard-boiled manner of Hemingway and the proletarian writers), he notes that "despite the notion that its rhythms were those of everyday speech, I found that when compared with the rich babel of idiomatic expression around me, a language full of imagery and gesture and rhetorical canniness, it was embarrassingly austere." In its place he sought a language and form that were richer, more varied, and more mysterious, full of wordplay and allusion, metaphoric in plot as well as verbal style, so as to convey the fluidity and complexity of the world as he had experienced it. In its form as well as narrative line, *Invisible Man* would exemplify the vernacular process through which American culture had explored its contradictions, including its racial conflicts.

One of Ellison's most strongly held views was that race itself is little more than a mystification, that skin color and blood kinship are trivial markers – of little help in explaining the complexity of human culture. Ellison's aim was to put aside "the insidious confusion between race and culture which haunts this society." Whether seen as a source of pride (by nationalists), of shame (by racists), or of solidarity (by communal boosters), race alone determines little about what human beings can achieve. It is not a fate to which individuals have been ineluctably condemned, or an essence that defines or delimits them. In his response to Irving Howe, he complains that "Howe makes of 'Negroness' a metaphysical condition, one that is a state of irremediable agony which all but engulfs the mind." Ellison's pragmatic response – to Howe, to Baldwin, to white supremacists and black nationalists alike – is that identity is forged rather than given, created rather than determined by biology or social statistics. "It is not skin color which makes a Negro American but cultural heritage as shaped by the American experience."

For Ellison the construction of identity is analogous to the hard work of making art, involving a mixture of personal discipline and subtle cultural influences. In *Invisible Man,* he gives us an anonymous protagonist with no identity except what others are continually trying to impose on him, no strategy except his eagerness to please. In the whole spectrum of postwar fiction he is the ultimate outsider, telling his story from his underground lair. But through most of the novel he is also the character who most wanted to be an insider, to fit in and be accepted. The novel's episodic structure, prismatic language, and fluid technique reflect the process through which he tests and gradually sheds these imposed definitions, with all the illusions that came with them.

Like Voltaire's Candide, whose experience continually belies his teacher's insistence that this is "the best of all possible worlds," Ellison's protagonist is an unshakeable innocent, immature, eager to get ahead, trained in the habits of deference and humility through which blacks in America had traditionally gotten by. But life itself, full of surprises, repeatedly tells him otherwise, beginning with the death of his grandfather, who, after a long, quiet, humble existence, calls himself a spy and a traitor in the enemy's country, and urges him to "overcome 'em with yeses, undermine 'em with grins, agree 'em to death and destruction." Near the end of the book, the hero decides bitterly to do the same: "I'd let them swoller me until they vomited or burst wide open. . . . I'd yes them until they puked and rolled in it. All they wanted of me was one belch of affirmation and I'd bellow it out loud. Yes! Yes! YES! That was all anyone wanted of us, that we should be heard and not seen, and then heard in one big optimistic chorus of yassuh, yassuh, yassuh!"

The whole novel is a testing of his grandfather's double message of humility and enmity, of seeming accommodation and inner resistance, the first of many such messages he takes in without fully understanding them. The scene with his grandfather is also the prototype of Ellison's semiallegorical method. Like the heroes of other picaresque novels, the young man is less a full-blooded character than a convenience of an often symbolic, occasionally surreal plot. As in the riff just quoted, Ellison uses narrative as a freewheeling vehicle for ideas, wordplay, wild satire, ideological burlesque, and striking realistic detail. His description of the characters passing through the Men's House in Harlem, for example, is an acidly etched inventory of people living out their dreams and illusions; it is a miniature human comedy of the whole Harlem scene. His grandfather's death scene, however, is not realistic but stylized and emblematic – a piece of comic and tragic argument, that gives us a gritty version of a general view of life. His grandfather's words serve as a chorus or leitmotif recurring from episode to episode. The novel is tied together by many other such texts that reappear musically, a theme and variations marking the stages of the narrator's progress. Another text like this is "To Whom It May Concern – Keep This Nigger-Boy Running," which the boy understands as the implicit message he carries with him as he tries to make his way in the world. In so many other words, that is exactly what it is. At every step, he is given the illusion of progress but is actually meant to keep running in place, to get nowhere. Only by breaking with received messages, socially ascribed roles, conventional restraints, and respectable ambitions does he begin to come into his own.

The typical bildungsroman explores the passage from innocence to experience, a process by which the naïve or callow protagonist becomes the substantial person who narrates the book. The hero of *Invisible Man,* however, ends up nowhere, in a state of articulate hibernation, in a well-lit Dostoyevskyan hole in the ground, not in Harlem but in some "border area" where he can see without being seen. The novel is not about the shaping of a life but the unshaping of illusions, about achieving a new awareness of who and what you are. When the hero eventually puts his innocence behind him – the naïveté he had resumed in nearly every episode – it is not to make a life but to shed all the false lives for which he had been pointlessly striving. Along with the "running" metaphor, this suggests *Invisible Man*'s kinship to other picaresque fiction discussed in the previous chapter, such as *The Catcher in the Rye, On the Road, Lolita,* and *Rabbit, Run.* In these novels, the protagonist's deepest need is not to become a success, to settle into an ordered life, but to escape the one he already has – not to take on responsibility but to slough it off. Like Holden Caulfield, Ellison's hero eventually sees through the phoniness of nearly everyone around him, the fakery inherent in social role playing. He rejects the 1950s mantra of maturity, the demand for affirmation, and reaches for something that makes him an outsider, even a pariah. He wants to live his discontent, even if it is only half understood.

One thread of *Invisible Man* is Ellison's lively mockery of every kind of respectability, black or white, corporate or communist, middle class or working class. The good white citizens who organize the "battle royal" are lechers and sadists, treating the black boys like gladiators in a Roman arena. At college the young man tries but fails to live by the visionary ideals of the Founder and Dr. Bledsoe. Expelled, he learns what they really add up to – a way of manipulating whites into thinking that you serve and respect them. Up north, the trustee Emerson's son opens his eyes (for the moment) to how he is being jerked around. But the young Emerson is a parody of a well-meaning white liberal – patronizing, neurotic, and self-absorbed; the man urges him to study the earlier Emerson's ideas about self-reliance and seeks plaintively to be his friend – but ends up asking him to serve as his valet.

Each episode is dominated by just such a false god exacting tribute, a would-be mentor trying to determine his path. "Everyone seemed to have some plan for me, and beneath that some more secret plan." At the paint factory he is under the authority of an old Uncle Tom, Lucius Brockway, underpaid, overqualified, submissive to whites, and vicious to other blacks, especially those connected with the union. After an explosion out of Fritz Lang's science-fiction masterpiece *Metropolis,* he enters a surgical "white" world and is treated by men who subject him to surreal experiments, prob-ing his sense of reality. "I fell to plotting ways of short-circuiting the machine." By trying to deprive him of his identity, to lobotomize him, they unwittingly open him up to a new, more fluid sense of identity that will flourish in the big city.

At the other extreme are the few characters who nurture him without an agenda of their own, or simply help open his eyes. Trueblood's tragi-comic tale of incest introduces him to the earthy world of the shacks and sharecropper cabins that lie outside the field of vision of the respectable college. When he shows this world to one of the white trustees, he is cast out – for introducing a touch of reality onto a painted set. Another helpful figure is the vet who echoed his grandfather's advice as he headed north: "Play the game, but don't believe in it – that much you owe yourself." In Harlem he boards with Mary, whose maternal concern is as anchored and authentic as Trueblood's ribald comedy of love and lust. She is a warm-hearted specimen of the common people, the substratum of personal real-ity that social theories tend to ignore or suppress. Each of the hero's false mentors claims to be putting him in touch with history, but it is only a conveyor belt toward an unwanted future, an abstract process that takes no account of his wishes or needs. "Look at me! Look at *me!*" he finally shouts, in what could be the motto for the whole novel. "Everywhere I've turned somebody has wanted to sacrifice me for my good – only *they* were the ones who benefited."

In one of the novel's richest scenes, he buys baked yams from a Harlem street vendor and is flooded with nostalgia for the home he left behind, a distant pastoral world he has been taught to rise above. Yet going back to this early world is no answer. He *must* see its value – must accept the com-mon life, the sensory plenitude from which he sprang – but also must put it behind him. Just as the college is the false Eden from which he must fall in order to become himself, Mary's home is only a temporary shelter from the swirl of the city streets. Eating the yams makes him not only homesick but reflective. "What a group of people we were, I thought. Why, you could cause us the greatest humiliation simply by confronting us with something we liked." This leads him to a delicious fantasy in which he accuses Bledsoe of being "a shameless chitterling eater! . . . of relishing hog bowels!"

Bledsoe would disintegrate, disinflate! With a profound sigh he'd drop his head in shame. He'd lose caste. The weekly newspapers would attack him. The captions over his picture: *Prominent Educator Reverts to Field-Niggerism!* . . . In the South his white folks would desert him. . . . He'd end up an exile washing dishes at the Automat.

This goes on much longer – it is the kind of wild riff that marks the hero's moments of recognition – and it leads to a moral: "to hell with being ashamed of what you liked." But the mind keeps turning, and within a page or two he begins to see the limits of the yam view of life. "Continue on the yam level and life would be sweet – though somewhat yellowish. Yet the freedom to eat yams on the street was far less than I had expected upon coming to the city. An unpleasant taste bloomed in my mouth now as I bit the end of the yam and threw it into the street; it had been frost-bitten." In the end, he typically resolves his conflict with an outrageous pun: "I yam what I yam."

This yam scene is one of several turning points at the center of the book. It is preachy – Ellison is always making his points – yet full of the sensory exuberance that gives this novel its gusto. Much of the commentary on the novel has focused on the brilliant set pieces of the first half, which can be seen a dark comic American equivalent of *The Pilgrim's Progress*. But readers have sometimes stumbled over the seemingly over-long Brotherhood sections that follow, which are clearly based on Ellison's (and Wright's) experiences with the Communist party. Yet it is only here and in the Harlem riots that follow – that Ellison begins to pull the many threads together, bringing the novel to an exhilarating conclusion. Just as the hero must leave Mary behind, he must give up the sanctuary of the Men's House, a temple of hollow propriety and foolish dreams and ambitions. (The Men's House is Ellison's version of the Harlem Y, where he first stayed when he came to the city in 1936.) By dumping the foul contents of a cuspidor over the head of a Baptist reverend whom he takes for Bledsoe, the hero throws away the crutch that protected him from a world "without boundaries" – from Harlem and the city. If in earlier episodes he is slowly shedding illusions, only to deal with new ones immediately afterward, in this part of the novel he gradually yields to the flux as he comes to recognize and relish his own invisibility. In his own way he enacts the process of self-making described in Ellison's (and Emerson's) essays.

The narrator's growth of awareness, his willingness to go with the urban flow, is played out through metaphors, such as the images of blindness and vision that run through the whole novel: the blindfolded boys at the battle royal, the college sermon about the Founder by the blind preacher Barbee, the torn photograph of a boxer who had been blinded in the ring, and finally the glass eye of Jack, the Brotherhood leader, which pops out at an unfortunate moment and reminds us of the limits of *his* vision. In the Brotherhood, the young man learns to see beyond race, as Richard Wright did among the Communists, but he is mocked and chastized when what he sees does not fit the current line. The Brotherhood liberates him at first, introducing him to a wider world, giving him both work to do and a fully developed set of ideas, along with a sense of hope, a solidarity with others. But finally it tries, like every other institution he gets entangled with, to impose its outlook on him. The Brotherhood pretends to have a scientific grasp of history; it claims to know what Harlem needs better than Harlem itself. But this is ultimately shown up as another example of whites patronizing blacks – and of inflexible organizations stifling spontaneity and individuality.

As the novel's Epilogue makes clear, Ellison is giving us a black-accented version of the anticonformist discourse of the 1950s, the social critique of the lonely crowd and the organization man. But because he is black, the narrator is faceless in a special and vivid way. He is invisible because no one really *sees* him; the Brotherhood recruits him but does not want him to think. "You made an effective speech," they tell him. "But you mustn't waste your emotion on individuals, they don't count. . . . History has passed them by." Though they object when he makes any appeal to color, he wonders whether he is being used simply because he is black. "What was I, a man or a natural resource?"

The second half of *Invisible Man* is also closely linked to midcentury novels and memoirs about the disillusionment with Communism, including Koestler's *Darkness at Noon,* Wright's *American Hunger* (the suppressed second half of *Black Boy*), and the collective volume *The God That Failed,* which included both Koestler and Wright along with Ignazio Silone and others. Since Ellison was young and marginal to the Harlem branch of the party and Wright was famous and central to the party's work among blacks, it is fair to assume that this part of *Invisible Man* is heavily indebted to Wright's experiences, as described in both *American Hunger* and Ellison's "Remembering Richard Wright." There Ellison expresses gratitude to

Wright for his willingness to confide in him about his problems with the party, "especially his difficulty in pursuing independent thought." When the narrator is brought up on trial, the charges echo those that had been directed against Wright – that he trusts his own judgment over the party's, that he speaks *for* blacks rather than *to* them, that he is too concerned with race. *Invisible Man* goes far beyond the anti-Communist genre, however, for the narrator's disillusionment is part of a larger process of casting off misconceptions and closely exploring his own identity.

When the narrator decides that his political mentors are simply white men with yet another plan for him, he realizes that even in the Brotherhood he needs to live a double life. He learns to live within a shifting sense of who he actually is. Standing before an audience on his party assignment, decked out in a new suit and a new name, he experiences a sense of vertigo, as if caught with his identity down. He fears that he might forget his name or be recognized by someone in the audience. "I bent forward, suddenly conscious of my legs in new blue trousers. But how do you know they're your legs? . . . For it was as though I were looking at my own legs for the first time – independent objects that could of their own volition lead me to safety or danger." He feels that he is standing simultaneously at opposite ends of a tunnel, both in the old life he has left behind and in a new world that is still disturbingly vague and unformed.

This was a new phase, I realized, a new beginning, and I would have to take that part of myself that looked on with remote eyes and keep it always at the distance of the campus, the hospital machine, the battle royal – all now far behind. Perhaps the part of me that observed listlessly but saw all, missing nothing, was still the malicious, arguing part; the dissenting voice, my grandfather part; the cynical, disbelieving part – the traitor self that always threatened internal discord. Whatever it was, I knew that I'd have to keep it pressed down.

Like so much else in the novel, this at once exemplifies and parodies Emersonian notions of self-transformation. As a spokesman for the Brotherhood, the narrator is shedding his old skin, exercising his power over language and people. Yet he is also simply playing another assigned role, keeping the dissenting parts of himself "pressed down." With a flash of panic he sees that "the moment I walked out upon the platform and opened my mouth I'd be someone else." But he also senses that he would become simply a party hack with an assumed name, someone arbitrarily forced to deny his past.

Only when he puts on dark green glasses and is everywhere taken for Rinehart, the hustler and trickster, the man of many faces and roles, is he willing to step outside history, acknowledge his invisibility, and yield to the fluidity of the world around him. Both the Brotherhood and the nationalists – personified by Ras the Exhorter, with his impassioned Marcus Garveyite rhetoric of racial pride – are locked into the hard lines of history as they see it. Only Rinehart, who is everywhere and nowhere at once, can negotiate the chaos of the ghetto, the boundary-free world of modern urban identity.

Could he be all of them: Rine the runner and Rine the gambler and Rine the briber and Rine the lover and Rinehart the Reverend? Could he himself be both rind and heart? What is real anyway? . . . His world was possibility and he knew it. He was years ahead of me and I was a fool. The world in which we lived was without boundaries. A vast seething, hot world of fluidity, and Rine the rascal was at home. Perhaps *only* Rine the rascal was at home in it.

This is the novel's version of the malleable, self-fashioned identity that Ellison invokes in his essays, a way of stepping out of imposed roles or shaping them to your needs. His friend Tod Clifton, the poster boy for the Harlem Brotherhood, has turned his back on the organization and plunged out of history. In Midtown he hawks Sambo dolls, whose fine strings symbolize how he himself felt manipulated. When Tod is shot down by a policeman, the narrator must find another, less suicidal way of reclaiming his individuality. Rinehart, the man of the city, provides him with a clue. "My entire body started to itch, as though I had been removed from a plaster cast and was unused to the new freedom of movement." He sees that compared to the South, where everyone knew him, the urban world can offer him freedom. "How many days could you walk the street without encountering anyone you knew, and how many nights? You could actually make yourself anew. The notion was frightening, for now the world seemed to flow before my eyes. All boundaries down, freedom was not only the recognition of necessity, it was the recognition of possibility."

Many of the midcentury works of deradicalization convey a wounded quality, a sense of apocalyptic combat, as in Whittaker Chambers's *Witness* (1952), or a mournful sense of loss, as in much of *The God That Failed.* Many former radicals portrayed Communism as a lost or spoiled idealism, something precious they would never be able to recover. But a heady exhilaration spills over in the last hundred pages of *Invisible Man,* the thrill of a man reclaiming his own life – the food that embarrassed him, the experiences that formed him, the music "that touched upon something deeper than protest, or religion." What does the Brotherhood know of "the gin mills and the barber shops and the juke joints and the churches. . . . and the beauty parlors on Saturdays when they're frying hair. A whole unrecorded history is spoken there." For these people it was not the

Brotherhood but Rinehart, with his dodges and disguises, his endlessly resourceful maneuvers, that represented "a principle of hope, for which they gladly paid. Otherwise there was nothing but betrayal."

The narrator reasserts his solidarity with those who lie outside history, the "transitory ones": "birds of passage who were too obscure for learned classification, too silent for the most sensitive recorders of sound." As in his recognition of a world "without boundaries," Ellison, through his character, is expressing his commitment to becoming an artist, at once shaping his own identity and keeping in touch with common experience. The Brotherhood's line, like other white views of Negro life, is enjoined from above, not experienced from below. "It was all a swindle, an obscene swindle. They had set themselves up to describe the world. What did they know of us, except that we numbered so many, worked on certain jobs, offered so many votes, and provided so many marchers for some protest parade of theirs." As he recognizes how he has been used, his Dostoyevskyan sense of humiliation helps him reclaim his own experience:

I began to accept my past and, as I accepted it, I felt memories welling up within me. It was as though I'd learned suddenly to look around corners; images of past humiliations flickered through my head and I saw they were more than separate experiences. They were me; they defined me. I was my experiences and my experiences were me, and no blind men, no matter how powerful they became, even if they conquered the world, could take that, or change one single itch, taunt, laugh, cry, scar, ache, rage or pain of it.

Through images of sight and insight, he gives us what seems like the novel's actual point of origin, the writer's own germinal moment of recognition that catapults him from the blindness of politics, ideology, and sociological abstraction to a grasp of the complexity of his own experience. Suddenly, all his old mentors merge into a single figure trying to bend him to their will – an external force that must be overthrown. "I looked around a corner of my mind and saw Jack and Norton and Emerson merge into one single white figure. They were very much the same, each attempting to force his picture of reality upon me and neither giving a hoot in hell for how things looked to me. I was simply a material, a natural resource to be used." This is Ellison's declaration of independence, his personal emancipation proclamation. The thrill he feels in writing it we also feel in reading it, not least because it provides the novel with such a strong formal resolution.

Did Ellison imagine that ordinary people, especially black people, could find freedom in the same way, by recognizing that reality and identity are malleable, that they were free to create themselves? Yes, for he believed that blacks have a culture in which they already have done so. He disliked deterministic visions of entrapment like the portrait of Bigger Thomas in *Native Son* and insisted that Richard Wright, in creating Bigger, had not done justice to his own wide experience. But Ellison's emphasis was always on *imaginative* freedom within political and social *un*freedom, within limits that could be only partly transcended. Writing about *The Great Gatsby* he describes "the frustrating and illusory social mobility which forms the core of Gatsby's anguish," yet he argues that the novel's black readers could not make Gatsby's mistakes. Accepting the National Book Award for *Invisible Man*, Ellison appealed instead to the shape-changing figure of Proteus as his paradigm for coping with America's "rich diversity and its almost magical fluidity and freedom." In his essays he tells us repeatedly that the effort that creates art – that requires craft, discipline, and a mastery over reality – is the same as the process that shapes individual identity and ultimately culture itself.

In one of many discursive texts set into *Invisible Man*, the narrator remembers a literature teacher's comments on Stephen Dedalus in Joyce's *Portrait of the Artist as a Young Man*:

Stephen's problem, like ours, was not actually one of creating the uncreated conscience of his race, but of creating the *uncreated features of his face*. Our task is that of making ourselves individuals. The conscience of a race is the gift of its individuals who see, evaluate, record. . . . We create the race by creating ourselves and then to our great astonishment we will have created something far more important: We will have created a culture.

Since *Invisible Man* is in many ways modeled on Joyce, and since Joyce himself highlights the word *race*, this is an especially momentous statement of purpose. *Invisible Man* is linked not only to the postwar discourse of anti-Communism but to the closely related defense of liberal individualism and cultural pluralism in the work of such social critics as Lionel Trilling, Reinhold Niebuhr, and Arthur Schlesinger, Jr. The case Trilling makes for the complexity and inwardness of art over the simplifications of ideology is echoed by both Baldwin and Ellison, yet Ellison gives it a radical – not a conservative – edge. His arguments for the diversity of both black and American life, for a cultural rather than a strictly political approach, for discipline and self-mastery, and for an acceptance of complexity and contradiction have in recent years provided such black artists and intellectuals as Albert Murray, Toni Morrison, Michael Harper, Wynton Marsalis, James Alan McPherson, Stanley Crouch, Gerald Early, and Henry Louis Gates, Jr. with a vigorous alternative to both black nationalism and Marxism.

Powerful as Ellison's essays are, his novel is even more impressive, a veritable *Ulysses* of the black experience, rich with folklore, verbal improvisation, mythic resonance, and personal history, in his words "a raft of hope, perception and entertainment" that does justice to the variety of African American life. Though it is a novel of the civil rights years, its perspective is neither integrationist nor rights-oriented but cultural. As angry as any text of black nationalists, it charts an odyssey through a whole way of life, a study of attitudes rather than abuses, deliberately written, as he recalled much later, in a voice of "taunting laughter," in a tone "less angry than ironic." The effort to go beyond anger and ideology to discover a common core of black experience is itself ideological, for there were many fifties attempts to pass beyond ideology that also appealed to "experience." Ellison does not simply proclaim an end to ideology, however; he enacts it. He was trying to avoid writing "another novel of racial protest instead of the dramatic study in comparative humanity which I felt any worthwhile novel should be."

The novel is rich with moments that are neither wholly realistic nor wholly allegorical but an emblematic mixture of both, such as the yam-eating scene or the hero's one-man uprising at the Men's House or the splendid vision of Ras on a great black horse, dressed in the garb of an Abyssinian chieftain, with fur cap, shield, and cape ("a figure more out of dream than out of Harlem"). Ras makes great speeches, but when the narrator, defending himself, throws a spear that locks his jaws together, Ellison is doing something that few other postwar novelists could get away with – creating a charged image that is at once an event, a metaphor, and a statement. Baldwin, in "Notes of a Native Son," had looked at the Harlem riots of 1943 through the lens of his own family history; Ellison, no less effectively, makes it emblematic of all the cross-currents of African American life. In *Invisible Man,* Marcus Garvey foreshadows the Black Panthers, thirties Marxism anticipates postsixties Marxism, and a midcentury conception of America's cultural diversity proves remarkably germane to an end-of-century debate over pluralism and multiculturalism. Summing up every ideology roiling the turbulent waters of black life, Ellison wrote a great ideological novel, perhaps the single best novel of the whole postwar era, at once his own inner history and the complex paradigm of a diverse and braided culture.

PHILIP ROTH: THE PRODIGAL SON OF THE JEWS

Philip Roth is by far the youngest writer discussed in this chapter, the only one whose mind was formed by the aftermath of World War II – by patriotism, prosperity, and social mobility – not by the Depression. Born in Newark in 1933, he was a generation younger than the writers invariably linked with him, Malamud and Bellow. He grew up without their memories of poverty, without immigrant Yiddish echoing in his ears. Yet he lived in a kind of ghetto nonetheless, a lower-middle-class Jewish neighborhood, where he attended nearly all-Jewish schools. Immigration had been sharply curtailed in the 1920s, but the children of immigrants, even as they assimilated, lived in largely homogeneous neighborhoods. In short, Roth grew up in an ethnically segregated yet pervasively American world, almost a textbook example of the kind of rich subculture that Ralph Ellison celebrates in his essays. It was a hybrid culture, in which American civics lessons, sports, dating rituals, radio programs, celebrity cults, and Hollywood myths were grafted onto ethnic roots. This was a world Roth would satirize but also idealize throughout his career.

Like Ellison, Roth developed an intimate knowledge of this culture – the speech, the mores, the cast of mind of those formed by it; like Ellison, too, he makes a great point of the "*Americanness*" of his identity. "My larger boyhood society cohered around the most inherently American phenomenon at hand – the game of baseball," he writes in his memoir, *The Facts: A Novelist's Autobiography* (1988), and goes on to compare the reassuring leathery smell of his mitt to his orthodox grandfather's well-worn phylacteries. Later in the book, after years of living in a mostly gentile world, he falls in with a group of educated Jewish friends who encourage his taste for farcical improvisations out of the background they all share. They were

an audience knowledgeable enough to discern, even in the minutest detail, where reportage ended and Dada began and to enjoy the ambiguous overlap. Unembarrassed by unrefined Jewish origins, matter-of-factly confident of equal American status, they felt American *through* their families' immigrant experiences rather than in spite of them and delighted in the shameless airing of extravagant routines concocted from the life we had all grown up with.

This is Roth himself, twenty years afterward, describing how he came to write *Portnoy's Complaint* (1969), still fending off charges of vulgarity and Jewish self-hatred that had been lodged against him ever since his first stories. Roth's literary debut came with a book that was almost as controversial, *Goodbye, Columbus* (1959), a novella and five stories acclaimed in reviews by Saul Bellow, Irving Howe, and Alfred Kazin but attacked by self-annointed spokesmen for the Jewish community.

Goodbye, Columbus had few of the Dada extravagances of *Portnoy's Complaint,* but it showed a superb ear for Jewish American speech and a wicked eye for satiric detail. This Roth was a realist, a student of Henry

James, not a fabulist like Bernard Malamud and I. B. Singer or a ruminative intellectual living mostly in his own mind, like Bellow. Outside the comedians of the Borscht Belt, no one could convey the full flavor of a garish Jewish wedding like Roth. The title novella relies on James's technique of building a scene obliquely through dialogue and seemingly neutral description. But Roth had also learned from Mary McCarthy's sexual frankness and well-developed sense of the ridiculous, her way of accumulating lethal details to cast a cold eye on the lives of her characters. For Roth, the Patimkins are not simply a family but social specimens, suburban Jews who have not yet lost their rough edges or their roots in the ghetto. Their lives are at once comically Jewish and stereotypically American.

Because the Patimkins made a great deal of money during the war, when "no new barracks was complete until it had a squad of Patimkin sinks lined up in its latrine," they were able to move from Newark to Short Hills, though their business remains in the old Jewish neighborhood, now largely black. Roth's protagonist, Neil Klugman, is seeing their daughter Brenda, a student at Radcliffe. They also have a jock son, just graduated from Ohio State, for whom they are planning the ultimate wedding, as well as a younger daughter who is spoiled and petulant. They have tennis lessons; a country-club membership; a second refrigerator (their old one from Newark) in the finished basement, reserved for fruit; and a cornucopia of sporting goods that seems to grow on trees:

Outside, through the wide picture window, I could see the back lawn with its twin oak trees. I say oaks, though fancifully, one might call them sporting-goods trees. Beneath their branches, like fruit dropped from their limbs, were two irons, a golf ball, a tennis can, a baseball bat, basketball, a first-baseman's glove, and what was apparently a riding crop.

Seen with this kind of coldly amused precision, suburbia is the promised land of the Jews, the postwar marker of wealth, success, and acceptance. Yet the Patimkins have stored all their old furniture in the attic, either as a reminder of their origins or as something to fall back on. Neil looks at them through a poor boy's eyes, with mixed feelings of cultural superiority and class anger. He works at the Newark Public Library and lives modestly with his Aunt Gladys in the old Jewish section of Newark. As his name suggests, Neil is also something of an intellectual, a "clever man," a bit too facile in his condescension. When he mentions Buber to Mrs. Patimkin, she wants to know whether he is orthodox or conservative. He is put off by the Patimkins' materialism, for he has a social conscience, which shows in his solicitude toward a young black boy who keeps coming to the library to look at a book about Gauguin.

Still, bringing culture to the black ghetto is not exactly Neil's prime motivation. Neil wants Brenda, but a Brenda detached from the values and middle-class inhibitions of her family. When he pushes her to go to the Margaret Sanger Clinic for a diaphragm, he makes his reasons clear:

> "Brenda, I want you to own one for . . . for the sake of pleasure."
> "Pleasure? Whose? The doctor's?"
> "Mine," I said.

When Brenda leaves the diaphragm at home, where her mother discovers it, Neil suggests that she is unconsciously siding with her parents, looking for a way to thwart him or end the affair.

> "It's you who's confusing things," Brenda said. "You act as though I wanted her to find it."
> I didn't answer.

"Goodbye, Columbus" is not particularly bold or frank by later standards, but for the 1950s it was a daring story; it handles sex with a combination of self-will and self-righteousness that would become central to Roth's writing. Greater sexual freedom, the growing acceptance of sex as personal gratification rather than conjugal bliss, was an integral yet controversial part of postwar culture, brought into the open by the Kinsey reports of 1948 and 1953. In *Grand Expectations,* the historian James T. Patterson attaches it to the expanding culture of consumption. Neil's condemnation of Brenda for thwarting him is a mild one, but he attacks her with unshakeable self-assurance, a sense of entitlement. When the book first appeared, it seemed surprising that anyone could indict and dismiss someone on a presumption of her *unconscious* motives. Surely this was an appalling way of using Freudian logic – to assign blame, to feel misused. This would not be the first time one would need to take a reverse angle on Roth's heroes, to look at them from the viewpoint of the accused woman. Roth's great literary gifts were always matched by glaring blind spots, especially in his treatment of women. His protagonists were prone to paranoia, self-righteousness, a mixture of overweening need and intense suspicion, and a fear of being deceived, overwhelmed, or devoured. From *Goodbye, Columbus* and *My Life as a Man* (1974) to *I Married a Communist* (1998), Roth's heros are prone to feel victimized or betrayed by the women in their lives. The same aggrieved feelings would come into play in Roth's response to his critics, especially the Jewish critics – from the rabbis and other professional Jews who, perhaps obtusely, criticized his early stories to Irving Howe, who recanted his early praise and derided Roth in a 1972 essay. More than a decade later, Roth struck back by lampooning Howe as a sleazy, fast-talking pornographer in *The Anatomy Lesson.*

Compared to the works of Malamud and Bellow, nearly twenty years his senior, Roth's fiction speaks for the second generation. For Roth and his contemporaries, the pressure to rebel against the parents, including his literary parents, is matched by an urgent need for their approval; a loving immersion in ethnic Jewishness is balanced by a boundless contempt for the ghetto's provinciality, its limited horizons. Roth's work is not all of a piece, and it passes through several different phases, but the protagonists – from Neil Klugman and Alexander Portnoy to Peter Tarnopol (in *My Life as a Man,* Nathan Zuckerman (in *The Anatomy Lesson,* 1983, and other works of the Zuckerman saga), and Mickey Sabbath (in *Sabbath's Theater,* 1995) – tend to be variations on the same figure, roughly the same age and from the same background as the author. Like so many other second-generation males working out conflicts of identity, the Rothian figure needs to escape and to return home, needs to transgress yet also to be recognized as the most upright man who ever lived. Portnoy himself, preaching on a text from Freud ("The Most Prevalent Form of Degradation in Erotic Life," 1912), is caught between his mother and his lovers, his memories of tenderness and his raging libido, his not very convincing work on human rights and his convincing yet tormented assertion of his own rights. He tells his analyst, Dr. Spielvogel, that he is "torn by desires that are repugnant to my conscience, and a conscience repugnant to my desires," thus reminding us how verbal he is, how prepared to overwhelm everything, including his own pain, in a torrent of words.

The Rothian hero is a man defending himself, beset and put upon, but also someone in conflict with himself, exposed and vulnerable. Roth's work arrived at a confessional moment in American literature, when the barriers of privacy and discretion had been breached, when Robert Lowell was publishing *Life Studies* and Allen Ginsberg was completing *Kaddish,* but also when sex and the body were coming out into the open, not only with the publication of banned classics by D. H. Lawrence and Henry Miller but in learned but utopian works of cultural theory such as Herbert Marcuse's *Eros and Civilization* (1955) and Norman O. Brown's *Life Against Death* (1959), with its dithyrambic coda on "The Resurrection of the Body." Well-mannered young writers like Updike and Roth were slow to pick up on this explicit treatment of sex as personal salvation, certainly slower than Norman Mailer or James Baldwin. But by the late sixties, with Updike's *Couples* and Roth's *Portnoy,* they had marched to the head of the class.

Roth was not the only one to describe his generation as prematurely mature, burdened by too great a sense of moral responsibility. Roth and

Updike wrote on the cusp between two generations in a world whose values were rapidly changing. The writers' own conflicted feelings infuse Roth's early stories and Updike's *Rabbit, Run* with an edgy creative tension. For Rabbit this takes shape as a contrast between the luminous past and the humdrum present, between duty and the need for freedom, between settling into the rut of marriage and fatherhood and intimations of something beyond, something transcendent that sex might enable him to recapture. For Portnoy this is expressed through the Freudian clash between civilization and its discontents, between the mores of the tribe and the stubborn resistance of the individual will. This conflict was what brought Roth so much grief from his Jewish critics.

Neil Klugman is equally repelled by the vulgarity of the newly rich (the Patimkins and their country-club set) and the small-mindedness of the poor (his nagging, moralistic Aunt Gladys). He looks down at everyone indiscriminately: Old World Jews have no more appeal to him than grasping suburbanites. Even his co-workers at the library are shown up as narrow, rigid pedants with no imagination and no future. But at the end he is glad to leave Brenda and return to work on the Jewish New Year, as if to show that the library is his true synagogue. Only the black boy, who elicits his sentimental sympathy for the Other, is exempt from judgment: with his wide-eyed affection for Gauguin, the boy is an island of simplicity in a sea of decadence and compromise. Like the Columbus of the title, he stands for an earlier, more innocent America, Fitzgerald's "fresh green breast of the new world."

The other stories in *Goodbye, Columbus,* though well crafted, depend even more schematically on the author's own quarrel with the Jews. "Epstein," the most sexually explicit story, foreshadows the less buttoned-up writer Roth would eventually become. In the end, however, it is little more than a farcical anecdote about an aging Jewish businessman who develops an embarrassing rash on his private parts. Roth cruelly mocks Epstein's unappetizing wife, with her blue-veined thighs and drooping breasts. Poor Epstein reaches out for a new life by sleeping with a widowed neighbor, but this autumnal love affair is cut off by his outraged spouse, who spies what she thinks is venereal disease; by an unfeeling family that believes that sex is only for the young; and finally by an ill-timed heart attack that pulls Epstein back to the living death of his stale marriage. This is a young man's view of middle age.

Roth is as harsh on the nonconforming young of his own generation as he is mocking of the sexuality of their elders. Epstein's leftist daughter reads Howard Fast and specializes in social protest; her folksinger boyfriend shows no inclination to find a real job. Along with a visiting nephew, they are all disgusted by the old man's behavior and become witnesses to his shame. "Epstein" is written with a touch of pathos and empathy compared to the other stories. "The Conversion of the Jews" gives us Roth's quarrel with the Jews in a purer form. Ozzie, a boy in Hebrew school with a name right out of the pop culture of the fifties, gets into frequent trouble by questioning his teachers. Finally, when he is inadvertently hit, he races up onto the roof and threatens to jump, to become a "martyr," unless the offending party, the intolerant Rabbi Binder, and everyone around him acknowledge that "God can make a child without intercourse."

Ozzie is confused and amused by what is soon happening around him, but the story itself is more deliberate. By "catechizing" the rabbi, his classmates, his own mother, and even the old custodian who belongs to another generation, by forcing them to get down on their knees as they repeat after him, Ozzie is making comedy out of some very dark moments of Jewish history, when Jews were forced to choose between death and mass conversion. Roth identifies with the young rebel turning the tables on his sanctimonious teachers. Assimilated Jewish writers often recalled their flimsy religious education as bigoted and narrow-minded. The *melamed* or Hebrew teacher in Michael Gold's *Jews Without Money* (1930) was a prototype of filth, ignorance, and corporal punishment, and Rabbi Binder is his distant, more respectable successor. Ozzie takes special pleasure in seeing Yakov Blotnik, the mumbling custodian, "for the first time in his life upon his knees in the Gentile posture of prayer," for he suspects the old man "had memorized the prayers and forgotten all about God." The story claims to speak for tolerance and nonviolence ("You should never hit anybody about God," says Ozzie), but its transparent purpose is to rub the noses of the assembled Jews in their *in*tolerance, their lack of enlightenment within a modern, enlightened nation.

By far the most controversial story in *Goodbye, Columbus* was "Defender of the Faith," a finely textured piece of writing that embarrassed some Jews when it found a wide audience in the genteel pages of *The New Yorker*. It reaches impressively outside Roth's own Newark, focusing on a Jewish sergeant, Nathan Marx, a hero of the European war, who is repeatedly played upon by a Jewish recruit for special privileges. When he realizes that this man, Sheldon Grossbart, has pulled strings to keep from being shipped off to the Pacific, Marx pulls strings of his own to make sure he *is* sent out. The story ends with a twist of moral ambiguity as Marx realizes the enormity of what he has done. As the other recruits think nervously about their fate, he hears Grossbart behind him, swallowing hard, accepting his. "And then, resisting with all my will an impulse to turn and seek pardon for my vindictiveness, I accepted my own." But this twist provides little more than protective coloration for the main theme of Roth's narrative.

The story tells how an assimilated Jew, said to be a war hero but also someone with a Jewish conscience, a man who is vulnerable to an appeal to Jewish solidarity, casts off the tribal claims made by a more stereotypical Jew – an operator, a malingerer, probably a coward. Malamud typically used such an ethnic Jew – the marriage broker, Salzman, in "The Magic Barrel," Susskind in "The Last Mohican" – to show up the limitations of the more deracinated Jew: the confusions of identity, the pallid intellectuality. Roth does exactly the opposite: to him the challenge for the assimilated Jew is to fend off any appeal to ethnic kinship, even at some cost to his conscience.

Despite his name ("big beard"), there is nothing spiritual about Grossbart, nothing but manipulation and grubby self-interest. "Stop whining," Marx keeps telling him, "stand on your own two feet, Sheldon," as the man draws him into an intimacy he resists and dislikes. Nathan Marx, whose name combines the universalism of Lessing's Nathan the Wise and Karl Marx, is the real defender of the faith, not the faith of the Jews but of the Enlightenment, as embodied in the colorblind meritocracy of America and its citizen army. "The young man had managed to confuse himself as to what my faith really was," he says of one of Grossbart's friends, a soldier whose glasses give him "the appearance of an old peddler who would gladly have sold you the rifle and cartridges that were slung all over him." (In such later novels as *The Counterlife* (1987) and *Operation Shylock* (1993), Roth would become even more explicit in defending "diasporism" against the tribal claims of Zionists.)

American isolationists in the 1940s contended that the war was being fought for the Jews, was incited by the Jews, yet Jewish boys would somehow manage to avoid fighting it. Nathan Marx, of course, belies this canard, but we must take it on faith – his heroic combat days are over before the story begins. But the devious Sheldon Grossbart seems to confirm the libel, just as Portnoy fleshes out the caricature of the lustful Jew defiling WASP womanhood. Indeed, *Portnoy's Complaint* picks up Roth's quarrel with his people where *Goodbye, Columbus* leaves off. Roth's response to his Jewish critics in such essays as "Writing About Jews" (1963) and "Imagining Jews" (1974) – both collected in *Reading Myself and Others* (1975) – is that these types really exist, that Jews are unduly sensitive to criticism, and, finally, that previous Jewish writers, especially Malamud and Bellow, had erred in the opposite direction, portraying Jews as *too* spiritual, too asexual, too moral – always as victims rather than agents, never as the victimizers they can also become.

Implying that America has essentially solved the problem of anti-Semitism, Roth insists that since Jews are no longer threatened, they can be less sensitive about their image and give up their "timidity – and paranoia" (a curious argument from someone who would later grow so sensitive to criticism). He maintains that Jews must unlearn ghetto habits of fear, deference, and self-restraint that made sense only when their lives and welfare were in danger. This is very close to the theme of *Invisible Man,* as Roth himself acknowledges. Ellison's book shows us how the protagonist gradually emancipates himself from deference, from an eagerness to ingratiate himself, which is another version of the ghetto mentality. Yet by the late sixties, Roth's hero had as much Grossbart as Marx in him: his fiction turned more vulgar and ethnic, and "Imagining Jews" shifts this defense in a subtler direction. Malamud and Bellow, he says, consistently identify their Jewish characters, such as those in *The Assistant, The Magic Barrel,* and *The Victim,* with renunciation and self-abnegation, while saving appetite and self-will for non-Jewish characters like Henderson or Frank Alpine or more Americanized Jews, like the Chicago-born Augie March. Put more succinctly in *Portnoy's Complaint,* Roth's goal is to "put the Id back in Yid," to create the willful, transgressive Jewish protagonist of a new generation, transcending old fears and moral scruples of the ghetto.

Despite a remarkable continuity in Roth's work through four decades, the 1960s reshaped his fiction in decisive ways. It brought out the figure of the sexual outlaw already implied by the desperate Epstein and the sanctimonious Neil Klugman. His first two novels, *Letting Go* (1962) and *When She Was Good* (1967), still written under the sign of Henry James, were perfectly readable but unspeakably grim. The entanglements of their characters made the books seem aimless and shapeless. Their textured realism could do but scant justice to the spectacle Roth was seeing all around him, the carnival Tom Wolfe describes in his early journalism, the political confrontations Mailer describes in *his* journalism, the sight of a whole culture actually letting go. Though *Portnoy* became one of the literary milestones of the sexual revolution, Roth repeatedly cited other sources: the inspired mimicry of stand-up routines that took him back to his Jewish childhood, the heated atmosphere and satiric rage stirred up by the Vietnam War, and even his first wife's wild fabrications and "lunatic imagination," which

rendered absolutely ridiculous my conventional university conceptions of fictional probability and all those elegant Jamesian formulations I'd imbibed about proportion and indirection and tact. . . . Without doubt she was my worst enemy ever, but, alas, she was nothing less than the greatest creative-writing teacher of them all, specialist par excellence in the aesthetics of extremist fiction.

This last point may be little more than a piece of creative invention, a small appendage to *My Life as a Man,* with its frantic account of his unhappy marriage; the links to *Portnoy* seem questionable. Superficially, *Portnoy* seems to reflect the new sexual freedom that really took off with the licensing of the first contraceptive pill in 1960. But despite its confessional frankness and wild, unihibited vaudevillean tone, it is less about transgression than about Portnoy's inability to transgress. At war with the Jewish superego, the old incubus of morality, *Portnoy* is as much about guilt as about sex. If Malamud made a specialty of Jewish suffering, Roth's characters suffer from their failure to live, to be spontaneous; from their conflict between conscience and desire. "This is my life, my only life," Portnoy tells his analyst, "and I'm living it in the middle of a Jewish joke. . . . Is this the Jewish suffering I used to hear so much about?" He complains that he cannot smoke, drink, do drugs, borrow money, or even play cards. "Sure I say *fuck* a lot, but I assure you, that's about the sum of my success with transgressing." Even at fourteen Portnoy recalls being sick to death of the "saga of *his people* . . . sucking and sucking on that sour grape of a religion! Jew Jew Jew Jew Jew Jew!" He is fed up with the pompous rabbi who enunciates every syllable. "It is coming out of my ears already, the saga of the suffering Jews. Do me a favor, my people, and stick your suffering heritage up your suffering ass." Yet what is Portnoy but a suffering Jew, whining up a verbal storm, feeling the pangs of liberation as his forebears suffered the traumas of repression?

The uninhibited freedom that Portnoy cannot quite realize in his behavior he achieves in his language, ranting against Jews and gentiles alike, caricaturing his parents, railing against women, and giving an epic account of his youthful feats of masturbation. *Portnoy's Complaint* is a series of set pieces that remain wonderfully funny when they deal with family, childhood, and masturbation but turn dark and self-lacerating in the portrayal of his adult life. Few readers recall the last third of the novel, which grows quite ugly in Portnoy's frantic vituperation against *goyim* and women, anticipating the sense of grievance and bitter disappointment that dominates later books like *My Life as a Man, The Anatomy Lesson,* and *Sabbath's Theater.*

Irving Howe suggested in 1972 that "the cruelest thing anyone can do with *Portnoy's Complaint* is to read it twice," but the funny parts of the book, with their wonderful range of voices – the parents, their ass-licking son, the pompous rabbi, the horny teenagers – hold up very well, like great radio sketches. As an analytic patient, Portnoy does his stand-up routines lying down, but his rolling riffs and wild exaggerations never lose touch with reality. Ten years earlier, Roth had interrupted the wedding scene in "Goodbye, Columbus" with a long monologue by Mr. Patimkin's less successful brother, Leo, the kind of sad sack other Jewish writers might have put at the center of the story. Roth uses him only as a momentary foil to his brother's family, to the Jews who have made it, but his voice, his muted self-pity, his coarseness and wistfulness, seem absolutely authentic, certainly more authentic than Neil's own narration, which reaches us through a filter of irony and literary decorum. Though Portnoy may be Neil ten years later, his voice is enlivened by the mimicry and pathos, the shifting kaleidoscope of emotions, that we heard from poor Leo but never from Neil himself.

Sometimes Portnoy's mimicry can seem like virtuosity for its own sake, more Woody Allen than Céline, as in his send-up of his parents, the same mother and father he used to keep in stitches with his "imitations." ("I used to leave them in the aisles at mealtime – my mother once actually wet her pants, Doctor, and had to go running in hysterical laughter to the bathroom from my imitation of Mister Kitzel on 'The Jack Benny Show'.") His voice can sound whiny and crude, out of a perverse need to shock and disturb us, but it can also be rich and complex in its shifting emotional tones, especially in his warm memories of a childhood that remained the real anchor of his life, though also perhaps the source of his later despair. (Later, in *American Pastoral*, it was precisely Roth's idealization of the postwar world of 1949 that led him to give so grim a picture of 1969, the same year *Portnoy* appeared.)

Portnoy is grounded not in kinky sex but in Proustian recollections of childhood and youth, as in this description of the *shvitz* or steam bath to which his father would take him:

The moment he pushes open the door the place speaks to me of prehistoric times, earlier even than the era of the cavemen and lake dwellers that I have studied in school, a time when above the oozing bog that was the earth, swirling white gasses choked out the sunlight, and aeons passed while the planet was drained for Man. I lose touch instantaneously with that ass-licking little boy who runs home after school with A's in his hand, the little over-earnest innocent endlessly in search of the key to that unfathomable mystery, his mother's approbation, and am back in some sloppy watery time, before there were families such as we know them, before there were toilets and tragedies such as we know them, a time of amphibious creatures, plunging brainless hulking things, with wet meaty flanks and steaming torsos.

This prose is the kind of rich supple instrument that, starting with *The Ghost Writer,* would transform Roth's later work from vivid caricature to subtle sensory evocation. When he was not working up routines about his histrionic mother, about fucking the family's dinner, about his Jewish nose, or about his penis falling off, Roth, like Norman Mailer during the same period, was beginning to explore how a language closer to speech could accommodate new resources of metaphor and syntax. Yet it is a literary language, not Ellison's vernacular, with complex sentences that grow musical and fluent when they deal with the remembered past. Though Roth's writing never became as baroque as Mailer's new style, it developed shades and resonances that paved the way for his experiments in metafiction and autobiography in the 1980s and 1990s. In a sense this complex style, with its self-conscious metaphors and its concern with perspective, grew out of Roth's old apprenticeship to Henry James.

It is significant that this long passage evokes the primeval world of the fathers against the cultural aspirations, the "good" behavior, the need for approval, which he associates with the mother. A matching passage near the end of the book recalls the baseball games of his childhood, in which the men of the neighborhood seemed to be showing him the only life he would ever need to know, the sweat-filled, rough-hewn world of ordinary Jewish males, muscular, gamy, and profane with insult and ridicule. What a contrast to the narcissism of his adult life, he thinks, *"Oh, so alone! Nothing but self! Locked up in me!"* It is not only free of punishing self-consciousness but it is a world without gentiles, a world without women, especially the gentile women he pursues so urgently, with such disastrous results. At the Turkish bath, pounding and punishing their flesh, purging themselves of the cares of their daily lives, "they appear, at long last, my father and his fellow sufferers, to have returned to the habitat in which they can be natural. A place without *goyim* and women."

These are Portnoy's fantasies as well as his memories, especially his fantasy of not becoming the person he is, not having the problems with women he has always had. Roth's tone is too subtle to allow for any simple reading. But these passages add to one's feeling that the key figure in the book is the stoical, eternally constipated father rather than the cartoonish, overbearing mother. This helps explain why, in sharp contrast to the mocking fury of Roth's early books, his later works would devote their most evocative prose to father figures (in *The Ghost Writer* and *I Married a Communist*) or to his actual father, by then old and dying (in *The Facts* and *Patrimony*, 1991). A blistering hostility toward both women and *goyim* disfigures the second half of *Portnoy's Complaint*. He lampoons the *shikses* and their families for their holiday customs, their repressed emotions, their physical beauty, their dignity. Yet to him "these people are the *Americans*, Doctor. . . . these blond-haired Christians are the legitimate residents and owners of this place." They represent the infinitely desirable, infinitely detestable Other, and Portnoy pines for their acceptance even as he longs to exact his vengeance.

The young Portnoy's mute attraction to the gentile girls across the lake, whom he sees ice-skating, is his attraction to America, the world of Henry Aldrich and Oogie Pringle that he knows from the movies and the radio. This is his desire simply to be ordinary, to belong. At thirteen, "skating behind the puffy red earmuffs and the fluttering yellow ringlets of a strange *shikse* teaches me the meaning of the word *longing*. . . . I learn the meaning of the word *pang*." Despite the irony and self-mockery that mingle with this longing, the overall effect is poignant. But Portnoy sniffing around the home of his first college girlfriend is a less attractive sight, for the scene is distorted by the venom and craving of the outsider. Later, he dumps her without warning. His affair with a blond New England WASP whom he dubs "The Pilgrim" is even less edifying. Getting her to suck his cock becomes the mission of his life, his way of bringing down the whole Social Register. In a more genial moment, he confesses to his doctor that "I don't seem to stick my dick up these girls, as much as I stick it up their backgrounds – as though through fucking I will discover America. *Conquer* America – maybe that's more like it."

In contrast to the ambiguous lure of such women, which is sensual yet also social, the world of the father is the solid, reassuring world of the Jewish family. "I naively believed as a child that I would always have a father present," Roth writes in *The Facts*, "and the truth seems to be that I always will." To be reconciled at last with the father, to play the role of the loving and successful Jewish son, is also "to become the hero one's father failed to be." Part of Roth still recoils from this belated return to the fold. Getting the last word in *The Facts*, Roth's transgressive alter ego, Nathan Zuckerman, denounces him for taking "a tone of reconciliation that strikes me as suspiciously unsubstantiated," and for trying to show "that your parents had a good son who loved them." He blames this not simply on the impulse to seem good, to look moral, but on Roth's "separating the facts from the imagination and emptying them of their potential dramatic energy." As devil's advocate he urges him not even to publish this memoir, which Roth is said to have written for therapeutic reasons while recovering from a breakdown. In this internal dialogue, Zuckerman refuses to see that the good-boy side of Roth – the man as devoted to his parents as he is to the Jews – is as vital to him as the side that Zuckerman usually embodies. The moral outlaw in Roth always longs for acceptance, even as he wants to shock and outrage.

Zuckerman's intervention is part of Roth's long campaign against reading his fiction as a transcription of his life, a campaign that began with *My Life as a Man* and went into high gear with the alternate narratives of *The Counterlife* and the interplay of memoir and commentary in *The Facts*.

Having been accused of the sin of confessional writing, of simply *being* his characters, unable to invent anything, he was determined to show how he embroidered his memories with dramatic projections and richly imagined alternatives. This led him belatedly into the company of such postmodernists as John Barth, Donald Barthelme, Robert Coover, and Thomas Pynchon, who were examining the premises of fiction while wondering how it could ever get written. If the chapters of *The Counterlife* read like alternate versions of the same story, the full title of his memoir, *The Facts: A Novelist's Autobiography,* plays on the ambiguous relationship between memory and imagination. Although Roth can be accused of being obsessed by his critics – his books are full of characters who tell him, quite sensibly, to let it go – his need to defend himself eventually led him onto new fictional terrain, risky, probing, and analytical, with subtle and ingenious variations that are also deeply felt. Like other postmodernists, his best imaginative flights were fueled by paranoia. His books turned insecurity into art.

Portnoy's Complaint made Roth rich and famous even as it summarized one side of the extremist fiction of the fifties and sixties. The civil rights movement, the growing youth culture, the campus uprisings and urban riots, the stealthy escalation of the Vietnam War, the new sexual freedom both among the young and in the suburbs, the spread of feel-good drugs like marijuana and hallucinogens like LSD, the growing impact of rock music, and the new ethos of the counterculture divided Americans along new lines and altered their private as well as their public life. Television amplified everything, from the look of the counterculture and the high jinks of the young to the racial conflicts of the South and the horrors of the Vietnam War. The official accounts of the war were far different from what people already knew. Americans felt lied to and manipulated, and this undermined their traditional respect for authority, even their sense of reality. All this was reflected in American fiction as obliquely as the Holocaust and the bomb had been assimilated a generation earlier. Already in 1961 Roth had complained that fiction as he knew it could hardly equal the American reality, which was more bizarre and extreme than anything a writer could credibly invent. As the decade went on, writers increasingly lost confidence that conventional fiction could do justice to what was unfolding before them. In this frustration at having to compete with the daily news, they turned from fiction to journalism, or from fifties realism to black humor. American fiction grew paranoid and apocalyptic, finding new combinations for outrageous comedy and unmitigated horror.

Reflecting the new challenge to authority yet seeking new ground from which to write, journalists, novelists, and poets found an anchor in the first person, as Salinger and the Beats had done before them, as Whitman,

Thoreau, and Emily Dickinson had done before them. Life imitated art as the countercultural young took on the spirit of the books they admired, such as *The Catcher in the Rye, Catch-22, On the Road,* and *One Flew Over the Cuckoo's Nest.* The antinomian mood of American letters revived as part of the new culture of carnival, youthful rebellion, political protest, and anxious moral witness. Roth's work, which had begun in the rebellion of American sons against immigrant fathers, found its place as part of the larger uproar in American life, which became a new conflict of generations.

Roth had found a new voice in *Portnoy's Complaint,* but he was not sure how to use it. The book "determined every important choice I made during the next decade," he says in *The Facts.* It rekindled the hostility of his Jewish critics, fueling Roth's own sense of grievance, which would later become central to the trilogy of novels he called *Zuckerman Bound* (1979–85), where Nathan Zuckerman, the author of some controversial stories and one scandalous novel, muses endlessly on the injuries that women, critics, and other insensitive readers have inflicted on him. In the decade between *Portnoy* and the first of these books, *The Ghost Writer,* Roth seemed genuinely lost. His satire on Nixon, *Our Gang* (1971), ran out of steam after the first chapter. *The Breast* (1972) and *The Great American Novel* (1973) were completely misconceived. *The Professor of Desire* (1977) was simply a feeble retread of *Portnoy,* with some swipes at his critics. His self-absorption lost its comic edge.

Only *My Life as a Man,* his almost incredible account of his first marriage, has some of the great confessional energy of *Portnoy,* besides being his first venture into telling a story analytically, through multiple perspectives. Unfortunately, these do not include any credible effort to explore the viewpoint of the outrageous wife, as the irrepressible Zuckerman points out after Roth retells the same story in *The Facts.* "If you want to reminisce productively," says Roth's alter ego, "maybe what you should be writing, instead of autobiography, are thirty thousand words from Josie's point of view. *My Life as a Woman. My Life as a Woman with That Man.*"

Roth had never been the kind of writer who could project himself imaginatively into another point of view, especially that of his "worst enemy ever." Roth's conflicts come to a head in the frantic pages of *The Anatomy Lesson,* where he even makes a plausible case for giving up writing. The confessional mode, he feels, has run out of steam for him, turned into navel gazing – his bad back, his reviewers, what next? "Fiction about losing my hair? I can't face it. Anybody's hair but mine." "Either there was no existence left to decipher or he was without sufficient imaginative power to convert into his fiction of seeming self-exposure what existence had now become. . . . He could no longer pretend to be anyone else." From this clumsy beginning, however, Roth makes his problem his subject. By the mid-1980s he developed a dialogue around it, which contributed to the intellectual density, the sheer intelligence of his late work. Such books as *The Counterlife, The Facts, Operation Shylock,* and *Sabbath's Theater* bring the critical debate about his work into the work itself. In an ingenious moment at the end of *The Counterlife,* the protagonist's wife withdraws from the novel, tired of being reduced to one of the "fictive propositions" in his "argumentative books." Roth's motive for this play on fact and fiction may be defensive, but he seems genuinely puzzled by the man he was, the writer he became, the way he was seen. He brought the spirit of the essay, the spirit of intellectual dialogue, into his fiction. As a novelist of ideas, he came to rival Bellow himself.

Belying Fitzgerald's dictum that there are no second acts in American lives, Roth managed to reinvent himself in every decade. *The Ghost Writer* freed him from the need to be outrageous, just as *Portnoy,* ten years earlier, had freed him from the need to be decorous. *The Counterlife,* in turn, liberated Nathan Zuckerman from his exclusive concern with himself, giving him both a wider historical purview (in the sections set in England and Israel) and a set of alternative lives. With the idea of the "counterlife" – the life you imagine rather than the life you live – the book became a meditation on fiction that assuaged both the voices of his critics and his own need for vindication. Soon literary honors flowed his way, his first since *Goodbye, Columbus,* and Jewish honors as well, as Roth was welcomed back like the prodigal son who had finally returned to the fold. *The Ghost Writer* was an especially important breakthrough. Roth's sense of injury still burned in the book, but Zuckerman also manages to look back benignly at the mentors of his early years, including Malamud and Bellow, and even at the Jewish iconology represented by Anne Frank and the Holocaust. This side of the book is not only mellow, it is magically evocative. The richly detailed treatment of the older writers eventually became the warm filial tone of *Patrimony,* and soon Roth was almost a beloved elder statesman of Jewish and American letters. As if unsettled by all this acceptance, Roth turned around in *Sabbath's Theater* (1995) and published the ugliest, most deliberately offensive book he had ever written.

Perhaps a product of the health problems and emotional crises that Roth passed through in the late eighties and early nineties, *Sabbath's Theater* reads like a work of profound self-loathing. After the mellow books that preceded it, Roth returns with a vengeance to the Theater of Cruelty, the need to shock. The book is a bitter retrospective on a career as a transgressive artist, and it smells of panic and hatred in the face of aging and dying. Roth had written in *The Facts* of helping his father as he is "trying to die. . . . [T]hat's his job now and, fight as he will to survive, he understands, as he always has, what the real work is." *Patrimony* was a quietly authentic account of how that work was done, almost an act of restitution on Roth's part. Mickey Sabbath's "real work" is also to die; he fails, but along the way he manages to make everyone in his life as miserable as he is.

Sabbath's life is an inspired metaphor for the dark side of Roth's career, as well as a belated eulogy for the transgressive moment in American art in the 1960s. This was when Sabbath had his brief moment of glory, doing street theater with finger puppets that tested the boundaries of both art and propriety. At Sabbath's theater, "the atmosphere was insinuatingly anti-moral, vaguely menacing, and at the same time, rascally fun." Sabbath had also worked with live actors, especially his first wife, but felt that their real personalities created an intrusive human presence that diminished the purity of his art. The puppets, on the other hand, offer him perfect control, the kind a novelist has, as compared to a dramatist.

Part of the metaphor is Sabbath's lewd use of his fingers, which not only control the puppets but give their own little performance to entice members of the audience. Sabbath's story is one long bout of sexual excess and compulsion, beginning with the whores who initiate him as a teenage sailor in South American ports and finally grinding down, some fifty years later, as he jerks off into the panties of an old friend's daughter. Sabbath's married but insatiable Croatian mistress is a female version of himself, with a "great taste for the impermissible," and she talks compulsively about the performance of her other lovers. But she dies early in the novel, and this begins to close the book on the frenzied sexuality that long ago took the place of his art. Sabbath's agile fingers are now crippled by arthritis. Fired years earlier from a teaching job for seducing a student, dependent for money on a wife he despises, he vents his grief and fury in the cemetery after dark, keening for his mistress and pissing on her grave.

Fearing revenge from her policeman son, Sabbath flees their small New England town and returns to New York, the scene of his short-lived fame thirty years earlier. Sabbath's days in New York, living on the kindness of friends, are one long attempt to hit bottom. He does all he can to degrade himself yet to remain somehow unbowed, to live the last of his days as defiantly, as outrageously, as he had lived in his prime. His friend tells him that he is a relic of an earlier era, someone who is "kept fresh by means of anarchic provocation": "Isn't it tiresome in 1994, this role of rebel-hero? What an odd time to be thinking of sex as rebellion. . . . [Y]ou persist in quarreling with society as though Eisenhower is president!" Now the street performers of Sabbath's day have been replaced by homeless bums and beggars, the puppets of his Indecent Theater by warm, childlike Muppets. Briefly,

Sabbath too turns panhandler, begging on the subway, searching for another way to degrade himself and thus to savor a new experience.

Looking back over his life, Sabbath regrets not his provocations but his timidity, his meekness. Roth gives Sabbath's memories a testamentary quality, a tone of ultimate defiance. "To everyone he had ever horrified, to the appalled who'd considered him a dangerous man, loathsome, degenerate, and gross, he cried, 'Not at all! My failure is failing to have gone far *enough!* My failure is not having gone *further!*'" Sabbath had lived the life of the artist-hero but had actually produced little. "He'd paid the full price for art, only he hadn't made any. He'd suffered all the old-fashioned artistic sufferings – isolation, poverty, despair, mental and physical obstruction – and nobody knew or cared. . . . He was just someone who had grown ugly, old, and embittered, one of billions." But Sabbath's disappointment, his debasement, his very anonymity are meant to give his plight a more universal quality. He hears his late mother saying to him, "This is human life. There is a great hurt that everyone has to endure." Clearly this is the key line of the book, which is a work of great pain but also immense self-pity.

The novel's epigraph is from *The Tempest* – Prospero's valediction, "Every third thought shall be my grave" – but its atmosphere comes straight out of *King Lear*; it is the story of an old man raving and raging against life. The last pages are close to unbearable as Sabbath, wearing both a yarmulke and an American flag, returns to his mistress's grave in the hope that her son will kill him, for he has been repeatedly defiling it. All passion spent, he will stage his suicide as a final joke, his last piece of entertainment. "He had not realized how very long he'd been longing to be put to death. He hadn't committed suicide, because he was waiting to be murdered." But the policeman-son refuses to play the role assigned to him, and simply dumps him on the road, the figure of the Wandering Jew who cannot die, an Ancient Mariner living under the sign of Cain. "How could he leave? How could he go? Everything he hated was here." This is how the book ends.

In its fierce antinomian energy yet its sense of devolution and disintegration, *Sabbath's Theater* may or may not have been Roth's momentary retrospective on his career. It raised his battles with his critics to a level of cosmic principle. It resurrected the romantic image of the scorned and embattled artist while highlighting its futility. In the end Sabbath wonders,

What had happened to his entire conception of life? It had cost him dearly to clear a space where he could exist in the world as antagonistically as he liked. Where was the contempt with which he had overridden their hatred; where were the laws, the code of conduct, by which he had labored to be free from their stupidly harmonious expectations?

It would be absurd to identify Sabbath with Roth but equally absurd not to see him as a projection of Roth. *Sabbath's Theater* is an ugly, brilliant book, a dark, paranoid book, an execration in the face of critics who had long since stopped criticizing, a gauntlet thrown down to feminists who had long since stopped caring. If Ellison's work, after taking us through every kind of emotional and ideological excess, represents the ultimate victory of moderation, the triumph of the center, *Sabbath's Theater* brings us back to the old apocalyptic fury. With its deliberate evocation of a fragile moment of transgressive art, now thirty years passed, it can also be seen as the last novel of the 1960s, combining the frantically beleaguered hero of *Herzog* with the surreal fantasies of *An American Dream* and the sexual and verbal excess of *Portnoy*. It is hard to say why Jewish writers were led to produce such works of masculine megalomania and self-pity, but it is easy to see how they answered to the intoxicated spirit of the moment. For "the new mutants" of the counterculture, as Leslie Fiedler called them in 1965, gender differences were beginning to break down, but not for Bellow, Mailer, and Roth, who were writers at the barricades of the gender wars as well as the culture wars. Their novels of the 1960s obliquely refracted the anxieties and confrontations of the era, to which *Sabbath's Theater* would come as an immense, angry footnote.

AFTER THE SOUTHERN RENASCENCE

John Burt

INTRODUCTION

WHEN IN 1958 C. Vann Woodward defined "the distinctive character of the southern heritage," he did not turn, as an earlier generation of historians might have done, to such things as an attachment to land and to a traditional paternalist culture (and a distrust of capitalism, equality, and modernity generally) but to a historical burden of unsolved problems about which complex moral and cultural experiences have accreted much as layers of pearl do around a particle of sand. Specifically, Woodward argued, Southerners have never been able to comfort themselves with the illusion that history is only something that happens to other peoples, that the cycles of guilt and sorrow, resentment and revenge, or rise and fall, which are the matter of historical consciousness, are something from which they have been exempted. Southerners have never been able to imagine that they had a claim on the legacy of innocence, success, and prosperity, accepted unearned by elite white Northerners. The burden of Southern history is a legacy as well, however, since those who bear it may bring to the general culture a circumspection, a sense of the irony of history, and a moral humility that may temper the crusading self-righteousness and soaring political and economic ambitions of the general culture without sacrificing the virtues that culture wishes to serve.

Woodward's "The Search for Southern Identity" is very much a product of the civil rights era, but it is also a product of the Cold War. It does not describe a South recognizable to such antebellum defenders of the South as George Fitzhugh or to Thomas R. Dew or to such postwar idealizers as Ulrich Phillips or Sidney Lanier. It does describe, though, how the special moral problems of Southern history can, if they are brooded on without extenuation or histrionics, provide occasions for developing the kind of mature political consciousness American culture of the Cold War era was supposed – not just by Woodward but by Reinhold Niebuhr and many others – to lack. Woodward sought, without evasion, to take up the challenge to the white South that the civil rights era posed. The chastened reflectiveness about their allegiances that Woodward describes in progressive Southerners like himself has a national role, however, not just a

Southern one, that of persuading the nation to think twice before destroying the world in order to save it. The idealized Southerner Woodward describes holds in mind two contradictory facts: the necessity of moral engagement and skepticism about a crusading politics that, when it is not a stalking horse for expedience and power, often risks entanglement in a moral panic that undoes its aims.

The character type Woodward describes may not be found in such representative Southern figures as Thomas Jefferson, or in Jefferson's shadow and specter, John C. Calhoun. Whatever the role the character type Woodward described played in Southern politics, however, it can be abundantly observed in the literary life of the 1950s. It is most closely represented in Robert Penn Warren, to whom Woodward's *The Burden of Southern History* is dedicated, and with whose historical fictions Woodward is engaged in a complex dialogue. Certainly similar characters, in whom idealism and skepticism are engaged in a subtle dance, are common in the fiction of Southerners of that period – as for instance in Gavin Stevens of *Intruder in the Dust* (1948) and in Stevens's later echoes, Atticus Finch of Harper Lee's *To Kill a Mockingbird* (1960) and Lawyer Barrett of Walker Percy's *The Second Coming* (1980).

The writers with whom this chapter is concerned gained their reputation as novelists as the civil rights movement began to win legal and political victories, and in different ways Warren, Flannery O'Connor, Eudora Welty, and Percy wrestled with the special problems of that era. They also had to consider, however, as the generation before them did, what the cost would be if solutions to the special problems of the South were to cause the South itself to vanish. Even in Faulkner's *Requiem for a Nun* (1951), the tin-roofed shack is vanishing, but it is the tract house that is taking its place. The concrete repressions of the segregation era, always in tension with (and, as Woodward reminds us, directed against) a tradition of personal relations among people of different races, give way not to racial peace but to the more complete if less violent cultural alienation between the races one finds in the contemporary North.

Except for Warren, who was a writer of the Renascence generation, the four writers this chapter centers on also were the inheritors of a rich but problematic literary tradition from the preceding generation, from Faulkner most of all, but also from Katherine Anne Porter, Ellen Glasgow, Caroline Gordon, and Allen Tate, whose work represented a profound break with Southern literary traditions of the nineteenth century. Asked by an interviewer to account for the Southern Renascence, the extraordinary burst of literary creativity that happened in the South in the quarter century following the First World War, Robert Penn Warren noted that cultures often go through periods of literary excitement when they are on the brink of a profound cultural and political change, although the literary ferment subsides once the change is fully under way; the literature of the Southern Renascence, no less than the great novels of the Russian nineteenth century or the writings of the Celtic Twilight, are all the works of provincial cultures facing imminent modernization and express the ambivalent feelings that attend on modernization.

World War I is the traditional starting point of the Southern Renascence. World War I might not have ushered in material prosperity, and if anything it sharpened racism, but it did break the stranglehold of loyalty politics that had paralyzed Southern letters – driving out George Washington Cable, and forcing Mark Twain into irony and evasion – for the preceding fifty years. Certainly the Fugitive Movement – many of whose principals were returned veterans – could not have happened without the First World War.

In different ways, the major writers of the Southern Renascence expressed the divided allegiances of a not-yet-modernized culture. The village culture Ellen Glasgow depicted in *Vein of Iron* (1935) is if anything more rigid and repressive than similar village cultures described by Sinclair Lewis or Sherwood Anderson, but when the protagonist leaves that life for the economically and sexually fast life of the city during and after World War I, her criticism of the repressiveness of provincial life is considerably modified. In Porter's Miranda stories the weight of family history – most of it tawdriness romanticized into tragedy – is something the protagonist is, like Quentin Compson, nearly suffocated by; but Porter also ironizes the debunked version of the story Miranda comes to accept, and the life Miranda runs to, in wartime Denver, is so empty and so alienated that her near death in the great influenza pandemic of 1918 comes almost as a relief. Even Ernest Hemingway is not Porter's equal in portraying the grayness – balanced by a romanticized sexual rebelliousness – of wartime culture. Stark Young or Caroline Gordon also have little nostalgia for the Old South, yet both worry about the consequences of the passing of an agrarian and provincial way of life.

The grand tragedy of Allen Tate's *The Fathers* (1938) is ironically tangled in the cultural transformations that the novel predicts. The novel turns on one of the staples of Southern fiction, a white Southerner's repeated betrayals of his unacknowledged mixed-race half brother. George Posey, one of the two fathers of the title, sells his half brother Jim in order to buy a horse and is later unable to protect him when Jim is subjected, for reasons of complicated family politics, to a false charge of rape. The novel's lines of allegiance are tangled, for the betraying white brother, unlike his counterparts in Cable, Twain, and Faulkner, stands for secular capitalist modernity, not for the traditional South. Despite his cultural politics, however, George Posey throws his lot in with the Confederacy. Traditional Southern agrarianism is represented by the other father of the title, George's father-in-law Major Buchan, whose ideals are shown in the course of the novel to be played out and stale. Major Buchan, ironically, remains loyal to the Union, and he is rewarded by having his house burned by Union soldiers who assume, because of his class, that his loyalties lie elsewhere. When Lacey Buchan, the novel's protagonist, chooses his spiritual father, George Posey, over his biological one, Major Buchan, one may wonder what it is that moves Lacey to that choice, since Posey is finally so repulsive a character, but one has no doubt why Tate had Lacey make that choice, because Lacey's choice is the choice of assimilation to the modern, which Tate believes and fears will be the South's choice, too.

All of the authors treated here must come to terms not just with the political legacy of the South, and with the literary legacy of the Renascence generally, but also with the specific legacy of Faulkner, whose greatest work was behind him by the time he won the Nobel prize in 1950, but whose example rose to greatest prominence only in his last years. Before Faulkner won the Nobel prize, his reputation in the United States was chiefly as the author of lurid and risqué novels over which responsible critics shook their heads and clucked about "decadence," but he had considerable fame in France, where Sartre considered him among the great masters of English prose fiction. Although the *New York Times* was dismayed at the Nobel committee's choice, and although Faulkner's major novels, all out of print in 1950, had won him such a meager income that he had attempted to support himself, without much success, as a Hollywood scriptwriter, the publication of Malcolm Cowley's *The Portable Faulkner* in 1946 began to mark the place for him in the American literary canon that was fully established by the time Cleanth Brooks published *William Faulkner: The Yoknapatawpha Country* in 1963. *Go Down, Moses* (1942) and *Intruder in the Dust* (1948) are perhaps the last of Faulkner's novels that bear comparison with *Absalom! Absalom!* (1936) and *Light in August* (1932). The wit and brio of *The Hamlet* (1940) continues, however, in the diminished later novels of the Snopes trilogy, *The Town* (1957), and *The Mansion* (1959); in *Requiem for a Nun* (1951), Faulkner attempted a serious revision and reconsideration of his sexual nightmare *Sanctuary* (1931). The one completely new development in Faulkner's work, *A Fable* (1954), which retells the Gospel story as a mutiny in France during the First World War, is, relative to his best work, labored and turgid. The memorable scene in which the Devil, a German officer, flies across no-

man's land to discuss with his Allied counterparts how to end the unauthorized cease-fire that has spread through the trenches, however, is as
charged a scene as anything else in Faulkner.

Each of the major Southern authors who came to fame in the years after
World War II turns to a different other author for lessons in the art of fiction that could not have been learned from Faulkner. Warren, Faulkner's
contemporary as a writer but his junior as a novelist, learns at least as
much from Joseph Conrad as from Faulkner, Eudora Welty from Virginia
Woolf, Flannery O'Connor from Nathanael West and Georges Bernanos,
Percy from F. Scott Fitzgerald, Reynolds Price from Welty. The tie to
Faulkner is strongest perhaps in Cormac McCarthy, whole paragraphs of
whose *The Orchard Keeper* (1965) and *Outer Dark* (1968) could have been
taken from Faulkner. The Faulkner who matters to McCarthy, though, is
not the Faulkner of *Light in August* or *Absalom! Absalom!* but the more
lurid and ironical Faulkner of *Sanctuary* and *As I Lay Dying*. McCarthy's
most striking novel, *Outer Dark,* is a darkly comic parody of the Gospel
story. In it, Rinthy Holme bears her brother Culla's child, and sets out
looking for it after, the brother having left it for dead in the woods, the
child is rescued by an itinerant tinker. Culla in turn sets out looking for
Rinthy, and both have a series of horrific adventures. Throughout the
novel, their paths are shadowed by three murderous strangers, a kind of
gruesome Holy Trinity, who, after forcing Culla to eat human flesh, murder the child before his eyes. In later novels, McCarthy has turned away
from Faulkner, and he has accomplished this chiefly by turning away from
Southern subject matter.

Shelby Foote's early novels are also closely in Faulkner's line. *Tournament*
(1949) concerns the rise and fall, in a fictional Jordan County in which several of Foote's other novels are set, of the charismatic and energetic Hugh
Bart, who is, in turn, a farmer, a sheriff, a major planter, a great hunter,
and a gambler. Hugh Bart has Thomas Sutpen's energy and ambition, and
like Sutpen, he spends that energy on small change. Unlike Sutpen, Bart is
not a great evildoer, but he fades into age aware of having spent himself
greatly but having never discovered anything worthy of the kind of intensity he has given to everything he has done. Foote was freed from
Faulkner's influence by turning away from fiction entirely to write his
greatest work, his monumental three-volume *The Civil War: A Narrative*
(1958–1974). Foote's Civil War history is novelistic in its feel for character, its eye for telling anecdotes, its management of sequence and pace, and
its ability to contrast different narrative perspectives. At the same time,
Foote never has any personages say anything they did not actually say, and
he scrupulously avoids projecting himself into their minds, even in ways

that are within the traditional rules of narrative history. *The Civil War: A Narrative* belongs in the great tradition of narrative histories, alongside William Prescott's *The Conquest of Mexico* and Francis Parkman's *France and England in North America*.

Possibly the most interesting example of how an artist of the post-Faulkner generation came to terms with him is provided by the case of Will Barrett in Walker Percy's *The Last Gentleman* (1966) and *The Second Coming* (1980). The moral decline of Will Barrett's family – the great-grandfather singlehandedly stood off the Ku Klux Klan; the father, trapped between love and irony, committed suicide; and Will himself seems to be a drifter and humorist – clearly reflects Percy's sense of the history of his own family. He is also working through his own literary role, however, as the author of the satyr-play that follows the great tragedy: like the authors of the satyr-plays, Percy must find a way to do justice to the horrifying and mesmerizing themes of the tragedy without slighting his own more affirmative if apparently more modest calling.

Throughout *The Second Coming,* Will broods on the love and despair that drove his father to suicide. His thoughts obsessively revisit a hunting accident he had had with his father in the swamps of Georgia. Flushing two quail from the brush, his father had "accidentally" shot him, and then himself, although neither were killed at this time. Will remembers, however, that his father had reloaded before taking the second shot and that their guide had found *three* spent shells at the site. The father had fired both barrels of the shotgun at Will, but had flinched at the last moment and so had not hit him with a lethal shot. Reflecting on this, he concludes that the father had recognized in the son a despair and unfitness for the world like his own and had tried to kill him in order to spare the son a life like the father's own.

The hunting scenes in *The Second Coming* repeat, without irony, similar scenes in *The Bear* and *Aleck Maury, Sportsman*. Clearly in working out Will's relationship with his father, Percy is also working out his relationship with Faulkner, Caroline Gordon, and with the earlier generation of Southern novelists in general. The father is very pointedly armed with the weapon Gordon had lovingly given to Aleck Maury, an ancient Greener shotgun. In the elder Barrett's anguished love of Will, one sees the pull of the tragic values, and the tragic dignity, of a cultural generation Percy loves and hates, honors, and must separate himself from. It is the predicament of most of the writers in the South of his time.

Ironically, that predicament may be the result of the passing of some of the worst features of Southern politics – of the end of the distinctive Southern agony over race and its replacement by anonymous Northern-style racism, the end of distinctively Southern kinds of agrarian poverty, the end of distinctively Southern kinds of class politics. One of the things modernization brought to the South was the freedom not to tell different versions of the same story. Clearly, contemporary writers in the South such as Reynolds Price, Barry Hannah, Bobbie Ann Mason, or Ellen Gilchrist have been given a wider rein than their predecessors. No longer huddled in the tight circle of inherited griefs and grievances, Southern writers, or rather, writers who live in the South, will have many different stories, but they will be stories that do not have much to do with each other, not growing out of the same dense network of obsessions. Having a common history is having a common story, and having a common story is having the same shame to live down or live past. The end of the Southern Renascence has not left the South silent – no human place is silent – but it may have left it not the South.

2

❦

ROBERT PENN WARREN

ROBERT Penn Warren's literary career began before the publication of *The Waste Land* and ended after Robert Lowell and many poets of the generation following had died. Like Thomas Hardy, Warren has a distinguished reputation both as a poet and as a novelist, winning the Pulitzer prize in both genres (and twice in poetry). As with Hardy, his poetry, for which he was appointed the first poet laureate of the United States, is his principal claim to fame for those who know him best, but his fiction is better known to readers at large. He distinguished himself as well as a critic and as a teacher, coauthoring with Cleanth Brooks *Understanding Poetry* (1938), the textbook that taught two generations of college students how to read poetry and that symbolizes for the literary criticism of the present day that figment of the retrospective imagination now called New Criticism. Warren also was a considerable essayist on politics and history, and he made a mark as a biographer and as a dramatist as well. Few white Southerners of his generation thought as seriously or in as sustained a way as Warren did about the problems of racism during the last years of legal segregation of the races in the South and the first years of legal integration.

Growing up in Guthrie, Kentucky, a railroad junction on the Tennessee border where he was born in 1905, Warren was a precocious student (he skipped two grades in school) and was subjected to considerable hazing, including one incident, discovered by a recent biographer, in which local toughs actually hanged him. At the age of 15, after graduating from high school and studying an additional year in nearby Clarksville, Tennessee, Warren received an appointment to the United States Naval Acadamy in Annapolis, but an accident cost him the use of one eye and forced his parents to send him to Vanderbilt University instead.

It turned out to be a fortunate accident. Warren never became, as he had wanted to be, "the Admiral of the Pacific Fleet," but he did study with the poet John Crowe Ransom and befriend the poet Allen Tate, and he became associated with the circle of intellectuals at Vanderbilt in those days, including H. C. Nixon and Frank Owsley, a group known in its early years as the Fugitive circle, from the little magazine that Warren edited during its brief life, and later, after their thought took a political turn, as the Agrarians. The chief concerns of the Fugitives were poetic, and in Warren's poems of this period one sees him learning a subject matter and a stance from Hardy and from A. E. Housman, and one can watch him assimilate new influences from his study of the Metaphysical poets and from his interest in poetic Modernism. The Fugitives were very eager to repudiate the self-pitying romanticism about the Old South that loyalty politics forced on Southern poets during the years between Reconstruction and the First World War: the Fugitive, John Crowe Ransom announced in their opening manifesto, flees from nothing faster than from that. The Fugitives played a major role, both in their own poetry and in their criticism, in introducing the poetry and thought of T. S. Eliot into American culture, and later generations of poets, including talents as diverse as Robert Lowell and Randall Jarrell, learned poetry from their example.

The "New South" movement, which sought to bring industrial development to the South, and to quell racism and class division and other social problems in the South by means of the prosperity that was supposed to follow in development's wake, is associated with Henry Grady and the Atlanta *Constitution* beginning in the 1880s, but its chief intellectual heirs were progressive historians and such social thinkers as W. J. Cash, V. O. Key, Howard Odum, and W. T. Couch of the University of North Carolina. Increasingly through the 1920s, the circle in Nashville came to see itself in opposition to the Carolinians and to the "New South," which they felt would sacrifice devotion to nature, to the human scale, and to the traditional, all in the interest of a capitalist ethic of accumulation and secularism that would obliterate their identity as Southerners. Particularly under pressure arising from the Scopes trial and the essays of H. L. Mencken, the thought of the Nashville circle took on a defensive tone, seeking to vindicate Southern habits of thought and to repudiate the pressure to reject them in favor of Northern ones.

The result was a complex, little understood, and to some extent poorly thought through movement known as Agrarianism, whose chief manifestos, *I'll Take My Stand* and *Who Owns America? A New Declaration of Independence,* appeared in 1929 and 1936, respectively. Agrarianism did not represent a nostalgia for the plantation economy of the Old South, but it did seek to use a Jeffersonian romanticism about the life of the farmer to describe Southern traditions opposed to what they took to be Northern traditions of individualism, capitalist exploitation of people and land, and alienation from history and nature. In some ways, Agrarianism was the last gasp of that traditional Southern conservatism that Eugene Genovese described, although it learned more from Thomas Jefferson, the traditional enemy of most Southern conservatives, than from Calhoun. It is difficult to piece together a coherent ideological program from Agrarianism, however, because the Agrarians had various positions on many specific issues, especially on racial politics. Particularly in the immediate aftermath of the stock market crash that happened after *I'll Take My Stand* was conceived, Agrarianism demands to be seen against other crank economic theories of the 1930s, such as the Townsend Pension plan and Huey Long's Share Our Wealth program. The Agrarians probably learned more from Tolstoy and Yeats, however – who also spoke in defense of traditional agrarian cultures as they were on the brink of assimilation into the metropolitan economy – than from any particularly Southern source, and what they argued resembles, as its authors well knew, the positions taken by defenders of many other provincial traditional cultures on the uncomfortable brink of modernity.

Warren's contribution to the first volume was "The Briar Patch," which includes a thinly argued defense of racial segregation – although not of legal, educational, or economic inequality – which he would repudiate in short order and which was to haunt him considerably over the following years. The principal claim of the essay was that industrialization would not of itself solve the problem of racism, because factory owners would use competition between white and black labor to hold wages down, as they were already doing in the North, and racism would increase as a result. He notes that the segregation of unions in the North both plays into the hands of the owners and increases the racist resentments of white workers. For either the black or the white poor to get ahead, both must see that their interests are tied, and Warren argues that this can be more easily done in an agrarian society, in which people confront each other as individuals, than in an industrial one, where they see each other en masse. Warren does employ some stereotypical language, and he does not challenge the doctrine of "separate but equal," but he does at least insist on taking the "equal" part of that doctrine seriously. Warren also cautiously presents another possibility: "Something else may be added: what the white workman must learn, and his education may be as long and laborious as the negro's, is that he may respect himself as a white man, but, if he fails to concede the negro equal protection, he does not properly respect himself as a man." In the context of Warren's argument about how employers play on racism to drive down wages, it is hard to see his defense of segregation in public accommodations as other than a strategic concession.

Warren's first book, *John Brown: The Making of a Martyr*, was also a product of 1929. Like similar "Confederate" biographies written by Allen Tate and Andrew Nelson Lytle over the same years, the book is full of nervous defensiveness about Southern politics and history, stereotypical thinking about racial issues, and a certain amount of special pleading as well, but some of its themes remain important for Warren's two greatest novels, *All the King's Men* (1946) and *World Enough and Time* (1950), and his profound if uneven narrative poem *Brother to Dragons* (1953 and 1979).

Chief among the elements that would matter for Warren's later work is the figure of John Brown himself, the first of many murderous political idealists in Warren's writings. Warren's Brown is more venal and more banal than Warren's other hero-villains. Warren records his financial double-dealing with glee, and portrays him more as a con man of the order of Twain's Duke and Dauphin than as an idea-mad terrorist. This is a particularly damaging strategy against Brown, since it deprives his defenders of their view of him as a man who did wrong but who was always motivated by right. Warren does not scant Brown's bloodthirstiness, either. Although Brown's contemporary hagiographers did not positively know of his involvement in the dismemberment of pro-slavery farmers at the Pottawatomie Massacre (Brown's son did not confirm that it was Brown's doing until O. G. Villard's biography, years after the event), Warren shows that relatively accurate contemporary accounts of the event were in fact available, and that the accounts Brown's defenders chose to believe, many of them confected by their pet journalist James Redpath, were transparently incredible even at the time. Despite this, even Warren is not immune to Brown's personal magnetism. Warren confesses to a fascination with Brown – not merely to straightforward repulsion – continuously from this book, through his 1961 *The Legacy of the Civil War,* to the interviews he granted through the last years of his career. So powerful is Warren's sense that Brown's violence is somehow a backhanded testimony to the stringency of the moral demands placed on human beings by their relationship to transcendent values that Warren, here as elsewhere, is sometimes, like Milton, of the Devil's party without knowing it.

Warren's feelings are much less complicated about Brown's defenders Thoreau and Emerson, whose largely foolish pronouncements about Brown Warren mocks as typical of self-righteous, bloody-minded Yankeedom. In Thoreau and Emerson, however, Warren finds also the opponents against whom he intellectually defines himself. He often later – echoing his friend, critic R. W. B. Lewis – describes American literature as a struggle between Emerson and Thoreau on the one hand and Hawthorne and Melville (and himself) on the other. His quarrel with Emerson, both in his political prose, and in such poems as his slashing 1966 work "Homage to Emerson," turns on his criticism of Emerson's belief in the perfectability of the human being. Optimism about human nature, in Warren's view, is not only a mistake but the kind of mistake that most lends itself to becoming the agent of the fallenness it denies. Those who seek to exempt themselves from a general vision of human complicity in moral and political evil are likely also to lack the circumspection that might save them from the enraged acts that affirm their complicity in human evil despite everything.

It would have been easy for Warren to have used this Hawthornesque sense of human fallenness as a rationalization for political passivity, as Hawthorne himself did: if all political acts are undone by the ironies of history and if stern attempts at righting wrongs wind up making more wrongs to be righted, then why do anything at all? Warren does not take this step in *John Brown,* however, choosing to idealize the figure of Abraham Lincoln – an odd turn enough for so apparently unreconstructed a book – whom Warren sees as someone acutely aware of the ironies of political idealism without for all that losing his ability to act in the political world.

Warren's two later political books, *Segregation: The Inner Conflict in the South* (1956) and *Who Speaks for the Negro?* (1965), are in different ways profound meditations on the political changes overtaking the South, and the United States, during the years after the *Brown v. Board of Education of Topeka* decision. The second book is of particular interest, since in it Warren interviewed almost all of the major leaders of the civil rights movement and caught them just at that moment when the legal victories of the movement were mostly won and the movement had begun to turn to more intractable social and economic concerns. It also captured that moment when the leadership that had taken the movement through the desegregation era was beginning to be supplanted by harsher figures for whom racial integration was not necessarily a good thing. Warren also, by serendipity, happened to be one of the last people to interview Malcolm X before his assassination, and unlike many white journalists, Warren was able to see in Malcolm X something other than the nightmare projection of his own guilt. Warren's own presence in these books, judicious without being judgmental, eager for reform but eager also to avoid a morally panicked repudiation of all things Southern, frank about himself without either extenuation or theatrics, is a good model of the political cast of mind Warren most admired.

The political novels of Warren's major phase more often turn on class conflict than on racial conflict, and racial issues are more directly at issue only in such lesser later novels as *Band of Angels* (1955) and *Wilderness* (1960). *Band of Angels* is a classic "tragic mulatto" novel, whose protagonist discovers that she is of mixed race only when she is seized by her father's creditors at her father's funeral. Manty Starr's tribulations in wartime Louisiana and postwar Kansas, and her relationships with her master (played in the motion picture by Clark Gable, who had earlier played Rhett Butler in *Gone with the Wind*), her slave lover, and her Union officer husband, are both politically and melo-dramatically tangled. *Wilderness* (1960), takes an idealistic German Jewish immigrant through the 1863 New York City Draft Riots, to the dreary winter quarters of General Meade's army, to the bloody, stalemated battle of the Wilderness the next May, a battle whose confusions and slaughter – at one point forest fires swept over the battlefield and incinerated the wounded – are throughout Warren's career seen by him as emblematic of the realities of idealistically motivated war.

Warren's most charged work on racial questions is also his most flawed, the book-length poem *Brother to Dragons,* which Warren published in completely different versions in 1953 and 1979. The 1953 version is the only major poetic work of the "period of poetic silence" Warren entered in 1943, to emerge with a radically different prosody, voice, and concerns in his pathbreaking volume *Promises* of 1957. *Brother to Dragons* is closer to the intellectual world of the major novels, and it is particularly close to the last of those novels, *World Enough and Time* (1950). Published immediately before the *Brown* decision, *Brother to Dragons* is not only an anguished meditation on the history of racism and the ways in which it insinuates itself into even the most profoundly egalitarian American traditions; it also broods on the conquest and extermination of the Native American peoples, the corruption and exploitation of the West, and the repression of labor during the Detroit strikes of the Depression years. Warren's notes clearly show him also to be using the poem to think through the issues raised by the Holocaust and the atomic bomb. He studied Hannah Arendt's *The Origins of Totalitarianism* deeply during the composition of the poem and extracted passages from that book to help him clarify his own thoughts about the outbreak of metaphysical evil in political life. Warren's book is also in a not very indirect way a meditation on the ironies of Cold War–era politics: the poem is intended as a critique of the American sense of national innocence, which Warren fears may lead America, although legitimately in conflict with totalitarian powers, into a self-righteousness for which there is a high moral price to be paid in unreflecting brutality and in ends-justify-the-means expedience.

Brother to Dragons concerns the true story of how two nephews of Thomas Jefferson, Lilburn and Isham Lewis, murdered their slave George at Smithland, Kentucky, on the morning before the great New Madrid earthquake of 1811. The Lewises had bricked up the dismembered remains of George in a chimney, which the earthquake threw over. Some days later, the local sheriff, having witnessed a dog chewing an obviously human bone, investigated the case and determined to charge the Lewises with the murder. It was illegal, the legal historian Mark Tushnet reminds us, to murder slaves, although it was very difficult to convict masters of the offense. Before they could be arrested, the Lewis brothers arranged to shoot each other over the grave of their recently deceased mother, but the suicide pact went awry, and only the principal murderer, Lilburn, was killed. In the poem, Lilburn tricks the weak Isham into killing him, but in the actual event, the fact that Isham was not killed too was accidental. Isham escaped from the area, and legend has it that he was one of the small number of American casualties at the Battle of New Orleans.

Warren is moved by the fact that Jefferson never felt able to comment upon the Smithland tragedy in any way. In the poem, the shade of Jefferson is confronted by Warren, RPW, himself (or rather a fierce, unforgiving specter of RPW), who seeks, with equal parts cynicism and hysteria, to throw in his face the history of the country that claims to have been founded on Jefferson's principles. The Jefferson he confronts, however, is not an enlightenment believer in human perfectability but an anguished and embittered ghost, unable to rest because of his inability to respond to the ugly conclusions about America and about human nature that the Lewis case presents. Reflecting on his authorship of the Declaration of Independence, Jefferson compares his grand idea of freedom to the half-human, half-beast Minotaur: the Declaration embodies not a more than human value but a violating illusion that debases what it appears to exalt. He compares the high cultural professions of his own Enlightenment to the refined perversions of Pasiphaë, as if the atmosphere of cultivation of that era were not a denial of our animal nature but merely a new and kinky way of asserting it. Culture is the "infatuate machine of her invention," in which Pasiphaë waits, "laced, latched, thonged up and humped for joy."

Jefferson's own vision of the possibility of human perfection he sees not as contradictory to his complicity in evil as a slaveholder and a man but as somehow the agent of that complicity, as if the spiritual pride of that vision drives the complicity (the following quotations are from the 1953 version):

> Yes, then I met the beast. Well, better, indeed,
> Had it been the manifest beast and the circumstantial
> Avatar of destruction. But no beast then: the towering
> Definition, angelic, arrogant, abstract,
> Greaved in glory, thewed with light, the bright
> Brow tall as dawn. I could not see the eyes.
> So seized the pen, and in the upper room,
> With the excited consciousness that I was somehow
> Purged, rectified, and annealed, and my past annulled
> And fate confirmed, wrote. And the bell struck
> Far off in darkness, and the watch called out.

> Time came, we signed the document, went home.
> Slept, and I woke to the new self, and new doom.
> I had not seen the eyes of that bright apparition.
> I had been blind with light. That was my doom.
> I did not know its eyes were blind.

In the course of the poem, Jefferson is brought to see, by the shade of his sister Lucy (Lilburn's mother) that his own horrified recoil from Lilburn's evil is, in its moral panic and its rage, a kind of proliferation of evil as much as it is a reaction against it. Lucy argues that in striking down George, Lilburn struck not at George but at his inability to face what he had been doing to George, at his own inner evil. In refusing to recognize his inner kinship with people like Lilburn, Lucy argues, Jefferson compounds his crime.

In the poem's climactic moments, Lucy urges Jefferson to take Lilburn's hand, which Jefferson is ultimately persuaded to do. Warren is often considered something of a Calvinist, in that he shares the Calvinist's dark skepticism about human nature, but the Calvinist, for all his skepticism about human nature, also believes in the notion of God's spontaneous and mysterious grace, which makes human redemption possible when it seems least likely. Warren offers nothing like this in *Brother to Dragons,* offering instead only the sad wisdom of fallenness, which keeps us from serving evil in the act of fighting it:

> The recognition of complicity is the beginning of innocence.
> The recognition of necessity is the beginning of freedom.
> The recognition of the direction of fulfillment is the death of the self,
> And the death of the self is the beginning of selfhood.
> All else is surrogate of hope and destitution of spirit.

This claim bears on more than merely the specific conflicts on which the poem turns, but its particular bearing is clearly on the early Cold War sense of America's prophetic calling among nations and its sense of moral exemption from history.

The early novels of Warren's major phase are informed in easy to specify ways by the concerns of his Agrarian period. *Night Rider* (1939) concerns the actual turn-of-the-century attempt of oppressed tobacco growers in the Tennessee–Kentucky border regions to resist the power of the tobacco buyers by setting up a cooperative. The result was the "Black Patch War," a major civil disturbance that took place partly in Warren's native Guthrie and that was ultimately put down by the army. Unable to enlist all of the growers in their association and unable to dictate to the buyers without doing so, the association takes to intimidating the holdouts, first by threatening them, then by scraping their seedling beds, and finally by burning warehouses. The violence spills over into racial violence, until the Night Riders are brutalizing African Americans as much as intimidating holdouts from the association, and the movement finally collapses in fratricidal struggle.

In outline, *Night Rider* is a social realist novel of a familiar 1930s kind, having some kinship with *Native Son* (1940) and *The Grapes of Wrath* (1939) and having some affinities even with such older naturalist novels as Frank Norris's *The Octopus* (1901). The social realist concerns of the novel are crossed with concerns of another sort, however.

The protagonist, a lawyer named Percy Munn, whom the narrator derisively always calls Mr. Munn, is drawn to political action by motives unlike those that drive characters in conventional naturalist novels but that one may find in Conrad: he feels that those with political commitments have some essential reality or moral seriousness that he feels the lack of in himself, and he is drawn to the association as a way of proving to himself that he is morally alive. Reluctantly giving a speech at an association rally, Mr. Munn becomes swept up by his sense of the lives of the poor farmers he is speaking to and finds himself caught up in a position of authority in a political movement. Munn is thrilled by his new role, and in the service of a self-betraying hunger for reality, he leads the association into worse and worse violence, rapes his wife, and has a destructive affair with the daughter of a friend. At the final moment, however, he is unable to kill Senator Tolliver, who had turned against the association when things got ugly, and instead rushes out to receive the fire of the men who have been seeking to arrest him. Munn's sparing of Tolliver is the one moment of moral clarity that Warren allows him: in refusing to kill someone he has power over and reason to kill, Munn acts on what is to Warren always the first motivation of ethical people: a recognition that they are morally akin even to their worst adversaries.

Like *Night Rider, At Heaven's Gate* (1943) is based on real events, the rise and fall of the corrupt Nashville financier Rogers Clarke Caldwell (who also plays a role in Peter Taylor's 1986 *A Summons to Memphis*). Here again, Warren's precursor is not so much Faulkner as Conrad; one might think of *At Heaven's Gate* as *The Financier* as it might have been had it been written by Conrad rather than by Theodore Dreiser. The novel turns more on the host of characters who are drawn into the orbit of Bogan Murdock's operation than it does on Murdock himself, and the result is a kaleidoscopic novel in which a complicated action is presented through many points of view and in many different styles. One central character is Jerry Calhoun, a protégé of Murdock's who sacrifices his freedom and his integrity on Murdock's behalf, whose father's farm is foreclosed on by Murdock, and who finally goes to jail for Murdock's financial misdeeds. The design of the novel evinces more complicated feelings about the other chief protagonist, Murdock's daughter Sue. Sue is an instance of a common Southern character, the tragic, sexually promiscuous daughter of a powerful family. She stands in a line that includes Candace Compson of *The Sound and the Fury* (1929) and Peyton Loftis of William Styron's *Lie Down in Darkness* (1951). As Sue passes sexually from Jerry Calhoun to the labor organizer Jason Sweetwater to Slim Sarrett, a poet, boxer, literary critic, and closeted gay, we see her as alternately driven and manipulative, and only her murder by Sarrett enables the reader to sort out very complicated feelings about her. Interspersed throughout the novel is the Narrative of Ashby Wyndham, a poor wandering evangelist whose story intersects with the main story at several points. Alone in the novel, Ashby Wyndham understands the entanglement of guilt and redemption that here, as in *Night Rider,* is at the novel's center.

Warren's most important novel, *All the King's Men* (1946), was the product of many years of thinking about the Huey Long dictatorship of 1930s Louisiana. Although he had no personal contact with the Kingfish, he had ample opportunity to observe his kingdom, for during the Long years Warren founded *The Southern Review* (with Cleanth Brooks and Charles Pipkin) and taught at Louisiana State University (LSU). Despite its being a product of Long's plan to develop LSU into a major institution of learning, *The Southern Review* was by no means a Longite organ, and Huey, uncharacteristically perhaps (after all, he called the plays of the LSU football team), left it alone. Nevertheless, when would-be reformers finally swept Long's successors out of office in 1942, among their first acts was to close *The Southern Review,* ostensibly as a wartime necessity, and to divert the money that was supposed to be providing a promotion for Warren into the care and feeding of Mike the Tiger, the LSU mascot. In a small way, then, Warren's flight from the South, to teaching positions at the University of Minnesota and at Yale, was the result of the end of the Long regime in Louisiana.

In less comical moments, Warren would remember the aura of violence and tension apparent even at LSU. He has remarked of those years that he had then the rare opportunity of seeing History (with a capital *H*) unfolding before him. He recalls his sense that poor people, black and white, around the country – gas station attendants in Nevada, for instance – felt in the desperate years of the Depression a personal stake in Long's political progress. Even late in life, Warren thought of Long as a figure who, however much was wrong with him, must be taken seriously. (Ernest J. Gaines makes the same point in *The Autobiography of Miss Jane Pittman* [1971].)

Although Warren did not seriously begin working on the novel until the autumn of 1940, he had been attempting to write about the Long dictatorship since at least the middle 1930s, when he was drafting a highly stylized verse tragedy called *Proud Flesh,* in which the fall of a governor called Governor Talos, after the Yron Groome in Book V of Spenser's *The Faerie Queene,* is described by a chorus of motorcycle policemen and surgeons and other masked men. The play only slightly resembles the novel that was to follow many years later; for one thing, it lacks Jack Burden, the novel's protagonist, and centers instead on a character (pointedly called Dr. Amos) who seems to be a precursor of the novel's Adam Stanton.

Sinclair Lewis had portrayed his version of Huey Long as a sinister buffoon in *It Can't Happen Here* (1940). Characters modeled on Huey Long are made of similar pasteboard in Hamilton Basso's *Sun in Capricorn* (1942), in Adria Locke Langley's *A Lion Is in the Streets* (1945), and in Robert Rossen's Oscar-winning 1949 film of *All the King's Men.* By contrast, Warren's Willie Stark is no clown, is not merely a greedy party boss, and is never even a venally corrupt figure. Most important of all, Stark is never exactly a dictator, not even in the ways that Long was a dictator. Warren always stoutly if implausibly denied that Willie Stark was based on Huey Long; Willie does differ from Huey in important particulars. Willie's worst political crimes are limited to blackmailing his opponents with the threat to reveal what is after all only the truth about their conduct; Willie never, as Huey did, calls out the National Guard to threaten the local police, and he never threatens, as Huey did, to overturn his enemies by force.

If Willie is not Huey, neither is he Hitler or Stalin: written as it was during the American struggle with these two charismatically evil totalitarian leaders, *All the King's Men* has almost nothing to say about mass politics of a totalitarian kind, dealing instead in class conflicts that are of a specifically Southern variety and in political pathologies that are characteristic of democratic rather than of totalitarian rule. It is not a meditation on the metaphysical evil of the international scene of the 1930s and 1940s; it is an analysis of some of the characteristic tensions of Southern politics between Reconstruction and the civil rights era.

All the King's Men takes place against the background of the conflict between a conservative Bourbon lowland elite that has ruled the state in its own interest for decades (but which sees itself as public minded and honorable) and a populist upland represented by demagogues who bring to politics the ugly energy of their constituents' resentments (among which is a hot, race-hatred style of racism contrasting with the cooler, hierarchical racism of the Bourbons) but who also do genuinely speak for their people. This conflict among different varieties of white people Warren sees as one of the keys of Southern politics from the Civil War until the 1970s. The conflict between Bourbon and highlander goes back long before 1860 –

one sees traces of it as early as William Byrd's *History of the Dividing Line* written circa 1728, published in 1866) – but certainly the conflict played a major role in the internal politics of the Confederacy, in which the high-landers were often Unionists, and profoundly shaped the politics of the Reconstruction era up through the victory of the populist demagogues in the 1890s and the imposition of legal racial segregation that followed. Warren's sense of the complex, three-sided dance played out among the African Americans and the two white factions closely resembles that set forth by C. Vann Woodward in *Origins of the New South* (1951). Warren's Willie Stark is a populist demagogue of the sort common to Southern poli-tics between the 1890s and the 1960s.

Given the legacy bequeathed to him by populist race baiters like Tom Watson and James K. Vardaman, it is surprising how little interest Willie Stark has in playing race loyalty politics. It was the populists, after all, who had finally disenfranchised the African American voters, whose realis-tic support of the Bourbons as the lesser of two evils made their votes the Bourbons' margin of victory until the ballot was taken from their hands, and it was the populists who imposed formal segregation of the races. It is in the priority he gives to class over racial politics that Willie Stark most resembles Huey Long, who, whatever his racial feelings, did not often use race baiting for political ends, at least relative to other populist dema-gogues, and who did make sure that the benefits of his social programs were felt by black and white alike. Indeed, race baiting is more often the strategy of Willie's enemies, as for instance when the courthouse gang in Mason City whips up hostility against African American labor as a way of stampeding popular feeling against Willie and steering a lucrative con-struction contract to one of their cronies.

Willie represents not only a specifically Southern but also a more gener-ally American political problem: that popular rule in times of angry urgency and public need is vulnerable to those who will undermine the institutional structures and restraints on which free government depends in order to serve the pressing needs of the people. Willie claims through-out the book to have no moral motivations at all and to be interested only in power, but this claim is a strategic one: he means by it only to turn the elevated rhetoric of his opponents against them. In more reflective moments, he sees himself as compelled to trample on the niceties of politi-cal process by his sense of the urgency of the economic sufferings he is called on to answer.

[The law is] like a single-bed blanket on a double bed and three folks in the bed and a cold night. There ain't ever enough blanket to cover the case, no matter how much pulling and hauling, and somebody is always going to nigh catch pneumonia. Hell, the law is like the pants you bought last year for a growing boy, but it is always this year and the seams are popped and the shankbones to the breeze. The law is always too short and too tight for growing humankind. The best you can do is do something and then make up some law to fit and by the time that law gets on the books you would have done something different.

When Willie describes himself as motivated only by a desire for power, what he is really doing is claiming to be someone who has brushed away sterile and conformist moral illusions in the service of something he thinks of as morally primary. Willie's amorality is rejection of conventional morality in favor of an unstated moral aim immanent in revolutionary political acts. An unstated moral aim like this always becomes fuzzy, however, as soon as one looks hard at it, for the expedient always defend themselves in exactly Willie's language, and nothing Willie can do can shake the suspicion that he is merely one of them after all. That is why Willie is unnerved when it occurs to him that he may in fact finally be the amoral power-monger he had earlier so gleefully proclaimed himself to be.

Worse yet, the heroic transgressor Willie wishes to be may ultimately be different from the sleaze only in having so great a measure of narcissism in his nature that even he is gulled by his own Tartuffery. In such a figure – Jeremiah Beaumont in *World Enough and Time* is a better example of it than Willie Stark is – we genuinely cannot tell his basest motives from his noblest ones. Such figures are dangerous, because their virtues are stalking horses for their vices, but they are formidable as well, because their virtues are just genuine enough to demand from them the unreserved homage of rash acts. The more seriously heroic transgressors seek to take their role, the more they are driven to extremities by the need to distinguish between their own nobility and their own baseness.

Indeed, what finally undoes Willie is his attempt to do one unambiguously good thing that will prove to himself that he has despite everything served justice all along. The plot of *All the King's Men* is very intricate and so densely connected that it is hard to summarize it without going into too much detail. Willie is concerned for much of the novel with a huge charity hospital project, which he conceives of in the wake of a scandal in the state auditor's office. The scandal in the auditor's office leads to a political crisis in which Willie is nearly impeached, but it is not to impress the public in the face of the scandal that Willie seizes upon the idea of the hospital, for even after he has beaten down the impeachment attempt, he focuses obsessively on the hospital project. He is building the hospital, this is to say, not to restore the public's faith in him but to restore his own faith in himself. He has to prove to himself that his motives are good, and every time the project comes up, there is an edge of hysteria to his voice. This is why

Willie refuses even to make the kinds of pragmatic compromises, the deal making and the palm greasing that one might have assumed would be second nature to him, in the hospital project. Of course, though, one of the things you cannot prove to yourself is the purity of your own motives, for once you doubt your own motives, the things you do to prove yourself to yourself provide only further occasions for the suspicion of bad faith.

The project is morally entangled from the beginning. To bring the famed surgeon Adam Stanton into the project, Willie has his press secretary Jack Burden, who is also Adam's childhood friend, apply pressure on him. Jack is essentially a blackmailer who strongarms Willie's opposition by discovering embarrassing information about them. Jack overcomes Adam's resistance by revealing to him that Adam's father, Governor Stanton, had covered up the corruption of his family friend Judge Irwin. Jack also reveals Judge Irwin's corruption to Adam's sister Anne, who is a former sweetheart of Jack's, and Jack's revelation deepens the affair with Willie that Anne has already entered into. Later, political complications cause Willie to send Jack to put pressure directly on Judge Irwin. When Jack confronts Judge Irwin with what he knows, the judge does not give in, but commits suicide instead.

Judge Irwin's suicide has profound effects. Its most profound effect is on Jack, for it moves Jack's mother to reveal to him that Judge Irwin, not Ellis Burden, is his actual father, and this in turn sets off the train of moral reflections that transform his character in ways to be examined later. Judge Irwin's suicide also has important political consequences for Willie, in that it forces him to strike a bargain with a group of corrupt contractors with ties to his contemptible lieutenant governor, Tiny Duffy. When Willie's surly, foolish son, Tom, is paralyzed in a football accident, however, Willie suffers a fit of moral revulsion over this deal and calls it off. Tiny, angered by Willie's treachery, then reveals to Adam Stanton that Willie has been having an affair with his sister Anne, causing Adam to kill Willie in a jealous rage. Willie's death is in a complicated way the consequence of his attempt to prove to himself that he is not the moral relativist he has always said he is.

Warren finds it hard to take a simple stance on the issues Willie raises. The law as it stands, Warren concedes to Willie, is incapable of responding to the urgent sufferings of the people and is largely the instrument of those who have an interest in their suffering. At the same time, to step outside the law in the name of a higher law, or in the name of the people, or in the name of the pseudo-god History, is to enter a realm of chaos where values consume themselves and acts become undone by irony. This is the situation described by Captain Vere in *Billy Budd,* but Warren differs from

Melville in that Melville presents the case both of Vere and of the officers who would decide otherwise in a strongly convincing light, but for Warren, justice and law are always in tension with each other, and neither available position escapes crushing problems, yet the choice of not making a decision is also unavailable. Facing this crux is both Willie's greatness and his tragedy. Jack Burden's summation is eminently fair:

> I must believe that Willie Stark was a great man. What happened to his greatness is not the question. Perhaps he spilled it on the ground the way you spill a liquid when the bottle breaks. Perhaps he piled up his greatness and burnt it in one great blaze in the dark like a bonfire and then there wasn't anything but dark and the embers winking. Perhaps he could not tell his greatness from ungreatness and so mixed them together that what was adulterated was lost. But he had it. I must believe that.

Jack Burden's situation is a deeper version of the tangle of ironies in which Willie is caught, because Jack, unlike Willie, must ultimately do things that are positively evil. A child of the privileged aristocracy of the Gulf Coast, Jack is alienated from that aristocracy, primarily by his sense of the self-servingness of their moral postures, but also by his disgust with his mother, who collects husbands and furniture in the same way. Jack's two motivations are reflections of each other, although it would be a mistake to see Jack's political objections to Burden's Landing life as merely a projected version of his difficulties with his mother. Unable to complete his doctoral thesis, he puts his skills as a historian to work in digging up incriminating information with which to blackmail Willie's opponents. Jack is a lost soul, but the critique he presents of his family and his friends is completely credible, and it is not only because he is a lost soul, and not only because he wishes to outrage his family, that he serves Willie, although like Mr. Munn he feels himself somehow deficient in connection to real life and turns to politics as a way of satisfying his hunger for essential reality.

Jack Burden is probably the only character in Western literature who is redeemed by causing his father's death. What redeems him, however, is not that he discovers a strong wicked father in the place of the weak good father he had thought he had, the once lawyer, now evangelist, Ellis Burden. What redeems him is his discovery that when Judge Irwin could have saved himself by revealing to Jack that he is his father, he chose to face up to what he had done instead. What Jack learns from this is that although the judge is corrupt, and although his corruption is a deep fact about him, it is not the only fact about Judge Irwin, and in facing what he has done as he does, he shows a kind of courage and also precisely the kind of nobility we were most inclined to deny him. Armed with this knowledge, that we are all fallen but that fallenness is not the only fact about us,

Jack comes to recognize his own complicity in evil. Given the chance to expose Duffy's role in the assassination of Willie Stark to Willie's body-guard, who would certainly have taken revenge, Jack has a vision of Duffy winking at him, and, rebuked by that vision, he is unable to take revenge. Jack's refusal of revenge is parallel to Mr. Munn's refusal to kill Senator Tolliver in *Night Rider* and to Jefferson's agreeing to take Lilburn Lewis's hand in *Brother to Dragons.*

Jack also responds to his recognition of complicity in a more troubling way, by lying to his mother about whether Judge Irwin was in trouble when he committed suicide. Jack's lie is modeled on Marlow's lie at the end of Conrad's *Heart of Darkness,* and it is meant to be generous, because it shields his mother from the knowledge of Irwin's corruption. It is also self-serving, though, since it shields Jack from his mother's condemnation as well. Mrs. Burden has already accused Jack of causing Irwin's death, so it does not really take him off the hook, and furthermore, he has also con-fessed his complicity to us, who finally matter a great deal more than Mrs. Burden does; ultimately, we have to extend to Jack the kind of generosity he extends to Duffy (and, posthumously, to Irwin) – otherwise, we are like him at his worst.

The recognition of complicity as a central moral act is presented far dif-ferently in the story of Cass Mastern, Ellis Burden's Civil War–era kins-man and the subject of Jack's uncompleted dissertation. Cass's friend and patron Duncan Trice discovers his affair with Trice's wife Annabelle and commits suicide in a way that only Annabelle will know for sure is a sui-cide, leaving his wedding ring on his pillow as a kind of message to her. Annabelle's slave Phebe finds the ring, however, and Annabelle, unable to live with Phebe's knowledge, sells her down the river. Unable to find Phebe to buy her, and unable to assuage his guilt by freeing his own slaves in Mississippi, Cass courts death by serving in the Confederate army but not carrying a gun, finding peace only in the kinship he feels with the other suffering souls, from North and South, who die with him in a mili-tary hospital outside of Atlanta.

Whether complicity can be recognized in a less self-destructive way is something the novel leaves open. Cass dies and seems to enjoy the narrator's respect. Jack survives, yet his final acts are ambiguous – but finally, the novel wishes to affirm the possibility of political right despite the ironies of history and the entanglements of political acts. Jack Burden at the end of the novel is in a situation rather like that of the protagonist at the end of *Invisible Man* (1952), which Warren's later friend Ralph Ellison began writ-ing in 1944. Jack's commitment to Willie is like the Invisible Man's com-mitment to the Brotherhood: we cannot doubt that either springs from

political motives that the novelist finds to be as credible at the end of the
novel as he did at the beginning. At the same time, the political institutions that are supposed to represent those values keep falsifying them, and
the commitments that are supposed to ground the character's sense of his
own reality keep imprisoning or betraying the identity they had promised
to realize. As the Invisible Man in the later novel decides despite everything
that he must ultimately emerge from the hole in which he has hidden himself and take up a new political task, however, so Jack Burden is shaken by
the ironies of politics but not paralyzed by them, and in the last few pages
of the novel, having retreated to his home to lick his wounds, Jack chooses
– in the summer of 1939 – to "go into the convulsion of the world, out of
history into history and the awful responsibility of Time." *All the King's Men*
is not a reflection on the totalitarian politics of the 1940s, but rather, like
Invisible Man, a chastened but still committed reflection on the values that
had moved the political fiction of the 1930s.

World Enough and Time (1950) is by contrast a book that completely
despairs of the politics it is nevertheless obsessed with. The novel had its
origins in a historical murder case, the Sharp-Beauchamp murder case of
1820s Kentucky, which had earlier been the subject of Edgar Allan Poe's
play *Politian* and of novels by William Gilmore Simms, Charles Fenno
Hoffman, and Thomas Holley Chivers. *The Confessions of Jeroboam O.
Beauchamp* had been given to Warren by Katherine Anne Porter, who correctly saw that it was material perfectly suited for him, but the novel
changes the details of the Kentucky Tragedy in many significant ways. For
one thing, Sharp and Beauchamp were both partisans of the conservative
Anti-Relief party, not of the radical Relief party. For another thing, in the
historical account Beauchamp's wife, the former Ann Cook, successfully
committed suicide in Beauchamp's cell. Beauchamp was hanged, and the
escape to the swamplands that occupies the last quarter of the novel never
happened. Principally, the novel differs from the historical account in that
the actual Beauchamp seems to have been little more than a self-pitying
killer, but the fictional Beaumont, for all his viciousness and for all his self-
deceit, is still not without nobility and not without eloquence.

The young Jeremiah Beaumont is raised from poverty and trained in
the law by an older patron, Colonel Cassius Fort. On learning that Fort
had seduced an abandoned young woman named Rachel Jordan in another
county, Beaumont resolves, sight unseen, to marry the woman and to murder Col. Fort. Beaumont's resolution is as impulsive as this blunt summary
shows it to be, but it is complicated by his nervous moral self-doubt. On
one hand, he is stung into making his resolution by a friend who accuses
him of not feeling the proper outrage about what Col. Fort has done

because he is Col. Fort's creature. Beaumont chooses to murder Col. Fort in order to prove to himself that he has pure motives, and the violence of his ambitions is a way of shouting down his sense of being morally impure. At the same time, he always doubts whether his quest is either rational or moral. It is a sign of Beaumont's hysteria that he treats these quite reasonable doubts as signs of moral weakness, and his efforts to suppress his doubts spur him to outdo himself in displays of moral stringency.

After a courtship in which his profession of serving Rachel masks a large amount of bullying of her, he persuades her to marry him and extorts from her the demand that he murder Fort. Here again, his position is very complicated: he coerces Rachel into sharing his obsession, but he also knows that Rachel's demand has no meaning if she made it only because he demanded that she do so, for he cannot prove his own moral heroism to himself unless he does what Rachel genuinely wishes him to do.

Rachel's doubts about his lunatic plan place him in a quandary, for if Rachel does not really want to be avenged, then his own ambitions as an avenger arise from vanity rather than from moral purity. Beaumont draws the sting of this thought by treating Rachel's doubts as one more sign of the damage Col. Fort did to her and therefore as one more thing to be avenged by him. Beaumont believes that he knows what Rachel really wants, and in seeing her doubts as a sign of her confusion he imagines that he serves her best by coercing her, since what he coerces her into is what she most deeply wants anyway, despite her doubts. From his point of view, his coercion of Rachel is in a strange way the instrument of her freedom, since what she would do if left to herself would be a betrayal of herself. Impulsive and even insane as Beaumont's thoughts are, they are the all-too-natural consequences of combining the belief that one is crucially morally invested in another with the belief that one has a special insight, penetrating even that other person's self-deceits and moments of weakness, into what that other person is finally all about. All vocations that depend on answering the hidden inwardness of other people are subject to the same cruxes.

Before Beaumont can carry out his project, a political crisis intervenes. Driven by the economic chaos that followed the crash of 1819, the legislature passes a debt-relief bill that relieves the pressure on debtors by expropriating creditors. A near civil war follows, in which Beaumont and Fort both take the side of the Relief party. The state supreme court overturns the debt-relief statute, however, and the legislature retaliates by appointing a new court to take its place. Skirmishing breaks out between partisans of the New Court and partisans of the Old Court. Col. Fort, fearing chaos from the overturning of the court, changes sides and supports the Old Court, and Fort and Beaumont run on opposite sides in the state elections.

A pamphlet appears in which Fort is accused of having fathered Rachel's dead child. Another pamphlet appears in which the child is said to have been fathered by one of Rachel's slaves. Spurred by this charge, Beaumont finally murders Fort on the evening before Fort is to announce a solution to the political problem that he believes would satisfy both parties. (The second pamphlet turns out to have been the work of New Court partisans who wished to force Beaumont into the murder. This detail is apparently historical: the real Jeroboam Beauchamp was maneuvered into murdering Colonel Solomon Sharp by a pamphlet making the same accusation against his wife, and that pamphlet, too, probably originated among members of his own faction.) After a trial in which both sides engage in and are entangled in a web of complicated deceits, Beaumont is convicted.

In Beaumont's underground jail cell after the trial, Beaumont and his wife attempt suicide and humiliatingly fail to die. They both escape to the marshy area between the Tennessee and Cumberland Rivers, where they lead degraded lives with the gang of the river bandit La Grande Bosse. After Rachel's death, Beaumont, aware of all of his errors and seeking to do penance for them, correctly sees his sense of moral calling as arising from selfhood and learns that morals begin with the sacrifice of selfhood. Bitterly, he also realizes that sacrifice of selfhood was what he had always thought he was doing, and that nobody can successfully distinguish between the deepest selflessness and the worst vanity. He attempts to return to Lexington to face his punishment, but, in the novel's nastiest and most ironic turn, he is captured and beheaded by bounty hunters instead. Unable to distinguish finally between selflessness and vanity, heroism and monstrousness, freedom and compulsion, Beaumont in the last paragraph of his confessions wonders bitterly, "Was all for naught?" The narrator, who sees that what has entangled Beaumont is not merely the consequence of his private neurosis but also entangles all morally heroic vocations, is unable to answer his question.

The novel's politics are extremely dark: the New Court partisans are violent people, extremist figures who are capable of anything and whose measures cannot help but collapse into chaos and self-destruction, yet only they are taken by the narrator with any moral seriousness, since their Old Court opponents are repressive, corrupt, and (with a few exceptions) entirely self-serving. The New Court is mad, but at least it is justice that has maddened them. At the same time, they are infected with that desire for moral perfection and with that vision of themselves as agents of the absolute that is for Warren always the way that good harnesses itself to the service of evil.

Beaumont's moral hysteria is entangled with a sexual one. His rage for political purity is also a rage for sexual purity, and his hostility to Fort as an agent of the Old Court is uncomfortably close to his hostility to Fort as the seducer of Rachel. As with Hamlet, Beaumont's contempt for fallenness is also contempt for sexuality, and it expresses itself in an obsession with sexual purity that is, again like Hamlet's, deeply permeated with misogyny and sadism. Like Aylmer in Hawthorne's "The Birth Mark," Beaumont cannot distinguish between his sense of his wife's sexual past and his sense of human mortality and the moral corruption of the world. Warren also gives Beaumont Aylmer's sexually charged fantasies about the birthmark that stains Rachel Jordan's face. The desire for sexual purity in this book is not a desire to escape from sexuality altogether; it is a refined perversion, in that disgusted by sex and unable to think of anything else, Beaumont takes, despite that disgust, a kind of dark pleasure both in outraging the disgust by means of sexual excess and in rejecting sexuality in sadistic and sexually charged ways. Like Angelo in Shakespeare's *Measure for Measure,* Beaumont is no mere hypocrite, who says one thing about sex and does another; he is someone whose sexual repressions and whose sexual aggressiveness are different forms of the same thing, someone for whom repression and sadism are identical.

Beaumont's feelings are made clear in his repeated references to a childhood fascination with an illustration from Foxe's *Book of Martyrs.* In the illustration, which he remembers after the important turning points in his relationship with Rachel, a young women is tied cruelly to a post "so that the bonds seemed to crush her sweet flesh and her face lifted up while the flames rose about her." Beaumont's three mutually exclusive but equally compelling responses to this picture capture the inner relationships among idealism, repression, and sadism:

> Sometimes the strange fancy took me that I might seize her from the flame and escape with her from all the people who crowded about for her death. At other times it seemed that I might throw myself into the fire to perish with her for the very joy. And again, my heart leaping suddenly like a fish and my muscles tight as at the moment when you wait to start a race, I saw her standing there bound, with no fire set, and I myself flung the first flaming faggot and could not wait to see her twist and strive against the tight bond in the great heat and toss her head with the hair falling loose to utter a cry for the first agony.

Despite all this, the narrator, a historian seeking to reconstruct the story, never allows us merely to dismiss Beaumont as a fanatic and a pervert and thus to dissociate ourselves from the problem he represents, for it is his virtues, not his vices, that drive Beaumont into his worst acts. The narrator implies that there is no credible alternative to Beaumont's world, in which one is driven mad by a correct assessment of the world's fallenness and an urgent and morally serious (if destructive and morally self-repeal-ing) attempt to respond to that fallenness, for the only alternative is the modern world of the historian's own day, in which we are not capable of Beaumont's crimes because we do not value anything enough to commit such crimes on its behalf. The novel gives us only the choice between the world of Beaumont's obsessions and the empty and meaningless world of the narrator's ironies, and the narrator's bitter self-contempt makes it clear that his own world is an even less respectable one than Beaumont's. Of our attempt to pity Beaumont as a kind of pervert, the narrator writes:

> That idea would have struck him as ridiculous, as worse than ridiculous, for it would rob him of the last shred of pride as the author of his own ruin and leave him alone without identity, staring into the blank face of suffering. The idea would have been ridiculous to him, for in the end he did not ask for pity, at least not human pity. But pity at the price of his self-respect is what we are most ready to give him. For with us pity for others is the price we are anxious to pay for the privilege of our self-pity.

The connection between Beaumont's sexual and political problems is the opposite of that which Freud might have proposed: it would be reductive to treat Beaumont's political idealism as merely a reflection of his repressive sadism. Quite the reverse, Beaumont's sexual and political problems are parallel consequences of the same thing, of the angry desire to be more than human, of the panic that ensues on his inability to assimilate the fact that human beings are radically fallen. The novel has tragic dignity only because despite everything, Beaumont really does have nobility. Even its dignity, however, is the dignity of a life-denying and life-destroying desire to evade the discrediting entanglements of human life. Beaumont has genuine eloquence in the novel, but his eloquence is always somehow tied to his melancholy and erotically charged love of death. As a child, he had wandered in the limestone caves of Kentucky, and remembering those wanderings as he describes his imprisonment in an underground jail cell, he describes the caves with the grave, death-haunted beauty that is the root of his credibility as a speaker:

> So I lay there, and breathed the limey, cool, inward smell of the earth's bowels, which is not like any smell common to the superficies, though in spots dank and unvisited by the sun. It is a smell cleanly and rich, not dead and foul but pregnant with secret life, as though you breathed the dark and the dark were about to pulse. And while I lay there, I thought how I might not be able to return, but would lie there forever, and I saw how my father might at that moment be standing in a field full of sun to call my name wildly and might run to all my common haunts to no avail. I felt a sad pity for him, and for all who ran about thus seeking in the sun and shade. But I felt no terror. It was like a dream of terror with the terror drained away, and the dark was loving kindness.

World Enough and Time does not offer even the qualified consolations Warren was to offer in *Brother to Dragons,* that the recognition of complicity is the beginning of wisdom. Instead, *World Enough and Time* leaves us, as does *Measure for Measure,* at a complete impasse. It is the most despairing novel of politics in the American tradition.

After *World Enough and Time,* Warren's investment shifts to poetry, although he continued to publish novels until the 1970s. One finds in his greatest poems that longing for a point of view beyond suffering and time, and beyond humanity, in which we can see what we are without extenuation or deceit. Warren finds that point of view, the point of view that eluded both Jeremiah Beaumont and his narrator, in his 1974 poem, "Evening Hawk."

> From plane of light to plane, wings dipping through
> Geometries and orchids that the sunset builds,
> Out of the peak's black angularity of shadow, riding
> The last tumultuous avalanche of
> Light above pines and the guttural gorge.
> The hawk comes.
>
> His wing
> Scythes down another day, his motion
> Is that of the honed steel-edge, we hear
> The crashless fall of stalks of Time.
> The head of each stalk is heavy with the gold of our error.
>
> Look! look! he is climbing the last light
> Who knows neither Time nor error, and under
> Whose eye, unforgiving, the world, unforgiven, swings
> Into shadow.
>
> Long now,
> The last thrush is till, the last bat
> Now cruises in his sharp hieroglyphics. His wisdom
> Is ancient, too, and immense. The star
> Is steady, like Plato, over the mountain.
>
> If there were no wind we might, we think, hear
> The earth grind on its axis, or history
> Drip in darkness like a leaking pipe in the cellar

3

❦

CARSON McCULLERS

WHEN AT TWENTY-THREE Carson McCullers came to fame in 1940 with *The Heart Is a Lonely Hunter,* her first readers thought they knew very well what to make of her. With Erskine Caldwell (and with a completely misread William Faulkner), she was described as a member of the Southern Gothic school, a purgatorial figment of the Northern imagination to which Flannery O'Connor was also consigned. Of her second novel, *Reflections in a Golden Eye* (1941), *Time* magazine said, with characteristic fatuity, that it "is the Southern school at its most Gothic, but also at its best. It is as though William Faulkner saw to the bottom of matters which merely excite him, shed his stylistic faults, and wrote it all out with Tolstoyan lucidity." By the time of *Clock Without Hands* (1961), her fame had faded considerably, and now few critics put her in the first rank even of Southern writers of her own generation. She did have considerable influence, however; Tennessee Williams's *The Glass Menagerie* (1945), in its sense of emotional thwartedness and its concern with the overpowering misery and hidden obsessions of its characters, owes a great deal to McCullers, as does the brooding lyricism and pungent sexual strangeness of Truman Capote's first novel *Other Voices, Other Rooms* (1948). (Indeed, Idabell Thompkins in the latter novel could be the blood sister of Mick Kelly in *The Heart Is a Lonely Hunter.*)

Now that her fame has largely dissipated, it is easier to bring her considerable virtues as a writer into focus. For one thing, it is clear that McCullers learned little from Faulkner or Caldwell or any of her other putative masters but learned a great deal from Sherwood Anderson, and, through Sherwood Anderson, from Chekhov. For another thing, it is also clear that for all her affection for grotesque and peculiar characters, in *The Heart Is a Lonely Hunter* she also learned a great deal from the social realist writers of the 1930s and absorbed many of their political values even if she did not absorb their representational techniques. One also sees in retrospect that in *Reflections in a Golden Eye* there is a large unacknowledged debt to Lawrence. For all of her interest in the contemporary politics of the South, McCullers did not share a tragic sense of history or a mythic sweep with Warren or with Faulkner or even with Styron, focused as she was on the pathos of the predicaments of individual characters.

Much of the power of *The Heart Is a Lonely Hunter* arises from the sense that the characters are, despite considerable interactions among them, almost entirely unknown to each other, engaged intensely as they are in totally private concerns so absorbing that they are unaware that they are not shared by everybody else. This world of grotesque, slightly pathetic loners, each wrapped up in their own obsessive stories, is recognizably the world of Sherwood Anderson's *Winesburg, Ohio* (1918), and the atmosphere of repressed unorthodox sexuality that pervades the novel owes something to Anderson as well. What McCullers most owes to Anderson is the gently compassionate point of view she occupies as a narrator who is uniquely able to comprehend characters who are mysteries to themselves and to each other.

If the stories of the characters loosely intersect, joined only by the author's perspective on them, the characters themselves believe that their stories are connected by their mutual concern with the deaf-mute John Singer, to whom they all tell their stories, and whom they all believe understands them better than they understand themselves. Singer, whose boardinghouse room they all visit when he is not at work for a jeweler, is in fact kind and patient and forbearing with all of the characters, and because of his generosity they each assume they have from him the sympathy and comprehension they crave. They attribute to him the knowingness that eager, egocentric talkers always attribute to silent, attentive people; his deafness gives him in their minds a kind of heightened hearing, as blindness is said to give epic poets second sight.

In fact, Singer's letters reveal that he is puzzled by almost all of the people who pour out their stories to him. The central attachment of Singer's life is also completely unknown to his friends. Singer had for a long time been passionately invested in another deaf-mute named Spiros Antonapoulos, a mentally ill and also mentally retarded young man who worked in his cousin's fruit shop and whose own chief concern seems to be with filching sweet things to eat. The relationship is certainly erotically charged, but Antonapoulos is essentially a presexual person who is not really capable of affection for anybody and sees Singer mostly as a source of sweets. When Antonapoulos becomes demented enough to be a financial burden to his cousin, he is shipped off to a mental asylum, and Singer, devastatingly lonely for his friend, moves into the Kelly boardinghouse.

Among the memorable obsessives in the novel is Mick Kelly, the daughter of Singer's landlord, a tough-minded, rather masculine girl on the brink of puberty. She has some talent as a painter, although what she likes to paint are things like boiler explosions, riots, and birds falling out of the sky with broken backs. Her primary talent, and passion, is for music, however, for "MOTSART" to begin with, and later for Beethoven. As the novel unfolds, we gradually see her musical awakening, from her comical attempts to make a ukelele into a violin, to her composition of tunes in her notebook, to her setting out to compose her Symphony No. 1. McCullers is not rewriting *The Song of the Lark,* however; she does not imagine a musical career for Mick. In fact, Mick's musical talent resembles her father's talent for repairing watches, which he does with painstaking skill and obsessive, but rather unremunerative, intensity.

Mick's musical awakening parallels her sexual awakening. Few authors have captured the physical awkwardness of adolescence as McCullers has. Mick has a developing relationship with Harry Minowitz, a Jewish neighbor with whom she plots to assassinate Hitler and with whom she has a sexual fling near the end of the novel, although neither seems to have a very clear idea of what sex is about. By the end of the novel, Mick is working in the five-and-dime to support her parents' family, and despite her intense vitality, she will ultimately become one more character thwarted by small-town life.

Biff Brannon is the proprietor of an all-night diner patronized by Singer and most of the other characters. He has a testy relationship with his wife Alice, who complains about his management of the diner, and with his sister-in-law Lucile Wilson, who is emotionally dependent on her wastrel husband Leroy. Biff collects, files, and indexes newspapers, and his home is filled with them. After Alice suddenly dies, Biff redecorates his home so as not to remind him of her, but he also becomes fascinated with his wife's *agua florida,* which he begins to wear.

Jake Blount is an itinerant labor organizer who seems to have wandered into this novel from Steinbeck or from Michael Gold. He has traveled all over the South and is consumed with bitterness about his inability to organize the mill workers, who treat him with contempt, which drives him to drink, which earns him further contempt. His speeches are strongly persuasive, however, and it is hard to imagine that McCullers does not partly share his politics. At the end of the novel, after Singer's death, a racial riot breaks out at the carnival where he maintains a flying jenny, and he chooses to leave town.

The most complicated character in the novel is Dr. Benedict Mady Copeland, an African American physician. He is strongly concerned with the interests of his people, and in his conviction, and in his anger, he resembles Blount. Where he differs from Blount is in having tangled relations with his family, who think of him as demanding and cruel. His son Willie cooks at Biff Brannon's diner, and his daughter Portia cooks at the

Kelly's boardinghouse. Will and Portia live with Portia's husband Highboy, but they have very strained relations with their father, who thinks of them not only as failures but as betrayers of his ideals. Like Blount, Dr. Copeland is very influenced by Marx, after whom he has named a son (who, inevitably, calls himself not Karl but Buddy).

Dr. Copeland meets Blount at Singer's room, and they ought to have something in common. (Actually, they had crossed paths shortly before: to stir up an integration incident, Blount, in a drunken inspiration, had grabbed Dr. Copeland from the street and pulled him into Brannon's diner, but Dr. Copeland, divining Blount's intentions, evaded them angrily.) When they do get together, they quarrel over whether race or class is the greater source of oppression, and each leaves angry, but aware also of an opportunity missed.

Dr. Copeland's affairs are brought to a head when his son Willie, to his father's disgust, is arrested after a brawl at a brothel and sent to prison. Willie is mistreated in jail so badly that his feet have to be amputated. When Dr. Copeland, who is himself dying of tuberculosis, goes to see the local judge to seek redress, he is beaten by the police and jailed.

All of the tenuous connections among the characters break when Singer, having discovered that Antonapoulos has died of nephritis, kills himself in despair. Dr. Copeland agrees to allow his family to take him for rest in the country, but it is clear that his death is what is in prospect. Jake escapes the riot at the carnival and seeks Dr. Copeland again, but finding that the doctor has already left town, he leaves town to resume his wanderings. Mick Kelly bitterly reflects that her work at Woolworth's has drained the music from her, and Biff Brannon waits for the sun to come up in his empty diner.

McCullers never quite matched the achievement of *The Heart Is a Lonely Hunter*. Although *The Ballad of the Sad Café* (1946) and *The Member of the Wedding* (1951) were well received, probably her strongest other novel is *Reflections in a Golden Eye* (1941), a story of sexual intrigue on a peacetime army base in the South. The standoff between an impotent Captain Penderton and his very ignorant but very sensuous wife Leonora, is matched in intensity only by the standoff between Leonora's neighbor and lover, the brutal and philistine Major Langdon, to whom Captain Penderton is also attracted, and his music-loving but neurasthenic wife Alison, who in despair mutilates herself sexually early on, and is tended by an affected Filipino houseboy, with whom she entertains fantasies of running away. The stalemate is broken by the appearance of a mysterious Private Williams, who, in a scene Lawrence could have imagined, wanders naked onto the scene after Captain Penderton has been run away with by Leonora's unruly and magnificent horse. Williams captures the horse, and ever after this prowls the Penderton household secretly at night, crouching in entranced fascination by the side of the sleeping Leonora. Alison Langdon discovers him there, but nobody believes her story, and she is packed off to an asylum, where she immediately dies. Williams, still haunting the Penderton house, is finally (in a hypnotic scene) murdered by Captain Penderton. In capturing the numbing quality of life in an army post, *Reflections in a Golden Eye* might be compared with James Jones's *From Here to Eternity* or William Styron's *The Long March,* but its sexual charge, at once horrified and fascinated, puts it in a class by itself.

4

FLANNERY O'CONNOR

F LANNERY O'Connor's passionate religious convictions were the central fact of her intellectual and aesthetic life, vastly outweighing in her view any of the ways her sensibility was shaped by her gender, her region, or her race. Although like the Agrarians of the preceding generation O'Connor saw the South as if not resisting the rush to an alienating, secular, and capitalist modernity, at least as not yet totally given over to it, she never sentimentalized the vocation of the subsistence farmer and did not have romantic ideas about traditionalism generally. She was as bitterly critical of the urban habit of life and of secular culture as the Agrarians were, and those characters who represented for her a modern, cosmopolitan, secular, Northern-oriented consciousness, such characters as Rayber of *The Violent Bear It Away*, Asbury Fox of "The Enduring Chill," Julian of "Everything That Rises Must Converge," or Hulga Hopewell of "Good Country People," were subjected to a ruthless satire.

To say that religious issues mattered more to O'Connor than political ones did is not to say that O'Connor was blind to the political and cultural transformation of the South of her day, or that she had nothing to say about the integration struggle that was proceeding throughout the years of her career, although she never wrote about it as Warren did in *Segregation: The Inner Conflict in the South* and *Who Speaks for the Negro?* or as Welty did in "Where Is the Voice Coming From?" O'Connor's "Everything That Rises Must Converge" is set during the period immediately after the integration of buses, and contrasts, with irony in both directions, the attitudes toward race of the progressive Julian and his racist mother. Julian is accompanying his mother on the bus to her weight reduction class at the YMCA, because she will no longer travel alone now that buses have been integrated. Julian broods on ways to score a point against his mother on the subject, and his mother makes a series of remarks that make her ignorant but sentimental views clear. An African American child and his mother board the bus. Julian notes with delight that the mother wears exactly the same hat his own mother is wearing. Rather than being taken aback by this, the mother gives the child a penny. Offended by the sentimentality of her gesture, the child's mother wallops Julian's mother with her fist. Julian is about to read his mother a lecture about her condescension, but to his horror she has a stroke and dies on the scene, calling for her African American mammy. The point of the story seems to be to remind reform-oriented people not to lose sight of the humanity of those they would reform: Julian may well be right that his mother is foolish, but her gesture is not unfriendly and she deserves better than she gets, especially from Julian.

The materialism and deracination of the modern culture of which O'Connor is critical is a consequence of its secularism, and it is at secularism, rather than at materialism or at the rejection of tradition, that O'Connor aimed most of her criticism. In her story "Good Country People," the protagonist is a young woman who, like O'Connor herself, after becoming disabled, had to return to the South so that her aging mother could take care of her. The young woman, Hulga Hopewell, is a representation of the kind of person O'Connor herself might have become had she entertained different convictions. In the North, Hulga, who had changed her name from Joy in order to vex her mother, had studied philosophy and come to the conclusion that there is no God, and that only things like convention and sexual guilt keep us from seeing through religious illusions and grasping our existential freedom. In Hulga's case, as in Julian's and Asbury's and many others of O'Connor's Modern Young People, there is something adolescent about their rejection of their religion and about their rejection of the South: they often seem to be showing their slower-minded parents a thing or two, and O'Connor often catches them in the act of delivering carefully rehearsed set-piece speeches to them. Hulga meets a traveling Bible salesman named (appropriately, as it turns out, Manley Pointer), who seems to her to be naïve both in his traditional morality and in his religious convictions. She sets out to awaken him to modernity by seducing him and then using his sexual guilt to free him from his bondage to Jesus. When she climbs up to the barn loft for the tryst she has arranged, however, she finds that Pointer has brought a hollowed out Bible, whiskey, condoms, and obscene playing cards to the event, and he even manages to steal her wooden leg. She says that she does not believe in God, he remarks, but he, he goes on to say, has been believing in nothing since he was born. What this means is that Hulga does not really know what it is to live in a world without God, and that that world is not grand and free as she imagines it to be, but tawdry and small and vicious and full of people like Manley Pointer.

What O'Connor valued in Southern culture was the way in which even its crassest and most vulgar corners were still haunted by the living and all-demanding presence of Jesus. Unlike Caroline Gordon or Walker Percy,

O'Connor was not a convert to Catholicism, yet the character of her faith, at least when it expresses itself in her fiction, seems more radically Protestant than Catholic, insofar as faith is disclosed primarily to the inner light through intense experiences of emotional upheaval neither originating in nor shaped by the pastoral traditions of religious institutions.

O'Connor repeatedly, in essays and in her letters, addressed the subject of the deep differences she perceived between Catholic and Protestant sensibilities. When a Protestant hears a voice, she says, he assumes that it is the voice of God and does its bidding, but when a Catholic hears a voice, he assumes that it could be either the voice of God or the Devil and goes to the Church for guidance about whether to listen to it or not. The crucial difference is that for a Protestant sensibility, divine grace is a turbulent emotional experience, an experience that, like love, has unmistakable power and authority, but – also like love – is fleeting and sometimes subject to paralyzing self-doubt. For a Catholic sensibility, divine grace is a legal state, more like marriage than like love, which one enters by means of rituals performed by an institutional authority. The Catholic version of grace is stable and temperate in ways that states of pure feeling are not, but it also lacks the same unmistakable inward pull. O'Connor was sympathetic to Protestantism because she took the religious experiences at its center to be genuine, although unstable and likely either to run amok or to run stale. The inward authority of Protestantism, she says, is open at both ends, to atheism on one hand, because it rejects all authorities, but also to faith, because it will follow the leadings of the spirit. O'Connor wrote about Protestants, she says, because their sense that grace is an emotional experience forces them to work out the problems of their faith in dramatic ways. Since fiction is the drama of the emotions, the cruxes of Protestant faiths, O'Connor argues, are easier to make fiction of than the cruxes of Catholicism are. Whether this claim is true or false, O'Connor without question was deeply attracted to the emotional intensity, and to the mystical inwardness, of the Protestant prophets she wrote about.

O'Connor was repeatedly fascinated by moments in which characters have an intense but annihilating confrontation with the Absolute. In her story "Greenleaf," Mrs. May, a somewhat snobbish and materialistic farm wife, seems to be granted a moment of vision at the instant of her being gored to death by her tenant's bull. Her death has an unmistakable sexual edge to it (the story in places seems to burlesque D. H. Lawrence), and a class edge as well. Mrs. May has throughout the story been mightily concerned with keeping her tenant Mrs. Greenleaf's shabby bull from among her cows. Mrs. May's contempt for Mrs. Greenleaf combines a class-based distaste for emotionally charged religious practices with an equally class-based sexual fastidiousness: she is particularly put out by Mrs. Greenleaf's habit of cutting out morbid clippings from the newspaper, burying them in the yard, and throwing herself over them, writhing and moaning and crying out "Oh, Jesus! Stab me in the heart!" O'Connor knows a great deal about the relationships between farmers and their tenants, and between white farmers and their black employees, but the sociological accuracy of her story as well as its dark comedy (after all, Mrs. May does get stabbed in the heart) are subordinated to a religious purpose.

In her most famous short story, "A Good Man Is Hard to Find," a fussy and indeed somewhat ridiculous grandmother, traveling with her put-upon son's family and with his bratty children, causes a car wreck that places them in the hands of an escaped murderer. The murderer calls himself "the Misfit" because he cannot make his sense of what he has done fit with his sense of the far worse things God has done to him. The Misfit explains to the grandmother as he casually orders his gang to take her son's family off and shoot them, that he kills out of his despairing sense of being in a spiritual crux. On the one hand, the death of Jesus made experience in the world meaningful and therefore it cannot merely be wasted in pursuit of pleasures such as killing somebody or burning down his house – "No pleasure but meanness," he says. On the other hand, Jesus' delay in returning to the earth makes it unclear to him whether his original promise meant anything. The Misfit's predicament is clearly intended to be darkly comic version of Pascal's Wager. Under the pressure of her own imminent death, the grandmother, not so much in an attempt to save her life as in an awed recognition of the Misfit's humanity, reaches out to him, proclaiming that he is one of her lost children. The Misfit is unable to bear this and immediately shoots her in a kind of panic, but the reader is meant to see that the grandmother's recognition is a genuine transformation of a soul that had never taken itself seriously as a soul until faced with death. As the Misfit says, "She would of been a good woman if it had been somebody there to shoot her every minute of her life."

O'Connor complained in her letters that she wrote for all those people who have the idea that God is dead, and she wrote in her essays that she used violent and shocking stories as a means of astonishing her readers into faith only because they could not be reached by any other means, comparing the extremity of her stories to the loud voice one must use in speaking to the nearly deaf. O'Connor writes religious fiction to an audience that is not only unbelieving but also in a state of radical bad faith. Few authors, indeed, have approached their readers so aggressively.

From early on, O'Connor was acutely and bitterly sensitive to what Northern readers expected out of Southern writers, and she made no pretense that her real audience was Southern and religious like herself. She was aware that Faulkner's major novels were out of print when he won the Nobel prize and were seen as kinky, lurid, and informed by reactionary politics. She was aware also that what the Northern reader expected was a sort of freak show, populated by mental defectives who suffer from pellagra, marry their cousins, and lynch black people for amusement. This is precisely what such writers as Erskine Caldwell were serving up, but Thomas Wolfe did not fully resist the temptation in *The Web and the Rock* (1939), and even the relatively recent novel *Deliverance* (1970), by James Dickey, deals in the same themes. Complicating these expectations is the further assumption that such novels were sociologically accurate: Northern readers are supposed to be at once shocked, titillated, and assured of their own moral superiority by such books.

O'Connor seems to have deliberately courted this misunderstanding. She always professed no interest in producing sociologically accurate books (although in fact there is a great deal of sociologically accurate detail), and she withdrew her first novel from publication by Rinehart over the editor's demand that the novel be more realistic. O'Connor always insisted that her principal characters were grotesques, that average Southerners do not in fact put their eyes out with lye or drown their cousins so as to resist the temptation to baptize them. She also insisted, however, that her object was not the rather base thrill that she associated with the Southern gothic but was instead the apprehension of the absolute, an ambition that seemed to her, as to Hawthorne, to require the invention of extreme characters and extreme situations. She reveled in Hawthorne's description of himself as a romancer, rather than a novelist, and she always pointed out that her characters were extreme not in the way Erskine Caldwell's characters are but in the way Ethan Brand and Ahab and Joe Christmas are extreme. Somehow or other, her claims had difficulty sticking in the popular mind: as late as the 1970s the jacket blurb of *The Violent Bear It Away* described it as a chronicle of three generations of a demented Southern family, obsessed with guilt and driven to violence.

O'Connor's first and best novel, *Wise Blood* (1952), was largely written in the North, after she completed her master of fine arts degree at the State University of Iowa, while she was a fellow at Yaddo in New York and later a tenant of Robert and Sally Fitzgerald. While she was completing the book, she suffered the first attack of the systemic lupus that was to force her to return to her mother's house in Milledgeville, Georgia, and that ultimately killed her. The book is best seen as a sophisticated intellectual satire on religious issues, analogous to Swift's *A Tale of a Tub* or Blake's *The Marriage of Heaven and Hell*.

The protagonist, Hazel Motes, returns from World War II to find his family and his native hamlet to have vanished. While serving in various deserts during the war, he had studied his soul and come to the conclusion that it did not exist. Having discovered this good news, his first ambition is to outrage the sensibilities of his fierce grandfather, an evangelist who had traveled over three counties "with Jesus hidden in his head like a stinger," and who had had something to do with Motes's persistent, although persistently denied, sense of sexual guilt. In his youth, after seeing a naked woman in a casket, he had put broken glass in his shoes for weeks. He had also been intensely disappointed – this actually is the beginning of the crisis of his faith that comes to a culmination during the war – that God had taken no notice either of his guilt or of his remorse.

Motes travels to the city and tries in various ways to assert his complete freedom from Christianity, living briefly with a prostitute ("Mrs. Leora Watts! Friendliest bed in town!") and buying a ruinous old car that he invests with symbolic force ("A man that's got a good car don't need no Justification!"). What he winds up doing is becoming the evangelist he keeps denying he is, preaching from the hood of his car the word of the Church Without Christ, whose doctrines are a broad but nevertheless cutting parody of Sartre. He picks up disciples, whom he rejects, including the slutty daughter of a panhandling evangelist who pretends to have blinded himself for Jesus and whose faith Motes cannot outrage because he is not really a believer in the first place. He also rejects as a disciple a dim youth named Enoch Emery, who had been visiting the zoo to hurl insults at the primates in order to prove to himself that he is smarter than they are, and who responds to Motes's call for a New Jesus, who will prove to us that we are born only once, by stealing a wizened little mummy from a glass case in the MVSEVM. Rejected by Motes, Emery winds up stealing a gorilla suit from a man advertising a movie about Gonga, the Giant Jungle Monarch, so that he, too, can be a new kind of man. If Motes is a burlesque of Sartre, Emery is a burlesque of Darwin.

Motes's most threatening would-be disciple is a con-man evangelist who calls himself Onnie Jay Holy. When Motes, having the integrity of his convictions, rejects his offer of a lucrative partnership, Holy sets up a rival church with Hazel's own doctrines called the Holy Church of Christ Without Christ. Holy dresses up a derelict named Solace Layfield, who looks like Motes, to be its prophet. Motes, in a rage not so much because of Layfield's parody of him as because of his sense that Layfield is not a heroic unbeliever but a down-at-heels believer (and therefore a hypocrite), runs him over with his car.

The murder of Layfield is the turning point of the novel. Motes attempts to flee town, but his car is destroyed by a comic highway patrolman. Suddenly feeling the sense of uncleanness and fallenness he had denied, Hazel blinds himself with lye and wraps himself in barbed wire. Strangely, at this moment Motes becomes transformed in the narrator's eyes from a parodic to a prophetic figure, someone "whose eyes hold more because they have no bottom." What Motes seems to have discovered is that real atheism is venal and small, something befitting Onnie Jay Holy, and that he himself, almost despite himself, had been attesting not to God's death but to his incomprehensibility. Motes's would-be atheism was at bottom an ascetic mysticism, an iconoclasm so profound that it prohibits not only graven images of God but even the very thought.

The sense that modern atheism is still Christ haunted is central to O'Connor's second novel, *The Violent Bear It Away* (1960). The protagonist, Francis Marion Tarwater, is an angry, provincial young man who owes something to Huckleberry Finn and something to Holden Caulfield. As with Hazel Motes, the experience that launches him into the novel is a moment of theological disappointment: he had been raised in the woods by his great-uncle, Mason Tarwater, to be a prophet, but he is humiliated that the prophetic task appointed to him by the old man, that he baptize his mentally retarded cousin, Bishop, seems too small for his vocation. Young Tarwater is further humiliated by God's failure to show him a sign to prove his calling to him. Rejecting the old man's demand, fortified by whiskey from the old man's still, and prompted by a mysterious Friend who materializes out of his own voice and who turns out to be the Devil, Tarwater burns down the house, believing that the old man's body is still inside it, and sets off for the city to be initiated by his uncle Rayber into the secular life.

Tarwater no sooner meets Rayber than he rejects his tutelage as thin, lifeless, and false. Rayber has the most mechanical of intellects – he is a designer of psychological tests, and to call his every remark psychobabble is a polite understatement. (He has cast a long shadow in contemporary literature, however, since the character Schoolteacher in Toni Morrison's *Beloved* (1987) is modeled closely on him.) Rayber has great plans: he will rescue the boy from the old man's influence. Rayber, too, had been stolen from his venal parents by the old man and instructed in prophecy. Rayber thinks of the old man as having done something akin to child abuse to the both of them, and he has conducted his own life with rigorous, narrow, and rather cold discipline, choosing an empty life over what strikes him as an insane one. Rayber sees Tarwater's task of baptizing Bishop as a kind of compulsion, and he goes into terrific and – to O'Connor – ludicrous psychological detail about it. He also seeks to reform the boy's education, taking him to the museum "to meet his ancestor the fish" and taking him out to eat a different unappetizing kind of foreign cuisine every night.

Tarwater's Friend is a more powerful figure. For one thing, unlike Rayber, he has wit and insight. He correctly points out that there is vanity in the old man's sense of his vocation. Furthermore, he has two telling arguments that he repeatedly deploys. First, he argues that nothing Tarwater may advance as a sign of his own vocation cannot be explained in one way or another. When, Bishop having suddenly escaped from Rayber and jumped into a fountain, the sun comes out and places an aureole around his head, the Friend replies, "Well, that's your sign . . . The sun coming out from under a cloud and falling on the head of a dimwit. Something that could happen fifty times a day without no one being the wiser." When Tarwater gets his first glimpse of Cherokee Lake, in which he will be asked to baptize Bishop, and the lake is described as "so unused it might only the moment before have been set down by four strapping angels for him to baptize the boy in," the Friend replies, tellingly, "Steady. Everywhere you go you'll find water. It wasn't invented yesterday."

The Friend's other argument concerns Tarwater's freedom. Adopting Rayber's theory that Tarwater's urge to baptize Bishop amounts to a clinical compulsion, he demands that Tarwater do something to prove his own freedom. Now once somebody doubts your freedom, absolutely nothing you can do suffices to demonstrate it, since what you do to demonstrate your freedom is always motivated by the desire to create a plausible excuse for fulfilling your compulsions. The Friend's two arguments are both versions of the same argument: that in a world where causal explanations are complete, there is no room for transcendentals like personal freedom or the divine plan.

The Friend demands that Tarwater prove – by drowning Bishop instead – that he is not compelled to baptize Bishop. Tarwater does drown Bishop but finds that despite himself he has baptized him while drowning him. The freedom that Tarwater believes he has won turns sour on him immediately. Called on to declare his new independence to a shopkeeper who upbraids him, he is shocked to hear a torrent of obscenities rushing out of his own mouth. (This moment is modeled on an earlier moment of illusory freedom in American literature, the freedom Dimmesdale thinks he has bought for himself in the forest scene in *The Scarlet Letter*.) Tarwater is picked up by a mysterious driver, a materialization of the Friend, who drugs and sodomizes him.

Recovering himself, Tarwater burns the woods where he has been violated and returns to the old man's farm, where he discovers that he had not in fact burned the old man's body, since it had been buried by the old man's African American friend, Buford Munson, while Tarwater was making free with his great-uncle's whiskey. Having made this discovery, Tarwater has a vision in which he is told to warn the children of God of the speed of God's mercy, and he sets back off to the city to take up his prophetic vocation.

O'Connor had no sooner published the book than she felt compelled to explain that it is not a book about obsession but a book about baptism, and that Mason Tarwater, not Rayber, speaks for her values. That there is still considerable critical controversy about the book – it turns now not on what O'Connor meant but on what the book does – should be no wonder, because the book is almost designed to be misinterpreted, as if Northern secular readers are dared to identify their point of view with Rayber's. The issue is deeper than this, however, since the critical controversies are only repetitions of the very arguments played out between Tarwater and the Friend, and the Friend's arguments are unanswerable not because they are correct but because it is in the nature of the questions of faith to pose unanswerable problems to the intellect.

5

❦

EUDORA WELTY

WHEN Eudora Welty was a young woman just out of the University of Wisconsin and Columbia Business School, she briefly was a "publicity agent, junior grade" for the Works Progress Administration, and in that capacity she traveled over the eighty-two counties of Mississippi, bringing her Kodak with her on bookmobile routes, into juvenile courts, and into Holiness Churches. Republishing those photographs many years later in *One Time, One Place* (1971) – she pointedly calls them "snapshots," not only to make clear the casual and amateurish way she took them but also to make clear the relaxed, personal, one-on-one quality of the relationship between the people on both sides of the lens – she reflects that although these pictures were taken in the depth of the Depression, she was grateful that her beginner's luck gave her what a more practiced method could not have given, "the blessing of showing me the real State of Mississippi, not the abstract state of the Depression." In particular, she finds that the pictures she took conveyed more about their subjects than any thesis about the South she might have been attempting to prove.

It was with great dignity that many other portrait sitters agreed to be photographed, for the reason, they explained, that this would be the first picture taken of them in their lives. So I was able to give them something back, and though it might be that the picture would be to these poverty-marked men and women and children a sad souvenir, I am almost sure that it wasn't all sad to them, wasn't necessarily sad at all. Whatever you might think of those lives as symbols of a bad time, the human beings who were living them thought a good deal more of them than that. If I took picture after picture out of simple high spirits and the joy of being alive, the way I began, I can add that in my subjects I met often with the same high spirits, the same joy. Trouble, even to the point of disaster, has its pale, and these defiant things of the spirit repeatedly go beyond it, joy the same as courage.

Welty's remarks here are aimed at those who have been trained up to certain reflex expectations about pictures of the South by Walker Evans and James Agee's *Let Us Now Praise Famous Men* (1941). She also has in mind all those readers who ask, with an air of knowing already what they should get, "Tell us about the South," or of demanding, as Welty remembered a stranger who called her long distance one midnight demanding, "All right, Eudora Welty, what are you going to do about it?" Concerning her many pictures of African American people, she describes the temptation to use them to demonstrate a Claim about Race in the South as if that temptation were something ulterior, something that ignores, even tramples, the humanity of particular people with particular lives: "I wished no more to indict anybody, to prove or disprove anything by my pictures, than I would have wished to do harm to the people in them, or have expected any harm from them to come to me."

Welty feels under some pressure, as Faulkner, Warren, O'Connor, and others all did, to preach against some of the manifest evils of her time and place, and she feels under the pressure of some of those evils, also. She is eager, however, to resist what she describes in her essay "Must the Novelist Crusade?" as "generalities that clank when wielded," and which "make too much noise for us to hear what people might be trying to say. They are fatal to tenderness, and are in themselves non-conductors of any real, however, modest, discovery of the writer's own heart." Welty's argument, it is important to note, is not that authors should not have political commitments or that they should not respond to the moral issues of their time and place. Her argument is not against politics but against the Political Novel, and her argument against it is not that it is political but that it is political in wrong ways, obliterating the personhood of the novelist's subjects, who become generalities, not people, and obliterating the personhood of the novelist's own voice, which becomes the voice of a crowd: personhood on both sides is the first thing politics and art ought each to respect, and, failing that respect, the political novel fails both as politics and as novel.

The medium of the novelist's art, Welty says, is not argument but feeling. Feeling conveys the human force of convictions in a nuanced way that is not only more persuasive than argument but also ultimately fairer, since it reaches also into the question of what feelings really mean (when played on the pulse) and articulates political values in the place where their meanings are ultimately to be tested anyway, in the feeling lives of people.

One way to see what Welty has in mind is to notice how peculiar and alive Phoenix Jackson, the protagonist of her early story "A Worn Path," seems to be. The plot of the story is very simple: an elderly African American woman makes her way steadily through the woods and along the old Natchez Trace past many vicissitudes to fetch medicine for her grandson, for whom she has had to make this journey regularly since he swallowed lye three years before. Despite the fact that the journey is one she frequently makes, she must face down a number of difficulties, some of them merely obstructions, some of them seemingly the uncanny opposition the world puts up to indomitable spirits.

What the story turns on is not only her courage but also her strangeness, her peculiar combination of vulnerability and self-sufficiency. Passing through a swampy area, she is surprised and knocked over by a strange dog. Momentarily losing consciousness, she is helped to her feet, still partly in dream, by what seems to be a real hunter, although he has a hint of the uncanny about him: he could have just stepped in from "Little Red Riding Hood," but whether he is a version of the hunters or of the wolf is never entirely clear, because he is always helpful and menacing in the same breath. Having rescued her from the dog – which his own dog fights with – he ridicules her mildly, and suggests that she should give up on her errand and return home. Then, distracted by the dogs, he loses a coin, which Phoenix picks up. The coin is treated in the story as a kind of mystic token, and it will finally be used to buy a paper windmill for the grandson. When the hunter returns, he idly threatens her in a way that is both the manner of a bullying white man and the manner of a folktale spook. She thinks he is threatening her over the coin, but his reply indicates that that is not the reason and that the threat is a kind of test. The mild dignity with which she replies makes more political points than one might at first suspect:

> The man came back, and his own dog panted about them. "Well, I scared him off that time," he said, and then he laughed and lifted his gun and pointed it at Phoenix.
>
> She stood straight and faced him.
>
> "Doesn't the gun scare you?" he said, still pointing it.
>
> "No, sir, I seen plenty go off closer by, in my day, and for less than what I done," she said, holding utterly still.
>
> He smiled, and shouldered the gun. "Well, granny," he said, "you must be a hundred years old, and scared of nothing. I'd give you a dime if I had any money with me. But you take my advice and stay home, and nothing will happen to you."
>
> "I bound to go on my way, mister," said Phoenix. She inclined her head in the red rag. Then they went in different directions, but she could hear the gun shooting again and again over the hill.

Welty's fundamental impulses are comic and familiar, but to say this is not to say that she does not know fallen human nature. The hand with which Welty writes "Lily Daw and the Three Ladies," in which three well-meaning but buffoonish women maneuver the protagonist into a mental asylum, is as light a hand as that with which she describes the vanities and bickering that drive the narrator to her final expedient in "Why I Live at the P. O.," but the sinister undertones of the first story are still unmistakable. Officious and unconsciously sinister busybodies are something of a stock in trade for Welty and give her stories some of the sense of the repressiveness of small-town life we associate with the work of Sherwood Anderson. For example, in *Losing Battles* (1970), Miss Lexie, a former student assigned to take care of her ailing teacher Miss Julia, ignorantly and with the best of intentions imprisons and brutalizes her. There is much broad, even slapstick comedy in *Losing Battles*: a young man who is not only innocent but "an innocent" returns from prison to a family reunion but spends much of it extricating, from a perilous position on a cliff's edge, the car of the judge who sent him to prison. The novel also pays close attention, however, to the pressure the family puts on the convict's wife, a schoolteacher who feels born for better things than her husband's comical family can give her, and who, like many daughters-in-law in Welty, feels the force of the family's disapproval.

Darkest of all are the conformity pressures on Miss Eckhart, the outcast piano teacher of "June Recital" from Welty's 1949 sequence of related stories, *The Golden Apples*. Miss Eckhart is isolated from the rest of the townsfolk of the appropriately named Morgana by her culture: she is the only Lutheran, and more pointedly, the only German, in town. The former is an issue that drives a low-intensity but continuous conflict in Welty: Baptists and Methodists are engaged in a delicate class struggle with each other in which the place of a lone Lutheran is hard to define. As a German American during World War I, Miss Eckhart is ostracized as a possible enemy sympathizer. She is also set aside from the rest by her interest in high culture: her respectable students are interested in culture chiefly as an expression of their gentility, and although Miss Eckhart is also ruthlessly genteel, she has an emotional investment in music that is all the more intense for all of the other repressed feelings that go into it.

We are given a few glimpses into Miss Eckhart's inner life. She has a dark relationship with her invalid mother, who once ridicules her during a lesson and whom she then brutally slaps in front of her students. She develops a powerful but repressed attachment to a shoe salesman who plays the cello in the movie theater. Nothing comes of the relationship, but when the salesman dies in an accident, she leaps into his grave at the funeral. After this, she is attacked and possibly raped by a black man; she suffers the opprobrium of the community for not leaving it afterward. Finally, she is intensely invested in Virgie Rainey, a poor girl who is her best student. Virgie treats her own talent with some contempt, and, aware of the power she has over her teacher, plays rather sadistically on Miss Eckhart's vulnerability.

At the story's climax, presented to us through the eyes of two young people who live next door (one of them a former student), Miss Eckhart returns to the now-abandoned house where she used to board and give lessons. Virgie Rainey is upstairs, making love to a sailor. It is not certain that Miss Eckhart knows that Virgie and the sailor are in the house, but that knowledge would clearly not have changed her course. Miss Eckhart carefully arranges newspapers around the downstairs parlor, in a kind of parody of the decorations she used to arrange for recitals, and sets them on fire. Two clownish passersby notice the fire and put it out before it spreads. Miss Eckhart then sets fire to her hair. Bound by the two clowns, Miss Eckhart is hustled off to the lunatic asylum in Jackson, Mississippi. On her way down the street, she and Virgie Rainey meet face to face, but each coldly refuses to acknowledge the other.

Welty's second, and greatest, novel, *Delta Wedding* (1946) concerns the family politics of the Fairchilds, a well-to-do family in the Delta region of Mississippi, the flat, fertile region along the Mississippi River between Memphis and Vicksburg. The Fairchilds are gathering for the wedding of their daughter, Dabney. In depicting the bustle and to-do of a complicated family centering on a generous but exhausted woman in late middle age, the novel clearly owes something to Virginia Woolf's *To the Lighthouse,* and the scenes in which Ellen Fairchild bakes a cake and sees that act as somehow metaphorically holding her scattered family together look back unmistakably to the *boeuf en daube* prepared by Mrs. Ramsay in *To the Lighthouse.* The gender politics of the novels are strongly different, in that while Woolf's Mr. Ramsay is domineering and egocentric, the Fairchild men are for the most part amiable but not terribly perceptive people who leave most of the real business to their wives, and the crucial conflicts in the book are mostly among the women. In both novels, the conflicts among the characters are subordinated to a deeper conflict between the characters and life, which in both novels is a dark force that raises up human energies only to dissipate them; in both novels, life is not the opponent of death but part of that wheel of life-into-death on which all of the characters, without their consent and sometimes without even their knowledge, are slowly being broken.

Life as a destroyer in Woolf's novel is dreamy and sensuous, and the passages in which the deaths of the principal characters surface are written with a rich and suggestive lyricism reminiscent of the early Tennyson (for whom indulgence in lyricism was also a kind of dreamy surrender to dissolution), and through Tennyson to Keats, who, hearing the nightingale, was "half in love with easeful death." Life-into-death feels very different in Welty's novel, for its characteristic air is not cool and dreamy but rank and intoxicating. Welty's meditations on life as a richness that ultimately runs to rot are somehow also meditations on what seems to her to be a feminine sexual destiny. For example, in the scene where the bride Dabney, riding her horse in the morning, turns off to look at the bayou and is unsettled by the thought that eyes are watching her from under the black water, it is not hard to see that what Dabney is facing is at once a vision of decay and a vision of her own sexual maturity and the world of ripeness and decay that she is shortly to enter as a grown woman.

There were more eyes than hers here – frog eyes – snake eyes? She listened to the silence and then heard it stir, churn, churning in the early morning. She saw how the snakes were turning and moving in the water, passing across each other just below the surface, and now and then a head horridly sticking up. The vines and the cypress roots twisted and grew together on the shore and in the water more thickly than any roots should grow, gray and red, and some roots too moved and floated like hair. On the other side, a turtle on a root opened its mouth and put its tongue out. And the whirlpool itself – could you doubt it? doubt all the stories since childhood of people white and black who had been drowned there, people that were dared to swim in this place, and of boats that would venture to the center of the pool and begin to go around and everybody fall out and go to the bottom, the boat to disappear? A beginning of vertigo seized her, until she felt herself leaning, leaning toward the whirlpool.

The nine-year-old protagonist, Laura McRaven, comes to the wedding desperately hungry for love. Her mother has recently died, and her father, although a sympathetic figure, is regarded by everyone as inept and incapable of bringing her up properly. For much of the novel, Laura's need is unanswered because the family is so swept up in the chaos of its ongoing life that she seems barely to be noticed. Things change for Laura before the end of the novel: her cousins keep tactlessly reminding her that she cannot be a flower girl at Dabney's wedding because her mother has just died, but the cousin who will play this part comes down with the chicken pox and she gets to do it after all, and almost as an afterthought Ellen – who also announces that she is pregnant again – decides to take Laura in for the long term.

Laura's feeling that she is somehow outside of the circle of The Fairchilds is shared by almost everybody else in the novel. Even Ellen, who is the vital center of the book, is nevertheless only a Fairchild by marriage and regards them with equal amounts of pity and puzzlement. Dabney, who is regarded by her sister Shelley with bitter envy as more of a Fairchild than she is, nevertheless is marrying the overseer Troy Flavin, a man not of her class and furthermore, a man whom she barely knows, as a way of outraging her family.

It is the two male uncles of the bride who seem most to experience the odd sense of being at the same time at the center and at the periphery of the family. Uncle Denis, whose death has haunted the family imagination for years, is the figure on whom all of the family's hopes were set, but there is also a crushing unconscious cruelty about the family's love of Denis, and he responds by drinking too much, living too quickly, and dying young, after marrying the mentally unstable Virgie Lee. Uncle George, always in the shadow of Denis, marries beneath him to escape the burden of his family's love and moves away to put distance between him and them.

At the novel's opening, George's wife (referred to throughout as "that Robbie Reid") has just left him. Some days before, he and she and the rest had been at a family picnic. They were crossing a railroad trestle when the Yazoo-Delta train came, and everybody jumped for safety, except for Maureen, the cruel, mentally retarded daughter of Denis and Virgie Lee whose foot was stuck in the tracks. George, risking his life, stayed to help Maureen. George's heroic act enrages Robbie, who feels that he endangered himself only because his family expected he would do so. George is in fact always being tenderly bullied by his female kin and knows it, and the fact that he does what they wish despite his knowledge of what is really going on only compounds his betrayal of Robbie in his wife's eyes.

The Fairchilds never experience life, Robbie feels, because nothing happens to them that they do not draw the sting of by transmuting it into a romantic or amusing story. We hear several versions of the story of the incident of the trestle retold often enough – and hilariously enough – by different members of the family to be sure that there is justice in Robbie's charge. Mythologizing the story keeps death out of it, but it also devalues the story and its protagonists, and in refusing this, Robbie believes she is standing up for a kind of earnestness about life that the Fairchilds are incapable of.

The Fairchilds are, as Robbie says they are, people who simply cannot see when they are walking on the edge of an abyss, and danger and violence keep encroaching on the story in ways that the characters never comprehend. There are the always present reminders of real tragedies – Denis's death, the murder of an early Fairchild as he came out on the Natchez Trace, a bloody quarrel in the preceding generation about a cotton gin – but all of these are neutralized by becoming family mythology. There is also an ongoing crisis among their African American servants, in which a young woman named Pinchy is going through a religious conversion called "coming through," which seems also to be a kind of sexual trauma that somehow provokes the men around her into violence. (Troy winds up settling this crisis with disturbing nonchalance with his pistol.) There is the strangely beautiful runaway girl, whom Ellen meets in the woods (and whom George also meets, and sleeps with), who is fleeing in disgrace from somewhere unknown to the deeper disgrace of Memphis and who is in fact run down and killed by the Yazoo-Delta late in the novel. Although her motives are completely self-centered, and although it is hard to imagine what else George could have done in the trestle scene, Robbie is right that the train could have killed George, and she is right to see in everybody's refusal to see this fact a kind of devaluation of George and a kind of unseriousness about life.

What Robbie finally discovers is that George's act on the trestle was purely spontaneous, not the result of his surrendering to his family. Indeed, to have done otherwise would have been in its own way to remain a prisoner to his family, since to be required to resist them under all circumstances would also be to remain under their thumb. This reconciliation sets off a chain of other reconciliations, which give the final chapters of the novel something of the symmetry of Shakespearean comedy.

The novel ends in joy, not merely in the tentative victory over chaos that ends *To the Lighthouse*. As in Woolf's novel though, the victory here is not a victory for all time, for the joy of the novel is not the joy of one who triumphs over life's darkness, nor is it the joy of one who can, Fairchildlike, ignore it blissfully; it is the joy of someone who knows all the worst things about life and is not daunted by them, the kind of joy one can only call tragic joy.

Except for *The Optimist's Daughter* (1972), Welty's other novels are more broadly comic. *The Ponder Heart* (1953) and *Losing Battles* (1970) are high-spirited works, with equal parts slapstick, Southwestern humor, and fairy tale, although there is a barely acknowledged strain of tragedy in the latter. *The Robber Bridegroom* (1942) retells the Grimm fable in the context of Natchez Trace folk history, including in the story larger-than-life and grotesque versions of some of the real Natchez Trace bandits, such as the Harp brothers, and some of the folk traditions of the keelboatmen, such as the "half-horse half-alligator" Mike Fink. Clement Musgrove, a fairy-tale innocent, does not know that Jamie Lockhart, whom he asks to rescue his daughter Rosamond, is himself the man who has stolen her, but Jamie does not know that the girl Clement hires him to find is the girl he has already kidnapped and fallen in love with. The novel works out a series of dual identities and mistaken identities with humor and brio. In the dual view the novel takes of Jamie Lockhart, who is at once a sexual aggressor and an idealized hero, the novel thinks through, in ways that resemble the classic fairy tale Beauty and the Beast, feminine ambivalences about masculine sexuality.

The spareness of *The Optimist's Daughter* (1969; revised 1972) sets it apart from Welty's other works. Laurel McKelva, a war widow, returns to Mount Salus, Mississippi, to take Judge McKelva, her father, to New Orleans for an operation to repair a torn retina. Laurel's mother is dead, and Judge McKelva has married Fay, a frivolous and self-centered woman younger even than Laurel who sees Judge McKelva's operation mostly as a matter of personal inconvenience to her. During his convalescence, throughout which he becomes mysteriously weaker and more passive, Judge McKelva unexpectedly dies. Although it is not clear whether Fay actually causes the old man's death, his sudden turn for the worse happens just when Fay, against the doctor's orders, attempts to pull him out of bed to force him to attend the Mardi Gras. Far from feeling guilt over what she has done, Fay is enraged with Laurel for allowing the nurse to pull her from the room and enraged with the judge for allowing himself to die on her birthday. When Fay and Laurel return to Mount Salus for the funeral, the family friends descend on the house, offending Fay with their memories of Laurel's mother, and offending Laurel, too, by making all of the arrangements without her. While the friends outdo each other with romanticized stories about Judge McKelva, Fay makes a sordid display of herself at the wake in front of her numerous vulgar relatives from Texas, whom Fay had denied the existence of, and finally Fay pointedly has the judge buried far from the family plot, so that he will not be buried with his first wife.

Alone in the house after Fay's departure with her family, and after a rather alienating conversation with her old friends, with whom she now has little in common except pretending to have something in common, Laurel discovers a bird trapped in the house (traditionally, as we learn from a similar scene in *Delta Wedding,* a very bad omen). She compares it to herself, trapped in her former life, and she wonders if her desire to confront Fay for what she is, or her desire to tell the whole story to the only person who might understand it all, her dead mother, is merely another version of Fay's own vice, the perpetual desire to "make a scene."

Later, she finds the letters from her parents' courtship and reflects about her mother's single life in Virginia, how her mother never forgave herself when her own mother died, how her father (Laurel's mother's father) had cried out "Don't let them tie me down!" just before his death at Johns Hopkins. (These last, we read in Welty's memoir *One Writer's Beginnings* (1984), are incidents in Welty's own family history.) These thoughts lead Laurel to bitter memories of her own mother's dying days. She remembers her mother's anger with the judge for his inability to help her, her mother's increasing despair, and her father's inability to put other than the best face on the situation, his "optimism," which the mother took as a kind of betrayal.

Laurel sees the connection between what her father had suffered in both his marriages. Fay had been her mother's nightmare, a projection both of her mother's fear of the judge's optimism and of her jealousy of him. The judge's marriage to Fay is exactly the kind of betrayal of his first wife, the kind of refusal to take her seriously, that his optimism had been. Fay's inability to respond to the gravity of the judge's illness is only an extreme version of his own earlier inability: it is the story of his first marriage with the genders reversed and with tragedy transposed into debasing farce. Laurel reflects sadly and poignantly on her own life, wondering to what extent her survival is a betrayal of the dead parallel to her father's and step-mother's betrayals. She dreams how once, traveling with her husband, she came on the confluence of the Ohio and Mississippi Rivers, which seemed to her an image of the whole promise of married life. This vision makes her sense all the sharper of being betrayed by life, and of having, by living, betrayed her husband: "As far as Laurel had ever known, there had not happened a single blunder in their short life together. But the guilt of out-living those you love is justly to be borne, she thought. Outliving is some-thing we do to them. The fantasies of dying could be no stranger than the fantasies of living. Surviving is perhaps the strangest fantasy of all."

Only after having worked through all these thoughts is Laurel able to free the trapped bird. When Fay returns unexpectedly, just as Laurel is preparing to depart for Chicago, they have a confrontation over a bread-board that Laurel's husband had made for her mother, an object that Fay has scarred and abused and that seems to stand for all those loyalties and generosities that Fay will never understand. Laurel is at the point of strik-ing Fay on the head with the board when noon strikes, and Laurel lowers the board, aware that she cannot rebuke Fay without resembling her, and that as a survivor she is already more like Fay than she had been ready to admit. Survival is betrayal, for Laurel no less than for Fay. The novel is set pointedly during the Lenten period, and clearly Laurel's moment of recog-nition when the clock strikes is parallel to Peter's recognition of his own intimate betrayal at the moment when the cock crows three times. Only in backing down does Laurel become aware that the past is out of reach but that memory will never be, whatever Fay may do.

Welty's subject, from *Delta Wedding* through *The Optimist's Daughter* and beyond, is finally the elusiveness and painful mystery of love, of conflu-ence. Welty never captured better the sense of simultaneous urgency and longing, of simultaneous faith and despair, than in the climax of her early story "A Still Moment," in which Audubon, the traveling evangelist Lorenzo Dow, and the bandit James Murrell are brought up short by the vision of a heron:

What each of them had wanted was simply *all*. To save all souls, to destroy all men, to see and to record all life that filled this world – all, all – but now a single frail yearning seemed to go out of the three of them for a moment and to stretch toward this one snowy, shy bird in the marshes. It was as if three whirlwinds had drawn together at some center, to find there feeding in peace a snowy heron. Its own slow spiral of flight could take it away in its own time, but for a little it held them still, it laid quiet over them, and they stood for a moment unburdened. . . .

6

❦

NOVELS OF RACE AND CLASS

BOTH *Intruder in the Dust* (1948) and *To Kill a Mockingbird* (1960) set out to be stories about race and turn into stories about class. Because *To Kill a Mockingbird* is in some ways a stripped-down revision of *Intruder in the Dust,* it shows its hand more starkly and thus makes a clearer statement about the price of its central strategies. Written with the Emmett Till case in mind and with the Scottsboro Boys case in the background, *To Kill a Mockingbird* turns on the unsuccessful attempt of a widowed, slightly eccentric, morally decent small-town lawyer, Atticus Finch, to defend a young African American man, Tom Robinson, who has been falsely accused of rape in the south Alabama town of Maycomb during the Depression.

To Kill a Mockingbird is narrated by Atticus's daughter Scout, a shrewd, vital, feisty, tomboy rather on the model of Mick Kelly in *The Heart Is a Lonely Hunter.* The naïveté and sensitivity of the narrator serves a political purpose, because there is no better way to make clear the irrationality of racism than to attempt to make sense of it to someone like Scout. Scout herself has to learn to make her way in a very flawed and dangerous world, and her own developing insight and courage are meant to model a younger generation that may repair some of the problems of the world they inherit.

Much of the early part of the novel does not concern the trial at all but rather the attempts of Scout, her brother Jem, and her friend Dill, to lure the recluse Boo Radley out of his house. The children are full of mythology about him, and although Boo Radley is white, the specter they imagine him to be is meant to model the compound of fear and ignorance that is, in the novel's view, the main component of racial prejudice. What Boo Radley is really like is made clear early on in the novel: he leaves presents in a hollow tree for children that he does not seem to know are bent on tormenting him, and, unseen, he also gives Scout a blanket to warm herself with when she stands in the cold to watch a burning house.

The children, like Atticus Finch himself, are presented as being on easy and familiar terms with the African American people they know. In particular, they are close to the family cook Calpurnia, who is not precisely a stereotypical mammy but who is always presented in an idealized way as a stern model of good sense and charitable feelings. In one particularly pointed scene, the children accompany her to her church, where they are gradually made comfortable. The incident has two purposes: first, to demonstrate the kinship of religious and moral feelings among black and white and the possibility of close relationships among them (this lesson is presumably aimed at Southern readers), and second, to demonstrate that people of good sense and warm feelings in the South are capable despite everything of liking each other (this lesson is presumably aimed at Northern readers).

Harper Lee arranged the details of the rape case in such a way as to make it as unambiguous as possible. One need only compare the use E. M. Forster made of similar material in *A Passage to India* to see how simple, even simpleminded, the case is in this novel. The facts of the case are this: Mayella Ewell, the daughter of a very grubby and shiftless poor white family, has been making sexual advances to Tom Robinson, whom she has been calling into her house on the pretext of doing chores for her. Tom is perfectly aware of the danger of his position and makes every effort, within the bounds of politeness (crossing which would involve him in other dangers) to evade her. Here again, Lee's novel takes the easy way out. Compare how Richard Wright handled the scenes between Bigger and Mary, his accidental victim, in *Native Son,* for instance, or the scenes between the protagonist and Sybil in *Invisible Man.* Lee is so eager to make Tom Robinson a completely unambiguous victim that he winds up being a completely flat, even stereotyped, character in ways that even Harriet Beecher Stowe's Uncle Tom never is. While Mayella is acting in a particularly forward way, her father, Bob Ewell, catches sight of her through the window. He beats her severely, and she, to exculpate herself, claims that Robinson was assaulting her.

It is clear that nobody much believes Mayella's story, at least among the articulate people in the novel who talk about it, but a jury of poor white country people brings in a guilty verdict in short order, possibly not out of ignorance so much as out of naked race loyalty. Scout and Jem want nothing to do with this kind of loyalty politics. Indeed, they sneak into the courthouse to watch the trial from the Colored section, in the balcony. The "decent people" do not do much better than the country people, however, since not even Atticus will denounce the standing order in public, although the judge (in appointing Finch, rather than some lesser lawyer, to take the case) had in covert ways made his feelings clear, as did the sheriff, in preventing the crowd from lynching Robinson before the trial.

Unable to do anything in public other than fall in line behind Bob Ewell's story, nobody much stands up for Robinson, who is later killed in prison. Bob Ewell also knows, however, that nobody really believes his story, although nobody will say so, and he winds up suffering more shame than so lumpen a character would normally be expected to feel. Stung by the accusation that nobody will even voice but that he sees in everybody's expression, he vows to harm Atticus. What he tries to do is to assault Scout and Jem, but he is mysteriously killed before he can actually do them harm. The killer turns out to be Boo Radley, but to protect him Sheriff Tate agrees to the fiction that Ewell slipped and stabbed himself.

The two cases of convenient fictions are in a way parallel: agreeing not to hold an inquest into the killing of Ewell is somehow a recompense for agreeing not to question his transparently incredible allegation against Tom Robinson. The idea is that given a chance to do so that would not require them to shout it out in public, the decent people will be able to do the decent thing, although they might not do the same if they had to do so in the open. It is at best an ambiguous defense of such people, although it is perhaps a fair enough description of how people behave under the tyranny of opinion. At least there are the Atticus Finches, who will take somewhat more of a chance, although even they know which risks are pointless and which are not.

The main thrust of the book is its claim about the power of a common recognition of humanity to call people back to their senses. Boo Radley turns out not to be a ghoul. Dolph Raymond, who is said to be an alcoholic and keeps an African American mistress, in fact drinks only Coca-Cola and pretends to be an alcoholic so that none of the townspeople will figure out that he really does love his mistress. Walter Cunningham, leading a mob intending to lynch Tom Robinson before his trial, is recognized by Scout as the father of a boy in her grade in school, and he is so abashed by this that he comes to himself. The price of all this humanity, however, is that Bob Ewell seems to be the only racist in Maycomb and the one man responsible for all of the ugly history of racism in America. Treating racism as a disease primarily of "poor white trash" is as old a strategy as there is – it was a common staple of Bourbon politics after the end of Reconstruction. Perhaps it was the very availability of the strategy, that made the glaring exception to the author's charity invisible to her.

The crudity of *To Kill a Mockingbird* may seem obvious, but even *Intruder in the Dust* does not totally resist the temptation to seek a solution to racism by replacing it with class conflict, as if black and white could get along if they could unite against ignorant white people, as if the denizens of Beat Four, the Workitts and the Gowries and the Ingrums, were chief inventors of racism in Yoknapatawpha. Faulkner knows better than this in other books – in *Absalom! Absalom!* most especially. At least in the defendant, Lucas Beauchamp (a mixed-race descendent of Carothers McCaslin of *Go Down, Moses* [1942]), Faulkner creates a credible African American character, which is to say a character who is larger than the most obvious designs his author has on him. In his dignity, his stubbornness, his shrewdness, even in his crank angularity, he announces himself as a man who can hold his own; he is formidable, unidealized, and in no way a projection of the author's pity or guilt.

This is not to say that he is not in his own way as mythological a creation as Joe Christmas or Sam Fathers. A novelist always runs risks when characters take on mythological force. When characters come to stand for abstractions, they tend to become less human and tend also to become the creatures of authorial ulterior motives. In making Lucas so unmistakably himself, so much a creature with his own agenda, Faulkner forswears the kinds of ulterior motive that might have been evident in his creation of more mythologically charged characters. To use a character to forswear an ulterior motive, however, is in its way a no less ulterior use of a character. How can anybody really prove, however, that they have nothing to prove? That is an unanswerable question, and like most unanswerable questions, a meaningless one. How the will escapes its own ulterior motives is a mystery as old as St. Augustine, who noted that the corruptions of a corrupt will corrupt even the will to purify itself. One cannot will one's self out of one's own will any more than one can will one's self into sleep or can just "be one's self" by main force in front of a stranger with a camera. Augustine wills for a better will than the one he wills with, but that is finally the gift of grace, not of will. That said, the best route to grace is giving it. It suffices that Lucas Beauchamp is vital enough a creation that whatever one says about him leaves something unsaid. That is as good a definition of acknowledged humanity as one can come by.

The reader is lead through the novel by young Chick Mallison, who is like Scout Finch, old enough to see the injustices of his world and young enough to still be offended by them. He had four years earlier learned from Lucas the same lesson Faulkner wishes to teach us: having fallen in a frozen creek while hunting for rabbits, he is rescued by Lucas — or rather Lucas prevents his incompetent friends from drowning him in the act of saving him. As Chick's clothes dry, Lucas's peremptoriness having forbidden Chick to be fastidious about stripping in a strange house, he sees about him all the signs of Lucas's rectitude and self-possession: his fine suit, his gold toothpick, the grotesque antique pistol inherited from his white grandfather, and his air of arrogant imperturbability, which the narrator at once admires and is amused by. Lucas gives him what Chick later understands to be his own dinner, but when Chick attempts to pay him for his

trouble, Lucas tartly refuses the money (since it would establish a hierarchical relationship between them) and steadfastly subverts Chick's
attempts to even the accounts between them by sending him gifts by
matching him gift for gift in a kind of potlatch of racial equality.

When Lucas is arrested for the murder of Vinson Gowrie, Chick finally
believes he has found the means to even the score between them. He brings
his uncle Gavin Stevens in to defend Lucas, but Lucas is not forthcoming
with Stevens. For one thing, Lucas knows that Stevens proposes to plea-bar-
gain the case. For another thing, Lucas knows that if he takes the direct
route and asks Stevens to have Gowrie's body exhumed, Stevens will anyway not be able to go to the racist and lawless hill country of Beat Four and
ask them to disinter a white man to save the life of a black one. Stevens,
with the help of Sheriff Hampton and hunter Will Legate, manages to
arrange a guard for Lucas so that he will not be lynched, but Lucas characteristically refuses even to allow Stevens to guard him that night personally,
because he knows that Stevens will talk all night and he feels he needs his
sleep. Having dismissed Gavin Stevens, Lucas enlists Chick Mallison to dig
up Gowrie's body, which, he says, will have a bullet wound that could not
have been made by Lucas's own recently fired unwieldy ancient Colt pistol.
Chick is aided in his nocturnal adventure by his African American playmate
Aleck Sander and by the most interesting and comical of Faulkner's stubborn and eccentric elderly ladies, Miss Habersham, who is a descendent of
one of the founding families of Jefferson, and who was also a childhood
friend of Lucas's deceased wife Mollie.

What the three discover in Gowrie's grave is the body of Jake
Montgomery, but when they return the next day with Sheriff Hampton,
they discover in the grave not Jake but nobody at all. This comic turn of
events winds up solving the case, for both bodies are shortly discovered in
the quicksand of a nearby creek, and the bullet wound in Gowrie's body
can only have been made by the Luger pistol of his brother Crawford.
Vinson had learned that his brother was pilfering lumber, and that Lucas
had seen the pilferer at work. Hearing of this, Crawford had solved both
his problems by murdering Vinson and framing Lucas for the murder, but
Montgomery, Crawford's partner in the lumber scam, guessing what had
happened and seeking to blackmail Crawford, had been in the act of digging Vinson up when Crawford surprised him at the grave and killed him
only a few minutes before Chick and his party arrived at the same place.

The vindicated Lucas comically replays with Stevens the earlier scene of
refusing to be the object of the other's generosity that he had played out
with Chick: arriving at Stevens's office, he demands to pay him for his
legal services. When Stevens seeks to evade the evening of accounts by

naming a fee of only two dollars, Lucas punctiliously counts out the amount in pennies and asks for his receipt.

As in *To Kill a Mockingbird,* the upright lawyer makes a case that the white people of the South are capable of addressing the problem of their own racism without self-righteous interference from the North. Stevens makes the further claim that if racial justice is imposed from without rather than arrived at from within, the consequence will be the destruction of the South as a distinct organic culture and the absorption of the South into a miscellaneous and anonymous America, which Stevens views with distaste. African American culture, Stevens feels, is no less threatened by omnivorous Americanism than the culture of the white South is. Warren was to brood about similar things in *Segregation: The Inner Conflict in the South* and in *Who Speaks for the Negro?,* where he worries that a completely assimilated America will be a place where all American cities are as alike and as sterile as their airports are. In the latter book, written at the beginning of an upsurge of nationalist feeling in the black community, Warren interviews many African American intellectuals who also equate cultural assimilation with cultural suicide. Stevens's defense of the homogeneous cultures of the black and white South against the polyglot world of the North turns on the transparently silly claim, however – silly because it justifies anything, and silly because it more easily justifies politics opposed to Stevens's than it does his own – that "only from homogeneity comes anything of a people or for a people of durable and lasting value."

Stevens spends a great deal of time rearing up on his hind legs and speechifying, and it is hard to know how seriously to take him. After all, left to himself, he would have botched the case, and not only Lucas but also Chick repeatedly makes a fool of him. On the other hand, Stevens's views are not far removed from those Faulkner expressed in a soon-repudiated, drunken interview in 1956. Certainly Faulkner shares Stevens's distaste for the unearned sense of moral superiority he believes Northerners enjoy over Southerners, and certainly both resist the idea that the only way the South can give up racism is to become the North. Certainly, too, Stevens speaks for Faulkner when he credits the white and the black Southerner alike with resisting the lure of the Northern trinity of materialism, mediocrity, and conformism. Stevens argues that Southerners themselves must do justice lest it be done for them, for if justice is done for them by the imposition of federal power, the North will wind up inflaming the decent and the indecent Southerner alike into a suicidal defense of their region's identity. He further argues that the North's intervention will excite a racist orgy in which its own unacknowledged racism will play a large part. Many Southerners made similar arguments, but Stevens's presentation of them – in an italicized, two-page sentence fragment in the midst of a six-page sentence – sounds so unhinged (only the first half appears here) that it could easily pass for the malicious parodies of Faulkner sometimes sponsored by literary magazines:

– to defend not Lucas nor even the union of the United States but the United States from the outlanders North East and West who with the highest of motives and intentions (let us say) are essaying to divide it at a time when no people dare risk division by using federal laws and federal police to abolish Lucas's shameful condition, there may not be in any random one thousand Southerners one who really grieves or even is really concerned over that condition nevertheless neither is there always one who would himself lynch Lucas no matter what the occasion yet not only of that nine hundred ninety-nine plus that other first one making the thousand whole again would hesitate to repulse with force (and one would still be that lyncher) the outlander who came down here with force to intervene or punish him, you say (with sneer) You must know Sambo well to arrogate to yourself such calm assumption of his passivity and I reply I don't know him at all and in my opinion no white man does but I do know the Southern white man not only the nine hundred and ninety-nine but that one other too because he is our own too and more than that, that one other does not exist only in the South, you will see allied not North and East and West and Sambo against a handful of white men in the South but a paper alliance of theorists and fanatics and private and personal avengers plus a number of others under the assumption of enough physical miles to afford a principle against and possibly even outnumbered a concorded South which has drawn recruits whether it would or no from your own back-areas, not just your hinterland but the fine cities of your cultural pride your Chicagoes and Detroits and Los Angeleses and wherever else live ignorant people who fear the color of any skin or shape of nose save their own and who will grasp this opportunity to vent on Sambo the whole sum of their ancestral horror and scorn and fear of Indian and Chinese and Mexican and Carib and Jew, you will force us the one out that first random thousand the nine hundred and ninety-nine out of the second who do begrieve Lucas' shameful condition and would improve it and have and are and will until (not tomorrow perhaps) that condition will be abolished to be not forgotten maybe but at least remembered with less of pain and bitterness since justice was relinquished to him by us rather than torn from us and forced on him both with bayonets, willynilly into alliance with them with whom we have no kinship whatever in defence of a principle which we ourselves begrieve and abhor . . .

It is finally the hill people of Beat Four who are stigmatized in *Intruder in the Dust.* Despite Chick Mallison's fleeting recognition of the humanity of old Gowrie's grief for his son at the second exhumation, despite Stevens's admission that the inhabitants of Beat Four have been cheated and exploited by their more prosperous neighbors, and despite Stevens's recognition that the cravenness and complicity of the rest of Yoknapatawpha County is as necessary to a lynching as the rage of Beat Four is, the Beat Four people finally all remain vicious figures of fun. In *Intruder in the Dust* no less than in *To Kill a Mockingbird,* the ability of the white Southern characters to work out the racial difficulties depends on a kind of class scapegoating that in practice cannot but exacerbate the kinds of resentments the novels are ostensibly claiming can be easily laid to rest. It is not for nothing that when Twain attempted to think through similar problems in *Huckleberry Finn,* he recognized that the crucial relationship is between Jim and the son of Pap Finn, not between Jim and the son of the small-town aristocrat. The big flaw of the two novels at hand was in failing to see that it is Huck and his kind who need to be written into the solution.

7

❧

NOVELS OF SLAVERY AND
RECONSTRUCTION

MARGARET WALKER'S *JUBILEE*

ARGARET Walker's original claim to fame was as the first
African American woman to win the Yale Younger Poets prize,
for *For My People* in 1942. Much later, after a career as a professor at Jackson State University in Mississippi (Walker, with Ernest Gaines,
is one of the few major African American writers to make her career in the
South), she published *Richard Wright: Daemonic Genius* (1980), a controversial, very unsympathetic biography of Richard Wright, who was a former
friend of hers. Her most durable reputation, however, is for *Jubilee* (1966),
a thoroughly researched novel about slavery and Reconstruction, partly
based on the recollections of her own maternal great-grandmother,
Margaret Duggans Ware Brown.

Tangled feelings are rife in *Jubilee.* The protagonist, Vyry, is the daughter
of her master, John Morris Dutton, of Dawson, Georgia, and his slave Sis
Hetta, who later dies in childbirth bearing another of Dutton's children.
Dutton maintains a relationship of false heartiness and cheer with Jake,
Hetta's husband, who is not fond of Vyry. After Hetta's death, Vyry is sent to
the Big House, both to learn to cook under the tutelage of Aunt Sally and to
serve as a playmate for her half sister, Lillian. Dutton is a feckless and irresponsible man who does not acknowledge Vyry, although finally he seems to
be less the villainous tyrant than a bluff, rather foolish squire. In fact,
because he is more interested in state politics, he does not even pay close
attention to the workings of his plantation. He often does intercede against
the tyranny and cruelty of Grimes, his overseer, for whom he has class contempt, and against the petty sadism of his wife, Big Missy, however.

Grimes's cruelty to the slaves in his charge has something to do with his
own class resentment against his employer. Walker resists the class scapegoating one finds in Lee, however, describing a complex tangle of class and
racial politics like that Faulkner described in *Absalom! Absalom!* Walker goes
out of her way to point out that his standard of living is only a notch higher

than that of the slaves he oversees and that during thin times, the poor whites who skulk at the edges of the plantation economy may not even fare, materially at least, so well as that. In one memorable incident, Grimes, while Dutton is away at the legislature, demands that one of Dutton's favorites, Grandpa Tom, harness one of Dutton's prize horses to pull a plow. Tom, aware that Dutton would not permit this and that Grimes has no right to ask it, refuses. Grimes, enraged as much by the favor Dutton shows Tom as by Tom's refusal, beats Tom unconscious and shoots him to death, an offense for which he is never punished.

Big Missy's cruelties are pettier but very galling; she is consumed by self-pity over the state of her marriage, and like many people who think of themselves as disempowered even as they wield considerable power, she has an endless capacity for small, vicious cruelties against those she can hold in terror. At one point, she hangs Vyry by the wrists in a closet, mostly for being Dutton's child. At another, she makes all the house servants take ipecac every day for weeks so she can determine who has been stealing her preserves. This kind of thing makes her feel immensely practical, and she and Grimes often congratulate each other with how much more worldly they are than Dutton is.

There is also a communal hysteria over poisoning. As with so many other things, laziness and passivity prevent Dutton, who knows better, from intervening. His active participation in it is limited to selling the cook Sally, which he later regrets, admitting that he was foolish to have been stampeded by his wife and by Grimes, who attributes the death of his own child by disease to black magic. All of the slaves, however, are made to witness a public execution of two cooks who were convicted of poisoning their master. Dutton makes no effort to recover Sally or otherwise repair the damage caused by his complicity.

In the midst of all this, Vyry develops a very close relationship with her half sister Lillian, who fully and without shame acknowledges her as family. Vyry's relationship with Lillian and other collateral relatives of the Dutton family, which persists long after slavery, is one of the more interesting if controversial features of the novel, which insists upon underlining the intimate if ambivalent human relationships among slaves and masters.

Against her master's wishes, Vyry marries (although not legally, since she is a slave) a free blacksmith named Randall Ware, with whom she has two children. He has connections with local white opponents of slavery and with the underground railroad, but he is forced to flee, and in the confusion, he and Vyry are separated, Vyry ultimately being recaptured.

The Civil War brings a series of misfortunes to the Dutton household. Dutton himself, returning from the Confederate constitutional convention in Montgomery, is injured in a carriage accident, and dies, bitter and raving, from the resulting infection. He had much earlier promised to set Vyry free before his death. During his illness, he taunts her about this, as a way of proving to himself that he is still alive, and, completely insane for his last few days, leaves the task undone at his death. Dutton's son Johnnie is wounded at Chickamauga and returns home to die of infection. His servant, out of loyalty to him, makes sure to deliver him to his family before escaping to freedom, even though his doing this puts him somewhat at risk. Lillian's fiancé Kevin, who, unlike Johnnie, is no enthusiast for the Confederate cause, is killed at Olustee by a soldier of the famous 54th Massachusetts Regiment. Big Missy, after a horrific visit to the Andersonville prison camp, and after mortgaging all her property to invest in Confederate bonds, suffers a stroke. Walker captures vividly the weariness and the decay of Confederate nationalism over the war years; her treatment is at least comparable to that Caroline Gordon gives of the same subjects in *None Shall Look Back*. Most striking of all is that despite everything they have done, and without finally changing her views about them, the narrator is not without pity for the miserable deaths the Duttons undergo.

Walker's treatment of the immediate aftermath of emancipation is very ambivalent: Vyry and Lillian plan to cultivate the land for food crops, but their plans are disrupted by passing Union soldiers, who assault both of them. Vyry is rescued by a passing former slave named Innis Brown, who loves her but whom at first she looks down on, partly for reasons of color, and partly because he does not have the education and sophistication that Randall Ware had had. Ware, however, is missing, and because of a long illness does not return to Dawson until after Vyry and Brown have left.

Lillian was clubbed with a musket during the assault, and she is feeble-minded for the rest of the novel. Taking charge, Vyry arranges for Lillian's aunt, Lucy Porter, to come from their home in Georgiana, Alabama, to take Lillian and care for her. Vyry and Innis Brown set out to make a new life in Alabama and have several trials before they finally are able to establish themselves. They first attempt to farm a rich bottomland, which turns out to be flooded every year. They then take over a farm on shares from a miserable white family, only to discover that the owner forges charges for them against the company store and plans to put them into impossible fraudulent debt.

Next they move to Troy, Alabama, where Innis works in a sawmill and Vyry works for a white family named Jacobson. The Jacobsons take an interest in them, and although they are often patronizing, they ultimately help them set up another small farm and comfort them after they are burned out of that farm by the Ku Klux Klan. Once again Walker goes out of her way to see Vyry's relations with white people as complicated and human on both sides.

Ultimately Vyry and her family move to Butler County, Alabama, but Vyry, wary of being burned out again, does not wish to put up a new house there. Vyry does reestablish contact with Lillian's Aunt Lucy, and, on a visit to her, discovers that Lillian is permanently insane. Lucy Porter's family, like the Jacobsons before them, looks after the interests of Vyry's family.

Vyry by this time is supplementing her income by selling eggs to poor whites in Greenville, Alabama. She is able to go into all neighborhoods, because she is able to pass for white, and in so doing she hears considerable amounts of racist gossip. She assists a poor white woman with an extremely difficult birth and learns from her that she thinks that African Americans have tails. When Vyry proves otherwise, the woman is astonished and ashamed and becomes Vyry's fast friend, and when she learns of Vyry's reluctance to build a new house she recruits a crew of white people, including some of the racist gossipers, to raise her a house. This story, so startlingly at odds with the drift of the class politics of its time, is so incredible that it can only be founded on an actual experience.

The house-raising sets up the moral conclusion of the novel. Lucy Porter discovers that there is increasing friction between Innis Brown and Vyry's son (by Randall Ware) Jim, who looks down on Innis because of his color and who seeks an education that Jim will not pay the school tax to provide. Innis, enraged by Jim's unwillingness to do the kind of work on the farm that he does, whips Jim severely. Lucy, outraged by Innis's behavior, has her husband bear this news back to Dawson, where he goes to prevent Grimes from seizing the old Dutton plantation. There he discovers Randall Ware, who had returned to Dawson after Vyry's departure. Ware had served in the legislature during Reconstruction but afterward had been chiseled out of much of his considerable property by bullying white people, especially by the ever-grasping Grimes, and had hidden in his blacksmith shop while the Klan killed his apprentice.

Hearing of the fight between Jim and Innis, Ware comes to Greenville to reclaim his child. Vyry has by this time provisionally reconciled Jim and Innis, and there are a few moments of tense confrontation between her two husbands. Vyry casts in her lot with Innis Brown but agrees to let Randall Ware take Jim off to be educated at a normal school in Selma. She also has an intense political quarrel with Randall Ware, who is angrily antiwhite, and rebukes Vyry for her dependency on white people like the Porters: "the white man is your natural enemy and he regards you as his natural enemy.

It's just that simple." Vyry takes vigorous exception to this and to his attempt to play on loyalty politics. He says that she refuses to hate white people only because she is herself half white. She is especially shocked when he ridicules Lillian. She ends the argument by giving a moving speech about forgiveness and Christian charity, of which the narrator remarks that

> She was, in that night, a spark of light that was neither of the earth nor September air, but eternal fire. Yet it was not that she stood there in pride for them to worship her or be in awe of her deep integrity. She was only a living sign and mark of all the best that any human being could hope to become. In her obvious capacity for love, redemptive and forgiving love, she was alive and standing on the highest peaks of her time and human personality. Peasant and slave, unlettered and untutored, she was nevertheless the best true example of the motherhood of her race, an ever present assurance that nothing could destroy a people whose sons had come from her loins.

This speech marks, in the author's view, the moral high point of the novel, but it also marks *Jubilee* as a work of its time and as a glimpse into the road not taken.

WILLIAM STYRON'S *THE CONFESSIONS OF NAT TURNER*

The Confessions of Nat Turner provoked so acrid a controversy when it was published in 1967 that the air of scandal still clings to it. Partly, the scandal was a matter of timing. Styron had in fact been meditating on the book since 1942, and had the book appeared then, its fate would certainly have been far different. As the civil rights movement hardened into the Black Power movement, however, such figures as Nat Turner – whose contemporary fame, Eugene Genovese pointed out, is ironically enough largely owing to Styron's book – became risky to criticize. (In Daniel Panger's *Ol' Prophet Nat,* published the same year, he is accorded more sympathetic treatment than Styron gives him.)

Much of the controversy turned on Styron's use of historical materials. Styron did not claim to be writing a history but "a meditation on history," but it is clear at this distance that he used what materials were available to him conscientiously. Styron did make extensive and critical use, for example, of T. R. Gray's problematic pamphlet reporting Turner's original confessions, and of available secondary works such as William Sidney Drewry's 1900 *The Southampton Insurrection,* originally a doctoral thesis written under the influence of the now-discredited Dunning school of Southern historians.

The source materials present obvious difficulties. Indeed, in the novel, Styron thematizes some of the difficulties of assessing them. In particular,

Gray himself plays a major role in the novel, the florid paste gems of his rhetoric and ostentatious legal erudition contrasting with the grossness of his complexion (Styron pays a lot of attention to pockmarks and pimples and peeling skin on the faces of his white characters) and the crudeness of his behavior (he prefaces one particularly grandiloquent speech by lifting his thigh off his seat and farting). Styron describes Gray this grossly chiefly as a way of indicating that Gray's account is contaminated by self-serving and racism, but Styron's relationship with Gray's text is vexed, since for all of its faults it was just about the only primary material available to him. Despite a great deal of noise about folk traditions concerning Nat Turner made by critics at publication time, those folk traditions turned out largely to be figments of the critics' imagination and wishful thinking. Other issues over which the novel was faulted – such as for ignoring T. W. Higginson's claim that Turner had a wife – have turned out on examination to turn on speculations with far less warrant than any of the liberties Styron took with his materials.

The issue was not in reality the book's general portrayal of slavery in Southampton County, Virginia, which nobody could claim was an idealized one. The scene in which Nat's mother is raped by the overseer McBride (who threatens her with a broken bottle) is the equal of any scene of plantation horror one reads anywhere. Indeed, Styron's picture of slavery seems seedier and nastier than Margaret Walker's, and almost without exception the slaveholders in Walker's book are far more sympathetic than the slaveholders in Styron's. Styron does present a range of masters, however, from the morally anguished but ineffectual Samuel Turner, who promises Nat freedom but does not deliver it, to the filthy Reverend Eppes, to the loutish and illiterate Thomas Moore, to the crude but not totally inhuman Joseph Travis.

Styron did take one general historical liberty, for he presents Samuel Turner as a far more prosperous figure than he was in real life. Styron explained that because of the importance of the plantation to an understanding of slaveholding culture, he felt it was necessary to imagine Nat as living on at least one plantation, although in fact by Turner's time, Southampton County had become an exhausted and impoverished backwater in which few slaveholders owned more than half a dozen slaves and in which the principal product was no longer tobacco but apple brandy. For the most part, Styron does not deal in generalities about slavery or the plantation economy but in the particular conditions of southside Virginia, although the decrepitude and disorder of the society he describes generally resembles those that Frederick Law Olmsted described in his travels though the backwaters of the South.

The novel develops with particular care Nat's changing feelings toward Samuel Turner, the one white man for whom he comes to feel actual hate rather than merely a visceral dislike. Turner is presented as representing a kind of Virginia slaveholder that was becoming rarer as the legacy of the Revolution faded, the slaveholder who, like Jefferson, despised slavery and groped about wishfully and ineffectually for ways to end it. (His debates with his bluff, hardheaded, even rather brutish brother, recall the debates on the same subjects between Cass and Gilbert Mastern in *All the King's Men*.) Like Jefferson, Turner is a colonizationist, but unlike Jefferson, he does not minimize the intellectual and moral capacities of his slaves. His family encourages Nat's learning to read, and he promises to teach Nat the trade of carpentry and to free him once he knows that trade well enough to support himself. Samuel Turner, like Jefferson, is also so entangled in debt, however, that he is powerless to free his slaves. Having made the initial devil's bargain with slavery, Turner is forced down the slippery slope into uglier and uglier measures. Pressure from his creditors leads Turner to sell Nat's close friend Willis. Samuel sharpens the blow by bungling the transaction in such a way that Nat himself winds up delivering Willis to the trader. One by one, all of his slaves are sold, with Samuel explaining in each case that by selling one he is holding off the bankruptcy that would force the sale of them all, and that by selling them off piecemeal he can at least make sure that what slaves he sells he sells to masters he knows about. None of these expedients saves Turner's Mill, and it is not the least sign of Turner's blundering and blindness that when his estate is broken up for sale, he thinks he has given Nat (whom he had earlier promised to teach a trade and to free) a good start toward his freedom by selling him to the rancid Eppes, who chiefly wishes to rape Nat but ultimately settles for attempting to work him to death instead.

The principal issue on which the controversy turned was on Styron's portrayal of Nat Turner himself. The irony of this is that although Nat is not the heroic stalwart Styron's critics demanded, he is no demonic villain either, and he is certainly more sympathetic than the figure who appears in Gray's confessions, who is more interested in racial war than in liberation of slaves (he sacrifices many tactical advantages in order to kill more people, for instance) and who, in his visions, and, even more, in his astonishing egocentricity, is in general more like an anti-messiah than like Malcolm X. Styron's Turner is a chiliastic figure, a destructive mystic. This view of him does accord with the purport of Nat's apocalyptic visions, which Styron takes straight from Gray. Styron's Nat is actually far different from Gray's, however; he is ultimately a tragic figure, neither heroic nor demonic, and he has an eloquence, a reflectiveness, and a humanity that Styron denies to almost every other character in the book.

The contours of Nat's character seem most closely derived from Robert Penn Warren's Jeremiah Beaumont, and the interplay of sympathy and hostility in Styron's treatment of him resembles Warren's practice in *World Enough and Time*. In particular, the lyricism and gravity of Nat's narration derives from Beaumont. Consider the book's opening paragraph, in which Nat recounts a recurring dream he has while awaiting execution (the dream, incidentally, closely resembles a dream President Lincoln had while returning from Richmond the week before his assassination):

Above the barren, sandy cape where the river joins the sea, there is a promontory or cliff rising straight up hundreds of feet to form the last outpost of land. One must try to visualize a river estuary below this cliff, wide and muddy and shallow, and a confusion of choppy waves where the river merges with the sea and the current meets the ocean tide. It is afternoon. The day is clear, sparkling, and the sun seems to cast no shadow anywhere. It may be the commencement of spring or perhaps the end of summer; it matters less what the season is than that the air is almost seasonless – benign and neutral, windless, devoid of heat or cold. As always, I seem to be approaching this place alone in some sort of boat (it is a small boat, a skiff or maybe a canoe, and I am reclining in it comfortably; at least I have no sense of discomfort nor even of exertion, for I do not row – the boat is moving obediently to the river's sluggish seaward wallow), floating calmly toward the cape past which, beyond and far, deep blue, stretches the boundless sea. The shores of the river are unpeopled, silent; no deer run through the forests, nor do any gulls rise up from the deserted, sandy beaches. There is an effect of great silence and of even greater solitude, as if life here had not so much perished as simply disappeared, leaving all – river shore and estuary and rolling sea – to exist forever unchanged like this beneath the light of a motionless afternoon sun.

Nat's psychology in many ways resembles Beaumont's as well. For one thing, he is intensely withdrawn from other people, especially from other slaves. Nat's aloofness, especially from the other conspirators, is a detail repeatedly insisted on in Gray's account, but in Gray that aloofness serves for Nat a political purpose, that of wrapping him in the kind of mystery that would overawe his disciples and keep them under his control. In Styron, the aloofness arises at least as much from a kind of class prejudice, and, more than this, from a fundamental fastidiousness that is linked here, as in Warren's novel, with the protagonist's sense of his prophetic role.

Styron also insists also on Nat's sexual fastidiousness, partly because he finds no mention in Gray of Nat's having close attachments to any women outside of his immediate family. Repression and sexual shame are linked with Nat's sense of his prophetic vocation: here, as in *World Enough and*

Time, having a high moral calling and having a horror of sexuality are related facts, although in neither novel is a case made that the political and religious calling of the protagonist is simply a consequence of his sexual inhibitions. Both Nat and Beaumont also link repression and sadism so closely that they are sometimes hard to distinguish.

Nat's rape fantasies are one of the most controversial features of the novel, since they seem to replay a classic white Southern nightmare. Although Styron presents these fantasies as an element of the enraged desire for revenge and freedom, however, he also notes that neither Nat nor any of his confederates, including his demonic shadow Will, who seems to talk of nothing else, actually rapes anybody during the revolt. In their immediate literary context, Nat's rape fantasies, like Beaumont's vision of the female martyr in the flames, are in a strange way sexually charged rejections, bitter rejections, of sexuality itself. They are the expression of a racial and political predicament, but they are also a consequence of that strange mixture of idealization and disgust with which prophetic characters think about sex. Nat's sadism, like Beaumont's, is the product of his disgusted recognition that he is a sexual creature like everyone else; sadism appears to cast sex away, to be directed against sexuality, but it is of course sexually charged, as if sexuality not only turns ugly under repression but turns the means of repression to sexual ends.

In an act of racial abnegation and self-contempt, Nat had long idealized Emmaline, the daughter of one of his masters. Part of this idealization is contempt for himself as a sexual creature. When he overhears Emmaline secretly having sex with a cousin she despises (and when he learns, from what she angrily tells the cousin, that she had been so obsessed by an earlier love affair that she allowed her then-lover to sell her body), Emmaline becomes the object of ever more violent fantasies, which reflect back on her the violence of the self-contempt that had informed Nat's earlier idealization of her.

Nat's overhearing of Emmaline's affair is an instance of a theme Styron repeats several times: even when they are not the objects of their masters' sexual urges, slaves are always face-to-face with the hidden sexual lives of their masters, and they provide, to that extent, occasions for sexual shame, which leads to further sadism on the masters' part. For instance, Nat's confederate Hark is viciously hated by his young owner Putnam Travis because Hark caught him in a homosexual embrace with a young friend.

Homosexual experiences play a surprisingly large part in the novel, although Styron does not treat them in themselves as explaining or explaining away anything about Nat's insurrection. One of Nat's owners, a stingy, malodorous, down-at-heels Baptist preacher named Reverend

Eppes, frequently attempts to rape him. Even Eppes's revival services are replete with a sexual charge that is not far from the surface, and Nat, like Swift before him, describes in these services an inner link between religious enthusiasm and sexual excess. Nat's own one white convert to Jesus, Ethelred T. Brantley, whom he baptizes as white people pelt them both with stones and offal, is a young man cast out from his community for making homosexual advances. Brantley was a real person, but he is not specifically described as a homosexual in Gray, although Styron's inference from the ambiguous language in Gray's text is not totally implausible. Eppes's and Brantley's styles of homosexual experience are to be contrasted with Nat's own sexual experience with Willis, which is tender and loving, although Nat feels revulsed afterward, and Nat's taking up his calling as a clergyman immediately follows, in reaction. Styron makes a strong distinction between the homosexual experiences of his black and white characters: in the case of the white characters, the experience has something to do with their status as wielders of power, and Nat's revulsion from them is at least partly revulsion from their power. By contrast, Styron describes Nat's homosexual experience with Willis as arising in a strange way from Nat's repression of sexual feelings in general; it is not a straightforward expression of sexual feelings so much as where those feelings turn under repression. Styron's treatment of homosexual themes may be unpersuasive, but it is not without nuance, and the relationship between Nat and Willis provides in any event one of the rare moments of pure emotional generosity Nat gives or experiences from anyone.

The key relationship in the novel, in which sexual and racial and political tensions all cross, is Nat's relationship with Margaret Whitehead, which was the focus of much of the controversy about the novel. The historical Nat Turner describes himself in Gray's account as having bungled the killing of several other people, who were finally killed by his confederate Will, but the only person among the fifty-odd killed by the insurrectionaries who was killed by Nat himself was the actual Margaret Whitehead. There is no evidence to suggest any relationship between the historical Nat and the historical Margaret, although in the small world of 1830s Southampton they probably knew each other. In developing a relationship between them out of the tantalizing detail in Gray, Styron attempts to face down one of the sexual nightmares that has long haunted the racial imagination of white people, the avoidance of which would have been a failure of nerve. Styron's treatment of this relationship is finally no riskier than Wright's treatment of the relationship between Bigger and Mary in *Native Son,* but where Bigger sees only the danger that Mary has unawares led him into, and where Mary really has no insight into Bigger but sees him only as the projection of her own progressive political values, there is a thwarted possibility of human acknowledgment on both sides in the relationship between Nat and Margaret. (It is this possibility that distinguishes the relationship here from the relationship between Joe Christmas and Joanna Burden in Faulkner's *Light in August,* another novel with which *The Confessions of Nat Turner* is engaged in a complicated dance.)

What actually happens in the novel between them is quite minimal: they have a few conversations in which Margaret consults his expertise about the Bible and describes for him a masque she wrote at school, and they rescue an injured turtle. Margaret is a thoughtful, warmhearted, well-read young woman; she is naïve and charming, and she also radiates a sexual glow that she does not have the self-knowledge to understand. She makes it clear in her few conversations with Nat that she is sympathetic to African Americans and opposes slavery. It is also clear, although Margaret never acknowledges this even to herself, that she has come to love Nat. Her attraction to Nat is not merely a matter of prurient racist sexual curiosity, nor is it a girlish infatuation. She sees in Nat the one person she knows who is a reader, who has a profound religious nature, and who is alive to the poetry of the Bible, the one person, that is, with whom she feels some real spiritual kinship. She sees in Nat, in short, all of the human depth and human possibilities that Styron was accused of denying him.

Nat hates her for this. His hatred is paradoxical but not at all irrational. For one thing, he knows that without intending it, Margaret is tempting him to do things that would risk his life. For another thing, his own feeling for her, not just his attraction to her, involves him in risks he resents being presented with. Most important of all, her acknowledgment of him threatens his ability to hold his own in the world. One of the ways Nat keeps his head above water is by investing himself in a role that insulates him from suffering; so long as he is playing out the role "slave" to the white people (or the role "prophet" to himself) he is invulnerable to the world because he can master its rules. When Margaret offers him human acknowledgment, however, he is placed in a position of inner vulnerability to which none of the rules he understands applies: he must be Nat to Margaret, not merely "slave," and he must see Margaret as Margaret, not merely as "white woman." Margaret presents to Nat precisely the challenge the grandmother presents to the Misfit in O'Connor's "A Good Man Is Hard to Find," when she suddenly says to the Misfit that he is, despite everything, one of her children. Nat responds exactly as the Misfit does, and for the Misfit's reasons.

Nat bungles the killing of Margaret as he bungles them all. One of the reasons Styron depicts Nat as an incompetent killer is that Gray does, but there are other reasons as well, reasons that inhere in the kind of novel *The Confessions of Nat Turner* is. Prophetic figures in fiction frequently learn that actual killings are not the redemptive and magnetizing acts they envision themselves committing: the nausea that overtakes Nat in the act of killing is a sign of his humanity, not of his weakness. Nat is also nearly eclipsed, during the actual rebellion, by his demonic shadow Will, a brutal – but also a brutalized – figure who holds Nat in contempt for his inability to kill. Styron had little to go on about the historical Will (except for Gray's testimony that Will completed the killings Nat could not). Will represents the ways in which social upheavals release energies that swamp the designs of their projectors and turn in directions that they ultimately have no say in. Styron emphasizes Nat's shaky control over his rebels, and what follows is not a disciplined revolution but a generalized spree of killing punctuated by such scenes as that of a young rebel urinating into the mouth of a dead elderly woman, and that of the resurgent slaveholders impaling a slave woman on a post. Styron also emphasizes the ironies that overtake the rebellion as well. Although there is no evidence in Gray that loyal slaves actively participated in the suppression of the revolt, Styron's inference accords with well-known incidents of slave revolts in Brazil and the Caribbean, and there is evidence in Gray that some white people who survived the killings did so because their slaves hid them.

Will leaves Nat to kill Margaret, but his stabbing of her fails to kill her. Her last confrontation with Nat, in which she asks him to finish killing her to end her pain, is haunting: Margaret, who gazes up at Nat in "a grave and drowsy tenderness," seems in no way undone by terror. Even as Nat is in the act of killing her, she persists in seeing him as himself and not as a specter. The killing somehow deflates him, and when shortly after this a young girl escapes, spreading the alarm that later allows the rebellion to be suppressed, it is Nat himself, the only person who saw her slip away, who chooses, in his weariness and despair, to let her go.

Margaret's act has crucial moral consequences. During his captivity, Nat is God-abandoned and unable to pray. He insists, though, against pressure from Gray, that his sense of being abandoned by God does not mean that even in the face of the failure of his revolt and the bloody repression that follows it he regrets or has reason to regret his leading it, nor does he feel compunction for the killings he ordered. On his way to his execution, he has a final tender vision of Margaret, which releases in him the ability to pray. Why is this vision of Margaret – so like the final appearance of that other Margaret in the last scene of Goethe's *Faust* – so redemptive? Why does it move him to say that he would have "spared her that showed me Him whose presence I had not fathomed or maybe never even known"? Nat at the end does not regret hatred and killing; what he regrets is personalizing hatred, blinding himself to love, and what redeems him is the recognition of a personal love that makes its own way despite everything. This love may not change the world, and it is of course powerless against the violence of history, but it does demand to be seen for what it is.

ERNEST J. GAINES'S *THE AUTOBIOGRAPHY OF MISS JANE PITTMAN*

The Autobiography of Miss Jane Pittman (1971) is presented as the recollections of its title character over the years from the close of the Civil War to the beginning of the civil rights movement. The novel is episodic and does not turn on one central moral crisis, but it does capture something of the sweep of ninety years of African American history. Gaines was raised in Point Coupée Parish, Louisiana, and teaches at the University of Southwestern Louisiana in Lafayette; the history he captures is specifically Louisiana history, not the history of the African American experience in general, but in its respect for the particulars, it does the kind of justice to historical experiences that only fiction does.

The novel is written in dialect, but its dialect is never obtrusive or stigmatizing, partly because it is suggested sparingly. Jane Pittman is more often the narrator than the protagonist, but the energy of her personality, the tartness of her judgments, and the humanity of her insight into even unsympathetic characters holds together the disparate episodes of the book and suggests a moral point of view about the matter of history.

When the novel opens, Jane is a little girl on the Bryant plantation, and there she is known as Ticey. She is given a new name, Jane Brown, by a passing Union soldier, a Corporal Brown, who in an offhanded way promises to intervene if her master ever beats her again. The promise is immediately put to the test: when she refuses to answer to the name Ticey to her mistress, the mistress beats her senseless, then orders her husband either to sell her or to kill her. He does neither, choosing to send her into the fields to keep her out of harm's way, but she is Jane Brown to everybody after that.

It turns out to be the master himself, after the end of the war, who announces the emancipation. He offers the prospect of farming on shares to those who choose to stay, and also offers a rather pointless present of apples and potatoes to those who choose to leave. Many, knowing that since they no longer have money value to white people they risk being killed, choose to stay, but Jane, with many others, sets out for the North (once the direction is pointed out to her) to look for the mysterious Brown.

The party of wandering, newly freed slaves runs into trouble almost immediately, being attacked by a gang of patrollers and Confederate veterans, who kill many of them. Jane survives the attack, and, taking charge of an orphaned little boy named Ned, to whom she gives her own new last name, sets out again to search for Ohio and Mr. Brown. She winds up never leaving Louisiana, which, she discovers after many sadly comic episodes, is much larger than she had thought it was. On the way, she meets, but refuses the patronage of, a white woman traveling back to her plantation, who tells her that there is no Ohio, or if there is, it is not what she thinks it is. When an old man who befriends them calculates that it will take them thirty years to get to Ohio (and that they are headed in the wrong direction anyway), by which time the one among the many thousands of Mr. Browns they are looking for may be dead, she is totally undeterred. Finally, they come under the protection of a poor old white man who, despite the crabbing of his wife, will not take no for an answer:

> "Y'all look beat," the man said to me.
> His name was Job; the people told us later.
> "We was going to Ohio," I said. "My little friend here got tired."
> "He look it," Job said.

Job takes them to the plantation of a carpetbagger named Bone, who is also a Republican politician. Through his eyes, Jane sees the final years of Reconstruction. One of the curiosities she observes is the spectacle of African American Democrats, who were a rarity but who also were an important swing constituency as Republican power collapsed in the South. (Martin R. Delany, for instance, the antislavery radical who wrote *Blake, or the Huts of America,* later became a Democrat.) When the collapse happens, Bone loses his plantation to the original owner, one Colonel Dye, and Ned, taking the surname Douglass, after Frederick Douglass, sets out for Kansas, becoming one of the Exodusters.

Jane chooses not to follow Ned to Kansas, and instead informally marries Joe Pittman, a horsebreaker whose skills are so in demand that he is able to leave the Dye place for a position near the Texas–Louisiana border. Jane becomes obsessed with the idea that a particular wild horse will kill him; having failed to secure the intercession of a hoodoo, she tries to set the horse loose, but Joe is killed attempting to recapture it.

After Joe Pittman's death, Jane returns to the St. Charles River valley, where she is joined by Ned, who has a family and an education, and who, after serving in the Spanish-American War, wishes to set up a school for

African Americans. He runs into political trouble and is assassinated after an eloquent sermon on the bank of the river.

Gaines could have handled the assassination the easy way, by making the assassin either faceless or a demonic clown like Bob Ewell in *To Kill a Mockingbird*. In one of the more remarkable twists of the novel, though, he chooses to make the assassin, a down-at-heels Cajun gunslinger named Albert Cluveau, not only fully believable but also fully human. Before the assassination, he had been Jane's long-time fishing partner. He thinks of himself as her friend, and to her silent amazement, he keeps telling her, in a dispassionate and detached way, of the many people he had killed. She takes him more or less as he takes himself; she judges him, that is to say, but she is also interested by him.

When Cluveau warns her, secretly, that the white people are putting pressure on him to kill Ned, he feels ashamed and can barely face her – so ashamed that she feels a stab of pity for him. When he makes it clear that he will kill Ned if he is made to, however, she faints, and Cluveau, in possibly the novel's oddest turn, is shocked and worried about her health.

He does kill Ned, however, and Jane curses him, saying that when the chariot of hell comes rattling for him, people will hear his screaming all over the parish. Cluveau – like the Pyncheons – believes that Jane has somehow hexed him, and he torments his family with his fears so badly that his daughter comes to Jane to ask her to remove the curse. Jane had not put a curse on him to begin with, however, and she leaves him to his bad conscience, from which he finally dies raving. Jane's humanity denies her the satisfaction of revenge: "I had always thought I wanted to hear Cluveau scream. I had told myself that ever since he killed Ned. But that had happened so long ago, and now I couldn't help but feel sorry for Cluveau – 'specially Adeline there."

The story of Ned is essentially repeated at the end of the novel in the killing of Jimmy, who has been leading a demonstration against segregation. The thematic center of the novel, however, is in two stories of interracial relationships that separate these two killings. Both stories involve Tee Bob Samson, the son of the owner of the plantation where Jane becomes a cook after the death of Ned.

Tee Bob is very close to – idolizes, in fact – his mixed-race half brother Timmy Henderson, who has more of the robust and transgressive personality of his father, Robert Samson. Timmy keeps leading Tee Bob into riskier and riskier sorts of mischief, subtly challenging the racial barrier as well as testing his half brother's mettle. In the course of these misadventures, Tee Bob breaks his arm in a riding accident. Seizing the opportunity, the cruel overseer Tom Joe, who hates Timmy both for himself and for the Samson in him, beats Timmy senseless. In doing this, Tom Joe satisfies both his racially motivated hatred of Timmy and his class resentment of Timmy's father, Robert Samson. When Samson's wife calls on her husband to punish Tom Joe for beating Timmy, Samson refuses to do so, refusing to defend a black person against a white one even when the black person is his own son. Samson not only forces Timmy to leave the plantation, he also denies him the chance to say good-bye to Tee Bob, who for this reason carries a smouldering resentment of his father for the rest of the novel.

Tee Bob is a curious figure – a vulnerable, sensitive young man who can never quite internalize the racist habits of thinking that are second nature to everyone else. Gaines imagines him as a white victim of racism, and his attachment to Timmy sets him up for his tragic love of the mixed-race schoolteacher Mary Agnes LeFabre.

Gaines arranges the attachment with considerable care: Mary Agnes, who knows the rules and who is furthermore a character whose stiffness and formality is a sign that she has no particular insight into her own feelings, does not encourage him and denies to herself that she knows what he feels for her. He, in turn, is so inhibited, so guilty, and so intent on not being the predatory white man seeking sexual favors from a black woman that he remains practically walled up within his manners. His family completely misunderstands what he is about – they think he is merely "sowing his wild oats" – and they arrange a marriage for him with an eligible planter's daughter. When the day of the party at which his engagement is to be announced arrives, he flees to Mary Agnes's house and begs her to leave with him. Then confusion breaks out, which leads most people to believe that he has raped her, and Tee Bob, locking himself in the library of his house, kills himself with a letter opener as his father tries to break down the door.

At this point, Tee Bob's godfather, Jules Raynard, a man of insight and delicacy, recovers his suicide note and pieces together what has really happened. From Tee Bob's suicide note he learns that Mary Agnes had not led Tee Bob on. Fortified by this, he stands off Tee Bob's friends (and Robert Samson), who are prepared to cast the whole blame on Mary Agnes. He learns from Mary Agnes that, contrary to first appearances, Tee Bob did not rape her: he had attempted to pull her from the door, and she fell in the struggle, but he did not rape her. This last detail enables Jules to reconstruct what finally drove Tee Bob to kill himself: when Mary Agnes fell, he saw her face, and he saw in her face that for a flash of an eye she expected, even invited, him to make love to her. What drives him to suicide, this is to say, is not Mary Agnes's rejection of him but their mutual inability to escape imprisoning preconceptions about interracial relationships.

The key to the problem is that Mary Agnes both loved Tee Bob and refused to acknowledge it, even to herself. If she had acknowledged her love, paradoxically, the disaster would have been worse, since she would in that case have borne, in the public eye at least, the responsibility for Tee Bob's suicide. This is why Tee Bob, in his last act of generosity, had made it clear that she had in no way led him on. At the same time, Jules Raynard guesses, and he is clearly right, that Tee Bob knew that Mary Agnes had feelings for him of which she was at once aware and unaware.

Mary Agnes's feelings for Tee Bob Samson bear very close comparison to Margaret Whitehead's feelings for Nat Turner in *The Confessions of Nat Turner*. Both women feel a strong and legitimate love – not merely an attraction – for someone across a racial barrier. Neither acknowledges that love, even to herself, but in both cases, the object of that love knows it implicitly, and in ways that are also on their own side totally unacknowledged, longs to return it. Each relationship is brought up short by the failure of mutual acknowledgment. Each relationship, from the moment of that failure, inflames a racial stereotype that the relationship had been intended to undermine – the black and white versions, respectively, of the cliché of interracial rape. Both *The Autobiography of Miss Jane Pittman* and *The Confessions of Nat Turner* tell tragic stories of racial oppression. They also tell stories of love so thwarted that it does not even know itself as love.

8

WALKER PERCY

WALKER Percy's novels are the artistic play of a disciplined intellectual with widespread scientific and philosophical knowledge. A friend from youth of the novelist and historian Shelby Foote, Percy was raised largely in the family of his uncle, William Alexander Percy, whose *Lanterns on the Levee: Memoirs of a Planter's Son* (1941) captures the intellectual life of a genteel, romantic, public-minded, scholarly, culturally conservative white Southerner, an outspoken opponent of the Ku Klux Klan and of racist violence (but not of racial segregation) such as Faulkner had portrayed in Gavin Stevens. Percy remembered his "Uncle Will" with affection, but he was also acutely aware of the limitations of the cast of mind his uncle represented and could not bring himself to rely on the mixture of secular traditionalism and fatalism (held in check by noblesse oblige) his uncle lived by.

Percy's original interests were scientific and medical, leading him to study chemistry at the University of North Carolina and to earn his medical degree from Columbia University in 1941. He also had, during this period, a deep intellectual investment in psychoanalysis, undergoing three years of analysis while in medical school. All of this changed when, during his residency as a pathologist at Bellevue Hospital, he contracted tuberculosis from an autopsy patient, and, quarantined for an extended period, began a serious course of philosophical and religious study. The ultimate fruits of this study were his return to the South (he lived in Covington, Louisiana, for most of his life), and his conversion to Roman Catholicism.

Like Flannery O'Connor, Percy's return to the South and his religious commitments were at least sharpened by the experience of serious illness. O'Connor's convictions were fully formed before her first attack of the systemic lupus erythrematosis that finally killed her, however, her illness only intensifying the dark, mystical, and transgressive faith she already had. By contrast, Percy's religious convictions were completely changed by his illness, although before and after his conversion the cast of his intellect was reflective, invested in the scientific and philosophical issues of his time, and intellectually temperate.

In the early 1950s, before his novelistic career took hold, Percy began publishing articles about psychoanalysis and the philosophy of language in psychiatric and philosophical journals, whose professional literature he kept abreast of and to which he made formal and informal contributions frequently, collecting both his professional and popular essays on these subjects in two late volumes, *The Message in the Bottle* (1975) and *Lost in the Cosmos* (1983). Percy's essays on the philosophy of language make clear the profound difference between his Catholicism and the prophetic, visionary Catholicism of Flannery O'Connor on one hand and the traditionalist, conservative Catholicism of Caroline Gordon on the other. The chief concern in the essays is with the limitations of the view of the human being that informs twentieth-century psychology (not just Watson and Skinner, but also Freud), contemporary philosophy of science (not just Carnap and Ayer but also Wittgenstein), and contemporary linguistics (not just Bloomfield and Morris but also Chomsky). Percy's view – which comes to him most directly from Ernst Cassirer, Suzanne K. Langer, and C. S. Peirce, but which also comes to him in different ways from Kierkegaard and Aquinas – is that all of these disciplines err when they treat the human being as essentially an animal species responding to its environment.

Symbolic forms by nature involve human beings in concerns, such as moral responsibilities to other people or the purpose of life or the proper way to lead it, which cannot be correctly rendered in the formalism of adaptive responses to an environment. These concerns must be seen as inquiries after a true account of meaning and being, and these inquiries in turn cannot proceed without epistemological and moral engagement with other people. For example, the work of the behavioral psychologist cannot be described in a behaviorist way, since the behaviorist does not think of himself or herself as responding to an environment but as establishing a claim about the world that he or she hopes to demonstrate as scientifically true to a community of other scientists. Likewise, the psychoanalyst sees the patient as essentially the creature of drives and repressions and sees what the patient says only as strategic interventions in the quarrel of drives and repressions, but at the same time the psychoanalyst sees psychoanalytic theory, and his or her own acts under the guidance of that theory, not as responsive to the working out of his or her own psychodynamics but as true claims about the world, assertions about external reality that are fundamentally different in logical kind from anything the patient says.

Percy is eager to provide an account of meaning (both in its lowercase-letter and in its uppercase-letter sense), which can take into consideration the limitations of the existing scientific descriptions without at the same time devoting itself to Kantian or Hegelian or Heideggerian quests after absolute being. Whatever meaning is, he maintains, it is capable of being described rigorously without being treated in the reductive ways it is treated by logical positivism, or by the philosophy of language of the later Wittgenstein, or by semiotics. It is his search for a disciplined account of meaning, tempted neither by scientism nor by mysticism, that underlies his respect for the Schoolmen. The same concerns also underlie his social criticism – expressed in similar language in his essays and in his novels – for Percy believes that it is the inability of contemporary culture to provide a satisfactory account of meaning that leads people to seek the sense of being alive, which an account of meaning ought to provide, in ersatz extreme experiences such as the pursuit of power or of orgasm.

The consequence of a materialist view of human nature is estrangement from God and estrangement from self. All fallen people are, by definition, estranged from God, and for this reason estrangement is not, for Percy, a historical fact about modern people but a moral fact about human nature. What is different about the present is that contemporary culture – and especially those parts of contemporary culture that, like psychoanalysis or behaviorist psychology, attempt to describe what are essentially moral and metaphysical experiences in a biological or physical formalism in which moral and metaphysical concerns are unreal – estranges us from the language in which alienation from God can even be comprehended as a serious problem. The consequence of that estrangement is a life in which moral deadness alternates with a moral panic that never succeeds in vanquishing the deadness although it seeks ever more extravagant ways of doing so.

Materialist views of human nature have political consequences. Like Anthony Burgess in A Clockwork Orange, Percy is very nervous about mechanical attempts – such as through operant conditioning – to manipulate people in the service of some presumed social good, because moral aims cannot be served except through moral reflection. Percy's most naked statement about the dangers of treating human beings as objects even in the service of a moral program is in his very flawed last novel, The Thanatos Syndrome (1987), in which an attempt to reform people's behavior and raise their intelligence by dissolving heavy sodium in the water supply runs disastrously astray, raising people's ability to calculate and to remember facts (the projectors of this novel seem to be descendants of Dickens's Professor Gradgrind as much as of Swift's Laputans) but also making them incapable of hearing nuances in language and lowering sexual inhibitions to the point of producing an epidemic of child abuse. The novel was written against the background of a large number of child-abuse scandals in day-care centers, but it also recalls the 1950s political quarrels over fluorida-tion of the water supply – still a subject of paranoid concern in far-right circles. The society Percy fears from the triumph of materialist views of human nature is a society of Raybers, except that its people are not para-lyzed like Rayber (or like Alex under treatment in *A Clockwork Orange*) but instead are capable – because their awareness of their tender motivations blinds them to their own acts – of doing anything.

Throughout *The Thanatos Syndrome,* Percy repeats a phrase Flannery O'Connor had used about Hawthorne's Aylmer (another well-intentioned meddler in human nature who was not prepared for the unintended conse-quences of his acts): when tenderness is detached from the source of ten-derness, its logical outcome is terror and the gas chamber. Psychologist Robert Coles, to whom the book is dedicated, also broods upon O'Connor's phrase, and it is worth reflecting on its meaning. Tenderness detached from the source of tenderness is a moral motive detached from the divine. The reason that tenderness is a source of terror is that detachment from the divine is also detachment from circumspection about fallen human nature: in our rage to perfect ourselves we lose sight of how easily we turn the best things – like religion itself – to the worst uses. Only the divine is always in a position to rebuke us when our certainty about being in the right ren-ders us most dangerous.

Percy's South is far different from that of the preceding two generations of writers. It is not, as it was for Faulkner, a precinct set aside from the rest of America by its traditionalism and communalism, a region haunted by the giant specters of guilt and defeat and a history it must, but cannot ever, come to terms with and make amends for. It is not the Jesus-mad-dened brand saved from the secular burning that O'Connor writes of, nor the region sobered into a stern and rigorous self-consciousness by wrestling with an intractable moral problem that Warren describes. In his self-interview "Questions They Never Asked Me (So He Asked Them Himself)," Percy ridicules the idea of a South with "the storytelling tradi-tion, sense of identity, tragic dimension, community, history, and so forth," describing instead the South as he experienced it as a culture of well-fed vulgarians who do not read much or think much, but who at least leave one alone to do one's own work and "don't come up to you, press your hand and give you soulful looks."

Percy's South is religious in the way most of America is, in that better than nine of ten profess to believe in God but at the same time expect God to mind his own business except when he is busy assuring them a life of unreflective Babbitry. His world is not one of white tenant farmers, black sharecroppers, and Bourbon aristocrats, but of shopping centers, Howard Johnson motels, faux-Tudor houses set on golf courses, and "restored" plantations through which camera-toting Northerners are given guided tours by appropriately costumed faithful retainers. His characters are Southerners only in nostalgic ways; they do not feel that desperate combination of love and guilt for their region that Quentin Compson felt, but they do love to go to Mardi Gras balls and to wear rebel colonel hats at the Chevrolet dealership. It is a racist world, but one that has replaced outright cruelty (as Percy remarks in his essay "A Novel About the End of the World") with a shabby indifference that may be even more destructive; Percy's white Southerners are racists not in the dramatic old Southern way but in the chilly and impersonal way of Northerners late and soon. It is a despairing world also, but it does not despair in the characteristically Southern way: the grim stoical fatalists, characters like Will Barrett's father in *The Last Gentleman* (1966), who might have walked from Faulkner's world into Percy's, are relict survivors of an earlier era, like the gingko or the metasequoia. Their place has been taken by those who cannot despair because the everydayness of suburban life denies them the reflectiveness to name what they are feeling as despair.

Percy's first, and still best-known, novel, *The Moviegoer* (1961), won him the National Book Award, to the immense chagrin of his publisher, Alfred A. Knopf, who was pulling for another book on his list, and to the surprise of the reviewers. The protagonist of *The Moviegoer,* John Bickerson ("Binx") Bolling, is a familiar type in American literature, the comically alienated idler whose idleness is a critique of the pointlessness of everybody else's industry. The character type has a long literary history, going back at least to Irving, and characters as diverse as Hawthorne's Miles Coverdale, Melville's Ishmael, Thoreau's persona in *Walden,* Fitzgerald's Nick Carraway, and Todd Andrews of Barth's *The Floating Opera* are some of its avatars.

Like Nick Carraway, Binx Bolling is a stockbroker, and a stockbroker not from conviction but merely because it is a job he does not have to take seriously as work. Also like Nick Carraway, he holes up in an out-of-the-way place, choosing to live in the lower-middle-class neighborhood of Gentilly rather than in the Garden District of New Orleans, where the rest of his family lives. He is a keen and gleeful observer of the little turns of posture and voice that disclose the illusions of particular character types. Like Nick Carraway, he delights in satirical thumbnail descriptions of passing acquaintances, and although he is proud of the bite and perceptiveness of his own observations, he also feels a little flush of wonder at the variousness of human kinds. Here is how he describes a young woman he sees, and momentarily lusts after, on a bus:

She is a strapping girl but by no means too big, done up head to toe in cellophane, the hood pushed back to show a helmet of glossy black hair. She is magnificent with her split tooth and her Prince Val bangs split on her forehead. Gray eyes and wide black brows, a good arm and a fine swell of calf above her cellophane boot. One of those solitary Amazons one sees on Fifty-seventh Street in New York or in Nieman Marcus in Dallas. Our eyes meet. Am I mistaken or does the corner of her mouth tuck in ever so slightly and the petal of her lower lip curl out ever so richly? She is smiling – at me! My mind hits upon half a dozen schemes to circumvent the terrible moment of separation. No doubt she is a Texan. They are nearly always bad judges of men, these splendid Amazons. Most men are afraid of them and so they fall victim to the first little Mickey Rooney that comes along. In a better world I should be able to speak to her: come, darling, you can see that I love you. If you are planning to meet some little Mickey, think better of it.

Binx is oppressed by the sense of the "everydayness" of life, and, at least since the moment of his wounding during the Korean War, has been on a "search" for something different from the everyday. Binx feels the malady of the quotidian at various times: when he sits in a large car, for instance (his snappy little MG is for a while an exception), or when he hears public figures orate (in identical language) about the Uniqueness and Dignity of the Individual on the television program "This I Believe," or when he overhears earnest talk about Satisfactory Relationships and a Meaningful Vocation. Even his own wounding in Korea is more an occasion for puzzlement than of clarification for him.

Binx is a "moviegoer" because he is perpetually going to moviehouses rather than living as his family thinks he ought. The other characters, especially his morally earnest Aunt Emily, who keeps expecting him to "find himself" and put to use his putative "flair for research," see his moviegoing as a retreat from reality, but the lives they are leading are scarcely more real than Binx's, except that they do not recognize that the uneasiness they keep feeling is the despair of an unreal life, the despair that Kierkegaard describes as incapable of recognizing itself as despair. Movies do not offer Binx an alternative reality; he delights in their falseness and zestfully recounts the glaringly artificial plots of a dozen movies in the course of the book. In their transparent falsehood they offer him not a road to truth but a way of withholding himself from other things that are equally false but false in less obvious ways.

Now in the thirty-first year of my dark pilgrimage on this earth and knowing less than I ever knew before, having learned only to recognize merde when I see it, having inherited no more from my father than a good nose for merde, for every species of shit that flies – my only talent – smelling merde in every quarter, living in fact in the very century of merde, the great shithouse of scientific humanism where needs are satisfied, everyone becomes an anyone, a warm and creative person, and prospers like a dung beetle, and one hundred percent of people are humanists and ninety-eight percent believe in God, and men are dead, dead, dead; and the malaise has settled like a fall-out and what people really fear is not that the bomb will fall but that the bomb will not fall – on this my thirtieth birthday, I know nothing and there is nothing to do but fall prey to desire.

The "desire" Binx talks about here is his other refuge from everydayness, the experience of random sexual passion. Binx is not in fact a formidable seducer, although he suffers much from the lust of the eye. He eyes a succession of brisk, pretty secretaries at his brokership, and his failed amours with Sharon, his current secretary, who holds him expertly at arm's length and who is more than a match for him physically, make for some of the best comic writing in the book.

His relationship with his cousin Kate Cutrer is another matter, for Kate has a despair about life rather like Binx's, except that it is unrelieved by an ironic sensibility. Even in Binx's angriest passages – such as the one above about his nose for *merde* – his tongue is ever so slightly in his cheek, and even in his most cutting descriptions of people there is always an undercurrent of affection. Kate had been on the brink of marriage, but she and her fiancé suffered a car accident in which he was killed. Like Binx's father, who became real to himself only *in articulo mortis,* Kate learns from the accident that the emotional heightening that comes from the presence of death is a kind of substitute for the sense of reality that a life sunk in everydayness must lack.

Have you noticed that only in time of illness or disaster or death people were so kind and helpful and *solid?* Everyone pretended that our lives until that moment had been every bit as real as the moment itself and that the future must be real too, when the truth was that our reality had been purchased only by Lyell's death. In another hour or so we had all faded out again and gone our dim ways.

Her family puts her under the care of the comically named psychiatrist Merle Mink, who keeps trying to return her to the well-adjusted everydayness she is most eager to escape. She also attempts suicide, although whether she wants to die is not clear; from her point of view, what she wants to do is to stop not living.

On an impulse, Kate flees with Binx to Chicago, where he is to address a stockbroker's convention. The romantic flight does not work out, however; for one thing, Binx botches the sexual encounter between them, putters around at the convention, and takes Kate on a failed reunion with the man who had saved his life in Korea. Binx returns to New Orleans, on Ash Wednesday, with his tail between his legs, to face the rebuke of his wrathful aunt, but Kate and Binx decide to get married, and Binx decides to study medicine. Just as they do so, Binx spots an African American businessman coming down the steps from having received the Ash Wednesday ashes in church. Binx contemplates the odd mix of the worldly and the unworldly in his nature and wonders if the same mix can be found in Kate and himself. He has not exactly found a solution to the spiritual problem that he began with – Percy characters do not – but he has not despaired of it either, and the very cautious illumination he receives is at least enough to persuade him that if he does not know the meaning of experience, at least he does not know for sure that it is meaningless.

Percy's second novel, *The Last Gentleman* (1966), is a more complicated and ambitious work, and also a broader satire. Like *The Violent Bear It Away,* it is harshly critical of "scientific humanism" and ultimately turns on a baptism. Will Barrett is the scion of a distinguished Southern family, but a family in moral decline: his great grandfather (like Percy's ancestors) singlehandedly stood off the Ku Klux Klan, his grandfather wished he might have done such a thing but could not make himself sure it was the most honorable thing to do, and his father, caught between honor and irony, committed suicide (like Percy's own father). After dropping out of Princeton, Will, having completed the descent from heroism into paralyzed irony that his grandfather began, works as a "humidification engineer" at Macy's. He also suffers from amnesiac fugues. The amnesiac fugues have something to do with his "abstraction," his withdrawal from the world of meaning into the world of purely factual knowledge, the world governed not by God but by the dials and meters of the humidifiers he spends his days in the basement of Macy's peering at.

Will becomes drawn to a brother and sister and follows or chases them from New York, through the South, and west to New Mexico. The brother, Jamie Vaught, is a brilliant and sensitive young man, fascinated by mathematics and by philosophy, who is dying of leukemia. It falls to Will to equip him with what he needs to face death. Will has to evade several choices prepared for Jamie by members of his family. He must turn his back on Jamie's Babbit of a father and his paranoid anti-Semitic mother, and on the teachings of his sister-in-law Rita Vaught, who is an enthusiast for American Indian religions and has other interests that we would nowadays refer to as New Age. Jamie also is offered the self-sacrificing and even saintly Catholicism of his sister Val, who serves a parish of African Americans so poor that they have the reputation of being depraved. Jamie also must resist the counsel of his brother Sutter, once a doctor and now a coroner who treated his depressed patients by making them stay on the terminal ward until they decided that their lives were

bearable after all, and who now, disgusted by the various kinds of inauthenticity he sees around him, devotes himself to sex, to alcohol, and to
thoughts of suicide.

Percy makes the kind of investment in Jamie that James does in Milly
Theale, and for the same reasons. If it is easy to see in Will an ironist like
Percy himself, it is hard also to avoid seeing in Jamie, who is, like Percy, a
scientist and who, like Percy, is brought to a hunger for deeper things by
illness, a reflection not so much of what Percy is but of what Percy would
prefer to have been, someone who perhaps made a less ironic use of a spiritual opportunity than Percy himself did. The conflict between Rita and
Val over baptizing Jamie that ensues also ties this novel to *The Violent
Bear It Away,* and Rita's political and religious opinions – and emotional
coldness – owe something to O'Connor's Rayber as well.

After numerous misadventures, the novel concludes in Sante Fe,
where Will discovers that Jamie is dying and that Sutter intends to commit suicide shortly after Jamie dies. Jamie and Sutter both prevail on
Will to call Val with this news (for some reason they are both too proud
to make this call themselves), and Val persuades Will to make sure that
Jamie is baptized should he die before she can get there. With comic difficulty, since he is neither Catholic nor the next of kin, Will persuades
the resident priest, Father Boomer, to baptize Jamie at the brink of
death. Jamie is suffering diarrhea the whole time and keeps trying to get
out of bed, and it is far from clear that Jamie understands the questions
that Father Boomer asks him, although the ambiguous and already-
undercut responses he gives are about all that Percy ever gives in the way
of satisfactions of spiritual quests. It does suffice, however, to persuade
Sutter to postpone his suicide, and to that extent Will's act is an act of
grace after all.

Percy completed Will Barrett's story in his second-to-last novel, *The
Second Coming* (1980), but its plot seems a somewhat sentimental retelling
of *The Moviegoer.* Percy's best novel, *Love in the Ruins* (1971), by contrast,
broke new ground for him. A comic dystopian fantasy and political satire,
Love in the Ruins (subtitled *The Adventures of a Bad Catholic at a Time Near
the End of the World*) is set in a Louisiana in which the cultural conflicts of
the 1960s have continued unchecked for a few decades. There is very little
that is especially Southern about the world of the novel, for it describes a
generic commercial America in desuetude. Cars that nobody has the skill
to repair any longer litter the landscape, and shopping centers destroyed
in racial riots have been given over to the rats and the raccoons; vines
seem to be rapidly enveloping everything, even the bottles of liquor in
still-busy bars.

The Catholic church has split into three parts. The right-wing American Catholic Church is a parody of Catholicism under the moral leadership of Cardinal Spellman, which celebrates Property Rights Sunday, plays "The Star-Spangled Banner" at the elevation of the Host, and is headquartered in Cicero, Illinois, a center of Northern working-class racism in the 1960s. The Dutch Schismatics, whose priests marry and work in politics, are a parody of what will be called liberation theology. The disconsolate remnant, including the protagonist, is still loyal to Rome.

The political parties have also split along lines that reflect the cultural and political divisions of the 1960s. The Republicans have become the Knotheads, a militantly and self-righteously Christian party chiefly concerned with protecting its money interests. The Democrats have become the Lefts, or the Leftpapasane party (for "Liberty, Equality, Fraternity, The Pill, Atheism, Pot, Anti-pollution, Sex, Abortion Now, Euthanasia," its key values). The political divisions are cultural ones, too: the Knotheads watch only Disney movies and reruns of the Ice Capades; the Lefts watch only pornography but are vaguely bored by it. Each suffers characteristic malaises: the Lefts suffer from Angelism, a tendency to leave this world for a world of pure thought from which they are incapable of descending (which is why the Lefts so often suffer vertigo, morning terror, and, despite their professions of sexual liberation, impotence), and the Knotheads suffer from rage (chiefly over threats to their property or self-esteem) and large-bowel complaints. Left doctors tend to be sex therapists, and Knothead doctors – among whom are numbered Spiro Agnew – tend to be proctologists. The country is also mired in a fifteen-year war between corrupt, oligarchic South Ecuador and brutal, socialist North Ecuador, and the Knotheads and the Lefts take opposite sides in the quarrel, although it is clear that there is not much to choose between them.

Two groups in *Love in the Ruins* have opted out of the quarrel between the Lefts and the Knotheads: the Bantus, who seem to be essentially the Black Panther party of the 1960s and who live out in the Honey Island Swamp, from which they mount raids on golf courses and shopping centers; and the Choctaws, who are essentially 1960s hippies who live in chickees in the swamp and cultivate marijuana.

The protagonist – the "bad Catholic" of the subtitle – is a neurophysiologist named Dr. Thomas More, and he tells us that he is collaterally related to the saint. More works in Fedville, a federal complex consisting of a medical school, a geriatric rehabilitation center (which practices euthanasia on uncooperative patients by allowing them to stimulate the pleasure centers of their brains until they lose interest in eating), and a sex therapy clinic. More is neither Knothead nor Left and treats both parties with an irony qualified by some personal affection for their adherents. He also suffers both Angelism and large-bowel complaints, and he is simultaneously a doctor and a patient at the lunatic asylum in Fedville. (More is truly a man for all seasons.) He is involved with women from both factions: an ignorant assistant in the sex therapy clinic named Moira Schaffner and the horse-riding, cello-playing daughter of a proctologist, Lola Rhoades. He is also watched over by his brisk Georgia Presbyterian nurse, Ellen Oglethorpe, who expends a great deal of effort attempting to keep her difficult employer out of trouble.

More had earlier won fame by noticing the effects of "heavy sodium," which releases inhibitions so that people's real selves come out. Now More has invented what he calls a "quantitative-qualitative ontological lapsometer," with which he is able to diagnose people's moral and philosophical problems by taking electrical readings of various parts of their brains. The promise of the ontological lapsometer is that it enables More to heal the Cartesian split between mind and body without reducing either to the other. It also gives him an empirical grasp on moral and cultural problems without treating those problems as merely biological epiphenomena. The lapsometer, in short, is precisely the machine the author of the essays in *The Message in the Bottle* would have most loved to invent: a machine that enables one to describe the human being in a rigorous way as both a body and a spirit, as subject both to the laws of nature and to the laws of freedom.

More no sooner tests his machine than he is tempted to sign it over to the Devil, who appears as Art Immelmann, a pharmaceutical salesman who reeks simultaneously of body odor and deodorant, who cannot understand figurative language, and who has mysterious connections both with the federal government and with the Nobel committee. In a fit of pique (his director has refused him funding), More signs the rights to the lapsometer over to Immelmann, who comes into possession of a number of the devices. Immelmann alters the devices so that they not only diagnose states of mind but alter them as well, and chaos begins to break out between Knothead and Left, whose differences Immelmann sets out to systematically exacerbate.

Several political events converge at this point. For one thing, the president and vice-president (a moderate Knothead and a moderate Left) are planning to speak at a joint rally on the Fourth to try to make peace among them. Knothead extremists are preparing to march on Fedville, the Left stronghold, and Left extremists are preparing to return the favor. Furthermore, the lapsometers that Immelmann uses have begun to start chain reactions in the salt domes, which, if they do not start a nuclear explosion will at least spread mood-altering heavy sodium through the atmosphere, with chaotic effects More can predict.

The Bantus, meanwhile, have planned to seize, on that day, all of the houses on the Paradise Estates Golf Course in order to gain control of a television transmitter. To do this, they are planning to kidnap the cheerleading squad from the segregated Valley Forge Academy, but they wind up, through a mishap, with a busload of their formidable mothers instead. Bantu snipers have been harassing More for several days in order to force him out of his house on the golf course, and More's friend Victor Charles, whose mother is one of More's patients, discreetly warns him that he would be wiser to stay out of his house over the holidays. More winds up in an abandoned Howard Johnson motel with Moira, Lola, and Ellen. Attempting to evade yet another Bantu sniper, More blunders into the middle of their operation.

Percy clearly plays with fire in all of the Bantu episodes of the novel. More has several run-ins with Knothead racists in the course of the novel, in one of which he is required to save Victor Charles from their wrath. More has no use for the Bantus, whose pseudo-African terminology strikes him as not far different from the inventions of the New Agers in Fedville. (This is no accident, since Uru, the Bantu leader, is a once and future professor from the University of Michigan.) The distinction between Victor Charles's Christianity (and his lack of a generalized hatred of white people, which seems to follow from that Christianity) and the ersatz vodun of Uru (which is tied to his much harder edged view of white people both as a group and individually) is in More's view the distinction also between African American culture and politics in the South and in the North. This is one of the ways in which *Love in the Ruins* announces itself to be the work of a Southerner.

Uru would as soon have More killed, but the saintly Victor Charles rescues him, and, after a great deal of low comedy, More manages to escape his captivity to discover that Moira and Lola have gone their separate ways, left and right. More encounters Immelmann, who attempts to compel him and Ellen to depart with him, but More vanquishes Immelmann with a last-second prayer to his ancestor, St. Thomas More. In the novel's broadly satiric conclusion, More marries Ellen, the political tensions between Left and Knothead subside, and the Bantus, who turn out to be living on oil land, strike it rich and take up golf.

Like *The Magic Mountain* or, for that matter, *Invisible Man, Love in the Ruins* is a novel whose ironies cut in almost all of the available directions, and no position, left or right, escapes the author's ridicule entirely. Like Ellison in *Invisible Man,* however, the author is not satisfied with irony as a political position and resolves, even in the face of his ironic recognitions, to turn his face in an idealistic political direction. At the end of the novel, we learn that Victor Charles – whom More meets at Mass, where they pray for "our poor unhappy country" – is running for Congress. Victor asks More to be his campaign manager (he has assembled Bantus, Choctaws, Knotheads, and Lefts under his banner) and he is reviving the old Democratic party, that irrational but national coalition, the party of both Medgar Evers and L. Q. C. Lamar.

This conclusion is odd, but it is odd in a familiar way, since it is borrowed from the conclusion of *All the King's Men,* where Jack Burden, despite the harrowing political experiences he has been through, experiences that one might think would cost him his idealism, nevertheless finds himself enlisted in the campaign of Hugh Miller, the former attorney general who will be asked to clean up the corrupt state of affairs Willie Stark left behind and to fulfill the promises, and live up to the genuine greatness, that Jack insists despite everything that Willie had. Percy's conclusion in *Love in the Ruins* is a delicate homage to the political insight, and political decency, of Warren. It is also, however, the closing of a chapter of literary history, since the political ironies of *Love in the Ruins* and its pale sequel *The Thanatos Syndrome* (1987) are not for the most part specifically Southern, and although the conclusions' idealism is qualified and compromised, it is not chastened in the way Warren or C. Vann Woodward would recognize as specifically Southern either.

9

❦

REYNOLDS PRICE

R EYNOLDS Price has distinguished himself as a writer of short stories, as a playwright, as a poet, as a biblical translator, as an
essayist and critic, and as a memoirist, but it is on his novels that
his reputation hangs. Because the middle 1990s are the peak of his
career, it is hazardous to make claims about the shape of his work, but
his twenty-seven books over the last thirty-odd years have shown a powerful consistency in their aesthetic and in their governing concerns.
Whether Price will be the last of the great novelists of the Southern
Renascence tradition depends chiefly on who follows him, but his
proudly old-fashioned practice of the Southern novel, always traditional
but never derivative, places his work squarely and unapologetically in
Southern fiction's main line of descent. The inheritance of Southern fiction in some way resembles the inheritance of the burdened and entangled family histories it so often describes, but if Price is the last of a
dynasty, he never, perhaps uncharacteristically in Southern dynastic stories, thinks of himself as the troubled and ironic heir of a legacy he both
loves and fears. Walker Percy, like his own Will Barrett, and Peter
Taylor, like his own Phillip Carver, see themselves as comically or wistfully belated. Neither Price nor his own Hutchins Mayfield, however,
proud as they are of their ability to render keen and complex judgments,
think of themselves as latecomers in any way; indeed, both rather hard-
headedly insist that the traditional resources at their disposal are fully up
to the exigencies of the present day.

In his 1972 essay "Dodo, Phoenix, or Tough Old Cock," Price causti-
cally rejects the proposition that "the South" is no more, and that with the
end of "the South," the Southern Renascence has ended also. For one thing,
although the modernization and "uglification" of the South has made
Birmingham nearly "as difficult to breathe in as Gary," the South nevertheless still presents that living tension between country and city, permanent and transient, that Price, like the Agrarians before him, thinks of as
an essential condition for novels. For another thing, all of the old problems
of the South, however tired literary journalists may be of them, were as
alive in the 1950s as in the 1850s and will be a part of living memory for

years to come – and so was a fiercely insisted on history, repeated in the schoolboy warfare of many six-year-olds the region over:

> If such encounters do not, in fifteen years or so, prove to have been intense, mysterious, scarring enough to produce their own novelists (whose work will feed at the same dugs as Faulkner's or Warren's or Welty's), then claim that Southern fiction is dead. For whatever new subjects, new forms of life the new South is offering (and to me they seem either developments of the old or copies of standard American types), the old South will go on offering its life as subject for another fifty years at least – the working life of those who are children in it now. Not *offering* but *imposing,* and those apprentice novelists upon whom it imposes itself must invent new tools for seeing and controlling its intent on their lives or smother in silence – or turn to the fiction of game and puzzle which is presently cranking-up in younger regions already gone to desert.

Price usually shrugs off the inevitable comparisons with Faulkner by noting that if the apples of Cézanne resemble the apples of Chardin, they do so mostly because both artists have seen apples. Sometimes he takes a more aggressive view of his relationship with Faulkner, however. Early in *The Promise of Rest* (1995), Hutchins Mayfield, like Price a professor of English at Duke University, chides Faulkner for his fascination with mythic rather than realistic African American characters and with his inability to portray ordinary family life, mothers who do not crush their children, or responsible fathers. Despite the defensive tone here, it would be wrong to call this a list of Price's own contributions, although in Rosacoke Mustian, who appears in various novels and stories over almost thirty years, and in the protagonist of *Kate Vaiden* (1986), Price invents some of the most vital female heroines since James's Isabel Archer. Few of Price's characters are good fathers and mothers – least of all Hutch and Ann Mayfield – but issues of responsible fatherhood and motherhood are ones that many of Price's characters, unlike so many other characters in American fiction, do wrestle with as best they can; for all of their difficulties, what they are in quest of, what their novels turn on, is a kind of emotional and intellectual adulthood, a mature ability to rise to the responsibilities of love, family, and work that concerns all too few other major American authors.

The literary parent whom Price will acknowledge is Eudora Welty, from whom Price learned his central theme, the tug of war between the hunger for love and the fear of dissolution of one's separate identity, a conflict that goes on in all intimate relationships. (Price passed on the same lessons to Anne Tyler, whom he taught as a college freshman at Duke.) Focused as he is on issues he shares with Welty, however, Price rarely sounds like her. For one thing, he does not share her interest in the narrative techniques of high modernism. For another thing, although there is plenty of comedy in Price, he rarely displays the high spirits and super-abundant narrative energy one finds even in Welty's darkest books. Indeed, in the most stylistically striking of Price's books, *The Surface of Earth,* even his most elaborate prose is grave and indirect and not only sober but repressed.

Price shares with O'Connor and Percy a serious commitment to Christianity, which expresses itself in the intense fascination with the divine magnetism of Jesus he feels in Mark's Gospel, which he translated. In general, the quality of Price's faith derives as much from Milton, to whom he has devoted a seminar every year of his teaching life, as from any Southern source. He describes himself as an orthodox but not fundamentalist Christian. What this means is that Price beholds, in the literary testimony of the Gospels, the presence of a power that cannot be merely literary to him. From that presence he derives the conviction that history is meaningful, that divine care, while obscured, is never to be despaired of, and that most of the grand facts of human endurance and commitment and courage arise from humanity's sense of that care. This transforming power Price does not see abstractly, as Walker Percy does, but as something personal and intimate, as O'Connor does. There is nothing of O'Connor's prophetic rage or furious antimodernism, however, in Price's Christianity, and there is nothing of Percy's sexual fastidiousness and cultural conservatism either.

As with Percy and O'Connor, Price's faith has been shaped, although not created, by an experience of life-threatening illness. In 1984, with twelve books already behind him, Price began to suffer neurological symptoms of what was then considered a fatal case of spinal cancer; exploratory surgery revealed a pencil-thick, ten-inch-long tumor too intricately braided into his spinal cord to remove by the knife. A rigorous course of radiotherapy did nothing to destroy the tumor or to relieve the scorching pain it caused, but it damaged his spinal cord enough to paralyze him forever. Price's 1994 account of his illness and recovery, *A Whole New Life,* describes his struggle candidly and with a moral clarity earned by day-to-day small acts of courage and a stubborn religious faith.

In the midst of all this, Price taught most of his classes; wrote a book of poems, *The Laws of Ice* (1986), which appeared two days after his final surgery; wrote several plays, one of whose original productions he supervised; and wrote his best regarded novel, *Kate Vaiden,* for which he won the National Book Critics' Circle Award in 1986.

Kate Vaiden may be the novel for which Price is remembered, for in a succinct and totally unostentatious way it connects the concerns of many of his other works and provides the most mature statement of his central themes. The tension between destructive merging and preservation of identity has been of interest to Price throughout his career. *Kate Vaiden* stands at the intersection of two different kinds of treatment of this theme in Price's oeuvre: the forgiving and ultimately comic treatment in all of his Rosacoke Mustian novels, *A Long and Happy Life* (1962), *A Generous Man* (1966), and *Good Hearts* (1988); and the harsh, almost vampiric style of love described in the trilogy *A Great Circle* (1975, 1981, 1995).

No novel bears fewer traces of the difficulties under which it was composed than does *Kate Vaiden*. Despite the darkness of its plot, the novel is borne up by the energy and vitality of Kate's narration. Kate is an attractive and credible narrator because she is in no hurry to extenuate the acts she is ashamed of, but she is also interested in simple candor and avoids bathing in self-blame. Although she is given ample grounds on which to judge other characters harshly, there are few characters whose point of view so repulses her that she is incapable of seeing how the world looks to them. What is more, Kate is determined to live, as few of the major characters of the trilogy are, and she is determined to love life despite whatever it offers. She keeps her generosity intact under the kinds of challenge that might seem to make that generosity a liability, but her poise is no less genuine for being hard earned; her even, reflective, unjudgmental narration is the work of a sensibility tempered by a suffering that she will never make too much of.

Kate does not know the crucial event in her own story, why her father killed her mother and himself during Kate's eleventh year, until nearly the end of the novel. What we know about the murder is puzzling, because the relationship between Dan and Frances Vaiden seems to be close and warm, and Kate is aware of nothing untoward, although Dan, from intense need of Frances, occasionally bursts into scorching anger with her. Kate's tender and comical stories about her parents' courtship are drawn in detail from the courtship of Price's own parents. (Frances also resembles Price's mother in being raised by an elder sister and her hard-handed brother.) When Frances' brother Taswell dies in a motorcycle accident, however, Dan refuses to go to the funeral. The quarrel that follows seems at first to be one common to many couples – Dan complains that Frances is too close to her own family and alienated from his – but almost immediately they are in much deeper water than that.

> Dan said "Everybody that's ever known me known all I feel, one minute to the next. I've never been sure of you for one clear second."
> Frances waited a long time. Then she told him "That's the saddest thing I ever heard."
> Dan said "That is not the same as saying I'm wrong."

What is at issue here seems to be Dan's overpowering, indeed obliterating love of Frances. Kate had always worried that she somehow came between her parents, that their love was too stiflingly close for there to be any room for her. The tension between blistering need and the hunger for separateness seems to Kate to be the key to Dan's later act. This is why Kate can never bring herself to hate her father, why she always treats him with bewildered pity.

To attend Taswell's funeral, Kate and her mother go to Macon, North Carolina, Price's own hometown, to the house of Frances's sister Caroline Porter, who had raised Frances from childhood. The next day, Frances makes a "Penny Show" for Kate, lining a hole in the ground with funeral flowers, then protecting it with a plate of glass and concealing the glass under a thin layer of dirt. It is the last time Kate sees her, for at this point Frances's nephew Swift begs her to go to Taswell's grave with him. Swift is described as someone whose face is "so alive you couldn't watch it long," and he has that same searing need of love Dan has. Frances is all too glad to go, and Swift cruelly points out to the disappointed Kate that "I loved her years before you came." While they are gone, Dan arrives unexpectedly from Greensboro, looking for Frances, and takes off immediately for the cemetery, in quest of her, leaving Kate behind.

The next thing Kate knows, Dan has murdered Frances. Growing up in Macon with Caroline and her husband Holt, Kate gradually outgrows the stigma of her parents' death. She develops a close relationship with the Porter's African American cook, Noony, who, in a remarkable scene, explains the facts of life to her on the afternoon of Kate's first menstrual period. Kate's relative Fob Foster and his African American hired man Tot take a paternal interest in her and take her fox hunting. Fob also gives her a considerable amount of money so that she can ultimately be independent. Fob's generosity, his encouragement of Kate to make something of herself, his intense closeness to an African American employee, and even his fox hunting, are all drawn from Price's real-life distant cousin, Macon Thornton, although the erotic element in Fob's relationship to Tot is missing from Price's description of the conspicuously celibate Thornton.

In high school, Kate becomes sexually involved with an older classmate, Gaston Stegall, who is the son of Fob's tenant and who seems to be the primary romantic attachment of her life. Gaston graduates from high school in 1943 and dutifully volunteers for the marines. During basic training, however, he commits suicide, and the circumstances are strange enough that it is unclear to Kate whether what Gaston had lost faith in was the marines or his love for her.

After Gaston's death, Kate is driving home from a shopping trip with Swift when he suddenly, remarking how much she looks like her mother, drives off in a different direction, and, throwing his knowledge of her three-year affair with Gaston Stegall in her face, seems to make an incestuous proposition to her. He loses his nerve and backs down, and Kate does not reveal what Swift has done. Nevertheless, she runs away from home almost immediately afterward, seeking Caroline's other son Walter in Norfolk. (The flight to the home of a brother in Norfolk is another detail drawn from Price's family life: his mother did the same.)

Walter has been alienated from his father for years and is something of a pariah in Macon, yet at the same time everybody speaks of him as warm and sweet. What his family cannot tolerate is that Walter is gay. Walter desperately but generously loves an orphaned distant relative named Douglas Lee, whom he took from the orphanage and raised. Douglas has an ugly and possessive side: he had stabbed Walter in a fit of jealousy when Walter reestablished ties with his family. Despite her better judgment, Kate becomes sexually involved with Douglas behind Walter's back. When Kate learns that she is pregnant by Douglas, she presses Walter to break this news to Douglas, since Kate is afraid of him. It is Walter, not Douglas, who brings her Douglas's proposal of marriage.

Unable to face the strangeness of this, Kate flees the house. Douglas stabs Walter, who had accused him of taking advantage of Kate, and vanishes. Douglas reappears the next day and asks Kate to flee with him to Raleigh, but Kate jumps from the train as it passes through Macon, leaving Douglas to his own devices. She has her baby in Macon, and she names him Daniel Lee Vaiden, after both Dan Vaiden and Douglas Lee. Douglas Lee continues to ask her to marry him, and they have a botched reunion in which Kate again loses her nerve. Eventually his letters to her peter out, after it becomes clear that he is chiefly after the savings that Fob had given her.

When Kate reads in a Raleigh paper that blind piano tuner Whitfield Eller, for whom Douglas has been driving, has been stabbed, she knows that it is Douglas who has stabbed him. Eller loves Douglas, however, and covers for him, although he does let it slip to Kate, who has taken Douglas's place as his driver, that Douglas stabbed him because he would not lend him money. Ultimately, Douglas returns to Raleigh, where he kills himself in Eller's bathtub. Moved by this, Eller proposes marriage to Kate, who rejects him.

In leaving Eller, Kate turns her back on love, but she does this because she is aware how scorching a thing love is, what it did to Gaston, to Walter, and most of all to Dan and Frances Vaiden. She also turns her back on young Lee, however, seeking to cut her ties with a trammeling past and live a completely anonymous life. She succeeds at this, becoming a legal secretary in Raleigh, where forty largely uneventful years pass for her.

When, years later, her diagnosis with cervical cancer leads her to look for Lee she is understandably uncertain about what kind of reception will await her. She learns from Noony, who rebukes her with abandoning them all and with abandoning Lee, that Holt and Caroline are dead. Noony will not tell her where Lee is, other than that he served in Vietnam and is still alive. Stymied by Noony, Kate manages to track down Swift, who is under restraint in a nursing home. Swift tells her that Walter is also dead, and that Lee is a commander in the navy.

Swift also tells her why her parents died as they did: Dan had discovered some days before that Frances had had a long-standing affair with her nephew, Swift, and seeing her sitting with Swift at the cemetery was more than he could bear. Kate resists the urge to recriminate, telling Swift that Frances had a part in whatever happened as well. She even, somewhat more strangely, forgives him for his long-ago propositioning of her. Swift then tells her that he had discovered and hidden a letter to Kate that her father had left behind before he departed for Macon. In the letter, Dan had told Kate in a veiled way that something terrible is likely to happen, although the outcome is not certain. This, of course, Kate already knows, but what she did not know is the love Dan had also had for her. It comes to her that in begetting Lee she has not been merely botching together an improvised life but has done something that in some way atones for her father's act. Inspired, she discovers that although Walter has recently died, he still has a telephone listing in Norfolk. Calling this, she gets an answering machine and hears on it what she has never heard before, the voice of her grown son.

Kate Vaiden manages to capture many of Price's themes in a small compass, but it is in *The Surface of Earth* (1975) and its two sequels, *The Source of Light* (1981) and *The Promise of Rest* (1995), that Price writes his most ambitious work. The first book of the trilogy is by a long shot the strongest, perhaps because it was the fruit of over twenty years of work. It is an intense novel of anguished family life, much in the vein of *The Sound and the Fury,* covering four generations of the Mayfield and Kendal families. The flavor of the novel is clear in its first pages, when, on a spring evening in 1903, Bedford Kendal, with grim relish, tells his children Eva, Rena, and Kennerly how Thad Watson, their mother's father, immediately after his wife had died in childbirth strode into the room where she lay and shot himself over her body. They blame Thad for her death, and his own death does not prompt them to relent toward him. They also know that their mother – the newborn child of the story – blames herself, and they are not inclined to disagree. This is the first of a series of hard births in the novel, and in the very unforgiving commentary on it by the Kendal children one sees the harsh kinship of love and death, intimacy and reproach, candor and brutality that characterizes the trilogy.

That very evening, as if to point the moral, Eva elopes with her Latin teacher, the much older Forrest Mayfield. Her family disowns her, and Kennerly goes so far as to return her letters unopened. Forrest and Eva live in Bracey, Virginia, with Forrest's widowed sister Hatt Shorter, in troubled intensity. Forrest wants more of Eva than any living person can give, and to explain that love, Forrest tells of the nameless despairing hunger that drove his alcoholic and sexually predatory father. Eva comes to feel this same despairing love for her mother, from whom she had been aloof before her marriage.

At the point of death from a difficult childbirth, Eva has Forrest write her tidings to her mother. Far from being mollified by what might have been a deathbed appeal, Eva's mother, telling nobody of Eva's news, walks calmly into her kitchen and drinks lye, leaving behind a searing note to Eva: "I do not want to live in a world that will harbor and succor a heart like yours." She also rebukes Eva for "seeking the sole satisfaction of *body*" and suggests that Eva adopt the chastity she herself had adopted after Eva was born.

Eva returns home to Fontaine, North Carolina, after this, and her marriage to Forrest is over. (Eva's elopement with her teacher, and her abandonment of him, but not her mother's suicide, are drawn from the life of Price's own maternal aunt.) The infant, named Rob after Forrest's father, remains behind with Eva, although Eva is so wrapped up in her relationship with her father that she scarcely has love to spare for Rob, who is instead loved, with perhaps frightening intensity, by his aunt Rena and by Sylvie, the family cook.

Having lost Eva, Forrest recovers a different family. Aunt Veenie, his aged family servant, tells him that her great-grandson Grainger Walters is a grandson of Forrest's wastrel father, old Rob. Forrest wishes to take Grainger into his family, as a way of taking responsibility for his father's racial and sexual transgressions, but Veenie makes him promise never to tell Grainger about his ancestry. She is seeking to prevent Grainger from hoping for too much from the Mayfield family, who do not often deliver on their promises and do not in fact deliver on them fully to Grainger. She is also seeking, however, to prevent him from having to play a complicated role in the African American community, too, and here again she fails, since Forrest almost immediately, unable to keep such crucial knowledge from Grainger, breaks his oath.

Not having a Bible to swear on, Veenie makes Forrest take this oath on a photograph, which she tells him afterward is of old Rob, his father, whom Forrest has never seen. Veenie has secretly known where old Rob is for the last thirty years, and, having drawn out Forrest's promise, she rewards him by giving him his father's address. Veenie thus gives fathers to both Forrest and Grainger.

Once he has gathered in Grainger, who will be the son to him that young Rob will never be, Forrest goes to his dying father in Richmond, where he is under the care of a dutiful, much younger woman named Polly Drewry. Old Rob has broken many hearts and many ties, but under Polly's care, he seems to have come to a resting place at last. Rob has with him, as a sort of emblem of the ties he has broken but that still remain with him, his wedding ring, which Forrest sends to Eva in an unsuccessful attempt to reconcile with her. This ring plays a talismanic role in the trilogy, passing from old Robinson Mayfield, Forrest's father, to Forrest, to Grainger Walters, to young Rob's son Hutch, to Hutch's wife Ann Mayfield, back to Forrest's lover Polly Drewry, and finally, via Grainger and Hutch one last time at the end of *The Promise of Rest,* to Raven Bondurant, the last so far of the line.

Old Rob also has an uncanny collection of bark carvings of the men and women he has known. The carving that he calls "Pa" but that seems to stand for old Rob himself – it has a working penis – makes an odyssey over the trilogy that roughly parallels that made by his wedding ring, binding together the various characters but also haunting them. The tenuous coming to terms that Forrest will work with Rob, whom he does not know, Forrest will later repeat with young Rob, who does not know him. Young Rob will repeat the same act with his son Hutch, whom he, too, will have abandoned.

After Forrest's reconciliation with old Rob, the action skips forward to 1921, beginning with young Rob's high school graduation. Rob has been raised by Eva but does not really know the story of what transpired between her and Forrest. He has grown into something of a sexual predator, like his grandfather. As in his mother's life, the day of his high school graduation is a day of sexual trauma. He attempts to coerce his girlfriend Min Tharrington into sex, but she refuses him. Instead he sleeps with Flora, Sylvie's cousin, inaugurating a characteristic pattern of parallel sexual involvements across racial lines. Sylvie rebukes him, but she also wearily concedes that she knows him all too well to expect much different from him.

Rob rejects his whole Kendal connection and leaves home. Forrest is now living with Polly in Richmond and teaching in a normal school for African American children. Forrest's work and his relationship with Polly are, in unstated ways, part of the general atonement he is seeking for his family's sins, but his life in Richmond complicates his relation to his obligations, since Grainger, having quarreled with Polly over Forrest's love, has decamped to live in Bracey. Grainger has also married a woman named Gracie, who has left him. We learn later that Grainger's knowledge of his kinship to Forrest is what destroyed his marriage, partly because he treats Gracie with contempt because she is darker than he is, partly because he never longs for Gracie's love the way he longs for Forrest's.

The result of this complex arrangement is that Grainger, who was supposed to be a son to Forrest, instead becomes a father to young Rob, for when Rob comes to Hatt's house in Bracey, looking for Forrest, whom he has never seen, he finds Grainger in his place. Almost at first sight Grainger picks up and follows Rob to Goshen, Virginia, where Rob has a job building a road.

In Goshen, Rob continues his alcoholic sexual misadventures on both sides of the color line, courting Rachel Hutchins, the daughter of his landlord Raven Hutchins, but also sleeping with Della, who is the maid for the Hutchinses' ramshackle hotel and spa. Rachel is extremely vulnerable, having been hospitalized in Lynchburg for a nervous condition in which she suffered the delusion of being pregnant, but she writes Alice, the daughter of her Lynchburg doctor to whom she has a lesbian attachment, that she is prepared to take Rob as he is, come what may. (Rachel's delusion of pregnancy, and her generosity as well, Price borrowed from the life of his own aunt, Ida Drake.) Grainger is alarmed by Rob's behavior, however, and writes Forrest to ask him to intervene.

The outcome of Forrest's intervention is that Rob proposes marriage to Rachel. Forrest and Grainger bless the wedding and look to it to change the unhappy love history of their family. In a way, it works, since even Gracie returns to Grainger for the ceremony and attempts for some months to mend fences and live with him under Rob and Rachel's roof.

For much of the marriage that follows, Rob works at Forrest's school in Richmond and they are happier than most Mayfields get to be. When in July 1929 Rob returns to Fontaine for old Bedford Kendal's death, he resumes his relationship with Min Tharrington, however. Ironically, the next day, when Rachel arrives, he and Rachel beget their one child, who will be Hutchins Mayfield.

A break in the action follows, and when the story resumes, in June 1944, we find that Rachel had died in giving birth to Hutchins in 1930 and that Rob is now living in Raleigh with Min Tharrington. Forrest has been dead a matter of weeks. Rob has just lost a teaching job because of his drinking, particularly in the wake of Forrest's death. When, after years of living with him, Min demands that he either marry her or leave, he puts her off and travels to Fontaine in search of another teaching position.

There he looks to be reunited with Hutch, whom he had left in Fontaine with Grainger. He toys with the idea of establishing a new life for himself in Fontaine that would include Min as well as Hutch and Grainger.

Rob makes an uneasy peace with Sylvie, with Grainger, and with Hutch and goes off to see the school superintendent about a position. Grainger has little faith that Rob can redeem himself. Rob tells the wary Hutch that at the actual moment of Rachel's death he was outside the house, getting a drink from a bottle he kept in his car; Grainger, who was waiting in the car, told him to promise to God that if Rachel lived, he would give up drink and infidelity. (Price's own birth was very hard, and his father, up to that point a serious alcoholic, made the same promise, which by and by he was able to keep.) Hearing this story, Hutch asks Rob to keep the promise, however belatedly, that Grainger had asked of him.

Still uncertain about what he will ultimately do, Rob takes Hutch with him to Richmond to settle Forrest's affairs. Rob is overcome by the task and goes on a drinking binge. Hutch is disgusted by the sight of his naked, drunken father and abandons him, writing to Grainger, telling him that he plans to go to Goshen to see old Raven Hutchins and inviting Grainger to join him there. In Goshen, he discovers that Raven has died, but he meets his father's old lover Della, to whom Raven had given his hotel. Della, knowing that she probably would not be allowed to keep the hotel anyway, gives it to Hutch, who decides that he will manage the hotel himself, with Della and Grainger's help. Rob shows up repentant, and Della reconciles him to Hutch. Thinking through his life, Rob decides that it had, despite all his botching, a shape and a meaning given to it by all the people who had loved him, not just Min and Rena and Polly, but also Grainger and Eva and most especially Rachel. He decides to finally keep the promise Grainger had demanded of him when Rachel lay dying and to return to Richmond to try to put his life back together. Grainger decides to stay with Hutch, and old Rob's ring, which Gracie had given back to Rob and which Rob gave back to Grainger, is given by Grainger, tenderly, to Hutch.

Neither of the other two novels of the trilogy have the obsessiveness of *The Surface of Earth,* but they do work out a tentative resolution to its issues, and they are broadly parallel to each other. *The Source of Light* (1981) and *The Promise of Rest* (1995) also lack the large temporal sweep of *The Surface of Earth,* each novel dealing with events of about a year's duration, and each turning on a significant death in the family.

When *The Source of Light* opens, in the spring of 1955, Hutch has just finished teaching at a prep school in the Shenandoah Valley and is preparing for a year's study at Oxford before entering graduate school. He is engaged to Ann Gatlin, but he is very hesitant about his commitment to her. Ann has reason to doubt him, since he not only chooses to make his love for her second to his professional ambitions (like the protagonist of *Love and Work* [1968]) but is even rather cool about the idea of her coming to England to visit him. One reason for Hutch's ambivalence is that he has recently begun a sexual relationship with Strawson Stuart, one of his students. Straw's intensity and vitality make him seem more like a Mayfield than the reserved and cautious Hutch, and he is willing to take considerable risks for Hutch if Hutch will only give him loyalty. Straw also has other sexual ties, most especially to an older woman named Estelle Llewellyn, whom he makes pregnant, and who, completely against his wishes, procures an abortion for herself. Hutch is no less hesitant about his relationship with Straw than he is about his engagement with Ann.

What Hutch does not know as he sets off for England is that Rob has been diagnosed with lung cancer. Rob does tell Eva, and even Polly, but he keeps the news from Hutch, partly because he does not know how long it will take and does not want Hutch to rush back from Europe just to wait him out, but also because he does not want to put Hutch to the test. Polly gives Rob's news to Ann, but Rob himself writes to Ann to prevent her from telling Hutch. This evasion, so easy to begin but as time passes by so much more complicated to end, ultimately puts all of the characters, but especially Ann, in an increasingly false position with Hutch.

In England, Hutch has a number of sexual adventures with members of both sexes, from Marlene Pickett, an Oxford prostitute, to Lew Davis, a young Welshman returning for a quick trip to Wales to help him decide whether to continue living in Canada or to return home. With Lew, Hutch travels to Tintagel Castle and to the Scilly Isles, where Hutch conceives of a poem retelling the Tristan legend. He also has an affair with an Oxford stonemason, James Nichols. Hutch's involvement with James pulls in a different imaginative direction from his involvements with Straw and with Lew. The latter two represent a kind of spiritual intensity that is totally involved in the present and totally consuming. Love for either of those young men is tied up with a high vision of an artistic vocation, but what draws Hutch to James is James's longing for his daughter's love. James teaches Hutch the importance of family love, and in particular the importance of having children, an ethos somewhat at odds with the ethos of heroic eroticism represented by Hutch's other two male lovers. Love for James, because it is tied to a vision of love for family, is also tied to a more temperate vision of the artistic vocation; James represents, this is to say, the same sort of engagements and entanglements that Ann does. It is Hutch's love for James that makes it clear that in this novel the distinction between heroic and temperate visions of the artistic life does not map squarely onto the distinction between homosexual and heterosexual love, nor does it even map squarely onto the distinction between not having children and having them.

At Christmastime, Hutch is reunited with Ann in Rome, but their meeting is troubled, and although he gives her old Rob's ring, he is unwilling to spell out exactly what his relationship with Ann will be. They befriend a rather lost American airman, Rowlet Swanson, who is attracted to Ann and not sure how committed Hutch is to her. Only hours after Hutch finally gives Ann the ring, Rowlet wakes them to tell Hutch that he has an urgent call from America.

The call is from Grainger in Fontaine, the one person able to break through the impasse surrounding Rob's illness. Learning the truth from Grainger, Hutch also learns that Ann knew the whole story, and he is angered by what he feels is her betrayal of him. He does not ask her to return to Fontaine, but they do make love that last night, and the narrator tells us that Ann immediately knows that she is with child. Before he leaves, however, Hutch practically gives Ann to Rowlet, and very shortly after his departure, Ann and Rowlet have a brief affair.

Hutch is finally reconciled with Rob by the time of his death, and at the moment of his death, Price, rather daringly in a realistic novel, describes the event from Rob's point of view. Hutch offers to let Straw live on the Kendal property outside of town, where Grainger will also live, and Grainger persuades Hutch to bury Rob on the same property. Ann belatedly arrives, and Hutch breaks to Straw the news of his impending marriage. Even having made the decision to remain engaged to Ann, Hutch, to Grainger's amazement, decides to return to England without her.

Left alone in Richmond, and pregnant, Ann decides with reason not to place much faith in Hutch's love and begins to search for an abortionist. She asks Straw, whose girlfriend she knows had an abortion, how to get one, but Straw, who had wanted the child, is offended and not only refuses to help her but also writes an angry letter to Hutch complaining that Hutch must have told Ann something that Straw had only told Hutch in confidence. Grainger, sensible as ever, persuades Straw not to send the letter. Ann keeps Hutch as much in the dark about her plans as she had earlier kept him in the dark about his father's illness and indeed writes him an ambiguous letter that only by a hair stops short of breaking off with him entirely. Here Grainger again intervenes, uneasy about keeping Ann's secret. Hutch is angry and disoriented and ready as always to bolt, but James Nichols persuades him that if he still loves Ann, he must not let the opportunity slip. Ann and Hutch reconcile, and, with painful slowness, but also real generosity, forgive each other. Ann tells Hutch that she gave old Rob's ring to Polly at the time of her abortion, and Hutch, perhaps ominously, asks Polly to keep the ring as a token of thanks for her taking care of Ann during that hard winter. Polly refuses the gift but agrees to keep the ring for safekeeping and blesses the marriage that is to come, such as it is, between Ann and Hutch.

When *The Promise of Rest* opens, in the spring of 1993, Ann and Hutch are separated. Hutch believes that Ann is motivated by a desire for a separate life and career advancement, but Ann in fact believes that Hutch's long-ago choice of her over Straw was an act of moral cowardice.

Both are alienated from their son Wade, who lives in New York City with his African American lover, Wyatt Bondurant. Ann cannot come to terms with Wade's sexual orientation. What comes between Wade and Hutch is different, however: Wyatt has a general hatred of white people, from which even Wade is not fully exempt, and their relationship turns on a complex dynamic in which racial guilt, desire, and simple will to power over one's loved ones all play a part.

Wyatt's particular hostility to Hutch is different from his general hostility to white people, for he is angered by the fact that Hutch has never acknowledged Grainger as his family in other than compromised and partial ways. Wyatt has no use for Grainger either, whom he thinks of as submissive and cowardly. Wade knows that Wyatt has this partly wrong, but when Wyatt demands that he choose between Hutch and himself, Wade chooses Wyatt. For some years, Wade will not even answer Hutch's telephone calls, and the alienation between them persists even after Hutch learns that Wade is suffering from AIDS.

When Hutch visits Grainger to celebrate his hundred and first birthday, Grainger, who has kept in touch with Wade, rebukes Hutch for allowing Wade to suffer his illness alone. Grainger tells him that Wade's disease has progressed far enough to blind him. Straw, now married and living on the old Kendal property, takes care of Grainger, and he too has heard, from Grainger, of Wade's condition. Together, they prevail on Hutch to telephone Wade. Hutch learns from Wade that Wyatt has killed himself a few weeks before. Hutch will later learn that Wyatt did this because he discovered that he was the source of Wade's infection. Hutch prevails on Straw to set out with him for New York City to retrieve Wade. Straw insists that Hutch call Ann and tell her the whole story first, because he is aware that Hutch would like to monopolize Wade's last weeks, keeping Ann as far out of Wade's death as Eva had kept him out of Rob's.

At Wade's apartment the next day, they meet Ivory Bondurant, who has been helping take care of Wade, who tells them why Wyatt shot himself. Ivory is magnetic and plain speaking, and she approaches Hutch with tough skepticism, but she does not shut him out, and despite her harshness she treats him with some sympathy. They also meet the bright and energetic volunteer worker Jimmy Boat, who is from Georgia and who in contrast to Ivory is delighted to see them. Part of the difference between them is what Price sees as the difference between African American cultures North and South, but Boatie's brisk efficiency also assures Hutch that Wade has at least been in trained hands, and Boatie gives essential help to Hutch and Straw as they prepare Wade for the trip back to North Carolina.

Back home, Hutch arranges for Wade's care and is given help by a straight student, Hart Salter, who comforts Wade by letting him touch his naked body, and by a gay one, Maitland Moses, who obliges Wade when Wade wishes to prove to himself that he is still connected to sexual life by listening as Mait and his lover make love in the room.

When Wade and Hutch, with difficulty, come to visit Grainger, Wade asks to have his ashes scattered in a clear place in a stream that Grainger had made for him years before. For the occasion of this trip, Wade persuades Hutch to let Ann play more of a role in his care, which Hutch, painfully, agrees to, and when on the return trip Wade develops a fever that turns out to be pneumonia, Ann and Hutch gingerly work out a modus operandi. Ann never fully reconciles herself to Wade's sexual orientation, however. Hutch also keeps in touch with Ivory Bondurant, who keeps a mysterious distance from him but also treats him with the kindness one gives to people whom one wishes well but never expects to see eye to eye with.

As he did in *The Source of Light,* Price narrates the moment of death from the dying person's point of view. Wade asks after Ivory. He senses Wyatt's presence. Boatie, who has come down to be with him, senses it as well, and tells him that now everyone he loves is there. Wade replies, mysteriously, "That's a lie. Thanks anyhow." Then he wanders into death, where he is welcomed by Rob Mayfield. Hutch, immediately after the death, senses Wyatt's anguished presence in the room, and after a moment of painful hesitation, gives Wade up to him.

What Wade's last words mean is made clear only much later. Hutch is in something of a quandary about where Wade's ashes are to be scattered, because Wade had at different times asked to be scattered on Grainger's stream or to be with Wyatt's remains, up North. Grainger, in his one explicit claim of kin in the trilogy, delicately asks that Wade's ashes be scattered on the stream. Ivory Bondurant writes, saying that she will accept whatever Hutch decides to do. Knowing that Wade has held something back, Ivory sends Hutch a letter that Wade had given to her to send to his parents after his death. In the letter, Wade explains that he and Ivory had been lovers just after her divorce and before he met her brother Wyatt, and that the chances are that he is the father of Ivory's child. Ivory and her child, this is to say, are the loved ones who were missing from the deathbed scene.

Ivory does not know how Hutch will take this news, and she is not certain he will welcome her to Wade's funeral. Hutch is in fact overjoyed about it, although he is also cautious not to ask Ivory for a closer relationship with the boy than she is willing to allow. Ivory also makes it clear that the boy's paternity is not certain, but the fact that he is named Raven, which is both Hutch's and Wade's actual first name, gives some sign of what her best judgment is. Young Raven does come down for the funeral with Ivory, and although the tentatively reconciled Mayfields want Ivory to know that the choice is hers, they make it clear that they wish to accept both Raven and her as family. It is Raven and Hutch who distribute Wade's ashes on the stream. At the last minute, Grainger gives Hutch old Rob's wedding ring, which has circulated back to him, and tells him to do with it only what he thinks is right. What Hutch does is to give the ring to Raven. It is a beautiful gesture of reconciliation across racial lines and it does not promise more than it can give: Hutch knows very well he may never see Raven again. It moves Hutch to mentally compose a part of a poem that testifies that the consolation of this moment may not be everything, but it is at least something:

> This child knows the last riddle and answer.
> They wait far back in these mineshaft eyes
> Till he concedes your right to know them,
> Which may be never.

PETER TAYLOR

PETER Taylor has had two separate careers, one, stretching from the mid-1950s to the mid-1980s, as a writer of short stories, the other, commencing in 1986 with *A Summons to Memphis,* as a novelist. The métier of his stories is upper-middle-class life in middle Tennessee. He has a special gift, in such stories as "A Wife of Nashville" and "Cookie," for portraying the complicated relationships between upper-middle-class white families and their African American cooks. He also is a master of tales of delicate grotesquerie and sexual uneasiness in such stories as "A Spinster's Tale," and "Venus, Cupid, Folly, and Time," tales that owe some of their strangeness of atmosphere to Carson McCullers but that are also presented with a restraint and understatement unlike that of any other writer of the Southern tradition. Finally, in such stories as "Heads of Houses," and "In the Miro District," Taylor captures generational conflicts that are also cultural conflicts, and, since the children are usually less self-consciously Southern than the adults, regional conflicts as well.

In *A Summons to Memphis,* Taylor also treats a generational quarrel that is also a regional one, in that the entanglement of the protagonist's family history is also an entanglement with his native region, and fleeing the former is a way of fleeing the latter. The novel provides a metaphorical way of describing the literary predicament of a belated generation of Southern novelists, a generation that must sever its consuming ties with the Renascence generation but must also risk its vitality as novelists if it succeeds in breaking the tie.

Phillip Carver, the narrator, is an editor in late middle age, living in New York City with Holly Kaplan, his much younger live-in lover. He thinks of himself as having more or less settled all of the issues of his complicated childhood in Tennessee and of having made his peace with his family (from which he fled in the middle of the night some decades before). In fact, though, there is something stale, even dead, about his life, that he not only cannot articulate but is not even fully aware of; only the indirection and extreme restraint of his language gives any sign that there is something missing. He thinks of what is really detachment from life as if it were understanding and good sense and the good taste never to throw a scene. He describes New York as the place where he has made his life, but for all of his professed satisfaction with that life and his pointed contrasts with the unhappy life he left behind in Tennessee, it seems clear that he is somehow inwardly thwarted, that he is more camping out in New York than living as a New Yorker.

When he receives two urgent messages to return to Memphis from his spinster sisters Jo and Betsy, he is in a vulnerable state, because Holly Kaplan has left him for reasons he will not go into, and therefore he pays more attention to his sisters' demands than he might otherwise have done. His sisters have long been something of an embarrassment to him. They are successful businesswomen – they run a real estate business – and they ought to have become settled into a respectable middle age. They dress in the flamboyant and revealing clothing of women thirty years younger than they are, however, and they continually frequent the nightclubs of the Memphis area with men who are many years their junior. (Phillip spends disconcerting amounts of detail describing their overweight legs and over-ripe bosoms.) Phillip tries to treat his sisters' exploits with humor, but he is clearly mortified, all the more so because they describe their lives to him as if they were exciting and wicked, as if the places they were frequenting were 1920s speakeasies rather than the kind of lounge where drinks are served with a little paper umbrella.

Their very elderly father has recently been seen frequenting the same places in the company of very much younger women. The sisters have been describing the old man's misadventures in much apparently lighthearted detail, but in fact he is rather fuddled and confused (on one memorable night, after "attempting to dance," he gropes and blunders his way into the ladies' room by mistake), and the sisters seem to be taking a perverse pleasure in watching their father make a fool of himself. Phillip ought to have been alarmed by all this, but he either does not or will not see what is happening.

What finally alarms the sisters is their father's sudden intention to marry one Clara Stockwell. The issue at first appears to be a threat to their inheritance, but in fact there are deep but glossed-over conflicts among all of the members of the family. Many years earlier, in 1931, George Carver, the father, had been financially ruined in Nashville by a close friend, the financier Lewis Shackleford. (Shackleford is probably modeled on the actual Rogers Clarke Caldwell, who was the model also for Bogan Murdock in Warren's *At Heaven's Gate*.) Reeling from this, the father had decided to pull up stakes and move his family to Memphis. The family feels acutely the difference between the genteel, horsey, restrained culture of Nashville and the vulgar and grubby river culture of Memphis. As the father keeps up the pretenses of Nashville propriety, the mother gradually sinks into thirty years of invalidism. The move to Memphis – as well as the father's suspicion and rigidity – breaks up the romance between Betsy and her fiancé. The father's possessiveness over his daughters also chases away Jo's one romantic attachment, and the father later, during the run-up to World War II, travels to Chattanooga to break up the one relationship, with a young woman named Clara Price, that Phillip ever intended to bring to marriage.

All of the children, but especially the daughters, are in fact burning with resentment of their father, which is why they aided Phillip in his initial escape to New York and why (to quote Phillip's at once detached and brutal language)

They were so useful to my brother George and me whenever we wished to achieve some degree of independence for ourselves. George was in Father's law firm for a while but since he was unhappy there he pretended he had been drafted into the Army, though actually he volunteered and went off to war. My sisters helped him deceive Father in the matter and made it possible for him to go off to Europe and get himself killed, which I assume had become his own chief purpose in life.

When Phillip arrives in Memphis, he learns from his father not only that is he too late to prevent the wedding but that it is going to take place that very day. The father is overjoyed at Phillip's arrival and in many ways makes it impossible for Phillip to perform his errand. Influenced by his father's high spirits, Phillip decides that his father needs rescuing not from Clara Stockwell but from Jo and Betsy. He arrives too late even for this, however, because Clara does not arrive for the wedding, having been scared off by the sisters.

Having retreated back to New York, where he is reconciled with Holly, Phillip also seeks to reconcile himself with his father. He is summoned again by his sisters, to accompany his father on a visit to Owl Mountain, near Chattanooga. There, apparently with a mind to upset the old man, the sisters have engineered an "accidental" fleeting encounter between Phillip and his Chattanooga sweetheart Clara Price. Phillip is just absorbing this information when his father and Lewis Shackleford meet for the first time since 1931, and instantly, despite everything, become fast friends again.

Six weeks later, Phillip is summoned to Memphis a third time, this time to prevent his father from going to Nashville for a long visit with Lewis Shackleford. He is uncertain about whether he will thwart the old man or rescue his father from his sisters (who have moved back into the family home, the more easily to keep their father under control). He blocks his father's car in the driveway, but before he decides what he will finally do, a call comes in from Nashville, which the sisters say (lying, apparently) is the announcement of Shackleford's death. Phillip returns again to New York, and shortly afterward, his father dies. He tells us how he has come to serenely accept his life there and to appreciate the relief it offers him from life in Memphis, but the bitter quotation from Hardy in his last paragraph gives the lie to this:

> Those places mean nothing to us nowadays. And surely there is nothing in the world that can interfere with the peace and quiet of life in our tenth-floor apartment. I have the fantasy that when we get too old to continue in the magazine and book trade the two of us, white-haired and with trembly hands, will go on puttering amongst our papers and books until when the dusk of some winter day fades into darkness we'll fail to put on the lights in these rooms of ours, and when the sun shines in next morning there will be simply no trace of us. We shall not be dead, I fantasize. For who can imagine he will ever die? But we won't for a long time have been 'alive enough to have the strength to die.' Our serenity will merely have been translated into a serenity in another realm of being. How else, I ask myself, can one think of the end of two such serenely free spirits as Holly Kaplan and I?

Phillip Carver in New York, free of history, free of guilt, free of family, free of having a story, free even of life: a better emblem of what it is, to a Southern writer at least, to have worked free of a vexing Southern burden cannot be imagined.

POSTMODERN FICTIONS, 1960–1990

Wendy Steiner

RETHINKING POSTMODERNISM

In *The Anatomy Lesson,* Philip Roth's Zuckerman – who has authored a book that sounds suspiciously like *Portnoy's Complaint* – receives a letter from the editors of his old college newspaper. They "wanted to interview him about the future of his kind of fiction in the post-modernist era of John Barth and Thomas Pynchon." Because Zuckerman is in the hospital suffering undiagnosed pain, the editors have sent a list of written questions: "*1. Why do you continue to write? 2. What purpose does your work serve? 3. Do you feel yourself part of a rearguard action in the service of a declining tradition?*"

These are not questions of the sort to cheer an ailing writer, but they do summarize the elitist view of post-1960s fiction. From this standpoint, Zuckerman's humor and ethnicity and his lack of esoteric technique and political commitment demote his work to a "rearguard action, in the service of a declining tradition." Roth locates this attitude in the self-important undergraduate editors of *The Anatomy Lesson* (1983), but it is still pervasive in intellectual circles. The metaphor of the rearguard (and its correlate, the avant-garde) and the assignment of the "postmodernist era" to John Barth and Thomas Pynchon are symptomatic of a conception of literary history that itself should be labeled "a rearguard action in the service of a declining tradition," for the student editors are speaking the language of modernism, the aesthetic ideology of the early twentieth century.

In the authoritative narrative that modernism told about itself, there was a "high road" of art, a stylistically innovative line in which poetry was the predominant genre and Hemingway and Faulkner the experimentalist giants in the sphere of prose. Fiction by leftists, women, minorities, or traditionalists was interesting for documentary reasons, but generally outside the march of technical discovery. This view produced the label "High Modernism" for the masterful, innovative works of the early twentieth century and equated artistic history with a progressive development in which the works participating were the great works.

The notion of history as an experimental line is obviously a vast simplification of the cacophony of competing voices at work in the first half of the century. As such, it has considerable elegance and intellectual convenience for those attempting to understand modernism as a literary period. Applied to contemporary literature, the approach has produced a parallel ambiguity in the term *postmodernism*: it means both the stylistically innovative writing from the 1960s to the 1990s, such as that by Pynchon or Barth, and the literature of the period as a whole. The move to equate experimental postmodernism with the overall post-1960 period is equivalent to that equating High Modernism with modernism in general: the technically self-conscious line becomes a synecdoche for the whole period.

The reduction of aesthetic history to the history of style is a particularly modernist legacy. As Malcolm Bradbury noted, "the historically modern has its logical outcome precisely in style." We can see this tendency in all the arts; indeed, the application of the avant-garde metaphor in the visual arts set the pattern for such thinking elsewhere. In painting, this line runs from Cézanne to Cubism, Futurism, and the abstraction of Kandinsky, Malevich, and Mondrian; the American Abstract Expressionism of the 1940s and 1950s; and the Minimal and Conceptual Art of the 1960s and 1970s. Each of these movements, so the story goes, eliminated nonessential pictorial elements – perspective and other realist conventions, the temporal and spatial unity of the represented world, the represented world as such, and finally even paint and canvas – in order to produce "pure painting." Such painting would be universal: not tied to any particular culture or time, ahistorical, impersonal. Its focus was the formal essence of painting.

In America, a strong ideology grew up to explain and support this view of art – the critical formalism of Clement Greenberg and his students. "Greenberg argued that the one true course in modern painting was the course of 'self-definition,' through which every element that was not essential to the art of painting must be ruthlessly eliminated. No 'painterly' striving for emotional or atmospheric effects, no recognizable images, and above all no illusionistic spatial depth that might divert attention from the essential *flatness* of the canvas support, the 'integrity of the picture plane.'" Greenberg's influence on critics and artists was profound, and the view that twentieth-century art was the story of the progressive elimination of impurities and the exploration of technical means has been widely accepted. In America in particular, it has made the Dadaist, Surrealist, and Realist movements of the early century virtually invisible.

The state of affairs in architecture is parallel. The twentieth century was dominated by a functionalist aesthetic in which "form follows function" (Louis Sullivan), "less is more" (Mies van der Rohe), and the aim is "to find beauty in form" (Adolf Loos). By eliminating ornamentation, this architecture attempted to simplify the functional diversity of buildings, so that structure and formal means would be the single focus.

When Le Corbusier called the modern home "a machine for living," moreover, he was making explicit the fundamental metaphor behind this line of architectural thought – the mechanical world of the factory. However, this cold functionalism had its ethical thrust. By avoiding the "waste" of ornament and by setting an example of functional and aesthetic integration, modernist architecture was meant to inaugurate a new social age. The inhabitants of these perfect buildings were to be reorganized by their dwellings, made productive members of society, remade in the image of good design.

Modern architecture was programmatically antihistorical, obscuring its references to earlier styles. Like modernist painting, it aimed at universal values, transpersonal significance, and eternal validity: the single best solution to a particular problem. This development, from Sullivan and Loos to Bauhaus and the International Style, generally characterized architecture from the early years of the century until about 1970, during which time it is often hard to distinguish office buildings from universities, convents, or apartment houses. The cleanness of design; the stress on form; and the use of slick glass, steel, polished stone, and concrete produced the uniformity of the American city as we now know it.

Umberto Eco, scholar and author of such best-selling novels as *The Name of the Rose* (1980), has summarized the progress of the experimental line in the various arts:

The avant-garde destroys, defaces the past. . . . Then (it) goes further, destroys the figure, cancels it, arrives at the abstract, the informal, the white canvas, the slashed canvas, the charred canvas. In architecture and the visual arts, it will be the curtain wall, the building as stele, pure parallelepiped, minimal art; in literature, the destruction of the flow of discourse, the Burroughs-like collage, silence, the white page; in music, the passage from atonality to noise to absolute silence.

By the 1960s and early 1970s, however, the "high" universalist line of aesthetic development appeared to be in desperate straits. The experimentalism of Hemingway and Faulkner had hardened into a much-imitated orthodoxy. Continued attempts at innovation among prose writers were so far removed from public approbation as to appear a lunatic fringe of the counterculture. "Serious" novelists were frustrated, unwilling to keep reproducing earlier formulas and yet unable to see where the experimental line now led. Leslie Fiedler, Philip Roth, Susan Sontag, and John Barth all proclaimed at this time that the novel was dead. In Barth's influential essay, "The Literature of Exhaustion," we find the central term for the dilemma – generic exhaustion, "the used-upness of certain forms or exhaustion of certain possibilities." The only thing left for a novelist to do, according to this line of thought, was to parody the act of novel writing.

Thus, Barth begins his "Life-Story" as follows: "What a dreary way to begin a story he said to himself. . . . Another story about a writer writing a story! Another regressus in infinitum! Who doesn't prefer art that at least overtly imitates something other than its own processes?"

Pynchon's short story "Entropy" turns this aesthetic angst into a general anxiety about the future of the world, whose energy is slowly but surely winding down. Pynchon pictures a jazz quartet improvising without a piano – that is, without root chords. "What one does in such a case is, one *thinks* the roots," but then, one might as well think everything, and that is just what this quartet – without instruments or sound – proceeds to do. Like the Conceptual Art of the time, the purest formal solution is silence, thought, the formlessness of pure form. This is also the most boring solution, and the topic of ennui was rampant in 1960s art and criticism.

From the hindsight of the mid-1970s, the experimental writer and critic Raymond Federman summed up the ideology of exhaustion:

> Writing about fiction today, one could begin with the usual clichés – that the novel is dead; that fiction is no longer possible because real fiction happens, every-day, in the streets of our cities, in the spectacular hijacking of planes, on the Moon, in Vietnam, in China (when Nixon stands on the Great Wall of China), and of course on television (during the news broadcasts); that fiction has become use-less and irrelevant because life has become much more interesting, much more incredible, much more dramatic than what the moribund novel can possibly offer. And one could go on saying that fiction is now impossible (as so many theoreti-cians and practitioners of fiction have demonstrated) because all the possibilities of fiction have been used up, exhausted, abused, and therefore, all that is left, to the one who still insists on writing fiction, is to repeat (page after page, *ad nauseam*) that there is nothing to write about, nothing with which to write, and thus sim-ply write that there is nothing to write.

In the visual arts, people also felt that experimentalism was moribund and therefore that art was dead. Donald Judd, a sculptor in fluorescent light, was quoted in 1974 as saying, "It looks like painting is finished." Dan Flavin, another Minimalist, stated that "The term 'avant-garde' ought to be restored to the French Army where its manic sense of futility propi-tiously belongs. It does not apply to any American art that I know about."

The "death of architecture" occurred in less metaphoric terms, accord-ing to Charles A. Jencks:

> Modern Architecture died in St. Louis, Missouri on July 15, 1972 at 3:32 p.m. (or thereabouts) when the infamous Pruitt-Igoe scheme (a low-income housing pro-ject), or rather several of its slab blocks, were given the final *coup de grace* by dyna-mite. . . . Its Purist style, its clean, salubrious hospital metaphor, was meant to instill, by good example, corresponding virtues in the inhabitants. Good form was

to lead to good content, or at least good conduct; the intelligent planning of abstract space was to promote healthy behavior. . . . Alas, such simplistic ideas, taken over from philosophic doctrines of Rationalism, Behaviorism, and Pragmatism, proved as irrational as the philosophies themselves.

Gloria Naylor's powerful fiction, *The Women of Brewster Place* (1980), shows the apocalyptic dismemberment of a less well intentioned housing development at the hands of the women who inhabit it.

The thinking behind the notion of exhaustion is peculiarly mechanistic, reducing art to a single function and aim, and thus to an extremely narrow range of possibilities. It assumes that art progresses along only one line and that, as Charles Jencks put it, "every new form limits the succeeding innovations in the same series." Anything not conforming to the central aim of the series is outside it – that is, outside the main line of artistic development. As we have seen, that leaves out a great deal: socially committed fiction, surrealist painting, Art Deco architecture, to mention only some previously marginalized movements.

In literature, the purist argument leads to a main line of aesthetic activity that is utterly male and white. Critics who equate postmodernism with technical experiment – for example, Jerome Klinkowitz – unselfconsciously produce a strikingly gender- and race-restricted canon: John Barth, John Hawkes, Gilbert Sorrentino, Thomas Pynchon, William Gass, Donald Barthelme, Jerzy Kosinski, Ronald Sukenick, Raymond Federman, Richard Coover, and Kurt Vonnegut. Even Joseph Heller and Philip Roth are included more often than are female or minority writers. As late as 1980, John Barth, in dividing fiction into the premodern, the modern, and the postmodern (with an arrow marking the avant-garde and therefore the artistically privileged works at any given moment), labels *premodern* the works of "most of our contemporary American women writers of fiction, whose main literary concern, for better or worse, remains the eloquent issuance of . . . secular news reports."

The usual explanation offered for the absence of women and minorities from the high-art line is that they started later and therefore are still going through the realist phase that many mainstream writers traversed in the nineteenth century. This might be termed the "ontology recapitulates philogeny" argument, where an art is seen as an obligatory sequence of periods in which particular problems are formulated, explored, and exhausted. After each period, a new problem logically unfolds. In the case of the novel, first, it had to perfect its adequacy to historical and psychological reality; then, it had to experiment with its technical means; and now, it contemplates the end of stylistic innovation by ironically commenting on the act of novel writing. If women and minorities keep developing at their current rate, they, too, can expect to reach this advanced state in a few generations!

The arbitrariness of this history and the violence it does to the complexity of artistic activity at any given time are obvious, as art is equated with only a tiny portion of what is being produced, read, and enjoyed. Yet we have all been schooled in the "high" approach and abandon it only with great difficulty. It is a tremendous convenience. The world of art and the university have cooperated in establishing this hierarchy: the best art is that which questions its formal constraints; the best audience is that capable of appreciating such art. Perhaps the single most revolutionary development in literature from 1970 to the present has been the questioning of these assumptions, with the result that the literary canon and audience have been broadened, the categories within "high art" multiplied, and the meaning of artistic history reassessed.

To see how this shift came about, we must consider the ideas contributing to the notion of exhaustion, for they spawned both the experimental line of postmodernism and the broad heterogeneity of the postmodern period as a whole. As I have already stated, in all the arts, modernism produced a preoccupation with formal means and a corresponding devaluation of representation, culminating in the logical absurdity of aesthetic silence and invisibility. This "crisis in representation," as Fredric Jameson has called it, is directly related to the 1960s' fascination with the medium of communication in general – language.

The 1960s was a great period of "linguistic imperialism," when models developed for the study of language were applied to virtually every subject in the humanities and social sciences. It was not only that everything could be described in terms applicable as well to language; artists and theorists were claiming that there was no reality independent of language. Ihab Hassan, a critic and early theorist of postmodernism, described this position: "For the Romantics, the voice of the poet was the voice of *all*; for us it is the voice of *no one*. . . . We blend, in short, into the postmodernist attitude, which holds that the author is but a 'moment of convergence of different voices which flow into a text,' a 'somewhat fortuitous crystallization of language.'" Subjectivity and objectivity dissolve; everything is a mere tissue of words; writing is no longer a mirror of reality. As William Gass stated, "There are no descriptions in fiction, there are only constructions." All of writing, speech, and social life are merely a function of language.

Jacques Ehrmann, a Yale scholar who had an important influence both inside the academy and among writers, explained this word-centered world in his famous essay, "The Death of Literature":

One can no longer say that the poet is at the *origin* of his language, since it is language which creates the poet and not the reverse. Nor can one say henceforth that poetry depends upon the *intention* of the poet. . . . Poetry (or fiction) is therefore not to be found *within* texts of a given (conventional) type but, virtual and diffuse, within language itself, that is, in the relationship between writer and writing, reading and reader, and, even more generally, in the play of all communication.

Of course, Ehrmann's essay was considered an extreme view when it appeared, but it combined a number of ideas that were givens of the "exhaustion" position. Meaning is a transaction between the text and the author or reader; it is not *in* the text, waiting to be extracted by the clever analyzer, but is a product of the act of interpretation. As a result, the meaning of a work changes constantly. Since all meaning works this way, literature is just one case of communication, and indeed, Ehrmann goes on, it is hard to say what separates the act of reading a sonnet from the act of reading a telephone directory. Everything we encounter is a text, and our interactions with it constantly produce meaning. Finally, since language creates the poet and not the reverse, "the criterion of 'originality' of artistic production is both modified and contested. To write would be first of all to quote." In one form or another, these notions lie at the heart of virtually all contemporary literature. They also form the basis of the French theorizing about language and art that displaced the entrenched New Critical formalism of the 1940s, 1950s, and 1960s in America. Just as the literature of exhaustion was the culmination of the preceding modernist purism, in the realm of criticism, linguistically centered structuralism and poststructuralism outdid New Critical formalism at its own game.

The disappearance of the boundary between literature and nonliterature was matched in the 1960s by a whole series of category confusions. Tom Wolfe, who earned a doctorate in American studies at Yale, popularized the claim that journalism and literature might be stylistically indistinguishable. As he wrote in his essay, "The New Journalism," "it was possible in non-fiction, in journalism, to use any literary device, from the traditional dialogisms of the essay to stream of consciousness, and to use many different kinds simultaneously, or within a relatively short space . . . to excite the reader both intellectually and emotionally." Since novelists were boring the reader to death writing about the exhaustion of writing, journalists now "would wipe out the novel as literature's main event."

It was not only journalists who exploited this fact–fiction ambiguity. Norman Mailer gave his *Armies of the Night* (1968) the subtitle *History as a Novel, the Novel as History,* and Truman Capote's *In Cold Blood* (1965), though claimed by the New Journalism, was as much a novelistic feat. By the time of Mailer's *The Executioner's Song* (1979), the confusion between fiction and journalism had become one of the most productive devices in the repertoire of the postmodern novel.

It was not only new journalists and fiction writers who were proclaiming the indistinguishability of fact and fiction. In the early 1970s, the historian Hayden White advanced an elegant and influential argument urging that we "consider historical narratives as what they most manifestly are – verbal fictions, the contents of which are as much invented as found and the forms of which have more in common with their counterparts in literature than they have with those in the sciences." If the novel is as "true" as any kind of narrative, historical narratives are as much imaginative products as any novel.

If this point can be maintained for public histories, why should it not apply as well to personal ones? The boundary between autobiography and the novel virtually disappeared in the postmodern period, with countless first-person narrators, or Mailer's third-person presentations of Mailer. Always the theorist of such dilemmas, John Barth wrote in "Life-Story": "He being by vocation an author of novels and stories it was perhaps inevitable that one afternoon the possibility would occur to the writer of these lines that his own life might be a fiction, in which he was the leading or an accessory character."

The most important "proof" of the merging of fact and fiction, however, was the Holocaust; indeed, "post-Holocaust" literature is one of the names sometimes given to postmodernism. In Nazi Germany, the unimaginable became real. The job of assimilating this nightmare had barely begun in 1960s fiction, and even with D. M. Thomas's *The White Hotel* (1981), William Styron's *Sophie's Choice* (1979), and other harrowing novels of recent years, the Holocaust is still an "unspeakable" reality. It is the message Zuckerman's nice Jewish mother leaves him at her death, a word that masks a scream. The scholar George Steiner wrote in "The Retreat from the Word" of the shrinking of the sphere of the verbal after the war, the unspeakable thought of Auschwitz, and hence the expansion of the domain of silence. What had seemed a specifically European horror, however, suddenly came home with Vietnam. As the reportage of that war increased, Americans felt themselves implicated in events of equal horror to the Holocaust, surpassing the ugliness of any fictional imaginings.

The philosophical outlook underlying category confusions and the retreat into silence is existentialism, and its literary expression is the absurd. John Barth's paraphrase of his character Todd Andrews's position in *The Floating Opera* (1956) summarizes the point of view with typical Barthian succinctness: "1. There is no ultimate justification for any action. 2. Continuing to live is a variety of action. 3. Therefore etc." This syllogism underlies much postmodern art, in high and popular forms alike (for instance, the films of Woody Allen). One of the major tasks of postmodernism has been writing anyway, finding an answer to the existentialist analysis beyond suicide or willed forgetting, filling in Todd Andrews's "etc." We shall see some of the ways of coping that developed, but these are still temporizing moves. As late as 1986, Ihab Hassan offered this explanation of postmodernism: "We have killed our gods – in spite or lucidity, I hardly know – yet we remain ourselves creatures of will, desire, hope, belief. And now we have nothing – nothing that is not partial, provisional, self-created – upon which to found our discourse."

You will have noted by now how frequently fiction is quoted here for explanations of theoretical issues, and theory, for expressions of aesthetic attitudes. The confusion of criticism and art is perhaps the most striking of the "category mistakes" informing postmodernism. There has probably never before been so marked a connection between writers and the academy or so fluid a boundary between literature and its description. When literature is left with only the task of exploring its limits, the functions of artist and critic merge.

The novel is a particularly appropriate context for this merger. As Charles Newman wrote, the novel "is, in fact, the oldest of abstract forms, the first mixed-media. Its thrust from the beginning has been aleatory – syncretic, not synthetic – held together by the tension of its own formal contradictions, testimony both to the interpenetrability of experience and the necessity for recombinant expression." Contemporary theory tends to view the novel this way, as the most anarchic of genres, effortlessly incorporating any kind of discourse – letters, ads, poetry, historical documents, and so forth – into its complex structure. The organic and formalist criticism prevalent in this century before 1970 was singularly unable to deal with the novel, concentrating instead on the structural integrity of poetry. With the revival of M. M. Bachtin's work in the 1970s and 1980s, critics gained the vocabulary and historical perspective to theorize the novel – now seen as growing out of Menippean satire and other "dialogic" forms, where disparate voices interact to expose conflicts in ideas and experience. This notion of the heterogeneous and conflictual structure of the novel is perfectly in keeping with postmodernist needs, and it is not surprising that the period should have both developed a new theory of the novel and elevated the genre to the most important vehicle of literary expression.

Faced with these complexities—an art of diminished possibilities, the confusion of history, journalism, and criticism with the self-enclosed fictive world, an all-engulfing view of language, and unappeasable existential dread—art reacted, if you will forgive this oversimplification, in one of two ways. Either it continued under the assumptions familiar in modernism, claiming that it was postmodern by virtue of its extreme reduction of representation and its exploitation of formal means, or it practiced a new kind of inclusion, a humor and amplitude taking it far from modernism. When John Hawkes said that he "began to write fiction on the assumption that the true enemies of the novel were plot, character, setting, and theme," he was indicating his early involvement in modernist reductionism. Raymond Federman's justification for disrupting authorial viewpoint is even further entrenched in the past. "[N]o longer being manipulated by an authorial point of view, the reader will be the one who extracts, invents, creates a meaning and an order for the people in the fiction. . . . The writer . . . will stand on equal footing with the reader in their efforts to *make sense* out of the language common to both of them, *to give sense* to the fiction of life. In other words, as it has been said of poetry, fiction, also, will not only mean, but it will be!" Federman is quoted here at some length to show the lack of irony in his call for a "thing-novel," parallel to Archibald MacLeish's "A poem should not mean/But be" urged *five decades* earlier. Surely we may admit that the experimental line of American fiction has become retrograde. It is the move toward semantic and stylistic breadth, diversity, and humor in Pynchon, Roth, Morrison, Robinson, and Proulx that marks the vital (though specifically not progressive) arm of postmodern writing.

These two responses to the exhaustion of modernism can be seen readily in the other arts. In painting, Minimalism continued the reductivism of the purist line. Dan Flavin stated in 1967, "We are pressing downward toward no art – a mutual sense of psychologically indifferent decoration – a neutral pleasure of seeing known to everyone." Likewise, Frank Stella's geometric, shaped canvases are meant to stand as "something that was stable in a sense, something that wasn't constantly a record of your own sensitivity." Impersonality, universality, and reduction are still the rationale for such visual art.

In contrast, the pop art of Andy Warhol, Roy Lichtenstein, and others was a flagrant attempt to defy the century's main line of pictorial experimentation. Pop art is obviously representational, borrowing from advertising, the comics, the movies, high art, and anyplace else where "canned," popularly recognizable images can be found. This art was deliberately banal, disdaining the high, spiritual claims of abstract expressionism and conceptual art. It was also funny, creating incompatibilities of style and subject matter, redoing Picasso with Ben Day dots, or van Doesburg with line drawings. Rather than accepting the inevitability of boredom in a world where there was nothing to do but repeat and to meditate on one's repetition, Pop art revitalized repetition in Warhol's multiple reproductions of the same image – Marilyn Monroe, Jackie Kennedy, Campbell's soup cans – and in Lichtenstein's recontextualizing of familiar images – his comic-book sequences and his "artist's studio" collocations.

In its campy, outrageous way, pop art presented a wholly new approach to existential dread and the fear of technology, as they had been expressed in such modernist works as Walter Benjamin's "The Work of Art in the Age of Mechanical Reproduction." In an interview, Warhol stated, "I think everybody should be a machine. I think everybody should like everybody." The interviewer replied, "Is that what Pop Art is all about?" He answered, "Yes. It's liking things." "And liking things is like being a machine?" "Yes, because you do the same thing every time. You do it over and over again." "And you approve of that?" "Yes, because it's all fantasy." Turning the machine and repetition into the stuff of fantasy is a cryptic formulation of the postmodern task. The real work of this period is to get beyond the logic of existentialism as interpreted by modernism and to forge a new – though not innocent – modus operandi for art.

The frequency of references to Art Deco, Surrealism, and Dada among Pop artists indicates their reconfiguring of the high modernist canon. At the same time, their technical innovations (silk screen, projectors, Ben Day dots enlarged from the comics, vivid air-blown paint) make them every bit as serious formal "experimenters" as the most reductivist painters. Humor, ironic historical reference, the merging of high and popular sources, the reinterpretation of "exhaustion," and the creation of a new tension between representational and formal means were the opening into the "broad postmodernism" of the 1970s, 1980s, and 1990s. Suddenly, in Robert Rauschenberg's and Jasper Johns's collages and in Photo-Realism, Graffiti Art, and Neo-Expressionism, painters were dealing again with the tensions between depicting the world and the act of depiction. In a sphere in which only one, ever-narrowing path supposedly marked high art, a multiplicity of inconsistent approaches has now emerged. As Richard Marshall wrote in *American Art Since 1970,* "The art of this period is most frequently described as 'pluralistic,' implying a variety of styles, media, forms, and ideas that seem fractured and disjointed, with no single expressive mode dominating. One way of approaching the early and mid-1970s is to view it as an explosion of fragments, each containing different ideas, materials, intents, and forms, all flying away from the reductive, rigid, restrictive, and seemingly impersonal aspects of Minimalism." Minimalism, then, became just one of the competing movements and not the characteristic line of development. In the 1980s and 1990s, photography, performance art, videos, and multimedia installations expanded the diversity of artistic practice yet further.

In architecture, postmodernism enshrines a similar pluralism. In the years following the symbolic murder of the International Style in the Pruitt-Igoe explosion, designers virtually reversed the tenets of the earlier movement. Whereas modernist functionalism and purism had forbidden ornament, eclectic historical reference, and internal inconsistency, postmodern architecture was a congeries of ornamental elements and historical-stylistic references. Philip Johnson topped his AT&T skyscraper with a gigantic Chippendale pediment; Charles Moore built the Piazza Italia in New Orleans as a rococo profusion of arches, columns, fountains, and neon lights, in gorgeous, garish colors; Michael Graves designed houses with empty window frames erected on the roof and fanciful elements incongruously combined. Rather than the "inarticulate building" of the International Style, as Charles Jencks termed it, where architectural principles became so universal that a factory and a convent might be all but indistinguishable, postmodernism produced Robert Venturi's "difficult whole," in which buildings signify their functions and at the same time indicate their multifarious relations to the history of architecture preceding them.

Like Pop art, postmodernism reinterprets the earnestness and nobility of modernism with humor and irony. Whereas the Bauhaus artist Theo van Doesburg wrote in 1924 that "the proper tendency of the machine . . . is as the unique medium of . . . social liberation," postmodernism – or Ornamentalism, as it is sometimes called – uses the machine where it must, but welcomes the return of craft, of the handmade, precious object.

Ornamentalism permits us to laugh at ourselves, an honest and liberating act. It provides a means of dealing in imagination with our culture, of filtering the monstrously contradictory facts of our existence. Ornamentalism contains its own ideas about what things are and what things ought to be . . . but it does not insist on any correspondence between those ideas and some ultimate truth. Ornamentalism is, in part, a process of demystification, of retreat from Modernist claims to an exclusive means of salvation in a complicated world. The force of Ornamentalism, its strength and originality, lie in its abandonment of the machine aesthetic and its simultaneous ability to keep contradictions alive and explicit in the forms created. . . . Ornamentalism dances on the surface of technology, using it but denying its aura.

To Mies's austere "Less is more," Robert Venturi quipped, "Less is a bore."

Charles Jencks once suggested that this new architectural phase be called "Neo-Art Nouveau." Though the name never caught on, it does capture the spirit of the postmodern. "Neo-Art Nouveau" indicates the return of the aesthetic function so important in Art Nouveau, and in its Neo-Nouveau joke it exemplifies postmodernism's ironic play of style against style, period against period, and innovation against nostalgia.

The similarity of these characteristics to postmodern painting and literature is striking: they all involve an investigation of the functional and
semantic richness of their arts. Moreover, they all create a reversal of the
categories of the conventional and experimental. Art Nouveau architecture
was dominated by sensuous ornamentation. The radical move of functionalism was to eliminate ornament, to equate the aesthetic with formal or
structural beauty. Now, in postmodernism, after over sixty years of this
prohibition, it is an utterly progressive act to use ornament, even though
one does so with the knowledge that that ornament belongs to the past.
Likewise, in painting one might characterize impressionism as the culmination of the search for pictorial representation. The revolutionary gesture
of, say, Picasso in the 1907 *Demoiselles d'Avignon* was to balance the representational function against an equally urgent insistence on the form and
materiality of the pictorial medium. After over fifty years of increasing
semantic depletion in painting, one could hardly imagine a more startling
painterly move than to stencil a famous photograph of a movie star over
and over again on a canvas; yet this return of representation, through its
insistence on mechanical reproduction and simple repetition, also signifies
its difference from premodernist representational art.

Postmodern fiction, as we shall see, involves a parallel inversion of convention and radical experiment, with the sense that the revived premodern
is recovered only at a historical and ironic distance. Before we turn to fiction, however, there are some developments in television that are relevant
to this discussion. Unlike painting and architecture, television is one of
the "arts" that is perceived as posing a threat to literature. The reasons are
obvious: in most American homes, when people are in, the television is on;
most people spend much more time watching TV than reading. Though
book sales have risen, one wonders how many of the books bought are
actually read, especially by younger audiences brought up on videos,
action games, and the unvaried choices of cable TV. It is not surprising
that the harshest critics of the "electronic media" are high-culture writers
and their champions in academia, although the new possibilities for the
dissemination of knowledge on the Internet are drawing some of these
Luddites into the electronic age.

The subject of television tends to bring out rather extraordinary contradictions. For example, Ihab Hassan blamed TV and the computer for promoting "a paradoxical view of consciousness as information and history as
happening." Since Pynchon and other fine postmodern writers play on just
this theme, it is hard to see why it is so objectionable. Ronald Sukenick, a
hard-line experimentalist, sounded like a psychological realist of the last
century when he stated that "television can give us the news; fiction can best

express our response to the news. No other medium – especially not film – can so well deal with our strongest and often most intimate responses to the large and small acts of our daily lives." Just as often, such critics of literary experiment as Sven Birkerts blame the electronic media for "minimalist" writing: "The byte-sized perceptions, set in an eternal present, are the natural effluence of an electronically connected, stimulus-saturated culture."

Television is clearly the last frontier of tolerance for the literary establishment; yet TV is a better guide to the variety of this writing than one would think. During the period, an interesting mix of social commitment and intertextual complexity has characterized TV, and it is just this combination that marks postmodern fiction. The phenomenal success of *M*A*S*H,* a well-written and -acted comedy series about an American medical team in the Korean War, indicates the popular taste for examining the human cost of war, particularly in light of Vietnam. The police show *Cagney and Lacey* had policewomen encountering a special set of problems because of their gender. The show was kept running by a public outcry when the network tried to remove it, an indication of the importance that viewers attached to this subject. The social impact of later series was even greater, with *Murphy Brown's* depiction of unwed motherhood provoking Vice President Dan Quayle's censure, and the uncloseting of the eponymous character in *Ellen* helping to normalize lesbianism in public consciousness.

The police series *Hill Street Blues* and the hospital shows *St. Elsewhere* and *E. R.* introduced new and complex narrative strategies to TV. In any given episode, numerous characters figure in relatively independent plots that are usually not resolved in a single night. The shows proceed soap-opera–style in a sequence of snippets from intersecting lives. These shows are pervaded with allusions to other television series, with confusions of actor and role, and with other metareferences that make the project of TV viewing as much an insider's game as postmodern cinema and literature.

The promotion of the "soaps" to prime-time slots is perhaps the inspiration for this stylistic paradigm, although *Dallas, Falcon Crest,* and *Dynasty* were not usually as intertextual as *St. Elsewhere.* The evening soaps became the closest thing to an international culture, with *Dallas* broadcast in virtually every continent but Antarctica. Audiences enjoyed the stylized, pop quality of the characters and action, caring about the villains and martyrs but recognizing them as pasteboard figures – a double consciousness essential to postmodern high and popular culture.

Miami Vice, a 1980s police series, did more to familiarize the American public with the look of postmodern architecture than any other cultural source. Its premise is straight out of Camus or Sartre, with a certain low-brow pretentiousness: that the world is meaningless and pervaded with cruelty, that crime and justice are all but indistinguishable, and that all we can do is make gestures of love and compassion that are inevitably swamped by the violence and hatred around us. The show was full of references to pop culture – rock music, reggae, the world of show business, other TV shows, and especially videos. In fact, *Miami Vice* was like an extended video – all image, but exploring image as the only thing we have left. It was at times witty, humorous, and quite intelligent, although, after the first few years of production, it deteriorated badly. To experience the sophistication of postmodern pop, one could do worse than watch an early episode of *Miami Vice.*

We come now to postmodern fiction. Just as in painting, where some artists continue as if modernism were still in force and others upset and reverse the course of pictorial development, in literature we have a similar paradox: a conservative experimentalism and a radical traditionalism. On the one hand, we have Ihab Hassan quoting Emerson to the effect that "Speech is of Time, Silence is of Eternity"; Ronald Sukenick proposing that the book page should be considered a visual structure like that of field painting; and Raymond Federman proposing that a novel should cancel itself as it goes along and that the new fiction "will not only mean, but it will be!" We find Marc Saporta publishing a box of loose pages out of which readers can make their own novels. In John Barth's "Frame-Tale" (1968), the reader cuts off, folds, and pastes the tale into a Möbius strip reading interminably "Once upon a time there was a story that began." William Burroughs designed *Nova Express* (1964) and *The Ticket That Exploded* (1962; 1967) to be read by folding a page down the middle, placing it over another page, and reading across. Formal experiment was still a force in fiction in the 1960s and into the 1970s.

From the 1970s on, however, we see a turn toward "sociological" or thematic, rather than formal, experimentation in the novel. These works by women, blacks, homosexuals, and other nonaesthetically defined groups might inspire Barth's withering characterization as "secular news reports," but ultimately, they embody the assumptions of postmodernism every bit as fully as the more obvious, esoteric, and largely unread "neomodernists" do. What happened was that an extraordinarily talented array of writers responded in new ways to the modernist givens – the existential sense of the absurd, the arbitrariness of historical description, the importance of the medium of language in shaping thought and action. Without ignoring or denying these facts, they insisted on the validity of personal experience as an alternative to angst and hyperrationality.

This moment in literary history might be likened to the encounter between the eighteenth-century empiricist Bishop Berkeley and the man of letters Samuel Johnson. Berkeley had "proven" that we cannot know that there is a world beyond us, that the most intensely "real" sensations, such as pain, are utterly unsharable and therefore unverifiable, and that knowledge depends finally on a leap of faith. It is this fact that Lucky in Beckett's *Waiting for Godot* registers: "the dead loss per head since the death of Bishop Berkeley being to the tune of one inch four ounce per head approximately by and large more or less to the nearest decimal good measure round figures." Dr. Johnson offered a refutation to Berkeley's position by kicking a stone and showing his pain to demonstrate that the stone was "there." Then as now, this "simple-minded," pragmatic philistinism has a certain force. It affirms the unquestionability of human pain. In the watershed moment of the late 1960s, the elegant despair of the postmodern formalists was rewritten through the pain, the subjectivity, the stubborn self-validation of writers who might previously have been relegated to a merely popular or retrograde taste.

Another way to see this development is to consider John Barth's early novel *The End of the Road* (1958). Its hero, Jacob Horner, cannot come to any decisions because one choice is as good as another under the universal perspective that he has adopted. "Consequently," he has an affair with his best friend's wife, who becomes pregnant and dies during a botched abortion. Jacob is left trying to cope with this experience through the "mythotherapy" of a psychiatrist. This work might be labeled "High Exhaustion." We can imagine the postmodern revolution as a switch in viewpoint to the best friend's wife – so easily disposed of in the novel. In postmodernism, she seizes control of the plot, asserting her needs and expressing what it is to live with a man – in a world – in which one choice is as good as another, and therefore in which victimization and pain become merely part of the existential condition. We might recall poor Zuckerman, reading the pronouncements of the sophisticated young editors as he lies in bed, sunk in pain and enforced silence.

What these scenarios reveal is that the absolute boundary between the two visions – between "high" postmodernism and women's, ethnic, or minority art – is a fiction maintained by a mind-set lodged in modernism. According to it, any exploration of a societal dilemma other than white male existential angst is a throwback to the nineteenth-century novel, or rather, there is no progressive existential angst that is not white, male, and ethnically unmarked. Anyone reading the really powerful works of the last few decades, however – Thomas Pynchon's *The Crying of Lot 49,* John Hawkes's *Travesty,* Toni Morrison's *Beloved,* Marilynne Robinson's *Housekeeping,* Philip Roth's *The Anatomy Lesson,* and E. Annie Proulx's *The Shipping News* – cannot help but see the commonality of postmodern concerns in work that is labeled experimental, feminist, black, or Jewish writing.

As a brief example of this generalizing of issues, we might take Toni Morrison's *Sula* (1973). The narrator in *Sula* blames the plight of a black community specifically on the ambiguity of language. The blacks received their land when a slavemaster fulfilled his promise to a freed slave by tricking him into taking the infertile hillside as his farm. The master says that he

> had hoped to give him a piece of the Bottom. The slave blinked and said he thought valley land was bottom land. The master said, "Oh, no! See those hills? That's bottom land, rich and fertile."
>
> "But it's high up in the hills," said the slave.
>
> "High up from us," said the master, "but when God looks down, it's the bottom. That's why we call it so. It's the bottom of heaven – best land there is."

Perspective changes the meaning of words – God's perspective versus man's – but there is nothing innocent about this reversal. It is power that drives the variability of meaning. The analysis of language as a function of political power is a repeated topos in minority fiction. It is the practical reality behind the linguistic vertigo of the absurd.

Sula contains other elements straight out of existentialism. A character "blasted and permanently astonished by the events of 1917" (the first world war) establishes "National Suicide Day" in his town, when like-minded people march about carrying bells and draping nooses about their necks in a comic-absurd celebration of the utter meaninglessness of existence. The gratuitous violence of *The Stranger* pervades *Sula,* but at the same time *Sula* insists on the affect lying beneath the apparent indifference or cheerfulness of its characters. There is only apparent anesthesia, blankness; the reader must learn to see the pain beneath, as if a valley man who happened to be up in the hills watched a woman dancing:

> The black people watching her would laugh and rub their knees, and it would be easy for the valley man to hear the laughter and not notice the adult pain that rested somewhere under the eyelids, somewhere under their head rags and soft felt hats, somewhere in the palm of the hand, somewhere behind the frayed lapels, somewhere in the sinew's curve. He'd have to stand in the back of Greater Saint Matthew's and let the tenor's voice dress him in silk, or touch the hands of the spoon carvers (who had not worked in eight years) and let the fingers that danced on wood kiss his skin. Otherwise the pain would escape him even though the laughter was part of the pain.

The great postmodern novels that we shall be examining bear no resemblance to the "hieratic," "aloof," "Olympian" tone of high modernism, but they proceed from a startlingly similar analysis. Philip Roth's *The Anatomy Lesson* is a deep exploration of the meaning of pain, with its pitifully inadequate definition, "To miss. To feel the absence of" presented in some of the funniest writing in English. In *Linden Hills* (1985), Gloria Naylor has a woman character prick her belly with a pin each time she speaks, rubbing the cut with indelible ink; thus, speech becomes a wound and a mark made permanent by the ink of writing. Recalling the machine in Kafka's "The Penal Colony," Naylor's inked wounds are as eloquent an advocacy of silence as the most experimentalist work of exhaustion.

The broadening of the postmodern analysis across the varieties of contemporary fiction implies a new understanding of audience. As with modernist architecture, high modernist literature had associated aesthetic with ethical values. It is no longer tenable, however, to validate anyone morally on the grounds of tastefulness. George Steiner has pointed out that under Nazism, dedication to the highest "humanistic" interests was compatible with genocide, and Susan Sontag and Leslie Fiedler, that the entire artistic tradition of the West is corrupted by a hyperrationalism and imperialism that are akin to the aggression of bourgeois capitalist nations. Though we still accord respect to those who read sophisticated literature we do not accord them any ethical superiority as a result. It is also harder now to stratify the reading audience – morally and intellectually – into those who are in sympathy with the experimental line and those who manage only "lesser," easier works. First, no audience today subsists on a steady diet of Coover, Barth, and Powers, or even Pynchon and DeLillo, and no one would generalize from these writers to an overall view of contemporary writing (as people did with Eliot, Pound, and Joyce).

Second, in modernism, much as there was a single leading aesthetic line, there was a single prestige audience. Postmodernism is built on the assumption that audience is a multiple and much less hierarchical construct. Even prestige readers are expected to have more catholic taste than were the intelligentsia of earlier years. The constant juxtaposition of stylistic levels in Thomas Pynchon, Philip Roth, Norman Mailer, Carol Hill, and Harold Robbins – esoteric allusion next to slapstick and pop – encode a pluralistic notion of audience and reception like that in postmodern painting and architecture. Readers cannot get by anymore with a purely high-art literary experience. Indeed, the abandonment of the attempt at "universality" of meaning is itself an argument for the notion that a work of art appeals in vastly different ways to different readers. This is one reason why the sociological categories of race and gender have recently been so much stressed. It is not only that different types of readers each have their own type of novel to read (women's, black, gay, white-middle-class-bourgeois, and so forth) or that different readers read the same text differently (although of course they do). Rather, any reader is really a multiplicity of reading types trained by his or her experience with electronic and print media and by the heterogeneity of contemporary life.

Because of all these uncertainties and complexities, the relation between the work and its audience is often one of the central topics of fiction. Norman N. Holland found the most salient characteristic of postmodernism to be its "calling into question the relationship between its audience and itself." Sometimes this questioning involves considerable violence, as when John Hawkes's narrator-protagonist addresses the other occupants of his car in *Travesty* (1976). Like the reader, these figures are never heard, although the speaker responds to their fear, discomfort, and nausea as he drives them – and by implication, us – toward a smash-up from which there will be no survivors. In contrast, Alice Walker's *The Color Purple* (1982) implies not aggression but desperate separation from the reader, with its letters addressed to a sister whose answers are secretly confiscated. Eventually, the heroine starts addressing her letters to God, and though she finally gets to read what her sister has written her and affirms her communion with God, the greater part of the book dramatizes the terrible futility and suffering involved in the attempt to communicate.

Postmodernism commonly thematizes the act of reading. If meaning is the result of an interaction between text and reader, then the drama of postmodern literature is the drama of interpretation. Thus, the heroine of Pynchon's *The Crying of Lot 49* (1966) sifts through vast amounts of evidence in order "to project a world." Edmund White's *Nocturnes for the King of Naples* (1978) recalls the medieval exegesis of the Song of Solomon to come to an understanding of homosexual love. At all levels of the contemporary novel, detective plots proliferate, because they are so overtly related to issues of interpretation. The detective's investigation of a crime models the reader's construing of a fiction, and so the analogy of crime and writing becomes obvious. As Stefano Tani has argued, "When we get to metafictional anti-detective novels . . . the detective is the reader who has to make sense out of an unfinished fiction that has been distorted or cut short by a playful and perverse 'criminal,' the writer."

The focus on the reader finds its critical parallel in reader response theory. The aim here is to determine how the reader deals with the work rather than what the work in itself is, to show that readings are grounded in the historical, social, and psychological contexts of their audience. As Jonathan Culler pointed out, however, "it proves no easier to say what is in *the* reader's or *a* reader's experience than is in the text. . . . The result is not a new foundation but stories of reading." A good many of the most striking postmodern fictions, for example, *The Color Purple, The Crying of Lot 49,* or *Linden Hills,* like the archetypal case of Nabokov's *Pale Fire* (1962), might aptly be called "stories of reading."

The focus on the reader, the themes of violence and objectification, and the intermingling of low and high taste have propelled pornography to the center of postmodern literature. The liberal treatment of sex in literature began with modernism, in Judge Woolsey's historic decision on *Ulysses* and the breakthroughs of D. H. Lawrence. Nevertheless, Henry Miller's novels were not openly available in the States until the 1960s, and in the introduction to *Slow Learner,* Pynchon mentions the constraint of the fifties as provoking a general self-censorship among writers. The 1960s institutionalized sexual license in literature and established it as a free-speech issue. With the publication of Vladimir Nabokov's *Lolita* (1955), Terry Southern's *Candy* (France, 1958; United States, 1964), and Gore Vidal's *Myra Breckenridge* (1968), the 1970s opened on a scene in which pornography and aesthetic theorizing coalesced in the best-seller.

Pornography was important not simply because it could now be published. Leslie Fiedler claimed that "all those writers who have helped move Porn from the underground to the foreground have in effect been working towards the liquidation of the very conception of pornography; since the end of Art on one side means the end of Porn on the other. And that end is now in sight, in the area of films and Pop songs and poetry, but especially in that of the novel." It is certainly true that the category of pornography seems less and less meaningful in recent serious fiction, but even more important for postmodernism than this relativization of moral distinctions is pornography's validization of personal fantasy. The pornographic work is an unfettered "alternate world," as significant a display of game playing and linguistic power as any genre of postmodern fiction. Pornography makes literal the metaphor of plot as sexual act and the critical cliché of "narrative desire."

Many feminists, however, would not approve of this characterization, having argued since at least the 1960s that pornography violates the rights of women. Whereas publishing and selling pornographic literature are certainly related to the right to free expression, protection from victimization seems an even more compelling right. When in May 1986, Hugh Hefner, the creator and promoter of the *Playboy* empire, faced the closure of several of his clubs and the banning of his magazine from convenience stores, he claimed that the 1980s were a new age of conservatism paralleling the 1950s. Feminists argued that a governmental commission's finding that pornography is a source of violence against women was a radically progressive act. Censorship thus becomes both conservative and progressive, depending on one's point of view. What is at issue is the same clash between the existential subject and the newly empowered object that we discussed in connection with *The End of the Road.* Pornography is important in postmodernism because it creates the most blatant clash between imaginative power and physical victimization.

In this period, mainstream women writers began publishing sexually explicit texts. Erica Jong's *Fear of Flying* (1973) and Margaret Atwood's eerie *The Handmaid's Tale* (1985), as much as John Rechy's *City of Night* (1963), John Updike's *Couples* (1968), or Stephen Schneck's *The Nightclerk* (1983), reveal the centrality of transgressive writing at this time. Pornography is a special case of "nonimpersonal" literature, writing that creates an overt appeal to the reader. Thus, when Roth's Zuckerman, posing as the unrepentant publisher of a salacious journal called *Lickety Split,* asks his female driver if he offends her on feminist grounds, she answers, "Privacy is as good a cause as pornography, you know. No, I don't find you unacceptable because I'm a God damn feminist. It's because I'm a human being." The fact that she is wearing black leather boots and a uniform does not solidify her humanity with the reader, but her point takes the pornography question beyond the usual issues of victimization and free speech. Since Stephen Dedalus (and therefore Aquinas) in *A Portrait of the Artist as a Young Man,* the impersonality of a text has been judged as a sign of its universalism and hence its value, whereas the personal has been equated with the pornographic. The postmodern shift revalidates the personal and in the process reproblematizes the issue of pornography.

The inclusiveness of postmodernism is apparent in the literary canon that it has constructed. Just as T. S. Eliot remade the history of English writing for modernism, postmodern writers reconstituted the literary canon, concentrating not on poetry, as Eliot had, but on the "great tradition" of the novel: Daniel Defoe, Henry Fielding, Jane Austen, Charles Dickens, George Eliot, Honoré de Balzac, Gustav Flaubert, Leo Tolstoy, Henry James. This line, propounded in the twenties and thirties by R. D. Leavis and reaffirmed in universities ever after was still the canon for Wayne Booth's *The Rhetoric of Fiction* (1961) and remains so for very traditional reading lists in university courses today.

The canon of postmodernism, however, is really a multiplicity of historical constructs. The experimentalists and many less technically oriented writers have rejected the focus on psychology and societal milieu of the great tradition in favor of the humor, perversity, and intelligence of Laurence Sterne, the Marquis de Sade, William Blake, le Comte de Lautréamont, Alfred Jarry, Gertrude Stein, the James Joyce of *Finnegans Wake,* Henry Miller, Samuel Beckett, Jorge Luis Borges, the French New Novel, and

Vladimir Nabokov. The suddenness of this canon shift is apparent in the treatment of Sterne. *Tristram Shandy* has long been considered the sport of the eighteenth-century novel – idiosyncratic and anachronistically self-referential. Early in the century, when the Russian Formalist Victor Shklovsky concluded his essay, "Art as Technique," with the assertion that *"Tristram Shandy* is the most typical novel in world literature," one took his point as a logical extrapolation from the modernist concern with style, though in light of the great tradition one could hardly imagine a less "typical novel." Today the reaction is quite different. As Ronald Sukenick wrote, "I'll bet that the multifaceted, antisequential, surrational *Tristram Shandy* is closer to the truth of your experience these days than *Robinson Crusoe.*"

Many women writers and feminist scholars, in contrast, have become archaeologists, unearthing a buried canon of women's writing. Alice Walker, for example, returns us to slave narratives, the novels and anthropological research of Zora Neale Hurston, and the writing of Colette, Jean Toomer (a man sympathetic to women, according to Walker), Anaïs Nin, Virginia Woolf, and Tillie Olsen. This historical reconstruction is not limited to women; the Harlem Renaissance has been newly studied as well. Nineteenth-century white women's novels, such as Charlotte Perkins Gilman's *The Yellow Wallpaper* (1899), have entered the university curriculum. One of the most striking achievements of this activity has been the "discovery" of Hurston's *Their Eyes Were Watching God* (1937), which went from a forgotten footnote of the Harlem Renaissance to an undisputed classic of modernist writing in less than a decade of commentary. Though these works were all written before postmodernism, their popular reception has come only in this period, and thus, in terms of their reception, they are postmodern products. A marked effect of this recovery of the past has been to revise modernism, elevating many texts outside the high tradition to the status of classics. As this process continues, it will be more and more difficult to experience the modernist canon as modernism viewed it; it is all but impossible, for example, to accord Hemingway the sympathy and centrality that he used to command.

Another of the interesting "discoveries" of contemporary fiction is Henry Miller. From the bad boy of American letters – a pornographer banned in Boston for his scandalous prose – Miller has emerged for a variety of novelists as a major source of postmodern ideology. Roth and Pynchon allude to him in some of their most hilarious moments, and Sukenick wrote that "Henry Miller is for American novelists what Whitman is for American poets. The source of his vitality is the current that began flowing when he reconnected our art with our experience. Experience begins with the self and Miller put the self back into fiction."

The comprehensiveness of Miller's vision, his frenetic synthesizing, the range of his language – from obscenity to sublime metaphor and back in the space of a sentence – and his ability to enjoy himself in the face of utter absurdity and meaninglessness make him a fitting model for many writers today. As he said in *Tropic of Capricorn* (1930), "Everything that happens, when it has significance, is in the nature of a contradiction. . . . I was a contradiction in essence."

The embracing of contradiction, the rejection of the either/or, is one of the most often-repeated formulas of postmodernism. Not the either/or but the both/and – this was a refrain of the Pop artists, John Cage, and Robert Rauschenberg. Pynchon's characters search for a world not divided into the binary opposites of logic but allowing for "middles" – statements that are both true and false at once. Federman imagined a fiction of the future in which "all forms of duality will be negated – especially duality: that double-headed monster which, for centuries now, has subjected us to a system of values, an ethical and aesthetical system based on the principles of good and bad, true and false, beautiful and ugly." The aim of this destruction of dualism is not to create confusion but to have the novel more faithfully mirror the current state of reality – or this is the claim of the various fictionists advocating the both/and. It is also the way philosophers discuss the contemporary state of knowledge. According to Paul K. Feyerabend, knowledge is "an ever increasing ocean of mutually incompatible (and perhaps even incommensurable) alternatives, each single theory, each fairy tale, each myth that is part of the collection forcing the others into greater articulation and all of them contributing, via this process of competition, to the development of our consciousness. Nothing is ever settled, no view can ever be omitted from a comprehensive account."

This sense of plenitude and comprehensiveness gave new energy to the novel after the exhaustion hypothesis of the 1960s. By the 1980s, virtually every writer and critic who had proclaimed the novel dead had written a retraction – for example, Barth's "The Literature of Replenishment" (1980) or Fiedler's "The Death and Rebirths of the Novel" (1982). Jerome Klinkowitz even named his introduction to postmodern fiction "The Death of the Death of the Novel." The explanation these writers offer for their earlier pessimism is that it was the modernist novel or sometimes the "great tradition" that was worn out, and that the turning inward, the exploration of the conditions of novel making, created a whole new system of possibilities.

The empowerment of new voices has left that exploration open to an unusually heterogeneous array of writers. Recent novelists, starting from seemingly incompatible assumptions, have produced a fictional discourse as broad, variegated, and yet interconnected as the worldview they propose. Like Sukenick's therapeutic "Psychosynthesis" in 98.6 (1975), literary practice is now "based on the Mosaic Law. The Mosaic Law is the law of mosaics[:] a way of dealing with parts in the absence of wholes."

A literary history based on such a law would accept the fact that history changes according to the teller, that the past is a creative construction on the part of interested voices, and that history is more properly a plural than a singular sphere. To think historically is thus to become like the Soviet historian in the joke – someone who can predict the past. To predict the past, to "project a world" as Pynchon's Oedipa Maas would put it, is to imagine a believable – though not unique – picture of time gone by.

Such an approach implies a certain humility (and exhilaration) for anyone writing a history of the contemporary novel, but it also provides a key to our conceptualization of recent fiction. Novels have always styled themselves as alternate histories, from *Tom Jones* to *Armies of the Night*. We might thus examine postmodern fiction as a field of interested stories predicting the past – not a line of stylistic "progress" but a plenitude of prophesies about the fast-fleeting now. As Jean-François Lyotard advises us, "*Post modern* would have to be understood according to the paradox of the future (*post*) anterior (*modo*)." It is this Janus-like historical situation and the variety of audience appeals that create the excitement of postmodern fiction.

2

❦

FABLES OF THE FETISH

I N 1970, THE WRITING DISEASE had been diagnosed as exhaustion, and
practitioners were busily at work to find a cure. One approach was to
analyze the condition itself, to explore the various symptoms and sub-
tleties of the postmodern state. The "High Postmodernism" usually identified with Thomas Pynchon, John Barth, John Hawkes, Donald
Barthelme, and Kurt Vonnegut was the result, and the investigations of
these writers in many respects coincided. What was wrong with the novel,
they concluded, was its rootedness in modernism, an ideology that
fetishizes the work of art. A revitalized novel would be a novel written and
received not as a neurotic fetish à la Freud or a commodified fetish à la
Marx but as an opening, a doorway to communication.

The use of *fetish* here is prompted by postmodern novelists themselves,
several of whom refer specifically to the formulations of the term in Freud
or, less directly, in Marx. Marx took the term *fetish* from religion, where it
refers to a statue or other cult object to which believers attribute the same
powers as those of the spirits that the fetish object represents.
Accordingly, Marx characterized the commodity fetish as a bourgeois
attempt to make a religion out of mere material objects, noting the peculiar fact that we speak and act as if commodities "had" value. In the commodity, "the social character of men's labour appears to them as an
objective character stamped upon the product of that labour." What is in
fact a social relation is understood as a property of things; the process by
which labor links people together is obscured, translated into an impersonal ratio of objects.

The confusion of sign and thing, the displacement of social relations
onto objects, and the attribution of spiritual value to the inanimate commodity all have direct bearing on the modernist vision of art. Modernism
enshrined the belief that art could provide a quasireligious experience; it
stressed the object status of the work of art – that is, its material medium
and style; it conceived of aesthetic meaning and value as existing *in* the
artwork; and it minimized the social factors – the writer, reader, extra-
artistic reality, and language code – that are essential to the very production of meaning. In the modernist period, the artwork was seen as a

commodity, a reification of value that both preserves that value for reader-consumers and locks it away from them through its esoteric difficulty. Postmodernism, in contrast, insists on the fluidity of the artwork in the social dynamics of reading. It is a concerted effort to instruct the reader in the folly of fetishism and the empowerment and interest that can arise instead for the enlightened interpreter.

If Marx's use of the term *fetish* suggests the economic and political dangers of treating art as a commodity, Freud provided the postmodernists with a psychological view of the problem. He explained the fetishist as a boy who is so threatened at the discovery that his mother has no penis (and hence that he might be deprived of his, too) that he constructs a substitute for it in her foot, shoe, garter, and so on. His fetish allows him both to give up the belief in her phallus and to retain it, for the fetish is both different from a phallus and a version of it. The fetish "now inherits the interest which was formerly directed to its predecessor. But this castration has set up a memorial to itself in the creation of this substitute." The paradoxical thinking surrounding the fetish allows one to compensate for absence and death, but in the process the fetishist forgets that the fetish also memorializes loss. As such, it is a very suggestive analogue for the decadent and modernist view of art.

The sense of living at the end of an age, of making do with diminished possibilities, blossomed in the aestheticism of the late nineteenth century. The response of the Decadents to the "departure of the gods" and the withdrawal of meaning was to turn to art as a repository of value, a substitute for what was missing in other areas of life. Their legacy to the twentieth century was the fetishizing of the aesthetic experience, the belief in art for its own sake. If modernism bemoaned the unavailability of such consolation from art, at the same time the whole effect of the movement and its criticism was to produce an overdetermined, self-reflexive aesthesis in which value, intensity, and meaning would be caught in the work – reinforcing each other to produce a "little world" of heightened experience. As observer, passive participant, voyeur, the reader would know transcendence, but only mediately. And though this might be cold comfort, it was comfort nonetheless. Hemingwayesque, the reader learned to take satisfaction where he or she could find it.

Postmodernists tended to reject this fetishization because it is such a deluded compensation for loss. In Thomas Pynchon's first novel, *V.* (1963), for example, the fetish is decisively and grotesquely dismissed. The lady V. and a fifteen-year-old dancer named Mélanie have a decadent love affair in the heyday of modernism. In an orgy of voyeurism and fetishism, they pose in costumes and gaze at each other in mirrors. Mélanie is starring in a bal-

let in which she plays a Chinese princess who is first ravaged by an invad-
ing army and then impaled on a spear – what amounts to a huge metal
penis. On opening night, having forgotten the chastity belt device that
was to protect her, she actually is impaled and dies. Her death signals the
impossibility of using art to replace the missing penis in the fetishistic
theater of art. Pynchon uses the ballet to make this point because it is the
modernist image par excellence of perfect presence, of the banishing of the
boundary between actor and act, knower and known, and all dualistic
opposites. Yeats's key formula for aesthetic transcendence, "How can we
know the dancer from the dance?" is directly criticized here, because the
aesthetic fetish is exposed as such – a substitute, a last-ditch effort, a sign
not of transcendence but of death. Art is artificial. One cannot use it to
correct a situation it symptomizes.

The revolutionary move of postmodernism is to undercut the earlier
fetishism. It is thus particularly ironic that critics have justified postmodernist experimentalism through the rhetoric of the early twentieth-century
avant-garde: the stress on style, technique, and medium. In fact, contemporary experimentalists foil the text's ability to function as an internally
valuable object, a self-reflexive replacement for departed meaning, or even
an exemplification of the failure of value. They do so by characterizing
such attitudes as unhealthy, subverting the metaphor of the textual fetish
or love object to the point of its undoing. In postmodern fiction, modernist aesthesis is a delusory state akin to neurosis and depersonalization.

Thus, Pynchon, Barth, Hawkes, and other experimentalists set up the
temptation of the fetish and then subvert it. They push us toward the
fetish and then destroy or invalidate it, as if it were necessary to have modernist aesthetics acknowledged and in place in order for a new stage of
understanding to occur. This is one reason why the romance is such a crucial literary mode in contemporary fiction. It is about the behavior surrounding the fetish – the Holy Grail or beautiful princess or
self-understanding that seem so precious to the questor that they nullify
all quotidian reality. Postmodernism asserts that the quest for value should
not end in the establishment of a substitute that both is and is not what
we lack – in other words, that metaphor, allegory, and ultimately art are
not adequate solutions to loss.

The analogy between fetish and artwork is not gratuitous, as the perennial use of Narcissus's image in the pool as a symbol of painting indicates.
All art invites the contradictory thinking of the fetish. It is an institutionalized splitting of belief, since its truth status is so paradoxical. A work of
art both represents the world and bears no responsibility for the accuracy
of that representation; it does not lie, but neither does it tell the truth.

What art does, and what the romance does most markedly, is to allow us to have our cake and eat it too, to experience loss in a form so full and so satisfying that, to reverse Eliot's formulation, it gives with the famishing. Aesthesis, necessary to the romance quest, cannot be its end, however, for like any determinate end it can lead only to repetition, redundancy, and death. To fixate ourselves on art for its own sake is to replay the decadent scenario of the late nineteenth century.

John Hawkes undoes the aesthetic fetish through a merger of pornography and self-reflexiveness. Though his play on the traditional novelistic elements of plot, character, setting, and theme recalls the modernist concentration on technique at the expense of reference, his writing is very different from modernist fiction. His subjects are violence and eroticism, his plots are peculiar oneiric refashionings of other fictions – Westerns, thrillers, pornography, the nouveau roman – and his settings, though specific and often exotic (Greece, the South Pacific, French chateau country) are misty fantasy worlds that put no realistic pressure on the plot. Unlike Pynchon, whose settings and floating narrative line are often equally dreamlike, Hawkes shows no counterpull in the direction of historicism. His writing is like Freudian dreamwork; it elides reality in favor of the fetishized worlds of literature, philosophy, and the body.

Although Hawkes unblushingly evokes this world of wish fulfillment, he disdains the sentimentality and weakness that normally invest it with value. All institutions surrounded by conventional responses – the affective spurs that Milan Kundera in *The Unbearable Lightness of Being* (1984) defines as kitsch – in Hawkes are shorn of ordinary feeling. As a result, the reader feels victimized, exposed to a harrowing or titillating sequence of events in which affect is ignored or belittled. In "Notes on Violence," Hawkes says that he "rejects sympathy for the ruined members of our lot, revealing thus the deepest sympathy of all." It is this reversal – profound emotion conveyed as coldness or anesthesia – that is the most interesting aspect of his work, along with his remarkable verbal facility. It is not accidental that he cites Camus as an important influence.

Hawkes's first novel, *The Cannibal,* was published in 1949 and was followed by a steady stream of critically acclaimed – though otherwise ignored – fictions. Most of them have appeared with New Directions, a pathbreaking publishing house under the leadership of the late James Laughlin, who was responsible for keeping many of the major figures of the twentieth-century avant-garde available to the public.

In Hawkes's work we see the significance of the fetish for postmodernism. Hawkes is a master of the fixation, dwelling on tattoos, rituals, and visual compulsions. In *Innocence in Extremis* (1985), for example, a novel full of incest and intrigue in a French chateau, an "Old Gentleman" poses his granddaughter on a horse so as to produce a beautiful composition. Controlling the shadows and the angle of the sun, the position of the seated audience, and even the direction of the horse's head, he allows the spectators to see only the girl's right side. By placing her legs on the left of the horse, he "created for her audience the illusion of a legless rider seated in perfect balance upon her horse. The fact that she appeared to have no legs was . . . the incongruity without which the congruous whole could not have achieved such perfection." This perverse tripping up of perfection in order to make perfection possible is analogous to Hawkes's technique of stalling affect in order to release it. It is the basis for his verbal eroticism. This contradiction—simultaneous loss and gain—is the very essence of the fetish, its compensation for what is absent by an inadequate replacement. Like other postmodernists, Hawkes equates art with the fetish as the legacy of modernism, and derides, deprecates, and undermines this aesthetic compensation for the absence of a meaningful world.

One of the clearest presentations of Hawkes's fetishistic eroticism is his trilogy, *The Blood Oranges* (1971); *Death, Sleep and the Traveler* (1974); and *Travesty* (1976). The first two appear to be unredeemed soft pornography; they titillate the reader while violently foisting him or her away. *The Blood Oranges* is the story of two married couples, one practicing unbounded sexual freedom, the other, monogamous marriage. They meet on a Greek island and become variously entangled, until the conventional husband locks his wife in a chastity belt and then commits suicide.

The novel is an ironic, highly ambiguous examination of the notion of sexual liberation and its relation to art. One of modernism's achievements was to force the courts and the public to accept sexuality in art on the grounds of imaginative freedom and "redeeming social value," and Hawkes alludes to that victory in his epigraph, a somewhat maudlin plea for sexual license taken from Ford Madox Ford's *The Good Soldier* (1915): "Is there then any terrestrial paradise where, amidst the whispering of the olive-leaves, people can be with whom they like and have what they like and take their ease in shadows and in coolness?" This primitivist image of sexual pleasure Hawkes exposes in all its sentimentality. He turns the erotic paradise of the Greek island – of sentimentalized art – into an ideological struggle between the conventional moralism of the suicide, who is a photographer (a fetishist of still images), and the libertinism of the protagonist. There is always a snake in the garden, and that snake may be not only the rigidity of the "straight" world but the insensitivity of "liberated innocence." Pure wish fulfillment is an impossibility in life and in art, for it willfully excludes the one fact that can never be forgotten – death.

The next novel in the trilogy, *Death, Sleep and the Traveler,* goes more deeply into the ideology of eroticism as a fetishistic substitution for fulfillment. A married couple exploring the intricacies and varieties of sexuality have formed a triangle with a lover critical of the husband's attitude to pornography. A psychiatrist, the lover asks the husband, Allert, whether he does not find pornography boring. Ursula, the wife, answers: "For you and me . . . Allert's pornography would be intolerable. You and I do not filter life through fantasy." Later, she adds, "Allert's theory is that the ordinary man becomes an artist only in sex. In which case pornography is the true field of the ordinary man's imagination." Here sexuality, pornography, fantasy, art, and imagination merge. It is in sexuality, Allert proposes, that the panacea of the aesthetic fetish becomes universal.

Allert tells many dreams to Ursula, and since he is also the narrator, the dream narration is often indistinguishable from that of the novel as a whole. His enactment of his sexual imaginings is echoed in this merging of waking "reality" and dream. Thus, when the psychiatrist chides Allert that the pornographic fantasies in his collection "are not even real," this assessment seems not only bullying but wrong. The three characters are themselves living out a pornographic fantasy, which in turn is a pornographic fantasy for the reader. This amounts to a postmodern formula: a paradox involving a confusion of logical or epistemological levels turns out to be "in fact" the case. Where we are aware of the artificiality, the distance of the text from our lives, we find ourselves most roused by it, appearing to interact with it.

Hawkes pushes the device further. The psychiatrist lover dies of a heart attack as the three relax in a sauna, and later Allert goes off by himself on a cruise, abandoned to "death, sleep, and the anguish of lonely travel." In his dreamlike narration, Allert reveals that he has thrown a girl, whom he had taken as a lover, out the ship's porthole. He has since been tried for murder and has gotten off with the help of Ursula. The crime is "real" but presented in such a dreamlike fashion that it has no reality next to the psychiatrist's violent death. The book ends with Allert's assertion, "I am not guilty," and indeed, he neither feels guilt nor has been pronounced guilty. Inner and outer reality nullify his responsibility for this act, and likewise the reader, who has willingly proceeded with these fantasies, reversing reality and dream and accepting moral and epistemological disorientation, is both innocent and implicated in a crime through his or her very attention. Allert himself is such a reader, a reader of pornography and a deployer of attention. His name in English means Alan, we are told, but it is also "a repository for the English word 'alert,' as if the name is a thousand-year-old clay receptacle with paranoia curled in the shape of a child's skeleton inside. I myself have always been quietly alert." This quiet alertness is the reader's amoral affliction, created by the fetishistic feeding and famishing of the text.

The third novel in the trilogy, *Travesty,* crystallizes the issues even more clearly. It is as if *The Blood Oranges* were an idyll perfected by its tinge of tragedy; *Death, Sleep and the Traveler* were a meta-idyll, its tragedy commenting on the idyll and the idyll invalidating the tragedy; and *Travesty,* finally, a deliberate allegory of the whole process. In *Travesty,* the analogy between eroticism and reading is the central theme. The plot of the book is a literal drive toward death, the novel's speaker (there is no narrator) delivering a monologue that is his conversation with his best friend and his own daughter, passengers in his expensive car. He explains that he is taking them on a ride from which "there shall be no survivors," for it will end with the car's slamming into a stone wall at high speed. Thus, they will enter "the toneless world of highway tragedy" as opposed to "travesty," a pair of literary modes in which "design" is matched against "debris." "In its own way, it is a form of ecstasy, this utter harmony between design and debris."

We might note that this is the very "ecstasy" that animates Andy Warhol's "Disaster" works. In one, a photo of a gory traffic accident is silk-screened over and over again on a canvas to produce a beautiful design. The image of an atomic bomb or an electric chair are the repeated elements in others. In his *Lavender Disaster* or related works like *Three Deaths Eleven Times in Orange,* Warhol reveals the shocking implication of design in debris, creating artistic ecstasy and undermining it in the same gesture.

The engine propelling Hawkes's plot toward its end is Honorine, the driver's wife and the friend's mistress, "the lady of the dark chateau." She is their muse, for the lover Henri is a poet. As the epigraph from Michel Leiris states, "I am imbued with the notion that a Muse is necessarily a dead woman, inaccessible or absent; that a poetic structure – like the canon, which is only a hole surrounded by steel – can be based only on what one does not have; and that ultimately one can write only to fill a void or at the least to situate, in relation to the most lucid part of ourselves, the place where this incommensurable abyss yawns within us." Both muse and canon are fascinating voids in need of filling – fetishes in the purest sense. Obediently, Hawkes assembles a formidable canon in this book – Michel Leiris, Albert Camus, William Wordsworth, Alain Robbe-Grillet, Jean-Paul Sartre, Vladimir Nabokov – while his muse, asleep and dreaming in the family chateau, is an absent presence driving all of us on toward the ending. "Your Muse, my clarity," her husband describes her, and his "clairvoyance" is the state he values above everything. It is necessary for skillful driving, writing, and reading.

Clarity is the version of existentialist heroism depicted in Camus's *The Myth of Sysiphus* (1942), when the damned sinner, condemned for eternity to push a boulder up a rock and watch it fall down again, understands his situation and goes off after the boulder anyway. The speaker in *Travesty* is an existentialist teacher, forcing his passengers and his readers toward lucidity, and yet the cruelty of this training, its utter inhumanity, suggests that Hawkes's book might very properly be read as a travesty of French existentialist art and the modernism out of which it springs.

As the driver's clarity, Honorine exerts a fascination through her status as a fetish, a beautiful object perfected by incongruity. She is the perfect châtelaine, well dressed and groomed, well suited to her life, a good friend and mother. "Everything about such a person suggests the bearded father, the hand prepared well in advance to tend the sumptuous roses, a certain intelligence in the eyes, but finally the undeniable indications of the female life that is destined, after all, for unfulfillment – which is not interesting." This impression is utterly false, though, belied by a remarkable tattoo located on Honorine's abdomen, a tattoo of grapes overlying the fruits beneath it. A sexual promised land, Honorine is a pure erotic fantasy, a symbolic doubling of sexuality, desire signifying itself.

Moreover, like all fetishes, she is presented as static, though that stasis provokes the most violent reactions. The speaker imagines her dreaming in her bed in the chateau. The stillness of that image preceding the "accident" corresponds to the stillness of the design-debris following it. As a child, the speaker had been fascinated by pictures of accident victims and erotica, and now he is thrilled at the idea of the people in the car imagining the pattern of remains they will leave on the highway. As the car rushes past a cemetery, the driver notes that they see "that small village of the dead" as if "from a stationary vehicle parked in our empty wind-blown, golden field directly across from that small, excellent example of our morbid artistry." Here motion and stasis reverse, the racing car becomes stationary, and one suspects a pun with *stationery* – letters, writing. This book tells the story of a speeding car aiming at a crash and prophesies silence and a pattern of still remains – all of this an analogy to the process of writing or reading. Artistry is the gesture toward emptiness, silence, stasis, and death: "cessation is what we seek, if only because it alone is utterly unbelievable."

For this reason, the speaker must rewrite Wordsworth's formula for poetry, "the spontaneous overflow of powerful emotion recollected in tranquility." His aesthetic "drive" rests not in memory's tempering of the past but in the bolstering of emotion with idea, with the flaw of travesty that does not mar but perfects. He is producing not a Wordsworthian recollection but "an animated revery," "emotional expression stiffened with the bones of thought." The book is itself an example of the travesty it describes, a corsetting of the fleshy overflow of feeling, a pornographic tease disciplining raw affect.

The central Wordsworthian spot of time in *Travesty* is perfectly consistent with this thinking. When the speaker was just getting to know Honorine long ago, he drove his fast car through a village on the way to see her. An old poet was standing by the street holding the hand of a striking young girl. The speaker's staring at the girl so infuriated the old poet that he glared at the approaching car and shook his umbrella at it. The speaker raced at the girl and passed her, not knowing whether he had struck her. This is an event that "defined me, thrilled me, convinced me of the validity of the fiction of living, but which I have now forgotten." The immediate action of *Travesty*, however, is a structural re-creation of that very episode: the driver, a poet, and a young woman – the daughter in the backseat, whom the driver has just humiliated with a recounting of the obscene game of Carrots. He hopes to rationalize the trauma of the death ride with the "explanation" offered in his recitation of the past: "emotional expression stiffened with the bones of thought." Instead of the completeness of the Wordsworthian merging of language and experience, the spot of time in Hawkes is an obscene and ambiguous puzzle.

The book is a formula, in this way, for Hawkes's idea of art. Like so much of postmodernism, it is a redoing of romanticism and the neoromanticism of modernism, an unsentimentalized recasting of the comfort art brings into an ugly, willed, and perverse attempt to have one's cake and eat it too. If one has the stomach for such a tough feast, then Hawkes provides it, though for many, one fears, it is enough to spoil the appetite for good. The text always tempts the reader to take it at face value, to accept it as pornography for the literati, or philosophy for the eroticist. Thus, like the violent fantasies of Jerzy Kosinski, Hawkes's work can seem like a lapse into the fetish rather than a warning against it, becoming formulaic, overly clever, and at times pretentious. The mental discipline – the stiffening of thought – required to overcome this temptation is formidable.

Robert Coover's fictional experiments are even more subject to this danger. His *Universal Baseball Association, Inc., J. Henry Waugh, Prop.* (1968) is an elaborate allegory of life as baseball; *Pricksongs and Descants* (= Death Cunts [1969]) is a repetitive, antifeminist fable; and *The Public Burning* (1977), the most interesting of his novels, suffers from stylistic preciosity and self-consciousness. Ronald Sukenick's *Long Talking Bad Conditions Blues* (1979) is *The Sun Also Rises* of the 1970s and an interesting rewriting of that earlier work. In its reevocation of Hemingway, however, it often seems more like a return to modernism than a departure from it. Such works support the critics who explain postmodernism in modernist terms. They exemplify a nostalgic strain among the experimentalist postmoderns, viewing society regressively as a lost generation and art as technique.

Raymond Federman's theorizing is very much in this tradition. His novel *Take It or Leave It* (1976) is an exploration of typography as fate, a play on language in the tradition of James Joyce and Henry Miller. It tells a story of disconnection and disorientation interspersed with some acute theoretical and critical remarks, to the effect that the marriage of fiction and theory has not always been a happy one:

It was not going very well already in the kingdom of literature since le nouveau roman that great triumph of sing-my-ass we were going quite helpless copiously robbegrilladized semiotized . . . drifting on the lacanian raft derridean barge ship-wrecked in other words on the sea of fucked up literature where civilization can be measured assessed rather by the distance man places between himself and his excrement.

Jacques Derrida's notion of "differance" – the inevitable differing and deferring of signs from their meanings, and of art from reality – is the lesson of the postmodern fetish. For those still operating within the mind-set of modernism, it constitutes the tragedy of contemporary art.

Donald Barthelme, however, turns this situation into an occasion for wit. His *Snow White* (1967) is a romance based on the fairy tale of that name, brought up to date in terms of 1960s counterculture. In it, a beautiful girl, living with seven young men, longs for completion through the love of a handsome, existentially tormented writer. Here, in a much more humane way than in Hawkes, Barthelme indicates the relation of women to the fetish. Not only is Snow White herself a fetish object – beautiful, enthralling, a magnet for male response – but her dilemma is to have no other self-image than that. Longing for her prince to come, she experiences herself as incomplete, as an object needing to be perceived, vivified, loved by a destined mate. Given the death of destiny and the fundamental confusion among available princes, however, Snow White's prognosis is poor. The romance structure shamelessly evoked in this modern fairy tale, like that in Hawkes, Barth, Pynchon, and so many postmodernists, falls of its own weight, and yet the humor and irony that surround this collapse do not invalidate the gesture toward romance in the first place, the desperation of the search for value and some compensation for loss.

Snow White includes a questionnaire checking whether the reader has grasped salient aspects of the plot, asking advice for the following chapters, and soliciting opinions on crucial matters such as copyright legislation and the optimal number of shoulders for human beings. It also contains wonderful parodies of the literary canon, especially Eliot. Here, for example, Beckett and Shakespeare perform a duet as a character expresses horror at World War II atrocities: "Filthy Deutschmarks! That so eclipse the very mark and texture . . . That so eclipse the very mark and bosom of a man, that vileness herself is vilely o'erthrown. That so enfold . . . That so enscrap . . . Bloody Deutschmarks! that so enwrap the very warp and texture of a man, that what we cherished in him, vileness, is . . . Dies, his ginger o'erthrown. Bad pelf!" (Ellipses are Barthelme's.) The marriage of Shakespearean eloquence with Beckettian babble is entirely apt, paradoxical, funny.

Barthelme is best known for his short stories, collected in *Unspeakable Practices, Unnatural Acts* (1968), *City Life* (1970), and other volumes. Dramatizing absurdities in human relations, politics, and art, these fictions display an entertaining, deadpan puckishness. *The Dead Father* (1975), Barthelme's second novel, is about the displacement of the father and the quest for love, sex, and life that is actually a journey toward death. Embedded in the novel is a long, comical *Manual for Sons,* and the rest of the book is filled with Homeric/Joycean catalogues in a crazy mixture of myth and pop culture. Its comments on art are delectable. For example, on the tenth day of a gruesome sentence meted out by the Dead Father in a Gilbert-and-Sullivanesque attempt to make the punishment fit the crime, "the trifler is confined alone in a small room with the works of Teilhard de Chardin and the music of Karlheinz Stockhausen." Along with the humor and playfulness, however, Barthelme shows a fine sensitivity to language: "it is possible to admire the hair for a long time, many do, on a Sunday or other holiday or in those sandwich hours neatly placed between fattish slices of work." The "sandwich" aside is not crucial to either the action or the general tone of the novel; it is a surplus pleasure thrown in.

Other postmodernists, such as William Gaddis, for example, in his monumental *The Recognitions* (1955), have explored the intricacies and ironies of self-reflexiveness, but none has done so more publicly and programmatically than John Barth. With his many volumes of fiction; his writing instruction at Pennsylvania State University, State University of New York at Buffalo, and Johns Hopkins University; and his frequent essays in the *Atlantic Monthly* and the *New York Times Book Review,* Barth was held up during the 1960s and 1970s as the most prominent, skilled, and characteristic of the postmodernists, though the taste for his endless allegories of writing and exhaustion is now waning. His hilarious treatment of love both draws readers in and distances them from the text, in a more convivial version of Hawkes's antifetishism. Barth has a wicked sense of humor and a brilliantly disciplined intelligence; in the merging of irony and romance characteristic of late twentieth-century fiction, the balance in his work falls unsentimentally on the ironic.

Barth's first novel, *The Floating Opera* (1956), is programmatically existential. Its hero, Todd Andrews, who wishes to guard (guardedly) against a symbolic reading of his name, decides in the course of the book not to commit suicide. He has been troubled by the thought that all values are only relative, that his father is dead, that his own heart is probably diseased, that there is no reason to live. He has an affair with his friend's wife and may be the father of her child Jeannine. When he attempts suicide at the end, he is accidentally rescued by those who clear the gas out of the room, but also by his spontaneous and, to him, inexplicable concern for Jeannine, who has coincidentally fallen into convulsions. His confusion as to why he should care about a child in a world without meaning leads him to seek an answer. He realizes that if there is no reason to live there is equally no reason to commit suicide, and finds himself heartened by the fact that "there *are* relative values."

The eponymous Floating Opera, the minstrel showboat on which this fateful change of mind takes place, is an analogy to the novel itself – purportedly Todd's novel – which he writes to explain his change of heart. The novel has followed exactly the sequence of acts in the show, beginning with rather ponderous references to great literature, then proceeding through a certain amount of song and dance, and building to a catastrophe and gentle conclusion. The ingredients of Barth's fiction – existential angst, marital and readerly infidelity, a paralyzing limitlessness of possibilities, the incorporation of the novel into its own action, and the confusion of author, narrator, and character – are already in place with *The Floating Opera*. The influence of Beckett, Joyce, and Camus is obvious, soon to be augmented by Borges and Nabokov and the paradoxical games described in Douglas R. Hofstadter's *Gödel, Escher, Bach* (1979), a veritable handbook for the postmodern intellectual.

What is perhaps most remarkable in Barth's fiction is the variety of novelistic forms he attempts. *The Floating Opera* and *The End of the Road* (1958) are fairly conventional as novels, though very self-reflexive. Beginning with *The Sot-Weed Factor* (1960), however, Barth becomes more experimental. *The Sot-Weed Factor* is a historical novel written in the style of an eighteenth-century picaresque. It is full of disguises, hidden identities, false names, incest, and sexual exuberance in the tradition of Fielding. Its hero is initially unable to act because of the endless possibilities open to him. He decides finally to turn his sexual inabilities into a calling, that of the virgin poet. Accordingly, he sets sail for Maryland to become its poet laureate. Cured by the rites of the Sacred Eggplant, a Native American treatment for his sexual difficulties, he finally experiences love and then ceases to write good poetry. With its fusion of history, fantasy, and parody, *The Sot-Weed Factor* is a hilarious metafiction.

Barth's next work, *Giles Goat-Boy* (1966), subtitled *The Revised New Syllabus,* is a computer tape in six reels read out to the computer's son Giles. In it, a university curriculum becomes all of reality, and myth and cybernetics merge. As Barth writes in another novel, *Letters* (1979), "the 700-plus pages of *Giles Goat-Boy* have surfeited their author with that particular vein of 'transcendent parody' and (literally, of course) *sophomoric* allegory." After *Giles* came *Lost in the Funhouse: Fiction for Print, Tape, Live Voice* (1968), with its do-it-yourself Möbius strip called "Frame-Tale," reading endlessly, "Once upon a time there was a story that began," and its series of fresh starts, each in a new modal register.

Chimera (1972) follows – three novellas redoing *The Thousand and One Nights* and Greek mythology, each engendering the next, though not narratively continuous with it. "The Dunyazadiad" is the first and most appealing of the three, imagining the author as a genie (Genie) called up from the twentieth century by Scheherazade's (Sherry's) realization that "the key to the treasure *is* the treasure." The genie tells her *The Thousand and One Nights,* supplying her with stories to beguile her cruel husband so that she can stay alive. She accompanies them with innovative sexual exploits, witnessed by her sister Dunyazade (Doony), who is also her lover. "The Dunyazadiad," like most of Barth's work, is a story about the parallelism between lovemaking and fiction making, and the power relations between men and women and between authors and readers. It raises the issues of what "fidelity" to a text or author entails, who "originates" a work – author or reader – and what the nature of narrative power is in relation to existential dread. It is one of those sites in postmodern literature where a fiction writer seems to outdo the narratologist, revealing with hilarity and intellectual brilliance the relations among feminism, reception theory, and narrative.

After Sherry tells him a thousand and one stories, the King discontinues his nightly threat of death, and in celebration, marries Sherry's sister Doony to his brother, Shah Zaman, who is also thought to have been marrying and killing off young women. To stave off death at his hands, Doony promises the ultimate in lovemaking, which involves Shah Zaman's being bound hand and foot to the bed. She then tells him a story that, we realize, is the narrative of the one thousand and one nights we have just heard, and ends by revealing her intent to castrate Shah Zaman. He calls in his guards, who have been there all along, thus demonstrating that Doony wields no power over him that he has not willed. He then dismisses the guards, who return Doony's knife to her, and, remaining bound to the bed, he begs a boon: that he be allowed to tell *Doony* a story. He thus reverses yet again the power and gender relations between teller and audience. His initials, S. Z., call to mind Roland Barthes's treatise on narratology *S/Z* (1970; English translation, 1974), in which similar gender and power reversals proliferate, and the similarity of *Barth* and *Barthes* reinforces this association.

The story Shah Zaman tells is of the founding of a community of women: the Amazons (who turn up later in *Chimera* in "The Bellerophoniad"). He ends by revealing that his brother has known all along that Sherry was cheating on him with Doony and had allowed her, out of love, to do so. To accept infidelity, death, and impermanence and to embrace love is to learn that the "Key and the Treasure are the same." By implication, the failure of perfect understanding between author and reader is to be accepted as an occasion for laughter and love. The text still offers an invitation to perfect unity, to fetishistic reading – as Shah Zaman urges Doony, "Treasure me, treasure me" – but the fulfillment of this offer is deferred. The crowing of the cock interrupts the chapter before Doony can give her answer. "The Dunyazadiad" finishes with a frame tale in which the author extols *The Thousand Nights and a Night* and says, "If I could invent a story as beautiful," it would have Dunyazade and her bridegroom making love as equals. In saying this, however, he both performs the task and suggests it to be impossible, since he has had control of the invention all along. Barth almost allows us, in this novella, a rather beautiful feminist fable, a *Turandot* adjusted for indeterminacy.

Barth's next novel, the most massive of his mastodon-like productions, is *Letters* (1979), subtitled *An Old Time Epistolary Novel by Seven Fictitious Drolls and Dreamers Each of Which Imagines Himself Actual*. The seven drolls and dreamers are mostly characters from Barth's earlier novels who reveal their intertwined pasts and current involvements. The book begins with a letter from Lady Germaine Amherst inviting the Author to receive an honorary Doctor of Letters degree, which suggests to him the "doctoring of letters" that *Letters* is. He entangles his various characters in the design of this epistolary novel, making *them* its authors, and thus connecting the stylistic and thematic concerns of all of his past fiction.

The central action of the novel is the love of Ambrose Mensch, the novelist who takes the Author's place as the recipient of the Doctor of Letters, and Lady Germaine Amherst. Their love almost literally engenders this book (and the word *literally* in a book called *Letters* is not innocent). "*Conflict:* last-ditch provincial Modernist wishes neither to repeat nor to repudiate career thus far; wants the century under his belt but not on his back. *Complication:* he becomes infatuated with, enamored of, obsessed by a fancied embodiment . . . of the Great Tradition and puts her – and himself – through sundry more or less degraded trials . . . until he loses his cynicism and his heart to her spirited dignity and, at the *climax,* endeavors desperately, hopefully, perhaps vainly, to get her one final time with child: his, hers, theirs. (cc. Author)." "Cc. Author" indeed!

There is something heroic about tying everything one has ever written into a greater fiction: having the past enrich the future, as the motto of Marshyhope State University College reads, and all this on top of the history of the American Revolution and the Napoleonic wars. Brilliant as the effort is, however, its brilliance constantly degenerates into compulsiveness, and the "longeurs" of *Letters* are longer than almost anywhere else in literature. Barth went on to write *Sabbatical* (1982), "a half-assed autobiographic romance," as he termed it; *Tidewater Tales* (1987); and other novels that undermine the "facts" of history, painting, and literature. The intellectual range of his work is enormous, and the debunking of the decadent view of art as a self-enclosed world of perfect communication is as thoroughgoing – and ambiguous – as his play with love.

Kurt Vonnegut's writing constitutes an opposite pole to Barth's, if we imagine an experimentalist continuum running between them. Whereas Barth recapitulates history and his own previous novels within the affective constraints of a highly intellectual game, Vonnegut does so as an emotional liberal, with his political, aesthetic, and interpersonal assumptions laid bare, vulnerable for all to see. Barth's Author in *Letters* is a proper, colorless academic, whereas Vonnegut's "I" is himself. This "I" is a writer whose father was an architect, who grew up in Indianapolis, who witnessed the firebombing of Dresden, and who experienced the deaths of family members with the pained fatalism of his infuriating phrases, "So it goes" and "Hi ho." Unlike Barth, with his scholarly grasp of history and ancient mythology, Vonnegut exemplifies the fantasist side of postmodernism, using time warps, extraterrestrials, and miniaturized Chinese as analogues for the real-life incomprehensibilities of war, betrayal, and corruption. At his best, in *Mother Night* (1961), he is a truly hard-hitting ironist.

Vonnegut's work repeats certain themes, events, characters, and even phrases from novel to novel. Moreover, his fiction is always constructed the same way – out of short, somewhat disconnected episodes that gradually coalesce into a fully developed plot. *Mother Night,* for instance, is told in often outrageously incongruous episodes as "The Confessions of Howard W. Campbell, Jr.," but at the same time, its plot, once the reader puts it together, has all the suspense and surprise of a spy novel. Its dedication, "To Mata Hari," is not only funny but apt.

One of the central issues of *Mother Night* is the conflict between the personal and public spheres. The hero, Campbell, is an American-born writer living in Germany and married to an actress. He writes an erotic manuscript entitled *Memoirs of a Monogamous Casanova* to celebrate the "conquests of all the hundreds of women my wife, my Helga, had been. . . . There is not one word in it to indicate even the century or the continent of its origin." In this novel within a novel, the pair establish an imaginary Kingdom of Two in which they are totally absorbed in each other. This combination of pornography, high romance, and noncontingent value in Campbell's novel suggests a fetishizing of love that postmodernism likes to debunk.

As it turns out, however, the *Memoirs* are not a piece of sentimentality. Campbell's private writing is part of an overarching political aim, and the Kingdom of Two is in fact reality, for Campbell is an American spy whose cover is his job as a pro-Nazi radio propagandist. As he stirs up anti-Semitic hatred, the pauses and intonations in his talks transmit coded secrets essential to the American war effort. When Campbell's wife disappears during the war, her sister somehow manages to pass as Helga. She later confesses her identity to Campbell and they reestablish a Kingdom of Two, until Campbell discovers that she is actually a Soviet agent sent to kidnap him to Moscow. Helga is caught by the Americans and takes cyanide, claiming that she is dying for love. Impossible conflicts between love and politics, the private and public spheres, constantly recur. As Campbell complains, "The part of me that wanted to tell the truth got turned into an expert liar! The lover in me got turned into a pornographer! The artist in me got turned into ugliness such as the world has rarely seen before." The ironic contradictions that postmodernism revels in are here the stuff of personal tragedy.

Tempting as it is to accept the problem as a victimization by events, Campbell knows, however, that part of him desired his perversion. His spymaster argues that agents never take on their jobs for money or glory but because they enjoy playing their false roles. Campbell uses this truth to explain Nazism, in which otherwise kind, sensitive people promoted atrocities. Likewise, he preaches hatred and destruction, though with the excuse that no one could really accept what he said. He had intended, in fact, to be ludicrous, but people were too eager to hate to be able to see his humor.

The difficulty of discerning the comic and the ludicrous in a world gone mad is the challenge of Vonnegut's fiction. When Campbell is introduced to a Nazi youth group in New York, the Iron Guard of the White Sons of the American Constitution, he notes that they wear ribbons in a specially made buttonhole in their right lapel. He asks whether they get tailors to make the holes. "'Most tailors are Jews,' said Dr. Jones. 'We don't want to tip our hand.' 'Besides,' said Father Keeley, 'it's good for mothers to participate.'" As here, where the language of fascism merges with the language of the PTA, Vonnegut founds his comedy on the unnatural correspondences, the schizophrenia, of normal existence.

Slaughterhouse-Five, or The Children's Crusade: A Duty-Dance with Death (1969) again plays on the correspondence between history and fantasy. The hero, Billy Pilgrim, has come "unstuck" in time and travels instantaneously from the past to the present to the futuristic planet of Trafalmador, where he is kept in a cage in a zoo with a former porno star. Memory, actuality, and fantasy have equal reality for Billy, and the temporal jumps he makes are precisely those of the overall plot and of Vonnegut's fiction in general. Billy Pilgrim asks "Why me?" when the Trafalmadorians kidnap him in their spaceship, just as a soldier asks "Why me?" of his German captor during the Dresden episode. This correspondence is a kind of keyhole in time. The question itself, according to the Trafalmadorians, is the sort that only earthlings ask; wiser beings accept that everything must be as it is. Accordingly, though the author originally proposed to use the execution of a soldier caught stealing a teapot as the climax of the book, this event is reported on the last page as matter-of-factly as any of the other wild anticlimaxes. Billy's own death, foreseen by him, "occurs" two thirds of the way through the book. Even the death of the novel – the topic of a radio broadcast – is met with the fatalistic, though not callous, formula, "So it goes."

Breakfast of Champions (1973) is all about the death of the novel. Here a used-car mogul meets Ilgore Trout, a writer who has appeared in other Vonnegut novels. "Trout was the only character I ever created who had enough imagination to suspect that he might be the creation of another human being," says the narrator of *Breakfast of Champions*. Trout's book turns the used-car dealer into a homicidal maniac, because "Ideas or the lack of them can cause disease!" Likewise, the structure and context of fiction can cause people to behave abominably.

They were doing their best to live like people invented in story books. This was the reason Americans shot each other so often. It was a convenient literary device for ending short stories and books. . . . I resolved to shun storytelling. I would write about life. Every person would be exactly as important as any other. All facts would also be given equal weightiness. Nothing would be left out. Let others bring order to chaos. I would bring chaos to order, instead, which I think I have done.

Vonnegut does not quite achieve this, of course – there are still central and peripheral characters and events in his works – but the distribution of interest across his disjointed episodes and jokes goes a long way toward imitating the chaos and fragmentation of life.

Different as Hawkes, Barth, Vonnegut, and the others are, they do share a number of traits: the mixture of elaborate self-reflexivity, humor, and sex; the fixation on history and the bridging of past and present; the confusion of the boundary between fantasy and historical event; and the play with literary form, disjunction, and incongruity. These efforts constitute an examination – overt or unconscious – of the aesthetic and sexual fetish. The core of 1970s experimentalism is this "realizing" of literary exhaustion, the tempting critique of the depleted fetish object, art. Here lies the important difference between the experimental postmodernists and Thomas Pynchon. Though his work contains every one of the features mentioned above, it responds to them not with despair, frustration, ironic humor, or lascivious fascination – or at least not only with these emotions. Instead, Pynchon incorporates them into the world he depicts and he lays out the possibilities for action within it.

Pynchon began writing short stories in the late fifties while an undergraduate at Cornell University, and he has since published five novels: *V.* (1963), *The Crying of Lot 49* (1966), *Gravity's Rainbow* (1973), *Vineland* (1990), and *Mason & Dixon* (1997). The early short stories, collected in a volume entitled *Slow Learner* (1984), establish many of the themes of his later work; for example, the "spy story" "Under the Rose" is cannibalized in *V.* and *Gravity's Rainbow,* and the ideas in "Entropy" recur in *Lot 49.* Pynchon has, in addition, written a few essays for the *New York Times Book Review,* but apart from the occasional review, he has been known to the public only through his fiction. He went into hiding after college, and his whereabouts remained unknown until a web site appeared in 1996 claiming he lived in New York with his agent-wife and his children. Pynchon has outdone even J. D. Salinger as a postmodern recluse.

The only statement Pynchon published about his work appears in the introduction to *Slow Learner.* There he speaks of the temptation he felt as a young author to "'Make it literary,' a piece of bad advice I made up all by myself and then took." The play here on "Make it new," a slogan of modernism, is typical of Pynchon, who uses modernism as the major premise from which to proceed and diverge. By "literary" he seems to mean "allusive" – of Eliot and Hemingway in "Small Rain," and of a vast array of writers in his other work. Pynchon's novels, however, were not less "literary" than his stories; instead, the allusion in them seems better integrated into plot and theme, often itself becoming a theme.

In the introduction to *Slow Learner,* Pynchon also notes his fascination with the Surrealist concept of metaphor – the "simple idea that one could combine inside the same frame elements not normally found together to produce illogical and startling effects. What I had to learn later on was the necessity of managing this procedure with some degree of care and skill: any old combination of details will not do." As with "making it literary," the problem was to master the device rather than eliminate it.

Third, Pynchon claims he learned the following maxim from writing "Entropy": "get too conceptual, too cute and remote, and your characters die on the page." All of his writing is haunted by the conflict between idea and character, and this because of the central postmodern problem of how to relate theory to experience. Maybe this opposition explains why his characters sometimes carry over from one work to another, like heroes of medieval romance or comic books: they are embodiments of assumptions that perennially occupy their author, rather than unique psychological inventions like Flaubert's or James's characters. Pynchon clearly worries abut the abstraction of his work, and this concern leads him to belittle *The Crying of Lot 49,* "in which I seem to have forgotten most of what I thought I'd learned up till then." The heroine of this book, however, is no flatter than the hero of *Gravity's Rainbow,* and the action no more remote.

Rather, the problem is that the short, schematic *Lot 49* is brushing the boundaries of allegory, and Pynchon's whole literary stance is peculiarly antiallegorical – peculiarly, because at the same time Pynchon constructs all the elaborate conditions necessary for allegorical reading. *V.,* for example, is a veritable study of parallelism: the modern present and the fabled past; the above-ground of New York City with its disaffected, decadent Whole Sick Crew, and the underground world of the sewers with their alligator hunts and sorties of demented Jesuits preaching love and salvation to susceptible lady rats; the mundane boredom of Benny Profane's America and the romance of Malta or the "private colonies of the imagination" of the land of Vheissu. Benny's life is a "yo-yoing" between worlds, as the text describes it, a tense oscillation between opposites. Pynchon's work explores the tendency to proliferate levels, for, as a wonderful, anti-Wittgensteinian song of his explains, "If the world is all that the case is/ That's a pretty discouraging basis/ On which to pursue/ Any sort of romance." Romance, with its immersion in the problem of the fetish, its superimposition of fantasy on reality, and its polarization of values, is the only antidote to exhaustion.

For *V.,* adventure, love, engagement, and ultimately plot all depend on our constructing a world more complex than what the case is, and this construction is founded on the parallelism of worlds that composes allegory. Without such layering there is no romance, and one ends up like the Whole Sick Crew, living in an advanced state of decadence. Pynchon presents this decadence as a version of the literary exhaustion discussed in chapter 1 of this section. The Whole Sick Crew are beatniks, schlemiels, and avant-garde artists, one of whom is painting an ongoing series of *Cheese Danish* canvases. "They produced nothing but talk and at that not very good talk. A few like Slab actually did what they professed; turned out a tangible product. But again, what? Cheese Danishes. Or this technique for the sake of technique – Catatonic Expressionism. Or parodies of what someone else had already done. . . . This sort of arranging and rearranging was Decadence, but the exhaustion of all possible permutations and combinations was death." Pynchon is referring to Abstract Expressionism and Pop art, the exploration of formal means or trivial subjects even when these lead to pure redundancy. That both life and art could be a mere shuffling of variables, an exhaustion of possibilities, is the specter haunting *V.*'s central character Benny Profane. It is a situation that generates other worlds, allegorical layers, the wish-fulfillment realms of romance.

The trouble with projecting romance layers, however, is that these alternate worlds may themselves prove empty: simple mirrorings of the decadence that generated them. The character Stencil from the spy plot represents this possibility. He has devoted his whole adult life to a search analogous to the most orthodox romance quest for what he thinks might be a woman, V. From Malta to New York to the mythical Vheissu (perhaps, *"Wie heisst du?"* or *"V. heisst du"*), through all the vicissitudes of twentieth-century European history, he has looked for clues beginning with the letter *V* to an image that he became fixated on in his youth – Queen Victoria, the girl Victoria Wren, the rat Veronica, Vera Meroving, Helvig Vogelsand, Botticelli's Venus, the Maltese capital Valletta, the lost Vivaldi *Kazoo Concerto*. By the end of the book, however, he is no closer to finding V. or the "truth" about her. "Stencil sketched the entire history of V. that night and strengthened a long suspicion. That it did add up only to the recurrence of an initial and a few dead objects." Trying to stamp all of reality into a meaningful if compulsive pattern – trying to stencil it – to see his "grand Gothic pile of inferences" cohere, Stencil must always face the possibility that reality is a mere collocation, "a few dead objects." The "scattering" of characters, the literal bodily disassembly of the decadent False Priest in one episode, and the removable parts of characters – feet, eyes – express this ever-present possibility of fragmentation and disorder, of entropy, as Pynchon labels it in his short story and in *Lot 49*. On the one hand, we have the stenciled redundancy of a cookie-cutter psyche; on the other, the anarchic fragmentation of a mind that "can connect/ Nothing with nothing."

Almost any price is worth paying to avoid confronting a purely entropic vision, or even the tamer version of a mere cause-and-effect universe where everything runs by mechanical, inhuman laws. Thus, the narrator informs us that

No apologia is any more than a romance – half a fiction – in which all the successive identities taken on and rejected by the writer as a function of linear time are treated as separate characters. . . . So we do sell our souls, paying them away to history in little installments. It isn't so much to pay for eyes clear enough to see past the fiction of continuity, the fiction of cause and effect, the fiction of a humanized history endowed with "reason."

If continuity, cause and effect, and a humanized history are all fictions to be disdained then the alternative worlds of romance might equally be fabrications. The poet Fausto Maijstral implies as much when he formulates a theory of two worlds: the street and under the street, the kingdom of death and the kingdom of life. At the same time, he claims that he lives in the world of metaphor and therefore "is always acutely conscious that metaphor has no value apart from its function; that is as a device, an artifice." The assumptions behind reality are all fictions, but so are the romance artifices we build to belie them. Stencil, dedicated against all odds to the search for the romance ultimate, finally gives up his critical faculties and opts for blind faith. He ends up in an affair with a character called Veronica Manganese, sunk in a fetishistic nostalgia so deep that he becomes totally alienated from time and history, just as the capital of Malta, Valletta, from a distance deteriorates into a mere spectacle and is "assumed again into the textual stillness of her own history." This willed surrender to a fiction – either that of the romance underworld or the matter-of-fact reality in plain sight, appears as an unfortunate weakness, an abnegation of one's vitality in the game played out between the two worlds.

Benny Profane, still a schlemiel yo-yoing between worlds, emerges from the adventure with the antinomies intact. He has not found an answer or learned anything definitive about the meaning of life. To have learned would have been either to fall in with the underworld of metaphor or to accept and pump up formal reality. Either of these strategies involves a flat allegorical consciousness, in Pynchon's view, an $x = y$ logic.

V. tries to train the reader in the avoidance of such thinking. The *Cheese Danish* artist, Slab, in a bold attempt to separate himself from Catatonic Expressionism and simultaneously replace the cross in Western symbolism, paints a striking picture. It represents a foiled perpetual motion machine: a partridge in a pear tree that will die. The symbolism works as follows: the partridge eats the pears and its droppings fertilize the tree, causing the tree to grow taller and produce more pears for the partridge to eat, with the result that he will produce more droppings and so on ad infinitum. Since *perdix* means partridge (the "pear"/"per" being in the partridge as much as the partridge in the pear tree), a pun runs the machine, and possibly an obscene pun. At the top of the painting, however, Slab has placed a gargoyle with sharp fangs. As the tree grows, the partridge will one day be impaled on the gargoyle's teeth, for, as we are told, the bird has forgotten how to fly. "I detect allegory in all this," says Slab's interlocutor. "'No,' said Slab. 'That is on the same intellectual level as doing the Times crossword puzzle on Sunday. Phony. Unworthy of you.'" Allegorical readings reduce complexity, flatten levels, opt mechanically or sentimentally for a simplicity of meaning that is no longer available. The trick is to use the correspondence of levels while keeping them distinct.

Pynchon expresses this paradoxical antiallegorism through an elaborate theory of mirrors and voyeurism that culminates in the oddest episode of an extraordinarily odd book – the affair between the woman V. and the young dancer Mélanie discussed at the beginning of this chapter. Their relationship is pure decadence: Mélanie on the bed in exotic costume contemplates herself in a mirror with V. watching. "An adolescent girl whose existence is so visual observes in a mirror her double; the double becomes a voyeur. . . . She needs, it seems, a real voyeur to complete the illusion that her reflections are, in fact, this audience. With the addition of this other . . . comes consummation: for the other is also her own double." Voyeurism becomes narcissism, a doubling of the self. It is the construction of a fetish, the text asserts, that serves the Kingdom of Death, for it guarantees the correspondence of layers, the mechanical adequacy of illusion to reality. It prevents the honest confusion of a schlemiel like Benny Profane, who, like Kilroy, "was possibly the only objective onlooker in Valletta that night."

Pynchon goes to some trouble to identify Mélanie as a fetish. "Come, fétiche, inside," one character calls to her, and just in case she does not understand the term, Mélanie is given a definition. "Do you know what a fetish is? Something of a woman which gives pleasure but is not a woman. A shoe, a locket . . . une jarretière. You are the same, not real but an object of pleasure." Since Mélanie's nickname is "La Jarretière" (The Garter), the connection to the Freudian fetish is direct. The forming of fetishes is at the very essence of decadence, like the *Cheese Danish* works of Slab or the day-to-day existence of the Whole Sick Crew. "A decadence is a falling away from what is human," we are told. "Because we are less human, we foist off the humanity we have on inanimate objects and abstract theories."

Pynchon undermines this decadent strategy by revealing the inhumanity of the art used as a fetish. He symbolizes the lost penis of Freud's fetish with a theatrical or ˃ that is all too present: the phallic sword upon which Mélanie is mistakenly impaled in the ballet. Art's alleged compensation for loss turns out to be a kind of death. This revelation releases V. from her fixation and allows her to return to her elusive role as Other. In the process, the decadent theory of art as a replacement or compensation for life is totally discredited.

If art is not a compensation for loss and incommensurability, then what is its value? Pynchon explores this problem in his second novel, *The Crying of Lot 49*. There he continues his meditation on narcissism in an overt quest romance, with his heroine Oedipa Maas starting out on a trip to San Narciso. Once before, she had been faced with a solipsistic dilemma. She had seen a painting by the Surrealist Remedios Varo (another V.) of maidens locked in a tower, embroidering a tapestry that flowed out the windows to form the world outside. She knew then that she was also a captive maiden locked in the tower of herself. All of reality, all knowledge, she realized, is a function of the knowing self, but that self cannot account for its own nature. She may learn that the shape of reality is prescribed by the mind that constructs it, but that shaping mind remains utterly mysterious to itself.

Under the circumstances, Oedipa finds herself in the same dilemma as everyone else: forced to found the shape of reality on an arbitrary account of the mystery. "Such a captive maiden . . . soon realizes that her tower, its height and architecture, are like her ego only incidental: that what really keeps her where she is is magic, anonymous and malignant, visited on her from outside and for no reason at all." People have reacted to this fact by taking a leap of faith into religion, by going mad, by immersing themselves in some enthralling busywork such as making art, or by falling in love. For Oedipa, though, all of these are unheroic compromises. Her response is to sink into a thoughtless, anaesthetized existence as the suburban wife of a disc jockey.

What propels her out of this world is a posthumous request from an old lover, Pierce Inverarity. He makes her coexecutrix of his will and thus forces her to take on "interests." The need to execute Pierce's will sets Oedipa on an incredible quest to discover what his interests in fact were. In the process, she uncovers an underground world as elaborate as those in *V.*, full of disaffected splinter organizations who communicate through a secret mail system called W.A.S.T.E., the modern counterpart of a mysterious "Trystero System."

Names full of puns and symbolism, the multiplication of worlds, a heroine-questor sent to "execute a will" that becomes her own — all these are the standard devices of allegory, and yet Pynchon cuts the ground out from anyone intent on performing an allegorical interpretation of this book. As Oedipa uncovers more and more clues, she also finds more and more indications that the secret world might all be under Inverarity's control. By the time she exposes the intricate network of information and "leads," Oedipa is left with this set of possibilities: "Either you have stumbled . . . onto a secret richness and concealed density of dream. . . . Or you are hallucinating it. Or a plot has been mounted against you, so expensive and elaborate . . . so labyrinthine that it must have meaning beyond just a practical joke. Or you are fantasying some such plot, in which case you are a nut, Oedipa, out of your skull." Either there is a world outside her or she is deluding herself, or someone is trying to trick her into believing in a world outside herself or she is fantasizing that plot. The evidence for paranoia on either level is as compelling as that for reality, and Oedipa is left precisely where she started with the picture of the maidens locked in their tower – except that her response this time is not to retreat into indifference but to continue the quest, to "keep the ball bouncing," as Pierce Inverarity used to say.

Oedipa is in fact doing what one of the tower maidens in Varo's painting does, weaving a trap in the tapestry so that she can escape. *Embroidering the Terrestrial Cloak* is the central canvas of a triptych, whose third image shows the maiden and her lover fleeing from the tower toward a grotto. As in *The Crying of Lot 49,* we do not see them reaching the world of escape, but the process of their trying to do so is represented. Rather than a static, solipsistic view of reality and art, Varo's triptych shows how fetishistic repetition and self-absorption can be transformed into dynamic adventure, and how a self-enclosed visual object can become an open-ended narrative when it enters the life of a viewer or reader. To have formulated this response to the epistemological dilemma of modernity is Pynchon's great contribution to contemporary letters. The humor, honesty, and sophistication – the humanism – of his writing set a standard for artistic generosity.

The Crying of Lot 49 is particularly instructive in that it takes off so directly from high modernism. It is in many respects a rewrite of *The Waste Land.* Both texts examine solipsism as the source of our inability to know reality: Pynchon through the Varo painting and the trip to San Narciso, and Eliot through Bradley's tower where the key turns once in the lock and once only. Both works are concerned with our relation to history in a world of epistemological uncertainty. Eliot shows traditional plots of natural renewal and metamorphosis failing, historical documents and typological interpretation grown undependable, the cultural and political past left "a heap of broken images." Pynchon goes over the same ground but relativizes Eliot's position through his humor and archness. Both works are quest romances, making direct reference to the Grail legends. And, of course, with Pynchon's underground mail system named W.A.S.T.E., both works consider the viability of communication itself in a world where we cannot know that we know reality, ourselves, or each other.

The Waste Land and Lot 49, moreover, are riddled with literary allusion. The modernist Eliot uses it as a sign of the falling away of culture, of the meaningless debris remaining after value and faith have departed. The postmodern Pynchon reconstrues allusion as the merger of worlds, the magical point of contact between the present and the past, the mundane and the fabulous, flat reality and the multifarious underworld lurking beneath it. Like the pun or the surrealist metaphor, allusion is the occasion of miracle, erupting through context to reveal a truth independent of contingency. This rewriting of Eliot indicates Pynchon's departure from modernism, as does his robust low-culture voice, constantly undercutting the high seriousness of his themes, turning allegory into a rich, if bewildering, array of possibilities, and tempering modernist elitism and angst with humor and vitality.

If Lot 49 reveals Pynchon's relation to modernism, however, it also exploits the art of his own time, especially Pop art. Both thematize the narrow line between repetition and narrative cause and effect, boredom and frenetic emotion, bathos and meaning. Both are profoundly concerned with communication, the Trystero System having a real-life source in the late Pop artist Ray Johnson's New York Correspondence School of Art. In this unlikely institution, friends, artists, and chance contacts were drawn into a Dadaesque exchange of greetings, clippings, and miscellaneous information. Though John Barth would categorize such art as mere experimentalism, its openness to chance and its entertainment of the both/and rather than the binary either/or make it a proper opening to postmodernism. Pynchon gathers both the high art of the past and the experimentalism of the 1950s and 1960s into a recipe for future art.

Pynchon's third novel, Gravity's Rainbow, is a fleshing out of Lot 49's schematism into a long and often difficult work. Its hero, Tyrone Slothrop, is a slicker and more mature version of V.'s Benny Profane. He comes of a long line of New England Puritans, counting among his forebears one Constant Slothrop and one Variable. Since his initials are T. S., and assuming, as he notes, that they do not stand for "Tough Shit," Slothrop seems yet again a gesture toward T. S. Eliot. Gravity's Rainbow is Slothrop's long, involved quest for a technological Holy Grail: the fabulous erectile plastic Imipolex G and the Schwartzgerat or black device that will trigger the Germans' A4 Rocket to win World War II. Diving after a harmonica that has fallen down a toilet, Slothrop enters an alternate, Alice-in-Wonderland reality in which one wild adventure leads to another.

Slothrop's quest, however, is a frame-up, a psychological experiment run by mad scientists in London who need a "projective test," an unstructured stimulus onto which Slothrop will impose a structure. He is their target because he has been marking his sexual conquests with stars on a map of London, and the distribution of these stars mysteriously corresponds to that of the Germans' rocket strikes. Because Tyrone dates his stars, the scientists are able to discover that a "star always comes *before* its corresponding rocket strike." They deduce that Slothrop has some peculiar mental power enabling him to anticipate the enemy's rocket attacks, a power detecting effects before their causes, responses before stimuli. They attribute this power to Slothrop's paranoia:

Pavlov was fascinated with "ideas of the opposite." . . . Helping to distinguish pleasure from pain, light from dark, dominance from submission. . . . But when, somehow . . . you weaken this idea of the opposite, and here all at once is the paranoid patient who would be master, yet now feels himself a slave. . . . It is precisely the *ultraparadoxical phase* which is the basis of the weakening of the idea of the opposite."

When one of the scientists points out that some people feel the idea of cause and effect has been taken as far as it can go and that science must look for a broader set of assumptions if it is to continue, the suggestion is brushed aside as sentimental yin–yang rubbish. Thus, in order to establish Slothrop's ultraparadoxical reversals of cause and effect, the scientists create a paranoid situation. They engineer a vast plot involving the training of an octopus to attack a woman so that Slothrop can save her, have a passionate affair with her, and in the process be watched and manipulated. The scientists create the paranoia they wish to observe, reversing stimulus and response, becoming themselves ultraparadoxical. By implication, World War II as a whole might have been just such a logical reversal, a struggle caused by technology, generating a politics that was made to look like the real cause. Military technology did not arise to fulfill the needs of war, but war arose to fulfill the needs of technology. Thus, "politics was all theatre." This, of course, is a paranoid view.

The opposite of this idea is the acceptance of pure chance, randomness. As in all of Pynchon's fiction, we are confronted with the contrast between paranoid redundancy and deathlike entropy. Paranoia is much the more human choice: "Anti-paranoia, where nothing is connected to anything, [is] a condition not many of us can bear for long." The jovial Pig Bodine, who appeared in *V.* as well, assures Slothrop that *Everything* is some kind of a plot, man," but within a few pages he is mistaken for Slothrop and erroneously castrated by army doctors. Slothrop himself by the end of the book is being broken down and scattered by his experience, his Tarot pointing toward "no clear happiness or redeeming cataclysm." He has been merely a "pretext."

The A4 rocket is the focus for the book's symbolism because its flight involves a true merging of opposites, male and female, law and chance. "Ascending, programmed in a ritual of love . . . at Brennschluss it is done – the Rocket's purely feminine counterpart, the zero point at the center of its target, has submitted. All the rest will happen according to the laws of ballistics. The Rocket is helpless in it. Something else has taken over. Something beyond what was designed in." This something else is perhaps reality, the alterity beyond paranoid design; it sounds a lot like death as well. The analogy with sex is the central conceit of the book, Slothrop's erections and orgasms exactly correlated – by design or by chance – with the explosions of rockets, a physiological basis for behavior indeed.

The symbolism of the title involves these two possibilities. Gravity is what holds the world together, compacting its surface into the multiple levels of history (and allegory). "Gravity, taken so for granted, is really something eerie, Messianic, extrasensory in earth's mindbody . . . having hugged to its holy center the wastes of dead species." The rocket's ascent, however, is just the opposite of this centripetal impulse. The novel ends with a rocket blast. "This ascent will be betrayed to Gravity. But the Rocket engine, the deep cry of combustion that jars the soul, promises escape. The victim, in bondage to falling, rises on a promise, a prophesy, of Escape." The rocket's flight is a romance flight, a promise of individual control and assertion that must inevitably be betrayed by the reality of death, history, weight. And yet, when the rocket does come down at the end, it comes down into a "theatre," a world of fantasy and wish fulfillment.

The rainbow in the title is a humanization of the necessity of descent. It stands for light and beauty tamed by gravity/reality, but also fecundating the earthly necessity that draws it down. Slothrop stands by a crossroad watching a rainbow, "a stout rainbow cock driven down out of pubic clouds into Earth, green wet valleyed Earth, and his chest fills and he stands crying, not a thing in his head, just feeling natural." This passage, like many in the novel, creates a moment of poignance as rich and evocative as any in the great fictions of the past, and the love scenes are filled with a sensuousness and power not matched elsewhere in Pynchon's work. To his habitual Rabelaisian excess – the outrageous treatments of excretion, orgiastic eating, and sex – is added an intense, caring sensitivity, an abundant humanism that balances the cruelty and indifference of Slothrop's Theatre of War.

Gravity's Rainbow is a masterpiece, and yet, like that other case of an American encyclopedic novel, *Moby-Dick,* it presents enormous problems for the reader. Its narrative flows oneirically, as if produced by the drug Oneirine within it. Its most likely counterpart in the twentieth century is

James Joyce's *Ulysses,* and yet the experience of reading the two is utterly different. Joyce's work is divided into coherent chapters, each a rendering of all the rest through a new stylistic lens. Though Pynchon also plays with stylistic levels and variants (particularly in *V.* and *The Crying of Lot 49*), the chapter divisions of *Gravity's Rainbow* do not function as attentional and structural demarcations. The reader does not have the relief of such breaks and new beginnings.

In one passage, Pynchon gives us an image of *Gravity's Rainbow.* He begins with an echo of *The Waste Land*: the figures walking in a Dantean hell in their daily progress to work over London Bridge, as if the very structure of the novel were a vision of the tedious agony of modernity. "Who would have thought so many would be here? They keep appearing, all through this disquieting structure, gathered in groups, pacing alone in meditation, or studying the paintings, the books, the exhibits. It seems to be some very extensive museum, a place of many levels, and new wings that generate like living tissue – though if it all does grow toward some end shape, those who are here inside can't see it."

The end of this passage echoes Lorenzo's speech to Jessica in *The Merchant of Venice* about the music of the spheres. "Such harmony," he concludes, "is in immortal souls;/ But whilst this muddy vesture of decay/ Doth grossly close it in, we cannot hear it." As with divine harmony, we who live within the proliferating wings of Pynchon's museum cannot see the shape toward which the architecture tends, or toward which the novel tends either. The heroism it demands of the reader resembles that of Camus's Sysiphus. For unlike Joyce, whose *Ulysses* is a paradoxical play with closure, or a slick fabulator like John Barth, who presents the formulas of uncertainty with little of its emotion, Pynchon's *Gravity's Rainbow* is uncompromising in its indeterminacy and in its dramatization of the feel of this state. It leaves the reader with a never-ending responsibility to it – a text – in a life unfortunately filled with practical contingency. The reader's task is thus directly implicated in the impossible antinomies of Pynchon's art.

3

❧

THE END OF TRADITIONALISM

AT THE BEGINNING of the 1970s, "serious" American fiction was
defined in terms of two predominantly male camps: Thomas
Pynchon, John Barth, John Hawkes, and other "High
Postmodernists" on the one hand, and such literary traditionalists as Saul
Bellow, Norman Mailer, Joseph Heller, John Updike, Joyce Carol Oates,
John Cheever, and Philip Roth on the other. The most obvious difference
between the two groups was that the experimentalists worked on two levels – the fictive and the metafictive – spinning out stories that were simultaneously the stories of those stories. The traditionalists, though their
protagonists were often writers, valued the level of the primary fiction
above any musings about it and held up this involvement as a sign of their
humanism, their commitment to values. They explored the psychology of
class and ethnicity: the self-absorption of Bellow's Herzog, with his perpetual writer's block; the failed dreams of Mailer's early characters; the desperate, doomed attempts of Updike's "little man" in the Rabbit novels to
escape his meaningless life; the scandals and boredom of Oates's suburbs or
Cheever's small-town America; and the hilarious degradations of the second-generation American Jew, Roth's Portnoy. The novels were mostly
male in outlook and authorship, masterful in style but never calling attention to this mastery, and extremely appealing to their audience. This writing represented popular educated taste in 1970. It is surprising how dated
much of it now appears.

What is even more surprising is how inadequate the division between
experimental and traditional writing soon became. The survivors in the
traditionalist group, almost to a person, could not so easily be classed as
psychological or sociological fictionists as the 1970s progressed. Norman
Mailer, in a sequence of stunning works culminating in *The Executioner's
Song* (1979), tested the paradoxical limits of the fiction/reality opposition
so adroitly that one almost forgives him his egotism and impossibly chauvinist treatment of women. Joyce Carol Oates became a kind of traditionalist John Barth, parodying the historical novel in *The Bloodsmoor Romance*
(1982), Hemingway or Mailer in an essay on boxing, and a whole array of
forms and styles in other works. And Philip Roth's *The Anatomy Lesson*

(1983) is a comic masterpiece as fully "postmodern" as any novel by Pynchon. The merging of traditional and experimental approaches is so marked among writers just coming to maturity in the 1970s and 1980s that one would be hard pressed to categorize a Don DeLillo or Tim O'Brien as either one. Few important novelists now write without attention to both plot and metaplot, character and author/audience, history and the history of literature.

The historical events contributing to this shift were the Vietnam War and the domestic disruptions of the early 1970s – Watergate, racial strife, and the rise of feminism. Vietnam was perhaps the most decisive. The war was covered by an army of reporters, some of them writers of note. During the Tet Offensive alone there were between six hundred and seven hundred accredited correspondents in Vietnam. Beyond these, large numbers of public figures, politicians, academics, and people of conscience visited the war and wrote about it. Susan Sontag's "Trip to Hanoi" (1968), Daniel Berrigan's *Night Flight to Hanoi* (1968), Mary McCarthy's *Vietnam* (1967) and *The Seventeenth Degree* (1974), Hannah Arendt's *Crises of the Republic* (1972), and Noam Chomsky's *American Power and the New Mandarins* (1969), *At War with Asia* (1970), and *For Reasons of State* (1973) are just a few of the books intellectuals wrote to help stop the war. Antiwar sentiment penetrated every area of American culture, in the folk songs of Bob Dylan and Joan Baez; the rock 'n' roll of the Beatles, the Rolling Stones, and Jimi Hendrix; Pop art and the collages of Robert Rauschenberg and Jasper Johns; and in every aspect of university life. If the 1960s celebrated the "youth generation" – the population bulge produced after World War II – the reality that generation learned in its classes, parties, television news, and political rallies was a reality of violence and guilt unprecedented in American history.

In reading the reportage and fiction of the Vietnam War, one of course feels its similarity to the writing surrounding any war. The dehumanization, cruelty, and absurdity of the experience are the same as that presented in Stephen Crane, Ernest Hemingway, or Henry Miller. The disorientation of the returning soldier had already been memorialized in Gertrude Stein's phrase "the lost generation" and in Hemingway's fictions "Soldier's Home" and *The Sun Also Rises*. The plight of the lower classes and of blacks, who, as Clyde Taylor wrote, "died fighting in somebody else's war," was at least as deplorable in World War I as Vietnam. What sets this experience of war apart from the others was its relation to the commentary surrounding it. Again, propaganda and rhetoric are inevitable concomitants of battle, but the volume of the *verbal warfare* waged about Vietnam was unprecedented. This was not only America's longest war but its first televised war.

Correspondents traveled freely in the war zones, and the army and marines cooperated fully with them, much to the later embarrassment of the General Staff. Vietnam was a war fought on two fronts – Indochina and America; it was waged as much with words and pictures as with bombs and helicopters.

Just as with the civil rights movement, the media presented themselves in the role of honest observer in Vietnam, a force that would keep officials straight and the public involved. When the media were more and more blamed for the American defeat in Indochina, James Reston wrote that this accusation was "another way of challenging the whole idea of democracy." The fact that the press and television *could* be blamed for the loss of a war was the astonishing development in Vietnam. Because the antiwar movement demanded popular involvement and the media presented the horrors of battle more vividly and relentlessly than in any previous war, the *American* front in the Vietnam struggle became crucial. It changed history. In the pivotal Tet Offensive, the military reported an American victory and the media declared an American defeat. Because of the official lack of credibility by that point, the media's story was widely accepted, though it turned out to be mistaken. This interpretive vertigo precipitated the end of Lyndon Johnson's presidency.

As Michael Herr, the *Esquire* correspondent in Vietnam, wrote in *Dispatches* (1977), "sooner or later all of us heard one version or another of 'My Marines are winning this war, and you people are losing it for us in your papers.'" The whole population witnessed the conflict between official statement and eyewitness report, between the enormity of war and the government's optimistic statistics. The effect was to turn what before had been a strictly highbrow belief in the permeability of fiction and reality – so crucial to postmodern experimentalism – into a commonplace. The most esoteric, academic speculation was suddenly validated by everyday experience.

Virtually every article on Vietnam commented on this peculiar merging of reality and fiction. For example, both eyewitness reports and scholarly histories remark on the fact that people described Vietnam in terms of the movies. John Wayne's behavior in World War II adventure films was one of the most popular models, but even more fundamental was the notion that the war was a kind of performance. "It took me a month," Michael Herr wrote, "to lose that feeling of being a spectator to something that was part game, part show," and the sociologist Lloyd B. Lewis argued that American soldiers had been "taught by the media that experience was to be objectified and cast in terms of viewer and viewed."

When there were no swashbuckling heroes, though, when the enemy were often innocent children or whole towns of civilians, and when the dramatic spectacle turned out to be life-threatening to the viewer, people reacted with considerable disorientation. "I can come up with no connecting thread to tie events neatly together," Philip Caputo wrote in *A Rumor of War* (1977). Tim O'Brien's powerful memoir, *If I Die in a Combat Zone* (1973), relates how "things happened, things came to an end. There was no sense of developing drama." Ronald J. Glasser described this antifictive quality of experience in *365 Days* (1971): "There is no novel in Nam, there is not enough for a plot, nor is there really any character development." This war, taken at first as a script, refused to conform to anything in the movies or fiction.

Kurt Vonnegut's persona in *Slaughterhouse-Five* complains about this resistance of war to art and produces, as a result, a different kind of novel, plot, and character. For him, however, it is the sheer meaninglessness of the Dresden bombing that defies a conventional novelistic treatment. Certainly the spate of titles like Norman Mailer's *Why Are We in Vietnam?* (1967), Sam Brown and Len Ackland's *Why Are We Still in Vietnam?* (1970), and Norman Podhoretz's *Why We Were in Vietnam* (1982) suggests the same bewilderment. The universal tendency to act and interpret Vietnam in conformity with fictive models and the subsequent foiling of that tendency, made the soldier's and correspondent's experience not merely a brush with such existential truth as all war provides, but with linguistic relativism and postmodern verbal indeterminacy. For a good part of the 1970s, Vietnam writing was typically personal narrative; fiction seemed unable to handle it. Not till the late 1970s and the 1980s did the important novels and films about the war appear, and they took full cognizance of both the pressing need to see the war as fiction and the cruel frustration of this need.

The withdrawn invitation to fiction can be traced to the pervasiveness of the contemporary media, with their training of the public in the habits of voyeurism. Again, the aim of the media was anything but the creation of a merely voyeuristic populace. The slogan "The whole world is watching," chanted at the Democratic convention in 1968, was meant to instill responsibility in decision makers and public alike – the first because their actions had been made visible to the constituency whose desires they were elected to represent and whose moral sense they were sworn to uphold, the second because the act of watching should indicate commitment, caring, and participation. Voyeurism, in contrast, fetishizes the act of watching, making it into an end in itself, aestheticizing and fictionalizing what is viewed. The more that viewers watched the incessant coverage of Vietnam, however, the more powerless they felt to change it. Knowledge was definitely not power, and to go on watching anyway began to seem not ethical but prurient. Powerlessness and prurience proved more realistic assess-ments of the effects of war coverage than the responsibility and efficacy that leftists felt would automatically come of constant exposure.

Michael Herr describes the voyeuristic dilemma in *Dispatches*:

> I was there to watch. Talk about impersonating an identity, about locking into a role, about irony. I went to cover the war and the war covered me; an old story, unless of course you've never heard it. I went there behind the crude but serious belief that you had to be able to look at anything, serious because I acted on it and went, crude because I didn't know, it took the war to teach it, that you were as responsible for everything you saw as you were for everything you did. The problem was that you didn't always know what you were seeing until later, maybe years later, that a lot of it never made it in at all, it just stayed stored there in your eyes. Time and information, rock and roll, life itself, the information isn't frozen, you are.

The freezing of the self, the inability to process an overflow of bewildering information, and the transformation of the viewer from an actor on reality to a victim of it are concomitants of voyeurism. The only more powerful recent treatment of this theme is the work of Thomas Pynchon; it is the norm in experimental postmodernism.

With this in mind, we can perhaps understand the effectiveness of the Vietnam War Memorial. It is a long, winding, polished stone wall inscribed with the names of the soldiers who died in the war. There is no editorializing; no heroic idealization goes on, as in the Iwo Jima monu-ment commemorating the Marines slain in World War II. The Vietnam wall indicates that these were specific individuals, each with a different name, who died in a faraway war. The polished stone reflects the faces of those who read the names of the dead, and so the acts of reading, viewing, and mourning become part of the content of the memorializing itself. In a very literal sense, Vietnam was an exercise in voyeurism; never has a war so problematized the public's awareness of war.

Vietnam, then, was actualizing the claims of postmodern fiction: the inappropriateness of conventional notions of plot and character, the pecu-liarly tense relation between text and audience (war and public), and the intrusion of metaconcerns into any form of action. Just as experimental fic-tion focused on past history – political and literary – revising and relativiz-ing it, the effect of the Indochina War on writers was to make them reexamine earlier wars in its light. In fact, the most telling Vietnam fic-tions of the 1960s and early 1970s were not overtly about Vietnam at all: Joseph Heller's *Catch-22,* Pynchon's *Gravity's Rainbow,* and Vonnegut's *Slaughterhouse-Five,* all set in World War II; Richard Hooker's M*A*S*H (1968) set in the Korean War. These semitransparent allegories reinterpret the past, presenting quite new visions of the wars in question. At the same time, they tend to familiarize Vietnam by locating its anomalies in other wars. The striking humor of these books – in addition to their bitterness and pain – situates them in postmodernism and represents an attitude not yet possible for the Vietnam experience (although Robin Williams's comic film *Good Morning, Vietnam* (1987) and the Oscar-winning *Forrest Gump* (1994) might indicate the beginnings of a new attitude).

The war experience seemed to deny the possibility of character development and conventional plot structure in narrative. Thus, many personal memoirs read like a series of arbitrarily assembled episodes analogous to the disjointed juxtapositions found in Robert Rauschenberg's collages. *Dispatches* combines excerpts from the Beatles, *Ramparts* magazine, and high literature with helmet graffiti, slang, and press headlines. Herr uses this manic assemblage to express the widespread sense that one should see everything but that everything may not necessarily cohere into a manageable whole.

Perhaps the most sophisticated correspondence between postmodern experiment and Vietnam reportage is the relativization of the notion of cause and effect. The premise of *Gravity's Rainbow* is that Slothrop experiences responses before stimuli and effects before causes, and the madness of Vietnam made such reversals routine. Michael Herr, for example, describes the variety of Vietnam experience: some soldiers and correspondents got out quickly to save themselves, some continued on and were killed or suffered madness, and "some kept going until they reached the place where an inversion of the expected order happened, a fabulous warp where you took the journey first and then you made your departure." In Robert Mason's *Chickenhawk* (1983), the narrator acts out a totally respectable life in Vietnam. It is not until he gets home and suffers post-traumatic stress disorder that he tries drugs and eventually ends up arrested for smuggling them into the country. "I am currently free as of February 1983, appealing conviction. No one is more shocked than I." The disorientation and lack of control associated with drugs befall this soldier before he ever tries them; he then takes drugs as a kind of afterthought. In this light, *Gravity's Rainbow* appears not so much an imaginative triumph as one of the great documentary achievements of the Vietnam era.

The Vietnam experience thus went a long way toward normalizing postmodernist experiment, making it into a mimetic mode. Likewise, it led war novels and memoirs – stylistically conservative genres – to some very unconventional practices. Tim O'Brien's *Going After Cacciato* (1978), for example, is the story of a detachment sent to bring back a deserter. He leads them west through Indochina by staying just enough ahead to keep them in pursuit. Although it becomes clear that in following him the detachment will soon become guilty of desertion for leaving the theater of war without permission, they do so anyway, crossing Asia and then Europe until they end their quest in Paris. This funny picaresque is full of the feel of the absurd, until a surrealist excursion into dream at the end threatens to revise drastically the meaning of what came before. Other powerful Vietnam novels, such as Jayne Ann Philips's *Machine Dreams* (1984) and Bobbie Ann Mason's *In Country* (1985), use similarly unconventional strategies, as do the war films appearing in the late 1970s and the 1980s, *Apocalypse Now* (1979), *The Deer Hunter* (1978), and *Platoon* (1986).

The paradox that we have been observing – that the "contamination" of fiction by historical event led not to documentary art but to a demonstration of the relativism of truth and value – is nowhere more evident than in Joseph Heller's *Catch-22* (1961). Though Heller wrote it throughout the 1950s, and though it is frequently taught as the culmination of a novelistic tradition running from Ford Madox Ford through Hemingway, this work can more productively be seen as a prophetic precursor of postmodernism, along the lines of Pynchon's *V.* (1963) or Hawkes's novels of the 1960s. A World War II novel written in the 1950s and yet "describing" Vietnam, it is a fantasy made real by historical events, that at the same time undoes the very power of history to render the real. Its own history as a text embodies the reversals that Vietnam normalized.

Catch-22's treatment of World War II is full of anachronistic references to the McCarthy hearings and the Cold War, but it was at first not understood as a powerful historical comment. Its initial sales were not strong, and the early reviews described it as hypersophisticated, immoral, overly long, and lacking in "craft and sensibility." As the Vietnam War heated up, however, its sales took off, until by 1968 there were over two million copies in print. The phrase "catch-22" became so perfect a characterization of Vietnam and of the bureaucratic absurdity of Watergate that it passed into popular idiom and was canonized in the *Webster's Collegiate Dictionary*. Reaching anachronistically toward the past, this novel became a formula for the reality of the decades *after* it was written, a reality that Heller could not have predicted in the mid-1950s. His novel would have had an entirely different meaning and reception had there been no Vietnam. In this case, reality created the meaning of a text, the historical future invented the fictive past, and Pynchon's inversion of cause and effect became literal truth.

Written under the immediate influence of William Faulkner, Louise–Ferdinand Céline, and Vladimir Nabokov, *Catch-22* is the spiritual heir of Lewis Carroll, Franz Kafka, Surrealism, and the Theater of the Absurd. Like its experimentalist contemporaries, it is riddled with literary allusion, an example of a phenomenon that the book calls "seeing double." Its protagonist, Yossarian, malingering in the army hospital, decides to imitate a patient whose worst symptom is double vision. The doctor holds up a finger and asks the patient how many fingers he sees; the patient replies "two." At this, the patient is hustled into quarantine, since seeing everything twice is a serious condition. Yossarian tries out the same scenario and is likewise put in quarantine, but when his inspirational model dies, he immediately reverts to seeing everything single and is returned to combat duty. Double vision has its dangers, but every positive character in the book flirts with dualism.

The literary version of double vision is the historical echoing of texts: allusion. When Snowden, a pilot in Yossarian's plane, dies in combat, the narrator asks, "Where are the snowdens of yesteryear?" As the chaplain conducts a funeral service for Snowden, he catches a glimpse of Yossarian sitting naked in a tree and has an eerie feeling of déjà vu, as if he had seen such a naked tree sitter before – or maybe it is *jamais vu*. He is not sure, but Genesis or *Paradise Lost* could have suggested an answer. The return of the past into the present, of the literary tradition into the allusive text, is both a reenactment of the fall in which history entered human experience and a hopeful redemption of the present through its connection with what came before it. Allusions, those misty echoes of the past, give meaning to reality, even to a somewhat confused Anabaptist chaplain.

At the same time, however, there seems to be no knowledge more elusive in this book than the priority of one event to another, of memory to consciousness, of past to present. The book's episodes are arranged as a welter of temporal fixations, moments imprinted on the narrator's or Yossarian's mind that appear to the reader at first without explanation or chronological relation. As the narration goes on, these points are expanded, filled in with detail through repetition, returning over and over until they become replete with comic or tragic fullness. The reader's imperfect apprehension of "events," of a "plot" that occurs more as a pointillistic repetition than a developing line, forces him or her into a feeling of déjà vu, or sometimes denial: the *jamais vu*. Doubling, repetition, seeing everything twice become our way of knowing a world in which time and logic have departed.

The paradox of a *catch-22* involves a postmodern deconstruction of logical dualism: only a madman would want to take on the risks of combat, but the only way to get out of fighting is to be mad. If you report to the hospital even with the most extreme symptoms of insanity in order to be sent back home, your plan will not succeed, since your desire to go home is ipso facto a proof of your sanity. If you keep fighting, you will not be sent home either, since Colonel Cathcart keeps raising the number of missions on a tour of duty. No humane compromise is possible between the either/or's in this situation, but only a rattling back and forth that confirms the arbitrariness of power, the paranoid plot of experience. It is not until Yossarian follows the lead of the impish figure Orr (the symbolism of whose name is crucial) that he achieves any possibility of authentic action. Orr, an apparent fool, has spent his missions practicing crash landings on the water and survival techniques on a life raft. He disappears after a flight, only to turn up at the end of the book in neutral Sweden, from where he cannot be extradicted. We last see Yossarian striking off on his own like Huckleberry Finn or Orr, pursued by the Fury-figure of Nately's whore.

Like many experimentalist fictions, *Catch-22* tests out the power of the polar opposites, language and reality. What kind of world would we have if language controlled reality, or conversely, what would language be if it were utterly under our control? These questions used to be the province of nonsense works like *Alice in Wonderland,* where the phrase "mock turtle soup" could generate a creature called a Mock Turtle, or a willful character like Humpty-Dumpty could seize power and give things any name he wished. In both cases, the social compact and the historical evolution that create language are disregarded. The premise of a complete, determinant system in either language or reality, words or will, creates a nightmare, but a nightmare that can be swept away as easily as by Alice's waking.

In *Catch-22,* it is harder to wake up. The nonsense interrogation of the chaplain is almost a word-for-word transcript of Carroll's trial of the Knave of Hearts (though Heller claims not to have read the Alice books when he wrote *Catch-22*), but it is also an imitation of the McCarthy hearings. The novel demonstrates all the linguistic willfulness of nonsense: when the malicious power of naming is set off by Major Major's father – who cannot resist making his son into an echo, a redundance – the computer furthers his efforts by designating the son Major Major Major and later Major Major Major Major, as if there were no end to the proliferation of language once activated. In contrast, when the absurdity of war becomes normalized in people's thinking, it contaminates language to the point where nothing can be said that is not nonsense. The contemporary act of naming, that déjà vu of Adam in the Garden of Eden, always inaugurates a Fall, and the institutionalization of pure power does likewise. As in *The Crying of Lot 49,* the validating of polar opposites produces a debilitating seesaw of experience that obliterates individual authenticity, interest, and meaning, turning people into "soldiers in white," the totally bandaged, anonymous, interchangeable statistics lying immobile in a hospital bed with one bottle for fluid going in and another for fluid going out. Heller's novel bears an uncanny similarity to Carroll's nonsense and

Pynchon's postmodernist fantasy, with the small but urgent difference that Vietnam confirmed it in popular experience as real, a nightmare of history from which we could not awake.

Catch-22 was an extraordinary first novel. In each of his succeeding fictions, Heller worked out different problems: the tragic anomie of life in the advertising world in *Something Happened* (1974), the absurd humor of politics in *Good as Gold* (1979), the existential hilarity of the King David story in *God Knows* (1984). None of these had the impact of *Catch-22,* but their humor, erudition, and enormous literary skill produce a striking body of fiction.

Though Vietnam and the Watergate scandal were responsible for demystifying war, power, and heroism, they did resurrect a different kind of hero, familiar in American writing since Jefferson, Whitman, the muckrakers of the Gilded Age, and 1930s movies. This was the journalist, in his or her functions as on-the-spot observer and investigative reporter. The uncovering of the Pentagon Papers and the Watergate tapes by reporters whose research skills, contacts, and inexhaustible energy helped them to change history still seems heroic. Equally impressive was the bravery of correspondents covering the war abroad and the demonstrations at home. These people, though neither drafted nor themselves counterculture figures, put themselves at risk to get a story. The film *All the President's Men* (1976) indicates the public's fascination with such reporters as Bob Woodward and Carl Bernstein, portrayed by the superstars Robert Redford and Dustin Hoffman.

For Norman Mailer and other authors indoctrinated in the Hemingway myth of the writer-hero, these models were irresistible. Mailer not only participated in political demonstrations but wrote about them. His *Armies of the Night: History as a Novel, the Novel as History* (1968) documents the march on the Pentagon of a huge crowd of antiwar protesters, in which Mailer played – at least by his own account – a prominent role. In *Slaughterhouse-Five,* Vonnegut has a panelist on a talk show discussing the death of the novel say "that people couldn't read well enough anymore to turn print into exciting situations in their skulls, so that authors had to do what Norman Mailer did, which was to perform in public what he had written." This fictive claim, however, both underestimates the audience and overestimates Mailer's imaginative distance from the roles he enacted.

Playing out fictions was not just another expression of novelistic exhaustion but a popular demonstration of postmodern relativism. One of the effects of idealizing the reporter was an extreme and nonesoteric confusion of reality and fiction. The action was historical but told through fictive technique; the author was both a reporter and a heroic participant; and the author's belief in the totally fabricated nature of all storytelling – documentary or fictive – led him to report all the variability in the facts available to him. In *Armies of the Night,* the size of the crowd is estimated differently by each newspaper and government source, as is the responsibility for disorder and arrests. The boundary disappears between fact and fiction, between what is knowable and what knowledge is fabricated.

But then, however, Mailer took what is essentially a piece of political wit and invested it with existential conviction. He examined the life of Marilyn Monroe in *Marilyn* (1973) and showed how she not only constructed her image but was done in by what she had made – a merging of Frankenstein and his monster. Mailer's own relation to this process is always part of the story, for his writing is invariably a self-projection, an image of the artist-hero, a monstrous parasite on himself. *Advertisements for Myself* (1958) and *The Prisoner of Sex* (1971) are early instances of Mailer's public airing of these self-creations, and the logical vertigo that it produced increased with his work through the 1970s. In *The Executioner's Song* (1979), Mailer investigated the background, crimes, and prosecution of the murderer Gary Gilmore, producing over one thousand pages of narrative and himself doing much of the research and interviewing. The act of writing the book is part of the history told in it, along with Gilmore's transformation from a person to a media phenomenon. As the story goes on, Mailer's involvement with Gilmore increases; he is impressed with Gilmore's letters and with the quality of his mind. The brilliance of this murderer, who lived out a fictive plot and made himself its protagonist, seems infinitely attractive to its chronicler, and the narrative that Mailer constructs "after the fact" is one of the greatest pieces of reportage in English.

The Executioner's Song is an excellent illustration of the disorientation produced by New Journalistic techniques. It obviously makes very strong documentary claims, including factual minutia that sometimes strain the reader's patience. At the same time, however, its narrator is a pure ventriloquist, entering characters' minds at will and mimicking their very styles of thought, so that the reader reacts as if to the prose of Hemingway rather than the *New York Times.* Dipping so deeply into characters' interiority, the one subjectivity that Mailer leaves unpenetrated is that of Gilmore himself. Through this narrative lacuna, most dramatically apparent in the murder scenes, the book poses the problem of how to account for the deeds of a cold-blooded murderer.

The reader's task becomes that of interpreter. Every detail is a clue rather than a fact, and anything can become a symbol. Mailer insinuates the wildest of symbolic suggestions, including an opening scene with Gary and his cousin Brenda as children in an Edenic orchard, Brenda stealing forbidden fruit and falling from a branch into Gary's arms. Original sin is not even the strangest of the many causes Mailer offers for Gilmore's acts – family situation, prison treatment, karma, crimes committed in another life, Gilmore's possible descent from Harry Houdini. The murderer himself oscillates between claiming that "you always have a choice" and insisting that "it had to happen." All the explanations the book offers, all the "evidence" it gathers, point to contradictory and irresolvable possibilities: that Gilmore was sane or crazy, that he acted out of free will or was utterly determined, that society is responsible for the psychopath or that it is not, that events have causes and explanations or that they do not. The binary opposites proliferate, and the reader has no easier path to negotiate between these poles than does Oedipa Maas in *The Crying of Lot 49.*

Moreover, the issues of culpability and freedom are transferred from Gilmore to the reader in the course of the narration. Do Mailer's heavy symbolism and obtrusive narrative technique leave the reader free to judge the issues? Does our middle-class complacency ally us with the murder victims of Gary Gilmore or with the jury whose death sentence is presented as an act of murder? The stylistic self-consciousness of *The Executioner's Song,* its moral and epistemological indeterminacy, its confusion of cause and effect, and its involvement of the audience in the voyeuristic experience of reportage, tie this book to the most esoteric developments in postmodern experimentation. At the same time, the hints at an equation between Gilmore's prison life and Vietnam merge his case with the major interpretive conundrum of contemporary American experience.

What is most striking about this fusion of art and fact, however, is the literalness with which Mailer himself seemed to accept it. A short time later he learned of another convicted felon, Jack Abbott, who had written a manuscript entitled *In the Belly of the Beast* (1981), whose publication he arranged. He argued for the release of Abbott as well, on the grounds that anyone capable of writing such a work was clearly rehabilitated. Mailer and others stirred up so much public feeling on Abbot's behalf that the man was paroled, but within months, he again committed murder.

The connections among imagination, crime, and writing are so troubled here that one can hardly hope to sort them out. Yet there is something of the logical extension of an idea in such an anecdote, like Raskolnikov's murder in *Crime and Punishment.* If the author's invention is intense enough, he can create an intricate system of details that brings a plot to life. A murderer likewise works out details to bring about a criminal act, and if he or she is a writer to boot, the boundaries between creativity and

transgression seem very fragile indeed. When Mailer was cast as an assassinated artist in the film of E. L. Doctorow's *Ragtime* (film, 1981; novel,
1975), the confusion seemed complete, rather like Pynchon's Manni Di
Presso in *The Crying of Lot 49,* "a one-time lawyer who quits his firm to
become an actor. Who in this pilot plays . . . an actor become a lawyer
reverting periodically to being an actor. The film is in an air-conditioned
vault at one of the Hollywood studios, light can't fatigue it, it can be
repeated endlessly."

In the Gary Gilmore case, the opposition between fact and fiction
becomes relativized in a writer (Mailer) and a mode (reportage) that one
would not associate with experimental postmodernism. The sense that
reality is like a fiction and that fictions come true marked the 1960s and
1970s. Such powerful works as Truman Capote's *In Cold Blood* (1965) narrowed the distinction between reality and horror story, with its grotesque
documentation of a family murdered by escaped killers. It has the impact
– in terms of its violence – of Richard Wright's *Native Son* (1940) or
Flannery O'Connor's *A Good Man Is Hard to Find* (1955), but with the
added horror that these events occurred "as depicted." An anticipation of
this phenomenon is John Rechy's *City of Night* (1963), which presented
homosexual experience as an alienating picaresque, an endless series of
shocking or saddening episodes whose truth is both unquestionable and
irrelevant in the numbing accumulation of callousness and violation that
constitutes the story. Such works extended postmodern ideology and structure to narratives of all sorts, making untenable the boundary between
experimental and traditional fiction. Having himself enacted this idea,
Mailer proceeded, Barth-like, through a catalog of fictional types – the
mystical-historical recreation of *Ancient Evenings* (1983) or the detective
fiction of *Tough Guys Don't Dance* (1984) – apparently using genre as a
structural premise for each new experiment.

Writers focused not only on the oppression of criminals in this period
but also on the politically oppressed. The playwright Arthur Miller, as
president of the Penn Club, officially protested the treatment of Eastern
bloc writers, who often could not publish, express their views freely, or
emigrate. The forced expulsion of Aleksandr Solzhenitsyn in 1969 was a
cause célèbre among American intellectuals, and the public at large
devoured his *Gulag Archipelago* (1974–1977), *Cancer Ward* (1969), and *One
Day in the Life of Ivan Denisovich* (1962; translated, 1963). Solzhenitsyn's
Slavophilia, his withdrawal from the American public scene, and his obvious disgust with American life and democracy, expressed in his famous
Harvard address of 1978, eroded the public's adulation, but other East
Europeans have filled the gap. The Polish Nobel prize–winning poet

Czeslaw Miłosz came to the United States in the 1950s; the late Joseph Brodsky emigrated from Russia in the 1960s and won a Nobel prize in 1987. Since the Czech novelist Milan Kundera settled in Paris, his works have been translated into all major European languages, and *The Book of Laughter and Forgetting* (1980) and *The Unbearable Lightness of Being* (1984) became American best-sellers, the latter a fine motion picture (1987).

Though the Latin American novelists Carlos Fuentes, Gabriel García Márquez, Jorge Amado, and Federico García Lorca had just as decisive an influence on contemporary U.S. fiction, their effect, like that of their crucial source Jorge Luis Borges, was more on the highbrow taste and the experimental tendency in postmodernism. The East Europeans, carrying their heritage of Tolstoy, Dostoyevsky, Kafka, and most immediately Nabokov, assembled an audience across style levels. They combined the avant-garde sense of the macabre, the perverse, and the illogical with the reality of that vision in the Soviet system. For many American writers, Soviet artists seemed to live out in extreme form the contradictions and humorous inversions that characterize fiction from Pynchon to Mailer, but as with the nightmare reality of Vietnam, East European reality and writing were too literal an enactment of postmodernism to make Americans comfortable. The fictional "as if" is still crucial to maintain in the North American context, where the abandonment to complete irony has never been a psychological possibility. The romance – irony tension central to American postmodernism is also central to the contemporary American sensibility.

One of the most brilliant depictions of Eastern Europe from the American point of view is Philip Roth's *Prague Orgy*, a short epilogue completing the three-novel sequence of *Zuckerman Bound* (1985). Roth had set an episode of *The Professor of Desire* (1977) in Prague, playing on its Kafkaesque contradictions, but at the time he had not made the experimentalist leap of his later writing. In *Prague Orgy*, Zuckerman, successful author, visits Prague and dips into the Czech cultural scene. He is beset by a nymphomaniac actress whose father-in-law's wartime stories he has come to Prague to smuggle out of the country. Followed by the police and eventually "invited" to leave, he is inducted into the paranoid idiosyncrasies of the Prague intellectual: a literalization of irony and the absurd. There is just enough exaggeration in this piece to make it extremely funny, but the involuted behavior seems all too real.

Perhaps the most interesting thing about *The Prague Orgy* is its place in the Zuckerman series. After the relatively conventional *The Ghost Writer* and *Zuckerman Bound*, we come to the breakthrough of *The Anatomy Lesson*, the masterpiece of the trilogy, capped by the seeming afterthought of *The*

Prague Orgy. One can read this sequence as an epitome of the development of the American novel during the same period. The traditionalist concern with the difficulty and the psychological depths of ordinary existence give way in *The Anatomy Lesson* to a rewriting of those facts in terms of the absurdity, humor, and intellectual sophistication of postmodernism, and then, in *Orgy,* that postmodernism is reinscribed in the documentary actuality of Eastern bloc life. It is not that contemporary fiction follows the subtitle of Stanley Kubrick's film, *Dr. Strangelove: Or How I Learned to Stop Worrying and Love the Bomb* (1964). This formula – "how I learned to stop worrying and love X" – has been adapted to scores of uses in our culture and reflects the shift in attitude that separates, say, a T. S. Eliot from the recent Philip Roth. No one stopped worrying, though; people instead were learning to use that worry to more enjoyable ends.

One of the finest achievements of this rapprochement between postmodernism and traditionalism is Philip Roth's remarkable novel *The Anatomy Lesson.* The problem it explores is the meaning of pain – the fact that pain is paradigmatically a sign, a symptom, of something else – of disease, mental distress, guilt, unrealized needs. As the epigraph taken from a medical text asserts, however, "The chief obstacle to correct diagnosis in painful conditions is the fact that the symptom is often felt at a distance from its source." Undiagnosed pain, effects without discernable causes, signs pointing nowhere and hence everywhere – this is the state that Zuckerman must deal with and by extension that all of us must who live in a post-Holocaust world.

Beyond the causal enigma that pain poses, Zuckerman keeps insisting, is the unremitting and outrageous fact of pain itself – sensation, the body, Zuckerman's "corpus." The system of analogies that Roth constructs leads inexorably from pain to writing, the novelist's corpus expressing his relations to his family and therefore exacerbating those hurts, standing as a reified offshoot of his mind: a body in pain.

Most scandalously, pain is a sign of subjectivity, the unsharability of sensation, the hopeless isolation of experience. This stress on subjectivity puts Roth's work directly in conflict with High Modernism, as Zuckerman realizes in this contrast between himself and the poet Christopher Isherwood: "Isherwood is a camera with its shutter open; I am an experiment in chronic pain." Like Isherwood in *I Am a Camera* (1953), the modernist author is an observer, a sensitive plate upon which reality leaves its mark. In Eliot's image, the writer is a catalyst who, unaffected himself, precipitates a reaction between reality and text; in Joyce's terms, he is a God-like observer removed from the scene, callously paring his fingernails. In contrast, the postmodern writer – here, Roth – is an experiment in chronic pain, an expression of all that is personal, intimate, and individual. His is a pain unspecific in origin or prognosis. It is chronic, "of time." Moreover, Zuckerman is an *experiment* in this pain, a tentative essay into self-expression open to constant revision and reassessment. There could not be a more definitive break between the status of the modern and postmodern writer.

Because of the radical subjectivity of pain and its disconnection from its source, pain becomes a symbol of the problematics of novelistic meaning. *The Anatomy Lesson* opens with a proverbial formula, like that at the beginning of *Pride and Prejudice* and scores of other novels exploring the relation between traditional wisdom and the particularities of a given situation: "When he is sick, every man wants his mother; if she's not around, other women must do. Zuckerman was making do with four women." The passage from mother to other women to four other women is that from sentimentality to existential homelessness to comic excess. In the process, the orderly association of comfort with femininity comes into question. The succeeding paragraphs, full of "consequently"s and "that was how"s, describe a quite abnormal, unreasonable situation, a plot run not by logical contingency but by irrational perversity. Just as "The Collar," the title of the first section, refers both to Zuckerman's neck brace and George Herbert's metaphysical poem about God's subjugation of His servants, so the path from body to spirit is a grotesque and witty one, rather than a matter of direct causality. "Metaphysical poets pass easily from trivial to sublime," Zuckerman notes, and he himself slides with ease along the same tracks and back again into the trivial.

In the process, however, the very fabric of novelistic reasoning is disrupted. Is it his notorious hostility to his father that causes Zuckerman's guilty pain and freezes up his pen? Or is it his inability to deserve his mother's love? Or is it the four women now in his life – or the two wives gone by – whose love and kindness he could not earn or abide? Or the Holocaust, the unutterable unkindness of people to each other? The book has no answers to these questions, cannot even say whether they are the causes or effects of pain. After hiring or attracting an army of interpreters – professional and amateur – Zuckerman is no further enlightened than when the pain first hit. "The illness with a thousand meanings. They read the pain as his fifth book." From pain to corpus, the transformation is ironic and cruel, but since this *is* more or less Roth's fifth book about a Zuckerman-like character, it is quite an accurate assessment, or as much so as any explanation.

Chapter 1 of this section noted the importance of *The Anatomy Lesson* to the contemporary treatment of pornography. At the height of his pain- and drug-induced mania, Zuckerman takes on the persona of a pornographer who publishes a journal called *Lickety Split*. The name he gives to his proponent of sexual license is Milton Appel, who is actually the Jewish critic who had denounced Zuckerman's politics and humanity in a rankling review. "Je m'appelle Appel," Zuckerman quips, as much as to say, "Call me Ishmael," and since the pornographer's nightclub is called Milton's Millennia, Milton Appel becomes an embodiment of the Great Tradition of both America and England, symbolizing stern moral value, high seriousness, and transcendent, millennialist yearning. This is a tradition that Zuckerman desperately wishes to jettison, perceiving it as inimical to his project as a writer. "You lay hold of my comedy with your ten-ton gravity and turn it into a travesty!" he complains to the Irving Howe–like Appel.

Still *The Anatomy Lesson* displays an equally strong nostalgia for the authority and dignity of canonic literature. Zuckerman remembers his earliest writing, a fifth-grade essay on the history of his native New Jersey, in which he compares the progress of New Jersey waterways to his own artistic development. This pretentious move reveals the utter inability of his life to support a geographical metaphor. Unlike the oppressive John Milton, who successfully assimilated all of history, myth, and religion into his own experience, Zuckerman is locked within himself, a metaphor lacking a vehicle, a meaning without a signifier, a self bereft of relation to family, land, history, and audience.

In his problematic engagement with his audience, Roth exemplifies one of the most common characteristics of postmodern writing. *The Anatomy Lesson* is about the inside observer – the American Jew – whose public airing of that privileged insider's information appears to be an act of disloyalty. We recall from chapter 1 of this section the reaction of Zuckerman's female chauffeur to his pornographic ravings – that they were an insult not to her feminism but to her sense of privacy. Critics felt that Zuckerman (and Roth) had committed a parallel obscenity in publishing *Carnovsky* (*Portnoy's Complaint*, 1969), turning his Jewish New Jersey experience into a hilarious exposé that could fuel anti-Semitism. By creating a hero who is transparently himself and at the same time by acting out his critics'/readers' response in the parody figure of Milton Appel, Roth produces an autobiographical text in which he is both writer and audience. He enacts us; we read ourselves.

When one teaches *The Anatomy Lesson*, students invariably preface their comments with such autobiographical locators as, "I'm Jewish, so . . ." or "I'm not a Zionist, but . . ." or, the best, "I'm from New Jersey, and . . . ." This need that readers feel to place their own experience in relation to the text is one of its most remarkable achievements. No longer able to see our-

selves as members of a universal audience appealed to on grounds beyond
the "accidents" of our ethnicity, gender, religion, or region, we relate to
Roth's novel through our partiality, our specificity, the scandal of our readerly individuality. As Roth recycles his critical readership into novelistic
antagonists, we, too, are changed from audience to art in a circulation
meant to instruct us in the postmodern fluidity of fact and fiction.
Zuckerman's identity, the center of concern in this novel, is the painful
conflict between his imaginative freedom and the real-life reference of his
work, between self-expression and the interpretive history that ensues on
art's entrance into the public, communicative sphere.

Beyond his Miltonic and Melvillian tormentors, Zuckerman draws in a
host of other literary "fathers." He rides the El in Chicago as a student,
reading Eliot. He vows "to renounce renunciation – to reunite with the
race," like a revised Stephen Dedalus from Joyce's *A Portrait of the Artist as
a Young Man.* He claims that the painkiller "Percodan was to Zuckerman
what sucking stones were to Molloy – without 'em couldn't go on," and
in another appropriation of Beckett, Zuckerman claims that *Waiting for
Godot* is a normal day in an author's life "except you don't get Pozzo and
Lucky." He even explains his excessive vodka drinking on the plane to
Chicago as a "fear of flying." Zuckerman writes notes in his hospital bed
using a Magic Marker, *pace* Thomas Mann, and feels his world constrict-
ing to the agony of his wired-up mouth, a Conradian Congo. Shakespeare,
Sir Thomas Browne, Percy Bysshe Shelley, John Keats, and Rembrandt,
too – *The Anatomy Lesson* is a wild congeries of allusion, successfully transformed in Zuckerman's corpus. The only source that still offers up an
Oedipal resistance to his usurpation is the self-righteous Jewish champion
of the Great Tradition, and Zuckerman's revenge on him is devastating,
though the cost to himself is equally extreme. If we recall Ambrose
Mensch's attempts to beget one last offspring on Lady Germaine
Amherst, the embodiment of the Great Tradition in Barth's *Letters,* we
can see that Roth's anxiety is not his alone, but that of postmodernism as
a whole.

Zuckerman's struggle with the great moral tradition also recalls a passage from Barthelme's *Snow White.* One of the seven dwarfs states bravely,
"I will light that long cigar, that cigar that stretches from Mont St. Michel
and Chartres, to under the volcano. What is merely fashionable will fade
away, and what is merely new will fade away, but what will not fade away,
is the way I feel: analogies break down, regimes break down, but the way I
feel remains. I feel abandoned." Though the context for this statement is
heavily ironic, the conflict between the oppressive authority of the literary
past and the imperative of individual pain *is* to be taken seriously. One sets

a match to the novelistic tradition from Henry Adams to Malcolm Lowry to show its ephemerality next to the indisputable reality of pain, and this whether one is Donald Barthelme or Philip Roth.

In the manic reordering of literary history, in the contemplation of effects without causes, and in the focusing on pain as the ultimate reality, the experimental and the conventional branches of contemporary writing merge. Roth, whose early work seemed so clearly within the Jewish, angst-ridden tradition that he repudiates in *The Anatomy Lesson,* becomes in his latest novels an equally clear analogue to Barthelme or Pynchon, exemplars of the postmodern tradition that has supposedly made his work passé. When the editors of the student literary journal send the hospitalized Zuckerman a questionnaire about the threat of Pynchon and Barth, he faints. As *The Anatomy Lesson* itself demonstrates, however, it is old-style humanism, moral criticism, and narrow-minded censoriousness, rather than postmodern exuberance, that is the enemy. By the 1980s, many "conventional" novelists had learned the lessons of the postmodern innovators of the late 1960s and 1970s, so that increasingly the Pynchonesque lion and the Rothian lamb lie down together in the same bed.

Perhaps one of the clearest examples of this fusion of stylistic and "humanist" goals is the work of Don DeLillo. His fiction is an unsettling combination of anomie, crime, humor, and complex emotion, recalling, at times, the feel of John Hawkes's writing. *White Noise* (1985), one of DeLillo's most brilliant inventions, begins as a wry domestic comedy about the family life of a professor in a small college town. His wife and he live with children from their various marriages, coping with over-weight, career disappointments, housekeeping chores, and the fear of death. DeLillo's dinner-table dialogue is hilarious, catching all the nonse-quiturs, canonized misinformation, and loving destructiveness of family small talk. The hero's university life is equally absurd; he is a professor of Hitler Studies in a department devoted to this subject, of which he is the sole and founding member – this despite the fact that he knows barely any German. The novel progresses in this fashion until the hero discovers that his wife has been taking pills meant to allay her unbearable fear of death, and that she obtained these only by sleeping with the supplier. The protagonist is soon overcome by the fear of death himself when he is exposed to toxic fumes released in an environmental accident. He seeks out the supplier of his wife's pills and shoots him, the novel ending with his gazing out at an unnaturally beautiful sunset, reddened by toxic clouds released into the atmosphere. From domestic comedy to existential drama, to environmental disaster script, to crime novel, to ironized romance, *White Noise* is built on a generic cacophony suggested in its title. The novel is an exercise in interference, exploring at every level from dialogue to genre to plot the static that obscures messages and foils attempts at closure.

DeLillo associates this static, moreover, with pain, the unifying concern of postmodern fiction. In an interview with Thomas LeClair, he described the subway arcades beneath 14th Street in New York, where "you hear mostly Spanish and black English with bits of Yiddish, German, Italian, and Chinese, and then there's this strange, broken language. The language of the insane is stronger than all the others. It is the language of self, the pain of self." Eliot's rubble heap of Western culture here becomes the cacophony of the city and the broken ruins of the self, the individual – the partial, idiosyncratic one.

If we recall the major divisions of the novel circa 1970 – traditional, experimental, women's – *White Noise* utterly undercuts these categories. Its language is traditional, with a standard, omniscient narrator; characters whose speech is highly naturalistic; and a concern for the depth of feeling and the concrete detail of ordinary experience. At the same time, its themes – domesticity, environmentalism, the family, the problems of a woman's fulfillment and a man's attunement to her – ally it to feminist writing, and its wildly disjunctive novelistic genres identify it with experimentalism and innovation. This novel is an especially apt case of contemporary fiction, in that it merges existentialism, politics, and individual assertion. The great development of post-1970 writing is the normalizing of the previously esoteric world of Nietzsche, Camus, and Beckett in an accessible mirror of the ordinary.

4

❦

WOMEN'S FICTION: THE REWRITING
OF HISTORY

I N THE 1970s and 1980s, the modernist division between avant-garde
and traditional fiction was coming to an end. As relativism, indeterminacy, self-reflexiveness, and absurdity became generally recognizable as
a description of contemporary experience, experimentalism shifted from a
goal in itself to a vehicle for a redefined realism.

The normalizing of the experimentalist ethos – so important in novels
by men – was equally crucial for women writers. Beginning in about
1970, an unprecedented explosion of novels by and about women appeared
in print, a simple fact in itself, but one that represented a fundamental
change in the meaning of women's experience. By writing, by being published, by finding an audience receptive to their work, women de facto
redefined their status in our culture. They achieved a "voice" where before
they were voiceless; they wrote themselves into history – both political and
literary – when previously they had been strikingly absent from it.
Women writers found immediately relevant the postmodern tenet that
history is a construct serving an ideology and open to varying interpretation. The problem was how to appropriate the authority to tell stories of
the past, and how to structure them in such a way as to generate a different
kind of future.

The emergence of women's writing beginning in the 1970s constituted
both a literary and a political revolution. The formation of a community of
women readers entailed a major social realignment, and the process of
writing, of turning personal expression into public interpretation, had
direct political consequences. Women writers lived out a script in which
art changes history. In *Catch-22*, we saw how history can change art, producing a real-life situation that transformed a novel into prophecy. The
books that women wrote, by contrast, transformed reality, both by their
effect on their readership and by the very fact of their existence.

Aware of the historical significance of their writing, women often
include this theme, exploring the connection between fiction and history
and thus returning the novel to its eighteenth-century affinities with historiography. In this respect, they merge with the general effort of post-

modernists – Pynchon, Barth, Mailer, Roth – to test the boundaries between fiction and fact, between private and public fantasies.

Women's literature, however, draws the analogy to history in order to displace the established, male-dominated view of the past with a "her-story." In *Linden Hills* (1985), for example, Gloria Naylor contrasts an "objective," cold professor of history to a young (male) poet who alone has the sensitivity and compassion needed to tell the story of the community. He writes, "There is a man in a house at the bottom of a hill./ And his wife has no name." These lines are the poetic opening into the only kind of history adequate to the past and capable of changing the future – an act of poetic imagination, a personal writing, a merger of the aesthetic and the political.

The paradigmatic plot of such imagining is the recovery of the lost past, the wife who has no name. In giving her a name and a story, the female author achieves an identity as well: "In search of my mother's garden," Alice Walker writes, "I found my own." Thus, built into women's writing is a self-reflexiveness as intense as that among male postmoderns, for the story recovered is at the same time the story told. As with *The Anatomy Lesson,* the subject of these histories is the pain of subjectivity, the individual cut off from connection, expression, and the past. "I cannot recover from such an ending," the French feminist Michèle Causse wrote. "And I flirt with the conditional mood. I rewrite history."

Women's writing involved more than the production of new literary works. It led to the recovery of a suppressed female canon and to the politicizing of a female readership. It was both the cause and the material manifestation of a social revolution. Such writers as Alice Walker and Tillie Olsen have brought forgotten books to the public's attention: Zora Neale Hurston's *Their Eyes Were Watching God* (1937) and *I Love Myself When I Am Laughing* (not published until 1979), for example, or Rebecca Harding Davis's *Life in the Iron Mills* (1861). Female authors and academics have instituted classes in feminist literature and theory, integrated these texts into "standard" university courses, and created majors in Women's Studies. The canon of literature now routinely taught in colleges across America is a canon significantly "feminized," compared to its state in 1970.

The fate of women's literature has been closely tied to that of feminism in general. Crucial works in the "consciousness raising" of the American public were Simone de Beauvoir's *The Second Sex* (1949), Betty Friedan's *The Feminine Mystique* (1963), Kate Millett's *Sexual Politics* (1970), Germaine Greer's *The Female Eunuch* (1971), Adrienne Rich's *Of Women Born* (1976), Sandra Gilbert and Susan Gubar's *The Madwoman in the Attic* (1979), and the work of such French feminists as Hélène Cixous and Luce

Irigaray. These and a host of other scholarly and critical books provide the institutional framework and popular recognition necessary for "women's literature" to be taken seriously as a kind of writing. *The Norton Anthology of Literature by Women,* released in 1985, was a landmark publication in that it formalized a canon of female writing and made it easily accessible in textbook form.

Scholarly journals on women's issues, such as *Signs,* began to appear in the 1970s, along with new publishing houses – the Feminist Press in the United States, Virago Press in Great Britain – dedicated to the promotion of women's writing and the ideologies associated with what was claimed to be a female world view. This piece of publicity for the Feminist Press reveals some typical assumptions: "Founded in 1970, this . . . organization works to eliminate sexual stereotypes in books and schools and to provide literature with a broad vision of human potential. . . . Through publications and projects, the Feminist Press contributes to the rediscovery of the history of women and the emergence of a more humane society." Of special note here is the bidirectionality of time in the project of women's publishing: the idea that the reconstruction of a female past will change the future, that history and revolution are directly interconnected. This position bears an interesting relation to the ambiguity of postmodernism as a prophecy of the past or the projection of a world gone by, where the arbitrary, provisional interpretation of history creates a social consensus for the future. The political urgency of this move for women seems even more immediate than for most male postmodernists.

The widespread intellectual preoccupation with language in the 1960s and 1970s pervades feminism. Such writers as Adrienne Rich called for the formation of a women's language, an English that did not perpetuate "patriarchal" values. Feminists declared certain usages sexist, insisting that *man* is not a neutral substitute for *humankind* or *people,* and that the masculine pronouns *he, him,* and *his* should not be used to denote the general case, as in "Everyone wants his freedom." Some linguists countered that these constructions have nothing to do with gender bias but simply reflect the structure of language, which is entirely organized in binary oppositions (*big/little, over/under, p/b, he/she*), in which one element is "unmarked" – that is, capable of carrying the force of the whole category as well as its particular oppositional meaning. When we ask "How big is it?" we do not imply that "it" is big, whereas the marked "little" produces quite a different effect in the question "How little is it?" "Big" is unmarked; "little" is marked.

Feminists responded that the unmarked status of the masculine pronoun indicates the phallocentric bias of the entire Judeo-Christian tradition, and that women are either omitted or subsumed under male control

whenever *man* or *he* is used in the general sense of *people* or *one.* Many publishers and cultural institutions have accepted this argument, substituting
people, humankind, he or she, and sometimes the plural *they* in place of the
traditional usages. This feminist victory, aside from changing basic linguistic constructions, has begun to destabilize the very structure of the
binary opposition. It is hard to believe anymore in the innocence of the
unmarked element. If the postmodern experimentalists sought to abolish
the either/or because it produced a redundant, predictable universe, feminists did so because binarism enshrines hierarchy, and moreover a hierarchy
in which women always seem to be disadvantaged.

As this academic theorizing proceeded, a broader-based exploration of
feminism was underway in popular women's magazines. From *Vogue* to
Ladies Home Journal, from *Cosmopolitan* to *Better Homes and Gardens,* the topics of independence, careerism, physical fitness, grooming, motherhood,
and love were thrashed out across a spectrum of audiences covering virtually the whole American female population. The time-honored doctrine of
self-help fostered by such journals gained a new focus: to assimilate the
changing status of women to whatever the ideological stripe of the readership was, and to present this goal as a collective female enterprise. Popular
television series responded to the same need: *One Day at a Time,* about a
divorced woman raising two teenage daughters; *Cagney and Lacey,* exploring the special concerns of female cops; *Kate and Allie,* following the development of two divorced women with children who form a cooperative
household; and a whole raft of programs about career women. As a result of
the print and electronic media, there can be very few women in the United
States, if any, who are unaware of the women's movement, and none whose
lives have been untouched by it.

One of the central effects of feminism was a thorough and public analysis of the female condition. Anthropology, psychiatry, and world literature
were enlisted in this enterprise, and the resulting picture of women was
not encouraging. We might recall the male postmodernists in chapter 2 of
this section whose analysis of the status of women left little hope for ame-
lioration. John Barth's fable about female authoring, the "Dunyazadiad"
from *Chimera,* traces all female power to the permissiveness of men. John
Hawkes's Honorine in *Travesty* escapes the inevitably disappointing life of
women only through the tattooed doubling of narcissism, which makes
her mysterious and irresistible to men, and Pynchon's women in *V.* and *The
Crying of Lot 49* experience the same self-fetishization. In the movies of
Brian De Palma (*Dressed to Kill, Body Double*), women are the objects of
voyeurs, and voyeurism and victimization are treated as concomitants.

Gender politics and the "image of woman" are inescapable concerns for writers of either sex today.

Both psychoanalysts and writers have diagnosed the problem with the female state as narcissism, an inevitable "self-regarding." (Interestingly, this structure is built into the literary romance, the central genre of postmodernism, too). According to this scenario, woman, deficient in her sense of identity, turns compulsively inward, focusing on herself, objectifying herself, making herself into an object of male attention. It is striking how much agreement prevails on this issue between psychology and literature. The analyst Eugénie Lemoine-Luccioni, a follower of Jacques Lacan, wrote that woman "truly lives under the sign of abandonment: mother, father, child, husband, penis, the entire world deserts her . . . always divided, always deprived of half of herself, narcissistically divided between subject and object, an orphan in every way. In a word, narcissistic by structure and dedicated to a destiny of partition." Compare Donald Barthelme's campy Heideggerian rendition of the female condition: *"The psychology of Snow White:* What does she hope for? 'Someday my prince will come.' By this Snow White means that she lives her own being as incomplete, pending the arrival of one who will 'complete' her. That is, she lives her own being as 'not-with'. . . . The incompleteness is an ache capable of subduing all other data presented by consciousness."

Loss, incompleteness, partition, and narcissism: small wonder that women should have countered with a vision of self-containment. Carolyn Heilbrun's *Toward a Recognition of Androgyny* (1973) is one of several scholarly books on the topic, and the frequency of references to Amazonian cultures, for example, in Alice Walker's *The Color Purple,* indicates this yearning for completeness. The lesbianism of Adrienne Rich, Gloria Naylor, and Rita Mae Brown, the "womanism" of Alice Walker, and the separatism of radical feminists are all attempts to reconceive woman as whole and complete.

The utopianism and future orientation of this vision make it particularly appropriate to pastoral and science fiction. One of the most interesting works on gender wholeness, in fact, is Ursula Le Guin's "thought experiment," *The Left Hand of Darkness* (1969). A classic romance, the novel's plot is the quest of an envoy who has been sent to promote peace and trade with a planet of androgyns. Sophisticated and tolerant, the emissary nevertheless finds it virtually impossible to deal with their sexual ambiguity. "I tried to, but my efforts took the form of self-consciously seeing a Gethenian first as a man, then as a woman, forcing him into those categories so irrelevant to his nature and so essential to my own."

In this way, Le Guin exposes the binarist habit of mind so deeply ingrained in our thinking and attempts to relativize it. The name of the envoy, for example, is Genly Ai, the first name suggesting Latin *gens* – family, clan, collectivity. As a representative of the confederation of Ekumen, he is appropriately named for supraindividual concerns, yet the Gethenians, unable to pronounce *l*, call him "Genry" and thus introduce quite different associations: *gender* and *genre,* and hence splitting, separation, division. Likewise, his surname, Ai, is a homonym for both *I* and, as the book terms it, a cry of pain. Genly is an amalgam of community and individual subjectivity, of self-assertion and pain. If he can combine such polar opposites, the novel asks, why must sexual identity be understood in such an exclusionary fashion?

The book extends this query to the status of the narrator's gender and authority. The text of *The Left Hand of Darkness* is a congeries of fictive verbal sources – official records, ancient legends, anthropological reports, and Genly's narrative. This last is extremely subjective, stressing the undependability of facts and claiming that it is the style of telling that establishes truth. The narrator makes his "report as if I told a story. . . . The story is not all mine, nor told by me alone. Indeed I am not sure whose story it is." The assumptions here are precisely the opposite of those behind authoritative, official, conventionally male discourse, and yet Genly's status as male is essential to the plot.

Later on we read a report filed by an investigator who preceded Genly on Gethen. It is an impersonal ethnographic account of the Gethenians' sexual habits – their incest taboos and the concept of descent from the mother. There are other consequences of androgyny as well: shared childrearing; the elimination of war; the separation of identity from sex; and the absence of the Oedipal complex, rape, and a populace divided into the strong and the weak. When we learn, almost accidentally, that the writer of this impersonal, professional report is a woman, suddenly we are forced to examine whether we think of narrators as gendered, and what difference it makes that this one is a "she." Does the report sound self-interested in a way that it did not before? Is our acceptance of the authority of a document dependent on the sexual neutrality of its author? As with so many postmodern works, *The Left Hand of Darkness* implicates the reader in its action, making the relation of text to audience a crucial part of its thematics.

Le Guin also plays with epistemology – what it means to know. She makes the people of Genly's planet telepathic and the Gethenians prophetic. Thus, the bugbears of solipsism – the problem of knowing another's interiority and knowing the future – are both overcome, though not for the same beings. Neither of these achievements, however, creates happiness. Genly's ability to see into his lover's mind reveals the enormity of the other's pain, and what prophecy teaches the Gethenians is the utter uselessness of such knowledge, for the future is already known with absolute certainty: we shall die. "The unknown . . . the unforetold, the unproven, that is what life is based on. Ignorance is the ground of thought. Unproof is the ground of action. . . . The only thing that makes life possible is permanent, intolerable uncertainty: not knowing what comes next."

This paradoxical view of existence, built on the inevitability of death, is precisely the same as the one unfolded in Pynchon's work. When the either/or gives way to the both/and, information and interest burst through. Thus, the wise men of the land of Winter who have perfected Foretelling have "the completeness of a wild animal, a great strange creature who looks straight at you out of his eternal present." For all their wisdom, however, these men are still prone to petty political squabbles and unhappiness. Le Guin teaches a gendered alien to love an androgyn, but she does not find among the necessary outcomes of sexual inclusiveness a world of peace and happiness.

Most women's writing does not advocate androgyny or separatism. Since the literary romance and female psychology set up an inevitable connection among woman's loss, her incompleteness, and her narcissism, the challenge is to use those factors to transform the female condition. As a result, perhaps the most important fictive pattern underlying feminist writing is that of *Frankenstein* (authored, after all, by a woman, Mary Shelley), but a *Frankenstein* in which the scientist and monster are one. In chapter 3 of this section, we saw how this strategy applies to Norman Mailer's self-creations, but the goal there is the birthing of Mailer only. The feminist collapsing of creator and creation aims, instead, at refashioning an entire sex. It does so, paradoxically, through the most personal of all experiences – pain. Through the exploration of the particularity of women's lives, the telling of all those ignored, unremarkable stories of boredom, unfulfillment, and suffering, women become the subjects of art, women's lives become an object of public contemplation, and the "merely domestic" is elevated to the historical. As Adrienne Rich discovered, "I began . . . to feel that politics was not something 'out there' but something 'in here' and of the essence of my condition."

We can see this strategy in Rita Mae Brown's *Rubyfruit Jungle* (1973), in the heroine's choice of a film subject. Molly is a lesbian who is supporting herself through film school at New York University, where she is the only woman in her class. Her unsympathetic male professor and aggressive fellow students make it almost impossible for her to check out equipment and film, and so for her senior project she steals a camera and heads south in a bus to film Carrie, her poor, estranged foster mother. On project night, the students show their films.

> The one that drew the most applause was a gang rape on an imaginary Martian landscape. . . . All the men mumbled about what a profound racial statement it was. My film was last on the list. . . . There was Carrie speeding away in her rocking chair looking straight at the camera and being herself. No quick cuts to steals from Kenneth Anger, no tinfoil balls dropping out of the sky to represent nuclear hail – just Carrie talking about her life, the world today, and the price of meat. . . . The last thing she said in the film was, "I'm gonna turn this house into a big gingerbread cake with icing on the corners. Then when those goddamn bill collectors come after me I just tell 'em to break off a piece of the house and leave me alone. In time they eat the whole house," she chuckled, "then I'll be sittin' out in the sunshine that the good Lord made. I'll be out in the lilies of the field that's richer than all King Solomon's gold. That ain't a bad way to die when yer as old as I am." She laughed a strong, certain laugh and as that laugh died so did the light.

The contrast here between male avant-garde and female "domestic" art is archetypal for the 1970s. We recall John Barth's deprecation of women's writing as "secular news reports." The value to Molly of telling such a woman's story is profound. She returns to the family setting of her youth and the foster mother who rejected her for her lesbianism. She explores the life of a woman who, unrelated and formerly hostile to her, is still a closer approximation of her own life than anything represented in the male fantasies of high experimentalism. In the course of Molly's film, Carrie's pain and personal limitations become transformed into a vision of fortitude and even beauty whose very simplicity has the power to silence the forces that try to subdue it. In the telling of the lives of women (recall the title of the Canadian writer Alice Munroe's book, *The Lives of Girls and Women*), all women gain a voice and an identity. Here, the personal *is* the political.

To show the implication of individual women in the class "woman," writers have employed a form that goes back to Gertrude Stein – the "novel" made of narratives of several women. Flaubert's *Trois Contes* (1877) was the direct inspiration for Stein; Sherwood Anderson used the same composite strategy in *Winesburg, Ohio* (1919); Stein's *Three Lives* (1909) is a masterpiece of the form. In *Many Many Women* (1910), Stein set out to describe every kind of woman and every kind of relationship between women. Though the maniacal and mechanical nature of her project is comical, it is in extreme form the structure that other women (and some men) seem to have needed.

For example, Gloria Naylor's *The Women of Brewster Place* (1982) tells the stories of several black women who live in the same housing project. These begin as separate, juxtaposed tales, but gradually the life of each woman is so implicated in the others that they dream each other's lives and live out a collective – though imaginary – apocalypse. Alice Walker's *In Love and Trouble: Stories of Black Women* (1974) is a somewhat less cohesive attempt at the same transformation of the individual and personal into the general and collective. What we have in such works, in logical terms, is the super-imposition of intensive and extensive definitions of women. Extensively defined, woman is the totality of all individual women; intensively, she is the essence that all women share. What structures like *The Women of Brewster Place* do is to create an extensive definition: to know what *woman* is, one must see the specific *women* who live in a given group, as if in a soci-ological survey. Out of the multiplicity, though, arises a common identity, an intensive definition of woman as sufferer, comforter, and finally revolu-tionary, joining with her peers to tear down Brewster Place and the oppres-sive values it stands for. From aggregate to essence to political force, woman is transfigured in the strategy of the collective life.

In a parallel move, feminist scholars and writers have gone back to women's stories of the past to build both a canon of "women's literature" and models for future writing. Two texts have emerged as catalysts. For black female writers, probably no novel has been more influential than Zora Neale Hurston's *Their Eyes Were Watching God* (1937), and for white women, Kate Chopin's *The Awakening* (1899) has played a similar role. Both were quite forgotten until the 1970s, and both deal with a woman's gradual self-realization, but whereas Hurston's novel culminates in an extraordinary representation of fulfillment, Chopin's ends in the heroine's suicide.

Alice Walker has commented on this contrast between black and white writing in "Saving the Life That Is Your Own: The Importance of Models in the Artist's Life":

White American writers tended to end their books and their characters' lives as if there were no better existence for which to struggle. The gloom of defeat is thick. By comparison, black writers seem always involved in a moral and/or physical struggle, the result of which is expected to be some kind of larger freedom. Perhaps this is because our literary tradition is based on the slave narratives, where escape for the body and freedom for the soul went together, or perhaps this is because black people have never felt themselves guilty of global, cosmic sins.

Whether or not Walker's explanation is valid, black women's writing does seem more urgently revolutionary, depicting the destruction of repressive orders and the institution of new ways for women to live. Perhaps this dif-ference can be explained by the fact that in popular mythology, black women have nothing to lose. In the pecking order dominated by white men, white women come second, then black men, and finally black women. "De nigger woman," wrote Hurston, "is de mule uh de world."

Black women's novels, such as Toni Morrison's *Sula* (1973), chart the passage from the personal to the collective to the revolutionary. At first, the cost of independence is charged against the self: the matriarch Eva arranges for her leg to be hacked off so that she can collect enough insurance money to live her own life, and the girl Sula likewise cuts off her fingertip to frighten away some threatening boys. Through a series of violent, absurd lessons, however, Sula is released from this self-destructiveness into a self-affirming openness to experience:

As willing to feel pain as to give pain, to feel pleasure as to give pleasure, hers was an experimental life. . . . She had no center, no speck around which to grow. . . . She was completely free of ambition, with no affection for money, property or things, no greed, no desire to command attention or compliments – no ego. For that reason she felt no compulsion to verify herself – be consistent with herself.

Sula's achievement, a kind of Gideian or existential *disponibilité*, does not stop with herself. When she comes back to her old home, she sets the whole community right. Parents stop beating their children; husbands stop mistreating wives; nature itself seems kinder and more beautiful for her presence. Paradoxically, Sula is a social abomination, a denial of all the community represents. All men want her, even her best friend's husband, and yet their adultery is somehow not destructive. All women are jealous of her, and yet she improves their lives. When she dies, a harsh winter comes, bringing illness and the return of child abuse.

Sula's influence does not die with her, though. Her death mobilizes the townspeople and makes them rise up against their oppressors. Shadrack, a man crazed by World War I who celebrates National Suicide Day each year, sees Sula laid out in the mortuary and leads his antic followers to the mine where they had been shut out of work. They then tear down the mine, as Shadrack stands above the wild destruction ringing his bell, for the death of Sula is intolerable. Her freedom was the only model of individual success in the town – the experimental life – and resistant as they were, the community learned from it in spite of themselves. Sula teaches them revolt and self-assertion, and they express these in a form so archetypal – destroying the mine to the accompaniment of the madman's ringing of his doomsday bell – that we see the act as an apocalypse, an irreversible change.

The change is not left at the communal level. The book ends with Nel, Sula's oldest friend. Alienated because Sula has had an affair with her husband, she is returning home from Sula's funeral. As she walks, she realizes that her unhappiness stems from the loss not of her husband but of Sula and the promise of youth they shared. "'We was girls together,' she said as though explaining something. 'O Lord, Sula,' she cried, 'girl, girl, girlgirl-girl.' It was a fine cry – loud and long – but it had no bottom and it had no top, just circles and circles of sorrow." The realization of this woman's love gives Nel a voice after long silence and allows her to complete the circle of her life, although this is a circle of sorrow. The passage from Sula's intensely personal loneliness to the communal loss caused by her death to social revolution at the mine finally returns to the personal when Nel registers the loss of Sula and her own girlhood self.

The lyricism of the Nobel prize winner Toni Morrison and the intense imagistic logic of her plots have produced some of the most powerful fiction of our day, notably *The Bluest Eye* (1970), *Song of Solomon* (1977), and the masterpiece *Beloved* (1987), to which we shall return. More openly programmatic than Morrison, Alice Walker reached a larger mass of the American reading and viewing public during the 1970s and 1980s. *The Color Purple* (1982) won a Pulitzer prize and a National Book Award for Fiction and was made into a successful film by Stephen Spielberg. Other novels by Walker – *The Third Life of Grange Copeland* (1970) and *Meridian* (1976) – have been commercial and critical successes, and her scholarly work on Langston Hughes and Zora Neale Hurston has been widely influential in academia. Walker's career as a political activist, teacher, lecturer, critic, and fiction writer gives her work a practical range unusual in any writer. The feminist project she lives out involves the recovery of women's history, the female literary tradition, and the sense of self necessary for a full life. The relative ease with which literary, political, and psychological goals intersect in Walker's work indicates its profound contrast with the earlier literature of exhaustion.

Walker collected a number of her essays in a volume entitled *In Search of Our Mothers' Gardens: Womanist Prose* (1983). There she describes the omissions in her college education: courses in black fiction almost wholly devoid of female writers. Determined not to let this situation continue, Walker lays out a canon of "womanist" writers: Zora Neale Hurston, Jean Toomer (a man), Colette, Virginia Woolf, Anaïs Nin, and Tillie Olsen. Likewise, she used her fiction to teach black women their history, just as she had in the 1960s as a Head Start teacher. "How *do* you teach earnest but educationally crippled middle-aged and older women the significance of their past? How do you get them to understand the pathos and beauty of a heritage they have been taught to regard with shame? . . . It should have been as simple as handing them each a mirror, but it was not." The solution Walker invented was to encourage them to write their autobiographies. Thus, she instituted in a pedagogical setting the central literary strategy of women's writing today. The writing of the one becomes the writing of the many and in turn allows the one a place within a tradition of living voices.

What makes this interaction between history and the present so positive is its transformation of the seemingly hopeless diagnosis of female narcissism. A paradigmatic image of this metamorphosis appears in Walker's essay "Beyond the Peacock: The Reconstruction of Flannery O'Connor":

> Whenever I visit antebellum homes in the South, with their spacious rooms, their grand staircases, their shaded back windows that, without the thickly planted trees, would look out onto the now vanished slave quarters in the back, this is invariably my thought. I stand in the backyard gazing up at the windows, then stand at the windows inside looking down into the backyard, and between the me that is on the ground and the me that is at the windows, History is caught.

This striking interface of perspectives is the positive lesson of history, the fact that it presents two Alice Walkers endowed with completely different fates: the antebellum slave peering in and the contemporary black woman looking out. They regard each other through a temporal transparency made possible by historical awareness – a window rather than the opaque glass of a narcissistic mirror. Walker's image transforms solipsistic self-contemplation into empathy and fellow feeling. The interposition of history between Walker and her self-image releases her from the narcissism bequeathed to women by their psyches and their culture and turns her into an active force for change.

The immense popularity of Walker's novels was due to her crystalization of the basic themes of black feminism. *The Color Purple,* for example, develops a number of issues that became normative in such writing, especially the suppression of women's past and the male control of their bodies. The heroine Celie is made pregnant twice by the man she assumes is her father, and the baby born to her is each time taken away. With the second birth, she becomes sterile. Deprived of her children and of the very power to bear children, she begins the novel as a victim of patriarchy whose only outlet is the writing of letters to God. She waits for letters from her missionary sister Nettie but does not receive them, for when Celie is married off to a man who does not love her, he hides Nettie's letters from Africa in a trunk. With the disappearance of her children and of Nettie's words, all possibility for Celie's self-expression disappears. She becomes a writer with no audience but God, and it takes her a good part of the book to learn that God is not a male power but the beauty all around her.

Celie's salvation depends on the recovery of the past. In her first passionate love with Shug, her husband's mistress, she returns to the feelings of her youth and the tenderness that she felt for her lost babies. Shug also unearths Nettie's letters in the trunk, and with these, Celie regains an audience and a wholly new historical perspective. Nettie's letters tell of Africa, the sisters' racial past; they reveal as well that the children of the missionaries Nettie has accompanied are Celie's stolen boy and girl. These children — modern Americans raised in the timelessness of tribal Africa — experience a historical vertigo somewhat like what Alice Walker describes in her essay on Flannery O'Connor. The past that they inhabit forbids the education of girls and sanctions clitoridectomy to prevent female sexual pleasure. The parallel with Celie's present is clear — the suppression of her writing and the sterility and frigidity imposed on her by a male world. It is the blatancy of the African forms of this oppression that makes them so revealing.

Moreover, Africa itself is a place of historical disjunction. The Western missionaries are blacks who have come "home" to change that home, in effect to alienate Africans from their heritage. They are returning to their roots to pluck them out. At the same time, the capitalist road builders cutting through the jungle literally destroy the village. The roofleaf plant that was the basis of the Olinkas' economic and religious life cannot be grown any longer, and the builders mow down Nettie's round hut, the symbol of her wholeness, femininity, and identity.

Celie adopts a quilt pattern called Sister's Choice, symbolizing the freedom of action she gains by achieving this continuity with her past. A striking embodiment of this freedom is Shug, who loves both men and women, sings jazz, and writes her own songs. The book is careful to tie Shug into another historical tradition, that of jazz and the blues. Shug travels about giving performances and hobnobbing with the likes of Bessie Smith, Sophie Tucker, and Duke Ellington. This use of real people sets the fictive Shug in a living tradition that she embodies and extends through the creativity of her music and her style of loving. The faintly mythic quality of the rural south of the 1920s is countered by the documentary realism of the jazz references, just as the timeless African world is invaded by World War I and capitalist exploitation.

The Color Purple is virtually a formula for black women's fiction, including among its themes the suppression of women's writing and their bodies, the recovery of the African and black American past, the interconnection of sisterhood and self-determination, and the merging of myth and history. It is exemplary, also, in its treatment of history. Walker comments on this theme in her essay, "Writing *The Color Purple*":

I . . . knew *The Color Purple* would be a historical novel, and thinking of this made me chuckle. . . . A black male critic said he'd heard I might write a historical novel someday, and went on to say in effect: heaven protect us from it. The chuckle was because, womanlike (he would say), my 'history' starts not with the taking of lands, or the births, battles, and deaths of Great Men, but with one woman asking another for her underwear.

This sense that history changes through the intimacy of women is the premise we have been observing consistently in women's writing – that the personal and the communal, once observed and valued, constitute a political revolution. What is particularly striking about Walker's example, though, is its echo of Faulkner's note that *The Sound and the Fury* began with the image of a little girl with dirty drawers up in a tree. The intimacy of the view is the same, and so is its potential for scandal. Whereas the vision of Caddie's dirty drawers, however, expresses a masculine sense of woman as a transgressive, voyeuristic object, alien, without voice, and initiating a history of deracination and loss; Walker's image is one of sharing, of the opening up of communication, of the projection of the most homely of domestic subjects into a world-shattering moment.

Like Walker, Paule Marshall deals with the clash of cultures and the relation between private and political experience in her short stories and her novels: *Brown Girls, Brownstones* (1959); *The Chosen Place, the Timeless People* (1969); and *Praisesong for the Widow* (1983). Rather than the recovery of the African heritage, however, Marshall focuses on the cultural disjunctions between the West Indies and the United States, and often, as in the short story "To Da-Duh, in Memoriam," on the mutual incomprehension of generations of the same family raised in these different traditions. Marshall has the ability to create characters of such vivid intensity that they take on almost an independent existence. Their need to deal with extraordinary difficulties – sexual harassment, economic exploitation, familial cruelty – reveals the epic potential of ordinary people. The heroine of *Merle,* a brilliantly condensed version of *The Chosen Place, the Timeless People,* is an unforgettable figure, and Marshall's treatment of men, though they are not the central characters in her fiction, is equally sensitive.

Perhaps nowhere is the connection between the personal and the historical worked out more extensively than in Gloria Naylor's fiction. Already in *The Women of Brewster Place,* Naylor had produced a powerful image of the interchange between the two realms. A young mother whose child has died by electrocution is comforted by her neighbor Mattie. Holding the mother in her arms,

Mattie rocked her out of that bed, out of that room, into a blue vastness just underneath the sun and above time. She rocked her over Aegean seas so clean they shone like crystal, so clear the fresh blood of sacrificed babies torn from their mothers' arms and given to Neptune could be seen like pink froth on the water. She rocked her on and on, past Dachau, where soul-gutted Jewish mothers swept their children's entrails off laboratory floors. They flew past the spilled brains of Senegalese infants whose mothers had dashed them on the wooden sides of slave ships. And she rocked on. She rocked her into her childhood and let her see murdered dreams. And she rocked her back, back into the womb, to the nadir of her hurt.

To cure this pain one must recognize it and the whole history of women's suffering. To be born again, as this sorrowing mother is, one must recapitulate all that has come before and, in the process, turn the mute history of pain into an eloquent, life-giving balm.

Whereas Naylor shows women's love performing this recuperative act, man's history comes in for a very different treatment. In *Linden Hills* (1985), the official history of the community, now reaching its twelfth volume, is being written by a long-time resident of the housing development, Dr. Braithwaite. He has cut down the trees in front of his house and installed a Plexiglas window over an entire wall in order to observe everything that goes on, but though he can spy on the whole community, the one house invisible to him is the source of the community's tragedy. Braithwaite is a deluded voyeur who prides himself on his distance, his lack of involvement, and even his lack of power to change what he sees. When asked why he did nothing to stop a suicide next door, he answers, "I'm talking about not being able to stop the course of human history, a collective history or an individual one. . . . I know that I can only hope to record that knowledge, not rectify it."

The text immediately following reads *"After such knowledge, what forgiveness?"* This snippet from *Gerontion* is one of many lines quoted from T. S. Eliot's great contemplation of historical impotence, a knowledge (called "she") whose "giving famishes the craving," who "guides us by vanities" and gives either too soon or too late. Another modernist, Gertrude Stein, wrote, "Let me explain what history teaches. History teaches." This resignation to fate, to the impossibility of learning from the past to change the present, is unacceptable to Naylor. Her critique of objective history is also a critique of the vaunted impersonality and universality of modernist art, focused in the figure of Eliot. History must be built, constructed, in an act of intensely personal imagining. What one needs to build it is self-awareness, "that silver mirror God propped up in your soul."

Naylor uses this image of the mirror as part of a Faustian bargain that the inhabitants of Linden Hills have made with the devil figure of Luther Nedeed, their landlord. In exchange for prosperity, they have traded away their consciences and their self-awareness, and in the process, all hope of community, sharing, and love. At the center of Linden Hills, Nedeed has locked his wife and son in the basement because the son seems too light in color to be a Nedeed. The child dies after weeks of malnourishment, and the wife goes mad. She reads the neglected papers of earlier Nedeed women – compulsively recorded recipes and canning schedules, diaries that tell of oppression and sadistic mistreatment, and photographs in which a woman has systematically obliterated her own face. One Nedeed wife responded to her husband and son's oppression by refusing to talk unless required to do so. She marked her few ceremonial speeches by pricking her abdomen with a pin and coloring the wound with indelible ink, an utterly different kind of tattoo from that in Hawkes's *Travesty*, although the agency of male dominance lies behind both.

By examining these lost historical documents, the current Mrs. Nedeed gathers herself out of her sorrow and recalls her name, Willa Prescott Nedeed. She then reconstructs the personal history that landed her in this basement and looks at her image in a pan of water. For the first time in months she can sleep, and out of that mirror image she reconstructs an identity, and wakes, newly born. "It was a birth accompanied by the sound of thunder. . . . She stretched her arms and arched her back while fluttering her eyelids to awaken full grown into a sphere defined by the words *It's Christmas Eve, Mrs. Nedeed*." In this remarkable *Frankenstein* rebirth, Willa carries her dead son up the basement stairs, negotiates the door, and inadvertently starts a fire that burns the whole house down. By regaining the "silver mirror" God propped up in her soul, she ends five generations of tyranny.

While Willa's drama has been proceeding in the basement hell of Luther's house, above-ground the poet Willie has been descending through the Dantean circles of Linden Hills toward her. The correspondence of his name to Willa's is symptomatic of Naylor's strategy – the revelation of interconnectedness. Just as Willa recovers her identity through reading the lost writings of her dead predecessors, Willie goes about Linden Hills realizing the correspondence of all the lives he sees. What begins as a seemingly random picaresque becomes an intense experience with metaphor and symbol, and in social terms, with shared experience.

Naylor interweaves Willa's present with the past words of other Mrs. Nedeeds; likewise, Willie's yearnings merge with the blighted stories of Linden Hills, to the point where it is hard to see where one leaves off and the next begins. At one point, Willie dreams himself pursued by a voice importuning him to eat: "Willie, eat it." Two pages later, Willa in her basement reads of the attempts of a previous Mrs. Nedeed to win her husband's love by feeding him. Willa wonders, "Will he eat it?" Thus, Willie has dreamed Willa's words as if addressed to him. In the process, he has entered into her mind. It is this capacity for empathy that makes Willie the proper historian of Linden Hills and through that empathy, the model of what is needed to redeem the hell into which the inhabitants have fallen.

Braithwaite has written Willie into the next volume of the official history of Linden Hills, a counterchronicle to Naylor's book. The point is that these are two different kinds of history – his impotent to alter lives because predicated on *impersonality;* hers potent, because it not only tells individual stories but gives a theory of personal history, of the interweaving of all lives and the priority of self-examination to revolution. If the female condition was portrayed in the 1960s and 1970s as a desperate imprisonment in narcissism, such novelists as Naylor, Marshall, Walker, and Morrison are rewriting that narcissism as the first step toward liberation.

What we have been seeing in all these works is the crucial role of the past in situating and redirecting the present. Still, none of the novels we have discussed except *The Color Purple* could be called a historical novel, and even that one is not so strongly marked by its moment as to seem alien to the contemporary world. Toni Morrison's *Beloved* (1987), however, is a different matter. Set in the days of slavery, the book brings to life a historical mentality that persists nowadays only as a vestigial ache, a sense of dim horror and injustice like that of the Holocaust for those who did not live through it. Nowhere in fiction have the recovery from slavery and the adjustment to freedom been presented so dramatically: the painful dialectics of loss and memory, of repression and the imaginative opening to love.

Beloved is, amazingly, a ghost story. It tells of a slave family's plan to escape by crossing over the river into Ohio. The children are sent ahead, but before their mother Sethe can join them, she is forcibly held down and milked in a barn by white men and boys intent on discovering the aspects of her that are human as opposed to those that are animal. Pregnant, she is whipped for complaining of this treatment; she finally escapes to Ohio, delivering her baby en route. When the white men cross over to reclaim her, she tries to kill her children in order to free them from such abuse. She succeeds only with her elder baby daughter. Years later, after her returned lover chases the ghost of this baby from her house, the baby's spirit comes back as a young woman of the age she would have been had she lived. She seduces her mother's lover and forces him to leave, preying on her mother and sister. The ghost grows and flourishes as the mother and sister starve, until the community moves to assist them.

The pain of failed mothering is the central issue in this book. In slavery, protecting a child may involve killing her; love means loss; fostering means destroying. In this world of inversions, memories overtake reality, glutting themselves and starving out the impoverished present, so that by the end of the novel, the incongruity of a ghost in a historical novel does not seem a problem.

What *is* an issue is why storytelling should go on when it trafficks in the unbearable pain of memory, in losses that the novel terms "ungovernable" and "unspeakable." The ghost daughter, Beloved, thrives on the past. Her need for stories is as insatiable as memory itself. "Why was there nothing it refused?" Sethe wonders. "No misery, no regret, no hateful picture too rotten to accept? Like a greedy child it snatched up everything." Memory in the local speech is "rememory," an amalgam of *memory* and the verb *to remember,* as if the faculty were too active and too compulsively repetitive to submit to a mere abstract noun. At the end, when the ghost has been exorcised and the lovers reunited, the narrator chants, "It was not a story to pass on. . . . It was not a story to pass on. . . . This is not a story to pass on. . . . Beloved." The book is specifically this "passing on," this transmission, this death that is communication, and Sethe's future and ours depend on the digging up and "rememory" of the unspeakable past.

The character Beloved amounts to an allegory of memory, a demon returned to haunt and displace the present. Her very name is "all that is remembered" – the only word from the funeral's "Dearly Beloved" that remains with Sethe, the only word that would fit on the baby's tombstone, the lost word for what Sethe considers the best part of herself. Morrison embeds this steel armature of allegory in a novel so full of local color and so moving in its revelation of the inner lives of its characters that we are caught in a paradox. We read Beloved as a real being, and memory as a force so vital as to be a person – a selfish, greedy, insatiable adolescent who would totally overtake its parent's life. For Morrison to naturalize a ghost and transform us into nineteenth-century escaped slaves is an epic act of historical imagining. The past becomes not merely a political sphere of events and institutions to be learned – slavery, the Civil War, the formation of free black communities – but a psychological landscape to be inhabited. Like Louise Erdrich in *Love Medicine* and Marilynne Robinson in *Housekeeping,* Toni Morrison gives us access in *Beloved* to a forgotten world, and in the process bequeaths it to us as our own heritage.

Moreover, she does so not by ignoring the state of white, male fiction, but by taking off from it. She presents the birth of Beloved as a Beckettian passage from Sethe's womb to the grave. She mixes novelistic norms as violently as Don DeLillo in *White Noise,* mingling the ghost tale with the historical novel, dream narrative, and metastory. Her text runs the whole gamut of narrative modes, from omniscient storytelling to choral chanting. By stressing the role of the community in exorcising memory and by addressing the audience in the coda of the last two pages, Morrison turns the book from a story to an exhortation for readerly community. *Beloved* is a masterful conflation of feminist and postmodern aesthetic concerns. It demonstrates the central claim of this essay: that experimentalism, traditionalism, and women's writing merged in the major fictions of postmodernism.

A similar assertion might be made about *Love Medicine* (1984) by Louise Erdrich, a woman of mixed Native American and Caucasian ancestry. This, her first novel, is structured as a single story, with each chapter told from the perspective of a different character at a different historical moment. The characters belong to two interconnected families, and the Faulknerian weave of minds reveals the memories and the secrets that bind them. Thus, *Love Medicine* combines extensive with intensive definition, like Naylor's and Walker's collective storytelling. This strategy is particularly daring, because the characters provide so little stimulus to interpretation. Unlike the people of Linden Hills, they do not exteriorize their values in property, status, self-presentation, or careerist striving. They have dumb surfaces – "shells," as the text symbolizes them, that are in constant danger of cracking.

This schema of a blank exterior harboring a vulnerable inside appears in a system of imagery remarkable for its parasitism on conventional white symbolism. The book opens, for example, with June, the central figure in everyone's life, compared to an egg. It is Easter, and as the narrative shows her picked up in a bar, seduced in a car, and wandering away to her death in a snowstorm, the accompanying symbolism creates a different script for her. She is a peculiar mingling of Christ figure and Easter chick, wearing a top specifically termed a "shell," and "born" when the car door "cracks open" so that she can emerge a full-fledged walker on water. As the egg imagery continues, it draws in pies whose shells are irremediably cracked, and thus hints at Humpty-Dumpty, a broken egg who could not be put together again. This dizzying sequence of images – from pagan to Christian to nonsense literature – is typical of the subversive progress of *Love Medicine*'s symbolism. Similarly, the extensive fishing imagery links various female characters to Christ as a fisher of men, only to recast them as manipulators, reeling men in on their seductive lines.

These altered symbols are politically charged. Apples, for example, begin as signs of original sin, but in time signify Indians who have taken on white values: red on the outside and white underneath. The title of a painting of one of the tribe – *The Plunge of the Brave* – is a parody of "the home of the brave" from "The Star-Spangled Banner." It contains a terrible pun on the word *brave* that becomes a commentary on the privileged status of whites in American society. When one character tries to explain why he likes *Moby-Dick,* his companion cannot understand why anyone wants to read about "the white wail." By the end of *Love Medicine,* the egg, fish, apple, turtle, goose, and other images have become an array of totem objects, arising from white symbols but deliberately "misread" through an Indian frame of reference.

This distortion is not just a critique of the power structure of America but, more positively, a way for the Native Americans in the book to achieve a separate identity. *Love Medicine* shows how this perilous slippage of meaning endangers the Indian tradition. The central episode of the novel is the plan of a young man, Lipsha, to restore his grandfather's failing memory and love for his wife. Believing that he has "the touch," Lipsha decides to concoct a love medicine for his grandfather, which should be made out of goose hearts, since geese mate for life. He goes out to shoot some geese, but, unpracticed in hunting, he fails to shoot any, and unable to find one in the supermarket, he buys a frozen turkey with its innards wrapped in paper. He defrosts the heart, and then decides that it must be blessed. As the local priest and a nun refuse to do so, Lipsha steals some holy water, says his own words over the heart, and mixes it into his grandfather's food. His grandfather, suspicious, chokes on the heart and dies, and Lipsha concludes that he has underestimated the strength of his own "touch." This episode dramatizes the erosion of both the Indian and the Christian heritage, but Lipsha's faith in his magic mitigates the loss. By the end of the book, he discovers who his parents are and gains a new and exhilarating sense of identity.

The preoccupations of this book are strikingly consistent with other texts we have considered. Its central theme is memory and the recovery of lost histories and relationships. It deals with binarism in an almost programmatic fashion, with a pair of Indian twins separated as children, one brought up among whites and the other among his own people, and with the grandfather's two women, the domineering Marie and the pleasure-loving Lulu. Tattooing and wounding and stigmata express the same writing of pain on the body as in *The Executioner's Song* and *Linden Hills,* and as in so many contemporary novels, the oppressiveness of society leads to the self-destructive burning of a house. The characters' lives are paralleled to the Vietnam experience when an Indian returned from the war commits suicide. Erdrich draws the by now commonplace analogy between the creation of a community and the creation of a literary audience and experiments with narrative modes. In these ways *Love Medicine* takes virtually every characteristic of postmodern fiction and adapts it to the situation of the Native American woman.

Postmodern women's fiction is full of destroyed buildings. The Nedeed house in *Linden Hills* and Lulu's house in *Love Medicine* burn down; the mine in *Sula,* the housing development in *The Women of Brewster Place,* and the Olinka huts in *The Color Purple* are all torn down. These are images of the violence loosed when, in Langston Hughes's terms, a dream is deferred too long. Several of the objects destroyed are symbols of containment and domesticity and indicate the unsuitability of traditional roles and limits for women. What is interesting, too, is that the destruction of these symbols is the characteristic climax of minority women's writing. Though Marilynne Robinson's *Housekeeping* also culminates in the burning of a house, this violent representation of change is much more common in black fiction. White women, rather than following women's situation from loss through historical conscious- ness to a personal or collective apocalypse, stop at the exploration of loss, as if the model of Chopin's *The Awakening* were still definitive.

A whole cross-section of white female writers has fixed on this plot, from the disjointed narratives of Joan Didion to the academic irony of Alison Lurie and the lyricism of Anne Tyler. Didion's *Book of Common Prayer* (1977) tells of a woman whose daughter runs away, whose infant is born defective and dies, whose husband becomes incurably ill, whose friend – the narrator – has cancer, and who is herself killed by mistake in a Caribbean revolution – someone else's struggle for liberation. The charm, the beauty, the perfected femininity of this woman give her nothing but an enhanced opportunity to experience loss. Alison Lurie, in *The War Between the Tates* (1974), writes with biting sarcasm of the breakup and reconciliation of a couple, where neither home nor children nor spouse provides peace or fulfillment. In *Foreign Affairs* (1984), she presents two doomed love affairs, the one a classical romance between a handsome American professor and a beautiful British actress; the other, and the more central of the two, the story of a plain woman academic in her mid-fifties and a redneck from Oklahoma seeking his family roots. Both loves fail, largely because of the author's disdain for sentimentality. Like the fictions of British novelist Anita Brookner, Lurie's *Foreign Affairs* has won prizes and critical acclaim; apparently, something about these pathetic stories of loneliness and loss appeals strongly to the public and reviewers. The phenomenal success of Robert Waller's *The Bridges of Madison County* (1992) no doubt proceeds from the same sensibility.

A similar melancholy informs the masterful work of Anne Tyler. Her beautifully written and plotted novels – *Celestial Navigation* (1974), *Earthly Possessions* (1977), *Dinner at the Homesick Restaurant* (1982), *The Accidental Tourist* (1985) – explore an antiheroic view of experience. The major happen- ings of life are accidents rather than choices, and changes come about more by slow inurement than discrete acts of will. Tyler plays on the strangeness of family members to each other, their utter inability to understand each other. She also presents the isolation of sensitive and idiosyncratic figures, showing at the same time that everyone fits into these categories. With her affecting novels of outsiders and people of "limited horizons," she was one of the strongest female writers of the 1970s and 1980s.

Of course, much white women's writing pursues a recuperative goal analogous to that of black women. In Gale Godwin's *The Finishing School* (1984), the narrator sets out to become whole by recalling her past, the summer in which she was awakened to art, sexuality, and human sensitivity, and betrayed them in her immaturity. *Rubyfruit Jungle* likewise is a first-person narrative that retraces the course of a life in order to explain the narrator's strength and determination in the present. Lisa Alther's *Kinflicks* (1975) transforms a history of self-discovery, rebellion, frustration, and loss into a sort of comedy. It ends, "Like most of her undertakings, her proposed suicide had degenerated into burlesque. Apparently she was condemned to survival. . . . She left the cabin, to go where she had no idea." Like classical Bildungsromane, these novels end with the heroine launched, "lighting out" in an unknown direction that promises nothing specific except that old inhibitions or problems have been left behind. The achievement lies in the fact that there will be new possibilities.

The most notable source for such novels is Erica Jong's best-selling *Fear of Flying* (1973). At times hilarious, at times sad, this book is one of the first to depict female sexuality with the joyful abandon that James Joyce or Henry Miller gained for male writers earlier in the century. The heroine's sexual fantasizing culminates in the "zipless fuck," an image so necessary to modern culture that the phrase, like "catch-22," has now become a part of the language, even for those who have never heard of Jong's novel. The desire for pure sexual pleasure without practical contingencies or consequences, the achievement of the total control of a fantasy in which control is abandoned – these contradictory and assertive wishes inject a new humor and energy into women's writing. Though Jong's later books – like much of Joyce Carol Oates's massive oeuvre – are disappointingly mechanical, *Fear of Flying* stands as probably the most popular tale of female growth and liberation of the past twenty-five years. Its optimism and excitement pave the way for such books as Carol Hill's *The Eleven Million Mile High Dancer* (1985), which carries the fantasy one step further. It is a science-fiction dream of the liberated woman, its heroine an astronaut, physicist, beauty, and skilled roller skater who flouts the tiresome rules of the military and lives out a magical allegorical romance in which the forces of despair and evil are defeated by love.

Such unqualified success stories are seldom found in women's writing. More common is the frustration of Francine Prose's *Bigfoot Dreams* (1986) or Lorrie Moore's *Anagrams* (1986), both about well-educated women who cannot find satisfaction with men. The heroine of *Bigfoot Dreams,* a staff writer for a popular tabloid, produces "Demento Dentist Plants CB Radios in Malpractice Molars" as her first story. Despite her obvious journalistic skills, she is fired from the paper when her story about a fountain of youth, invented from a chance photograph, turns out to be true in every detail and the harassed subjects sue the paper. Deserted for the fifth time by her hippie husband, facing the imminent departure of her adolescent daughter, the heroine has nothing but her fantasies and alliterations to tide her through, to turn the world of failed love and permanence into the magical fulfillment of her wishes.

Anagrams is as wryly funny as *Bigfoot Dreams.* Its heroine is a teacher of poetry writing in a community college. For her, words are infinitely flexible structures capable of transforming themselves into puns and contradictions of the wildest sort: "I had *Lovesick* and *evil sock* scrawled in large letters. 'You're losing it, Benna. It must be your love life.' Eleanor leaned over and wrote *bedroom* and *boredom*; she had always been the smarter one." We eventually learn that this friend Eleanor and even Benna's daughter are permutations of Benna herself – imaginary people with whom the reader has lived on the same terms as the "real" characters in the book. The desolation of this woman beset by loss and loneliness is presented, however, as merely run-of-the-mill, the typical plight of smart women today.

More stylized and hip but equally funny is Tama Janowitz's *Slaves of New York* (1986). In the manner of the collective history, it tells a variety of stories of young artists and their friends whose lives are controlled by the expense and confusion of living in Manhattan. A Yuppie cult book, this fiction, like Jay McInerney's adolescent *Bright Lights, Big City* (1984) and other "Brat Pack" novels, depicts the dislocation of New York's gilded and not-so-gilded youth suffering not only from predictable identity crises and unhappiness but from an environment that utterly swamps them.

One of the most brilliant achievements of recent women's writing is Marilynne Robinson's *Housekeeping* (1980). Along with Morrison's *Beloved,* Roth's *Anatomy Lesson,* and Pynchon's *The Crying of Lot 49* and *Gravity's Rainbow, Housekeeping* both summarizes its period norms and supersedes them in exploring loss and the imaginative expansion of those who experience it. Robinson's first and only novel, *Housekeeping* is a meditation on the meaning of domesticity and the extension of domestic fiction to the scale of the epic. "My name is Ruth," the book opens, a feminine rewriting of "Call me Ishmael" that injects the epic struggle for identity and meaning with the pain of the foster daughter. The novel's allusive sources are the

Bible and the paradoxicalist Keats, and its emotive intensity is as great as the horizons it explodes.

Housekeeping is about the maintaining of bounds and their willed or unwilled dissolution. To keep house is to establish limits on the self, to create a boundary between the family and the outside world. All the routines – the cooking and the cleaning – are meant to make this identity enduring, to stave off time. The drudges of housekeeping, the two maiden great-aunts who come to take care of the narrator Ruth and her sister Lucille, "enjoyed nothing except habits and familiarity, the precise replication of one day in the next." A poet of housekeeping such as Ruth's grandmother experiences this routine as a divine rhythm: "Their lives spun off the tilting world like thread off a spindle, breakfast time, suppertime, lilac time, apple time." The book insists, however, that "this world purged of disaster and nuisance," like all replicas of heaven on earth, is doomed from the start.

The story of Ruth and Lucille's life is a story of loss:

> My name is Ruth. I grew up with my younger sister, Lucille, under the care of my grandmother, Mrs. Sylvia Foster, and when she died, of her sisters-in-law, Misses Lily and Nona Foster, and when they fled, of her daughter, Mrs. Sylvia Fisher. Through all these generations of elders we lived in one house, my grandmother's house, built for her by her husband, Edmund Foster . . . who escaped this world years before I entered it.

The story of the generations of elders is the "begats" of the Bible, a sequential list that should symbolize continuity but instead signals death and absence. To be fostered in this family is to be cared for as a foster child, a foundling. As the Fosters depart by accident, illness, desertion, or suicide, they slide actually or metaphorically into the lake that dominates the town of Fingerbone, leaving the girls finally under the care not of a Foster but a Fisher, a woman who dips into the lake of death and memory, and whose "housekeeping" gradually obliterates the boundaries between the house and the natural world outside it.

Housekeeping is almost entirely built of imagery, and its imagery is part of the theory of housekeeping itself. An image is a domestication of nature, a metaphoric transformation of a neutral object, for example, the lake that comes to stand for memory and death. Like imagery, housekeeping keeps the object world in line, manages it, and prevents it from a decay that would impinge upon our consciousness. Imagery maintains and tames memory, thus shaping family history, but it also puts limits on the imaginative embellishment of reality, limits that are as narrow or broad as the imagination of the housekeeper.

Words themselves are just such forces for order. There is something scandalous, then, about sequences of this sort: "She put our suitcases in the screened porch, which was populated by a cat and a matronly washing machine, and told us to wait quietly. Then she went back to the car and drove north almost to Tyler, where she sailed in Bernice's Ford from the top of a cliff named Whiskey Rock into the blackest depth of the lake." What do the cat, the washing machine, the direction of the drive, the name of the town or cliff have to do with the suicide flight of the car? They are detritus, like the suitcase, seat cushion, and lettuce that constitute the sole remains of the grandfather's train after it disappears into the lake. The world of things remains indifferent despite our best efforts; garbage is inescapable. Thus, like Pynchon, Robinson might be characterized as an antiallegorical writer. No matter how deep the symbolism and biblical allusion in *Housekeeping,* they always break down under the stubborn incommensurability of things and ideas. There is always something unassimilable left over, and yet the attempt to manage words and things is heroic. The imagistic reach of this book and the honesty of Ruth and her aunt Sylvie Fisher fill their idiosyncratic housekeeping with grandeur.

Even as creative a symbol maker as Sylvie, who "feels the life of perished things," participates in the decay of images. The energy she expends in turning the world into a playground of living forces keeps endangering the stability of homely images. The work of good housekeepers is to control things, to eliminate all but the useful, and to make them stable, unchanging, always the same. This task calls for a certain violence, a discarding of bad things and a taming and domesticating of good things, so that they will not participate in the world of death and decay. For Sylvie, however, everything is valuable in some way, so that housekeeping involves all of reality. Sylvie gradually obliterates the barrier between inside and outside, letting animals and dry leaves inside and turning the lights off at night to make the darkness continuous between the two worlds. She is the death of binary thinking.

Sylvie is also a transient. Before taking over the girls' care in the town of Fingerbone, she rides around the country in freight cars, experiencing randomness as an everyday fact. Her housekeeping, when she settles down, is not the management of things but their accumulation, since everything for her deserves to be preserved, to be incorporated into the house that is her life. In making us assent to Sylvie's viewpoint, in showing the continuity between respectable housekeeping and Sylvie's variety, Robinson naturalizes madness, taking the reader over, as Morrison does in *Beloved,* to a previously unimaginable state of mind.

Gradually we come to accept the fact that the boundary building of respectable domesticity destroys the home and family it was meant to protect. When the townspeople decide to take the girls away because Sylvie permits truancy, messiness, and transience, Sylvie frantically enacts the role of a conventional housekeeper. She and Ruth build a huge bonfire and burn up the accumulated garbage in the house, piles of newspapers and magazines, piles of memories. "It had never occurred to me," Ruth thinks as the newsprint burns, "that words, too, must be salvaged. . . . It was absurd to think that things were held in place, are held in place, by a web of words." To keep house involves destroying words, and similarly, the custody hearing determines that the girls should be removed from Sylvie's care – that one best preserves domestic values by obliterating the very premise of domesticity, the family. At this point, the last reason for conforming to the community's view of housekeeping is removed, and Ruth and Sylvie proceed to burn down their home. "Now truly we were cast out to wander and there was an end to housekeeping."

After fleeing across the bridge over the lake, Ruth and Sylvie ride the rail lines of the Northwest, tracing ever larger circles of horizon. The book ends with Ruth picturing the narrow horizons of her conventional sister Lucille, who is now grown up and living respectably in Boston. As Lucille sits in a restaurant, "Her water glass has left two-thirds of a ring on the table, and she works at completing the circle with her thumbnail." Lucille's circle is as wide as the diameter of a water glass; Ruth and Sylvie's, as broad as the Northwest. The loss and sadness lying behind the attempt to complete the circle is, however, the same.

Robinson invents a language of negation to express these opposites that is startling in its eloquence. The book ends

No one watching this woman smear her initials in the steam on her water glass with her first finger, or slip cellophane packets of oyster crackers into her handbag for the sea gulls, could know how her thoughts are thronged by our absence, or know how she does not watch, does not listen, does not wait, does not hope, and always for me and Sylvie.

Housekeeping is a willed forgetting, but as such it is inevitably a remembering, too. The difference between Lucille's loss and Ruth's, between theirs and that of the best homemakers in Fingerbone, is merely a matter of degree.

The idea of loss is expressed through a complicated system of imagery, all relating to the lake, a reflective surface with dark depths below, housing the dead. The lake's flooding has the power to take away perspective, and it is this ever-present fear of being swamped, of having all order obliterated, that makes people insist on housekeeping, on sanity. The security of sanity is just a matter of perspective, however, of which side of the lake, or window, you are looking through:

When one looks from inside at a lighted window, or looks from above at the lake, one sees the image of oneself in a lighted room, the image of oneself among trees and sky – the deception is obvious, but flattering all the same. When one looks from the darkness into the light, however, one sees all the difference between here and there, this and that.

Robinson puts a new twist in the meaning of narcissism. If *Housekeeping* and all recent women's novels are in some sense concerned with identity, then Robinson's image of the lake or lighted window complicates the issue. From the "right" side of the reflecting surface, the domestic side, we get a reassuring self-image, but if we look through the surface, we see only alterity, death, the untameable reality that is the not-us. Narcissism is the desperate expression of the need to write ourselves over the world. It is utterly natural and utterly doomed, for the reflecting surface is not stable enough to block out the depths behind it.

The persistence of thought and life is just this insistence on the surface. It is the world of imagination and the mind, and Robinson ties it to the visual or literary image itself:

The only true birth would be a final one, which would free us from watery darkness and the thought of watery darkness, but could such a birth be imagined? What is thought, after all, what is dreaming, but swim and flow, and the images they seem to animate? The images are the worst of it. It would be terrible to stand outside in the dark and watch a woman in a lighted room studying her face in a window, and to throw a stone at her, shattering the glass, and then to watch the window knit itself up again and the bright bits of lip and throat and hair piece themselves seamlessly again into that unknown, indifferent woman. It would be terrible to see a shattered mirror heal to show a dreaming woman tucking up her hair. And here we find our great affinity with water, for like reflections on water our thoughts will suffer no changing shock, no permanent displacement . . . they persist, outside the brisk and ruinous energies of the world. I think it must have been my mother's plan to rupture this bright surface, to sail beneath it into very blackness, but here she was wherever my eyes fell, and behind my eyes, whole and in fragments, a thousand images of one gesture, never dispelled but rising always, inevitably, like a drowned woman.

The mother, however, is not *like* a drowned woman; she *is* one. She continues to float up in Ruth's memories of that narcissistic gesture before the lighted window. As much as Ruth would like to break down the gulf that separates them – to shatter the glass of her mother's reflection and have their eyes meet – the window knits itself up again and the barrier between thought and presence remains. The imagistic richness of *Housekeeping* – fetishlike – expresses the seductive attraction of the surface world of imagination. What we should not forget is "the watery darkness and the thought of watery darkness" that lie behind this surface.

Robinson builds into this water imagery a political argument as pointed as that of any of the women discussed in this chapter. One of the central allusions of the book is the biblical account of Noah's flood. The aim of an imaginative liberation like Sylvie's is to turn one's house into an ark, a moveable boundary for the self floating on the waters of memory. However, the pain of this unanchoring is terrible. Far from glorifying Noah, Robinson directs us to his wife, who spent her time aboard the vessel bewailing all that had been lost and left behind. A traditional figure of mockery in world literature, Noah's wife has no name but comes down to us only as an antiheroic appendage of her husband. Robinson tells the lost story of Noah's wife, and that of Lot's wife, too, condemned for the caring that caused her to look backward. Likewise, Ruth's grandmother's obituary is a collage of pictures of her husband's train wreck, which callously omits any mention of her. The aim of *Housekeeping* is to recover and dignify all those lost lives, all those appended identities, by showing the grandeur of the unheroic backward glance.

The imagistic artistry of this book is unsurpassed in postwar fiction, but what one notices first about it is its language, a surface so rich and highly wrought that it becomes an analogue to the lake and the imagination. Here, one might pause to consider the claim that women's writing is a throwback to nineteenth-century realism, where conventional plot, theme, and characterization – the elements of Barth's "secular news report" – dominate stylistic and technical concerns. Indeed, if we consider the novels discussed in this chapter, the range of linguistic innovation is remarkable: the oneiric, imagistic richness of Robinson's prose; the array of narrative types in Le Guin's *The Left Hand of Darkness*; the thick allusion to modernist writing in Gloria Naylor; the ironic quotations from Dick and Jane readers in Toni Morrison's *The Bluest Eye*; the language that Morrison invents for the ghost in *Beloved*; the wild headlines of *Bigfoot Dreams* and the puns of *Anagrams*; Alice Walker's use of the epistolary form in *The Color Purple* (not the parodic reevocation of an eighteenth-century form that we see in Barth's *Letters* but an original refashioning of the very meaning of letter writing, of communication, and of women's authoring); and the picaresque string of episodes in *Linden Hills* that coalesce into a violent simultaneity, when the past letters and diaries and pictures enter the present.

These stylistic innovations differ from the writing of the extreme experimentalists of the 1960s and 1970s in that the style is never a focus of interest in itself. Contemporary female writers seem seldom to take language per se as their subject, or the state of literature or its history. Though language, literature, and aesthetic history enter all their writing, their central concern is the act of storytelling in a historical moment. Even as seemingly apolitical a book as *Housekeeping* depends on the current state of reality for the interpretation of its female world. This merging of social and aesthetic problematics is the great achievement of recent women's writing, and indeed of the postmodernism it so clearly embodies.

5

❧

CONCLUSION

THIS STUDY has described some of the remarkable changes in
American fiction since the late 1960s. At that time, the novel displayed three main tendencies. The one considered most artistically
important then was the playful experimentation of John Barth and Thomas
Pynchon, which struck critics as such a departure from the past that it was
labeled "postmodern." Now, at the end of the century, its connections to
such high modernists as James Joyce and Franz Kafka seem obvious, so that
this experimental wing of "postmodernism" may not quite merit its prefix.
In contrast to the experimentalists, such authors as Norman Mailer and
Philip Roth were producing a story- and character-centered literature that
seemed to have more in common with nineteenth-century realism than the
twentieth-century avant garde. The third category in the trio was just
emerging as a literary entity: women's fiction. Its aim was to rewrite history
so as to recast the importance of women in all areas of life, and it was
defined not in terms of literary affinities or differences (traditionalism,
experimentalism) but in terms of the gender of its authors.

Though the work of other groups – blacks, gays, Native Americans –
was being published in the late 1960s, it was usually not identified as
such. Scholars had not yet elaborated the historical and theoretical context
that would create a separate identity for such works, and in the late 1960s,
many critics were acutely uncomfortable with typologies determined by
ethnicity and gender. Thus the work of the black novelist Ishmael Reed
was treated as experimentalism and that of the gay author Edmund White
was seen as realism.

Women's writing was perhaps the first of the categories determined by
autobiographical factors to gain critical acceptance, though black literature was not far behind. The other two fictional types, experimentalism
and realism, belonged to an older critical thinking based on formal factors.
These were the legacy of the New Critics, who had addressed themselves
to the work rather than the author. By 1970, they had reached the end of
their long dominance in American English departments, but the post-
structuralists who followed them likewise proclaimed the "death of the
author." Women's writing was thus still a conceptual problem in 1970 for

many critics and scholars, and the typology of women's, experimentalist, and traditional fiction was obviously a temporary, "interparadigmatic" construction.

As time went on, these categories proved less and less adequate, as powerful novels combined characteristics from all three. As we have seen, the fictions of men and women, traditionalists and experimentalists alike, explored the literary romance and its relation to voyeurism, solipsism, and narcissism, rejecting the either/or of conventional binary thinking in favor of the inclusiveness of the both/and. Identity was depicted not as a heroic individualism, as in Pound or Camus or the lower-brow Ayn Rand, but as a social determinism by ethnicity, race, class, and gender. In the process, fiction and history often blended in a partial, personal writing. Gone was the universal stance of modernism, in which the "human condition" was detachable from a time and place. Even the reader was refused this neutral position. Late-twentieth-century novels include their audience within them, whether as a passenger in *Travesty*'s high-speed car crash or the heir to *Beloved*, "not a story to pass on."

Because of the merging of the three categories over the last three decades of the century, the term *postmodernism* makes more sense if used to cover all the writing of this period, rather than merely the experimentalism to which it at first referred. Experimentalism becomes only a particularly extreme case within the field of postmodern writing. Thus, though it might seem like a foolishly quietistic move to characterize the diverse fiction of Pynchon, Roth, and Robinson as elements of a coherent system, these novels are better understood through this totalizing gesture than according to categories that they constantly belie.

By the late 1990s, the hierarchy among the three tendencies had shifted. It is quite clear that experimentalism is no longer the leading edge of fiction. Several (usually white male) writers continue to publish long, game-oriented, self-reflexive novels – for example, Richard Powers's *The Gold Bug Variations* (1991), *Operation Wandering Soul* (1993), and *Galatea 2.2* (1995) and Thomas Pynchon's *Vineland* (1990) and *Mason & Dixon* (1997). Outside the United States, such metafictionists as Salman Rushdie, Italo Calvino, Gabriel García Márquez, and Julian Barnes are still enthusiastically received; in America, however, critical taste has moved on. To be sure, *Mason & Dixon* was on the *New York Times* Bestseller List when it appeared, for Pynchon remains one of the most esteemed American writers of the postwar era. However, the reviews were respectful but disappointed, as they were with Pynchon's previous book, *Vineland*. Though Richard Powers's fiction shows impressive intellect and emotional power, major literary prizes have eluded him, going instead to less hermetic authors. The era seems to be passing when the most revered fiction is also the most esoteric.

As early as 1980, critics registered this change. The December 14, 1980, *New York Times Book Review* asked, "As we move into the 80s, what is happening to fiction? Is it becoming more realistic and less experimental? Are writers more concerned with historical and nonfictional material and less interested in being 'self-referential,' in writing about writing? Are we really living . . . in a Golden Age of the American Novel?" As this history has tried to show, the issue was not experimentalism *versus* realism but some peculiar rapprochement of the two that spread across women's literature and the writing of other socially demarcated groups.

One could speculate about the causes of this change in taste. It is certainly the case that some of the practitioners of metafiction – Thomas Pynchon, Robert Coover, John Hawkes, John Barth, William Gass – have passed the prime of their careers. In *Vineland,* Pynchon's brilliance often degenerates into silliness and sentimentality, and the same is true of *Mason & Dixon,* which reads like Barth's *The Sot-Weed Factor* laboriously reprised for the 1990s. In this context, Richard Powers, still a young writer, seems especially anachronistic.

Beyond simply the aging of the experimentalists, however, the shift away from difficult fiction reflects a new public attitude to the arts and cultural experts. For a long time, the public treated academics' fondness for esoteric art as a professional tic – incomprehensible but ultimately harmless, since high art did not impinge much on their daily experience. Since the mid-1980s, however, this attitude has changed. A series of highly publicized scandals has undermined the modernist assumptions behind American high culture: openness about sex, ironic distance, the desirability of aesthetic complexity, the right of artists to challenge conventional beliefs, and even the distinction between art and reality. Every season seems to produce a new crop of aesthetic or academic controversies, from quarrels about "political correctness" to outrage against sexuality in art expressed by both leftist feminists and rightist reactionaries. Seldom has the conflict between the taste of the general public and the experts been more vividly dramatized than in these late-twentieth-century "culture wars." Whereas in midcentury such a rarified poet as T. S. Eliot could fill an American football stadium for a public reading, today an author must appeal to Oprah Winfrey to reach that level of public approbation, and her reading club has shown no interest so far in the likes of Pynchon or Powers.

The rigorous line between art and reality has become severely eroded. It sometimes seems as if the public has forgotten that the phrase "virtual reality" is an oxymoron. Virtuality, or at least the virtuality of art, now flows effortlessly into the actual, in part at least because advertising and political "spin" are so effective in manipulating symbols to "change reality." Web enthusiasts speak of their fantasy roles in Internet chatrooms as the most intensely real aspects of their lives, and large numbers of Americans believe that art directly affects behavior, despite all evidence to the contrary. For example, as of 1997, the actual crime rate in the United States has been dropping noticeably, whereas the amount of crime on television news and in the movies continues as high as ever. Nevertheless, everyone from the president of the United States to the average public-minded high school student claims that television and film violence promote crime. Similarly, pornography is blamed without proof for rape and the unequal status of women in the workplace. The burden of reality lies so heavily on art that a Nabokovian argument for aesthetic bliss through the freedom of fantasy comes across as callous irresponsibility.

Changes in the marketing of books have also contributed to the demise of esoteric fiction. However important this writing has been throughout the century, its success was always a matter of critical approbation rather than mass sales. However, market forces now make it more and more difficult for books aiming only at a succès d'estime to get into print in the first place. The expansion of the giant chains – Borders, Barnes & Noble, Waldenbooks – has swallowed up smaller operations or made them financially unviable. As a result, corporate buyers now choose what the American public will read, rather than the intellectuals and literati who did so before in their capacity as bookstore owners. Books must be marketable to succeed on the market, a tautology that has become a self-fulfilling prophecy about the relationship between popular taste and high fiction.

As the taste for metafiction has waned, the barriers between high and low fiction have become more permeable, but this is not to say that they have disappeared. It is not an accident that this study has almost completely ignored popular writing, despite the indisputable fact that formulaic detective stories, spy thrillers, science fiction, horror stories, romances, and westerns fill the shelves of bookstores in airports and supermarkets and malls. Equally important are the nonfiction genres that have recently merged with the field of fiction: memoirs, autobiographies, pop psychology, travel narratives, celebrity biographies, and even fitness manuals and cookbooks. These are an integral part of the field in which 1990s fiction is received. Many involve first-person or at least "personal" testimony of one sort or another, in which the contours of fiction and fact become indistinguishable.

It is important to realize the interaction between elite and popular genres, however separate they still remain. In the 1970s, American nonfiction best-sellers were typically Bibles, dictionaries, and sex manuals. By the end of this period, individual editions of the Bible had ceased to become best-sellers, since there were then so many competing translations and so many different groups targeted by the various editions that no single one could dominate the market. This is another manifestation of the switch from a "universal" to a group-targeted appeal that we have observed in high fiction.

Early 1970s best-seller lists register a sudden proliferation of sex manuals: *Everything You Wanted to Know About Sex but Were Afraid to Ask* (1969) by David Reuben; *The Sensuous Man* (1971) by "M"; and *Total Woman* (1973) by Marabel Morgan. This development reflects the easing of censorship in publishing and is a direct legacy of modernist fiction. The victory in the *Lady Chatterley's Lover* case in the 1960s virtually ended legal trials of literature in America and England; it was another modernist masterpiece, James Joyce's *Ulysses,* that had begun this liberalization in the 1930s with Judge Woolsey's famous opinion. Modernist fiction and the later fashion for self-help opened the way for the representation of sex in nonfiction.

Paperback pop fiction had a direct relation to the high tradition in that so much of it follows the plot structure of the literary romance. Erich Segal's *Love Story* topped the list two years in a row (1970 and 1971) and William P. Blatty's *The Exorcist* did so in 1974. Mario Puzo's *The Godfather* (1969) sold over ten million copies, and James Michener's romance sagas of exotic places were perennial financial blockbusters. The interplay between fiction and film was apparent by this time, too, a marketing symbiosis that has increased, if anything, in later decades.

The *New York Times* Bestseller List of December 13, 1987, reveals the tenuous connection between high and low fiction in popular taste. It contains *two* horror novels by Stephen King, a Danielle Steel romance, one of Garrison Keillor's sweetly wry accounts of growing up in the Midwest, a spy novel, a crime story, two historical novels of family passion, a science-fiction sequel to *2001: A Space Odyssey,* a children's Christmas book, humorous tales of an outdoorsman, a James Michener epic, and books by three of the authors discussed in previous chapters of this book – Toni Morrison, Tom Wolfe, and Kurt Vonnegut. The pattern is clear: pop fiction of all genres dominates the list, though established "high" artists occasionally reach a mass market.

Thus, any picture of contemporary fiction would be incomplete without reference to the brilliant horrors of King's *Pet Sematary* (1983) or *Christine* (1983), the western melancholy of Larry McMurtrey's *The Last Picture Show* (1966) or *Lonesome Dove* (1985), or for that matter Jacqueline Suzanne's lubricious adventure stories. "Serious writers" have themselves tried out popular genres. Joyce Carol Oates, Norman Mailer, and Tom Wolfe, for example, have produced works indistinguishable from mass fiction (respectively, *A Bloodsmoor Romance, Tough Guys Don't Dance,* and *Bonfire of the Vanities*) without endangering their status as artists.

The arrangement of titles in bookstores reflects the gulf between high and low writing. Whereas pop fiction is grouped according to genre (romance, mystery, science fiction), "serious novels" are sold under the undifferentiated heading of "literature." Pop fiction consumption is presumably genre driven, but the stigma attached to "formula fiction" is one of the strange hangovers of modernism in our day. It is hard to see why the work of Ursula Le Guin or John Le Carré should not be found under the heading of literature, and why conformity to genre norms is automatically "low."

The line between high and low culture is a reflection of a class consciousness that is particularly embarrassing to liberal and leftist intellectuals, as Martha Bayles's humorous "The 'New Yorker' Story," published in 1984 in *Harper's Magazine,* reveals. In it, a young writer named William has his career launched when the *New Yorker* accepts a piece of his fiction set in the Midwest, "somewhere out there in that endless, anomic, checkerboard flatness: that heartland without a heart to which his imagination keeps returning." He begins another story, this time with a leading character called Betty, a J. C. Penney's clerk from the same anomic heartland; but Betty very soon escapes her creator's control, developing a will of her own and a big-city sophistication and glamour. Thoughtfully, she picks up a remote-control transmitter and flicks on her Pioneer stereo system. William expects her to play Stockhausen, or possibly Schoenberg, but no, Betty turns on Muzak, the same Muzak she has heard in the mall.

> William leapt forward. "There, you *see?!? That's* why I want you back in J. C. Penney's! Because you have no *taste!*"
> Betty turns up the Muzak, then smiles. "Let me get this straight. There's no meaning in the world, so all experiences are equally pointless."
> William waves his arms. "If you want to discuss my world view, you're going to have to turn down that *garbage!*"

High taste is still the cachet to the literary world view, even if that view holds that all experience is equally valid – or equally meaningless. Despite the blatant violations of decorum in postmodern literature, it maintains a studious distance from low culture.

This fact still conditions our attitudes to short fiction. The epic scope of the novel is generally seen as more valuable than the smaller canvas of the short story, even though the short story has passed through the same high experimentalism as the novel. In the late 1960s and early 1970s, under the influence of Borges and the whole spectrum of aesthetic experimentation of the time, short stories violated every literary norm. *Anti-Story* (1971), edited by Philip Stevick, collects works under the following heads: Against Mimesis, Against Reality, Against Event, Against Subject, Against the Middle Range of Experience, Against Analysis, Against Meaning, Against Scale. Eugene Wildman's *Experiments in Prose* (1969) contains recognizable if nonnormative fiction, such as Donald Barthelme's stories, but also collages, photographic sequences, concrete poems, dialogues, and poster foldouts.

It is an indication of the short story's lack of critical stature that no one bemoaned or even proclaimed the "death of the short story" as a result of these violations. The disruption of the story was an obviously invigorating development, for 1950s works are notoriously self-imitating. "The Craft of Short Fiction" is a typical title for collections at this time, suggesting the story as a prose equivalent of the lyric poem – a perfectly shaped extension of modernist themes. When antistories, narrative experiments, Edward Gorey's camp illustrated tales, or Woody Allen's philosophical burlesques appeared, the story gained a playfulness and visuality that seemed no particular threat to an already marginalized subgenre.

In the 1980s, however, the short story briefly appeared to be in the vanguard of fiction. The brilliant pieces of Raymond Carver in *What We Talk About When We Talk About Love* (1981) and *Cathedral* (1983) carry a condensed power that led critics to characterize him as a "Minimalist." This term echoes the name of a visual arts movement whose reductivism pushed avant-garde modernism to a new extreme; however, Carver's writing is anything but abstract in its effect or meta-artistic in its meaning. He shows us emotion, disappointments, dissolving relationships. The deadpan simplicity with which he lets feelings emerge in his stories is reminiscent of the early Hemingway, without Hemingway's stylistic and ethical self-consciousness.

Carver is the writer most often cited in lists of Minimalists – those 1980s figures whose compression, lucidity, and technical craftsmanship differ so markedly from the obscurity and allusiveness of 1960s fiction. Called "new realists" by their proponents and the "Redneck Brigade" by detractors, Carver, Richard Ford, Ann Beattie, Bobbie Ann Mason, and Tobias Wolff produced fiction characterized by its "equanimity of surface": ordinary subjects treated by neutral narrators in a very brief scope. Minimalism differed from experimental postmodernism in its simplicity and de-emphasis of irony, though it is often as ambiguous and rich in meaning as the most esoteric metafiction. Carver in particular contrasted his work to the aridity of postmodernist experimentalism: "Too often such writing gives us no news of the world, or else describes a desert landscape . . . a place of interest only to a few scientific specialists."

Many of the Minimalists went on to become established fiction writers – for example, Richard Ford, who won the Pulitzer prize for fiction for

Independence Day (1995). Carver himself would undoubtedly have become a major figure if not for his unfortunate death in 1988. By the 1990s, none of these writers was known as a Minimalist any longer. The importance of the movement lay in its dramatization of changes that were already taking place in novel writing – in particular, the shift away from experimentalism as a goal in itself toward an integration of style, realist depth, and the recovery of previously ignored points of view.

By the mid-1990s, metafiction had declined in favor of the dramatization of personal voices in confessional modes. The memoir was becoming the master genre of the day. This nonfiction genre epitomizes the aim of women's literature to allow women a "voice," and its very publication is a political act. Memoirs from the 1990s tell supposedly true stories of oppression and violence that would not before have been printed or, indeed, believed. The first person, moreover, obliterates the boundary between objective truth and fictive subjectivity. The title of Mary Karr's brilliant memoir, *The Liar's Club* (1995), is paradigmatic.

So many memoirs by "ordinary people" were published by the mid-1990s that the media began to comment. In 1996, wrote Doreen Carvajal,

A retired high school teacher's memoir of his impoverished Irish childhood is No. 1 on the New York Times best-seller list [Frank McCourt's *Angela's Ashes*]. . . . The nation's publishers are preparing to release a torrent of confessionals that offer competing visions of anxiety. Rape, downsizing and disease. Depression and blue huckleberry jelly recipes. The "cellular memories" of a heart and lung transplant recipient who mysteriously developed her donor's zest for beer and fried chicken.

This sudden public interest in the personal testimony of "average citizens" has shifted the idea of the heroic decisively away from Aristotle's aristocrats and Warhol's celebrities to the AIDS sufferer, the assaulted girl child, the ordinary person who survived.

Though the memoir is a nonfiction genre, the trend toward confession has had an important influence on novelists. Whereas before they might have transformed personal traumas into sharable fantasies, many now present their traumas as bald fact. Kathryn Harrison followed her novel *Exposure* (1993), which was about imagined incest and rape, with the memoir *The Kiss* (1996), about her true-life experiences of incest and rape. After writing numerous novels about a fictive father, beginning with *Final Payments* (1978), Mary Gordon presented her real father in a memoir, *The Shadow Man* (1996). In the introduction she quipped, "I entered the cave of memory, which nowadays seems like a tourist trap in high season. Everyone's talking about memory: French intellectuals, historians of the

Holocaust, victims of child abuse, alleged abusers. It's a subject of conversation in the academy and on morning chat shows – even on A M radio."

As the critic Kirk Hughes has noted, daytime talk shows are themselves confessional genres in which guests and hosts reveal hidden truths about their lives. *The Oprah Winfrey Show* is perhaps the most extreme example of this television confessionalism. It is thus not surprising that Ms. Winfrey chooses novels for the Oprah Winfrey Book Club on the basis of their resemblance to the real-life confessions on her show. In 1996 she selected Toni Morrison's *Song of Solomon* (1979), a choice that resulted in the sale of half a million copies of the seventeen-year-old novel within a month. Never let it be said that fiction and nonfiction have separate developmental histories!

This interaction has produced a self-reflexiveness worthy of 1970s metafiction, in which novelists write true fiction about themselves as fiction-writers. The short-story writer Gary Krist described this effect in a 1997 essay in the Sunday *New York Times*:

A writer – call him "Gary Krist" – sits down and writes a novel about a writer – call *him* "Gary Krist" – who writes novels about writing novels.

Is this fiction? Imaginary memoir? Metafictional musing?

Well, yes. And whatever else it is, it seems to be an increasingly common ploy in contemporary fiction. David Leavitt's novella "The Term Paper Artist" and Paul Theroux's novel "My Other Life" are just the two most prominent recent examples of this phenomenon – fictions that feature the author as character, under his own name.

Not to be confused with straightforward memoirs, in which writers tell lies about themselves in the guise of nonfiction, these books frankly proclaim their fictionality. But unlike autobiographical novels, in which writers tell truths about themselves in the guise of fiction, they operate on a different level of coyness, playing more openly with the boundaries between actual fact and the products of imagination.

One might note in passing that David Leavitt had written a novel before *The Term Paper Artist* called *While England Sleeps* (1993) in which an episode so resembled one in the life of the British poet Stephen Spender that Spender sued Leavitt for plagiarism and had the book removed from store shelves. And Paul Theroux, best known as a travel writer, had published the nonfictional *My Secret History* (1990), even the title of which seems indistinguishable from his fictional *My Other Life*. In *My Secret History*, Theroux explains how he split his time between England and America and so acquired "two of everything." The English critics took him to task for this unseemly and inconsiderate confession. It is hard to decide whether a confession is a fictionalization of the self or a revelation of it, and critical response to these works has been caught in the confusion.

The proliferation of memoir has spread across all the literary (and visual) genres. In the 1996 nominations for the National Book Critics' Circle Awards, all five categories—criticism, general nonfiction, fiction, poetry, and autobiography/biography—could have been won by a confession. *Angela's Ashes* did win in the autobiography/biography category, swamping some very accomplished third-person lives (e.g., Peter Conn's *Pearl S. Buck*) that could not compete with the emotional power of the confession. As a result, the Book Critics' Circle debated, not for the first time, whether to split the category of autobiography/biography, and decided, also not for the first time, not to do so.

Even when 1990s fiction does not use the first person or make any gestures toward the nonfiction memoir, it often contains the same factors that have catapulted the confession to literary prominence. Some of the finest novels of the 1990s are about the inner suffering of ordinary people. In Stanley Elkin's *Mrs. Ted Bliss* (1995), the last years of a Jewish widow in Miami take on the tragic grandeur of an epic. Perhaps the most powerful novel of the 1990s, Annie Proulx's *The Shipping News* (1992), reveals just this extraordinary beauty in the unpromisingly ordinary.

Like the imaginative leap of *Mrs. Ted Bliss,* in which a male author explores the mind of an old lady, *The Shipping News* is a female author's exploration of a male character. This is a man so inarticulate and so beaten down at the beginning that he can hardly be said to have a point of view. Moreover, he is a man who, unlike his wild wife, loves and nurtures his children. His name is Quoyle, the word for a coil of rope, and the novel, inspired by a handbook on knots, is about the process of acquiring human ties, of progressing from isolation to belonging and finally love. Like countless heroines of recent fiction, Quoyle achieves this growth by learning to tell stories, and indeed, by having his journalistic reports published in the local paper, "The Shipping News." Perhaps not since Benjie in Faulkner's *The Sound and the Fury* (1929) has there been such an unpromising hero, and not for a very long time in fiction has the potential for growth seemed so miraculous.

Proulx's prose is itself a miracle. The book begins with a language as matter-of-factly painful as Quoyle's life:

Hive-spangled, gut roaring with gas and cramp, he survived childhood; at the state university, hand clapped over his chin, he camouflaged torment with smiles and silence. Stumbled through his twenties and into his thirties learning to separate his feelings from his life, counting on nothing. He ate prodigiously, liked a ham knuckle, buttered spuds.

By the end of the book, though, Quoyle's spiritual expansion is matched in Proulx's triumphal prose: a visionary symbolism instinct with hope.

Water may be older than light, diamonds crack in hot goat's blood, mountain-tops give off cold fire, forests appear in mid-ocean, it may happen that a crab is caught with the shadow of a hand on its back, that the wind be imprisoned in a bit of knotted string. And it may be that love sometimes occurs without pain or misery.

Like *Housekeeping, The Shipping News* exceeds any formulaic view of its moment in literary history, and yet, it has much to tell us about this period, too. Its respect for individual experience, for the ordinary, is consistent with the confessional 1990s, and it deals with existential despair in a way that the early postmodernists did not anticipate. It is true that for both, the meaninglessness of experience can be met only by the assertion of individual interest. This is the lesson that Pierce Inverarity teaches Oedipa Maas from the grave – to keep the ball bouncing, to take on "interests." For Proulx, however, the strategies of coping are not hyperrationality, paradox, and the absurd but a kind of nurturing steadfastness. She stays with the nonheroic until it is imbued with grandeur. The miracle here is not Pynchon's collision of worlds through the magic of language but the patient quantitative gains of personal growth that suddenly produce a qualitative leap in value. If this period of fiction opened with metafictional fireworks, it closes with the extraordinary commonplace of love.

EMERGENT LITERATURES

Cyrus R. K. Patell

FROM MARGINAL TO EMERGENT

Wittman Ah Sing, the protagonist of Maxine Hong Kingston's novel *Tripmaster Monkey: His Fake Book* (1989), has a problem. Named for the great poet of American individualism and steeped in American cultural history, Wittman wants to be a latter-day Jack Kerouac, but to his chagrin, he comes to realize that the real Kerouac would never have seen him as a protégé. To Kerouac, Wittman could only have been another Victor Wong, preserved for posterity in Kerouac's novel *Big Sur* (1962) as "little Chinese buddy Arthur Ma." In other words, Wittman wants to be an American Artist – he wants to carve a place for himself in American cultural history – but finds that first he must disengage himself from the subordinate place that American culture has made for him on the basis of his ethnicity.

Wittman's manic narrative registers the pain of being caught between two cultures, of being increasingly drawn away from the Chinese culture of his ancestors, which he admires, by the dominant, mainstream culture of Whitman, Kerouac, Marilyn Monroe, and the University of California at Berkeley, which he also admires. Wittman wants to define an identity for himself that can truly be called "Chinese American," but to do so he must prevent his Chinese inheritance from being transformed into a safely exotic form of cultural residue: he must prevent the "Chinese" from being marginalized by the "American." Wittman's goal is to create a form of public art that can redefine what it means to be "Chinese American" – redefine it for himself, his community, and the larger culture of which both he and his community are a part. In the course of the novel, Wittman discovers that his cultural identity is necessarily hybrid, and he suspects that every American identity is, in fact, necessarily hybrid, though mainstream American culture has worked hard to deny that fact.

Tripmaster Monkey thus dramatizes the predicament faced by all of America's minority cultures, whether they are oriented around ethnicity or around sexuality: how to transform themselves from marginal cultures into emergent cultures capable of challenging and reforming the mainstream. This conception of cultural emergence draws upon Raymond Williams's analysis of the dynamics of modern culture, an analysis that has served as the foundation for minority discourse theory in the 1990s. In *Marxism and Literature* (1977), Williams characterizes culture as a constant struggle for dominance in which a hegemonic mainstream – what Williams calls "the effective dominant culture" – seeks to defuse the challenges posed by both residual and emergent cultural forms. According to Williams, residual culture consists of those practices that are based on the "residue of . . . some previous social and cultural institution or formation" but continue to play a role in the present, whereas emergent culture serves as the site or set of sites where "new meanings and values, new practices, new relationships and kinds of relationships are continually being created." Both residual and emergent cultural forms can only be recognized and indeed conceived in relation to the dominant: each represents a form of negotiation between the margin and the center over the right to control meanings, values, and practices.

As a result, the newness that Williams associates with emergent culture is a matter of perspective: what is new is what looks new from the vantage point of the dominant. So it should not surprise us to discover that some cultural forms that we might designate as emergent are, in fact, hundreds, perhaps even thousands, of years old. For example, elements of homosexual experience played an important role in the cultures of classical Greece and Rome and of medieval Islam, but gay and lesbian culture remains in an emergent and oppositional position in the United States today because it has never been accepted by the mainstream and continues to be legislated against in many areas of the country. "The project of our enemies is to keep us from falling in love," writes Paul Monette in his memoir *Becoming a Man: Half a Life Story* (1992): "It has always been thus, the history writ by straight boys who render us invisible, as if we were never there. . . . If you isolate us long enough and keep us ignorant of each other, the solitary confinement will extinguish any hope we have of finding our other half." We find a similar assault on a minority's sense of community in a moment from Leslie Marmon Silko's *Ceremony* (1977) when the narrator describes the character Auntie's worldview: "An old sensitivity had descended in her, surviving thousands of years from the oldest times, when the people shared a single clan name and they told each other who they were; they recounted actions and words each of their clan had taken, and would take; from before they were born and long after they died, the people shared the same consciousness." But Auntie feels that Christianity has "separated the people from themselves; it tried to crush the single clan name, encouraging each person to stand alone, because Jesus Christ would save only the individual soul." The holistic communitarianism that Auntie longs for is ancient, but in Silko's novel it becomes an alternative that can be transformed into a site of new resistance.

For many emergent ethnic American writers, the foundations of these sites of resistance are laid on non-European mythological beliefs and stories. Native American authors draw upon what remains of their tribal cultures, in part because tribal ways represent an integral part of their personal identities, but also because their depictions of tribal cultures help to preserve those cultures, not simply in memory but as living cultures. The novelist N. Scott Momaday's Kiowa name is Tsoai-talee, which means "Rock-tree Boy," a reference to Momaday's being taken as an infant to Tsoai, a place sacred to the Kiowas that appears on U.S. maps as Devil's Tower, Wyoming. The name connects Momaday to a Kiowa legend that he was told by his great-grandmother and that he tells this way in his memoir *The Names* (1976):

Eight children were there at play, seven sisters and their brother. Suddenly the boy was struck dumb; he trembled and began to run upon his hands and feet. His fingers became claws, and his body was covered with fur. There was a bear where the boy had been. The sisters were terrified; they ran, and the bear after them. They came to the stump of a great tree, and the tree spoke to them. It bade them climb upon it, and as they did so it began to rise into the air. The bear came to kill them, but they were just beyond its reach. It reared against the tree and scored the bark all around with its claws. The seven sisters were borne into the sky, and they became the stars of the Big Dipper.

Momaday tells interviewers that he imagines himself to be the reincarnation of that boy and uses storytelling to enable himself to explore what it means to live under the sway of a legend: "All things can be accepted, if not understood, if you put them into a story. It is exactly what the Kiowas did when they encountered that mysterious rock formation. They incorporated it into their experience by telling a story about it. And that is what I feel that I must do about the boy bear." Momaday's writing reenacts the story-making that loomed so large in the lives of his ancestors; its very existence represents a way of resisting both the cultural eradication pursued by the U.S. government in the nineteenth century and the cultural mummification wrought by those whose images of the Indian remain rooted in nineteenth-century stereotypes.

Other emergent ethnic writers give prominence within their fictions to figures or places that embody the ideas of subversion and resistance. One such figure is the trickster, who appears throughout Native American tribal mythologies in such manifestations as Coyote, Crow, Jay, Hare, Loon, Raven, Spider, Wolverine, and Old Man. Sometimes a heroic, even godlike figure, the trickster can also be a liar and a cheater, a fool and a bungler, but he is almost always connected to the telling of stories. In *Love Medicine* (1984; expanded edition, 1993) and *The Bingo Palace* (1994),

Louise Erdrich draws on Chippewa tales of the trickster Nanabozho to create figures of both comedy and subversion in Gerry Nanapush, a member of the radical American Indian Movement (AIM), who has a knack for escaping from prison by squeezing into unimaginably small spaces, and his son, Lipsha Morissey, who embarks on a vision quest for three days and ends up having visions of American fast food. Maxine Hong Kingston sets a trickster figure at the heart of *Tripmaster Monkey*; alluding to Wu-Chengen's sixteenth-century Chinese folk novel *Hsi Yu Chi* (translated into English as *The Journey to the West*), Wittman Ah Sing calls himself "the present-day U.S.A. incarnation of the King of the Monkeys." Wu-Chengen's Monkey King, Sun Wu Kong, is a master of transformation, undergoing seventy-two of them in the course of his story, and Wittman seeks to revolutionize American literature by tapping into Sun Wu Kong's transformative powers, particularly those that arise from his ability to tell tales. The Native American writer Gerald Vizenor (Chippewa) draws attention to the parallels between the Native American and Chinese trickster traditions in his novel *Griever: An American Monkey King in China* (1987), whose protagonist, Griever de Hocus, a visiting professor at Zhou Enlai University in Tianjin, is described as a "mixedblood tribal trickster, a close relative to the oldmind monkeys." Elsewhere, Vizenor has argued that the trickster is a natural resource for both Native American tribal narratives and for postmodernism because he is the embodiment of deconstructive strategies – "chance and freedom in a comic sign" – and thus disrupts and resists institutionally sanctioned ways of reading.

For Chicano writers, the most potent deployment of mythical belief has been the collective reimagining of Aztlán, the Chicano homeland. In the Nahuatl language of ancient Mexico, *Aztlán* means "the lands to the north" and it is used by Chicanos today to refer to what is now the Southwestern United States. In his essay "Aztlán: A Homeland Without Boundaries" (1989), the novelist Rudolfo A. Anaya writes that "the ancestors of the Aztecs named their homeland Aztlán, and legend placed it north of Mexico. Aztlán was the place of origin, the *sipapu,* the Eden of those tribes. There they came to a new relationship with their god of war, Huitzilopochtli, and he promised to lead them in their migration out of Aztlán." That migration southward led to the establishment of the new Aztec nation of Tenochtitlán, which would eventually be conquered by Cortés in 1521. For all of its bloodthirstiness, the Spanish conquest of Mexico ironically resulted in a true melting pot, a nation less obsessed than its northern neighbor with ideas of blood purity, and thus most Mexicans and Chicanos are products of the fusion of both Native American and Spanish bloodlines and cultures.

It is no accident that the rebirth of interest in Aztlán occurred in tandem with the rise of the Chicano Movement during the 1960s, a time when, according to Anaya, the "absorption of the Chicano into the mainstream American culture was occurring so quickly that unless we re-established the covenants of our ancestors our culture was threatened with extinction." Seeking Chicano origins in Aztlán was a way of emphasizing the Native American roots of Chicano identity and thus of deemphasizing its roots in the Spanish conquistadors, the first invaders and occupiers of America, forerunners in that sense of the U.S. government. "The naming of Aztlán," writes Anaya, "was a spontaneous act which took place throughout the Southwest," which was codified at the Chicano Youth Conference held in Denver, Colorado, in March 1969. The document adopted at the Conference, *"El Plan Espiritual de Aztlán,"* concludes with this declaration:

> Brotherhood unites us and love for our brothers makes us a people whose time has come and who struggle against the foreigner "Gabacho," who exploits our riches and destroys our culture. With our hurt in our hands and our hands in the soil, We Declare the Independence of our Mestizo Nation. We are a Bronze People with a Bronze Culture. Before the world, before all of North America, before all our brothers in the Bronze Continent, We are a Nation, We are a Union of free pueblos, We are Aztlán.

The modern invocation of the myth of Aztlán thus represents the conscious deployment of an ancient myth of origin for the purpose of political and cultural resistance. In 1972, the radical dramatist Luis Valdez coedited an activist anthology of Mexican American literature entitled *Aztlán.* Anaya entitled his second novel *Heart of Aztlán* (1976) and pushed the mythopoetic techniques used in his prize-winning debut *Bless Me, Ultima* (1972) even further; in *Heart of Aztlán,* myth becomes not just a way of interpreting the world but a way of revolutionizing it.

The potential for resistance is a crucial component of cultural emergence: according to Raymond Williams, a truly emergent culture must be "substantially alternative or oppositional" to the dominant, and it is an article of faith among minority discourse theorists that the experience of antagonism toward the dominant culture is an experience that all U.S. minority cultures share.

This section of *The Cambridge History of American Literature* focuses on prose writings produced by Asian American, Chicano, Native American, and gay and lesbian authors since 1940. These are the literatures that have thus far provided the most fertile ground for minority discourse theorists within American studies, but the aim here is to treat them as case studies in the dynamics of emergent literature generally. Whether they are based

on ethnicity, race, or sexuality, minority cultures all find themselves in a
struggle to avoid being dominated and co-opted – in Williams's parlance,
"incorporated" – by the mainstream, and it is this shared experience that
underwrites and even necessitates a comparative approach to minority discourse. A comparative approach that emphasizes the similarities between
various emergent cultures, without losing sight of their salient differences,
can serve as an antidote to the divide-and-conquer strategy that attempts
to set U.S. minorities into antagonistic relationships with one another as a
way of defusing their antagonism to the mainstream.

Contained within the mental image of the crushing nature of Christianity
that Auntie evokes in Silko's *Ceremony* is an insight that Frantz Fanon
articulates in *The Wretched of the Earth* (1961), a text that has also become a
staple of minority discourse theory. Colonizers, argues Fanon, inflict cultural damage on those whose lands and minds they invade. Indeed, perhaps the most insidious forms of damage occur well after the bombs have
been dropped, the houses burned, and the bodies buried. Recalling the
powerful force exerted by Hollywood during her childhood in the
Philippines, the Filipino American writer Jessica Hagedorn reflects:

> Even though we also studied Tagalog, one of our native languages . . . , and read
> some of the native literature . . . , it was pretty clear to most of us growing up in
> the fifties and early sixties that what was really important, what was inevitably
> preferred, was the aping of our mythologized Hollywood universe. The coloniza-
> tion of our imagination was relentless and hard to shake off. Everywhere we
> turned, the images held up did not match our own. In order to be acknowledged,
> we had to strive to be as American as possible.

Named for a derogatory stereotype of Filipinos, Hagedorn's novel *Dogeaters*
(1990) depicts the culture of the Philippines as the quintessential damaged culture, transformed by its encounter with America into an empty
simulacrum that eschews its native forms in order to model itself on the
sham culture depicted in Hollywood movies. The novel begins in "the air-
conditioned darkness of the Avenue Theater, . . . Manila's 'Foremost! First-
Run! English Movies Only!' theater," where one of the novel's central
characters, a young girl named Rio Gonzaga, sits with her "blond" "mestiza" cousin, Pucha, the two of them "enthralled" as they watch Jane
Wyman, Rock Hudson, and Gloria Talbott in *All That Heaven Allows*: "we
gasp at Gloria's cool indifference, the offhand way she treats her grieving
mother. Her casual arrogance seems inherently American, modern, and
enviable." Written in a present-tense pastiche of first-person narrative,
third-person narrative, and fictional newspaper accounts, as well as actual

quotations from the Associated Press, from a poem by José Rizal, from a speech by William McKinley, and from Jean Mallat's ethnographic study *The Philippines* (1856), *Dogeaters* depicts a thinly veiled version of the corrupt regime presided over by Ferdinand and Imelda Marcos from 1965 to 1986. Casual arrogance marks the novel's depiction of the repressive social apparatus: the military regime led by General Nicasio Ledesma is ruthless, brutal, and efficient in its use of torture, rape, and murder to eliminate the enemies of the President and the First Lady. But even more powerful in ensuring the regime's dominance is the culture's ideological apparatus, which operates through religion, education, and (perhaps most powerfully) popular culture.

Dogeaters permits us to enter the thoughts of characters from the full spectrum of social classes: from Madame First Lady to the theater cashier Trinidad Gamboa, from Severo Alacran, the richest man in the Philippines, to the junkie mulatto deejay Joey Sands. Linked together through a series of violent events that culminates in an assassination, these characters are even more tightly bound together by their common fascination with the movies. "What would life be without movies?" the First Lady asks an American journalist off the record. "Unendurable, *di ba?* We Filipinos, we know how to endure, and we embrace the movies. With movies, everything is okay *lang*. It is one of our few earthly rewards." Linking its characters together through violence and pop culture, the novel suggests that violence and pop culture are themselves inextricably linked. The entire country is addicted to the radio soap opera *Love Letters,* and Rio tells us in the novel's first chapter that "without fail, someone dies on *Love Letters*. There's always a lesson to be learned, and it's always a painful one. Just like our Tagalog movies." The connection is vividly dramatized in the novel's most chilling scene, a gang rape carried out by military officers and a presidential aide while *Love Letters* plays in the background.

American culture colonizes abroad. It colonizes at home, too. Remembering Raymond Williams's conception of modern culture as a dynamic process, as a constant struggle in which a hegemonic mainstream seeks to defuse the challenges posed by both residual and emergent cultural forms, we must recognize that within its own boundaries a dominant culture seeks to colonize the imaginations of those whom it has marginalized. Mainstream American culture teaches gays and lesbians that they are perverts and deviants; it constructs "Americanness" and "homosexuality" as opposites and encourages gays and lesbians to remain closeted, to assimilate quietly – "don't ask, don't tell." In *Becoming a Man,* Monette describes the experience of being made to feel like an enemy of the culture, a spy in one's native land:

I speak for no one else here, if only because I don't want to saddle the women and men of my tribe with the lead weight of my self-hatred, the particular doorless room of my internal exile. Yet I've come to learn that all our stories add up to the same imprisonment. The self-delusion of uniqueness. The festering pretense that we are the same as they are. The gutting of all our passions till we are a bunch of eunuchs, our zones of pleasure in enemy hands. Most of all, the ventriloquism, the learning how to pass for straight. Such obedient slaves we make, with such very tidy rooms.

Mainstream U.S. culture fosters an oppositional relationship with gay culture by luring gay men and women into mimicking its thinking by "halving the world into *us* and *them*," even as it attempts to keep gay culture divided by making it difficult for gay men and women to acknowledge one another openly.

The experience of being in the closet is akin to the experience of cultural hybridity – the feeling of being caught between cultures – that ethnic Americans undergo when they are taught to deny the parts of themselves that lie outside of mainstream U.S. culture. Tayo, the protagonist of Silko's *Ceremony,* remembers what he was told at the VA hospital: "the white doctors had yelled at him – that he had to think only of himself, and not about the others, that he would never get well as long as he used words like 'we' and 'us.'" Like many late-twentieth-century Native American writers, Silko conceives of Indian culture and history as primarily communitarian in nature and therefore set against the grain of the American national culture's celebration of individualism. So Tayo thinks to himself that he has "known the answer all along, even while the white doctors were telling him he could get well and he was trying to believe them: medicine didn't work that way, because the world didn't work that way." Kingston's Wittman Ah Sing finds himself in an analogous position in *Tripmaster Monkey,* sitting in the unemployment office watching "a cartoon about going for a job interview" that gives him hints about "good grooming," which turn out to include the following pieces of advice: "COME ALONE to the interview. DO NOT take friends or relatives with you." Wittman immediately realizes the nature of the message implicit in these dicta: "An X through my people. Adios, mis amigos. . . . An American stands alone. Alienated, tribeless, individual. To be a successful American, leave your tribe, your caravan, your gang, your partner, your village cousins, your refugee family that you're making the money for, leave them behind. Do not bring back-up."

What Monette, Silko, and Kingston are confronting here is a logic that is dominant within American culture, a logic that is founded upon *ontological individualism,* the belief that the individual has an a priori and primary reality and that society is a derived, second-order construct. This logic relies on the idea, as the political theorist Jon Elster puts it, that "all social phenomena – whether process, structure, institution, or *habitus* – can be explained by the actions and properties of the participating individuals." From Ralph Waldo Emerson to John Rawls, American theorists of individualism have typically sought to shift the ground of inquiry from culture and society to the individual, translating moments of social choice into moments of individual choice. This strategy is a literal application of the motto *e pluribus unum* – "from many, one" – which expresses the idea that the American nation is formed through the union of many individuals. In the hands of thinkers like Emerson and Rawls, the customary sense of this motto is reversed: they move from the many to the one, to the single individual, paring away differences in order to reach a common denominator that will allow them to make claims about all individuals. And one of the most powerful claims that American culture makes about individuals is that sexuality, ethnicity, and cultural hybridity are contingent, incidental, and ultimately irrelevant aspects of individual identity.

Richard Rodriguez's controversial autobiography *Hunger of Memory: The Education of Richard Rodriguez* (1982) makes a powerful case for the applicability of this model of identity formation to individuals designated as minorities by mainstream American culture. Arguing that class is the true dividing line in American culture, Rodriguez argues that middle-class Americans of all races and ethnicities who are in a position to think like individualists should do so. His opposition to both bilingual education and affirmative action (which have made him unpopular among Chicano activists) is based on the belief that such remedies are unnecessary for middle-class individuals who have the opportunity to participate in America's culture of individualism.

The benefits – and the potential losses – that result from this stance can be seen most poignantly in Rodriguez's rendering of what is the classic situation for the ethnic minority subject: being forced to choose between the culture of his parents and the dominant culture that surrounds him. Having summoned the courage to raise his hand and speak up in class, Rodriguez tells us that "at last, at seven years old, I came to believe what had been technically true since my birth: I was an American citizen." This gain, however, entails a loss: "the special feeling of closeness at home was diminished" by "the dramatic Americanization" that he and his siblings underwent: "gone was the desperate, urgent, intense feeling of being at home; rare was the experience of feeling individualized by family intimates. We remained a loving family but we were greatly changed. No longer so close; no longer bound tight by the pleasing and troubling knowledge of our public separateness." For Rodriguez, the loss is completely offset by the gain. It is never, for him, really a question of choosing between two equally viable cultural groups. There is only one group – the dominant group – and it is one to which he does not belong. In other words, Rodriguez presents himself from the outset as "tribeless," and he conceives of emergence not as a struggle between cultures but as a process of personal metamorphosis. It is in this shifting of the ground of analysis from the group to the individual that *Hunger of Memory* proves itself to be a classic account of American self-making, a contribution to the Emersonian and Rawlsian traditions of American liberalism.

The last pieces of advice that the cartoon offers to Wittman Ah Sing deal with the question of language: "SPEAK clearly and answer questions honestly. BE business-like and brief." The cartoon exhorts its audience to present a public self that is likely to succeed in mainstream culture, and it is the development of this public self that Rodriguez charts in his autobiography. In arguing against bilingual education, Rodriguez writes:

Today I hear bilingual educators say that children lose a degree of "individuality" by becoming assimilated into public society. . . . But the bilingualists simplistically scorn the value and necessity of assimilation. They do not seem to realize that there are *two* ways a person is individualized. So they do not realize that while one suffers a diminished sense of *private* individuality by becoming assimilated into public society, such assimilation makes possible the achievement of *public individuality*.

The achievement of this public individuality has a price: "it would never again be easy," Rodriguez tells us, "for me to hear intimate family voices." But it is a price that Rodriguez is willing to pay, though he nonetheless tries to minimize its cost, naturalizing this split between private and public individuality by ascribing it to the "inevitable pain" of growing up: "The day I raised my hand in class and spoke loudly to an entire roomful of faces, my childhood started to end." Childhood is indeed full of pain, and children often find themselves at odds with their families, but what is different about the particular pain that Rodriguez describes is that it is the product of the dominant culture's attempt (in Wittman Ah Sing's phrase) to put an X through his people. Almost in passing, Rodriguez tells us that "the bilingualists insist that a student should be reminded of his difference from others in mass society, his heritage." But "heritage" is a subject upon which Rodriguez chooses not to dwell, setting it aside without further comment. The price for the achievement of his public individuality, then, is alienation from family, ancestors, and heritage. What Rodriguez fails to points out is that it is only members of minority cultures who must pay this particular price.

In seeking to portray class as the primary determinant factor in American life, Rodriguez must deny his identity as an ethnic hybrid (and, though this is not made explicit in the text, his identity as a gay man). He is thus forced to inflict damage not only upon himself – by sacrificing his "private individuality" – but also upon his family. In a later essay he describes the beginning of his Americanization as his "emergence as a brat" and admits that he "determined to learn English, initially, as a way of hurting [his parents]." Rodriguez's autobiographical writings provide a case study in the ways that America's minority cultures internalize the damage inflicted on them by mainstream culture. There is a tension in Rodriguez's text between the argument he is making – about the primacy of class over ethnicity as a determinant of identity – and the ethnically inflected episodes that he uses to illustrate it.

Hunger of Memory is indeed an emergent text: it transforms American liberalism because it asserts the right of a person of color to participate in the American liberal tradition, a right recognized in theory but not yet fully realized in practice. Paradoxically, however, it can assert this right only by denying the relevance of its author's racial, ethnic, and sexual identity. In other words, the text is forced to abjure the very qualities that make it emergent. Because Rodriguez's aim is not to transform mainstream American culture but rather to detail a strategy for becoming part of it, he seeks to naturalize what other authors might represent as a process of cultural damage. Rodriguez chooses to describe the hardships he has undergone as fundamentally like hardships that any American faces when trying to achieve a public voice. But his text leaves us with the uncomfortable feeling that what it is recording – almost despite itself – is the damage specifically inflicted upon minorities by mainstream American culture.

To put Rodriguez's rhetorical strategies in perspective, we might compare *Hunger of Memory* to another text that portrays the inevitability of Americanization, John Okada's novel *No-No Boy* (1957). The novel's protagonist, Ichiro, has suffered the humiliation of being interned in a camp with other Japanese Americans and decides, when he is later drafted, not to serve in the American army. Ichiro has chosen to side with his nonassimilationist mother, and he goes to prison for it. Returning home to Seattle after the war, Ichiro thinks to himself what he is unable to say to his mother, that there was a time when "we were Japanese with Japanese feelings and Japanese pride and Japanese thoughts because it was all right then to be Japanese and feel and think all the things that Japanese do even if we lived in America." But then there came a time when I was only half Japanese because one is not born in America and raised in America and taught in America and one does not speak and swear and drink and smoke and play and fight and see and hear in America among Americans in American streets and houses without becoming American and loving it. But I did not love enough, for you were still half my mother and I was thereby still half Japanese and when the war came and they told me to fight for America, I was not strong enough to fight you and I was not strong enough to fight the bitterness which made the half of me which was you bigger than the half of me which was America and really the whole of me that I could not see or feel.

This passage, taken from a long interior monologue in the middle of the novel's first chapter, embodies the novel's recognition of the extent to which Japanese Americans suffer from what observers of Asian American culture have called "the dual identity" or "dual personality," the idea that the "Asian" and the "American" are incompatible selves at war with one another within the Asian American individual. Trapped within a logic of either/or, Okada's protagonist believes that he must choose either to be Japanese or to be American. What *No-No Boy* explores is the deep regret that Ichiro feels after his release, the sense that he has made a mistake, that he has chosen wrongly. And he comes to believe that he has chosen foolishly because what appeared to be a choice was, in fact, never really a choice. *No-No Boy* portrays resistance to assimilation as futile, but it differs from *Hunger of Memory* because it openly explores the pain of cultural hybridity, which it understands as a state of violence. *No-No Boy* thus anticipates a narrative strategy that has proven to be central to the project of producing emergent literature in late-twentieth-century America.

This strategy is to understand hybridity as a crucial fact about identity and to depict the ontology of hybridity as an ontology of violence. Writers such as N. Scott Momaday, Leslie Marmon Silko, Oscar Zeta Acosta, Jessica Hagedorn, Maxine Hong Kingston, and Paul Monette depict characters who seem to embody within themselves the violence implicit in Williams's conception of culture as struggle. For example, the mixed-blood war veteran Abel in Momaday's *House Made of Dawn* (1968) experiences his mixed blood as a clash between contradictory frames of reference, a clash that fractures his consciousness, leading him to treat wartime combat as if it were ritual, and ritual as if it were actual combat. The vicious schoolyard beating of a "meek, nervous kid" by a group of "Irish toughs" is an unforgettable incident that occurs early in Monette's memoir *Becoming a Man*; later, when threatened by a "football jock" two years older than he, Monette describes himself as "a prisoner who spills all the secrets as soon as he sees the torture room, before the first whip is cracked." Being in the closet is for Monette an experience of pain: "When you finally come out, there's a pain that stops, and you know it will never hurt like that again, no matter how much you lose or how bad you die." Worst of all, he finds that being in the closet has made him internalize the hatred directed toward him: "it makes me sick to hate the way my enemies hate."

"Decolonization," writes Fanon, "is always a violent phenomenon." Gay and lesbian texts share with texts of ethnic emergence a preoccupation with the violence of living on the margins of American culture. In fact, many gay and lesbian activists believe that gay studies, queer theory, and the gay rights movement should pattern themselves on "the ethnic model" in order to gain political power. The problem with this strategy, as Dana Takagi points out in her contribution to the anthology *Asian American Sexualities: Dimensions of the Gay & Lesbian Experience* (1996), is "the relative invisibility of sexual identity compared with racial identity. While both can be said to be socially constructed, the former are performed, acted out, and produced often in individual routines, whereas the latter tends to be more obviously 'written' on the body and negotiated by political groups." This caveat – about the extent to which identities like "Asian American" or "gay and lesbian" can be considered performative – is an important one. But it applies to bodies and not texts, to authors rather than their work. For all texts are "performed, acted out, and produced . . . in individual routines"; all of them represent a decision either to "pass" as mainstream or to present themselves as "emergent." In this sense, both ethnic and gay writers share the dilemma that addles Kingston's poet-protagonist at the end of the first chapter of *Tripmaster Monkey*: "Does he announce now that the author is – Chinese? Or, rather, Chinese-American? And be forced into autobiographical confession. Stop the music – I have to butt in and introduce myself and my race." Whether the question is race, ethnicity, or sexuality – and we could perhaps argue for the inclusion of gender and class as well – the dilemma is that of the marginalized author who would be emergent.

Kingston's novel suggests that the dilemma of whether to introduce one's race was not something that Herman Melville faced: "'Call me Ishmael.' See? You pictured a white guy, didn't you?" Some queer theorists might beg to differ, however, arguing that texts like *Benito Cereno* and *Billy Budd* bear the signs of struggle evident when a gay writer chooses to pass for straight: one of the major subjects in Melville studies during the 1990s has been the question of whether the author was, in fact, gay. Melville, it seems, may have been closer to the margins of American culture than the canonical tradition would have us believe.

For gay and lesbian writers, being emergent entails both establishing the literary right to explore the dynamics of gay life – in particular the dynamics of gay eroticism – and "outing" those gay authors who have been assimilated into the mainstream literary canon with no acknowledgment of the impact that their sexualities may have had upon their literary art. Part of the project of American queer theory in the 1980s and 1990s has been to locate the closets within the texts of such writers as Melville, Henry James, and Willa Cather, to understand what Eve Kosofsky Sedgwick has called "the epistemology of the closet." Judith Fetterley, for example, has argued that the power of Cather's *My Ántonia* is "connected with its contradictions" and that "these contradictions are intimately connected to Cather's lesbianism." Unable to write freely about lesbian desire, Cather finds a "solution to the inherent contradiction between American and lesbian" by conflating the two and portraying the land both as female and as an object of desire: according to Fetterley, "in the land, Cather successfully imagined herself; in the land, she imagined a woman who could be safely eroticized and safely loved." Such rereadings of canonical authors have a double effect: first, they demonstrate the existence of a long-standing tradition of gay and lesbian writing upon which openly gay writers can now draw; second, they demonstrate the extent to which mainstream American culture has been shaped by gay sensibility. It is no accident, these critics argue, that America's bard, Walt Whitman, was a homosexual: who better to embody the ideology of individualism than a gay man cut off from the rest of his "tribe" (to use Paul Monette's word)?

Whether Whitman looms as a force of liberation or constraint depends, however, upon an author's subject position. To Paul Monette, who uses one of Whitman's *Calamus* poems ("I Hear It Was Charged against Me") as the epigraph for *Becoming a Man,* he is a forefather to be cherished and emulated. For Maxine Hong Kingston, however, Whitman represents the canonical American tradition – so full of the writings of white men – that places the emergent ethnic writer into an oppositional position. Whitman is a precursor to be admired but appropriated.

Emergent ethnic writers, however, often find themselves forced to do violence not only to the tradition of canonical American texts, but also to the literary, mythological, and cultural traditions that have given them the opportunity to be "emergent" in the first place. Thus, for example, Frank Chin has accused Kingston of attacking Chinese civilization by rewriting some of its fairy tales and myths. The novelist and critic Paula Gunn Allen (Laguna) has accused Leslie Marmon Silko (Laguna) of violating Native American religious and ethical traditions by transcribing and interpolating into her written texts stories that are meant to be spoken – and spoken only within a clan for specific purposes. Writers like Kingston and Silko take a dynamic view of traditional myth, however, believing it to be not a static relic of the past but an ongoing process in the present. Kingston declares, in a personal statement included in a volume of essays on her autobiographical fantasia *The Woman Warrior: Memoirs of a Girlhood Among Ghosts* (1976):

Sinologists have criticized me for not knowing myths and for distorting them; pirates correct my myths, revising them to make them conform to some traditional Chinese version. They don't understand that myths have to change, be useful or be forgotten. Like the people who carry them across oceans, the myths become American. The myths I write are new, American.

Silko provides a similar answer to critics like Allen, an answer embodied in the character of Betonie, the medicine man in *Ceremony,* who includes newspapers and telephone books among his implements of magic. Betonie says:

The people nowadays have an idea about the ceremonies. They think the ceremonies must be performed exactly as they have always been done. . . . They think that if a singer tampers with any part of the ritual, great harm can be done, great power unleashed. . . . At one time the ceremonies as they had been performed were enough for the way the world was then. But after the white people came, elements in this world began to shift; and it became necessary to create new ceremonies. I have made changes in the rituals. The people mistrust this greatly, but only this growth keeps the ceremonies strong.

For writers like Silko and Kingston, tampering with the myths and unleashing great power often means bringing to bear techniques of literary representation drawn from canonical American literature. Like Wittman Ah Sing, most of the emergent ethnic writers considered in this section of the *Cambridge History* have been educated in American universities and have read widely in canonical American literature and the Western literary tradition; many hold professorships of literature or creative writing in universities today. The Chicano critic Hector Calderón has commented that although Chicano literature "may inform the dominant culture with an alternative view of the world filtered through myth and oral storytelling or offer an oppositional political perspective, this is done so from within educational institutions. Almost all Chicana and Chicano writers of fiction have earned advanced degrees in the United States." We must realize, writes Calderón, "how institutionally Western" Chicano literature is. According to Rolando Hinojosa, who like Américo Paredes, teaches at the University of Texas at Austin, "Chicano Literature, which at times passed itself off as a people's literature . . . is actually a child of us, the academicians who make up one of the last privileged classes in our native land." As a result of both their training and their teaching, these authors, like Kingston's Wittman, find themselves deeply influenced by canonical traditions of American, English, and European literature, and the literature they produce is almost necessarily a hybrid of mainstream and ethnic forms.

Drawing from both the center and the margins of American literary culture, however, does not guarantee that these writers will be able to appeal to either constituency. Mid-twentieth-century ethnic writers like Jade Snow Wong, Monica Sone, and José Antonio Villarreal solved the problem of audience by writing in a realist style addressed primarily toward a white readership, a solution that comes to seem less appealing as emergent literatures gain the self-confidence that accompanies literary recognition. "I am really a megalomaniac," says Maxine Hong Kingston, "because I write for everybody living today and people in the future; that's my audience, for generations." Her audience, she claims, includes "everyone" – not only Chinese Americans, but also her "old English professors of the new criticism school in Berkeley," as well as "those who are not English majors and don't play literary games." Aware that her writing "deals with a culture that has not adequately been portrayed before," Kingston reveals that she consciously "work[s] on intelligibility and accessibility" when revising her manuscripts. Yet in an essay entitled "Cultural Mis-readings by American Reviewers," written after the publication of *The Woman Warrior,* Kingston registers the artistic problems involved in bringing these different audiences together. Many of her reviewers, she laments, "praise[d] the wrong things": unfamiliar with many of the historical, cultural, and social contexts that inform *The Woman Warrior,* many reviewers "measur[ed] the book . . . against the stereotype of the exotic, inscrutable, mysterious oriental." To Kingston, such responses demonstrate the failure of her text: "the critics who said how the book was good because it was, or was not, like the oriental fantasy in their heads might as well have said how weak it was, since it in fact did not break through that fantasy."

What must the emergent ethnic writer do to break through the stereotypical assumptions of Eurocentric readers? In the essay, Kingston claims that the process of heightening "intelligibility and accessibility" does *not* include "slow[ing] down to give boring exposition, which is information that is available in encyclopedias, history books, sociology, anthropology, mythology." After all, she claims, "I am not writing history or sociology but a 'memoir' like Proust. . . . Some readers will have to do some background reading." Her second volume, *China Men* (1980), however, makes a greater attempt to educate her non-Chinese and non–Chinese American readers, because, as she told an interviewer, the reviews of *The Woman Warrior* "made it clear that people didn't know the history – or that they thought I didn't. While I was writing *China Men,* I just couldn't take that tension any more." In her second book, Kingston shifts the balance between myth and history: the mythical imagination of *The Woman Warrior* is tempered in *China Men* by the desire to heighten the historical texture of the narrative. Most telling of all is the decision to include a brief interchapter entitled "The Laws," in which she lists and comments wryly upon pieces of legislation that have affected Chinese Americans, beginning with the Burlingame Treaty of 1868. "The Laws" is not sociology and it is not boring, but its inclusion does register Kingston's frustration with readers who have not done their background reading and who are content to read her texts from the vantage point of Orientalism. What "The Laws" is designed to demonstrate is that Kingston's characters cannot be safely exiled to the exotic realms of myth; they exist in history – in U.S. history – and they have been the victims of nationally sanctioned injustice.

Kingston's dilemma is a familiar one to writers and critics of emergent fiction, who often claim that this fiction has a special relation to history. The Chicano critic Ramón Saldívar contends, for example, that history is "the decisive determinant of the form and content of [Chicano] literature" and therefore "cannot be conceived as . . . mere 'background' or 'context'"; it is, instead, "the subtext that we must recover" if we wish to understand Chicano writing. For many critics of our generation, however, this description of the interconnection between history and literature applies not only to Chicano writing or even to emergent writing more generally but rather to *all* writing; for the historicist critic, history is the subtext that we must recover if we wish to understand *any* literary text fully. Rather than possessing a special relationship to history, the emergent text simply reminds us forcefully of what is true of every text: that it is marked by the historical context – or rather by the multiple, intersecting historical contexts – from within which it arose.

It should come as no surprise that the claims made by minority discourse theorists about emergent fiction have come to seem banal to historicists in the late 1990s because emergent ethnic writing (and the criticism that it fostered) played a crucial role in the much-discussed "turn to history" that took place in American literary and cultural studies in the early 1980s. Scholars of ethnic writing have long recognized that the formalism that characterized New Criticism, structuralism, and deconstruction implicitly depends on the existence of a particular Eurocentric interpretive community. The close reading skills taught at most American high schools and universities prove inadequate to the challenges posed by emergent literature; they do not, for example, help a reader to do more than scratch the surface of a text like N. Scott Momaday's *The Way to Rainy Mountain* (1969), which the Native American novelist and essayist Michael Dorris has described as "a classic of traditional Kiowa literature." Although the text is written in English, Dorris contends that "it cannot be understood without major reference to its tribal symbol system. It may misleadingly

appear, like much oral literature when written down, simple and straightforward and the non-Kiowa reader who approaches the work in isolation
will likely miss much of its depth and hence most of its beauty and significance." In short, emergent ethnic writing teaches us about the inseparabil-
ity of text and cultural context, and the contribution of minority discourse
theory to late-twentieth-century historicism is one of the ways in which
Wittman Ah Sing has forced us to reread Walt Whitman, to recall that as
a gay man writing about sexuality Whitman was – and, in this respect,
still is – an emergent writer.

Part of the project of emergent writing in the United States is to create
what Dorris has called "self-history": history written from within particular
communities whose stories are either excluded or distorted by the "standard
history" of the nation. American history, as commonly construed, is the history of a nation; self-history is the history of a particular people, a history
that typically stretches much further back in time than the founding of the
United States and often originates in territories that lie outside of its boundaries. Gay history, a field that came into being only after the 1969 Stonewall
rebellion, has necessarily been a field of self-history: as Paul Monette suggests in *Becoming a Man,* mainstream history has always been "writ by
straight boys who render us invisible, as if we were never there." One of the
field's founding texts was a collection of primary documents entitled *Gay
American History* (1976), edited by Jonathan Katz, whose qualifications for
the undertaking were the result not of a doctorate in history but rather of
years spent as a gay activist. The current task of gay history is to lift into visibility the homosexual elements of all cultures – ancient and modern – that
have hitherto been hidden from view by standard history.

Ethnic self-history, however, must distinguish itself not only from standard history but also from the academic subdiscipline known as "ethnohistory," which often provides a wealth of information about ethnic
communities but cannot substitute for ethnic self-history because it tends to
represent an outsider's point of view. Ethnohistory is generally written from
without: according to the anthropologist Harold Hickerson, ethnohistory

consists of the use of primary documents – library and archival materials – to gain
knowledge of a given culture as it existed in the past, and how it has changed. . . .
In its broadest sense, ethnohistory employs a number of research techniques to see
in what way the present-day culture is similar or dissimilar to ancestral cultures,
to what degree, in other words, the culture has changed, and what the distinctive
historical factors were in determining such change.

It is a telling fact about the practice of ethnohistory that the discipline
arose in the early 1950s as a result of Congress's passage of the Indian

Claims Commission Act in 1946, which gave Native Americans the right to claim redress for losses of land incurred as the result of the U.S. government's violation of laws, treaties, or "standards of fair and honorable dealings." To carry out its mandate, the commission enlisted anthropologists to use historical sources in order to determine whether certain Indian tribes had occupied particular territories, whether they had received fair value for those lands upon removal, and whether those now claiming redress were their rightful descendants. The journal *Ethnohistory* was founded in 1954, primarily to serve scholars engaged in the study of relations between white and Native American cultures.

For many emergent ethnic writers, both "American history" and ethnohistory are things that they learn in school; ethnic self-history is what they learn at home or in the streets of their neighborhoods. Paula Gunn Allen has contrasted the education that she received in school (where she was "treated to bloody tales" of "savage Indians" killing "hapless priests and missionaries" and taught "that Indians were people who had benefited mightily from the advanced knowledge and superior morality of the Anglo-Europeans") with the understanding "derived" from her "daily experience of Indian life" and from the teachings of her "mother and the other Indian people who raised" her. The narrator of Fae Myenne Ng's *Bone* (1993) reflects, "We know so little of the old country. We repeat the names of grandfathers and uncles, but they have always been strangers to us. Family exists only because somebody has a story, and knowing the story connects us to a history." Ethnic self-history, in other words, is intimately connected to personal narrative, and as a result, autobiography and autobiographical fiction have played a formative role in the emergence of Native American, Asian American, and Chicano literatures.

Some ethnic autobiographies, like Rodriguez's *Hunger of Memory,* Jade Snow Wong's *Fifth Chinese Daughter* (1945), or Monica Sone's *Nisei Daughter* (1953), devote themselves to charting a process of assimilation into the mainstream of American life. They adopt the individualistic perspective traditionally associated with the Western tradition of autobiography that dates back at least to Rousseau's *Confessions* (and possibly to Augustine's), charting individual development as a process of conversion that leads to a sense of self-autonomy. They belong in a history of American emergent literatures because, despite their assimilative stances, they dramatize and document the damage inflicted on minority cultures in the United States by the mainstream. In contrast, autobiographies like *The Woman Warrior,* Ernesto Galarza's *Barrio Boy* (1971), or *America Is in the Heart* (1946) by the Filipino immigrant Carlos Bulosan describe development in collective rather than individualistic terms; they set themselves against the grain of Western autobiography. Although Bulosan concludes his text with what seems to be a ringing affirmation of the American dream, expressing his "desire to know America, and to become a part of her great tradition, and to contribute something toward her final fulfillment," his conception of that "fulfillment" has little to do with the laissez-faire individualism typically associated with the American Dream. What Bulosan seeks is "the enlargement of the American Dream," and what his autobiography charts is the development of feelings of communal solidarity. Late in the autobiography, Bulosan recalls attending a meeting in Los Angeles with "several cannery workers: Japanese, Mexicans, Filipinos, and white Americans," and coming to the realization that "there was the same thing in each of them that possessed me: their common faith in the working man. . . . Then it came to me that we are all fighting against one enemy: Fascism. It was in every word and gesture, every thought." Indeed, the image that brings about Bulosan's final reverie on the promise of America is the sight of "Filipino pea pickers in the fields" stopping to wave as the bus that Bulosan is riding passes by.

The history of Native American autobiography sets these two forms in a developmental relation while reenacting the shift from ethnography to ethnic self-history. The first full-length autobiography published by a Native American, William Apess's *A Son of the Forest. The Experience of William Apes, a Native of the Forest* (1829), is quite literally a conversion narrative. George Copway, a Canadian Ojibwa who moved to the United States in 1846 after becoming a Methodist minister, mixes ethnography with conversion narrative in *The Life, History, and Travels of Ka-ge-ga-gah-bowh* (1847), which contains detailed, if slightly romanticized, accounts of Ojibwa tribal customs as well as the story of Copway's conversion to Christianity. Charles Eastman's two autobiographies, *Indian Boyhood* (1902) and *From the Deep Woods to Civilization* (1916), stress the formative influence not of the Santee Sioux customs according to which he was raised by his paternal grandmother and uncle, but rather the Christian humanism that he learned at U.S. universities. Apess, Copway, and Eastman are exceptions rather than the rule for nineteenth- and early-twentieth-century Native American autobiography. They write rather than speak their autobiographies. The bulk of nineteenth-century Native American personal narratives were transcriptions of oral accounts, and they were presented to the white reading public as specimens of ethnography. Prominent examples include J. B. Patterson's *Life of Black Hawk* (1833), S. M. Barrett's *Geronimo's Story of His Life* (1906), and perhaps the most famous of these accounts, *Black Elk Speaks, Being the Life Story of a Holy Man of the Oglala Sioux, as Told Through John G. Neihardt* (1932). Although scholars believe that Neihardt sought to capture the Lakota chief's narrative as faithfully as he could, he nevertheless took liberties with the oral account, including the addition of the text's famous opening and closing paragraphs. Instead of Neihardt serving as Black Elk's amanuensis, we have Black Elk serving as the vehicle for Neihardt's vision of Native America. In contrast to these personal narratives, in which both the individuality and the representativeness of the subject are effaced by the mediation of a white interpreter, late-twentieth-century autobiographical texts like N. Scott Momaday's *The Way to Rainy Mountain* (1969) and *The Names* (1976) and Leslie Marmon Silko's *Storyteller* (1981) begin with the individual voices of their authors, but quickly expand to incorporate the polyvocality of tribal traditions.

Autobiography and autobiographical fiction have also played a formative role in the emergence of gay and lesbian American literature. With the advent of the gay liberation movement in the aftermath of the Stonewall rebellion (1969) came a new literary genre: the "coming-out" narrative. Anthologies of personal accounts like *The Lesbian Path* (1980) and *The Coming Out Stories* (1980) found an immediate audience within the gay community; Audre Lorde's "biomythography" *Zami: A New Spelling of My Name* (1982) and Paul Monette's *Becoming a Man* gained national critical attention. The early 1980s saw the rise of what might be called the gay male bildungsroman, whose central act was often a boy's coming out to his parents. Prominent examples of the genre include Edmund White's *A Boy's Own Story* (1980), Robert Ferro's *The Family of Max Desir* (1983), and David Leavitt's *The Lost Language of Cranes* (1986), in which a son and father come out to one another. Like many ethnic autobiographies, coming-out narratives map the individual onto the collective: they tell individual and occasionally idiosyncratic stories that often turn on the realization that the narrator's experience is shared by a broad community of other individuals. The act of coming out is often performative rather than constative; that is, the act of coming out to one's family and friends is often the very act that signals and brings about the embracing of one's homosexual identity. Likewise, the emergence of the coming-out narrative as a major genre of writing has helped to bring about the existence of an openly gay American literature and to provide crucial encouragement to gay Americans still locked in their closets. The fact that literary coming-out narratives may have practical effects is made evident at the end of the anthology *Growing Up Gay/Growing Up Lesbian* (1994), which includes one appendix listing "books, magazines, and videos that may be of special interest to young adults" and a second appendix listing such "resources" as hot lines and support groups for gay youth. The collective nature of gay personal narrative and autobiographical fiction has only been strengthened with the advent of a second major genre, the AIDS narrative, which includes both nonfictional accounts such as Monette's *Borrowed Time* (1988), an account of the death of his lover Roger Horwitz, and novels such as Ferro's *Second Son* (1988) and Monette's *Afterlife* (1990).

Perhaps because many Native American tribal cultures are matriarchal, matrilineal, and traditionally tolerant of homosexuality and transvestism, Native American feminist writers like Leslie Marmon Silko, Louise Erdrich, or Paula Gunn Allen have not been subjected to the kind of withering attacks that Asian American and Mexican American feminists and gay writers have received from their straight male counterparts. In the work of such writers as Maxine Hong Kingston or the gay Chicano novelists Arturo Islas and John Rechy, the claims of ethnicity occasionally come into conflict with the claims of gender or sexuality. These writers are doubly marginalized: by mainstream American culture on the basis of ethnicity, and by both mainstream American culture and their own ethnic subcultures on the basis of gender or sexuality. The playwright and novelist Frank Chin has bitterly attacked Kingston for choosing the claims of feminism over the claims of ethnicity in *The Woman Warrior*. He accuses her of betraying her culture and of playing to Western stereotypes that undermine Chinese masculinity. Similarly, in an autobiographical collection of poems, essays, and stories entitled *Loving in the War Years: Lo Que Nunca Pasó Por Sus Labios* (1983), the lesbian Chicana feminist Cherríe Moraga takes aim at the misogyny that prevents a true sense of "Chicano community" from being achieved: "There is a deeper love between and amongst our people that lies buried between the lines of the roles we play with each other. . . . Family is *not* by definition the man in a dominant position over women and children. . . . The strength of our families never came from domination. It has only endured in spite of it – like our women." Misogyny, however, is not the only problem for writers like Moraga, who are multiply marginalized. Women of color encounter discrimination from men of color on the basis of gender, and from other women on the basis of color. The groundbreaking anthology *This Bridge Called My Back: Writings by Radical Women of Color* (1983), which Moraga edited together with Gloria Anzaldúa, began as "a reaction to the racism of white feminists." Dedicated to the task of demonstrating that "we are not alone in our struggles nor separate nor autonomous but that we – white black straight queer female male – are connected and interdependent," the anthology brings together prose and poetry by straight and gay African American, Asian American, Chicana, Latina, and Native American women. Moraga and Anzaldúa describe *This Bridge Called My Back* "as a revolutionary tool falling into the hands of people of all colors." It is a text that demonstrates that the goal of setting emergent American literatures into a comparative framework – a framework that highlights similarity without losing sight of difference – is not just a scholarly imperative but also a cultural necessity: it is the necessary precursor to the reconception of the idea of "America" that is the goal of emergent writers in the United States.

Anzaldúa has written what, in both formal and thematic terms, is arguably the most radical autobiography produced by a late-twentieth-century American emergent writer. *Borderlands/La Frontera: The New Mestiza* (1987) is a hybrid text written partly in prose and partly in poetry, partly in English and partly in Spanish, and it brings the issue of hybridity immediately to the fore. "I am a border woman," writes Anzaldúa in the book's preface: "I grew up between two cultures, the Mexican (with a heavy Indian influence) and the Anglo (as a member of a colonized people in our own territory). I have been straddling that *tejas*-Mexican border, and others, all my life. It's not a comfortable territory to live in, this place of contradictions. Hatred, anger and exploitation are the prominent features of this landscape." Motivated by her "preoccupations with the inner life of the Self, and with the struggle of that Self amidst adversity and violation," Anzaldúa's text demonstrates that for someone like her – the book's jacket describes her as "a Chicano *tejana* lesbian-feminist poet and fiction writer" – personal narrative is political narrative: to understand her personal identity she must unearth the mythic and historical foundations upon which it is built and explore a complex cultural inheritance drawn from the civilizations of the Aztec, the Spaniard, and the Anglo. Hers is an identity wracked by the contradictions of race, ethnicity, gender, and sexuality, but – like Walt Whitman before her – she embraces these contradictions. One of Anzaldúa's poems imagines the borderlands as a space where mainstream systems of classification break down: "To live in the Borderlands means you / are neither *hispana india negra españa / ni gabacha, eres mestiza, mulata,* half-breed." *Borderlands/La Frontera* depicts the borderlands as a place of unspeakable violence, but also a place of incredible promise, a place that cannot be tamed by hegemonic culture, a place where new selves and kinds of selves can be born: "To survive the Borderlands/ you must live *sin fronteras* / be a crossroads."

For writers and critics of late-twentieth-century emergent American literatures, the borderlands have become a powerful trope. What these literatures have in common is the desire to negotiate the borderlands between traditional cultures, to live without frontiers, to become a crossroads where Wittman Ah Sing (Chinese American *and* American playwright) can meet Walt Whitman (American bard *and* gay American) in order to collaborate in the making of what Whitman called "the greatest poem" – America itself.

2

※

COMPARATIVE RACISM AND THE
LOGIC OF NATURALIZATION

IN N. Scott Momaday's *House Made of Dawn,* the Native American protagonist, Abel, is brutally beaten without provocation by a Chicano
policeman named Martinez. Richard Rubbio, the Chicano protagonist
of José Antonio Villarreal's *Pocho* first learns about racism by observing the
way his friends discriminate against a Japanese boy named Thomas.
Midway through John Okada's *No-No Boy,* a young Japanese American
veteran named Kenji realizes that instead of finding ways to unite to
achieve common goals, America's minority cultures continually find ways
to discriminate against one another and even against their own members:

The Negro who was always being mistaken for a white man becomes a white man
and he becomes hated by the Negroes with whom he once hated on the same side.
And the young Japanese hates the not-so-young Japanese who is more Japanese
than himself, and the not-so-young, in turn, hates the old Japanese who is all
Japanese and, therefore, even more Japanese than he.

Kenji tries to find a "pattern" that can be "studied" so that "answers" can
be "deduced," but all he is able to conclude is that "the world was full of
hatred." What he does not manage to articulate is the fact that the dis-
unity of America's marginalized cultures, evident in these three novels, is
no accident.

It is, instead, the result of a divide-and-conquer strategy of comparative
racism, in which racial and ethnic groups are measured against not only
the gold standard of Anglo-Saxon "whiteness" but also against one
another, so that they can be assigned positions of relative inferiority. These
positions shift over time depending on the threat that these groups are
seen to pose to the mainstream. For example, from the mid- to the late
nineteenth century, the Chinese were seen as a "degraded" race while the
Japanese were held in relative esteem; by the end of World War II, these
positions had been reversed. Comparative racism has been an abiding feature of popular discourse and (until relatively recently) of legislation in the
United States, and nowhere more evident than in the late-nineteenth-cen-

tury debates and acts surrounding the question of which nonwhite immigrants and resident aliens should be allowed to become citizens of the United States.

The nativism of this period put into place strategies of repression that would continue to affect Asian Americans, Mexican Americans, and Native Americans well into the twentieth century. The 1940s began with the Chinese Exclusion Act of 1882 still in effect and the Bureau of Indian Affairs (BIA) still trying to craft an "Indian New Deal" that could at least partially remedy the disastrous effects of the Dawes Act of 1887, which had attempted to bring about an end to tribal ownership of lands. The decade would be marked by sanctioned racism in the U.S. armed forces, the anti-Hispanic zoot suit riots in Los Angeles, and the evacuation and internment of U.S. residents of Japanese origin during World War II. To make sense, then, of the situations faced by these three minority cultures in 1940, we must look back into the nineteenth century and learn to see it with the eyes of an emergent writer. The task of showing what nineteenth-century U.S. history looked like to those pushed to the margins of American culture has proven to be central to the project of emergent American writing after 1940. Describing his "first impulse" in writing the young-adult novel *Morning Girl* (1992), which portrays the lost Taino tribe, Michael Dorris argues that "if we concede the explication of our past, on any level, to those who have no investment in its accurate and sympathetic portrayal, we are giving up much more than the exploration of roots. We are abandoning the future to which we are uniquely entitled." The project of emergence, which by definition is all about the future, turns out also to be very much about the past.

❧

The first U.S. Naturalization Act (1790) enabled "free white persons" who had been in the United States for as little as two years to be naturalized in any U.S. court. Immigrant blacks – and later immigrant Asians – were not intended to be naturalized, and the act made no citizenship provisions for nonwhites who were born in the United States. Whether a free black could be a citizen depended on the state in which he or she was living, until the ratification of the Fourteenth Amendment in 1868 established uniform national citizenship.

Mexican Americans, however, had already learned that mere citizenship does not guarantee the protection of rights for those who are nonwhites. As a result of the Treaty of Guadalupe Hidalgo, which ended the Mexican-American War in 1848, Mexico ceded all of its territories north of the Rio Grande to the United States, territories that spanned the present-day states of Arizona, California, Nevada, New Mexico, Utah, and half of Colorado. Though approximately 2,000 of the area's Spanish-speaking residents chose to relocate to Mexico, more than 80,000 remained on their lands and automatically became American citizens, though they were allowed to maintain their language and cultural traditions. Article IX of the treaty guaranteed Mexicans remaining in the Southwest "the enjoyment of all the rights of citizens of the United States according to the principles of the Constitution; and in the meantime shall be maintained and protected the free enjoyment of their liberty and property, and secured in the free exercise of their religion without restriction." Gloomily commenting on the signing of the treaty, the Mexican diplomat Manuel Crescion Rejón predicted that "our race, our unfortunate people will have to wander in search of hospitality in a strange land, only to be ejected later. Descendants of the Indians that we are the North Americans hate us, their spokesmen depreciate us, even if they recognize the justice of our cause, and they consider us unworthy to form with them one nation and one society."

The Mexicans who stayed to become American citizens were treated as second-class citizens: they constituted an ethnic minority within American national culture, and they were soon victimized by unscrupulous white Americans. "A pre-Civil War type of carpetbagger moved into the territory to make his fortune," writes the Chicano fiction writer and scholar Américo Paredes, "preying upon the newly created Americans of Mexican descent. The Mexican's cattle were killed or stolen. The Mexican was forced to sell his land; and if he did not, his widow usually did after her husband was 'executed' for alleged cattle rustling. Thus did the great Texas ranches and the American cattle industry begin." Naturalized Mexicans in California, too, found themselves treated as second-class citizens. Though they outnumbered Anglos in the territory at first, the discovery of gold near John Sutter's mill led to a massive influx of migrants to California. In 1849, the Mexican population of California was 13,000, while the Anglo population had ballooned to 100,000. As a result, Anglos were able to control the state legislature and enact discriminatory laws aimed at Mexicans. An antivagrancy act popularly referred to as the "Greaser Act" defined as "vagrants" all persons "commonly known as 'Greasers' or the issue of Spanish or Indian blood . . . and who [were] armed and not peaceable and quiet persons"; a foreign miner's license tax of twenty dollars per month was in effect a tax on miners perceived to be Mexicans, since the bulk of the fees collected were taken from Spanish-speaking miners, including those who were in fact U.S. born citizens of Mexican extraction.

The roots of twentieth-century Chicano literature lie in the tradition of resistance that originated during this period as a response to what Mexican

Americans still consider to be the "occupation" of America by the U.S. government. The period that began with the Texas uprising and closed with the Mexican Revolution of 1910 was the heyday of the Mexican American *corrido,* a form of folk song that came to dominate the popular culture of the Southwest. The *corrido* is a narrative ballad, generally composed anonymously and sung or spoken to musical accompaniment. Related to ballad forms such as the *copla,* the *décima,* and the *romance,* which had been brought by the Spanish to Mexico, the *corrido* flourished during the hundred years that followed the Texas uprising, particularly in the border region south of Texas where relations between Mexican and Anglo-Americans were particularly troubled. In contrast to earlier ballad forms, which generally dealt with incidents from daily life, the *corrido* emphasizes drama and conflict, particularly the resistance of an individual to forces of oppression. True to its name, which is derived from the verb *correr,* "to run," the *corrido* generally offers a swiftly paced story, most often told in stanzas of four eight-syllable lines. In his groundbreaking study of the *corrido,* *"With His Pistol in His Hand": A Border Ballad and Its Hero* (1958), Américo Paredes argues that the "balladry of the Lower Border [was] working toward a single type: toward one form, the *corrido,* toward one theme, border conflict; toward one concept of the hero, the man fighting for his right with his pistol in his hand." Paredes's study, which is often cited by the first generation of Chicano writers as a major influence, focuses on the most famous of these ballads, *"El corrido de Gregorio Cortéz"* ("The Ballad of Gregorio Cortéz), which attacks the racism and lawlessness of Anglo-Americans by recounting the story of a Mexican American cowboy – a *vaquero* – who avenges his brother's murder at the hands of an Anglo sheriff. These verses demonstrate the way in which this representative *corrido* contrasts the intelligence and courage of the *vaquero* with the stupidity and cowardice of the Anglo cowboy:

> In the ranch corral
> they managed to surround him.
> A little more than 300 men
> and there he gave them the slip.
>
> There around Encinal
> from all that they say
> They had a shoot-out
> and he killed another sheriff.
>
> Gregorio Cortéz said,
> with his pistol in his hand,
> "Don't run, you cowardly Rangers
> from one lone Mexican."

> He turned toward Laredo
> without a single fear,
> "Follow me, you cowardly Rangers,
> I am Gregorio Cortéz."

Taken together, the variants of the Cortéz *corrido* have been described by the critic Raymund Paredes as "a kind of Mexican American epic that pulls together the basic themes of contemporary Mexican American writing: ethnic pride, a forceful rejection of unflattering Anglo stereotypes, and, through celebration of Cortéz's marvelous *vaquero* skills, an affirmation of the Mexican American's rootedness in the Southwest."

In 1876, Porfirio Díaz engineered a coup and became president of Mexico. In order to help finance the industrialization of agriculture, mining, and transportation, the Díaz government encouraged investment by North Americans, who were benefiting from the expansion of the U.S. economy during the decades after the Civil War. Industrialization – in particular the building of 15,000 miles of railroad track between 1880 and 1910 – transformed the Mexican economy, bringing about the decline of the communal village and forcing many peasants to become migrant workers; increasingly these workers, called *braceros,* traveled across the border to work in the United States. The *braceros* often competed with freed slaves for work, and like the Chinese, they were identified by white Americans as equivalent to blacks and treated in a similarly discriminatory fashion. In addition, they shared with Chinese sojourners the sense that they were merely transient residents of the United States: according to Américo Paredes, "the Mexican immigrant's sense of continuing to 'pass through' after twenty years or more of residence in the United States contributed to his problems, since he remained a perennial visitor in a foreign country, without children born in the United States in his own way of thinking." The sufferings of the *bracero* were also captured in the stanzas of the *corrido,* which began to bear titles like *"Los Deportados"* ("The Deported Ones"), *"La Discriminación," "Los Engancahdos"* ("The Work Gang"), and *"Tristes Quejas de un Bracero"* ("A Bracero's Complaint").

The outbreak of the revolution of 1910 produced what Américo Paredes calls "the Greater Mexican heroic *corrido,*" but the theme of border conflict continued to dominate Mexican American balladry. What the Mexican Revolution did produce was a massive influx of new *braceros* who would fill the need for cheap foreign labor created after the Chinese Exclusion Acts of 1882, 1892, and 1902 and the U.S. government's "Gentleman's Agreement" with Japan in 1907 combined to curtail the flow of working-class Asians into the Western states.

I'm going to tell you, gentleman,
all about my sufferings.
Since I left my country,
to come to this nation.

It must have been about ten at night,
the train began to whistle.
I heard my mother say,
"There comes that ungrateful train
that is going to take my son."

"Good-bye to my beloved mother.
Give me your blessings.
I am going abroad,
where there is no revolution."

These lines from the *corrido "El Deportado"* ("The Deportee"), recorded by Los Hermanos Buñuelos in 1929, are typical of the shift that occurred in the border ballad during this period of immigration. It is thought that as many as 100,000 Mexican immigrants entered the United States during the years surrounding the Mexican Revolution; with the outbreak of the First World War in 1914, a second wave of immigration began that would bring over one million Mexican immigrants to the United States by the end of the 1920s. Throughout this period, as its subject shifted from the *vaquero* to the *bracero*, the *corrido* remained the primary cultural form through which the suffering of Mexicans in United States found expression. *"El Deportado"* concludes with these verses addressed to the people of Mexico:

Oh my beloved countrymen,
I suffered a lot.

The light skinned men are very wicked.
They take advantage of the occasion.
And all the Mexicans
are treated without compassion.

There comes a large cloud of dust,
with no consideration.
Women, children and old ones
are being driven to the Border.
We are being kicked out of this country.

Good-bye beloved countrymen,
we are being deported.
But we are not bandits,
we came to work.

I will wait for you in my homeland,
there is no more revolution.
Let's leave my dear friends,
we will be welcomed
by our beautiful nation.

Taken together, what *"El Corrido de Gregorio Cortéz"* and *"El Deportado"* demonstrate is that the abiding theme of the Mexican American *corrido* is the racial oppression suffered at the hands of Anglo-Americans who sought to deny Mexican American citizens their rights and to exploit poor Mexicans seeking to better their fortunes in the United States.

❦

The Chinese Exclusion Acts and the Gentleman's Agreement with Japan that created the labor shortage in the western states at the turn of the century were intended to end a period of Asian immigration that began in 1849. White Easterners and Europeans were not the only ones lured to California by the discovery of gold at Sutter's Mill: 325 Chinese migrants arrived in California that year to participate in the Gold Rush, followed the next year by 450 of their compatriots. Starting in 1851, however, the number of Chinese emigrating to California began to rise dramatically, with more than twenty-five hundred arriving that year and more than twenty thousand arriving in 1852, bringing the total of Chinese immigrants to about twenty-five thousand. By 1870, there were approximately sixty-three thousand Chinese in the United States, the majority of them (seventy-seven percent) living in California. By 1890, three years after the Dawes Act, there were 107,488 "Chinese" living in the United States. (In the U.S. census, *Chinese* was a racial definition that included both immigrants from China and their descendants.)

The Chinese men who first emigrated to the United States in the mid-nineteenth century were known as *gam saan haak,* "travelers to the Gold Mountain," and they thought of themselves as sojourners. At first, these Chinese men were welcomed as visitors who could assist in fostering California's economic growth; mid-nineteenth-century accounts referred to these Chinese migrants as "Celestials" (since China was often called the Celestial Empire). California's leading newspaper, the San Francisco *Daily Alta California,* wrote in 1852 that "quite a large number of the Celestials have arrived among us of late. . . . Scarcely a ship arrives that does not bring an increase to this worthy integer of our population. The China boys will yet vote at the polls, study in the same schools and bow at the same altar of our own countrymen." The governor of California, John

McDougal, told the legislature at the beginning of 1852 that the Chinese constituted "one of the most worthy classes of our newly adopted citizens – to whom the climate and the character of these lands are peculiarly suited" – apparently failing to remember that Chinese were prohibited from becoming American citizens by the 1790 Naturalization Act, which restricted the privilege of naturalization to "white" immigrants. Throughout the 1850s, California's popular press contained numerous articles presenting favorable portraits of Chinese immigrants.

These views, however, were not shared by white workers with whom the Chinese were competing for jobs. As early as the spring of 1852, there was considerable anti-Chinese sentiment among white miners, and their agitation led to the passage of a new foreign miners' license tax, which appeared to apply to all immigrant miners but was in reality aimed specifically at the Chinese. It stipulated that a monthly tax of three dollars was to be paid by any miner who did not intend to become an American citizen, an intent that the Chinese were prohibited from having. "In California," wrote Mark Twain in *Roughing It* (1872), a Chinese man "gets a living out of old mining claims that white men have abandoned as exhausted and worthless – and then the officers come down on him once a month with an exorbitant swindle to which the legislature has given the broad, general name of 'foreign' mining tax, but is usually inflicted on no foreigners but Chinamen." This miner's tax remained in place until it was theoretically abolished by the Civil Rights Act of 1870.

In "The Grandfather of the Sierra Nevada Mountains," from *China Men,* Maxine Hong Kingston imagines the sojourner's life that her grandfather Ah Goong led while working for the Central Pacific Railroad. It was one of Ah Goong's "peculiarities," Kingston writes, "that he heard the crackles, bangs, gunshots that go off when the world lurches; the gears on its axis snap. Listening to a faraway New Year, he had followed the noise and came upon the blasting in the Sierras. . . . The Central Pacific hired him on sight; chinamen had a natural talent for explosions." Chinese migrants had begun to work in greater and greater numbers for the Central Pacific Railroad when profits from mining started to decrease in the early 1860s. By 1867, there were 12,000 Chinese working for the line, representing ninety percent of its entire workforce.

Kingston's story depicts Ah Goong's experiences during the strike of 1867, which took place after the railroad proposed to raise wages four dollars per month (to thirty-five) while requiring Chinese workers to work ten-hour rather than eight-hour shifts. Five thousand Chinese workers walked out, demanding wages of forty-five dollars (a raise of fourteen dollars) and a

workday equal in length to that of white workers: "Eight hours a day good
for white man, all the same good for Chinamen" was their slogan. Because
the white workers did not join the strike and because the railroad managed
to cut off the strikers' food supply, the matter was settled in nine days, and
the final compromise was a four-dollar raise and an eight-hour shift. "The
China Men went back to work quietly," writes Kingston. "No use singing
and shouting over a compromise and losing nine days' work." What was a
cause for celebration was the completion of the railroad in 1869; Kingston
describes the scene at Promontory Point when the two tracks were connected at last: "A white demon in top hat tap-tapped on the gold spike, and
pulled it back out. Then one China Man held the real spike, the steel one,
and another hammered it in." Contemporary commentators noted the contribution made to the project by the Chinese: "The dream of Thomas
Jefferson, and the desires of Thomas Hart Benton's heart," wrote one magazine writer in an essay called "Manifest Destiny in the West," "have been
wonderfully fulfilled, so far as the Pacific Railroad and the trade with the
old world of the East is concerned. But even they did not prophesy that
Chinamen should build the Pacificward end of the road." Ah Goong has
misguidedly purchased worthless papers from a "Citizenship Judge," but it
is "having built the railroad" that makes him feel truly American.

Although Chinese workers were first hired by the railroad in February
of 1865, Kingston places Ah Goong with the railroad in the spring of
1863, allowing her to write that Ah Goong was also hired "because there
were not enough workingmen to do all the labor of building a new country" and to add wryly that "some of the banging" that Ah Goong heard
"came from the war to decide whether or not black people would continue
to work for nothing." The link between Chinese and blacks here is not
idle, for as Ronald Takaki has argued, racial characteristics previously associated only with blacks were easily transferred to the Chinese, because
many of the Europeans and Americans who were coming to California
from the East had never seen a Chinese person before. They therefore simply assumed that the Chinese were equivalent to the nonwhite peoples
with whom they *were* familiar: Indians and blacks. After a change in editorial leadership, the *Daily Alta California* proclaimed in 1853, "We have a
class here . . . who have most of the vices of the African and they are
numerous in both town and country. We allude to the Chinese. Every reason that exists against the toleration of free blacks in Illinois may be
argued against that of the Chinese here." White miners often referred to
the Chinese as "nagurs" and described them along with blacks as savage,
childlike, lustful – in short, physically and morally inferior. California's
stereotype of African Americans was nearly identical to that found in the

South, because there were relatively few blacks in California in the 1850s: the black population of approximately 2,200 in 1852 was less than a tenth of the Chinese population, and it is thought that the stereotypes of blacks found in the popular press were imported by white Southerners who moved to California during the Gold Rush, and who represented approximately one third of the total population of California at the time. But because antiblack racism had been a part of the national consciousness for so long, it provided a ready-made template for the description and judgment of other peoples of color.

This use of antiblack racism as a standard of reference occurred not only in the popular press but in legal discourse as well. California law treated blacks, Indians, and Chinese equally – equally inferior to whites. Mark Twain, that keen critic of American slavery, also documented the systematic racism directed at Chinese in *Roughing It*: "Any white man can swear a Chinaman's life away in the courts, but no Chinaman can testify against a white man. Ours is the 'land of the free' – nobody denies that – nobody challenges it. (Maybe it is because we won't let other people testify.) As I write, news comes that in broad daylight in San Francisco, some boys have stoned an inoffensive Chinaman to death, and that although a large crowd witnessed the shameful deed, no one interfered."

In the 1854 case of *People v. Hall,* the court based its opinion on section fourteen of an 1850 law regulating criminal proceedings according to which "no black or mulatto person, or Indian, shall be allowed to give evidence in favor of, or against a white man." Attempting to include Chinese under the rubric *Indian,* the court argued first that the term *Indian* originated in Columbus's mistaken belief that he had reached one of the "Islands of the Chinese Sea" when he arrived at Hispaniola and was therefore always intended to signify inhabitants of Asia, and second that it was a common belief among ethnologists that the Indian and "the Mongolian, or Asiatic," belonged to "the same type of the human species." In other words, said the court, "the name of Indian, from the time of Columbus to the present day, has been used to designate, not alone the North American Indian, but the whole of the Mongolian race, and that the name, though first applied probably through mistake, was afterward continued as appropriate on account of the supposed common origin."

The court, however, did not stop there. It bolstered its argument by speculating about the intentions of the original Naturalization Act of 1790 when it used the term *free white persons,* stating, "We are of the opinion that the words 'white,' 'Negro,' 'mulatto,' 'Indian,' and 'black person' wherever they occur in our Constitution and laws, must be taken in their generic sense, and that, even admitting the Indian of this continent is not of the Mongolian type, that the words 'black person' in the 14th section [of the 1850 law], must be taken as contradistinguished from white, and necessarily excludes all races other than the Caucasian." As a result of this twisted logic, Chinese were prevented from being able to give testimony for or against whites until 1872, when the 1850 law was repealed. What is important to note is that "black" here is an inclusive category constructed on the basis of physical characteristics. As we shall see, both the definition and the construction of this category will have shifted by the time of the Chinese Exclusion Act in 1882.

Chinese immigrants protested being equated with Indians and free blacks. In 1855, a merchant named Lai Chun-Chuen, writing on behalf of the San Francisco Chinese business community, upbraided white Americans for describing Chinese people as if they were "the same as Indians and Negroes." Arguing that Native Americans knew "nothing about the relations of society," since they wore neither clothes nor shoes and lived in caves, Lai pointed out that the Chinese had a wealthy civilization that dated back more than a thousand years, with long traditions of civil government and philosophy. "Can it be possible," he asked, "that we are classed as equals with this uncivilized race of men?" Three years earlier, a Chinese community leader named Norman Asing had asked a similar question in the pages of the *Daily Alta California.* Writing an open letter to the governor of California, John Bigler, who had just given a special message to the legislature on the evils of Chinese immigration, Asing "remind[ed]" Bigler that "when your nation was a wilderness, and the nation from which you sprung *barbarous,* we exercised most of the arts and virtues of civilized life; that we are possessed of a language and a literature, and that men skilled in science and the arts are numerous among us; that the productions of our manufactories, our sail, and workshops, form no small commerce of the world. . . . We are not the degraded race you would make us."

Yet not only did white Americans continue to depict the Chinese as a degraded race, but they also began to present blacks as far less degraded in comparison. For example, in 1877, the California legislature sent a "memorial" to the United States Congress offering advice on the question of limiting Chinese immigration. Comparing blacks in the eastern states with Chinese immigrants in California, the memorial notes that "the free Negro speaks our language, . . . grows up among us, worships the same God as ourselves, and is accustomed to our institutions." The Chinese, on the other hand, constitute a race that "is utterly a stranger to our language, to the fundamental principles of enlightened religion, to our consciousness of moral obligations, and, with a few individual exceptions, even to a sense of the most common proprieties of life." Blacks, in other words, are well-behaved and well-acculturated compared to the Chinese, and yet the eastern states find "the presence of a comparatively small population of [free blacks] exceedingly annoying, and fraught with dangers not only to the peace of their own community, but to the harmony between their laws and the constitutional policy of the National Legislature." How much worse, then, is California's plight, confronted as she is by the "unlimited influx of a race which already comprises the eighth part of her entire population," a race that seems completely alien.

So alien, in fact, that at the California constitutional convention in 1887 – the year of the Dawes Act – a delegate named John F. Miller could declare: "Were the Chinese to amalgamate at all with our people, it would be the lowest most vile and degraded of our race and the result of that amalgamation would be a hybrid of the most despicable, a mongrel of the most detestable that has ever afflicted the earth." Miscegenation between blacks and whites is bad, apparently, but miscegenation between Chinese and whites would be a horror.

Things had looked promising for Chinese immigrants in 1868, when the United States and China signed the Burlingame Treaty, in which the two nations agreed that they would "cordially recognize the inherent and inalienable right of man to change his home and allegiance, and also the mutual advantage of the free migration and emigration of their citizens and subjects respectively from the one country to the other for purposes of curiosity, of trade, or as permanent residents." Maxine Hong Kingston uses this excerpt from the treaty as the headnote for "The Laws" section of *China Men,* but her first entry immediately undercuts this seemingly idealistic piece of governmental rhetoric, juxtaposing it to the fact that 1868 was also the year in which "40,000 miners of Chinese ancestry were Driven Out." Although the Fourteenth Amendment was also enacted in 1868 to guarantee that "naturalized Americans have the same rights as native-born Americans," Kingston points out that this guarantee was soon denied to Asian Americans by the Nationality Act of 1870, which limited naturalization to "white persons and persons of African descent." In broadening the 1790 Naturalization Act, which had been rendered anachronistic by the abolition of slavery, Congress pointedly rejected the more general, color-blind phrase "persons," which was advocated by a group of radical Republicans led by Senator Charles Sumner of Massachusetts. The debates over the 1870 act made it clear that the new phraseology was pointedly designed to exclude Chinese from citizenship. The act thus created a third category to which Chinese immigrants were relegated: "aliens ineligible to citizenship," a category that was reinforced by the provisions of the Chinese Exclusion Act twelve years later, which made the Chinese the only ethnic group that could not emigrate freely to the United States. They would remain ineligible until 1943 when the Chinese exclusion laws were finally repealed by Congress.

What made the Chinese seem so alien to white Americans? We can gain some insight into the underlying logic of this claim, and of the Chinese Exclusion Act, by looking at the series of legislative acts that led to the granting of citizenship to Native Americans in 1887. During the period of nineteenth-century Chinese emigration to the United States, Native Americans were also denied the privileges of citizenship, but in 1871 the federal government passed the first in a series of laws designed to assimilate Indians by weaning them from their tribal orientation, a process that would lead to the conferral of citizenship rights by the Dawes Act sixteen years later. What Congress did in 1871 was to endorse a policy that treated Indians as individuals and wards of the government and ceased to recognize the legal standing of tribes. The weaning process continued in 1883 when the judicial powers of chiefs were dissolved and transferred to a system of federal courts. Finally, in 1887, the Dawes Act, which Theodore Roosevelt described as "a mighty pulverizing engine to break up the tribal mass," formally dissolved tribes as legal bodies and redistributed tribal lands among families and unmarried individuals. Heads of families were allotted 160 acres, individuals 80 acres, with the stipulation that the lands were to be held in trust for 25 years without taxation, so that the Indians could learn to profit from the land and to assume the responsibilities that landholding entailed, including the payment of taxes. Once the twenty-five years had elapsed, the Indians would become full owners of their allotments, free to sell or lease them, or – if they could not pay their taxes – to lose them.

The Dawes Act was passed in response to the efforts of reformers like Helen Hunt Jackson, whose 1881 tract *A Century of Dishonor* and 1884 novel *Ramona* had publicized the unjust treatment of Native Americans. Most reformers had decided by 1887 that the only alternative to assimilation for the American Indian was extermination. The Dawes Act was intended to speed that process of assimilation by bringing to an end the tribal system, with its economy based on hunting and gathering, and introducing Native Americans to an individualistic conception of social life and a capitalistic understanding of land use and agriculture. Addressing the Lake Mohonk Conference of the Friends of the Indians in 1886, the president of Amherst College, Merill E. Gates, argued that "to bring him out of savagery into citizenship we must make the Indian more intelligently selfish before we can make him unselfishly intelligent. We need to awaken in him wants. . . . Discontent with the teepee and the starving rations of the Indian camp in winter is needed to get the Indian out of the blanket and into trousers – and trousers with a pocket in them, and with a pocket that aches to be filled with dollars." During the debate over the Dawes Act, Texas Senator Samuel Bell Maxey objected to the bill's provision for Indian citizenship: "Look at your Chinamen, are they not specifically excepted from the naturalization laws?" Maxey hoped that the treatment of Chinese immigrants might serve as a precedent for reining in the rights of Native Americans. The provision stood, however, because natives – unlike the Chinese – were considered capable of eventual assimilation. According to historian Frederick Hoxie, the Dawes Act was "made possible by the belief that Indians did not have the 'deficiencies' of other groups [such as the Chinese]: they were fewer in number, the beneficiaries of a public sympathy and pity, and [were considered] capable of advancement." In other words, like African Americans, Natives were considered reeducable. Being capable of advancement meant being capable of learning the lessons of individualism and laissez-faire capitalism necessary for assimilation into mainstream American culture.

In the second volume of his 1893 study, *The American Commonwealth,* British historian James Bryce writes that "the circumstance of colonial life, the process of settling the western wilderness, the feelings evoked by the struggle against George III, all went to intensify individualism, the love of enterprise, and the pride in personal freedom" in the United States. In Bryce's analysis, individualism and its related values are not uniquely American; he argues that the American "State governments of 1776 and the National government of 1789 started from ideas, mental habits, and administrative practice generally similar to those of contemporary England." Americans, however, do not acknowledge the origins of this aspect of their social thought. "From that day to this," writes Bryce, "individualism, the love of enterprise, and the pride in personal freedom, have been deemed by Americans not only their choicest, but their peculiar and exclusive possessions."

Bryce was, essentially, confirming the analysis offered half a century earlier by another famous European observer of American culture, Alexis de Tocqueville. In the second volume of *Democracy in America,* published in 1840, Tocqueville wrote that "'individualism' is a word recently coined to express a new idea. Our fathers only knew about egoism." Henry Reeve, the translator of the American edition, felt obliged to comment on his use of the term: "I adopt the expression of the original," he wrote in a footnote, "however strange it may seem to the English ear, . . . because I know of no English word exactly equivalent to the expression." The term *individualisme* had been coined in France during the 1820s, and it was deployed by both counterrevolutionary and socialist thinkers as a critique of

Enlightenment thought. It is in this negative sense that Tocqueville uses the term *individualism* in the second volume of *Democracy in America*. Tocqueville defines it as "a calm and considered feeling which disposes each citizen to isolate himself from the mass of his fellows and withdraw into the circle of family and friends; with this little society formed to his taste, he gladly leaves the greater society to look after itself." According to Tocqueville, egoism "springs from a blind instinct," while "individualism is based on misguided judgment rather than depraved feeling." The distinction, however, ultimately becomes moot: "Egoism sterilizes the seeds of every virtue; individualism at first only dams the spring of public virtues, but in the long run it attacks and destroys all the others too and finally merges in egoism."

American thinkers, however, were already in the process of appropriating and redefining the term *individualism*. In 1839, the year before Tocqueville's second volume appeared, the anonymous author of a piece in the *Democratic Review* entitled "The Course of Civilization" described the "history of humanity" as "the record of a grand march . . . at all times tending to one point – the ultimate perfection of man. The course of civilization is the progress of man from a state of savage individualism to that of an individualism more elevated, moral and refined." Two years later, in the first American review of *Democracy in America,* which appeared in the *Boston Quarterly Review,* an anonymous author inverts Tocqueville's argument in order to appropriate the term *individualism* and endow it with a positive connotation. Regarding individualism as the driving force behind American society, the reviewer describes it as "that strong confidence in self, or reliance upon one's own exertion and resources." The author applauds what Tocqueville laments, arguing that "it is the artificial classification of mankind, into certain unfounded castes of the high and the low, the learned and the ignorant, patricians and plebeians, priests and laymen, princes and subjects . . . rather than the free scope of personal or individual peculiarities, which has enfeebled, and thereby corrupted the race." Individualism, by destroying the chains forged by aristocratic society and forcing each individual to rely on "the inherent and profound resources of his own mysterious being," has actually created a new "organic unity of the collective race." Individualism is thus perceived not as a destructive vice that dams the spring of public virtues but rather as the source of all public virtue and, ultimately, as the mechanism through which America will fulfill its promise.

According to the logic of this rhetoric, then, blacks and Indians can be assimilated into the white race if they can learn the lessons of individualism; thus, what makes the Chinese so alien is not their particular physical or genetic characteristics but their refusal to accede to the principles of individualism. Lai Chun-Chuen and Norman Asing argue that the Chinese are a civilized race with a long history and that they should therefore be distinguished from blacks and Indians. Their wish is granted, though not in the way that they hoped. For that long history of civilization is, in fact, precisely the problem. Unlike African Americans or Native Americans, the Chinese have too much civilization. The Chinese "race," concludes an 1885 report by the San Francisco Board of Supervisors, "is one that cannot readily throw off its habits and customs" and the "fact that these customs are so widely at variance with our own, makes the enforcements of our laws and compulsory obedience to our laws necessarily obnoxious and revolting to the Chinese." In other words, unlike blacks and Indians, the Chinese have a culture that puts them at odds with American individualism, and it is a culture that cannot simply be "pulverized," to recall Teddy Roosevelt's expression.

Some thirty years earlier, in 1853, the *Daily Alta California* complained that the Chinese were more clannish than American blacks and morally inferior to them, as if being "clannish" were a sign of moral inferiority. The same logic can be found in the California legislature's 1877 memorial to the U.S. Congress. The self-sacrifice and cooperation necessary for the Chinese to survive in a culture hostile to them are portrayed as signs that the Chinese are a "degraded" race: "Chinese labor ranks no higher in the public respect than slave labor. Its compensation is so low in proportion to the necessities of life in California that the white laborer cannot compete with the Chinaman." Noting that "the larger portion of the Chinese has been engaged in mining," the memorial states that "during the early years after the discovery of gold in this State, when our population was sparse, and when there was no lack of rich surface mines, the American and European miner experienced no hardship from the presence of the Chinese." Later, however,

when the rich surface diggings became more and more exhausted, and the chances of generous reward for individual labor in mining claims became rare, the antipathies of our own race against the Mongolians were aroused, and grew daily stronger in proportion as the mines occupied by Mongolians became of increasing importance to American citizens or Europeans, who sought the means of a modest and toilsome subsistence for a permanent settlement upon our soil.

Competition is the name of the game in American individualism, but the Chinese get no credit for competing well because they are not motivated by "the chances of generous reward for individual labor." Their willingness to settle for less and to pursue communal rather than individual goals has given them, seemingly, an unfair advantage. And the memorial continues: "in the cities too hostility toward the Chinese is increasing because in several industries white workingmen cannot compete with the Chinese": white workers, "being unable to maintain a decent and civilized subsistence upon wages which afford the Chinaman a comfortable living, were compelled, in every case where Chinese competition made its appearance, to retire from their profession and abandon its exercise to their Chinese competitors." The frugality of the Chinese is thus depicted not as a form of Franklinian virtue but rather as a vice.

In the 1885 San Francisco Board of Supervisors report, the depiction of this supposed vice is intensified to the point of hyperbole. The report likens frugality to opium smoking, gambling, and prostitution:

Compel the Chinamen by municipal laws which are not only enacted but enforced, to live like our own race; prevent them from burrowing and crowding together like vermin; enforce cleanliness in mode of life; break up opium dens and gambling hells; restrict the number of inhabitants in any given block in the city; enforce upon this people, so far as may be possible by every legitimate method that can be devised, a cost of living that shall approach as nearly as possible that of the ordinary white laborer.

What lies behind this hyperbole is a fear that is implicit in both the memorial and the supervisors' report: that Chinese frugality and communitarianism will turn out to foster a vice within American individualism itself, a vice that could ultimately destroy the American way. According to the memorial, Chinese practices bring about the "degradation of labor and the impoverishment of the laboring classes," both of which it describes as "poisons which destroy the lifeblood of a republic." A few pages later it becomes clear how this happens, as the memorial admits that

the presence of hordes of Mongolians would at present undoubtedly be advantageous to the capitalist and the manufacturer. These classes, although very necessary to the development of a young State, are generally not as careful of the preservation of the principles of freedom and of the exclusion of every element dangerous to the maintenance and the purity of republican institutions, as they are anxious of reaping immediate and unusual profits.

In other words, the presence of a frugal community like the Chinese threatens to foster the selfishness that Tocqueville believed lay at the heart of American individualism. Chinese communitarianism will prove to be a "poison" that will destroy American individualism from within.

Deemed incapable as a race of understanding or practicing individualism, the Chinese were denied the ability to become naturalized citizens and as a result denied the ability to be fully fledged bearers of individual rights. There is perhaps no better illustration of the intimate link between

American individualism and American racism than the case of the *People v. Washington* in 1869, in which a mulatto was indicted for the robbery of a Chinese man named Ah Wang, on the basis of testimony from Chinese witnesses. The Civil Rights Act of 1866 had guaranteed all citizens equality before the law with respect to their personal liberty. Included in the definition of citizens were all persons born within the United States and not subject to a foreign power. The main thrust of the act was to guarantee blacks the same rights as whites. The law stipulated that citizens of every race and color, without regard to previous condition of servitude, should have "the same right, in every State and Territory, to the full and equal benefit of all laws and proceedings for the security of person and property as is enjoyed by white citizens." On appeal, the Supreme Court overturned the mulatto Washington's conviction, reasoning that since California law explicitly excluded Chinese testimony against whites, then extending equality to blacks meant giving them the same right to be protected from Chinese testimony. In this case, "black" was no longer a category that signified all nonwhite as it had in the earlier case of the *People v. Hall.* Now "white" was a category that signified those whose rights would be protected, a category that pointedly excluded the Chinese. When the Dawes Act conferred citizenship rights on Native Americans in 1887, *white,* rather than *black,* would prove to be the more inclusive term. In both popular and legal discourse, then, where *black* once signified "all non-whites," *white* came to signify – at least, temporarily – "all non-Chinese." What this analysis suggests, of course, is not that blacks had a legal or cultural standing equal to that of whites, since this was also an era of virulent antiblack discourse in which black citizenship rights gained after the Civil War were significantly eroded. Instead what is demonstrated by this pattern of rhetoric – with its unthinkable equation of whites and blacks – is the depth of white hatred for the Chinese.

❦

The ultimately devastating effect of the Dawes Act on Native American tribal culture is dramatized in Louise Erdrich's novel *Tracks* (1988), the third novel in the tetralogy that includes *Love Medicine, The Beet Queen* (1987), and *The Bingo Palace* (1994). *Tracks* is a "historical novel" in the conventional sense of the term. The dated chapters carefully establish the time of the novel as the years 1912–24 and the events of the novel correspond to documented historical occurrences: the outbreaks of tuberculosis that afflicted North Dakota from 1891 to 1901 and the battles over Indian land rights that erupted after the implementation of the Dawes Severalty Act. Unlike Kingston, Erdrich never names the pieces of legislation that set in motion the events of the novel. In *China Men,* Kingston discusses legislation explicitly in order to get across the idea that standard national history and ethnic self-history tell very different stories, and the book throws its weight behind ethnic self-history by relegating its overtly historical material to a single interchapter. *Tracks* emphasizes ethnic self-history even further by suppressing standard national history, including it only by implication.

Like many novels written by Native American writers, *Tracks* dramatizes the collision of two different ways of understanding the nature of history and time. The dating of its chapter by season and year juxtaposes the Western linear sense of time that assigns sequential numbers to each year with the cyclical conception of time identified with the changes of season and stressed in many Native American cultures. In addition, the time period covered in each chapter is also described by its specific Indian name. Thus, the first chapter is called "Winter 1912: *Manitou-geezisohns*: Little Spirit Sun." The opening paragraph also dramatizes the collision of these two conceptions of time and history:

We started dying before the snow, and like the snow, we continued to fall. It was surprising there were so many of us left to die. For those who survived the spotted sickness from the south, our long fight west to Nadouissioux land where we signed the treaty, and then a wind from the east, bringing exile in a storm of government papers, what descended from the north in 1912 seemed impossible.

Identifying each of the events described in this paragraph with one of the directions links the prose here to traditional Native American creation myths, which stress the role played by the four directions, a link that proves ironic since what the narrator is describing is the destruction of his tribe. The paragraph's description of written materials such as "the treaty'" and the "storm of government papers" points to another distinction between native and Western modes of historiography. Native self-history is transmitted orally through storytelling, while Western history is transmitted through written accounts. Moreover, Western history is to a large extent a history of the written word and of the ways in which writing has been used to effect cultural change. *Tracks* dramatizes the defeat of the native culture of storytelling by a Western culture of documents. Native historiography must give way to Western historiography, a pattern embodied by the use of the date "1912" at the end of the novel's first paragraph to puncture the sense of mythical time with which the paragraph begins. Erdrich shares this understanding of the difference between Native American culture and U.S. culture with a great many other Native American authors. For example, Paula Gunn Allen has argued that "there is some sort of connection between colonization and chronological time. There is a connection between factories and clocks, and there is a connection between colonial imperialism and factories. There is also a connection between telling Indian tales in chronological sequences and the American tendency to fit Indians into the slots they have prepared for us." She notes that she had difficulty with publishers because she "chose Indian time over industrial time as a structuring device" in *The Woman Who Owned the Shadows* (1983), her first novel.

It is no accident that *Tracks* begins in 1912, twenty-five years after the Dawes Act, for though the novel does not mention the act by name, its plot revolves around the struggles of the Turtle Mountain Chippewa to keep their allotments from falling into the hands of timber companies and to maintain a sense of tribal identity. *Tracks* focuses particularly on the plight of Nanapush's adopted daughter, Fleur Pillager, whose choice allotment on the banks of Lake Matchimanito is ultimately lost, in part through the connivance of "government Indians" like Bernadette Morissey who are eager to assimilate and to profit from the misfortunes of fellow tribe members. Intended to bolster Native American land ownership, the Dawes Act ended up sabotaging it instead, inadvertently opening up areas previously reserved for Indians to white settlement. Many Indians, like Fleur Pillager, lost their allotments because they could not pay their taxes; others lost their allotments after pledging them as security for loans to buy goods, while others were conned into selling their allotments well below fair market value. The U.S. government abetted the erosion of Indian ownership with the 1906 Burke Act, which shortened the twenty-five-year trust period for Indians deemed "competent," enabling them to sell (or lose) their lands that much more quickly, and in 1917 the ironically named commissioner of Indian affairs, Cato Sells, issued a "Declaration of Policy" stipulating that all Indians with more than one half white blood would be automatically defined as competent, given U.S. citizenship, and required to pay taxes on their allotments. Linda Hogan's first novel, *Mean Spirit* (1990), dramatizes the aftermath of the Dawes Act in Oklahoma, where white oilmen, acting in tandem with government agents, cheated and, if necessary, murdered Indians whose allotments happened to have become valuable because of the discovery of oil. "They had ideas about the Indians," Hogan writes about the government clerks distributing land royalty checks, "that they were unschooled, ignorant people who knew nothing about life or money." The U.S. government has imposed the lessons of individualism and capitalism on Native American culture, but whites resent it when the Indians are not only willing but able to implement those lessons: "In the background, a surly clerk in a white shirt piped up and said to another one, out loud,

'Hell, some of them buy three cars. We don't have that kind of money, and we're Americans.'" Hogan uses moments of magical realism to embody the wonder and power of Native American culture, but these moments are no match for the realism that embodies the hypocrisy of white culture, whose mean spirit reduces the culture and life of Native America – quite literally – to "nothing more than a distant burning."

It is estimated that between 1887 and 1934, when the Wheeler-Howard Indian Reorganization Act ended the policy of allotment and once again recognized tribal ownership of lands, more than sixty percent of tribal lands were lost to railroads, cattlemen, timber companies, and land corporations: before 1887, 139 million acres were held in trust for Indians in the form of reservations; by 1934 only 48 million acres of land were still under Native American control, and many Native Americans were left landless.

❦

African and Native Americans were not the only ethnic groups to whom Chinese and Chinese Americans were unfavorably compared. Many white Americans believed that the Japanese were a far superior race to the Chinese, a fact borne out by the writing careers of the Eaton sisters, Edith and Winnifred. Using the pseudonym Sui Sin Far, Edith Eaton (1865–1914) became the first writer to attempt an "inside" representation of Chinese American lives. Eaton was the daughter of an English merchant named Edward Eaton and a Chinese woman named Grace Trepesis, who was abducted from home at the age of three or four and eventually adopted by an English missionary family in Shanghai. She emigrated with her parents and five siblings from Macclesfield, England, to the United States in 1874, because her father's family disapproved of his marriage to a Chinese woman, and the family eventually settled permanently in Montreal, Canada, where Edith's sister Winnifred was born in 1875. Ultimately, the Eatons had sixteen children, two of whom died during childhood. Edith herself contracted rheumatic fever as a child; the disease weakened her constitution and eventually contributed to her early death at the age of forty-nine. She nevertheless pursued a career in journalism, publishing her first article, "A Trip in a Horse Car," in the Montreal magazine *Dominion Illustrated* in 1888. Eaton adopted the pseudonym Sui Sin Far (literally, "water fragrant flower") when she began publishing short stories in the mid-1890s. Her short fiction was collected into a volume entitled *Mrs. Spring Fragrance* (1912), which received generally favorable reviews. The New York *Independent* wrote that "the conflict between occidental and oriental ideals and the hardships of American immigration laws furnish the theme for most of the tales" and suggested that a reader "has his mind widened by becoming acquainted with novel points of view." Generally more conservative, the *New York Times* wrote that "Miss Eaton has struck a new note in American fiction," though its praise was qualified with the suggestion that this note had not been "struck . . . very surely, or with surpassing skill." Admitting, however, that "it has taken courage to strike it at all," the *Times* reviewer argues that Eaton's goal of "portray[ing] for readers of the white race the lives, feelings, sentiments of the Americanized Chinese on the Pacific coast, of those who have intermarried with them, and of the children who have sprung from such unions" is "a task whose adequate doing would require well-nigh superhuman insight and the subtlest of methods." This sentiment indicates just how resistant white Americans were to the idea that they shared a common humanity with the Chinese, who were routinely vilified as being subhuman.

Further evidence of this vilification can be found in an anecdote that Sui Sin Far recounts in her autobiographical essay "Leaves from the Mental Portfolio of an Eurasian" (1909). Sitting at a dinner party given by the man who employs her as a stenographer, she listens, aghast, to this exchange:

My employer shakes his rugged head. "Somehow or other," says he, "I cannot reconcile myself to the thought that the Chinese are humans like ourselves. They may have immortal souls, but their faces seem to me to be so utterly devoid of expression that I cannot help but doubt."

"Souls," echoes the town clerk. "Their bodies are enough for me. A China man is, in my eyes, more repulsive than a nigger."

"They always give me such a creepy feeling," puts in the young girl with a laugh.

"I wouldn't have one in my house," declares my landlady.

"Now, the Japanese are different altogether. There's something bright and likeable about those men," continues Mr. K.

A miserable, cowardly feeling keeps me silent. I am in a Middle West town. If I declare what I am, every person in the place will hear about it the next day. The population is in the main made up of working folks with strong prejudices against my mother's countrymen. The prospect before me is not an enviable one – if I speak. I have no longer an ambition to die at the stake for the sake of demonstrating the greatness and nobleness of the Chinese people.

Mr. K. turns to me with a kindly smile.

"What makes Miss Far so quiet?" he asks.

"I don't suppose she finds the 'washee washee men' particularly interesting subjects of conversation," volunteers the young manager of the local bank.

With great effort, I raise my eyes from my plate. "Mr. K.," I say, addressing my employer. "The Chinese people may have no souls, no expression in their faces, be altogether beyond the pale of civilization, but whatever they are, I want you to understand that I am – I am Chinese."

There is silence in the room for a few minutes. Then Mr. K. pushes back his plate and standing up beside me, says:

"I should not have spoken as I did. I know nothing whatever about the Chinese. It was pure prejudice. Forgive me!"

I admire Mr. K.'s moral courage in apologizing to me; he is a conscientious Christian man, but I do not remain much longer in the little town.

This story both captures the depth of white American prejudice against the Chinese and also conveys a sense of the nature of Sui Sin Far's activism: her speech tacitly accepts the superiority of white civilization. Earlier in the essay, Eaton has described a childhood fight against white children who yell epithets like "yellow-face, pig-tail, rat-eater" at her and her brother: "They pull my hair, they tear my clothes, they scratch my face, and all but lame my brother; but the white blood in our veins fights valiantly for the Chinese half of us," and they are able to report later on to their mother that they have "won the battle." The assumption that the white blood is stronger than the Chinese underwrites Sui Sin Far's activism. She seems to believe that her hybrid identity makes her better able to champion the cause of the Chinese in America: later in the essay, she writes, "I meet many Chinese persons, and when they get into trouble am often called upon to fight their battles in the papers. This I enjoy." Eaton's syntax embodies her cultural situation: she is sympathetic to "Chinese persons," wishes to fight their battles, but writing primarily for a white audience and feeling empowered by her white blood, she describes other Chinese Americans in the third person, as "they" rather than "we."

The title of Eaton's essay, "Leaves from the Mental Portfolio of an Eurasian," recalls the title of an extremely popular book by Fanny Fern (Sara Willis Payson), *Fern Leaves from Fanny's Portfolio* (1853), and it indicates Eaton's affinity with nineteenth-century women writers of domestic fiction. Her writings expose the hardships suffered not only by Chinese Americans but also by women, particularly women of the working class. It is this characteristic that has led scholars of Asian American literature to see her as a forerunner of Maxine Hong Kingston, whose writing also offers a two-pronged critique of American culture. At the same time, however, the title of her book, *Mrs. Spring Fragrance,* suggests a hint of the exoticism that Sui Sin Far manipulates throughout her writings, particularly in the flowery language with which she translates Chinese names and expressions into English, and in the physical appearance of the book, which was printed on paper embossed with a design that any reader would deem "Chinese" and featured a vermilion cover stamped with gold letters and representations of the moon, lotus flowers, and a dragonfly. Although such devices might seem to be at odds with Eaton's often bitterly ironic representations of the hardship of Chinese American life, we might compare Eaton's use of these strategies to the deployment of sentimentality in novels like Harriet Beecher Stowe's *Uncle Tom's Cabin* (1852) and Fern's *Ruth Hall* (1855). Eaton lures white readers in by catering to their Orientalist expectations, which are then not dashed but cunningly transformed as the stories unfold.

Later in the essay, Eaton takes up the idea suggested in the anecdote by her employer that "the Japanese are different altogether." Once its ports had been forcibly opened to Western trade by Admiral Perry in 1854, Japan (in contrast to China) embraced the idea of modernization on the Western model and drew upon the scientific and technological expertise of experts from the West; Japan's military forced China to cede both Korea and Taiwan in 1895 and ten years later defeated Russia. These victories gained Japan the respect of Western nations, and the country's domestic prosperity meant that relatively few of its citizens were seeking to emigrate to the United States. Americans like Eaton's employer could idealize the Japanese because they had practically no contact with them. Eaton notes that because "Americans [have] for many years manifested a much higher regard for the Japanese than for the Chinese, several half Chinese young men and women, thinking to advance themselves, both in a social and business sense, pass as Japanese." In fact, Eaton's younger sister, Winnifred, would do precisely that – at least as a writer – adopting an ostensibly Japanese pseudonym, Onoto Watanna, and inventing a suitable biography, which claimed that she was born in Nagasaki the daughter of a Japanese noblewoman. Winnifred had a longer career than her sister: after publishing what is thought to be the first novel published by an Asian American, *Miss Nume of Japan* (1899), she would write a dozen more novels, a fictionalized autobiography, and a biography of her sister Sara. Winnifred did not restrict herself to Asian or Asian American subjects: for example, *The Diary of Delia: Being a Veracious Chronicle of the Kitchen with Some Sidelights on the Parlour* (1907) purports to be the journal of one Delia O'Malley, housekeeper to the Wooley family, and is written in Irish American dialect, and Winnifred's final novel, *His Royal Nibs* (1925), recounts the adventures of Cheerio, an English painter on a ranch in Alberta who finds himself inspired by Native American subjects and ultimately gains the love of the rancher's daughter. In contrast to her sister Edith, Winnifred's goal was not to challenge the expectations of her readers but to write popular fiction; her novels and autobiography both reflect and take advantage of popular stereotypes of both Asians and women.

The fact that China was held in relatively low esteem by the U.S. government in comparison to Japan during this period can be seen in the different responses offered by the United States to rising immigration from the two countries. The Burlingame Treaty was eventually suspended in

1881, and the following year Congress passed the first Chinese Exclusion Act, which prevented Chinese laborers, whether skilled or unskilled, from entering the continental United States for ten years. This ban was extended for another ten years in 1892 by the Geary Act and then extended indefinitely in 1904 with the prohibition enlarged to include Hawaii and the Philippines. In contrast to this unilateral attempt to limit immigration from China, the United States sought to work with the Japanese government when the flow of immigrants from Japan rose precipitously to 127,000 in 1907: the two nations signed a "Gentleman's Agreement," according to which Japan voluntarily limited the number of its citizens that it would allow to emigrate legally.

❦

The Chinese Exclusion Act lessened but did not stop the flow of Chinese to the United States: new immigrants managed to enter the country through illegal border crossings and, after 1906, through an elaborate system of immigration fraud that took advantage of the conjunction of a loophole in American law and a natural disaster. The Fourteenth Amendment had stipulated that "all persons born . . . in the United States" were to be citizens, including people of Chinese ancestry. The great San Francisco earthquake and fire of 1906 destroyed nearly all of the birth records pertaining to Chinese immigrants, enabling many Chinese aliens to claim American citizenship fraudulently. Some of these "paper sons" returned to China to bring their sons back to the United States, but a great number of them stayed in China and sold their forged certificates of return to other Chinese, who could then bring their sons, nephews, and cousins to the United States.

The idea of the "paper son" whose identity is constructed from half-truths designed to circumvent U.S. immigration laws has become a major motif in Chinese American fiction. In *China Men,* Kingston imagines her father's first trip to the United States:

BaBa would go with two sets of papers: bought ones and his own, which were legal and should get him into the Gold Mountain according to American law. But his own papers were untried, whereas the fake set had accompanied its owners back and forth many times. These bought papers had a surname which was the same as our own last name – unusual luck: he would be able to keep the family name. He would carry his diplomas, and if they did not work, he would produce the fake papers.

Leila, the narrator of Ng's *Bone,* writes that her stepfather "saved every single scrap of paper. I remember his telling me about a tradition of honoring paper, how the oldtimers believed all writing was sacred." She reflects that her stepfather was "right to save everything. For a paper son, paper is blood." Family history thus exists in two versions, the official public history of paper sons and the secret private history of true familial relations, though frequently the versions mingle so that what is true and what is made up are no longer separable: "I'm the stepdaughter of a paper son," Leila says, "and I've inherited this whole suitcase of lies. All of it is mine. All I have are those memories, and I want to remember them all."

Kingston's BaBa is detained at San Francisco's Angel Island, where he is repeatedly interrogated by the "Immigration Demons," who ask about the number of pigs his family owned in 1919, the number of steps on the back stoop of the family house, when he cut off his queue, what his relatives' addresses in the United States had been – all the while "look[ing] into his eyes for lies." Because "he had an accurate memory" and thus manages to keep his answers consistent from session to session, he is finally allowed into the United States. BaBa's experience is meant to be representative: after the passage of the exclusion act, all prospective Chinese immigrants arriving at San Francisco Bay were led to the "Tongsaan Matau," the China Dock, where they were processed for immigration in a notorious detention center that they referred to as the "Muk uk" or "Wooden Barracks"; the miserable condition of the facility led to its replacement in 1910 by the Angel Island facility. It was not uncommon for those who were awaiting processing to be detained for several weeks, months, or even longer, and detainees were prohibited from leaving the compound or meeting any visitors from the outside. To express their feelings of loneliness and despair, many of these detainees wrote lines of poetry on the walls of the barracks, which were copied down in the 1930s by two detainees and thus survive today. The two poems that follow are typical:

So, liberty is your national principle;
Why do you practice autocracy?
You don't uphold justice, you Americans,
You detain me in prison, guard me closely.
Your officials are wolves and tigers,
All ruthless, all wanting to bite me.
An innocent man implicated, such an injustice!
When can I get out of this prison and free my mind?

A weak nation can't speak up for herself.
Chinese sojourners have come to a foreign country.
Detained, put on trial, imprisoned in a hillside building;
If deposition doesn't exactly match: the case is dead and in a bind.
No chance for release.

My fellow countrymen cry out injustice:
The sole purpose is strict exclusion, to deport us all back to Hong Kong.
Pity my fellow villagers and their flood of tears.

What many of these poems demonstrate is an understanding not only of the principles of American democracy but also the stipulations of the Burlingame Treaty, and they voice the despair of discovering that they were foolish to believe that either would be upheld.

Kingston's description of U.S. officials as "Immigration Demons" alludes to the countermythology that Chinese immigrants developed in response to their own demonization by white Americans. Many of the sojourners who returned to China represented their trip to the Gold Mountain as a difficult and dangerous errand into a wilderness peopled by savages. Indeed, much as William Bradford did in his *History of Plymouth Plantation* (1630), Chinese sojourners mythologized the harshness of life in America. Lee Chew, whose personal narrative was included in Hamilton Holt's *Life Stories of (Undistinguished) Americans, As Told by Themselves* (1906) refers to "Chinese prejudice against Americans" and recalls "the wild tales that were told about them in our village." Described by Holt as a "representative Chinese business man of New York," Chew protests that "the treatment of Chinese in this country is all wrong and mean" but argues nonetheless that "Americans are not all bad, nor are they wicked wizards." He notes, however, that not all Chinese immigrants share his opinion: "some of the Chinese, who have been here twenty years and who are learned men, still believe that there is no marriage in this country, that the land is infested with demons and that all the people are given over to general wickedness."

The idea that marriage did not exist in the United States was, however, effectively true for Chinese men. From the mid-nineteenth century through at least the end of World War II, the Chinese population in the United States was overwhelmingly male: for example, there were 11,794 Chinese in California in 1852, but only 7 of them were women. In 1870, the ratio of Chinese men to women in the United States was fourteen to one; by 1920, it had improved to seven to one, and twenty years later it was slightly under three to one. Women were left behind because the expense of paying their passage would have decreased the profitability of the sojourn, and women from the better classes tended to have bound feet that would prove to be a severe handicap on an arduous journey. In addition, wives who stayed behind were thought to provide a form of insurance for the families who depended on the money that husbands and sons sent back to China. According to one Chinese woman, "The mother wanted her son to come back. If wife go to America, then son no go back home and no send money." Chinese American men also suffered from American culture's obsession with miscegenation: they were prohibited by law from marrying white women. As a result, the Chinese Exclusion Act of 1882 caused the Chinese American population to undergo a long decline by freezing its lopsided gender ratio in place, essentially creating a population of bachelors in which young men were always outnumbered by old.

U.S. immigration laws thus had the effect of masculinizing Chinese American culture; at the same time, however, U.S. naturalization laws had the effect of feminizing Chinese Americans: with the granting of citizenship to nonwhite groups in the 1870s and 1880s, men of Chinese extraction – and indeed of Asian extraction generally – were treated by the United States as if they were women. This legal conception was reinforced by popular stereotypes that portrayed "chinamen" as naturally (in other words, racially) suited only to feminized, service-oriented jobs such as laundry washing and table waiting. "The Chinese laundryman does not learn his trade in China," Lee Chew complained: "There are no laundries in China. The women there do the washing in tubs and have no washboards or flat irons. All the Chinese laundrymen here were taught in the first place by American women just as I was taught." With the enfranchisement of women by the Nineteenth Amendment in 1919, the legal standing of Asian American men was further eroded, and even after the enfranchisement of Chinese Americans in 1943, the stereotype of the effeminate Asian American man would continue to be pervasive and damaging. Frank Chin has argued that throughout the period leading up to World War II, "the stereotype came out of the laws, out of the schools, out of the white literary lights of the time, out of the science, out of the comics, movies, and radio night and day." As a result, not only white Americans but also many Chinese Americans came to internalize it, and according to Chin, early Chinese American writing represented "Chinese men" almost exclusively as "emasculated and sexually repellent."

3

❦

NISEI SONS AND DAUGHTERS

AOMI Nakane, the narrator of Joy Kogawa's novel *Obasan* (1981), looks at the box of journals, letters, and government documents that she has received from her Aunt Emily and thinks to herself, "Crimes of history . . . can stay in history. What we need is to concern ourselves with the injustices of today." Naomi calls her activist aunt "a word warrior" and "a crusader," and the papers chronicle the shocking treatment of Japanese Canadians by the Canadian government during and after World War II. Aunt Emily is a *Nisei,* a second-generation Japanese North American (the term *Nisei* being a combination of the Japanese character *sei* meaning "generation" and a prefix signifying "second"), and she sees herself as a Canadian betrayed by Canada. But Emily is not the aunt – the *obasan* – to whom the novel's title refers. Naomi's *obasan* is her Aunt Aya, whose husband Isamu has just died, bringing about the reunion of the surviving members of Naomi's extended family with which the novel will conclude.

Obasan is an *Issei,* a first-generation Japanese immigrant, and she has none of Emily's brash outspokenness. "How different my two aunts are," Naomi thinks to herself: "One lives in sound, the other in stone." Obasan's stoicism keeps her from expressing, perhaps even from feeling, the outrage that engulfs Emily: "Obasan was not taking part in the conversation. When pressed, finally she said that she was grateful for life. 'Arigatai. Gratitude only.'" As the novel opens, Naomi finds herself wishing, like Obasan, to forget the hardships that she, her family, and all Japanese Canadians endured during World War II, because "what is past recall is past pain"; she thinks to herself that "questions from all these papers, questions referring to turbulence in the past, are an unnecessary upheaval in the delicate ecology of this numb day," the day after her uncle's death.

As the day and the novel continue, however, Naomi finds herself reading through these papers and supplementing the stories that they tell with her own recollections and nightmares. Kogawa based the character of Aunt Emily in large part upon the activist Muriel Kitagawa (1912–72), a columnist for the *New Canadian* whose family was one of those permitted to leave British Columbia and resettle in Toronto. Portions of Aunt Emily's journal are slightly revised transcriptions of Kitagawa's writing, most notably the moving essay "This Is My Own, My Native Land!" in which Kitagawa contemplates Walter Scott's poem "The Lay of the Last Minstrel"; the essay is included in a collection of Kitagawa's wartime letters and other writings entitled *This Is My Own: Letters to Wes & Other Writings on Japanese Canadians, 1941–1948* (1985). Kogawa's prefatory note acknowledges the use of documents and letters from the public archives of Canada, and the permissions page of the novel states that it "is based on historical events, and many of the persons named are real." Aware that "facts" can be "an encumbrance to the fiction," Kogawa nevertheless told an interviewer that "they still insist on being present." The writer's task, according to Kogawa, is to create a "vision" that can enable "documents and facts . . . to direct our prejudiced hearts," and vision, she claims, "comes from relationship. Facts bereft of love direct us nowhere." The expository prose of Emily's documents provides the necessary historical framework for the reader who is unacquainted with the treatment of Japanese Canadians during the war, but insofar as they also force Naomi to confront her own buried memories, the documents also serve to underwrite the mixture of lyrical narrative modes that captivated early reviewers of the novel. One of these reviewers praised the novel's "finely honed craft" and likened it to "an extended poem," claiming that its "language alone is almost a sufficient reward." History emerges as the force that brings the imagination alive.

The literature produced after 1940 by North American writers of Japanese descent differs from the other literatures we are considering here because it is so dominated by a single historical moment: World War II. During the war, both the U.S. and Canadian governments would relocate and intern individuals of Japanese origin residing within their borders, regardless of whether they were aliens or citizens, and ultimately the United States would take the extreme step of dropping atomic bombs on Hiroshima and Nagasaki. At the heart of this literature is the plight of the *Nisei,* who find themselves caught between the culture of their parents and the culture of their birth, drawn to both but at home in neither. The history of Japanese North Americans during and after World War II may serve as a case study in the dynamics of hybridity, demonstrating why it is that so many writers of emergent fiction view hybridity as a state of psychological, and frequently physical, violence.

The nature of the *Nisei*'s ambivalence is captured in the entry that Charles Kikuchi, a resident of Berkeley, California, made in his journal on December 7, 1941:

Pearl Harbor. We are at war! Jesus Christ, the Japs bombed Hawaii and the entire fleet has been sunk. I just can't believe it. I don't know what in the hell is going to happen to us, but we will all be called into the Army right away . . . I think of the Japs coming to bomb us, but I will go and fight even if I think I am a coward and I don't believe in wars but this time it has to be. I am selfish about it.

Taken out of context, these might seem like the words of young white racist, but as his name suggests, Kikuchi was in fact a *Nisei.* The journal entry expresses the fears that were on the minds of many *Nisei* in the days that followed Japan's bombing of Pearl Harbor: "The next five years will determine the future of the Nisei. . . . If we are ever going to prove our Americanism, this is the time. . . . The Anti-Jap feeling is bound to rise to hysterical heights, and it is most likely that the Nisei will be included as Japs. . . . I don't know what to think or do."

Similar feelings of bewilderment and apprehension can be found in other texts written by *Nisei* about their wartime experiences. In her memoir *Nisei Daughter* (1953), Monica Sone describes the contentment and optimism that she had just begun to feel before the attack on Pearl Harbor disrupted her life: "Father had found this marvelous big barn of a house on lovely Beacon Hill from where we could see the east morning mist rising from Lake Washington in the east, a panoramic view of Puget Sound and the city in the west. In such a setting, my future rolled out in front of me, blazing with happiness. Nothing could possibly go wrong now." This picture of tranquillity disintegrates on the very next page, however, as Sone describes her reaction when a friend bursts into her living room to tell her family about the attack: "I felt as if a fist had smashed my pleasant little existence, breaking it into jigsaw puzzle pieces. An old wound opened up again, and I found myself shrinking inwardly from my Japanese blood, the blood of an enemy. I knew instinctively that the fact that I was an American by birthright was not going to help me escape the consequences of this unhappy war." Toshio Mori describes a similar scene in his short story "Slant-Eyed Americans" (1949):

Mother's last ray of hope paled and her eyes became dull. "Why did it have to happen? The common people in Japan don't want war, and we don't want war. Here the people are peace-loving. Why cannot the peoples of the earth live peacefully?"

"Since Japan declared war on the United States it'll mean that you parents of American citizens have become enemy aliens," I said.

"Enemy aliens," my mother whispered.

American by birth but Japanese to those inclined to judge solely by outward appearance, the *Nisei* had good reason to fear that they and their families would be mistreated in the aftermath of Japan's declaration of war. They had only to think about the experience of their parents, the *Issei,* the first generation of Japanese immigrants. Although a few Japanese nationals had entered the United States after the Civil War, Japanese immigration did not begin in earnest until 1885, when the Japanese government began to give its citizens official permission to emigrate. Before 1890, there were approximately 3,000 immigrants from Japan to the mainland United States, but between 1891 and 1900 that number jumped up to 27,000; by 1924 (when the Asian Exclusion Act was passed) a total of 275,000 Japanese had emigrated to the U.S. mainland. It is important to put these numbers in perspective, however, by noting that the Japanese constituted a very small minority during the period between 1890 and the Second World War, never more than 2.1 percent of the California population or more than 0.02 percent of the total U.S. population, which numbered 130 million in 1940. Nevertheless, like the Chinese before them, these Japanese immigrants were eventually perceived as a threat by labor leaders on the West Coast, and in 1900 each of the three major political parties in California – Democrat, Populist, and Republican – publicly opposed immigration from Asia.

Unlike China, at the end of the nineteenth century Japan was an emerging world power, and during the 1890s, its government monitored the treatment of Japanese nationals in the United States, believing Japan's prestige as a nation would be damaged if it allowed its emigrants to be exploited as the Chinese and other Asians had been. In 1905, President Theodore Roosevelt, though privately sympathetic to many of the arguments made in favor of Japanese exclusion, nevertheless informed the government in Tokyo that "the American Government and the American People have not the slightest sympathy with the outrageous agitation against the Japanese," adding that "while I am President the Japanese will be treated just exactly like other civilized peoples." Seeking a political solution that could mollify both the Japanese government and anti-Japanese public opinion in California, Roosevelt negotiated the so-called Gentleman's Agreement with Japan, which consisted of six notes exchanged between the two governments in late 1907 and early 1908, in which the Japanese agreed to limit immigration to the United States. Presented to Californians as the equivalent of an exclusion act, the Gentleman's Agreement actually allowed the Japanese American population to more than double during the next twenty years and shifted the gender balance of the Japanese American population from being overwhelmingly male in 1908 to nearly even by 1924. The Japanese American community referred to the years following the Gentleman's Agreement as *yobiyose-jidai,* "the period of summoning": the agreement not only enabled married Japanese men resident in the United States to send for their wives and children but also permitted resident Japanese bachelors to acquire "picture brides" by proxy. The hardship endured by Japanese women who immigrated to the United States under these circumstances is movingly dramatized in Yoshiko Uchida's novel *Picture Bride* (1987), which tells the story of the marriage between Hana Omiya and Taro Takeda, "the lonely man who had gone to America to make his fortune in Oakland, California"; the novel begins with her immigration in 1917 and ends with their internment at the Topaz Relocation Center, where Taro is mistakenly shot by a camp guard.

Japanese immigration followed the pattern already established by the Chinese: most of the early Japanese immigrants to the United States were young men who tended to regard themselves as sojourners, exiled from Japan in order to earn money but determined to return some day to their homeland without being contaminated by their exposure to American culture. This attitude is presented as one of the primary characteristics of the *Issei* in many of the autobiographies and novels written by *Nisei* after the war. For example, when Ichiro, the *Nisei* protagonist of John Okada's *No-No Boy,* asks his father, "What made you and Ma come to America?" the answer he receives is simple: "We came to make money." Ichiro thinks to himself that the *Issei* "rushed to America with the single purpose of making a fortune which would enable them to return to their own country and live adequately." Despite the fact that "their sojourns were spanning decades instead of years," these *Issei* "continued to maintain their dreams by refusing to learn how to speak or write the language of America and by living among their own kind and by zealously avoiding long-term commitments such as the purchase of a house." Thinking about his parents' friends the Kumasakas, Ichiro remembers that before World War II they had "lived in cramped quarters" above their dry-cleaning shop "because, like most of the other Japanese, they planned some day to return to Japan and still felt like transients after thirty or forty years in America." When he learns that they have decided to buy a house, Ichiro is "impressed" because it "could only mean that the Kumasakas had exchanged hope for reality and, late as it was, were finally sinking roots into the land from which they had previously sought not nourishment but only gold." In contrast, Ichiro's parents are resolute in the determination to return to Japan; even after the end of the war, Ichiro's father still believes that the family will be returning to Japan – "very soon."

Because they regarded themselves simply as sojourners, many of the early *Issei* had little interest in integrating themselves into American society. As a rule they spoke little English. Ichiro reflects that

his parents, like most of the old Japanese, spoke virtually no English. On the other hand, the children, like Ichiro, spoke almost no Japanese. Thus they communicated, the old speaking Japanese with an occasionally badly mispronounced word or two of English; and the young, with the exception of a simple word or phrase of Japanese which came fairly effortlessly to the lips, resorting almost constantly to the tongue the parents avoided.

In Hisaye Yamamoto's short story "Seventeen Syllables" (1949), the language gap between *Issei* and *Nisei* is emblematic of a larger cultural divide. The *Nisei* daughter Rosie pretends to appreciate the haiku that her mother has just composed, because she is ashamed to reveal just how shaky her command of Japanese really is: "The truth was that Rosie was lazy; English lay ready on the tongue but Japanese had to be searched for and examined, and even then put forth tentatively (probably to meet with laughter). It was so much easier to say yes, yes, even when one meant no, no." Remembering a haiku written in English and French that she has seen in a magazine and that delighted her –

> *It is morning, and lo!*
> *I lie awake, comme il faut,*
> *sighing for some dough.*

– Rosie reflects on the problem of translating not only from one language to another but from one culture to another: "how to reach her mother, how to communicate the melancholy song? Rosie knew formal Japanese by fits and starts, her mother had even less English, no French. It was much more possible to say yes, yes." Avoiding situations in which they would have to speak English, the *Issei* kept themselves isolated. In Hawaii, they lived in the camps reserved for Japanese workers on the sugar plantations; on the mainland, they lived either on small farms in rural areas or else in ethnic enclaves like the "Lil' Yokohama" that Toshio Mori describes in his collection of short stories *Yokohama, California* (1949).

The oppressiveness of the *Issei*'s attempt to replicate Japanese culture on American soil is one of the subjects of Milton Murayama's novel *All I Asking for Is My Body* (1975), which depicts life in the sugar cane plantations of Hawaii in the 1930s as seen through the eyes of a young *Nisei* named Kiyoshi Oyama. The novel portrays *Issei* life as authoritarian and feudal in its insistence on social hierarchy and the priority of familial needs over the needs of the individual. Kiyoshi's elder brother, Toshio, the family's "number one son" chafes against the Japanese way of life imposed on the family by his parents: "Goddam old futts, they still think they in Japan!" he fumes, after complaining that his mother treats his father "like he was a *tonosama* (feudal lord)." Number-one sons like Tosh are expected to work for years alongside their fathers in order to pay off their family's debts. In requiring his son to forgo his education to work with him in the cane fields, Tosh's father is simply replicating what was done to him, perpetuating a system that he believes to be part of the natural order of things. Tosh's grandfather had returned to Japan from Hawaii, taking with him all of the money that his family had earned over the years, leaving Tosh's father and mother not even a month's subsistence, in order to pay back his debts in Japan and to establish a new business for himself and the rest of the family, a business that is destroyed the next year in the Tokyo earthquake. Tosh regards his grandfather as a "thief," but his mother defends the grandfather's actions: "[Your] father was number one son, and a filial number one son. . . . Grandfather cried with gratitude when he left. He said he couldn't ask for more filial children. We did all we could for him. That's filial piety."

For these *Issei,* to be called "filial" is to receive the greatest compliment a parent can bestow, but the novel depicts these kinship relations not as bonds of familial love but as economic obligations: "Every child must repay his parents," Tosh's mother tells him. Believing that they are passing on to their children a dream of self-sufficiency and enterprise, these *Issei* are instead saddling the next generation with a legacy of indentured servitude, and Tosh describes his situation in terms that recall the slave system of the American South: "Shit, all I asking for is my body. I doan wanna die on the plantation like these other dumb dodos."

Murayama later described the central theme of his novel as "the Japanese family system vs. individualism, the plantation system vs. individualism." These systems are so stifling that the bombing of Pearl Harbor actually becomes the mechanism that frees both Tosh and Kiyo. Despite all of his "crabbing," Tosh has internalized *Issei* values and thus turned down the opportunity to pursue a career in boxing; the war ironically gives him the upper hand over his domineering father, whose inability to speak English forces him to cede authority to his son. Tosh becomes the head of the family, the one who issues orders that must be obeyed: "Your Japanese flag in the *tansu* [dresser]. Burn it or bury it. Hide all your Japanese books in the chicken coop. Don't talk Japanese when there're any non-Japanese around." In contrast, Kiyo, always the more tolerant and more accommodating of the brothers, is the one who leaves the family behind: learning to cheat at dice, he wins enough money to pay off the family debt and asserts his individuality by joining the armed forces to fight for the United States.

The *Issei* in Murayama's and Okada's novels live in a fantasy world in which Japan can do no wrong: Tosh and Kiyo's father refuses to admit that the Japanese army committed atrocities during the military operation that the rest of the world refers to as "the rape of Nanking"; Ichiro's mother refuses to believe that Japan has lost World War II. Not all *Issei* shared this perspective, however; in a secret report commissioned by the State Department as war with Japan became seemingly inevitable, Curtis B. Munson provided the following description of the *Issei*:

First generation Japanese. Entire cultural background Japanese. Probably loyal romantically to Japan. They must be considered, however, as other races. They have made this their home. They have brought up children here, their wealth accumulated by hard labor is here, and many would have become American citizens had they been allowed to do so. They are for the most part simple people.

Two prominent *Nisei* autobiographers have presented portraits of their parents that fit Munson's description. Monica Sone relates that her father had "succumbed to the fever which sent many young men streaming across the Pacific to a fabulous new country rich with promise and opportunities," chief among which was the opportunity "to continue his law studies at Ann Arbor, Michigan." In *Desert Exile: The Uprooting of a Japanese Family* (1982), Yoshiko Uchida describes her father's desire "to go to Yale and eventually to become a doctor"; unlike most *Issei* men, Dwight Takashi Uchida was actually going to the United States to be reunited with his family, in this case with his mother and his sister.

But even those *Issei* like Uchida who did wish to settle in the United States permanently and assimilate into American culture knew that accepting the United States as their home did not mean that the United States would accept them in turn. Prevented by the 1870 Naturalization Act from becoming citizens, the *Issei* were also prevented from owning land or even leasing it for more than three years by California's Alien Land Law Act of 1913 (which would remain in effect for nearly fifty years). Hisaye Yamamoto recalls that "our family and other farm families we knew moved quite frequently. . . . The availability of land to lease came down in a kind of pipeline from other Japanese, usually friends of the family who had come from the same area in Japan. So there was this kind of floating community that we belonged to, with village and prefectural picnics every year." And, she adds, "There wasn't much mingling with the white community, although there were probably some lasting contacts formed with some landlords, business people, neighbors." Isolated by a white culture that accused *them* of being isolationist, the *Issei* realized that it was only through their children, who were U.S. citizens by birth, that they might be said to have a future in America. The *Nisei,* it was hoped, would be a "bridge" (*kakehashi*) between the United States and Japan, "intermediaries" who could serve as cultural interpreters and promote better understanding between the two cultures.

Many *Issei* parents, however, hedged their bets by registering their children as citizens of Japan. For example, eighty-four percent of the *Nisei* living in the Pacific coast and Rocky Mountain states in 1926 were registered as Japanese citizens, and in 1940 over half of all the *Nisei* in the United States were registered as Japanese citizens. Understanding the precariousness of their situation as unnaturalizable aliens in a country where they were constantly subjected to racial discrimination, many *Issei* wanted to be able to take their children with them in the event that they might be forced to return to Japan and to give their children the option of returning there on their own. Although many *Issei* sent their children to Japanese-language schools, some parents took the further step of sending their children to Japan in order to learn about Japanese culture firsthand; these so-called *Kibei* tended to live in Japan for several years before returning to the United States. In the December 7, 1941, entry of his journal, Charles Kikuchi worries about "Kibei spies" perpetrating "sabotage," though a *Kibei* friend later assures him that "Kibei are loyal." Indeed, many *Kibei* returned to the United States with a renewed appreciation for the country of their birth.

The Munson report's description of the *Issei* concludes with the observation that "their age group is largely 55 to 65, fairly old for a hard-working Japanese," and it goes on to note that the *Nisei* range in age from "1 to 30 years." In fact, the gap in age between the *Issei* and *Nisei* generations was wider and more pronounced than that between the first and second generations in other immigrant communities for two reasons. First, the flow of Japanese male immigrants to the United States was cut off precipitously in 1908 as the result of the "Gentleman's Agreement" between the U.S. and Japanese governments. Japanese women continued to emigrate until the 1921 "Ladies Agreement" led Japan to prohibit the emigration of "picture brides," virtually ending Japanese immigration to the United States. The 1924 Immigration Act ended Japanese immigration altogether. Second, Japanese immigrant men tended to marry rather late in life: only after years of scrimping and saving would an *Issei* man send back to Japan for a bride. As a result, between the *Issei* and the *Nisei* there was nearly an entire generation missing: in 1930, for example, the average ages of *Issei* men and women were forty-two and thirty-five, respectively, while the average age of *Nisei* boys and girls was ten.

The absence of younger *Issei* whom the *Nisei* could regard as peers exacerbated the cultural generation gap that one expects to see between first- and second-generation immigrants, and this gap was further heightened by the fact that the *Issei,* who were ineligible for U.S. citizenship, tended to remain culturally and politically oriented toward Japan, while the *Nisei,*

U.S. citizens by virtue of their birth on U.S. soil, were culturally and politically oriented toward the United States. The Munson report described the
Nisei as the "second generation who have received their whole education in
the United States and usually, in spite of discrimination against them and
a certain amount of insults accumulated through the years from irresponsible elements, show a pathetic eagerness to be American," which puts them
"in constant conflict with the orthodox, well disciplined family life of their
elders." In *Desert Exile,* Yoshiko Uchida remembers that she and her Nisei
friends "were sometimes ashamed of the Issei in their shabby clothes, their
rundown trucks and cars, their skin darkened from years of laboring in
sun-parched fields, their inability to speak English, their habits and the
food they ate."

In effect, each Japanese American community contained two distinct
subcultures, *Issei* and *Nisei.* Toshio Mori's story "Miss Butterfly" (1939)
captures the cultural divide that separates the *Issei* and the *Nisei.* In the
story, a homesick old *Issei* named Hamada-*san* asks his friend's two *Nisei*
daughters, Sachi and Yuki, to put on kimonos and perform a traditional
Japanese dance for him before they rush off to a high school dance. The
girls reluctantly agree, and their performance of the *odori* momentarily
seems to bear out Hamada-*san*'s belief that when dressed in kimonos,
"Nisei girls . . . are the most beautiful women in the world," because "your
eyes brighten up, your figure becomes symmetrical, your gestures move
naturally." For Sachi and Yuki, however, dancing in kimonos can only be
artificial; what is natural to them is the "social dance" that their father
describes as a "popular American pastime." The end of the story leaves
Hamada-*san* sitting "mutely" as his friend continues to read the newspaper
and smoke: "He could have gone outside for a breath of fresh air but did
not move. His eyes took in the phonograph, the record albums, the spots
where the girls danced, and the room that was now empty. In the silence
he heard the clock ticking." As the story's title suggests, the traditional
Japanese culture that Hamada-*san* wishes to preserve is as doomed by its
encounter with American ways as Puccini's Cio-cio-*san* is by her encounter
with the American officer Pinkerton.

Hamada-*san*'s night out is one of those experiences that Sherwood
Anderson describes in *Winesburg, Ohio* as an "adventure," and Mori frequently acknowledged Anderson as a formative influence. Dismayed by
the stereotypical portrayal of Japanese and Japanese Americans in popular
novels like Peter B. Kyne's *The Pride of Palomar* (1921) or J. P. Marquand's
Mr. Moto Is So Sorry (1938), Mori addressed himself primarily to a white
audience and sought to create more accurate representations of his fellow
Japanese Americans by adapting some of the storytelling techniques that

Anderson used to depict the lives of his characters in *Winesburg, Ohio.* The dance provides an Andersonian moment in which we see Hamada-*san* dreaming of "the old Japan," "becoming alive," and exclaiming to the girls, "I shall never forget this performance."

One of the impulses behind Mori's writing is to document and preserve a way of life that must inevitably pass away – the world of the *Issei.* "As a whole, I thought the Issei were more interesting, stronger characters than the Nisei," Mori told an interviewer in 1975. "Nisei as a whole didn't associate much with the Issei. They were struggling to become good obedient American citizens so that they could be accepted as part of American life." As sympathetic as Mori is to the situation of the *Issei,* however, the thrust of his stories is to dramatize the inevitability and indeed the desirability of the combination of Japanese culture and American culture that the *Nisei* represents. In "The Sweet Potato" (1941), two friends who have spent their summer arguing "about the problem of the second generation of Japanese ancestry" and worrying that they're "not getting anywhere" go to the Fair at Treasure Island, where they meet "an old white lady" and her son who have done what the two *Nisei* have not: visited Japan. Speaking Japanese, the old lady tells her favorite story, about "the big earthquake" and how "a Japanese family whom [they] did not know, found a single sweet potato" and shared it with them. "That potato was really sweet," the son says, and the end of the story finds the four of them "forgetting time and place," sitting and talking "for a long time as if we had known one another a good many years," while those around them "looked curiously at us, wondering what we had in common." What they have in common – what all of Mori's characters, Japanese and white, have in common – is their shared humanity, a theme that runs throughout all of Mori's stories and particularly the wartime stories about the internment experience.

Mori became a published author at the age of twenty-eight, when his story "The Brothers" appeared in *Coast* magazine, a San Francisco publication modeled on the *New Yorker.* A parable about two young Japanese boys who fight over possession of their father's old desk, the story caught the eye of William Saroyan, who took it upon himself to become Mori's literary mentor. Encouraged by Saroyan, Mori managed to place stories in a variety of publications, and a collection of stories entitled *Yokohama, California* was scheduled for publication by Caxton Printers in the spring of 1942, with an introduction by Saroyan. The book's title acknowledges Mori's debt to *Winesburg, Ohio,* and Anderson's book plays a prominent role in the story "Akira Yano," where it serves as the basis for the friendship between the story's narrator and its title character, who dreams of being a successful prose writer like Anderson.

Some of Mori's stories depict characters who resemble Anderson's "grotesques," characters whose paralyzed lives are marked and summed up by those moments of "adventure." In "The Seventh Street Philosopher," the third story in *Yokohama, California,* Mori tells the story of Motoji Tsunoda's attempt to arrange for a lecture by Akegarasu, "the great philosopher of Japan" who was "touring America, lecturing and studying and visiting Emerson's grave." When the visit falls through, Tsunoda decides to give the lecture himself, and he remains undaunted despite the fact that after waiting an hour past the time given for the start of the lecture, the audience numbers only eleven ("counting the two babies"). "It was wonderful," the narrator tells us, "the spectacle; the individual standing up and expressing himself, the earth, the eternity, and the audience listening and snoring, and the beautiful auditorium standing ready to accommodate more people." Sherwood Anderson might have ended the story there, but Mori's narrator steps back at the end of the story to offer this generous interpretation of what he has told us: "there was something worth while for everyone to hear and see, not just for the eleven persons in the auditorium but for the people of the earth: that of his voice, his gestures, his sadness, his patheticness, his bravery, which are of common lot and something the people, the inhabitants of the earth, could understand, sympathize for awhile." The occasional bumpiness of Mori's prose, evident in this passage, led Saroyan to write, at the very outset of his introduction, "Of the thousands of unpublished writers in America there are probably no more than three who cannot write better English than Toshio Mori. His stories are full of grammatical errors. His use of English, especially when he is most eager to say something good, is very bad. Any high-school teacher of English would flunk him in grammar and punctuation." Despite the disclaimer, however, Saroyan describes Mori as "one of the most important new writers in the country at the moment" and calls him "a natural born writer."

Mori's stories are designed to demonstrate that the phrase "Yokohama, California" is not an oxymoron. The narrator of "Lil' Yokohama" begins his vignette by affirming that in "our community, we have twenty-four hours every day . . . and morning, noon, and night roll on regularly just as in Boston, Cincinnati, Birmingham, Kansas City, Minneapolis, and Emeryville" and then narrows his focus to a particular day, the day of the "big game" between the Alameda Taiiku and the San Jose Asahis, as if to ask, What could be more American than baseball in the afternoon? Or else, for those with a little more knowledge of Japanese culture, How different can the United States and Japan be if they share the same national pastime? Mori had, in fact, considered trying to become a professional baseball player and was even given a tryout by the Chicago Cubs, but he turned to writing after receiving encouragement from his English teacher at Oakland High School.

Many of Mori's stories depict the struggles of the writer – not "the Japanese American writer" but simply "the writer." Though he does make reference to his situation as a Japanese American bachelor being nagged by his elders to marry, the narrator of "Confessions of an Unknown Writer" (1936) is far more concerned with his ability to pursue his vocation as a writer. Worried that he is nothing but a "dead-beat," the narrator sits in his mother's room holding used copies of *"Story, Harper, New Yorker, Atlantic Monthly, Fiction Parade, Scribner's* and *Writer's Digest"* that he has bought for a "nickel apiece," "thinking of names and dates. Dreiser wrote his *Sister Carrie* at twenty-eight; Thomas Wolfe began at twenty-eight; Dostoyevsky at twenty-five; Saroyan at twenty-four." Worried throughout the story that he is nothing but a "fool," the narrator realizes at the end how "natural" it is for him "to sit before the typewriter and face the challenge of a white paper and life," convinced that he "will go on writing" and that "being a fool will not stop one from becoming what nature had intended him to be." Mori has been called a "universalist" by critics of Asian American literature, because his ultimate aim is the depiction not simply of the Japanese American condition but of the human condition. In the story "1936," titled for the year of its composition, Mori writes, "I wanted to do everything, I wanted to know women, I wanted to know the white people, the minds of my generation and people, the Nisei, the nature of our parents, the Issei, the culture of Japan, the culture of America, of life as a whole."

Unlike Mori, however, many other *Nisei* wished to distinguish themselves from what they viewed as the backwardness of the *Issei*. This desire found public expression in the policies of the Japanese American Citizens League (JACL), a political organization that excluded *Issei* from membership because they were not U.S. citizens. The goal of the JACL was to demonstrate that Japanese Americans were true-blue Americans, despite their ostensibly Japanese faces. The organization's official creed, written in 1940 by Mike Masaoka in the face of escalating tensions between the United States and Japan, is an oath of loyalty to the United States:

I am proud that I am an American citizen of Japanese ancestry, for my very background makes me appreciate more fully the wonderful advantages of this nation. I believe in her institutions, ideals and traditions; I glory in her heritage; I boast of her history; I trust in her future. She has granted me liberties and opportunities such as no individual enjoys in this world today. She has given me an education befitting kings. She has entrusted me with the responsibilities of the franchise. She has permitted me to build a home, to earn a livelihood, to worship, think, speak and act as I please – as a free man equal to every other man.

Although some individuals may discriminate against me, I shall never become bitter or lose faith, for I know that such persons are not representative of the American people. True, I shall do all in my power to discourage such practices, but I shall do it in the American way – above board, in the open, through courts of law, by education, by proving myself to be worthy of equal treatment and consideration. I am firm in my belief that American sportsmanship and attitude of fair play will judge citizenship and patriotism on the basis of action and achievement, and not on the basis of physical characteristics. Because I believe in America, and I trust she believes in me, and because I have received innumerable benefits from her, I pledge myself to do honor to her at all times and all places; to support her constitution; to obey her laws; to respect her flag; to defend her against all enemies, foreign and domestic; to actively assume my duties and obligations as a citizen, cheerfully and without any reservations whatsoever, in the hope that I may become a better American in a greater America.

Deeply individualistic in its outlook, the JACL's creed denied that racism was a pervasive social phenomenon, ascribing it instead to the actions of a few ignorant individuals.

The attack on Pearl Harbor occurred just after dawn on Sunday, December 7, 1941. The Japanese warplanes destroyed or damaged 19 ships and killed approximately 2,300 Americans. The next day, the *Los Angeles Times* described California as "a zone of danger" and urged a response to the perceived threat from U.S. residents of Japanese extraction: "We have thousands of Japanese here. . . . Some, perhaps many . . . are good Americans. What the rest may be we do not know, nor can we take a chance in the light of yesterday's demonstration that treachery and double dealing are major Japanese weapons." The *Times*'s rhetoric was restrained in comparison to that of many other West Coast papers, which frequently referred to the Japanese not only as "Nips" but also as "yellow vermin" and "mad dogs." Even the *Times,* though, would eventually succumb to the anti-Japanese frenzy being fomented by the press, as this excerpt from a January editorial indicates: "A viper is nonetheless a viper wherever the egg is hatched – so a Japanese American, born of Japanese parents – grows up to be a Japanese, not an American." The anti-Japanese hysteria was by no means limited to the West Coast press, as syndicated columnists began with increasing stridency to urge that drastic measures be taken against Japanese Americans. "I am for the immediate removal of every Japanese on the West Coast to a point deep in the interior," wrote Henry McLemore, a syndicated columnist for Hearst newspapers. "I don't mean a nice part of the interior either. Herd 'em up, pack 'em off and give 'em the inside room in the badlands." Walter Lipmann published an article entitled "The Fifth Column on the Coast" in the *Washington Post* in which he urged that Japanese Americans be removed from the Pacific Coast, which he described as "a combat zone" that was "in imminent danger of a combined attack from within and without." One of the most shocking published responses to Pearl Harbor came two days after the attack from the nationally syndicated columnist Westbrook Pegler, who suggested that the United States should follow the lead of its enemies by incarcerating subversive Germans, Italians, and "alien Japanese" in concentration camps and executing "100 victims selected out of [these] concentration camps" whenever a single American hostage was murdered by Axis forces.

The public climate of anti-Japanese xenophobia that resulted from the hysterical editorializing of the press made it easy for the head of the newly created Western Defense Command, Lieutenant General John L. DeWitt, to make a case for the evacuation and internment of Japanese resident aliens and Japanese Americans. Historians now agree that the internment was a matter of politics rather than military necessity. The Munson report, delivered to Roosevelt precisely a month before the attack on Pearl Harbor, had concluded that "there will be no armed uprising of Japanese" in the United States:

Japan will commit some sabotage largely depending on imported Japanese as they are afraid of and do not trust the Nisei. There will be no wholehearted response from Japanese in the United States. . . . For the most part the local Japanese are loyal to the United States or, at worst, hope that by remaining quiet they can avoid concentration camps or irresponsible mobs. We do not believe that they would be at least any more disloyal than any other racial group in the United States with whom we went to war.

In a subsequent investigation carried out in January 1942, Lieutenant Commander K. D. Ringle of the Office of Naval Intelligence reached a similar conclusion, stating that because only about thirty-five hundred resident Japanese in the United States could be considered military threats, there was no need for mass evacuation. The FBI had already come to this conclusion: three days after Pearl Harbor, J. Edgar Hoover informed the administration that he now had in custody "practically all" of the potentially subversive individuals whom he had planned to arrest. Significantly, General Delos Emmons, the military governor in Hawaii, which had a much higher proportion of Japanese residents than California, viewed the imposition of martial law as a sufficiently drastic and effective step and refused to support the secretary of the navy's call for internment in Hawaii.

DeWitt chose to ignore the conclusions reached by Munson, Ringle, and Hoover, as well as the precedent set by Emmons in Hawaii. Claiming that there were "approximately 288,000 enemy aliens" within the 8 states included in the Western Defense Command, DeWitt claimed to "have little confidence that the enemy aliens are law-abiding or loyal in any sense of the word." DeWitt was a sixty-one-year-old army bureaucrat, who specialized in logistics and had, twenty years earlier, prepared a plan for the militarization of Hawaii in the event of war that included not only the imposition of martial law but also the internment of citizens as deemed necessary by the military. DeWitt was also a racist, and his final recommendation to the Secretary of War Henry Stimson on February 14, 1942, justified evacuation in racial terms:

In the war in which we are now engaged racial affinities are not severed by migration. The Japanese race is an enemy race and while many second and third generation Japanese born on United States soil, possessed of United States citizenship, have become "Americanized," the racial strains are undiluted. . . . It therefore follows that along the vital Pacific Coast over 112,000 potential enemies, of Japanese extraction, are at large today.

Five days later, Roosevelt signed Executive Order 9066 into law, bringing about the removal of over one hundred twenty thousand individuals of Japanese ancestry, approximately seventy-seven thousand of them citizens of the United States, from their homes and communities.

The order is a marvel of rhetorical discretion. It mentions no specific ethnic or racial groups, no specific locations. Citing the fact that "the successful prosecution of the war" required "every possible protection against espionage and against sabotage," the order "authorize[s] and direct[s] the Secretary of War" and his

Military Commanders . . . to prescribe military areas in such places and of such extent as he or the appropriate Military Commander may determine, from which any or all persons may be excluded, and with respect to which, the right of any person to enter, remain in, or leave shall be subject to whatever restrictions the Secretary of War or the appropriate Military Commander may impose in his discretion.

The order further specifies that such excluded persons may be given "transportation, food, shelter, and other accommodations as may be necessary . . . to accomplish the purposes of this order."

Although the language of Executive Order 9066 was elliptical and nonspecific, the public relations campaign that accompanied it made it clear to the press and thus to the public that the "military area" in question was California and the "persons" to be "excluded" were resident Japanese aliens and Japanese Americans, because they posed a significant threat to national security. The "accommodations" that they were given turned out to be "relocation centers" in California, Utah, Idaho, Wyoming, Arizona,

Colorado, and Arkansas, where some evacuees would be interned for as many as four years. These centers were publicly referred to as "concentration camps," until the use of that term became unfashionable after the discovery of the Nazi death camps. In fact, Roosevelt himself had used the term – as early as 1936 – in a memorandum to the chief of naval operations, in which he suggested "that every Japanese citizen or non-citizen on the island of Oahu who meets . . . Japanese ships or has any connection with their officers or men should be secretly but definitely identified and his or her name placed on a special list of those who would be the first to be placed in a concentration camp in the event of trouble." Although the American camps were by no means death camps – nearly all of the 1,862 internees who died in the relocation centers died of natural causes – they were nonetheless places where innocent individuals were deprived of their rights, confined against their will, and surrounded by barbed wire and armed guards.

Toshio Mori and Hisaye Yamamoto were among those who were evacuated and interned under the provisions of Executive Order 9066. In the aftermath of the bombing of Pearl Harbor, Caxton postponed the publication of Mori's *Yokohama, California* indefinitely, and Mori and his family were evacuated to the Tanforan Assembly Center in San Bruno, which had once been a racetrack, and ultimately assigned to the Topaz, Utah, relocation center. During this period, Mori's younger brother Kazuo continued to serve in the all-*Nisei* U.S. Army unit that he had joined before the war; he would suffer a serious head injury at the Italian front that would leave him paralyzed and confined to a wheelchair. Yamamoto had a similar experience: she was interned in Poston, Arizona, where she worked for the camp newspaper, the *Poston Chronicle,* as a columnist and editor, and also published a serialized mystery entitled "Death Rides the Rails to Poston." She worked during one summer as a cook in Springfield, Massachusetts, under the auspices of a government program designed to resettle *Nisei* in the east but returned to Poston after receiving news that her nineteen-year-old brother Johnny had died while fighting for the U.S. Army in Italy. Yamamoto recalled this traumatic event in a piece entitled "Life and Death of a Nisei GI: After Johnny Died," which was published shortly after the war in the *Los Angeles Tribune,* a black newspaper where Yamamoto worked as a columnist and rewrite person: "After Johnny died, one kind soul insisted that now I had experienced all a Japanese in America could and that I must put it all down in a book for all the world to read." Although her response was instead to throw the notes urging her to write about Johnny into the wastebasket where "they made a hauntingly lovely thud," it was a bequest from Johnny's insurance that allowed her to devote herself to writing fiction full time after the publication of her first story, "The High Heeled Shoes," in *Partisan Review* in 1948.

During his internment at Topaz, Mori helped to edit the official camp magazine *Trek,* which appeared three times before most of its editors relocated east. Mori stayed on and published a fourth issue entitled *All Aboard.* Mori became involved with *Trek* after its editors published his story "Tomorrow Is Coming, Children," which became the first story in the revised manuscript of *Yokohama, California* that was finally published in 1949. Appearing in *Trek* in both Japanese and English versions, "Tomorrow Is Coming, Children," is a story told by an *Issei* woman to her grandchildren, Johnny and Annabelle, while they are at a relocation center. She recounts her journey to the United States and her life in San Francisco – her "dream city" – where, she recalls, she first "began to feel at home" because of the company of "a little neighbor, the white American wife of a Japanese acrobat." Minimizing the injustice of her treatment by the U.S. government, the grandmother tells Johnny and Annabelle that although it is "terrifying," although "it upsets personal life and hopes," war has "its good points too," because it forces you to "become positive," to "choose sides." What war has given her, she says, "is the opportunity to find where her heart lay. To her surprise her choice had been made long ago, and no war will sway her a bit." What she realizes is that America is where she belongs and where she wants to be buried. In his introduction to the 1985 republication of *Yokohama, California,* Lawson Fusao Inada describes the inclusion of this story as "Caxton's attempt to soften history, to start with bygones and get into the book in a positive way." A second story added for the publication of *Yokohama, California* appears near the end of the volume. Entitled "Slant-Eyed Americans," it is an autobiographical story that begins on the day that Pearl Harbor was bombed and ends with the departure of the narrator's younger brother Kazuo for the war. "Give your best to America," a family friend tells Kazuo. "Our people's honor depends on you Nisei soldiers." Though not the final story in the collection, "Slant-Eyed Americans" signals the impending destruction of Lil' Yokohama that is already implicit in the internment setting of the collection's first story.

In what would prove to be a sign of things to come, at least as far as his writing career was concerned, Mori discovered upon returning from Topaz to his hometown of San Leandro that nearly two hundred stories that he had stored in a barn there had been destroyed by bookworms. *Yokohama, California* received some good reviews from the mainstream press when it appeared, but Albert Saijo, writing for the Japanese American weekly *Crossroads,* condemned the book along with other *Nisei* writing as marred by "muddled intelligence . . . sentimentality . . . and poor craftsmanship." During the next three decades, despite the fact that he reportedly wrote five novels and several hundred stories, and continued to publish stories in magazines and fiction journals, Mori received little attention and continued to work in obscurity. In the mid-1970s, however, his work came to the attention of several writers and critics who were eager to construct a new Asian American literary canon, leading to its inclusion in a number of anthologies of Asian American literature. A novel, *Woman from Hiroshima,* which portrays an *Issei* woman modeled on Mori's mother, was published by a small press in 1978, and the following year a collection entitled *The Chauvinist and Other Stories* appeared with an introduction by Hisaye Yamamoto.

Nothing embodied the paradoxes and contradictions of Nisei identity more clearly than did the federal government's attempt to draft *Nisei* internees into the U.S. Army during the later stages of the war, and it is this policy and its aftereffects that are the subjects of John Okada's novel, *No-No Boy.* Initially, all young Japanese men, including *Nisei,* were classified 4-C – enemy aliens – but in October 1942, the director of the Office of War Information recommended to President Roosevelt that *Nisei* be recruited for the war effort in order to help combat "Japanese propaganda" characterizing the war as "a racial war." In February 1943, not quite a year after signing Executive Order 9066, President Roosevelt issued a public statement in support of the army's plan to recruit an all-*Nisei* combat unit of approximately five thousand men drawn from Hawaii and the mainland. "No loyal citizen of the United States," Roosevelt proclaimed, "should be denied the democratic right to exercise the responsibilities of his citizenship, regardless of his ancestry. . . . Americanism is not, and never was, a matter of race or ancestry."

For the *Nisei* internees, the announcement that *Nisei* volunteers were being recruited by the U.S. Army was the ultimate irony. In *Nisei Daughter,* Monica Sone describes a friend's reaction to the news: "What do they take us for? Saps? First, they change my army status to 4-C because of my ancestry, run me out of town, and now they want me to volunteer for a suicide squad so I could get killed for this damn democracy. That's going some, for sheer brass!" Asked how he can justify looking for volunteers from among those whose rights as citizens have been violated, the army recruiter who visits Sone's camp can only say, "The evacuation occurred, and right or wrong, it's past. Now we're interested in your future. The War Department is offering you a chance to volunteer and to distinguish yourselves as Japanese-American citizens in the service of your country." Adapting an existing questionnaire designed for aliens, the army produced a form to be given to male draft-age *Nisei,* at the heart of which were these two questions:

27. Are you willing to serve in the armed forces of the United States on combat duty, wherever ordered?

28. Will you swear unqualified allegiance to the United States of America and faithfully defend the United States from any or all attack by foreign and domestic forces, and forswear any form of allegiance to the Japanese emperor, to any other foreign government, power or organization?

Of the 21,000 *Nisei* men who were eligible for the draft, 22 percent (4,600) would be known as "no-no boys" because they answered these two questions with a no, a qualified yes, or a blank. Only a relatively small number of the *Nisei* who answered yes to questions 27 and 28 actually volunteered – 1,208 out of approximately 10,000 eligible – and in January 1944 the Selective Service reclassified *Nisei* who had answered yes from 4-C to 1-A and began issuing draft registration notices.

Okada based Ichiro, the protagonist of *No-No Boy,* on Hajiime Akutsu, who was one of forty-four internees from Camp Minidoka imprisoned at McNeil Island for resisting the draft. Okada himself was not a no-no boy: born and raised in Seattle, he volunteered for the military after graduating from Scottsbluff Junior College and spent the war, as Frank Chin puts it in his afterward to a reprint edition of the novel, "hanging out of an airplane over Japanese-held islands asking their occupants in their own language to give up."

In *No-No Boy,* Okada explores what it means to live in a state of cultural hybridity, which is depicted as violent and even monstrous. Toward the end of the long interior monologue that dominates the first chapter of the novel, Ichiro realizes how alienated he is from the Japanese fundamentalism embodied by his mother: "I do not understand you who were the half of me that is no more and because I do not understand what it was about that half that made me destroy the half of me which was American and the half which might have become the whole of me if I had said yes I will go and fight in your army because that is what I believe and want and cherish and love." Ichiro's sense of his bifurcated identity is gruesomely literalized at the climax of the novel by the fate of his friend Freddie, who also refused to serve in the U.S. Army. Trying to escape from Bull, a *Nisei* veteran who hates all no-no boys, Freddie dies when his car crashes into another:

A Japanese youth . . . came running in. Flushed with excitement, he exclaimed to Ichiro: "What a mess! Didja see it? Poor guy musta been halfway out when the car smacked the building. Just about cut him in two. Ugh!" He hastened into the phone booth.

Equally monstrous is the fate of Ichiro's friend Kenji, a "yes-yes" boy wounded by machine-gun fire, whose fate embodies the slow erosion of the

Japanese American self under the pressure of American racism. Kenji's leg, amputated below the knee, will not heal; Ichiro describes it to himself as "a leg that was eating itself away until it would consume the man himself in a matter of a few years," and by the end of the novel, Kenji is dead.

Particularly poignant is the plight of *Nisei* veterans who return to find that the country they fought to protect has little interest in fighting for them or protecting their rights. These veterans continue to wear their army uniforms and medals in civilian life, so that everyone around them will know that they served, that they were not enemy aliens, internees, or no-no boys. The novel dramatizes the fact that racism ultimately renders no-no boys and yes-yes boys equal in the eyes of mainstream America. The novel, however, ends on a note of muted hopefulness, willfully extracted from a scene of violence and pain:

A glimmer of hope – was that it? It was there, someplace. He couldn't see it to put it into words, but the feeling was pretty strong.

He walked along, thinking, searching, thinking and probing, and, in the darkness of the alley of the community that was a tiny bit of America, he chased that faint and elusive insinuation of promise as it continued to take shape in mind and in heart.

Like the narrator of Carlos Bulosan's *America Is in the Heart,* Ichiro refuses to give up on the America he carries within himself, an America as yet unrealized in the United States.

Perhaps because it did not provide the ringing affirmation of the American way that many Japanese Americans perceived to be necessary in the aftermath of World War II, Okada's novel was not a popular success. "At the time we published it," wrote Charles Tuttle, the publisher of the book's first edition, "the very people whom we thought would be enthusiastic about it, mainly the Japanese-American community in the United States, were not only disinterested but actually rejected the book." In contrast, Monica Sone's *Nisei Daughter* ends on a note of complete acceptance and forgiveness, as the narrator tells her mother, "I don't resent my Japanese blood anymore. I'm proud of it, in fact, because of you and the Issei who've struggled so much for us. It's really nice to be born into two cultures, like getting a real bargain in life, two for the price of one. The hardest part, I guess, is the growing up, but after that, it can be interesting and stimulating. I used to feel like a two-headed monstrosity, but now I find that two heads are better than one." She argues that "the war and the mental tortures we went through" have given the *Nisei* "a clearer understanding of America and its way of life, and we have learned to value her more." The final chapter of Sone's book is an example of the *Nisei*'s eagerness to prove themselves American, a restatement of Mike Masaoka's JACL creed. Arguing that "Masaoka's visionary language has crept into Nisei art," Frank Chin has charged that "the Nisei came out of the camps manufactured, trained, and indoctrinated in the loathsome stereotypes of Asia, Japan, and yellow immigrants. They came out of the desert to outwhite the whites and fulfill racial fantasies."

In the aftermath of Michi Weglyn's revisionist history of internment, *Years of Infamy: The Untold Story of America's Concentration Camps* (1976), more recent *Nisei* writing has been less willing to forgive the injustice perpetrated against them by their own government. "Instead of directing anger at the society that excluded and diminished us," writes Yoshiko Uchida, "such was the climate of the times and so low our self-esteem that many of us Nisei tried to reject our own Japaneseness and the Japanese ways of our parents." Sone herself, in the preface to the 1979 reissue of her autobiography, takes a far more activist stand, praising President Gerald Ford for rescinding Executive Order 9066 in 1976, charging the Supreme Court with "overlook[ing] the vital American principle that consideration of guilt and punishment is to be carried out on an individual basis and is not to be related to the wrongdoing of others," and urging Japanese Americans to pursue the issue of redress.

In 1979, Congress enacted legislation creating the Commission on Wartime Relocation and Internment of Civilians, which was appointed in the last days of the Carter administration. Its report, *Personal Justice Denied,* was released early in 1983 and contained this summary of its findings:

The promulgation of Executive Order 9066 was not justified by military necessity, and the decisions which followed from it – detention, ending detention and ending exclusion – were not driven by analysis of military conditions. The broad historical causes which shaped these decisions were race prejudice, war hysteria and a failure of political leadership. Widespread ignorance of Japanese Americans contributed to a policy conceived in haste and executed in an atmosphere of fear and anger at Japan. A grave injustice was done to Americans and resident aliens of Japanese ancestry who, without individual review or any probative evidence against them, were excluded, removed, and detained by the United States during World War II.

Shortly before the expiration of its legislative mandate, the commission issued five recommendations to Congress on the subject of redress: (1) a joint resolution of Congress signed by the president apologizing for the injustices committed by the U.S. government as a result of its policy of evacuation and internment; (2) presidential pardons for those who were convicted of violating statutes related to the evacuation; (3) the recommendation that the executive branch look generously on applications by

Japanese Americans for the restitution of benefits and entitlements taken away during the war on the basis of ethnicity; (4) the appropriation of money to establish a special foundation to "sponsor research and public educational activities" in order to promote better understanding of the history of internment; and (5) an appropriation of $1.5 billion to cover the cost of funding recommendation four and of making one-time redress payments of $20,000 to those who were excluded. After five years of debate over the issue of whether monetary compensation was appropriate and if so in what amount, a bill enacting the redress provisions was passed in 1988. The first payments – to the oldest of the camp survivors – were made in 1990.

4

꽃

LEGACIES OF THE SIXTIES

HE Native American poet Simon Ortiz (Acoma Pueblo) describes the decade of the 1960s as "inspirational," "creative," and "invigorating," because it was a "worldwide phenomenon of third-world peoples decolonizing themselves and expressing their indigenous spirit, especially in Africa and the Americas." And, Ortiz argues, this "process of decolonizing includes a process of producing literature." Describing "the condition of the Chicano" in 1972, Luis Valdez, the director of the radical Teatro Campesino, writes, "Our people are a colonized race, and the root of their uniqueness as Man lies buried in the dust of conquest. In order to regain our corazon, our soul, we must reach deep into our people, into the tenderest memory of their beginning." And then he quotes the poet Alurista:

> . . . razgos indigenas
> the scars of history on my face
>   and the veins of my body
> that aches
>   vomito sangre
> y llora libertad
>   I do not ask for freedom
> I AM freedom. . .

What many Native American, Asian American, and Chicano writers learned from the experiences of the 1960s is that literature has a crucial role to play in the formation of ethnic identity and the creation of ethnic pride. Asked to compare the so-called Native American Renaissance to the "Harlem Renaissance in black writing," N. Scott Momaday pointed to Dee Brown's best-selling revisionist historical account *Bury My Heart at Wounded Knee* (1970), researched and written during the 1960s, as a watershed; according to Momaday, the publication of Brown's book created "a sudden disposition to understand the experience of the American Indian. The kind of burgeoning that we're talking about really happened in the publishing world rather than in any sort of social or political arena."

꽃

Chicano critics like Juan Bruce-Novoa, Raymund Paredes, and Ramón Saldívar tend to conceive of Chicano literature as an emergent literature that consciously defines itself against mainstream Anglo-American culture. Saldívar argues that "the narrative writings of Chicano women and men must be understood as different from and in resistance to traditional American literature, yet must also be understood in their American context, for they take their oppositional stance deliberately, in order to offer readers a reformulation of historical reality and contemporary culture." Most agree, too, with Bruce-Novoa's suggestion in the introduction to his study *Chicano Authors: Inquiry by Interview* (1980) that the "emergence" of "Chicano literature is a recent phenomenon" that was to a large extent "a by-product of the Chicano Movement, the socio-political civil rights struggle begun in the mid-1960's by and on behalf of people of Mexican descent living in the United States."

José Antonio Villarreal's *Pocho* (1959), the first novel by a Mexican American author to be published by a mainstream American publishing house, uses the world of the *corridos* (ballads) like *"Gregorio Cortéz"* as its point of departure. Taking its title from the Mexican epithet for an Americanized Chicano, the novel is a *Kunstlerroman* that tells the story of Richard Rubbio, a Mexican American boy growing up in California whose father, Juan, was a companion of the legendary Pancho Villa and a hero of the Mexican Revolution. When the novel opens, however, the Mexican Revolution is long past – if not in years, then in spirit: Villa has retired, his rival General Alvaro Obregón has become president of Mexico, and Juan Rubbio feels a disillusionment that embodies the loss of revolutionary fervor. Rubbio is a figure from the heroic *corrido*: the first scene of the novel presents him striding into a cantina in Ciudad Juárez, flirting with a young woman, and then deliberately insulting and shooting her lover. Once his identity is discovered by the soldiers who arrest him, Rubbio is treated with respect, even reverence, by the general in command at Juárez, an older man who feels emasculated and useless in the postrevolutionary political climate. By the end of the chapter, however, it is clear that the day of the heroic *corrido* and of men like Rubbio is over: when Rubbio learns that Villa has been killed, he resigns himself to eking out a living in the United States, "mourn[s] deeply for the loss of his god," and dreams of the day that he and his family can return to Mexico. In his heart, he knows that he is now "one of the lost ones."

After the first chapter, the novel shifts its focus almost exclusively to Rubbio's son, Richard, leaving behind the world of the *corrido* for the world of the *pocho*. Left behind, too, is the fusion of individual and communal values that characterizes the *corrido*: the culture into which Richard is born is a culture that valorizes individualism above all. Growing up among Anglos in Santa Clara, California, Richard experiences what sociologists call "structural assimilation": most of Richard's close friends are Anglos and his steady girlfriend is a white girl from Nordic and Portuguese stock. Like Joyce's *Portrait of the Artist as a Young Man* (1916), upon which it was modeled, *Pocho* presents a protagonist who attempts to forge an identity for himself, first by exploring his heritage as a Roman Catholic, then by attempting to understand his historical situation as a member of a colonized people (which for Richard means firsthand knowledge of union halls, strikes, and strike-related violence, as well as racial discrimination), and of course by coming to terms with the sexual feelings that accompany adolescence and young adulthood. Richard's development into a young man who decides that he wants to become a writer is set against the gradual disintegration of his family, and Richard comes to realize that he cannot "give [the] institution [of marriage] the importance it had falsely taken on through the centuries. Marriage, per se, was not life, nor could it govern life." Richard's process of assimilation is complete when he rejects both the "codes of honor" by which his father lives and the Catholic faith that is so important to his mother, substituting instead a set of ideas about honor and faith that arise from his own personal experience. This "cultural assimilation" culminates when Richard declares to himself, late in the novel: "I can be a part of everything . . . because I am the only one capable of controlling my destiny. . . . Never – no, never – will I allow myself to become a part of a group – to become classified, to lose my individuality." At the end of *Pocho,* Richard takes up his father's old vocation – he joins the U.S. armed forces – but it is a gesture that represents the final break with the culture of Mexico that his father still embraces.

Chicano critics disagree about the role that *Pocho* has played in Chicano literary history. Because of its obvious embrace of the tradition of the *Kunstlerroman,* its linguistic style (which is firmly rooted in standard American English), and its assimilative stance (which resembles the one that Richard Rodriguez would later adopt), *Pocho* has been called "an American book with Mexican American characters and themes" and disparaged as "the kind of book" that subsequent "Mexican American writers neither admired nor wanted to write." On the other hand, because subsequent landmark Chicano novels like Anaya's *Bless Me, Ultima* and Acosta's *The Autobiography of a Brown Buffalo* (1972) would also adopt the framework of the story of the writer's apprenticeship and because it treats themes that would become staples of later Chicano writing – immigration, Catholic culture, Mexican sexual taboos, the effects of assimilative pressure on the traditional Mexican family – *Pocho* has also been called "the first Chicano novel" and "a paradigmatic Chicano narrative."

The etymology of the term *Chicano* is still hotly disputed among Chicano scholars. The most likely derivation is from *Mexicano,* with the *x* pronounced the way it was at the time of the Spanish conquest, as *sh.* The term *Chicano,* which came to prominence during the student movements of the 1960s, has not been universally accepted by those whom it is intended to describe, however. According to the critic José Limón, "Almost immediately after . . . [its] public appearance within the student movement, the term set off controversy and debate within the larger U.S.–Mexican community. The general reaction ranged from indifference to outright rejection and hostility." Various other terms have gained currency in different regions, however: for example, *Hispano* and *Spanish American* have been the preferred terms in southern Colorado and northern New Mexico, while *Mexicano* has been widely accepted in south Texas and in many of the border regions.

Equally hard to define is the so-called Chicano Movement – *La Causa* – which arose during the early 1960s in tandem with other movements aimed at gaining civil rights for disenfranchised minority groups. We might locate the origins of this widespread and diffuse set of social issues in the strike that became known as *La Huelga,* a word that originally signified rest, repose, relaxation from work. In 1962, César Chávez founded the National Farm Workers Association (NFWA) in Delano, California; the NFWA would eventually become the United Farm Workers (UFW). On September 16, 1965, the *campesinos* of the NFWA voted to join the Filipino grape pickers who were on strike. *La Huelga* would last for five years and gain national attention with the grape boycott begun in New York in 1968. On a two-hundred-fifty-mile pilgrimage to the state capitol, Sacramento, Chávez and his fellow strikers issued a document called "The Plan of Delano," which declared "the beginning of a social movement in fact and not in pronouncements. We seek our basic, God-given rights as human beings." It was a moment of solidarity among oppressed groups: "The strength of the poor," declared the plan, is "in union. We know that the poverty of the Mexican or Filipino worker in California is the same as that of all farm workers across the country, the Negroes and poor whites, the Puerto Ricans, Japanese and Arabians; in short, all of the races that comprise the oppressed minorities of the United States."

Out of the UFW came El Teatro Campesino, a bilingual theater company established by Luis Valdez in 1965 "to teach and organize Chicano farm workers." In an account contained in an anthology of Chicano writing entitled *Aztlán: An Anthology of Mexican American Literature* (1972) that he coedited with Stan Stiner, Valdez recalls starting "in a broken-down shack in Delano, California, which was the strike office for César Chávez'[s] farm workers' union" by hanging "signs around people's necks, with the names of familiar character types: scab, striker, boss, etc. They started to act out everyday scenes on the picket line. These improvisations quickly became satirical. More people gathered around and started to laugh, to cheer the heroes and boo the villains; and we had our first show." In plays such as *Los Vendidos* (1967), *The Militants* (1969), and *Soldado Raso* (1971), Valdez updated Mexican and Spanish dramatic forms to dramatize issues that were important to the membership of the UFW. Their preferred form was the comic *acto,* a one-act play of less than half an hour that, according to Valdez, dealt "with the strike, the union and the problems of the farm worker." Satirizing the opponents of the UFW, the Teatro toured across the country in 1967 "to publicize the strike, performing at universities, in union halls and civic auditoriums, at New York's Village Theater, at the Newport Folk Festival and in the courtyard of the U.S. Senate Building in Washington, D.C.," receiving an Obie award in 1968 "for creating a workers' theater to demonstrate the politics of survival." Valdez argued that "Chicano theater must be revolutionary in technique as well as content. It must be popular, subject to no other critics except the pueblo itself; but it must also educate the pueblo towards an appreciation of social change, on and off the stage." In 1969, the Teatro filmed a version of *I Am Joaquin,* an epic poem written in 1967 by another hero of the Chicano Movement, Rodolfo "Corky" Gonzales, who founded the Crusade for Justice in Colorado. In 1970, Valdez introduced a second genre, the *mito* (myth), which he described as "a parable that unravels like a flower Indio fashion to reveal the total significance of a certain event." With its combination of parable and ritual, the *mito* allowed the Teatro to present longer narratives and to explore the Indian elements of Chicano identity. In 1971, Valdez published *Actos: The Teatro Campesino,* a collection of *actos* written between 1965 and 1971. "We will consider our job done," he wrote the next year, "when every one of our people has regained his sense of personal dignity and pride in his history, his culture, and his race."

Drawing on the cultural energies let loose by El Teatro Campesino, a group of Chicano academics at the University of California, Berkeley, founded Quinto Sol Publications in 1969 to make works by Chicano authors available. Seeking to foster the growth of an identifiable Chicano literature, Quinto Sol began by publishing a journal called *El Grito,* which the novelist Tomás Rivera described in 1980 as the "one milestone" to date in Chicano literature, and two years later it produced the first anthology of

Chicano creative writing, *El Espejo/The Mirror* (1st edition, 1969), edited by Octavio Romano-V. and Herminio Rios-C., leading Rivera to remark to the critic Juan Bruce-Novoa that the Chicanos were the first people to have an anthology before they had a literature. The writers who became associated with Quinto Sol were self-conscious experimenters who sought to break down boundaries between fiction and nonfiction, poetry and prose in order to capture the modern-day Chicano experience while remaining true to the folk traditions that arose in Mexico and the Southwest. Many Chicano poets sought to take advantage of their bilingualism, blending Spanish and English in their poetry. The very existence of Quinto Sol gave Chicano authors a sense of empowerment.

In 1970, the publishers established *El Premio Quinto Sol,* a cash prize designed to establish a canon of Chicano novels; the project lasted for three years and its recipients – Tomás Rivera, Rudolfo Anaya, and Rolando Hinojosa – would become what Juan Bruce-Novoa has called "the Chicano Big Three," still the most widely read and studied of Chicano novelists. As inspirational as Villarreal's *Pocho* was to a generation of Chicano writers, by 1970 its assimilationist vision had come to seem problematic and even outdated. The blurb on the back cover of the paperback edition published in 1970 offers this apology: "To many young Mexican-Americans who seek an identity rooted in their own cultural heritage, the pocho represents much of what they, the Chicanos, are trying to change." In his introduction to the paperback edition, Ramón Ruiz damns the novel with faint praise, arguing that *Pocho* "has immense historical value for today's reader," because it "documents the intellectual-emotional evolvement of Mexican-Americans in a chronological sense." For Ruiz, Villarreal's handling of his protagonist's plight is outdated, and he concludes his introduction by championing the ideological point of view espoused by the newly christened Chicanos:

In rebellion against his dual heritage, Richard stands defenseless, an insecure and beaten young man. Here Villarreal reveals the gulf that time and events have built between his generation of Mexican-Americans and chicanos. No longer are chicanos "lost" Richards. The militant and not-so-militant young with Spanish surnames have started to build, not just a regional political movement, but an identity to replace that sense of inferiority that settled down upon Richard in his lonely battle with reality.

According to Raymund Paredes, "To its largely Anglo readership, *Pocho* was a moving portrait of a necessary if painful process of assimilation. To a Mexican American audience, awash in a rising tide of ethnic pride, however, *Pocho* was a story of terrible loss. . . . [It] was precisely the kind of book a new generation of Mexican American writers neither admired nor wanted to write."

The first Quinto Sol prize was awarded to Tomás Rivera's novelistic collection of sketches about migrant workers, . . . *y no se lo tragó la tierra* (. . . *and the Earth Did Not Part,* 1971), which epitomized the Quinto Sol sensibility. Unlike *Pocho,* which depicts the displacement of traditional Chicano values by the individualist ideology of Anglo-America, *Tierra* portrays the survival of those values in the face of discrimination and economic hardship. According to Rivera, while he was writing *Tierra,* "The Chicano Movement was una fuerza total ya [a complete power already] in the university and so forth. I wanted to document, somehow, the strength of those people I had known" – the migrant workers of the period 1945 to 1955. Influenced by the writings of such experimentalists as William Faulkner, James Joyce, John Dos Passos, and Juan Rulfo, *Tierra* is a novel in the sense that Sherwood Anderson's *Winesburg, Ohio* might be considered a novel, and it begins on a note that briefly recalls the magical realism of Rulfo or such Latin American "boom" writers as Jorge Luís Borges and Gabriel García Márquez:

Aquel año se le perdió. A veces trataba de recordar y ya para cuando creía que se estaba aclarando todo un poco se le perdían las palabras. Casi siempre empezaba con un sueño donde despertaba de pronto y luego se daba cuenta de que realmente estaba dormido. Luego ya no supo is lo que pensaba había pasado o no.

[That year was lost to him. At times he tried to remember, and just about when he thought everything was clearing up some, he would be at a loss for words. It almost always began with a dream in which he would suddenly awaken and then realize that he was really asleep. Then he wouldn't know whether what he was thinking had happened or not.]

Magical realism is not the dominant mode of *Tierra,* however: what Rivera learns above all from the Rulfo of *El llano en llamas* (*The Burning Plain,* 1953) or *Pedro Páramo* (1955) is a sense of irony, detachment, and spareness.

The rest of *Tierra* consists of twelve sketches, each representing a month of the narrator's "lost year" and each preceded by an interchapter in the manner of Hemingway's *In Our Time,* with a concluding sketch in which the narrator attempts to "discover and rediscover and piece things together." The sketches portray the harshness of the Chicano migrant's life: in *"Los niños no se aguantaron"* ("The Children Couldn't Wait"), a foreman accidentally shoots a young boy who has taken an unauthorized water break; in *"Los quemaditos"* ("The Little Burn Victims"), three children burn to death while left alone in a migrant worker's shack because "the owner didn't like children in the fields doing mischief and distracting their parents"; in *"Cuando lleguemos"* ("When We Arrive"), we hear the thoughts of workers crammed into a truck: "When we get there I'm gonna see about getting a good bed for my vieja. Her kidneys are really bothering her a lot nowadays. Just hope we don't end up in a chicken coop like last year, with that cement floor. Even though you cover it with straw, once the cold season sets in, you just can't stand it. That was why my rheumatism got so bad, I'm sure of that." Although like Villarreal's *Pocho, Tierra* seems to focus on one young man's search for self-understanding, Rivera's narrator, like Anderson's George Willard, floats through the different sketches, some of which are told in the first person, others in the third: the effect is less that of the traditional bildungsroman than the portrayal of collective experience. What happens to the Chicano bildungsroman as it moves from Villarreal to Rivera is that it becomes a form in which what is at stake is the development not simply of the individual protagonist but also of the community and culture to which he belongs. In novels of development like *Tierra* and Sandra Cisneros's *The House on Mango Street* (1983), as well as autobiographies like Ernesto Galarza's *Barrio Boy,* individual identity and communal identity develop simultaneously and are inseparably intertwined.

The winner of the third Quinto Sol prize, Rolando Hinojosa's *Estampas del valle y otras obras* (*Sketches of the Valley and Other Works,* 1973) shares certain features with Rivera's *Tierra*; it is written in Spanish, makes use of the *estampa* or sketch form popularized by Julio Torri in Mexico, and takes as its setting southern Texas. Unlike Rivera's irony, which is always tinged with melancholy and bitterness, Hinojosa's irony is tinged with humor as he describes human behavior that ranges from the heroic to the depraved. Where Rivera limited himself to the experience of migrant farm workers, Hinojosa aims to portray a far more representative version of Chicano life, which proves ultimately to be Faulknerian in its sweep.

Set in Klail City, a fictional town in the Rio Grande Valley, *Estampas del valle* consists of four different kinds of narrative: twenty portraits of the valley and its inhabitants by Jehú Malacara; six accounts of Badleamar Cordero's stabbing to death of Ernesto Tamez; a chronicle devoted to the lives of Texas Mexicans; and Rafa Buenrostro's recollections of his schooling and of his experiences in the Korean War. *Estampas* would prove to be the first in a series of novels – the *Klail City Death Trip* series – devoted to the depiction of "Belken County." Hinojosa's second novel, *Klail City y sus alrededores* (1976) was awarded the prestigious award for best novel of the year by the Cuban publishing house La Casa de las Américas; it was published in English in the United States in 1977 with the Spanish title *Generaciones y semblanzas* (Generations and Biographies). The series continued in 1978 with an extended verse narrative entitled *Korean Love Songs,* followed by *Mi querido Rafa (Dear Rafe,* 1981), *Rites and Witnesses* (1982), *Partners in Crime* (1985), *Claros varones de Belken/Fair Gentlemen of Belken County* (1986), and *Becky and Her Friends* (1989). Influenced by the narrative styles of both Faulkner and García Márquez, the *Klail City Death Trip* series continues the project begun by Américo Paredes in his study of "The Ballad of Gregorio Cortéz": it offers a critique of the Anglo cultural mythologies surrounding the Texas Rangers in particular and the borderlands of the Southwest in general while creating a massive historical fiction that has the effect of ennobling Chicano history. It also dramatizes the linguistic evolution of the cultures that it depicts: the Spanish of *Estampas del valle* gives way to the explicit bilingualism of *Mi querido Rafa,* which is followed by the English of *Rites and Witnesses,* whose protagonists – Jehú Malacara and Rafa Buenrostro – are enmeshed in the larger culture of the United States. "In the first two or three works," Hinojosa told an interviewer, "I focus mainly on the Texas-Mexican. But as both Rafe Buenrostro and Jehú Malacara grow up and go into the Army, the University of Texas and the workplace, they're coming into the Anglo world." In a sense, the *Klail City Death Trip* series also continues the project of Rivera's *Tierra*: it emerges, finally, as a massive bildungsroman in which both the young boys and the valley community introduced in *Estampas del valle* reach maturity in the midst of an individualistic dominant culture without sacrificing their ties to collective history and identity.

Sandwiched between Rivera and Hinojosa as winners of the Quinto Sol prize was Rudolfo A. Anaya, whose *Bless Me, Ultima* (1972) is written in English. Like *Pocho, Bless Me, Ultima* focuses on the experiences of a young boy who aspires to be a writer. Set in New Mexico just after World War II, the novel also maps the ways in which a community responds to cultural change both within and without. Antonio Marez is a boy who embodies liminality, torn as he is between the two different subcultures from which his parents hail. His father is a *llanero,* a man of the plains who "had been a vaquero all his life, a calling as ancient as the coming of the Spaniard to Nuevo Méjico." His mother, however, is the "daughter of a farmer," who "could not see the beauty in the llano and . . . could not understand the coarse men who lived half their lifetimes on horseback." The novel's first-person narrative includes italicized passages depicting the dreams of the young Antonio, whose boyhood is profoundly influenced by his friendship with the old *curandera* (folk healer) Ultima, who comes to stay with the family as the novel opens. Through Ultima, Antonio learns about pre-Christian forms of spirituality and knowledge that do not supplant but instead supplement the Christian teachings that he learns in school and at church. Both Ultima and her apprentice Antonio are mediating forces in the novel: through them, the novel's oppositions – between father and mother, *llanero* and farmer, Christian and non-Christian – are synthesized into a dialectical relationship. Toward the end of the novel, we see signs of the encroachment of Anglo culture onto the Chicano world of Antonio's youth, most pressingly in the form of the apocalyptic threat of the atomic bomb, being tested by the U.S. government in New Mexico. What Antonio feels he has learned from Ultima is "that the tragic consequences of life can be overcome by the magical strength that resides in the human heart." Although early critics of the novel faulted it for the evasion of the materiality of history seemingly evident in such statements, *Bless Me, Ultima* proves to be as deeply political as either Rivera's or Hinojosa's writings. What the novel ultimately suggests is that the fusion of spiritual traditions will enable Antonio not only to mediate conflicts within his community but also to help that community maintain its sense of identity and coherence in the face of a consuming Anglo culture.

The Quinto Sol prize project succeeded in establishing the core of a Chicano canon, but as the critic Juan Bruce-Novoa has argued, it was a canon constructed around the desire to present a positive image of Chicanos and their culture. Excluded were the works of such writers as John Rechy, whose novels focus on questions of gay rather than Chicano identity, or Oscar Zeta Acosta, whose social satire refuses to exempt Chicano pieties. Even Tomás Rivera fell victim to the desire to promote communally correct portraits of Chicano life: the Quinto Sol editors are thought to have rejected "Pete Fonseca," now considered to be one of his finest stories, because it was deemed unflattering to Chicanos.

Critics who justified omitting Rechy's best-selling novel *City of Night* (1963) from a list of Chicano classics because the novel's perspective and subject matter are far more influenced by Rechy's sexuality than by his ethnicity could not use the same logic to exclude Acosta's writings. Published in 1972, the same year as *Bless Me, Ultima,* Acosta's picaresque novel *The Autobiography of a Brown Buffalo* depicts the adventures of a Chicano lawyer from Los Angeles who drops out of his profession to embark on journey through the Southwest trying to discover the roots of his "fucked up identity," ingesting copious amounts of drugs and alcohol along the way before ending up in a jail in Ciudad Juárez. Written in a style reminiscent of the "gonzo" journalism of Hunter S. Thompson, who was one of Acosta's good friends, *Brown Buffalo* begins by confronting the reader with the physical presence of its narrator, Oscar, in a manner designed to foreshadow the interplay of ethnicity and narcissism that will mark the text as a whole:

I stand naked before the mirror. Every morning of my life I have seen that brown belly from every angle. It has not changed that I can remember. I was always a fat kid. I suck it in and expand an enormous chest of two large hunks of brown tit. . . . But look, if I suck it in just a wee bit more, push the bellybutton up against the back; can you see what will surely come to pass if you but rid yourself of this extra flesh? Just think of all the broads you'll get if you trim down to a comfortable 200. . . . I enter the bathroom and struggle to the toilet. With my large, peasant hands carefully on the rim of white, I descend to my knocked knees. I stare into the repository of all that is unacceptable and wait for the green bile, my sunbaked face where my big, brown ass will soon sit.

The comma between "big" and "brown" in the description of Oscar's "ass" is emblematic: bigness and brownness emerge as the axes upon which both his identity and his narrative locate themselves. Fined and released by a Mexican judge in Ciudad Juárez who tells him to "go home and learn to speak your father's language," told by an immigration officer at the border, "You don't look like an American, you know?" – Oscar finds himself at the end of the novel back where he began: "I stand naked before the mirror. I cry in sobs. My massive chest quivers and my broad shoulders sag. I am a brown buffalo lonely in a world I never made." What Oscar realizes at the end of his odyssey is that he is "neither a Mexican nor an American. I am neither a Catholic nor a Protestant. I am a Chicano by ancestry and a Brown Buffalo by choice." Refusing to build his personal identity around the ready-made template signified by *Chicano,* Oscar chooses to define a new hybrid identity for himself and to build a new cultural identity around it.

The individualism of this stance surfaces throughout Acosta's second novel, *The Revolt of the Cockroach People* (1973), which opens with Oscar leading a Chicano Militant demonstration at a Los Angeles Roman Catholic church. In the second chapter, Oscar describes the moment, lying awake in bed, in which he determined to become a radical, after thinking about a humiliating incident of racial discrimination that he suffered while in high school: "That night I get no sleep. My brain goes off like explosives and by dawn I have made innumerable resolutions. I will change my name. I will learn Spanish. I will write the greatest books ever written. I will save the world. I will show the world what is what and who the fuck is who. Me in particular." Angry at the dominant culture's mistreatment of Chicanos in general and himself in particular, Oscar rechristens himself "Buffalo Z. Brown," meets César Chávez, participates in the bombing of a supermarket, runs for sheriff of Los Angeles Country, and describes himself as a "professional revolutionary."

Throughout the novel, however, Oscar's animosity shifts back and forth between the dominant culture and the Chicano Movement itself. Oscar's commitment to the movement is intermittent: after his unsuccessful run for

sheriff, he decides to "drop out again," going to Acapulco to visit his brother
Jesus and pursue a sybaritic existence. He returns only after the death of the
Chicano journalist Roland Zanzibar, a fictionalized version of Ruben Salazar,
a prominent Chicano television anchorman in Los Angeles, who was killed
by the police while covering the first National Chicano Moratorium to
protest the Vietnam War. While defending the demonstrators known as the
Toomer Flats Seven, Oscar is accused of "directing the activities of the
Chicano Liberation front," in particular "the bombings during the riots,"
but Oscar laughs and portrays himself not as a leader but as a victim: "Those
guys wouldn't do what I told them to do if their lives depended on it. They
are *vatos locos! Nobody* tells crazy guys what to do. . . . It is *they* who have driven me to this brink of madness. It is they who are watching and wondering
and complaining about me. *I* am the sheep. *I* am the one being used"
[ellipses in original]. The Militants are suspicious of Oscar because he has
received a book offer: "That I would think to make money off the struggle
for freedom of the Cockroaches has made some people whisper traitor, *ven-
dido, tio taco,* uncle tom and a capitalist pig to boot." But Oscar sees himself
filling the shoes left empty by the death of Zanzibar; echoing Walt
Whitman, he writes, "I shouted it to the rooftops: we *need* writers, just like
we need lawyers. Why not me? I *want* to write." Oscar's motives prove to be
overdetermined at the end of *Revolt*: self-aggrandizement, revolutionary fervor, and the profit motive merge. After his successful defense of the Toomer
Flats Seven, believing that he has "helped start a revolution to burn down a
stinking world," Oscar opts out once again, deciding to "split with the
Chicanos" in order "to carry on the species and my own Buffalo run as long
as I can" – and to write his memoirs. The end of the novel promises that
more of Oscar's story will soon be told, but *Revolt of the Cockroach People*
would have no sequel: in June 1974 Acosta left Mazatlán, Mexico, on a
friend's boat and was never heard from again.

Acosta's identification with the mainstream counterculture, including
his appropriation of Hunter S. Thompson's narrative stylistics, has led a
number of Chicano critics to argue that he was not an authentic Chicano
writer: Raymund Paredes, for example, argues in an essay included in the
Modern Language Association (MLA) collection *Three American Literatures*
(1982) that "Chicano literature is that body of work produced by United
States citizens and residents of Mexican descent for whom the portrayal of
their ethnic experience is a major concern." To Paredes, Acosta is problematic because although he does seem to attempt "to retrieve his ethnic heritage, . . . the reader is struck by the superficiality of his quest and the
flimsiness of the foundation upon which he hopes to build his ethnic identity." What Paredes takes for granted here is that ethnic identity must lie

at the core of a Chicano's personal identity if he is to be a true Chicano, for surely Acosta fulfills both criteria that Paredes designates for Chicano literature: Acosta's novels devote considerable space to representing the psychological damage inflicted upon a Mexican American because of his ethnicity. What truly makes Acosta problematic is his refusal to grant the ethnic component of his identity primacy: he writes explicitly at the end of *Brown Buffalo* that his "single mistake has been to seek an identity with any one person or nation or with any part of history." Acosta's novels finally insist on the need for individualism, and insofar as individualism is a dominant component of mainstream American ideology, this insistence places both the author and his novels at odds with Chicano culture. Despite its countercultural stance, therefore, Acosta's writing has far more in common with Villarreal's *Pocho* than it does with such Chicano bildungsromans as Rivera's *Tierra* or Anaya's *Bless Me, Ultima*.

Kenneth Lincoln describes the "reemergence" of Native American literature as a "written renewal of oral traditions translated into Western literary forms." The poet Simon Ortiz (Acoma Pueblo) identifies N. Scott Momaday (Kiowa), Vine Deloria, Jr. (Sioux), and James Welch (Blackfeet-Gros Ventre) as the writers who initiated a tradition of written Native American literature that did not exist before. After producing a privately published study of Kiowa myths entitled *The Journey of Tai-Me* in 1967, Momaday published his novel *House Made of Dawn* the following year; in 1969, it was awarded the Pulitzer prize. The Pulitzer jury's decision took author, publisher, and reading public by surprise: according to Momaday's biographer Matthias Schubnell, "Momaday at first refused to believe the news, and some of the senior editors at Harper and Row could not even remember the novel." James Welch describes Momaday's winning the Pulitzer as a crucial turning point: "suddenly people started to notice Indian literature, [and] the way kind of opened for Indians; . . . younger people who didn't think they had much of a chance as a writer, suddenly realized, well, an Indian can write." Momaday's novel coincided with a renewal of political and social activism among American Indians that gained national attention with the publication of Deloria's *Custer Died for Your Sins* (1969), Dee Brown's *Bury My Heart at Wounded Knee* (1970), and the occupation of Alcatraz Island from 1969 to 1971.

The 1960s saw the creation of a new pan-Indian consciousness exemplified by the Chicago Conference of 1961, which brought together hundreds of Indians from different tribes to discuss issues of common interest. Calling on the U.S. government to respect the treaties that it had made with Indian tribes and to cease taking "our lands . . . for a declared public purpose," the conference's "Declaration of Indian Purpose" recognizes that differences among tribes are less important in the present moment than a sense of Indian solidarity: "in the beginning the people of the New World, called Indians by accident of geography, were possessed of a continent and a way of life. In the course of many lifetimes, our people had to adjust to every climate and condition from the Arctic to the torrid zones. In their livelihood and family relationships, their ceremonial observances, they reflected the diversity of the physical world they occupied." Moving here from a sense of the collective "people of the New World" to a sense of the "diversity" of Indian tribes, the declaration finally describes American Indians in collective terms again in recognizing "the complexities which beset a people moving toward new meaning and purpose." The goal of the document is to "ask for assistance, technical and financial, for the time needed, however long that may be, to regain in the America of the space age some measure of the adjustment [the Indians] enjoyed as the original possessors of their native land." Studying the situation of Native Americans in 1961, the United States Commission of Civil Rights concluded that Indians were being subjected to discrimination and infringement of opportunity in such areas as voting, employment, education, housing, and justice. In the aftermath of the commission's report, Native Americans made slow gains throughout the 1960s in the area of civil rights, and in 1968 Congress passed the Indian Civil Rights Act, which guaranteed to Native Americans rights that white Americans had always taken for granted, such as freedom of speech, press, and religion (the sacramental use of peyote had been protected by the U.S. Supreme Court four years earlier); the rights of assembly and petition; and protection against the seizure of property without just compensation.

Dissatisfied both with the rate of improvement under federal programs that were often implemented incompletely and with the imperious attitude of the Bureau of Indian Affairs (BIA), which continued to wield a substantial amount of power over Native American programs, off-reservation and urban Indians formed a variety of different activist organizations to supplement the existing National Congress of American Indians and the National Indian Youth Conference. Of these new organizations, the most militant was the American Indian Movement (AIM), founded in Minneapolis in 1968 by two members of the Chippewa tribe, Dennis Banks and George Mitchell, who were later joined by a third Chippewa, Clyde Bellecourt. Originally intended simply to assist Indians who were moving from upper-Midwest reservations to cities (particularly to protect them from selective law enforcement and unequal justice), AIM increasingly devoted itself to agitating on behalf of restoration of Indian lands illegally seized by the federal government and of bona fide application of the Indian civil rights law. The tactics used by AIM and other groups ran the gamut of political action, from peaceful demonstration to the seizure of land and buildings and occasionally armed resistance to the authorities.

The increase in Indian militancy can be measured by comparing the 1961 Chicago Conference's "Declaration of Indian Purpose" to "A Proclamation from the Indians of All Tribes, Alcatraz Island, 1969," released after Indian activists occupied Alcatraz (since 1963, no longer used as a federal prison) and claimed their right to the island (which had been declared surplus property by the federal government) under the Fort Laramie Treaty of 1868, which allowed any male Indian over eighteen whose tribe was a party to the treaty to file for a homestead on government land. Five years earlier, Sioux activists had attempted to claim Alcatraz Island under federal law, staging a sit-in (complete with lawyers) that the national media described as "wacky." "Looking back, I'm not surprised," writes the Indian activist Russell Means in his autobiography *Where White Men Fear to Tread* (1995):

White America has always trivialized Indian people. . . . Our treaty wasn't "wacky," it was the law of the land. . . . The lawyers filed suit to press our claim on Alcatraz, but eventually the case was thrown out. There was no legal basis for the judge's refusal to hear the suit, but in those days there was so much racism that no one cared. It would be five more years before another group of Indians took over Alcatraz – and then the white man knew we were serious.

The Alcatraz proclamation addresses itself to "the Great White Father and All his People" and begins: "We, the native Americans, re-claim the land known as Alcatraz Island in the name of all American Indians by right of discovery." Designed to express dissatisfaction with the federal government's trusteeship of native lands, the document proposes to offer a "treaty" to the U.S. government:

We will purchase said Alcatraz Island for twenty-four dollars (24) in glass beads and red cloth, a precedent set by the white man's purchase of a similar island about 300 years ago. We know that $24 in trade goods for these 16 acres is more than was paid when Manhattan Island was sold, but we know that land values have risen over the years. Our offer of $1.24 per acre is greater than the 47 cents per acre the white men are now paying the California Indians for their land.

We will give to the inhabitants of this island a portion of the land for their own to be held in trust by the American Indian Affairs and by the Bureau of Caucasian Affairs to hold in perpetuity – for as long as the sun shall rise and the rivers go down to the sea. We will offer them our religion, our education, our life-ways, in order to help them achieve our level of civilization and thus raise them and all their white brothers from their savage and unhappy state. We offer this treaty in good faith and wish to be fair and honorable in our dealings with all white men.

The occupation of Alcatraz Island drew wide national and international attention, and public support lasted until 1971, when federal officials found that they could remove the protesters from the island with little public outcry. Indian militancy did not end with the removal of protesters from Alcatraz: in 1972, during the so-called Broken Treaties Caravan to Washington, protesters occupied the BIA building, destroying federal records and other pieces of public property. And in 1973, led by members of AIM, armed Indians occupied the village of Wounded Knee, made famous by Dee Brown's book, which concludes by describing the horrific massacre of Sioux men, women, and children by the Seventh Cavalry in 1890.

Momaday's *House Made of Dawn* participates in this new sense of pan-Indian consciousness by bringing together Kiowa, Navajo, and Walotowa (Jemez Pueblo) mythic and oral traditions. The novel is framed with the traditional Walotowa formula words for "opening" (*Dypaloh*) and "closing" (*Qtsedaba*), and the bulk of the novel's prologue offers an image of a Walotowa ceremony, the annual footrace of the "runners after evil." But the first paragraph of the prologue also draws from another set of beliefs and rituals:

> *Dypaloh.* There was a house made of dawn. It was made of pollen and of rain, and the land was very old and everlasting. There were many colors on the hills, and the plain was bright with different-colored clays and sands. Red and blue and spotted horses grazed in the plain, and there was a dark wilderness on the mountains beyond. The land was still and strong. It was beautiful all around.

This first paragraph (and the novel's title) allude to a chantway – the Navajo Night Chant – a healing ritual that the novel's protagonist, Abel, will encounter after his relocation to Los Angeles, sung to him by his Navajo friend Ben Bennally:

> *Tséghi.*
> House made of dawn,
> House made of evening light,
> House made of dark cloud,
> House made of male rain,
> House made of dark mist,
> House made of pollen,
> House made of grasshoppers,
> Dark cloud is at the door.
> The trail out of it is dark cloud.
> The zigzag lightning stands high upon it.

Male deity!
Your offering I make.
I have prepared a smoke for you.
Restore my feet for me,
Restore my legs for me,
Restore my body for me,
Restore my mind for me.
This very day take out your spell for me.
Your spell remove for me.
You have taken it away for me;
Far off it has gone.
Happily I recover.
Happily my interior becomes cool.
Happily I go forth.
My interior feeling cool, may I walk.
No longer sore, may I walk.
Impervious to pain, may I walk.
As it used to be long ago, may I walk.
Happily may I walk.
Happily, with abundant dark clouds, may I walk.
Happily, with abundant showers, may I walk.
Happily, with abundant plants, may I walk.
Happily, on a trail of pollen, may I walk.
Happily may I walk.
Being as it used to be long ago, may I walk.
May it be beautiful before me,
May it be beautiful below me,
May it be beautiful above me,
May it be beautiful all around me.
In beauty it is finished.

According to Navajo belief, health depends on a harmonious and integrated psyche, with little distinction made between physical and mental
illness, and a state of health is conceived as a state of beauty and accord. An
individual who is isolated or alienated – from his tribe, from the land – is
thus a sick individual, and the rituals of healing center on reintegrating
this isolated or alienated individual into the organic unity of the universe.

Abel is doubly isolated and alienated. He is a mixed blood who "did not
know who his father was. His father was a Navajo, they said, or a Sia, or an
Isleta, an outsider anyway, which made him and his mother and [his
brother] Vidal somehow foreign and strange." Abel's inability to fit into
the ceremonial life of the village is exemplified and magnified by his violation of the ritual of the Bakyush eagle hunt: feeling sorry for the captive
eagle, he strangles her. But Abel is also isolated and alienated because he is
a contemporary American Indian in a white-dominated culture, unable to
adjust to the frames of reference offered first by the government boarding

school to which he is sent and then the U.S. Army into which he is drafted. Moreover, assimilating into white American society, even if it were possible, would mean accepting an ideology based in individualism that runs counter to all of his tribe's traditional beliefs. Returning home, nearly psychotic after his experiences in the Second World War, Abel is sent to prison for the ritual murder of an albino who has humiliated him during a Walotowa ceremony and then is relocated to the urban ghetto of Los Angeles, where he encounters the Indian preacher John Big Bluff Tosamah. He befriends Ben Bennally, a young urban Navajo, as well as a white social worker named Milly, who becomes his lover, and is finally beaten nearly to death by a Mexican American policeman for refusing to pay protection money. Lying near death, he begins to understand the significance of both the Navajo healing chant and the Walotowa footrace, to understand why he has "lost his place . . . and was even now reeling on the edge of the void."

In the story that accompanies the Navajo Night Chant, Crippled Boy and Blind Boy, left behind when the tribe must migrate and thus all but left for dead, help each other to climb a cliff, where they meet the Holy People who teach them the healing Night Chant. Momaday's Abel is a combination of these two figures: not blind but mute and therefore – in his culture of storytelling and oral tradition – crippled.

Abel's inability to speak is a powerful emblem of his alienation from his tribe and from himself, and it lies at the center of the novel's consideration of the nature of human language. Commenting on the expression "white man speaks with forked tongue," Momaday once told an interviewer that the expression "seems to me to reach farther into basic perceptions than most of us would understand at first. It is, unwittingly or not, a sensitive commentary upon the way in which the Indian and the non-Indian look at language." *House Made of Dawn* dramatizes the differences between Indian and non-Indian understandings of language that result from the Indian's participation in traditions of oral literature. The Indian "Priest of the Sun," the "Right Reverend John Big Bluff Tosamah," preaches a sermon on the opening line of Genesis: *In principio erat Verbum* – "In the Beginning was the Word." The sermon quickly becomes an indictment of "the way in which the white man thinks of [language]":

The white man takes such things as words and literatures for granted, as indeed he must, for nothing in his world is so commonplace. On every side of him there are words by the millions, an unending succession of pamphlets and papers, letters and books, bills and bulletins, commentaries and conversations. He has diluted and multiplied the Word, and words have begun to close in upon him. He is sated and insensitive; his regard for language – for the Word itself – as an instrument of creation has diminished nearly to the point of no return. It may be that he will perish by the word.

Obviously, however, the novel – first, by virtue of its simply being a novel – does not eschew "the white man['s] . . . literatures" altogether, for if *House Made of Dawn* owes a formal debt to the Walotowa, Navajo, and Kiowa traditions on which it draws, it also owes a debt to the modernist experimentalism of Faulkner, Joyce, and Lawrence, since it relies heavily on such techniques as flashbacks, interior monologue, multiple narrators, and typographical differentiation. According to Paula Gunn Allen, Joyce was one of the few Western writers whose writing could embody something like a Native American mythic space – the kind of mythic space that "make[s] you dance" – and, "if it weren't for Joyce," she suggests, "we wouldn't have Momaday." (Allen credits Gertrude Stein with playing a similar role for her.) Drawing from both Native American oral traditions and high modernist written traditions, *House Made of Dawn* – both in its form and in its subject – captures both the pain and the potential power of cultural hybridity, and it would become a model for later Native American writers. According to the Abnaki writer Joseph Bruchac, Momaday's novel "opened the eyes of a new generation of Native American writers. They read the novel and heard the deeper meanings of its powerful writing: a person caught between cultures can, despite the deepest of problems, find a way to survive, a road which circles out of the past, 'The House Made of Dawn,' and ends in understanding."

Leslie Marmon Silko, who has been called "the first Native American woman to publish a full-length novel," was one member of that new generation of Native Americans writing in the wake of *House Made of Dawn,* and in many respects her first novel, *Ceremony* (1977), seems to be a response to and even a rewriting of Momaday's novel. Both novels are set primarily in the pueblos of the Southwest, and like Momaday's Abel, Silko's protagonist, Tayo, is not a full-blooded Indian: Abel was a mixed blood, but Tayo is even further outside the tribal norm, because he is a half-breed, taken in by his aunt "to conceal the shame of her younger sister."

Weaving together fragments of Laguna Pueblo and Navajo mythology, Silko tells the story of Tayo's return to the Laguna Pueblo from combat in the Pacific during the Second World War. He has been released from a veterans' hospital but still suffers from a complex form of guilt: he blames himself for failing to protect his beloved half brother Rocky, upon whom all of his family's hopes had been placed; for causing the drought that has been afflicting the Laguna Pueblo; and finally for bringing about the death of his beloved uncle Josiah, to whom he left the task of managing an entire herd of Mexican spotted cattle and whose face he saw in the faces of every Japanese soldier that he killed.

As in Momaday's novel, Tayo's redemption comes through his participation in a healing ceremony. When the traditional ceremonies of the tribal elders fail to mend Tayo's injured and alienated psyche, he is sent to the revisionist Navajo medicine man Betonie, whose hazel eyes and Mexican ancestry make him a hybrid figure like Tayo. Betonie is distrusted by traditionalists because he makes use of modern implements – such as phone books – in his ceremonies. Like *House Made of Dawn,* Silko's novel thus makes crucial use of Navajo ceremonial tradition, but the myth that undergirds the novel is the story of Ts'its'tsi'nako – referred to variously as Thought Woman, Spider Woman, and Grandmother Spider – the author of all thought and all stories. "She is sitting in her room / thinking of a story now," we are told in the poetic lines that begin the novel; "I'm telling you the story / she is thinking." The life-force of the universe is thus a feminine principle, and it is contrasted in the novel with the death-force, the "witchery," that is associated with technology, white culture, and the masculine violence embodied by the veterans who return home from the war, particularly Emo, Tayo's nemesis.

Tayo's ceremony can be completed only with a quest:

"One night or nine nights won't do it any more," the medicine man said; "the ceremony isn't finished yet." He was drawing in the dirt with his finger. "Remember these stars," he said. "I've seen them and I've seen the spotted cattle; I've seen a mountain and I've seen a woman."

The woman turns out to be Ts'eh, a member of the Montaña family who lives with her brother on Mount Taylor, the Laguna sacred mountain, and who helps Tayo to recover his lost cattle. What *Ceremony* presents that *House Made of Dawn* does not is a vision of the power of the creative and curative powers of the female principle, which is always allied with and generated by the land. Near the end of the novel, Tayo thinks to himself, "we came out of this land and we are hers," and he realizes, "They had always been loved. He thought of her then; she had always loved him, she had never left him; she had always been there."

Tayo's nemesis, the war veteran Emo, who carries around a bag of teeth taken from Japanese corpses, represents a countermyth invented by Silko: he is the embodiment of "the witchery," the novel's mythic explanation for the genesis of white culture. Betonie tells Tayo, "That is the trickery of the witchcraft":

They want us to believe all evil resides with white people. Then we will look no further to see what is really happening. They want us to separate ourselves from white people, to be ignorant and helpless as we watch our own destruction. But white people are only tools that the witchery manipulates; and I tell you, we can deal with white people, with their machines and their beliefs. We can because we invented white people; it was Indian witchery that made white people in the first place.

The novel then presents an account of the witchery, which takes place "Long time ago / in the beginning" when "there were no white people in this world" and "nothing European." The witch people get together for a storytelling contest, and one of them tells a story about "white skin people / like the belly of a fish / covered with hair," who "see only objects" when they look at the world, for whom "the world is a dead thing." This story-teller wins the contest, but other witches ask that the story be taken back: "what you said just now – it isn't so funny . . . Call that story back." It is too late, however, because words and stories have efficacy; they have creative power:

> . . . the witch just shook its head
> at the others in their stinking animal skins, fur and feathers.
> *It's already turned loose,*
> *It's already coming,*
> *It can't be called back.*

White culture is thus portrayed as the product of witchery, and white ideology is seen as mechanistic because it values technology over nature and brings violence into the world. Thus Emo, too, is a victim: white culture has made him a sociopath by recruiting him for its war and then shunning him as an outsider afterward. It is only when Tayo can reject the temptation to kill Emo, can renounce the violence that is Emo's way of life, that Tayo is finally cured. It is, finally, the rejection of violence that proves to be the culmination of Tayo's ceremony.

Ceremony is a critique of American individualism. When he first meets Betonie, Tayo remembers what he has been told in the hospital: "That he had to think only of himself, and not about the others, that he would never get well as long as he used words like 'we' and 'us.'" Even though he wants to believe them, however, Tayo already knows that they are wrong, "because the world didn't work that way. His sickness was only part of something larger, and his cure would be found only in something great and inclusive of everything." White culture attempts to recruit Native American culture to its individualistic conception of the world, but when he finally takes up the role of storyteller at the end of the novel, Tayo signals that he has successfully resisted and reinserted himself into the communal life of his tribe.

Unlike *House Made of Dawn* and *Ceremony,* James Welch's first two novels, *Winter in the Blood* (1974) and *The Death of Jim Loney* (1979), are set in the Northwest and offer a far bleaker vision of Native American life. Asked to comment on the storytelling tradition in these novels, Welch says first of all that they "are written in the Western, European-American tradition," in part because they lack the moral that Welch associates with "the storytelling tradition of traditional Indians." Welch is a mixed blood, Blackfeet on his father's side and Gros Ventre on his mother's, and in *Winter in the Blood* he draws on both traditions ironically. Standing Bear, the first husband of the narrator's grandmother, is a Blackfeet warrior who meets his doom while leading his people away from the "Long Knives" – federal soldiers – "in a futile raid on the Gros Ventres, who were also camped in the valley." The Montana Blackfeet were reputedly the fiercest tribe on the Great Plains, the last tribe to negotiate a truce with the U.S. government, but those days of heroic resistance are long gone in Welch's novel. All that remains are memories of humiliation, as this sardonic added detail – typical of Welch's black humor – makes clear: "When the survivors [of the raid] led [Standing Bear's] horse into camp, his eldest son killed it and the family lived off the meat for many days. The horse was killed because Standing Bear would need it in the other world; they ate it because they were starving."

Welch's novel seems to draw on Blackfeet and Gros Ventre traditions in other ways as well, but always ironically. The ever-unnamed narrator may represent an updating of the Blackfeet tradition that forbade one to speak one's own name to others. The fact that he is thirty-two years old may signify that he is about to embark on a vision quest: according to Gros Ventre tradition, when a man reaches thirty-two he must go on a vision quest, look for a wife, and attempt to qualify for initiation in a Crazy Lodge via the "crying for pity ritual." At the beginning of Welch's novel, however, the narrator has seemingly found a wife, a Cree woman that he has brought home, only to have her run away with his shotgun and his razor. The narrator does in fact set out on several trips to neighboring towns, throughout the novel, ostensibly to recover her and his belongings, and the result is several absurdist encounters that seem unlikely to result in any revelation. Welch denies that he modeled the novel after a vision quest, as many critics have suggested, and he argues that a vision quest is no longer possible for a twentieth-century Indian like the narrator:

in the real vision quest the people went to seek a vision and from that vision they would know how to conduct themselves, not only in their everyday lives but in things that really counted for them, like in battle they'd been courageous.

Depending upon which power animal appeared to them, they would take the attributes of that animal, so if a raven came to them, they would probably become farseeing. . . . So, a traditional vision quest always had a particular thing it sought and then once the vision came it had almost a practical aspect; then you could use the power that the vision represented.

Winter in the Blood is a modern-day vision quest in the same way that Joyce's *Ulysses* (1922) is a modern-day epic. Welch's style has as much in common with the black humor of Faulkner's *As I Lay Dying* (1930) as it does with the trickster tales to which it is often compared, and the climax of the novel, in which the narrator struggles to rescue a cow caught in the mud, seems reminiscent of those moments in Faulkner's narratives – such as the flood in "Old Man" – when humans find themselves overmatched in their battle with the elements. The narrator of *Winter in the Blood* does learn something about his identity: he learns that he is not a half-breed but is in fact a full-blood Blackfeet, but what difference this will make in his life is unclear at the end of the novel. The narrator begins the novel feeling alienated: "The distance I felt came not from country or people; it came from within me. I was as distant from myself as a hawk from the moon. And that was why I had no particular feelings toward my mother and grandmother. Or the girl who had come to live with me." The ending of the novel tells us little about whether the narrator's experiences will ultimately thaw this winter in his blood.

Unrelieved by the comic moments that leaven the sardonic realism of *Winter in the Blood,* Welch's second novel, *The Death of Jim Loney,* is a bleak narrative that portrays the liminal space between white culture and Native American culture as an existential no-man's-land from which its protagonist cannot escape. Like both *House Made of Dawn* and *Ceremony,* Jim Loney is a hybrid character, in this case a half-breed who is abandoned by his parents – his white father, Ike, and his mother, Eletra Calf-Looking – and he finds that he can feel no connection to either parent or to either of their cultures. Accidentally killing his high school rival Myron Pretty Weasel while the two are hunting, Loney lets the tribal police believe he has committed murder and allows himself to be shot in Mission Canyon, a site believed to be a gateway into the next life. Welch's novels eschew the richly textured mythic substructures that undergird Momaday's *House Made of Dawn* and Silko's *Ceremony* in favor of a more stripped-down narrative style reminiscent of Hemingway.

In their different ways, Momaday, Silko, and Welch create hybrid novels that bring together Native American oral traditions with the powerful legacy of American modernist writing, as if to assert that the Native American novel will not conform to critical expectations that have linked ethnic writing to realism. Like Villarreal's *Pocho, House Made of Dawn* stands at the head of a novelistic tradition, but the two novels could not be more different stylistically. Inspired in part by Joyce's *Portrait of the Artist as a Young Man, Pocho* belongs to the tradition of autobiographical realism that was the norm for American ethnic writing in the first half of the twentieth century. *House Made of Dawn,* however, has less in common with *Pocho* than it does with Henry Roth's *Call It Sleep* (1934), long regarded as an anomaly within American ethnic writing because of its formal experimentalism. *Call It Sleep* gained national recognition only after it was rediscovered and reissued in paperback in 1964, becoming a national best-seller. Roth's novel found its audience in the mid-1960s, the same cultural moment that produced Momaday's *House Made of Dawn,* and significantly, both novels are inconceivable without the prior example of Joyce – not the Joyce of *Portrait,* however, but the Joyce of *Ulysses.* What *Call It Sleep* and *House Made of Dawn* have in common with each other, as well as with Silko's *Ceremony* and Welch's *Winter in the Blood* and *The Death of Jim Loney,* is that they are revisionist novels that revise in two directions: they bring ethnic traditions to bear on modernist writing and modernist experimentalism to bear on ethnic writing.

Formal experimentation marks the work of the novelist and essayist Gerald Vizenor, who finds a natural affinity between Native American oral traditions and literary postmodernism. A mixed-blood Indian who is an enrolled member of the Anishinabe (Chippewa) tribe, Vizenor sees in the ambiguity of mixed blood an opportunity to be seized rather than a problem to be solved. Momaday, Silko, and Welch portray their mixed-blood characters as pained figures who can avoid tragedy only by resolving the ambiguities of their identities. In contrast, Vizenor's mixed-bloods are tricksters who revel in ambiguity and marginality, and they are portrayed as comic rather than tragic characters. Vizenor takes issue with the analysis of tribal tricksters presented by anthropologists such as Paul Radin, who claims that the trickster "possesses no values, moral or social" and "knows neither good nor evil yet is responsible for both." For Vizenor, the trickster – no matter how disruptive he or she may prove to be – is always "a compassionate and imaginative character." In the prologue to *The Trickster of Liberty: Tribal Heirs to a Wild Baronage* (1988), Vizenor writes:

The Woodland trickster is a comic trope; a universal language game. The trickster narrative arises in agonistic imagination; a wild venture in communal discourse, an uncertain humor that denies aestheticism, translation, and imposed representations. The most active readers become obverse tricksters, the waver of a coin in a tribal striptease.

Like the novels of John Hawkes, Vizenor's narratives are designed to produce discomfort in his readers through sudden shifts in narrative reality and through jarring depictions of graphic violence and explicit, often perverse, sexuality.

As in many traditional trickster narratives, the comedy of Vizenor's novels is frequently dark and sardonic. His first novel, *Darkness in Saint Louis Bearheart* (1978, republished in 1990 as *Bearheart: The Heirship Chronicles*), is a postmodern frame tale that begins with an elliptical account of the takeover of the Washington office of the Bureau of Indian Affairs by radicals from the American Indian Movement. A young militant woman discovers a manuscript written by an old shaman-turned-bureaucrat named Saint Louis Bearheart, and it is this manuscript that will serve as the bulk of the novel that we are going to read. "What is your book about?" she asks Bearheart, and he replies, "Sex and violence." Bearheart's manuscript is a bleakly futuristic account of a time when the U.S. government orders the cutting of forest preserves, forcing Proude Cedarfair to abandon the sacred grove of cedars that his family has protected for generations. Cedarfair and his wife Rosina embark on a pilgrimage, joined by a strange band of companions that includes "thirteen weird and sensitive women" poets living in a communal "scapehouse"; a little man named Bigfoot who possesses an enormous uncircumcised penis that the poets have nicknamed "president jackson"; a homosexual tribal lawyer and his lover; a tribal historian named Wilde Coxswain; and a woman named Lilith Mae, whose lovers are her two pet boxer dogs. The manuscript's loosely connected series of episodes are a mixture of reimagined trickster tales, such as the story of the Evil Gambler, whose defeat brought back the rains, and contemporary fables that dramatize the plight of Native Americans, such as the poisoning of Belladonna Darwin-Winter Catcher, who can conceive of her "tribal identity" only as a series of inherited clichés. Such clichés are examples of what Vizenor calls "terminal creeds," belief systems that subject the world to static definitions, and it is the goal of his novel to disrupt and transform the terminal creeds that are poisoning Native American cultures. The novel ends with a transformative moment that pays homage to N. Scott Momaday: near the Walatowa Pueblo that provides the setting for much of *House Made of Dawn,* Proude Cedarfair and his companion Inawa Biwide reach the "vision window" that allows them "to enter the fourth world as bears," like the boy in Momaday's retelling of the Kiowa legend of the origin of the Big Dipper.

Vizenor's subsequent novels have become increasingly abstract and elliptical, full of passages that seem more appropriate to literary theory than fiction and structured around what Vizenor (following Jean-François

Lyotard) calls "wisps of narratives." In an essay entitled "Trickster Discourse," Vizenor quotes Lyotard's suggestion that "the people do not exist as a subject but as a mass of millions of insignificant and serious little stories that sometimes let themselves be collected together to constitute big stories and sometimes disperse into digressive elements." Like Proude Cedarfair, who leaves his reservation to lead a band of pilgrims and ultimately leaves the present world behind, Vizenor's writing increasingly abandons the rootedness in place and the particularity of tribal affiliation that marks so much Native American writing. Steeped in post-structuralist literary theory, Vizenor's fiction, like his critical writing, is full of puns and jargon; it is deliberately inaccessible and almost compulsively self-referential. His "novel" *The Trickster of Liberty* consists of what look like outtakes from his earlier novels, episodes that will make little sense to readers who are not already participants in Vizenor's discursive enterprise. Speaking of Bagese, a tribal woman who "became a bear last year in the city," the narrator of Vizenor's *Dead Voices: Natural Agonies in the New World* (1992) says, "I pretended to understand, but some of her stories were obscure and she never responded to my constant doubts," a sentiment no doubt echoed by many of Vizenor's readers. What Vizenor has done, however, is to push the insights of emergent literature to an extreme: his fiction accepts and welcomes the violence of cultural hybridity, and he does not shy away from depicting scenes that may leave even his most sympathetic readers feeling assaulted. His goal is to transform words into "word-arrows" that can serve as weapons in what the subtitle of Bearheart's manuscript calls "the cultural word wars."

Although the Anishinabe novelist Louise Erdrich is frequently described as postmodern by literary critics, her novels bear relatively little resemblance to those of Vizenor. In comparison to Vizenor, Erdrich writes in a neorealist mode that is firmly rooted in palpable depictions of place and character. The word *heir* occurs repeatedly in Vizenor's writing, but of the two novelists it is Erdrich who is more interested in portraying the generational histories of the Anishinabe people. The tetralogy that begins with *Love Medicine* and includes *The Beet Queen* (1986), *Tracks* (1988), and *The Bingo Palace* (1994) charts some eighty years in the life of the Turtle Mountain Chippewa Reservation in North Dakota, juxtaposing different narrative voices in the manner of Faulkner's *As I Lay Dying* (1930). A word that consistently recurs in critics' descriptions of Erdrich's prose is *lyrical,* and her lyricism has the effect of heightening the real without pushing it into the surreal. It gives her rendering of mythical elements the same palpability as her rendering of contemporary social problems, while allowing her to question frames of reference that her readers might otherwise take for granted. In *Tracks,* for example, Erdrich's lyrical style enables her to present Catholic belief and Anishinabe legend on equal footing, with just a hint that of the two, it may be Catholicism that is the more fantastic. Erdrich, like Vizenor, seeks to challenge shibboleths of mainstream culture, but her novels are gently, rather than aggressively, subversive of readers' expectations.

Erdrich draws upon some of the same tribal traditions that inspire Vizenor, in particular the trickster figure Nanabozho, who serves as the archetype upon which such characters as Old Nanapush, Moses Pillager, Gerry Nanapush, and Lipsha Morrissey are patterned. Like Vizenor, she works primarily in the comic mode; in a 1989 interview with the television journalist Bill Moyers, Erdrich suggested that "the one universal thing about Native Americans from tribe to tribe" may be "survival humor," the ability to "live with what you have to live with" and "to poke fun at people who are dominating your life and your family," in part by recognizing that "the most serious things have to be jokes." In the episode to which the title *Love Medicine* refers, Lipsha Morrissey's ad hoc updating of an Anishinabe ritual intended to renew his grandparents' love for one another and restore his grandfather's memory has an aura of slapstick about it, yet it results in the grandfather's death by choking. Erdrich's comic irony, however, lacks the savagery of Vizenor's, and her depictions of violence rarely seem designed to be an assault on her reader. In Erdrich's novels, storytelling serves less as a mechanism for disruption and subversion than as a way of preserving spirituality, creating community, and ensuring survival. In her novel *Tales of Burning Love* (1996), Erdrich presents four Great Plains women who, like Scheherezade or the characters in *The Decameron,* must tell stories in order to stay alive, in this case to stay awake and keep themselves from freezing to death or suffocating in their snow-bound car. As its title suggests, sexuality is a central theme in *Tales of Burning Love,* as it is in all of Erdrich's novels, yet it is not the barren sexuality portrayed by Vizenor. Among the prominent Native American novelists, Erdrich emerges as the one most interested in exploring the dynamics of love and sexuality and the extent to which relationships between men and women might serve as a basis for the renewal of culture.

Momaday, Silko, Welch, Vizenor, and Erdrich represent the core of the canon of Native American prose fiction that has arisen in the last thirty years, and their combined influence can be seen in the work of a writer like Sherman Alexie, whose novels draw liberally from the styles they pioneered: his short-story collection *The Lone Ranger and Tonto Fistfight in Heaven* (1993) uses a variety of narrative personae to portray reservation life in the Northwest with the same flashes of dark comedy that mark Erdrich's novels; his first novel, *Reservation Blues* (1995), draws on the mythical overtones seen in the novels of Momaday, Silko, and Erdrich; and his second novel, *Indian Killer* (1996), is a gritty urban work set in Seattle that seems indebted above all to Welch.

Midway through *Indian Killer*, a well-to-do white man named Daniel Smith searches among Seattle's homeless Indian population for his emotionally disturbed adopted son, John, an Indian whose tribal heritage was kept secret by the adoption agency. "He spent most of the day in downtown Seattle," Alexie writes, "but never found anybody, white or Indian, who had ever heard of an Indian named John Smith, though they all knew a dozen homeless Indian men." Then we get this list:

> "Yeah, there's that Blackfeet guy, Loney."
> "Oh, yeah, enit? And that Laguna guy, what's his name? Tayo?"
> "And Abel, that Kiowa."

This reference to the protagonists of novels by Welch, Silko, and Momaday is a Native American novelist's in-joke, but it also suggests one of *Indian Killer*'s powerful insights: that all Native Americans are in some fundamental way homeless, victims of displacement, dispossession, and cultural damage. The young Native American activist Marie Polatkin, one of the protagonists of Alexie's novel, believes "that homeless people were treated as Indians had always been treated. Badly. The homeless were like an Indian tribe, nomadic and powerless . . . so a homeless Indian belonged to two tribes, and was the lowest form of life in the city."

The lives of the Native American protagonists of *Indian Killer* can be seen as parables of the cultural damage suffered by Native Americans as a result, first, of the European conquest of the Americas, and later of the U.S. government's attempts to assimilate Native Americans into mainstream American culture. John Smith, for example, is taken from his teenage mother and his reservation at birth, raised by two loving and liberal white parents, and baptized a Catholic. Regarded by the teachers at the St. Francis Catholic School (in which he is one of four nonwhite students) as "a trailblazer, a nice trophy for St. Francis, a successfully integrated Indian boy," John eventually proves himself to be quite the opposite, a schizophrenic who finds himself at home nowhere. John Smith thus embodies the physical displacement of the U.S. government's policy of Indian Removal in the midnineteenth century and the process of detribalization through which the U.S. government sought to assimilate Native Americans by weaning them from their tribal orientation. The fact that John is so emotionally damaged despite his liberal parents' efforts both to make him feel loved and to teach him Native American history is a signal that the cultural damage perpetrated by the U.S. government will not so easily be undone.

The title of Alexie's novel refers to a serial killer who is stalking, scalping, and otherwise mutilating white men in Seattle. The killings spawn a cycle of racially motivated violence, as whites begin to beat innocent Indians, and Indians launch unprovoked attacks on innocent and indeed sympathetic whites. As the violence escalates, the power of the so-called Indian Killer seems to grow:

A full moon. A cemetery on an Indian reservation. On this reservation or that reservation. Any reservation, a particular reservation. The killer wears a carved wooden mask. Cedar, or pine, or maple. The killer sits alone on a grave. The headstone is gray, its inscription illegible. There are many graves, rows of graves, rows of rows. The killer is softly singing a new song that sounds exactly like an old one. As the killer sings, an owl silently lands on a tree branch nearby. The owl shakes its feathers clean. It listens. The killer continues to sing, and another owl perches beside the first. Birds of prey, birds of prayer. . . .

The killer spins in circles and, with each revolution, another owl floats in from the darkness and takes its place in the tree. Dark blossom after dark blossom. The killer sings and dances for hours, days. Other Indians arrive and quickly learn the song. A dozen Indians, then hundreds, and more, all learning the same song, the exact dance. The killer dances and will not tire. The killer knows this dance is over five hundred years old. . . . The killer plans on dancing forever. The killer never falls. The moon never falls. The tree grows heavy with owls.

This passage is taken from the novel's concluding chapter, which is entitled "A Creation Story." Late in the novel, Marie Polatkin suggests that "maybe this Indian Killer is a product of the Ghost Dance. . . . Maybe this is how the Ghost Dance works." Later on, she tells the police, "[I]f some Indian is killing white guys, then it's a credit to us that it took over five hundred years for it to happen. And," she says, "there's more[:] Indians are dancing now, and I don't think they're going to stop." Decolonization here is, indeed, a violent phenomenon.

As the twentieth century comes to a close, the Native American novel seems to have become darker and more pessimistic. The hopes for change that marked Native American culture as a result of the revolutionary fervor of the 1960s seem to have been worn down, overtaken perhaps by the desire for entrepreneurial success that motivates Erdrich's Lyman Lamartine in *Love Medicine* and *The Bingo Palace*. Although Erdrich maintains her faith in the healing powers of human love and traditional Native American beliefs, she seems increasingly to be the exception rather than the rule. The shift in Leslie Marmon Silko's work may perhaps be an indication of the direction in which the Native American novel is headed. The healing of wounds that takes place at the end of *Ceremony* with Tayo's disavowal of violence and the departure of his nemesis, Emo, is replaced in Silko's massive second novel, *Almanac of the Dead* (1991), by a sense that the evil represented by men like Emo is resilient and powerful and not so easily dismissed. In form and subject matter, *Almanac* is as difficult and jarring as any of Vizenor's novels, but it lacks Vizenor's sense of the comic. Described by Silko as a "763-page indictment for five hundred years of theft, murder, pillage, and rape," *Almanac* portrays a nightmarish world of violence, sexual perversion, and corruption at every level of society, a world in which the "witchery" has won out. None of the characters in *Almanac* are capable of love, and few of them seem capable even of hatred. The triumph of individualism has created a hierarchical, mechanistic, misogynist culture, in which the ontological norm might well be the stupor of the drug addicts who abound throughout the novel. If there is any hopefulness in *Almanac of the Dead,* it is perhaps in the novel's conviction that the Eurocentric regimes that now rule the Americas are destined to be overthrown.

Silko told an interviewer in 1992 that "*Almanac* spawned another novel about a woman who is a serial killer" whose victims are only "policemen and politicians." It was, she said, "way more radical than *Almanac,*" but she set it aside because she believed that it was too soon "to serve the narrative again on something so hard." Asked by the interviewer "what happened to the nice, charming Leslie Silko who used to write poems," Silko laughed and described "what happened" as "classic," simply a matter of "development," the result of "reading, learning," and emerging from a "sheltered" life. What Silko sees in her own life is the inevitability of encountering the violence that is inherent in cultural emergence, a violence that is increasingly being given life in the Native American novel, embodied in characters like Vizenor's tricksters, Alexie's Indian Killer, and Silko's drug addicts, sadists, and serial killer–to-come. The revolutionary politics that have always been a thread in the Native American novel seem now to be more pressing and aggressive than ever.

❧

For Asian Americans, the 1960s offered a different legacy. Considered unassimilable aliens until World War II, Asian Americans would in the aftermath of the war become cast in the role of the "model minority," in contradistinction to those minorities – particularly African Americans and Chicanos – who were growing increasingly militant in their calls for social equality. According to the literary scholar Elaine Kim, Asian Americans were portrayed by the white mainstream during the 1960s as "restrained, humble, and well-mannered, a people who respect law, love education, work hard, and have close-knit, well-disciplined families."

This shift in stereotypical portrayals of Asian Americans may well have begun with the success of Earl Derr Biggers's six Charlie Chan novels, which appeared between 1925 and 1932, all published in novel form after being serialized in the *Saturday Evening Post,* and which provided an alternative to Sax Rohmer's sinister Fu Manchu. "Sinister and wicked Chinese are old stuff," Biggers would claim, "but an amiable Chinese on the side of law and order has never been used." Charlie Chan became a phenomenon, with forty-eight Chan films produced by four different studios featuring six different non-Chinese actors as the detective who solves crimes in exotic settings both in Chinatown and abroad.

The image of Chinatown as a place of mystery – exotic but safe – would become the basis for a genre of writing that might be called the "Chinatown Book," first made popular by Leong Gor Yun's *Chinatown Inside Out* (1938). In the introduction to *Aiiieeeee!* (1974), the first anthology of Asian American writing, Frank Chin, Jeffery Paul Chan, Lawson Fusao Inada, and Shawn Hsu Wong argue that *"Chinatown Inside Out* was obviously a fraud," noting that "the author's name 'Leong Gor Yun,' means 'two men' in Chinese." Consisting of what Chin et al. identify as "items cribbed and translated from the Chinese-language newspapers of Chinatown in San Francisco tied together with Charlie Chan/Fu Manchu images and the precise logic of a paranoid schizophrenic," *Chinatown Inside Out* fooled "even scholars of Chinese America," who failed to notice "the awkward changes of voice and style, the differences between the outright lies and the rare facts," and the clue contained in the author's pen name. *Chinatown Inside Out* would prove influential, becoming the source for the novel *Chinatown Family* (1948), written by Chinese émigré Lin Yutang, which presents an idealized portrait of Chinese American family life that draws on the model of the Horatio Alger success story, suggesting that success can be achieved through a mixture of hard work and well-deserved good fortune.

Autobiographical accounts published by Asian Americans in the 1940s, when China was an ally of the United States against Japan, tend to reinforce the idea that Chinese people were in fact assimilable. Pardee Lowe's *Father and Glorious Descendant* (1942) belittles Chinese culture as "alien" and "strange," while presenting the United States as "God's own country"; the dust jacket presented the book as an example of why the United States should "assimilate her loyal minorities" and noted that Lowe "enlisted in the U.S. Army shortly after delivering the manuscript of the book." Jade Snow Wong's autobiography, *Fifth Chinese Daughter* (1945), adopts the alternative but complementary strategy of Orientalizing Chinatown, making it seem exotic but safe. Wong's book was a financial success, reprinted several times in paperback and translated into a variety of languages. The influence of the "Chinatown book" would continue to be felt in the 1960s. S. W. Kung, a Chinese émigré, would cite Lin's *Chinatown Family* as an influence on his study *Chinese in American Life* (1962); Calvin Lee, a former assistant dean at Columbia University, would cite both Leong Gor Yun and S. W. Kun in describing his assimilation into white American society in *Chinatown U.S.A.* (1965). Betty Lee Sung's *Mountain of Gold: The Story of the Chinese in America* (1967) praises Chinese Americans for not being "overly bitter about prejudice" but lamented their tendency to gather in ethnic enclaves instead of dispersing themselves around the country to "reduce the degree of visibility." Like both Pardee Lowe and Jade Snow Wong, Sung blames Chinese Americans themselves for adding to their hardships.

In a revised version of the *Aiiieeeee!* introduction published in the MLA anthology *Three American Literatures,* Chin et al. have argued that "much of Asian-American literary history is a history of a small minority being cast into the role of the good guy in order to make another American minority look bad. In World War II the Chinese were used against the Japanese." Citing both a *Newsweek* article entitled "The Japanese-American Success Story: Outwhiting the Whites" (June 21, 1971) and the "favorable reception" accorded Sung's *Mountain of Gold* and Daniel I. Okimoto's *American in Disguise* (1970), Chin et al. contend that "today, the Chinese- and Japanese-Americans are used to mouth the white racist cliches of the fifties." They note that Sung's book, which "went through two printings of 7,500 and in 1971 was issued in a paperback edition," is "the only book by a Chinese-American still in print" in 1974. An article published in *U.S. News and World Report* at the end of 1966 suggested that the Chinese could serve as a model for African Americans and other "troublesome minority groups," because they have managed to succeed "on their own" despite past "hardships" that would "shock those now complaining about the hardships endured by today's Negroes." Praising Chinatown as "the safest place" in New York City, where residents "stay out of trouble" and "overcome their handicaps quietly," the article proclaims:

At a time when it is being proposed that hundreds of billions be spent to uplift Negroes and other minorities, the nation's 300,000 Chinese are moving ahead on their own . . . with no help from anyone else. Still being taught in Chinatown is the old idea that people should depend on their own efforts . . . not a welfare check . . . in order to reach America's "promised land."

Originally published by Howard University Press in 1974 but reprinted the following year in a paperback edition by Anchor Books, *Aiiieeeee!* sets itself against both the stereotype of Asian Americans as the model minority, lamenting that "seven generations of suppression under legislative racism and euphemized white racist love have left today's Asian-Americans in a state of self-contempt, self-rejection, and disintegration." As of 1975, the book's editors claim, fewer than "ten works of fiction and poetry have been published by American-born Chinese, Japanese, and Filipino writers," not because "in six generations of Asian-Americans there was no impulse to literary or artistic self-expression" but because mainstream American publishers were interested in publishing only those works written by Asian Americans that were "*actively inoffensive* to white sensibilities."

Aiiieeeee! was intended to counter the accepted wisdom that a literature that could be called "Asian American" simply did not exist; in an essay describing the genesis of the anthology, Chin et al. wryly cite the different reasons given for this lack: "Sung says we're working too hard to write; Kung says we were too low class to write; Okimoto says we were too full of self-contempt to write and that if we could write we would have nothing to say. All three had obviously let their library cards lapse." Describing their method of "searching the past for works" as more "serendipitous" than "scientific," they write: "We found John Okada on the shelf of a grocery store; Louis Chu we found in the card catalog of the Oakland Public Library; Toshio Mori we found on the shelf of a used book store we'd gone into seeking shelter on a rainy day in Berkeley." After a polemical introduction entitled "Fifty Years of Our Own Voice," *Aiiieeeee!* offers its readers selections from Carlos Bulosan's semiautobiographical account of a Filipino migrant worker's life, *America Is in the Heart* (1946); Diana Chang's novel *The Frontiers of Love* (1956); Louis Chu's novel *Eat a Bowl of Tea* (1961); Momoko Iko's drama *The Gold Watch*; Toshio Mori's collection of stories, *Yokohama, California* (1949); and John Okada's novel *No-No Boy* (1957), as well as stories by Wallace Lin, Oscar Peñaranda, Sam Tagatac, and Hisaye Yamamoto and writings by editors Frank Chin, Jeffery Paul Chan, and Shawn Hsu Wong. "My writer's education owes a big debt to this first *Aiiieeeee!*," writes Filipino American writer Jessica Hagedorn:

The energy and interest sparked by *Aiiieeeee!* in the Seventies was essential to Asian American writers because it gave us visibility and credibility as creators of our own specific literature. We could not be ignored; suddenly, we were no longer silent. Like other writers of color in America, we were beginning to challenge the long-cherished concepts of a xenophobic literary canon dominated by white heterosexual males. Obviously, there was room for more than one voice and one vision in this ever-expanding arena.

In 1990, the editors of *Aiiieeeee!* produced a sequel entitled *The Big Aiiieeeee!*, which restricted itself to Chinese American and Japanese American literature, despite the fact that it contained twice as many writers as the original volume. In narrowing its focus, *The Big Aiiieeeee!* contributed to the perception that "Asian American literature" essentially consists of literature by Chinese and Japanese Americans, with sporadic contributions by writers of Southeast Asian and Asian Indian descent.

Implicit in the logic of both *Aiiieeeee!* anthologies, as it was in the Quinto Sol prize project, was the desire to establish a canon of writings that would promote nonstereotypical depictions of Asian Americans, a goal that was shared by the Combined Asian Resources Project (CARP), in which Chin, Chan, and Wong all participated. The introduction to *The Big Aiiieeeee!* denounces the adoption by Asian American writers of autobiography, which they claim is a form that can only "ventriloquiz[e] the same old white Christian fantasy of little Chinese victims of 'the original sin of being born to a brutish, sadomasochistic culture of cruelty and victimization' fleeing to America in search of freedom from everything Chinese and seeking white acceptance." Arguing that "every Chinese American book ever published in the United States of America by a major publisher has been a Christian autobiography or autobiographical novel," they present a list of works that must be excluded from any Asian American canon, beginning with Yung Wing's *My Life in China* (1909), moving through Leong Gor Yun's *Chinatown Inside Out,* Pardee Lowe's *Father and Glorious Descendant,* and Jade Snow Wong's *Fifth Chinese Daughter* and concluding with Maxine Hong Kingston's *The Woman Warrior: Memoirs of a Girlhood Among Ghosts* (1976), *China Men* (1980), and *Tripmaster Monkey: His Fake Book* (1989) and Amy Tan's *The Joy Luck Club* (1989) – because they "all tell the story that Will Irwin, the Christian social Darwinist practitioner of white racist love, wanted told in *Pictures of Old Chinatown* (1908) about how the 'Chinese transformed themselves from our race adversaries to our dear subject people.'" They identify only "four works by Chinese American authors" that "do not suck off the white Christian fantasy of the Chinese as a Shangri-La people": two published by "major publishing houses" – Diana Chang's *The Frontiers of Love* (1956) and Louis Chu's *Eat a Bowl of Tea* (1961) – and two written by editors of the anthologies – Shawn Wong's novel *Homebase* (1979) and Frank Chin's collection of short stories, *The Chinaman Pacific & Frisco R.R. Co.* (1988).

What appeals to Chin and his coeditors about a work like *Eat a Bowl of Tea* is its author's refusal to present either Chinese or Chinese American culture as exotic: Chu portrays the last vestiges of bachelor society in New York's Chinatown from the inside, from the point of view of the waiters, barbers, and laundrymen who comprised it. His Chinatown is, as Chin et al. put it, "drab, even boring." Chu was born in Toishan but emigrated at the age of nine with his family to Newark, New Jersey; he served in the

U.S. Army during World War II and returned to China shortly thereafter to marry. *Eat a Bowl of Tea* chronicles the transformation of New York's Chinatown from a community of bachelors to a community of young families by telling the story of an old "bachelor" named Wah Gay and his son, Ben Loy. After decades working as a waiter, Wah Gay has established himself as the proprietor of the "Money Come club house," a dingy basement where Wah Gay and other lonely "bachelors" convene to play mahjong. Technically not a bachelor, Wah Gay has a wife in China, whom he married twenty-five years earlier during a brief return visit and whom he has not seen since: "Each time he had received a letter from his wife he began to relive the past. He knew it was not right to let the old woman stay in the village by herself. He often wondered, during lonely moments, if perhaps some day he and Lau Shee would have a joyous reunion." What takes the place of actual families in the lives of these old men are memberships in clan associations and tongs, and sex with prostitutes.

When the novel opens, their son, born in China but now living in the United States, has also returned to his native village to marry the daughter of his father's friend Lee Gong; unlike his father, however, Ben Loy is able to bring his bride, Mei Oi, back with him because of the repeal of the Exclusion Act and a subsequent law permitting Chinese brides of American citizens to enter the United States on a nonquota basis (facts left unstated by the novel). Mei Oi's presence proves highly disruptive to Chinatown's bachelor society: Ben Loy, an experienced frequenter of prostitutes, becomes impotent in the face of what he conceives to be his wife's "purity"; Mei Oi is seduced by an unscrupulous bachelor named Ah Song, causing a scandal throughout Chinatown; Wah Gay cuts off the seducer's ear in revenge and is saved from jail only when fellow members of the Sing On tong compel Ah Song to withdraw the charges he has filed with the police. Ultimately, Wah Gay and Lee Gong leave Chinatown to spare themselves further humiliation, Ah Song is ostracized by the tong for five years, and the young couple relocate to San Francisco. Ben Loy's impotence becomes a trope for the sterility of Chinese American bachelor society, a sterility created by the racist policies of the U.S. government. Ben Loy breaks the cycle of impotence: what cures him is not simply the bitter bowl of tea prescribed by an herbalist he visits but his forgiveness of his wife and his acceptance of the child she has borne that is not his by blood but will be his by choice. In moving from New York to San Francisco, Ben Loy and Mei Oi move to the cultural heart of Chinese America, and the conclusion of the novel promises reunion and regeneration, as the couple plan to invite their estranged fathers to the hair-cutting party for their second child. Realistic in its rendering of Cantonese figures of speech into English, naturalistic in its sexual frankness, *Eat a Bowl of Tea* did not achieve popular success or critical recognition during Chu's lifetime, but it has become an inspiration to Asian American artists like Chin and the director Wayne Wang, whose film version of the novel was released in 1988.

Unlike the Quinto Sol prize project, which managed to build the core of a Chicano canon around Rivera, Anaya, and Hinojosa, *The Big Aiiieeeee!* failed to solidify an Asian American canon centered around the work of Chang, Chu, Okada, Wong, and Chin. Members of CARP were influential in bringing about the University of Washington Press's Asian American Studies series, which issued new editions of Bulosan's *America Is in the Heart,* Okada's *No-No Boy,* Chu's *Eat a Bowl of Tea,* and Sone's *Nisei Daughter* between 1973 and 1979. But it is Maxine Hong Kingston who is the most widely taught Asian American writer.

To render the hostility that Chin et al. feel for Kingston's writing comprehensible, we remember that CARP devoted itself to dismantling the two seemingly contradictory but pervasive myths about Asian Americans: either that they are temporary "sojourners" determined to remain unassimilable or that they represent a "model minority" within American culture, docile and eager to assimilate. For the members of CARP and in particular for Frank Chin, both of these myths represent a threat to Asian American culture because they represent a threat to Asian American masculinity. What bothers Chin et al. most about Charlie Chan is the fact that he walks with "the light dainty step of a woman," asexual at best, at worst feminized and emasculated. Seeing this emasculated Chinese man as the core stereotype of Asian Americans, Chin has described himself as a "Chinatown cowboy," thus asserting both the possibility of a Chinese American masculinity and rooting that masculinity in the history of the American West. A second strand to his argument has been the desire to distinguish Chinese Americans from Chinese, as a way of dissociating Chinese Americans from what he conceives to be the mainstream American view of Chinese culture as unmanly: "The Asian culture we are supposedly preserving is uniquely without masculinity; we are characterized as lacking daring, originality, aggressiveness, assertiveness, vitality, and a living art and culture."

The desire to focus on the importance of Asian American masculinity to American history, embodied by the image of the Chinese worker building the railroad and opening up the American West, is the guiding theme behind the long essay by Chin included in *The Big Aiiieeeee!,* "Come All Ye Asian American Writers of the Real and the Fake," in which Chin attacks Maxine Hong Kingston, Amy Tan, and David Henry Hwang for perpetuating the stereotype of the feminized Asian American male. Arguing that "it is an article of white liberal American faith today that Chinese men, at their best are effeminate closet queens like Charlie Chan and, at their worst, are homosexual menaces like Fu Manchu," Chin concludes that it is "no wonder that David Henry Hwang's derivative *M. Butterfly* won the Tony for best new play of 1988. The good Chinese man, at his best, is the fulfillment of white male homosexual fantasy, literally kissing white ass."

Chin has gone so far as to argue that the comparatively large number of Asian American women writers and their commercial success also pose a threat to Asian American manhood. These beliefs result in a misogynist current that runs through the selections chosen in *The Big Aiiieeeee!*. Elaine Kim has argued that "aside from Toshio Mori, few Asian American male writers have attempted multidimensional portrayals of Asian American women," whereas such Asian American women writers as Noriko Sawada, Emily Cachapero, Wakako Yamauchi, Eleanor Wong Telemaque, and Hisaye Yamamoto have "demonstrated a profound sympathy for an understanding of their men." Not surprisingly, these writers are appreciated by Chin and his coeditors because, as Kim suggests, their efforts "complement the efforts of male writers to correct distortions and omissions about Asian American men."

For Chin, however, Maxine Hong Kingston represents the enemy, a critically and commercially successful writer whose subject is the double disenfranchisement of Chinese American women, who are second-class citizens within both American culture and Chinese American culture. Kingston is like the sister who airs family problems in public, outside of the sanctity of the home. Both Chin and Kingston share the goal of combating the stereotypical views of Asian Americans established by mainstream American culture, but in Kingston's writing this is only part of the story: she also depicts the relegation of Chinese American women to second-class status within both American *and* Chinese American culture. In Kingston's writing, the claims of ethnicity and gender occasionally conflict, and she does not always assign the claims of ethnicity first priority. Her writing dramatizes the deleterious effects of both white American discrimination against Chinese Americans *and* of Chinese American misogyny and homophobia.

The Big Aiiieeeee!'s prejudices have rendered it more useful as a historical document than as a state-of-the-art collection of Asian American writing. In the realm of fiction, that distinction belongs to Jessica Hagedorn's collection *Charlie Chan Is Dead* (1993), which represents itself as "the first anthology of Asian American fiction by a commercial publisher" in the United States and includes selections from forty-eight writers, not only Chinese and Japanese but also Filipino, Korean, and Asian-Indian

American. Like both *Aiiieeeee!* collections, *Charlie Chan Is Dead* seeks to move beyond the stereotype of the model minority. "Charlie Chan is indeed dead, never to be revived," writes Elaine Kim in the preface to the anthology. "Gone for good his yellowface asexual bulk, his fortune-cookie English, his stereotypical Orientalist version of 'the [Confucian] Chinese family.'" As if in tacit rebuke of the *Aiiieeeee!* editors, Hagedorn's introduction proclaims finally:

> For many of us, what is personal is also political, and vice versa. We are asserting and continually exploring who we are as Asians, Asian Americans, and artists and citizens of what Salman Rushdie calls "a shrinking universe." The choice is more than whether to hyphenate or not. The choice is more than gender, race, or class. First generation, second, third, fourth. Uncle Tom or Charlie Chan. And the language(s) we speak are not necessarily the language(s) in which we dream.

These words point to the inadequacies of our current conceptions of what it means to be "Asian" or "Asian American"; they seem to call for a new universalism grounded in the recognition and articulation of difference. And they highlight an issue that seems very likely to become central to the study of emergent ethnic literature in the United States: the issue of language.

Of the writers discussed in this section of the *Cambridge History,* it is the Hispanic Americans who have most fully explored the creative possibilities of their bilingualism. Some of the central works of Chicano literature – for example, Tomás Rivera's *. . . y no se lo tragó la tierra* and Rolando Hinojosa's *Estampas del valle y otras obras* – were written in Spanish, and Hinojosa has continued to move freely between both Spanish and English in his fiction. It is therefore already impossible to write a history of emergent American literatures that focuses exclusively on English-language writings, and it is likely that the next major history of American literature will include even more texts written in languages other than English. Several of the essayists in King-Kok Cheung's anthology *An Interethnic Companion to Asian American Literature* (1997) feel bound to comment that their accounts are partial and incomplete because they are limited to texts written in English. This linguistic gap in the field of American studies is currently being addressed by scholarly efforts like the *Recovering the U.S. Hispanic Literary Heritage Project* and Harvard University's Longfellow Institute, which (according to its mission statement) "has set itself the task to identify, and to bring back as the subject of study, the multitudes of culturally fascinating, historically important, or aesthetically interesting texts that were written in languages other than English." These texts range "from works in indigenous Amerindian languages, Portuguese, Spanish, French,

Dutch, German, Yiddish, Russian, Chinese, and Japanese, to Arabic and French texts by African Americans." The *Longfellow Institute Anthology of Literature of the United States* will be the first in a series of volumes that will present these texts in bilingual editions or English translations.

Multilingualism seems likely to join, perhaps even to supplant, multiculturalism at the cutting edge of American literary study and force scholars to seek out *contemporary* emergent texts written in other languages, such as Pan Xiujuan's Chinese-language story, "Abortion" (1979), in which a group of sweatshop workers in San Francisco openly discusses the economic reasons to terminate a pregnancy; or the work of GUMIL *(Gunglo Dagiti Mannurat nga Ilokana iti Hawaii)*, the Association of Ilokano Writers in Hawaii, which chooses to cultivate writing in the Ilokano language of the Philippines. These writers examine the conflict between mainstream and margin that is the hallmark of emergent literature, but they write for the margin, with little regard for whether the mainstream is watching. Even if the recovery of earlier non-English U.S. ethnic texts does not encourage contemporary emergent writers to produce texts in languages other than English, it is still likely to have an effect on their future writings, since many of them supplement their childhood knowledge of ethnic traditions with knowledge gained from reading and research: how could a writer like Maxine Hong Kingston resist making use of a tradition of American Chinese-language sources if such a tradition suddenly became available?

Ethnic writing will play an increasingly visible role in the landscape of American fiction because critics, publishers, and readers have begun to realize that some of the most vital American writing is going on in texts written by ethnic American authors. The fields of Asian American and Hispanic American fiction in particular seem destined to become broader and more wide ranging. "Asian American literature" has typically meant "Chinese and Japanese American Literature" in practice, as embodied by the narrowed focus of *The Big Aiiieeeee!* anthology in comparison to its predecessor. In recent years, however, Filipino American writing has been given a boost by Hagedorn's work, and Korean American fiction has risen in prominence after the glowing reviews that greeted Chang-Rae Lee's first novel, *Native Speaker* (1995), which may turn out to do for Korean American fiction what Momaday's *House Made of Dawn* did for writing by Native Americans. South Asian American fiction has not yet coalesced as a distinct literary field: in its nascent stages, it has been dominated by Bharati Mukherjee, who lived in Canada from 1966 to 1980 before emigrating to the United States, and by two Canadian writers of South Asian descent, Rohinton Mistry and Michael Ondaatje. Given the increasing critical and commercial recognition accorded to ethnic writing in the late

1990s, it seems likely that the rubric of Asian American literature in the future will also include writings by Americans of Bangladeshi, Burmese, Cambodian, Indonesian, Laotian, Nepalese, Thai, and Vietnamese descent.

Writings by Chicano authors have dominated discussions of fiction by Hispanic Americans, in part because of the conscious attempts to found a Chicano literary canon described above, and in part because Chicano literary scholars have been prominent participants in the development of minority discourse theory. Though centered from the outset on the work of male authors, the Chicano canon is already shifting to include writings by Gloria Anzaldúa, Ana Castillo, Denise Chávez, Sandra Cisneros, and Cherríe Moraga. At the moment, Chicano fiction outstrips the fiction produced by writers of Puerto Rican American, Cuban American, and Dominican American descent both in sheer volume and in critical attention, but this situation is likely to change in the near future. Puerto Rican American literature still remains best known for "Nuyorican" poetry, though any incipient canon of Puerto Rican American fiction would have to be centered on Nuyorican prose: Piri Thomas's personal narrative *Down These Mean Streets* (1978) remains a classic of Hispanic American literature, whereas the most famous and most accomplished Nuyorican fiction writer is a woman, Nicholasa Mohr, whose stories and novel, *Nilda* (1986), dramatize the difficulty of growing up in situations of cultural hybridity. With the commercial success of Oscar Hijuelos's *The Mambo Kings Play Songs of Love* (1989) and the critical accord given to Cristina García, Cuban American fiction seems to be entering a new stage of development. The best known Dominican American writer is Julia Alvarez, whose novel *In the Time of the Butterflies* (1994) was a finalist for the National Book Critics' Circle Award. The commercial and critical success already achieved by these writers suggests an impending expansion of the field of non-Chicano Hispanic American literature, though Alvarez herself is wary of such a prediction: there is a danger, she has argued, that America as "a consumer culture" will simply "consume its latest ethnicity: literature and music and food. Then make a chain store out of it. . . . You know, disposable culture." Thus, she predicts that once again "the doors will close on people who are the wrong color, come from the wrong place. Those battles will still have to be fought."

5

❧

REFUSING TO GO STRAIGHT

NOTHER shift in the study of emergent American literatures that seems inevitable is a closer affiliation between the fields of ethnic literature and gay and lesbian literature, between minority discourse theory and queer theory. Understanding the ways in which the dynamics of emergence both change and do not change when the literature in question orients itself around sexuality rather than ethnicity is a conceptual task that is pressing in both of these fields.

Gay writing has, of course, been around since at least the time of Socrates and Sappho, but the idea of a self-constituted field called "gay and lesbian literature" did not exist before the era of gay liberation that began in 1969 and could not have existed before the latter part of the nineteenth century. The labels *gay, lesbian,* and *homosexual* take for granted a relatively recent idea: namely, the idea of sexual orientation, according to which same-sex erotic attraction, if present, constitutes an abiding and defining characteristic of personal identity. Indeed, it is thought that the term *homosexuality* did not exist before 1869, when it appeared in a pamphlet written by Karl Maria Kertbeny entitled "An Open Letter to the Prussian Minister of Justice." Classical Greek has no word for "homosexual" because ancient Greek culture understood sexuality as a matter of preference rather than orientation, liable to change from occasion to occasion – at least as far as men were concerned. Describing the sexual practices of ancient Greece in *The Use of Pleasure* (1985), Michel Foucault argues that "the notion of homosexuality is plainly inadequate as a means of referring to an experience, forms of valuation, and a system of categorization so different from ours. The Greeks did not see love for one's own sex and love for the other sex as opposites, as two exclusive choices, two radically different types of behavior." The idea of "homosexuality" is also inadequate to describe the sexual practices of many Native American cultures whose languages contain words that express sexual categories for which there are no equivalents in European cultures.

The course of scientific research into the nature of homosexuality was profoundly influenced by Richard von Krafft-Ebing's treatise *Psychopathia Sexualis* (1886), which depicted homosexuality as a pathological condition.

Krafft-Ebing devoted a hundred pages in the first edition of the treatise to a discussion of "antipathic sexual instinct"; he would adopt Kertbeny's term *homosexualität* in subsequent editions. Rejecting the contention that homosexuality was in any way "natural," he argued that the only "natural" sexuality was procreative, heterosexual sexuality. A prominent dissenter from Krafft-Ebing's position was Sigmund Freud, who wrote in his "Letter to an American Mother" (1935) that although "homosexuality is assuredly no advantage . . . it is nothing to be ashamed of, no vice, no degradation, it cannot be classified as an illness; we consider it to be a variation of the sexual function produced by a certain arrest in development. Many highly respectable individuals of ancient and modern times have been homosexuals, several of the greatest men among them." Freud never formulated a coherent, fully-developed theory of homosexuality and the fact that the homosexuals who came to him for treatment were suffering from mental illness led many of his followers to ignore his belief that "homosexual persons are not sick," a statement written in 1903 in a letter to the Viennese newspaper *Die Zeit.* "Homosexuals are essentially disagreeable people," wrote the psychoanalyst Edmund Bergler in *Homosexuality: Disease or Way of Life?* (1956), adding that "there are no healthy homosexuals."

By 1956, however, American attitudes toward homosexuality were beginning to change, in large part due to the furor created by the publication of Alfred Kinsey's *Sexual Behavior in the Human Male* (1948). Trained as an entomologist, Kinsey began his research into human sexuality inadvertently, when he supervised an interdepartmental course on marriage at Indiana University in 1938 and found himself serving as an unofficial counselor to students seeking advice for sexual problems. After consulting the prevailing scientific literature on human sexuality, Kinsey discovered that "in many of the published studies of sex there were obvious confusions of moral values, philosophic theory, and scientific fact." The notes that Kinsey kept on his students' problems soon proved to be more extensive than the case studies found in the sources that he had consulted in putting his course together, and they led him to conceive the project that resulted in *Sexual Behavior in the Human Male.* Although falling short of the planned one hundred thousand case histories, the study eventually drew upon in-depth interviews with more than twenty thousand individuals, interviews that lasted between ninety minutes and two hours and covered as many as five hundred questions.

Kinsey's results, disputed by most of his contemporaries, showed a far more widespread incidence of homosexuality than anyone had suspected. Thirty-seven percent of Kinsey's male subjects had at least one postadolescent homosexual experience leading to orgasm, with the rate climbing to

50 percent among men who remained unmarried until age 35; 12.5 percent of the men reported having periods of at least 3 years in which homosexual activity predominated, and 4 percent reported being exclusively homosexual throughout adulthood. Although Kinsey and his team were themselves initially skeptical about the results, Kinsey finally concluded that "persons with homosexual histories are to be found in every age group, in every social level, in every conceivable occupation, in cities and on farms, and in the most remote areas of the country." Moreover, the data disputed the fixity of sexual orientation that most medical theories about homosexuality took as an article of faith. Kinsey eventually developed what became known as the Kinsey Scale that ranked individuals from 0 to 6 according to proportions of homosexual experience, with individuals ranked 0 being "exclusively heterosexual with no homosexual experience" and those ranked 6 being "exclusively homosexual." The proportions among women, published in 1953 in *Sexual Behavior in the Human Female*, were lower but still statistically significant: by age 30, 25 percent of women interviewed had "recognized erotic responses to other females"; by the age of 45, 13 percent of women reported experiencing orgasm with another woman. Kinsey stressed that most of the lesbians interviewed led "normal" lives: they included "many assured individuals who were happy and successful in the homosexual adjustments, economically and socially well established in their communities and, in many instances, persons of considerable significance in the social organization."

Most behavioral scientists and psychiatrists dismissed Kinsey's study as methodologically flawed, often distorting Kinsey's numbers in the process. But the study provided crucial impetus for the formation of organizations devoted to the pursuit of equal rights for gays and lesbians, providing scientific evidence that they were not deviants and perverts but instead an oppressed American minority.

This is the plea made by Edward Sagarin in his landmark study *The Homosexual in America* (1951), published under the pseudonym Donald Webster Cory. Describing twenty-five years of experience as a homosexual, Sagarin refers to homosexuals as "the unrecognized minority," and he makes an analogy to the situation of other oppressed marginalized groups:

We are a minority, not only numerically, but also as a result of a caste-like status in society. . . . Our minority status is similar, in a variety of respects, to that of national, religious, and other ethnic groups: in the denial of civil liberties; in the legal, extra-legal and quasi-legal discrimination; in the assignment of an inferior social position; in the exclusion from the mainstreams of life and culture; in the development of a special language and literature and a set of moral tenets within our group.

The Homosexual in America documents the hostility, discrimination, and persecution that gay men faced, as well as the variety of homosexual lifestyles and the richness of emerging gay social institutions. Sagarin's book is a polemic addressed to the general reader, but in his final chapter, he addresses himself directly and "only" to the reader who is gay: "My story is yours, just as your story is mine, no matter how divergent our paths of life, no matter how sharp our disagreement on the specific aspects of life." Ultimately, the book is designed to foster gay culture's transition from a state of marginalization to a state of emergence: confident that "the combined efforts of many will surely effect a beneficial change," Sagarin concludes, "The future belongs to all who will have it. It is yours and mine, and it belongs to all worthy men of good will. I am confident that you, like so many others who are gay, will utilize the years ahead to good advantage, undismayed and undefeated, inspired by the knowledge that your temperament can make you a better person and this a better world."

The year 1951 was marked not only by the publication of *The Homosexual in America* but also by the formation of the Mattachine Society in Los Angeles by Harry Hay and Rudi Gernreich. Named after a society of court jesters in medieval Italy who presented veiled political satires, the society sought to promote social and political change in the face of persecution brought on by the McCarthyist linking of homosexuality to Communism. The previous year, a Senate subcommittee investigating "Employment of Homosexuals and Other Sex Perverts in Government" had concluded that homosexuals were "perverts" and that "the lack of emotional stability which is found in most sex perverts and the weakness of their moral fiber, makes them susceptible to the blandishments of the foreign espionage agent." The report claimed that "one homosexual can pollute a Government office," proposing therefore that all homosexuals be purged from government and disclosing that in the three preceding years, homosexuality had been used as the basis for turning down 1,700 applicants for government jobs, as well as for forcing the resignation or dismissal of 420 government workers and 4,380 members of the military.

Ironically, three of the founding members of the Mattachine Society – Hay, Bob Hull, and Chuck Rowland – had in fact been members of the Communist party, and they used its organizational structure as a model for their new society, creating a hierarchical system of cells that emphasized secrecy. The Mattachine Society described itself as "homophile," a term coined to stress loving relations rather than sexuality, and its aim was to educate other homosexuals about their status as an oppressed minority and to affirm the validity of a homosexual identity. In their founding statement of "Missions and Purposes," the society pledged to develop a highly ethical homosexual culture . . . paralleling the emerging cultures of our fellow-minorities – the Negro, Mexican, and Jewish Peoples. The Society believes homosexuals can lead well-adjusted, wholesome and socially productive lives, once ignorance, and prejudice, against them is successfully combatted [sic], and once homosexuals themselves feel they have a dignified and useful role to play in society.

The gay historian John D'Emilio has pointed out that although the Mattachine Society was "not the first homophile movement in the U.S.," its foundation "does mark the start of an *unbroken* history of homosexual and lesbian organizing that continues until this day."

The Mattachines gained national attention when one of their members, Dale Jennings, was arrested in 1952 for "lewd and dissolute" behavior after being bullied by an undercover police officer into inviting him home. Jennings's lawyer admitted that his client was indeed a homosexual but said that he was innocent of wrongdoing because he had not engaged in any actual sexual contact with the officer; simply being a homosexual, in other words, was not a crime. The jury deadlocked, leading to the dismissal of the case. The Mattachine Society's ad hoc Citizens' Committee to Outlaw Entrapment proclaimed the outcome of the trial "a great victory for the homosexual minority." The first issue of *ONE*, a magazine founded by several Mattachine members and edited by Jennings, appeared in January 1953; with a national circulation reaching two thousand in a matter of months, it helped to spread the word about the society. Later in the year, however, the Mattachine Society held its first convention, which resulted in a change of leadership, an anticommunist stance, and a new policy of accommodationism that would define Mattachine policy for over a decade. The policy of the new leadership was to argue that homosexuals and heterosexuals were alike in every way save for what they did in bed, and they stressed that gay sexuality was a private and relatively unimportant matter. Jennings and Rowland continued to work for *ONE*, publishing several withering attacks on the Mattachines, and although these attacks would cease once Jennings and Rowland left the magazine, *ONE*'s outlook would remain more radical than the society's, and it would eventually metamorphose into One, Inc., an organization that included both gay men and lesbians.

In 1955, Del Martin and Phyllis Lyon got together with three other lesbian couples in San Francisco to form the first lesbian political association. Named the Daughters of Bilitis (DOB) after an erotic poem by Pierre Louÿs entitled "Songs of Bilitis," the organization was founded as a social club – "a *safe* place, where we could meet other women and dance," according to Lyon – but it soon became an activist organization. Its statement of purpose described the DOB as "a women's organization for the purpose of promoting the integration of the homosexual into society"; a 1959 article from its monthly magazine, the *Ladder,* describes the prototypical Daughter of Bilitis as a "thoughtful, public spirited, responsible type" and described the DOB as "an organization for social, not anti-social, ends." The Mattachine Society, the DOB, and One, Inc. would remain the dominant forces in the homophile movement through the middle of the 1960s, but their frequent infighting and conflicts with one another prevented the movement from transcending its grassroots origins and becoming a truly national enterprise.

In addition to the publication of *The Homosexual in America* and the foundation of the Mattachine Society, the year 1951 also saw the publication of a short story by James Baldwin entitled "Outing," his first published story devoted to a homosexual theme. The story centers on a day spent together at a church picnic by two boys, one of whom begins to realize that he has sexual feelings for the other. The theme of an adolescent's awakening into gay sexuality is explored further in Baldwin's autobiographical first novel, *Go Tell It on the Mountain* (1953), though it is overshadowed by the novel's treatment of the roles played by family history and race relations in the formation of its protagonist's identity. By 1956, when his second novel, *Giovanni's Room,* appeared, Baldwin had published his first collection of nonfictional work, *Notes of a Native Son* (1955), which confirmed his literary reputation and established him as an important African American cultural commentator. Set in Paris, where Baldwin had moved in 1948 and would live on and off for the rest of his life, *Giovanni's Room* focuses on the love affair between two men, a white American named David and an Italian named Giovanni. The ambivalence that marked the story "Outing" reappears here in the form of David's guilty recollections, in which he blames himself for setting in motion the train of events leading to Giovanni's imminent execution for the accidental murder of a bar owner. In abandoning Giovanni, David shows himself to have internalized his culture's normative expectations of heterosexuality, refusing to face up to the validity of his private erotic feelings for other men. Attempting to live a lie by promising to marry his girlfriend, Hella, David cannot keep himself from seeking solace in a gay bar, where Hella discovers him and abandons him to a life of thwarted loneliness. The novel presents a gloomy picture of gay life, in which erotic relationships between men are doomed to be short and unsatisfactory, and homosexuality is portrayed as something akin to illness.

The lack of prominent black characters in *Giovanni's Room* and its overt treatment of homosexuality disappointed many of Baldwin's readers, though Baldwin was generally spared harsh public criticism, perhaps because of his position as a prominent African American writer. The reception of Baldwin's novel *Another Country* (1962) was another matter, however. A complex novel that explicitly links racial and sexual protest in an effort to show that homophobia is a form of bigotry as heinous as racism, *Another Country* is set in New York City and focuses on the interwoven lives of eight characters with diverse economic, regional, racial, and sexual backgrounds; its prescient multiculturalism suggests that this circle of characters should be read as a microcosm of contemporary American society. In the years between *Giovanni's Room* and *Another Country,* Baldwin had changed his ideas about homosexuality, no longer presenting homosexual panic as inevitable. In the later novel, homosexuality and heterosexuality exist as equally viable – and equally problematic – forms of romantic attachment. To be sure, contemporary life in *Another Country* is bleak and the novel's gay characters do suffer, but Baldwin suggests that this suffering can lead to self-knowledge and redemption. Although the novel became a best-seller, reviews of *Another Country* were generally negative, with favorable commentary almost exclusively reserved for its portrayal of racism. Baldwin would come under fire from writers of the Black Arts Movement, who deplored his analogy between racism and homophobia. In *Soul on Ice* (1968), Eldridge Cleaver would accuse Baldwin of "a shameful, fanatical fawning" love of whites that made him an unfit spokesperson for African Americans. Baldwin refused to capitulate to what he viewed as reverse racism, referring to himself as "an American writer" rather than a "black writer" and exploring gay themes in two subsequent novels, *Tell Me How Long the Train's Been Gone* (1968) and *Just Above My Head* (1979).

The year 1963 marked a watershed of sorts for gay and lesbian fiction because of two best-selling novels that featured gay and lesbian protagonists. Mary McCarthy's *The Group* was the year's second biggest seller for fiction and would sell over three million copies during the next fifteen years. Although it was written by a prominent heterosexual author and left the details of lesbian sexuality largely to the reader's imagination, the novel demonstrated that lesbianism could be an acceptable subject for mainstream fiction. Its central character, Lakey, a woman who dresses in violet suits and has an affair with a baroness, is a strong-minded romantic heroine who cannot be dismissed either by "the Group" of Vassar graduates to which she belongs or by McCarthy's readers. Lakey's career represents a glamorous rejection of the idea – dramatized by Radclyffe Hall's landmark lesbian novel *The Well of Loneliness* (1928) – that homosexuality is a form of perversion or sickness.

The same cannot be said of John Rechy's *City of Night* (1963), which reached number one on best-seller lists in New York and California, and number three nationally, despite savage reviews from publications like the

New York Times, the *New Republic,* and the *New Yorker.* The novel originated
in a letter intended for a friend in Evanston, Illinois, describing a stay in
New Orleans during Mardi Gras; Rechy rescued the unmailed letter from
the trash, reworked it into a story called "Mardi Gras," and sent it to the
Evergreen Review. Don Allen, one of the *Review*'s editors, wrote back, admiring
the story and asking whether it was part of a novel. "I had never intended to
write about the world I had first seen on Times Square," Rechy writes in the
introduction to a 1984 reprinting of the novel. "'Mardi Gras' for me
remained a letter. But thinking this might assure publication of the story, I
answered, oh, yes, indeed, it was part of a novel and 'close to half' finished."
The story appeared in the sixth issue of *Evergreen,* the first of several pieces
that appeared in the journal and attracted the notice of such writers as
Norman Mailer and James Baldwin. Allen helped Rechy to procure a contract for the novel from Grove Press, which appealed to Rechy because it was
"publishing the best of the modern authors – and battling literary censorship." (At the time that Rechy was writing *City of Night,* Grove was involved
in defending its edition of Henry Miller's *Tropic of Cancer* [1934], with its
scenes of graphic heterosexual sex, from obscenity charges.)

   At first, Rechy resisted the call of his novel, returning to what he called
his "streetworld," until a friend and patron urged him to return to El Paso
"where it had begun." Therefore, Rechy writes,

I returned to my mother's small house and wrote every day on a rented
Underwood typewriter. My mother kept the house quiet while I worked. After
dinner, I would translate into Spanish and read to her (she never learned English)
certain passages I considered appropriate. "You're writing a beautiful book, my
son," she told me.

Rechy's "beautiful book" presented a frank depiction of life as a hustler in
the gay underworlds of New York, Los Angeles, and New Orleans. Its first
chapter suggests a Freudian explanation for its unnamed Mexican American
narrator's homosexuality: a childhood marked by a "father's inexplicable
hatred" and a "mother's blind carnivorous love." The novel alternates
between two types of narrative: chapters labeled "City of Night" that detail
the unnamed Mexican American narrator's wanderings and vivid character
sketches that introduce us to the narrator's friends and customers. As soon
as we get to know one of these characters, a "City of Night" chapter moves
us away and forward. The effect of this alternation is to put the reader in the
position of the hustler, whose acquaintances are brief and whose life is
marked by rootlessness. The hustlers' lives are depicted as joyless and alienated, in part because they construct their identities around the idea that
they are not really queer if they engage in homosexual relations only for the

money. The novel's penultimate chapter, a portrait entitled "Jeremy: White Sheets" that introduces us to a character who offers the narrator true love and affection, ends with the narrator's compelling Jeremy to have sex with him to create distance rather than closeness: "The orgasms have made us strangers again. All the words between us are somehow lost, as if, at least for this moment, they have never been spoken." The narrator thinks to himself, "Yes, maybe you're right. Maybe I could love you. But I won't," and he returns to "the grinding streets."

Many of the themes of *City of Night* would resurface in Rechy's later writings. If the first novel depicts the lives of men who hustle at least in part in order to avoid coming to terms with their identities as homosexuals, Rechy's less pessimistic second novel, *Numbers* (1967), depicts an ex-hustler named Johnny Rio who now indulges in only casual sex but still finds himself constrained by a conventional view of masculinity, in which he must assert his manhood by dominating others: the "numbers" whom he seduces in Griffith Park must perform fellatio on him with no reciprocation. Unlike the earlier novel, however, *Numbers* suggests that the protagonist's inability to exist in a loving relationship arises from his particular view of masculinity rather than from his identity as a homosexual. The suffocating mother returns in *This Day's Death* (1969), which depicts the arrest of a Texas man during a vice raid in Griffith Park, a man whose life is defined by his role as the dutiful son of a dying mother. *The Sexual Outlaw: A Documentary* (1977) features a bifurcated narrative that alternates between realistic and often nearly pornographic passages describing the adventures of a hustler named Jim, and expository passages that ruminate upon society's negative constructions of homosexuality. Rechy's critique of heteronormative discourses in the meditative sections of the book is reinforced by the juxtaposition of erotic gay narrative centered on Jim, even as it depicts the ways in which homosexuality depends upon heterosexuality: gay culture as depicted in *The Sexual Outlaw* is a truly emergent culture, one that defines and structures itself through its antagonistic relationship to a dominant mainstream heterosexual culture. *The Sexual Outlaw* is Rechy's most overtly political book, and it is characteristic of the militant stance that began to characterize gay and lesbian culture in the aftermath of the Stonewall rebellion in 1969.

The Stonewall rebellion came on the heels of two years of increasing gay and lesbian activism. In 1967, a police campaign against Los Angeles gay bars sparked a demonstration on Sunset Boulevard that was the largest of the decade. In New York, student homophile leagues were founded at Columbia by Robert A. Martin and at New York University (NYU) by

Rita Mae Brown; the Columbia group became radicalized by the general campus unrest the following year and picketed a psychiatric seminar on homosexuality held on campus. Then, on the night of Friday, June 27, 1969, New York City police raided a gay bar called the Stonewall, the sixth such raid in three weeks. This time, however, the response was different. The novelist Edmund White described the scene in a letter to his friends Ann and Alfred Corn:

> Well, the big news here is Gay Power. It's the most extraordinary thing. It all began two weeks ago on a Friday night. The cops raided the Stonewall, that mighty Bastille which you know has remained impregnable for three years, so brazen and conspicuous that one could only surmise that the Mafia was paying off the pigs handsomely. . . . A mammoth paddy wagon, as big as a school bus, pulled up to the Wall and about ten cops raided the joint. The kids were all shooed into the street; soon other gay kids and straight spectators swelled the ranks to, I'd say, about a thousand people. . . . Someone shouted "Gay Power," others took up the cry – and then it dissolved into giggles. A few more prisoners – bartenders, hat-check boys – a few more cheers, someone starts singing "We Shall Overcome" and then they started camping on it. A drag queen is shoved into the wagon; she hits the cop over the head with her purse. The cop clubs her. Angry stirring in the crowd. The cops, used to the cringing and disorganization of gay crowds, snort off. But the crowd doesn't disperse . . .
>
> Some adorable butch hustler boy pulls up a *parking meter,* mind you, out of the pavement, and uses it as a battering ram (a few cops are still inside the Wall, locked in). . . . Finally the door is broken down and the kids, as though working to a prior plan, systematically dump refuse from waste cans into the Wall, squirting it with lighter fluid, and ignite it. Huge flashes of flame and billows of smoke.

With the aid of riot police and two fire engines, the crowd was eventually dispersed, but the demonstrations would continue through the weekend. On June 29, the Mattachine Action Committee issued a flier calling for organized resistance. The gay liberation movement was born.

For lesbian fiction writers in the years surrounding the Stonewall rebellion, liberation meant rejecting Radclyffe Hall's portrayal of lesbianism as a sickness. Many lesbian writers depicted what amount to lesbian utopias that provide an alternative to the pathologies generated within mainstream, patriarchal culture. For example, 1972 saw the publication by a commercial press of *Patience and Sarah* by Isabel Miller (pseudonym for Alma Routsong), which had been published privately three years earlier as *A Place for Us.* The novel imagines two nineteenth-century women who leave patriarchal culture behind to build a farm in upstate New York. The protagonist of Elana Nachman's *Riverfinger Woman* (1974) fantasizes about making a movie with her lover that will demystify lesbianism for heterosexuals, "so that people would see that lesbians are beautiful," that "there is nothing, nothing at all unnatural about them," that "they too can have weddings and be in the movies." Both novels epitomize the kind of communitarian feeling that marks the lesbian novel after Stonewall.

An exception to this rule is the novel that is still the most famous fictional treatment of lesbianism since *The Well of Loneliness,* Rita Mae Brown's *Rubyfruit Jungle* (1973), which makes use of both the picaresque and the bildungsroman to tell the story of Molly Bolt, a self-described "bastard" adopted by a German American family. Molly's name suggests both the rootless freedom of Twain's Huckleberry Finn and the ironic appropriation of a male world of building and construction. Molly's intelligence and ambition set her apart from the rest of her working-class family, whereas her lesbianism places her on the margins of American culture, kept at arm's length even by the radicals of the 1960s: "My bitterness was reflected in the news, full of stories about people my own age raging down the streets in protest," she tells us at the end of the novel. "But somehow I knew my rage wasn't their rage and they'd have run me out of their movement for being a lesbian anyway." The novel's title refers to one of Molly's sexual fantasies: "When I make love to a woman," she says late in the novel, "I think of their genitals as a ruby fruit jungle, [because] women are thick and rich and full of hidden treasures, and besides that, they taste good." Even when her bigoted mother disowns her and calls her "a stinking queer," Molly refuses to fall into the self-loathing that marks protagonists of earlier lesbian novels. Traveling to New York, Molly earns a degree in filmmaking from NYU, graduating *summa cum laude* as a result of the unfashionable but brilliant senior project that she chooses to present, "a twenty-minute documentary of one woman's life" – her mother's life, as it turns out. Molly's lesbianism becomes both a source of personal pride and the wellspring of her artistic vision. "I wish the world would let me just be myself," she tells us finally, "but I knew better on all counts. I wish I could make my films. That wish I can work for. One way or another I'll make those movies and I don't feel like having to fight until I'm fifty. But if it takes that long then watch out world because I am going to be the hottest fifty-year-old this side of the Mississippi." Molly's story thus embodies the Emersonian values of reliance and self-making, but it also serves as a parable of the transformation of marginalization into emergence.

Liberation is also a central theme in fictions about male homosexuality produced in the aftermath of the Stonewall rebellion. Some novelists, like Patricia Nell Warren and Armistead Maupin, take up the project embodied by Christopher Isherwood's *A Single Man* (1964), which depicted the life of a middle-aged, middle-class man, a life that in its very ordinariness implicitly attacked the idea that gay men were effeminate, deviant, and predatory.

Warren's novels *The Front Runner* (1974), *The Fancy Dancer* (1976), and *The Beauty Queen* (1978) seek to demystify homosexuality by presenting stories of self-discovery in a resolutely realistic and conventional narrative style. In its depiction of the relationship between a track coach and one of his athletes, *The Front Runner* challenges the idea that gay relationships are necessarily ephemeral and dominated by an obsession with sexual experience. The unhappiness of Warren's gay characters arises not from some inner sickness but from social persecution. Indeed, Tom Meeker, the gay Roman Catholic priest who is the protagonist of *The Fancy Dancer* comes to understand that the alienation and suffering that gay people endure gives them a special and valuable perspective: "In spite of the pressures on them, or maybe because of the pressures, gay people had found the ability to explore and express a richness of inner human experience that straight people had somehow missed. The Church would impoverish herself to the degree that She refused to tap this richness." Maupin's *Tales of the City* (1978), which was successful enough to generate six sequels and to be adapted for television, presents the intertwined homosexual and heterosexual lives of San Francisco's elite society in a way that demonstrates the existence of a shared culture with idiosyncrasies and foibles that make it a target for satire. Maupin treats homosexuality as simply one aspect of personality, and often it is not the most important or defining aspect.

Occasionally in Maupin's fiction, the quest for a meaningful relationship leads only to sex, an idea that links his work to the strain of post-Stonewall gay fiction that takes its cue from Rechy's *City of Night* and seeks literary liberation through the exploration of gay sexuality. Two prominent books that chronicle the promiscuity of life in the urban gay fast lane are Larry Kramer's *Faggots* and Andrew Holleran's *Dancer from the Dance,* both published in 1978. Narrating the attempts of a New York screenwriter named Fred Lemish to find a love relationship in the three days before his fortieth birthday, *Faggots* depicts a milieu of gay men who lead successful professional lives but whose personal lives are desperate and lonely. Many of the men whom Fred encounters during his weekend-long search are single, dreaming of an ideal lover, some are so traumatized by their homosexuality that they can manage only brief, anonymous encounters, followed by bouts of guilt and self-loathing; and those few in relationships are dissatisfied and generally unfaithful. "Of all the 2,639,857 faggots in the New York City area," Kramer writes, "2,639,857 think primarily with their cocks." The response to Kramer's novel within the gay community was largely negative: "Everyone hates it," wrote the novelist Felice Picano in his journal. "Not only because it's politically retrograde or repulsive (which it is), not only because it's slanderous, self-hating, homophobic (which it is), but also because it's poorly written, even after four years of writing and one of editing." Holleran's novel offers a similarly bleak view of the way in which promiscuity thwarts gay men's ability to have meaningful relationships, but it was celebrated by the gay press because its depiction of glamorous, self-destructive lives seemed to evoke both the lyricism of F. Scott Fitzgerald and the acerbic wit of Evelyn Waugh. Holleran's narrator describes the men who come to dance at the Twelfth Floor club as "the romantic creatures in the city. . . . If their days were spent in banks and office buildings, no matter: Their true lives began when they walked through this door – and were baptized into a deeper faith, as if brought to life by miraculous immersion. They lived only for the night." The novel is profoundly ambivalent about the lives it depicts, both drawn to and repulsed by the "doomed queens" who populate its pages. Several years later, the adjective *doomed* would take on a meaning that neither Holleran nor any of his peers could have imagined in 1978.

Stonewall might have initiated gay America's emergence from its cultural closet, but it took the AIDS epidemic to make *homosexual* a household word. In 1980, the U.S. medical community was puzzled by the unusually high number of men in their thirties and forties who had contracted what were thought to be rare diseases: Kaposi's sarcoma, a form of cancer generally only seen in elderly patients; toxoplasmosis, a brain disease transmitted by an animal parasite; and a form of pneumonia caused by *Pneumocystis carinii*. Two things linked most of these men together: their immune systems were malfunctioning and they were gay. Researchers believed that these illnesses were the result of a single syndrome, which they called "gay-related immune disorder" (GRID); it was referred to frequently as "the gay plague." Because it was perceived to be something that affected only homosexuals, the syndrome was all but ignored by the U.S. media; it would take the death in 1985 of Rock Hudson, a prominent actor whose homosexuality had been hidden from the general public, to alert the U.S. public to the severity of the problem. By then it had a new name, "acquired immune deficiency syndrome" (AIDS), and it was known to be caused by a virus dubbed the "human immunodeficiency virus" (HIV), which could infect any individual, regardless of his or her sexual orientation, because it was spread through the exchange of bodily fluids or through the use of infected needles. A year before Hudson's death, the truly catastrophic proportions of the epidemic had begun to emerge with the introduction of a blood test for HIV.

Promiscuous gay men were reluctant to change their lifestyles, many feeling that their identities as gay men were dependent on the free expression of their sexuality. An article in the *New York Native* in 1982 entitled,

"We Know Who We Are: Two Gay Men Declare War on Promiscuity,"
begins with the declaration that

Those of us who have lived a life of excessive promiscuity on the urban gay circuit
of bathhouses, backrooms, balconies, sex clubs, meat racks, and tearooms know
who we are. We could continue to deny overwhelming evidence that the present
health crisis is a direct result of the unprecedented promiscuity that has occurred
since Stonewall, but such denial is killing us. Denial will continue to kill us until
we begin the difficult task of changing the ways in which we have sex.

The pamphlet's authors, Richard Berkowitz and Michael Cullen, conclude
with a plea: "The 13 years since Stonewall have demonstrated tremendous
change. So must the next 13 years." The following year they published the
first safe-sex manual, "How to Have Sex in an Epidemic." The question of
whether to celebrate gay sexuality despite the AIDS epidemic remains a
charged one for male homosexual writers. Such AIDS novels as Paul
Monette's *Afterlife* (1990) and *Halfway Home* (1991) implicitly reject the
"excessive promiscuity" of novels like Rechy's *City of Night* and *Numbers* or
Holleran's *Dancer from the Dance* and *The Beauty of Men* (1996). According
to the novelist Edmund White, AIDS has produced "a new prudishness
about sex" among some gay novelists and critics, as if "gay erotic literature
is somehow *unworthy* of the gay community, which should now be ready to
produce its world-class geniuses of the stature of Tolstoy or Flaubert."
White, however, has argued that gay novelists have an obligation to write
about gay sexuality, not only because "every male thinks about sex once
every 30 seconds, a frequency seriously underrepresented in serious fiction," but also because sexuality – promiscuous sexuality – is so intimately
bound to a gay man's emotional life. In White's novel *The Farewell
Symphony* (1997), the narrator reflects that

the phrase "anonymous sex" might suggest unfeeling sex, devoid of emotion.
And yet, as I can attest, to hole up in a room at the baths with a body after having opened it up and wrung it dry, to lie, head propped on a guy's stomach just
where the tan line bisects it, smoke a cigarette and talk to him late into the
night and early into the morning about your childhood, his unhappiness in love,
your money worries, his plans for the future – well, nothing is more personal,
more emotional.

White is the most prominent of the writers who belonged to the gay
literary circle that called itself the Violet Quill, a group whose collective
career encapsulates the history of gay culture from Stonewall through the
AIDS epidemic. In addition to White, the Violet Quill consisted of
Andrew Holleran, Felice Picano, Michael Grumley, Robert Ferro,

Christopher Cox, and George Whitmore. In addition to seeing each other often at gay literary and social functions, the writers met several times during 1980–1 to read and critique one another's work. White remembers the impetus for the meetings coming from Ferro and Grumley, lovers who had met one another at the University of Iowa Writers' Workshop. Holleran had been a classmate of theirs, and the Violet Quill was an attempt to create a reading group that could provide the kind of practical and stylistic advice that straight writers and editors seemed unable to offer. The group fell apart after Ferro took exception to Whitmore's story "Getting Rid of Robert," which Ferro regarded as an attack on his relationship with Grumley (although the particulars of the story seem to have closer parallels to White's breakup with Cox).

In many respects, the lives of the group's members embody the dynamics of the era of gay liberation. White and Cox were both present at Stonewall. Picano's journal (excerpted in David Bergman's collection *The Violet Quill Reader*) offers a glimpse of the liberated lifestyles of New York and Fire Island, whereas Whitmore's autobiographical novel *The Confessions of Danny Slocum* (1980; revised edition, 1985) offers an account of the trials of gay sexuality. Ferro and Grumley's relationship lasted for twenty years; each eventually succumbed to AIDS, which has also claimed the lives of Whitmore and Cox. White, who is HIV positive, has transformed the tetralogy that was to have begun with the autobiographical novels *A Boy's Own Story* (1982) and *The Beautiful Room Is Empty* (1988) into a trilogy that concludes with *The Farewell Symphony* (1997). *The Beautiful Room* ended with an account of the Stonewall rebellion, which would have served as the midpoint in the story of gay liberation, "the most important event in our lives." Now, however, it serves as the close of the second act of a tragedy that chronicles, according to White, how gay men "were oppressed in one generation, liberated in the next, and wiped out in the next."

AIDS forced mainstream America to discuss homosexuality openly; it forced gay America to leave the relative safety of gay neighborhoods and gay bars to demonstrate and pursue political action. ACT UP, the political action group devoted to AIDS issues, adopted the slogan "Silence = Death." In "Out of the Closet, on to the Bookshelf," an essay written for the *New York Times Magazine* in 1991, White remembers returning to the United States the previous year from Paris to find that his "literary map had been erased," because so many distinguished gay writers had fallen victim to AIDS. "The paradox," he writes, is that AIDS, which destroyed so many of these distinguished writers, has also, as a phenomenon, made homosexuality a much more familiar part of the American landscape." Eleven years earlier, the same *New York Times* was loath to review works by gay writers and seemed to pan them whenever it did. In March 1980, Felice Picano wrote in his journal that "gay literature is still a hotly disputed subject – *The New York Times,* for example, doesn't seem to believe it exists," and he reflected on the fact Edmund White, whose first novel, *Forgetting Elena* (1973) had been "highly praised, extolled even in *The New York Times,*" had been "reviled in reviews since he came out [of the closet]." By 1991, gay literature had made its way onto the literary map. "The grotesque irony," writes White in "Out of the Closet,"

is that at the very moment so many writers are threatened with extinction gay literature is healthy and flourishing as never before. Perhaps the two contradictory things are connected, since the tragedy of AIDS has made gay men more reflective on the great questions of love, death, morality and identity, the very preoccupations that have always animated serious fiction and poetry. Or perhaps AIDS has simply made gay life more visible. As a result even straight readers are curious to read books about this emerging troubled world that throws into relief so many of the tensions of American culture.

White's prognostications were borne out by the following year's National Book Awards: Dorothy Allison's *Bastard Out of Carolina* was a finalist in the fiction competition, and Paul Monette's *Becoming a Man* won the award for nonfiction.

Despite its increased visibility, however, gay and lesbian literature remains the least assimilated and most oppositional of America's emergent literatures. Gays and lesbians are, after all, the only one of the groups discussed here whose rights are not fully protected; indeed, the practice of homosexuality is still a criminal offense in many areas of the United States. But the Stonewall rebellion marked a watershed moment in American culture, bringing an end to what Jill Johnston describes in her book *Lesbian Nation* (1973) as "that awful life of having to choose between being a criminal or going straight." As Johnston puts it, "We were going to legitimize ourselves as criminals." A quarter-century later, the project of gay emergence remains incomplete, and gay and lesbian literature retains that oppositional edge, remaining like Rita Mae Brown's Molly Bolt, unbowed and fiercely determined.

6

❦

BEYOND HYBRIDITY

AS THE INTRODUCTION to this volume makes clear, the task of the current *Cambridge History of American Literature* differs significantly from that of its predecessors. Rather than seeking to identify, consolidate, and canonize an American literary tradition, this history arises from a cultural moment marked not by consensus but "dissensus." Its task, therefore, is to "redraw the boundaries of the field" of American literary scholarship, opening up the canon to expansion and redefinition by acknowledging that literary history must be "a multivocal, multifaceted scholarly, critical, and pedagogic enterprise" driven by "the energies of heterogeneity." The recognition that the American literary tradition must necessarily be conceived as heterogeneous has dictated one of the ways in which this *Cambridge History* differs from previous efforts: namely, its inclusion of this section's comparative approach to emergent American literatures.

When the next multivolume literary history of the United States is written sometime during the next century, it will no doubt still need to include a section or set of sections on emergent literatures, because it seems unlikely that American culture will, in the intervening years, cease to marginalize nonwhites and nonheterosexuals. What we learn from Raymond Williams's analysis of cultural dynamics is that human culture has always been the product of conflict and has always depended for its coherence on the identification of certain peoples, ideas, and practices as Other. Whether we believe that this is an abiding and eternal feature of human culture or instead look forward to the day when human cultures will no longer achieve consensus through the demonization of difference, we must recognize that American culture thus far has given no sign that it is about to render Williams's model obsolete; moreover, if we have reason to be hopeful that marginalization on the basis of gender is a practice that will soon wither away, we have far less reason to hope that ethnicity, race, and sexuality will cease to be reasons for discrimination against individuals. After all, this section of the *Cambridge History of American Literature* is being completed in a year when the president of the United States felt compelled to close his State of the Union Address with a plea against racism and other forms of discrimination, observing that "we still see evidence of abiding bigotry and intolerance, in ugly words and awful violence, in burned churches and bombed buildings."

Emergent literatures challenge familiar ways of classifying and categorizing texts and people: they are arenas where new genres and identities, new sets of meanings and practices are negotiated, articulated, and tested. As a result, we might expect the next literary history of the United States to reflect both new relationships to the dominant mainstream and new configurations within the field of emergent American literature. Almost inevitably, the task of this literary history will be to move beyond the model of hybridity, to ask what happens when two or more emergent categories are located in a single identity or text. What happens when the model of hybridity represents an oversimplification of reality? To understand hybridity, we have had to make a transition from an understanding based on "either/or" to an understanding based on "both/and." Increasingly, however, to understand emergence in American culture, we must move beyond the duality implicit in the hybrid model of "both/and" to a model that captures the interplay of multiple hybrid states. Ethnicity, race, gender, sexuality, class – any one of these categories can be used as the starting point for the examination of hybrid identity. But what happens when we put all of these variables into play? That is the question that writers and critics of emergent literature are asking with ever-increasing urgency as the century comes to its end.

Historically, the concept of hybridity was a conceptual leap forward for emergent writers, critics, and theorists, opening up what Homi K. Bhabha has called "the Third Space of enunciation." Like much early post-structuralist literary criticism, emergent American literatures set themselves the task of identifying and deconstructing modes of binary thinking in which the two halves of an opposition are not created equal. For many emergent writers, this process meant understanding the ways in which they and those like them were portrayed as different, incomprehensible, inscrutable, uncivilized – in short, portrayed as "others" who could not be assimilated. Leslie Marmon Silko told an interviewer that "all writing from those considered Other by the powers of life and death has some similarities. But that includes gay people, immigrants, people who have maybe been insane. Maybe when you come back from having been insane, you're Other." Certainly, many emergent writers have depicted the experience of being "Other" as an experience akin to insanity: witness Silko's own Tayo, Momaday's Abel, Acosta's Brown Buffalo, Okada's Ichiro, Alexie's Indian Killer.

One response to this problem of binary thinking was simply to reverse the polarity of an oppressive opposition, rendering positive what the culture typically portrayed as negative, powerful what the cultural typically designated as weak. This strategy can be found in nineteenth-century domestic and sentimental novels like *Uncle Tom's Cabin,* in which gentleness, docility, and love of family – traits portrayed as characteristic of both women and blacks – prove to be sources of power because they make those who possess them better Christians. Similarly, a novel like Silko's *Ceremony* finds transformative strength in what it takes to be non-Western tribal traditions, shifting the balance of power away from individualism toward a holistic communitarianism, away from male aggression toward female nonviolence.

Another approach to the dismantling of binary oppositions is to deny the validity of a particular opposition. Frank Chin devotes his writing to refuting the idea that Asian Americans are necessarily the victims of an "identity crisis" in which they are forced to choose between two opposed and incompatible identities – the Asian and the American. Chin's stories and plays depict a Chinatown that is dying because it provides no models of "manhood" for its younger generation: Tam Lum, the protagonist of Chin's play *Chickencoop Chinaman,* says, "I'm a Chickencoop Chinaman. My punch won't crack an egg, but I'll never fall down." Chin's dramas of beset Asian American manhood look back to a more heroic era in which Chinese men were men: in an essay entitled "Confessions of a Chinatown Cowboy (1972)," he writes wistfully about Ben Fee, "a word-of-mouth legend, a bare-knuckled unmasked man, a Chinaman loner out of the old West, a character out of Chinese sword-slingers, a fighter," now "forgotten" in "his hometown, Chinatown San Francisco." Asserting that the cultural mythologies of China, with its "sword-slingers," and the United States, with its gunslinging loners, are fundamentally alike, Chin claims a place for Asian American men within the archetype of the American rugged individualist. In thus denying the opposition between American and Asian forms of masculinity, Chin moves away from the necessity to choose implicit in the idea of an "identity crisis" toward a conception of cultural hybridity in which the Asian and the American fuse into a seamless whole.

The problem again is that this account of identity is still a drastic oversimplification. For Chin, the only identities that matter are the "American" and the "Asian," and he vilifies those Asian Americans who try to assert the primacy of other categories such as gender or sexuality. Chin's aim is not to reconceptualize American identity but simply to reconfigure it, to enable it to accommodate his vision of Asian masculinity. Not only has Chin thus accepted the general premise of binary thinking, but he has also accepted some of the particular premises of the opposition he is seeking to refute, namely its misogyny and homophobia. It comes as no surprise, therefore, that Chin must necessarily attack the writings of Amy Tan, David Henry Hwang, and Maxine Hong Kingston, which refuse to give primacy to the vicissitudes of Asian American masculinity in their depictions of Asian American identity.

It should also come as no surprise that it is Kingston's and not Chin's work that has captured the imaginations of the vast majority of scholars and students of Asian American literature. Whereas Chin's work remains rooted in the vagaries of binary thinking, Kingston's work dramatizes the limitations of the available models of hybrid identity and seeks to move beyond hybridity to a more complex model of heterogeneous identity. The model of hybridity simply does not account for a character like the protagonist of Mukherjee's *Jasmine* (1989), who constantly reinvents herself in ways that defy binary thinking: from Jyoti, the Hindu girl from provincial India, she transforms herself into Jasmine, the wife of a progressive thinker who teaches her to shun traditional Hindu ways; into the widowed Jase, au pair to Duff and lover of Taylor, an urban academic from whom she learns about Americanization; and finally into Jane, the wife of a middle-aged banker in rural Iowa, whose child she is carrying as she continues her journey west at the end of the novel. Jasmine describes her own transformations as "genetic" and those of her adopted Vietnamese son Du as "hyphenated," by which she means that he has had more freedom to make life choices than does she.

Nor does the model of hybridity account for the complexities of a writer like John Rechy; indeed, it leads one critic to conclude that "Rechy's essay 'El Paso del Norte' certainly should be considered Chicano literature, but his novel *City of Night,* which is virtually devoid of ethnic content, probably should not." Rechy is a marginalized member of a marginalized group, but should we think of him as a gay man marginalized within the gay community by his ethnicity, or as a Chicano marginalized with the Chicano community by his sexuality? In different moments and in different texts, one of these two descriptions is probably more accurate than the other. To understand which is more accurate and why, in any given instance, we will probably have to turn to history, specifically to gay history and Chicano history and to the differences between them. In our efforts to move beyond hybridity and to find the common ground that can create the solidarity that leads to social change, we must be careful not to lose sight of salient differences between emergent groups, differences produced not by the theoretical dynamics of cultural emergence but rather by the practical turns and twists of history.

Feminists and queer theorists remind us that group identities – whether they arise from race, ethnicity, gender, sexuality, or class – are not additive when it comes to particular individuals. As Dana Takagi puts it, "Marginalization is not as much about the quantities of experience as it is about the qualities of experience." Nothing reveals to us these qualities of experience better than the literary text, nor can we fully appreciate the complexities of the literary texts produced by America's emergent traditions without reading them side by side, observing where they meet and where they part ways. Only when our literary experience encompasses the worlds of Abel, Molly Bolt, Brown Buffalo, Paul Monette, Naomi Nakane, Fleur Pillager, Richard Rubbio, Tayo, Wittman Ah Sing, and a host of others – only then will we truly understand the quality of the American experience, which is more contradictory and contains more multitudes than even Walt Whitman ever imagined.

Oscar Zeta Acosta was born in El Paso, Texas, in 1935 but moved with his family to Riverbank (now part of Modesto), California, at the age of five. After attending Oakdale Joint Union High School, Acosta turned down a music scholarship to the University of Southern California, instead enlisting in the United States Air Force (as a member of the Air Force Band), primarily so that he could continue to be involved with an Anglo woman whose parents disapproved of him. After their relationship ended a year later, Acosta sought solace in religion, converting from Catholicism to the Baptist faith and becoming a preacher. Shipped to Panama in part because of his overzealous attempts to convert other Catholic soldiers, Acosta became a minister at a leper colony and was honorably discharged from the air force in 1956. After a suicide attempt prompted by his loss of faith, Acosta met Betty Daves in a Modesto hospital and married her shortly thereafter. In 1965, the then-divorced Acosta began studying law at night at San Francisco Law School and became an attorney for the East Oakland Legal Aid Society. Two years later, he quit his law practice to wander around the Southwest in search of a vision; after being briefly jailed in Mexico, Acosta assumed a new identity – Buffalo Z. Brown – and became a political activist in Los Angeles and a leader of the Chicano Movement. In 1969, he met his second wife, Socorro Anguiniga. After unsuccessfully running for Los Angeles County sheriff (as an independent, on an anarchist platform) in 1970, Acosta befriended Hunter S. Thompson and accompanied him on the trip that would be preserved for posterity in Thompson's *Fear and Loathing in Las Vegas*. In June 1974, he disappeared in Mazatlán, Mexico and was never seen again.

Acosta's two best-known works are his novels, *The Autobiography of a Brown Buffalo* (1972) and *The Revolt of the Cockroach People* (1973). A selection of autobiographical essays, short fiction, and letters can be found in *Oscar "Zeta" Acosta: The Uncollected Works* (1996). "The concepts of integration, assimilation and acculturation describe historical relationships between Africans, Orientals and Europeans, persons all foreign to this land," Acosta writes in the 1969 essay "Racial Exclusion": "Despite the lack of organization or of truly national leaders, despite the inability to articulate his rage, the Mexican-American claims the Southwest by right of prior possession, by right of ancestry. . . . The Mexican will not perish for lack of dreams; for whatever the outcome, the young Chicano presently dreams of Zapata while reading his Che."

SHERMAN ALEXIE (SPOKANE–COEUR D'ALENE, 1966–)

Born of mixed Spokane–Coeur d'Alene heritage, Sherman Alexie grew up on the Spokane reservation on the Washington–Idaho border. After attending an all-white high school near the reservation, Alexie enrolled at Gonzaga University in Spokane and then Washington State University, where he began writing poetry that quickly appeared in a number of poetry journals. In 1992, the Hanging Loose Press published his first book, *The Business of Fancydancing,* a collection of poems and short stories that was reviewed on the front page of the *New York Times Book Review.* He has since published another collection of short stories, *The Lone Ranger and Tonto Fistfight in Heaven* (1993), and two novels, *Reservation Blues* (1995) and *Indian Killer* (1996). He has left the reservation and now lives with his family in Seattle. "I always knew I'd be leaving the reservation," Alexie told the *Boston Globe.* "I had the scout mentality. Some Indians should stay on the reservation, but I'm not one of them," though he qualifies that assertion by adding, "But it's home; that's where my people are." Inspired by writers like Leslie Marman Silko and Louise Erdrich, Alexie finds himself disgusted by mainstream stereotypes of contemporary Indian life – and by Native writers who pander to them. "There are plenty of Indian writers out there doing this Four-Directions-Corn-Pollen-Eagle-Feather crap, [but] we don't live that way. What we're dealing with on our reservation is uranium pollution, alcoholism, suicide. We're worried about a job, about eating, about political corruption – just like everybody else. Nobody has time to sit around and rub a crystal."

Alexie has recently turned his attention to filmmaking: his screenplay for the film *Smoke Signals* (1998) was based on several of the stories from *The Lone Ranger and Tonto Fistfight in Heaven,* and he is currently developing a film version of his novel *Indian Killer.* In the introduction to the published version of his shooting script for *Smoke Signals,* Alexie writes that "screenplays are more like poetry than like fiction" because they "rely on imagery to carry the narrative, rather than the other way around." He describes filmmaking as an integral part of his plans for the future: "I love movies more than I love books, and believe me, I love books more than I

love every human being, except the dozen or so people in my life who love
movies and books just as much as I do . . . I knew that no matter what else
happened during the making of *Smoke Signals,* I was going to make movies
for the rest of my life."

Born in 1939 to a Lebanese father who served as lieutenant governor of
New Mexico and a Laguna Pueblo mother, Paula Gunn Allen spent much
of her childhood at Laguna and, like her cousin Leslie Marmon Silko, is a
member of the tribe. She earned a doctoral degree in American studies
from the University of New Mexico in 1975, and taught at the
University of California, Berkeley, before becoming professor of English
at the University of California, Los Angeles. She has received a fellowship
from the National Endowment for the Arts (1978) and the Native
American Prize for Literature (1990). Allen first drew national attention
with her poetry, which she began writing during the 1960s under the
auspices of the poet Robert Creeley. She cites among her influences Percy
Bysshe Shelley, John Keats, Gertrude Stein, Allen Ginsberg, Audre
Lorde, Adrienne Rich, and Denise Levertov. She also credits N. Scott
Momaday's Pulitzer prize–winning novel, *House Made of Dawn* (1968),
with bringing her back to herself and making her realize that her experiences as a Native American woman could serve as a viable and valuable
subject for poetry and fiction. Allen's works include *Shadow Country*
(poems, 1982), *The Woman Who Owned the Shadows* (1983), *The Sacred
Hoop: Recovering the Feminine in Native American Indian Traditions* (criticism, 1986), *Wyrds* (poetry, 1987), *Skin and Bones: Poetry 1979–87*
(poetry, 1988), and *Spider Woman's Granddaughters* (editor, anthology,
1989). "I have a lot of voices in my work," Allen says. "I'm a poet and a
short-story writer and an essayist and a scholar because I have so many
different personae in me and not just one. I don't think anyone is just one
thing, but I really can't be because my father is very different from my
mother, who is very different from my grandmother, who is very different
from my grandfather. . . . Also, I was raised on Indian music, Arabic
music, Roman Catholic music, Mexican music – so those cadences are all
there inside me."

Julia Alvarez was born in the Dominican Republic in 1951 and immigrated with her family to the United States in 1960 when her father's

involvement with underground efforts to overthrow dictator Rafael Trujillo was discovered by Dominican authorities: "My parents brought me here when I was ten. Back then, you came here and the price for getting into this American dream was that you cut the cord. There was a part of me I was cut off from. It became a secret, hidden part of me that only got affirmed when I went home to my parents or went back to the island." She received a bachelor's degree from Middlebury College and a master's from Syracuse University. Alvarez's first novel, *How the Garcia Girls Lost Their Accents* (1991), describes the experiences of four sisters who belong to a family much like her own. It begins with a vignette about thirty-nine-year-old Yolanda's return to the Dominican Republic and moves backward in time to the days before the family began its exile. *In the Time of the Butterflies* (1994), which was a finalist for the National Book Critics' Circle Award, presents a fictionalized account of the three Mirabel sisters, Dominican political activists who were murdered in 1960 under orders from Trujillo, an event that helped to galvanize the insurrection that would lead to Trujillo's assassination the following year. Her third novel, *¡Yo!* (1996), continues the story of the García family, describing the family's outrage when Yolanda publishes a successful autobiographical novel. *¡Yo!* expands the earlier novels' use of multiple perspectives, presenting the voices of twenty-five people – sisters, relatives, a landlady, a therapist, old boyfriends – who knew Yolanda "when." Alvarez has taught at Phillips Andover Academy, the University of Vermont, George Washington University, and the University of Illinois. She is currently a professor of English at Middlebury. *Homecoming: New and Collected Poems* was published in 1996. "I am a Latina who writes, but not one who writes only for Latinos," Alvarez has said. "The bad part of being a 'Latina writer' is that people want to make me into a spokesperson. There is no spokesperson!" Alvarez exclaims. "There are many realities, different shades and classes. . . . And I have to believe that the best stuff will stay and will add to what it is to be an American and to be a human being."

RUDOLFO A. ANAYA (1937–)

Rudolfo A. Anaya was born in Pastura, New Mexico, and grew up in nearby Santa Rosa. His early experiences there would provide the backdrop for his first and still best-known novel, *Bless Me, Ultima* (1972), which was awarded the Quinto Sol prize. After the eighth grade, he moved with his parents to Albuquerque, where he attended Washington Junior High and graduated from Albuquerque High School in 1956. He received both a bachelor's and a master's degree in English literature from the University

of New Mexico; he served as director of counseling at the University of
Albuquerque and in 1974 joined the faculty of the University of New
Mexico, where he is now professor of English emeritus. After the success of
Ultima, Anaya wrote two novels in quick succession: *Heart of Aztlán*
(1976), which portrays the loss of traditional rural values that results when
a family is forced to move from the small town of Guadalupe to a *barrio* in
downtown Albuquerque, and *Tortuga* (1979), which returns to the world
of *Bless Me, Ultima* to tell the story of a young boy who is nicknamed
Tortuga ("Turtle") after he is paralyzed and placed in a body cast.
Subsequent works of fiction include *The Silence of the Llano: Short Stories*
(1982); *The Legend of La Llorona* (1984); *The Adventures of Juan Chicaspatas*
(1985); and *Lord of the Dawn: The Legend of Quetzalcoatl* (1987). *Albuquerque*
(1992) is the first in a projected quartet of novels; it was followed in 1995
by the mystery novel *Zia Summer.* Anaya is also the author of the travel
narrative *A Chicano in China* (1986) and two plays, *The Season of La Llorona*
(1987) and *Matachines* (1992); he is also editor of *Aztlán: Essays on the
Chicano Homeland* (1989). *The Anaya Reader,* a collection of fiction, plays,
poems, and essays, was published in 1995.

   "In the sixties, when I first began to work," Anaya has said, "I used
Anglo American writers as role models. But I really couldn't get my act
together until I left them behind. They had a lot to teach me and I don't
underestimate that – you're learning whether you're reading a comic book
or Hemingway or Shakespeare or Cervantes – but I couldn't tell my story
in their terms. And it wasn't until I said to myself, let me shift for myself,
let me go stand on my earth, coming out of my knowledge, and tell the
story then and there – that's where Ultima came in. She opened my eyes as
she opens Antonio's eyes at the beginning of the book, for the first time; so
I sat down to write the story *Bless Me, Ultima,* thinking in Spanish though
I wrote it in English. And it worked, because I was creating what to me
was a reflection of that real universe that I knew was there."

GLORIA ANZALDÚA (1942–)

Gloria Anzaldúa grew up in the borderlands near the Rio Grande in South
Texas, working as a child in the fields with her parents, who were ranchers
and sharecroppers. Describing herself as a "dyke" – or more particularly as
"a Chicano *tejana* lesbian-feminist poet and fiction writer" – Anzaldúa
found herself subjected to racism at school and sexism and homophobia at
home and in her community, gradually coming to feel more at home in the
lesbian feminist community, despite the fact that it was predominantly
white. In *Borderlands/La Frontera: The New Mestiza* (1987), she brings

together autobiographical fiction, essays, and poetry in order to explore what it means to live between cultures, to chart not only the "actual physical borderlands" of the United States–Mexico border, but also "the psychological borderlands, the sexual borderlands and the spiritual borderlands [that] are not particular to the Southwest." The anthology *This Bridge Called My Back: Writings by Radical Women of Color* (1981, 1983), which Anzaldúa co-edited with Cherríe Moraga, was awarded the Before Columbus Foundation American Book Award. Anzaldúa has also edited a collection of essays, poems, stories, and informal pieces by women of color entitled *Making Face, Making Soul/Haciendo Caras* (1990). She has taught at various universities, including San Francisco State University, Vermont College of Norwich University, and the University of Texas at Austin. "I want to take the attention away from the center and place it on the periphery and the margin," Anzaldúa has said in an interview. "Once that displacement happens, there is no center. One of the fears that a lot of academics have with multicultural education and with people like myself is that they will be replaced. But they are wrong. I'm not interested in *replacing* them but in *displacing* them – from the center."

JAMES BALDWIN (1924–1987)

Born on August 2, 1924, in New York City to a poor, unmarried twenty-year-old mother, James Baldwin described his childhood as "the usual bleak fantasy": his family was poor; he was abused by his stepfather and bullied by his peers because of his effeminate manner and diminutive size. At fourteen, alarmed by what he perceived as his own sexual depravity, Baldwin underwent a spiritual conversion and became for a while a Pentecostal minister who preached at evangelical churches in Harlem and environs. Baldwin left both Harlem and the church in 1942, moving downtown to Greenwich Village, and tried to write, selling his first short story, "Previous Condition" in 1947. Troubled by a growing awareness of his homosexual feelings, Baldwin fled to Paris with only forty dollars and no knowledge of French. He would live there on and off for the rest of his life.

In Paris, Baldwin completed his autobiographical first novel, *Go Tell It on the Mountain* (1953), and in 1955 published a collection of essays, reviews, and journalistic articles entitled *Notes of a Native Son*. His 1956 novel *Giovanni's Room* was an attempt to come to terms with his homosexuality through the vehicle of fiction, which set aside the interest in the problem of race that had marked his earlier writings. His novel *Another Country* (1962) combined the themes of race and sexuality, exploring the intertwined lives of several biracial and bisexual couples. The following year, Baldwin became a national celebrity and a major figure in the civil rights movement with the publication of *The Fire Next Time,* a remembrance of Baldwin's years as a preacher together with an account of the rise of the Black Muslims. The title comes from a warning to the white race: "God gave Noah the rainbow sign, no more water, the fire next time." Subsequent works included an unproduced screenplay for Alex Haley's *The Autobiography of Malcolm X,* which was published as *One Day, When I Was Lost* (1971), and an autobiographical essay, *No Name in the Street* (1972), which laments what Baldwin considered to be America's failure to heed the message that he and others (such as Martin Luther King, Jr. and Malcolm X) had sought to bring. In his final, autobiographically inflected novel, *Just Above My Head* (1979), Baldwin once again combined the problems of racism and homosexuality in telling the story of the difficult life and death of a gay African American gospel singer. Baldwin died of cancer in France in 1987. "Once I found myself on the other side of the ocean," Baldwin told an interviewer, "I could see where I came from very clearly, and I could see that I carried myself, which is my home, with me. You can never escape that. I am the grandson of a slave, and I am a writer. I must deal with both."

RITA MAE BROWN (1944–)

Rita Mae Brown likes to say that she had "illegitimate parents." Born to an unwed couple, Brown was adopted and raised by a poor family in York, Pennsylvania. In 1955, her family moved to Fort Lauderdale, Florida, where Brown attended pubic schools; in 1962, she attended the University of Florida but was expelled the following year for being a lesbian. After moving to Manhattan, she received a bachelor's degree from New York University (NYU) and studied at the New York School of Visual Arts; she received a doctorate from the Institute of Policy Studies in Washington, D.C. in 1973. Her early years form the basis for her semiautobiographical first novel *Rubyfruit Jungle* (1973). As a student at NYU, she was politically active in the emerging gay liberation movement, helping to found a homophile league at NYU in 1968; she also published two collections of feminist poetry, *The Hand That Cradles the Rock* (1971) and *Songs to a Handsome Woman* (1973). Brown's second novel, *In Her Day* (1976), drew on the same interest in the lives of working-class people, the psychological experiences of women, and the marginalization of lesbians and homosexuals that animated *Rubyfruit Jungle.* Her third novel, *Six of One* (1978), published with the aid of a fiction grant from the National Endowment for the Humanities, was more mainstream in its orientation, presenting the lives of the eccentric residents of a small town on the border of Pennsylvania and Maryland, a setting to which Brown would return in her novel *Bingo* (1988).

During the late 1970s, Brown began a well-publicized affair with tennis star Martina Navratilova; the two moved in together in 1979 but broke up two years later. Their relationship became the basis for the roman à clef *Sudden Death,* which uses the depiction of life on the women's tennis circuit to reexplore the themes of the feminist essays collected in *A Plain Brown Rapper* (1976). Brown's subsequent works include the more mainstream regionalist novels *Southern Discomfort* (1982) and *High Hearts* (1986); three mystery novels written "with" her cat, Sneaky Pie; *Starting from Scratch: A Different Kind of Writer's Manual* (1988); the lesbian-themed novel *Venus Envy* (1993); and *Dolley: A Novel of Dolley Madison in Love and War* (1994).

CARLOS BULOSAN (1911–1956)

Carlos Bulosan was born on November 2, 1911, in Mangusmana, Binalonan, Pangasinan in the Philippines, at a time when the Philippines had become a U.S. colony in the aftermath of the Filipino–American War (1898–1902). Bulosan emigrated to the United States in 1930, landing in Seattle, Washington, at the height of the Great Depression. Working in California in restaurants and on farms, Bulosan grew to know the life of the itinerant worker that was the lot of most Asians in America during the 1930s. He became involved in union organizing and served as the editor of a bimonthly workers' magazine called the *New Tide* in 1934, which put him in touch with progressive writers such as Louis Adamic, William Saroyan, William Carlos Williams, and Richard Wright.

Recovering from tuberculosis and kidney problems from 1936 to 1938, Bulosan steeped himself in the works of progressive and radical writers such as Theodore Dreiser, James Farrell, Mahatma Gandhi, Maxim Gorky, Nicolas Guillen, Lillian Hellman, Nazim Hikmet, Karl Marx, George Bernard Shaw, Agnes Smedley, Edgar Snow, John Steinbeck, Walt Whitman, and José Rizal, the so-called father of Filipino literature. While in the hospital, Bulosan began composing vignettes that depicted the suffering of the economically dependent and outcast; these satiric fables were collected in *The Laughter of My Father* (1944). His best-known work, the autobiographical novel *America Is in the Heart,* was published in 1946. A collection of essays, stories, and poems entitled *On Being Filipino: Selected Writings of Carlos Bulosan* was published in 1995. "The writer is also a citizen," wrote Bulosan in an essay entitled "The Writer as Worker," "and as a citizen he must safeguard his civil rights and liberties. Life is a collective work and also a social reality. Therefore the writer must participate with his fellow man in the struggle to protect, to brighten, to fulfill life. Otherwise he has no meaning – a nothing."

ANA CASTILLO (1953–)

Ana Hernandez Del Castillo was born in Chicago, which she has described affectionately as "a double-standard, double-crossing, hyphenated-American megametropolis. . . . If it doesn't make you sentimental, it makes you smart." Castillo published her first book of poetry, *Zero Makes Me Hungry,* in 1972, the year she graduated from Northeastern Illinois University. Her formally experimental first novel, *The Mixquiahuala Letters,* was published by the Bilingual Press in 1986; it consists of a series of letters written by a California Chicana poet named Teresa to her white friend Alicia, which evokes the two women's changing attitudes toward life, work, love, and their relationship to each another. Not only is the text full of narrative gaps (since only one side of the correspondence is presented), but it is also unresolvable at the level of plot, since it offers three different tables of contents – one for "the conformist," one for "the cynic," and one for "the quixotic" – each of which presents a different ordering of the letters and thus different outcomes for the story that the text tells.

Castillo dedicated *Letters* to "the master of the game, Julio Cortázar," and her second novel, *Sapogonia* (1990), makes extensive use of magical realism, presenting a mythic, politically troubled mestizo homeland, "a distinct place in the Americas where all mestizos reside, regardless of nationality, individual racial composition, or legal residential status." Her novel *So Far from God* (1993) is set in contemporary New Mexico and draws its inspiration from the telenovelas of Spanish-language television; its title refers to a remark made by the Mexican dictator Porfirio Díaz: "Poor Mexico. So far from God – and so near the United States!" Castillo has also published *Massacre of the Dreamers: Essays on Xicanisma* (1994) and a collection of short stories, *Loverboys* (1996). She has also edited the collection *Goddess of the Americas = La diosa de las Americas: Writings on the Virgin of Guadalupe* (1996). After spending a number of years in the western United States, Castillo moved back to Chicago in 1995. "I learned a lot about the world being from Chicago," she has written, "not the least being fearlessness of mean weather, but also: to speak Portuguese, to dance the samba and merengue, to eat Indian curry rice with my fingers, and to wrap a sari. At home, I spoke poor Mexicans' Spanish, but out in Chicagoland, I trained my ear to detect the nuances of Spanish used by people from Mayagüez to Matamoros."

DIANA CHANG (1934–)

Born in New York City to a Chinese father and a Eurasian mother, Diana Chang grew up in China, where her family lived until the end of World War II. She returned to New York to attend high school and majored in English at Barnard College, where she wrote poetry that was published in literary journals. After receiving a fellowship from the John Hay Whitney Foundation, Chang published *The Frontiers of Love* (1956), the first novel to be published by a American-born Chinese American. Although *The Frontiers of Love* focuses on the experiences of Eurasian characters, her subsequent novels – *A Woman of Thirty* (1959), *A Passion for Life* (1961), *The Only Game in Town* (1963), *Eye to Eye* (1974), and *A Perfect Love* (1978) – all feature Caucasian characters and are indebted primarily to European modernism and existentialism rather than Chinese cultural history. A poet and painter as well as a novelist, Chang taught creative writing at Barnard College until 1989. "All of us are Chinese some of the time," says the narrator of the short story "Falling Free," which Chang adapted into a radio play that was broadcast on National Public Radio; "Other times, I'm a Calvinist, familiar with dimity and yokes. My favorite summer dress is Danish, my gold ring Greek, my face cream French, my daydreams I can't place. For someone so unsure of who I am, from time to time I have such definite statements to make."

DENISE CHÁVEZ (1948–)

Denise Chávez lives and writes in the house where she was born in Las Cruces, New Mexico. "We'd spend summers in west Texas with my aunt," Chávez has said. "It was very hot, so we couldn't go out, but my aunt had an incredible library – fairy tales, science fiction, philosophy. My sister liked the Oz stories; I liked books of psychological torment." She received a bachelor's degree in drama from New Mexico State University and a master's degree in drama from Trinity University in Dallas, as well as a master's in creative writing from the University of New Mexico. Her first novel, *Face of an Angel* (1994), draws on her experiences waiting tables during graduate school to tell the story of Sovieda Dosamantes, a divorced and widowed waitress who compiles a frank and earthy waitress's handbook. On the dust jacket of the novel, Sandra Cisneros describes Chávez as a "chismosa par excellence – a gossip, a giver-away of secrets, a teller of tales our mama told us not to tell."

Chávez's collection of short stories, *The Last of the Menu Girls,* was published by the Arte Publico Press in 1986. A dramatist whose plays have been

produced at the Edinburgh Festival in Scotland and Joseph Papp's Festival
Latino de Nueva York, Chávez cites among her influences *Oedipus Rex,*
Restoration comedy, Chekhov, Brecht, Gabriel García Marquez, and *Gone
with the Wind,* as well as *Dialing for Dollars* and supermarket tabloids. She
feels particularly indebted to Rudolfo A. Anaya, who became her friend and
mentor: "When I first realized there was a writer, Rudolfo Anaya, who lived
in New Mexico, I couldn't believe it. The ground shook! A Chicano writer
who lives in New Mexico and has been published! All the books I had seen
by Chicano writers were family memoirs with bad art, or cookbooks."

FRANK CHIN (1940–)

"I was born in Berkeley, California, in 1940, far from Oakland's
Chinatown where my parents lived and worked," writes Frank Chin in an
autobiographical essay. "I was sent away to the Motherlode country where
I was raised through the War. Then back to Chinatowns Oakland and San
Francisco." In 1961, he received a fellowship from the University of Iowa
Writers' Workshop; he later worked as a television writer in Seattle. His
first play, *The Chickencoop Chinaman,* won the East West Players playwrit-
ing contest in 1971 and was produced by New York's American Place
Theatre the following year. Three years later, the American Place produced
his second play, *The Year of the Dragon,* which was dedicated to the memory
of Louis Chu and John Okada; the production was videotaped for PBS's
Theater in America series. The two plays were published together in a single
volume in 1981. Chin is the author of a volume of short stories entitled
The Chinaman Pacific & Frisco R.R. Co. (1988) and the novels *Donald Duk*
(1991) and *Gunga Din Highway* (1994). He also coedited the anthologies
Aiiieeeee! and *The Big Aiiieeeee!* In "Come All Ye Asian American Writers of
the Real and the Fake," the controversial essay that introduces *The Big
Aiiieeeee!,* Chin lambastes writers like David Henry Hwang, Maxine Hong
Kingston, and Amy Tan for "distorting" the Chinese mythological tradition and "playing up" to Western stereotypes of Chinese culture. "This is a
white racist country," Chin has said, "and the white racist writers get published and those who are willing to falsify Chinese culture get published
and those who are not have a more difficult time of it. . . . In the 50s I had
a novel kicking around that it was suggested by a publisher I turn into an
autobiography to make it more saleable. I said no." *Gunga Din Highway* is
Chin's attempt to make use of Chinese mythology in a way that is "real"
rather than "fake." Chin's collection *Bulletproof Buddhists and Other Essays*
was published in 1998.

LOUIS CHU (1915–1970)

Born in Toishan, China, on October 1, 1915, Louis Chu immigrated to the United States at the age of nine. He attended high school in New Jersey and earned a bachelor of arts degree from Upsala College and a master of arts degree from New York University, with further graduate work at the New School for Social Research. He went on to work for the New York City Department of Welfare and later became director of a social center. He served as executive secretary for the Soo Yuen Benevolent Association and hosted a radio program called *Chinese Festival.* His novel, *Eat a Bowl of Tea* (1961), was adapted for the screen by director Wayne Wang and released in 1988.

SANDRA CISNEROS (1954–)

Although she was born and raised in Chicago's Latino neighborhoods, Sandra Cisneros's childhood was marked by long visits to the home of her father's family in Mexico City. Because she was the only daughter in a family with six sons, Cisneros received special attention from her mother, who made sure that her daughter had a library card before she was even able to read. Cisneros began writing poetry in grade school and eventually earned a bachelor's degree in English from Loyola University of Chicago. She was a student at the University of Iowa Writers' Workshop, where she received a master of fine arts degree in 1978. Her master's thesis, a collection of poetry, would eventually be revised, expanded, and published as *My Wicked Wicked Ways* (1987). Although she began to write short stories and sketches while at Iowa, her first published volume was a collection of poems, *Bad Boys* (1980), which was published as part of a series of Chicano chapbooks. Her 1983 collection of fiction *The House on Mango Street* was originally published by a publishing house specializing in Latino and Latina literature, but when the book received an American Book Award from the Before Columbus Foundation and was adopted as part of Stanford University's new multicultural core curriculum, Cisneros came to the attention of mainstream publishing houses. Random House published a revised version of *Mango Street* in 1991, along with Cisneros's second collection, *Woman Hollering Creek and Other Stories.* A third book of poetry, *Loose Woman,* and a children's book, *Hairs = Pelitos,* were both published in 1994. Most of Cisneros's writings dramatize the experience of growing up as part of the Latino working class in Chicago and are largely autobiographical. According to Cisneros, "All fiction is nonfiction. Every piece of fiction is based on something that really happened."

MICHAEL DORRIS (1945–1997)

Michael Dorris was born in Louisville, Kentucky, the only child of Mary Besy Dorris and Jim Dorris, who was killed at the end of the Second World War. Part Modoc Indian, Dorris graduated *cum laude* from Georgetown University with a bachelor's degree in English and classics. Awarded a Woodrow Wilson fellowship and a Danforth graduate fellowship, Dorris entered Yale University in 1967 as a graduate student in the department of history of the theater, but switched programs the following year to pursue a master's of philosophy in anthropology, which he received in 1971. Dorris served as an assistant professor of anthropology in 1971–72, before joining the Dartmouth College faculty. There he served as founding chairman of the Native American Studies Department, a post he held until 1989, when he resigned in order to devote more time to writing.

While at Dartmouth, Dorris met Louise Erdrich, who had enrolled in the college in 1972 as a member of its first co-educational class, returning nine years later as a writer-in-residence. The two were married in 1981 and began a literary collaboration that resulted in the publication of the novels *Love Medicine* (1984) and *The Beet Queen* (1986) under Erdrich's name and *Yellow Raft on Blue Water* (1987) under Dorris's name. Dorris told an interviewer in 1987, "We tell other writers we collaborate, and they say 'Mmmmm' in a doubtful way. There's no actual name for it, I guess. But we both feel a part of all these books. We each write the book with our name on it. The initial idea comes from the person with his name on it. [Then,] once you write the first sentence, the first paragraph, the first chapter, you give it to the other one, and they go over it with a red pencil, crossing out, writing in new words, making exclamation points for something good or a star, if you're lucky, or NO in big letters. You get back this saved draft, and then the arguments begin." One of their friends, the novelist Martin Cruz Smith, described them as "a twin star system," adding, "I can't think of another pair of writers who work like that."

Three children resulted from Dorris and Erdrich's marriage, joining the three Native American children whom Dorris had adopted before his marriage to Erdrich. The eldest of these adopted children, Abel, suffered from fetal alcohol syndrome, and Dorris chronicled Abel's struggles in *The Broken Cord* (1989), which received the National Book Award for Nonfiction. In 1991, he and Erdrich jointly published *The Crown of Columbus,* a novel that imagines the arrival of Columbus through Native American eyes, and *Route Two,* a travel memoir. The year was marred by tragedy, however, when Abel was killed in a car accident. Dorris's other two adopted children, Jeffrey and Madeline, also struggled with problems related to fetal alcohol syndrome and eventually became estranged from Dorris and Erdrich; in 1995, the couple pressed charges for extortion against Jeffrey, after he sent them a threatening letter demanding money. The couple went into virtual hiding, moving first to Montana and then to Minneapolis, keeping their whereabouts as secret as possible. Jeffrey's first trial resulted in a hung jury, in the second, he was acquitted of the charges against Dorris, while the charges against Erdrich resulted in another hung jury.

Friends of the couple say that Dorris never fully recovered from the death of Abel and the experience of testifying against Jeffrey. Others say that the move to the Midwest left Dorris feeling cut off from the community he had established at Dartmouth. For whatever reasons, he became subject to bouts of depression, and his marriage to Erdrich foundered. The couple separated in 1996. Dorris took his own life in 1997, despondent over allegations of child abuse.

EDITH MAUD EATON (SUI SIN FAR) (1865–1914)
WINNIFRED EATON (ONOTO WATANNA) (1875–1954)

The Eaton sisters, Edith and Winnifred, were the first Asian American writers of fiction. They were the daughters of an English merchant named Edward Eaton and a Chinese woman named Grace Trefusius, who was abducted from home at the age of three or four and eventually adopted by an English missionary family in Shanghai. Because Edward Eaton's family disapproved of his marriage to a Chinese woman, he emigrated with his wife and six children from Macclesfield, England, to the United States in 1874. The family eventually settled permanently in Montreal, Canada, where Winnifred was born in 1875. Ultimately, the Eatons had sixteen children, two of whom died during childhood. Edith herself contracted rheumatic fever as a child; the disease weakened her constitution and eventually contributed to her early death at the age of forty-nine. She nevertheless pursued a career in journalism, publishing her first article, "A Trip in a Horse Car," in the Montreal magazine *Dominion Illustrated* in 1888. Eaton adopted the pseudonym Sui Sin Far (literally, "water fragrant flower"), when she began publishing short stories in the mid-1890s. Always an activist in her writings, Edith Eaton wrote short fiction and essays that dramatized the difficulties Asian Americans and Eurasians faced in a discriminatory society dominated by whites. In 1912, her stories were collected into a volume entitled *Mrs. Spring Fragrance.* Eaton died two years later in Montreal; her headstone in the Protestant Cemetery, erected by the Chinese community, is inscribed with the motto *"Yi bu wong hua"* – "The righteous one does not forget China."

Unlike her sister Edith, Winnifred chose to take advantage of the fact that Japanese were regarded with far more favor than were the Chinese by most late-nineteenth-century Americans. She adopted an ostensibly Japanese pseudonym, Onoto Watanna and let it be known that she had been born in Nagasaki to a Japanese noblewoman. Winnifred had a longer career than her sister: after publishing what is thought to be the first novel published by an Asian American, *Miss Nume of Japan* (1899), she would write a dozen more novels, a fictionalized autobiography entitled *Me,* and a biography of her sister Sara. Winnifred did not restrict herself to Asian or Asian American subjects, creating an Irish protagonist in *The Diary of Delia: Being a Veracious Chronicle of the Kitchen with Some Sidelights on the Parlour* (1907) and describing the adventures of an English painter on a ranch in Alberta in her final novel, *His Royal Nibs* (1925). In contrast to her sister Edith, Winnifred's goal was not to challenge the expectations of her readers but to write popular fiction, and her novels and autobiography both reflect and take advantage of popular stereotypes of Asians and women.

LOUISE ERDRICH (ANISHINABE, 1954–)

Louise Erdrich was born in Little Falls, Minnesota, in 1954 to an Anishinabe (Chippewa) mother and a father of German descent. Erdrich spent her childhood in Wahpeton, North Dakota, where her father and mother were teachers in an Indian school run by the Bureau of Indian Affairs. Her childhood was punctuated by frequent visits to her maternal grandparents on the Turtle Mountain Chippewa Reservation in North Dakota. At the age of eighteen, Erdrich won a scholarship to Dartmouth College, which had just created a new program in Native American studies. At Dartmouth, where she was a member of the first coeducational class, Erdrich published stories and poems in literary magazines and won prizes for her writing. She received her bachelor's degree in 1976 and then took on a series of different jobs – schoolteacher, waitress, short-order cook, flagger at a construction site – before earning a master of fine arts degree in creative writing at Johns Hopkins University in 1980. In 1981, she became writer-in-residence at Dartmouth and married Michael Dorris, a writer and anthropologist who was a professor of Native American studies at the university. Erdrich and Dorris collaborated on several writing projects, including *Yellow Raft on Blue Water* (1987), which was published under Dorris's name. Erdrich's first novel, *Love Medicine* (1984; revised edition, 1993), was named the best work of fiction by the National Book Critics' Circle. Together with its sequels *The Beet Queen* (1986), *Tracks* (1988), and *Bingo Palace* (1994), *Love Medicine* chronicles the intertwined lives of several Native American and European-immigrant families through three generations.

Though Erdrich says that she does not consider herself an "ethnic writer," her novels powerfully dramatize the hardships of reservation life and the struggles of Native Americans in the Northwest to maintain their cultural traditions while adapting to the demands of modern industrial American society. Built from vignettes told by different narrative voices, the novels blend humor, irony, and sadness in an attempt to undermine the stereotypical portrayals of Native Americans that have become a staple of American popular culture. Her other works include a volume of poetry, *Jacklight* (1984); the novel *The Crown of Columbus* (1991) and the travel book *Route Two* (1991), both written in collaboration with Dorris; a memoir entitled *The Blue Jay's Dance: A Birth Year* (1995); and the novel *Tales of Burning Love* (1996). Erdrich had separated from Dorris at the time of his suicide in early 1997.

CRISTINA GARCÍA (1958–)

Cristina García was born in Havana, Cuba, in 1958 but grew up in New York City. Growing up in largely Jewish neighborhoods with few other Latinos, García recalls feeling that her "Cubaness was very private. It didn't have much to do with the rest of my life. The worlds didn't overlap till I started writing." Indeed, she notes, "I read Kafka and *Madame Bovary* before I read García Marquez and Borges." She attended Barnard College and the School of Advanced International Studies at Johns Hopkins University. She decided to write fiction after working as a correspondent for *Time* magazine in San Francisco, Miami, and Los Angeles. Her first novel, *Dreaming in Cuban* (1992), which was nominated for the National Book Award, depicts the different ways in which three generations of women from a Cuban family react to the Cuban Revolution: from the pro-Castro grandmother who waits by the Cuban shore with her binoculars intent on "spot[ting] another Bay of Pigs invasion before it happened" to the Cuban American punk granddaughter, who mocks her mother's hatred for Castro. Her second novel, *The Agüero Sisters* (1997), describes the reunion in Miami of two Cuban sisters, estranged for thirty years after one of them flees for the United States in the wake of the revolution, both of whom are burdened by a family history marked by mystery and tragedy. Both novels display a fascination with what García describes as "the stories people told themselves to get by," with "what happens when memory and nostalgia and loss get all wrapped up together."

JESSICA HAGEDORN (1949–)

"When I think of my home now," writes Jessica Hagedorn, "I mean three places. The San Francisco Bay area really colored my work. New York is where I live. But Manila will always have a hold on me. What is the threshold of my dreams? I really don't think of myself as a citizen of one country, but as a citizen of the world." Hagedorn was born in the Philippines but emigrated to the United States in 1963, settling in San Francisco, where she graduated from high school in 1967. Knowing early in her life that she "always wanted to work in theatre – as a performer, a writer, a director," Hagedorn chose not to attend college, enrolling instead in the American Conservatory Theatre's training program. Her first poems were published in 1972 in *Four Young Women,* edited by Kenneth Rexroth. During the 1970s, however, Hagedorn's primary interest was rock 'n' roll (more precisely, a combination of rock and theater), and she put together a band called the West Coast Gangster Choir that performed in colleges and universities in northern California.

Moving to New York in 1978, Hagedorn established herself as a performance artist, working in a number of different media. In 1981, she transformed a song written for the Gangster Choir into the performance piece *Tenement Lover: no palm trees / in new york city,* which was directed by Thulani Davis and later published in revised form in *Between Worlds: Contemporary Asian-American Plays* (1990), edited by Misha Berson. She is the author of two novels, *Dogeaters* (1990) and *The Gangster of Love* (1996), and the editor of an anthology of Asian American writing entitled *Charlie Chan Is Dead* (1993).

OSCAR HIJUELOS (1951–)

Oscar Hijuelos was born on the Upper West Side of New York in 1951, the son of Cuban immigrants. His father, Pascual, had been a country gentleman with a small inheritance, but in the United States, he worked as a hotel dishwasher and cook; he died when Hijuelos was seventeen. Hijuelos's mother, Magdelena, was a housewife who wrote poetry in secret. Hijuelos published his first story at the age of eight in a Catholic magazine for children: "It was a short story that, in many ways, laid out all my themes very early in life," he says. "It was about a scientist who goes to the moon, convinced that it's made of cheese. Once there, he picks up a piece of the moon and bites into it – and it turns out to be rock." He was forced to learn to speak English while hospitalized for two years as a child for kidney disease; a similar episode appears in his autobiographical first novel, *Our House in the Last World* (1983), where a young boy is locked in a closet by a nurse who refuses to let him out until he says "Open the door" in English. When Hijuelos finally returned home, he was no longer fluent in Spanish, his parents' primary language.

Hijuelos claims to have found his vocation when a girlfriend gave him a short story by Donald Barthelme to read. After transferring from the community college he was attending to New York's City College, Hijuelos sought out Barthelme (who was teaching there) and was accepted into the creative writing program. Barthelme and Susan Sontag became his mentors. Pursuing his writing while working in advertising after his graduation from college, Hijuelos began writing the stories and sketches that would become his first novel during the late 1970s; the positive reception accorded to *Our House* when it was published in 1983 enabled Hijuelos to win a fellowship from the National Endowment for the Arts and the American Academy of Arts and Letters Rome Prize. His second novel, *The Mambo Kings Play Songs of Love* (1989) told the story of two brothers, Cesar and Nestor Castillo, recent Cuban immigrants to New York who become fixtures of the city's Latino music scene, hoping to make it big. Bawdy and masculine in its narrative style, *Mambo Kings* won the Pulitzer prize for fiction and was nominated for the National Book Award and the National Book Critics' Circle Award. Subsequent novels include *The Fourteen Sisters of Emilio Montez O'Brien* (1993), Hijuelos's attempt to "imagine the feminine side" after the aggressive masculinity of *Mambo Kings,* and *Mr. Ives' Christmas* (1995), which recounts one man's attempt to come to terms with the senseless murder of his son by another teenager.

ROLANDO HINOJOSA (1929–)

Rolando Hinojosa is a true child of the borderlands, born the son of a Mexican American father and an Anglo American mother in the southern Rio Grande valley of Texas. His father's family traces its roots in the area to the 1740s. Hinojosa served in the Korean War and then received a doctorate in Spanish literature. After serving as chairman of Chicano studies at the University of Minnesota, Hinojosa switched disciplines in the early 1980s and joined the University of Texas at Austin as professor of English. Hinojosa's books tell the story of the fictional south Texas county of Belkin with the aim of keeping alive the unique cultural forms of the Texas–Mexico borderlands. In Hinojosa's novels, as in the novels of William Faulkner, history is revealed through communal stories and oral traditions, and Hinojosa constantly experiments with form, writing in both Spanish and English (sometimes within a single text), relying heavily on interpolated newspaper accounts and legal documents designed to reveal the unreliability of the written word. Works in the Belken County series include: *Estampas del valle y otras obras* [*Sketches of the Valley and Other Works*] (1973); *Klail City y sus alrededores* (1976; published in the United States as *Generaciones y semblanzas* [*Generations and Biographies*], 1977); *Korean Love Songs* (poetry, 1978); *Mi querido Rafa* (*Dear Rafe,* 1981); *Rites and Witnesses* (1982); *Partners in Crime* (1985); *Claros varones de Belken/Fair Gentlemen of Belken County* (1986); and *Becky and Her Friends* (1990). *The Roland Hinojosa Reader: Essays Historical and Critical* was published in 1984.

LINDA HOGAN (CHICKASAW, 1947–)

Born in Colorado in 1947, Hogan has lived most of her life in Colorado and Oklahoma, which provide the primary settings for her fiction, poetry, and essays. A member of the Chickasaw tribe, Hogan received a master of arts degree in creative writing in 1978 from the University of Colorado and now teaches at the University of Colorado–Boulder. She is the recipient of many awards, including a 1986 National Education Association grant for fiction, and a Guggenheim Fellowship (1991–93). Hogan relates that even as a child, she was aware that the history of her people was missing from textbooks, and much of her writing is devoted to remembering and preserving that history. Hogan describes her first book of poetry, *Calling Myself Home* (1978), as an attempt to meditate upon the "dissonance" between her own background and mainstream U.S. culture. Her novel *Mean Spirit* (1990) is a mixture of history and fiction that chronicles the destruction of Indian culture in Oklahoma after the oil boom of the 1920s. She credits the writers Meridel LeSueur and Tillie Olsen, among others, with helping to understand how to weave together her creative impulses and her politics. Her other works include the novels *Solar Storms* (1995) and *Power* (1998) and several volumes of poetry: *Daughters, I Love You* (1981), *Eclipse* (1983), and *Seeing Through the Sun* (1985).

ANDREW HOLLERAN (1943–)

Andrew Holleran attended Harvard University, served in West Germany with the U.S. Army, and briefly attended law school, which he abandoned in favor of the University of Iowa Writers' Workshop. There he met Robert Ferro, who would become a lifelong friend and fellow member of the Violet Quill literary circle. His novel *Dancer from the Dance* (1978) was lauded by both the gay and the mainstream press when it was published and was one of the first breakthrough gay novels. Its self-consciously beautiful rhetorical style recalls the prose of F. Scott Fitzgerald's *The Great Gatsby* and *Tender Is the Night* and Evelyn Waugh's *Brideshead Revisited.* Indeed, the first chapter of *Dancer* is full of allusions to those novels, and the relationship between the novel's narrator and its doomed protagonist, Malone, is clearly patterned on Fitzgerald's portrayal of the relationship between Jay Gatsby and Nick Carraway. Moreover, like Fitzgerald in *Tender Is the Night,* Holleran takes his title from a work of romantic lyric poetry, in this case Yeats's "Among School Children." *Dancer from the Dance* chronicles life among the gay fast crowd in the years before the AIDS epidemic; in the preface to the second edition of the novel, Holleran writes that *Dancer* has become "a period novel," adding that "nothing in this novel . . . prepares us for what happened afterward in reality – that reality which far outstripped anything a poet could dream unless it is Edgar Allan Poe. . . . This book is sort of a time-capsule, composed in a prelapsarian state." Holleran's subsequent works include the novels *Nights in Aruba* (1983) and *The Beauty of Men* (1996), as well as *Ground Zero* (1988), a collection of essays on the AIDS epidemic. "Someday writing about this plague may be read with pleasure, by people for whom it is a distant catastrophe," Holleran predicts at the end of the first essay in *Ground Zero,* "but I suspect the best writing will be nothing more, nor less, than a lament: 'We are as wanton flies to the gods; they kill us for their sport.' The only other possible enduring thing would be a simple list of names – of those who behaved well, and those who behaved badly, during a trying time."

DAVID HENRY HWANG (1957–)

David Henry Hwang was born in Los Angeles in 1957. "When I was very young," he writes, "twelve or thirteen, I thought my grandmother was dying, and I decided to get her family stories down on paper. I'd sit with her and do these oral histories, and then I wrote a twelve-year-old's equivalent of a novel. It was distributed to all the members of my family and highly praised, and that was it." As a student at Stanford University, Hwang discovered that he was far more interested in drama than in prose fiction and in 1978, during the summer after his sophomore year, he had the opportunity to study playwriting with Sam Shepard and a number of other playwrights at the Padua Hills Playwrights Festival.

Hwang's first play, *FOB (Fresh Off the Boat),* a comedy about a young Chinese immigrant's attempts to adapt himself to Los Angeles culture, was produced during the Bay Area Playwrights Festival, where it was seen by Joseph Papp and given a full production at the 1979–80 New York Shakespeare Festival. *FOB* won an Obie award and became the first play in Hwang's self-proclaimed "Chinese-American" trilogy, which also includes the absurdist farce *Family Devotions* and *The Dance and the Railroad,* both written in 1981. In 1988, Hwang became the first Asian American dramatist to win a Tony award with *M. Butterfly,* a hit Broadway play based on the true story of a love affair between a French diplomat and his "mistress," a Chinese opera star who turns out to be a man in drag and a spy. Other works include *The House of Sleeping Beauties* (1983), the companion pieces *The Sound of the Voice* and *As the Crow Flies* (1986), *Rich Relations* (1986), and *Golden Child* (1996), as well as two librettos written for Philip Glass, *1000 Airplanes on the Roof* (1988) and *The Voyage* (1992).

ARTURO ISLAS (1938–1991)

Born in El Paso, Texas, Arturo Islas graduated from Stanford University in 1960 with a degree in literature, one of two nonwhite students in a graduating class of over a thousand. He received his doctorate from Stanford in 1970 and remained there as an English professor until the time of his death, producing the novels *The Rain God* (1984) and *Migrant Souls* (1990). A sickly child, Islas contracted polio, which left him with a permanent limp. In the early 1970s, after one of his favorite uncles was beaten to death, Islas began to write about his family; by 1974, he had completed a first draft of *The Rain God,* an autobiographical novel in which a literature teacher named Miguel Chico Angel reflects upon his family's life in the fictional town of Del Sapo, Texas. Elegiac and haunting, *The Rain God* would go unpublished for ten years. "His rejection letters read like a course in Anglo stereotypes of the Mexican American," wrote his friend and fellow critic Paul Skenazy: "There is not enough barrio life or violence in the novel; there is no reading public for the work of a Mexican American; the book lacks the voice of protest and political rage that should be part of any work from a so-called minority population." Finally, in 1984, the novel was published by the Alexandrian Press, a small firm in Palo Alto, and it received a warm critical reception. It was a finalist for the Bay Area Book Reviewer's Association Award for fiction and won the award for best work of fiction from the Border Regional Library Conference.

"We are *migrants,*" Islas had written in the letter that accompanied the manuscript of *The Rain God* from publisher to publisher, "proud of our heritage and proud of our contributions to North American life. Why does the establishment continue to ignore us?" *Migrant Souls* (1991), the second volume in a projected trilogy about the Angel clan, was marked by a more activist sensibility, laced with pointed observations about the perils of growing up Mexican in a *gringo* country. Published by a mainstream house and reviewed in the mainstream press, *Migrant Souls* was less well received than its predecessor. "One hopes this book signals a new commitment by U.S. publishing houses to the Mexican-American novel," wrote the reviewer for the *Nation,* adding, "If the third installment of the Islas trilogy fulfills the promise contained in the first, *Migrant Souls* will be seen as a small disappointment on a profound and long-overdue literary journey into the heart of Latino America." Islas, however, would not live to complete his Angel trilogy; his unfinished third novel, edited by Paul Skenazy and published posthumously as *La Mollie and the King of Tears,* turns to a fleetingly mentioned minor character from *Migrant Souls* – a jazz musician named Louie Mendoza – who delivers a vivid first-person monologue laced with allusions to old Hollywood films.

In the fall of 1985, Islas learned that his ex-lover, Jay Spears, was sick with AIDS. The two corresponded and became reconciled before Spears's death in December 1986. A little over a year later, Islas learned that he, too, was HIV positive. "I'm still learning how to write a novel," Islas told an interviewer shortly before his death. "I wish I had more time. . . . I got started real late and I'm not going to have time to complete."

MAXINE HONG KINGSTON (1940–)

Maxine Hong Kingston was born in Stockton, California, and was educated at the University of California, Berkeley, where she studied journalism and education. After her graduation, she married fellow student Earll Kingston and in 1965 began a career teaching high school English, first in California and then in Hawaii. She joined the faculty of the University of Hawaii in 1977, a year after the publication of her first book *The Woman Warrior: Memoirs of a Girlhood Among Ghosts* (1976), which was awarded the National Book Critics' Circle Award for nonfiction. In 1978, *Time* magazine named *The Woman Warrior* one of the ten best nonfiction books of the 1970s; its sequel, *China Men* (1980), won the National Book Award for nonfiction. Both books blend autobiography, cultural history, and mythology as they chart the lives of several generations of Kingston's family. Kingston's first novel, *Tripmaster Monkey: His Fake Book,* which was published in 1989, evokes the world of artists and social activists in the San Francisco Bay Area during the 1960s as it tells the story of a Chinese American beatnik (who bears a striking resemblance to one of Kingston's most outspoken critics, Frank Chin) and his attempt to create an authentic Chinese American drama. Kingston has received the *Mademoiselle* award (1977), a writing fellowship from the National Endowment for the Arts (1980), and a Guggenheim Fellowship (1981). Since 1990, Kingston has taught creative writing in the English Department at the University of

California, Berkeley. A stage version of *The Woman Warrior* was produced in Berkeley in 1994.

In an interview with Arturo Islas, Kingston said, "There is an expectation among readers and critics that I *should* represent the race. I don't like hearing non-Chinese people say to a Chinese person, 'Well, now I know about you because I have read Maxine Hong Kingston's books.' Each artist has a unique voice. Many readers don't understand that. The problem of how representative one is will only be solved when we have many more Chinese American writers. Then readers will see how diverse our people are. Black writers have already surmounted the problem."

JOY KOGAWA (1935–)

Joy Kogawa was born in Vancouver, British Columbia, to *Issei* parents. Her father worked as an Anglican clergyman. The family was evacuated to Slocan in 1942 and in 1945 moved to Coaldale, Alberta. Since then, Kogawa has lived in Calgary, Grand Forks, Moose Jaw, Ottawa, and Toronto. She has served as writer-in-residence at the University of Ottawa and worked as a writer for the Canadian prime minister's office. She is the author of five volumes of poetry: *The Splintered Moon* (1968), *A Choice of Dreams* (1974), *Jericho Road* (1977), *Six Poems* (1978), and *Woman in the Woods* (1985). Her first novel, *Obasan* (1982), tells the story of the evacuation and relocation of Naomi Nakane, a five-year-old Japanese Canadian girl and her family. A sequel, *Itsuka,* was published in 1992 and centers on Naomi's participation in the Canadian movement for redress. According to Kogawa, "minority groups, oppressed groups, women, all have parallel political realities. They're interchangeable somehow. Men within minority groups are oppressed, as women are in the mainstream. In fact, middle-class women, bourgeois women, are oppressors of minority men. So there is a kind of interchangeableness of the victim role." She adds that "one of the problems we have" in North America is competition to be the victim: "whether we're women or whoever we are of the various minority groups, we become competitors for center stage. That tends to nullify a lot of the change we could bring about if we could identify with and assist one another. . . . We do not promote real change until we see the ways in which we are the victimizers." Her third novel, *The Rain Ascends,* was published in Canada in 1995.

NICHOLASA MOHR (1938–)

The daughter of parents who immigrated to the United States from Puerto Rico during the Second World War, Nicholasa Mohr grew up in the Bronx and attended the Art Students League, the Brooklyn Museum Art School, and the Pratt Center for Contemporary Printmaking, eventually becoming a prominent graphic artist. Asked by her art agent to write about the experience of growing up Puerto Rican and female in the Bronx, Mohr began to write stories. Her first published work, the novel *Nilda* (1986), describes life in the Bronx as seen by a ten-year-old girl and is written in a simple style appropriate to a child's point of view. The novel was listed by the *New York Times* as one of its outstanding books of the year. Three of Mohr's later works – *Felita* (1979), *Going Home* (1986), and *All for the Better* (1993), a biography of Evelina Antonetty – are in fact intended for an adolescent audience, and the stories in *El Bronx Remembered* (1986) and *In Nueva York* (1988) all emphasize the everyday dilemmas faced by their central characters in order to counter the sensationalistic stereotypes of Puerto Ricans as criminals and gang members. Her collection *Rituals of Survival*: *A Woman's Portfolio* (1986) presents vignettes of six different adult Puerto Rican women who differ in age, class, sexual preference, and lifestyle; all of these women struggle to break out of the roles designated for them by their families and their communities because of their gender. Mohr cites among her favorite writers Raymond Carver, Denise Chávez, Tillie Olsen, Ishmael Reed, and Alice Walker.

N. SCOTT MOMADAY (KIOWA, 1934–)

N. Scott Momaday was born on February 27, 1934, in Lawton, Oklahoma, to Alfred M. Momaday, a traditional Kiowa artist, and Natachee Scott, whose paternal grandfather was Cherokee. In *The Names* (1976), Momaday records his memories of growing up near Rainy Mountain, Oklahoma, of moving during the Second World War to Hobbs, New Mexico, and of settling down eventually in Jemez Pueblo. He attended reservation, public, and parochial schools before enrolling at the University of New Mexico, where he received a bachelor's degree in political science. Momaday earned a doctorate in comparative literature from Stanford University in 1963, where he was strongly influenced by his teacher and friend Yvor Winters, writing his dissertation on the nineteenth-century anti-Transcendental poet Frederick Goddard Tuckerman. Momaday has taught at the University of California at Santa Barbara and at Berkeley, at Stanford University, and at the University of Arizona. His novel *House Made of Dawn* (1968) was awarded the Pulitzer prize in 1969. Other works include *The Way to Rainy Mountain* (1969), *The Ancient Child* (1990), and *In the Presence of the Sun*: *Stories and Poems, 1961–1991* (1992). In addition to traditional Kiowa stories and oral narratives, Momaday cites the Bible,

William Shakespeare, Herman Melville, Emily Dickinson, James Joyce, William Faulkner, and Isak Dinesen as the most significant of his many influences. Among many honors, Momaday has received an Academy of American Poets Prize (1962), a Guggenheim Fellowship (1966–7), and a grant from the National Institute of Arts and Letters (1970).

Words, Momaday has said, "are beautiful. Words are intrinsically powerful, and there is magic in that. Words come from nothing into being. They are created in the imagination and given life on the human voice. You know, we used to believe – and I'm talking now about all of us, regardless of our ethnic backgrounds – in the magic of words. The Anglo-Saxon who uttered spells over his fields so that the seeds would come out of the ground on the sheer strength of his voice knew a good deal about language, and he believed absolutely in the efficacy of language. That man's faith – and, may I say, wisdom – has been lost upon modern man, by and large. It survives in the poets of the world, I suppose, the singers. We do not know what we can do with words. But as long as there are those among us who try to find out, literature will be secure; literature will remain a thing worthy of our highest level of human being."

PAUL MONETTE (1945–1995)

Born in Lawrence, Massachusetts, Paul Monette was educated at Phillips Andover Academy and Yale University, receiving his bachelor of arts degree in 1967. His first volume of poetry, *The Carpenter at the Asylum,* was published in 1975. After coming out in his late twenties, Monette met Roger Horwitz, who would be his partner for the next twenty years. His first novel, *Taking Care of Mrs. Carroll* (1978) depicts a character inspired by Marlene Dietrich and recounts what Monette called "the camp and romanticism of the gay scene in the '60s and early '70s." In *The Gold Diggers* (1979) and *The Long Shot* (1981), Monette explores relationships between gay men and straight women; both novels, he claimed, "are about friendship and making a family that is not a blood family, but a chosen one."

After Horwitz died of AIDS in 1986, Monette wrote copiously about their years of battling the disease together in *Borrowed Time* (1988) and reflected upon his own battles to cope with the loss of a lover in *Love Alone* (1988). These memoirs made Monette one of the most visible AIDS activists of the late 1980s, and he would continue to explore the subject of AIDS in his novels *Afterlife* (1990) and *Halfway Home* (1991). Monette's autobiography, *Becoming a Man: Half a Life Story,* was awarded the National Book Award for nonfiction in 1992. He died of AIDS three years later. "Has anything ever been quite like this?" Monette asks in *Borrowed Time.* "Bad enough to be stricken in the middle of life, but then to fear your best and dearest will suffer exactly the same. Cancer and the heart don't sicken a man two ways like that. And it turns out all the certainties of health insurance and the job that waits are just a social contract, flimsy as the disappearing ink it's written in. I have oceans of unresolved rage at those who ran from us, but I also see that plague and panic are inseparable. And nothing compares."

CHERRÍE MORAGA (1952–)

"I am the very well-educated daughter of a woman who, by the standards in this country, would be considered largely illiterate," writes Cherríe Moraga in "La Güera." "My Mother was born in Santa Paula, Southern California, at a time when much of the central valley there was still farm land. Nearly thirty-five years later, in 1948, she was the only daughter of six to marry an anglo, my father." Moraga was born in Whitter, California, to Joseph Lawrence and Elvira Moraga. "Born with the features of my Chicano mother, but the skin of my Anglo father, I had it made." It took her years – and the admission of her lesbianism – to appreciate what it meant for her mother to be brown: "When I finally lifted the lid to my lesbianism, a profound connection with my mother reawakened in me. It wasn't until I acknowledged and confronted my own lesbianism in the flesh that my heartfelt identification with and empathy for my mother's oppression – due to being poor, uneducated, and Chicano – was realized. My lesbianism is the avenue through which I have learned the most about silence and oppression."

In 1981, Moraga coedited the groundbreaking anthology, *This Bridge Called My Back: Writings by Radical Women of Color* (with Gloria Anzaldúa). "I am a white girl gone brown to the blood color of my mother," she writes in one of the poems included in that anthology, "speaking for her through the unnamed part of the mouth/the wide-arched muzzle of brown women . . ." During the same year, Moraga helped to found the Kitchen Table: Women of Color Press, which was intended to publish the work of women writers – particularly women writers of color – who might otherwise be unable to get their work into print. Kitchen Table would publish the second edition of *Bridge* in 1983, which fell out of print when its original publisher, feminist Persephone Press based in Watertown, Massachusetts, went out of business. In 1983, Moraga also published her collection *Loving in the War Years: Lo Que Nunca Pasó Por Sus Labios,* as well as *Cuentos: Stories by Latinas,* which she coedited with Alma Gómez. In the preface to the second edition of *Bridge,*

Moraga argues that "the political writer . . . is the ultimate optimist, believing people are capable of change and using words as one way to try and penetrate the privatism of our lives. A privatism which keeps us back and away from each other, which renders us politically useless."

TOSHIO MORI (1910–1980)

Born in Oakland, California, Toshio Mori became a published author at the age of twenty-eight, when his story "The Brothers" appeared in *Coast* magazine, a San Francisco publication modeled on the *New Yorker.* Encouraged by William Saroyan, who took it upon himself to become Mori's literary mentor, Mori placed stories in a variety of publications, and a collection of stories entitled *Yokohama, California* was scheduled for publication by Caxton Printers in the spring of 1942. Publication was postponed because of the onset of the Second World War, and during the war, Mori was interned at the Topaz concentration camp, where he collaborated with other writers and artists on the camp magazine, *Trek. Yokohama, California* was eventually published in 1949, but Mori remained obscure until his fiction was rediscovered and reprinted in several anthologies during the 1970s. A second collection, *The Chauvinist and Other Stories,* appeared in 1978 with an introduction by Hisaye Yamamoto, and his novel *Woman from Hiroshima* appeared in 1980 and was given the Honor Award from the Women's International League for Peace and Freedom the following year.

BHARATI MUKHERJEE (1940–)

Bharati Mukherjee was born in Calcutta to an upper-middle-class Brahmin family. She attended a convent school run by Irish nuns in India and received further education in England and Switzerland. She moved to the United States in 1961 to attend the University of Iowa Writers' Workshop, where she received a master of fine arts degree in creative writing and doctorate in English and comparative literature. From 1966 to 1980, she lived in Canada with her husband, the Canadian writer Clark Blaise, but finally grew tired of the persistent racism, manifested in both verbal and physical abuse, that she encountered there. The couple emigrated to the United States in 1980. Her collection *The Middleman and Other Stories* (1988) won the National Book Critics' Circle Award. In addition to the short-story collection *Darkness* (1985), she is also the author of the novels *Wife* (1975), *The Tiger's Daughter* (1971), *Jasmine* (1989), *The Holder of the World* (1993), and *Leave It to Me* (1997), as well as two books of nonfiction, *Days and Nights in Calcutta* (1977) and *The Sorrow and the*

Terror: The Haunting Legacy of the Air India Tragedy (1987), both coauthored with Clark Blaise. She has received grants from the National Endowment for the Arts and the Guggenheim Foundation for fiction. She has taught creative writing at Columbia University, New York University, and Queens College and currently holds a distinguished professorship at the University of California, Berkeley.

FAE MYENNE NG (1956–)

Fae Myenne Ng was born in San Francisco and attended both the University of California at Berkeley and Columbia University. While growing up in San Francisco's Chinatown, she took note of her neighbors' practice of sending their relatives' bones back to China for burial. "I was very moved by this bone ritual when I was a child," Ng told an interviewer for the *Chicago Tribune* in 1993. According to Ng, the "old-timers" saw America as a place to work and China as home. "They came to this country to make a living and to bring it home and to raise their families, but in the end they couldn't do that. The working class . . . find themselves at the end of their lives in these SRO (single room occupancy) hotels with only their pennies. It was very important to make this journey back home after death. They talked about it. It was dreamed of. That moved me." Ng called her debut novel *Bone* to honor that tradition; its publication in 1993 was the culmination of ten years of work, a period during which she supported herself by working as a temp and as a waitress. She also received a fellowship from the National Endowment of the Arts.

In an essay that appeared in the *New Republic* shortly after the publication of *Bone*, Ng wrote, "It's that same old, same old story. We all have an immigrant ancestor, one who believed in America; one who, daring or duped, took sail. The Golden Venture emigrants have begun the American journey, suffering and sacrificing, searching for the richer, easier life. I know them; I could be one of their daughters. Like them, my father took the sacrificial role of being the first to venture. Now, at the end of his life, he calls it a bitter, no-luck life. I have always lived with his question, Was it worth it? As a child, I saw the bill-by-bill payback and I felt my own unpayable emotional debt. Obedience and Obligation: the Confucian curse." *Bone* represents an attempt to begin repaying this debt. Ng's parents do not read English, but, she says, "I've been able to tell them that the heart of the book celebrates the kind of hard work immigrants have put into this country as a way and an effort of setting up a foundation, a place for us to stand. I think that gives them comfort, because it helps them to understand that their labor and their sacrifices are appreciated."

JOHN OKADA (1923–1971)

Born in the Merchants Hotel in the Pioneer Square district of Seattle with the help of a Japanese midwife, John Okada attended the University of Washington, where he received a bachelor's degree in English. He later received a master's in English at Columbia University, where he met his wife, Dorothy. During World War II, he served as a sergeant in the U.S. Air Force. After the war, John and Dorothy were married and John attended the University of Washington again, earning a second bachelor's degree, this one in library science. Okada worked as an assistant in the Business Reference Department of the Seattle Public Library and later moved to Detroit for a better-paying job in the hope that he would have more time to work on his writing. He died unexpectedly of a heart attack in 1971.

After Okada's death, his widow offered his manuscripts, notes, and correspondence to the Japanese American Research Project at University of California, Los Angeles. They were uninterested. The editors of the anthology *Aiiieeeee!* had "rediscovered" Okada's novel *No-No Boy* (1957) the previous year and included an excerpt from the novel. By the time two of the editors, Frank Chin and Lawson Inada, finally met Okada's widow in Los Angeles, they were too late to reclaim the rest of his unpublished oeuvre. "John would have liked you," she told them. "You two are the first ones who ever came to see about his work," and she said that "the people I tried to contact about it never answered, so when I moved I burned it, because *I have him in my heart.*" Among the burned items was Okada's "other novel, about the *Issei,* which we both researched, and which was almost finished."

AMÉRICO PAREDES (1915–)

Américo Paredes was born in Brownsville on the Texas–Mexico border in 1915. In 1934, one of his early poems won first place in a state contest sponsored by Trinity College in San Antonio, and the following year he began publishing poetry in the San Antonio newspaper *La Prensa.* Paredes did his graduate work at the University of Texas at Austin. His doctoral thesis on the Mexican *corrido* was published in 1956 as *"With His Pistol in His Hand": A Border Ballad and Its Hero,* and it proved to be extremely influential for the first generation of Chicano writers. In 1989, Paredes was given the Charles Frankel Prize by the National Endowment for the Humanities in recognition of his "outstanding contributions to the public's understanding of the texts, themes, and ideas of the humanities." In 1994, the Arte Publico Press published Paredes's novel *George Washington Gomez,* a historical bildungsroman written during the Depression that anticipates Jose Antonio Villarreal's groundbreaking *Pocho* in its modernist evocation of the passing of the heroic era celebrated by the *corrido*. Paredes's later novel, *The Shadow* (1998), dramatizes a soldier's attempt to adjust to life in postrevolutionary Mexico. Other works include *The Hammon and the Bean and Other Stories* (1994); *Humanidad: Essays in Honor of George I. Sanchez* (1977); the folklore collection *Uncle Remus Con Chile* (1993); *Between Two Worlds* (1994), a collection of poetry; and *Folklore and Culture on the Texas-Mexican Border* (1995), a collection of essays first published between 1958 and 1987. Paredes is now professor emeritus of English at the University of Texas at Austin.

JOHN RECHY (1934–)

John Rechy was born in El Paso, Texas, the son of a Scottish father and a Mexican mother who had fled from Mexico during the purges conducted by Pancho Villa. Rechy began writing stories at the age of eight, started a novel about the French Revolution at thirteen, and wrote copiously throughout his teenage years. Rechy studied journalism at Texas Western College and the New School for Social Research in New York, and "read a lot, eclectically; my favorite writers," he wrote in the introduction to a reissue of his first novel, *City of Night* (1963), "included Euripides, Faulkner, Poe, Margaret Mitchell, Lorca, Melville, Jeffers, Hawthorne, Camus, Milton, Ben Ames Williams, Dickens, Emily Brontë, Nietzsche, Dostoyevsky, Chekhov, Donne, Gide, Henry Ballamann, Giraudoux, Pope, Djuna Barnes, Tennessee Williams, Proust, Joyce, Frank Yerby, Dos Passos, Thomas Wolfe, Capote, Mailer, James Jones, Henry James, Gertrude Stein, Beckett, Farrell, Nabokov, Kathleen Winsor, Swift." After serving in Germany in the U.S. Army, Rechy moved to New York with the intention of enrolling in Columbia University; instead, he discovered the "streetworld" of Times Square, beginning a period of hustling and drifting that would provide the raw material for *City of Night* and his subsequent novels *Numbers* (1967), *This Day's Death* (1969), and *Rushes* (1979), as well as for the nonfictional "documentary" *The Sexual Outlaw* (1977). Rechy continues to resist adopting the label of "gay writer," and his most recent novels – *Marilyn's Daughter* (1988), *The Miraculous Day of Amalia Gomez* (1991), and *Our Lady of Babylon* (1996) – feature protagonists who are heterosexual women.

TOMÁS RIVERA (1935–1984)

Tomás Rivera was born into a family of migrant farmworkers in the south Texas town of Crystal City. Each year the family would leave Crystal City in mid-April, looking for farm work as far north as Minnesota, returning to

Texas in early November. Rivera's childhood experiences as a farmworker would provide the raw material for his novel . . . *y no se lo tragó la tierra* (. . . *And the Earth Did Not Part*), published in 1971 and awarded the first Quinto Sol prize (a third edition, retranslated and published in 1991, was given the title . . . *And the Earth Did Not Devour Him*). Rivera's formal education began in Spanish-speaking schools, and he became fluent in English only when he was in the fifth grade. In 1954, Rivera entered junior college in Texas, and four years later he received his bachelor of science degree in English education from Southwest Texas State University. After teaching English and Spanish in various Texas high schools, Rivera returned to Southwest Texas State, where he received a master of education degree in 1964; he earned a doctorate in romance literatures in 1969 from the University of Oklahoma. The rest of his career was spent rising in the ranks of academia: after serving as associate professor of Spanish at Sam Houston State University, he became professor of Spanish and director of foreign languages at the University of Texas, San Antonio, in 1971, eventually rising to the rank of vice president for administration. In 1978, he assumed the position of executive vice president at the University of Texas, El Paso, moving a year later to the University of California, Riverside, where he served as chancellor until his death from a heart attack on May 16, 1984.

Despite his early renown as a fiction writer, Rivera gave priority to his role as an educator and was concerned throughout his career with advancing educational opportunities for minorities. In addition to *Tierra,* he published five short stories (two of which were episodes originally intended for the novel) and twenty-six poems, including an epic entitled "The Searchers." He is reputed to have been working on a second novel, *La casa grande del pueblo* (*The People's Mansion*) at the time of his death. *Tomás Rivera: The Complete Works* was published by the Arte Publico Press in 1992.

RICHARD RODRIGUEZ (1944–)

Richard Rodriguez was born into a family of Mexican immigrants living near San Francisco. Unable to speak English when he entered school, Rodriguez became an outstanding student, receiving a bachelor of arts degree from Stanford University, doing graduate work at Columbia University and the Warburg Institute in London (under the auspices of a Fulbright Fellowship), and completing his doctorate in Renaissance literature at the University of California, Berkeley. He received a fellowship from the National Endowment for the Humanities in 1976. Rodriguez discusses his educational career – and his reasons for abandoning the study of Renaissance literature – in the much anthologized essay "The Achievement of Desire," from his controversial autobiography, *Hunger of Memory: The Education of Richard Rodriguez* (1982). Rodriguez's career in journalism has included work as an associate editor with the Pacific News Service in San Francisco, as an essayist for the *MacNeil/Lehrer News Hour* on PBS, and as a contributing editor for *Harper's* magazine and for the opinion section of the *Los Angeles Times*. He is also the author of *Mexico's Children* (1991) and *Days of Obligation: An Argument with My Mexican Father* (1992), which was nominated for the Pulitzer prize in nonfiction.

In *Hunger of Memory,* Rodriguez argues that it is class, rather than race or ethnicity, that is the primary shaper of American identity; he leaves the issue of sexuality out altogether. In *Days of Obligation,* however, he includes an essay entitled "Late Victorians," a moving meditation on San Francisco's gay culture in the age of AIDS, that constitutes a literary coming out. "To grow up homosexual," he writes, "is to live with secrets and within secrets. In no other place are those secrets more closely guarded than within the family home. The grammar of the gay city borrows metaphors from the nineteenth-century house. 'Coming out of the closet' is predicated upon family laundry, dirty linens, skeletons. . . . I live in a tall Victorian house that has been converted to four apartments; four single men."

LESLIE MARMON SILKO (1948)

Leslie Marmon Silko was born on the Laguna Pueblo Reservation in 1948 in the same house in which her father was born. Her great-grandfather, Robert Gunn Marmon, was a trader who settled at Laguna Pueblo with his brother Walter; both men became important figures in the community, and Robert was even elected to a term as its governor. Hailing from mixed Laguna, Mexican, and Anglo ancestry, Silko was aware that her family nonetheless held a marginal place in the Laguna community. Silko became particularly attuned to the ways in which individual and communal identities are built through shared stories and traditions. She earned a bachelor of arts degree *magna cum laude* in English from the University of New Mexico in 1969 and attended law school there for several semesters with the intent of spending her life fighting the injustices perpetrated against Native American peoples. Silko's first published story, "The Man to Send Rain Clouds" (1969) was written for a creative writing class at the University of New Mexico that changed her life: it showed Silko that the writing she had pursued as an avocation could actually become the vocation through which she could dramatize and thus combat injustice. Her works include a volume of poetry, *Laguna Woman* (1974); *Storyteller* (1981), a collection of autobiographical poetry and prose; *With the Delicacy and Strength of Lace* (1985), a selection of her correspondence with the poet James Wright; and the novels *Ceremony* (1974) and *Almanac of the Dead* (1991). She was awarded a MacArthur Foundation fellowship in 1981 and has taught at Navajo Community College, Many Farms, Arizona; at the University of New Mexico; and at the University of Arizona. Paula Gunn Allen is a cousin.

SUI SIN FAR *(see Edith Maud Eaton)*

AMY TAN (1952–)

"As soon as my feet touched China, I became Chinese," says Amy Tan, who was born in Oakland, California, in 1952 and first visited China in 1987. Tan grew up in the San Francisco Bay Area before attending high school in Montreux, Switzerland. She holds a master's degree in linguistics from San Jose State University and worked as a consultant to programs for disabled children before turning to freelance writing. Her father emigrated to the United States in 1947, her mother two years later, shortly before Shanghai fell under Communist control. Her mother was forced to leave behind three daughters from a previous marriage, an episode that plays a central role in Tan's acclaimed first novel *The Joy Luck Club* (1989), which was a finalist for both the National Book Award and the National Book Critics' Circle Award and was made into a movie by director Wayne Wang in 1993.

Wartime hardship, the oppression of women by traditional Chinese culture, and the relationship between Chinese mothers and Chinese American daughters also lie at the heart of her second novel, *The Kitchen God's Wife*, whereas the relationship between sisters – one Chinese, one Chinese American – lies behind her third novel, *The Hundred Secret Senses* (1995). All three novels were national and international best-sellers; *The Joy Luck Club* has been translated in nineteen languages, including Chinese.

LUIS VALDEZ (1940–)

Born in Delano, California, on June 26, 1940, Luis Valdez was the second of ten children; because his parents were migrant farmworkers, his schooling was continually interrupted as his family followed the season crops. He nevertheless managed to excel in school and at an early age developed an interest in puppet shows, which he would create and stage for his friends and neighbors. His interest in theater bloomed while he was a student at San Jose State College, where his first full-length play, *The Shrunken Head of Pancho Villa*, was produced in 1964, the year of his graduation. The following year, after working with the San Francisco Mime Troupe, Valdez founded El Teatro

Campesino, a bilingual theater company that aimed "to teach and organize Chicano farm workers." Composed largely of striking farmworkers, with Valdez serving as its artistic director and resident playwright, El Teatro Campesino began by performing brief sketches called *actos* that dramatized the struggles of farmworkers. In 1967, Valdez decided to leave the farmworkers' union to concentrate on the theater and to free himself to explore Chicano themes beyond the struggles in the fields. During the same year, he composed his first *mito, Dark Root of a Scream,* a myth-play about Vietnam. In 1968, the Teatro received an Obie award for its work.

In 1971, the Teatro established itself as a resident company in the rural village of San Juan Batista, California, which has become its permanent home, and Valdez began to explore the idea of adapting traditional Mexican *corridos* for the stage, an experiment that eventually resulted in *La Carpa de los Rasquachis* (*The Tent of the Underdogs*), which was produced in 1973 at the Fourth Annual Chicano Theater Festival in San Jose, California. It would become one of the Teatro's signature pieces, performed on U.S. and European tours for several years. With *La Carpa de los Rasquachis* on tour, Valdez began an association with a major regional theater company, the Center Theater Group of Los Angeles, coproducing the play *Zoot Suit,* which opened during the summer of 1978. *Zoot Suit* brought together the forms with which Valdez had been working previously – the *acto,* the *mito,* and the *corrido* – to dramatize the events surrounding the Sleepy Lagoon Murder Trial of 1942 and the subsequent Zoot Suit Riots in Los Angeles. The play broke previous records for Los Angeles theater, playing to sold-out houses for nearly a year, and on March 25, 1979, it became the first Chicano play to open on Broadway. The success of *Zoot Suit* brought about another transformation of El Teatro Campesino, from a theater troupe with a full-time roster of actors to a producing company that contracted with actors and other professional talent for individual productions only.

Valdez adapted and directed *Zoot Suit* for the movies in 1981, signaling a further shift in his own career. Valdez would go on to direct the film *La Bamba,* which would become a major hit in the summer of 1987. Valdez has said that when he first "drove up to the studio gate, the guard . . . told me that the pastries were taken to a certain door. The only other Mexican he ever saw delivered the pastries." Valdez also adapted his show *Corridos* (1983) for PBS in 1987; the star of the production, which was renamed *Corridos: Tales of Passion and Revolution,* was Linda Ronstadt, with Valdez himself providing the narration.

"Chicano theatre," Valdez wrote in 1970, "is first a reaffirmation of LIFE. That is what all theatre is supposed to be, of course; but the limp, superficial, gringo seco productions in the 'professional' American theatre (and the college and university drama departments that serve it) are so antiseptic, they are antibiotic (anti-life). The characters and life situations emerging from our little teatros are too real, too full of sudor, sangre and body smells to be boxed in. Audience participation is no cute production trick with us; it is a pre-established, pre-assumed privilege." Valdez's genius has been his ability to develop as an artist – becoming a professional, working in regional theater, then on Broadway, and then in film and video – without losing sight of the antiestablishment edge that animated his early *actos*. In the early 1990s, he helped to form the Latino Writers Group, whose aim is to encourage Hollywood studios to produce more films written by Chicanos and Latinos.

JOSÉ ANTONIO VILLARREAL (1924–)

José Antonio Villarreal's parents emigrated to the United States in 1921, bringing with them their three children, one of whom died shortly after the family's arrival in Texas. The father, José Heladio Villarreal, had been a Villista for seven years. The family moved to California in 1922, and José Antonio was born two years later in Los Angeles. Ultimately, the Villarreals would bear seventeen children, three boys and fourteen girls; twelve of the children survived. For most of the 1920s, Villarreal's parents were migrant workers, and they moved the family throughout the state following the seasonal crops. In 1930, they settled in Santa Clara, where Villarreal began to attend school; it was in school that he learned to speak English, having spoken nothing but Spanish as a young child. He describes the experience of "growing up in the San Francisco Bay region" as "an important factor in my development as a human being," because the region "was at that time the most democratic portion of America." After spending four years in the U.S. Navy, Villarreal received his bachelor of arts in English literature in 1950 from the University of California at Berkeley. He has taught in the English departments of the University of Santa Clara, the University of Colorado–Boulder, and the University of Texas at El Paso. In 1973, he "repatriated" himself, moving with his wife and children to Mexico City and becoming a Mexican citizen.

Villarreal modeled his first novel, *Pocho* (1959), on Joyce's *Portrait of the Artist as a Young Man*, drawing liberally from his family's experiences in order to tell the story of a young writer's apprenticeship. It was the first novel by a Mexican American author to be published by a mainstream U.S. publishing house; the novel appeared in a Spanish translation in 1994. His second novel, *The Fifth Horseman* (1974), returned to the world that the Rubbios leave behind in *Pocho*: its story begins in Mexico on the eve of the 1910 revolution and follows the career of a hero of the revolution who finally chooses to leave his beloved Mexico and seek asylum in the United States rather than remain and participate in the Mexican army's betrayal of its revolutionary ideals. In portraying this generation of Mexican refugees as heroic and idealistic, *The Fifth Horseman* deliberately sets itself against the negative stereotype of refugees prevalent in both the United States and Mexico in the aftermath of the revolution. A third novel, *Clemente Chacon,* which recounts a day in the life of an insurance executive whose roots lie in the shantytowns of Ciudad Juárez, was published in 1984. *Two Sketches,* "The Last Minstrel in California" and "The Laughter of My Father," appeared in 1992 in the anthology *Iguana Dreams: New Latino Fiction,* edited by Delia Poey and Virgil Suarez; "The Laughter of My Father" is dedicated to the memory of Carlos Bulosan. "I do not believe that there ever will be a Chicano literature that can be separate from American literature," Villarreal told an interviewer in 1979, "and that makes it directly traceable to English literature. I say this because we write in English for the most part, and when we do not, we translate it into English. We have been educated in English, the major part of our reading history is English. . . . [W]e are by style, form and technique extremely traditional and adhere very strongly to the tradition of American letters."

GERALD VIZENOR (ANISHINABE, 1934–)

Born in Minneapolis in 1934 of mixed French and Anishinabe (Chippewa) heritage, Gerald Vizenor had a difficult childhood, scarred both by the family's poverty and his father's still-unsolved murder in 1936. At the age of 18, a few months before his high school graduation, Vizenor dropped out to join the U.S. Army, serving in Japan for three years. He later studied at New York University and the University of Minnesota, where he received his bachelor's degree in 1960 and later pursued graduate studies. During his graduate career, Vizenor pursued an interest in haiku poetry, and his collection of haiku, *Two Wings the Butterfly* was privately published in 1962. He would eventually publish five more books of haiku, most recently *Matsushima: Pine Islands* (1984). At the same time, he began collecting and re-rendering poems and stories from the Anishinabe tribal tradition, publishing the collection *Summer in the Spring: Lyric Poems of the Ojibway* in 1965; a revised edition, including stories from the collection *anishinabe adisokan: Tales of the People* (1970), was published in 1993 by the University of Oklahoma Press with the new subtitle *Anishinabe Lyric Poems and Stories.*

During the mid-1960s, he turned away from writing and became heavily involved with both tribal and Minneapolis politics, working as a social worker and as the executive director of the American Indian Employment and Guidance Center. His interest in tribal politics eventually led him back to writing and work as a journalist. A volume of collected articles and editorials, *Tribal Scenes and Ceremonies,* was published in 1976, and subsequent collections of journalistic and mixed-genre writings include *Wordarrows: Indians and Whites in the New Fur Trade* (1978), *The People Named Chippewa: Narrative Histories* (1984), and *Crossbloods: Bone Courts, Bingo, and Other Reports* (1990). In 1978, Vizenor began his teaching career with a one-year appointment at Lake Forest College in Illinois; he is currently professor of literature and American studies at the University of California, Santa Cruz, having also taught at Berkeley, Oklahoma, Minnesota, and Tianjin University in China. In 1978, Vizenor published his first novel, *Darkness in Saint Louis Bearheart* (reissued in 1990 as *Bearheart: The Heirship Chronicles*), a futuristic satire about a spiritual pilgrimage that challenges both stereotypes of Native Americans and the limits of conventional sexual morality. Subsequent works include four novels, *Griever: An American Monkey King in China* (1987), *The Trickster of Liberty: Tribal Heirs to a Wild Baronage* (1988), *The Heirs of Columbus* (1991), and *Dead Voices: Natural Agonies in the New World*; the autobiography *Interior Landscapes: Autobiographical Myths and Metaphors* (1990); and collections of short stories. All of Vizenor's writings draw inspiration both from Native American trickster mythology and from the formal experimentation of postmodernist writing as they explore the nature of mixed-blood identity and the role of mixed-bloods in contemporary Native culture. Vizenor's goal is to force his readers into sharing with him the act of creating meaning: "The page is not sacred," he has said. "It's what we send to the page that is sacred. . . . You have to go get it, find it, put it on the page. It has to be active. . . . The reader has to be engaged. The reader has to act."

ONOTO WATANNA *(see Winnifred Eaton)*

MICHI WEGLYN (1929–)

Born in the small farming town of Brentwood, California, Michi Weglyn and her family were interned during the Second World War at the Gila Relocation Center in Arizona, where Weglyn contracted tuberculosis. After recovering from the disease, Weglyn went on to become costume designer for *The Perry Como Show,* a weekly variety show on network television. Her book *Years of Infamy: The Untold Story of America's Concentration Camps* (1976) is a history book that is credited with changing Asian American history. Using primary documents to reconstruct the history of Japanese internment, Weglyn – who holds no advanced degree – was the first to make the significance of the Munson report clear; her book is not an "objective" piece of history writing, but rather a passionate, angry account that placed responsibility for internment at the highest levels of the U.S. government.

JAMES WELCH (BLACKFEET–GROS VENTRE, 1940–)

James Welch was born in Browning, Montana, on November 18, 1940, of mixed blood – Gros Ventre on his father's side, Blackfeet on his mother's. He attended schools on the Fort Belknap Reservation (Gros Ventre and Assiniboine) and on the Blackfeet Reservation, before moving to Minneapolis, where he graduated from high school and attended the University of Minnesota for a year. He received a bachelor of arts from the University of Montana and has taught at both the University of Washington and Cornell University. His works include a book of poetry, *Riding the Earthboy 40* (1971); *Killing Custer: The Battle of the Little Bighorn and the Fate of the Plains Indians* (1994), cowritten with Paul Stekler; and several novels: *Winter in the Blood* (1974), *The Death of Jim Loney* (1979), *Fool's Crow* (1986), *The Indian Lawyer* (1990).

EDMUND WHITE (1940–)

Edmund Valentine White III was born in Cincinnati in 1940 and received a bachelor of arts degree from the University of Michigan in 1962. One of the original members of the Violet Quill literary circle, he has taught literature and creative writing at Yale, Johns Hopkins, New York University, and Columbia University; was a full professor of English at Brown University; and served as executive director of the New York Institute for the Humanities. He has received a Guggenheim Fellowship, the Award for Literature from the National Academy of Arts and Letters, and the National Book Critics' Circle Award for *Genet: A Biography* (1993).

White's first novel, *Forgetting Elena* (1973), a baroque fantasy set in a mysterious place much like Fire Island, was praised by such literary celebrities as John Ashbery, Vladimir Nabokov, and Gore Vidal; though less fantastic in style, his second novel, *Nocturnes for the King of Naples* (1978), is still a rhetorical tour de force, taking the form of an extended apologia of a younger man to his older ex-lover. If these two novels betray the playful influence of Nabokov's literary dandyism, White's later, autobiographical novels *A Boy's Own Story* (1982), *The Beautiful Room Is Empty* (1988), and *The Farewell Symphony* adopt the more sober sensibility of Christopher Isherwood. "It's as though I peeled away the fantasy layer, in a style that was extremely ornate and appropriate to that particular vision," White told an interviewer. "Then

I was ready to deal with the painful reality of my youth in a more direct way. If my goal now was to tell the truth, I wasn't going to disguise it with a style that was very rhetorical." White's other works include the novel *Caracole* (1985) as well as three works of nonfiction: *The Joy of Gay Sex: An Intimate Guide for Gay Men to the Pleasures of a Gay Lifestyle* (1977, with Charles Silverstein), *States of Desire: Travels in Gay America* (1980), and *The Burning Library: Essays* (1994). White was found to be HIV positive in 1985.

SHAWN HSU WONG (1949–)

Shawn Hsu Wong was born in Oakland, California, and grew up in Berkeley. He studied for two years at San Francisco State University before attending the University of California at Berkeley as a pre-med, though he soon decided to become not a doctor but a writer. "I was in college and 19 years old," Wong remembers. "I'd been writing about a year when I realized that I was the only Asian-American writer I knew of." It was in Berkeley that Wong joined forces with Jeffery Paul Chan and Frank Chin in an attempt to recover the lost history of writing by Asian Americans. They began by interviewing a local greenhouse owner named Toshio Mori. Wong returned to San Francisco State for graduate work and was hired at the age of twenty-two to teach Asian American literature at Mills College. He received his master of fine arts degree in 1974, the same year in which the groundbreaking anthology *Aiiieeeee!*, edited by Chan, Chin, Wong, and Lawson Fusao Inada, was published by Howard University Press. A second anthology, *The Big Aiiieeeee!*, would appear in 1990.

Wong's first novel, a bildungsroman entitled *Homebase*, was turned down by six publishers before it was finally accepted for publication by Ishmael Reed in 1979. It was the first novel published in the United States by an American-born Chinese male, and it received both the Pacific Northwest Booksellers Award and a Washington State Governor's Writers Day Award. His second novel, *American Knees*, was published in 1995. Wong has also received a fellowship from the National Endowment of the Arts and is currently chair of the English department at the University of Washington, where he has taught since 1984. In 1996, Wong published a new collection, entitled *Asian American Literature: A Brief Introduction and Anthology*, which rectifies some of the more pointed omissions of *The Big Aiiieeeee!* by including writers like Maxine Hong Kingston and Amy Tan, as well as works by Asian Americans of Filipino, Vietnamese, and South Asian descent.

"I attended the second grade in Taiwan," Wong writes in the introduction to the 1996 anthology. "Given my last name, this is perhaps not a startling revelation. What was startling about this experience was that I was born in Oakland, California, and I spoke no Chinese, and in Taiwan, I was enrolled in an all-American, predominantly white U.S. Navy school. When my mother and I boarded the bus on the first day of school, the children chanted, 'No Chinese allowed!' I thought they were referring to my mother." Similar moments of cultural conflict and contradictions recur throughout both of Wong's novels. Rainsford, the young Chinese American narrator of *Homebase,* is obsessed by a desire to understand the life experiences of his ancestors who helped to build the American railroads, "my grandfathers, fathers, all without lovers, without women, struggling against black iron with hands splintered from coarse cross ties." The feeling of reconciliation that he discovers at the end of his novel remains incomplete: America has become a "homebase" in which Rainsford can sense his father's presence everywhere, but he remains cut off from Chinese American women – *that* reconciliation lies somewhere in the future. In contrast, *American Knees* is an adult love story that dramatizes the ways in which racial issues dominate even the erotic lives of its Asian American characters. "There's a sense," Wong says in describing the novel, "that when Asian Americans get together and talk about relationships, they talk about race – not just male-female relationships, but race, too."

HISAYE YAMAMOTO (1921–)

Hisaye Yamamoto was born in Redondo Beach, California, the child of Japanese immigrants. She began her writing career as a teenager and was a regular contributor to a number of Japanese American newspapers before the Second World War. In 1942, she was interned with her family for three years in the Poston, Arizona, concentration camp, where she published a serialized mystery and served as a reporter and columnist for the camp newspaper, the *Poston Chronicle.* Working from 1945 to 1948 for the *Los Angeles Tribune,* an African American weekly, Yamamoto began to publish short stories in national journals and received a John Hay Whitney Foundation Opportunity Fellowship in 1950. Like N. Scott Momaday, she found an advocate in Yvor Winters, who encouraged her to accept a writing fellowship at Stanford University, but she decided instead to work as a volunteer at a Catholic Worker rehabilitation farm on Staten Island in New York State from 1953 to 1955. After marrying Anthony DeSoto, she returned to Los Angeles. A master of short fiction, Yamamoto writes in a deceptively simple style that makes extensive use of irony and understatement. Her abiding subjects are the conflict between generations, particularly the inability of *Issei* parents to communicate with their *Nisei* children, and the Japanese American woman's struggle for self-expression and fulfillment. She was awarded an American Book Award for Lifetime Achievement from the Before Columbus Foundation in 1986. Her book *Seventeen Syllables and Other Stories* was published in 1988.

WAKAKO YAMAUCHI (1924–)

Wakako Yamauchi was born in the town of Westmoreland in California's Imperial Valley. Her father was a farmer, and Yamauchi turned to reading and writing as a way of escaping from the monotony and isolation of farm life. In 1942, she and her family were interned at the Poston, Arizona concentration camp in 1942, where she met and befriended the *Nisei* writer Hisaye Yamamoto. Married in 1948 to Chester Yamauchi, Wakako took up writing only in the late 1950s, once her daughter Joy had begun to attend school. Although she found herself unable to get her writing published in magazines and journals, she was able to place her work in the *Rafu Shimpo,* Los Angeles's Japanese American vernacular newspaper, in exchange for working there as an illustrator. Between 1961 and 1975, Yamauchi abandoned writing to pursue painting, returning to it only after being encouraged by Yamamoto to send samples of her written work to the group that was putting together the first *Aiiieeeee!* anthology. In 1974, Yamauchi was convinced by director Mako to write a stage adaptation of her story "And the Soul Shall Dance," written in 1959 and included in the *Aiiieeeee!* anthology, and the play later won the Los Angeles Critics' Circle Award for best new play of 1977 and was produced for public television. Describing *And the Soul Shall Dance,* Yamauchi has said, "I didn't consciously decide I was going to write the play from the point of view of the women. But my mother was a feminist in her time, and she always made me feel that I was somebody. Japanese men were very chauvinistic, especially in those days, but women had a way of adapting things, of handling the men. That's one of the things I wanted to show, that feeling we had: 'You can step on us, but you haven't got us yet!'"

Her second play, *The Music Lessons* (1977), was adapted from her short story "In Heaven and Earth." Both plays focus on the second period of Japanese emigration to the United States, from 1908 to 1924, and the hardships faced by the *Issei.* Other plays include *12-1-A* (1982), *The Memento* (1984), and *The Chairman's Wife* (1990). Yamauchi has received four Rockefeller Foundation playwriting grants. A collection of her work, entitled *Songs My Mother Taught Me: Stories, Plays, and Memoir,* was published in 1994.

CHRONOLOGY
1940–1990

Jonathan Fortescue

	American Literary Texts	American Events, Texts, and Arts	Other Events, Texts, and Arts
1940	Faulkner, William (1897–1962), *The Hamlet* (novel)	President Franklin Roosevelt reelected for third term.	Radar invented in Scotland.
	Glaspell, Susan (1882–1948), *The Morning Is Near Us* (drama)	Congress passes law requiring alien residents to register with the U.S. government. 29.5 million households in the U.S. own a radio.	Germany invades Norway, Denmark, Belgium, and Paris.
	Hemingway, Ernest (1899–1961), *For Whom the Bell Tolls* (novel)	First compulsory peacetime draft in U.S. begins.	Leon Trotsky is assassinated in Mexico.
	Hughes, Langston (1902–1967), *The Big Sea* (autobiography)	Woody Guthrie writes "This Land Is My Land" (folk song)	Germany, Italy, and Japan sign an alliance for mutual protection.
	McCullers, Carson (1917–1967), *The Heart Is a Lonely Hunter* (novel)	*Philadelphia Story* (film) directed by Geroge Cukor.	Japan invades Indochina.
	Odets, Clifford (1906–1963), *Night Music* (drama)	*The Great Dictator* (film) directed by Charlie Chaplin.	Brecht, Bertolt (1898–1956), *The Good Woman of Setzuan* (drama)
	Williams, Tennessee (1911–1983), *Battle of Angels* (drama)		
	Wright, Richard (1908-1960), *Native Son* (novel)		
1941	Agee, James (1909–1955), *Let Us Now Praise Famous Men* (documentary narrative)	Lend-Lease Act signed with Britain.	Germany and Italy combine to invade the Balkans.
	Fitzgerald, F. Scott (1896–1940), *The Last Tycoon* (novel, published posthumously)	Advent of common use of pencillin.	Germany bombs London and invades Russia.
	McCullers, Carson (1917–1967), *Reflections in a Golden Eye* (novel)	Coal and steel workers lead protracted strikes.	Borges, Jorge Luís (1899–1986), *The Garden of Forking Paths* (fiction)
	Odets, Clifford (1906-1963), *Clash by Night* (drama)	Federal Communications Commission licences television broadcasting.	
		Japan bombs Pearl Harbor. U.S. declares war on Axis powers.	

Welty, Eudora (1909–), *A Curtain of Green* (fiction)

1942

Faulkner, William (1897–1962), *Go Down, Moses* (fiction)

Glaspell, Susan (1882–1948), *Norma Ashe* (novel)

McCarthy, Mary (1912–1989), *The Company She Keeps* (fiction)

Welty, Eudora (1909–), *The Robber Bridegroom* (novel)

1943

Rand, Ayn (1905–1982), *The Fountainhead* (novel)

Mitchell, Joseph (1908–1998), *McSorley's Wonderful Salon* (published essay)

Warren, Robert Penn (1905–1989), *At Heaven's Gate* (novel)

Wolfert, Ira (1908–1997), *Tucker's People* (novel)

Welty, Eudora (1909–), *The Wide Net* (fiction)

1944

Bellow, Saul (1915–), *Dangling Man* (novel)

Brown, Harry (1917–1986), *A Walk in the Sun* (novel)

Hersey, John (1914–1993), *A Bell for Adano* (novel)

Citizen Kane (film) directed by **Orson Welles.**

Executive Order 9066 sends Japanese Americans to internment camps.

U.S. Supreme Court finds Georgia labor laws violate the Thirteenth Amendment.

First nuclear chain reaction produced in the labs of Enrico Fermi at University of Chicago.

U.S. government forbids racial discrimination by war contractors.

U.S. government begins to collect paycheck withholding tax.

Pollock, Jackson (1912–1956), *Mural* (painting)

Oklahoma premiers on Broadway.

Casablanca (film) directed by **Michael Curtiz.**

Franklin Roosevelt reelected to a fourth term as president.

Congress passes the GI Bill of Rights.

Communist party of the U.S. reconfigures itself into Communist Political Association.

Battle of the Coral Sea: first naval fight conducted only by airplane.

Battle of Midway: first major defeat of Japanese navy.

Battle of El Alamein forces German retreat out of North Africa.

Camus, Albert (1913–1960), *The Stranger* (novel); *The Myth of Sisyphus* (essay)

Russians push back German invasion at Battle of Stalingrad.

American and British forces invade Sicily.

Mussolini deposed.

Sartre, Jean-Paul (1905–1980), *Being and Nothingness* (essay; English, translation 1956)

D-Day: Allied Forces invade Normandy on June 6.

Allied forces march toward Berlin and score several victories in the Pacific.

American Literary Texts	American Events, Texts, and Arts	Other Events, Texts, and Arts
Miller, Arthur (1915–), *The Man Who Had All the Luck* (drama) **Williams, Tennessee** (1911–1983), *The Glass Menagerie* (drama)	Government freezes prices on rationed domestic goods to prevent inflation. **Myrdal, Gunnar** (1898–1987), *An American Dilemma* (nonfiction) *Double Indemnity* (film) directed by **Billy Wilder.**	Germans launch V-2 rockets toward London. **Borges, Jorge Luís** (1899–1986), *Fictions* **Sartre, Jean Paul** (1905–1980), *No Exit* (drama)

1945

American Literary Texts	American Events, Texts, and Arts	Other Events, Texts, and Arts
Glaspell, Susan (1882–1948), *Judd Rankin's Daughter* (novel) **Himes, Chester B.** (1909–1984), *If He Hollers Let Him Go* (novel) **Miller, Arthur** (1915–), *Focus* (novel) **Vidal, Gore** (1925–), *Williwaw* (novel) **Wong, Jade Snow** (1922–), *Fifth Chinese Daughter* (personal narrative) **Wright, Richard** (1908–1960), *Black Boy* (autobiography)	U.S. Senate ratifies United Nations charter. Franklin Roosevelt dies. Harry Truman becomes president. President Truman annouces the "Fair Deal" social policy. Tupperware is invented. *The Lost Weekend* (film) directed by **Billy Wilder.** **Dizzy Gillespie** (1917–1993) and **Charlie Parker** (1920–1955) record *Groovin' High, Ko Ko* (jazz).	Victory in Europe: May 8, V-E Day. U.S. drops atomic bombs on Hiroshima and Nagasaki. Victory in Japan: August 14, V-J Day. Nazi leadership tried in Nuremberg for crimes against humanity (1945–49). **Brecht, Bertolt** (1898–1956), *The Caucasian Chalk Circle* (drama)

1946

American Literary Texts	American Events, Texts, and Arts	Other Events, Texts, and Arts
Bulosan, Carlos (1913–1956), *America Is in the Heart* (personal narrative) **McCullers, Carson** (1917–1967), *The Member of the Wedding* (novel) **O'Neill, Eugene** (1888–1953), *The Iceman Cometh* (drama)	Atomic Energy Commission created. In a speech in Fulton, Missouri, Winston Churchill says that an "Iron Curtain" divides eastern and western Europe. Hobbs bill passed, preventing unions from interfering with interstate commerce.	Joseph Stalin warns of anti-Communist threat to Russia. Communists in Indochina resist the reassertion of French rule. British and French forces pull out of Lebanon.

Petry, Ann (1911–1997), *The Street* (novel)

Ward, Theodore (1907–), *Our Lan'* (drama)

Warren, Robert Penn (1905–1989), *All the King's Men* (novel)

Welty, Eudora (1909–), *Delta Wedding* (novel)

1947 Bellow, Saul (1915–), *The Victim* (novel)

Burns, John Horne (1916–1953), *The Gallery* (novel)

Himes, Chester B. (1909–1984), *Lonely Crusade* (novel)

Miller, Arthur (1915–), *All My Sons* (drama)

Motley, Willard (1912–1965), *Knock on Any Door* (novel)

Stafford, Jean (1915–1979), *The Mountain Lion* (novel)

Trilling, Lionel (1905–1975), *The Middle of the Journey* (novel)

Williams, Tennessee (1911–1983), *A Streetcar Named Desire* (drama)

U.S. Marines put down prison riot at Alacatraz.

Congress passes the Indian Claims Commission Act.

First houses are built in Levittown, New York, as suburban housing tracts rise on periphery of U.S. cities.

The Big Sleep (film) directed by **Howard Hawks**

Marshall Plan proposed.

President Truman consolidates armed forces into the new Department of Defense and announces commitment to fight communism in foreign nations (Truman Doctrine).

Central Intelligence Agency founded.

Congress passes Taft-Hartley Labor Act in an effort to limit power of organized labor.

The long-playing, or LP, record is invented.

Transistor is invented.

Chuck Yeager breaks the sound barrier in a rocket plane.

Charlie Parker (1920–1955) records *Quasimado* (jazz)

British Labor Party nationalizes health care.

Beauty and the Beast (film) directed by **Jean Cocteau**

Open City (film) directed by **Roberto Rossellini**

India and Pakistan gain independence from United Kingdom.

Civil war in Greece and Soviet actions against Turkey cause U.S. to send aid.

The U.S. becomes trustee of Pacific islands once claimed by Japan.

Camus, Albert (1913–1960), *The Plague* (novel)

Frank, Anne (1929–1945), *Diary of a Young Girl* (autobiography)

Kawabata, Yasunari (1899–1972), *Snow Country* (novel)

Mann, Thomas (1875–1955), *Doktor Faustus* (novel)

American Literary Texts	American Events, Texts, and Arts	Other Events, Texts, and Arts
1948 Capote, Truman (1924–1984), *Other Voices, Other Rooms* (novel)	Harry Truman reelected president.	State of Israel created.
Cozzens, James Gould (1903–1978), *Guard of Honor* (novel)	Television becomes a national phenomenon (number of stations grows from 11 to 65).	Burma becomes a sovereign nation. Organization of the American States (OAS) founded.
Faulkner, William (1897–1962), *Intruder in the Dust* (novel)	Alger Hiss indicted for espionage.	World Health Organization founded.
Mailer, Norman (1923–), *The Naked and the Dead* (novel)	Mine workers strike but return to work after the federal government levies heavy fines.	Communists win Czechoslovakian elections and take over country.
Shaw, Irwin (1913–1984), *The Young Lions* (novel)	President Truman desegregates the armed forces.	Soviets blockade West Berlin. Americans airlift supplies to the city.
Vidal, Gore (1925–), *The City and the Pillar* (novel)	de Kooning, Willem (1904–1997), *Asheville* (painting)	U.S. puts down peasant-communist uprising in the Philippines.
Williams, Tennessee (1911–1983), *Summer and Smoke* (drama)	Kinsey, Alfred (1894–1956), *Sexual Behavior in the Human Male* (sociology)	Mahatma Ghandi is assassinated. Holograph invented in Britain.
Lin Yutang (1895–1976), *Chinatown Family* (novel)		
1949 Algren, Nelson (1909–1981), *The Man with the Golden Arm* (novel)	Housing Act supports low-income housing development.	NATO founded. Mao Tse-Tung establishes Communist rule in China.
Bowles, Paul (1910–), *The Sheltering Sky* (novel)	U.S. courts convict eleven members of the U.S. Communist party for supporting the overthrow of the federal government.	Soviets explode their first atomic bomb.
Capote, Truman (1924–1984), *The Tree of Life* (short stories)	Barber, Samuel (1910–1981), *Knoxville: Summer of 1915* (classical music)	J. F. J. Cade introduces lithium for treatment of manic depression.
Hawkes, John (1925–), *The Cannibal* (novel)		de Beauvoir, Simone (1908–1986), *The Second Sex* (nonfiction)
Miller, Arthur (1915–), *Death of a Salesman* (drama)		
Mori, Toshio (1910–), *Yokohama, California* (fiction)		

Welty, Eudora (1909–), *The Golden Apples* (short stories)

Yamamoto, Hisaye (1921–), "Seventeen Syllables" (story, collected in 1988)

1950 Hemingway, Ernest (1899–1961), *Across the River and into the Trees* (novel)

Kerouac, Jack (1922–1969), *The Town and the City* (novel)

Salinger, J. D. (1919–), "For Esmé – with Love and Squalor" (short story)

Warren, Robert Penn (1905–1989), *Wild Enough and Time* (novel)

Williams, Tennessee (1911–1983), *The Rose Tattoo* (drama)

Johnson, Philip (1906–), *Glass House* (architecture)

Schlesinger, Arthur, Jr. (1917–), *The Vital Center* (nonfiction)

The Third Man (film) directed by Carol Reed

U.S. Army takes over the railroads to prevent strike.

Senator Joseph R. McCarthy incites fear of Communism as head of Permanent Subcommittee on Investigations.

House Committee on Un-American Activities accuses broad spectrum of citizens of subversive activity.

45 million households own a radio. Sales of televisions reach 1 million.

Riesman, David (1909–), *The Lonely Crowd* (nonfiction)

All About Eve (film) directed by Joseph K. Mankiewicz

The Men (film) directed by Fred Zinneman

Borges, Jorge Luís (1899–1986), *The Aleph* (fiction)

Orwell, George (1903–1950), *Nineteen Eighty-four* (novel)

Sartre, Jean Paul (1905–1980), *Nausea* (novel, French publication in 1938)

The Bicycle Thief (film) directed by Vittorio De Sica

North Korea invades South Korea. Korean War begins.

Klaus Fuchs arrested for espionage.

American military advisors arrive in South Vietnam.

Ionesco, Eugène (1912–1994), *The Bald Soprano* (drama)

Lessing, Doris (1919–), *The Grass Is Singing* (novel)

	American Literary Texts	American Events, Texts, and Arts	Other Events, Texts, and Arts
1951	Bowles, Paul (1910–), *The Delicate Prey and Other Stories* (fiction)	Julius and Ethel Rosenberg sentenced to death for treason.	Korean War escalates as United Nations sends in additional ground troops.
	Capote, Truman (1924–1984), *The Glass Harp* (novel)	Alger Hiss sentenced to prison for espionage.	Arab League begins economic blockade of Israel.
	Faulkner, William (1897–1962) *Requiem for a Nun* (novel)	Twenty-second Amendment to the Constitution limits the presidency to two terms in office.	Argentinian President Peron seizes control of South America's most respected newspaper, *La Prensa*.
	Jones, James (1921–1977), *From Here to Eternity* (novel)	President Truman removes General Douglas MacArthur from command of forces in Korea after the general advocates use of atomic weapons to help win Korean War.	Dublin's Abbey Theater burns down.
	McCullers, Carson (1917–1967), *The Ballad of the Sad Café* (novel)		Camus, Albert (1913–1960), *The Rebel* (drama)
	Mailer, Norman (1923–), *Barbary Shore* (novel)		*Forbidden Games* (film) directed by **René Clement**
	Nabokov, Vladimir (1899–1977), *Conclusive Evidence* (memoir)	First transcontinental television broadcast.	
	Salinger, J. D. (1919–), *Catcher in the Rye* (novel)	Levittown, New York, reaches full capacity as suburban growth continues.	
	Styron, William (1925–), *Lie Down in Darkness* (novel)	Arendt, Hannah (1906–1975), *The Origins of Totalitarianism* (nonfiction)	
		Sagarin, Edward (pseudonym of Donald Webster Cory) (1913–), *The Homosexual in America* (nonfiction)	
		CBS begins to telecast *I Love Lucy* (1951–1957).	

1952		
Chambers, Whittaker (1901–1961), *Witness* (memoir)	McCarren-Walter Act assembles previous immigration legislation into a uniform code that reaffirms restrictionist policies.	China begins forcible collectivization of agricultural, industrial and cultural institutions.
Childress, Alice (1920–), *Gold Through the Trees* (drama)	U.S. Army seizes steel mills to prevent labor strike.	Beckett, Samuel (1906–1989), *Molloy* (novel), *Malone Dies* (novel)
Ellison, Ralph (1914–1994), *Invisible Man* (novel)	U.S. explodes first hydrogen bomb.	Calvino, Italo (1923–1985), *The Cloven Viscount* (novel, English translation 1962)
Hemingway, Ernest (1899–1961), *The Old Man and the Sea* (novel)	Dwight D. Eisenhower elected president.	Waugh, Evelyn (1903–1966), *Men at Arms* (novel)
O'Connor, Flannery (1925–1964), *Wise Blood* (novel)	First performance of **John Cage**'s *4'33"* (music)	
	Singing in the Rain (film) directed by **Gene Kelley** and **Stanley Donen**	

1953		
Baldwin, James (1924–1987), *Go Tell It on the Mountain* (novel)	Earl Warren appointed chief justice of the U.S. Supreme Court.	Korean War ends.
Bellow, Saul (1915–), *The Adventure of Augie March* (novel)	President Eisenhower creates the Department of Health, Education, and Welfare.	Joseph Stalin (1880–1953) dies.
Cheever, John (1912–1982), *The Enormous Radio and Other Stories* (short stories)	New York public schools terminate contracts for teachers for suspected affiliation with the Communist party.	The nations of the European Coal and Steel Community (France, West Germany, Holland, Belgium, Italy, Luxembourg) draft a limited political federation. Birth of the European Economic Community.
Miller, Arthur (1915–), *The Crucible* (drama)	Attorney General Hubert Brownell, Jr. emphasizes the dangers of illegal immigration.	Beckett, Samuel (1906–1989), *Waiting for Godot* (drama), *The Unnameable* (novel)
Paterson, Louis (1923–), *Take a Giant Step* (drama)	Local television stations begin educational programming.	Milosz, Czeslaw (1911–), *The Captive Mind* (nonfiction)
Sone, Monica (1919–), *Nisei Daughter* (personal narrative)		
Welty, Eudora (1909–), *The Ponder Heart* (novel)		
Williams, Tennessee (1911–1983), *Camino Real* (drama)		

	American Literary Texts	American Events, Texts, and Arts	Other Events, Texts, and Arts
1954	Faulkner, William (1897–1962), *A Fable* (novel) Odets, Clifford (1906–1963), *The Flowering Peach* (drama) Vidal, Gore (1925–), *Messiah* (novel)	James Watson and Francis Crick discover the structure of DNA. Kinsey, Alfred (1894–1956), *Sexual Behavior in the Human Female* (sociology) U.S. Supreme Court desegregates public schools in *Brown v. Topeka*. Joseph Welch turns the tide of public sentiment against Senator Joseph McCarthy. *On the Waterfront* (film) directed by Elia Kazan Monk, Thelonious (1917–1982), records *'Round Midnight*.	Wittgenstein, Ludwig (1889–1951) *Philosophical Investigations* (nonfiction) *Tokyo Story* (film) directed by Yasujiro Ozu Golding, William (1911–1993), *Lord of the Flies* (novel) *The Seven Samurai* (film) directed by Akira Kurosawa *Pather Panchali* (film) directed by Satyajit Ray
1955	Baldwin, James (1924–1987), *Notes of a Native Son* (memoir) Gaddis, William (1922–), *The Recognitions* (novel) Mailer, Norman (1923–) *Deer Park* (novel) Miller, Arthur (1915–), *A View from the Bridge* (drama) Nabokov, Vladimir (1899–1977), *Lolita* (novel) O'Connor, Flannery (1925–1964), *A Good Man Is Hard to Find* (short stories)	Rosa Parks protests segregation on buses in Montgomery, Alabama. AFL & CIO merge with a combined membership of ~ 15 million. Congress grants Eisenhower powers to protect Formosa against Communist China. U.S. agrees to help train South Vietnamese Army.	Egypt, under Gamal Abdel Nasser, seizes the Suez Canal. Warsaw Pact signed. Argentinian military ousts Juan Peron from office. Delegates at Asian-African Conference at Bandung call for an end to European colonial domination.

Federal economists report that income levels, employment rate, and building starts reach new highs.

Joseph Salk's vaccine for polio proves effective.

First major Beat reading at the Six Gallery in San Francisco.

Blackboard Jungle (film) directed by Richard Brooks

Rebel Without a Cause (film) dir. Nicholas Ray

CBS begins to telecast *The Honeymooners* (1955–1956) and *Gunsmoke* (1955–1975), whose 633 episodes make up the longest run for a dramatic series on television.

First transatlantic telephone cable.

Soviet Army crushes social unrest in Hungary.

Highway Act signed. Government starts to build Interstate Highway System.

U.S. Supreme Court finds segregation laws violate the Fourteenth Amendment.

Southern congressmen join together to protest desegregation rulings.

Color television becomes commercially available.

Alfred Woolson, last surviving Civil War veteran, dies.

Universal Copyright Convention begins.

Lévi-Strauss, Claude (1908–), *Tristes Tropiques* (anthropology)

Robbe-Grillet, Alain (1922–), *Voyeur* (novel, English translation 1958)

Waugh, Evelyn (1903–1966), *Officers and Gentlemen* (novel)

Umberto D (film) directed by Vittorio De Sica

Boulez, Pierre (1925–), *Le Marteau sans Maître* (music)

Beckett, Samuel (1906–1989), *Endgame* (drama)

Camus, Albert (1913–1960), *The Fall* (novel)

Genet, Jean (1910–1986), *The Balcony* (drama)

American Literary Texts	American Events, Texts, and Arts	Other Events, Texts, and Arts
1957 Warren, Robert Penn (1905–1989), *Segregation* (essay) Agee, James (1909–1955), *A Death in the Family* (novel, published posthumously) Cheever, John (1912–1982), *The Wapshot Chronicle* (novel) Cozzens, James Gould (1903–1978), *By Love Possessed* (novel) Faulkner, William (1897–1962), *The Town* (novel) Kerouac, Jack (1922–1969), *On the Road* (novel) McCarthy, Mary (1912–1989), *Memories of a Catholic Girlhood* (memoir) Mailer, Norman (1923–), "The White Negro" (essay) Malamud, Bernard (1914–1986), *The Assistant* (novel) Nabokov, Valdimir (1899–1977), *Pnin* (novel) Okada, John (1924–1971), *No-No Boy* (novel) O'Neill, Eugene (1888–1953), *A Moon for the Misbegotten* (drama), *A Touch of the Poet* (drama)	Dwight D. Eisenhower reelected president. *Invasion of the Body Snatchers* (film) directed by **Don Siegel** *The Searchers* (film) directed by **John Ford** President Dwight D. Eisenhower creates the Commission on Civil Rights. Congress passes the Civil Rights Law, first such legislation since Reconstruction. Arkansas Governor Orval E. Faubus leads riots against desegregation. President Eisenhower sends in the National Guard to restore order. Senate exposes leaders of AFL-CIO for misuse of union funds. Union members respond against leaders. U.S. redoubles its efforts in the space race. Schools shift curriculums to emphasize the sciences. Laser is invented. *12 Angry Men* (film) directed by **Sidney Lumet**	**Mishima, Yukio** (1925–1970), *The Temple of the Golden Pavilion* (novel) *The Seventh Seal* (film) directed by **Ingmar Bergman** Soviet Union launches Sputnik I, the first man-made satellite. **Achebe, Chinua** (1930–) *Things Fall Apart* (novel) **Barthes, Roland** (1915–1980), *Mythologies* (nonfiction) **Calvino, Italo** (1923–1985), *The Baron in the Trees* (novel, English translation 1959) **Mahfouz, Naguib** (1912–), *The Cairo Trilogy* (novels [1956–1957]) **Poulenc, Francis** (1899–1963), *Dialogues of the Carmelites* (music)

Rand, Ayn (1905–1982), *Atlas Shrugged* (novel)

Salinger, J. D. (1919–), "Zooey" (novella)

Williams, Tennessee (1911–1983), *Orpheus Descending* (drama)

1958

Barth, John (1930–), *The End of the Road* (novel)

Berger, Thomas (1924–), *Crazy in Berlin* (novel)

Capote, Truman (1924–1984), *Breakfast at Tiffany's* (novel)

Foote, Shelby (1916–), *The Civil War* [1958–1974] (historical narrative)

Kerouac, Jack (1922–1969), *The Dharma Bums* (novel); *The Subterraneans* (novel)

Malamud, Bernard (1914–1986), *The Magic Barrel* (short stories)

Nabokov, Vladimir (1899–1977), *Nabokov's Dozen* (short stories)

Williams, Tennessee (1911–1983), *Suddenly Last Summer* (drama)

1959

Bellow, Saul (1915–), *Henderson the Rain King* (novel)

Brown, Norman O. (1913–), *Life Against Death* (essay)

Witness for the Prosecution (film) directed by Billy Wilder

Jack Paar begins to host *The Tonight Show* (1957–1962).

Congress creates NASA.

U.S. Navy nuclear submarine passes beneath the North Pole.

U.S. government launches its first orbital satellite.

National Airlines begins first domestic passenger-jet service.

Gailbraith, John Kenneth (1908–), *The Affluent Society* (economics)

van der Rohe, Mies (1886–1969) and Philip Johnson (1906–), *Seagram Building* (architecture)

Vertigo (film) directed by Alfred Hitchcock

Alaska and Hawaii admitted to the union as the forty-ninth and fiftieth states.

Labor-Management Disclosure and Report Act, designed to remove rack-

Nikita Khrushchev becomes premier of the Soviet Union.

China begins "The Great Leap Forward," an agrarian reform that leads to widespread starvation.

British Overseas Airways begins first transatlantic passenger-jet service.

Beckett, Samuel (1906–1989), *Krapp's Last Tape* (drama)

Fuentes, Carlos (1928–), *Where the Air Is Clear* (novel)

Mishima, Yukio (1925–1970), *Confessions of a Mask* (personal narrative)

Pinter, Harold (1930–), *The Birthday Party* (drama)

Wiesel, Elie (1928–), *Night* (personal narrative)

Fidel Castro becomes premier of Cuba.

Communist China invades Tibet.

Böll, Heinrich (1917–1985), *Billiards at Half-Past Nine* (novel)

American Literary Texts	American Events, Texts, and Arts	Other Events, Texts, and Arts
Burroughs, William (1914–1997), *Naked Lunch* (novel)	eteers from unions, passes in Congress.	Calvino, Italo (1923–1985), *The Nonexistent Knight* (novel, English translation 1962)
Faulkner, William (1897–1962), *The Mansion* (novel)	Congressional inquiry reveals the fixing of results on television quiz shows.	Robbe-Grillet, Alain (1922–), *In the Labyrinth* (novel, English translation 1960)
Gelber, Jack (1932–), *The Connection* (drama)	Integrated circuit is invented.	Vasconcelos, José (1882–1959), *The Flame* (nonfiction)
Hansberry, Lorraine (1930–1965), *A Raisin in the Sun* (drama)	Wright, Frank Lloyd (1867–1959), *Guggenheim Museum in Manhattan* (architecture)	*Black Orpheus* (film) directed by Marcel Camus
Kerouac, Jack (1922–1969), *Doctor Sax* (novel), *Maggie Cassidy* (novel)	*Some Like It Hot* (film) directed by Billy Wilder	*Breathless* (film) directed by Jean-Luc Godard
Lowell, Robert (1917–1977) *Life Studies* (memoir)	CBS begins to telecast *The Twilight Zone* (1959–1963).	*The 400 Blows* (film) directed by François Truffaut
Mailer, Norman (1923–), *Advertisements for Myself* (memoir and essays)	NBC begins to telecast *Bonanza* (1959–1973).	
Marshall, Paule (1929–), *Brown Girl, Brownstones* (novel)	Miles Davis (1926–1991) and John Coltrane (1926–1967) record *Kind of Blue* (jazz)	
Roth, Philip (1933–), *Goodbye, Columbus* (fiction)		
Villareal, José Antonio (1924–), *Pocho* (novel)		
Williams, Tennessee (1911–1983), *Sweet Bird of Youth* (drama)		
1960 Albee, Edward (1928–), *The Zoo Story* (drama), *The Sandbox* (drama)	Student sit-ins become a popular form of political protest.	OPEC (Organization of Petroleum Exporting Countries) founded.
Barth, John (1930–), *The Sot-Weed Factor* (novel)		
Faulkner, William (1897–1962), *The Mansion* (novel)		

Goodman, Paul (1911–1972), *Growing Up Absurd* (essay)

Kerouac, Jack (1922–1969), *Tristessa* (novel)

Kopit, Arthur (1937–), *Oh Dad, Poor Dad, Mama's Hung You in the Closet and I'm Feeling So Sad* (drama)

Lee, Harper (1926–), *To Kill a Mockingbird* (novel)

O'Connor, Flannery (1925–1964), *The Violent Bear It Away* (novel)

Richardson, Jack (1935–), *The Prodigal* (drama)

Updike, John (1932–) *Rabbit, Run* (novel)

Warren, Robert Penn (1905–1989), *Wilderness* (novel)

Williams, Tennessee (1911–1983), *Period of Adjustment* (drama)

1961   Albee, Edward (1928–), *The American Dream* (drama), *The Death of Bessie Smith* (drama)

Baldwin, James (1924–1987), *Nobody Knows My Name* (novel)

Chu, Louis (1915–1970), *Eat a Bowl of Tea* (novel)

Heller, Joseph (1923–), *Catch-22* (novel)

Four African Americans make headines when they refuse to move from an all-white lunch counter in Greensboro, North Carolina

Act of Bogotá begins U.S. subsidization of Latin America.

U.S. launches Echo I, first communications satellite and Tiros I, first weather satellite.

Nixon versus Kennedy: first nationally televised presidential debate.

John F. Kennedy elected president, first Roman Catholic to hold this office.

Hoffmann Larouche Pharmeceutical markets first benzodiazapine for treatment of anxiety.

Johns, Jasper (1930–), *Painted Bronze* (sculpture)

The Bay of Pigs: small military force botches invasion of Cuba.

Alan Shepard becomes first American to fly in outer space.

Public concern about nuclear war spreads: President John F. Kennedy announces that U.S. should build shelters for radioactive fallout "for every American as rapidly as possible."

Nationalist movements in Africa result in 19 newly sovereign nations, 14 of which were French colonies.

Communist guerillas begin to agitate in South Vietnam.

Ionesco, Eugène (1912–1994), *Rhinocerous* (drama)

Laurence, Margaret (1926–1987), *This Side Jordan* (novel)

Pinter, Harold (1930–), *The Caretaker* (drama)

La Dolce Vita (film) directed by Federico Fellini

L'Avventura (film) directed by Michelangelo Antonioni

Communists build Berlin Wall to separate east sector of city from the west sector.

Soviets begin to provide economic assistance to Cuba.

South Africa withdraws from British Commonwealth.

American Literary Texts	American Events, Texts, and Arts	Other Events, Texts, and Arts
McCullers, Carson (1917–1967), *Clock Without Hands* (novel)	Peace Corps founded.	Arab League admits Kuwait, after Iraq walks out of session.
Miller, Arthur (1915–), *The Misfits* (screenplay)	Indian activists from several tribes come together at the "Chicago Conference" and issue a Declaration of Indian Purpose.	Amado, Jorge (1912–), *Gabriela, Cloves, and Cinnamon* (novel)
Percy, Walker (1916–1990), *The Moviegoer* (novel)	Freedom Rides to protest segregation begin in the Deep South.	Beckett, Samuel (1906–1989), *Happy Days* (drama)
Williams, Tennessee (1911–1983), *Night of the Iguana* (drama)	*A Raisin in the Sun* (film) directed by **Dan Petrie**	Fanon, Frantz (1925–1961), *The Wretched of the Earth* (essay)
Wright, Richard (1908–1960), *Eight Men* (short stories, published posthumously)		Foucault, Michel (1926–1984), *Madness and Civilization* (nonfiction)
Vonnegut, Kurt (1922–) *Mother Night* (novel)		Waugh, Evelyn (1903–1966), *Unconditional Surrender* (novel)
Yates, Richard (1926–1992), *Revolutionary Road* (novel)		

1962

American Literary Texts	American Events, Texts, and Arts	Other Events, Texts, and Arts
Albee, Edward (1928–), *Who's Afraid of Virginia Woolf?* (drama)	John Glenn becomes first American to orbit the earth.	Egypt and Saudi Arabia support opposite sides in Yemen civil war.
Baldwin, James (1924–1987), *Another Country* (novel)	César Chávez founds the National Farm Workers Association, later called United Farm Workers (UFW).	U.S. and Russia support creation of neutral political state in Laos.
Burroughs, William (1914–1997), *Nova Express* (novel)	James Meredith matriculates as first black student at the University of Mississippi.	Algerian Moslems sign truce with colonial government after 70-year civil war in which more than 250,000 people died. Algerians then vote for independence.
Faulkner, William (1897–1962), *The Reivers* (novel)	Cuban missile crisis.	Pope John XXIII convenes Vatican II in Rome and calls for Christian unity.
Jones, James (1921–1977), *The Thin Red Line* (novel)	U.S. Supreme Court finds that official prayers in public schools are unconstitutional.	
Kennedy, Adrienne (1931–), *Funnyhouse of a Negro* (drama)		

Kerouac, Jack (1922–1969), *Big Sur* (novel)

Kesey, Ken (1935–), *One Flew Over the Cuckoo's Nest* (novel)

Nabokov, Vladimir (1899–1977), *Pale Fire* (novel)

O'Neill, Eugene (1888–1953), *More Stately Museums* (drama, unexpurgated text published 1988)

Price, Reynolds (1933–), *A Long and Happy Life* (novel)

Yates, Richard (1926–1992), *Eleven Kinds of Loneliness* (novel)

AT&T launches Telstar I and begins to relay television broadcasts between U.S. and Europe.

Psychiatric study reveals that viewers of a movie that shows a knife fight are more willing to inflict pain than are viewers of an educational film.

Carson, Rachel (1907–1964), *Silent Spring* (nonfiction)

Kung, S. W. (1905–), *Chinese in American Life* (nonfiction)

Lichtenstein, Roy (1923–), *Comic Strips* (painting)

Warhol, Andy (1928–1987), *Campbell Soup Can* (painting)

The Manchurian Candidate (film) directed by **John Frankenheimer**

Johnny Carson begins to host *The Tonight Show.*

Burgess, Anthony (1917–1993), *A Clockwork Orange* (novel)

Britten, Benjamin (1913–1976), *War Requiem* (music)

Fuentes, Carlos (1928–), *La muerte de Artemes Cruz* (novel)

Lessing, Doris (1919–), *The Golden Notebook* (novel)

Lévi-Strauss, Claude (1908–), *The Savage Mind* (anthropology)

Lawrence of Arabia (film) directed by **David Lean**

Ngo Ding Diem, president of South Vietnam, is assassinated.

Soviet Union sends first women into space.

Treaty between U.S., Britain, and Soviet Union bans all but underground nuclear tests.

1963
Baldwin, James (1924–1987), *The Fire Next Time* (essay)

Fornes, Maria Irene (1930–), *Tango Palace* (drama, written in 1960)

Kerouac, Jack (1922–1969), *Visions of Gerard* (novel)

Martin Luther King delivers "I have a dream" speech.

President John F. Kennedy is assassinated.

Vice-President Lyndon Johnson assumes office of the president.

Medger Evers, civil rights leader, is assassinated.

American Literary Texts	American Events, Texts, and Arts	Other Events, Texts, and Arts
McCarthy, Mary (1912–1989), *The Group* (novel) Mailer, Norman (1923–), *The Presidential Papers* (novelistic journalism) Malamud, Bernard (1914–1986), *Idiots First* (fiction) Pynchon, Thomas (1937–), *V.* (novel) Rechy, John (1934–), *City of Night* (novel) Updike, John (1932–), *The Centaur* (novel) Vonnegut, Kurt (1922–), *Cat's Cradle* (novel)	Treaty signed against atmospheric tests of atomic bombs. Julia Child introduces haute cuisine to America on the television show *The French Chef*. Friedan, Betty (1921–), *The Feminine Mystique* (nonfiction) Harrington, Michael (1928–), *Other America* (nonfiction)	Military leaders of Dominican Republic overthrow the first legally elected president in 38 years, Juan D. Bosch. Audio cassette invented in Holland. Böll, Heinrich (1917–1983), *The Clown* (novel) Oë, Kenzaburo (1935–), *Hiroshima Notes* (memorial narrative) Havel, Václav (1936–), *The Garden Party* (drama, translated, 1969) *8½* (film) directed by Federico Fellini *High and Low* (film) directed by Akira Kurosawa
1964 Albee, Edward (1928–), *Tiny Alice* (drama) Baldwin, James (1924–1987), *The Amen Corner* (drama), *Blues for Mister Charlie* (drama) Baraka, Amiri (1934–), *The Slave* (drama), *The Toilet* (drama), *Dutchman* (drama) Bellow, Saul (1915–), *Herzog* (novel) Ellison, Ralph (1914–1994) *Shadow and Act* (essays) Gelber, Jack (1932–) *On Ice* (novel)	Gulf of Tonkin incident leads to escalation of Vietnam War. President Lyndon Johnson signs civil rights bill, which forbids discrimination in voting, employment, and public services. He declares "War on Poverty." Medicare set up by law.	Communist China explodes its first nuclear device. Apartheid government of South Africa arrests Nelson Mandela for subversive activity. Leonid Brezhnev and Aleksei Kosygin depose Khrushchev as leader of the Soviet Union.

Romania asserts autonomy from Soviet control of its industry and foreign policy.

The Beatles tour the U.S. and begin the "British Invasion" of rock 'n' roll.

Böll, Heinrich (1917–1951), *1947 to 1951* (fiction)

Laurence, Margaret (1926–1987), *The Stone Angel* (novel)

Lessing, Doris (1919–), *Children of Violence* (novel, vol 2. published 1965)

Oë, Kenzaburo (1935–), *A Personal Matter* (novel)

Stan Getz, João and Astrid Gilberto record "The Girl from Ipanema" (bossa nova).

The Gospel According to Saint Matthew (film) directed by **Pier Pasolini**

Winston Churchill (1874–1965) dies.

U.S. uses napalm bombs for first time in Vietnam.

U.S. begins to use B-52s to bomb Vietnam.

Lyndon Johnson reelected president of the U.S.

Escobedo v. Illinois: U.S. Supreme Court rules that persons accused of crimes have the right to counsel, and that evidence acquired without proper cause is inadmissable in court.

U.S. spacecraft Ranger 7 takes first detailed photographs of the moon.

IBM introduces OS/360, the first widely used computer operating system. Music synthesizer invented.

Marcuse, Herbert (1898–1979), *One-Dimensional Man* (nonfiction)

John Coltrane (1926–1967) records *A Love Supreme* (jazz)

Dr. Strangelove or: How I Learned to Stop Worrying and Love the Bomb (film) directed by **Stanley Kubrick**

Malcom X is assassinated.

President Lyndon Johnson signs Voting Rights Act, Higher Education Act.

Alabama state troopers and Dallas County deputies attack civil rights marchers from Selma to Montgomery.

Hemingway, Ernest (1899–1961), *A Moveable Feast* (memoir)

Hansberry, Lorraine (1930–1965), *The Sign in Sidney Brustein's Window* (drama)

The Living Theater produces *The Brig* (drama), *Mysteries* (drama)

Miller, Arthur (1915–), *After the Fall* (drama)

Selby, Jr., Hubert (1928–), *Last Exit to Brooklyn* (novel)

Shepard, Sam (1943–), *Cowboys* (drama), *The Rock Garden* (drama)

Wilson, Lanford (1937–), *Home Free* (drama), *Balm in Gilead* (drama), *Madness of Lady Bright* (drama)

1965   **Baldwin, James** (1924–1987), *Going to Meet the Man* (short stories)

Baraka, Amiri (1934–), *The System of Dante's Hell* (novel)

American Literary Texts	American Events, Texts, and Arts	Other Events, Texts, and Arts
Bullins, Ed (1936–), *Clara's Ole Man* (drama), *Dialect Determinism* (drama)	President Lyndon Johnson sends in troops to protect marchers.	U.S. military intervenes in Dominican Republic.
Fornes, Maria Irene (1930–), *Promenade* (drama), *Successful Life of 3* (drama, published 1968)	Blacks riot in Watts, California, for five days in August.	China commits itself to fomenting Communist revolution abroad.
Kerouac, Jack (1922–1969), *Desolation Angels* (novel)	U.S. begins regular bombing of North Vietnam and brings in more ground forces.	Houari Boumedienne deposes Ben Bella as leader of Algeria.
Kosinski, Jerzy (1933–1991), *The Painted Bird* (novel)	Hart-Celler Act amends McCarran-Walter Act and abolishes national origin as a basis for discrimination against immigration.	Albert Schweitzer (1875–1965) dies. Unmanned Soviet spacecraft crashes into the lunar surface.
McCarthy, Cormac (1933–), *The Orchard Keeper* (novel)	Student protest against ROTC, military recruitment, and military funding of research on college and university campuses.	Aleksei Leonov becomes first human to walk in space.
Miller, Arthur (1915–), *Incident of Vichy* (drama)		Pinter, Harold (1930–), *The Homecoming* (drama)
Mitchell, Joseph (1908-1998), *Joe Gould's Secret* (profile)		Stoppard, Tom (1937–), *Rosencrantz and Guildenstern Are Dead* (drama)
Owens, Rochelle (1936–), *Futz* (drama, written 1958, published 1968)	Arno Penzias and Robert Wilson, physicists, discover background cosmic radiation that later proves to be evidence for the theory that the universe began from a single point – the Big Bang Theory.	
Porter, Katherine Anne (1890–1980), *The Collected Stories of Katherine Anne Porter* (fiction)		
Schneck, Stephen (1933–), *The Nightclerk* (novel)		
Shepard, Sam (1943–), *Icarus' Mother* (drama), *Chicago* (drama)	New law prohibts the burning of draft cards in protest of the Vietnam War.	
Warren, Robert Penn (1905–1989), *Who Speaks for the Negro?* (essay)		

Williams, Tennessee (1911–1983), *Slapstick Tragedy* (drama)

Wilson, Lanford (1937–), *The Rimers of Eldritch* (drama), *This Is the Rill Speaking* (drama)

1966 Albee, Edward (1928–), *A Delicate Balance* (drama)

Barth, John (1930–), *Giles Goat-Boy* (novel)

Capote, Truman (1924–1984), *In Cold Blood* (novelistic journalism)

McMurtrey, Larry (1936–), *The Last Picture Show* (novel)

Nabokov, Vladimir (1899–1977), *Speak, Memory* (memoir)

Ozick, Cynthia (1928–), *Trust* (novel)

Percy, Walker (1916–1990), *The Last Gentleman* (novel)

Price, Reynolds (1933–), *A Generous Man* (novel)

Pynchon, Thomas (1937–), *The Crying of Lot 49* (novel)

Shepard, Sam (1943–), *La Turista* (drama)

Federal government requires tobacco companies to put health warning label on cigarette packs.

First photographs of Mars, sent by Mariner 4, reveal no signs of life.

Bob Dylan causes outrage when he switches from acoustic to electric guitar at Newport Folk Festival.

Now (National Organization for Women) founded.

U.S. Supreme Court finds in *Miranda v. Arizona* that police must inform suspects of their constitutional rights.

Huey Newton and Bobby Seale found the Black Panther Party.

Race riots wrack Chicago, Cleveland, Brooklyn, Omaha, Baltimore, San Francisco, and Jacksonville during July heat wave.

Whites throw stones at Martin Luther King, Jr. during march in Chicago.

Edward Brooke of Massachusetts is the first black elected to U.S. Senate in 85 years.

Mao Tse-Tung launches Cultural Revolution in China.

Hendrik F. Verwoerd, prime minister of South Africa and designer of apartheid, is assassinated.

General Suharto deposes President Sukarno of Indonesia.

Ferdinand Marcos is elected president of the Philippines.

Amado, Jorge (1912–), *Doña Flor and Her Husbands* (novel)

Rhys, Jean (1890–1979), *Wide Sargasso Sea* (novel)

Andrei Rublev (film) directed by **Andrei Tarkovsky**

Blow-Up (film) directed by **Michelangelo Antonioni**

American Literary Texts	American Events, Texts, and Arts	Other Events, Texts, and Arts
Susann, Jacqueline (1921–1974), *Valley of the Dolls* (novel)	The *New York World-Telegram and Sun*, the *N.Y. Journal-American*, and the *New York Herald Tribune* merge. New paper folds in 1967 and leaves New York with only 3 newspapers.	
Walker, Margaret (1915–), *Jubilee* (novel	Gemini 6 and Gemini 7 make first rendevous in outer space and fly in formation for 6 hours.	
	Venturi, Robert (1925–), *Complexity and Contradiction in Architecture* (nonfiction)	
	The Sound of Music (film) dir. Robert Wise	
1967 **Barthelme, Donald** (1931–), *Snow White* (novel)	Thurgood Marshall sworn in as first black justice on the U.S. Supreme Court.	Israel seizes the Sinai Penisula in Six-Day War.
Burroughs, William (1914–1977), *The Ticket That Exploded* (novel)	U.S. population passes 200 million.	Civil war breaks out in Nigeria and Congo.
Jones, James (1921–1977), *Go to the Widowmaker* (novel)	Race riots sweep through the cities of U.S. throughout the summer.	Sixty-two countries ratify a treaty that limits the use of outer space for military purposes.
McCarthy, Mary (1912–1989), *Vietnam* (journalism)	Congress denies Adam Clayton Powell his seat because of misuse of funds.	Leonid Brezhnev denounces Mao's lack of Communism in a television broadcast.
Momaday, N. Scott (1934–), *The Journey of Tai-Me* (Kiowa myths)	U.S. begins to build anti-ballistic missile (ABM) defense system.	
Oates, Joyce Carol (1938–), *A Garden of Earthly Delights* (novel)	U.S. admits it bombed civilian targets in North Vietnam.	

Thomas, Piri (1928–), *Down These Mean Streets* (personal narrative)

Rechy, John (1934–), *Numbers* (novel)

Styron, William (1925–), *Confessions of Nat Turner* (novel)

Vidal, Gore (1925–), *Washington, D.C.* (novel)

1968 Albee, Edward (1928–), *Quotations from Chairman Mao Tse-Tung* (drama), *Box* (drama)

Baldwin, James (1924–1987), *Tell Me How Long the Train's Been Gone* (novel)

Barth, John (1930–), *Lost in the Funhouse* (short stories)

Barthelme, Donald (1931–), *Unspeakable Practices, Unnatural Acts* (short stories)

Bellow, Saul (1915–), *Mosby's Memoirs and Other Stories* (short stories)

Coover, Robert (1932–), *The Universal Baseball Association, Inc.: J. Henry Waugh Prop.* (novel)

Didion, Joan (1934–), *Slouching Towards Bethlehem* (essays)

Probe reveals CIA has set up dummy foundations to give money to student organizations.

First human heart transplant.

Sung, Betty Lee (1924–), *Mountain of Gold: The Story of Chinese in America* (nonfiction)

Bob Dylan (1941–) releases "Blonde on Blonde" (music)

The Graduate (film) directed by Mike Nichols

Robert Kennedy assassinated.

Martin Luther King assassinated.

American Indian Movement founded, a militant organization seeking reparation for lost lands and broken treaties.

Senator Eugene McCarthy bids for presidential nomination on an anti–Vietnam War platform.

Kerner Commission reports white racism is chief cause of unrest among African Americans.

Riots rock Democratic Party Convention and streets of Chicago.

Students riot on several university and college campuses in protest of the Vietnam War.

The secession of the region of Biafra from Nigeria leads to civil war. Famine follows as Nigeria wins war and deprives region of food.

García Márquez, Gabriel (1928–), *One Hundred Years of Solitude* (novel, English translation 1970)

The Beatles release *Sergeant Pepper's Lonely Hearts Club Band* (music) and surpass Bing Crosby as all-time biggest sellers of recorded music.

Communist troops in Vietnam launch Tet Offensive.

Battle of Saigon.

Soviets invade Czechoslovakia to suppress move toward liberalism, democracy, and capitalism.

Romania agrees to a cultural exchange with the U.S.

Students in Warsaw riot in support of Czechoslovakia.

The superpowers sign Nuclear Nonproliferation Treaty.

Student protests in France balloon into riots and civil disobedience involving 10 million people.

American Literary Texts	American Events, Texts, and Arts	Other Events, Texts, and Arts
Exley, Frederick (1929–1992), *A Fan's Notes* (novel)	Shirley Chisholm, of New York, is first black woman elected to Congress.	Students protest in Mexico against presence of military on university campuses.
Foreman, Richard (1937–), *Angelface* (novel)	*Hair* (musical) premiers on Broadway.	Pope Paul VI bans the use of artificial birth-control methods by
Living Theater presents *Paradise Now* (performance art)	**Berrigan, Daniel** (1921–), *Night Flight to Hanoi* (nonfiction)	Catholics.
McCarthy, Cormac (1933–), *Outer Dark* (novel)	**Cleaver, Eldridge** (1935–), *Soul on Ice* (nonfiction)	Quebec separtist groups merge to form Parti Quebecois.
McCarthy, Mary (1912–1989), *Hanoi* (journalism)	**Grotowski, Jerzy** (1933–), *Towards a Poor Theater* (non-fiction)	Canada nationalizes health care.
Mailer, Norman (1923–), *The Armies of the Night* (novelistic journalism), *Miami and the Siege of Chicago* (novelistic journalism)	*Planet of the Apes* (film) directed by **Franklin Schaffner**	**Handke, Peter** (1942–), *Kaspar* (drama)
Miller, Arthur (1915–), *The Price* (drama)	**Stanley Kubrick**	**Havel, Václav** (1936–), *The Memorandum* (drama), *The Increased Difficulty of Concentration* (drama)
Momaday, N. Scott (1934–), *House Made of Dawn* (novel)	*2001: A Space Odyssey* (film) directed by	
Oates, Joyce Carol (1938–), *Expensive People* (novel)	CBS begins to telecast *Hawaii Five-O* (1968–1980), which becomes the longest running police drama on television.	
Open Theater presents *The Serpent* (drama)		
Performance Group presents *Dionysus 69* (performance art)		
Updike, John (1932–), *Couples* (novel)		
Vidal, Gore (1925–), *Myra Breckinridge* (novel)		
Wolfe, Tom (1931–), *The Electric Kool-Aid Acid Test* (New Journalism)		

1969

Baraka, Amiri (1934–), *Four Black Revolutionary Plays* (drama)

Coover, Robert (1932–), *Pricksongs and Descants* (short stories)

Kopit, Arthur (1937–), *Indians* (drama)

LeGuin, Ursula (1929–), *The Left Hand of Darkness* (novel)

Marshall, Paule (1929–), *The Chosen Place, the Timeless People* (novel)

Momaday, N. Scott (1934–), *The Way to Rainy Mountain* (novel)

Nabokov, Vladimir (1899–1977), *Ada, or Ardor* (novel)

Oates, Joyce Carol (1938–), *them* (novel)

Open Theater presents *Terminal* (performance piece)

Puzo, Mario (1920–), *The Godfather* (novel)

Roth, Philip (1933–), *Portnoy's Complaint* (novel)

Stafford, Jean (1915–1979), *Collected Stories* (fiction)

Susann, Jacqueline (1921–1974), *The Love Machine* (novel)

Vonnegut, Kurt (1922–), *Slaughterhouse Five* (novel)

Chicano Youth Conference

Stonewall rebellion: Gays resist the abuse of the New York Police Department.

Troop dissent in Vietnam makes the news in the U.S.

U.S. Supreme Court orders Southern states to quit resisting the integration of public schools.

250,000 anti–Vietnam War protestors march to Washington, D.C.

Woodstock Music Festival (rock 'n' roll) in upper New York state draws over 500,000 people.

Apollo 11 reaches the moon; Neil Armstrong is first man to touch the lunar surface.

ARPAnet, predecessor of the Internet, goes on line.

Public Broadcasting System established.

Saturday Evening Post ends publication (1821–1969).

Physicist John Wheeler coins the term *black hole* for superdense areas in outer space.

Vietnam peace talks begin.

My Lai massacre of 1968 becomes public knowledge.

Rhodesia severs ties with Britain; white minority writes new constitution.

Military junta in Brazil deposes President Arthur da Costa e Silva.

Soviet Union and China clash in border war.

Charles DeGaulle resigns as French president after losing a vote of confidence.

Canada passes law that gives its speakers the right to speak French as well as English.

Socialist government wins power in West German Bundestag. Willy Brandt becomes chancellor.

Britain ends capital punishment.

Videotape cassette invented in Japan.

Solzhenitsyn, Aleksander (1918–), *Cancer Ward* (novel)

1970

American Literary Texts	American Events, Texts, and Arts	Other Events, Texts, and Arts
Angelou, Maya (1928–), *I Know Why the Caged Bird Sings* (novel)	Chomsky, Noam (1928–), *American Power and the New Mandarins* (essays)	U.S. invades Cambodia. Civil War in Jordan.
Barthelme, Donald (1931–), *City Life* (short stories)	Reuben, David (1933–), *Everything You Wanted to Know About Sex But Were Afraid to Ask* (non-fiction)	Salvador Allende Gossens, a Marxist, wins presidential election in Chile.
Bellow, Saul (1915–), *Mr. Sammler's Planet* (novel)	*Easy Rider* (film) dir. **Dennis Hopper**	Military junta in Argentina deposes Juan Carlos Onganía.
Breuer, Lee (1937–), *The Red Horse Animation* (drama)	*Midnight Cowboy* (film) dir. **John Schlesinger**	Gamal Abdel Nasser (1918–1970) dies a day after he brokers end to
Brown, Dee (1908–), *Bury My Heart at Wounded Knee* (historical narrative)	Miles Davis (1926–1991) records *In a Silent Way*.	civil war in Jordan. Anwar Sadat succeeds him.
Bullins, Ed (1936–), *It Bees Dat Way* (drama), *The Duplex* (drama)	U.S. gross national product is twice what it was in 1960.	Thor Heyerdahl and the crew of *Ra II* successfully sail in a reed boat
Hemingway, Ernest (1899–1961), *Islands in the Stream* (novel, published posthumously)	National Guardsmen kill 4 student pro-testors at Kent State University.	from Morocco to Barbados to prove that ancient Egyptians could
	Water Quality Improvement Act passed.	have visited the New World.
	National Air Quality Act passed.	
	Environmental Protection Agency established.	
	U.S. Supreme Court rules manufacturers must pay women on assembly lines equal pay for equal work.	
	Militants accidentally blow up town-house in Greenwich Village where they were making bombs.	

Mamet, David (1947–), *Lakeboat* (drama, published 1981)

Morrison, Toni (1931–), *The Bluest Eye* (novel)

Shepard, Sam (1943–), *Operation Sidewinder* (drama, published 1974)

Walker, Alice (1944–), *The Third Life of Grange Copeland* (novel)

Welty, Eudora (1909–), *Losing Battles* (novel)

Wilson, Lanford (1937–), *Lemon Sky* (drama)

Floppy disk invented.

National Public Radio established.

Chomsky, Noam (1928–), *At War with Asia* (nonfiction)

Millett, Kate (1934–), *Sexual Politics* (nonfiction)

Okimoto, Daniel I. (1942–), *American in Disguise* (nonfiction)

Five Easy Pieces (film) directed **Bob Rafelson**

M*A*S*H (film) directed by **Robert Altman**

Vital Alzar and his crew sail a long raft from Ecuador to Australia to prove that South American Indians could have sailed across the Pacific.

Yukio Mishima (1925–1970) commits *seppuku* (ritual suicide) after haranguing Japanese Army for its failure to live up to the Samurai tradition.

1971

Bullins, Ed (1936–), *The Fabulous Miss Marie* (drama), *New England Winter* (drama)

DeLillo, Don (1936–), *Americana* (novel)

Doctorow, E. L. (1931–), *The Book of Daniel* (novel)

Gaines, Ernest (1933–), *The Autobiography of Miss Jane Pittman* (novel)

Galarza, Ernesto (1905–), *Barrio Boy* (personal narrative)

Hawkes, John (1925–), *The Blood Oranges* (novel)

Kerouac, Jack (1922–1969), *Pic* (novel)

Kosinski, Jerzy (1933–1991), *Being There* (novel)

The *New York Times* publishes the Pentagon Papers, which reveal the actual level of U.S. involvement in Vietnam.

Twenty-Sixth Constitutional Amendment lowers the voting age to 18.

Computer microprocessor invented.

NASDAQ founded.

U.S. cuts dollar free from the price of gold.

Amtrak begins operation with the goal to revitalize passenger rail service.

Over 1,000 state troopers storm Attica Prison to quell prisoner riots.

Chile refuses compensation to U.S. firms after taking over their copper mines.

Bangladesh declares independence from Pakistan.

Communist China gains United Nations membership after over 20 years of unsuccessful applications.

Idi Amin deposes Milton Obote as leader of Uganda.

Protestants and Catholics renew violence in Ulster, Ireland; 172 civilians and soldiers die during the year.

American Literary Texts	American Events, Texts, and Arts	Other Events, Texts, and Arts
Mailer, Norman (1923–), *Of a Fire on the Moon* (nonfiction), *A Prisoner of Sex* (personal narrative)	Comfort, Alex (1920–), *The Joy of Sex* (nonfiction)	The Big Four (U.S., France, Britain, Soviet Union) agree to reduce the political focus on Berlin and approach easy access to West Berlin.
Ozick, Cynthia (1928–), *The Pagan Rabbi* (fiction)	Greer, Germane (1939–), *The Female Eunuch* (nonfiction)	
Percy, Walker (1916–1990), *Love in the Ruins* (novel)	Rawls, John (1921–), *A Theory of Justice* (moral philosophy)	
Rabe, David (1940–), *The Basic Training of Pavlo Hummel* (drama), *Sticks and Bones* (drama)	CBS begins to telecast *All in the Family* (1971–1979)	
Updike, John (1932–), *Rabbit Redux* (novel)		
Wilson, Robert (1941–), *Deafman Glance* (drama)		
1972 Acosta, Oscar (1935–1974), *The Autobiography of a Brown Buffalo* (novel)	Burglars break into Democratic National Committee offices in the Watergate Hotel.	Arab terrorists kill Israeli athletes at Munich Olympic Games.
Anaya, Rudolfo (1937–), *Bless me, Ultima* (novel)	SALT I treaty limits the number of ICBMs that the Cold War superpowers may possess.	Britain begins direct rule of Northern Ireland.
Aztlán: An Anthology of Mexican American Literature, edited by Luis Valdez et al.	Détente between U.S. and Soviet Union.	Communists launch massive offensive southward across the Demilitarized Zone in Vietnam.
Barth, John (1930–), *Chimera* (novella)	J. Edgar Hoover (1895–1972), director of the FBI since 1924, dies.	Japan and China sign treaty ending technical state of war that had existed for over 40 years.
Mamet, David (1947–), *Duck Variations* (drama, published 1978)	Native American militants known as "Indians of All Tribes" seize Alcatraz Island and occupy it for 19 months.	European Common Market expands from 6 to 10 members, but currency problems weaken unity movement.
Miller, Arthur (1915–), *The Creation of the World and Other Business* (drama)	U.S. and Canada sign treaty to clean up the Great Lakes.	
Miller, Isabel (1924–), *Patience and Sarah* (novel)		
Shepard, Sam (1943–), *The Tooth of Crime* (drama)		

Singer, Isaac Bashevis (1904–1991), *Enemies: A Love Story* (novel)

Welty, Eudora (1909–), *The Optimist's Daughter* (novel)

Williams, Tennessee (1911–1983), *Small Craft Warnings* (drama)

Wilson, Robert (1941–), *Overture to Ka Mountain* (drama)

1973   Acosta, Oscar (1935–1974), *The Revolt of the Cockroach People* (novel)

Brown, Rita Mae (1944–), *Rubyfruit Jungle* (novel)

Kerouac, Jack (1922–1969), *Visions of Cody* (novel)

Mailer, Norman (1923–), *Marilyn* (novelistic journalism)

Morrison, Toni (1931–), *Sula* (novel)

O'Brien, Tim (1946–), *If I Die in a Combat Zone* (personal narrative)

Pynchon, Thomas (1937–), *Gravity's Rainbow* (novel)

Rabe, David (1940–), *The Orphan* (drama)

Vidal, Gore (1925–), *Burr* (novel)

Calvino, Italo (1923–1985), *Invisible Cities* (fiction, English translation 1974)

Handke, Peter (1942–), *A Sorrow Beyond Dreams* (memoir)

Mishima, Yukio (1925–1970), *Spring Snow* (novel, first English translation)

Environmental Protection Agency bans the use of the pesticide DDT.

The Dow Jones average closes above 1,000 points for the first time.

Pocket calculator invented.

Compact disk (CD) invented; the CD becomes commonly available in 1983.

Bobby Fisher is the first American to win the World Chess Championship.

CBS begins to telecast *The Waltons* (1972–1981).

Supreme Court rules in *Roe v. Wade* that states may not prohibit abortions.

Watergate scandal embroils President Richard M. Nixon.

U.S. and Vietnam sign cease-fire agreement.

Military draft ends.

Militants from American Indian Movement seize church at Wounded Knee and demand investigation into broken treaties.

Gas crunch follows OPEC's decision to ban exports to the U.S.

Vice-President Sprio Agnew resigns to face charges of tax evasion.

Military coup in Chile overthrows President Salvador Allende Gossens.

Arab–Israeli War.

Arab members of OPEC ban exports of oil to the U.S.

President Juan Peron returns to power in Argentina after 20 years in exile.

Leonid Brezhnev visits the U.S.

Francisco Franco steps down as leader of Spain.

Great Britain, Ireland, and Denmark join the European Common Market.

Computed axial tomography (CAT) scan invented in England.

American Literary Texts	American Events, Texts, and Arts	Other Events, Texts, and Arts
Vonnegut, Kurt (1922–), *Breakfast of Champions* (novel) Walker, Alice (1944–), *In Love and Trouble* (short stories) White, Edmund (1940–), *Forgetting Elena* (novel) Williams, Tennesee (1911–1983), *Outcry* (drama) Wilson, Lanford (1937–), *The Hot l Baltimore* (drama)	Chomsky, Noam (1928–), *For Reasons of State* (essay) Geertz, Clifford (1926–), *The Interpretation of Cultures* (anthropology) Heibrun, Carolyn (1926–), *Toward a Recognition of Androgyny* (nonfiction) Johnston, Jill (1929–), *Lesbian Nation* (nonfiction) *Mean Streets* (film) directed by **Martin Scorsese**	Amis, Martin (1949–), *The Rachel Papers* (novel) Mishima, Yukio (1925–1970), *Runaway Horses* (novel, first English translation), *Temple of Dawn* (novel, first English translation) *The Last Tango in Paris* (film) directed by **Bernardo Bertolucci**
1974 *Aiiieeeee!: An Anthology of Asian-American Writing*, edited by Frank Chin et al. Angelou, Maya (1915–), *Gather Together in My Garden* (personal narrative) Baldwin, James (1924–1987), *If Beale Street Could Talk* (novel) Dillard, Annie (1945–), *Pilgrim at Tinker Creek* (essays) Hawkes, John (1925–), *Death, Sleep and the Traveler* (novel) Jong, Erica (1942–), *Fear of Flying* (novel) Lurie, Alison (1926–), *The War Between the Tates* (novel)	U.S. Supreme Court orders President Nixon to turn over White House tapes. President Richard M. Nixon resigns because of Watergate scandal. Vice-President Gerald Ford assumes office of the president and pardons Richard M. Nixon. Freedom of Information Act passed. Three members of the Symbionese Liberation Army kidnap Patty Hearst, the granddaughter of newspaper baron William Randolph Hearst.	India explodes its first nuclear device. Soviets deport Aleksandr Solzhenitsyn to West Germany. Arab nations end oil embargo against the U.S. Arab nations support Yasir Arafat as leader of Palestinian Arabs. Liberals overthrow military dictatorship in Portugal. Böll, Heinrich (1917–1983), *The Lost Honor of Katarina Blum* (novel) Brandão, Ignacio de Loyola (1936–), *Zero* (novel, English translation 1983)

Mamet, David (1947–), *Sexual Perversity in Chicago* (drama)

Pirsig, Robert M. (1928–), *Zen and the Art of Motorcycle Maintenance* (personal narrative)

Prose, Francine (1947–), *The Glorious Ones* (novel)

Roth, Philip (1933–), *My Life as a Man* (fiction)

Shepard, Sam (1943–), *Geography of a Horse Dreamer* (drama)

Tyler, Anne (1941–), *Celestial Navigation* (novel)

Welch, James (1940–), *Winter in the Blood* (novel)

1975

Albee, Edward (1928–), *Seascape* (drama)

Alther, Lisa (1944–), *Kinflicks* (novel)

Barthelme, Donald (1931–), *The Dead Father* (novel)

Bellow, Saul (1915–), *Humboldt's Gift* (novel)

Doctorow, E. L. (1931–), *Ragtime* (novel)

Mailer, Norman (1923–), *The Fight* (nonfiction)

Mamet, David (1947–), *American Buffalo* (drama)

Merriam, Eve (1916–), *Out of Our Father's House* (drama)

Murayama, Milton (1923–), *All I Asking for Is My Body* (novel)

CIA director William Colby testifies that the Nixon Administration authorized the CIA to destabilize the Chilean economy in order to weaken Salvador Allende Gossens political position.

Riots wrack Boston as busing begins to enforce racial integration in the public schools.

Muhammad Ali beats George Foreman in a boxing match in Kenya, regaining the heavyweight title he lost when he refused to enter military service during the Vietnam War.

Last American troops pull out of Vietnam.

John Mitchell, H. R. Haldeman, and John Ehrlichmann are found guilty of Watergate cover-up.

"Blue-Ribbon" panel reveals illegal CIA operations abroad and invasions of the privacy of U.S. citizens.

U.S. agrees to sell wheat to the Soviet Union.

Jimmy Hoffa, Teamsters Union leader, disappears, apparently murdered.

Carey, Peter (1943–), *The Fat Man in History* (novel)

Mishima, Yukio (1925–1970), *Decay of the Angel* (novel, first English translation)

Indira Ghandi declares state of emergency in India and limits civil freedoms.

Pol Pot and the Khmer Rouge depose the government of Cambodia.

U.S. Apollo and Russian Soyuz spaceships dock together in outer space.

Fuentes, Carlos (1928–), *Terra nostra* (novel)

Levi, Primo (1919–1987), *The Periodic Table* (meditations)

American Literary Texts	American Events, Texts, and Arts	Other Events, Texts, and Arts
	Wilson, Lanford (1937–), *The Mound Builders* (drama)	Venturi, Robert (1925–), and Rauch, John, Tucker House (architecture) *Nashville* (film) directed by Robert Altman	García Márquez, Gabriel (1928–), *The Autumn of the Patriarch* (novel, English translation 1976)
1976	Anaya, Rudolfo (1937–), *Heart of Aztlán* (novel)	Bicentennial of U.S. Declaration of Independence	Argentinian military overthrows government of Argentina.
	Angelou, Maya (1928–), *Singin and Swingin and Gettin Merry Like Christmas* (personal narrative)	House and Senate Intelligence Committees reveal that the CIA and the FBI continue to violate the privacy of U.S. citizens.	North and South Vietnam join to form Socialist Republic of Vietnam.
	Carver, Raymond (1939–1988), *Will You Please Be Quiet, Please* (short stories)	James (Jimmy) Carter elected president.	Mao Tse-Tung (1894–1976) dies.
	DeLillo, Don (1936–), *Ratner's Star* (novel)	Vikings I and II land on the surface of Mars.	Rhodesia agrees to end white minority rule.
	Federman, Raymond (1928–), *Take It or Leave It* (fiction)	Federal court releases Patty Hearst after 14 months in prison; she had helped her kidnappers rob a bank.	Spanish citizens vote overwhelmingly to reform the national government toward democracy and bring an end to Franco policies.
	Hawkes, John (1925–), *Travesty* (novel)	A mysterious bacterium in a hotel's air-conditioning system kills 29 members at the American Legion Conference in Philadelphia; illness now known as Legionnaire's disease.	Mario Soares, leader of Portugal's Socialist party, becomes president of Portugal.
	Kingston, Maxine Hong (1940–), *The Woman Warrior* (novel)	Howe, Irving (1920–1993), *World of Our Fathers* (nonfiction)	Britain and France begin to fly the Concorde, a supersonic passenger jet, across the Atlantic ocean in less than 4 hours.
	Kovic, Ron (1946–), *Born on the Fourth of July* (personal narrative)		*Seven Beauties* (film) directed by Lina Wertmuller
	Momaday, N. Scott (1934–), *The Names* (memoir)		
	Rabe, David (1940–), *Streamers* (drama)		
	Rich, Adrienne (1929–) *Of Woman Born* (essay)		
	Shepard, Sam (1943–) *Angel City* (drama), *Suicide in B-flat* (drama)		

Vidal, Gore (1925–), *1876* (novel)

Walker, Alice (1944–), *Meridian* (novel)

Weglyn, Michi (1926–), *Years of Infamy: The Untold Story of America's Concentration Camps* (nonfiction)

Glass, Philip (1937–), and Wilson, Robert (1941–), *Einstein on the Beach* (opera)

Rocky (film) directed by John G. Avildsen

Taxi Driver (film) directed by Martin Scorsese

President Jimmy Carter raises the Energy Department to Cabinet level and declares "war" on energy waste.

President Jimmy Carter pardons draft evaders from the Vietnam War.

U.S. government passes bill that regulates the strip-mining of coal; companies are required to repair the earth after the mining is finished.

Apple Computer introduces Apple II, the first commercially successful personal computer.

World Trade Center in Manhattan is completed.

Roots (television miniseries), based on novel by Alex Haley (1921–) about

Conservatives gain power in Israel under Menachem Begin.

China lifts ban on the music of Beethoven.

Vatican bars women from the priesthood.

Mararjai Desai beats Indira Ghandi in election in India.

Pakistani military deposes President Zulfikar Bhutto and social discord follows.

South Africa makes severest crackdown in 20 years on public protest by black majority.

Oë, Kenzaburo (1935–), *Teach Us to Outgrow Our Madness* (fiction)

1977   Bullins, Ed (1936–), *DADDY!* (drama)

Caputo, Philip (1941–), *A Rumor of War* (personal narrative)

Cheever, John (1912–1982), *Falconer* (novel)

Coover, Robert (1932–), *The Public Burning* (novel)

Didion, Joan (1934–), *Book of Common Prayer* (novel)

Herr, Michael (1950–), *Dispatches* (personal narrative)

Mamet, David (1947–), *The Water Engine* (drama)

Miller, Arthur (1915–), *The Archbishop's Ceiling* (drama)

Morrison, Toni (1931–), *Song of Solomon* (novel)

Rechy, John (1934–), *The Sexual Outlaw: A Documentary* (documentary narrative)

American Literary Texts	American Events, Texts, and Arts	Other Events, Texts, and Arts
Silko, Leslie Marmon (1948–), *Ceremony* (novel)	slavery, captures then largest television audience in history.	Gorecki, Henryk (1933–), *Third Symphony* (music)
Tyler, Anne (1941–) *Earthly Possessions* (novel)	*Star Wars* (film) directed by **George Lucas**	
Williams, Tennessee (1911–1983), *Vieux Carré* (drama)	*Annie Hall* (film) directed by **Woody Allen**	
Wright, Richard (1908–1960), *American Hunger* (personal narrative, published posthumously)		
1978 Cheever, John (1912–1982), *The Stories of John Cheever* (fiction)	Congress agrees to cede control of the Panama Canal to Panama in 1999.	Shah of Iran declares martial law as social protests increase.
Holleran, Andrew (1943–), *Dancer from the Dance* (novel)	U.S. Supreme Court finds racial quotas unconstitutional in *Bakke v. University of California.*	Camp David Accord leads to peace between Israel and Egypt.
Jones, James (1921–1977), *Whistle* (novel)	Californians pass Proposition 13, which slashes property taxes 57% and	Red Brigade terrorists kidnap and kill Aldo Moro, former Italian prime minister
King, Stephen (1947–), *The Stand* (novel, revised 1994)	severely limits future increases. It becomes a model for similar propositions in other states.	Civil war wracks several African nations.
Kramer, Larry (1935–), *Faggots* (fiction)	Nationwide coal miners strike.	First test-tube baby born in England.
Mori, Toshio (1910–), *Woman from Hiroshima* (novel)	Stagflation besets U.S. economy. First	Amis, Martin (1949–), *Success* (novel)
O'Brien, Tim (1946–), *Going After Cacciato* (novel)	major setback for Keynesian economic policy.	Angelo, Ivan (1936–), *A Festa* (novel, English translation 1982)
Shepard, Sam (1943–), *Buried Child* (drama), *Tongues* (drama, with Joseph Chaikin)	Mapplethorpe, Robert (1946–1989), *Photographs* (photography)	Pym, Barbara (1913–1980), *The Sweet Dove Died* (novel)
White, Edmund (1940–), *Nocturnes for the King of Naples* (fiction)		

750

Wilson, Lanford (1937–), *Fifth of July* (drama)

Wolfe, Tom (1931–), *The Right Stuff* (historical narrative)

1979   Albee, Edward (1928–), *The Lady from Dubuque* (drama)

Baldwin, James (1924–1987), *Just Above My Head* (novel)

Breuer, Lee (1937–), *A Prelude to a Death in Venice* (drama)

Fierstein, Harvey (1954–), *Torch Song Trilogy* (drama)

Henley, Beth (1952–), *Crimes of the Heart* (drama)

Hurston, Zora Neale (1903–1960), *I Love Myself When I Am Laughing* (collection)

McCarthy, Cormac (1933–), *Suttree* (novel)

Mailer, Norman (1923–), *The Executioner's Song* (novelistic journalism)

Miller, Arthur (1915–), *The American Clock* (drama)

Mori, Toshio (1910–), *The Chauvinist and Other Stories* (fiction)

Valdez, Luis (1940–), *Zoot Suit* (musical)

The Deerhunter (film) directed by **Michael Cimino**

Halloween (film) directed by **John Carpenter**; first "slasher" film

CBS begins to telecast *Dallas* (1978–1991).

Three Mile Island nuclear reactor partially melts down and releases radioactive gases.

U.S. government bails out financially strapped Chrysler Corporation.

U.S. and Soviet Union sign SALT II.

U.S. Supreme Court rules that state laws that require husbands but not wives to pay alimony are unconstitutional.

Vernon Jordan, president of the National Urban League, says blacks are on the verge of disaster as jobs leave the inner city.

The CIA admits it used satellites to spy on American students engaged in antiwar campaigns.

Ayatollah Khomeini takes over Iran and seizes American hostages.

Soviet Army invades Afghanistan.

Ugandan exiles overthrow the brutal dictator Idi Amin.

Vietnamese Army helps overthrow Pol Pot, Communist leader of Cambodia.

Civil unrest continues in Zimbabwe despite the creation of the nation's first black majority government.

General Agreement on Tarifs and Trades (GATT) devised.

Böll, Heinrich (1917–1983), *The Safety Net* (novel)

Calvino, Italo (1923–1985), *If on a Winter's Night a Traveler* (novel, English translation 1981)

	American Literary Texts	American Events, Texts, and Arts	Other Events, Texts, and Arts
	Roth, Philip (1933–), *The Ghost Writer* (novel)	The orbit of Skylab, U.S. space station, erodes and the station falls apart over Australia.	Iraq–Iran War (1980–1988) begins.
	Shepard, Sam (1943–), *Savage Love* (drama, with Joseph Chaikin)	A team of scientists announces the successful repair of a genetically damaged cell by injecting new genetic material into the cell.	Zimbabwe, formerly Rhodesia, becomes independent state.
	Styron, William (1925–), *Sophie's Choice* (novel)		Lech Walesa leads shipyard worker strike in Poland. The workers win right to form independent trade unions.
	Welch, James (1940–), *The Death of Jim Loney* (novel)	Mass suicide of followers of the Reverend Jim Jones at the People's Temple in Jonestown, Guyana.	
	Williams, Tennessee (1911–1983), *A Lovely Sunday For Crevecoeur* (drama)	*Breaking Away* (film) directed by **Peter Yates**	Eco, Umberto (1932–), *The Name of the Rose* (novel, English translation 1983)
	Wilson, Lanford (1937–), *Talley's Folley* (drama)		Kundera, Milan (1929–), *The Book of Laughter and Forgetting*
	Wong, Shawn (1949–), *Homebase* (novel)		
1980	*The Coming Out Stories* (personal narratives), edited by Susan Wolfe et al.	First appearance in U.S. of cases of acquired immunodeficiency syndrome (AIDS).	
	Kingston, Maxine Hong (1940–), *China Men* (novel)	Americans worry about year-long captivity of hostages in Iran.	
	Mann, Emily (1952–), *Still Life* (drama, published 1996)	U.S. boycotts the Olympic games in Moscow because of Soviet invasion of Afghanistan.	
	Percy, Walker (1916–1990), *The Second Coming* (novel)	Ronald Reagan elected president.	
	Robinson, Marilynne (1944–), *Housekeeping* (novel)	Massive toxic waste problem found in Love Canal, New York.	
	Shepard, Sam (1943–), *True West* (drama)		

White, Edmund (1940–), *A Boy's Own Story* (novel)

Whitmore, George (1945–), *Confessions of Danny Slocum* (personal narrative)

1981 Abbott, Jack (1944–), *In the Belly of the Beast* (personal narrative)

Carver, Raymond (1939–1988), *What We Talk About When We Talk About Love* (short stories)

Kogawa, Joy (1935–), *Obasan* (fiction)

Morrison, Toni (1931–), *Tar Baby* (novel)

Roth, Philip (1933–), *Zuckerman Unbound* (novel)

Silko, Leslie Marmon (1948–), *The Storyteller* (prose and poetry)

Updike, John (1932–), *Rabbit Is Rich* (novel)

Williams, Tennessee (1911–1983), *Something Cloudy, Something Clear* (drama)

Obsessed fan kills former Beatles member John Lennon.

Ordinary People (film) directed by **Robert Redford**

Raging Bull (film) directed by **Martin Scorsese**

82% of American households own a color television set; Nielsen ratings show that the average American watches 29 hours of television per week.

Space shuttle *Columbia* takes maiden voyage.

Sandra Day O'Connor is first woman appointed to U.S. Supreme Court.

President Ronald Reagan supports increased military spending in lieu of social programs.

Two-year string of murders of young African American children ends when police arrest Wayne B. Williams.

Obsessed fan of the film *Taxi Driver* tries to kill President Ronald Reagan.

IBM introduces the personal computer (PC).

MacIntyre, Alasdair (1929–), *After Virtue* (moral philosophy)

Iran frees American hostages.

Moslem extremists assassinate Egyptian President Anwar Sadat.

Polish government declares martial law and arrests Solidarity union leaders.

Rushdie, Salman (1947–), *Midnight's Children* (novel)

Birgit Haas Must Be Killed (film) directed by **Laurent Heynemann**

Mephisto (film) directed by **Istvan Szabo**

Pixote (film) directed by **Hector Babenco**

	American Literary Texts	American Events, Texts, and Arts	Other Events, Texts, and Arts
1982	Bellow, Saul (1915–), *The Dean's December* (novel) Hinojosa-Smith, Rolando (1929–), *Rites and Witnesses* (fiction) Mamet, David (1947–), *Edmond* (drama) Naylor, Gloria (1950–), *The Women of Brewster Place* (fiction) Norman, Marsha (1947–), *'night, Mother* (drama) Rodriguez, Richard (1944–), *Hunger of Memory* (personal narrative) Tyler, Anne (1941–), *Dinner at the Homesick Restaurant* (novel) Uchida, Yoshiko (1921–1992), *Desert Exile: The Uprooting of a Japanese Family* (personal narrative) Vidal, Gore (1925–), *Creation* (novel) Walker, Alice (1944–), *The Color Purple* (novel) Wilson, Lanford (1937–), *Angels Fall* (drama)	*Raiders of the Lost Ark* (film) directed by **Stephen Spielberg** NBC begins to telecast *Hill Street Blues* (1981–1987). AT&T relinquishes control of its Bell phone subsidiaries. President Ronald Reagan announces plan to fight the organized trade in illegal narcotics. Large antinuclear demonstration in Central Park, New York City. Ten-year fight to ratify Equal Rights Amendment fails. Senate passes bill that virtually eliminates busing to achieve racial integration. Unemployment in the U.S. reaches its highest point (10.8%) since 1940. First permanent artificial heart implanted in a human. *Blade Runner* (film) directed by **Ridley Scott** *E. T.* (film) directed by **Steven Spielberg** *Tron* (film) directed by **Steven Lisberger**	Israel invades Lebanon to remove terrorist camps. Britain defeats Argentina in battle for Falkland Islands; the defeat leads to the downfall of military dictatorship in Argentina and the restoration of democracy. Violence continues in Guatemala, Nicaragua, and El Salvador. Polish people continue to support the Solidarity labor movement; Lech Walesa, its leader, is released from jail. Leonid Brezhnev (1907–1982) dies.

1983

Allen, Paula Gunn (1939–), *The Woman Who Owned the Shadows* (novel)

Carver, Raymond (1939–1988), *Cathedral* (fiction)

Cisneros, Sandra (1954–), *The House on Mango Street* (fiction)

Fornes, Maria Irene (1930–), *Mud* (drama)

Hinojosa-Smith, Rolando (1929–), *Sketches of the Valley and Other Works* (fiction, originally published in Spanish in 1973 as *Estampas del valle y otras obras*)

Kennedy, William (1928–), *Ironweed* (novel)

Mamet, David (1947–), *Glengarry Glen Ross* (drama)

Marshall, Paule (1929–), *Praisesong for the Widow* (novel)

Mason, Robert (1946–), *Chickenhawk* (personal narratives)

Moraga, Cherríe (1952–), *Loving in the War Years* (personal narratives)

Roth, Philip (1933–), *The Anatomy Lesson* (novel)

Shepard, Sam (1943–), *Fool For Love* (drama)

1984

Bellow, Saul (1915–), *Him with His Foot in His Mouth and Other Stories* (fiction)

Erdrich, Louise (1954–), *Love Medicine* (novel)

Gibson, William (1948–), *Neuromancer* (novel)

260 U.S. marines killed in terrorist attack in Lebanon.

U.S. launches inquiry to find the cause of AIDS.

U.S. increases defense spending as tensions with the Soviet Union increase.

Sally Ride becomes first American woman to travel in outer space.

Congress passes a law to prevent Social Security from going bankrupt.

Residents of Chicago elect Harold Washington as the city's first African American mayor.

New York Philharmonic Horizons Festival is a rallying cry for a return to tonality in classical music.

Final episode of *M*A*S*H* (television series) airs and garners then largest television audience ever.

Huge deficit spending by the federal government and real estate speculation bolster the national economy.

150 million people on the verge of starvation as extreme drought strikes Africa.

Lech Walesa wins Nobel peace prize for his leadership of the Solidarity labor strike in Poland.

Yuri Andropov succeeds Leonid Brezhnev as leader of Soviet Union.

Unrest continues in Latin America; Reagan administration funds several rebel groups.

Souza, Márcio (1946–), *Mad Maria* (novel, English translation 1985)

Fanny and Alexander (film) directed by Ingmar Bergman

El Norte (film) directed by Gregory Nava

Entre Nous (film) directed by Diane Kurys

Sugar Cane Alley (film) directed by Euzhan Palcy

Soviet Union and Warsaw Pact nations boycott the Olympic games in Los Angeles in retaliation for 1980 boycott by U.S.

American Literary Texts	American Events, Texts, and Arts	Other Events, Texts, and Arts
Godwin, Gale (1937–), *The Finishing School* (novel)	Geraldine Ferraro first woman nominated as candidate for vice-president.	Indira Ghandi assassinated by two of her own bodyguards.
Heller, Joseph (1923–), *God Knows* (novel)	CIA admits mining harbors in Nicaragua.	Amis, Martin (1949–), *Money* (novel)
Lurie, Alison (1926–), *Foreign Affairs* (novel)	Ronald Reagan reelected president.	Kincaid, Jamaica (1949–), *Annie John* (novel)
McInerney, Jay (1955–), *Bright Lights, Big City* (novel)	Astronauts on space shuttle are first humans to float in space without tether connecting them to spaceship.	Kundera, Milan (1929–), *The Unbearable Lightness of Being* (novel)
Norman, Marsha (1947–), *Traveller in the Dark* (drama)	Interest in "String Theory" revives as a way to describe the fundamental physical properties of the universe.	*Home and the World* (film) directed by Satyajit Ray
Pynchon, Thomas (1937–), *Slow Learner* (fiction)	Apple Computer introduces the Mcintosh, first personal computer with a graphical user interface.	*The Killing Fields* (film) directed by Roland Joffe
Rabe, David (1940–), *Hurlyburly* (drama)	NBC begins to broadcast *The Cosby Show* (1984–1992).	
Vidal, Gore (1925–), *Lincoln* (novel)	*Tightrope* (film) directed by Richard Tuggle	
1985 Chute, Carolyn (1947–), *The Beans of Egypt, Maine* (novel)	Microsoft Corporation introduces Windows operating system.	Mikhail Gorbachev becomes General Secretary of the Soviet Union and announces new policies of *glasnost* and *perestroika*.
DeLillo, Don (1936–), *White Noise* (novel)	General Electric agrees to buy RCA in largest corporate merger outside the oil industry.	Live-Aid Rock Concert broadcast to 152 countries in effort to raise money for starving people of Africa.
Hawkes, John (1925–), *Innocence in Extremis* (novel)		
Hill, Carol (1942–), *The Eleven Million Mile High Dancer* (novel)		

Kitagawa, Muriel (1912–1974), *This Is My Own* (personal narrative)

McCarthy, Cormac (1933–), *Blood Meridian* (novel)

McMurtrey, Larry (1936–), *Lonesome Dove* (novel)

Mann, Emily (1952–), *Annulla, an Autobiography* (drama, earlier version 1977, published 1988)

Mason, Bobbie Ann (1940–), *In Country* (novel)

Naylor, Gloria (1950–), *Linden Hills* (novel)

Rivera, Tomás (1935–), *And the Earth Did Not Devour Him* (personal narrative, originally published in 1971 as . . . *Y no se lo tragó la tierra*, (translated by Rolando Hinojosa-Smith)

Shepard, Sam (1943–), *A Lie of the Mind* (drama)

Tyler, Anne (1941–), *The Accidental Tourist* (novel)

Wilson, August (1945–), *Ma Rainey's Black Bottom* (drama)

1986 Auster, Paul (1947–), *The New York Trilogy* (fiction)

Ellison, Ralph (1914–1994), *Going to the Territory* (fiction)

Ford, Richard (1944–), *The Sportswriter* (novel)

Hemingway, Ernest (1899–1961), *The Garden of Eden* (novel)

E. F. Hutton, one of the nation's largest brokerage houses, pleads guilty to financial misdealings.

Congress passes weakened Gramm-Rudman Bill to try to limit federal budget deficits; the Supreme Court declares it unconstitutional in 1987.

Reagan administration continues massive arms buildup and wins approval of MX missile, an ICBM stored on rails and shuttled between silos.

Brazil (film) directed by Terry Gilliam

Witness (film) directed by Peter Weir

ABC begins to telecast *Moonlighting* (1985–1989)

Space shuttle *Challenger* explodes.

U.S. imposes economic sanctions on South Africa because of apartheid.

U.S. bombs Libya in retaliation for terrorist bombing of disco in West Berlin.

Arab terrorists threaten the security of travelers in a series of highjackings and murders around the Mediterranean.

Carey, Peter (1943–), *Illywhacker* (novel)

García Márquez, Gabriel (1928–), *Love in the Time of Cholera* (novel)

Trials for human rights violations in Argentina; President Raul Alfonsín leads effort to resolve political issues of the "dirty war."

U.S. continues to provide military support for unrest in Latin America.

American Literary Texts	American Events, Texts, and Arts	Other Events, Texts, and Arts
Howe, Tina (1937–), *Coastal Disturbances* (drama)	William Rehnquist appointed chief justice of the U.S. Supreme Court. Tax Reform Law passes.	Soviet leader Mikhail Gorbachev releases Andrei Sakharov, a dissident Russian physicist, from internal exile.
Janowitz, Tama (1957–), *Slaves of New York* (fiction)	Crack cocaine first appears and quickly becomes associated with an increase in violent crime in America's cities.	President Ferdinand Marcos of the Philippines flees into exile amid the downfall of his corrupt government.
Leavitt, David (1961–), *The Lost Language of Cranes* (novel)	*Blue Velvet* (film) directed by **David Lynch**	An explosion damages the Chernobyl nuclear power plant and releases radioactive material into the Ukraine countryside.
Mohr, Nicholasa (1938–), *Nilda* (novel)		
Moore, Lorrie (1957–), *Anagrams* (novel)		
Prose, Francine (1947–), *Bigfoot Dreams* (novel)		
Taylor, Peter (1917–), *A Summons to Memphis* (novel)		
Wilson, August (1945–), *Fences* (drama)		

1987

American Literary Texts	American Events, Texts, and Arts	Other Events, Texts, and Arts
Auster, Paul (1947–), *In the Country of Last Things* (novel)	Iran Contra Scandal reveals Reagan administration traded weapons for cash to fund covert operations in Latin America.	Margaret Thatcher becomes first prime minister of Britain since 1820 to win a third term.
Barth, John (1930–), *Tidewater* (novel)	In January, the Dow Jones Industrial average closes above 2,000 for the first time.	South Korea drafts new constitution.
Bellow, Saul (1915–), *More Die of Heartbreak* (novel)	Dow Jones Industrial average plummets a record 508 points in October.	Doctors at Third International Conference on AIDS warn that the disease is spreading rampantly in the Third World.
Erdrich, Louise (1954–), *The Beet Queen* (novel)	U.S. becomes world's largest debtor nation with a total debt over $500 billion. In 1980, U.S. was world's largest creditor nation.	Failure to detect a civilian aircraft in Russian airspace leads to upheaval in Soviet military.
Ford, Richard (1944–), *Rock Springs* (fiction)		Vincent Van Gogh's *Sunflowers* sells at auction for $39.9 million.
Hinojosa-Smith Rolando (1929–), *Klail City* (novel, originally published in Spanish in 1976 as *Klail city y sus andredores*)		
Mamet, David (1947–), *Speed-the-Plow* (drama), *House of Games* (film)		

Morrison, Toni (1931–), *Beloved* (novel)

Percy, Walker (1916–1990), *The Thanatos Syndrome* (novel)

Roth, Philip (1933–), *The Counterlife* (novel)

Vizenor, Gerald (1934–), *Griever: An American Monkey King in China* (novel)

Wallace, David Foster (1962–), *The Broom of the System* (novel)

Clean Water Bill passes over Reagan veto.

Surgeon General C. Everett Koop endorses the advertising of condoms on television.

Legal battle occurs between biological parents and surrogate mother, who was artificially inseminated with the couple's fertilized egg, for the custody of Baby M.

U.S. Department of Commerce announces that inventors may patent new forms of genetically engineered animal life.

Drabble, Margaret (1939–), *The Radiant Way* (novel)

Tampopo (film) directed by **Juzio Itami**

1988   Chin, Frank (1940–), *The Chinaman Pacific & Frisco R. R. Co.* (fiction)

DeLillo, Don (1936–), *Libra* (novel)

Roth, Philip (1914–1994), *The Facts* (autobiography)

Erdrich, Louise (1954–), *Tracks* (novel)

Mamet, David (1947–), *Things Change* (drama)

Monette, Paul (1945–), *Borrowed Time* (memoir)

Price, Reynolds (1933–), *Good Hearts* (novel)

White, Edmund (1940–), *The Beautiful Room Is Empty* (novel)

Congress passes law that greatly increases penalites for insider trading on Wall Street.

President Ronald Reagan vetoes ethics bill that would have tightened restrictions on political lobbying.

Jesse Jackson is first African American to make serious bid for party nomination for president.

George Bush is elected president.

Heat wave brings U.S. worst drought in 50 years.

Terrorists blow up Pan Am Flight 103 over Scotland.

Soviet Union withdraws from Afghanistan.

Carey, Peter (1943–), *Oscar and Lucinda* (novel)

Eco, Umberto (1932–), *Foucault's Pendulum* (novel, English translation 1989)

Rushdie, Salman (1947–), *Satanic Verses* (novel); Moslem extremists call for the author's death.

American Literary Texts	American Events, Texts, and Arts	Other Events, Texts, and Arts
	NASA finds that the ozone layer is declining in thickness.	*Red Sorghum* (film) directed by **Zhang Yimou**; new wave of filmmaking from mainland China arrives.
	1.4 million illegal aliens register under a one-time federal amnesty.	
1989 **Auster, Paul** (1947–), *Moon Palace* (novel)	Investment firm Drexel Burnham Lambert pleads guilty to insider trading, pays $650 million fine.	Poland has first free elections.
Hijuelos, Oscar (1951–), *The Mambo Kings Play Songs of Love* (novel)		Berlin Wall is torn down.
Irving, John (1942–), *A Prayer for Owen Meany* (novel)	U.S. invades Panama and deposes Manuel Noriega.	Warsaw Pact dissolves; Communists lose power in eastern Europe.
Kingston, Maxine Hong (1940–), *Tripmaster Monkey: His Fake Book* (novel)	L. Douglas Wilder becomes first black governor of Virginia since the era of Reconstruction.	Chinese Army crushes public rebellion in Tianamen Square.
Mukherjee, Bharati (1940–), *Jasmine* (novel)	Savings and loan crisis; government bails out banks strapped with bad loans after real estate bubble of the 1980s burst.	**Amis, Martin** (1949–), *London Fields* (novel)
Tan, Amy (1952–), *The Joy Luck Club* (novel)		**García Márquez, Gabriel** (1928–), *The General in His Labyrinth* (novel)
Wallace, David Foster (1962–), *Girl with Curious Hair* (fiction)	Stocks score big gains at year's end as rally that lasts into 1990s begins.	**Taylor, Charles** (1931–), *The Sources of the Self* (moral philosophy)
	NBC begins to telecast *Seinfeld* (1989–1998).	

1990

Auster, Paul (1947–), *The Music of Chance* (novel)

Guare, John (1938–), *Six Degrees of Separation* (drama)

Hagedorn, Jessica (1949–), *Dogeaters* (novel)

Johnson, Charles (1948–), *The Middle Passage* (novel)

Monette, Paul (1945–), *Afterlife* (novel)

Updike, John (1932–), *Rabbit at Rest* (novel)

Wilson, August (1945–), *The Piano Lesson* (drama)

Americans with Disabilities Act passed.

Hate Crimes Statistics Act requires federal government to keep records of offenders who commit crimes motivated by racial, ethnic, or sexual bias.

Dow Jones industrial average reaches 3,000 points.

96% of American households own a color television set.

Fox begins to telecast *The Simpsons* (1990–).

Iraq invades Kuwait.

South Africa dismantles apartheid.

Reunification of Germany begins.

Republics of the Soviet Union demand independence from Russia.

Sandinistas and Contras hold elections in Nicaragua.

McEwan, Ian (1948–), *The Innocent* (novel)

BIBLIOGRAPHY

This selected bibliography is drawn from lists provided by the contributors to this volume. It represents works that they have found to be especially influential or significant. The bibliography does not include dissertations, articles, or studies of individual authors. We have also excluded primary sources, with the exception of certain collections that present materials that have been generally unknown or inaccessible to students and scholars.

Acuna, Rodolfo. *Occupied America: A History of Chicanos.* 3rd ed. New York: Harper & Row, 1988.

Adam, Barry D. *The Rise of a Gay and Lesbian Movement.* New York: Twayne Publishers, 1995.

Aldridge, John W. *After the Lost Generation: A Critical Study of the Writers of Two Wars.* New York: McGraw-Hill, 1951.

Allen, Frederick Lewis. *The Big Change: America Transforms Itself, 1900–1950.* New York: Harper & Brothers, 1952.

Allen, Paula Gunn, ed. *Studies in American Indian Literature: Critical Essays and Course Designs.* New York: Modern Language Association of America, 1983.

Allen, Paula Gunn. *The Sacred Hoop: Recovering the Feminine in American Indian Traditions.* Boston: Beacon, 1986.

Alter, Robert. *Partial Magic: The Novel as a Self-Conscious Genre.* Berkeley: University of California Press, 1975.

Anaya, Rudolfo A., and Francisco A. Lomeli, eds. *Aztlan: Essays on the Chicano Homeland.* Albuquerque, NM: Academia/El Norte Publications, 1989.

Apter, Emily, and William Pietz, eds. *Fetishism as Cultural Discourse.* Ithaca, NY: Cornell University Press, 1993.

Arteaga, Alfred, ed. *An Other Tongue: Nation and Ethnicity in the Linguistic Borderlands.* Durham: Duke University Press, 1994.

Baker, Houston A., Jr., ed. *Blues, Ideology, and Afro-American Literature: A Vernacular Theory.* Chicago: Chicago University Press, 1984.

Baker, Houston A., Jr., ed. *Three American Literatures: Essays in Chicano, Native American, and Asian-American Literature for Teachers of American Literature.* New York: Modern Language Association of America, 1982.

Bakhtin, Mikhail M. *Rabelais and His World.* Trans. Helene Iswolsky. Bloomington: Indiana University Press, 1984.

Balassi, William, John F. Crawford, and Annie O. Eysturoy, eds. *This Is About Vision: Interviews with Southwestern Writers.* Albuquerque: University of New Mexico Press, 1990.

Barone, Michael. *Our Country: The Shaping of America from Roosevelt to Reagan.* New York: The Free Press, 1990.

Barth, John. *The Friday Book: Essays and Other Nonfiction.* New York: Putnam's, 1984.

Barthes, Roland. *S/Z.* [Paris: Editions du Seuil, 1970.] Trans. Richard Miller. New York: Farrar, Straus and Giroux, 1974.

Bates, Milton J. *The Wars We Took to Vietnam: Cultural Conflict and Storytelling.* Berkeley: University of California Press, 1996.

Baudrillard, Jean. *Seduction.* [Paris: Editions Galilee, 1979.] Trans. Brian Singer. New York: St. Martin's Press, 1990.

Baumbach, Jonathan. *The Landscape of Nightmare: Studies in the Contemporary American Novel.* New York: New York University Press, 1965.

Bawer, Bruce. *Diminishing Fictions: Essays on the Modern American Novel and Its Critics.* Saint Paul: Graywolf Press, 1988.

Beauvoir, Simone de. *The Second Sex.* [Paris: Gallimard, 1949.] Trans. H. M. Parshley. New York: Modern Library, 1968.

Bergman, David, ed. *The Violet Quill Reader: The Emergence of Gay Writing After Stonewall.* New York: St. Martin's Press, 1994.

Bergman, David. *Gaiety Transfigured: Gay Self-Representation in American Literature.* Madison, WI: University of Wisconsin Press, 1991.

Bernstein, Alison R. *American Indians and World War II: Toward a New Era in Indian Affairs.* Norman: University of Oklahoma Press, 1991.

Bhabha, Homi K. *The Location of Culture.* London: Routledge, 1994.

Bhabha, Homi K., ed. *Nation and Narration.* London: Routledge, 1990.

Biskind, Peter. *Seeing Is Believing: How Hollywood Taught Us to Stop Worrying and Love the Fifties.* New York: Pantheon Books, 1983.

Blasius, Mark, and Shane Phelan, eds. *We Are Everywhere: A Historical Sourcebook in Gay and Lesbian Politics.* New York: Routledge, 1997.

Bloom, Harold. *The Anxiety of Influence: A Theory of Poetry.* New York: Oxford University Press, 1973.

Boelhower, William Q. *Through a Glass Darkly: Ethnic Semiosis in American Literature.* New York: Oxford University Press, 1987.

Bone, Robert A. *The Negro Novel in America.* New Haven: Yale University Press, 1965.

Booth, Wayne C. *The Rhetoric of Fiction.* Chicago: University of Chicago Press, 1961.

Boyer, Paul. *By the Bomb's Early Light: American Thought and Culture at the Dawn of the Atomic Age.* New York: Pantheon, 1985.

Bradbury, John M. *The Fugitives: A Critical Account.* Chapel Hill: University of North Carolina Press, 1958.

Branch, Taylor. *Parting the Waters: America in the King Years, 1954–1963.* New York: Simon & Schuster, 1988.

Brinkmeyer, Jr., Robert H. *Three Catholic Writers of the Modern South.* Jackson, MS: University Press of Mississippi, 1985.

Brooks, Cleanth. *The Hidden God: Studies in Hemingway, Faulkner, Yeats, Eliot, and Warren.* New Haven, CT: Yale University Press, 1963.

Brown, Dee A. *Bury My Heart at Wounded Knee: An Indian History of the American West.* New York: Holt, Rinehart & Winston, 1970.

Bruce-Novoa, Juan. *Chicano Authors: Inquiry by Interview.* Austin: University of Texas Press, 1980.

Bruce-Novoa, Juan. *RetroSpace: Collected Essays on Chicano Literature, Theory, and History.* Houston: Arte Publico Press, 1990.

Bruchac, Joseph. *Survival This Way: Interviews with American Indian Poets.* Tucson: University of Arizona Press, 1987.

Calderón, Héctor, and José David Saldívar, eds. *Criticism in the Borderlands: Studies in Chicano Literature, Culture, and Ideology.* Durham, NC: Duke University Press, 1991.

Camus, Albert. *The Myth of Sisyphus.* [Paris: Gallimard, 1942; 1st American ed. 1955.] Trans. Justin O'Brien. New York: Vintage, 1991.

Caramello, Charles. *Silverless Mirrors: Book, Self & Postmodern American Fiction.* Tallahassee: University Presses of Florida, 1983.

Cash, Wilbur J. *The Mind of the South.* New York: Random House, 1941.

Caute, David. *The Great Fear: The Anti-Communist Purge Under Truman and Eisenhower.* New York: Simon & Schuster, 1978.

Chafe, William H. *The Unfinished Journey: America Since World War II.* New York: Oxford University Press, 1986.

Chan, Jeffrey Paul, Frank Chin, Lawson Fusao Inada, and Shawn Wong, eds. *The Big Aiiieeeee!: An Anthology of Chinese American and Japanese American Literature.* New York: Meridian, 1991.

Chan, Sucheng. *Asian Americans: An Interpretive History.* Boston: Twayne Publishers, 1991.

Chan, Sucheng. *Entry Denied: Exclusion and the Chinese Community in America, 1882–1943.* Philadelphia: Temple University Press, 1991.

Chase, Richard. *The American Novel and Its Tradition.* New York: Doubleday, 1957.

Chauncey, George. *Gay New York: Gender, Urban Culture, and the Making of the Gay Male World, 1890–1940.* New York: HarperCollins/Basic Books, 1994.

Cheung, King-Kok, ed. *An Interethnic Companion to Asian American Literature.* New York: Cambridge University Press, 1997.

Cheung, King-Kok. *Articulate Silences: Hisaye Yamamoto, Maxine Hong Kingston, Joy Kogawa.* Ithaca, New York: Cornell University Press, 1993.

Coltelli, Laura. *Winged Words: American Indian Writers Speak.* Lincoln: University of Nebraska Press, 1990.

Commission on Wartime Relocation and Internment of Citizens. *Personal Justice Denied: Report of the Commission on Wartime Relocation and Internment of Civilians.* Washington, D. C.: U.S. Government Printing Office, 1982.

Conkin, Paul K. *The Southern Agrarians.* Knoxville: University of Tennesee Press, 1988.

Cornell, Stephen E. *The Return of the Native: American Indian Political Resurgence.* New York: Oxford University Press, 1988.

Cowan, Louise. *The Fugitive Group: A Literary History.* Baton Rouge: Louisiana State University Press, 1959.

Cowley, Malcolm. *The Flower and the Leaf: A Contemporary Record of American Writing Since 1941.* Ed. Donald W. Faulkner. New York: Viking, 1985.

Cowley, Malcolm. *The Literary Situation.* New York: Viking, 1954.

Crossman, Richard, ed. *The God That Failed.* New York: Harper, 1950.

Culler, Jonathan D. *On Deconstruction: Theory and Criticism After Structuralism.* London: Routledge and Kegan Paul, 1983.

D'Emilio, John. *Sexual Politics, Sexual Communities: The Making of a Homosexual Minority in the United States, 1940–1970.* Chicago: University of Chicago Press, 1983.

Derrida, Jacques. *Writing and Difference.* [Paris: Editions du Seuil, 1967.] Trans. Alan Bass. Chicago: University of Chicago Press, 1978.

Daniels, Roger. *Coming to America: A History of Immigration and Ethnicity in American Life.* New York: HarperCollins, 1990.

Daniels, Roger. *Prisoners Without Trial: Japanese Americans in World War II.* New York: Hill and Wang, 1993.

Dearborn, Mary V. *Pocahontas's Daughters: Gender and Ethnicity in American Culture.* New York: Oxford University Press, 1986.

Dickstein, Morris. *Gates of Eden: American Culture in the Sixties.* Cambridge, MA: Harvard University Press, 1997.

Diggins, John Patrick. *The Proud Decades: America in War and Peace, 1941–1960.* New York: W. W. Norton, 1988.

Duberman, Martin B., Martha Vicinus, and George Chauncey, Jr., eds. *Hidden from History: Reclaiming the Gay and Lesbian Past.* New York: Penguin/New American Library, 1989.

Duberman, Martin B. *Stonewall.* New York: Dutton, 1993.

Eco, Umberto. *Postscript to the Name of the Rose.* Trans. William Weaver. New York: Harcourt Brace Jovanovich, 1984.

Eisinger, Chester E. *Fiction of the Forties.* Chicago: University of Chicago Press, 1963.

Ellison, Ralph. *The Collected Essays of Ralph Ellison.* Ed. John F. Callahan. New York: Modern Library, 1995.

Fanon, Frantz. *The Wretched of the Earth.* Trans. Constance Farrington. New York: Grove Press, 1963.

Federman, Raymond, ed. *Surfiction: Fiction Now and Tomorrow.* Chicago: Swallow Press, 1975.

Ferraro, Thomas J. *Ethnic Passages: Literary Immigrants in Twentieth-Century America.* Chicago: University of Chicago Press, 1993.

Feyerabend, Paul K. *Against Method: Outline of an Anarchistic Theory of Knowledge.* London: NLB, 1975.

Fiedler, Leslie A. *Love and Death in the American Novel.* New York: Stein and Day, 1966.

Fishman, Robert. *Bourgeois Utopias: The Rise and Fall of Suburbia.* New York: Basic Books, 1987.

Fokkema, Donwe and Hans Bertens, eds. *Approaching Postmodernism.* Amsterdam: John Benjamins Press, 1986.

Foster, Hal, ed. *Postmodern Culture.* London: Pluto Press, 1985.

Friedan, Betty. *The Feminine Mystique.* New York: Norton, 1963.

Gass, William H. *Fiction & the Figures of Life.* Boston: Nonpareil Books, 1971.

Gates, Henry Louis, Jr., and Cornel West. *The Future of the Race.* New York: A. A. Knopf, 1996.

Gates, Henry Louis, Jr. *The Signifying Monkey: A Theory of Afro-American Literary Criticism.* New York: Oxford University Press, 1988.

Genovese, Eugene. *Roll, Jordan, Roll: The World the Slaves Made.* New York: Pantheon Books, 1974.

Gilbert, James B. *Another Chance: Postwar America, 1945–1968.* Philadelphia: Temple University Press, 1981.

Gilbert, James B. *A Cycle of Outrage: America's Reaction to the Juvenile Delinquent in the 1950s.* New York: Oxford University Press, 1986.

Gilbert, Sandra M., and Susan Gubar. *The Madwoman in the Attic: The Woman Writer and the Nineteenth-Century Literary Imagination.* New Haven: Yale University Press, 1979.

Gilbert, Sandra, and Susan Gubar. *The Norton Anthology of Literature by Women: The Tradition in English.* New York: Norton, 1985.

Goldman, Eric F. *The Crucial Decade – and After: America, 1945–1960.* New York: Vintage Books, 1960.

Gonzales-Berry, Erlinda, ed. *Paso Por Aqui: Critical Essays on the New Mexican Literary Tradition, 1542–1988.* Albuquerque: University of New Mexico Press, 1989.

Goodman, Paul. *Growing Up Absurd: Problems of Youth in the Organized System.* New York: Random House, 1960.

Goulden, Joseph C. *The Best Years, 1945–1950.* New York: Atheneum, 1976.

Graebner, William. *The Age of Doubt: American Thought and Culture in the 1940s.* Boston: Twayne Publishers, 1991.

Graff, Gerald. *Literature Against Itself: Literary Ideas in Modern Society.* Chicago: University of Chicago Press, 1979.

Gray, Richard J. *The Literature of Memory: Modern Writers of the American South.* Baltimore: Johns Hopkins University Press, 1977.

Guttmann, Allen. *The Jewish Writer in America: Assimilation and the Crisis of Identity.* New York: Oxford University Press, 1971.

Hagedorn, Jessica, ed. *Charlie Chan Is Dead: An Anthology of Contemporary Asian American Fiction.* New York: Penguin Books, 1993.

Hassan, Ihab H. *The Dismemberment of Orpheus: Toward a Postmodern Literature.* Madison, WI: University of Wisconsin Press, 1982.

Havard, William C., and Walter Sullivan, eds. *A Band of Prophets: The Vanderbilt Agrarians after Fifty Years*. Baton Rouge: Louisiana State University Press, 1982.

Hawkins, Peter S. *The Language of Grace: Flannery O'Connor, Walker Percy and Iris Murdoch*. Cambridge, MA: Cowley Publications, 1983.

Heilman, Robert B. *The Southern Connection: Essays*. Baton Rouge: Louisiana State University Press, 1991.

Hendin, Josephine. *Vulnerable People: A View of American Fiction Since 1945*. New York: Oxford University Press, 1978.

Hodgson, Godfrey. *America in Our Time*. Garden City, NY: Doubleday, 1976.

Hoffman, Daniel, ed. *Harvard Guide to Contemporary American Writing*. Cambridge, MA: Harvard University Press, 1979.

Hofstadter, Douglas. *Godel, Escher, Bach: An Eternal Golden Braid*. New York: Basic Books, 1979.

Holder, Alan. *The Imagined Past: Portrayals of Our History in Modern American Literature*. Lewisburg, PA: Bucknell University Press, 1980.

Holman, Clarence H. *The Immoderate Past: The Southern Writer and History*. Athens, GA: University of Georgia Press, 1977.

Hom, Marlon K. *Songs of Gold Mountain: Cantonese Rhymes from San Francisco Chinatown*. Berkeley: University of California Press, 1987.

Howe, Irving. *The Critical Point: On Literature and Culture*. New York: Horizon Press, 1973.

Howe, Irving. *Decline of the New*. New York: Horizon Press, 1970.

Hoxie, Frederick E. *A Final Promise: The Campaign to Assimilate the Indians, 1880–1920*. Lincoln: University of Nebraska Press, 1984.

Huerta, Jorge A. *Chicano Theater: Themes and Forms*. Ypsilanti, MI: Bilingual Press, 1982.

Hughes, Robert. *American Visions: The Epic History of Art in America*. New York: Alfred A. Knopf, 1997.

Humphries, Jefferson, ed. *Southern Literature and Literary Theory*. Athens, GA: University of Georgia Press, 1991.

Hutcheon, Linda. *Narcissistic Narrative: The Metafictional Paradox*. London: New York Routledge, 1984.

Hyman, Stanley Edgar. *Standards: A Chronicle of Books for Our Time*. New York: Horizon Press, 1966.

Jackson, Kenneth T. *Crabgrass Frontier: The Suburbanization of the United States*. New York: Oxford University Press, 1985.

JanMohamed, Abdul R., and David Lloyd, eds. *The Nature and Context of Minority Discourse*. New York: Oxford University Press, 1990.

Jaskoski, Helen, ed. *Early Native American Writing: New Critical Essays*. Cambridge, MA: Cambridge University Press, 1996.

Jay, Karla, and Joanne Glasgow, eds. *Lesbian Texts and Contexts: Radical Revisions*. New York: New York University Press, 1990.

Jencks, Charles A. *The Language of Post-Modern Architecture*. New York: Rizzoli, 1977.

Jensen, Robert, and Patricia Conway. *Ornamentalism.* New York: Clarkson N. Potter, 1982.

Jones, Peter G. *War and the Novelist: Appraising the American War Novel.* Columbia, MO: University of Missouri Press, 1976.

Karl, Frederick R. *American Fictions, 1940–1980: A Comprehensive History and Critical Evaluation.* New York: Harper & Row, 1983.

Karnow, Stanley. *In Our Image: America's Empire in the Philippines.* New York: Random House, 1989.

Katz, Jonathan Ned. *Gay American History: Lesbians and Gay Men in the U.S.A.* New York: Penguin/Meridian, 1976.

Kazin, Alfred. *Bright Book of Life: American Novelists and Storytellers from Hemingway to Mailer.* Boston: Little, Brown, 1973.

Kazin, Alfred. *Contemporaries.* Boston: Little, Brown, 1962.

Kim, Elaine H. *Asian American Literature: An Introduction to the Writings and Their Social Context.* Philadelphia: Temple University Press, 1982.

King, Richard H. *A Southern Renaissance: The Cultural Awakening of the American South, 1930–1955.* New York: Oxford University Press, 1980.

Klein, Marcus. *After Alienation: American Novels in Mid-Century.* Chicago: University of Chicago Press, 1978.

Klein, Marcus, ed. *The American Novel Since World War* II Greenwich, CT: Fawcett Publications, 1969.

Klinkowitz, Jerome. *Literary Disruptions: The Making of a Post-Contemporary American Fiction.* Urbana, IL: University of Illinois Press, 1975.

Krupat, Arnold. *The Voice in the Margin: Native American Literature and the Canon.* Berkeley: University of California Press, 1989.

Lauter, Paul. *Canons and Contexts.* New York: Oxford University Press, 1991.

LeClair, Thomas, and Larry McCaffery, eds. *Anything Can Happen: Interviews with Contemporary American Novelists.* Urbana, IL: University of Illinois Press, 1983.

Leuchtenburg, William E. *A Troubled Feast: American Society Since 1945.* Boston: Little, Brown, 1973.

Lewis, Richard W. B. *The American Adam: Innocence, Tragedy and Tradition in the Nineteenth Century.* Chicago: University of Chicago Press, 1955.

Lilly, Mark, ed. *Lesbian and Gay Writing: An Anthology of Critical Essays.* Philadelphia: Temple University Press, 1990.

Lim, Shirley Geok-lin, and Amy Ling, eds. *Reading the Literatures of Asian America.* Philadelphia: Temple University Press, 1992.

Limon, John. *Writing After War: American War Fiction from Realism to Postmodernism.* New York: Oxford University Press, 1994.

Lincoln, Kenneth. *Native American Renaissance.* Berkeley: University of California Press, 1983.

Ling, Amy. *Between Worlds: Women Writers of Chinese Ancestry.* New York: Pergamon Press, 1990.

Lingeman, Richard. *Don't You Know There's a War On?: The American Home Front, 1941–1945.* New York: G. P. Putnam's Sons, 1970.

Lowe, Lisa. *Immigrant Acts: On Asian American Cultural Politics.* Durham, NC: Duke University Press, 1996.

Lyotard, Jean François. *The Postmodern Condition: A Report on Knowledge.* Trans. Geoff Bennington and Brian Massumi. Minneapolis: University of Minnesota Press, 1984.

Mailer, Norman. *Advertisements for Myself.* New York: G. P. Putnam's Sons, 1959.

Maitino, John R., and David R. Peck, eds. *Teaching American Ethnic Literatures: Nineteen Essays.* Albuquerque: University of New Mexico Press, 1996.

Margolies, Edward. *Native Sons: A Critical Study of Twentieth-Century Negro American Authors.* Philadelphia: J. B. Lippincott, 1968.

Marshall, Richard. *American Art Since 1970.* New York: Whitney Museum, 1984.

May, Lary, ed. *Recasting America: Culture and Politics in the Age of Cold War.* Chicago: University of Chicago Press, 1989.

McHale, Brian. *Postmodernist Fiction.* New York: Methuen, 1987.

Meier, Matt S., and Feliciano Ribera. *Mexican Americans, American Mexicans: From Conquistadors to Chicanos.* New York: Hill & Wang, 1993.

Memmi, Albert. *The Colonizer and the Colonized.* Trans. Howard Greenfield. New York: Orion Press, 1965.

Miller, Douglas T., and Marion Nowak. *The Fifties: The Way We Really Were.* Garden City, NY: Doubleday, 1977.

Mondimore, Francis Mark. *A Natural History of Homosexuality.* Baltimore: Johns Hopkins University Press, 1996.

Moraga, Cherríe, and Gloria Anzaldúa, eds. *Making Face, Making Soul = Haciendo Caras: Creative and Critical Perspectives by Women of Color.* San Francisco: Aunt Lute Foundation Books, 1990.

Morris, Jan. *Manhattan '45.* New York: Oxford University Press, 1973.

Murphy, Timothy F., and Suzanne Poirier, eds. *Writing AIDS: Gay Literature, Language, and Analysis.* New York: Columbia University Press, 1993.

Murray, David. *Forked Tongues: Speech, Writing and Representation in North American Indian Texts.* London: Pinter Publishers, 1990.

Navasky, Victor S. *Naming Names.* New York: Viking Press, 1980.

Newman, Charles H. *The Post-Modern Aura: The Act of Fiction in an Age of Inflation.* Evanston, IL: Northwestern University Press, 1985.

Omi, Michael, and Howard Winant. *Racial Formation in the United States: From the 1960s to the 1980s.* New York: Routledge and Kegan Paul, 1986.

O'Neill, William L. *American High: The Years of Confidence, 1945–1960.* New York: The Free Press, 1986.

Patterson, James T. *Grand Expectations: The United States, 1945–1974.* New York: Oxford University Press, 1996.

Payne, James Robert, ed. *Multicultural Autobiography: American Lives.* Knoxville: University of Tennessee Press, 1992.

Pells, Richard H. *The Liberal Mind in a Conservative Age: American Intellectuals in the 1940s and 1950s.* New York: Harper & Row, 1985.

Podhoretz, Norman. *Doings and Undoings: The Fifties and After in American Writing.* New York: Farrar, Straus and Giroux, 1964.

Putz, Manfred, and Peter Freese, eds. *Postmodernism in American Literature: A Critical Anthology.* Darmstadt: Thesen Verlag, 1984.

Radin, Paul. *The Trickster: A Study in American Indian Mythology.* New York: Philosophical Library, 1956.

Riesman, David, with Nathan Glazer and Reuel Denney. *The Lonely Crowd: A Study of the Changing American Character.* New Haven: Yale University Press, 1961.

Roth, Philip. *Reading Myself and Others.* New York: Farrar, Straus and Giroux, 1975.

Rubin, Louis D., Jr., and Robert D. Jacobs, eds. *Southern Renascence: The Literature of the Modern South.* Baltimore: Johns Hopkins University Press, 1953.

Rubin, Louis D., Jr. *Writers of the Modern South: The Faraway Country.* Seattle: University of Washington Press, 1963.

Ruoff, A. LaVonne Brown, and Jerry W. Ward, Jr., eds. *Redefining American Literary History.* New York: Modern Language Association of America, 1990.

Ruoff, A. LaVonne Brown, ed. *American Indian Literatures: An Introduction, Bibliographic Review, and Selected Bibliography.* New York: Modern Language Association of America, 1990.

Saldivar, Ramon. *Chicano Narrative: The Dialectics of Difference.* Madison: University of Wisconsin Press, 1990.

Sarris, Greg. *Keeping Slug Woman Alive: A Holistic Approach to American Indian Texts.* Berkeley: University of California Press, 1993.

Schapiro, Meyer. *Modern Art, 19th and 20th Centuries.* New York: George Braziller, 1978.

Schaub, Thomas H. *American Fiction in the Cold War.* Madison: University of Wisconsin Press, 1991.

Schlesinger, Arthur M., Jr. *The Vital Center: The Politics of Freedom.* Boston: Houghton Mifflin, 1962.

Schorer, Mark. *The World We Imagine: Selected Essays.* New York: Farrar, Straus and Giroux, 1968.

Scruggs, Charles. *Sweet Home: Invisible Cities in the Afro-American Novel.* Baltimore: Johns Hopkins University Press, 1993.

Sedgwick, Eve Kosofsky. *Epistemology of the Closet.* Berkeley: University of California Press, 1990.

Shechner, Mark. *After the Revolution: Studies in the Contemporary Jewish-American Imagination.* Bloomington: Indiana University Press, 1987.

Sheed, Wilfrid. *The Morning After: Selected Essays and Reviews.* New York: Farrar, Straus and Giroux, 1971.

Shell, Marc, and Werner Sollors, eds. *Longfellow Institute Anthology of Literature of the United States in Languages Other than English.* Baltimore: Johns Hopkins University Press, 1997.

Simpson, Lewis P. *The Dispossessed Garden: Pastoral and History in Southern Literature.* Athens: University of Georgia Press, 1972.

Simpson, Lewis P. *The Fable of the Southern Writer.* Baton Rouge: Louisiana State University Press, 1994.

Singh, Amritjit, Joseph T. Skerrett, Jr., and Robert E. Hogan, eds. *Memory and Cultural Politics: New Approaches to American Ethnic Literatures.* Boston: Northeastern University Press, 1996.

Singh, Amritjit, Joseph T. Skerrett, Jr., and Robert E. Hogan, eds. *Memory, Narrative, and Identity: New Essays in Ethnic American Literatures.* Boston: Northeastern University Press, 1994.

Sollors, Werner. *Beyond Ethnicity: Consent and Descent in American Culture.* New York: Oxford University Press, 1986.

Solotaroff, Theodore. *The Red Hot Vacuum and Other Pieces on the Writing of the Sixties.* New York: Atheneum, 1970.

Stewart, John L. *The Burden of Time: The Fugitives and Agrarians.* Princeton, NJ: Princeton University Press, 1965.

Sullivan, Walter. *Death by Melancholy: Essays on Modern Southern Fiction.* Baton Rouge: Louisiana State University Press, 1972.

Summers, Claude J., ed. *The Gay and Lesbian Literary Heritage: A Reader's Companion to the Writers and Their Works, from Antiquity to the Present.* New York: Henry Holt, 1995.

Sunahara, Ann Gomer. *The Politics of Racism: The Uprooting of Japanese Canadians During the Second World War.* Toronto: James Lorimer and Company, 1981.

Swann, Brian, and Arnold Krupat, eds. *I Tell You Now: Autobiographical Essays by Native American Writers.* Lincoln: University of Nebraska Press, 1987.

Takaki, Ronald T. *A Different Mirror: A History of Multicultural America.* Boston: Little, Brown, 1993.

Tani, Stefano. *The Doomed Detective: The Contribution of the Detective Novel to Postmodern American and Italian Fiction.* Carbondale: Southern Illinois University Press, 1984.

Tanner, Tony. *City of Words: American Fiction, 1950–1970.* New York: Harper & Row, 1971.

Thornton, Russell. *American Indian Holocaust and Survival: A Population History Since 1492.* Norman: University of Oklahoma Press, 1987.

Tomkins, Calvin. *Off the Wall: Robert Rauschenberg and the Art World of Our Time.* Garden City, NY: Doubleday, 1980.

Trilling, Lionel. *Beyond Culture: Essays on Literature and Learning.* New York: Viking Press, 1965.

Trilling, Lionel. *The Liberal Imagination: Essays on Literature and Society.* New York: Scribner, 1950.

Truman, Harry S. *Memoirs.* 2 vols. Garden City, NY: Doubleday, 1956.

TuSmith, Bonnie. *All My Relatives: Community in Contemporary Ethnic American Literatures.* Ann Arbor: University of Michigan Press, 1993.

Tytell, John. *Naked Angels: The Lives and Literature of the Beat Generation.* New York: McGraw-Hill, 1976.

Vidal, Gore. *United States: Essays, 1952–1992.* New York: Random House, 1993.

Walker, Alice. *In Search of Our Mothers' Gardens: Womanist Prose.* San Diego: Harcourt, Brace, Jovanovich, 1983.

Waugh, Patricia. *Metafiction: The Theory and Practice of Self-Conscious Fiction.* London: Methuen, 1984.

Weglyn, Michi. *Years of Infamy: The Untold Story of America's Concentration Camps.* New York: Morrow Quill Paperbacks, 1980.

White, Edmund. *The Burning Library: Essays.* New York: Alfred A. Knopf, 1994.

Whitfield, Stephen J. *The Culture of the Cold War.* Baltimore: Johns Hopkins University Press, 1996.

Whyte, William H., Jr. *The Organization Man.* New York: Simon & Schuster, 1956.

Wiget, Andrew. *Native American Literature.* Boston: Twayne Publishers, 1985.

Wolfe, Tom, and E. W. Johnson, eds. *The New Journalism.* New York: Harper & Row, 1973.

Wong, Hertha D. *Sending My Heart Back Across the Years: Tradition and Innovation in Native American Autobiography.* New York: Oxford University Press, 1992.

Wong, Sau-ling Cynthia. *Reading Asian American Literature: From Necessity to Extravagance.* Princeton, NJ: Princeton University Press, 1993.

Woodward, Comer Vann. *Origins of the New South.* Baton Rouge: Louisiana State University Press, 1951.

Wu, Cheng-Tsu, ed. *"Chink!": A Documentary History of Anti-Chinese Prejudice in America.* New York: World Publishing, 1972.

Zimmerman, Marc. *U.S. Latino Literature: An Essay and Annotated Bibliography.* Chicago: MARCH/Abrazo Press, 1992.

INDEX